Praise for *Javascript® Bible*

"*JavaScript® Bible* is the definitive resource in JavaScript programming. I am never more than three feet from my copy."

— Steve Reich, CEO, PageCoders

"This book is a must-have for any web developer or programmer."

— Thoma Lile, President, Kanis Technologies, Inc.

"Outstanding book. I would recommend this book to anyone interested in learning to develop advanced Web sites. Mr. Goodman did an excellent job of organizing this book and writing it so that even a beginning programmer can understand it."

— Jason Hensley, Director of Internet Services, NetVoice, Inc.

"Goodman is always great at delivering clear and concise technical books!"

— Dwayne King, Chief Technology Officer, White Horse

"*JavaScript® Bible* is well worth the money spent!"

— Yen C.Y. Leong, IT Director, Moo Mooltimedia, a member of SmartTransact Group

"A must-have book for any internet developer."

— Uri Fremder, Senior Consultant, TopTier Software

"I love this book! I use it all the time, and it always delivers. It's the only JavaScript book I use!"

— Jason Badger, Web Developer

"Whether you are a professional or a beginner, this is a great book to get."

— Brant Mutch, Web Application Developer, Wells Fargo Card Services, Inc.

"I never thought I'd ever teach programming before reading your book [*JavaScript® Bible*]. It's so simple to use — the Programming Fundamentals section brought it all back! Thank you for such a wonderful book, and for breaking through my programming block!"

— Susan Sann Mahon, Certified Lotus Instructor, TechNet Training

"Danny Goodman is very good at leading the reader into the subject. *JavaScript® Bible* has everything we could possibly need."

— Philip Gurdon

"An excellent book that builds solidly from whatever level the reader is at. A book that is both witty and educational."

— Dave Vane

"I continue to use the book on a daily basis and would be lost without it."

— Mike Warner, Founder, Oak Place Productions

"*JavaScript® Bible* is by *far* the best JavaScript resource I've ever seen (and I've seen quite a few)."

— Robert J. Mirro, Independent Consultant, RJM Consulting

JavaScript® Bible

Seventh Edition

JavaScript® Bible

Seventh Edition

Danny Goodman
Michael Morrison
Paul Novitski
Tia Gustaff Rayl

WILEY

Wiley Publishing, Inc.

JavaScript® Bible, Seventh Edition

Published by
Wiley Publishing, Inc.
10475 Crosspoint Boulevard
Indianapolis, IN 46256
www.wiley.com

Copyright © 2010 by Wiley Publishing, Inc., Indianapolis, Indiana

Published simultaneously in Canada

ISBN: 978-0-470-52691-0

Manufactured in the United States of America

10 9 8 7 6 5 4 3 2 1

No part of this publication may be reproduced, stored in a retrieval system or transmitted in any form or by any means, electronic, mechanical, photocopying, recording, scanning or otherwise, except as permitted under Sections 107 or 108 of the 1976 United States Copyright Act, without either the prior written permission of the Publisher, or authorization through payment of the appropriate per-copy fee to the Copyright Clearance Center, 222 Rosewood Drive, Danvers, MA 01923, (978) 750-8400, fax (978) 646-8600. Requests to the Publisher for permission should be addressed to the Permissions Department, John Wiley & Sons, Inc., 111 River Street, Hoboken, NJ 07030, (201) 748-6011, fax (201) 748-6008, or online at http://www.wiley.com/go/permissions.

Limit of Liability/Disclaimer of Warranty: The publisher and the author make no representations or warranties with respect to the accuracy or completeness of the contents of this work and specifically disclaim all warranties, including without limitation warranties of fitness for a particular purpose. No warranty may be created or extended by sales or promotional materials. The advice and strategies contained herein may not be suitable for every situation. This work is sold with the understanding that the publisher is not engaged in rendering legal, accounting, or other professional services. If professional assistance is required, the services of a competent professional person should be sought. Neither the publisher nor the author shall be liable for damages arising herefrom. The fact that an organization or web site is referred to in this work as a citation and/or a potential source of further information does not mean that the author or the publisher endorses the information the organization or web site may provide or recommendations it may make. Further, readers should be aware that Internet web sites listed in this work may have changed or disappeared between when this work was written and when it is read.

For general information on our other products and services please contact our Customer Care Department within the United States at (877) 762-2974, outside the United States at (317) 572-3993 or fax (317) 572-4002.

Wiley also publishes its books in a variety of electronic formats. Some content that appears in print may not be available in electronic books.

Library of Congress Control Number: 2010923547

Trademarks: Wiley and the Wiley logo are trademarks or registered trademarks of John Wiley & Sons, Inc. and/or its affiliates, in the United States and other countries, and may not be used without written permission. JavaScript is a registered trademark of Oracle America, Inc. All other trademarks are the property of their respective owners. Wiley Publishing, Inc. is not associated with any product or vendor mentioned in this book.

To Tanya, with whom I share this loving orbit with Briar and Callum in our own cozy Klemperer rosette.
— Paul Novitski

To my husband, Edward, whose love, support, and encouragement kept me going through this and all my adventures, and to the memory of my parents who inspired me to step out in faith.
— Tia Gustaff Rayl

About the Authors

Danny Goodman is the author of numerous critically acclaimed and best-selling books, including *The Complete HyperCard Handbook, Danny Goodman's AppleScript Handbook, Dynamic HTML: The Definitive Reference*, and *JavaScript & DHTML Cookbook*. He is a renowned authority on and expert teacher of computer scripting languages. His writing style and pedagogy continue to earn praise from readers and teachers around the world.

Michael Morrison is a writer, developer, toy inventor, and author of a variety of books covering topics such as Java, C++, Web scripting, XML, game development, and mobile devices. Some of Michael's notable writing projects include *Faster Smarter HTML and XML, Teach Yourself HTML & CSS in 24 Hours*, and *Beginning Game Programming*. Michael is also the founder of Stalefish Labs (www.stalefishlabs.com), an entertainment company specializing in unusual games, toys, and interactive products.

Paul Novitski has been writing software as a freelance programmer since 1981. He once taught himself BASIC in order to write a machine language disassembler so that he could lovingly hack Wang's OIS microcode. He has focused on internet programming since the late '90s. His company, Juniper Webcraft, produces HTML-strict websites featuring accessible, semantic markup, separation of development layers, and intuitive user interfaces. He knows the righteousness of elegant code, the poignancy of living on the bleeding edge of wilderness, the sweet melancholy of mbira music, and the scorching joy of raising twin boys.

Tia Gustaff Rayl is a consultant who does development and training in database and Web technologies. Most recently she has published courseware for XHTML, CSS, JavaScript, and SQL. It comes as no surprise to those who know her that she began her software career with degrees in English and Education from the University of Florida. As is usual for most newcomers to the field, her introduction to computing was maintaining software. She went on to a long-standing career in the software industry in full life cycle system, application, and database development; project management; and training for PC and mainframe environments. In the mid-nineties she worked on early Web-enabled database applications, adding JavaScript to her repertoire. She continues to take on development projects to maintain her code-slinging skills. If she had any spare time (and money) she would go on an around-the-world cruise with her husband and two dogs.

About the Technical Editor

Benjamin Schupak holds a master's degree in computer science and has more than 11 years of professional programming experience for large corporations and U.S. federal departments. He lives in the New York metro area and enjoys traveling.

Credits

Executive Editor
Carol Long

Project Editor
John Sleeva

Technical Editor
Benjamin Schupack

Production Editor
Rebecca Anderson

Editorial Director
Robyn B. Siesky

Editorial Manager
Mary Beth Wakefield

Marketing Manager
Ashley Zurcher

Production Manager
Tim Tate

Vice President and Executive Group Publisher
Richard Swadley

Vice President and Executive Publisher
Barry Pruett

Associate Publisher
Jim Minatel

Project Coordinator, Cover
Lynsey Stanford

Proofreaders
Maraya Cornell, Word One New York
Sheilah Ledwidge, Word One New York

Indexer
Robert Swanson

Cover Designer
Michael E. Trent

Cover Image
© Joyce Haughey

Acknowledgments

My gratitude for being given the opportunity and the latitude to work on this immense tome extends to Carol Long of Wiley, editor John Sleeva, Carole Jelen at Waterside Productions, Julian Hall, my partner in crime at Juniper Webcraft, and, above all, my sweet, loving, supportive, and nearly homicidal spouse Tanya Wright, all of them long-suffering and all to be commended for not actually throttling me in the course of this overlong birthing. The solid foundation of research and explication established by Danny Goodman and his past collaborators in previous editions is awesome and I am humbled to have been able to help move this great body of knowledge forward to the next step. Tia Gustaff Rayl, who with wings spread and sparks flying rode in to the rescue, has been a kick in the pants to work with; she's smart and funny, but more than that she is gifted with the precise serendipity and good taste to share a birthday with me.

—Paul Novitski

I have been blessed with the support of many people who have reviewed my work and encouraged me along the way. I could never have done any of this without the devoted support of my husband, Edward. I love him without cease and thank God for bringing him into my life. I have been blessed by the remarkable patience of an incredibly tolerant immediate and extended family, as well as amused friends, who put up with my "Hi, I love you. Don't talk to me right now." way of answering the phone and greeting visitors at the door. My husband, family and friends are the ones who sacrificed the most for this book. Thank you all. I want to thank Paul for being great to work with and for his wry sense of humor which left me on the floor laughing just when I most needed a lift. I want to thank my editor, John Sleeva, who with great patience and humor guided me through the maze of the publishing world. I also want to thank Rebecca Anderson and Maraya Cornell for forcing me to be a better writer. Finally, I want to thank Miss Bigelow, my 11th and 12th grade English teacher, who instilled within me a great respect and love for the written word.

—Tia Gustaff Rayl

Contents at a Glance

Contents at a Glance

Contents

Contents

Contents

Contents

Contents

Contents

Introduction

This seventh edition of the *JavaScript Bible* represents knowledge and experience accumulated over fifteen years of daily work in JavaScript and a constant monitoring of newsgroups for questions, problems, and challenges facing scripters at all levels. Our goal is to help you avoid the same frustration and head-scratching we and others have experienced through multiple generations of scriptable browsers.

While the earliest editions of this book focused on the then-predominant Netscape Navigator browser, the browser market share landscape has changed through the years. For many years, Microsoft took a strong lead with its Internet Explorer, but more recently, other browsers that support industry standards are finding homes on users' computers. The situation still leaves an age-old dilemma for content developers: designing scripted content that functions equally well in both standards-compliant and proprietary environments. The job of a book claiming to be the "bible" is not only to present both the standard and proprietary details when they diverge, but also to show you how to write scripts that blend the two so that they work on the wide array of browsers visiting your sites or web applications. Empowering you to design and write good scripts is our passion, regardless of browser. It's true that our bias is toward industry standards, but not to the exclusion of proprietary features that may be necessary to get your content and scripting ideas flowing equally well on today's and tomorrow's browsers.

Organization and Features of This Edition

Like the previous three editions of the *JavaScript Bible*, this seventh edition contains far more information than can be printed and bound into a single volume. The complete contents can be found in the electronic version of this book (in PDF form) on the CD-ROM that accompanies the book. This edition is structured in such a way as to supply the most commonly needed information in its entirety in the printed portion of the book. Content that you use to learn the fundamentals of JavaScript and reference frequently are at your fingertips in the printed version, while chapters with more advanced content are in the searchable electronic version on the CD-ROM. Here are some details about the book's structure.

Part I: Getting Started with JavaScript

Part I of the book begins with a chapter that shows how JavaScript compares with Java and discusses its role within the rest of the World Wide Web. The web browser and scripting world have undergone significant changes since JavaScript first arrived on the scene. That's why Chapter 2 is devoted to addressing challenges facing scripters who must develop applications for both single- and cross-platform browser audiences amid rapidly changing standards efforts. Chapter 3 introduces some tools you can use to compose your pages and scripts, while Chapter 4 delves into the nitty-gritty of how to use JavaScript to run in a wide variety of browsers.

Part II: JavaScript Tutorial

All of Part II is handed over to a tutorial for newcomers to JavaScript. Ten lessons provide you with a gradual path through browser internals, basic programming skills, and genuine browser scripting, with an emphasis on industry standards as supported by most of the scriptable browsers in use today. Exercises follow at the end of each lesson to help reinforce what you just learned and challenge you to use your new knowledge (you'll find answers to the exercises in Appendix D, on the CD-ROM). The goal of the tutorial is to equip you with sufficient experience to start scripting simple pages right away while making it easier for you to understand the in-depth discussions and examples in the rest of the book.

Part III: JavaScript Core Language Reference

Reference information for the core JavaScript language fills Part III. In all reference chapters, a compatibility chart indicates the browser version that supports each object and object feature. Guide words near the tops of pages help you find a particular term quickly.

Part IV: Document Objects Reference

Part IV, the largest section of the book, provides in-depth coverage of the document object models as implemented in today's browsers, including the object used for modern Ajax applications. As with the core JavaScript reference chapters of Part III, these DOM chapters display browser compatibility charts for every object and object feature. One chapter in particular, Chapter 26, contains reference material that is shared by most of the remaining chapters of Part IV. To help you refer back to Chapter 26 from other chapters, a shaded tab along the outside edge of the page shows you at a glance where the chapter is located. Additional navigation aids include guide words near the tops of most pages to indicate which object and object feature is covered on the page. Note that the Objects Reference begun in Part IV of the book continues in Part VI on the CD, with an additional 13 chapters of reference material.

Part V: Appendixes

Appendix A offers a JavaScript and Browser Objects Quick Reference. Appendix B provides information about using the CD-ROM that comes with this book, which includes numerous bonus chapters and examples.

Part VI: Document Objects Reference (continued)

Beginning the portion of the book that resides only the accompanying CD, Part VI continues the document objects reference discussions that begin in Part IV by providing an additional 13 chapters of reference material.

Part VII: More JavaScript Programming

Chapters 46–51 discuss advanced JavaScript programming techniques, including data-entry validation, debugging, and security issues.

Part VIII: Applications

The final ten chapters of the book, available only on the CD-ROM, feature sample applications that cover the gamut from calendars to puzzles.

Part IX: Appendixes (continued)

The final three appendixes provide helpful reference information. These resources include a list of JavaScript reserved words in Appendix C, answers to Part II's tutorial exercises in Appendix D, and Internet resources in Appendix E.

CD-ROM

The CD-ROM is a gold mine of information. It begins with a PDF version of the entire contents of this seventh edition of the *JavaScript Bible*. This version includes bonus chapters covering:

- Dynamic HTML, data validation, plug-ins, and security
- Techniques for developing and debugging professional web-based applications
- Ten full-fledged JavaScript real-world applications

Another treasure trove on the CD-ROM is the Listings folder where you'll find over 300 ready-to-run HTML documents that serve as examples of most of the document object model and JavaScript vocabulary words in Parts III and IV. All of the bonus chapter example listings are also included. You can run these examples with your JavaScript-enabled browser, but be sure to use the index.html page in the Listings folder as a gateway to running the listings. We could have provided you with humorous little sample code fragments out of context, but we think that seeing full-fledged HTML documents (simple though they may be) for employing these concepts is important. We encourage you to manually type the script listings from the tutorial (Part II) of this book. We believe you learn a lot, even by aping listings from the book, as you get used to the rhythms of typing scripts in documents.

Be sure to check out the Chapter 4 listing file called evaluator.html. Many segments of Parts III and IV invite you to try out an object model or language feature with the help of an interactive workbench, called The Evaluator — a *JavaScript Bible* exclusive! You see instant results and will quickly learn how the feature works.

The Quick Reference from Appendix A is in PDF format on the CD-ROM for you to print out and assemble as a handy reference, if desired. Adobe Reader is also included on the CD-ROM, in case you don't already have it.

Prerequisites to Learning JavaScript

Although this book doesn't demand that you have a great deal of programming experience behind you, the more web pages you've created with HTML, the easier you will find it to understand how JavaScript interacts with the familiar elements you normally place in your pages. Occasionally, you will need to modify HTML tags to take advantage of scripting. If you are familiar with those tags already, the JavaScript enhancements will be simple to digest.

To learn JavaScript, you won't need to know server scripting or how to pass information from a form to a server. The focus here is on client-side scripting, which operates independently of the server after the JavaScript-enhanced HTML page is fully loaded into the browser. However, we strongly believe that a public web page should be operational in the absence of JavaScript, so any dynamic functionality that looks up results or modifies the content of a page should interact with a server-side script fundamentally. After that foundation is laid, we add JavaScript to make a page faster, easier, or more fun. So although you don't need to know server-side scripting in order to learn JavaScript, for serious web work you should either learn a server-side scripting language such as PHP in addition to JavaScript or look for server-side programmers to complement your client-side scripting abilities.

The basic vocabulary of the current HTML standard should be part of your working knowledge. You should also be familiar with some of the latest document markup standards, such as XHTML and Cascading Style Sheets (CSS). Web searches for these terms will uncover numerous tutorials on the subjects.

If you've never programmed before

Don't be put off by the size of this book. JavaScript may not be the easiest language in the world to learn, but believe us, it's a far cry from having to learn a full programming language such as Java or C. Unlike developing a full-fledged monolithic application (such as the productivity programs you buy in stores), JavaScript lets you experiment by writing small snippets of program code to accomplish big things. The JavaScript interpreter built into every scriptable browser does a great deal of the technical work for you.

Programming, at its most basic level, consists of nothing more than writing a series of instructions for the computer to follow. We humans follow instructions all the time, even if we don't realize it. Traveling to a friend's house is a sequence of small instructions: Go three blocks that way; turn left here; turn right there. Amid these instructions are some decisions that we have to make: If the stoplight is red, then stop; if the light is green, then go; if the light is yellow, then floor it! (Just kidding.) Occasionally, we must repeat some operations several times (kind of like having to go around the block until a parking space opens up). A computer program not only contains the main sequence of steps, but it also anticipates what decisions or repetitions may be needed to accomplish the program's goal (such as how to handle the various states of a stoplight or what to do if someone just stole the parking spot you were aiming for).

The initial hurdle of learning to program is becoming comfortable with the way a programming language wants its words and numbers organized in these instructions. Such rules are called syntax, the same as in a living language. Computers aren't very forgiving if you don't communicate with them in the specific language they understand. When speaking to another human, you can flub a sentence's syntax and still have a good chance that the other person will understand you. Not so with computer programming languages. If the syntax isn't perfect (or at least within the language's range of knowledge), the computer has the brazenness to tell you that you have made a syntax error.

The best thing you can do is just accept the syntax errors you receive as learning experiences. Even experienced programmers make mistakes. Every syntax error you get — and every resolution of that error made by rewriting the wayward statement — adds to your knowledge of the language.

If you've done a little programming before

Programming experience in a procedural language, such as BASIC, may actually be a hindrance rather than a help to learning JavaScript. Although you may have an appreciation for precision in syntax, the overall concept of how a program fits into the world is probably radically different from JavaScript's role. Part of this has to do with the typical tasks a script performs (carrying out a very specific task in response to user action within a web page), but a large part also has to do with the nature of object-oriented programming.

If you've programmed in C before

In a typical procedural program, the programmer is responsible for everything that appears on the screen and everything that happens under the hood. When the program first runs, a great deal of code is dedicated to setting up the visual environment. Perhaps the screen contains several text entry fields or clickable buttons. To determine which button a user clicks, the program examines the coordinates of the click and compares those coordinates against a list of all button coordinates on the screen. Program execution then branches out to perform the instructions reserved for clicking in that space.

Object-oriented programming is almost the inverse of that process. A button is considered an object — something tangible. An object has properties, such as its label, size, alignment, and so on. An object may also contain a script. At the same time, the system software and browser, working together, can send a message to an object — depending on what the user does — to trigger the script. For example, if a user clicks in a text entry field, the system/browser tells the field that somebody has clicked there (that is, has set the focus to that field), giving the field the task of deciding what to do about it. That's where the script comes in. The script is connected to the field, and it contains the instructions that the field carries out after the user activates it. Another set of instructions may control what happens when the user types an entry and tabs or clicks out of the field, thereby changing the content of the field.

Some of the scripts you write may seem to be procedural in construction: They contain a simple list of instructions that are carried out in order. But when dealing with data from form elements, these instructions work with the object-based nature of JavaScript. The form is an object; each radio button or text field is an object as well. The script then acts on the properties of those objects to get some work done.

Making the transition from procedural to object-oriented programming may be the most difficult challenge for you. But when the concept clicks — a long, pensive walk might help — so many light bulbs will go on inside your head that you'll think you might glow in the dark. From then on, object orientation will seem to be the only sensible way to program.

By borrowing syntax from Java (which, in turn, is derived from C and C++), JavaScript shares many syntactical characteristics with C. Programmers familiar with C will feel right at home. Operator symbols, conditional structures, and repeat loops follow very much in the C tradition. You will be less concerned about data types in JavaScript than you are in C. In JavaScript, a variable is not restricted to any particular data type.

With so much of JavaScript's syntax familiar to you, you will be able to concentrate on document object model concepts, which may be entirely new to you. You will still need a good grounding in HTML to put your expertise to work in JavaScript.

If you've programmed in Java before

Despite the similarity in their names, the two languages share only surface aspects: loop and conditional constructions, C-like "dot" object references, curly braces for grouping statements, several keywords, and a few other attributes. Variable declarations, however, are quite different, because JavaScript is a loosely typed language. A variable can contain an integer value in one statement and a string in the next (though we're not saying that this is good style). What Java refers to as methods, JavaScript calls methods (when associated with a predefined object) or functions (for scripter-defined actions). JavaScript methods and functions may return values of any type without having to state the data type ahead of time.

Perhaps the most important Java concepts to suppress when writing JavaScript are the object-oriented notions of classes, inheritance, instantiation, and message passing. These aspects are simply non-issues when scripting. At the same time, however, JavaScript's designers knew that you'd have some hard-to-break habits. For example, although JavaScript does not require a semicolon at the end of each statement line, if you type one in your JavaScript source code, the JavaScript interpreter won't balk.

If you've written scripts (or macros) before

Experience with writing scripts in other authoring tools or macros in productivity programs is helpful for grasping a number of JavaScript's concepts. Perhaps the most important concept is the idea of combining a handful of statements to perform a specific task on some data. For example, you can write a macro in Microsoft Excel that performs a data transformation on daily figures that come in from a corporate financial report on another computer. The macro is built into the Macro menu, and you run it by choosing that menu item whenever a new set of figures arrives.

Some modern programming environments, such as Visual Basic, resemble scripting environments in some ways. They present the programmer with an interface builder, which does most of the work of displaying screen objects with which the user will interact. A big part of the programmer's job is to write little bits of code that are executed when a user interacts with those objects. A great deal of the scripting you will do with JavaScript matches that pattern exactly. In fact, those environments resemble the scriptable browser environment in another way: They provide a finite set of predefined objects that have fixed sets of properties and behaviors. This predictability makes learning the entire environment and planning an application easier to accomplish.

Formatting and Naming Conventions

The script listings and words in this book are presented in a `monospace font` to set them apart from the rest of the text. Because of restrictions in page width, lines of script listings may, from time to time, break unnaturally. In such cases, the remainder of the script appears in the following line, flush with the left margin of the listing, just as it would appear in a text editor with word wrapping turned on. If these line breaks cause you problems when you type a script listing into a document yourself, we encourage you to access the corresponding listing on the CD-ROM to see how it should look when you type it.

As soon as you reach Part III of this book, you won't likely go for more than a page before reading about an object model or language feature that requires a specific minimum version of one browser or another. To make it easier to spot in the text when a particular browser and browser version is required, most browser references consist of an abbreviation and a version number. For example, WinIE5 means Internet Explorer 5 for Windows; NN4 means Netscape Navigator 4 for any operating system; Moz stands for the modern Mozilla browser (from which Firefox, Netscape 6 or later, and Camino are derived); and Safari is Apple's own browser for Mac OS X. If a feature is introduced with a particular version of browser and is supported in subsequent versions, a plus symbol (+) follows the number. For example, a feature marked WinIE5.5+ indicates that Internet Explorer 5.5 for Windows is required at a minimum, but the feature is also available in WinIE8 and probably future WinIE versions. If a feature was implemented in the first release of a modern browser, a plus symbol immediately follows the browser family name, such as Moz+ for all Mozilla-based browsers. Occasionally, a feature or some highlighted behavior applies to only one browser. For example, a feature marked

NN4 means that it works only in Netscape Navigator 4.x. A minus sign (e.g., WinIE-) means that the browser does not support the item being discussed.

The format of HTML markup in this edition follows HTML5 coding conventions, but also adheres to many XHTML standards such as all-lowercase tag and attribute names.

Note   **Tip**

Caution   **Cross Reference**

Note, Tip, Caution, and Cross-Reference icons occasionally appear in the book to flag important points or suggest where to find more information.

JavaScript® Bible

Seventh Edition

Part I

Getting Started with JavaScript

JavaScript's Role in the World Wide Web and Beyond

Many of the technologies that make the World Wide Web possible have far exceeded their original goals. Envisioned at the outset as a medium for publishing static text and image content across a network, the Web is forever being probed, pushed, and pulled by content authors. By taking for granted so much of the "dirty work" of conveying the bits between server and client computers, content developers and programmers dream of exploiting that connection to generate new user experiences and practical applications. It's not uncommon for a developer community to take ownership of a technology and mold it to do new and exciting things. But with so many web technologies — especially browser programming with JavaScript — within reach of everyday folks, we have witnessed an unprecedented explosion in turning the World Wide Web from a bland publishing medium into a highly interactive, operating system–agnostic authoring platform.

The JavaScript language, working in tandem with related browser features, is a web-enhancing technology. When employed on the client computer, the language can help turn a static page of content into an engaging, interactive, and intelligent experience. Applications can be as subtle as welcoming a site's visitor with the greeting "Good morning!" when it is morning in the client computer's time zone — even though it is dinnertime where the server is located. Or, applications can be much more obvious, such as delivering the content of a slide show in a one-page download while JavaScript controls the sequence of hiding, showing, and "flying slide" transitions as we navigate through the presentation.

Of course, JavaScript is not the only technology that can give life to drab web content. Therefore, it is important to understand where JavaScript fits within the array of standards, tools, and other technologies at your disposal. The alternative technologies described in this chapter are HTML, Cascading Style Sheets (CSS), server programs, and plug-ins. In most cases, JavaScript can work side by side with these other technologies, even though the hype can make them sound like one-stop shopping places for all your interactive needs. (That's rarely the case.) Finally, you learn about the origins of JavaScript and what role it plays in today's advanced web browsers.

3

Competing for Web Traffic

Web page publishers revel in logging as many visits to their sites as possible. Regardless of the questionable accuracy of web page hit counts, a site consistently logging 10,000 dubious hits per week is clearly far more popular than one with 1,000 dubious hits per week. Even if the precise number is unknown, relative popularity is a valuable measure. Another useful number is how many links from outside pages lead to a site. A popular site will have many other sites pointing to it — a key to earning high visibility in web searches.

Encouraging people to visit a site frequently is the Holy Grail of web publishing. Competition for viewers is enormous. Not only is the Web like a 50 million–channel television, but also, the Web competes for viewers' attention with all kinds of computer-generated information. That includes anything that appears onscreen as interactive multimedia.

Users of entertainment programs, multimedia encyclopedias, and other colorful, engaging, and mouse-finger-numbing actions are accustomed to high-quality presentations. Frequently, these programs sport first-rate graphics, animation, live-action video, and synchronized sound. By contrast, the lowest-common-denominator web page has little in the way of razzle-dazzle. Even with the help of Dynamic HTML and style sheets, the layout of pictures and text is highly constrained compared with the kinds of desktop publishing documents you see all the time. Regardless of the quality of its content, an unscripted, vanilla HTML document is flat. At best, interaction is limited to whatever navigation the author offers in the way of hypertext links or forms whose filled-in content magically disappears into the web site's server.

Other Web Technologies

With so many ways to spice up web sites and pages, you can count on competitors for your site's visitors to do their darnedest to make their sites more engaging than yours. Unless you are the sole purveyor of information that is in high demand, you continually must devise ways to keep your visitors coming back and entice new ones. If you design for an intranet, your competition is the drive for improved productivity by colleagues who use the internal web sites for getting their jobs done.

These are all excellent reasons why you should care about using one or more web technologies to raise your pages above the noise. Let's look at the major technologies you should know about.

Figure 1-1 illustrates the components that make up a typical dynamic web site. The core is a dialog between the server (the web host) and the client (the browser); the client requests data and the server responds. The simplest model would consist of just the server, a document, and a browser, but in practice web sites use the other components shown here, and more.

The process begins when the browser requests a page from the server. The server delivers static HTML pages directly from its hard drive; dynamic pages are generated on-the-fly by scripts executed in a language interpreter, such as PHP, but likewise delivered by the server to the client, usually in the form of HTML markup. For example, a server-side database can store the items of a catalog, and a PHP script can look up those data records and mark them up as HTML when requested by the browser.

The downloaded page may contain the addresses of other components: style sheets, JavaScript files, images, and other assets. The browser requests each of these, in turn, from the server, combining them into the final rendering of the page.

A JavaScript program is inert — just another hunk of downloaded bits — until it's received by the browser, which validates its syntax and compiles it, ready for execution when called upon by the

HTML page or the human user. It's then part of the web page and confined to the client side of the sever-client dialog. JavaScript can make requests of servers, as we'll see later, but it cannot directly access anything outside of the page it's part of and the browser that's running it.

FIGURE 1-1

The components of a typical dynamic web site.

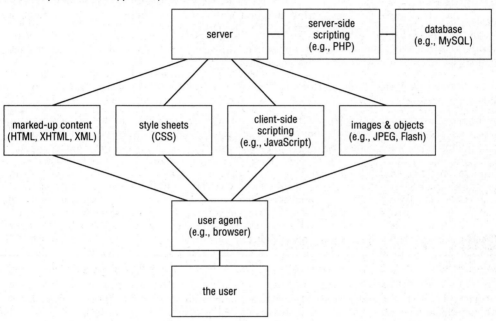

Hypertext Markup Language (HTML and XHTML)

As an outgrowth of SGML (Standard Generalized Markup Language), HTML brings structure to the content of a page. This structure gives us handles on the content in several important ways:

- Markup transforms a sea of undifferentiated text into discrete parts, such as headlines, paragraphs, lists, data tables, images, and input controls. Structure augments the meaning of the content by establishing relationships between different parts: between headline and subhead; between items in a list; between divisions of the page such as header, footer, and content columns. The semantics of a page are important to every reader: visual browsers for the sighted, vocal and Braille browsers for the visually impaired, search engines, and other software that parses the page, looking for a comprehensible structure.

- The browser transforms some marked-up structures into objects with particular behaviors. An image spills out rows of pixels in visually meaningful patterns. A form control accepts input from the user, while a button submits those form control values to the server. A hyperlink can load a new page into the browser window. These different types of objects would not be possible without some form of markup.

- The way a page is presented on screen, in Braille, or in speech, is determined by a style sheet that points to elements on the page and assigns appearance, emphasis, and other attributes. Every browser comes with a default style sheet that makes headlines, body text, hyperlinks, and form controls look a particular way. As web developers, we create our own style sheets to override the browser defaults and make our pages look the way we want. A style sheet tells the browser how to render the HTML page by referring to the document's markup elements and their attributes.

- Most importantly for the topic at hand, HTML markup gives JavaScript ways to locate and operate on portions of a page. A script can collect all the images in a gallery, or jump to a particular paragraph, because of the way the document is marked up.

Clearly, HTML markup and the way we handle it are critical to a document's structure and meaning, its presentation, and its successful interaction with JavaScript. While all the details of how best to use HTML are outside the scope of this book, it's clear that you'll want to hone your markup skills while you're learning JavaScript. Even the best script in the world can fail if launched on faulty, sloppy, or unplanned markup.

In the early years of web development, back before the turn of the century, in that medieval era now known as "the 90s," web designers didn't have much consciousness about markup semantics and accessibility. Pages were marked up in any way that would produce a desired visual presentation, relying on the default styling of the browser and without regard for the sensibility of the markup. A developer might choose an h4 tag simply in order to produce a certain size and style of font, regardless of the document's outline structure, or use data table markup for non-tabular content, simply to force the page layout to align. Required spaces and faux spacer images were mashed into the real content merely to tweak the appearance of the page: how things *looked* took complete precedence over what things *meant*. Fortunately, today that perspective seems quaintly old-fashioned, but unfortunately, there are still thousands of people producing pages that way and millions of pages left over from that dark era, their finger bones clutching at our sleeves and urging us to join them in their morbid pastime. It is one goal of this book to encourage you to code like a modern, living mammal, and not like a fossil.

Relegating HTML to the category of a tagging language does disservice not only to the effort that goes into fashioning a first-rate web page, but also to the way users interact with the pages. To our way of thinking, any collection of commands and other syntax that directs the way users interact with digital information is *programming*. With HTML, a web-page author controls the user experience with the content just as the engineers who program Microsoft Excel craft the way users interact with spreadsheet content and functions.

Version 4.0 and later of the published HTML standards endeavor to define the purpose of HTML as assigning context to content, leaving the appearance to a separate standard for style sheets. In other words, it's not HTML's role to signify that some text is italic but rather to signify *why* we might choose to italicize it. For example, you would tag a chunk of text that conveys emphasis (via the `<em>` tag) or to mark its purpose (`<span class="title">`) separately from the decision of how to format it with the style sheet. This separation between HTML markup and CSS presentation is an extremely powerful concept that makes the tweaking and redesign of web sites much faster than in the old days of inline styling and `<font>` tags.

XHTML is a more recent adaptation of HTML that adheres to stylistic conventions established by the XML (eXtensible Markup Language) standard. No new tags come with XHTML, but it reinforces the notion of tagging to denote a document's structure and content. While for several years XHTML was seen as the next stage of evolution of HTML toward the holy grail of a universal XML markup for documents, that promise has failed to deliver, in part because Microsoft, with its enormous share of the browser market, has consistently declined to accommodate XHTML served correctly as `application/xhtml+xml`. Nearly all XHTML documents today are served as `text/html`, which means that browsers treat them as just more HTML "tag soup." Perhaps the only advantage gained by using XHTML markup is the stricter set of rules used by the W3C HTML Validator (`http://validator.w3.org`), which checks to make sure that all tags are closed in XHTML documents, but isn't so fussy with HTML with its looser definitions.

For convincing arguments against the use of XHTML served as `text/html`, read "Sending XHTML as text/html Considered Harmful," by Ian Hickson (`http://hixie.ch/advocacy /xhtml`) and "Beware of XHTML," by David Hammond (`http://www.webdevout.net /articles/beware-of-xhtml`).

More recently, HTML5 has been growing in the Petri dishes of the World Wide Web Consortium (W3C). While modern browsers have only just begun to implement some of its features, HTML5 is considered by many to offer a more promising future than the seemingly abandoned XHTML. HTML5 offers an enriched vocabulary of markup tags compared to version 4, the better to align the markup language with the uses to which HTML is put in the real world.

Because HTML 4.01 is the prevailing markup language for the web today, the HTML samples in this book are compatible with HTML 4.01, except for those that illustrate newer HTML5 elements such as `canvas`. With the proper `DOCTYPE`, the samples should validate as HTML5. They are easily convertible to XHTML1.0 with a few simple transforms: change the `DOCTYPE`, add `lang` attributes to the HTML element, and close empty elements such as `input` and `link` with `/>`. It's our hope that this will make the samples useful to folks heading up either HTML or XHTML paths, and also make the book more future-friendly as HTML5 comes into its own.

Cascading Style Sheets (CSS)

Specifying the look and feel and speech of a web page is the job of Cascading Style Sheets (CSS). Given a document's structure as spelled out by its HTML markup, a style sheet defines the layout, colors, fonts, voices, and other visual and aural characteristics to present the content. Applying a different set of CSS definitions to the same document can make it look and sound entirely different, even though the words and images are the same.

(CSS 2.1 is the version of the W3C style sheet specification most widely supported by today's user agents. Aural style sheets that let us assign voices and other sounds to the markup of a web page are a module of the CSS 3 specification and, at this writing, are supported only by Opera and the FireVox extension to Firefox, although other browsers are sure to follow.)

Mastery of the fine points of CSS takes time and experimentation, but the results are worth the effort. The days of using HTML tables and transparent "spacer" images to generate elaborate multicolumn layouts are very much on the wane. Every web developer should have a solid grounding in CSS.

The learning curve for CSS can be steep because of the inconsistent support for its many features from one browser to the next. You can make your life much easier by triggering *standards mode* in the browser, whereby it adheres more closely to the W3C CSS specification. We recommend triggering standards mode by using a correct `DOCTYPE` at the top of your markup, such as one of these:

`HTML 4.01 Strict:`

```
<!DOCTYPE HTML PUBLIC "-//W3C//DTD HTML 4.01//EN"
    "http://www.w3.org/TR/REC-html40/strict.dtd">
```

`HTML 5:`

```
<!DOCTYPE html>
```

XHTML 1.0 Strict:

```
<!DOCTYPE html PUBLIC "-//W3C//DTD XHTML 1.0 Strict//EN"
    "http://www.w3.org/TR/xhtml1/xhtml1-strict.dtd">
```

For a clear explanation of DOCTYPE switching, read Eric Meyer's essay "Picking a Rendering Mode" (http://www.ericmeyeroncss.com/bonus/render-mode.html).

Server-side programming

Web sites that rely on database access, or change their content very frequently, incorporate programming on the server that generates the HTML output for browsers and/or processes forms that site visitors fill out on the page. Even submissions from a simple login or search form ultimately trigger some server process that sends the results to your browser. Server programming takes on many guises, the names of which you may recognize from your surfing through web development sites. PHP, ASP, .NET, JSP, and ColdFusion are among the most popular. Associated programming languages include Perl, Python, Java, C++, C#, Visual Basic, and even server-side JavaScript in some environments.

Whatever language you use, the job definitely requires the web-page author to be in control of the server, including whatever *back-end* programs (such as databases) are needed to supply results or massage the information coming from the user. Even with the new, server-based web site design tools available, server scripting is often a task that a content-oriented HTML author will need to hand off to a more experienced programmer.

Client-side JavaScript is not a replacement for server-side scripting. Any web site that reacts dynamically to user actions or that saves data must be driven by server-side scripting, even if JavaScript is used in the browser to enhance the user's experience. The reasons are simple: First, JavaScript itself cannot write to files on the server. It can help the user make choices and prepare data for upload, but after that it can only hand off data to a sever-side script for database updating. Second, not all user agents run JavaScript. Screen readers, mobile devices, search engines, and browsers installed in certain corporate contexts are among those that don't invoke JavaScript, or that receive web pages with the JavaScript stripped out. Therefore, your web site should be fully functional with JavaScript turned off. Use JavaScript to make the browsing experience faster, cooler, or more fun when it's present, but don't let your site be broken if JavaScript isn't running.

As powerful and useful as server-side scripting can be, its speed of interaction with the user is limited by the speed of the Internet connection between server and user agent. Obviously, any process that results in updating data on the server must include some client-server dialog, but there are many aspects of user interaction that, with the help of JavaScript, can take place entirely within the browser — form validation and drag-&-drop are two examples — then update the server when the response-sensitive process is complete.

One way that server programming and browser scripting work together is with what has become known as *Ajax* — Asynchronous JavaScript and XML. The "asynchronous" part runs in the browser, requesting XML data from, or posting data to, the server-side script entirely in the background. XML data returned by the server can then be examined by JavaScript in the browser to update portions of the web page. That's how many popular web-based email user interfaces work, as well as the draggable satellite-photo closeups of Google Maps (http://maps.google.com).

Working together, server programming and browser scripting can make beautiful applications together. You'll want to write in a server-side language such as PHP, or team up with someone who does, to lay the foundations for the JavaScript-enhanced pages you'll be creating.

Of helpers and plug-ins

In the early days of the World Wide Web, a browser needed to present only a few kinds of data before a user's eyes. The power to render text (tagged with HTML) and images (in popular formats such as GIF and JPEG) was built into browsers intended for desktop operating systems. Not wanting to be limited by those data types, developers worked hard to extend browsers so that data in other formats could be rendered on the client computer. It was unlikely, however, that a browser would ever be built that could download and render, say, any of several sound-file formats.

One way to solve the problem was to allow the browser, upon recognizing an incoming file of a particular type, to launch a separate application on the client machine to render the content. As long as this helper application was installed on the client computer (and the association with the helper program was set in the browser's preferences), the browser would launch the program and send the incoming file to that program. Thus, you might have one helper application for a MIDI sound file and another for an animation file.

Beginning with Netscape Navigator 2 in early 1996, software *plug-ins* for browsers enabled developers to extend the capabilities of the browser without having to modify the browser. Unlike a helper application, a plug-in can enable external content to blend into the document seamlessly.

The most common plug-ins are those that facilitate the playback of audio and video from the server. Audio may include music tracks that play in the background while visiting a page, or live (streaming) audio, similar to a radio station. Video and animation can operate in a space on the page when played through a plug-in that knows how to process such data.

Today's browsers tend to ship with plug-ins that decode the most common sound-file types. Developers of plug-ins for Internet Explorer for the Windows operating system commonly implement plug-ins as ActiveX controls — a distinction that is important to the underpinnings of the operating system, but not to the user.

Plug-ins and helpers are valuable for more than just audio and video playback. A popular helper application is *Adobe Acrobat Reader,* which displays Acrobat files that are formatted just as though they were being printed. But for interactivity, developers today frequently rely on the *Flash* plug-in by Macromedia (now owned by Adobe). Created using the Flash authoring environment, a Flash application can have active clickable areas and draggable elements, animation, and embedded video. Some authors simulate artistic video games and animated stories in Flash. A browser equipped with the Flash plug-in displays the content in a rectangular area embedded within the browser page. A variant of JavaScript called *ActionScript* enables Flash to interact with the user and components of the HTML page. Like JavaScript, ActionScript gets access to outside resources by making data-read and -write requests of the server. YouTube.com is a popular example of a web site with richly integrated Flash.

One potential downside for authoring interactive content in Flash or similar environments is that if the user does not have the correct plug-in version installed, it can take some time to download the plug-in (if the user even wants to bother). Moreover, once the plug-in is installed, highly graphic and interactive content can take longer to download to the client (especially on a dial-up connection) than some users are willing to wait. This is one of those situations in which you must balance your creative palette with the user's desire for your interactive content.

Another client-side technology — the Java applet — was popular for a while in the late 1990s, but has fallen out of favor for a variety of reasons (some technical, some corporate-political). But this has not diminished the use of Java as a language for server and even cellular telephone programming, extending well beyond the scope of the language's founding company, Sun Microsystems.

JavaScript: A Language for All

Sun's Java language is derived from C and C++, but it is a distinct language. Its main audience is the experienced programmer. That leaves out many web-page authors. Java's preliminary specifications in 1995 were dismaying. How much more preferable would have been a language that casual programmers and scripters who were comfortable with authoring tools such as Apple's once-formidable Hyper-Card and Microsoft's Visual Basic could adopt quickly. As these accessible development platforms have shown, nonprofessional authors can dream up many creative applications, often for very specific tasks that no professional programmer would have the inclination to work on. Personal needs often drive development in the classroom, office, den, or garage. But Java was not going to be that kind of inclusive language.

Spirits lifted several months later, in November 1995, when we heard of a scripting language project brewing at Netscape Communications, Inc. Born under the name *LiveScript,* this language was developed in parallel with a new version of Netscape's web server software. The language was to serve two purposes with the same syntax. One purpose was as a scripting language that web server administrators could use to manage the server and connect its pages to other services, such as back-end databases and search engines for users looking up information. Extending the "Live" brand name further, Netscape assigned the name *LiveWire* to the database connectivity usage of LiveScript on the server.

On the client side — in HTML documents — authors could employ scripts written in this new language to enhance web pages in a number of ways. For example, an author could use LiveScript to make sure that the user had filled in a required text field with an e-mail address or credit card number. Instead of forcing the server or database to do the data validation (requiring data exchanges between the client browser and the server), the user's computer handles all the calculation work — putting some of that otherwise-wasted computing horsepower to work. In essence, LiveScript could provide HTML-level interaction for the user.

LiveScript becomes JavaScript

In early December 1995, just prior to the formal release of Navigator 2, Netscape and Sun Microsystems jointly announced that the scripting language thereafter would be known as JavaScript. Though Netscape had several good marketing reasons for adopting this name, the changeover may have contributed more confusion to both the Java programming world and HTML scripting world than anyone expected.

Before the announcement, the language was already related to Java in some ways. Many of the basic syntax elements of the scripting language were reminiscent of the Java style. However, for client-side scripting, the language was intended for very different purposes than Java — essentially to function as a programming language integrated into HTML documents rather than as a language for writing applets that occupy a fixed rectangular area on the page (and that are oblivious to anything else on the page). Instead of Java's full-blown programming language vocabulary (and conceptually more difficult-to-learn object-oriented approach), JavaScript had a small vocabulary and a more easily digestible programming model.

The true difficulty, it turned out, was making the distinction between Java and JavaScript clear to the world. Many computer journalists made major blunders when they said or implied that JavaScript provided a simpler way of building Java applets. To this day, some new programmers believe JavaScript is synonymous with the Java language: They post Java queries to JavaScript-specific Internet newsgroups and mailing lists.

The fact remains that client-side Java and JavaScript are more different than they are similar. The two languages employ entirely different interpreter engines to execute their code.

Enter Microsoft and others

Although the JavaScript language originated at Netscape, Microsoft acknowledged the potential power and popularity of the language by implementing it (under the JScript name) in Internet Explorer 3. Even if Microsoft might prefer that the world use the VBScript (Visual Basic Script) language that it provides in the Windows versions of IE, the fact that JavaScript is available on more browsers and operating systems makes it the client-side scripter's choice for anyone who must design for a broad range of users.

With scripting firmly entrenched in the mainstream browsers from Microsoft and Netscape, newer browser makers automatically provided support for JavaScript. Therefore, you can count on fundamental scripting services in browsers such as Opera or the Apple Safari browser (the latter built upon an Open Source browser called KHTML). Not that all browsers work the same way in every detail — a significant challenge for client-side scripting that is addressed throughout this book.

JavaScript versions

The JavaScript language has its own numbering system, which is completely independent of the version numbers assigned to browsers. The Mozilla Foundation, successor to the Netscape browser development group that created the language, continues its role as the driving force behind the JavaScript version numbering system.

The first version, logically enough, was JavaScript 1.0. This was the version implemented in Navigator 2, and the first release of Internet Explorer 3. As the language evolved with succeeding browser versions, the JavaScript version number incremented in small steps. JavaScript 1.2 is the version that has been the most long lived and stable, currently supported by Internet Explorer 7. Mozilla-based browsers and others have inched forward with some new features in JavaScript 1.5 (Mozilla 1.0 and Safari), JavaScript 1.6 (Mozilla 1.8 browsers), and JavaScript 1.7 (Mozilla 1.8.1 and later).

Each successive generation of JavaScript employs additional language features. For example, in JavaScript 1.0, arrays were not developed fully, causing scripted arrays not to track the number of items in the array. JavaScript 1.1 filled that hole by providing a constructor function for generating arrays and an inherent `length` property for any generated array.

The JavaScript version implemented in a browser is not always a good predictor of core language features available for that browser. For example, although JavaScript 1.2 (as implemented by Netscape in Netscape Navigator 4) included broad support for regular expressions, not all of those features appeared in Microsoft's corresponding JScript implementation in Internet Explorer 4. By the same token, Microsoft implemented `try-catch` error handling in its JScript in Internet Explorer 5, but Netscape didn't include that feature until the Mozilla-based Netscape Navigator 6 implementation of JavaScript 1.5. Therefore, the language version number is an unreliable predictor in determining which language features are available for you to use.

Core language standard: ECMAScript

Although Netscape first developed the JavaScript language, Microsoft incorporated the language in Internet Explorer 3. Microsoft did not want to license the Java name from its trademark owner (Sun Microsystems), which is why the language became known in the Internet Explorer environment as

JScript. Except for some very esoteric exceptions and the pace of newly introduced features, the two languages are essentially identical. The levels of compatibility between browser brands for a comparable generation are remarkably high for the core language (unlike the vast disparities in object model implementations discussed in Chapter 25, "Document Object Model Essentials").

As mentioned, standards efforts have been under way to create industry-wide recommendations for browser makers to follow (to make developers' lives easier). The core language was among the first components to achieve standard status. Through the European standards body called ECMA, a formal standard for the language was agreed to and published. The first specification for the language, dubbed ECMAScript by the standards group, was roughly the same as JavaScript 1.1 in Netscape Navigator 3. The standard (ECMA-262) defines how various data types are treated, how operators work, what a particular data-specific syntax looks like, and other language characteristics. A newer version (called version 3) added many enhancements to the core language (version 2 was just version 1 with errata fixed).

The current version of the ECMAScript specification is known as ECMAScript, Fifth Edition, published online at www.ecma-international.org. To quote the ECMA, "The Fifth Edition codifies de facto interpretations of the language specification that have become common among browser implementations and adds support for new features that have emerged since the publication of the Third Edition. Such features include accessor properties, reflective creation and inspection of objects, program control of property attributes, additional array manipulation functions, support for the JSON object encoding format, and a strict mode that provides enhanced error checking and program security."

If you are a student of programming languages, you will find the document fascinating; if you simply want to script your pages, you might find the minutia mind-boggling.

All mainstream browser developers have pledged to make their browsers compliant with the ECMA standard. The vast majority of the ECMAScript standard has appeared in Navigator since version 3 and Internet Explorer since version 4, and as new features are added to the ECMA standard, they tend to find their way into newer browsers as well. The latest version of ECMAScript is version 5. The previous edition, the 3rd, has been supported in all mainstream browsers for the past few years.

Note
Even as ECMAScript, Fifth Edition was in the works, The Mozilla Foundation and Microsoft were implementing comparable versions of JavaScript 2.0 and JScript, respectively. An extension to ECMAScript called E4X (ECMAScript for XML) was finalized in late 2005 and is implemented in browsers based on Mozilla 1.8.1 or later (for example, Firefox 2.0). The Adobe ActionScript 3 language, which is used in the development of Flash animations, fully supports E4X. E4X is a significant addition to JavaScript because it makes XML (Extensible Markup Language) a native data type within the syntax of the language, making the processing of data in XML format much easier. XML is the data format used by many data exchange processes, including Ajax (see Chapter 39). ∎

JavaScript: The Right Tool for the Right Job

Knowing how to match an authoring tool to a solution-building task is an important part of being a well-rounded web site author. A web designer who ignores JavaScript is akin to a plumber who bruises his knuckles by using pliers instead of the wrench from the bottom of the toolbox.

By the same token, JavaScript won't fulfill every dream. The more you understand about JavaScript's intentions and limitations, the more likely you will be to turn to it immediately when it is the proper tool. In particular, look to JavaScript for the following kinds of solutions:

- Getting your web page to respond or react directly to user interaction with form elements (input fields, text areas, buttons, radio buttons, checkboxes, selection lists) and hypertext links
- Distributing small collections of database-like information and providing a friendly interface to that data
- Controlling multiple-frame navigation, plug-ins, or Java applets based on user choices in the HTML document
- Preprocessing data on the client before submission to a server
- Changing content and styles in modern browsers dynamically and instantly, in response to user interaction
- Requesting files from the server, and making read and write requests of server-side scripts

At the same time, it is equally important to understand what JavaScript is *not* capable of doing. Scripters waste many hours looking for ways of carrying out tasks for which JavaScript was not designed. Most of the limitations are intentional, to protect visitors from invasions of privacy or unauthorized access to their desktop computers. Therefore, unless a visitor uses a modern browser and explicitly gives you permission to access protected parts of his or her computer, JavaScript cannot surreptitiously perform any of the following actions:

- Setting or retrieving the browser's preferences settings, main window appearance features, action buttons, and printing capability
- Launching an application on the client computer
- Reading or writing files or directories on the client computer (with one exception: cookies)
- Writing directly to files on the server
- Capturing live data streams from the server for retransmission
- Sending secret e-mails from web site visitors to you (although it can send data to a server-side script capable of sending email)

Web site authors are constantly seeking tools that will make their sites engaging (if not cool) with the least amount of effort. This is particularly true when the task of creating a web site is in the hands of people more comfortable with writing, graphic design, and page layout than with hard-core programming. Not every webmaster has legions of experienced programmers on hand to whip up some special, custom enhancement for the site. Neither does every web author have control over the web server that physically houses the collection of HTML and graphics files. JavaScript brings programming power within reach of anyone familiar with HTML, even when the server is a black box at the other end of a telephone line.

Developing a Scripting Strategy

IN THIS CHAPTER

How leapfrogging browser developments help and hurt web developers

Separating the core JavaScript language from document objects

The importance of developing a cross-browser strategy

If you are starting to learn JavaScript at this point in the history of scriptable browsers, you have both a distinct advantage and a disadvantage. The advantage is that you have the wonderful capabilities of mature browser offerings from Microsoft, The Mozilla Foundation (under brand names such as Firefox, Netscape, and Camino), Apple, and others at your bidding. The disadvantage is that you have not experienced the painful history of authoring for older browser versions that were buggy and at times incompatible with one another due to a lack of standards. You have yet to learn the anguish of carefully devising a scripted application for the browser version you use, only to have site visitors send you voluminous email messages about how the page triggers all kinds of script errors when run on a different browser brand, generation, or operating system platform.

Welcome to the real world of scripting web pages with JavaScript. Several dynamics are at work to help make an author's life difficult if the audience for the application uses more than a single type of browser. This chapter introduces you to these challenges before you type your first word of JavaScript code. Our fear is that the subjects we raise may dissuade you from progressing further into JavaScript and its powers. But as developers ourselves — and some of us have been using JavaScript since the earliest days of its public prerelease availability — we dare not sugar-coat the issues facing scripters today. Instead, we want to make sure you have an appreciation for what lies ahead to assist you in learning the language. We believe that if you understand the big picture of the browser-scripting world as it stands today, you will find it easier to target JavaScript usage in your web application development and be successful at it.

Browser Leapfrog

Browser compatibility has been an issue for authors since the earliest days of the web gold rush — long before JavaScript. Despite the fact that browser developers and other interested parties voiced their opinions during formative stages of standards development, HTML authors could not produce a document that appeared the same, pixel by pixel, on all client machines. It may have been one thing to establish a set of standard tags for defining heading levels and line breaks, but it was rare for the actual rendering of content inside those tags to look identical on different brands of browsers on different operating systems.

Then, as the competitive world heated up — and web browser development transformed itself from a volunteer undertaking into profit-seeking businesses — creative people defined new features and new tags that helped authors develop more flexible and interesting-looking pages. As happens a lot in any computer-related industry, the pace of commercial development easily surpassed the studied progress of standards. A browser maker would build a new HTML feature into a browser and only then propose that feature to the relevant standards body. Web authors were using these features (sometimes for prerelease browser versions) before the proposals were published for review.

When the deployment of content depends almost entirely on an interpretive engine on the client computer receiving the data — the HTML engine in a browser, for example — authors face an immediate problem. Unlike a stand-alone computer program that can extend and even invent functionality and have it run on everyone's computer (at least for a given operating system), web content providers must rely on the functionality built into the browser. This led to questions such as, "If not all browsers coming to my site support a particular HTML feature, then should I apply newfangled HTML features for visitors only at the bleeding edge?" and "If I do deploy the new features, what do I do for those with older browsers?"

Authors who developed pages in the earliest days of the Web wrestled with these questions for many HTML features that we today take for granted. Tables and frames come to mind. Eventually, the standards caught up with the proposed HTML extensions — but not without a lot of author woe along the way.

Despite the current dominance of the Microsoft Internet Explorer browser on the dominant Windows operating system, the number of browsers that people use is not shrinking. Several recent browsers, including the modern Netscape, Firefox, and Camino browsers, are based on an Open Source browser called Mozilla. The Macintosh operating system includes its own Apple-branded browser, Safari (released in 2003). And the independent Opera browser also has a home on some users' computers. All of these non-Microsoft browser makers obviously believe that they bring improvements to the world to justify their development — building better mousetraps, you might say.

Duck and Cover

Today's browser wars are fought on different battlegrounds than in the early days of the Web. The breadth and depth of established web standards have substantially fattened the browser applications — and the books developers read to exploit those standards for their content. On one hand, most developers clamor for deeper standards support in new browser versions. On the other hand, everyday users care little about standards. All they want is to have an enjoyable time finding the information they seek on the Web. Most users are slow to upgrade, holding out until their favorite sites start breaking in their ancient browsers.

Industry standards don't necessarily make the web developer's job any easier. For one thing, the standards are unevenly implemented across the latest browsers. Some browsers go further in their support than others. Then, there are occasional differences in interpretation of vague standards details. Sometimes the standards don't provide any guidance in areas that are vital to content developers. At times, we are left to the whims of browser makers who fill the gaps with proprietary features in the hope that those features will become de facto standards.

As happens in war, civilian casualties mount when the big guns start shooting. The browser battle lines shifted dramatically in only a few years. The huge market-share territory once under Netscape's command came under Microsoft's sway. More recently, however, concerns about privacy and security on the Windows platform have driven many users to seek less vulnerable browsers. Mozilla Firefox has so far been the biggest beneficiary in the search for alternatives. Although a fair amount of authoring common ground exists between the latest versions of today's browsers, uneven implementation of the newest features causes the biggest problems for authors wishing to deploy on all browsers. Trying to define the common denominator may be the toughest part of the authoring job.

Compatibility Issues Today

Allow us to describe the current status of the compatibility situation among the top three browser families: Microsoft Internet Explorer, browsers based on Mozilla, and Apple Safari. The discussion in the next few sections intentionally does not get into specific scripting technology very deeply; some of you may know very little about programming at this point. In many chapters throughout this book, we offer scripting suggestions to accommodate a variety of browsers.

Separating the core JavaScript language from document objects

Although early JavaScript authors initially treated client-side scripting as one environment that permitted the programming of page elements, the scene has changed as the browsers have matured. Today, a clear distinction exists between specifications for the core JavaScript language and for the elements you script in a document — for example, buttons and fields in a form (see Figure 2-1).

FIGURE 2-1

The document object model is the programming interface between the HTML or XML document and the JavaScript programming language.

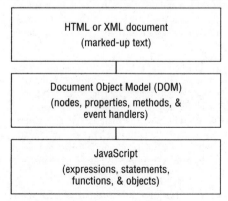

On one level, this separation is a good thing. It means that one specification exists for basic programming concepts and syntax that could become the programming language in any number of other environments. You can think of the core language as basic wiring. When you know how electric wires work, you can connect them to all kinds of electrical devices. Similarly, JavaScript today is used to wire together elements in an HTML document. Tomorrow, operating systems could use the core language to enable users to wire together desktop applications that need to exchange information automatically.

At the ends of today's JavaScript wires inside browsers are the elements on the page such as paragraphs (p), images (img), and input fields (input). In programming jargon, these items are known as *document objects*. By keeping the specifications for document objects separate from the wires that connect them, you can use other kinds of wires (other languages) to connect them. It's like designing telephones that can work with any kind of wire, including a type of wire that hasn't been invented yet. Today, the devices can work with copper wire or fiber-optic cable. You get a good picture of this separation in Internet Explorer, whose set of document objects can be scripted with either JavaScript or VBScript. The same objects can be connected with either of those two different sets of wiring.

The separation of core language from document objects enables each concept to have its own standards effort and development pace. But even with recommended standards for each factor, each browser maker is free to extend the standards. Furthermore, authors may have to expend more effort to devise one version of a page or script that plays on multiple browsers, unless the script adheres to a common denominator (or uses some other branching techniques to let each browser run its own way).

Core language standard

Keeping track of JavaScript language versions requires a brief history lesson. The first version of JavaScript (in Netscape Navigator 2) was version 1, although that numbering was not part of the language usage. JavaScript was JavaScript. Version numbering became an issue when Navigator 3 was released. The version of JavaScript associated with that Navigator version was JavaScript 1.1. The first appearance of the Navigator 4 generation increased the language version one more notch with JavaScript 1.2.

Microsoft's scripting effort contributes confusion for scripting newcomers. The first version of Internet Explorer to include scripting was Internet Explorer 3. The timing of Internet Explorer 3 was roughly coincidental to Navigator 3. But as scripters soon discovered, Microsoft's scripting effort was one generation behind. Microsoft did not license the JavaScript name. As a result, the company called its language JScript. Even so, the HTML tag attribute that lets you name the language of the script inside the tags could be either JScript or JavaScript for Internet Explorer. Internet Explorer 3 could understand a JavaScript script written for Navigator 2.

During this period of dominance by Navigator 3 and Internet Explorer 3, scripting newcomers were often confused because they expected the scripting languages to be the same. Unfortunately for the scripters, there were language features in JavaScript 1.1 that were not available in the older JavaScript version in Internet Explorer 3. Microsoft improved JavaScript in IE3 with an upgrade to the .dll file that gives IE its JavaScript syntax. However, it was hard to know which .dll is installed in any given visitor's IE3. The situation smoothed out for Internet Explorer 4. Its core language was essentially up to the level of JavaScript 1.2, as in early releases of Navigator 4. Almost all language features that were new in Navigator 4 were understood when you loaded the scripts into Internet Explorer 4. Microsoft still officially called the language JScript.

While all of this jockeying for JavaScript versions was happening, Netscape, Microsoft, and other concerned parties met to establish a core language standard. The standards body is a Switzerland-based organization originally called the European Computer Manufacturer's Association and now known simply as ECMA (commonly pronounced "ECK-ma"). In mid-1997, the first formal language specification was agreed on and published (ECMA-262). Due to licensing issues with the JavaScript name, the body created a new name for the language: ECMAScript.

With only minor and esoteric differences, this first version of ECMAScript was essentially the same as JavaScript 1.1, used in Navigator 3. Both Navigator 4 and Internet Explorer 4 officially supported the ECMAScript standard. Moreover, as happens so often when commerce meets standards bodies, both browsers went beyond the ECMAScript standard. Fortunately, the common denominator of this extended core language is broad, lessening authoring headaches on this front.

JavaScript version 1.3 was implemented in Netscape Navigator 4.06 through 4.7x. This language version is also the one supported in IE5, 5.5, and 6. A few new language features are incorporated in JavaScript 1.5, as implemented in Mozilla-based browsers (including Navigator 6 and later). A few more core language features were added to JavaScript 1.6, first implemented in Mozilla 1.8 (Firefox 1.5, and yet more to JavaScript 1.8 in Firefox 3).

In practice, so many browsers in use today support all but a few leading-edge features of the Mozilla browsers, that JavaScript version numbers are mostly irrelevant. Other compatibility issues with older browsers will likely get in your way before core language problems do. The time has come to forget about elaborate workarounds for the inadequacies of the oldest browsers.

Document object model

If prevalent browsers have been close to one another in core JavaScript language compatibility, nothing could be further from the truth when it comes to the document objects. Internet Explorer 3 based its document object model (DOM) on that of Netscape Navigator 2, the same browser level it used as a model for the core language. When Netscape added a couple of new objects to the model in Navigator 3, the addition caused further headaches for neophyte scripters who expected those objects to appear in Internet Explorer 3. Probably the most commonly missed object in Internet Explorer 3 was the image object, which lets scripts swap the image when a user rolls the cursor atop a graphic — *mouse rollovers,* they're commonly called.

In the level 4 browsers, however, Internet Explorer's DOM jumped way ahead of the object model that Netscape implemented in Navigator 4. The two most revolutionary aspects of IE4 were the ability to script virtually every element in an HTML document and the instant reflow of a page when the content changed. This opened the way for HTML content to be genuinely dynamic without requiring the browser to fetch a rearranged page from the server. NN4 implemented only a small portion of this dynamism, without exposing all elements to scripts or reflowing the page. It introduced a proprietary layering concept that was abandoned at the end of the Navigator 4.x lifetime. Inline content could not change in NN4 as it could in IE4. Suffice it to say that IE4 was an enviable implementation.

At the same time, a DOM standard was being negotiated under the auspices of the World Wide Web Consortium (W3C). The hope among scripters was that after a standard was in place, it would be easier to develop dynamic content for all browsers that supported the standard. The resulting standard — the W3C DOM — formalized the notion of being able to script every element on the page, as in IE4. But it also invented an entirely new object syntax that no browser had used. The race was on for browsers to support the W3C DOM standards.

An arm of the Netscape company called Mozilla.org was formed to create an all-new browser dedicated to supporting industry standards. The engine for the Mozilla browser became the basis for the all-new Navigator 6. It incorporated all of the W3C DOM Level 1 and a good chunk of Level 2. Mozilla 1.01 became the basis for the Netscape 7 browser, whereas Netscape 7.1 was built on the Mozilla 1.4 generation. In the summer of 2003, Netscape's parent company, AOL Time Warner, decided to end further Netscape-branded browser development. The work on the underlying Mozilla browser, however, continues under an independent organization called The Mozilla Foundation.

Mozilla-based browsers, and others using the same engine (such as Firefox and Camino), continue to be upgraded and released to the public. The Mozilla engine arguably offers the most in-depth support for the W3C DOM standards.

Even though Microsoft participated in W3C DOM standards development, IE5 and 5.5 implemented only some of the W3C DOM standard — in some cases, just enough to allow simple cross-browser scripting that adheres to the standard. Microsoft further filled out W3C DOM support in IE6, but chose to omit several important parts. Despite the long time gap between releases of IE6 and IE7, the latter included no additional W3C DOM support — much to the chagrin of web developers. IE8 finally did some significant catching up with the W3C DOM specification, with a switch to put IE8 back into IE7-compatibility mode for support of legacy scripts.

The Apple Safari browser has raced forward in its comparatively short life to offer substantial W3C DOM support. This is especially true of version 2, which was first released as part of Mac OS X version 10.4.

With this seemingly tortuous history of DOM development and browser support leading to the present day, you may wonder how anyone can approach DOM scripting with hope of success. Yet you'd be amazed by how much you can accomplish with today's browsers. You'll certainly encounter compatibility issues along the way, but this book will guide you through the most common problems and equip you to tackle others.

Laying a good foundation with markup

When the HTML markup on a page conforms to uniform public standards, browsers from different manufacturers tend to treat it similarly. However, in order to support the millions of web pages from past years, browsers also take a stab at guessing the author's intent when the markup differs from the specs. Because this sort of "guessing," for the most part, isn't prescribed in the HTML standards, the various browser manufacturers have come up with their own very different solutions. Therefore, you will get more consistent results and build more bullet-proof sites if your markup is easily parsable and error-free.

We encourage you produce markup that conforms to the W3C specification — for example, the HTML 4.01 spec at `http://www.w3.org/TR/html4/`. It's a good idea to rely on tools such as the W3C HTML Validator (`http://validator.w3.org/`) to check your markup against the standard. Beyond that, be consistent in your own work even when the spec is loose — for example, we suggest that you close all tags such as `td` and `li` even if the spec and the Validator don't require it. Examine and mimic the kind of markup produced by JavaScript using DOM methods, and you'll be doing fine.

Cascading Style Sheets

Navigator 4 and Internet Explorer 4 were the first browsers to claim compatibility with a W3C recommendation called *Cascading Style Sheets Level 1 (CSS1)*. This specification provided designers an organized way to customize the look and feel of a document (and thus minimized the HTML in each tag). As implementations go, NN4's had a lot of rough edges, especially when trying to mix style sheets and tables. But IE4 was no angel, either, especially when one compared the results of style sheet assignments as rendered in the Windows and Macintosh versions of the browser (developed by two separate teams).

CSS Level 2 adds more style functionality to the standard; IE6, Mozilla-based browsers, and Safari support a good deal of Level 2 (albeit unevenly) with the latest versions, such as Mozilla 1.8+ and

Safari 2+, and they are beginning to support CSS Level 3 features. Rendering of styled content is more harmonious among browsers, largely thanks to guidelines about how styles should render. Complex layouts, however, still need careful tweaking from time to time because of different interpretations of the standard.

JavaScript plays a role in style sheets in IE4+, Mozilla, and Safari because those browsers' object models permit dynamic modification to styles associated with any content on the page. Style sheet information is part of the object model and therefore is accessible and modifiable from JavaScript.

Standards compatibility modes (DOCTYPE switching)

Both Microsoft and Netscape/Mozilla discovered that they had, over time, implemented CSS features in ways that ultimately differed from the published standards that came later (usually after much wrangling among working-group members). To compensate for these differences and make a clean break to be compatible with the standards, the major browser makers decided to let the page author's choice of `<!DOCTYPE>` header element details determine whether the document was designed to follow the old way (sometimes called *quirks mode*) or the standards-compatible way. The tactic, known informally as *DOCTYPE switching,* is implemented in Internet Explorer 6 and later, Internet Explorer 5 for the Mac, and all Mozilla-based browsers.

Although most of the differences between the two modes are small, there are some significant differences between them in Internet Explorer 6 and later, particularly when styles or DHTML scripts rely on elements designed with borders, margins, and padding. Microsoft's original box model measured the dimensions of elements in a way that differed from the eventual CSS standard.

To place the affected browsers in CSS standards-compatible mode, you should include a `<!DOCTYPE>` element at the top of every document that specifies one of the following statements:

```
<!DOCTYPE HTML PUBLIC "-//W3C//DTD HTML 4.0 Transitional//EN"
        "http://www.w3.org/TR/REC-html40/loose.dtd">

<!DOCTYPE HTML PUBLIC "-//W3C//DTD HTML 4.0 Frameset//EN"
        "http://www.w3.org/TR/REC-html40/frameset.dtd">

<!DOCTYPE HTML PUBLIC "-//W3C//DTD HTML 4.0//EN"
        "http://www.w3.org/TR/REC-html40/strict.dtd">

<!DOCTYPE html PUBLIC "-//W3C//DTD XHTML 1.0 Transitional//EN"
        "http://www.w3.org/TR/xhtml1/DTD/xhtml1-transitional.dtd">

<!DOCTYPE html PUBLIC "-//W3C//DTD XHTML 1.0 Frameset//EN"
        "http://www.w3.org/TR/xhtml1/DTD/xhtml1-frameset.dtd">

<!DOCTYPE html PUBLIC "-//W3C//DTD XHTML 1.0 Strict//EN"
        "http://www.w3.org/TR/xhtml1/DTD/xhtml1-strict.dtd">

<!DOCTYPE html PUBLIC "-//W3C//DTD XHTML 1.1//EN"
        "http://www.w3.org/TR/xhtml11/DTD/xhtml11.dtd">
```

Be aware, however, that older versions of Internet Explorer for Windows, such as Internet Explorer 5 or Internet Explorer 5.5, are ignorant of the standards-compatible mode and will use the old Microsoft quirks mode regardless of your `<!DOCTYPE>` setting. Still, using the standards-compatible mode DOCTYPE is more likely to force your content and style sheets to render similarly across the latest browsers.

Dynamic HTML and positioning

Perhaps the biggest improvements to the inner workings of the Level 4 browsers from both Netscape and Microsoft revolved around a concept called *Dynamic HTML (DHTML)*. The ultimate goal of DHTML was to enable scripts in documents to control content, content position, and content appearance in response to user actions. To that end, the W3C organization developed another standard for the precise positioning of HTML elements on a page, as an extension of the CSS standards effort. The CSS-Positioning recommendation was later incorporated into the CSS standard, and both are now part of CSS Level 2. With positioning, you can define an exact location on the page where an element should appear, whether the item should be visible, and what stacking order it should take among all the items that might overlap it.

IE4+ adheres to the positioning-standard syntax and makes positionable items subject to script control. Navigator 4 followed the standard from a conceptual point of view, but it implemented an alternative methodology involving an entirely new, and eventually unsanctioned, tag for layers. Such positionable items were scriptable in Navigator 4 as well, although a lot of the script syntax differed from that used in Internet Explorer 4. Fortunately for DHTML authors, Mozilla, through its adherence to the CSS standard, is more syntactically in line with the DHTML style properties employed in IE4+.

Of more interest these days is the ability to modify the inline content of a web page without reloading the entire page. Fundamental standards from the W3C DOM Level 1 are supported by a wide range of browsers, including IE5+, Mozilla, Safari, and Opera. You can accomplish quite a lot using the same basic syntax across all of these browsers. Some challenges remain, however, as you'll see throughout this book.

Developing a Scripting Strategy

How do you create web pages that work well across the board? Browsers representing the latest generation contain a hodgepodge of standards and proprietary extensions. Even if you try to script to a common denominator among today's browsers, your code probably won't take into account the earlier versions of both the JavaScript core language and the browser DOMs.

The true challenge for authors is determining the audience for which scripted pages are intended. Each new browser generation not only brings with it new and exciting features you are probably eager to employ in your pages, but also adds to the fragmentation of the audience visiting a publicly accessible page. It can take months for the latest upgrade of a browser to supplant the previous version among its users, and some people seldom or never upgrade unless the new browser comes via a new computer or operating system upgrade. As a result, web developers are writing for an incredibly mixed audience of browser makes and models, including some of the latest mobile devices that don't support JavaScript. Add to that all the user agents that aren't visual browsers, such as screen readers and search engines. How to cope?

Graceful degradation and progressive enhancement

At this stage in the history of scriptable browsers, most web surfers arrive at our sites with browsers equipped with support for at least simple W3C DOM and DHTML capabilities. But "most" isn't everyone by a long shot, so it is our obligation to apply scripting in the additive, or value-added, manner known as *progressive enhancement*. By this we mean that your pages should convey their primary information to nonscriptable browsers designed for users with vision or motor-skill impairments, as well as less-feature-rich browsers built into the latest cellular phones. On top of that, your scripting efforts can give visitors with recent scriptable browsers a more enjoyable experience — better interactivity, faster performance, and a more engaging presentation. You will not only be contributing to the state of the art, but also carrying on the original vision of scripting in the browser.

In an early stage of the Web's evolution, many web site developers included the fancy features of the latest browser releases without much concern for folks who hadn't upgraded their browsers or switched from brand X to brand Y. This meant that a lot of new web sites were cosmetically — or, worse, functionally — broken for a lot of visitors. It was common to see banners explaining that "this website is viewed best in" such-and-such a browser, and it was left to the visitor to put up with the mess, or to install a new browser.

Over the years, web site producers have acquired two exciting new features that have changed our approach to browser support: the online business model and the social conscience. Excluding potential web site visitors from both commercial and non-profit sites is recognized as fiscally unwise. Excluding users of assistive technology is regarded as unjust — not to mention actionable in an increasing number of jurisdictions. As web developers, our concern isn't just a few obsolete browsers that can't run JavaScript. There are many other user agents that don't or can't support scripting, including search engines, some mobile devices, and some screen-readers and other assistive UAs. A lot of people simply turn off JavaScript support in their browsers. Some corporate firewalls strip JavaScript out of incoming web pages so that even entirely JavaScript-capable browsers within the organization do not see it or run it. Web stats are all over the map, but some estimates of the percentage of web site visitors who run without JavaScript for all of these reasons are 10% or higher. Even if it were only 1%, it would be significant. Imagine that you're holding the front door for customers at a physical storefront, and you choose to slam the door in the face of one out of every hundred people who approach. How long would you keep your job?

Graceful degradation is an approach to system design that provides fall-backs in case of failure. In web design, this means providing a lower level of appearance or functionality if the user agent can't handle any of the advanced technology that makes up the page. The problem with graceful degradation is the way it's been incorporated into site production. Developers who cut their teeth in the bad old days, and those who were trained by them, continued to build sites primarily for the most advanced and well-equipped browsers and then, as a final step or retrofit, tried to accommodate the rest. This approach adds a lot of work to the final stages of a project for the sake of a minority of users, so in the real world of web design, graceful degradation is often sacrificed due to all-too-common limits on time, money, and altruism. The result is an Internet full of web sites that still fail very *ungracefully* for a significant number of potential visitors.

Progressive enhancement is a newer approach that does justice to graceful degradation. A web site is first designed to run in all user agents, and then enhancements are added to make the user's experience faster or richer if they're using a more sophisticated browser. This ensures essential functionality for every reader (human or machine) and supports the fancy browsers without sacrificing the simpler ones. It puts the vegetable course before the dessert and the horse before the cart. It makes sure the car has a working engine before adding the chrome and the sound system.

One way we manifest the principle of progressive enhancement in our work is by building pages that work in the absence of JavaScript. This might seem like heresy in a JavaScript "Bible," but the bottom line is that JavaScript is one of many tools we use to accomplish our work. No single tool is so shiny and clever that it should upstage the real star of the show — the web site visitor.

Separation of development layers

Another important principle in modern web design is the separation of layers of development. The main layers we work with are the content of a page (such as text and image names), its structure in HTML markup, its behavior in JavaScript, and its presentation in CSS (see Figure 2-2). The more you can keep these layers separate, the easier it will be to build, modify, and re-use your work.

FIGURE 2-2

Four layers of client-side web development.

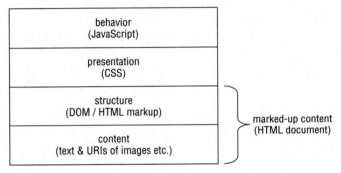

Old-school web pages are easy to spot: just look at the HTML source, and you'll see JavaScript and styling attributes embedded in the markup. This is like a house built with the wiring and pipes embedded in cement walls. If you want to change or replace the wiring, you've got a real mess on your hands. These cemented pages are redundant, since identical features on different pages require the same bloated markup to be downloaded each time. For that reason, they're also slower to download.

With separated layers, each component file is fairly trim and fast to download, and if the same style sheet or JavaScript script applies to more than one page, as is often the case, the response time is even faster since the browser caches (stores) files it has already fetched from the server. Web site development and redesign are also made more efficient because several people can work on different layers without stepping on one another's toes. It becomes possible to develop *modules* of markup, script, and style that can more easily be tweaked and re-used for future projects.

Separate development layers aren't unrelated. Just the opposite, in fact: the style sheet and JavaScript code refer to and depend on the HTML markup structure, tags, and attributes. They are hands whose fingers are designed to mesh perfectly, but they are still separate hands.

The first step in separating layers is literally to create separate files for your HTML, JavaScript, and CSS. (The HTML files you'll see in this book are already combinations of markup and content, which, in the everyday world of web production, are often a merger of HTML templates and database fields performed by a server-side script.)

Separation of layers is also an approach we can take to our scripting logic. JavaScript has the ability to write a chunk of cemented markup and text to a document in one operation, but if we separate the new structural elements from their content in our script, we end up with code that is easier to debug and re-use, and that contains fewer errors. Similarly, JavaScript can directly tweak the styling of an element on a page, changing its color or size or position, but instead, if we simply assign an id or class that is separately defined in the style sheet, then a graphic designer can change that presentation without anyone having to modify the JavaScript.

Further reading

Progressive Enhancement: Paving the Way for Future Web Design, by Debra Chamra
`http://hesketh.com/publications/articles/progressive-enhancement-paving-the-way-for/`

Graceful Degradation & Progressive Enhancement, by Tommy Olsson
`http://accessites.org/site/2007/02/graceful-degradation-progressive-enhancement/`

Progressive enhancement, in Wikipedia
`http://en.wikipedia.org/wiki/Progressive_enhancement`

Selecting and Using Your Tools

I n this chapter, you set up a productive script writing and previewing environment on your computer and learn where to find valuable resources on the Web. We also produce sample HTML, JavaScript, and CSS files to demonstrate how to use these tools to create real web pages.

Because of differences in the way various personal computing operating systems behave, we present details of environments for two popular variants: Windows (95 through XP) and Mac OS X. For the most part, your JavaScript authoring experience will be the same regardless of the operating system platform you use — including Linux or Unix. Although there may be slight differences in font designs, depending on your browser and operating system, the information remains the same. Most illustrations of browser output in this book are made from the Windows XP versions of Internet Explorer and Firefox. If you run another browser or version, don't fret if every pixel doesn't match the illustrations in this book.

IN THIS CHAPTER

How to choose basic JavaScript authoring tools

How to set up your authoring environment

How to enter a simple script to create a web page

The Software Tools

The best way to learn JavaScript is to type the HTML and scripting code into documents in a text editor. Your choice of editor is up to you, although we provide some guidelines for choosing.

Choosing a text editor

For the purposes of learning JavaScript in this book, avoid WYSIWYG (What You See Is What You Get) web page authoring tools such as FrontPage and Dreamweaver. These tools may come in handy later for molding your content and layout. But the examples in this book focus more on script content (which you must type anyway), so there isn't much HTML that you have to type. Files for all complete web page listings in this book (except for the tutorial chapters) also appear on the companion CD-ROM.

27

An important factor to consider in your choice of editor is how easy it is to save standard text files with an `.html` filename extension. In the case of Windows, any program that not only saves the file as text by default, but also enables you to set the extension to `.htm` or `.html`, prevents a great deal of problems. If you use Microsoft Word, for example, the program tries to save files as binary Word files — something that no web browser can load. To save the file initially as a `.txt` or `.html` extension file requires mucking around in the Save As dialog box. This is truly a nuisance.

Perhaps more importantly, a word processor such as Microsoft Word opens with a lot of default settings that may make desktop publishing easier but can frustrate a programmer, such as inserting spaces around words and automatically replacing straight quotes with curly quotes. Setting its defaults to make it programmer-friendly will make it less useful as a word processor.

Finally, we urge you not to create documents in Word and "save them as a web page." This will generate an HTML document that will look much like the word processing document on which it's based, but the actual HTML coding it produces will be bloated and redundant — a far cry from the sleek and elegant code that we hope you will be producing after you read this book. Word just isn't the right tool for this job.

Nothing's wrong with using bare-essentials text editors. In Windows, that includes the Word-Pad program or a more fully featured product such as Visual Studio or the shareware editor called TextPad. For Mac OS X, the bundled TextEdit application is also fine. Favorites among Mac HTML authors and scripters include BBEdit (Bare Bones Software) and SubEthaEdit (`www.codingmonkeys.de/subethaedit`).

Choosing a browser

The other component that is required for learning JavaScript is the browser. You don't have to be connected to the Internet to test your scripts in the browser. You can perform all testing offline. This means you can learn JavaScript and create cool, scripted web pages with a laptop computer — even on a boat in the middle of an ocean.

The browser brand and version you use are up to you. Because the tutorial chapters in this book teach the W3C DOM syntax, you should be using a recent browser. Any of the following will get you through the tutorial: Internet Explorer 5 or later (Windows or Macintosh); any Mozilla-based browser (including Firefox, Netscape 7 or later, and Camino); Apple Safari; and Opera 7 or later.

Note
Many example listings in Parts III and IV of this book demonstrate language or document object model (DOM) features that work on only specific browsers and versions. Check the compatibility listing for that language or DOM feature to make sure you use the right browser to load the page. ■

Setting Up Your Authoring Environment

To make the job of testing your scripts easier, you want to have your text editor and browser running simultaneously. You need to be able to switch quickly between editor and browser as you experiment and repair any errors that may creep into your code. The typical workflow entails the following steps:

1. Enter HTML, JavaScript, and CSS into the source documents in the text editor.

2. Save them to disk.

3. Switch to the browser.

    4. Do one of the following:

- If this is a new document, open the file through the browser's Open menu.
- If the document is already loaded, reload the file into the browser.

Steps 2 through 4 are actions you will take frequently. We call this three-step sequence the *save-switch-reload* sequence. You will perform this sequence so often as you script that the physical act will quickly become second nature to you. How you arrange your application windows and effect the save-switch-reload sequence varies according to your operating system.

In web site production, after you tweak your markup, style sheet, and scripts to your liking on your own computer, you'll upload them to your server using an FTP (File Transfer Protocol) program.

There are also online editors, but for now let's keep it simple. One of the advantages of doing your work off-line on your own computer is that you don't even have to have an active Internet connection during this stage of web site development.

Windows

You don't have to have either the editor or browser window maximized (at full screen) to take advantage of them. In fact, you may find them easier to work with if you adjust the size and location of each window so that both windows are as large as possible, while still enabling you to click a sliver of the other's window. Or, you can leave the taskbar visible so you can click the desired program's button to switch to its window (see Figure 3-1). A monitor that displays more than 800×600 pixels certainly helps in offering more screen real estate for the windows and the taskbar.

FIGURE 3-1

Editor and browser window arrangement in Windows XP.

In practice, however, the Windows Alt+Tab task-switching keyboard shortcut makes the job of the save-switch-reload steps outlined earlier a snap. If you run Windows and also use a Windows-compatible text editor (which more than likely has a Ctrl+S file-saving keyboard shortcut), you can effect the save-switch-reload sequence from the keyboard with your the left hand: Ctrl+S (save the source file), Alt+Tab (switch to the browser), and Ctrl+R (reload the saved source file).

As long as you keep switching between the browser and the text editor via Alt+Tab task-switching, either program is always just an Alt+Tab away.

Mac OS X

In Mac OS X, you can change between your text editor and browser applications via the Dock, or, more conveniently, by pressing ⌘+Tab. As long as you stay in those two applications, the other program is only one ⌘+Tab away (see Figure 3-2).

With this setup, the save-switch-reload sequence is a simple affair:

1. Press ⌘+S (save the source file).
2. Press ⌘+Tab (switch to the browser).
3. Press ⌘+R (reload the saved source file).

To return to editing the source file, press ⌘+Tab again.

FIGURE 3-2

Editor and browser window arrangement on the Macintosh screen.

Reloading issues

For the most part, a simple page reload is enough to let you test a revised version of a script right away. But sometimes the browser's cache (with its default settings) can preserve parts of the previous page's attributes when you reload, even though you have changed the source code. To perform a more thorough reload, hold down the Shift key while clicking the browser's Reload/Refresh button. Alternatively, you can turn off the browser's cache in the preferences area, but that setting may negatively affect the overall performance of the browser during your regular web surfing.

Validate, Validate, Validate

You can save yourself hours of debugging by checking to make sure your HTML is valid. If your markup is flawed, chances are your JavaScript and CSS will not work as expected, because they both depend on HTML elements (tags) and their attributes. The more closely your markup matches the industry-standard specs, the more likely it is that you'll get consistent results across browsers that are all approaching the holy grail of web standards conformance. You should always proofread your own code, of course, but an automated validation tool helps for large, complicated pages, and for programmers who are still learning all the rules for correct markup.

The World Wide Web Consortium (W3C), which wrote the HTML specification, has developed just such a validator. It checks a page with the rules specific to the DOCTYPE that begins the page. Besides catching our typos, an added advantage of running the Validator is that it helps us learn the fine points of HTML markup. Now repeat after me: The Validator Is My Friend.

The W3C Validator is at http://validator.w3.org/. It offers three ways to input your markup — by entering its online URL, by uploading the .html file from your computer, and by copying and pasting the markup into the Validator directly. Then, click the Check button and read the results. Often, a single error of markup will result in several items in the Validator error report. If it found any errors in your markup, make the necessary corrections and run your code through the Validator again until you get the green success banner.

Using the Validator will probably make you curious about the HTML specifications. You can read them on the W3C web site:

- **HTML 4.01:** http://www.w3.org/TR/html4/
- **HTML5:** http://www.w3.org/TR/html5/
- **XHTML 1.0:** http://www.w3.org/TR/xhtml1/

As time goes on, you'll discover other useful specs and validators out there, such as those for CSS (Cascading Style Sheets) and web accessibility guidelines:

- **CSS 2.1 Specification:** http://www.w3.org/TR/CSS21/
- **CSS Validation Service:** http://jigsaw.w3.org/css-validator/
- **Web Content Accessibility Guidelines:** http://www.w3.org/TR/1999/WAI-WEBCONTENT-19990505/
- **Web Accessibility Evaluation Tools:** http://www.w3.org/WAI/ER/tools/

Creating Your First Script

To demonstrate how we'll use these tools, let's create a classic "Hello, World" page in three stages: first as plain HTML, then augmented with JavaScript, and finally styled with CSS.

For the sake of simplicity, the kind of scripts we're building now are the kind that run automatically, immediately after the browser loads the HTML page. Although all scripting and browsing work here is done offline, the behavior of the page is identical if you place the source file on a server and someone accesses it through the web.

To begin, open your text editor and your browser. Also run Windows File Manager/Macintosh Finder to create a folder in which to save your scripts.

Stage 1: static HTML

Create a new text file and enter the markup in Listing 3-1.

LISTING 3-1

Source Code for hello-world.html

```html
<!DOCTYPE html>
<html>
   <head>
      <meta http-equiv="content-type" content="text/html;charset=utf-8">
      <title>Hello, World</title>
   </head>
   <body>
      <h1>Hello, World</h1>
      <p>This is HTML.</p>
   </body>
</html>
```

Save this file to your hard drive as `hello-world.html`, and open it in your browser. Figure 3-3 shows the page as it appears in the browser after you're finished. The precise appearance (or voice, if you're using a screen-reader) may vary slightly from one browser to the next, since at this point we're relying on the default style sheet in the browser to render the page.

The `head` of this page contains two required elements: a `meta` tag that declares the MIME type and character set, and a `title`. The `body` consists of a headline and a paragraph of text, pure and simple.

Stage 2: connecting with JavaScript

Now let's add JavaScript to the page. Create a new text file on your computer and enter Listing 3-2. Be sure and spell everything exactly, including upper- and lowercase:

LISTING 3-2

Source Code for hello-world.js

```javascript
var today = new Date();
var msg = "This is JavaScript saying it's now " + today.toLocaleString();
alert(msg);
```

FIGURE 3-3

The static HTML file displayed in a browser.

Save this file as `hello-world.js`. It consists of just three JavaScript statements: the first gets the current date, the second composes a brief message, and the third displays the message.

To enable this JavaScript program to act on your HTML document, add a new `script` tag to the `head` section of the HTML (shown highlighted in Listing 3-3):

LISTING 3-3

Revised Source Code for hello-world.html

```
...
  <head>
    <meta http-equiv="content-type" content="text/html;charset=utf-8">
    <title>Hello, World</title>
    <script type="text/javascript" src="hello-world.js"></script>
  </head>
...
```

The HTML `script` element tells the browser the type and name of the script file to combine with the document. Because the `src` (source) attribute doesn't include a path, the system assumes it's in the same folder as the HTML file. Unlike the `meta` tag, every `<script>` tag must be closed with `</script>`.

When you save the new JavaScript file and the modified HTML file, reload the HTML file in your browser. It should look something like Figure 3-4.

FIGURE 3-4

A JavaScript alert().

The text we passed to `alert()` appears in what's called a *modal dialog*. "Modal" means that you can't do anything more with the application (your browser) until you close the dialog. Notice that the HTML headline and paragraph seem to have disappeared! No worries; they will appear as soon as you click OK on the modal dialog. Why? The browser renders the HTML file from top to bottom. It encounters the `script` tag in the `head` and runs the named JavaScript program before it renders the HTML `body`. In this case, the modal dialog produced by the `alert()` method halts the rendering of the rest of the page until we respond.

Stage 3: styling with CSS

Let's add some styling to the page so that you can see how HTML and CSS interact. Create a new text file on your computer and enter Listing 3-4:

LISTING 3-4

Source Code for hello-world.css

```css
h1
{
    font: italic 3em Arial;
}
p
{
    margin-left: 2em;
    font-size: 1.5em;
}
```

Save this file to your hard drive as `hello-world.css`.

This style sheet applies a particular font and color to all the h1 elements on the page, and a left margin and font-size to all the p elements. Of course, in our document, there is only one of each.

To enable this style sheet to affect your HTML document, add a `link` tag to the `head` section of the HTML (shown highlighted in Listing 3-5):

LISTING 3-5

Revised Source Code for hello-world.html

```html
...
  <head>
    <meta http-equiv="content-type" content="text/html;charset=utf-8">
    <title>Hello, World</title>
    <script type="text/javascript" src="hello-world.js"></script>
    <link type="text/css" rel="stylesheet" href="hello-world.css">
  </head>
...
```

The `link` element tells the browser the type, relationship, and name of the style sheet to combine with the document. Note that, like the `meta` tag and unlike the `script` tag, `link` is an "empty" tag and does not take a separate closing tag. Because the `src` (source) attribute doesn't include a path, the system assumes it's in the same folder as the HTML file. Every `<script>` tag must be closed with `</script>`.

When you save these files and reload the HTML document in your browser (and click OK on that modal dialog), it will look something like Figure 3-5.

35

FIGURE 3-5

A styled page.

JavaScript Essentials

W hen first learning to use JavaScript in the context of the web browser environment, it can be easy to confuse the objects of the JavaScript language with the document objects that we control with JavaScript. It's important to separate the language from the Document Object Model (DOM) to help you make important decisions when designing JavaScript-enhanced pages. You may come to appreciate the separation in the future if you use JavaScript for other object models, such as in server-side programming or scripting Flash animations. All the basics of the language are identical from one context to another; only the objects differ.

This chapter introduces many aspects of the core JavaScript language, particularly as they relate to deploying scripts in a world in which visitors to your pages may use a wide variety of browsers. Along the way, you'll receive additional insights into the language itself. Fortunately, browser differences, as they apply to JavaScript, have lessened considerably as modern browsers continue to inch closer to consistently supporting the JavaScript (ECMAScript) standard. You can find details about the JavaScript core language syntax in Part III.

IN THIS CHAPTER

How to combine JavaScript with HTML

How to accommodate different versions of JavaScript

Language highlights for experienced programmers

Combining JavaScript with HTML

Scriptable browsers offer several ways to include scripts or scripted elements in your HTML documents. Not all approaches are recommended in today's best practices, but it's useful to learn even the old-school techniques so that you can understand legacy code when you come across it on the Web.

<script> tags

We marry JavaScript code to an HTML document using a `<script></script>` tag set that specifies the scripting language through the `type` attribute. You can have any number of such tag sets in your document. We recommend that all your scripts be external files linked to the HTML:

```
<script type="text/javascript" src="example.js"></script>
```

However, you can also embed JavaScript directly into the HTML by wrapping it in a `<script>...</script>` tag:

```
<script type="text/javascript">
// JavaScript code goes here
</script>
```

There are distinct advantages to linking external JavaScript to HTML rather than embedding the scripts directly in the markup. The principal of *separation of development layers* encourages us to keep different aspects of a document apart, typically in separate, linked files. Doing so facilitates cleaner development, faster downloads, and more modular, re-purposable code that can be much easier to modify than mixtures of technologies cemented together in a single file.

Linking to script libraries (.js files)

The advantages of linking to external JavaScript files become immediately obvious when the same script needs to run on more than one page of a site. If the script were embedded in the HTML markup, each page would be bloated with redundant content, and modifying the script would necessitate repeating the same changes in more than one file. In contrast, linking to an external file adds only a single line to each HTML file, and the external JavaScript file can be modified just once to immediately affect every page that includes it. Another plus is that, by separating the script code from the HTML document, you will not have to worry about comment-hiding or CDATA section tricks (see below).

Such an external script file contains nothing but JavaScript code — no `<script>` tags, no HTML. The script file you create must be a text-only file. Its filename extension can be anything, but the common convention is to use `.js`. To instruct the browser to load the external file at a particular point in your regular HTML file, you add a `src` attribute to the `<script>` tag as follows:

```
<script type="text/javascript" src="example.js"></script>
```

If you load more than one external library, you may include a series of these tag sets in the head of the document.

Notice that the `<script></script>` tag pair is required, even though nothing appears between them. Don't put any script statements between the start and end tags when the start tag contains a `src` attribute.

How you reference the source file in the `src` attribute depends on its physical location and your HTML coding style. In the preceding example, the `.js` file is assumed to reside in the same directory as the HTML file containing the tag. But you can just as easily link to JavaScript files located in other directories on your server or on other domains entirely. Just as with an HTML file, if you want to refer to an absolute URL, the protocol for the file is `http://`.

```
<script type="text/javascript" src="../scripts/example.js"></script>
```

```
<script type="text/javascript" src="http://www.example.com/example.js"></script>
```

(A critical prerequisite for using script libraries with your documents is that your web server software must know how to map files with the `.js` extension to a MIME type of `application/x-javascript`. Test your web server and, if necessary, arrange for server configuration adjustments. It is rare that a modern server will not correctly recognize `.js` files.)

When a user views the source of a page that links in an external script library, code from the `.js` file does not appear in the window, even though the browser treats the loaded script as part of the current document. However, the name or URL of the `.js` file is plainly visible (displayed exactly as it appears in your source code). Anyone can open that file in their browser (using the `http://` protocol) to view the `.js` file's source code. In other words, an external JavaScript source file is no more hidden from view than JavaScript embedded directly in an HTML file. Nothing that your browser downloads to render a web page can be hidden from view.

Specifying the MIME type & language

Every opening `<script>` tag should specify the `type` attribute. `script` is a generic element indicating that the contained statements are to be interpreted as executable script and not rendered as HTML. The element is designed to accommodate any scripting language that the browser knows — in other words, for which it contains an interpreter. For example, Internet Explorer carries interpreters for both JScript (Microsoft's version of JavaScript) and VBScript.

```
<script type="text/javascript" src="example.js"></script>
<script type="text/vbscript" src="example.vb"></script>
```

Both of these scripts will be interpreted by IE, but a non-VBScript-aware browser such as Mozilla will attempt to interpret only the JavaScript file.

Specifying the language version

It is rarely necessary to specify which version of JavaScript you wish to invoke in your documents. If your script relies on the objects and methods of a recent version of JavaScript that some older browsers won't support, it's better to test for that support directly. For example:

```
// if this browser isn't DOM-aware, exit gracefully
if (!document.getElementById) return;

// now it's safe to use the DOM method
var oExample = document.getElementById("example");
```

However, it isn't always possible to test for the existence of language features at run-time. If the new feature is built into JavaScript's syntax, its mere presence in the script can stop the interpreter from compiling the script to the point where it can't even execute an if-test.

For example, take the E4X syntax introduced in JavaScript 1.6 (see Chapter 20, "E4X — Native XML Processing"):

```
var xAuthor = <name>
                 <first>George</first>
                 <last>Sand</last>
              </name>;
```

If you include this syntax in a script run by a browser that doesn't "know" E4X syntax, the script will simply not run, in some cases with no meaningful error message to alert the visitor or the developer. No code in the same script will run, even if it's within the abilities of the browser.

You can isolate the new syntax with a version-specific `type` attribute for the `script` element:

```
<script src="example-all.js" type="text/javascript"></script>
<script src="example-1-6.js" type="text/javascript;version=1.6"></script>
```

or:

```
<script type="text/javascript">
    // script for all browsers goes here
</script>
<script type="text/javascript;version=1.6">
    // script for browsers that know JavaScript 1.6 and later
</script>
```

Be aware, though, that specifying the version as a special flag is non-standard so not all browsers support it. In the specific case of E4X syntax, Mozilla has introduced another special flag for the `type` attribute: e4x=1 meaning, essentially, "E4X support = true."

```
<script src="example-e4x.js" type="text/javascript;e4x=1"></script>
```

The practical question then arises: If you have to wall off part of your script from older browsers, what alternative code do you give to those older browsers in place of the new code? And if you're writing that work-around code, why not let that be the only code? What advantage is there in writing the same logic in two different ways in the same script? It's a question to ponder when working with leading-edge language enhancements.

The deprecated language attribute

The `type` attribute is required for the `<script>` tag as of HTML 4, formally published in 1998. Earlier browsers recognized the `language` attribute instead of `type`. The `language` attribute is *deprecated*, which means that it's an outdated feature of the language, has been replaced by newer constructs, and may become obsolete in future versions of HTML. Browsers continue to recognize it in order to support legacy web pages, but there's no reason to use it in industry-standard web sites today. We include it here so that you'll understand it when you encounter it in old markup.

The `language` attribute allowed the scripter to write for a specific minimum version of JavaScript or, in the case of Internet Explorer, other languages such as VBScript. For example, the JavaScript interpreter built into Navigator 3 knows the JavaScript 1.1 version of the language; Navigator 4 and Internet Explorer 4 include the JavaScript 1.2 version. For versions beyond the original JavaScript, you could specify the language version by appending the version number after the language name without any spaces, as in:

```
<script language="JavaScript1.1">...</script>
```

```
<script language="JavaScript1.2">...</script>
```

The `type` attribute didn't gain browser support until Internet Explorer 5, Mozilla, and W3C DOM-compatible browsers. If you need to inform even older browsers which language and version of scripting you're using, you can specify both the `type` and `language` attributes in your `<script>` tags, as older browsers will ignore the `type` attribute:

```
<script type="text/javascript" language="JavaScript1.5">...</script>
```

Of course, if you're depending on features in JavaScript 1.5, you've forgone legacy browsers anyway. In this case, just take the forward-looking approach and test for modern methods at the beginning of the script.

The proprietary for and event attributes

Internet Explorer versions 4 through 7 offered a variation on the `<script>` tag that bound statements of a script to a specific object and an event generated by that object. In addition to the `language` attribute, the tag must include both `for` and `event` attributes (not part of the HTML specification). The value assigned to the `for` attribute was a reference to the desired object. Most often, this was simply the identifier assigned to the object's `id` attribute. The `event` attribute was the event handler name that you wanted the script to respond to. For example, if you designed a script to perform some action upon a `mousedown` event in a paragraph whose ID was `myParagraph`, the script statements were enclosed in the following tag set:

```
<script for="myParagraph" event="onmousedown" type="text/javascript">
...
</script>
```

Statements inside the tag set executed only upon the firing of the event. No function definitions were required.

Because the `for` and `event` attributes were proprietary creations of Microsoft, this way of binding an object's event to a script guaranteed that only Internet Explorer would execute the script when the named event occurred.

Even in its day, the `script for` tag was not a winner. Its attributes constituted a lot of source code overhead for each object's script, so it was never a very efficient technique for linking script statements to multiple objects and events. In addition, non-Internet Explorer and pre-Internet Explorer 4 browsers would execute the script statements as the page loaded, making this proprietary language feature impractical in any cross-browser script.

Old-school inline JavaScript

Back in the bad old days of "tag soup" web development, it was common practice to insert JavaScript statements right in the HTML markup:

```
<select id="nations" name="nations" onchange="doSomething(this);">
```

In that example, the `change` event for the control object `nations` is set to trigger the JavaScript statements provided: a custom function call. We'll show you how this works elsewhere in the book to help you read legacy code, but combining markup and scripting like that today is commonly considered to be "very '90s."

There are many disadvantages to inserting JavaScript into markup this way: it's awkward and expensive to change the markup or the scripting independently when they're this intermeshed; the downloaded markup is unnecessarily bloated and doesn't take full advantage of the centralized modularity of externally linked scripts; and user agents running versions of JavaScript that can't handle the code are unable to avoid the script.

In a modern page, this markup would be cleaned up to

```
<select id="nations" name="nations">
```

with the event handler assigned entirely in JavaScript with something like

```
AddEvent("nations", "change", doSomething);
```

where the `AddEvent()` function can cater to a variety of event models in different browsers, can be entirely separate from the markup to protect user agents that can't handle scripting, and can be firewalled by defensive if-tests to protect it from legacy JavaScript interpreters that don't play well with modern code.

Accommodating the JavaScript-incapable user agent

There are several categories of user agent that can't or don't support JavaScript, representing, by some accounts, some ten to fifteen percent of all internet usage today. These user agents include search engine spiders, mobile device browsers, browsers inside government and corporate firewalls that strip out script for security reasons, assistive technologies, and browsers in which, for any of a variety of reasons, their users have turned scripting off. There is sure to be a small number of legacy browsers still in use today that cannot run JavaScript or that support very early versions, but the vast majority of non-JavaScript-using internet visitors are using contemporary hardware and software.

It is our responsibility as web developers to acknowledge that JavaScript is an option, not a given, and to ensure that our pages are functional even in its absence. It's our mission to use JavaScript to enhance the visitor's experience and not to supply critical elements without which a page would be broken or dead in the water. We make sure that the HTML markup provides all the fundamental content, hyperlinks, and form fields, and that server-side scripting completes the dialog between client and server that is the core of the HTTP request model. Then, when JavaScript is running, it can morph the page, pretty up the user interface, and quicken the response time. That is the win-win model of modern web scripting.

The question then comes, how can we add JavaScript to an HTML document in a way that leaves the page fully functional when the script interpreter is not running, not present, or packing an obsolete version? Our tactics are several:

- We begin our scripts by testing for the presence of modern DOM methods such as `document.getElementById` in order to turn away obsolete versions of the JavaScript interpreter.
- We export JavaScript to external files and link them to the HTML document with `script` tags. User agents not running a scripting interpreter won't even go there.
- Corollary to the above, we omit JavaScript from event attributes in HTML tags, and instead use JavaScript to assign event handlers to page elements.
- If it is ever unavoidable to include JavaScript in the HTML document itself, enclose the script in HTML comments so that it won't be rendered by not-script-savvy browsers.

Let's take a moment to expand on that last point.

Commenting out script in HTML

Non-scriptable browsers do not know about the `<script>` tag. Normally,
tags that they don't understand. That's fine when a tag is just one line of HTM.
`<script>...</script>` tag pair can enclose any number of script statement lines.
compact browsers don't know to expect a closing `</script>` tag. Therefore, their natural n.
is to render any lines they encounter after the opening `<script>` tag. Seeing JavaScript code spm.
out onto a page is sure to confuse or erode the confidence of any visitor.

You can, however, exercise a technique that tricks most non-scriptable browsers into ignoring
the script statements: surround the script statements (inside the `<script>` tag set) with HTML
comment markers. An HTML comment begins with the sequence `<!–` and ends with `–>`.
Therefore, you should embed these comment sequences in your scripts according to the
following format:

```
<script type="text/javascript">
<!--
script statements here
//-->
</script>
```

JavaScript interpreters know to ignore a line that begins with the HTML beginning comment sequence
`<!--`, but they need a little help with the ending sequence. The close of the HTML comment starts
with a JavaScript comment sequence (`//`). This tells JavaScript to ignore the line; but a non-scriptable
browser sees the ending HTML symbols and begins rendering the page with the next HTML tag or
other text in the document. An older browser doesn't know what the `</script>` tag is, so the tag is
ignored and rendering resumes after that.

Commenting out script in XHTML as character data

If your document is marked up with XHTML, the comment syntax is significantly different:

```
<script type="text/javascript">
<!--//--><![CDATA[//><!--
    // script statements here
//--><!]]>
</script>
```

That's quite a mouthful and deserves a bit of explanation.

XHTML parsers are intolerant of `<` symbols that don't begin elements and `&` symbols that don't begin
HTML entities, yet these characters are commonplace JavaScript operators. The solution is to encase
your script statements in what is known as a *CDATA* (pronounced "see-day-tah") section:

```
<![CDATA[
    XHTML permits any character here including < and &
]]>
```

We can then add the HTML comment markers to stop legacy browsers from rendering the
script:

```
<script type="text/javascript">
<!--<![CDATA[
```

```
        // script statements here
   //--]]>
   </script>
```

However, we can't stop here because XHTML also obeys the `<!--` and `-->` comment tags and an XHTML-aware browser will ignore the CDATA section and not execute the script. So, we have to close the comment tag before the CDATA begins in order to satisfy XHTML:

```
   <!-- --><![CDATA[
```

and use `//` comment syntax to make most HTML parsers ignore the rest of that line:

```
   <!--//--><![CDATA[
```

Some HTML parsers will treat the line after `//` as a comment and others will close the comment area with `-->`, so we have to make the CDATA open-tag not show up. The technique we're using is to make the HTML parsers think it's a closed tag

```
   <![CDATA[>
```

but to keep XHTML from considering it closed we'll add another comment marker

```
   <![CDATA[//>
```

and open the block comment tag once more to stop some browsers from attempting to render the JavaScript code as plain text:

```
   <!--//--><![CDATA[//><!--
```

Finally, the CDATA close-tag is commented out for HTML parsers:

```
   //--]]>
```

Whew! That's some of the fun web developers get to have when making multiple standards play nicely with one another. How much cleaner to simply export the JavaScript to an external file!

The noscript tag

The noscript element is the converse of script. A JavaScript-aware browser will render the contents of the noscript block if scripting has been turned off or if the browser doesn't support a scripting language invoked by a script element in the document. (Significantly, a legacy browser that doesn't support scripting at all and doesn't recognize script-related tags will likewise render the contents of both script and noscript blocks, which is why we comment out the contents of a script block. A noscript block will therefore be rendered by all browsers when scripting is not supported.)

You can display any standard HTML within the noscript tag set. It is a block-level element that can contain paragraphs, lists, divisions, headings, and so on.

The conventional use of noscript is to present HTML content to display in the absence of scripting support — a message such as, "This page would be more interesting if viewed with JavaScript running," for example, or an HTML hyperlink to a page that provides content that would otherwise be inserted by Javascript.

That use of `noscript` has commonly been superseded in recent years by the practice of providing only the non-scripting markup in the HTML, then replacing or enhancing that structure with scripting. Rather than telling visitors that they ought to upgrade their browsers or turn on scripting, we begin with the assumption that they're looking at our pages with a user agent that they need or want to use and give them decent, functional pages; then use scripting to give JavaScript-capable browsers a nicer page. It seems unlikely that there is anyone today using a browser with scripting deliberately turned off, or running behind a corporate firewall that strips out scripting, or using a mobile device with no scripting support, who isn't aware of the additional delights that the internet has to offer with the help of JavaScript. An admonition to upgrade may have been useful advice back in the '90s, but today it seems condescending and redundant.

Listing 4-1 is an example of presenting different content to scriptable and non-scriptable browsers. The HTML includes a plain paragraph that everyone will see and another inside a `noscript` element that will only be seen by user agents that don't support scripting, have JavaScript turned off, or are running an old JavaScript interpreter that's not DOM-aware. The accompanying JavaScript inserts another paragraph that will only be revealed by user agents with running JavaScript interpreters that are aware of the W3C DOM methods `appendChild()` and `createTextNode()`.

LISTING 4-1

Presenting Different Content for Scriptable and Nonscriptable Browsers

`HTML: jsb-04-01.html`

```html
<!DOCTYPE html>
<html>
   <head>
      <meta http-equiv="content-type" content="text/html;charset=utf-8">
      <title>Presenting Different Content for Scriptable and
      Nonscriptable Browsers</title>
      <script type="text/javascript" src="../jsb-global.js"></script>
      <script type="text/javascript" src="jsb-04-01.js"></script>
   </head>
   <body>
      <h1>Presenting Different Content for Scriptable and Nonscriptable
      Browsers</h1>

      <p>This text will be revealed to everyone.</p>

      <noscript>
         <p>Only user agents that don't or can't support W3C DOM
         scripting will reveal this text.</p>
      </noscript>

   </body>
</html>
```

continued

LISTING 4-1   *(continued)*

```
JavaScript: jsb-04-01.js
// initialize when the page has loaded
addEvent(window, 'load', addText);

function addText()
{
        // ensure a DOM-aware user agent
        if (!document.appendChild || !document.createTextNode) return;

    // create a text node
    var oNewText = document.createTextNode("Only DOM-aware user agents ↵
running JavaScript will reveal this text.");

    // create a paragraph
    var oParagraph = document.createElement('p');

    // insert the text into the paragraph
    oParagraph.appendChild(oNewText);

    // insert the paragraph at the end of the document
    document.body.appendChild(oParagraph);
}
```

Hiding scripts (not!)

A common question from beginning JavaScript programmers is how to hide scripts from visitors to a page, perhaps to protect a cherished bit of clever code. The short answer is that this isn't possible. In order to run, client-side JavaScript must be downloaded with the page, and therefore is visible in the browser's source view. The URL for an external linked script can simply be pasted into a browser's address bar.

If you are worried about other scripters stealing your scripts, you could include a copyright notice in your source code. Not only are your scripts visible to the world, but so are a thief's scripts. This way, you can easily see when someone lifts your scripts verbatim. Of course, there's nothing stopping someone from copying your script and deleting the notice of ownership.

The most you can hope for along these lines is to *obfuscate* your code, or make it difficult, time-consuming, and tiresome for a human to read. Obfuscation techniques include removing carriage returns and unnecessary spaces and tabs, using meaningless function and variable names, using variables to hold commonly named objects, using Boolean logic in place of if and other syntactical branching, writing self-generating code, using recursion, fragmenting logic sequences into multiple nested function calls, and encoding text in decimal, hexadecimal, or octal expressions. At the end of the day, however, global-replacement, careful reading, and patience can expose the logic of any text-based script. The most productive use of a JavaScript obfuscator is simply to produce a "compressed" copy of a script using as few characters as possible for fast download of enormous scripts. However, even that use is questionable since external scripts are cached by the browser after the first download.

If keeping your source code private is a great concern, consider using another programming language that compiles to machine code. Because of the existence of *disassemblers* that turn machine language back into source code, compiling can be viewed as just another form of obfuscation, but it will certainly reduce the number of people willing to put effort into decoding it.

However, it's nearly impossible to conceal anything significant. Even if they can't read your script, good programmers can look at the way your software behaves and write a fresh script that accomplishes much the same thing. The time you take to try to conceal your script could be spent writing new, exciting code!

We suggest that you consider flipping the paradigm on its head. Instead of attempting to conceal your programming code, flaunt it! Add helpful comments to the source code, publish it on your blog and on programming web sites, and otherwise assist as many people as possible to learn about and use it. (Add a Creative Commons license to encourage people to copy your code and keep it free for public use.) If you gain a reputation as a clever and helpful programmer, people will come to you for more.

Scripting for different browsers

Cross-browser compatibility is a concern for every JavaScript programmer. Even though the most recent browsers are doing a decent job of providing a workable lowest common denominator of scriptability, you will still have to consider a range of JavaScript support, from the most advanced browser to the least. Even the differences between the latest Firefox and the latest Internet Explorer are significant. Planning for compatibility begins with deciding on your goals for various classes of user agent.

Building the foundation beneath the towers

The purpose of most web pages can be boiled down to "delivering particular content." Where one web site differs from another is the specific content being delivered and its "look and feel" — the graphic appearance of the page and the style of the user interface with which visitors request further information.

The principal of progressive enhancement guides us first to deliver the content from the server to the client in HTML markup, without relying on JavaScript for core functionality. A web site should be fully usable and navigable, with all its public content exposed to all user agents, including those that don't support scripting ... such as search engines! After that, we use JavaScript to enhance the visitor's experience and make it faster, easier, more attractive, or more fun in browsers with JavaScript enabled.

One of the consequences of considering JavaScript last instead of first in the planning process is that we'll often discover that much of a web site's functionality that we might have expected to hand over to JavaScript is instead handled perfectly well by other, more universally supported technologies. We should ask JavaScript to perform only those functions that are outside the reach of core browser functionality such as HTML rendering and CSS styling. For example, navigation links should be marked up as functional hyperlinks regardless of whether JavaScript adds any spice to the mix. Multi-level menus, pop-up dialogs, and roll-over image changes can often be implemented using just HTML and CSS, and therefore work for a broader audience.

Ajax (Asynchronous JavaScript and XML) is an interesting case in point. Often developers and even clients will choose Ajax to deliver content just because it's perceived to be sexy technology, but without pausing to consider whether it's really more useful, faster, or more effective than normal page navigation. Reading content from the server takes a certain amount of time regardless; if all the images on a page are already downloaded and therefore cached, it's only the HTML markup that will be the overhead of reading a new page, and that can be the smallest slice of a page. Navigating to individual pages to reveal different content means that visitors can easily bookmark and share links to specific chunks of content, which isn't normally true of Ajax-retrieved content. Just because we *can* use JavaScript for a particular purpose doesn't mean we have to or should.

Once the core page or site is planned in detail using server-side technologies and HTML/CSS downloads, we can plot out the remainder of the user interface with JavaScript — the sweet dessert that follows the entrée!

JavaScript can be used to add animation to an otherwise static presentation, replace a navigation link with an Ajax download of additional content, augment a button-click editing process with drag-and-drop, fancify a form, and so on. While adding these nice-to-haves, make sure that all the content you're providing through JavaScript is also accessible without scripting. If you find yourself adding critical content to the site that can only been retrieved using JavaScript, you know that you've gone too far. Step back, add the new content to the core web site, then resume your JavaScript planning.

Choosing your battles

Any public web site can, and ultimately will, be viewed using every sort of user agent in existence. Because the range of JavaScript support is so broad — ranging from Early Primitive to Leading Edge — it can be quite challenging, verging on impossible, to write for every browser that's got a JavaScript interpreter. Part of web development planning can therefore be viewed as 'choosing your battles' or a kind of triage — drawing the line between interpreters you'll support and those you won't, and language features you'll use and those you'll avoid. According to this approach, instead of spending time trying to write script that will run in ancient browsers, simply block them from the playing field and focus your attention on developing code for the modern ones.

If, as we recommend, you've engineered your site so that all the core content and functionality are provided by HTML delivered from the server, you won't have to feel negligent if you prevent legacy browsers from trying to run your script. Relax — everyone will be able to use your site. By limiting the JavaScript interpreters you support to the current crop of modern ones and shutting out the older ones, you can save yourself hours of painstaking development work for a small minority of visitors, a decision that can salvage your deadline, your budget, and your sanity.

For example, most of the scripts in this book begin with the simple if-test

```
if (!document.getElementById) return;
```

In other words, "if the JavaScript interpreter running in this browser does not know about the getElementById method of the document object, stop running this script." This one statement shuts out interpreters that are too old to know about modern Document Object Model methods, allowing you to write most of your code for a single audience. At the other end of the spectrum, you may wish to avoid, for now, using leading-edge JavaScript syntax such as E4X that will stop most current browsers cold in their tracks. The middle ground — ECMAScript 3- and W3C DOM2-aware browsers — constitutes the vast majority in use today, and presents a very comfortable compromise with relatively consistent language support.

In planning your application or web site, it makes far more sense to deliver a single stream of content that can be viewed through all user agents rather than duplicating content in different modes. The latter approach was sometimes used in years past, for a site using frames and a parallel no-frames version, for example. In case you have a notion of creating an application or site that has multiple paths for viewing the same content, don't forget that maintenance chores lie ahead as the site evolves. Will you have the time, budget, and inclination to keep all paths up to date? Despite whatever good intentions a designer of a new web site may have, in our experience, the likelihood that a site will be maintained properly diminishes rapidly with the complexity of the maintenance task.

That said, providing multiple channels does not necessarily mean a duplication of effort. A site may be marked up to navigate to separate pages to deliver different content, but when scripting is supported the site could deliver the same content using Ajax. Since both apparent channels of content come from the server, we could use Ajax to request the same data stream that each stand-alone page requests. When the data is changed on the server, say, by modifying text in a database, both the stand-alone page and the Ajax content injection change accordingly.

Object detection

The methodology of choice by far for implementing browser version branching is *object detection*. The principle is simple: If an object type exists in the browser's object model, it is safe to execute script statements that work with that object.

One example of object detection that you'll see in a lot of older scripts uses the images collection. A script can change the src attribute of an image — effectively replacing it with another image read from the server — only if the version of JavaScript running in the browser recognizes images as objects. Object models that implement images always include an array of image objects belonging to the document object. The document.images array always exists, even with a length of zero when no images are on the page. Therefore, if you wrap the image-swapping statements inside an if construction that lets browsers pass only if the document.images array exists, older browsers simply skip the statements:

```
function imageSwap(imgName, url)
{
    if (document.images)
    {
        document.images[imgName].src = url;
    }
}
```

Object detection works best when you use it to test for the same object you need to use. It can get you into trouble when you use it to make assumptions about browser version and support for language features other than the one being tested.

For example, Internet Explorer 4 introduced a document object array called document.all, which is used very frequently in building references to HTML element objects. Netscape Navigator 4, however, did not implement that array; instead, it had a document-level array object called layers, which was not implemented in Internet Explorer 4. Unfortunately, many scripters used the existence of these array objects not as prerequisites for addressing those objects, but as determinants for the browser version. They set global variables signifying a minimum version of Internet Explorer 4 if document.all existed and Netscape Navigator 4 if document.layers existed. This was dangerous because there was no way of knowing whether a future version of a browser might adopt the object of the other browser brand or eliminate a language feature. In fact, when the Mozilla-based Netscape version first arrived, it did indeed remove all the layers stuff, replacing it with W3C standards-based features. Tons of scripts on the web used the existence of document.layers to branch to Netscape-friendly code that didn't even use document.layers. Thus, visitors using Netscape 6 or 7 found that scripts either broke or didn't work, even though the browsers were more than capable of doing the job.

This is why we recommend object detection, not for browser version sniffing, but for object availability branching, as previously shown for images. Moreover, it is safest to implement object detection only when all major browser brands (and the W3C DOM recommendation) have adopted the object so that behavior is predictable wherever your page loads in the future.

49

Techniques for object detection include testing for the availability of an object's method. A reference to an object's method returns a value, so such a reference can be used in a conditional statement. For example, the following code fragment demonstrates how a function can receive an argument containing the string ID of an element and convert the string to a valid object reference for three different DOMs:

```
function myFunc(elemID)
{
    var obj;
        if (document.getElementById)
        {
            obj = document.getElementById(elemID);
        }
        else if (document.all)
        {
            obj = document.all(elemID);
        }
        else if (document.layers)
        {
            obj = document.layers[elemID];
        }

        if (obj)
        {
            // statements that work on the object
        }
}
```

With this object detection scheme, it doesn't matter which browser brand, version, or operating system support a particular way of changing an element ID to an object reference. Whichever `document` object property or method is supported by the browser (or the first one, if the browser supports more than one), that is the property or method used to accomplish the conversion. If the browser supports none of them, no further statements execute in this function. Keep in mind, however, that the first approach in this example is sufficient (and recommended) as the technique for obtaining all objects from an ID in modern browsers.

If your script wants to check for the existence of an object's property or method, you may also have to check for the existence of the object beforehand, if that object is not part of all browsers' object models. An attempt to reference a property of a nonexistent object in a conditional expression generates a script error. To prevent the error, you can cascade the conditional tests with the help of the && operator. The following fragment tests for the existence of both the `document.body` object and the `document.body.style` property:

```
if (document.body && document.body.style)
{
    // statements that work on the body's style property
}
```

This is the functional equivalent of:

```
if (document.body)
{
```

```
        if (document.body.style)
        {
            // statements that work on the body's style property
        }
    }
```

In both examples, if the test for `document.body` fails, JavaScript bypasses the second test.

One potential "gotcha" in using conditional expressions to test for the existence of an object's property is that if the property exists, but its value is zero or an empty string, the conditional test responds the same as it would if the property did not exist. To work around this potential problem, the conditional expression can examine the data type of the value to ensure that the property genuinely exists. A nonexistent property for an object reports a data type of `undefined`. Use the `typeof` operator (discussed in Chapter 22, "JavaScript Operators") to test for a valid property:

```
    if (document.body && typeof document.body.scroll != "undefined")
    {
        // statements that work on the body's scroll property
    }
```

We wholeheartedly recommend designing your scripts to take advantage of object detection in lieu of branching on particular browser name strings and version numbers. Scriptable features are gradually finding their way into browsers embedded in a wide range of nontraditional computing devices. These browsers may not go by the same names and numbering systems that we know today, yet such browsers may be able to interpret your scripts. By testing for browser functionality, your scripts will likely require less maintenance in the future.

Browser version detection

Years ago, before object detection caught on, the commonplace way to pilot a script through the rocky shoals of language support was *browser sniffing*. As described more fully in Chapter 42, "The Navigator and Other Environment Objects," your scripts can examine the `navigator` object to discover which make and model the current browser claims to be. After examining the browser's purported name and version number, a script can branch to different bits of logic specific to the various browsers available at the time. We don't use this technique any more, chiefly because browsers can and do lie about what they are, because browser version sniffing isn't future-proof, and because it's a hack — it tests for one thing in order to act on another.

Browser sniffing is like letting someone fly a jet because they say they're a pilot. They might not actually be a pilot just because they claim to be, and even if they are, they might have gotten their pilot's license before jets were invented. In contrast, with object detection, you find out if they know how to fly the particular aircraft at hand and you let them fly it only if they can — simple, direct, and foolproof.

Designing for Compatibility

Each new major release of a browser brings compatibility problems for page authors. It's not so much that old scripts break in the new versions (well-written scripts rarely break in new versions). The problems center on the new features that attract designers when the designers

51

forget to accommodate visitors who have not yet advanced to the latest and greatest browser version or who don't share your browser brand preference.

Catering only to the lowest common denominator can more than double your development time, due to the expanded testing matrix necessary to ensure a good working page in all operating systems and on all versions. Decide how important the scripted functionality you employ in a page is for every user. If you want some functionality that works only in a later browser, you may have to be a bit autocratic in defining the minimum browser for scripted access to your page; any lesser browser gets shunted to a simpler presentation of your site's data.

Another possibility is to make a portion of the site accessible to most, if not all, browsers, and restrict the scripting to the occasional enhancement that non-scriptable browser users won't miss. When the application reaches a certain point in the navigation flow, the user needs a more capable browser to get to the really good stuff. This kind of design is a carefully planned strategy that lets the site welcome all users up to a point, but then enables the application to shine for users of, say, W3C DOM–compatible browsers.

The ideal page is one that displays useful content in any browser but whose scripting enhances the experience of the page visitor — perhaps by offering more efficient site navigation or interactivity with the page's content. That is certainly a worthy goal to aspire to. But even if you can achieve this ideal on only some pages, you will reduce the need for defining entirely separate, difficult-to-maintain paths for browsers of varying capabilities.

Regardless of your specific browser compatibility strategy, the good news is that time tends to minimize the problem. Web standards have solidified greatly in the past few years, and browser vendors have made significant strides toward fully supporting those standards.

Dealing with beta browsers

If you have crafted a skillfully scripted web page or site, you may be concerned when a prerelease (or *beta*) version of a browser available to the public causes script errors or other compatibility problems to appear on your page. Do yourself a favor: Don't overreact to bugs and errors that occur in prerelease browser versions. If your code is well written, it should work with any new generation of browser. If the code doesn't work correctly, consider the browser to be buggy. Report the bug (preferably with a simplified test-case script sample) to the browser maker.

One exception to the "it's a beta bug" rule arose in the transition from Netscape Navigator 4 to the Mozilla engine (first released as Netscape Navigator 6). A conscious effort to eliminate a proprietary Netscape Navigator 4 feature (the <layer> tag and corresponding scriptable object) caused many Netscape Navigator 4 scripts to break on Moz1 betas (and final release). Had scripters reported the problem to the new browsers' developer (Mozilla), they would have learned about the policy change and planned for the new implementation. It is extremely rare for a browser to eliminate a popular feature so quickly, but it can happen. Stronger web standards have probably minimized the chances of this situation happening again any time soon.

It is often difficult to prevent yourself from getting caught up in a browser maker's enthusiasm for a new release. But remember that a prerelease version is not a shipping version. Users who visit your page with prerelease browsers should know that there may be bugs in the browser. That your code does not work with a prerelease version is not a sin; neither is it worth losing sleep over. Just be sure to connect with the browser's maker either to find out whether the problem will continue in the final release or to report the bug so that the problem doesn't make it into the release version.

Compatibility ratings in reference chapters

With the proliferation of scriptable browser versions since Navigator 2, it is important to know up front whether a particular language or object model, property, method, or event handler is supported in the lowest common denominator for which you are designing. Therefore, in this book, we include frequent compatibility ratings, such as the following example:

Compatibility: WinIE5+, MacIE5+, NN4+, Moz+, Safari+, Opera+, Chrome+

A plus sign after a browser version number means that the language feature was first implemented in the numbered version and continues to be supported in succeeding versions. A minus sign means that the feature is not supported in that browser. The browsers tested for compatibility include Internet Explorer for Windows and Macintosh, Netscape Navigator, Mozilla (including all browsers based on the Mozilla engine), Apple Safari, Opera, and Google Chrome. We also recommend that you print the JavaScript and Browser Object Quick Reference file shown in Appendix A. The file is on the companion CD-ROM in PDF format. This quick reference clearly shows each object's properties, methods, and event handlers, along with keys to the browser version in which each language item is supported. You should find the printout to be valuable as a day-to-day resource.

This is a great place to clarify what we mean by "all browsers based on the Mozilla engine." Once upon a time, *Mozilla* pretty much meant *Netscape*, but those days are long gone. Now there are several viable Mozilla-based browsers that fall under the Moz+ designation in the compatibility charts throughout this book, including Netscape, Firefox, Camino, SeaMonkey, Flock, and others.

Here we're using "Mozilla" to refer to the Gecko (née NGLayout) layout engine. The numbering systems of the individual browser brands are not synchronized to the underlying Mozilla engine versions, making it difficult to know exactly which browser supports what feature. The following table shows which individual browser brands and versions correspond to the Mozilla engine numbering system:

Mozilla	Netscape	Firefox	Camino
m18	6.0		
0.9.2	6.1		
0.9.4	6.2		
1.0.1	7.0		
1.2b		0.1	
1.3a		0.5	
1.4	7.1		
1.5		0.7	
1.7		1.0	
1.7.2	7.2		
1.7.5	8.0–8.1		
1.8		1.5	1.0
1.8.1	9.0	2.0	1.6.5

Mozilla	Netscape	Firefox	Camino
1.9		3.0	2.0
1.9.1		3.5	
1.9.2		3.6	
1.9.3		3.7	
2.0		4.0	

As you can see, Netscape 6.0 and 6.2 were based on Mozilla versions of less than 1. It is rare to see either of these versions "in the wild" these days. The focus, therefore, is on Moz1 and later. Thus, the compatibility charts use Moz1 as the baseline feature set.

In summary, when you see Moz+ in the compatibility charts, it ultimately resolves to Netscape 7 or later, Firefox 1 or later, and Camino 1 or later, to name the most popular Mozilla-based browsers currently in use.

Language Essentials for Experienced Programmers

In this section, experienced programmers can read the highlights about the core JavaScript language in terms that may not make complete sense to those with limited or no scripting experience. Here, then, is the quick tour of the essential issues surrounding the core JavaScript language:

- **JavaScript is a scripting language.** The language is intended for use in an existing *host environment* (for example, a web browser) that exposes objects whose properties and behaviors are controllable via statements written in the language. Scripts execute within the context of the host environment. The host environment controls which, if any, external environmental objects may be addressed by language statements running in the host environment. For security and privacy reasons, web browsers generally afford little or no direct access through JavaScript to browser preferences, the operating system, or other programs beyond the scope of the browser. The exception to this rule is that modern browsers allow deeper client access (with the user's permission) through trust mechanisms such as signed scripts (Mozilla) or trusted ActiveX controls (Microsoft).

- **JavaScript is object based.** Although JavaScript exhibits many syntactic parallels with the Java language, JavaScript is not as pervasively object-oriented as Java. The core language includes several built-in static objects from which working objects are generated. Objects are created through a call to a constructor function for any of the built-in objects plus the new operator. For example, the following expression generates a String object and returns a reference to that object:

```
new String("Hello");
```

Table 4-1 lists the built-in objects with which scripters come into contact.

TABLE 4-1

JavaScript Built-In Objects

Core Objects	Error Objects	XML Objects	JSON Object
Array[1]	Error[2]	Namespace[4]	JSON[5]
Boolean	EvalError[2]	QName[4]	
Date	RangeError[2]	XML[4]	
Function[1]	ReferenceError[2]	XMLList[4]	
Global	SyntaxError[2]		
Math	TypeError[2]		
Number[1]	URIError[2]		
Object[1]			
RegExp[3]			
String[1]			

[1] Although defined in ECMA Level 1, was first available in NN3 and IE3/J2.
[2] Defined in ECMA Level 3; implemented in Moz1.
[3] Defined in ECMA Level 3; implemented fully in NN4 and IE6.
[4] Defined in E4X; implemented in Mozilla 1.8.1 (Firefox 2.0).
[5] Defined in ECMA Level 5; implemented in Mozilla 1.9.1 (Firefox 3.5).

- **JavaScript is loosely typed.** Variables, arrays, and function return values are not defined to be of any particular data type. In fact, an initialized variable can hold different data type values in subsequent script statements (obviously not good practice but possible nonetheless). Similarly, an array may contain values of multiple types. The range of built-in data types is intentionally limited:
  - Boolean (true or false)
  - Null
  - Number (double-precision 64-bit format IEEE 734 value)
  - Object (encompassing the Array object)
  - String
  - Undefined
  - XML (in E4X)
- **The host environment defines global scope.** Web browsers traditionally define a browser window or frame to be the global context for script statements. When a document unloads, all global variables defined by that document are destroyed.
- **JavaScript variables have either global or local scope.** A global variable is initialized in var statements outside of all functions. In a web browser, it typically executes as the document loads. All statements in that document can read or write that global variable. A local variable is also initialized with the var operator but inside a function. Only statements inside that function may access that local variable.

- **Scripts sometimes access JavaScript static object properties and methods.** Some static objects encourage direct access to their properties or methods. For example, all properties of the Math object act as constant values (for example, Math.PI).

- **You can add properties or methods to working objects at will.** To add a property to an object, simply assign a value of any type to it. For example, to add an author property to a string object named myText, use:

```
myText.author = "Jane";
```

Assign a function reference to an object property to give that object a new method:

```
// function definition
function doSpecial(arg1)
{
    // statements
}
// assign function reference to method name
myObj.handleSpecial = doSpecial;
...
// invoke method
myObj.handleSpecial(argValue);
```

Inside the function definition, the this keyword refers to the object that owns the method.

- **JavaScript objects employ prototype-based inheritance.** All object constructors create working objects whose properties and methods inherit the properties and methods defined for the *prototype* of that object. Scripts can add and delete custom properties and methods associated with the static object's prototype so that new working objects inherit the current state of the prototype. Scripts can freely override prototype property values or assign different functions to prototype methods in a working object without affecting the static object prototype. But if inherited properties or methods are not modified in the current working object, any changes to the static object's prototype are reflected in the working object. (The mechanism is that a reference to an object's property works its way up the prototype inheritance chain to find a match to the property name.)

- **JavaScript includes a large set of operators.** You can find most operators that you are accustomed to working with in other languages.

- **JavaScript provides typical control structures.** All versions of JavaScript offer if, if...else, for, and while constructions. JavaScript 1.2 (NN4+, IE4+, and all modern mainstream browsers) added do while and switch constructions. Iteration constructions provide break and continue statements to modify control structure execution.

- **JavaScript functions may or may not return a value.** There is only one kind of JavaScript function. A value is returned only if the function includes a return keyword followed by the value to be returned. Return values can be of any data type.

- **JavaScript functions cannot be overloaded.** A JavaScript function accepts zero or more arguments, regardless of the number of parameter variables defined for the function. All arguments are automatically assigned to the arguments array, which is a property of a function object. Parameter variable data types are not predefined.

- **Values are passed by reference and by value.** An object passed to a function is actually a reference to that object, offering full read/write access to properties and methods of that object. But other types of values (including object properties) are passed by value, with no reference chain to the original object. Thus, the following nonsense fragment empties the text box when the onchange event fires:

```
function emptyMe(arg1)
{
    arg1.value = "";
}
...
<input type="text" value="Howdy" onchange="emptyMe(this)">
```

But in the following version, nothing happens to the text box:

```
function emptyMe(arg1)
{
    arg1 = "";
}
...
<input type="text" value="Howdy" onchange="emptyMe(this.value)">
```

The local variable (arg1) simply changes from "Howdy" to an empty string.

Note

The property assignment event handling technique in the previous example is a deliberate simplification to make the example very brief. It is generally better to use the more modern approach of binding events using the addEventListener() **(NN6+/Moz/W3C) or** attachEvent() **(IE5+) methods. A modern cross-browser event handling technique is explained in detail in Chapter 32, "Event Objects."** ■

- **Error trapping techniques depend on JavaScript version.** There was no error trapping in NN2 or IE3. Error trapping in NN3, NN4, and IE4 was event-driven in the web browser object model. JavaScript, as implemented in IE5+ and Mozilla, Safari, and other recent browsers, supports try-catch and throw statements, as well as built-in error objects that are not dependent on the host environment.

- **Memory management is not under script control.** The host environment manages memory allocation, including garbage collection. Different browsers may handle memory in different ways.

- **Whitespace (other than a line terminator) is insignificant.** Space and tab characters may separate lexical units (for example, keywords, identifiers, and so on).

- **A line terminator is usually treated as a statement delimiter.** Except in very rare constructions, JavaScript parsers automatically insert the semicolon statement delimiter whenever they encounter one or more line terminators (for example, carriage returns or line feeds). A semicolon delimiter is required between two statements on the same physical line of source code. Moreover, string literals may not have carriage returns in their source code (but an escaped newline character (\n) may be part of the string).

The Evaluator Sr.

The Evaluator Sr. is a tool you can use in succeeding chapters to help you learn both core JavaScript and DOM terminology. The Evaluator provides an interactive workbench to experiment with expression evaluation and object inspection. (In Chapter 8, "Programming Fundamentals, Part I," we will introduce a slimmed-down version we call The Evaluator Jr.)

Figure 4-1 shows the top part of the page. Two important features differentiate this full version from the Jr. version in Chapter 8.

FIGURE 4-1

The Evaluator Sr.

First, you can try some Mozilla secure features if you have Code Base Principles turned on for your browser (see Chapter 49, "Security and Netscape Signed Scripts," on the CD-ROM) and you check the Use Code Base Security check box (Netscape Navigator 4 or later/Moz only). Second, the page has several HTML elements preinstalled, which you can use to explore DOM properties and methods. As with the smaller version, a set of 26 one-letter global variables (a through z) are initialized and ready for you to assign values for extended evaluation sequences.

Copy the evaluator.html and evaluator.js files from the companion CD-ROM to a local hard disk and set a bookmark for it in all your test browsers. Feel free to add your own elements to the bottom of the page to explore other objects. We describe a version of The Evaluator for embedding in your projects as a debugging tool in Chapter 48, "Debugging Scripts" (on the CD-ROM), where you can learn more built-in functionality of The Evaluator.

Part II

JavaScript Tutorial

Your First JavaScript Script

I n this chapter, you write a simple script, the results of which you can see in your JavaScript-compatible browser.

Two common ways of teaching spoken human languages are a) grammar lessons leading to eventual conversation and b) immersion in conversation leading to eventual grammar lessons.

We like b). It's more fun (play enhances learning), you get to see results right away, and it more closely resembles the way we each learned our own native tongue. The grammar's always there to refer to, but let's kick things off to a good start by plunging in and making a little magic happen on the screen.

Don't worry about memorizing every command and detail of syntax discussed in this chapter. Instead, relax and watch how the HTML markup and JavaScript statements become what you see in the browser. The details will soak in more quickly if you're enjoying yourself.

We'll explain each line of code as we go along, although all the methods we use in this first tutorial will be explained in much greater detail later in the book. For now, just enter the scripts as presented and see that they do what they're supposed to do.

IN THIS CHAPTER

Creating a simple application consisting of an HTML page, a JavaScript script, and a CSS style sheet

What Your First Script Will Do

Our first tutorial script will insert the current date and time into a web page. (This is a further evolution of the "Hello, World" script we showed you in Chapter 3, "Selecting and Using Your Tools.") First, we'll create an HTML page that simply displays static content; then we'll add JavaScript to make it dynamic; and then we'll add styling to jazz it up.

It's worth noting that this sequence — building HTML structure and then adding dynamic JavaScript and CSS for presentation — is not useful merely when learning; it's also a very decent model for everyday, real-world web site production. It's part of a larger sequence of development that might

1) HTML structure
2) dynamic Javascript
   & CSS presentation

include information design, graphic design, wireframe and proof-of-concept, HTML markup, server-side scripting, CSS styling, and JavaScript. Although it might be tempting to jump to the scripting first, that's sort of like spreading the icing before the cake is baked. JavaScript, like CSS, needs to know its context — the structure of the page in which it's operating. Also, working in this sequence encourages us to adhere to the principle of progressive enhancement, whereby everyone can get something out of the fundamental page, but those with user agents (such as browsers) with more capabilities can get even more out of it. By starting with the HTML page, we ensure that it's complete and makes sense even without JavaScript.

These days most serious web production includes a server-side scripting language and database, such as PHP and MySQL, to provide the fundamental dynamic content as HTML markup. As server-side scripting is outside the realm of this book, we'll mention it from time to time, but we will otherwise assume a truly static HTML page.

Entering Your First Script

Launch your text editor and browser. You may also want to launch your standard file manager utility to monitor the files that you'll be creating in a folder on your computer.

We'll be working offline throughout this book. All operations will happen locally on your computer and without Internet connectivity. If your browser offers to dial your Internet service provider (ISP) or begins dialing automatically, you can cancel or quit the dialing operation. If the browser's Stop button is active, you can click it to halt any network searching it may try to do. You may receive a dialog-box message or page indicating that the URL for your browser's home page (usually the home page of the browser's publisher — unless you've changed the settings) is unavailable. That's fine. You want the browser open, but you don't need to be connected to your ISP. If you're automatically connected to the Internet through a local area network in your office or school, or through cable modem or DSL, that's also fine. However, you don't need the network connection for now.

Step 1: The HTML document

Figure 5-1 shows our first goal: a simple page with a headline and a paragraph of text. This is what our initial page will look like, allowing for differences in the way various browsers present content by default (in other words, that hasn't yet been styled by us).

Enter the following HTML markup into a new text file and save it (with UTF-8 character encoding) with the name `date-time.html`:

LISTING 5-1

HTML Markup for "Date & Time": date-time.html

```
<!DOCTYPE html>
<html>
    <head>
        <meta http-equiv="content-type" content="text/html;charset=utf-8">
        <title>Date &amp; Time</title>
    </head>
```

```
    <body>
        <h1>Date &amp; Time</h1>
        <p>It is currently <span id="output">now</span>.</p>
    </body>
</html>
```

FIGURE 5-1

Step 1: Static HTML page.

Note

Throughout this book, we will consistently use UTF-8 character encoding for our HTML files. A character encoding tells the browser how to display text characters, and the Unicode standard of UTF-8 is a splendid system that enables us to include virtually any world language in our HTML files. It will serve you well in your web site production.

From the start, get into the habit of saving your files with UTF-8 encoding. Many text editors enable you to choose the encoding in the Save As... dialog, as well as set the default encoding for future files so that you don't have to specify it each time. If your text editor doesn't give you this option, keep using it for now, but start looking around for another editor that will. ■

Now open the document in your browser. You can do this by double-clicking on the file in the file manager screen or by choosing Open or Open File in the File menu of your browser.

If you typed all lines as shown, the document in the browser window should look like the one in Figure 5-1 (with minor differences for your computer's operating system and browser version).

Let's examine the details of the document so that you understand some of the finer points of what the markup is doing.

DOCTYPE

```
<!DOCTYPE html>
```

The DOCTYPE tells the browser how to render the document. Which DOCTYPE you use greatly affects CSS styling and markup validation. The DOCTYPE we're using in this book is the one for HTML5, but you can replace it with either the DOCTYPE for HTML 4.01-Strict for validation purposes:

```
<!DOCTYPE html PUBLIC "-//W3C//DTD HTML 4.01//EN"
    "http://www.w3.org/TR/html4/strict.dtd">
```

or with the one for XHTML 1.0-Strict (along with a few other changes in markup style):

```
<!DOCTYPE html PUBLIC "-//W3C//DTD XHTML 1.0 Strict//EN"
    "http://www.w3.org/TR/xhtml1/DTD/xhtml1-strict.dtd">
```

Note

XHTML style, if you intend to follow its conventions, requires all lowercase tags and attribute names. While the listings in this book are HTML, which accepts either upper- or lowercase tags and attributes, we will use lowercase consistently in order to remain compatible with both standards.

XHTML also requires several modifications to the HTML we're using in these examples. For more details on this, see the Introduction. ∎

html

The markup continues:

```
<html>
    ...
</html>
```

The entire page will always reside inside the html element, which declares the type of markup. The html element has just two children, head and body.

head

```
<head>
    ...
</head>
```

The head element may contain a variety of child elements that convey information *about* a document but that are not normally rendered as document content. The head must have, at minimum, two children, a meta element defining the character set, and a title:

```
<meta http-equiv="content-type" content="text/html;charset=utf-8">
<title>Date &amp; Time</title>
```

`meta` tags are a lengthy topic unto themselves. For now, just enter this one exactly as above. HTML5 can accept a shorter version:

```
<meta charset="UTF-8">
```

However, the longer version works for all three markup types (HTML 4.01, HTML5, and XHTML 1.0). Note that the `meta` tag is "empty" and does not take a closing `</meta>` tag. All the information it conveys is in its attributes, here `http-equiv` and `content`.

`title`, on the other hand, does require a closing tag; together they surround their content. The title "Date & Time" is entered as `Date &amp; Time`, using the HTML entity `&amp;` for the ampersand. There are four characters that must always be converted to HTML entities if they appear in the *content* of the page — attribute values and the text enclosed by tags — in order not to confuse the parsing engine:

```
<    &lt;
>    &gt;
&    &amp;
"    &quot;
```

This last one is the straight double quote used in HTML markup, not the curly quotes common in typeset text.

body

```
<body>
   ...
</body>
```

The `body` element contains the document's content — its structure, text, images, multimedia objects, and so on.

headline

```
<h1>Date &amp; Time</h1>
```

We use the headline tags `h1` through `h6` to create an outline structure in a document. Ordinarily, a document page will have only one `h1` to reiterate the page title, with all other headlines, starting with `h2`, nested beneath.

In the bad old days, people chose headline tags purely for their default appearance. Today, we use them just as you would use the numbers in a nested outline structure, and we control the appearance of all text from the style sheet.

paragraph

```
<p>It is currently <span id="output">now</span>.</p>
```

Finally, this is the paragraph of text where JavaScript will insert the current date and time. The `span` element has an ID (`output`) that JavaScript will use to locate it so that our script can replace the contents of the span with the actual date and time.

So, that's the static HTML page. Even after we plug in the JavaScript, anyone looking at the page with a user agent that doesn't support JavaScript (such as a search engine), or that has it turned off, will see just what we're seeing here. The page isn't terrifically informative in its current state, but at least it isn't broken. For public web sites, scripting should add value to the page rather than be mission critical.

Step 2: Adding JavaScript

Next, let's create the JavaScript for our page. Now is a good time to instill some good JavaScript habits that will be important to you throughout all your scripting ventures. First, JavaScript is case-sensitive. Therefore, you must type every word in your script with the correct uppercase and lowercase letters. When a line of JavaScript doesn't work, look for the wrong case first. Always compare your typed code against the listings printed in this book and against the various vocabulary entries discussed throughout it.

Second, notice that each JavaScript statement ends in a semicolon. These trailing semicolons — which you can think of as periods at the end of sentences — technically are optional in JavaScript, but we strongly recommend that you use them to remove ambiguity from your scripts. If you someday investigate other programming languages such as PHP, Java, or C++, you'll find that those semicolons are required. All the JavaScript listings in this book use semicolons.

Create a second text file in your editor named `date-time.js` and enter the following script:

Note

A JavaScript comment is any text contained between a double forward slash (//) and the end of the current line, or between slash-asterisk (/*) and asterisk-slash (*/). Comments are ignored by the JavaScript interpreter and are added purely to help human readers understand what's going on in the code. Therefore, you don't have to enter the comments exactly as you see here, but we do recommend that you get in the habit of commenting your code. Other programmers and your own future self will appreciate it! ■

LISTING 5-2

JavaScript Code for "Date & Time": date-time.js

```
// tell the browser to run this script when the page has finished loading
window.onload = insertDateTime;

// insert the date & time
function insertDateTime()
{
        // ensure a DOM-aware user agent
        if (!document.getElementById) return;
        if (!document.createTextNode) return;

    // create a date-time object
    var oNow = new Date();

    // get the current date & time as a string
    var sDateTime = oNow.toLocaleString();

    // point to the target element where we want to insert the date & time
    var oTarget = document.getElementById('output');
```

```
    // make sure the target is found
    if (!oTarget) return;

// delete everything inside the target
while (oTarget.firstChild)
{
    oTarget.removeChild(oTarget.firstChild);
}

// use the date-time string to create a new text node for the page
var oNewText = document.createTextNode(sDateTime);

// insert the new text into the span
oTarget.appendChild(oNewText);
}
```

To connect this JavaScript file to the HTML file, we need to add a `script` element to the HTML head. Bring `date-time.html` back into your text editor and add the line highlighted below:

```
    ...
    <head>
        <meta http-equiv="content-type" content="text/html;charset=utf-8">
        <title>Date &amp; Time</title>
        <script type="text/javascript" src="date-time.js"></script>
    </head>
    ...
```

The `script` tag identifies the MIME type of the linked JavaScript file and gives its name (and path, in case it's not located in the same folder as the HTML file itself). This causes the browser to read the JavaScript file as it's building the document page. The JavaScript interpreter within the browser validates and compiles the script, and runs it immediately, even before the rest of the HTML document has been read.

Now let's walk through the JavaScript code line by line so that you can see what it's doing.

Triggering the event

Here's a problem: Our script is going to insert the date and time into a paragraph in the page, but the browser reads and runs our JavaScript code before it's had a chance to read the HTML body. The paragraph into which we want to insert the new content won't even exist yet in the browser's memory when the JavaScript starts running.

Our solution is simply to tell JavaScript not to perform the insertion until the document has been fully read into memory. We do this using the `onload` event. Elements of the page — called *objects* in the Document Object Model (DOM) — can be made sensitive to a number of events, such as the click of a mouse or the press of a key. The `onload` event of the `window` object is triggered when the document finishes loading into the browser.

```
    // tell the browser to run this script when the page has finished loading
    window.onload = insertDateTime;
```

```
// insert the date & time
function insertDateTime()
{
    ...
}
```

In this case, we're telling JavaScript to call the `insertDateTime()` function when the document has finished loading. The date and time insertion routine that depends on the document having loaded is thus deferred until the browser has the target paragraph in memory.

Ensuring a safe environment

Once the document finishes loading into the browser, the `window.onload` event has been triggered, and the `insertDateTime()` function is called, the first thing the script does is to make sure it's being interpreted by a modern browser that speaks the same language:

```
// ensure a DOM-aware user agent
if (!document.getElementById) return;
if (!document.createTextNode) return;
```

`getElementById()` and `createTextNode()` are two DOM methods we're using in this function that some old JavaScript interpreters won't understand. The exclamation mark (!) means "not," and `return` tells JavaScript to stop running the current function; so, the first statement means, "If you aren't aware of the `getElementById()` method for the `document` object, exit this function." If we didn't include these safeguards, a legacy browser or its JavaScript interpreter would likely crash when trying to run the code that follows.

A crash can be as minor as the JavaScript interpreter stopping cold (leaving us with a plain HTML page and no JavaScript functionality at all) or as major as the whole browser freezing up and needing to be rebooted. Neither event is welcome. For many pages, we'll be writing JavaScript to perform several tasks, some of which can be executed by legacy browsers and others that can't. We want to guide the browser around the parts it can't handle, so it will run the parts it can. Preventing old JavaScript versions from crashing on the reefs of modern methods is a hallmark of professional piloting.

We subscribe to the principles of *graceful degradation* and *progressive enhancement*, whereby browsers that can't take advantage of particular features are let down gently and allowed to do the best they can. A fundamental courtesy of scripts that interact with the DOM is to turn away legacy JavaScript interpreters that aren't DOM-aware.

The old-school way of checking for old JavaScript interpreters is *browser-sniffing*, which examines the browser type as reported by the `navigator` object. Unfortunately, these claims of identity can't be relied on. What can be trusted is the JavaScript interpreter's own knowledge of which methods it's capable of executing, and that's the principal safety feature we use today.

Generating the date and time

The text we're going to insert into this document is the current date and time (according to the clock in the user's computer). JavaScript makes this easy: we create a `Date` object and use one of its many methods to produce the string:

```
// create a date-time object
var oNow = new Date();
```

method

```
// get the current date & time as a string
var sDateTime = oNow.toLocaleString();
```

This code sets the variable oNow to a new Date object. Once we have that, we use its toLocaleString() method to output a text string containing something like:

```
Thursday, August 20, 2009 4:16:05 PM
```

We capture the date and time string in variable sDateTime, which we'll use in a moment to output to the page.

The beauty of the toLocaleString() method is that it outputs the date and time formatted according to the user's settings and in the user's time zone. If two people run this exact same code at the same moment on opposite sides of the earth, they're likely to get two different dates and times expressed in two different formats and in two different languages. You'll learn a lot more about the Date object in the chapters ahead, particularly Chapter 12, "Strings, Math, and Dates," and Chapter 17, "The Date Object."

Note

In this example script, oNow is a Date object and sDateTime is a text string. One of the zillion flavors of programming style is the so-called *Systems Hungarian notation* in which each variable name begins with an indication of its type — here o for object, s for string, i for integer, and so on. Naming variables like this is purely optional, and for the programmer's own benefit. JavaScript doesn't care what the names are, as long as no keywords or illegal characters are used. JavaScript is a "dynamically typed" language in which the same variable can be set arbitrarily with numeric, string, Boolean, and object reference values. Some programmers like to maintain only one type of value in each variable to help keep the code easy to manage and debug. Using Hungarian notation can make these artificial variable types easier to remember. ■

Finding the target

The next step is to insert the date and time into the document exactly where we want it. To do that, we need to:

1. Refer to the target span element.
2. Delete any text already inside the element.
3. Insert new text inside the element.

To refer to the output span, the script uses the industry-standard way to refer to any HTML element that has an ID attribute:

```
// point to the target element where we want to insert the date & time
var oTarget = document.getElementById('output');
```

The first statement locates the target element in the HTML page by its ID (output) and stores a reference to that object in variable oTarget. The HTML specification mandates that every element ID must be unique on the current page. Even if we accidentally use the same ID more than once on the page, the getElementById() method returns only the first instance. So, we know that this method will locate just one element (if it's there at all) — in this case, the span we marked up in the HTML:

```
<p>It is currently <span id="output">now</span>.</p>
```

Notice that when we call getElementById(), we specify the element's ID (output) but not its tag name (span). In the HTML markup we could move the attribute id="output" from the span to any other element within the page, and our script would attempt to operate on that element instead. If you think about it, that's pretty cool. It means that, even though the markup and the script have to agree about the target element's ID, the script can potentially operate regardless of which tags are used in the markup. It's that kind of flexibility that can make for some truly versatile JavaScript functions down the road.

If we omit or misspell the ID in the markup, getElementById() will return a null value. To cover our bases, we test for that:

```
// make sure the target is found
if (!oTarget) return;
```

Similarly to the previous if-tests, this one says, "If the variable oTarget doesn't exist or has a null value, return from this function." Adding such reality checks to a script will help make it bulletproof. Developing habits like this will really benefit you when you're juggling dozens of elements on a page or working on pages that have been generated by numerous people and processes.

This is an opportunity to warn the user in case something is seriously wrong — for example:

```
if (!oTarget) return alert("Warning: output element not found");
```

However, since in most cases there's really nothing that a typical web site visitor can do about a problem like this, it might be best for the script to stop quietly or find something else to do, such as notify the web master.

Deleting what's there

Our HTML document comes pre-populated with some text we want to replace:

```
<p>It is currently <span id="output">now</span>.</p>
```

We want to delete the text within the span and then insert new content. In the DOM that represents the contents of the page, the span is the *parent* of everything within it. Right now there's just a single *child* — the word "now" — but we'd like this script to run successfully even if the HTML is later modified to include other markup within the target element.

Figure 5-2 shows that paragraph from a DOM perspective. The p element has three children: two text nodes and the span. The span has just one child: a text node containing the value "now".

FIGURE 5-2

A DOM's-eye view of the date and time paragraph before insertion.

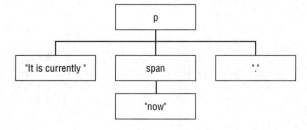

To remove the contents of the span, execute a little loop that deletes child elements one at a time, as long as there are any to delete:

```
// delete everything inside the target
while (oTarget.firstChild)
{
    oTarget.removeChild(oTarget.firstChild);
}
```

Given our current markup, this loop will execute just once. A while loop will repeat as long as the expression inside the parentheses tests true. When it begins, the property oTarget.firstChild is evaluated: Does the object oTarget have a first child node? The answer is yes (true) because the text node "now" is there. Inside the loop, the removeChild() method deletes that first child. Then JavaScript loops and asks the same question again: Does oTarget.firstChild exist? The answer is no (false), so JavaScript stops processing the while loop and resumes execution after the closing brace.

Inserting the date and time

Finally, we create a new node in the DOM that contains the text we want, and insert that into the span:

```
// use the date-time string to create a new text node for the page
var oNewText = document.createTextNode(sDateTime);

// insert the new text into the span
oTarget.appendChild(oNewText);
```

sDateTime is the string we generated from the Date object a few statements before. We call a method attached to the document object that creates a new text node with the date and time string as its value. At this point, the text node isn't yet part of the visible document content; it's waiting in the wings. We bring it on stage using the target element's appendChild() method.

The paragraph structure now looks like that shown in Figure 5-3. It's the same structural shape, but the span now has a new child.

FIGURE 5-3

The date and time paragraph after insertion.

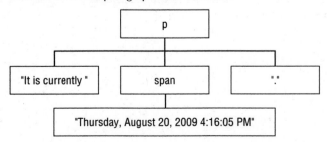

Debugging

When you've saved the JavaScript file and the HTML file with its script tag, you should be able to load the HTML page into your browser and see the word "now" replaced by the current date and time.

If you can't, take the time now to track down the problem and fix it. In the process, you'll learn important details about JavaScript that will help your future coding go faster and more smoothly.

Proofread the HTML markup and JavaScript code to make sure that they match the preceding listings. The two critical points in the markup will be the `script` tag and its attributes that point to the JavaScript file, and the `span` tag and its ID that JavaScript will look for. In the JavaScript file, make sure that every statement is spelled accurately, including spaces, punctuation, and upper- and lowercase letters.

If you are unsure about the HTML, it's always a good idea to validate it in the W3C HTML Validator, available at `http://validator.w3.org/`. Select either Validate by File Upload to upload the HTML file from your computer or Validate by Direct Input to copy and paste the HTML markup from your text editor into the Validator. At this writing, all the examples in this book with an HTML5 `DOCTYPE` will register one warning: `Using experimental feature: HTML5 Conformance Checker`. This is an informational message, not an error. Your goal is to get a green banner at the top of the Validator results page that says, `This document was successfully checked as HTML5!`

Check your browser's error console to see if it's reporting an error. If so, it will likely tell you the position of the error in the script file.

For further steps, see Chapter 48, "Debugging Scripts."

Step 3: Adding style

Finally, to illustrate how a third component of a typical web page ties in, let's add a simple style sheet to the mix. Style sheets tell the browser how the page should appear — everything from the layout to font choices to background colors.

Create a new text file in your editor, enter the following style sheet script, and save it as `date-time.css`:

LISTING 5-3

CSS Code for "Date & Time": date-time.css

```css
@charset "utf-8";

*
{
    margin: 0;
    font-family: sans-serif;
}
h1
{
    font-size: 10em;
    color: #DDF;
```

```
}
p
{
    position: absolute;
    top: 2.5em;
    left: 1.5em;
    font-size: 2em;
    font-weight: bold;
    color: #338;
}
#output
{
    font-style: italic;
    color: #C33;
}
```

To link this style sheet to the HTML file, add a link element to the HTML head. Bring date-time.html back into your text editor and add this line:

```
    ...
    <head>
        <meta http-equiv="content-type" content="text/html;charset=utf-8">
        <title>Date &amp; Time</title>
        <link href="date-time.css" rel="stylesheet" type="text/css" media="all">
        <script type="text/javascript" src="date-time.js"></script>
    </head>
    ...
```

Save the style sheet, save the modified HTML file, and reload the page in your browser. It should look pretty much like Figure 5-4.

Briefly, the style sheet is a list of rendering rules to be applied to the elements of the page. The basic syntax is as follows:

```
selector { property: value; [...] }
```

Our style sheet begins with a character-encoding directive:

```
@charset "utf-8";
```

Note that this matches the character encoding for the HTML file.

The * (wildcard) selector applies to all elements on the page. Here, it zeroes out default margins and sets the font-family for all text.

The h1 selector sets the headline font size to ten times the base font size (1em = 100% of base) and sets the font color to a pale blue with the RGB (red-green-blue) hexadecimal code of DDF.

The p selector applies to all paragraphs on the page (there is only one). The position, top, and left properties allow us to position the paragraph on top of the headline. We set the font weight to bold to make sure it's readable against the pale headline, and the text color to a dark blue with RGB #338.

73

FIGURE 5-4

Step 3: The styled page.

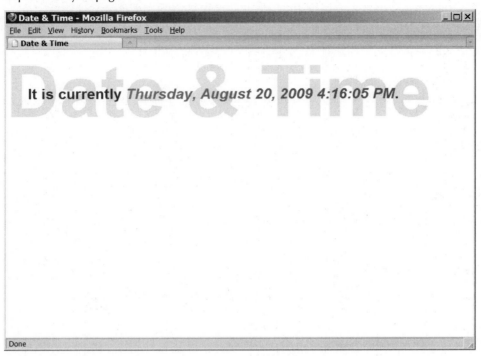

The #output selector applies to the element with an ID of output. Here, we change the font-style to italic and the text color to a dark red with RGB #C33. This element also inherits properties from its parent, including the bold font-weight.

To learn more about Cascading Style Sheets (CSS) go to www.w3.org/Style/CSS/.

Have Some Fun

Once you get this script working properly, play around with it a bit. Move the output ID from one element to another. Change the text that gets inserted. Get comfortable tweaking the markup, the script, and the style sheet to get effects that you want. After each change, save the file and reload the page in your browser to check your progress. Don't be afraid to make mistakes while you're learning. You can always undo a change that goes awry. Remember that play is the best way to learn!

Exercises

1. Perform a single cut-and-paste operation on the HTML markup in Listing 5-1 to cause JavaScript to replace the entire paragraph with the date and time, not just the span. *Hint:* After your edit, the paragraph will still contain text and a span element.

2. With the change of markup you've just made, consider the while loop in JavaScript Listing 5-2. Write out each step that the loop will take in deleting the contents of the paragraph.

3. Again given the HTML edit you made in Exercise 1, decide which change(s) to the style sheet in Listing 5-3 would be necessary in order to assign the paragraph the same font and color attributes that the span had before.

Browser and Document Objects

I n this chapter, you'll see several practical applications of JavaScript and begin to see how a JavaScript-enabled browser turns familiar HTML elements into objects that your scripts control. This tutorial teaches concepts and terminology that apply to modern browsers, with special focus on standards compatibility to equip you to work with today's and tomorrow's browsers. You should study this tutorial in conjunction with any of the following browsers: Internet Explorer 5 or later (Windows or Macintosh), any Mozilla-based browser (Firefox, Netscape 7 or later, or Camino), Apple Safari, or Opera 7 or later.

IN THIS CHAPTER

What client-side scripts do

What happens when a document loads

How the browser creates objects

How scripts refer to objects

What distinguishes one object from another

Scripts Run the Show

If you have authored web pages with HTML, you are familiar with how HTML tags influence the way content is rendered on a page when viewed in the browser. As the page loads, the browser recognizes angle-bracketed tags as formatting instructions. Instructions are read from the top of the document downward, and elements defined in the HTML document appear on-screen in the same order in which they appear in the document's source code. As an author, you do a little work one time and up front — adding the tags to text content — and the browser does a lot more work every time a visitor loads the page into a browser.

Assume for a moment that one of the elements on the page is a text input field inside a form. The user is supposed to enter some text in the text field and then click the Submit button to send that information back to the web server. If that information must be an Internet email address, how do you ensure the user includes the @ symbol in the address?

One way is to have a program running on the web server — such as one written in PHP, ASP, ColdFusion, or a Common Gateway Interface (CGI) language, such as Perl — inspect the submitted form data after the user clicks the Submit button and the form information is transferred to the server. If the user omits or forgets the @ symbol, the server-side program sends the page back to the browser — but this time with an instruction to include the symbol in the address. Nothing is wrong with this exchange, but it can mean a slight delay for the user in finding out that the address does not contain the crucial symbol. Moreover, the web server has to expend some of its resources to perform the validation and communicate back to the visitor. If the web site is a busy one, the server may try to perform hundreds of these validations at any given moment, probably slowing the response time to the user even more.

Now imagine that the document containing that text input field has some intelligence built into it that makes sure the text-field entry contains the @ symbol before ever submitting one bit (literally!) of data to the server. That kind of intelligence would have to be embedded in the document in some fashion — downloaded with the page's content so it can stand ready to jump into action when called upon. The browser must know how to run that embedded program. Some user action must start the program, perhaps when the user clicks the Submit button. If the program runs inside the browser and detects the lack of the @ symbol, an alert message should appear, to bring the problem to the user's attention. The same program should also be capable of deciding whether the actual submission can proceed or whether it should wait until a valid email address is entered in the field.

This kind of pre-submission data entry validation is but one of the practical ways JavaScript adds intelligence to an HTML document. Considering this example, you might recognize that a script must know how to look into what is typed in a text field; a script must also know how to let a submission continue and how to abort the submission. A browser capable of running JavaScript programs conveniently treats elements such as the text field as *objects*. A JavaScript script controls the action and behavior of objects, most of which you see onscreen in the browser window.

When to Use JavaScript

With so many web-oriented development tools and languages at your disposal, you should focus your client-side JavaScript efforts on tasks for which they are best suited. When faced with a web application task, we look to client-side JavaScript for help with the following requirements:

- **Data entry validation.** If form fields need to be filled out for processing on the server, we let client-side scripts prequalify the data entered by the user.

- **Serverless CGIs.** We use this term to describe processes that, were it not for JavaScript, would be programmed as CGIs on the server, yielding slower performance because of the interactivity required between the program and the user. This includes tasks such as small data collection lookup, modification of images, and generation of HTML in other frames and windows based on user input.

- **Dynamic HTML interactivity.** It's one thing to use DHTML's capabilities to position elements precisely on the page; you don't need scripting for that. But if you intend to make the content dance on the page, scripting makes that happen.

- **CGI prototyping.** Sometimes you want a server-side program to be at the root of your application because it reduces the potential incompatibilities among browser brands and versions. It may be easier to create a prototype of the CGI in client-side JavaScript. Use this opportunity to polish the user interface before implementing the application in your server-side script of choice.

- **Offloading a busy server.** If you have a highly-trafficked web site, it may be beneficial to convert frequently-used CGI processes to client-side JavaScript scripts. After a page is downloaded, the server is free to serve other visitors. Not only does this lighten server load, but users also experience quicker response from the application embedded in the page.

- **Adding life to otherwise-dead pages.** HTML by itself is pretty flat. Adding a blinking chunk of text doesn't help much; animated GIF images more often distract from, rather than contribute to, the user experience at your site. But if you can dream up ways to add some interactive zip to your page, it may engage the user and encourage a recommendation to friends or repeat visits.

- **Creating web pages that "think."** If you let your imagination soar, you may develop new, intriguing ways to make your pages appear "smart." For example, in the application Intelligent "Updated" Flags (Chapter 57 on the CD-ROM), you see how (without a server CGI or database) an HTML page can "remember" when a visitor last came to the page. Then, any items that have been updated since the last visit — regardless of the number of updates you've done to the page — are flagged for that visitor. That's the kind of subtle, thinking web page that best displays JavaScript's powers.

Note

Web pages and applications intended for public access should not rely exclusively on JavaScript to supply critical functions. Make sure that your primary data and web site functionality are accessible to visitors who have JavaScript turned off and to user agents that don't interpret JavaScript, such as search engines and mobile devices. Let your scripting enhance the experience for the majority of visitors who have JavaScript-enabled browsers, but don't let your web site be broken for the rest. ■

The Document Object Model

Before you can truly start scripting, you should have a good feel for the kinds of objects you will be scripting. A scriptable browser does a lot of the work of creating software objects that generally represent the visible objects you see in an HTML page in the browser window. Obvious objects include form controls (text boxes and buttons) and images. However, there may be other objects that aren't so obvious by looking at a page, but that make perfect sense when you consider the HTML tags used to generate a page's content — paragraph objects or frames of a frameset, for example.

To help scripts control these objects — and to help authors see some method to the madness of potentially dozens of objects on a page — the browser makers define a *document object model (DOM)*. In this context, a model is the organization of objects on the page.

Evolution of browser DOMs has caused much confusion and consternation among scripters due to a lack of compatibility across succeeding generations and brands of browsers. Fortunately, the DOM world is stabilizing around a formal specification published by the World Wide Web Consortium (W3C). Today's modern browsers continue to support some of the "old ways" of the earliest DOM because so much existing script code on the Web relies on these traditions continuing to work. (You'll see some of these in Chapter 11, "Forms and Form Elements.") But with the vast majority of browsers in use today supporting the basic W3C DOM syntax and terminology, scripters should aim toward standards compliance whenever possible.

HTML structure and the DOM

An important trend in HTML markup is applying markup solely to define the structure of a document and the context of each piece of content in the document. The days of using only HTML tags to influence the *appearance* of a chunk of text are drawing to a close. It is no longer acceptable to enclose a line of text in, say, an `<h1>` tag because you want the line to appear in the text size and weight that browsers automatically apply to text tagged in that way. An `<h1>` element has a special context

79

within a document's structure: a first-level heading. In today's HTML world, if you wish to display a stand-alone line of text with a particular style, the text would likely be in a simple paragraph (<p>) tag; the precise look of that paragraph would be under the control of a Cascading Style Sheet (CSS) rule. Current practice even frowns upon the application of <b> and <i> tags to assign boldface and italic styles to a span of text. Instead, surround the text with a contextual tag (such as the <em> element to signify emphasis), and define the CSS style you wish applied to any emphasized text in the document.

The result of applying strict structural design to your HTML tagging is a document that has a well-defined *hierarchy* of elements based on their nesting within one another. For example, a well-formed HTML 4.01 document has the following minimum elements:

- Document type declaration
- HTML
  - Head
    - Character encoding
    - Title
  - Body
    - Block-level content

The HTML markup for this empty document might look like this:

```
<!DOCTYPE HTML PUBLIC "-//W3C//DTD HTML 4.01//EN"
    "http://www.w3.org/TR/html4/strict.dtd">
<html>
    <head>
        <meta http-equiv="Content-Type" content="text/html;
charset=utf-8">
        <title></title>
    </head>
    <body>
        <p></p>
    </body>
</html>
```

Viewed as a family tree in which every child has just one parent, as shown in Figure 6-1, an HTML document must always have two children, DOCTYPE and html.

The DOCTYPE tells the browser which version of markup is being used, critical information for markup validation and the interpretation of style sheet rules. html has two required children, head and body. The head must minimally contain a meta element that specifies the character encoding and a title, and may also contain a variety of other children such as script and style sheet links. Elements in the head ordinarily don't appear as objects on the document page, but tell the browser how to configure the document, and can radically affect its appearance and behavior. The body contains the text, images, and other elements that we ordinarily think of as being page content; it must minimally contain at least one block-level element such as a headline, paragraph, or division.

Although we're using the much simpler DOCTYPE tag for HTML5 in this book,

```
<!DOCTYPE html>
```

FIGURE 6-1

Element hierarchy of an empty HTML 4.01 document.

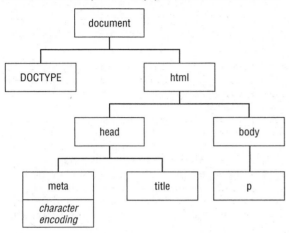

we adhere to the markup requirements for HTML 4.01 so that our HTML markup will validate, to the greatest extent possible, as both HTML 4.01 and HTML5 in order to provide valid examples for whichever branch of markup you choose to pursue.

The DOM in a browser window

As its name implies, the formal DOM focuses primarily on the HTML document and the content nested inside it. From a practical standpoint, however, scripters often need to control the environment that contains the document: the window. The window object is the top of the hierarchy that browser scripts work with. The basic structure of the object model in modern browsers (given an empty HTML document) is shown in Figure 6-2.

FIGURE 6-2

Basic object model for all modern browsers.

To give you a sense of the relationships among these top-level objects, the following describes their respective roles:

- `window` **object.** At the very top of the hierarchy is the window. This object represents the content area of the browser window where HTML documents appear. In a multiple-frame environment, each frame is also a window (but don't concern yourself with this just yet). Because all document action takes place inside the window, the window is the outermost element of the object hierarchy. Its physical borders contain the document.
- `navigator` **object.** This is the closest your scripts come to accessing the browser program, primarily to read the browser's claims of brand and version. This object is read-only, protecting the browser from inappropriate manipulation by rogue scripts; however, as you'll see, `navigator` can't be relied on to report the actual make, model, and version of the current browser.
- `screen` **object.** This is another read-only object that lets scripts learn about the physical environment in which the browser is running. For example, this object reveals the numbers of pixels high and wide available in the monitor.
- `history` **object.** Although the browser maintains internal details about its recent history (such as the list available under the Back button), scripts have no access to the details. At most, this object assists a script in simulating a click of the Back or Forward button.
- `location` **object.** This object is the primary avenue to loading a different page into the current window or frame. URL information about the window is available under very controlled circumstances so that scripts cannot track access to other web sites.
- `document` **object.** Each HTML document that gets loaded into a window becomes a `document` object. The `document` object contains the content that you are likely to script. Except for the `html`, `head`, and `body` element objects that are found in every HTML document, the precise makeup and structure of the element object hierarchy of the document depend on the content you put into the document.

When a Document Loads

Programming languages such as JavaScript are convenient intermediaries between your mental image of how a program works and the true inner workings of the computer. Inside the machine, every word of a program code listing influences the transformation and movement of bits (the legendary 1s and 0s of the computer's binary universe) from one RAM storage slot to another. Languages and object models are inside the computer (or, in the case of JavaScript and the DOM, inside the browser's area of the computer) to make it easier for programmers to visualize how a program works and what its results will be. The relationship reminds us of knowing how to drive an automobile from point A to point B without knowing exactly how an internal-combustion engine, steering linkages, and all that other internal "stuff" works. By controlling high-level objects such as the ignition key, gearshift, gas pedal, brake, and steering wheel, we can get the results we need.

Of course, programming is not exactly like driving a car with an automatic transmission. Even scripting requires the equivalent of opening the hood and perhaps knowing how to check the transmission fluid or change the oil. Therefore, now it's time to open the hood and watch what happens to a document's object model as a page loads into the browser.

A simple document

Figure 6-3 shows the HTML and corresponding object model for a document that we'll be adding to in a moment. The figure shows only the `document` object portion; the `window` object and its other top-level objects (including the document object) are always there, even for an empty document. When this page loads, the browser maintains in its memory a map of the objects generated by the HTML tags in the document. The body must contain block-level content, but we haven't added that yet.

FIGURE 6-3

Object map of an empty document.

```
<!DOCTYPE ...>
 <html>
  <head>
   <meta ...>
   <title></title>
  </head>
  <body>
   ...
  </body>
</html>
```

Add a paragraph element

Now, we modify the HTML file to include an empty paragraph element and reload the document. Figure 6-4 shows what happens to both the HTML and the object map, as constructed by the browser (changes shown in boldface). Even though no content appears in the paragraph, the <p> tags are enough to tell the browser to create that p element object. Also note that the p element object is contained by the body element object in the hierarchy of objects in the current map. In other words, the p element object is a *child* of the body element object. The object hierarchy matches the HTML tag containment hierarchy.

Add paragraph text

We modify and reload the HTML file again, this time inserting the text of the paragraph between the element's start and end tags, as shown in Figure 6-5. A run of text extending between tags is a special kind of object in the DOM called a *text node*. A text node always has an element acting as its container. Applying the official genealogy metaphor to this structure, this text node is a child of its parent p element. We now have a branch of the document object tree that runs several generations: document ⇨ html ⇨ body ⇨ p ⇨ text node.

Make a new element

The last modification we make to the file is to wrap a portion of the paragraph text in an <em> tag to signify emphasis for the enclosed text. This insertion has a large effect on the hierarchy of the p element object, as shown in Figure 6-6. The p element goes from having a single (text node) child to having three children: two text nodes with an element between them. In the W3C DOM, a text node cannot have any children and therefore cannot contain an element object. The bit of the text node now inside the em element is no longer a child of the p element, but a child of the em element. That text node is now a grandchild of the p element object.

Now that you see how objects are created in memory in response to HTML tags, the next step is to figure out how scripts can communicate with these objects. After all, scripting is mostly about controlling these objects.

FIGURE 6-4

Adding an empty paragraph element.

```
<!DOCTYPE ...>
 <html>
  <head>
   <meta ...>
   <title></title>
  </head>
  <body>
   <p></p>
  </body>
</html>
```

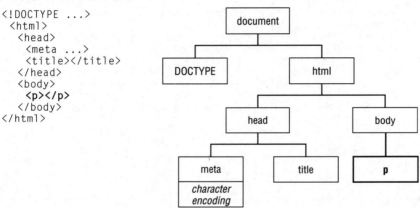

FIGURE 6-5

Adding a text node to the p element object.

```
<!DOCTYPE ...>
 <html>
  <head>
   <meta ...>
   <title></title>
  </head>
  <body>
   <p>This is the one and
   only paragraph.</p>
  </body>
</html>
```

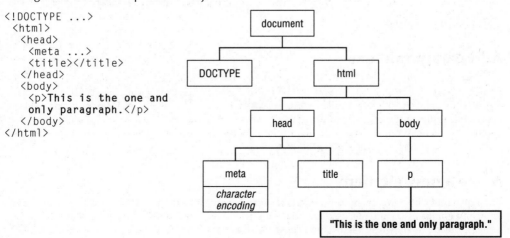

FIGURE 6-6

Inserting an element into a text node.

```
<!DOCTYPE ...>
 <html>
  <head>
   <meta ...>
   <title></title>
  </head>
  <body>
   <p>This is the <em>one
   and only</em>
   paragraph.</p>
  </body>
</html>
```

Object References

After a document is loaded into the browser, all of its objects are safely stored in memory in the containment hierarchy structure specified by the browser's DOM. For a script to control one of those objects, there must be a way to communicate with an object and find out something about it (such as "Hey, Mr. Text Field, what did the user type?"). To let your scripts talk to an object, you need a way to refer to that object. That is precisely what an *object reference* in a script does for the browser.

Object naming

The biggest aid in creating script references to objects is assigning a name to every scriptable object in your HTML. In the W3C DOM (and current HTML specification), the way to assign a name to an element is by way of the id attribute. This attribute is optional, but if you plan to use scripts to access an element in the page, it is most convenient to assign a name to that element's id attribute directly in the HTML code. Here are some examples of id attributes added to typical tags:

```
<p id="firstParagraph">

<img id="logo-1" src="images/logo.jpg" alt="Corporate Logo">

<div class="draggable" id="puzzle_piece">
```

The only rules about object IDs (also called *identifiers*) are that they:

- May not contain spaces
- May not contain punctuation except for the underscore, hyphen, period, and colon characters

85

- Must be inside quotes when assigned to the id attribute
- Must not start with a numeric character
- May not occur more than once in the same document

Think of assigning IDs as the same way as sticking name tags on everyone attending a conference meeting. To find a particular conference attendee whose name you know, you could wait at the entrance and scan each name tag until you find the name you're looking for, or you could bump around the attendees at random in the hope that you'll find a known name. But it would be more efficient if you had a way to target an attendee by name immediately — such as broadcasting the name on the public address system to the whole crowd.

Referencing a particular object

The W3C DOM provides that kind of instant access to any named element in the document. Here is the syntax you will use frequently in your browser scripting:

```
window.document.getElementById("elementID")
```

You substitute the ID of the element you wish to reference for elementID. For example, if you want to reference the paragraph element whose ID is firstParagraph, the reference would be

```
window.document.getElementById("firstParagraph")
```

JavaScript allows us to shorten this by omitting the window reference, so we often use this briefer form:

```
document.getElementById("firstParagraph")
```

Be careful! JavaScript is case sensitive. Be sure that you use uppercase for the three uppercase letters in the command and a lowercase *d* at the end, and that you spell the ID itself accurately as well.

The getElementById() command belongs to the document object, meaning that the entire document's collection of elements is subject to this instantaneous search for a matching ID. The dot — a traditional period character — is the JavaScript way of indicating that the item to the left of the dot (the document object here) has the item to the right of the dot (getElementById() here) as a resource to call upon whenever needed. Each type of object has a list of such resources, as you'll see in a moment (and as summarized in Appendix A).

id and name Attributes

Prior to the HTML 4.0 specification's introduction of the id attribute, scripts could access a handful of elements that also supported the name attribute. Elements supporting the name attribute are predominantly related to forms, images, and frames. You will see how name attributes work in forms in Chapter 11, "Forms and Form Elements." In fact, most browsers still require the name attribute for forms and form controls (text fields, buttons, and select lists) for their data to be submitted to a server. It is permissible to assign the same identifier to both the id and name attributes of an element, and, in fact, in XHTML it is recommended that an id and name assigned to the same element have the same value. For example:

```
<input type="text" id="firstname" name="firstname" />
```

Node Terminology

W3C DOM terminology uses metaphors to assist programmers in visualizing the containment hierarchy of a document and its content. One concept you should grasp early in your learning is that of a *node;* the other concept is the family relationship among objects in a document.

About nodes

Although the English dictionary contains numerous definitions of *node,* the one that comes closest to its application in the W3C DOM implies a knob or bump on a tree branch. Such nodules on a branch usually lead to one of two things: a leaf or another branch. A leaf is a dead end in that no further branches emanate from the leaf; the branch kind of node leads to a new branch that can itself have further nodes, whether they be leaves or more branches. When you define the structure of an HTML document, you also define a node structure (also called a *node tree*) in which the placement of branches and leaves depends entirely on your HTML elements and text content.

In the W3C DOM, the fundamental building block is a simple, generic node. But inside an HTML document, we work with special kinds of nodes that are tailored to HTML documents. The two types of nodes that scripts touch most often are *element nodes* and *text nodes.* These node types correspond exactly to HTML elements and the text that goes between an element's start and end tags. You've been working with element and text nodes in your HTML authoring, and you may not have even known it.

Look again at the simple document we've just assembled, along with its containment hierarchy diagram in Figure 6-7. All of the boxes representing HTML elements (html, head, body, p, and em) are element nodes; the three boxes containing the actual text that appears in the rendered document are text nodes. You saw in the transition from one long text node (Figure 6-5) to the insertion of the em element (Figure 6-6) that the long text node divided into three pieces. Two text node pieces stayed in the same position in the hierarchy relative to the containing p element. We inserted the new em element into the tree between the two text nodes and shifted the third text node one level away from the p element.

Parents and children

Looking more closely at the p element and its content in Figure 6-7, you can see that element has three child nodes. The first and last are of the text node type, whereas the middle one is an element node. When an element contains multiple child nodes, the sequence of child nodes is entirely dependent upon the HTML source code order. Thus, the first child node of the p element is the text node containing the text "This is the ". The em element has a single child text node as its sole descendant.

Element node children are not always text nodes; neither do branches always end in text nodes. In Figure 6-7, the html element has two child nodes, both of which are element nodes; the body element has one child node, the p element. A tag in the HTML indicates an element node, whether or not it has any child nodes. By contrast, a text node can never contain another node; it's one of those dead-end leaf type of nodes.

Notice that a child node is always contained by one element node. That container is the *parent* node of its child or children. For example, from the point of view of the em element node, it has both one child (a text node) and one parent (the p element node). A fair amount of W3C DOM terminology (which you'll meet in Chapter 25, "Document Object Model Essentials") concerns itself with assisting scripts starting at any point in a document hierarchy and obtaining a reference to a related node if necessary. For instance, if a Dynamic HTML script wants to modify the text inside the em element of Figure 6-7, it typically would do so by starting with a reference to the `em` element via the `document.getElementById()` command (assuming that the `em` element has an ID assigned to it) and then modifying the element's child node.

FIGURE 6-7

A simple HTML document node tree.

```
<!DOCTYPE ...>
 <html>
  <head>
   <meta ...>
   <title></title>
  </head>
  <body>
   <p>This is the <em>one
   and only</em>
   paragraph.</p>
  </body>
 </html>
```

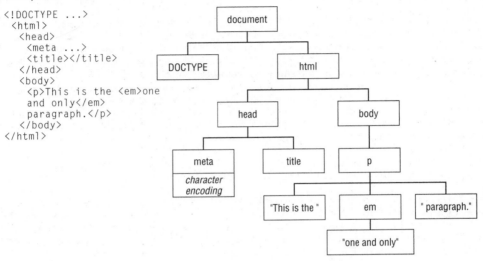

In case you're wondering, the `document` object at the top of the node tree is itself a node. Its place in the tree is special and is called simply the *document node.* Each loaded HTML document contains a single document node, and that node becomes the scripter's gateway to the rest of the document's nodes. It's no accident that the syntax for referencing an element node — `document.getElementById()` — begins with a reference to the `document` object.

What Defines an Object?

When an HTML tag defines an object in the source code, the browser creates a slot for that object in memory as the page loads. But an object is far more complex internally than, say, a mere number stored in memory. The purpose of an object is to represent some thing. In the browser and its DOM, the most common objects are those that correspond to elements, such as a text input form field, a table element, or the entire rendered body of the document. Outside the pared-down world of the DOM, an object can also represent abstract entities, such as a calendar program's appointment entry or a layer of graphical shapes in a drawing program. It is common for your browser scripts to work with both DOM objects and abstract objects of your own design.

Every type of DOM object is unique in some way, even if two or more objects look identical to you in the browser. Three very important facets of an object define what it is: what it "looks" like, how it behaves, and how scripts control it. Those three facets are properties, methods, and events (also known as handlers). They will play key roles in your future DOM scripting efforts. The Quick Reference in Appendix A summarizes the properties, methods, and events for each object in the object models implemented in the various browser generations.

Properties

Any physical object you hold in your hand has a collection of characteristics that defines it. A coin, for example, has shape, diameter, thickness, color, weight, embossed images on each side — and any number of other attributes that distinguish it from, say, a feather. Each of those features is called a *property*. Each property has a value of some kind attached to it (even if the value is empty or null). For example, the shape property of a coin might be *circle* — in this case, a text value. By contrast, the denomination property would most likely be a numeric value.

You may not have known it, but if you've written HTML for use in a scriptable browser, you have set object properties without writing one iota of JavaScript. Tag attributes are the most common way to set an HTML element object's initial properties. For example, the following HTML tag defines an input element object that assigns four property values:

```
<input type="button" id="clicker" name="clicker" value="Hit Me...">
```

In JavaScript parlance, then, the type property holds the word *button;* the id and name properties hold the same word, *clicker;* and the value property is the text that appears on the button label, *Hit Me ...* . In truth, a button input element has more properties than just these, but you don't have to set every property for every object. Most properties have *default values* that are automatically assigned if nothing special is set in the HTML, or later from a script.

The contents of some properties can change after a document has loaded and the user interacts with the page. Consider the following text input tag:

```
<input type="text" id="donation" name="donation" value="$0.00">
```

The id and name properties of this object are the same word: donation. When the page loads, the text of the value attribute setting is placed in the text field — the automatic behavior of an HTML text field when the value attribute is specified. But if a user enters some other text into the text field, the value property changes — not in the HTML, but in the memory copy of the object model that the browser maintains. Therefore, if a script queries the text field about the content of the value property, the browser yields the current setting of the property — which isn't necessarily the one specified by the HTML.

To gain access to an object's property, you use the same kind of dot-notation addressing scheme you saw earlier for objects. A property is a resource belonging to its object, so the reference to it consists of the reference to the object plus one more extension naming the property. Therefore, for the button and text object tags just shown, references to various properties are

```
document.getElementById("clicker").name
document.getElementById("clicker").value
document.getElementById("entry").value
```

Tip

JavaScript will fail or "abort" if it tries to reference the property of a non-existent element. Therefore, a safer, more bulletproof way of referencing these properties is to first test for the existence of the object:

```
var oClicker = document.getElementById("clicker");
    if (oClicker) var sName = oClicker.name;
```

or

```
var oClicker = document.getElementById("clicker");
    if (!oClicker) return;
var sName = oClicker.name;  ■
```

You might wonder what happened to the window part of the reference. It turns out that there can be only one document contained in a window, so references to objects inside the document can omit the window portion and start the reference with document. You cannot omit the document object from the reference, however.

Methods

If a property is like a descriptive adjective for an object, a *method* is a verb. A method is all about action related to the object. A method does something either to the object or with the object that affects other parts of a script or document. Methods are commands of a sort whose behaviors are tied to a particular object.

Internet Explorer References

Before the W3C DOM came into existence, Microsoft had created its own way of referencing element objects by way of their id attributes. You will find many instances of this syntax in existing code that has been written only for Internet Explorer 4 or later. The syntax uses a construction called document.all. Although there are a few different ways to use this construction, the most commonly applied way is to continue the dot notation to include the ID of the element. For example, if a paragraph element's ID is myParagraph, the IE-only reference syntax is

```
document.all.myParagraph
```

You can also omit the lead-in parts of the reference and simply refer to the ID of the element:

```
myParagraph
```

Be aware, however, that none of these approaches is supported in the W3C DOM standard. Both the IE-specific and W3C DOM reference syntax styles are implemented in IE5 or later. Also the document.all.elementId syntax cannot tolerate some of the valid HTML ID characters, such as hyphen, colon, and period, because JavaScript would interpret them as its own syntax.

Although it's important to be familiar with document.all in order to make sense of legacy code, you should stick to W3C DOM methods such as getElementById() in your own code to be compatible with forward-looking modern browsers.

Note

Note that the document.all syntax cannot tolerate any hyphens, colons, or periods in the ID. Although these are valid HTML IDs

```
my-paragraph
my.paragraph
my:paragraph
```

the resulting document.all expressions would cause JavaScript to give erroneous results or crash:

```
document.all.my-paragraph
document.all.my.paragraph
document.all.my:paragraph
```

Using the modern standard getElementById() is safer because the ID is always enclosed in quotation marks. ∎

An object can have any number of methods associated with it (including none at all). To set a method into motion (usually called *invoking a method*), a JavaScript statement must include a reference to it, via its object, with a pair of parentheses after the method name, as in the following examples:

```
var oForm = document.getElementById("orderForm");
oForm.submit();

var oEntry = document.getElementById("entry");
oEntry.focus();
```

The first is a scripted way of sending a form (named orderForm) to a server. The second gives focus to a text field named entry.

Sometimes a method requires that you send additional information with it so that it can do its job. Each chunk of information passed with the method is called a *parameter* or *argument* (you can use the terms interchangeably). The document.getElementById() method is one that requires a parameter: the identifier of the element object to be addressed for further action. This method's parameter must be in a format consisting of straight text, signified by the quotes around the identifier.

Some methods require more than one parameter. If so, the multiple parameters are separated by commas. For example, modern browsers support a window object method that moves the window to a particular *coordinate point* onscreen. A coordinate point is defined by two numbers that indicate the number of pixels from the left and top edges of the screen where the top-left corner of the window should be. To move the browser window to a spot 50 pixels from the left and 100 pixels from the top, the method is

```
window.moveTo(50,100)
```

As you learn more about the details of JavaScript and the document objects you can script, pay close attention to the range of methods defined for each object. They reveal a lot about what an object is capable of doing under script control.

Events

One last characteristic of a DOM object is the *event*. Events are actions that take place in a document, usually as the result of user activity. Common examples of user actions that trigger events include clicking a button or typing a character in a text field. Some events, such as the act of loading a document into the browser window or experiencing a network error while an image loads, are not so obvious.

Almost every DOM object in a document receives events of one kind or another — summarized for your convenience in the Quick Reference of Appendix A. Your job as scripter is to write the code that tells an element object to perform an action whenever the element receives a particular type of event. The action is simply executing some additional JavaScript code.

A simple way to begin learning about events is to apply one to an HTML element. Listing 4-1 shows a very simple document that displays a single button and a script that applies one event handler to the button. The event's name consists of the type of event (for example, click) preceded by the preposition *on* (as in, "on receiving the click event ... ": onclick).

LISTING 6-1

A Simple Button with an Event Handler

HTML: jsb-06-01.html

```html
<!DOCTYPE html>
<html>
    <head>
        <meta http-equiv="content-type" content="text/html;charset=utf-8">
        <title>A Simple Button with an Event Handler</title>
        <script type="text/javascript" src="jsb-06-01.js"></script>
    </head>
    <body>
        <form action="">
            <div>
                <button id="clicker">Click me</button>
            </div>
        </form>
    </body>
</html>
```

JavaScript: jsb-06-01.js

```javascript
// tell the browser to run this script when the page has finished loading
window.onload = applyBehavior;

// apply behavior to the button
function applyBehavior()
{
    // ensure a DOM-aware user agent
    if (document.getElementById)
    {
        // point to the button
        var oButton = document.getElementById('clicker');

        // if it exists, apply behavior
        if (oButton)
        {
```

```
            oButton.onclick = behave;
        }
    }
}

// what to do when the button is clicked
function behave(evt)
{
    alert('Ouch!');
}
```

When the browser loads the HTML page, it also loads the linked JavaScript file, compiles it, and begins to execute its instructions. In this case, the only instruction it will actually execute immediately is the window.onload statement because all the other statements are inside functions and won't execute until the functions are called by name. Only when the HTML page has finished loading (and when its DOM has been completely built) will our function applyBehavior() run. If the JavaScript interpreter that's running is aware of the DOM method getElementById(), the function uses it to look up the element with the ID of clicker. If found, it applies the onclick behavior to the button, telling it to execute the function behave() when clicked. When the user clicks the button, the behave() function issues an alert (a popup dialog box) that says, "Ouch!"

Cross-Reference

You will learn about other ways to connect scripting instructions to events in Chapter 25, "Document Object Model Essentials," and Chapter 32, "Event Objects." ■

Exercises

1. Which of the following applications are well suited to client-side JavaScript? Why or why not?
   a. Product catalog page that lets visitors view the product in five different colors
   b. A counter that displays the total number of visitors to the current page
   c. Chat room
   d. Graphical Fahrenheit-to-Celsius temperature calculator
   e. All of the above
   f. None of the above

2. Which of the following element IDs are valid in HTML? For each one that is invalid, explain why.
   a. lastName
   b. company_name
   c. 1stLineAddress
   d. zip code
   e. today's_date
   f. now:you-hear.this

3. Using the diagram from Figure 6-7 for reference, draw a diagram of the object model containment hierarchy that the browser would create in its memory for the following HTML. Write the script reference to the first paragraph element using W3C DOM syntax.

```
<!DOCTYPE html>
<html>
<head>
<meta http-equiv="content-type" content="text/html;charset=utf-8">
<title>Search Form</title>
</head>
<body>
<p id="logoPar"><img src="images/logo.jpg" height="90" width="300"
     alt="Logo"></p>
<div id="searchForm">
<form action="cgi-bin/search.pl" method="post">
<div>
<label for="searchText">Search for:</label>
<input type="text" id="searchText" name="searchText">
<input type="submit" value="Search">
</div>
</form>
</div>
</body>
</html>
```

4. Describe at least two characteristics that a text node and an element node have in common; describe at least two characteristics that distinguish a text node from an element node.

5. Write the HTML and JavaScript for a button input element named Hi, whose visible label reads Howdy, and whose action upon being clicked displays an alert dialog box that says, Hello to you, too!

Scripts and HTML Documents

C hapter 4, "JavaScript Essentials," covered many of the basics of how to combine JavaScript with HTML documents. This chapter's tutorial reviews how scripts are linked to HTML documents and what comprises a script statement. You also see how script statements can run when the document loads or in response to user action. Finally, you find out where script error information may be hiding.

Connecting Scripts to Documents

We use the `script` element to tell the browser to treat a segment of text as script and not as HTML. Whether our script is an external file linked to the HTML document or embedded directly in the page itself, the `<script>...</script>` tag set encapsulates the script.

Depending on the browser, the `<script>` tag has a variety of attributes you can set that govern the script. One attribute, `type`, advises the browser to treat the code within the tag as JavaScript. Some other browsers accept additional languages (such as Microsoft's VBScript in Windows versions of Internet Explorer). The following setting is one that all modern scriptable browsers accept:

```
<script type="text/javascript" ...>...<script>
```

Be sure to include the ending tag for the script. Your JavaScript program code goes either into an external file specified in the `src` attribute:

```
<script type="text/javascript" src="example.js"><script>
```

or between the two tags:

```
<script  type="text/javascript">
   one or more lines of JavaScript code here
</script>
```

If you forget the closing script tag, the script may not run properly, and the HTML elsewhere in the page may look strange.

The Old language Attribute

Another `<script>` tag attribute, `language`, used to be the way to specify the scripting language for the enclosed code. That attribute allowed scripters to specify the language version. For example, if the scripts included code that required JavaScript syntax available only in version 4 browsers (which implemented JavaScript version 1.2), the `<script>` tag used to be written as follows:

```
<script language="JavaScript1.2">...</script>
```

The `language` attribute was never part of the HTML 4.0 specification and is now falling out of favor. If W3C validation is one of your development concerns, you should be aware that the language attribute does not validate in strict versions of HTML 4.01 or XHTML 1.0. Older browsers that do not know the `type` attribute automatically default to JavaScript anyway. Use only the `type` attribute.

Tag positions

Where do these tags go within a document? The answer is anywhere they're needed in the document. Most of the time, it makes sense to include the tags nested within the `<head>...</head>` tag set; other times, it is essential that you drop the script into a very specific location in the `<body>...</body>` section.

In the following three listings, we demonstrate — with the help of a skeletal HTML document — some of the possibilities of `<script>` tag placement. Later in this lesson, you see why scripts may need to go in different places within a page, depending on the scripting requirements. In each example, we show two `script` tags – one a link to an external script and one for internal embedded scripting – just to show you how they both appear. In practice, it's most likely that you will consistently link only to external scripts.

Listing 7-1 shows the outline of what may be the most common position of a `<script>` tag set in a document: in the `<head>` tag section. Typically, the `head` is a place for tags that influence non-content settings for the page — so-called HTML *directive* elements, such as `<meta>` tags and the document title. It turns out that this is also a convenient place to plant scripts that are called in response to a page load or a user action.

LISTING 7-1

Scripts in the head

```
<html>
    <head>
        <title>A Document</title>
        <script type="text/javascript" src="example.js"></script>
        <script  type="text/javascript">
            //script statement(s) here
            ...
```

```
        </script>
    </head>
    <body>
    </body>
</html>
```

On the other hand, if you need a script to run as the page loads so that the script generates content in the page, the script goes in the `<body>` portion of the document, as shown in Listing 7-2.

LISTING 7-2

A Script in the body

```
<html>
    <head>
        <title>A Document</title>
    </head>
    <body>
        <script type="text/javascript" src="example.js"></script>
        <script  type="text/javascript">
            //script statement(s) here
            ...
        </script>
    </body>
</html>
```

It's also good to know that you can place an unlimited number of `<script>` tag sets in a document. For example, Listing 7-3 shows a script in both the head and body portions. This document needs the body script, perhaps to create some dynamic content as the page loads, but the document also contains a button that needs a script to run later. That script is stored in the head portion.

LISTING 7-3

Scripts in the head and body

```
<html>
    <head>
        <title>A Document</title>
        <script type="text/javascript" src="example.js"></script>
        <script  type="text/javascript">
            //script statement(s) here
            ...
        </script>
    </head>
    <body>
        <script type="text/javascript" src="example.js"></script>
```

continued

LISTING 7-3 *(continued)*

```
<script type="text/javascript">
    //script statement(s) here
    ...
</script>
</body>
</html>
```

Handling non-JavaScript browsers and XHTML

Only browsers that include JavaScript know to interpret the lines of code between the `<script>...</script>` tag pair as script statements rather than HTML text for display in the browser. This means that a pre-JavaScript browser or a simplified browser in a cell phone would not only ignore the tags, but also treat the JavaScript code as page content. The results can be disastrous to a page.

On the other hand, you don't have to worry about non-JavaScript browsers trying to execute externally linked scripts. That's one of the advantages of linking rather than embedding your scripts. The problem only arises when JavaScript code is embedded in the HTML document.

You can reduce the risk of older, non-JavaScript browsers displaying the script lines by enclosing the script lines between HTML comment symbols, as shown in Listing 7-4. Most nonscriptable browsers ignore the content between the `<!--` and `-->` comment tags, whereas scriptable browsers ignore the opening comment symbol when it appears inside a `<script>` tag set.

LISTING 7-4

Hiding Scripts from Most Old Browsers

```
<script type="text/javascript">
<!--
    //script statement(s) here
    ...
// -->
</script>
```

The odd construction right before the ending script tag needs a brief explanation. The two forward slashes are a JavaScript comment symbol. This symbol is necessary because JavaScript otherwise tries to interpret the components of the ending HTML symbol (`-->`). Therefore, while the forward slashes tell JavaScript to skip the line entirely, a non-scriptable browser simply treats those slash characters as part of the entire HTML comment to be ignored.

Although it's no longer really necessary to hide JavaScript in this way from older browsers, there are instances when a different type of hiding may be required. XML is more frequently being used to feed content to the browser, and often this is done using XHTML. In the XML world, all special characters need to be enclosed in a `CDATA` section, or else the file may be parsed incorrectly; at the very least, it will fail validation. Again, the trick is to enclose your script, but this time it will look like

Listing 7-5. You'll notice again that immediately before the closing script tag the JavaScript comment hides the closing of the CDATA section from JavaScript itself.

LISTING 7-5

Hiding Scripts From XML Parsers

```
<script type="text/javascript">
<![CDATA[
    //script statement(s) here
    ...
//]]>
</script>
```

Despite the fact that these techniques are often called *script hiding,* they do not conceal the scripts from human readers. All client-side JavaScript scripts are part of, or accompany, the HTML document, and they download to the browser just like all the other assets that make up the page. You can view the JavaScript source as easily as you can view the HTML document source. Do not be fooled into thinking that you can hide your scripts from prying eyes. Some developers *obfuscate* their scripts by removing all carriage returns and using nonsensical variable and function names, but this only slows down (and doesn't stop) any inquisitive visitor from reading and understanding the code.

Since it's not possible to truly hide your JavaScript programming from the public, you might as well flaunt it: sign the scripts you're proud of, include a copyright or Creative Commons notice of authorship in script comments, and encourage people who admire the script to come to you for more.

JavaScript Statements

Virtually every line of code in an externally linked file or that sits within a `<script>...</script>` tag pair is a JavaScript *statement* (except for HTML comment tags). To be compatible with the habits of experienced programmers, JavaScript accepts a semicolon at the end of every statement (the computer equivalent of a period at the end of a sentence). This semicolon is optional, but we strongly recommend that you use it consistently to avoid ambiguity. The carriage return at the end of a statement suffices for JavaScript to know that the statement has ended. It is possible, however, that in the future the semicolon will be required, so it's a good idea to get into the semicolon habit now.

A statement must be in the script for a purpose. Therefore, every statement does something relevant to the script. The kinds of things that statements do are

- Define or initialize a variable
- Assign a value to a property or variable
- Change the value of a property or variable
- Define or invoke an object's method
- Define or invoke a function routine
- Make a decision

If you don't yet know what all of these things mean, don't worry; you will, by the end of this tutorial. The point we want to stress is that each statement contributes to the scripts you write. The only statement that doesn't perform any explicit action is the *comment*. A pair of forward slashes (no space between them) is the most common way to include a single-line comment in a script:

```
// this is a one-line comment

var a = b;    // this comment shares a line with an active statement
```

Multiple-line comments can be enclosed in slash-asterisks:

```
/*
  Any number of lines are comments if they are
  bracketed by slash-asterisks
*/
```

You add comments to a script for the benefit of yourself and other human readers. They usually explain in plain language what a statement or group of statements does. The purpose of including comments is to remind you how your script works six months from now, or to help out another developer who needs to read your code.

When Script Statements Execute

Now that you know where scripts go in a document, it's time to look at when they run. Depending on what you need a script to do, you have four choices for determining when a script runs:

- While a document loads
- Immediately after a document loads
- In response to user action
- When called upon by other script statements

The determining factor is how the script statements are positioned in a document.

While a document loads: immediate execution

Listing 7-5 is a variation of your first script from Chapter 5, "Your First JavaScript Script." In this version, the script writes the current date and time to the page while the page loads. The `document.write()` method is a common way to write dynamic content to the page *during* loading. We call the kinds of statements that run as the page loads *immediate statements*. Care must be taken when you code scripts using `document.write()`. Once the page completes loading, any further `document.write()` statements create a new page, overwriting all the content you have carefully written.

LISTING 7-6

HTML Page with Immediate Script Execution

```
<!DOCTYPE html>
<html>
   <head>
      <meta http-equiv="content-type" content="text/html;charset=utf-8">
      <title>Date &amp; Time: Immediate Execution</title>
```

```
    </head>
    <body>
        <h1>Date &amp; Time: Immediate Execution</h1>
        <p>It is currently <span id="output">
        <script type="text/javascript">
            <!-- hide from old browsers
            var oNow = new Date();
            document.write(oNow.toLocaleString());
            // end script hiding -->
        </script>
        </span>.</p>
    </body>
</html>
```

In recent years, the use of document.write() has become mildly controversial. At the very least, it encourages bad structure in your document, mixing script with HTML. Good structure cleanly separates style (style sheets) and behavior (JavaScript) from the HTML markup. One issue with document.write() centers around the increased use of XML to feed content to the browser. XML documents must be well-formed. If a document.write() statement closes an element opened outside of it, or opens a new element, the XML document will fail to load because the browser will perceive it as malformed.

Another issue with document.write() centers around the DOM, especially with XHTML documents (which are served as XML). The use of document.write() means that the content will not be included in the DOM. The very important short story is that you will not be able to further manipulate such content with your JavaScript programs, limiting your dynamic response to the visitor's actions on your web page. This is an interesting conundrum because you might often choose to use document.write(), as we do in several examples in this book, to provide dynamic content, based on the browser environment, as the page loads.

Deferred scripts

The other three ways that script statements run are grouped together into what we call *deferred scripts*. To demonstrate these deferred script situations, we must introduce you briefly to a concept covered in more depth in Chapter 9, "Programming Fundamentals, Part II": the function. A *function* defines a block of script statements summoned to run some time after those statements load into the browser. Functions are clearly visible inside a <script> tag because each function definition begins with the word function followed by the function name (and parentheses). After a function is loaded into the browser (commonly in the head portion so that it loads early), it stands ready to run whenever called upon.

Run after loading

One of the most common times a function is called on to run is immediately after a page loads. Scripts using industry-standard DOM methods would fail if we attempted to operate on page elements before they appeared in the DOM, so we ask the browser to run the script only after the page has finished loading. The window object has an event handler property called onload. Unlike most event handlers, which are triggered in response to user action (for example, clicking a button), the window's onload event handler fires the instant that all of the page's components (including images, Java applets, and embedded multimedia) are loaded into the browser.

There are two cross-browser ways to connect the onload event handler to a function: via an object event property or an HTML event attribute. The object event property we prefer is shown in Listing 7-6. The assignment of the event handler is executed in immediate mode and attaches the desired function call to the load event of the window object. At this early point in page rendering, only the window object can be guaranteed to exist in the DOM.

In old-school web development, the window.onload event assignment was written right into the HTML, with the <body> element standing in to represent the window. Therefore, you can include the onload event attribute in the <body> tag, as shown in Listing 7-7. Recall from Chapter 6, "Browser and Document Objects," that an event handler can run a script statement directly. However, if the event handler must run several script statements, it is usually more convenient to put those statements in a function definition and then have the event handler *invoke* that function. That's what happens in Listing 7-7: When the page completes loading, the onload event handler triggers the done() function. That function (simplified for this example) displays an alert dialog box.

LISTING 7-7

Running a Script from the onload Event Handler

```html
<!DOCTYPE html>
<html>
    <head>
        <meta http-equiv="content-type" content="text/html;charset=utf-8">
        <title>An old-school HTML-based onload script</title>
        <script type="text/javascript">
            function done()
            {
                alert("The page has finished loading.");
            }
        </script>
    </head>
    <body onload="done()">
        <h1>An old-school HTML-based onload script</h1>
        <p>Here is some body text.</p>
    </body>
</html>
```

Don't worry about the curly braces or other oddities in Listing 7-7 at this point. Focus instead on the structure of the document and the flow. The entire page loads without running any script statements, although the page loads the done() function in memory so that it is ready to run at a moment's notice. After the document loads, the browser fires the onload event handler, which causes the done() function to run. Then the user sees the alert dialog box.

Although the HTML event attribute approach dates back to the earliest JavaScript browsers, the trend these days is to separate HTML markup from specifics of style (style sheets) and behavior (scripts). To the scripter's rescue come the equivalent event handler properties of objects. To get the onload attribute out of the <body> tag, you can instead assign the desired JavaScript function to the object's event as a property, as in:

```
window.onload = done;
```

Such statements typically go near the end of scripts in the head portion of the document. Note, too, that in this version, the right side of the statement is merely the function's name, with no quotes or parentheses. Because it is easier to learn about event handlers when they're specified as HTML attributes, most examples in this tutorial continue with that approach. We needed to show you the property version, however, because you will see a lot of real-life code using that format.

Run by user

Getting a script to execute in response to a user action is very similar to the preceding example for running a deferred script right after the document loads. Commonly, a script function is defined in the head portion, and an event handler in, say, a form element calls upon that function to run. Listing 7-8 includes a script that runs when a user clicks a button.

LISTING 7-8

Running a Script from User Action

```
<!DOCTYPE html>
<html>
   <head>
      <meta http-equiv="content-type" content="text/html;charset=utf-8">
      <title>An onclick script</title>
      <script type="text/javascript">
         function alertUser()
         {
            alert("Ouch!");
         }
      </script>
   </head>
   <body>
      Here is some body text.
      <form>
         <input type="text" name="entry">
         <input type="button" name="oneButton"
                value="Press Me!" onclick="alertUser()">
      </form>
   </body>
</html>
```

Not every object must have an event handler defined for it, as shown in Listing 7-8 — only the ones for which scripting is needed. No script statements execute in Listing 7-8 until the user clicks the button. The `alertUser()` function is defined as the page loads, and it waits to run as long as the page remains loaded in the browser. If it is never called upon to run, there's no harm done.

Called by another function

The last scenario for when script statements run also involves functions. In this case, a function is called upon to run by another script statement. Before you see how that works, it helps to read the next lesson, Chapter 8, "Programming Fundamentals, Part I." Therefore, we will hold off on this example until later in the tutorial.

Viewing Script Errors

In the early days of JavaScript in browsers, script errors displayed themselves in very obvious dialog boxes. These boxes were certainly helpful for scripters who wanted to debug their scripts. However, if a bug got through to a page served up to a nontechnical user, the error alert dialog boxes were not only disruptive, but also scary. To prevent such dialog boxes from disturbing unsuspecting users, the browser makers tried to diminish the visual impact of errors in the browser window. Unfortunately for scripters, it is often easy to overlook the fact that your script contains an error because the error message is not so obvious.

Not only does each browser have a different way of displaying error messages, but the display can differ from version to version. The method to display errors in each of the major browsers is covered in the section "Error Message Notification" in Chapter 48, "Debugging Scripts" on the CD-ROM. While you need to read that section before testing your code, we've included a sample error dialog box as it appears in IE5+ (see Figure 7-1) and one as it appears in Mozilla 1.4+ (see Figure 7-2). Keep in mind that script-error dialog boxes are not necessarily displayed by default in these and other browsers. You have to train yourself to monitor the status bar when a page loads and after each script runs.

FIGURE 7-1

The expanded IE error dialog box.

Understanding error messages and doing something about them is a very large subject, the complete discussion of which is in reserved for Chapter 48. During this tutorial, however, you can use the error messages to see whether you mistyped a script from a listing in the book.

FIGURE 7-2

The Mozilla 1.4 JavaScript console window.

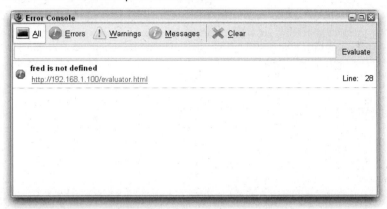

Scripting versus Programming

You may get the impression that scripting is easier than programming. *Scripting* simply sounds easier or more friendly than *programming*. In many respects, this is true. One of our favorite analogies is the difference between a hobbyist who builds model airplanes from scratch and a hobbyist who builds model airplanes from commercial kits. The "from scratch" hobbyist carefully cuts and shapes each piece of wood and metal according to very detailed plans before the model starts to take shape. The commercial kit builder starts with many prefabricated parts and assembles them into the finished product. When both builders are finished, you may not be able to tell which airplane was built from scratch and which one came out of a box of components. In the end, both builders used many of the same techniques to complete the assembly, and each can take pride in the result.

Thanks to implementations of the document object model (DOM), the browser gives scripters many prefabricated components with which to work. Without the browser, you'd have to be a pretty good programmer to develop your own application from scratch that served up content and offered user interaction. In the end, both authors have working applications that look equally professional.

Beyond the DOM, however, real programming nibbles its way into the scripting world. That's because scripts (and programs) work with more than just objects. Earlier in this lesson, we said that each statement of a JavaScript script does "something", and that "something" involves data of some kind. *Data* is the information associated with objects or other pieces of information that a script pushes around from place to place with each statement.

Data takes many forms. In JavaScript, the common incarnations of data are numbers, text (called *strings*), objects (derived from the object model or created with script), and `true` and `false` (called *Boolean values*).

Each programming or scripting language determines numerous structures and limits for each kind of data. Fortunately for newcomers to JavaScript, the universe of knowledge necessary for working with data is smaller than in a language such as Java or C++. At the same time, what you learn

105

about data in JavaScript is immediately applicable to future learning you may undertake in any other programming language; don't believe for an instant that your efforts in learning scripting will be wasted.

Because, deep down, scripting is programming, you need to have a basic knowledge of fundamental programming concepts to consider yourself a good JavaScript scripter. In the next two lessons, we set aside most of our discussion about the DOM and focus on the programming principles that will serve you well in JavaScript and future programming endeavors.

Exercises

1. Write the complete script tag set for a script whose lone statement is

   ```
   document.write("Hello, world.");
   ```

2. Build an HTML document, and include the answer to the previous question, such that the page executes the script as it loads. Open the document in your browser to test the results.

3. Add a comment to the script in the previous answer that explains what the script does.

4. Create an HTML document that displays an alert dialog box immediately after the page loads, and displays a different alert dialog box when the user clicks a form button.

5. Carefully study the document in Listing 7-9. Without entering and loading the document, predict

   a. What the page looks like without further styling

   b. How users interact with the page

   c. What the script does

   Then type the listing as shown into a text editor. Observe all capitalization and punctuation. Do not type a carriage return after the = sign in the upperMe function statement; let the line word-wrap as it does in the following listing. It's okay to use a carriage return between attribute name/value pairs, as shown in the first <input> tag. Save the document as an HTML file, and load the file into your browser to see how well you did.

LISTING 7-9

How Does This Page Work?

```
<!DOCTYPE html>
<html>
   <head>
   <meta http-equiv="content-type" content="text/html;charset=utf-8">
   <title>Text Object Value</title>
      <script type="text/javascript">
         function upperMe()
         {
            document.getElementById("output").value =
            document.getElementById("input").value.toUpperCase();
         }
```

```
        </script>
    </head>

    <body>
        Enter lowercase letters for conversion to uppercase:<br>
        <form name="converter">
            <input type="text" name="input" id="input"
                   value="sample" onchange="upperMe()" /><br />
            <input type="text" name="output" id="output" value="" />
        </form>
    </body>
</html>
```

Programming Fundamentals, Part I

The tutorial breaks away from HTML and documents for a while, as you begin to learn programming fundamentals that apply to practically every scripting and programming language you will encounter. Here, you start learning about variables, expressions, data types, and operators — things that might sound scary if you haven't programmed before. Don't worry. With a little practice, you will become quite comfortable with these terms and concepts.

IN THIS CHAPTER

What variables are and how to use them

Why you must learn how to evaluate expressions

How to convert data from one type to another

How to use basic operators

What Language Is This?

The language you're studying is called JavaScript. But the language has some other names that you may have heard. JScript is Microsoft's name for the language. By leaving out the *ava*, the company doesn't have to license the Java name from its trademark owner: Sun Microsystems.

A standards body called ECMA (pronounced "ECK-ma") now governs the specifications for the language (no matter what you call it). The document that provides all of the details about the language is known as *ECMA-262* (it's the 262nd standard published by ECMA). Both JavaScript and JScript are ECMA-262 compatible. Some earlier browser versions exhibit very slight deviations from ECMA-262 (which came later than the earliest browsers). The most serious discrepancies are noted in the core language reference in Part III of this book.

Working with Information

With rare exceptions, every JavaScript statement you write does something with a hunk of information — *data*. Data may be text information displayed onscreen by a JavaScript statement or the on/off setting of a radio button in a form. Each single piece of information in programming is also called a *value*. Outside of programming, the term *value* usually connotes a number of some kind; in the programming world, however, the term is not as restrictive.

A string of letters is a value. A number is a value. The setting of a checkbox (whether it is checked or not) is a value.

In JavaScript, a value can be one of several types. Table 8-1 lists JavaScript's formal data types, with examples of the values you will see displayed from time to time.

TABLE 8-1

JavaScript Value (Data) Types

Type	Example	Description
String	`"Howdy"`	A series of characters inside quote marks
Number	`4.5`	Any number not inside quote marks
Boolean	`true`	A logical true or false
Null	`null`	Devoid of any content, but a value just the same
Object		A software thing that is defined by its properties and methods (arrays are also objects)
Function		A function definition

A language that contains these few data types simplifies programming tasks, especially those involving what other languages consider to be incompatible types of numbers (integers versus real or floating-point values). In some definitions of syntax and parts of objects later in this book, we make specific reference to the type of value accepted in placeholders. When a string is required, any text inside a set of quotes suffices.

You will encounter situations, however, in which the value type may get in the way of a smooth script step. For example, if a user enters a number into a form's text input field, the browser stores that number as a string value type. If the script is to perform some arithmetic on that number, you must convert the string to a number before you can apply the value to any math operations. You see examples of this later in this lesson.

Variables

Cooking up a dish according to a recipe in the kitchen has one advantage over cooking up some data in a program. In the kitchen, you follow recipe steps and work with real things: carrots, milk, or a salmon filet. A computer, on the other hand, follows a list of instructions to work with data. Even if the data represents something that looks real, such as the text entered into a form's input field, once the value gets into the program, you can no longer reach out and touch it.

In truth, the data that a program works with is merely a collection of bits (on and off states) in your computer's memory. More specifically, data in a JavaScript-enhanced web page occupies parts of the computer's memory set aside for exclusive use by the browser software. In the olden days, programmers had to know the numeric address in memory (RAM) where a value was stored to retrieve a copy of it for, say, some addition. Although the innards of a program have that level of complexity, programming languages such as JavaScript shield you from it.

The most convenient way to work with data in a script is to first assign the data to a *variable*. It's usually easier to think of a variable as a basket that holds information. How long the variable holds the information depends on a number of factors. But the instant a web page clears the window (or frame), any variables it knows about are discarded.

Creating variables

You have a couple of ways to create a variable in JavaScript, but one way covers all cases properly. Use the `var` keyword, followed by the name you want to give that variable. Therefore, to *declare* a new variable called `myAge`, the JavaScript statement is

```
var myAge;
```

That statement lets the browser know that you can use that variable later to hold information or to modify any of the data in that variable.

To assign a value to a variable, use one of the *assignment operators*. The most common one by far is the equal sign. For example, if you want to assign a value to the `myAge` variable at the same time that you declare it (a combined process known as *initializing the variable*), use that operator in the same statement as the `var` keyword:

```
var myAge = 45;
```

On the other hand, if you declare a variable in one statement and later want to assign a value to it, the sequence of statements is

```
var myAge;
myAge = 45;
```

Use the `var` keyword for declaration or initialization — typically only once for the life of any variable name in a document.

A JavaScript variable can hold any value type. Unlike many other languages, you don't have to tell JavaScript during variable declaration what type of value the variable will hold. In fact, the value type of a variable can change during the execution of a program. (This flexibility drives experienced programmers crazy because they're accustomed to assigning both a data type and a value to a variable.)

Naming variables

Choose the names you assign to variables with care. You'll often find scripts that use vague variable names, such as single letters. Other than a few specific circumstances where using letters is a common practice (for example, using `i` as a counting variable in repeat loops in Chapter 9), you should use names that truly describe a variable's contents. This practice can help you follow the state of your data through a long series of statements or jumps, especially for complex scripts.

A number of restrictions help instill good practice in assigning names. First, you cannot use any reserved keyword as a variable name. That includes all keywords currently used by the language and all others held in reserve for future versions of JavaScript. The designers of JavaScript, however, cannot foresee every keyword that the language may need in the future. By using the kind of single words that currently appear in the list of reserved keywords (see Appendix C, on the CD-ROM), you always run a risk of a future conflict.

To complicate matters, a variable name cannot contain space characters. Therefore, one-word variable names are fine. Should your description really benefit from more than one word, you can use one of two conventions to join multiple words as one. One convention is to place an underscore character between the words; the other is to start the combination word with a lowercase letter and capitalize the first letter of each subsequent word within the name — referred to as *CamelCase* or *interCap* format. Both of the following examples are valid variable names:

```
my_age
myAge
```

Our preference is for the second version; it is easier to type and easier to read. In fact, because of the potential conflict with future one-word keywords, using multiword combinations for variable names is a good idea. Multiword combinations are less likely to appear in the list of reserved words.

Variable names have a couple of other important restrictions. Avoid all punctuation symbols except for the underscore character. Also, the first character of a variable name cannot be a numeral. If these restrictions sound familiar, it's because they're similar to those for HTML element identifiers described in Chapter 6.

Expressions and Evaluation

Another concept closely related to the value and variable is *expression evaluation* — perhaps the most important concept in learning how to program a computer.

We use expressions in our everyday language. Remember the theme song of "The Beverly Hillbillies"?:

Then one day he was shootin' at some food
And up through the ground came a-bubblin' crude
Oil, that is. Black gold. Texas tea.

At the end of the song, you find four quite different references (crude, oil, black gold, and Texas tea). They all mean oil. They're all *expressions* for oil. Say any one of them, and other people know what you mean. In our minds, we *evaluate* those expressions to mean one thing: oil.

In programming, a variable always evaluates to its contents, or value. For example, after assigning a value to a variable, such as

```
var myAge = 45;
```

any time the variable is used in a statement, its value (45) is automatically applied to whatever operation that statement calls. Therefore, if you're 15 years my junior, I can assign a value to a variable representing your age based on the evaluated value of myAge:

```
var yourAge = myAge - 15;
```

The variable, yourAge, evaluates to 30 the next time the script uses it. If the myAge value changes later in the script, the change has no link to the yourAge variable because myAge evaluated to 45 when it was used to assign a value to yourAge.

Expressions in scripts

You probably didn't recognize it at the time, but you have seen how expression evaluation came in handy in several scripts in previous chapters. Let's look at one in particular — from

Listing 5-6 — where a script writes dynamic text to the page as the page loads. Recall the second `document.write()` statement:

```
document.write(" of " + navigator.appName + ".");
```

Testing JavaScript Evaluation

You can begin experimenting with the way JavaScript evaluates expressions with the help of The Evaluator Jr. (see Figure 8-1), an HTML page you can find on the companion CD-ROM. (The Senior version is introduced in Chapter 4, "JavaScript Essentials.") Enter any JavaScript expression into the top text box, and either press Enter/Return or click the Evaluate button.

FIGURE 8-1

The Evaluator Jr. for testing expression evaluation.

The Evaluator Jr. has 26 variables (lowercase a through z) predefined for you. Therefore, you can assign values to variables, test comparison operators, and even do math here. Using the age variable examples

continued

continued

from earlier in this chapter, type each of the following statements in the upper text box, and observe how each expression evaluates in the Results field. Be sure to observe case sensitivity in your entries. The trailing semicolons are optional in The Evaluator.

```
a = 45;
a;
b = a - 15;
b;
a - b;
a > b;
```

To start over, click the Reload/Refresh button.

The `document.write()` method (remember, JavaScript uses the term *method* to mean *command*) requires a parameter in the parentheses: the text string to be displayed on the web page. The parameter here consists of one expression that joins three distinct strings:

```
" of "
navigator.appName
"."
```

The plus symbol is one of JavaScript's ways of joining strings. Before JavaScript can display this line, it must perform some quick evaluations. The first evaluation is the value of the `navigator.appName` property. This property evaluates to a string of the name of your browser. With that expression safely evaluated to a string, JavaScript can finish the job of joining the three strings in the final evaluation. The evaluated string expression is what ultimately appears on the web page.

Expressions and variables

As one more demonstration of the flexibility that expression evaluation offers, this section shows you a slightly different route to the `document.write()` statement. Rather than join those strings as the direct parameter to the `document.write()` method, you can gather the strings in a variable and then apply the variable to the `document.write()` method. Here's how that sequence looks, as you simultaneously declare a new variable and assign it a value:

```
var textToWrite = " of " + navigator.appName + ".";
document.write(textToWrite);
```

This method works because the variable, `textToWrite`, evaluates to the combined string. The `document.write()` method accepts that string value and does its display job. As you read a script or try to work through a bug, pay special attention to how each expression (variable, statement, object property) evaluates. As you learn JavaScript (or any language), you will end up scratching your head from time to time because you haven't stopped to examine how expressions evaluate when a particular kind of value is required in a script.

Data Type Conversions

We mentioned earlier that the type of data in an expression can trip up some script operations if the expected components of the operation are not of the right type. JavaScript tries its best to perform internal conversions to head off such problems, but JavaScript cannot read your mind. If your intentions differ from the way JavaScript treats the values, you won't get the results you expect.

A case in point is adding numbers that may be in the form of text strings. In a simple arithmetic statement that adds two numbers, you get the expected result:

```
3 + 3          // result = 6
```

But if one of those numbers is a string, JavaScript leans toward converting the other value to a string — thus turning the plus sign's action from arithmetic addition to joining strings. Therefore, in the statement

```
3 + "3"        // result = "33"
```

the stringness of the second value prevails over the entire operation. The first value is automatically converted to a string, and the result joins the two strings. Try this yourself in The Evaluator Jr.

If you take this progression one step further, look what happens when another number is added to the statement:

```
3 + 3 + "3"    // result = "63"
```

This might seem totally illogical, but there is logic behind this result. The expression is evaluated from left to right. The first plus operation works on two numbers, yielding a value of 6. But as the 6 is about to be added to the 3, JavaScript lets the stringness of the 3 rule. The 6 is converted to a string, and two string values are joined to yield 63.

Most of your concern about data types will focus on performing math operations like the ones here. However, some object methods also require one or more parameters of particular data types. Although JavaScript provides numerous ways to convert data from one type to another, it is appropriate at this stage of the tutorial to introduce you to the two most common data conversions: string to number and number to string.

Converting strings to numbers

As you saw in the preceding section, if a numeric value is stored as a string — as it is when entered into a form text field — your scripts may have difficulty applying that value to a math operation. The JavaScript language provides two built-in functions to convert string representations of numbers to true numbers: parseInt() and parseFloat().

There is a difference between integers and floating-point numbers in JavaScript. *Integers* are always whole numbers, with no decimal point or numbers to the right of a decimal. *Floating-point numbers,* on the other hand, have fractional values to the right of the decimal. By and large, JavaScript math operations don't differentiate between integers and floating-point numbers: A number is a number. The only time you need to be cognizant of the difference is when a method parameter requires an integer because it can't handle fractional values. For example, parameters to the scroll() method of a window require integer values of the numbers of pixels vertically and horizontally that you want to scroll the window. That's because you can't scroll a window a fraction of a pixel onscreen.

To use either of these conversion functions, insert the string value you wish to convert as a parameter to the function. For example, look at the results of two different string values when passed through the parseInt() function:

```
parseInt("42")          // result = 42
parseInt("42.33")       // result = 42
```

Even though the second expression passes the string version of a floating-point number to the function, the value returned by the function is an integer. No rounding of the value occurs here (although other math functions can help with that if necessary). The decimal and everything to its right are simply stripped off.

The parseFloat() function returns an integer if it can; otherwise, it returns a floating-point number, as follows:

```
parseFloat("42")        // result = 42
parseFloat("42.33")     // result = 42.33
```

Because these two conversion functions evaluate to their results, you simply insert the entire function wherever you need a string value converted to a number. Therefore, modifying an earlier example in which one of three values was a string, the complete expression can evaluate to the desired result:

```
3 + 3 + parseInt("3")  // result = 9
```

Converting numbers to strings

You'll have less need for converting a number to its string equivalent than the other way around. As you saw in the previous section, JavaScript gravitates toward strings when faced with an expression containing mixed data types. Even so, it is good practice to perform data type conversions explicitly in your code to prevent any potential ambiguity. The simplest way to convert a number to a string is to take advantage of JavaScript's string tendencies in addition operations. By adding an empty string to a number, you convert the number to its string equivalent:

```
("" + 2500)            // result = "2500"
("" + 2500).length     // result = 4
```

In the second example, you can see the power of expression evaluation at work. The parentheses force the conversion of the number to a string. A *string* is a JavaScript object that has properties associated with it. One of those properties is the length property, which evaluates to the number of characters in the string. Therefore, the length of the string "2500" is 4. Note that the length value is a number, not a string.

Operators

You will use lots of *operators* in expressions. Earlier, you used the equal sign (=) as an assignment operator to assign a value to a variable. In the preceding examples with strings, you used the plus symbol (+) to join two strings. An operator generally performs some kind of calculation (operation) or comparison with two values (the value on each side of an operator is called an *operand*) to reach a third value. This lesson briefly describes two categories of operators: arithmetic and comparison. Chapter 22, "JavaScript Operators," covers many more operators, but after you understand the basics here, the others are easier to grasp.

Arithmetic operators

It may seem odd to talk about text strings in the context of arithmetic operators, but you have already seen the special case of the plus (+) operator when one or more of the operands is a string. The plus operator instructs JavaScript to *concatenate* (pronounced "kon-KAT-en-eight"), or join, two strings together precisely where you place the operator. The string concatenation operator doesn't know about words and spaces, so the programmer must make sure that any two strings to be joined have the proper word spacing as part of the strings, even if that means adding a space:

```
firstName = "John";
lastName = "Doe";
fullName = firstName + " " + lastName;
```

JavaScript uses the same plus operator for arithmetic addition. When both operands are numbers, JavaScript knows to treat the expression as an arithmetic addition rather than a string concatenation. The standard math operators for addition, subtraction, multiplication, and division (+, -, *, /) are built into JavaScript.

Comparison operators

Another category of operator helps you compare values in scripts — whether two values are the same, for example. These kinds of comparisons return a value of the Boolean type: true or false. Table 8-2 lists the comparison operators. The operator that tests whether two items are equal consists of a pair of equal signs to distinguish it from the single-equal-sign assignment operator.

TABLE 8-2

JavaScript Comparison Operators

Symbol	Description
==	Equals
!=	Does not equal
>	Is greater than
>=	Is greater than or equal to
<	Is less than
<=	Is less than or equal to

Comparison operators come into greatest play in the construction of scripts that make decisions as they run. A cook does this in the kitchen all the time: If the sauce is too watery, add a bit of flour. You see comparison operators in action in Chapter 22.

Exercises

1. Which of the following are valid variable declarations or initializations? Explain why each one is or is not valid. If an item is not valid, how do you fix it so that it is?
   a. `my_name = "Cind";`
   b. `var how many = 25;`
   c. `var zipCode = document.getElementById("zip").value`
   d. `var 1address = document.("address1").value;`

2. Assume that the following statements operate rapidly in sequence, where each statement relies on the result of the one before it. For each of the statements in the sequence, write down how the `someVal` expression evaluates after the statement executes in JavaScript.

   ```
   var someVal = 2;
   someVal = someVal + 2;
   someVal = someVal * 10;
   someVal = someVal + "20";
   someVal = "Robert";
   ```

3. Name the two JavaScript functions that convert strings to numbers. How do you give the function a string value to convert to a number?

4. Type and load the HTML page and script shown in Listing 8-1. Enter a three-digit number in the top two fields, and click the Add button. Examine the code, and explain what is wrong with the script. How do you fix the script so that the proper sum is displayed in the output field?

LISTING 8-1

What's Wrong with This Script?

HTML: `jsb-08-01.html`

```html
<!DOCTYPE html>
<html>
   <head>
      <meta http-equiv="content-type" content="text/html;charset=utf-8">
      <title>Making Sums</title>
      <script type="text/javascript" src="../jsb-global.js"></script>
      <script type="text/javascript" src="jsb-08-01.js"></script>
   </head>
   <body>
      <h1>Making Sums</h1>
      <form action="addit.php">
         <p><input type="text" id="inputA" name="inputA" value="0"></p>
         <p><input type="text" id="inputB" name="inputB" value="0"></p>
         <p><input type="button" id="add" name="add" value="Add"></p>
         <p><input type="text" id="output" name="output"></p>
      </form>
   </body>
</html>
```

JavaScript: jsb-08-01.js

```javascript
// initialize when the page has loaded
addEvent(window, 'load', initialize);

function initialize()
{
    // do this only if the browser can handle DOM methods
    if (document.getElementById)
    {
        // point to critical elements
        var oInputA = document.getElementById('inputA');
        var oInputB = document.getElementById('inputB');
        var oButton = document.getElementById('add');
        var oOutput = document.getElementById('output');

            // if they all exist...
            if (oInputA && oInputB && oButton && oOutput)
            {
                // apply behaviors
                addEvent(oButton, 'click', addIt);
            }
    }
}

// add two input numbers & display result
function addIt()
{
    var value1 = document.getElementById("inputA").value;
    var value2 = document.getElementById("inputB").value;

    document.getElementById("output").value = value1 + value2;
}
```

5. What does the term *concatenate* mean in the context of JavaScript programming?

Programming Fundamentals, Part II

Your tour of programming fundamentals continues in this chapter with subjects that have more intriguing possibilities. For example, we show you how programs make decisions and why a program must sometimes repeat statements over and over. Before you're finished here, you also will learn how to use one of the most powerful information holders in the JavaScript language: the array.

Decisions and Loops

Every waking hour of every day, you make decisions of some kind; most of the time, you probably don't even realize it. Don't think so? Well, look at the number of decisions you make at the grocery store, from the moment you enter the store to the moment you clear the checkout aisle.

No sooner do you enter the store than you are faced with a decision. Based on the number and size of items you intend to buy, do you pick up a hand-carried basket or attempt to extricate a shopping cart from the metallic conga line near the front of the store? That key decision may have impact later, when you see a special offer on an item that is too heavy to put in the handbasket.

Next, you head for the food aisles. Before entering an aisle, you compare the range of goods stocked in that aisle with items on your shopping list. If an item you need is likely to be found in this aisle, you turn into the aisle and start looking for the item; otherwise, you skip the aisle and move to the head of the next aisle.

Later, you reach the produce section in search of a juicy tomato. Standing in front of the bin of tomatoes, you begin inspecting them one by one — picking one up, feeling its firmness, checking the color, looking for blemishes or signs of pests. You discard one, pick up another, and continue this process until one matches the criteria you set in your mind for an acceptable morsel. Your last stop in the store is the checkout aisle. "Paper or plastic?" the clerk asks. One more decision to make. What you choose affects how you get the groceries from the car to the kitchen, as well as your recycling habits.

During your trip to the store, you go through the same kinds of decisions and repetitions that your JavaScript programs encounter. If you understand these frameworks in real life, you can look into the JavaScript equivalents and the syntax required to make them work.

Control Structures

In the vernacular of programming, the kinds of statements that make decisions and loop around to repeat themselves are called *control structures*. A control structure directs the execution flow through a sequence of script statements based on simple decisions and other factors.

An important part of a control structure is the *condition*. Just as you may travel different routes to work depending on certain conditions (for example, nice weather, nighttime, whether you're attending a soccer game), so, too, does a program sometimes have to branch to an execution route if a certain condition exists. Each condition is an expression that evaluates to true or false — one of those Boolean data types mentioned in Chapter 8. The kinds of expressions commonly used for conditions are expressions that include a comparison operator. You do the same in real life: If it is true that the outdoor temperature is less than freezing, you put on a coat before going outside. In programming, the comparisons are strictly comparisons of numeric values and character strings.

JavaScript provides several kinds of control structures for different programming situations. Three of the most common control structures you'll use are if constructions, if...else constructions, and for loops.

Chapter 21 covers in great detail other common control structures you should know. For this tutorial, however, you need to learn about the three common ones just mentioned.

if constructions

The simplest program decision is to follow a special branch or path of the program if a certain condition is true. Formal syntax for this construction follows. Items in italics get replaced in a real script with expressions and statements that fit the situation.

```
if (condition)
{
    statement[s] if true
}
```

Don't worry about the curly braces yet. Instead, get a feel for the basic structure. The keyword, if, is a must. Between the parentheses goes an expression that evaluates to a Boolean (true/false) value. This is the condition being tested as the program runs past this point. If the condition evaluates to true, one or more statements inside the curly braces execute before the program continues with the next statement after the closing brace. If the condition evaluates to false, the statements inside the curly braces are ignored, and processing continues with the next statement after the closing brace.

The following example assumes that a variable, myAge, has had its value set earlier in the script (exactly how is not important for this example). The conditional expression compares the value myAge against a numeric value of 13:

```
if (myAge < 13)
{
    alert("You are not yet a teenager.");
}
```

In this example, the data type of the value inside myAge must be a number so that the proper comparison (via the <, or less than, comparison operator) does the right thing. For all instances of myAge less than 13, the nested statement inside the curly braces runs and displays the alert to the user. After the user closes the alert dialog box, the script continues with whatever statement follows the entire if construction.

if . . . else constructions

Not all program decisions are as simple a the one shown for the if construction. Rather than speci-fying one detour for a given condition, ya might want the program to follow either of two branches depending on that condition. It is a fine ut important distinction. In the plain if construction, no special processing is performed when the condition evaluates to false. But if processing must follow one of two special paths, you need the i...else construction. The formal syntax definition for an if...else construction is as follows:

```
if (condition)
{
    statement[s] if tre
}
else
{
    statement[s] if flse
}
```

Everything you know about the condon for an if construction applies here. The only difference is the else keyword, which provides alternative path for execution to follow if the condition evalu-ates to false.

As an example, the following if..lse construction determines how many days are in February for a given year. To simplify the der the condition simply tests whether the year divides equally by 4. (True testing for this value inclu special treatment of end-of-century dates, but we're ignoring that for now.) The % operator symbs called the *modulus operator* (covered in more detail in Chapter 22). The result of an operation withis operator yields the remainder of division of the two values. If the remainder is zero, the first valuivides evenly by the second.

```
var febDays;
var theYear = 2010;
    if (theYear % 4 =0)
    {
        febDays = 29;
    }
    else
    {
        febDays = 28
    }
```

The important point to see frors example is that by the end of the if...else construction, the febDays variable is set to eith 8 or 29. No other value is possible. For years evenly divisible by 4, the first nested statement runs all other cases, the second statement runs. Then processing picks up with the next statement afte if...else construction.

Repeat Loops

Repeat loops in real life generally mean the repetition of a series of steps until some condition is met, thus enabling you to break out of that loop. Such was the case earlier in this chapter, when you looked through a bushel of tomatoes for the one that came closest to your ideal tomato. The same can be said for driving around the block in a crowded neighborhood until a parking space opens up.

A *repeat loop* lets a script cycle through a sequence of statements until some condition is met. For example, a JavaScript data validation routine might inspect every character that you enter in a form text field to make sure that each one is a number. Or, if you have a collection of data stored in a list, the loop can check whether an entered value is in that list. When that condition is met, the script can break out of the loop and continue with the next statement after the loop construction.

The most common repeat loop construction used in JavaScript is called the for loop. It gets its name from the keyword that begins the construction. A for loop is a powerful device because you can set it up to keep track of the number of times the loop repeats itself. The formal syntax of the for loop is as follows:

```
for ([initial expression]; [condition]; [update expression])
{
    statement[s] inside loop
}
```

The square brackets mean that the item is optional. However, until you get to know the for loop better, we recommend designing your loops to use three items inside the parentheses. The *initial expression* portion usually sets the starting value of a counter variable. The *condition* — the same kind of condition you saw for if constructions — defines the condition that forces the loop to stop going around and around. Finally, the *update expression* is a statement that executes each time all the statements nested inside the construction complete running.

A common implementation initializes a counting variable, i; increments the value of i by 1 each time through the loop; and repeats the loop until the value i exceeds some maximum value, as in the following:

```
for (var i = startValue; i <= maxValue; i++)
{
    statement[s] inside loop
}
```

Placeholders startValue and maxValue represent any numeric values, including explicit numbers or variables holding numbers. In the update expression an operator we have not presented yet. The ++ operator adds 1 to the value of i each time the update expression runs at the end of the loop. If startValue is 1, the value of i is 1 the first time through the loop, 2 the second time through, and so on. Therefore, if maxValue is 10, the loop repeats itself 10 times (in other words, as long as i is less than or equal to 10). Generally speaking, the statements inside the loop use the value of the counting variable in their execution. Later in this lesson, show how the variable can play a key role in the statements inside a loop. At the same time, you will how to break out of a loop prematurely and why you may need to do this in a script.

Functions

In Chapter 7, you saw a preview of the JavaScript function. function is a definition of a set of deferred actions. Functions are invoked by event handlers statements elsewhere in the script.

Whenever possible, good functions are designed for reuse in other documents. They can become building blocks you use over and over again.

If you have programmed before, you can see parallels between JavaScript functions and other languages' subroutines. But unlike some languages that distinguish between procedures (which carry out actions) and functions (which carry out actions and return values), only one classification of routine exists for JavaScript. A function is capable of returning a value to the statement that invoked it, but this is not a requirement. When a function does return a value, the calling statement treats the function call like any expression — plugging in the returned value right where the function call is made. We will show some examples in a moment.

Formal syntax for a function is as follows:

```
function functionName ( [parameter1]...[,parameterN] )
{
    statement[s]
}
```

Names you assign to functions have the same restrictions as names you assign to HTML elements and variables. You should devise a name that succinctly describes what the function does. We tend to use multiword names with the CamelCase or interCap (internally capitalized) format that start with a verb because functions are action items, even if they do nothing more than get or set a value.

Another practice to keep in mind as you start to create functions is to keep the focus of each function as narrow as possible. It is possible to generate functions that are literally hundreds of lines long. Such functions are usually difficult to maintain and debug. Chances are that you can divide the long function into smaller, more tightly focused segments.

Function parameters

In Chapter 4, you saw how an event handler invokes a function by calling the function by name. A typical call to a function, including one that comes from another JavaScript statement, works the same way: A set of parentheses follows the function name.

You also can define functions so that they receive parameter values from the calling statement. Listing 9-1 shows a simple script in which a statement passes text data to a function at the same time that it calls the function.

LISTING 9-1

Calling a Function from an Event Handler

HTML: jsb-09-01.html

```
<!DOCTYPE html>
<html>
   <head>
      <meta http-equiv="content-type" content="text/html;charset=utf-8">
      <title>Passing a Parameter to a Function</title>
      <script type="text/javascript" src="jsb-09-01.js"></script>
   </head>
```

continued

125

LISTING 9-1 *(continued)*

```
    <body>
        <h1>Passing a Parameter to a Function</h1>
    </body>
</html>
```

JavaScript: jsb-09-01.js

```
// display a personalized greeting
function greeting(sName)
{
    alert("Hello, " + sName + "!");
}

greeting("Chris");
```

Parameters (also known as *arguments*) provide a mechanism for handing off a value from one statement to another by way of a function call. If no parameters occur in the function definition, both the function definition and the call to the function have only empty sets of parentheses (as shown in Chapter 4, Listing 4-2).

When a function receives parameters, it assigns the incoming values to the variable names specified in the function definition's parentheses. Consider the following script segment:

```
function sayHelloFirst(a, b, c)        → Passing 3 strings as
{                                         parameter
    alert("Say hello, " + a);
}
sayHelloFirst("Gracie", "George", "Harry");
sayHelloFirst("Larry", "Moe", "Curly");
```

After the function is defined in the script, the next statement calls that very function, passing three strings as parameters. The function definition automatically assigns the strings to variables a, b, and c. Therefore, before the alert() statement inside the function ever runs, a evaluates to "Gracie", b evaluates to "George", and c evaluates to "Harry". In the alert() statement, only the a value is used, and the alert reads

```
    Say hello, Gracie
```

When the user closes the first alert, the next call to the function occurs. This time through, different values are passed to the function and assigned to a, b, and c. The alert dialog box reads

```
    Say hello, Larry
```

Unlike other variables that you define in your script, function parameters do not use the var keyword to initialize them. They are automatically initialized whenever the function is called.

Variable scope

Speaking of variables, it's time to distinguish between variables that are defined outside and those that are defined inside functions. Variables defined outside of functions are called *global variables;* those defined inside functions with the `var` keyword are called *local variables.*

A global variable has a slightly different connotation in JavaScript than it has in most other languages. For a JavaScript script, the globe of a global variable is the current document loaded in a browser window or frame. Therefore, when you initialize a variable as a global variable, it means that all script statements in the page (including those inside functions) have direct access to that variable's value via the variable's name. Statements can retrieve and modify global variables from anywhere in the script. In programming terminology, this kind of variable is said to have *global scope* because every statement on the page can see it.

It is important to remember that the instant a page unloads itself, all global variables defined in that page disappear from memory forever. If you need a value to persist from one page to another, you must use other techniques to store that value (for example, as a global variable in a framesetting document, as described in Chapter 27, "Window and Frame Objects," or in a cookie, as described in Chapter 29, "The Document and Body Objects." Although the `var` keyword is usually optional for initializing global variables, we strongly recommend that you use it for all variable initializations to guard against future changes to the JavaScript language.

In contrast to the global variable, a local variable is defined inside a function. You already saw how parameter variables are defined inside functions (without `var` keyword initializations). But you can also define other variables with the `var` keyword (absolutely required for local variables; otherwise, they become recognized as global variables). The scope of a local variable is only within the statements of the function. No other functions or statements outside functions have access to a local variable.

Local scope allows for the reuse of variable names within a document. For most variables, we strongly discourage this practice because it leads to confusion and bugs that are difficult to track down. At the same time, it is convenient to reuse certain kinds of variable names, such as `for` loop counters. These are safe because they are always reinitialized with a starting value whenever a `for` loop starts. In order to nest one `for` loop inside another, you need to specify a different loop-counting variable in the nested loop.

To demonstrate the structure and behavior of global and local variables — and show you why it can get confusing to reuse most variable names inside a script — Listing 9-2 defines two global variables and a local one. For the purposes of this illustration, we intentionally use bad form by initializing a local variable that has the same name as a global variable.

LISTING 9-2

Global and Local Variable Scope Demonstration

HTML: `jsb-09-02.html`

```html
<!DOCTYPE html>
<html>
   <head>
      <meta http-equiv="content-type" content="text/html;charset=utf-8">
      <title>Global and Local Variable Scope</title>
```

continued

LISTING 9-2   *(continued)*

```
    <script type="text/javascript" src="jsb-09-02.js"></script>
  </head>
  <body>
    <h1>Global and Local Variable Scope</h1>
  </body>
</html>
```

JavaScript: jsb-09-02.js

```
var Boy = "Charlie Brown";   // global
var Dog = "Snoopy";          // global

// using improper design to demonstrate a point
function demo()
{
   // local variable with the same name as a global
   var Dog = "Gromit";

   alert(Dog + " does not belong to " + Boy + ".");
}

// use global variables
alert(Dog + " belongs to " + Boy + ".");

// use global & local variables
demo();
```

When the page loads, the script initializes the two global variables (Boy and Dog) and defines the demo() function in memory. Inside the function, a local variable is initialized with the same name as one of the global variables: Dog. In JavaScript, such a local initialization overrides the global variable for all statements inside the function. (But note that if we had omitted the var keyword from the local initialization, the variable Dog inside the function would have referred to the global variable — i.e., "Gromit".)

The script displays two alert dialogs. The first to appear concatenates the two global variables to display:

```
Snoopy belongs to Charlie Brown.
```

The second dialog, invoked by calling the function demo() in the last line of the script, occurs inside the demo() function and therefore uses the local variable Dog instead of the global one:

```
Gromit does not belong to Charlie Brown.
```

Curly Braces

Despite the fact that you probably rarely — if ever — use curly braces ({ }) in your writing, there is no mystery to their usage in JavaScript (and many other languages). Curly braces enclose blocks of statements that belong together. Although they do assist humans who are reading scripts in knowing what's going on, curly braces also help the browser know which statements belong together. You always must use curly braces in matched pairs.

You use curly braces most commonly in function definitions and control structures. In the function definition in Listing 9-2, curly braces enclose three statements (including the comment line) that make up the function definition. The closing brace lets the browser know that whatever statement comes next is a statement outside the function definition.

Physical placement of curly braces is not critical. (Neither is the indentation style you see in the code we provide.) The following function definitions are treated identically by scriptable browsers:

```
function sayHiToFirst(a, b, c)
{
    alert("Say hello, " + a);
}
function sayHiToFirst(a, b, c) {
    alert("Say hello, " + a);
}

function sayHiToFirst(a, b, c) {alert("Say hello, " + a);}
```

Throughout this book, we use the style shown in the first example because we find that it makes lengthy and complex scripts easier to read — especially scripts that have many levels of nested control structures. However, this aspect of scripting style is highly personal and varies from one programmer to another — even among the co-authors of this book!

Arrays

The JavaScript array is one of the most useful data constructions you have available to you. You can visualize the structure of a basic array as though it were a single-column spreadsheet. Each row of the column holds a distinct piece of data, and each row is numbered. Numbers assigned to rows are in strict numerical sequence, starting with zero as the first row. (Computers tend to start counting with zero.) This row number is called an *index*. To access an item in an array, you need to know the name of the array and the index for the row. Because index values start with zero, the total number of items of the array (as determined by the array's length property) is always one more than the highest index value of the array. More advanced array concepts enable you to create the equivalent of an array with multiple columns (described in Chapter 18). For this tutorial, we stay with the single-column basic array.

Data elements inside JavaScript arrays can be any data type, including objects. And unlike a lot of other programming languages, JavaScript allows different rows of the same array to contain different data types.

Creating an array

An array is stored in a variable, so when you create an array, you assign the new array object to the variable. (Arrays are objects that belong to the core JavaScript language rather than to the document object model [DOM].) A special keyword — new — preceding a call to the JavaScript function that generates arrays creates space in memory for the array. An optional parameter to the Array() function enables you to specify at the time of creation how many elements (rows) of data eventually will occupy the array. JavaScript is very forgiving about this because you can change the size of an array at any time. Therefore, if you omit a parameter when generating a new array, your script incurs no penalty.

To demonstrate the array creation process, we create an array that holds the names of the 50 U.S. states plus the District of Columbia (a total of 51). The first task is to create that array and assign it to a variable of any name that helps us remember what this collection of data is about:

```
var USStates = new Array(51);
```

At this point, the USStates array is sitting in memory like a 51-row table with no data in it. To fill the rows, we must assign data to each row. Addressing each row of an array requires a special way of indicating the index value of the row: square brackets after the name of the array. The first row of the USStates array is addressed as:

```
USStates[0]
```

To assign the string name of the first state of the alphabet to that row, use a simple assignment operator:

```
USStates[0] = "Alabama";
```

To fill in the rows, include a statement for each row:

```
USStates[0] = "Alabama";
USStates[1] = "Alaska";
USStates[2] = "Arizona";
USStates[3] = "Arkansas";
...
USStates[50] = "Wyoming";
```

(Note that the 51st array element has an index of 50 because we're starting with 0, not 1.)

Therefore, if you want to include a table of information from which a script can look up information without accessing the server, you include the data in the script in the form of an array creation sequence. When the script loads into the browser and the statements run, the data collection array is built and ready to go. Despite what appears to be the potential for a lot of statements in a document for such a data collection, the amount of data that must download for typical array collections is small enough not to affect page loading severely — even for dial-up users. In Chapter 18, you also see some syntax shortcuts for creating arrays that reduce source code character counts.

Accessing array data

The array index is the key to accessing an array element. The name of the array and an index in square brackets evaluates to the content of that array location. For example, after the USStates array is built, a script can display an alert with Alaska's name in it with the following statement:

```
alert("The largest state is " + USStates[1] + ".");
```

Just as you can retrieve data from an indexed array element, you can change the element by reassigning a new value to any indexed element in the array.

Parallel arrays

Now we show you why the numeric index methodology works well in JavaScript. To help with the demonstration, we generate another array that is parallel with the USStates array. This new array is also 51 elements long, and it contains the year in which the state in the corresponding row of USStates entered the Union. That array construction looks like the following:

```
var stateEntered = new Array(51);
stateEntered [0] = 1819;
stateEntered [1] = 1959;
stateEntered [2] = 1912;
stateEntered [3] = 1836;
...
stateEntered [50] = 1890;
```

In the browser's memory, then, are two data tables that you can visualize as looking like the model in Figure 9-1. We can build more arrays that are parallel to these for items such as the postal abbreviation and capital city. The important point is that the zeroth element in each of these tables applies to Alabama, the first state in the USStates array.

FIGURE 9-1

Visualization of two related parallel data tables.

USStates		stateEntered
"Alabama"	[0]	1819
"Alaska"	[1]	1959
"Arizona"	[2]	1912
"Arkansas"	[3]	1836
⋮	⋮	⋮
"Wyoming"	[50]	1890

If a web page included these data tables and a way for a user to look up the entry date for a given state, the page would need a way to look through all the USStates entries to find the index value of the one that matches the user's entry. Then that index value could be applied to the stateEntered array to find the matching year.

For this demo, the page includes a text entry field in which the user types the name of the state to look up. This methodology is fraught with peril unless the script performs some error checking in case the user makes a mistake. Let's not assume that the user always types a valid state name; instead, let's gracefully handle the circumstance in which they don't. (Don't ever assume that user input is valid in your web site's pages.) An event handler from either the text field or a clickable button calls a function that looks up the state name, fetches the corresponding entry year, and displays an alert message with the information. The function is as follows:

```
function getStateDate()
{
    var selectedState = document.getElementById("entry").value;
    for (var i = 0; i < USStates.length; i++)
    {
```

[handwritten annotations:] initial expression (start value) — condition (max value) — update expression (adds 1 to the value of i each time)

131

Handwritten margin notes (left): statement inside loop (if construction inside for loop)

```
if (USStates[i] == selectedState)
    {
        break;
    }
}

if (i < USStates.length)
    {
        alert(selectedState + " entered the Union in " + stateEn-
tered[i] + ".");
    }
    else
    {
        alert("Sorry, '" + selectedState + "' isn't a US state.");
    }
}
```

In the first statement of the function, we grab the value of the text box and assign the value to a variable, selectedState. This is mostly for convenience, so that we can use this shorter variable name later in the script. In fact, the usage of that value is inside a for loop, so the script is marginally more efficient because the browser doesn't have to evaluate that long reference to the text field each time through the loop.

The key to this function is in the for loop. Here is where we combine the natural behavior of incrementing a loop counter with the index values assigned to the two arrays. Specifications for the loop indicate that the counter variable, i, is initialized with a value of zero. The loop is directed to continue as long as the value of i is less than the length of the USStates array. Remember that the length of an array is always one more than the index value of the last item. Therefore, the last time the loop runs is when i is 50, which is both less than the length of 51 and equal to the index value of the last element. Each time after the loop runs, the counter increments by 1 (i++).

Nested inside the for loop is an if construction. The condition tests the value of an element of the array against the value typed by the user. Each time through the loop, the condition tests a different row of the array, starting with row zero. In other words, this if construction can be performed dozens of times before a match is found, but each time, the value of i is 1 larger than in the previous try.

The equality comparison operator (==) is fairly strict when it comes to comparing string values. Such comparisons respect the case of each letter. In our example, the user must type the state name exactly as it is stored in the USStates array for the match to be found. In Chapter 12, you learn about some helper methods that eliminate case and sensitivity in string comparisons.

When a match is found, the statement nested inside the if construction runs. The break statement is designed to help control structures bail out if the program needs it. For this application, it is imperative that the for loop stop running when a match for the state name is found. When the for loop breaks, the value of the i counter is fixed at the row of the USStates array containing the entered state. We need that index value to find the corresponding entry in the other array. Even though the counting variable, i, is initialized in the for loop, it is still alive and in the scope of the function for all statements after the initialization. That's why we can use it to extract the value of the row of the stateEntered array in the final statement that displays the results in an alert message.

If the entered state name doesn't match any of the values in the USStates array, the counter variable i increments to the length of the array (51) and the for loop terminates, leaving i equal to 51. From that we can easily tell whether we successfully found a state name match and display an error message if no match was found.

This application of a `for` loop and array indexes is a common one in JavaScript. Study the code carefully, and be sure you understand how it works. This way of cycling through arrays plays a role not only in the kinds of arrays you create in your code, but also in the arrays that browsers generate for the DOM.

Document objects in arrays

If you look at the `document` object portions of the Quick Reference in Appendix A, you can see that the properties of some objects are listed with square brackets after them. These are indeed the same kind of square brackets you just saw for array indexes. That's because when a document loads, the browser creates arrays of like objects in the document. For example, if your page includes two `<form>` tag sets, two forms appear in the document. The browser maintains an array of `form` objects for that document. References to those forms are

```
document.forms[0]
document.forms[1]
```

You can also capture this array using the DOM method `getElementsByTagName()`:

```
var aForms = document.getElementsByTagName('form');
```

and then refer to the form array items with:

```
aForms[0]
aForms[1]
```

Index values for objects are assigned according to the loading order of the objects. In the case of `form` objects, the order is dictated by the order of the `<form>` tags in the document. This indexed array syntax is another way to reference forms in an object reference. You can still use a form's identifier (`id` attribute) if you prefer — and we heartily recommend using object names wherever possible, because even if you change the physical order of the objects in your HTML, references that use names still work without modification. But if your page contains only one form, you can use the reference types interchangeably, as in the following examples of equivalent references to the `length` property of a form's `elements` array (the `elements` array contains all the form controls in the form):

```
document.getElementById("entryForm").elements.length
document.forms[0].elements.length
document.getElementsByTagName('form')[0].elements.length
```

In examples throughout this book, you can see that we often use the array type of reference to simple forms in simple documents. But in our production pages, we almost always use named references.

Exercises

1. With your newly acquired knowledge of functions, event handlers, and control structures, use the script fragments from this chapter to complete the page that has the lookup table for all the states and the years they entered into the union. If you do not have a reference book for the dates, use different year numbers, starting with 1800 for each entry. In the page, create a text entry field for the state and a button that triggers the lookup in the arrays.

2. Examine the following function definition. Can you spot any problems with the definition? If so, how can you fix the problems?

```
function format(ohmage)
{
    var result;
    if ohmage >= 1e6
    {
        ohmage = ohmage / 1e6;
        result = ohmage + " Mohms";
    }
    else
    {
        if (ohmage >= 1e3)
            ohmage = ohmage / 1e3;
            result = ohmage + " Kohms";
        else
            result = ohmage + " ohms";
    }
    alert(result);
```

3. Devise your own syntax for the scenario of looking for a ripe tomato at the grocery store, and write a `for` loop using that object and property syntax.

4. Modify Listing 9-2 so that it does not reuse the `Dog` variable inside the function.

5. Given the following table of data about several planets of our solar system, create a web page that enables users to enter a planet name and, at the click of a button, have the distance and diameter appear either in an alert box or (as extra credit) in separate fields of the page.

Planet	Distance from the Sun	Diameter
Mercury	36 million miles	3,100 miles
Venus	67 million miles	7,700 miles
Earth	93 million miles	7,920 miles
Mars	141 million miles	4,200 miles

Window and Document Objects

N ow that you have exposure to programming fundamentals, it is easier to demonstrate how to script objects in documents. Starting with this lesson, the tutorial turns back to the Document Object Model (DOM), diving more deeply into the objects you will place in many of your documents.

Top-Level Objects

As a refresher, study the hierarchy of top-level objects in Figure 10-1. This chapter focuses on objects of this level that you'll frequently encounter in your scripting: window, location, navigator, and document. The goal is not only to equip you with the basics so you can script simple tasks, but also to prepare you for the in-depth examinations of each object and its properties, methods, and event handlers, that you will find in Part IV, "Document Objects Reference." We introduce only the basic properties, methods, and events for objects in this tutorial. Examples in Part IV of the book assume that you know the programming fundamentals covered here in Part II.

The window Object

At the top of the object hierarchy is the window object. This object gains that exalted spot in the object food chain because it is the master container for all content you view in the web browser. As long as a browser window is open — even if no document is loaded in the window — the window object is defined in the current model in memory.

In addition to the content part of the window where documents go, a window's sphere of influence includes the dimensions of the window and all the stuff that surrounds the content area. The area where scrollbars, toolbars, the status bar, and (non-Macintosh) menu bar live is known as a window's *chrome*. Not every browser has full scripted control over the chrome of the main browser window,

IN THIS CHAPTER

What the window object does

How to access key window object properties and methods

How to trigger script actions after a document loads

The purposes of the location and navigator objects

How the document object is created

How to access key document object properties and methods

but you can easily script the creation of additional windows sized the way you want and with only the chrome elements you wish to display.

FIGURE 10-1

The top-level browser object model for all scriptable browsers.

Although the discussion of frames comes in Chapter 13, "Scripting Frames and Multiple Windows," we can now safely say that each frame is also considered a `window` object. If you think about it, that makes sense, because each frame can hold a different document. When a script runs in one of those documents, it regards the frame that holds the document as the `window` object in its view of the object hierarchy.

As you will learn in this chapter, the `window` object is a convenient place for the DOM to attach methods that display modal dialog boxes and adjust the text that displays in the status bar at the bottom of the browser window. A `window` object method enables you to create a separate window that appears onscreen. When you look at all of the properties, methods, and events defined for the `window` object (see Chapter 27, "Window and Frame Objects"), it should be clear why they are attached to window objects: Visualize their scope and the scope of a browser window.

Note

In the modern crop of browsers, the user is given the choice of opening web pages either in new *tabs* within one browser or in new *browser windows*, which are separate copies of the browser program on the desktop. JavaScript does not exert any control whatsoever over this choice, which remains the user's prerogative. Browser windows and browser tabs are both identically `window` objects to JavaScript. Efforts to control features such as window size and the appearance of toolbars will either fail or will frustrate the user's attempts to make their browser conform to their own personal usability standards. In other words, if you don't want to irritate web site visitors, don't try to mess with their settings. Trust users to manage their browsers. Focus your creative energies on the content and style of the page, not the window chrome. ■

Accessing window properties and methods

You can word script references to properties and methods of the `window` object in several ways, depending more on whim and style than on specific syntactical requirements. The most logical and common way to compose such references includes the `window` object in the reference:

```
window.propertyName
window.methodName([parameters])
```

A window object also has a synonym when the script doing the referencing points to the window that houses the document. The synonym is self. Then the reference syntax becomes

```
self.propertyName
self.methodName([parameters])
```

You can use these initial reference object names interchangeably, but we tend to reserve the use of self for more complex scripts that involve multiple frames and windows. The self moniker more clearly denotes the current window holding the script's document, and can make the script more readable — by us and by others.

Back in Chapter 6, "Browser and Document Objects," we indicated that because the window object is always there when a script runs, you can omit it from references to any objects inside that window. Therefore, the following syntax models assume properties and methods of the current window:

```
propertyName
methodName([parameters])
```

In fact, as you will see in a few moments, some methods may be more understandable if you omit the window object reference. The methods run just fine either way.

Creating a window

A script does not create the main browser window. A user does that by virtue of launching the browser or by opening a URL or file from the browser's menus (if the window is not already open). But a script can generate a large number of subwindows when the main window is open (and that window contains a document whose script needs to open subwindows).

The method that generates a new window is window.open(). This method contains up to three parameters that define window characteristics: the URL of the document to load, its name for target attribute reference purposes in HTML tags, and physical appearance (size and chrome contingent). We don't go into the details of the parameters here (they're covered in great depth in Chapter 27), but we do want to expose you to an important concept involved with the window.open() method.

Consider the following statement, which opens a new window to a specific size and with an HTML document from the same server directory that holds the current page:

```
var subWindow = window.open("define.html","def","height=200,width=300");
```

The important thing to note about this statement is that it is an assignment statement. Something gets assigned to that variable subWindow. What is it? It turns out that when the window.open() method runs, it not only opens that new window according to specifications set as parameters, but also evaluates to a reference to that new window. In programming parlance, the method is said to *return a value* — in this case, a genuine object reference. The value returned by the method is assigned to the variable.

Now your script can use that variable as a valid reference to the second window. If you need to access one of its properties or methods, you must use that reference as part of the complete reference. For example, to close the subwindow from a script in the main window, use this reference to the close() method for that subwindow:

```
subWindow.close();
```

137

If you issue `window.close()`, `self.close()`, or just `close()` in the main window's script, the method closes the main window (after confirming with the user), but not the subwindow. To address another window, then, you must include a reference to that window as part of the complete reference. This has an impact on your code because you probably want the variable holding the reference to the subwindow to be valid as long as the main document is loaded into the browser. For that to happen, the variable has to be initialized as a global variable, rather than inside a function (although you can set its value inside a function). That way, one function can open the window while another function closes it.

Listing 10-1 is a page that has a button for opening a blank new window and a button for closing that window from the main window. To view this demonstration, shrink your main browser window to less than full screen. Then, when the new window is generated, reposition the windows so you can see the smaller, new window when the main window is in front. (If you lose a window behind another, use the browser's Window menu to choose the hidden window.) The key point of Listing 10-1 is that the `newWindow` variable is defined as a global variable so that both the `makeNewWindow()` and `closeNewWindow()` functions have access to it. When a variable is declared with no value assignment, its initial value is `null`. A `null` value is interpreted to be the same as `false` in a condition, whereas the presence of any nonzero value is the same as `true` in a condition. Therefore, in the `closeNewWindow()` function, the condition tests whether the window has been created before issuing the subwindow's `close()` method. Then, to clean up, the function sets the `newWindow` variable to `null` so that another click of the Close button doesn't try to close a nonexistent window.

Note

The property assignment event-handling technique employed throughout the code in this chapter, and much of the book, is `addEvent()`, **a cross-browser event handler explained in detail in Chapter 32, "Event Objects."**

The `addEvent()` **function is part of the script file** `jsb-global.js`, **located on the accompanying CD-ROM in the** `Content/` **folder where it is accessible to all chapters' scripts.** ■

LISTING 10-1

References to Window Objects

HTML: `jsb-10-01.html`

```html
<!DOCTYPE html>
<html>
   <head>
      <meta http-equiv="content-type" content="text/html;charset=utf-8">
      <title>Window Open &amp; Close</title>
      <script type="text/javascript" src="../jsb-global.js"></script>
      <script type="text/javascript" src="jsb-10-01.js"></script>
   </head>
   <body>
      <h1>Window Open &amp; Close</h1>
      <form>
         <p>
            <input type="button" id="create-window" value="Create New Window">
            <input type="button" id="close-window" value="Close New Window">
         </p>
      </form>
```

```
    </body>
</html>
```

JavaScript: jsb-10-01.js

```
// initialize when the page has loaded
addEvent(window, 'load', initialize);

function initialize()
{
    // do this only if the browser can handle DOM methods
    if (document.getElementById)
    {
        // point to critical elements
        var oButtonCreate = document.getElementById('create-window');
        var oButtonClose = document.getElementById('close-window');

        // if they all exist...
        if (oButtonCreate && oButtonClose)
        {
            // apply behaviors
            oButtonCreate.onclick = makeNewWindow;
            oButtonClose.onclick = closeNewWindow;
        }
    }
}

var newWindow;

function makeNewWindow()
{
    newWindow = window.open("","","height=300,width=300");
}

function closeNewWindow()
{
    if (newWindow)
    {
        newWindow.close();
        newWindow = null;
    }
}
```

window Properties and Methods

The three methods for the window object described in this section have an immediate impact on user interaction by displaying dialog boxes of various types. They work with all scriptable browsers. You can find extensive code examples in Part IV for each property and method. You can also experiment with the one-statement script examples by entering them in the top text box of The Evaluator Jr. (from Chapter 8, "Programming Fundamentals, Part I").

One of the first questions that new scripters ask is how to customize the title bars, sizes, and button labels of these dialog boxes. Each browser maker dictates how these dialogs are labeled. Because tricksters have tried to use these dialog boxes for nefarious purposes over the years, browser makers now go to great lengths to let users know that the dialog boxes emanate from web page scripts. Scripters cannot alter the user interfaces of these dialog boxes.

window.alert() method

We use the `alert()` method many times in this tutorial. This window method generates a dialog box that displays whatever text you pass as a parameter (see Figure 10-2). A single OK button (whose label you cannot change) enables the user to dismiss the alert.

FIGURE 10-2

A JavaScript alert dialog box.

All three dialog-box methods are good cases for using a `window` object's methods without the reference to the window. Even though the `alert()` method technically is a `window` object method, no special relationship exists between the dialog box and the window that generates it. In production scripts, we usually use the shortcut reference:

```
alert("This is a JavaScript alert dialog.");
```

window.confirm() method

The second style of dialog box presents two buttons (Cancel and OK in most versions on most platforms) and is called a confirm dialog box (see Figure 10-3). More important, this is one of those methods that returns a value: `true` if the user clicks OK or `false` if the user clicks Cancel. You can use this dialog box and its returned value as a way to have a user make a decision about how a script progresses.

FIGURE 10-3

A JavaScript confirm dialog box (IE7/WinXP style).

Because the method always returns a Boolean value, you can use the evaluated value of the entire method as a condition statement in an `if` or `if...else` construction. For example, in the following code fragment, the user is asked about starting the application over. Doing so causes the `index.html` page to load into the browser.

```
if (confirm("Are you sure you want to start over?"))
{
    location.href = "index.html";
}
```

window.prompt() method

The final dialog box of the `window` object, the prompt dialog box (see Figure 10-4), displays a message that you set and provides a text field for the user to enter a response. Two buttons, Cancel and OK, enable the user to dismiss the dialog box with two opposite expectations: canceling the entire operation or accepting the input typed in the dialog box.

FIGURE 10-4

A JavaScript prompt dialog box (Safari 2 style).

The `window.prompt()` method has two parameters. The first is the message that acts as a prompt to the user. You can suggest a default answer in the text field by including a string as the second parameter. If you don't want any default answer to appear, include an empty string (two double quotes without any space between them).

This method returns one value when the user clicks either button. A click of the Cancel button returns a value of `null`, regardless of what the user types in the field. A click of the OK button returns a string value of the typed entry. Your scripts can use this information in conditions for `if` and `if...else` constructions. A value of `null` is treated as `false` in a condition. It turns out that an empty string is also treated as `false`. Therefore, a condition can easily test for the presence of real characters typed in the field to simplify a conditional test, as shown in the following fragment:

```
var answer = prompt("What is your name?","");
if (answer)
{
    alert("Hello, " + answer + "!");
}
```

In this example, the only time the `alert()` method is called is when the user enters something in the prompt dialog box and clicks the OK button.

load event

The `window` object reacts to several system and user events, but the one you will probably use most often is the event that fires as soon as everything in a page finishes loading. This event waits for images, Java applets, and data files for plug-ins to download fully to the browser. It can be dangerous to script access to elements of a document object while the page loads because if the object has not loaded yet (perhaps due to a slow network connection or server), a script error results. The advantage of using the `load` event to invoke functions is that you are assured that all document objects are in the browser's DOM.

The `load` event handler can be applied to the `window` object in several ways, depending on the browser and the circumstances:

```
window.addEventListener('load', functionName, false);
window.attachEvent('onload', functionName);
```

where `functionName` is the function you've written that you want to run as soon as the page has downloaded. (For a cross-browser event-adding function, see Chapter 32.) `addEventListener` and `attachEvent` can be called multiple times to add more than one function to the list to be executed when the page has loaded.

You can also apply the behavior directly to the element:

```
window['onload'] = functionName;
window.onload = functionName;
```

However, this usage dictates that there will be only one function to run when the page is loaded, replacing any event handler already assigned to the `window` object.

In old-school legacy web pages, you'll sometimes find the window event handler applied to the `body` element right in the HTML:

```
<body onload="functionName()">
```

(Even though you will come to associate the `<body>` tag's attributes with the `document` object's properties, it is the `window` object's event handlers that go inside the tag.) This embedding of JavaScript into the fabric of the HTML is considered poor usage today for several reasons: it doesn't let browsers that can't handle the scripting fail gracefully, it makes the HTML file heavier than it has to be, and it makes both the script and the markup messier and more time-consuming to modify. Separation of layers is the way to go.

Cross-Reference
For more on the `window.onload` event, see Chapter 27, "Window and Frame Objects." ∎

The location Object

Sometimes an object in the hierarchy represents something that doesn't seem to have the kind of physical presence that a window or a button does. That's the case with the `location` object. This object represents the URL loaded into the window. This differs from the `document` object (discussed later in this lesson): the document is the content of the page, while the location is its URL (Uniform Resource Locator or address).

A URL consists of many components that define the address and method of data transfer for a file. Pieces of a URL include the protocol (such as `http:`) and the hostname (such as `www.example.com`). You can access all these items as properties of the `location` object. For the most part, though, your scripts will be interested in only one property: the `href` property, which defines the complete URL.

Setting the `location.href` property is the primary way your scripts navigate to other pages:

```
location.href = "http://www.example.com/contact.html";
```

For pages outside the domain of the current page, you need to specify the complete URL. You can generally navigate to a page in your own web site by specifying a relative URL (that is, relative to the currently loaded page) rather than the complete URL with protocol and host information.

```
location.href = "contact.html";    // relative URL
```

If the page to be loaded is in another window or frame, the window reference must be part of the statement. For example, if your script opens a new window and assigns its reference to a variable named `newWindow`, the statement that loads a page into the subwindow is

```
newWindow.location.href = "http://www.example.com";
```

The navigator Object

Despite a name reminiscent of the Netscape Navigator-branded browser, the `navigator` object is implemented in all scriptable browsers. All browsers also implement a handful of properties that reveal the same kind of information that browsers send to servers with each page request. Thus, the `navigator.userAgent` property returns a string with numerous details about the browser and operating system. For example, a script running in Internet Explorer 8 in Windows XP receives the following value for the `navigator.userAgent` property:

```
Mozilla/4.0 (compatible; MSIE 8.0; Windows NT 5.1)
```

The same script running in Firefox 3.5.2 on a Macintosh reveals the following `userAgent` details:

```
Mozilla/5.0 (Macintosh; U; PPC Mac OS X 10.4; en-US; rv:1.9.1.2)
    Gecko/20090729 Firefox/3.5.2
```

Cross-Reference

See Chapter 42, "Navigator and Other Environment Objects" (on the CD), for more details about the `navigator` object and the meaning of the values returned by its properties. Unfortunately, it cannot be trusted to accurately report the actual user agent make, model, and version. It once was used extensively to branch script execution according to various browser versions. Chapter 25, "Document Object Model Essentials," describes more modern ways to detect the capabilities of the browser. ∎

The document Object

The `document` object holds the real content of the page. Properties and methods of the `document` object generally affect the look and content of the document that occupies the window. As you saw in Chapter 5, "Your First JavaScript Script," all W3C DOM-compatible browsers allow script access to the text contents of a page when the document has loaded. You've also seen that DOM methods let a script create content dynamically after the page has loaded. Many document object properties are arrays of other objects in the document, which provide additional ways to reference these objects (over and above the document.getElementById() method).

Accessing a document object's properties and methods is straightforward, as shown in the following syntax examples:

```
[window.]document.propertyName
[window.]document.methodName([parameters])
```

The window reference is optional when the script is accessing the document object that contains the script. If you want a preview of the long list of document object properties of IE or a Mozilla-based browser, enter document in the object text box of The Evaluator Jr. and press Enter/Return. The object's properties, current values, and value types appear in the Results box (as well as methods in Mozilla). Following are some of the most commonly used properties and methods of the document object.

document.getElementById() method

You met the document.getElementById() method in Chapter 5 when learning about the syntax for referencing element objects. This W3C DOM method is one you will use a lot. Get to know its finger-twisting name well. Be sure to honor the upper- and lowercase spelling of this all-important method.

The sole parameter of this method is a quoted string containing the ID of the element you wish to reference. The Evaluator Jr. page from Chapter 8 (and in the listings on the CD-ROM) has several element objects with IDs, including input, output, and inspector. Type this method in the top text box with each ID, as in the following example:

```
document.getElementById("output")
```

The method returns a value, which you typically preserve in a variable for use by subsequent script statements — for example:

```
var oneTable = document.getElementById("salesResults");
```

After the assignment statement, the variable represents the element object, allowing you to get and set its properties or invoke whatever methods belong to that type of object.

document.getElementsByTagName() method

getElementsByTagName() is a handy method for collecting an array of page elements that share the same tag name. For example, to get a list of all of the images on the page, we could call:

```
var aImages = document.getElementsByTagName('img');
```

Referring to an image by its position in an array of all images can be challenging — for example, if we want to work with an image gallery on a page that also contains miscellaneous images before and after the gallery. One of the advantages of using getElementsByTagName() is that it can gather a collection within any container element on the page:

HTML:

```
<div id="gallery">
    <h2>My Gallery</h2>
    <img src="bat.jpg" alt="bat">
    <img src="cat.jpg" alt="cat">
    <img src="hat.jpg" alt="hat">
</div>
```

JavaScript:

```
var oGallery = document.getElementById('gallery');
var aCollection = oGallery.getElementsByTagName('img');
```

The array aCollection() in this example then contains the three image objects (but not, of course, the h2 element). As you'll recall from the discussion of arrays in Chapter 9, "Programming Fundamentals, Part II," an index number inside an array's square brackets points to one of the elements in the array. To find out how many objects are in the collection, use

```
aCollection.length
```

Each object can be accessed by its offset into the array:

```
oImage = aImages[0];    // first image
oImage = aImages[1];    // second image
```

Other applications of this method might be to collect all the items in a list, all the hyperlinks (anchors) in a text block, or all the multimedia objects on a page.

document.forms[] property

Implemented back in pre-DOM days, the document.forms property of the document object contains an array of all form element objects in the document. Compare these two expressions:

```
var aForms = document.forms;
var aForms = document.getElementsByTagName('form');
```

One important difference is that the document.forms collection enables us to reference a particular form directly by its name, not just by its offset in the array. It isn't always practical to refer to a form by its index number. A dynamic web page might contain a varying number of forms depending on context, so the position of any one form on the page might change with circumstances. For example, a Search form that sits in the header chrome of every page of a web site might be suppressed on the Advanced Search page; a Join List form might be suppressed on the Contact page; and a page listing workshops might blossom with registration forms for selected workshops.

Scriptable browsers let you refer to a form more directly by its name or ID (that is, the identifier assigned to either the name or id attribute of the <form> tag):

```
<form id="formId" name="formName" ...>
```

The first way is by using the getElementById() method:

```
document.getElementById("formId")
```

The second way uses array syntax, applying the form's name or ID as a string index value of the array:

```
document.forms["formId"]
document.forms["formName"]
```

A third, even shorter way to refer to a `form` object by name is to append the name as a property of the `document` object, as in:

```
document.formName
```

However, this last technique works only if the `name` attribute omits several characters that are legal in HTML element names but illegal in JavaScript object names such as hyphen (-), period (.), and colon (:). (For more on this point, see Chapter 6.)

Any of these methodologies reaches the same object. We will primarily be using the DOM methods `getElementById()` and `getElementsByTagName()` throughout this book; however, the `document.forms` collection syntax, which dates back to the earliest scriptable browsers, is still valid in the most modern versions.

document.images[] property

Just as a document keeps track of forms in a special array property, the `document` object maintains a collection (array) of images inserted into the document by way of `<img>` tags. Images referenced through the `document.images` array may be reached by either numeric or string index of the `img` element's name. Just as with forms, the `name` attribute value is the identifier you use for a string index.

The presence of the `document.images` property indicates that the browser supports image objects and therefore scripting techniques such as image-swapping. Thus, you can use the existence of the property as a test condition to make sure the browser supports images as objects before attempting to perform any script action on an image. To do so, surround statements that deal with images with an `if` construction that verifies the property's existence, as follows:

```
if (document.images)
{
    // statements dealing with img objects
}
```

Older browsers skip the nested statements, preventing them from displaying error messages to their users.

In a typical, complex web page today, there are images in different sections used for very different purposes, and it doesn't often make sense to collect all the images on a page in a single array. In cases like this, it might be more convenient to use the DOM method `getElementsByTagName()` instead (see above).

document.createElement() and document.createTextNode() methods

Adding a new element to an HTML document consists of, at minimum, two steps:

1. Create the new element for the document.
2. Insert it exactly where you want it within the tree structure of the page.

The `document.createElement()` method lets you create a brand-new element object in the browser's memory. To specify the element you wish to create, pass the tag name of the element as a string parameter of the method:

```
var newElem = document.createElement("p");
```

You may also want to add some attribute values to the element, which you may do by assigning values to the newly created object's properties, even before the element becomes part of the document.

```
newElem.setAttribute("class", "intro");
```

This element can be inserted wherever you want in the document — for example, at the end:

```
document.body.appendChild(newElem);
```

These three lines of code generate a paragraph at the end of the document body:

```
<body>
...
<p class="intro"></p></body>
```

As you saw in the object hierarchy illustrations in Chapter 6, "Browser and Document Objects," an element object frequently needs text content between its start and end tags. The W3C DOM way to create that text is to generate a brand new text node via the `document.createTextNode()` method and populate the node with the desired text. For example:

```
var newText = document.createTextNode("Greetings to all.");
newElem.appendChild(newText);
```

resulting in:

```
<body>
...
<p class="intro">Greetings to all.</p></body>
```

As you can see, the act of creating an element or text node does not by itself influence the document node tree. You must invoke one of the various insertion or replacement methods to place the new text node in its element and place the element in the document, as you learned how to do in Chapter 5.

document.write() method

The `document.write()` method is another way of writing content to a document. It has the advantage of being "quick and dirty," but it also has several disadvantages:

- `document.write()` can add a piece of a web page only while the page is loading into the browser the first time. Any subsequent invocation of the method replaces the entire page.
- Because `document.write()` will insert any old block of text into the document, it enables sloppy programming habits and malformed markup, encourages the mixture of markup with content in scripting, and does not encourage the separation of development layers (structure from content).
- `document.write()` does not work with XHTML, a document type that doesn't permit its content to be modified during the initial parsing.

147

For these reasons we do not recommend that you use `document.write()` in your own code, though it's still useful to understand how it works in order to be able to read legacy code.

The `document.write()` method operates both in immediate scripts to create content in a page as it loads and in deferred scripts that create new content in the same window or in a different window. The method requires one string parameter, the HTML content to be written to the window or frame. Such string parameters can be variables or any other expressions that evaluate to a string. Very often, the written content includes HTML tags.

Bear in mind that after a page loads, the browser's *output stream* automatically closes. After that, any `document.write()` method issued to the current page opens a new stream that immediately erases the current page (along with any variables or other values in the original document). Therefore, if you wish to replace the current page with script-generated HTML, you need to accumulate that HTML in a variable and perform the writing with just one `document.write()` method. You don't have to clear a document explicitly and open a new data stream; one `document.write()` call does it all.

One last piece of housekeeping advice about the `document.write()` method involves its companion method, `document.close()`. Your script must close the output stream when it finishes writing its content to the window (either the same window or another). After the last `document.write()` method in a deferred script, be sure to include a `document.close()` method. Failure to do this may cause images and forms not to appear. Also, any `document.write()` method invoked later will only append to the page, rather than clear the existing content to write anew.

To demonstrate the `document.write()` method, we show two versions of the same application. One writes to the same document that contains the script; the other writes to a separate window. Type the code for each document in a new text editor file, save them, and open the `.html` file in your browser.

Listing 10-2 creates a button that assembles new HTML content for a document, including HTML tags for new document title and color attributes for the `<body>` tag. An operator in the listing that may be unfamiliar to you is `+=`. It appends a string on its right side to whatever string is stored in the variable on its left side. This operator is a convenient way to accumulate a long string across several separate statements. With the content gathered in the `newContent` variable, one `document.write()` statement blasts the entire new content to the same document, obliterating all vestiges of the content of Listing 10-2. The `document.close()` statement, however, is required to close the output stream properly. When you load this document and click the button, notice that the document title in the browser's title bar changes accordingly. As you click back to the original and try the button again, notice that the dynamically written second page loads much faster than even a reload of the original document.

LISTING 10-2

Using document.write() on the Current Window

HTML: `jsb-10-02.html`

```
<!DOCTYPE html>
<html>
   <head>
      <meta http-equiv="content-type" content="text/html;charset=utf-8">
      <title>Writing to Same Doc</title>
```

```
      <script type="text/javascript" src="../jsb-global.js"></script>
      <script type="text/javascript" src="jsb-10-02.js"></script>
   </head>
   <body>
      <h1>Writing to Same Doc</h1>
      <form>
         <p>
            <input type="button" id="rewritePage" value="Replace Content">
         </p>
      </form>
   </body>
</html>
```

JavaScript: jsb-10-02.js

```javascript
// replace the page with new markup
function reWrite()
{
 // assemble content for new window
 var newContent = '<!DOCTYPE html>';
 newContent += '<html>';
 newContent += '<head>';
 newContent += '<meta http-equiv="content-type"
    content="text/html;charset=utf-8">';
 newContent += '<title>A New Doc</title>';
 newContent += '<style type="text/css">';
 newContent += 'body { background-color: aqua; }';
 newContent += '</style>';
 newContent += '</head>';
 newContent += '<body>';
 newContent += '<h1>This document is brand new.</h1>';
 newContent += '<p>Click the Back button to see the original document.</p>';
 newContent += '</body>';
 newContent += '</html>';

 // write HTML to new window document
 document.write(newContent);
 document.close(); // close layout stream
}

// apply behaviors when document has loaded
function initialize()
{
 // do this only if the browser can handle DOM methods
 if (document.getElementById)
 {
    // point to the button
    var oButtonRewrite = document.getElementById('rewritePage');

      // if it exists...
      if (oButtonRewrite)
      {
```

continued

149

LISTING 10-2 *(continued)*

```
        // apply event handler
        addEvent(oButtonRewrite, 'click', reWrite);
      }
  }
}

// initialize when the page has loaded
addEvent(window, 'load', initialize);
```

In Listing 10-3, the situation is a bit more complex because the script generates a subwindow to which an entirely script-generated document is written.

Note
You will have to turn off pop-up window blocking temporarily to run this script. ∎

To keep the reference to the new window alive across both functions, the newWindow variable is declared as a global variable. As soon as the page loads, the onload event handler invokes the make-NewWindow() function. This function generates a blank subwindow. We added a property to the third parameter of the window.open() method that instructs the status bar of the subwindow to appear.

A button in the page invokes the subWrite() method. The first task it performs is to check the closed property of the subwindow. This property returns true if the referenced window is closed. If that's the case (if the user closed the window manually), the function invokes the makeNewWindow() function again to reopen that window.

With the window open, new content is assembled as a string variable. As with Listing 10-2, the content is written in one blast (although this isn't necessary for a separate window), followed by a close() method. But notice an important difference: Both the write() and close() methods explicitly specify the subwindow.

LISTING 10-3

Using document.write() on Another Window

HTML: jsb-10-03.html

```
<!DOCTYPE html>
<html>
   <head>
      <meta http-equiv="content-type" content="text/html;charset=utf-8">
      <title>Writing to Subwindow</title>
      <script type="text/javascript" src="../jsb-global.js"></script>
      <script type="text/javascript" src="jsb-10-03.js"></script>
   </head>
   <body>
      <h1>Writing to Subwindow</h1>
      <form>
```

```
        <p>
            <input type="button" id="writeSubwindow" value="Write to Subwindow">
        </p>
      </form>
   </body>
</html>
```

JavaScript: jsb-10-03.js

```javascript
var newWindow;

function makeNewWindow()
{
   newWindow = window.open("","","status,height=200,width=300");
}

function subWrite()
{
    // make new window if someone has closed it
    if (!newWindow || newWindow.closed)
    {
        makeNewWindow();
    }

   // bring subwindow to front
   newWindow.focus();

   // assemble content for new window
   var newContent = '<!DOCTYPE html>';
   newContent += '<html>';
   newContent += '<head>';
   newContent += '<meta http-equiv="content-type"
       content="text/html;charset=utf-8">';
   newContent += '<title>A New Doc</title>';
   newContent += '<style type="text/css">';
   newContent += 'body { background-color: aqua; }';
   newContent += '</style>';
   newContent += '</head>';
   newContent += '<body>';
   newContent += '<h1>This document is brand new.</h1>';
   newContent += '</body>';
   newContent += '</html>';

   // write HTML to new window document
   newWindow.document.write(newContent);

   // close layout stream
   newWindow.document.close();
}

// apply behaviors when document has loaded
function initialize()
{
```

continued

LISTING 10-3   *(continued)*

```
// do this only if the browser can handle DOM methods
if (document.getElementById)
{
    // point to the button
    var oButtonRewrite = document.getElementById('writeSubwindow');

        // if it exists...

        if (oButtonRewrite)
        {
            // apply event handler
            addEvent(oButtonRewrite, 'click', subWrite);
        }
    }
}

// initialize when the page has loaded
addEvent(window, 'load', initialize);
addEvent(window, 'load', makeNewWindow);
```

The next logical step after the document level in the object hierarchy is the form. That's where you will spend the next lesson.

Exercises

1. Which of the following references are valid, and which are not? Explain what is wrong with the invalid references.
   a. `window.document.form[0]`
   b. `self.entryForm.submit()`
   c. `document.forms[2].name`
   d. `document.getElementByID("firstParagraph")`
   e. `newWindow.document.write("Howdy")`

2. Write the JavaScript statement that displays an (annoying) dialog box welcoming visitors to your web page.

3. Write the JavaScript statement that executes while the page loads to display the same message from Question 2 to the document as an <h1>-level headline on the page.

4. Create a page that prompts the user for his or her name as the page loads (via a dialog box) and then welcomes the user by name in the body of the page.

5. Create a page with any content you like, but one that automatically displays a dialog box after the page loads to show the user the URL of the current page.

Forms and Form Elements

Most interactivity between a web page and the user takes place inside a form. That's where a lot of the interactive HTML stuff lives for every browser: text fields, buttons, checkboxes, option lists, and so on.

In this chapter, we discuss how to locate forms and their controls in the document tree, how to change them, how to examine the user's input, and how to submit a form or suppress submission if the input doesn't validate.

The Form object

A form and the input controls that go inside it are DOM objects with unique properties that other objects in the document don't have. For example, a form object has an `action` property that tells the browser where to send input values when a form is submitted. A `select` control (drop-down list) has a `selectedIndex` property that tells us which option has been selected by the user.

Our first step is to point to the form on the page. Here are three ways of doing this, all referring to the following abbreviated snippet of a page that contains three forms:

```
<div id="header">
    <form id="search" action="...">...</form>
    <form id="join-list" action="...">...</form>
</div>
    ...
    <form id="contact" action="...">...</form>
    ...
```

1. The DOM method `getElementById()`, as described in previous chapters, gives us a handle on a single, specific element on the page if we know its `id` attribute:

   ```
   var oForm = document.getElementById('search');
   ```

IN THIS CHAPTER

What the form object represents

How to access key form object properties and methods

How text, button, and select objects work

How to submit forms from a script

How to pass information from form elements to functions

In practice, using getElementById() suffices most of the time because web pages generally contain one or a very small number of unique forms which accomplish very different tasks; assigning them unique IDs in the markup is a natural.

2. The DOM method getElementsByTagName() delivers an array or collection of form objects with a given tag name:

```
var aForms = document.getElementsByTagName('form');
var oForm = aForms[0];  // get the first form on the page
```

As always, JavaScript arrays begin with the first item having an index of zero, so our collection of three forms can be addressed as array elements 0, 1, and 2.

It's worth pondering the usefulness of working with a collection of all the forms on a page. In order to locate a specific form from the collection, we would have to know its position among all the forms on the page (which could change in a rich, dynamic site) or we'd have to cycle through them looking for an identifier (which suggests using getElementById() in the first place).

One of the cool things about getElementsByTagName() is that it can give us a collection of objects within a particular parent other than the document element itself:

```
var oHeader = document.getElementById('header');
var aForms = oHeader.getElementsByTagName('form');
var oForm = aForms[0];
```

In this example, we're collecting all the forms in the "header" section of the document only.

Or imagine a page listing a series of workshops, each of which has its own separate registration form. We could collect an array of all those registration forms by first pointing to their parent div without worrying about other miscellaneous forms on the page confusing the mix.

3. The syntax document.forms is another way of collecting all the forms on the page that pre-dates today's DOM methods but is still supported by modern browsers, so as not to break legacy web sites.

```
var aForms = document.forms;
// then point to one form:
var oForm = aForms[0];
// or:
var oForm = aForms["search"];
// or:
var oForm = aForms.search;
```

Using this original "DOM Level 0" syntax, we can reference a form object either by its position in the array of forms contained in a document or by name (if you assign an identifier to the id or name attribute inside the <form> tag). If only one form appears in the document, it is still a member of an array (a one-element array) and is referenced as follows:

```
document.forms[0]
```

Or use the string of the element's name as the array index:

```
document.forms[formName]
```

Notice that the array reference uses the plural version of the word, followed by a set of square brackets containing the index number (zero is always first) or name of the element. Alternatively, you can use the form's name (not as a quoted string) as though it were a property of the `document` object:

```
document.formName
```

However, this last syntax works only if the form `id` or `name` doesn't include characters such as hyphens, periods, or colons that would confuse JavaScript. For example, the second form in our sample HTML above has the `id` of `join-list`:

```
var oForm = document.forms.join-list;
```

This looks to JavaScript like we're trying to subtract the value of a variable named `list` from a `form` object with the `id` of `join`. This statement would either stop JavaScript cold or produce a result of `NaN` (Not a Number). As a general rule, we recommend that you use syntax that puts element names in quotes.

Because there are so many ways to arrive at a `form` object, we'll often represent them in further examples with the label `formObject`.

Form as object and container

Because the modern DOM is backward-compatible with many of yesterday's conventions, the form object finds itself the matriarch of two different family trees at the same time. The modern DOM Level 2 specifies that the form is the parent of all of its child nodes, both element and text nodes, whereas the older DOM Level 0 makes the form the container for all of its form control objects only (`input`, `select`, `button`, and `textarea` elements). Figure 11-1 shows the structure of this DOM 0 hierarchy and its place relative to the `document` object. You'll see the effect this structure has on the way you reference form control elements in a moment.

FIGURE 11-1

DOM Level 0 hierarchy for forms and controls.

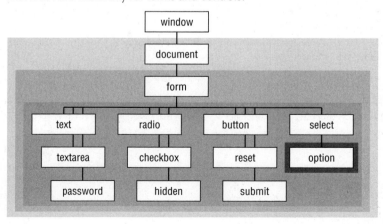

Let's illustrate the difference by diagramming the following snippet of HTML:

LISTING 11-1

Sample form markup

```
<form action="search.php" method="post">
    <p>
        <label for="inputSearch">Search for:</label>
        <input id="inputSearch" name="inputSearch" type="text" value="">
        <input id="submit" type="submit" value="Search">
    </p>
</form>
```

Figure 11-2 shows the DOM Level 2 tree for this markup. Note that it represents the entire content of that segment of the document. The carriage returns, tabs, and spaces between elements are text nodes (represented here by the shorthand "[whitespace]").

FIGURE 11-2

DOM Level 2 tree for a typical form.

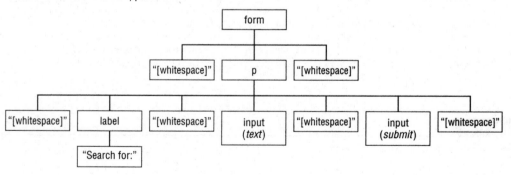

Figure 11-3 shows the DOM Level 0 tree for this same form. It includes only the input controls and omits the paragraph, the label, and the text nodes.

FIGURE 11-3

DOM Level 0 tree for the same form.

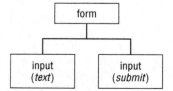

These two object trees are clearly useful for very different purposes. The DOM Level 2 tree can be used to read and write the entire document content with fine granularity. The DOM Level 0 tree makes it quick and easy to read and write the form controls only.

Please note that whether you're using DOM 0 or DOM 2 techniques in any given statement, the objects are the same. For example,

```
var oForm = document.getElementById('myForm');
var oControl = oForm.fritzy;
```

is perfectly valid JavaScript and will work fine if `fritzy` is the ID of an input control inside the form `myForm`.

In addition to a large collection of properties and methods it has in common with all HTML element objects, the form object features a number of items that are unique to this object. Almost all of these unique properties are scripted representations of the `form` element's attributes (`action`, `target`, and so on). Scriptable browsers allow scripts to change these properties under script control, which gives your scripts potentially significant power to direct the behavior of a form submission in response to user selections on the page.

Accessing form properties

Forms can be created from standard markup tags in the HTML page or by using DOM methods in JavaScript. Either way, you can set attributes such as `name`, `target`, `action`, `method`, and `enc-type`. Each of these is a property of a form object, accessed by all lowercase versions of those words, as in:

```
var sURL = formObject.action;
```

To change any of these properties, simply assign new values to them:

```
formObject.action = "http://www.example.com/cgi/login.pl";
```

These last two JavaScript statements could be re-stated using compound object references:

```
var sURL = document.getElementById('formName').action;
document.forms[0].action = "http://www.example.com/cgi/login.pl";
```

However, combining multiple operations into a single expression doesn't allow the script to test for validity along the way. Separating steps and testing as we go is a more bulletproof way to code:

```
var oForm = document.getElementById ('formName');
    if (!oForm)
    {
        // do something if the named form isn't found
    }
var sURL = oForm.action;
```

form.elements[] property

The `elements[]` property is a collection of all the input controls within a form. This is another array with items listed in the order their HTML tags appear in the source code. It is generally more efficient to refer to a single element directly using its ID, but sometimes a script needs to look through all of the elements in a form. For example, a form-validation routine might loop through every element checking to make sure that its value has been entered correctly by the user. A loop like that might not need to look at the text nodes and other elements that aren't form controls, and in fact it would have to perform a series of tests on each element it encountered to determine whether it were a control. In a case like this, using the elements[] collection is vastly more efficient.

The following code fragment shows the form.elements[] property at work in a for repeat loop that looks at every control element in a form to set the contents of text fields to an empty string. The script cannot simply barge through the form and set every element's content to an empty string because some elements may be types (for example, a button) whose value properties have different purposes.

```
var oForm = document.getElementById('registration-form');
    if (!oForm) return false;

for (var i = 0; i < oForm.elements.length; i++)
{
    if (oForm.elements[i].type == "text")
    {
        oForm.elements[i].value = "";
    }
}
```

In the first statement, we create the variable oForm that holds a reference to the desired form. We do this so that when we make many references to form elements later in the script, the typical length of each reference is much shorter (and marginally faster). We can use the oForm variable as a shortcut to building references to items more deeply nested in the form.

Next, we start looping through the items in the elements array for the form. Each form control element has a type property, which reveals what kind of form control it is: text, button, radio, checkbox, textarea, and so on. We're interested in finding elements whose type is text. For each of those, we set the value property to an empty string.

We're permitting compound expressions such as oForm.elements[i].type in this case because, having already tested to make sure the form exists, we can trust the DOM to deliver us a valid form control object with each iteration of the elements[] collection. Even if the form were empty of controls, the script wouldn't fail; if the elements[] collection were an empty array, the for loop above would simply terminate before its first iteration with no error because oForm.elements.length would be zero.

We'll return to forms later in this chapter to show you how to submit a form without a Submit button and how client-side form validation works.

Form Controls as Objects

Three kinds of HTML elements nested inside a <form> tag become scriptable objects in all browser DOMs. Most of the objects owe their existence to the <input> tag in the page's source code. Only the value assigned to the type attribute of an <input> tag determines whether the element is a text box, password entry field, hidden field, button, checkbox, or radio button. The other two kinds of form controls, textarea and select, have their own tags.

To reference a particular form control as an object, you can point directly to it using its `id` or `tagName` with DOM Level 2 methods, or, using DOM Level 0 syntax, build a reference as a hierarchy starting with the `document`, through the form, and then to the control. You've already seen how many ways you can reference merely the form part — all of which are valid for building form control references. But if you are using only the identifiers assigned to the form and form control elements (rather than the associated arrays of elements), the syntax is as follows:

```
document.getElementById(controlName)
```

or

```
document.formName.controlName
```

For example, consider the following simple form:

```
<form id="searchForm" action="cgi-bin/search.pl">
    <p>
        <input type="text" id="entry" name="entry">
        <input type="submit" id="sender" name="sender" value="Search">
    </p>
</form>
```

The following sample references to the text input control are all valid:

```
document.getElementById("entry")
document.searchForm.entry
document.searchForm.elements[0]
document.forms["searchForm"].elements["entry"]
document.forms["searchForm"].entry
```

Although form controls have several properties in common, some properties are unique to a particular control type or to related types. For example, only a `select` object offers a property that reveals which item in its list is currently selected. Checkboxes and radio buttons both have a property that indicates whether the control is currently set to on. Similarly, all text-oriented controls operate the same way for reading and modifying their content.

Having a good grasp of the scriptable features of form control objects is important to your success with JavaScript. In the next sections, you meet the most important form control objects and see how scripts interact with them.

Text-related input objects

Each of the four text-related HTML form elements — input elements of the `text`, `password`, and `hidden` types, plus the `textarea` element — is an element in the document object hierarchy. All but the hidden types are normally displayed on the page, enabling users to enter text and select options.

To make these form control objects scriptable in a page, you don't need to do anything special to their normal HTML tags — with the possible exception of assigning an `id` attribute. We strongly recommend assigning both unique IDs and names to every text-related form control element if your scripts will be getting or setting properties, or invoking their methods. IDs are handy for DOM manipulation and for associating labels with controls, and names are necessary for a form to function normally.

When a form is actually submitted to a server-side program, it is the control elements' name attributes that are sent to the server along with the elements' values.

For the visible objects in this category, event handlers are triggered from many user actions, such as giving a field focus (getting the text insertion pointer in the field) and changing text (entering new text and then leaving the field). Most of your text-field actions are triggered by the change of text (the onchange event handler). In current browsers, events fire in response to individual keystrokes as well.

Without a doubt, the single most-used property of a text-related element is the value property. This property represents the current contents of the text element. A script can retrieve and set its content at any time. Content of the value property is always a string. This may require conversion to numbers (see Chapter 8, "Programming Fundamentals, Part I") if text fields are used for entering values for math operations.

Text Object Behavior

Many scripters look to JavaScript to solve what are perceived as shortcomings or behavioral anomalies with text-related objects in forms. We want to single these out early in your scripting experience so that they do not confuse you later.

Most browser forms practice a behavior that was recommended long ago as an informal standard by web pioneers. When a form contains only one text input object, a press of the Enter/Return key while the text object has focus automatically submits the form. For two or more fields in browsers other than IE5/Mac and Safari, you need another way to submit the form (for example, a Submit button). This one-field submission scheme works well in many cases, such as the search page of most web search sites. But if you are experimenting with simple forms containing only one field, you can submit the form with a press of the Enter/Return key. Submitting a form that has no other action or target specified means the page performs an unconditional reload, wiping out any information entered into the form. You can, however, cancel the submission through an onsubmit event handler in the form, as shown later in this chapter. You can also script the press of the Enter/Return key in any text field to submit a form (see Chapter 32, "Event Objects").

To demonstrate how a text field's value property can be read and written, Listing 11-2 provides a complete HTML page with a single-entry field. When you enter text into the field and press Tab or Enter, the input text is made all uppercase.

LISTING 11-2

Getting and Setting a Text Object's value Property

HTML: jsb-11-02.html

```
<!DOCTYPE html>
<html>
   <head>
      <meta http-equiv="content-type" content="text/html;charset=utf-8">
      <title>Text Object value Property</title>
      <script type="text/javascript" src="../jsb-global.js"></script>
      <script type="text/javascript" src="jsb-11-02.js"></script>
```

```
    </head>
    <body>
        <h1>Text Object value Property</h1>
        <form id="UCform" action="make-uppercase.php">
            <p>
                <input type="text" id="converter" name="converter" value="sample">
            </p>
        </form>
    </body>
</html>
```

JavaScript: jsb-11-02.js

```
// initialize when the page has loaded
addEvent(window, 'load', initialize);

var oInput;    // (global) input field to make uppercase

// apply behaviors when document has loaded
function initialize()
{
    // do this only if the browser can handle DOM methods
    if (document.getElementById)
    {
        // apply event handler to the button
        oInput = document.getElementById('converter');
            if (oInput)
            {
                addEvent(oInput, 'change', upperMe);
            }

        // apply event handler to the form
        var oForm = document.getElementById('UCform');
            if (oForm)
            {
                addEvent(oForm, 'submit', upperMe);
            }
    }
}

// make the text UPPERCASE
function upperMe(evt)
{
        // consolidate event handling
        if (!evt) evt = window.event;

    // set input field value to the uppercase version of itself
    var sUpperCaseValue = oInput.value.toUpperCase();
    oInput.value = sUpperCaseValue;

    // cancel default behavior (esp. form submission)
        // W3C DOM method (hide from IE)
```

continued

LISTING 11-2   *(continued)*

```
    if (evt.preventDefault) evt.preventDefault();

  // IE method
  return false;
}
```

Here's how it works: When the page loads into the browser, the `initialize()` function applies event handlers to the form and to the input field it contains. The `onchange` event handler of both the form and the input field invokes the `upperMe()` function, which converts the text to uppercase.

Notice that the `oInput` variable, used to refer to the input field `converter`, is declared outside of all the functions and is therefore a global variable. This means that it's accessible from anywhere in the script. We've done this so that we can use it from two separate functions — `initialize()` and `upperMe()`. (In contrast to global variables, *local variables* are declared with `var` inside of a function and cannot be seen outside of the function in which they were declared.)

The core of the `upperMe()` function consists of two statements:

```
    var sUpperCaseValue = oInput.value.toUpperCase();
    oInput.value = sUpperCaseValue;
```

A lot goes on in the first statement of the function. The right side of the assignment statement performs a couple of key tasks. The reference to the `value` property of the object (`oInput.value`) evaluates to whatever content is in the text field at that instant. (Remember that `oInput` is that global variable that points to the input field `converter`.) Then that string is handed over to one of JavaScript's string functions, `toUpperCase()`, which converts the value to uppercase. The evaluated result of the right-side statement is then assigned to the second variable: `sUpperCaseValue`. Nothing has changed yet in the text box. That comes in the second statement, where the `value` property of the text box is assigned whatever the `sUpperCaseValue` variable holds. We've divided this logic into two statements for learning purposes so that you can see the process. In practice, you can combine the actions of steps 1 and 2 into one power-packed statement:

```
    oInput.value = oInput.value.toUpperCase();
```

The `onchange` event for the input field is what makes the text uppercase when you press Tab to navigate away from that field. Because this is a one-input-field form, the Enter key acts to submit the form, so we've set the form's `onsubmit` event to run the `upperMe()` function as well. In addition to making the text uppercase, that function also cancels the normal submit behavior. (More on event capture later in this chapter.)

If JavaScript is disabled or not supported by the user agent rendering this page, the entered text is submitted to a server-side program called `make-uppercase.php`, which presumably performs the uppercasing of the text as well.

Note

The function to assign event handlers throughout the code in this chapter and much of the book is `addEvent()`, a cross-browser event handler explained in detail in Chapter 32, "Event Objects."

The `addEvent()` function is located in the file `jsb-global.js` on the accompanying CD-ROM and is included in each HTML example with a `script` tag in the document `head`. ∎

The button input object

We use the button-type `input` element in many examples in this book. The button is one of the simplest objects to script. In the simplified object model of this tutorial, the button object has only a few properties that are rarely accessed or modified in day-to-day scripts. Like the text object, the visual aspects of the button are governed not by HTML or scripts but by the operating system and browser that the page visitor uses. By far the most useful event of the button object is the `click` event. It fires whenever the user clicks the button. Simple enough. No magic here.

The checkbox input object

A checkbox is also a simple element of the `form` object, but some of the properties may not be entirely intuitive. Unlike the `value` property of a plain button object (the text of the button label), the `value` property of a checkbox is any other text you want associated with the object. This text does not appear on the page in any fashion, but the property (initially set via the `value` attribute) might be important to a script that wants to know more about the purpose of the checkbox within the form.

For example, consider this:

```
<input type="checkbox" id="memory" name="remember-me" value="yup">
<label for="memory">Remember me on this computer</label>
```

If we check this checkbox and submit the form, the browser sends the server the name/value pair "remember-me" and "yup"; the label text "Remember me on this computer" appears on the screen but is not sent to the server.

The key property of a checkbox object is whether the box is checked. The `checked` property is a Boolean value: `true` if the box is checked, `false` if not. When you see that a property is a Boolean value, it's a clue that the value will be easy to use in an `if` or `if...else` conditional expression. In Listing 11-3, the value of the `checked` property determines which alert box the user sees.

LISTING 11-3

The Checkbox Object's checked Property

HTML: `jsb-11-03.html`

```
<!DOCTYPE html>
<html>
    <head>
        <meta http-equiv="content-type" content="text/html;charset=utf-8">
        <title>Checkbox Inspector</title>
        <script type="text/javascript" src="../jsb-global.js"></script>
        <script type="text/javascript" src="jsb-11-03.js"></script>
    </head>
    <body>
        <h1>Checkbox Inspector</h1>
        <form action="">
            <p>
                <input type="checkbox" id="checkThis" name="checkThis">
```

continued

163

LISTING 11-3   *(continued)*

```
        <label for="checkThis">Check here</label>
        <input type="button" id="inspectIt" value="Inspect Box">
    </p>
    </form>
  </body>
</html>
```

JavaScript: jsb-11-03.js

```javascript
// initialize when the page has loaded
addEvent(window, 'load', initialize);

var oCheckbox;    // checkbox object (global)

// apply behaviors when document has loaded
function initialize()
{
   // do this only if the browser can handle DOM methods
   if (document.getElementById)
   {
      // point to crucial elements
      oCheckbox = document.getElementById('checkThis');
      var oButton = document.getElementById('inspectIt');

         // if they exist, apply event handler
         if (oCheckbox && oButton)
         {
            addEvent(oButton, 'click', inspectBox);
         }
   }
}

// report the checked state of the checkbox
function inspectBox()
{
   if (oCheckbox.checked)
   {
      alert("The box is checked.");
   }
   else
   {
      alert("The box is not checked at the moment.");
   }
}
```

Checkboxes are generally used as preference setters rather than as action inducers. Although a checkbox object has an onclick event handler, a click of a checkbox should never do anything drastic, such as navigate to another page.

The radio input object

Setting up a group of radio objects for scripting requires a bit more work. To let the browser manage the highlighting and unhighlighting of a related group of buttons, you must assign the same `name` attribute to each of the buttons in the group. You can have multiple radio groups within a form, but each member of the same group must have the same name.

Assigning the same name to a form element forces the browser to manage the elements differently than if they each had a unique name. Instead, the browser maintains an array list of objects with the same name. The name assigned to the group becomes the name of the array. Some properties apply to the group as a whole; other properties apply to individual buttons within the group and must be addressed via array index references. For example, you can find out how many buttons are in a radio group by reading the `length` property of the group:

```
formObject.groupName.length
```

If you want to find out whether a particular button is currently highlighted via the same `checked` property used for the checkbox, you can access the button element by its position in the collection of same-named input fields:

```
formObject.groupName[0].checked
```

Listing 11-4 demonstrates several aspects of the radio-button object, including how to look through a group of buttons to find out which one is checked, and how to use the `value` attribute and corresponding property for meaningful work.

The page includes three radio buttons and a plain button. Each radio button's `value` attribute contains the full name of one of the Three Stooges. When the user clicks the button, the `onclick` event handler invokes the `fullName()` function. In that function, the first statement creates a shortcut reference to the form. Next, a `for` repeat loop looks through all the buttons in the `stooges` radio-button group. An `if` construction looks at the `checked` property of each button. When a button is checked, the `break` statement bails out of the `for` loop, leaving the value of the `i` loop counter at the number where the loop broke ranks. Then the alert dialog box uses a reference to the `value` property of the `i`th button so that the full name can be displayed in the alert.

LISTING 11-4

Scripting a Group of Radio Objects

HTML: jsb-11-04.html

```
<!DOCTYPE html>
<html>
    <head>
        <meta http-equiv="content-type" content="text/html;charset=utf-8">
        <title>Extracting Highlighted Radio Button</title>
        <script type="text/javascript" src="../jsb-global.js"></script>
        <script type="text/javascript" src="jsb-11-04.js"></script>
    </head>
    <body>
        <h1>Extracting Highlighted Radio Button</h1>
        <form action="stooges.php">
```

continued

LISTING 11-4   *(continued)*

```html
        <fieldset>
            <legend>Select your favorite Stooge:</legend>
            <p>
                <input type="radio" name="stooges" id="stooges-1"
                value="Moe Howard" checked>
                <label for="stooges-1">Moe</label>
            </p>
            <p>
                <input type="radio" name="stooges" id="stooges-2"
                value="Larry Fine">
                <label for="stooges-2">Larry</label>
            </p>
            <p>
                <input type="radio" name="stooges" id="stooges-3"
                value="Curly Howard">
                <label for="stooges-3">Curly</label>
            </p>
            <p>
                <input type="submit" id="Viewer" name="Viewer"
                value="View Full Name...">
            </p>
        </fieldset>
    </form>
  </body>
</html>
```

JavaScript: jsb-11-04.js

```javascript
// initialize when the page has loaded
addEvent(window, 'load', initialize);

var aStooges;   // radio button array (global)

// apply behaviors when document has loaded
function initialize()
{
    // do this only if the browser can handle DOM methods
    if (document.getElementById)
    {
        // point to crucial elements
        var oButton = document.getElementById('Viewer');
        var aForms = document.forms;
            if (aForms) aStooges = aForms[0].stooges;   // global variable

            // if they exist, apply event handler
            if (oButton && aStooges)
            {
                addEvent(oButton, 'click', showFullName);
            }
```

```
    }
}

// display the full name of the selected stooge
function showFullName()
{
    for (var i = 0; i < aStooges.length; i++)
    {
        if (aStooges[i].checked)
        {
            break;
        }
    }
    alert("You chose " + aStooges[i].value + ".");
}
```

The select object

The most complex form control to script is the select element object. As you can see from the DOM Level 0 form object hierarchy diagram (see Figure 11-1), the select object is really a compound object that contains an array of option objects. Moreover, you can establish this object in HTML to display itself as either a drop-down list or a scrolling list — the latter configurable to accept multiple selections by users. For the sake of simplicity at this stage, this lesson focuses on deploying it as a drop-down list that allows only single selections.

Some properties belong to the entire select object; others belong to individual options inside the select object. If your goal is to determine which item the user selects, and you want the code to work on the widest range of browsers, you must use properties of both the select and option objects.

The most important property of the select object itself is the selectedIndex property, accessed as follows:

        formObject.selectName.selectedIndex

This value is the index number of the currently selected item. As with most index counting schemes in JavaScript, the first item (the one at the top of the list) has an index of zero. The selectedIndex value is critical for enabling you to access properties of the selected option. Two important properties of an option item are text and value, accessed as follows:

        formObject.selectName.options[n].text
        formObject.selectName.options[n].value

The text property is the string that appears onscreen in the select object's list. It is unusual for this information to be exposed as a form object property because the HTML that generates a select object defines the text as an <option> tag's nested text. But inside the <option> tag, you can set a value attribute, which, like the radio buttons shown earlier, enables you to associate some hidden string information with each visible entry in the list.

To read the value or text property of a selected option most efficiently for all browsers, you can use the select object's selectedIndex property as an index value to the option. References for this kind of operation get pretty long, so take the time to understand what's happening here. In the following function, the first statement creates a shortcut reference to the select object. Then the

167

selectedIndex property of the select object is substituted for the index value of the options array of that same object:

```
function inspect()
{
    var oList = document.getElementById('choices');
        if (oList)
        {
            var sChosenItemValue = oList.options[oList.selectedIndex].value;
        }
    }
```

To bring a select object to life, use the onchange event handler. As soon as a user makes a new selection in the list, the script associated with the onchange event is run. Listing 11-5 shows a common application for a select object. Its text entries describe places to go in and out of a web site, and the value attributes hold the URLs for those locations. When a user makes a selection in the list, the onchange event handler triggers a script that extracts the value property of the selected option and assigns that value to the location.href object property to effect the navigation.

Of course, most of these new locations (web pages) won't already exist on your computer in the folder where the HTML page resides. When you select a location and your page attempts to relocate there, you'll see a "File not found" error page. Notice the intended page in the address bar, and then click the Back button to return to the sample form.

The form includes a submit button so that, when JavaScript is turned off or is non-existent in the user agent, the page still works by submitting the form to a server-side program to perform the redirection. Under JavaScript control, it can be argued that this kind of navigation doesn't need a separate Go button on the page, and in this example we've hidden the button from view using JavaScript to set its display style to "none." Note, however, that some people criticize the usability and accessibility of a select list that submits a form as soon as a selection is made. The argument is that since form submission isn't a normal function of a select list, adding that behavior with JavaScript will take some users by surprise and will switch them to a new page without their deliberate consent. Also, the list's behavior assumes that the user's first selection from the list is where they really want to go and doesn't allow for accidental selections, which anyone could make, but particularly those with motor-skill disabilities. Try this form with JavaScript turned off to see the difference for yourself.

LISTING 11-5

Navigating with a select Object

HTML: jsb-11-05.html

```
<!DOCTYPE html>
<html>
    <head>
        <meta http-equiv="content-type" content="text/html;charset=utf-8">
        <title>Select Navigation</title>
        <script type="text/javascript" src="../jsb-global.js"></script>
        <script type="text/javascript" src="jsb-11-05.js"></script>
    </head>
    <body>
```

```
      <h1>Select Navigation</h1>
      <form action="redirect.php" method="get">
         <p>
            <label for="urlList">Choose a place to go:</label>
            <select id="urlList" name="urlList">
               <option selected value="index.html">Home Page</option>
               <option value="store.html">Shop Our Store</option>
               <option value="policies.html">Shipping Policies</option>
               <option value="http://www.google.com">Search the Web</option>
            </select>

            <input type="submit" id="submit-button" value="Go">
         </p>
      </form>
   </body>
</html>
```

JavaScript: jsb-11-05.js

```
// initialize when the page has loaded
addEvent(window, 'load', initialize);

var oList;    // select list (global)

// apply behaviors when document has loaded
function initialize()
{
    // do this only if the browser can handle DOM methods
    if (document.getElementById)
    {
      // point to crucial elements
      oList = document.getElementById('urlList');
      oButton = document.getElementById('submit-button');

         // if they exist...
         if (oList && oButton)
         {
            // make the list dynamic
            addEvent(oList, 'change', goThere);

            // make the submit button disappear when JavaScript is running
            oButton.style.display = 'none';
         }
    }
}

// direct the browser to the selected URL
function goThere()
{
    location.href = oList.options[oList.selectedIndex].value;
}
```

Note

Recent browsers also expose the value **property of the selected option item by way of the** value **property of the** select **object. This is certainly a logical and convenient shortcut, and you can use it safely if your target browsers include IE, Mozilla-based browsers, and Safari.** ■

There is much more to the select object, including the ability to change the contents of a list in newer browsers. Chapter 37 covers the select object in depth.

Passing Elements to Functions with this

In all the examples so far in this lesson, when an event handler invokes a function that works with form elements, the form or form control is explicitly referenced by a global variable. But valuable shortcuts exist for transferring information about the form or form control directly to the function without having to declare global variables.

JavaScript features a keyword — this — that always refers to whatever object contains the script in which the keyword is used. For instance, if you attach a function to a button by its click event, then you click the button, the keyword this inside the function refers to the button itself. Using this is cool: it means having to use fewer global variables, lessening the chance that two independent scripts will someday use the same global variable name and mess up each other's logic, and it means that you can use the same generic function for multiple elements. Here's a simple example:

```
function identify()
{
    if (this.tagName)
    {
        alert('My tagName is ' + this.tagName);
    }
}
```

If you apply the identify() function to multiple elements on the page and then click them, each reports its tagName: P, LABEL, INPUT, FORM, BODY, etc.

Take a look at Listing 11-6. There are two functions that use the this keyword: processData(), which is attached to the submit button, and verifySong(), which is attached to the song name input field.

LISTING 11-6

Passing Elements to Functions with this

HTML: jsb-11-06.html

```
<!DOCTYPE html>
<html>
    <head>
        <meta http-equiv="content-type" content="text/html;charset=utf-8">
        <title>Beatle Picker</title>
        <script type="text/javascript" src="../jsb-global.js"></script>
```

```
    <script type="text/javascript" src="jsb-11-06.js"></script>
  </head>
  <body>
    <h1>Beatle Picker</h1>
    <form id="beatles-form" action="beatles.php" method="get">
      <p>
        <label>Choose your favorite Beatle:</label>
        <input type="radio" name="Beatles" id="radio1"
                    value="John Lennon" checked>
        <label for="radio1">John</label>
        <input type="radio" name="Beatles" id="radio2" value="Paul McCartney">
        <label for="radio2">Paul</label>
        <input type="radio" name="Beatles" id="radio3" value="George Harrison">
        <label for="radio3">George</label>
        <input type="radio" name="Beatles" id="radio4" value="Ringo Starr">
        <label for="radio4">Ringo</label>
      </p>
      <p>
        <label for="song">Enter the name of your favorite Beatles song:</label>
        <input type="text" id="song" name="song" value="Eleanor Rigby">
        <input type="submit" id="submit" value="Process Request...">
      </p>
    </form>
  </body>
</html>
```

JavaScript: jsb-11-06.js

```
// initialize when the page has loaded
addEvent(window, 'load', initialize);

// apply behaviors when document has loaded
function initialize()
{
    // do this only if the browser can handle DOM methods
    if (document.getElementById)
    {
        // point to crucial elements
        var oForm = document.getElementById('beatles-form');
        var oSong = document.getElementById('song');
        var oButtonSubmit = document.getElementById('submit');

            // if they all exist...
            if (oForm && oSong && oButtonSubmit)
            {
                // apply behavior to input field & button
                addEvent(oSong, 'change', verifySong);
                addEvent(oButtonSubmit, 'click', processData);
            }
    }
}
```

continued

LISTING 11-6   *(continued)*

```
// verify all input & suppress form submission
function processData(evt)
{
    // consolidate event handling
    if (!evt) evt = window.event;

  // point to the activated control's form ancestor
  var oForm = this.form;

  // see which radio button was selected
  for (var i = 0; i < oForm.Beatles.length; i++)
  {
    if (oForm.Beatles[i].checked)
    {
      break;
    }
  }

  // assign values to variables for convenience
  var sBeatle = oForm.Beatles[i].value;
  var sSong = oForm.song.value;

  // this is where a data lookup would go...
  alert("Checking whether " + sSong + " features " + sBeatle + "...");

    // cancel form submission
    if (evt.preventDefault) evt.preventDefault();
  return false;
}

// verify the song name when it's changed
function verifySong()
{
  // get the input song
  // ('this' is the object whose event handler called this function)
  var sSong = this.value;

  // this is where a data lookup would go...
  alert("Checking whether " + sSong + " is a Beatles tune...");
}
```

The function verifySong() wants access to the value entered into the song input field, so it uses this in the statement:

```
var sSong = this.value;
```

In other words, get the value of the current object (the input field) and assign it to the variable sSong. We're using this as a shortcut replacement for

```
var oInput = document.getElementById('song');
var sSong = oInput.value;
```

The function processData() needs to refer to several form elements, so it first takes advantage of the fact that every form element points to the form it belongs to with the form property:

```
var oForm = this.form;
```

Regardless of which input control this refers to, this.form points to the parent form. Then it can proceed to use object references such as oForm.Beatles and oForm.song to point to various controls within the form by name.

If you're a bit puzzled by the behavior of this script when you run it in your browser, here's an explanation of the programming logic behind what you experience. When you enter a new song title in the text box and exit the input field by pressing Tab or clicking elsewhere, the onchange event handler calls the verifySong() function, which displays an alert saying that it's checking the song. (It doesn't actually validate it against a database in this example.)

When you click the Process Request button, its onclick event handler calls the function processData(), which announces that it's checking to see if the entered song features the Beatle selected in the radio buttons above.

Now let's throw it two balls at once. Type a new song name in the input field, and then immediately click the Process Request button. You see only one alert — the verifySong() message that it's checking the song. Why don't you see both alerts? Because the button click action is interrupted by the onchange event handler of the text box. In other words, the button doesn't really get clicked, because the onchange alert dialog box comes up first. That's why you have to click the button for what seems to be a second time to get the song/Beatle verification. If you don't change the text in the field, your click of the button occurs without interruption, and the processData() verification takes place.

Note
Discrepancies between the ways that IE and other browsers handle event assignments and event processing require explanations beyond the scope of this tutorial. You'll meet them soon enough, however, beginning in Chapter 25, "Document Object Model Essentials," and again in Chapter 32, "Event Objects." ∎

Submitting and Prevalidating Forms

In an ordinary HTML document, we submit a form by clicking on a submit button; the browser then gathers up the values we entered or selected with the input controls and sends them to the specified URI. JavaScript lets us intercept that submit request, validate the input or do whatever else we need to do, and then either permit the form submission to proceed or cancel it so that we can guide the user to improve the input.

You can perform this sort of last-second validation of data or other scripting (for example, changing the form's action property based on user choices) in a function invoked by the form's onsubmit event handler. We'll go into substantial detail about validation routines in Chapter 46, "Data-Entry Validation," on the CD-ROM. For now, we just want to show you how the onsubmit event handler works.

To juggle the ways different browsers handle events, we need to use two techniques to cancel the event, corresponding exactly to the two techniques our addEvent() function uses to apply the event handlers in the first place:

```
// add an event to an element
function addEvent(elem, evtType, func)
{
   // first try the W3C DOM method
   if (elem.addEventListener)
   {
      elem.addEventListener(evtType, func, false);
   }
   // otherwise use the 'traditional' technique
   else
   {
      elem["on" + evtType] = func;
   }
}
```

Compare this to how the script in Listing 11-7 cancels the submit event:

```
function checkForm(evt)
{
     // consolidate event handling
     if (!evt) evt = window.event;
   ...
   // cancel form submission
     // W3C DOM method (hide from IE)
     if (evt.preventDefault) evt.preventDefault();
   // IE method
   return false;
   ...
}
```

For browsers compatible with the W3C DOM, the event is added with addEventListener(), and the form submission is cancelled with preventDefault(). Attempting to invoke a DOM method that the browser thinks doesn't exist causes a runtime error, so we protect the older and less capable browsers by testing first, to make sure the method exists for the event object.

For those less capable browsers, notably Internet Explorer, the event is added to the object by setting the event property (in this case, onsubmit), and form submission is cancelled simply by returning a false value from the function called by the event handler.

We'll get into all the whys and wherefores later in this book, but for now let's use this dual technique for handling events.

Listing 11-7 shows a page with a simple validation routine that ensures that all fields have something in them before allowing form submission to take place. The HTML marks up a form with four input fields and a submit button. Note that the action of the form element is the fictitious server-side program validate.php. If this page is delivered to a user agent not running JavaScript, the form will submit the input values to the server-side program for validation. Fundamental form validation must always happen server-side; we're duplicating that validation in client-side JavaScript to give the user a more immediate response to their actions. (Incidentally, that's one indicator of whether there's a typo in the script: if you submit this form with any of the input fields blank and the browser window attempts to bring up `validate.php`, you'll know that you probably made a typo while entering the HTML or JavaScript code because the script isn't blocking form submission.)

After the page loads, the script attaches the `checkForm()` function to the `onsubmit` event of the form. Note that we're not applying `onclick` behavior to the `submit` button; instead, we're letting the button do its normal job and we're intercepting the submission process at the form object itself.

When `submit` is clicked, the next normal step is for the browser to submit the form, but first it honors the `onsubmit` event handler and calls our function `checkForm()`. This function's principal job is to loop through all the form controls, looking for a blank input field. If it finds one, it displays an error message and cancels form submission.

Inside the loop, the `if` statement performs two tests. The first test is to make sure that we're examining form controls whose `type` properties are text (so as not to bother with, say, buttons). Next, it checks to see whether the value of the text field is empty. The `&&` operator (called a Boolean AND operator) forces both sides to evaluate to `true` before the entire condition expression inside the parentheses evaluates to `true`. If either subtest fails, the whole condition fails.

LISTING 11-7

Last-Minute Checking Before Form Submission

HTML: `jsb-11-07.html`

```html
<!DOCTYPE html>
<html>
   <head>
      <meta http-equiv="content-type" content="text/html;charset=utf-8">
      <title>Form Field Validator</title>
      <script type="text/javascript" src="../jsb-global.js"></script>
      <script type="text/javascript" src="jsb-11-07.js"></script>
   </head>
   <body>
      <h1>Form Field Validator</h1>
      <form id="theForm" action="validate.php" method="get">
         <p>Please enter all requested information:</p>
         <p>
            <label for="firstName">First Name:</label>
            <input type="text" id="firstName" name="firstName">
         </p>
         <p>
            <label for="lastName">Last Name:</label>
            <input type="text" id="lastName" name="lastName">
         </p>
         <p>
            <label for="age">Age:</label>
            <input type="text" id="age" name="age">
         </p>
```

continued

LISTING 11-7   *(continued)*

```
        <p>
            <label for="favoriteColor">Favorite Color:</label>
            <input type="text" id="favoriteColor" name="favoriteColor">
        </p>
        <p>
            <input type="submit" id="submit">
        </p>
    </form>
  </body>
</html>
```

JavaScript: jsb-11-07.js

```
// initialize when the page has loaded
addEvent(window, 'load', initialize);

// apply behaviors when document has loaded
function initialize()
{
    // do this only if the browser can handle DOM methods
    if (document.getElementById)
    {
        // point to the form
        var oForm = document.getElementById('theForm');

            // if it exists, apply the behavior
            if (oForm)
            {
                addEvent(oForm, 'submit', checkForm);
            }
    }
}

// when the form is submitted,
// check to make sure all input fields have been filled in
function checkForm(evt)
{
        // consolidate event handling
        if (!evt) evt = window.event;

    // 'this' is the current object, in this case the form
    for (var i = 0; i < this.elements.length; i++)
    {
        if (this.elements[i].type == "text" && this.elements[i].value == "")
        {
            alert("Fill out ALL fields.");

            // cancel form submission
                // W3C DOM method (hide from IE)
```

```
            if (evt.preventDefault) evt.preventDefault();
        // IE method
        return false;
    }
  }
  // allow form submission
  return true;
}
```

A word about submit()

The scripted equivalent of submitting a form is the form object's `submit()` method. All you need in the statement is a reference to the form and this method:

```
formObject.submit();
```

One quirky bit of behavior involving the `submit()` method and the `onsubmit` event handler needs explanation. Although you might think (and logically so, in our opinion) that the `submit()` method would be the exact scripted equivalent of the click of the real Submit button, it's not. The `submit()` method does not cause the form's `submit` event to fire at all. If you want to perform validation on a form submitted via the `submit()` method, invoke the validation in the script function that ultimately calls the `submit()` method.

So much for the basics of forms and form controls. In Chapter 12, you step away from HTML for a moment to look at more advanced JavaScript core language items: strings, math, and dates.

Exercises

1. Rework Listings 11-2, 11-3, 11-4, and 11-5 to use the `this` keyword instead of global variables.

2. For the following form (assume that it's the only form on the page), write at least 10 ways to reference the text input field as an object in all modern scriptable browsers.

    ```
    <form name="subscription" action="cgi-bin/maillist.pl" method="post">
     <p>
       <input type="text" id="email" name="email">
       <input type="submit">
     </p>
    </form>
    ```

3. Write a function that displays the value of an input field in an alert dialog box, plus the script that causes that function to be called when the input field is changed.

4. A document contains two forms, `specifications` and `accessories`. In the `accessories` form is a field named `acc1`. Write at least two different statements that set the contents of that field to `Leather Carrying Case`.

5. Create a page that includes a select object to change the background color of the current page. The property that you need to set is `document.body.style.backgroundColor`, and the three values you should offer as options are `red`, `yellow`, and `green`. In the `select` list, the colors should display as `Stop`, `Caution`, and `Go`.

Strings, Math, and Dates

For most of the lessons in the tutorial so far, the objects at the center of attention belong to the document object model (DOM). But, as indicated in Chapter 2, "Developing a Scripting Strategy," a clear dividing line exists between the DOM and the JavaScript language. The language has some of its own objects that are independent of the DOM. These objects are defined such that if a vendor wished to implement JavaScript as the programming language for an entirely different kind of product, the language would still use these core facilities for handling text, advanced math (beyond simple arithmetic), and dates. You can find formal specifications of these objects in the ECMA-262 recommendation.

Core Language Objects

It is often difficult for newcomers to programming — or even experienced programmers who have not worked with object-oriented languages before — to think about objects, especially when objects are attributed to things that don't seem to have a physical presence. For example, it doesn't require lengthy study to grasp the notion that a button on a page is an object. It has several physical properties that make perfect sense. But what about a string of characters? As you learn in this chapter, in an object-based environment such as JavaScript, "everything that moves" is treated as an object — each piece of data from a Boolean value to a date. Each such object probably has one or more properties that help define the content; such an object may also have methods associated with it to define what the object can do or what you can do to the object.

JavaScript objects that are not part of the DOM are called *core language objects*. You can see the full complement of them in the Quick Reference in Appendix A. This chapter focuses on the String, Math, and Date objects.

String Objects

You have used `String` objects many times in earlier lessons. A *string* is any text inside a quote pair. A quote pair consists of either double quotes (" ") or single quotes (' '). That JavaScript includes two types of quotes makes it easy to nest one string inside another. In the following example, the `alert()` method requires a quoted string as a parameter:

```
alert('You cannot lose.');
```

If the quoted expression includes an apostrophe, it's easy enough to switch the outer quotes to double:

```
alert("You can't lose.");
```

When the solution isn't so simple, as when both apostrophe and quotation mark appear in the quoted string, *escape sequences* come to the rescue. More on them in Chapter 15, "The String Object."

JavaScript imposes no practical limit on the number of characters that a string can hold. However, most older browsers have a limit of 255 characters for a script statement. This limit is sometimes exceeded when a script includes a lengthy string that is to become scripted content in a page. You need to divide such lines into smaller chunks, using techniques described in a moment.

You have two ways to assign a string value to a variable. The simplest is a basic assignment statement:

```
var myString = "Howdy";
```

This works perfectly well except in some exceedingly rare instances. You can also create a string object using the more formal syntax that involves the `new` keyword and a constructor function (that is, it constructs a new object):

```
var myString = new String("Howdy");
```

Whichever way you initialize a variable with a string, the variable receiving the assignment can respond to all `String` object methods.

Joining strings

Bringing two strings together as a single string is called *concatenation*, a term you learned in Chapter 8, "Programming Fundamentals, Part I." String concatenation requires one of two JavaScript operators. Even in your first close look at script, in Chapter 3, "Selecting and Using Your Tools," you saw how the addition operator (+) combines multiple strings into one:

```
var today = new Date();
var msg = "This is JavaScript saying it's now " + today.
    toLocaleString();
```

As valuable as the + operator is, another related operator can be even more scripter-friendly: +=. This operator is helpful when you are assembling large strings in a single variable. The strings may be so long or cumbersome that you need to divide the building process into multiple statements. Or you might decide to split the concatenation into several statements to help it make more sense to the human reader. The pieces may be combinations of *string literals* (strings inside quotes) and variable values. The clumsy way to do it (perfectly doable in JavaScript) is to use the addition operator to append more text to the existing chunk:

```
var msg = "Four score";
msg = msg + " and seven";
msg = msg + " years ago,";
```

But the += operator, called the *add-by-value operator*, offers a handy shortcut. The symbol for the operator is a plus and equal sign together. This operator means *append the stuff on the right of me to the end of the stuff on the left of me*. Therefore, the preceding sequence is shortened as follows:

```
var msg = "Four score";
msg += " and seven";
msg += " years ago,";
```

You can also combine the operators if the need arises:

```
var msg = "Four score";
msg += " and seven" + " years ago";
```

String methods

Of all the core JavaScript objects, the String object has the most diverse collection of methods associated with it. Many methods are designed to help scripts extract segments of a string. Another group, rarely used and now obsolete in favor of Cascading Style Sheets (CSS), wraps a string with one of several style-oriented tags (a scripted equivalent of tags for font size, font style, and the like).

In a string method, the string being acted upon becomes part of the reference followed by the method name:

```
myString.methodName();
```

All methods return a value of some kind. Most of the time, the returned value is a converted version of the string object referred to in the method call — but the original string is still intact. To capture the modified version, you need to assign the results of the method to a variable:

```
var result = myString.methodName();
```

The following sections introduce you to several important string methods available to all browser brands and versions.

Changing string case

Two methods convert a string to all uppercase or all lowercase letters:

```
var result = string.toUpperCase();
var result = string.toLowerCase();
```

As always, you must strictly observe the case of each letter of the method names if you want them to work. These methods come in handy when your scripts need to compare strings that may not have the same case (for example, a string in a lookup table compared with a string typed by a user). Because the methods don't change the original strings attached to the expressions, you can simply compare the evaluated results of the methods:

```
var foundMatch = false;
  if (stringA.toUpperCase() == stringB.toUpperCase())
  {
      foundMatch = true;
  }
```

String searches

You can use the `string.indexOf()` method to determine whether one string is contained by another. For example, say you've built a contact form on a web site that sends visitors' messages to the public relations department, but you want to carbon copy the ombudsman any messages containing the word "complaint." That word could occur anywhere within the long message string. In this case, you probably don't need to know exactly where the word occurs, just whether it's there.

The `string.indexOf()` method returns a number indicating the index value (zero-based) of the character in the larger string where the smaller string begins. The key point about this method is that, if no match occurs, the returned value is -1. To find out whether the smaller string is inside, all you need to test is whether the returned value is something other than -1.

Two strings are involved with this method: the shorter one and the longer one. The longer string is the one that appears in the reference to the left of the method name; the shorter string is inserted as a parameter to the `indexOf()` method. To demonstrate the method in action, the following fragment looks to see whether the input message contains the word 'complaint':

```
var sMsg = '';
var oInput = document.getElementById('message');
    if (oInput)
    {
        sMsg = oInput.value;
    }
var isComplaint = false;
    if (sMsg.indexOf("complaint") != -1)
    {
        isComplaint = true;
    }
```

The operator in the `if` construction's condition (`!=`) is the inequality operator. You can read it as meaning *is not equal to*.

Extracting copies of characters and substrings

To extract a single character at a known position within a string, use the `charAt()` method. The parameter of the method is an index number (zero-based) of the character to extract. When we say *extract*, we don't mean delete, but grab a snapshot of the character. The original string is not modified in any way.

For example, consider a script in a main window that is capable of inspecting a variable, `stringA`, in another window that displays map images of different corporate buildings. When the window has a map of Building C in it, the `stringA` variable contains `"Building C"`. In English the building letter is always at the 10th character position of the string (or number 9 in a zero-based counting world), so the script can examine that one character to identify the map currently in that other window:

```
var stringA = "Building C";
var bldgLetter = stringA.charAt(9);
    // result: bldgLetter = "C"
```

There are two similar methods — `string.substr()` and `string.substring()` — that enable you to extract a contiguous sequence of characters, provided that you know the starting position of the substring you want to grab. The difference between the two methods is that `string.substr()`

wants to know the length of the substring, whereas `string.substring()` wants to know the ending position of the substring:

```
string.substr(startingPosition [, length])
string.substring(startingPosition [, endingPosition])
```

Either method will extract everything up to the end of the original string if the second parameter (length or ending position) is omitted. The original string from which the extraction is made appears to the left of the method name in the reference. The starting and ending position parameters are index values (zero-based).

```
var stringA = "banana daiquiri";

var excerpt = stringA.substr(2,4);      // result: "nana"
var excerpt = stringA.substr(2);        // result: "nana daiquiri"

var excerpt = stringA.substring(2,6);   // result: "nana"
var excerpt = stringA.substring(2);     // result: "nana daiquiri"
```

String manipulation in JavaScript is fairly cumbersome compared with that in some other scripting languages. Higher-level notions of words, sentences, or paragraphs are absent. Therefore, sometimes it takes a bit of scripting with string methods to accomplish what seems like a simple goal. Yet you can put your knowledge of expression evaluation to the test as you assemble expressions that utilize heavily nested constructions.

For example, let's say you want to grab everything from a multiword expression except the first word:

```
var stringA = "The Painted Bird";
var firstSpace = stringA.indexOf(" ");
var excerpt = stringA.substring(firstSpace + 1);
    // result: excerpt = "Painted Bird"
```

Assuming that the first word can be of any length, the second statement uses the `string.indexOf()` method to look for the first space character. We add 1 to that value to serve as the starting index value for the `string.substring()` method. We omit the second `length` parameter in order to extract everything up to the end of `stringA`.

Creating statements like this one is not something you are likely to enjoy over and over again, so in Chapter 23, "Function Objects and Custom Objects," we show you how to create your own library of string functions that you can reuse in all of your scripts that need their string-handling facilities. More powerful string-matching facilities are also built into today's browsers by way of *regular expressions* (see Chapter 15, "The String Object," and Chapter 45, "The Regular Expression and RegExp Objects").

The Math Object

JavaScript provides ample facilities for math — far more than most scripters who don't have a background in computer science and math will likely use. But every genuine programming language needs these powers to accommodate clever programmers who can make windows fly in circles onscreen.

The `Math` object contains all these powers. This object is unlike most of the other objects in JavaScript in that you don't generate copies of the object to use. Instead, your scripts use the properties and methods of a single Math object. (Technically, one Math object actually occurs per window or frame, but this fact has no impact whatsoever on your scripts.) Programmers call this kind of fixed object a *static object*. That Math object (with an uppercase *M*) is part of the reference to the property or method. Properties of the Math object are constant values, such as pi and the square root of 2:

```
var piValue = Math.PI;
var rootOfTwo = Math.SQRT2;
```

Math object methods cover a wide range of trigonometric functions and other math functions that work on numeric values already defined in your script. For example, you can find which of two numbers is the larger:

```
var larger = Math.max(value1, value2);
```

Or you can raise one number to a power of 10:

```
var result = Math.pow(value1, 10);
```

More common, perhaps, is the method that rounds a value to the nearest integer value:

```
var result = Math.round(value1);
```

Another common request of the Math object is a random number. The Math.random() method returns a floating-point number between 0 and 1. If you design a script to act like a card game, you need random integers between 1 and 52; for dice, the range is 1 to 6 per die. To generate a random integer between 0 and any top value, use the following formula

```
Math.floor(Math.random() * (n + 1))
```

where n is the top number. (Math.floor returns the integer part — the digits to the left of the decimal point — of any floating-point number.) To generate random numbers between 1 and any higher number, use this formula

```
Math.floor(Math.random() * n) + 1
```

where n equals the top number of the range. For the dice game, the formula for each die is

```
newDieValue = Math.floor(Math.random() * 6) + 1;
```

To see this, enter the right part of the preceding statement in the top text box of The Evaluator Jr. and repeatedly click the Evaluate button.

The Date Object

Working with dates beyond simple tasks can be difficult business in JavaScript. A lot of the difficulty comes from the fact that dates and times are calculated internally according to *Greenwich Mean Time (GMT)* — provided that the visitor's own internal PC clock and control panel are set accurately. As a result of this complexity, better left for Chapter 17, "The Date Object," this section of the tutorial touches on only the basics of the JavaScript Date object.

A scriptable browser contains one global Date object (in truth, one Date object per window) that is always present, ready to be called upon at any moment. The Date object is another one of those static objects. When you wish to work with a date, such as displaying today's date, you need to invoke the Date object constructor function to obtain an instance of a Date object tied to a specific time and date. For example, when you invoke the constructor without any parameters, as in

```
var today = new Date();
```

the Date object takes a snapshot of the PC's internal clock and returns a Date object for that instant. Notice the distinction between the static Date object and a Date object instance, which contains an actual date value. The variable today contains not a ticking clock but a value that you can examine, tear apart, and reassemble as needed for your script.

Internally, the value of a Date object instance is the time, in milliseconds, from zero o'clock on January 1, 1970, in the GMT zone — the world standard reference point for all time conversions. That's how a Date object contains both date and time information.

You can also grab a snapshot of the Date object for a particular date and time in the past or future by specifying that information as parameters to the Date object constructor function:

```
var someDate = new Date("Month dd, yyyy hh:mm:ss");
var someDate = new Date("Month dd, yyyy");
var someDate = new Date(yyyy,mm,dd,hh,mm,ss);
var someDate = new Date(yyyy,mm,dd);
var someDate = new Date(GMT milliseconds from 1/1/1970);
```

If you attempt to view the contents of a raw Date object, JavaScript converts the value to the local time-zone string, as indicated by your PC's control panel setting. To see this in action, use The Evaluator Jr.'s top text box to enter the following:

```
new Date();
```

Your PC's clock supplies the current date and time as the clock calculates them (even though JavaScript still stores the date object's millisecond count in the GMT zone). You can, however, extract components of the Date object via a series of methods that you apply to a Date object instance. Table 12-1 shows an abbreviated listing of these properties and information about their values.

Caution

Be careful about values whose ranges start with zero, especially the months. The getMonth() **and** setMonth() **method values are zero based, so the numbers are 1 less than the month numbers you are accustomed to working with (for example, January is 0 and December is 11).** ■

You may notice one difference about the methods that set values of a Date object. Rather than returning some new value, these methods actually modify the value of the instance of the Date object referenced in the call to the method.

TABLE 12-1

Some Date Object Methods

Method	Value Range	Description
dateObj.getTime()	0-...	Milliseconds since 1/1/70 00:00:00 GMT
dateObj.getYear()	70-...	Specified year minus 1900; four-digit year for 2000+
dateObj.getFullYear()	1970-...	Four-digit year (Y2K-compliant); version 4+ browsers
dateObj.getMonth()	0-11	Month within the year (January = 0)
dateObj.getDate()	1-31	Date within the month
dateObj.getDay()	0-6	Day of week (Sunday = 0)
dateObj.getHours()	0-23	Hour of the day in 24-hour time
dateObj.getMinutes()	0-59	Minute of the specified hour
dateObj.getSeconds()	0-59	Second within the specified minute
dateObj.setTime(*val*)	0-...	Milliseconds since 1/1/70 00:00:00 GMT
dateObj.setYear(*val*)	70-...	Specified year minus 1900; four-digit year for 2000+
dateObj.setMonth(*val*)	0-11	Month within the year (January = 0)
dateObj.setDate(*val*)	1-31	Date within the month
dateObj.setDay(*val*)	0-6	Day of week (Sunday = 0)
dateObj.setHours(*val*)	0-23	Hour of the day in 24-hour time
dateObj.setMinutes(*val*)	0-59	Minute of the specified hour
dateObj.setSeconds(*val*)	0-59	Second within the specified minute

Date Calculations

Performing calculations with dates frequently requires working with the millisecond values of the Date objects. This is the surest way to compare, add, and subtract date values. To demonstrate a few Date object machinations, Listing 12-1 displays the current date and time and one way to calculate the date and time seven days from now.

LISTING 12-1

Date Object Calculations

HTML: jsb-12-01.html

```
<!DOCTYPE html>
<html>
   <head>
```

```
        <meta http-equiv="content-type" content="text/html;charset=utf-8">
        <title>Date Calculation</title>
        <script type="text/javascript" src="../jsb-global.js"></script>
        <script type="text/javascript" src="jsb-12-01.js"></script>
    </head>
    <body>
        <h1>Date Calculation</h1>
        <form id="date-form" action="date-calc.php">
            <p>
                <label for="today">Today is:</label>
                <input type="text" id="today" name="today" size="80">
            </p>
            <p>
                <label for="nextWeek">Next week will be:</label>
                <input type="text" id="nextWeek" name="nextWeek" size="80">
            </p>
            <p>
                <input type="submit" id="submit">
            </p>
        </form>
    </body>
</html>
```

JavaScript: jsb-12-01.js

```
// run script when the page has loaded
addEvent(window, 'load', calcDates);

// calculate dates and plug into document
function calcDates()
{
    var dTodaysDate = new Date();

    // plug in today
    var oToday = document.getElementById('today');
        if (oToday)
        {
            oToday.value = dTodaysDate;
        }

    // plug in next week
    var oNextWeek = document.getElementById('nextWeek');
        if (oNextWeek)
        {
            // today in milliseconds
            var msToday = dTodaysDate.getTime();

            // one week = 1000 milliseconds * 60 seconds * 60 minutes
            //            * 24 hours * 7 days
            var msOneWeek = 1000 * 60 * 60 * 24 * 7;
```

continued

LISTING 12-1   *(continued)*

```
        // next week in milliseconds
        var msNextWeek = msToday + msOneWeek;

        // next week as date object
        var dAWeekFromNow = new Date(msNextWeek);

        // plug in string value
        oNextWeek.value = dAWeekFromNow;
    }
}
```

The script first creates a new `Date` object and assigns it to the variable `dTodaysDate`. Then it displays the current date and time by setting the value of the input field `today` equal to `dTodaysDate`. Although you might expect that this would insert a copy of the `Date` object into the input field, what really happens is that it uses the `toString()` method of the `Date` object to output a string such as

```
    Sun Dec 05 2010 16:47:20 GMT-0800 (Pacific Standard Time)
```

Next, we display the date and time one week from now. To work with milliseconds, we start by assigning the current date and time in milliseconds to variable `msToday`. To add one week to this, we need to know how many milliseconds there are in a week: 1000 ms. per second, 60 seconds per minute, 60 minutes per hour, 24 hours per day, and seven days per week. The product of all these we store in variable `msOneWeek`. We add that week of milliseconds to the current date and time, and then use the result to create a new `Date` object, which we store in variable `dAWeekFromNow`. Displaying the resultant date and time is done the same way as before — simply by assigning the new `Date` object to an input field's `value` attribute.

To add time intervals to or subtract time intervals from a `Date` object, you can use a shortcut that doesn't require the millisecond conversions. By combining the date object's `set` and `get` methods, you can let the `Date` object work out the details. For example, in Listing 12-1, you could replace the "next week" logic with:

```
    dTodaysDate.setDate(dTodaysDate.getDate() + 7);
    oNextWeek.value = dTodaysDate;
```

Because JavaScript tracks the date and time internally as milliseconds, the accurate date appears in the end, even if the new date is into the next month. JavaScript automatically takes care of figuring out how many days there are in a month, as well as in leap years.

Many other-quirks and complicated behavior await you if you script dates in your page. As later chapters demonstrate, however, the results may be worth the effort.

Exercises

1. Create a web page that has one form field for entering the user's email address, and a Submit button. In the accompanying JavaScript script, write a presubmission validation routine that verifies that the text field contains the @ symbol used in all email addresses before you allow submission of the form.

2. Given the string `"Internet Explorer"`, fill in the blanks of the `string.substring` `()` method parameters here that yield the results shown to the right of each method call.

```
var myString = "Internet Explorer";
myString.substring(___,___)      // result = "Int"
myString.substring(___,___)      // result = "plorer"
myString.substring(___,___)      // result = "net Exp"
```

3. Consider this logic for extracting the part of a string that comes after the first word:

```
var stringA = "The Painted Bird";
var firstSpace = stringA.indexOf(" ");
var excerpt = stringA.substring(firstSpace + 1);
```

What will happen in this logic if `stringA` does not contain a space? Work out what you think should occur, then run the script to see if you're right.

4. Fill in the rest of the function in the listing that follows so that it looks through every character of the entry field and counts how many times the letter *e* (either upper- or lowercase) appears in the field. (Hint: All that is missing is a `for` repeat loop.)

```
var inputString = 'Elephantine';
var count = 0;

MISSING CODE

var msg = "The number of e's in '" + this.mainstring.value + "'";
msg += " is " + count;
alert(msg);
```

5. Create a page that has two fields and one button. The button should trigger a function that generates two random numbers between 1 and 6, placing each number in one of the fields. (Think of using this page as a substitute for rolling a pair of dice in a board game.)

6. Create a script that displays the number of days between today and next Christmas.

Scripting Frames and Multiple Windows

O ne of the attractive aspects of JavaScript for some applications on the client is that it allows user actions in one frame or window to influence what happens in other frames and windows. In this section of the tutorial, you extend your existing knowledge of object references to the realm of multiple frames and windows.

IN THIS CHAPTER

Relationships among frames in the browser window

How to access objects and values in other frames

How to control navigation of multiple frames

Communication skills between separate windows

Frames: Parents and Children

You've seen in earlier top-level hierarchy illustrations (such as Figure 6-2) that the window object is at the top of the chart. The window object also has several synonyms, which stand in for the window object in special cases. For instance, in Chapter 10, "Window and Document Objects," you learned that self is synonymous with window when the reference applies to the same window that contains the script's document. In this lesson, you learn the roles of three other references that point to objects behaving as windows: frame, top, and parent.

Loading an ordinary HTML document into the browser creates a model in the browser that starts out with one window object and the document it contains. The top rungs of the hierarchy model are as simple as can be, as shown in Figure 13-1. This is where references begin with window or self (or with document because the current window is assumed).

FIGURE 13-1

Single-frame window and document hierarchy.

To frame or not to frame?

Frames and iFrames are valid HTML and their use might be seen as desirable for accomplishing some tasks. However, frame-based web sites pose serious usability and accessibility issues that can make them less than ideal for general web site development.

The fundamental problem with framesets is that any given combination of framed pages is not directly addressable. That is, if you navigate through a frameset to bring up a particular combination of content in the frames, the URL in the browser's address bar will remain that of the parent frameset document, not that of the actual content you're viewing. This lack of unique addressing of frame-paged content prevents search engines from indexing content and prevents other people from publishing links to the framed content, bookmarking them on their computers, or sharing them in email. Framesets can also be disorienting or completely inaccessible for the users of mobile devices and assistive technology such as magnifiers and screen-readers.

Web usability expert Jakob Nielsen wrote "Why Frames Suck (Most of the Time)" back in 1996. The situation hasn't improved in all the years since.

Alternatives to frames that avoid these problems include using server-side scripting to combine multiple source pages, and using the CSS properties overflow: auto, to create fields of scrolling content, and position: fixed, to establish sections that don't move when the rest of the page scrolls.

In this book, we assume that you've considered the pros and cons of using frames and may have a web development problem — or mere curiosity — that requires their use. We want you to know how to manipulate them with JavaScript if you have to, and they make for great exercise in navigating the DOM, but we don't recommend their use in most circumstances.

The instant a framesetting document loads into a browser, the browser starts building a slightly different hierarchy model. The precise structure of that model depends entirely on the structure of the frameset defined in that framesetting document. Consider the following skeletal frameset definition:

```
<!DOCTYPE HTML PUBLIC "-//W3C//DTD HTML 4.01 Frameset//EN"
        "http://www.w3.org/TR/html4/frameset.dtd">
<html>
    <head>
        <meta http-equiv="Content-Type" content="text/html; charset=utf-8">
        <title>Title of all pages in this frameset</title>
    </head>
    <frameset cols="50%,50%">
        <frame name="leftFrame" src="somedoc1.html" title="Frame 1">
        <frame name="rightFrame" src="somedoc2.html" title="Frame 2">
        <noframes>
```

```
    . . .
  </noframes>
 </frameset>
</html>
```

This markup splits the browser window into two frames side by side, with a different document loaded into each frame. The model conveys both the structure (parent with children) and the layout (the relative sizes of the frames and whether they're set up in columns or rows). Because frames markup is not backward-compatible — it displays absolutely nothing in browsers that don't support frames — we also provide a no-frames alternative, which might be actual content or a hyperlink to a frameless page.

Framesets establish relationships among the frames in the collection. Borrowing terminology from the object-oriented programming world, the framesetting document loads into a *parent window*. Each of the frames defined in that parent window document is a *child frame*. Figure 13-2 shows the hierarchical model of a two-frame environment. This illustration reveals a lot of subtleties about the relationships among framesets and their frames.

FIGURE 13-2

Two-frame window and document hierarchy.

It is often difficult at first to visualize the frameset as a window object in the hierarchy. After all, with the exception of the URL showing in the browser's Location/Address field, you don't see anything about the frameset in the browser. But that window object exists in the object model. Notice, too, that in the diagram the framesetting parent window has no document object showing. This may also seem odd, because the window obviously requires an HTML file containing the specifications for the frameset. In truth, the parent window has a `document` object associated with it, but it is omitted from the diagram to better portray the relationships among parent and child windows. A frameset parent's document cannot itself contain most of the typical HTML objects such as forms and controls, so references to the parent's document are rarely, if ever, used.

If you add a script to the framesetting document that needs to access a property or method of that window object, references are like any single-frame situation. Think about the point of view of a script located in that window. Its immediate universe is the very same window.

Things get more interesting when you start looking at the child frames. Each of these frames contains a `document` object whose content you see in the browser window, and the structure is such that each frame's document is entirely independent of the other. It is as though each document lived in its own browser window. Indeed, that's why each child frame is also a window type of object. A frame has the same kinds of properties and methods as the `window` object that occupies the entire browser.

From the point of view of either child window in Figure 13-2, its immediate container is the `parent` window. When a `parent` window is at the top of the hierarchical model loaded in the browser, that window is also referred to as the `top` object.

References Among Family Members

Given the frame structure of Figure 13-2, it's time to look at how a script in any one of those windows can access objects, functions, or variables in the others. An important point to remember about this facility is that if a script has access to an object, function, or global variable in its own window, that same item can be reached by a script from another frame in the hierarchy (provided that both documents come from the same web server).

A script reference may need to take one of three possible routes in the two-generation hierarchy described so far: parent to child; child to parent; or child to child. Each of the paths between these windows requires a different reference style.

Parent-to-child references

Probably the least common direction taken by references is when a script in the parent document needs to access some element of one of its frames. Since the parent can contain one or more frames, the parent maintains an array of the child frame objects. You can address a frame by array syntax or by the name you assign to it with the `id` or `name` attribute inside the `<frame>` tag. In the following examples of reference syntax, we substitute a placeholder named `ObjFuncVarName` for whatever object, function, or global variable you intend to access in the distant window or frame. Remember that each visible frame contains a `document` object, which generally is the container of elements you script; be sure that references to the elements include `document`. With that in mind, a reference from a parent to one of its child frames can follow any one of these models:

```
[window.]frames[n].ObjFuncVarName
[window.]frames["frameName"].ObjFuncVarName
[window.]frameName.ObjFuncVarName
```

Numeric index values for frames are based on the order in which their `<frame>` tags appear in the framesetting document. You will make your life easier, however, if you assign recognizable names to each frame and use the frame's name in the reference.

Child-to-parent references

It is not uncommon to link scripts to the parent frameset document (in the `head` portion) that multiple child frames or multiple documents in a frame use as a common script library. Because they load in the frameset, these scripts load only once while the frameset is visible. If other documents from the same server load into the frames over time, they can take advantage of the parent's scripts without having to load their own copies into the browser.

From the child's point of view, the next level up the hierarchy is called the `parent`. Therefore, a reference from a child frame to items at the parent level is simply:

```
parent.ObjFuncVarName
```

If the item accessed in the parent is a function that returns a value, the returned value transcends the parent/child borders down to the child without hesitation.

```
var sValue = parent.FuncName();
```

When the parent window is also at the top of the object hierarchy currently loaded into the browser, you can optionally refer to it as the *top window,* as in:

```
top.ObjFuncVarName
```

Using the `top` reference can be hazardous if for some reason your web page gets displayed in some other web site's frameset. What if your top window is not the master frameset's top window? Therefore, we recommend using the `parent` reference whenever possible (unless you want your script to fail when nested inside an unwanted framer of your web site).

Child-to-child references

The browser needs a bit more assistance when it comes to getting a child window to communicate with one of its siblings. One of the properties of any window or frame is its `parent` (whose value is `null` for a single window). A reference must use the `parent` property to work its way out of the current frame to a point that both child frames have in common — the parent, in this case. When the reference is at the parent level, the rest of the reference can carry on as though it were starting at the parent. Thus, from one child to one of its siblings, you can use any of the following reference formats:

```
parent.frames[n].ObjFuncVarName
parent.frames["frameName"].ObjFuncVarName
parent.frameName.ObjFuncVarName
```

A reference from the other sibling back to the first looks the same, but the `frames[]` array index or `frameName` part of the reference differs. Of course, much more complex frame hierarchies exist in HTML. Even so, the object model and referencing scheme provide a solution for the most deeply nested and gnarled frame arrangement you can think of — following the same precepts you just learned.

Frame-Scripting Tips

One of the first mistakes that frame-scripting newcomers make is writing immediate script statements that call on other frames while the pages load. The problem here is that you cannot rely on the document loading sequence to follow the frameset source-code order. All you know for sure is that the parent document *begins* loading first. Regardless of the order of `<frame>` tags, child frames can begin loading in any sequence. Moreover, a frame's loading time depends on other elements in the document, such as images or Java applets.

Fortunately, you can use a certain technique to initiate a script when all the documents in the frameset are completely loaded. Just as the `load` event for a window fires when that window's document is fully loaded, a parent's `load` event fires after the `load` events in its child frames have fired. When you specify a `window.onload` event handler in a script linked to the frameset document, it's the equivalent of applying the event handler to the `frameset` element. That handler might invoke a function in the framesetting document that then has the freedom to tap the objects, functions, or variables of all frames throughout the object hierarchy.

Make special note that a reference to a frame as a type of window object is quite separate from a reference to the `frame` element object. An element object is one of those DOM element nodes in the document node tree (see Chapter 6, "Browser and Document Objects"). The properties and methods of this node differ from the properties and methods that accrue to a window-type object. It may be a difficult distinction to grasp, but it's an important one. The way you reference a frame — as a window object or element node — determines which set of properties and methods are available to your scripts.

Cross-Reference

See Chapter 26, "Generic HTML Element Objects," for a more detailed introduction to element node scripting. ■

If you start with a reference to the `frame` element object, you can still reach a reference to the `document` object loaded into that frame, but the syntax is different, depending on the browser. IE4+ and Safari let you use the same `document` reference as for a window; Mozilla-based browsers follow the W3C DOM standard more closely, using the `contentDocument` property of the frame element. To accommodate both syntaxes, you can build a reference as follows:

```
var docObj;
var frameObj = document.getElementById("myFrame");
  if (frameObj.contentDocument)
  {
      docObj = frameObj.contentDocument;
  }
  else
  {
      docObj = frameObj.document;
  }
```

About iframe Elements

The `iframe` element is supported as a scriptable object in IE4+, Mozilla-based browsers, and Safari (among other modern browsers). It is often used as a way to fetch and load HTML from a server without disturbing the current HTML page. It's not uncommon for an `iframe` to be hidden from view while scripts handle all the processing between it and the main document. (Today, the trick of asynchronously loading data from the server into an already-downloaded page is often accomplished using `XMLHttpRequest()` — see Chapter 39, "Ajax, E4X, and XML," on the CD.)

An `iframe` element becomes another member of the current window's `frames` collection, but you may also reference the `iframe` as an element object through W3C DOM `document` `.getElementById()` terminology. As with the distinction between the traditional frame-as-window object and DOM element object, a script reference to the `document` object within an `iframe` element object needs special handling. See Chapter 27, "Window and Frame Objects," for additional details.

Highlighting Footnotes: A Frameset Scripting Example

For a taste of inter-window scripting, consider a frameset that highlights a footnote in one frame when the corresponding link is clicked in the document text. Figure 13-3 shows what this frameset looks like, and Listing 13-1 provides the markup and scripting.

The three HTML files establish a frameset with two child frames, one for the main text and one for the footnotes. Clicking on a footnote link in the text brings the selected footnote to the top of the footnote frame. It does this by adding the element ID of the selected footnote to the 'hash' of the URL:

```
<a target="frameFootnotes" ↵
href="jsb-13-01-frame-footnotes.html#footnote-01">Footnote 1</a>
```

FIGURE 13-3

Highlighting Footnotes frameset.

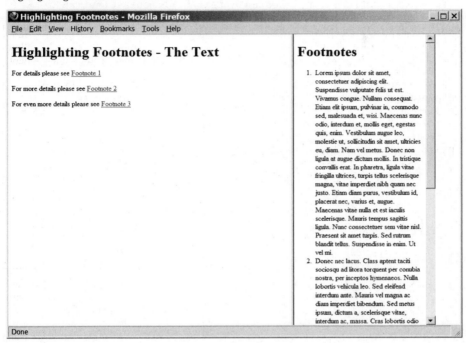

The `target` attribute identifies the child frame while the `href` specifies which document will appear in that frame. The final part of the `href` URL `#footnote-01` matches up with the footnote markup:

```
<li id="footnote-01">Lorem ipsum dolor ...
```

It is basic browser functionality that, when the ID of an element is set as the hash of a URL, the page scrolls up (if it can) to position that element at the top of the window.

JavaScript and CSS work together to highlight the selected footnote: when the user clicks on a footnote link in the text window, JavaScript assigns a "selected" class to the footnote element. CSS styles that class with a background color.

LISTING 13-1

Highlighting Footnotes

HTML: jsb-13-01-frameset.html

```
<!DOCTYPE HTML PUBLIC "-//W3C//DTD HTML 4.01 Frameset//EN"
    "http://www.w3.org/TR/html4/frameset.dtd">
<html>
    <head>
```

continued

LISTING 13-1   *(continued)*

```
    <meta http-equiv="Content-Type" content="text/html; charset=utf-8">
    <title>Highlighting Footnotes</title>
    <link href="jsb-13-01-frameset.css" rel="stylesheet"
        type="text/css" media="all">
  </head>
  <frameset cols="66%,33%">
    <frame name="frameText" src="jsb-13-01-frame-text.html" title="Frame 1">
    <frame name="frameFootnotes" src="jsb-13-01-frame-footnotes.html"
        title="Frame 2">
    <noframes>
      <body>
        <h1>Text with Footnotes</h1>
        <p>Proceed to <a href="jsb-13-01-frame-text-footnotes.html">
            combined text and footnotes</a>.</p>
      </body>
    </noframes>
  </frameset>
</html>
```

Stylesheet: jsb-13-01-frameset.css

```
/* limit the width of the page */
html
{
   width: 60em;
   max-width: 100%;
}
```

HTML: jsb-13-01-frame-text.html

```
<!DOCTYPE html PUBLIC "-//W3C//DTD HTML 4.01 Transitional//EN"
   "http://www.w3.org/TR/html4/loose.dtd">
<html>
  <head>
     <meta http-equiv="Content-Type" content="text/html; charset=utf-8">
     <title>Highlighting Footnotes - The Text</title>
     <script type="text/javascript" src="../jsb-global.js"></script>
     <script type="text/javascript" src="jsb-13-01-frame-text.js"></script>
  </head>
  <body>
     <h1>Highlighting Footnotes - The Text</h1>

     <p>For details please see <a target="frameFootnotes"
            href="jsb-13-01-frame-footnotes.html#footnote-01">Footnote 1</a></p>

     <p>For more details please see <a target="frameFootnotes"
            href="jsb-13-01-frame-footnotes.html#footnote-02">Footnote 2</a></p>
```

```
      <p>For even more details please see <a target="frameFootnotes"
            href="jsb-13-01-frame-footnotes.html#footnote-03">Footnote 3</a></p>

  </body>
</html>
```

JavaScript: jsb-13-01-frame-text.js

```javascript
// run script when the page has loaded
addEvent(window, 'load', initialize);

// global memory of the last footnote highlighted
var oFootnote = null;
var sFootnoteClass = '';

// apply behaviors when document has loaded
function initialize()
{
    // do this only if the browser can handle DOM methods
    if (document.getElementById)
    {
        // collect anchors
        var aAnchors = document.getElementsByTagName('a');

        // for each anchor...
        for (var i = 0; i < aAnchors.length; i++)
        {
            // get the target of the link
            var sTarget = aAnchors[i].getAttribute('target');

                // if there is a target and it's the footnotes frame
                if (sTarget && sTarget == 'frameFootnotes')
                {
                    addEvent(aAnchors[i], 'click', highlightFootnote);
                }
        }
    }
}

// highlight the selected footnote
function highlightFootnote()
{
        // restore previously highlighted footnote (if any)
        if (oFootnote)
        {
            oFootnote.className = sFootnoteClass;
        }

    // get the HREF of the clicked anchor
    var sHref = this.getAttribute('href');
```

continued

LISTING 13-1   *(continued)*

```
    // get the 'hash' of the URL
    var iHash = sHref.indexOf('#');
    // everything after the hash mark is the element Id
    var sFootnoteId = sHref.substr(iHash + 1);

    // the target of the link is the frame Id
    var sFrameId = this.getAttribute('target');

        // if the frame exists...
        if (parent[sFrameId])
        {
            // point to the indicated footnote
            oFootnote = parent[sFrameId].document.getElementById(sFootnoteId);
                // if it exists...
                if (oFootnote)
                {
                    // remember its original class to restore it later
                    sFootnoteClass = oFootnote.className;

                    // set its new class
                    oFootnote.className = 'selected';
                }
        }
}
```

HTML: jsb-13-01-frame-footnotes.html

```
<!DOCTYPE html PUBLIC "-//W3C//DTD HTML 4.01 Transitional//EN"
    "http://www.w3.org/TR/html4/loose.dtd">
<html>
    <head>
        <meta http-equiv="Content-Type" content="text/html; charset=utf-8">
        <title>Footnotes</title>
        <link href="jsb-13-01-frame-footnotes.css" rel="stylesheet"
            type="text/css" media="all">
    </head>
    <body>
        <h1>Footnotes</h1>

        <ol class="footnotes">
            <li id="footnote-01">Lorem ipsum dolor sit amet, consectetuer
adipiscing elit. Suspendisse vulputate felis ut est. Vivamus congue.
Nullam consequat. Etiam elit ipsum, pulvinar in, commodo sed, malesuada
et, wisi. Maecenas nunc odio, interdum et, mollis eget, egestas quis, enim.
Vestibulum augue leo, molestie ut, sollicitudin sit amet, ultricies eu, diam.
Nam vel metus. Donec non ligula at augue dictum mollis. In tristique convallis
erat. In pharetra, ligula vitae fringilla ultrices, turpis tellus scelerisque
magna, vitae imperdiet nibh quam nec justo. Etiam diam purus, vestibulum id,
```

placerat nec, varius et, augue. Maecenas vitae nulla et est iaculis scelerisque. Mauris tempus sagittis ligula. Nunc consectetuer sem vitae nisl. Praesent sit amet turpis. Sed rutrum blandit tellus. Suspendisse in enim. Ut vel mi.</li>

                                            `<li id="footnote-02">`Donec nec lacus. Class aptent taciti sociosqu ad litora torquent per conubia nostra, per inceptos hymenaeos. Nulla lobortis vehicula leo. Sed eleifend interdum ante. Mauris vel magna ac diam imperdiet bibendum. Sed metus ipsum, dictum a, scelerisque vitae, interdum ac, massa. Cras lobortis odio at augue. Aenean fermentum bibendum purus. Ut congue interdum turpis. Ut quis mi a ligula viverra hendrerit. Nulla facilisi. Nullam lacinia, ligula ac congue feugiat, risus diam fringilla tellus, condimentum volutpat eros risus sit amet dolor.`</li>`

                                            `<li id="footnote-03">`Proin et urna. Morbi in odio. In mauris tellus, tincidunt vitae, ultrices a, sollicitudin sit amet, nulla. Praesent consequat, lectus auctor imperdiet dapibus, risus turpis feugiat orci, sit amet tempus quam erat a purus. Nullam neque nulla, fringilla ut, dictum id, luctus placerat, urna. Sed vel velit. Fusce eget erat a quam auctor pulvinar. Phasellus vel neque eu risus feugiat sagittis. Nulla est. Duis sed massa. Duis ac leo quis sapien fringilla posuere. Nam facilisis lorem. Nullam bibendum, wisi quis ultrices bibendum, sem pede volutpat sem, ut ultrices odio nisl ut ligula. Cras ligula est, tempus et, tempus vitae, pretium eget, ipsum. Integer Blandit mattis wisi. Curabitur eget tellus at neque vulputate dignissim. Phasellus leo nibh, euismod ac, congue vel, interdum et, turpis. Fusce viverra aliquet wisi.`</li>`

```
      </ol>
   </body>
</html>
```

Stylesheet: jsb-13-01-frame-footnotes.css

```css
/* style the selected footnote */
ol.footnotes li.selected
{
    background-color: aqua;
}
```

Let's walk through the JavaScript to see how the highlighting works. The script is linked to the `frame-text.html` document because it's the act of clicking the links in that document that triggers the highlighting event. The `addEvent()` function call tells JavaScript to run the `initialize()` function when the document has loaded. That function loops through all the anchor elements in the document. If it finds a `target` attribute set to `frameFootnotes`, it applies the `onclick` event to run the function `highlightFootnote()`.

When the user clicks on one of these links in the document text, the `highlightFootnote()` function gives the anchor element the `selected` class. To make it easy to restore a link to its previous class name later, the script stores the current anchor element pointer and its class attribute in global variables `oFootnote` and `sFootnoteClass`. So, the first thing it does when a link is clicked is to restore the previously-clicked link, if any.

To set the `class` attribute of the footnote in the other child frame, the script needs to determine the names of the frame and the footnote element. The frame name is exactly the same as the `target` attribute of the link that's clicked. The footnote element is whatever element in the footnote frame has the ID equal to the hash at the end of the link's URL.

If the named frame exists and the named element exists, the script can safely save the element's existing class (if any) and set the class to `selected`. Finally, the style sheet linked to the footnotes document applies a background color to any footnote with the `selected` class.

There are two important scripting principles illustrated with Listing 13-1. First, the fundamental operation of this page — bringing the selected footnote to the top of the footnote frame — is handled entirely by HTML without any help from JavaScript. This ensures that the page will be usable when viewed with user agents that don't support JavaScript, such as mobile devices, or with browsers in which the user has disabled JavaScript. This is an example of *progressive enhancement*, which stipulates that our scripting efforts should enhance already functional pages rather than supplying mission-critical functionality. We want to improve the experience for those who are running JavaScript and not break the page for those who aren't.

Second, we're using JavaScript to indicate that the footnotes are "selected" but not how they should be styled. We could have scripted:

```
oFootnote.style.backgroundColor = 'aqua';
```

Instead, the styling is left to CSS. This is an example of *separation of development layers*, whereby HTML structure and content are kept separate from JavaScript behavior and CSS presentation. This mode of development makes it quick and easy to create new code, tweak existing code, and apply old code to new projects. For example, when the web site designer changes the look of the site — and rest assured nearly every site *will* be changed either during development or afterward — cosmetic changes should be within the grasp of someone who knows CSS, without requiring the services of a JavaScript programmer.

References for Multiple Windows

In Chapter 10 you saw how to create a new window and communicate with it by way of the `window` object reference returned from the `window.open()` method. In this section, we show you how one of those subwindows can communicate with objects, functions, and variables in the window or frame that creates the subwindow.

Every `window` object has a property called `opener`. This property contains a reference to the window or frame that held the script whose `window.open()` statement generated the subwindow. For the main browser window and frames therein, this value is `null`. Because the `opener` property is a valid window reference (when its value is not `null`), you can use it to begin the reference to items in the original window — just like a script in a child frame uses `parent` to access items in the parent document. (The `parent` keyword isn't used for a subwindow's opener, however.)

Listing 13-2 contains two documents that work together in separate windows. `jsb-13-02-main.html` displays a button that opens a smaller window and loads `jsb-13-02-sub.html` into it, and another button that closes the subwindow. The main window document also contains a text field that gets filled in when you enter text in a corresponding field in the subwindow.

Note

You may have to turn off pop-up blocking temporarily to experiment with these examples.

Because so many people have set their browsers to block pop-up windows, and because pop-ups can be so disorienting to folks using assistive technology such as screen readers, and simply irritating to everyone else, we don't recommend that you create subwindows with JavaScript in real-world applications — and especially not for any critical function. Instead, use other techniques, such as CSS pop-ups, that gracefully degrade to simple HTML navigation in the absence of styling and scripting. ■

In the main window's script, the openSubWindow() function generates the new window. Because the closeSubWindow() function needs to know which window to close, we store the pointer to the new window in a global variable.

LISTING 13-2

A Main Window Document

HTML: jsb-13-02-main.html

```
<!DOCTYPE html>
<html>
    <head>
        <meta http-equiv="content-type" content="text/html;charset=utf-8">
        <title>Opener</title>
        <script type="text/javascript" src="../jsb-global.js"></script>
        <script type="text/javascript" src="jsb-13-02-main.js"></script>
    </head>
    <body>
        <h1>Opener</h1>
        <form action="">
            <p>
                <input type="button" value="Open Sub Window" id="open-sub-window">
                <input type="button" value="Close Sub Window" id="close-sub-window">
            </p>
            <p>
                <label>Text incoming from subwindow:</label>
                <input type="text" id="output">
            </p>
        </form>
    </body>
</html>
```

JavaScript: jsb-13-02-main.js

```
// run script when the page has loaded
addEvent(window, 'load', initialize);

// global pointer to sub-window
var oSubWindow;
```

continued

LISTING 13-2   *(continued)*

```
// apply behaviors when document has loaded
function initialize()
{
    // do this only if the browser can handle DOM methods
    if (document.getElementById)
    {
        // point to button
        var oButton = document.getElementById('open-sub-window');

            // if it exists, apply behavior
            if (oButton)
            {
                addEvent(oButton, 'click', openSubWindow);
            }

        // point to button
        oButton = document.getElementById('close-sub-window');

            // if it exists, apply behavior
            if (oButton)
            {
                addEvent(oButton, 'click', closeSubWindow);
            }
    }
}

// open (create) sub window
function openSubWindow()
{
    // store sub-window pointer in global variable
    oSubWindow = window.open("jsb-13-02-sub.html", "sub", "height=200,width=300");
}

// close (destroy) sub window
function closeSubWindow()
{
        // if the sub-window has been opened, close it
        if (oSubWindow)
        {
            oSubWindow.close();
        }
}
```

HTML: jsb-13-02-sub.html

```
<!DOCTYPE html>
<html>
    <head>
        <meta http-equiv="content-type" content="text/html;charset=utf-8">
        <title>Sub-Document</title>
        <script type="text/javascript" src="../jsb-global.js"></script>
```

```html
    <script type="text/javascript" src="jsb-13-02-sub.js"></script>
  </head>
  <body>
    <h1>Sub-Document</h1>
    <form id="sendForm" action="">
      <p>
        <label for="input">Enter text to be copied to the main window:</label>
        <input type="text" id="input">
      </p>
      <p>
        <input type="button" value="Send Text to Opener" id="send-text">
      </p>
    </form>
  </body>
</html>
```

JavaScript: jsb-13-02- sub.js

```javascript
// run script when the page has loaded
addEvent(window, 'load', initialize);

// apply behaviors when document has loaded
function initialize()
{
    // do this only if the browser can handle DOM methods
    if (document.getElementById)
    {
        // point to button
        var oButton = document.getElementById('send-text');

            // if it exists, apply behavior
            if (oButton)
            {
                addEvent(oButton, 'click', copyToOpener);
            }
    }
}

// copy input text to output in parent
function copyToOpener()
{
    // find the input field in the current window
    var oInput = document.getElementById('input');

    // find the output field in the parent window
    var oOutput = opener.document.getElementById('output');

        // if they both exist, copy input text
        if (oInput && oOutput)
        {
            oOutput.value = oInput.value;
        }
}
```

All the action in the subwindow document stems from the onclick event handler assigned to the Send Text button. It triggers the copyToOpener() function, which assigns the subwindow input field's value to the value of the output field in the opener window's document. Remember, the contents of each window and frame belong to a document. Even after your reference targets a specific window or frame, the reference must continue helping the browser find the ultimate destination, which generally is some element of the document.

Just one more lesson to go before we let you explore all the details elsewhere in the book. We'll use the final tutorial chapter to show you some fun things you can do with your web pages, such as changing images when the user rolls the mouse over a picture.

Exercises

Before answering the first three questions, study the structure of the following frameset for a web site that lists college courses:

```
<html>
    <head>
       ...
    </head>
    <frameset rows="85%,15%">
        <frameset cols="20%,80%">
            <frame name="mechanics" src="history101M.html">
            <frame name="description" src="history101D.html">
        </frameset>
        <frameset cols="100%">
            <frame name="navigation" src="navigator.html">
        </frameset>
    </frameset>
    <noframes>
       ...
    </noframes>
</html>
```

1. Each document that loads into the description frame links to a JavaScript script that uses the onload event handler to store a course identifier value in the framesetting document's global variable currCourse. Write the function that sets this value to history101.

2. Draw a block diagram that describes the hierarchy of the windows and frames represented in the frameset definition.

3. Write the HTML markup and JavaScript statements located in the navigation frame that together perform two actions: load the file french201M.html into the mechanics frame, and load the file french201D.html into the description frame.

4. While a frameset is still loading, a JavaScript error message suddenly appears, saying, "window.document.navigation.form.selector is undefined." What do you think is happening in the application's scripts, and how can you solve the problem?

5. A script in a child frame of the main window uses window.open() to generate a second window. How can a script in the second window access the location object (URL) of the top (framesetting) window in the main browser window?

Images and Dynamic HTML

The previous eight lessons have been intensive, covering a lot of ground for both programming concepts and JavaScript. Now it's time to apply those fundamentals to learning more advanced techniques. We cover two areas here. First, we show you how to implement the ever-popular *mouse rollover,* in which images swap when the user rolls the cursor around the screen. Then we introduce you to techniques for modifying a page's style and content after the page has loaded.

Although image swapping on mouse rollover can be accomplished more easily using Cascading Style Sheets (CSS), we'll demonstrate how to do it with JavaScript because you'll probably see a lot of it in legacy scripts, and because it's a handy way to illustrate how to manipulate image objects.

IN THIS CHAPTER

How to pre-cache images

How to swap images for mouse rollovers

Changing style sheet settings

Modifying body content dynamically

The Image Object

One of the objects contained by the document is the Image object — supported in all scriptable browsers since the days of NN3 and IE4. Image object references for a document are stored in the object model as an array belonging to the document object. Therefore, you can reference an image by array index or image name. Moreover, the array index can be a string version of the image's name. All the following are valid references to an image object:

```
document.getElementById("imageName")
document.getElementsByTagName("img")[n]
document.images[n]
document.images["imageName"]
document.imageName
```

(The last reference will work only if imageName doesn't include any valid HTML ID characters that aren't permitted in JavaScript names, such as a hyphen or period.)

We are no longer constrained by ancient scriptable browser limitations that required an image be encased within an a element to receive mouse events. You may still want to do so if a click is intended to navigate to a new URL, but to use a visitor's mouse click to trigger local JavaScript execution, it's better to let the img element's event handlers do all the work.

Interchangeable images

The advantage of having a scriptable image object is that a script can change the image occupying the rectangular space already occupied by an image. In current browsers, the images can even change size, with surrounding content automatically reflowing around the resized image.

The script behind this kind of image change is simple enough. All it entails is assigning a new URL to the img element object's src property. The size of the image on the page is governed by the height and width attributes set in the <img> tag, and the height and width properties set in the style sheet. The most common image rollovers use the same size of image for each of the rollover states.

Pre-caching images

Images take extra time to download from a web server until they are stored in the browser's cache. If you design your page so that an image changes in response to user action, you usually want the same fast response that users are accustomed to in other programs. Making the user wait seconds for an image to change can detract from enjoyment of the page.

JavaScript comes to the rescue by enabling scripts to load images into the browser's memory cache without displaying the image, a technique called *pre-caching images*. The tactic that works best is to preload the image into the browser's image cache while the page initially loads. Users are less impatient for those few extra seconds when the main page loads, than they are waiting for an image to download in response to some mouse action. However, keep in mind that there is a balance. Today's audience tends to give a page less than 10 seconds to load before moving on. Although pre-caching images means a fast response to a mouse action, if you pre-cache too many images, you risk losing web site visitors before they can see your amazing image swapping in response to mouse actions.

Pre-caching an image requires constructing an image object in memory. An image object created in memory differs in some respects from the document img element object that you create with the <img> tag. Memory-only objects are created by script, and you don't see them on the page at all. But their presence in the document code forces the browser to load the images as the page loads. The object model provides an Image object constructor function to create the memory type of image object as follows:

```
var myImage = new Image(width, height);
```

Parameters to the constructor function are the pixel width and height of the image. These dimensions should match the width and height attributes of the <img> tag. Once the image object exists in memory, you can then assign a filename or URL to the src property of that image object:

```
myImage.src = "someArt.gif";
```

When the browser encounters a statement assigning a URL to an image object's src property, the browser fetches and loads that image into the image cache. All the user sees is some extra loading information in the status bar, as though another image were in the page. By the time the entire page loads, all images generated in this manner are tucked away in the image cache. You can then assign your cached image's src property, or the actual image URL, to the src property of the document image created with the <img> tag:

```
document.images[0].src = myImage.src;
```

or

```
document.getElementById("myImg").src = myImage.src ;
```

The change to the image in the document is instantaneous.

Listing 14-1 demonstrates a page that has one `<img>` tag and a select list that enables you to replace the image in the document with any of four pre-cached images (including the original image specified for the tag). If you type this listing, you can obtain copies of the four image files from the companion CD-ROM in the Chapter 14 directory of listings. (You still must type the HTML and code, however.)

LISTING 14-1

Pre-Caching Images

HTML: jsb-14-01.html

```
<!DOCTYPE html>
<html>
    <head>
        <meta http-equiv="content-type" content="text/html;charset=utf-8">
        <title>Image Object</title>
        <style type="text/css">
            img
            {
                height:90px; width:120px;
            }
        </style>
        <script type="text/javascript" src="../jsb-global.js"></script>
        <script type="text/javascript" src="jsb-14-01.js"></script>
    </head>
    <body >
        <h2>Image Object</h2>
        <img src="desk1.gif" id="thumbnail">
        <form>
            <select id="imageChooser">
                <option value="image1">Bands</option>
                <option value="image2">Clips</option>
                <option value="image3">Lamp</option>
                <option value="image4">Erasers</option>
            </select>
        </form>
    </body>
</html>
```

JavaScript: jsb-14-01.js

```
// initialize when the page has loaded
var oImageChooser;
addEvent(window, "load", initialize);
```

continued

LISTING 14-1   *(continued)*

```
function initialize()
{
   // get W3C DOM or IE4+ reference for an ID
   // imageChooser is the select element
   if (document.getElementById)
   {
      oImageChooser = document.getElementById("imageChooser");
   }
   else
   {
      oImageChooser = document.imageChooser;
   }

   addEvent(oImageChooser, 'change', loadCached);

}

// initialize empty array
var imageLibrary = new Array();
// pre-cache four images
imageLibrary["image1"] = new Image(120,90);
imageLibrary["image1"].src = "desk1.gif";
imageLibrary["image2"] = new Image(120,90);
imageLibrary["image2"].src = "desk2.gif";
imageLibrary["image3"] = new Image(120,90);
imageLibrary["image3"].src = "desk3.gif";
imageLibrary["image4"] = new Image(120,90);
imageLibrary["image4"].src = "desk4.gif";

// load an image chosen from select list
function loadCached()
{
   var imgChoice = oImageChooser.options[oImageChooser.selectedIndex].value;
   document.getElementById("thumbnail").src = imageLibrary[imgChoice].src;
}
```

As the page loads, it executes several statements immediately. These statements create an array that is populated with four new memory image objects. Each image object has a filename assigned to its src property. These images are loaded into the image cache as the page loads. Down in the body portion of the document, an <img> tag stakes its turf on the page and loads one of the images as a starting image.

A select element lists user-friendly names for the pictures while housing (in the option values) the names of image objects already pre-cached in memory. When the user makes a selection from the list, the loadCached() function extracts the selected item's value — which is a string index of the image within the imageLibrary array. The src property of the chosen image object is assigned to the src property of the visible img element object on the page, and the pre-cached image appears instantaneously.

Creating image rollovers

A favorite technique to add some pseudo-excitement to a page is to swap button images as the user rolls the cursor over them. The degree of change to the image is largely a matter of taste. The effect can be subtle (a slight highlight or glow around the edge of the original image) or drastic (a radical change of color). Whatever your approach, the scripting is the same.

When several of these graphical buttons occur in a group, we tend to organize the memory image objects as arrays, and create naming and numbering schemes that facilitate working with the arrays. Listing 14-2 shows such an arrangement for four buttons that control a slide show. The code in the listing is confined to the image-swapping portion of the application. This is the most complex and lengthiest listing of the tutorial, so it requires a bit of explanation as it goes along. It begins with a style sheet rule for each of the `img` elements located in a `controller` container.

LISTING 14-2

Image Rollovers

```
<!DOCTYPE html>
<html>
    <head>
        <meta http-equiv="content-type" content="text/html;charset=utf-8">
        <title>Slide Show/Image Rollovers</title>
        <style type="text/css">
            div#controller img {
                height: 70px; width: 136px; padding: 5px;
                }
        </style>
        <script type="text/javascript" src="../jsb-global.js"></script>
        <script type="text/javascript">
```

Only browsers capable of handling image objects should execute statements that pre-cache images. Therefore, the entire sequence is nested inside an `if` construction that tests for the presence of the `document.images` array. In older browsers, the condition evaluates to *undefined,* which an `if` condition treats as `false`:

```
if (document.images)
{
```

Image pre-caching starts by building two arrays of image objects. One array stores information about the images depicting the graphical buttons' off position; the other is for images depicting their on position. These arrays use strings (instead of integers) as index values. The string names correspond to the names given to the visible `img` element objects whose tags come later in the source code. The code is clearer to read (for example, you know that the `offImgArray["first"]` entry has to do with the First button image). Also, as you see later in this listing, rollover images don't conflict with other visible images on the page (a possibility if you rely exclusively on numeric index values when referring to the visible images for the swapping).

After creating the array and assigning new blank image objects to the first four elements of the array, we go through the array again, this time assigning file pathnames to the `src` property of each object stored in the array. These lines of code execute as the page loads, forcing the images to load into the image cache along the way:

```
// pre-cache all 'off' button images
var offImgArray = new Array();
offImgArray["first"] = new Image(136,70);
offImgArray["prev"] = new Image(136,70);
offImgArray["next"] = new Image(136,70);
offImgArray["last"] = new Image(136,70);

// off image array -- set 'off' image path for each button
offImgArray["first"].src = "firstoff.png";
offImgArray["prev"].src = "prevoff.png";
offImgArray["next"].src = "nextoff.png";
offImgArray["last"].src = "lastoff.png";

// pre-cache all 'on' button images
var onImgArray = new Array();
onImgArray["first"] = new Image(136,70);
onImgArray["prev"] = new Image(136,70);
onImgArray["next"] = new Image(136,70);
onImgArray["last"] = new Image(136,70);

// on image array -- set 'on' image path for each button
onImgArray["first"].src = "firston.png";
onImgArray["prev"].src = "prevon.png";
onImgArray["next"].src = "nexton.png";
onImgArray["last"].src = "laston.png";
```

Do you see the repeating pattern in the statements above? Instead of those statements, here's a way you could take advantage of the repeating pattern:

```
var offImgArray = new Array();
var onImgArray = new Array();
var ButtonArray = ["first", "prev", "next", "last"];

for (var i=0; i < ButtonArray.length; i++)
{
    var Button = ButtonArray[i];

    // pre-cache 'off' button image
    offImgArray[Button] = new Image(136,70);
    offImgArray[Button].src = Button + "off.png";

    // pre-cache 'on' button image
    onImgArray[Button] = new Image(136,70);
    onImgArray[Button].src = Button + "on.png";
}
```

As you can see in the following code, when the user rolls the mouse atop any of the visible document image objects, the onmouseover event handler invokes the imageOn() function, passing the name of the particular image. The `imageOn()` function uses that name to synchronize the `document.images` array entry (the visible image) with the entry of the in-memory array of on images from the `onImgArray` array. The `src` property of the array entry is assigned to the corresponding document image `src` property. At the same time, the cursor changes to look like it does over active links.

```
    }
    // functions that swap images & status bar
    function imageOn(imgName)
    {
        if (document.images)
        {
            document.images[imgName].style.cursor = "pointer";
            document.images[imgName].src = onImgArray[imgName].src;
        }
    }
```

The same goes for the `onmouseout` event handler, which needs to turn the image off by invoking the `imageOff()` function with the same index value.

```
    function imageOff(imgName)
    {
        if (document.images)
        {
            document.images[imgName].style.cursor = "default";
            document.images[imgName].src = offImgArray[imgName].src;
        }
    }
```

Both the `onmouseover` and `onmouseout` event handlers set the status bar text to a friendly descriptor — at least in those browsers that still support displaying custom text in the status bar. The `onmouseout` event handler sets the status bar message to an empty string.

```
    function setMsg(msg)
    {
        window.status = msg;
        return true;
    }
```

For this demonstration, we disable the functions that control the slide show. But we leave the empty function definitions here so they catch the calls made by the clicks of the links associated with the images.

```
    // controller functions (disabled)
    function goFirst()
    {
    }
    function goPrev()
    {
    }
    function goNext()
    {
    }
```

```
function goLast()
{
}
// event handler assignments
function init()
{
    if (document.getElementById)
    {
        oImageFirst = document.getElementById("first");
        oImagePrev = document.getElementById("prev");
        oImageNext = document.getElementById("next");
        oImageLast = document.getElementById("last");
    }
    else
    {
        oImageFirst = document.first;
        oImagePrev = document.prev;
        oImageNext = document.next;
        oImageLast = document.last;
    }

    addEvent(oImageFirst, 'click', goFirst);
    addEvent(oImageFirst, 'mouseover', function()
        {
            imageOn("first");
            return setMsg("Go to first picture");
        });
    addEvent(oImageFirst, 'mouseout', function()
        {
            imageOff("first");
            return setMsg("");
        });
    addEvent(oImagePrev, 'click', goPrev);
    addEvent(oImagePrev, 'mouseover', function()
        {
            imageOn("prev");
            return setMsg("Go to previous picture");
        });
    addEvent(oImagePrev, 'mouseout', function()
        {
            imageOff("prev");
            return setMsg("");
        });
    addEvent(oImageNext, 'click', goNext);
    addEvent(oImageNext, 'mouseover', function()
        {
            imageOn("next");
            return setMsg("Go to next picture");
        });
```

```
            addEvent(oImageNext, 'mouseout', function()
                {
                    imageOff("next");
                    return setMsg("");
                });
            addEvent(oImageLast, 'click', goLast);
            addEvent(oImageLast, 'mouseover', function()
                {
                    imageOn("last");
                    return setMsg("Go to last picture");
                });
            addEvent(oImageLast, 'mouseout', function()
                {
                    imageOff("last");
                    return setMsg("");
                });
            }

        // initialize when the page has loaded
        addEvent(window, "load", init);
    </script>
</head>

<body>
    <h1>Slide Show Controls</h1>
```

We elected to place the controller images inside a div element so that the images could be positioned or styled as a group. Each img element's onmouseover event handler (defined above) calls the imageOn() function, passing the name of the image to be swapped. Because both the onmouseover and onmouseout event handlers require a return true statement to work in older browsers, we combine the second function call (to setMsg()) with the return true requirement. The setMsg() function always returns true and is combined with the return keyword before the call to the setMsg() function. It's just a trick to reduce the amount of code in these event handlers.

```
        <div id="controller">
            <img src="images/firstoff.png" name="first" id="first" >
            <img src="images/prevoff.png" name="prev" id="prev" >
            <img src="images/nextoff.png" name="next" id="next" >
            <img src="images/lastoff.png" name="last" id="last" >
        </div>
    </body>
</html>
```

You can see the results of this lengthy script in Figure 14-1. As the user rolls the mouse atop one of the images, it changes from a light to dark color by swapping the entire image. You can access the image files on the CD-ROM, and we encourage you to enter this lengthy listing and see the magic for yourself.

FIGURE 14-1

Typical mouse rollover image swapping.

Rollovers Without Scripts

As cool as the rollover effect is, thanks to CSS technology, you don't always need JavaScript to accomplish rollover dynamism. You can blend CSS with JavaScript to achieve the same effect. Listing 14-3 demonstrates a version of Listing 14-2, but using CSS for the rollover effect, while JavaScript still handles the control of the slide show.

The HTML for the buttons consists of `li` elements that are sized and assigned background images of the off versions of the buttons. The text of each `li` element is surrounded by an `a` element so that CSS `:hover` pseudo-elements can be assigned. (Internet Explorer through version 7 requires this, whereas W3C DOM browsers recognize `:hover` for all elements.) When the cursor hovers atop an `a` element, the background image changes to the on version. The `onclick` event handler assignments remain in the script portion of the page, where they are performed after the page loads (to make sure the elements exist).

LISTING 14-3

CSS Image Rollovers

HTML: `jsb-14-03.html`

```
<!DOCTYPE html>
<html>
    <head>
        <meta http-equiv="content-type" content="text/html;charset=utf-8">
        <title>Slide Show/Image Rollovers</title>
        <link rel="stylesheet" href="jsb-14-03.css" type="text/css">
        <script type="text/javascript" src="../jsb-global.js"></script>
        <script type="text/javascript" src="jsb-14-03.js"></script>
```

```
        <script type="text/javascript">
        </script>
    </head>
    <body>
        <h1>Slide Show Controls</h1>
        <ul id="controller">
            <li id="first"><a href="#">First</a></li>
            <li id="prev"><a href="#">Previous</a></li>
            <li id="next"><a href="#">Next</a></li>
            <li id="last"><a href="#">Last</a></li>
        </ul>
    </body>
</html>
```

CSS: jsb-14-03.css

```
#controller {
    position: relative;
    }
#controller li {
    position: absolute; list-style: none; display: block;
    height: 70px; width: 136px;
    }
#controller a {
    display: block; text-indent: -999px; height: 70px;
    }

#first {
    left: 0px;
    }
#prev {
    left: 146px;
    }
#next {
    left: 292px;
    }
#last {
    left: 438px;
    }

#first a {
    background-image: url("firstoff.png");
    }
#first a:hover {
    background-image: url("firston.png");
    }
#prev a {
    background-image: url("prevoff.png");
    }
#prev a:hover {
    background-image: url("prevon.png");
    }
```

continued

217

LISTING 14-3 *(continued)*

```
#next a {
   background-image: url("nextoff.png");
   }
#next a:hover {
   background-image: url("nexton.png");
   }
#last a {
   background-image: url("lastoff.png");
   }
#last a:hover {
   background-image: url("laston.png");
   }
```

JavaScript: jsb-14-03.js

```
// controller functions (disabled)
function goFirst()
{
   alert("in gofirst");
}
function goPrev()
{
   alert("in goprev");
}
function goNext()
{
   alert("in gonext");
}
function goLast()
{
   alert("in golast");
}

// event handler assignments
function init()
{
   if (document.getElementById)
   {
      oImageFirst = document.getElementById("first");
      oImagePrev = document.getElementById("prev");
      oImageNext = document.getElementById("next");
      oImageLast = document.getElementById("last");
   }
   else
   {
      oImageFirst = document.first;
      oImagePrev = document.prev;
      oImageNext = document.next;
      oImageLast = document.last;
   }
```

```
    addEvent(oImageFirst, 'click', goFirst);
    addEvent(oImagePrev, 'click', goPrev);
    addEvent(oImageNext, 'click', goNext);
    addEvent(oImageLast, 'click', goLast);
}

// initialize when the page has loaded
addEvent(window, "load", init);
```

The need to wrap the li element text for Internet Explorer (which the CSS shifts completely off-screen, because we don't need the text) forces scripters to address further considerations. In this application, a click of an li element is intended to run a local script, not to load an external URL. But the a element's default behavior is to load another URL. The # placeholder shown in Listing 14-3 causes the current page to reload, which will wipe away any activity of the onclick event handler function. It is necessary, therefore, to equip each of the slide-show navigation functions with some extra code lines that prevent the a element from executing its default behavior. You'll learn how to do that in Chapter 32, "Event Objects." (It requires different syntax for the incompatible W3C DOM and IE event models.)

One other note about the CSS approach in Listing 14-3 is that there is no image pre-caching taking place. You could add the pre-caching code for the "on" images from Listing 14-2 to get the alternative background images ready for the browser to swap. That's a case of CSS and JavaScript really working together.

The javascript: Pseudo-URL

You have seen instances in previous chapters of applying what is called the javascript: pseudo-URL to the href attributes of <a> and <area> tags. This technique should not be used for public web sites that may be accessed by browsers with scripting turned off (for which the links will be inactive).

The technique was implemented to supplement the onclick event handler of objects that act as hyperlinks. Especially in the early scripting days, when elements such as images had no event handlers of their own, hyperlinked elements surrounding those inactive elements allowed users to appear to interact directly with elements such as images. When the intended action was to invoke a script function (rather than navigate to another URL, as is usually the case with a hyperlink), the language designers invented the javascript: protocol for use in assignments to the href attributes of hyperlink elements (instead of leaving the required attribute empty).

When a scriptable browser encounters an href attribute pointing to a javascript: pseudo-URL, the browser executes the script content after the colon when the user clicks the element. For example, the a elements of Listing 14-3 could have been written to point to javascript: pseudo-URLs that invoke script functions on the page, such as:

```
    <a href="javascript:goFirst()">
```

Note that the javascript: protocol is not a published standard, despite its wide adoption by browser makers. In a public web site that may be accessed by visitors with accessibility concerns (and potentially by browsers having little or no JavaScript capability), a link should point to a server

URL that performs an action (for example, through a server program), which in turn replicates what client-side JavaScript does (faster) for visitors with scriptable browsers.

Popular Dynamic HTML Techniques

Because today's scriptable browsers uniformly permit scripts to access each element of the document and automatically reflow the page's content when anything changes, a high degree of dynamism is possible in your applications. Dynamic HTML (DHTML) is a very deep subject, with lots of browser-specific peculiarities. In this section of the tutorial, you will learn techniques that work in Internet Explorer and W3C DOM-compatible browsers. We'll focus on two of the most common tasks for which DHTML is used: changing element styles and modifying document content.

Changing style sheet settings

Each element that renders on the page (and even some elements that don't) has a property called `style`. This property provides script access to all CSS properties supported for that element by the current browser. Property values are the same as those used for CSS specifications — frequently, a different syntax from similar settings that used to be made by HTML tag attributes. For example, if you want to set the text color of a `blockquote` element whose ID is `FranklinQuote`, the syntax is

```
document.getElementById("FranklinQuote").style.color = "rgb(255, 255, 0)";
```

Because the CSS `color` property accepts other ways of specifying colors (such as the traditional hexadecimal triplet — `#ffff00`), you may use those as well.

Some CSS property names, however, do not conform to JavaScript naming conventions. Several CSS property names contain hyphens. When that occurs, the scripted equivalent of the property compresses the words and capitalizes the start of each word. For example, the CSS property `font-weight` would be set in script as follows:

```
document.getElementById("highlight").style.fontWeight = "bold";
```

A related technique properly gives responsibility for the document design to CSS. For example, if you define CSS rules for two different classes, you can simply switch the class definition being applied to the element by way of the element object's `className` property. Let's say you define two CSS class definitions with different background colors:

```
.normal {background-color: #ffffff};
.highlighted {background-color: #ff0000};
```

In the HTML page, the element first receives its default class assignment as follows:

```
<p id="news" class="normal">...</p>
```

A script statement can then change the class of that element object so that the highlighted style applies to it:

```
document.getElementById("news").className = "highlighted";
```

Restoring the original class name also restores its look and feel. This approach is also a quick way to change multiple style properties of an element with a single statement.

Dynamic content via W3C DOM nodes

In Chapter 10, "Window and Document Objects," you saw the `document.createElement()` and `document.createTextNode()` methods in action. These methods create new document object model (DOM) objects out of thin air, which you may then modify by setting properties (attributes) prior to plugging the new stuff into the document tree for all to see.

As an introduction to this technique, we'll demonstrate the steps you would go through to add an element and its text to a placeholding `span` element on the page. In this example, a paragraph element belonging to a class called `centered` will be appended to a `span` whose `id` is `placeholder`. Some of the text for the content of the paragraph comes from a text field in a form (the visitor's first name). Here is the complete sequence:

```
var newElem = document.createElement("p");
newElem.className = "centered";
var newText = document.createTextNode("Thanks for visiting, " +
    document.forms[0].firstName.value);
// insert text node into new paragraph
newElem.appendChild(newText);
// insert completed paragraph into placeholder
document.getElementById("placeholder").appendChild(newElem);
```

After the element and text nodes are created, the text node must be inserted into the element node. Because the new element node is empty when it is created, the DOM `appendChild()` method plugs the text node into the element (between its start and end tags, if you could see the tags). When the paragraph element is assembled, it is inserted at the end of the initially empty `span` element. Additional W3C DOM methods (described in Chapter 26, "Generic HTML Element Objects," and Chapter 27, "Window and Frame Objects") provide more ways to insert, remove, and replace nodes.

Dynamic content through the innerHTML property

Prior to the W3C DOM specification, Microsoft invented a property of all element objects: `inner-HTML`. This property first appeared in Internet Explorer 4, and it became popular due to its practicality. The property's value is a string containing HTML tags and other content, just as it would appear in an HTML document inside the current element's tags. Even though the W3C DOM working group did not implement this property for the published standard, the property proved to be too practical and popular for modern browser makers to ignore. You can find it implemented as a de facto standard in Mozilla-based browsers and Safari, among others.

To illustrate the difference in the approach, the following code example shows the same content creation and insertion as shown in the previous W3C DOM section, but this time with the `innerHTML` property:

```
// accumulate HTML as a string
var newHTML = "<p class='centered'>Thanks for visiting, ";
newHTML += document.forms[0].firstName.value;
newHTML += "</p>";
// blast into placeholder element's content
document.getElementById("placeholder").innerHTML = newHTML;
```

Although the innerHTML version seems more straightforward — and makes it easier for HTML coders to visualize what's being added — the DOM node approach is more efficient when the document modification task entails lots of content. Extensive JavaScript string concatenation operations can slow browser script processing. Sometimes, the shortest script is not necessarily the fastest.

And so ends the final lesson of the *JavaScript Bible* tutorial. If you have gone through every lesson and tried your hand at the exercises, you are ready to dive into the rest of the book to learn the fine details and many more features of both the DOM and the JavaScript language. You can work sequentially through the chapters of Part III, "JavaScript Core Language Reference," and Part IV, "Document Objects Reference," but before too long, you should also take a peek at Chapter 48, "Debugging Scripts," to learn some important debugging techniques.

Exercises

1. Explain the difference between a document img element object and the memory type of an image object.

2. Write the JavaScript statements needed to pre-cache an image file named jane.jpg that later will be used to replace the document image defined by the following HTML:

   ```
   <img name="people" src="john.jpg" height="120" width="100" alt="people">
   ```

3. With the help of the code you wrote for question 2, write the JavaScript statement that replaces the document image with the memory image.

4. Backward-compatible img element objects do not have event handlers for mouse events. How do you trigger scripts needed to swap images for mouse rollovers?

5. Assume that a table element contains an empty table cell (td) element whose ID is forwardLink. Using W3C DOM node creation techniques, write the sequence of script statements that create and insert the following hyperlink into the table cell:

   ```
   <a href="page4.html">Next Page</a>
   ```

Part III

JavaScript Core Language Reference

The String Object

The tutorial in Chapter 8, "Programming Fundamentals, Part I," introduced you to the concepts of values and the types of values that JavaScript works with — features such as strings, numbers, and Boolean values. Chapter 12, "Strings, Math, and Dates," described several characteristics and methods of strings. In this chapter, you look more closely at the very important String data type, as well as its relationship to the Number data type. Along the way, you encounter the many ways in which JavaScript enables scripters to manipulate strings.

Note
Much of the syntax that you see in this chapter is identical to that of the Java programming language. Because the scope of JavaScript activity is much narrower than that of Java, you don't have nearly as much to learn for JavaScript as you do for Java. ■

String and Number Data Types

Although JavaScript is what is known as a "loosely typed" language, you still need to be aware of several data types, because of their impact on the way you work with the information in those forms. In this section, we focus on strings and two types of numbers.

Simple strings

A *string* consists of one or more standard text characters placed between matching quote marks. JavaScript is forgiving in one regard: You can use single or double quotes, as long as you match two single quotes or two double quotes around a string. A major benefit of this scheme becomes apparent when you try to include quoted text inside a string. For example, say that you're assembling a line of HTML code in a variable that you will eventually write to a new window that is completely controlled by JavaScript. The line of text that you want to assign to a variable is the following:

```
<input type="checkbox" name="candy" />Chocolate
```

To assign this entire line of text to a variable, you have to surround the line in quotes. But because quotes appear inside the string, JavaScript (or any language) has problems deciphering where the string begins or ends. By carefully placing the other kind of quote pairs, however, you can make the assignment work. Here are two equally valid ways:

```
result = '<input type="checkbox" name="candy" />Chocolate';
result = "<input type='checkbox' name='candy' />Chocolate";
```

Notice that in both cases, the same unique pair of quotes surrounds the entire string. Inside the string, two quoted strings appear that are treated as such by JavaScript. It is helpful stylistically to settle on one form or the other, and then use that form consistently throughout your scripts.

If the expression you're quoting contains both apostrophes and double quotes, you need to *escape* one or the other within the string, with a backslash:

```
Pat's favorite word is "syzygy."
result = "Pat's favorite word is \"syzygy.\""
result = 'Pat\'s favorite word is "syzygy."'
```

Because escaped characters aren't as easy to read and proofread, you might want to choose a quote character that doesn't appear in the expression you're quoting, if possible.

Building long string variables

The act of joining strings together — concatenation — enables you to assemble long strings out of several little pieces. This feature is very important for some scripting — for example, when you need to build an HTML page's specifications entirely within a variable before writing the page to another frame, with one statement. It is often unwieldy and impractical to include such lengthy information in a single string on one line of code, which is why you may want to build the large string out of substrings.

One tactic keeps the length of each statement in this building process short enough so that it's easily readable in your text editor. This method uses the add-by-value assignment operator (+=) that appends the right-hand side of the equation to the left-hand side. Here is a simple example, which begins by initializing a variable, newDocument, as an empty string:

```
var newDocument = "";
newDocument += "<!DOCTYPE html>";
newDocument += "<html>" ;
newDocument += "<head>";
newDocument += '<meta http-equiv="content-type"';
newDocument += ' content="text/html;charset=utf-8">';
newDocument += "<title>Prodigal Summer</title>";
newDocument += "</head>";
newDocument += "<body>";
newDocument += "<h1>Prodigal Summer</h1>";
newDocument += '<p class="byline">by Barbara Kingsolver</p>';
```

Starting with the second line, each statement adds more data to the string being stored in newDocument. You can continue appending string data until the entire page's specification is contained in the newDocument variable.

Note
Excessive use of the add-by-value operator involving large quantities of text can become inefficient. If you are experiencing slow performance when accumulating large strings, try pushing your string segments into items of an array (see Chapter 18, "The Array Object"). Then use the array's join() **method to generate the resulting large string value.** ■

Joining string literals and variables

In some cases, you need to create a string out of literal strings (characters with quote marks around them) and string variable values. The methodology for concatenating these types of strings is no different from that of multiple string literals. The plus-sign operator does the job. Therefore, in the following example, a variable contains a name. That variable value is made a part of a larger string whose other parts are string literals:

```
teamName = prompt("Please enter your favorite team:","");
var msg = "The " + teamName + " are victorious!";
alert(msg);
```

Some common problems that you may encounter while attempting this kind of concatenation include the following:

- Accidentally omitting one of the quotes around a literal string
- Failing to insert blank spaces in the string literals to accommodate word spacing
- Forgetting to concatenate punctuation after a variable value

Also, don't forget that what we show here as variable values can be any expression that evaluates to a string, including property references and the results of some methods. For example:

```
var msg = "The name of this document is " + document.title + ".";
alert(msg);
```

Special inline characters

The way string literals are created in JavaScript makes adding certain characters to strings difficult — primarily quotes, carriage returns, apostrophes, and tab characters. Fortunately, JavaScript provides a mechanism for entering such characters into string literals. A backslash symbol, followed by the character that you want to appear as inline, makes that task happen. For the "invisible" characters, a special set of letters following the backslash tells JavaScript what to do.

The most common backslash pairs are as follows:

- \" Double quote
- \' Single quote (apostrophe)
- \\ Backslash
- \b Backspace
- \t Tab

- \n New line
- \r Carriage return
- \f Form feed

Use these *inline characters* (also known as *escaped characters*, but this terminology has a different connotation for Internet strings) inside quoted string literals to make JavaScript recognize them. When assembling a block of text that needs a new paragraph, insert the \n character pair. Here are some examples of syntax using these special characters:

```
msg = "I say \"trunk\" and you say \"boot.\"";
msg = 'You\'re doing fine.';
msg = "This is the first line.\nThis is the second line.";
msg = document.title + "\n" + document.links.length + " links present.";
```

Technically speaking, a complete carriage return, as it was known in the days of the typewriter, is both a line feed (advance the line by one) and a carriage return (move the carriage all the way to the left margin). Although JavaScript strings treat a line feed (\n new line) as a full carriage return, you may have to construct \r\n breaks when assembling strings that go back to a cgi script on a server. The format that you use depends on the string-parsing capabilities of the cgi program. (Also see the special requirements for the textarea object in Chapter 36, "Text-Related Form Objects," on the CD.)

It's easy to confuse the strings assembled for display in textarea objects or alert boxes with strings to be written as HTML. In most cases, browsers ignore carriage returns or render them like spaces. For HTML strings, make sure that you use standard HTML tags, such as paragraphs (<p>...</p>) and line-breaks (<br>), rather than, or in addition to, the inline return or line feed symbols.

String Object

Properties	Methods
constructor	anchor()
length	big()
prototype[†]	blink()
	bold()
	charAt()
	charCodeAt()
	concat()
	fixed()
	fontcolor()
	fontsize()
	fromCharCode()[†]
	indexOf()

Properties	Methods
	`italics()`
	`lastIndexOf()`
	`link()`
	`localeCompare()`
	`match()`
	`replace()`
	`search()`
	`slice()`
	`small()`
	`split()`
	`strike()`
	`sub()`
	`substr()`
	`substring()`
	`sup()`
	`toLocaleLowerCase()`
	`toLocaleUpperCase()`
	`toLowerCase()`
	`toString()`
	`toUpperCase()`
	`valueOf()`

†Member of the static `String` object

Syntax

Creating a string object:

```
var myString = new String("characters");
```

Creating a string value:

```
var myString = "characters";
```

Accessing static `String` object properties and methods:

```
String.property | method([parameters])
```

stringObject

Accessing string object properties and methods:

```
string.property | method([parameters])
```

Compatibility: WinIE3+, MacIE3+, NN2+, Moz+, Safari+, Opera+, Chrome+

About this object

JavaScript draws a fine line between a string value and a string object. Both let you use the same methods on their contents, so that by and large, you do not have to create a string object (with the new String() constructor) every time you want to assign a string value to a variable. A simple assignment operation (var myString = "fred") is all you need to create a string value that behaves on the surface very much like a full-fledged string object.

Where the difference comes into play is when you want to exploit the "object-ness" of a genuine string object, which is explained further in the discussion of the string.prototype property, later in this chapter. You may also encounter the need to use a full-fledged string object when passing string data to Java applets. If you find that your applet doesn't receive a string value as a Java String data type, then create a new string object via the JavaScript constructor function before passing the value to the applet.

With string data often comes the need to massage string text in scripts. In addition to concatenating strings, at times you need to extract segments of strings, delete parts of strings, and replace one part of a string with some other text. Unlike many plain-language scripting languages, JavaScript is fairly low-level in its built-in facilities for string manipulation. This characteristic means that unless you can take advantage of the regular expression powers of IE4+/Moz1+ or advanced array techniques, you must fashion your own string handling routines out of the very elemental powers built into JavaScript. Later in this chapter, we provide several functions that you can use in your own scripts for common string handling in a manner fully compatible with older browsers.

As you work with string values, visualize every string value as an object, with properties and methods, like other JavaScript objects. JavaScript defines a few properties and a slew of methods for any string value (and one extra property for the static String object that is always present in the context of the browser window). The syntax is the same for string methods as it is for any other object method:

```
stringObject.method()
```

What may seem odd at first is that the *stringObject* part of this reference can be any expression that evaluates to a string, including string literals, variables containing strings, methods or functions that return strings, or other object properties. Therefore, the following examples of calling the toUpperCase() method are all valid:

```
"blah blah blah".toUpperCase()
yourName.toUpperCase() // yourName is a variable containing a string
window.prompt("Enter your name","").toUpperCase()
document.forms[0].entry.value.toUpperCase() // entry is text field object
```

A very important (and often misunderstood) concept to remember is that invoking a string method does not change the string object that is part of the reference. Rather, the method returns a string value, which can be used as a parameter to another method or function call, or assigned to a variable.

Therefore, to change the contents of a string variable to the results of a method, you must use an assignment operator, as in:

```
yourName = yourName.toUpperCase(); // variable is now all uppercase
```

Properties

constructor

Value: Function reference   Read/Write

Compatibility: WinIE4+, MacIE4+, NN4+, Moz+, Safari+, Opera+, Chrome+

The `constructor` property is a reference to the function that was invoked to create the current string. For a native JavaScript string object, the constructor function is the built-in `String()` constructor.

When you use the `new String()` constructor to create a string object, the type of the value returned by the constructor is `object` (meaning that the `typeof` operator returns `object`). Therefore, you can use the `constructor` property on an object value to see if it is a string object:

```
if (typeof someValue == "object" )
{
    if (someValue.constructor == String)
    {
        // statements to deal with string object
    }
}
```

Although the property is read/write, and you can assign a different constructor to the `String.prototype`, the native behavior of a `String` object persists through the new constructor.

Example

Use The Evaluator (see Chapter 4) to test the value of the `constructor` property. One line at a time, enter and evaluate the following statements into the top text box:

```
a = new String("abcd")
a.constructor == String
a.constructor == Number
```

Related Items: `prototype` property

length

Value: Integer   Read/Write

Compatibility: WinIE3+, MacIE3+, NN2+, Moz+, Safari+, Opera+, Chrome+

The most frequently used property of a string is `length`. To derive the length of a string, read its property as you would read the `length` property of any object:

```
string.length
```

stringObject.prototype

The `length` value represents an integer count of the number of characters within the string. Spaces and punctuation symbols count as characters. Any backslash special characters embedded in a string count as one character, including such characters as newline and tab. Here are some examples:

```
"Lincoln".length // result = 7
"Four score".length // result = 10
"One\ntwo".length // result = 7
"".length // result = 0
```

The `length` property is commonly summoned when dealing with detailed string manipulation in repeat loops. For example, if you want to iterate through every character in a string, and somehow examine or modify each character, you would use the string's length as the basis for the loop counter.

prototype

Value: String object   Read/Write

Compatibility: WinIE4+, MacIE4+, NN3+, Moz+, Safari+, Opera+, Chrome+

`String` objects defined with the `new String("`*stringValue*`")` constructor are robust objects compared to run-of-the-mill variables that are assigned string values. You certainly don't have to create this kind of string object for every string in your scripts, but these objects do come in handy if you find that strings in variables go awry. This happens occasionally while trying to preserve string information as script variables in other frames or windows. By using the `String` object constructor, you can be relatively assured that the string value will be available in the distant frame when needed.

Another benefit to using true `String` objects is that you can assign prototype properties and methods to all string objects in the document. A *prototype* is a collection of properties and methods that become part of every new object created after the prototype items are added. As an example, you may want to define a new method for transforming a string that isn't already defined by the JavaScript `String` object. Listing 15-1 shows how to create and use such a prototype.

Note

The property assignment event-handling technique employed throughout the code in this chapter, and much of the book, is `addEvent()`, a cross-browser event handler explained in detail in Chapter 32, "Event Object."

The `addEvent()` function is part of the script file `jsb-global.js`, located on the accompanying CD-ROM in the `Content/` folder, where it is accessible to all chapters' scripts. ■

LISTING 15-1

Using the String Object Prototype

HTML: `jsb-15-01.html`

```html
<!DOCTYPE html>
<html>
    <head>
        <meta http-equiv="content-type" content="text/html;charset=utf-8">
        <title>Using the String Object Prototype</title>
        <script type="text/javascript" src="../jsb-global.js"></script>
        <script type="text/javascript" src="jsb-15-01.js"></script>
    </head>
```

```
    <body>
        <h1>Using the String Object Prototype</h1>
        <form action="initialCap.php">
            <p>
                <label for="entry">Enter one or more words to be Initial Capped:</label>
            </p>
            <p>
                <input type="text" id="entry" name="entry" value="">
                <input type="button" id="do-it" value="Initial Caps">
            </p>
        </form>
    </body>
</html>
```

JavaScript: jsb-15-01.js

```
// initialize when the page has loaded
addEvent(window, 'load', initialize);

function initialize()
{
    // do this only if the browser can handle DOM methods
    if (document.getElementById)
    {
        // point to critical elements
        var oButton = document.getElementById('do-it');
        var oEntry = document.getElementById('entry');

            // if they all exist...
            if (oButton && oEntry)
            {
                // apply behavior to button
                addEvent(oButton, 'click', doIt);
            }
    }
}

// try out the new String method
function doIt()
{
    // point to input field
    var oEntry = document.getElementById('entry');

    // use the new method to update the input text
    oEntry.value = oEntry.value.initialCaps();
}


// add a new method to the String prototype
// to capitalize the first letter of each word

String.prototype.initialCaps = function()
```

continued

LISTING 15-1   *(continued)*

```
{
    // get the input text
    var sText = this.toString();

    // separate individual words
    var aWords = sText.split(' ');

    // capitalize each word
    for (var i = 0; i < aWords.length; i++)
    {
        var sInitial = aWords[i].charAt(0);
        var sRemainder = aWords[i].substr(1);
        aWords[i] = sInitial.toUpperCase() + sRemainder.toLowerCase();
    }

    // reassemble the array of words back into a string
    return aWords.join(' ');
}
```

Note
Many of the HTML example pages in this book include a form action to post input to a server-side PHP program — as a reminder that it's important to make sure that our pages can function even when JavaScript is not running. The server-side scripts themselves do not exist and are outside the scope of this book. If written, they would perform essentially the same operations as the JavaScript logic does. ■

The core of the JavaScript in Listing 15-1 is the last block, where we add the `initialCaps()` method to the `String` object prototype, and spell out what that method does. Similar to most object methods, this new one doesn't modify the original string itself, but rather returns a value we can use for any purpose we want. Here, we grab the contents of the input field `entry`, transform it with `initialCaps()`, and use that new value to reset the input field contents.

Modifying object prototypes is a powerful way to add new features to the JavaScript language on-the-fly.

In the next sections, we divide `String` object methods into two distinct categories. The first, parsing methods, focuses on string analysis and character manipulation within strings. The second group, formatting methods, is devoted entirely to assembling strings in HTML syntax for those scripts that assemble the text to be written into new documents or other frames.

Parsing methods
string.charAt(*index*)

Returns: One-character string

Compatibility: WinIE3+, MacIE3+, NN2+, Moz+, Safari+, Opera+, Chrome+

Use the *string*.charAt() method to read a single character from a string when you know the position of that character. For this method, you specify an index value in the string as a parameter to the method. The index value of the first character of the string is 0. To grab the last character of a string, mix string methods:

```
myString.charAt(myString.length - 1)
```

If your script needs to get a range of characters, use the *string*.substring() method. Using *string*.substring() to extract a character from inside a string is a common mistake — the *string*.charAt() method is more efficient.

Example

Enter each of the following statements into the top text box of The Evaluator:

```
a = "banana daiquiri"
a.charAt(0)      // result = 'b'
a.charAt(5)      // result = 'a' (the third 'a')
a.charAt(6)      // result = ' ' (space)
a.charAt(20)     // result = '' (empty string)
```

Related Items: *string*.lastIndexOf(), *string*.indexOf(), *string*.substring() methods

string.charCodeAt([*index*])
string.fromCharCode(*num1* [, *num2* [, ... *numn*]])

Returns: Integer code number for a character; concatenated string value of code numbers supplied as parameters

Compatibility: WinIE4+, MacIE4+, NN4+, Moz+, Safari+, Opera+, Chrome+

Conversions from plain language characters to their numeric equivalents have a long tradition in computer programming. For many years, the most common numbering scheme was the ASCII standard, which covers the basic English alphanumeric characters and punctuation within 128 values (numbered 0 through 127). An extended version with a total of 256 characters, with some variations, depending on the operating system, accounts for other roman characters in other languages, particularly accented vowels. To support all languages, including pictographic languages, and other non-Roman writing systems, a world standard called Unicode provides space for thousands of characters. All modern browsers work with the Unicode system.

In JavaScript, character conversions are handled by string methods. The two methods that perform character conversions work in very different ways syntactically. The first, *string*.charCodeAt(), converts a single string character to its numeric equivalent. The string being converted is the one to the left of the method name — and the string may be a literal string or any other expression that evaluates to a string value. If no parameter is passed, the character being converted is by default the first character of the string. However, you can also specify a different character as an index value into the string (first character is 0), as demonstrated here:

```
"abc".charCodeAt()   // result = 97
"abc".charCodeAt(0)  // result = 97
"abc".charCodeAt(1)  // result = 98
```

stringObject.fromCharCode()

If the string value is an empty string, or the index value is beyond the last character, the result is `NaN`.

To convert numeric values to their characters, use the `String.fromCharCode()` method. Notice that the object beginning the method call is the static `String` object, not a string value. Then, as parameters, you can include one or more integers, separated by commas. In the conversion process, the method combines the characters for all of the parameters into one string, an example of which is shown here:

```
String.fromCharCode(97, 98, 99)  // result "abc"
```

Note

Although most modern browsers support character values across the entire Unicode range, the browser won't properly render characters above 255 unless the computer is equipped with language and font support for the designated language. To assist with Unicode character display, all our HTML documents begin with declarations of UTF-8 character encoding. ■

FIGURE 15-1

Conversions from text characters to ASCII values and vice versa.

Example

Listing 15-2 provides examples of both methods on one page. Moreover, because one of the demonstrations relies on the automatic capture of selected text on the page, the scripts include code to accommodate the different handling of selection events, and the capture of the selected text in a variety of browsers.

After you load the page, select part of the body text anywhere on the page. If you start the selection with the lowercase letter "a," the character code displays as 97.

Try entering numeric values in the three fields at the bottom of the page. Values below 32 are ASCII control characters that most fonts represent as blanks or hollow squares. But try other values to see what you get. Notice that the script passes all three values as a group to the `String.fromCharCode()` method, and the result is a combined string. Thus, Figure 15-1 shows what happens when you enter the uppercase ASCII values for a three-letter animal name.

LISTING 15-2

Character Conversions

HTML: jsb-15-02.html

```html
<!DOCTYPE html>
<html>
  <head>
    <meta http-equiv="content-type" content="text/html;charset=utf-8">
    <title>Character Codes</title>
    <script type="text/javascript" src="../jsb-global.js"></script>
    <script type="text/javascript" src="jsb-15-02.js"></script>
  </head>
  <body>
    <h1>Character Codes</h1>

    <form action="show-string.php">
      <h2>Capturing Character Codes</h2>
      <p>Select any text on this page and see the character code of the first
      character.</p>
      <p>
        <label for="display">Character Code:</label>
        <input type="text" id="display" name="display" size="3" />
      </p>

      <h2>Converting Codes to Characters</h2>
      <p>
        <label for="entry1">Enter a value 0-255:</label>
        <input type="text" id="entry1" name="entry1" size="6" />
      </p>
      <p>
        <label for="entry2">Enter a value 0-255:</label>
        <input type="text" id="entry2" name="entry2" size="6" />
      </p>
      <p>
```

continued

stringObject.fromCharCode()

LISTING 15-2   *(continued)*

```
            <label for="entry3">Enter a value 0-255:</label>
            <input type="text" id="entry3" name="entry3" size="6" />
        </p>
        <p>
            <input type="button" id="showstr" value="Show String" />
            <label for="result">Result:</label>
            <input type="text" id="result" name="result" size="5" />
        </p>
    </form>
  </body>
</html>
```

```
JavaScript: jsb-15-02.js


// initialize when the page has loaded
addEvent(window, 'load', initialize);

// show character code when text is selected
addEvent(document, 'mouseup', showCharCode);


function initialize()
{
    // do this only if the browser can handle DOM methods
    if (document.getElementById)
    {
        // point to critical element
        var oButton = document.getElementById('showstr');

            // if it exists...
            if (oButton)
            {
                // apply behavior to button
                addEvent(oButton, 'click', showString);
            }
    }
}


// show the text characters represented by the numbers entered
function showString()
{
    var oEntry1 = document.getElementById('entry1');
    var oEntry2 = document.getElementById('entry2');
    var oEntry3 = document.getElementById('entry3');
    var oResult = document.getElementById('result');

    oResult.value = String.fromCharCode(oEntry1.value, oEntry2.value, oEntry3.value);
}
```

```
// display the character code of the selected text
// (first character only)
function showCharCode()
{
    var theText = "";
    var oDisplay = document.getElementById('display');

    // get the selected text using various browsers' methods
    if (window.getSelection)
    {
        theText = window.getSelection().toString();
    }
    else if (document.getSelection)
    {
        theText = document.getSelection();
    }
    else if (document.selection && document.selection.createRange)
    {
        theText = document.selection.createRange().text;
    }

    // display the result if any
    if (theText)
    {
        oDisplay.value = theText.charCodeAt();
    }
    else
    {
        oDisplay.value = " ";
    }
}
```

string.concat(*string2*)

Returns: Combined string

Compatibility: WinIE4+, MacIE4+, NN4+, Moz+, Safari+, Opera+, Chrome+

JavaScript's add-by-value operator (+=) provides a convenient way to concatenate strings. Most browsers, however, include a string object method that performs the same task. The base string to which more text is appended is the object or value to the left of the period. The string to be appended is the parameter of the method, as the following example demonstrates:

```
"abc".concat("def")  // result: "abcdef"
```

As with the add-by-value operator, the concat() method doesn't know about word spacing. You are responsible for including the necessary space between words if the two strings require a space between them in the result.

Related Items: Add-by-value (+=) operator

string.indexOf(*searchString* [, *startIndex*])

stringObject.lastIndexOf()

Returns: Index value of the character within *string* where *searchString* begins

Compatibility: WinIE3+, MacIE3+, NN2+, Moz+, Safari+, Opera+, Chrome+

Like some programming languages' offset string function, JavaScript's `indexOf()` method enables your script to obtain the position in the main string where a search string begins. Optionally, you can specify where in the main string the search should begin — but the returned value is always relative to the very first character of the main string. Like all string object methods, index values start their count with 0. If no match occurs within the main string, the returned value is -1. Thus, this method is also a convenient way to determine whether one string contains another, regardless of position.

Example

Enter each of the following statements (up to but not including the "*//*" comment symbols) into the top text box of The Evaluator (you can simply replace the parameters of the `indexOf()` method for each statement after the first one). Compare your results with the results shown below.

```
a = "bananas"
a.indexOf("b")      // result = 0 (index of 1st letter is zero)
a.indexOf("a")      // result = 1
a.indexOf("a",1)    // result = 1 (start from 2nd letter)
a.indexOf("a",2)    // result = 3 (start from 3rd letter)
a.indexOf("a",4)    // result = 5 (start from 5th letter)
a.indexOf("nan")    // result = 2
a.indexOf("nas")    // result = 4
a.indexOf("s")      // result = 6
a.indexOf("z")      // result = -1 (no "z" in string)
```

Related Items: *string*.`lastIndexOf()`, *string*.`charAt()`, *string*.`substring()` methods

string.`lastIndexOf(`*searchString*`[,` *startIndex*`])`

Returns: Index value of the last character within the *string* where *searchString* begins

Compatibility: WinIE3+, MacIE3+, NN2+, Moz+, Safari+, Opera+, Chrome+

The *string*.`lastIndexOf()` method is closely related to the method *string*.`indexOf()`. The only difference is that this method starts its search for a match from the end of the string (*string*.`length` - 1) and works its way backward through the string. All index values are still counted, starting with 0, from the front of the string. The examples that follow use the same values as in the examples for *string*.`indexOf()` so that you can compare the results. In cases where only one instance of the search string is found, the results are the same; but when multiple instances of the search string exist, the results can vary widely — hence the need for this method.

Example

Enter each of the following statements (up to, but not including the "*//*" comment symbols) into the top text box of The Evaluator (you can simply replace the parameters of the `lastIndexOf()` method for each statement after the first one). Compare your results with the results shown below.

```
a = "bananas"
a.lastIndexOf("b")     // result = 0 (index of 1st letter is zero)
a.lastIndexOf("a")     // result = 5
a.lastIndexOf("a",1)   // result = 1 (from 2nd letter toward the front)
a.lastIndexOf("a",2)   // result = 1 (start from 3rd letter working
```

```
                                        toward front)
a.lastIndexOf("a",4)   // result = 3 (start from 5th letter)
a.lastIndexOf("nan")   // result = 2 [except for -1 Nav 2.0 bug]
a.lastIndexOf("nas")   // result = 4
a.lastIndexOf("s")     // result = 6
a.lastIndexOf("z")     // result = -1 (no "z" in string)
```

Related Items: *string*.lastIndexOf(), *string*.charAt(), *string*.substring() methods

string.localeCompare(*string2*)

Returns: Integer

Compatibility: WinIE5.5+, MacIE-, NN6+, Moz+, Safari+, Opera+, Chrome+

The localeCompare() method lets a script compare the cumulative Unicode values of two strings, taking into account the language system for the browser. This method is necessitated by only a few human languages (Turkish is said to be one). If the two strings, adjusted for the language system, are equal, the value returned is zero. If the string value on which the method is invoked (meaning the string to the left of the period) sorts ahead of the parameter string, the value returned is a negative integer; otherwise the returned value is a positive integer.

The ECMA standard for this method leaves the precise positive or negative values up to the browser designer. NN6+ calculates the cumulative Unicode values for both strings and subtracts the string parameter's sum from the string value's sum. IE5.5+ and FF1+, on the other hand, return -1 or 1 if the strings are not colloquially equal.

Related Items: *string*.toLocaleLowerCase(), *string*.toLocaleUpperCase() methods

string.match(*regExpression*)

Returns: Array of matching substrings

Compatibility: WinIE4+, MacIE4+, NN4+, Moz+, Safari+, Opera+, Chrome+

The *string*.match() method relies on the RegExp (regular expression) object to carry out a match within a string. The string value under scrutiny is to the left of the dot, whereas the regular expression to be used by the method is passed as a parameter. The parameter must be a regular expression object, created according to the two ways these objects can be generated.

This method returns an array value when at least one match turns up; otherwise the returned value is null. Each entry in the array is a copy of the string segment that matches the specifications of the regular expression. You can use this method to uncover how many times a substring or sequence of characters appears in a larger string. Finding the offset locations of the matches requires other string parsing.

Example

To help you understand the *string*.match() method, Listing 15-3 provides you with a regular expression workshop. Three input controls let you set up a test: the first is for the long string, to be examined by the method; the second is for a regular expression; and the third is a checkbox that lets you specify whether the search through the string for matches should be case-sensitive. Some default values are provided, in case you're not yet familiar with the syntax of regular expressions (see Chapter 45 on the CD-ROM). After you click the "Execute match()" button, the script creates a regular expression object out of your input, performs the *string*.match() method on the big string, and

***stringObject*.match()**

reports two kinds of results to the page. The primary result is a string version of the array returned by the method; the other is a count of items returned.

```
LISTING 15-3
```

Regular Expression Match Workshop

HTML: jsb-15-03.html

```html
<!DOCTYPE html>
<html>
    <head>
        <meta http-equiv="content-type" content="text/html;charset=utf-8">
        <title>Regular Expression Match Workshop</title>
        <script type="text/javascript" src="../jsb-global.js"></script>
        <script type="text/javascript" src="jsb-15-03.js"></script>
    </head>
    <body>
        <h1>Regular Expression Match Workshop</h1>

        <form action="regexp-match.php">
            <p>
                <label for="string">Enter a main string:</label>
                <input type="text" id="string" name="string" size="60"
                value="Many a maN and womAN have meant to visit GerMAny." />
            </p>
            <p>
                <label for="pattern">Enter a regular expression to match:</label>
                <input type="text" id="pattern" name="pattern" size="25" value="\wa\w" />

                <input type="checkbox" id="caseSens" name="caseSens" />
                <label for="caseSens">Case-sensitive</label>
            </p>
            <p>
                <input type="button" id="button" value="Execute match()" />
                <input type="reset" />
            </p>
            <p>
                <label for="result">Result:</label>
                <input type="text" id="result" name="result" size="40" />
            </p>
            <p>
                <label for="count">Count:</label>
                <input type="text" id="count" name="count" size="3" />
            </p>
        </form>
    </body>
</html>
```

JavaScript: jsb-15-03.js

```javascript
// initialize when the page has loaded
addEvent(window, 'load', initialize);
```

```
function initialize()
{
    // do this only if the browser can handle DOM methods
    if (document.getElementById)
    {
        // point to critical element
        var oButton = document.getElementById('button');

            // if it exists...
            if (oButton)
            {
                // apply behavior to button
                addEvent(oButton, 'click', doMatch);
            }
    }
}

// perform regular expression match using input values
function doMatch()
{
    // gather input values
    var oString = document.getElementById('string');
    var sString = oString.value;

    var oPattern = document.getElementById('pattern');
    var oCaseSensitivity = document.getElementById('caseSens');
    var sFlags = 'g';   // g = find all
        if (!oCaseSensitivity.checked) sFlags += 'i';   // i = case-insensitive

    // create regular expression object
    var oRegExp = new RegExp(oPattern.value, sFlags);

    // perform match
    var aResult = sString.match(oRegExp);

    // display results
    var oResult = document.getElementById('result');
    var oCount = document.getElementById('count');

        // got matches?
        if (aResult)
        {
            oResult.value = aResult.toString();
            oCount.value = aResult.length;
        }
        else
        {
            oResult.value = "<no matches>";
            oCount.value = "";
        }
}
```

stringObject.replace()

The default value for the main string has unusual capitalization intentionally. The capitalization lets you see more clearly where some of the matches come from. For example, the default regular expression looks for any three-character string that has the letter "a" in the middle. Six string segments match that expression. With the help of capitalization, you can see where each of the four strings containing "man" is extracted from the main string. The following table lists some other regular expressions to try with the default main string.

RegExp	Description
man	Both case-sensitive and not
man\b	Where "man" is at the end of a word
\bman	Where "man" is at the start of a word
me*an	Where zero or more "e" letters occur between "m" and "a"
.a.	Where "a" is surrounded by any one character (including space)
\sa\s	Where "a" is surrounded by a space on both sides
z	Where a "z" occurs (none in the default string)

In the scripts for Listing 15-3, if the `string`.match() method returns `null`, you are informed politely, and the count field is emptied.

Related Items: RegExp object (see Chapter 45 on the CD-ROM)

string.replace(*regExpression, replaceString*)

Returns: Changed string

Compatibility: WinIE4+, MacIE4+, NN4+, Moz+, Safari+, Opera+, Chrome+

Regular expressions are commonly used to perform search-and-replace operations. In conjunction with the *string*.search() method, JavaScript's *string*.replace() method provides a simple framework in which to perform this kind of operation on any string.

A replace operation using RegExp requires three components. The first is the main string that is the target of the operation. Second is the regular expression pattern to search for. And third is the string to replace each instance of the text found by the operation.

```
stringToSearch.replace(pattern, replacementString);
```

For the *string*.replace() method, the main string is the string value, or object referenced, to the left of the period. This string can also be a literal string (that is, text surrounded by quotes). The regular expression to search for is the first parameter, whereas the replacement string is the second parameter.

The regular expression definition determines whether the replacement is of just the first match encountered in the main string, or all matches in the string. If you add the g flag to the end of the regular expression, then one invocation of the replace() method performs a global search-and-replace throughout the entire main string.

As long as you know how to generate a regular expression, you can easily use the *string* .replace() method to perform simple replacement operations. But using regular expressions can make the operation more powerful. Consider these soliloquy lines by Hamlet:

```
To be, or not to be: that is the question:
Whether 'tis nobler in the mind to suffer
```

If you wanted to replace both instances of "be" with "exist," you can do it in this case by specifying

```
var regexp = /be/g;
soliloquy.replace(regexp, "exist");
```

But you can't always be assured that the letters "b" and "e" will be standing alone as a word. What happens if the main string contains the word "being" or "saber"? The above example would replace the "be" letters in them as well.

Rescue comes from special characters that better define what to search for. In the example here, the search is for the word "be." Therefore, the regular expression surrounds the search text with word boundaries (the \b special character), as in

```
var regexp = /\bbe\b/g;
soliloquy.replace(regexp, "exist");
```

This syntax also takes care of the fact that the first two "be" words are followed by punctuation, rather than a space, as you may expect for a freestanding word. For more about regular expression syntax, see Chapter 45 on the CD-ROM.

Example

The page created by Listing 15-4 lets you practice with the *string*.replace() and *string*.search() methods, and regular expressions, in a friendly environment. The source text is a five-line excerpt from *Hamlet*. You can enter the regular expression to search on, and the replacement text as well. Note that the script completes the job of creating the regular expression object, so that you can focus on the other special characters used to define the matching string. All replacement activities act globally because the g flag is automatically appended to any expression you enter.

Default values in the fields replace the contraction 'tis with "it is" after you click the "Execute replace()" button (see Figure 15-2). Notice that the backslash character in front of the apostrophe of 'tis (in the string assembled in mainString) makes the apostrophe a non-word boundary, and thus allows the \B't regular expression to find a match there. As described in the section on the *string*.search() method, the button connected to that method returns the offset character number of the matching string (or -1 if no match occurs).

stringObject.replace()

FIGURE 15-2

Using the default replacement regular expression.

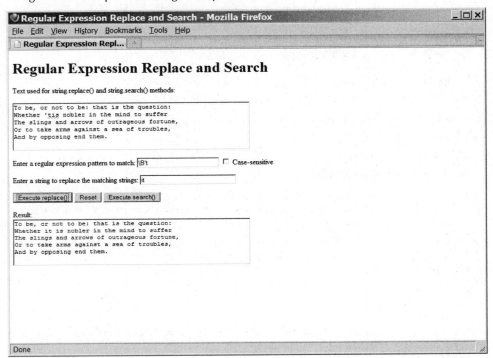

LISTING 15-4

Lab for *string*.replace() and *string*.search()

HTML: jsb-15-04.html

```html
<!DOCTYPE html>
<html>
   <head>
      <meta http-equiv="content-type" content="text/html;charset=utf-8">
      <title>Regular Expression Replace and Search</title>
      <script type="text/javascript" src="../jsb-global.js"></script>
      <script type="text/javascript" src="jsb-15-04.js"></script>
   </head>
   <body>
      <h1>Regular Expression Replace and Search</h1>

      <form action="regexp-replace.php">
         <p>
            <label for="source">Text used for string.replace() and
```

```
                              string.search() methods:</label>
        </p>
        <p>
            <textarea id="source" name="source" cols="60" rows="5">
To be, or not to be: that is the question:
Whether 'tis nobler in the mind to suffer
The slings and arrows of outrageous fortune,
Or to take arms against a sea of troubles,
And by opposing end them.
</textarea>
        </p>
        <p>
          <label for="pattern">Enter a regular expression pattern to match:</label>
          <input type="text" id="pattern" name="pattern" size="25" value="\B't" />

          <input type="checkbox" id="caseSens" name="caseSens" />
          <label for="caseSens">Case-sensitive</label>
        </p>
        <p>
          <label for="replacement">Enter a string to replace
                    the matching strings:</label>
          <input type="text" id="replacement" name="replacement"
                    size="30" value="it " />
        </p>
        <p>
          <input type="button" id="button-replace" value="Execute replace()"
                    onclick="doReplace(this.form)" />
          <input type="reset" />
          <input type="button" id="button-search" value="Execute search()"
                    onclick="doSearch(this.form)" />
        </p>
        <p>
          <label for="result">Result:</label><br />
          <textarea id="result" name="result" cols="60" rows="5"></textarea>
        </p>
      </form>
    </body>
</html>
```

JavaScript: jsb-15-04.js

```
// initialize when the page has loaded
addEvent(window, 'load', initialize);

function initialize()
{
    // do this only if the browser can handle DOM methods
    if (document.getElementById)
    {
      // check for critical elements
      var oSource = document.getElementById('source');
      var oPattern = document.getElementById('pattern');
```

continued

stringObject.replace()

LISTING 15-4   *(continued)*

```
        var oCaseSensitivity = document.getElementById('caseSens');
        var oReplacement = document.getElementById('replacement');
        var oButtonReplace = document.getElementById('button-replace');
        var oButtonSearch = document.getElementById('button-search');
        var oResult = document.getElementById('result');

            // if they all exist...
            if (oSource && oPattern && oCaseSensitivity && oReplacement
               && oButtonReplace && oButtonSearch && oResult)
            {
                // apply behaviors
                addEvent(oButtonReplace, 'click', doReplace);
                addEvent(oButtonSearch, 'click', doSearch);
            }
            else
            {
                alert('Critical element not found');
            }
    }
}


function doReplace()
{
    var sSource = document.getElementById('source').value;
    var sReplacement = document.getElementById('replacement').value;
    var sPattern = document.getElementById('pattern').value;
    var sFlags = 'g';    // g = find all; i = case-insensitive
        if (!document.getElementById('caseSens').checked) sFlags += 'i';

    // create regular expression object
    var oRegExp = new RegExp(sPattern, sFlags);

    // perform replace
    var sResult = sSource.replace(oRegExp, sReplacement);

    // display results
    document.getElementById('result').value = sResult;
}


function doSearch()
{
    var sSource = document.getElementById('source').value;
    var sPattern = document.getElementById('pattern').value;
    var sFlags = 'g';    // g = find all; i = case-insensitive
        if (!document.getElementById('caseSens').checked) sFlags += 'i';

    // create regular expression object
```

```
var oRegExp = new RegExp(sPattern, sFlags);

// perform replace
var sResult = sSource.search(oRegExp);

// display results
document.getElementById('result').value = sResult;
}
```

Related Items: *string*.match() method; RegExp object

string.search(*regExpression*)

Returns: Offset integer

Compatibility: WinIE4+, MacIE4+, NN4+, Moz+, Safari+, Opera+, Chrome+

The results of the *string*.search() method may remind you of the *string*.indexOf() method. In both cases, the returned value is the character number where the matching string first appears in the main string, or -1 if no match occurs. The big difference, of course, is that the matching string for *string*.search() is a regular expression.

Example

Listing 15-4, which illustrates the *string*.replace() method, also provides a laboratory to experiment with the *string*.search() method.

Related Items: *string*.match() method; RegExp object

string.slice(*startIndex* [, *endIndex*])

Returns: String

Compatibility: WinIE4+, MacIE4+, NN4+, Moz+, Safari+, Opera+, Chrome+

The *string*.slice() method resembles the method *string*.substring(), in that both let you extract a portion of one string and create a new string as a result (without modifying the original string). A helpful improvement in *string*.slice(), however, is that specifying an ending index value relative to the end of the main string is easier.

Using *string*.substring() to extract a substring that ends before the end of the string requires machinations such as the following:

```
string.substring(4, (string.length-2))
```

Instead, you can assign a negative number to the second parameter of *string*.slice() to indicate an offset from the end of the string:

```
string.slice(4, -2)
```

The second parameter is optional. If you omit the second parameter, the returned value is a string from the starting offset to the end of the main string.

stringObject.slice()

Example

With Listing 15-5, you can try several combinations of parameters with the *string*.slice() method (see Figure 15-3). A base string is provided (along with character measurements). Select from the different choices available for parameters, and study the outcome of the slice.

FIGURE 15-3

Lab for exploring the *string*.slice() method.

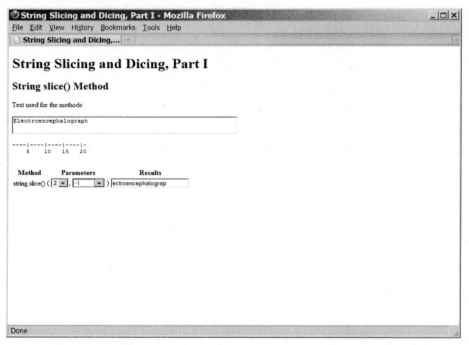

LISTING 15-5

Slicing a String

```
HTML: jsb-15-05.html
<!DOCTYPE html>
<html>
   <head>
      <meta http-equiv="content-type" content="text/html;charset=utf-8">
      <title>String Slicing and Dicing, Part I</title>
      <script type="text/javascript" src="../jsb-global.js"></script>
      <script type="text/javascript" src="jsb-15-05.js"></script>
   </head>
   <body>
   <h1>String Slicing and Dicing, Part I</h1>
```

```
        <b>String slice() Method</b>

        <form action="string-slice.php">
            <p>
                <label for="source">Text used for the methods:</label>
            </p>
            <p>
                <textarea id="source" name="source" cols="60" rows="1">
Electroencephalograph</textarea>
                <pre>
----|----|----|----|-
    5    10   15   20
                </pre>
            </p>

            <table>
                <thead>
                    <tr>
                        <th>Method</th>
                        <th>Parameters</th>
                        <th>Results</th>
                    </tr>
                </thead>
                <tbody>
                    <tr>
                        <td>string.slice()</td>
                        <td>(
                            <select id="parameter1" name="parameter1">
                                <option value="0">0</option>
                                <option value="1">1</option>
                                <option value="2">2</option>
                                <option value="3">3</option>
                                <option value="5">5</option>
                            </select>,
                            <select id="parameter2" name="parameter2">
                                <option>(None)</option>
                                <option value="5">5</option>
                                <option value="10">10</option>
                                <option value="-1">-1</option>
                                <option value="-5">-5</option>
                                <option value="-10">-10</option>
                            </select>
                        )</td>
                        <td>
                            <input type="text" id="result" name="result" size="25" />
                        </td>
                    </tr>
                </tbody>
            </table>
        </form>
    </body>
</html>
```

continued

251

stringObject.slice()

LISTING 15-5   *(continued)*

JavaScript: jsb-15-05.js

```javascript
// initialize when the page has loaded
addEvent(window, 'load', initialize);

function initialize()
{
   // do this only if the browser can handle DOM methods
   if (document.getElementById)
   {
      // check for critical elements
      var oSource = document.getElementById('source');
      var oParameter1 = document.getElementById('parameter1');
      var oParameter2 = document.getElementById('parameter2');
      var oResult = document.getElementById('result');

         // if they all exist...
         if (oSource && oParameter1 && oParameter2 && oResult)
         {
            // apply behaviors
            addEvent(oParameter1, 'change', showResults);
            addEvent(oParameter2, 'change', showResults);
         }
         else
         {
            alert('Critical element not found');
         }
   }
}


// execute the method and display the result
function showResults()
{
   // get source text
   var oSource = document.getElementById('source');
   var sSource = oSource.firstChild.nodeValue;

   // get paramaters
   var oParameter1 = document.getElementById('parameter1');
   var iParameter1 = parseInt(oParameter1.options[oParameter1.selectedIndex].value);

   var oParameter2 = document.getElementById('parameter2');
   var iParameter2 = parseInt(oParameter2.options[oParameter2.selectedIndex].value);

   // generate result & display it
   var oResult = document.getElementById('result');

      if (!iParameter2)
      {
```

```
    oResult.value = sSource.slice(iParameter1);
}
else
{
    oResult.value = sSource.slice(iParameter1, iParameter2);
}
}
```

Related Items: *string*.substr(), *string*.substring() methods

string.split("*delimiterCharacter*" [, *limitInteger*])

Returns: Array of delimited items

Compatibility: WinIE4+, MacIE4+, NN3+, Moz+, Safari+, Opera+, Chrome+

The split() method is the functional opposite of the array.join() method (see Chapter 18, "The Array Object"). From the string object point of view, JavaScript splits a long string into pieces delimited by a specific character, and then creates a dense array with those pieces. You do not need to initialize the array via the new Array() constructor. Given the powers of array object methods, such as array.sort(), you may want to convert a series of string items to an array to take advantage of those powers. Also, if your goal is to divide a string into an array of single characters, you can still use the split() method, but specify an empty string as a parameter. For some older browsers, such as NN3 and IE4, only the first parameter is observed.

In modern browsers, you can use a regular expression object for the first parameter, enhancing your power to find delimiters in strings. For example, consider the following string:

```
    var nameList = "Fred - 123-4567,Jane - 234-5678,Steve - 345-6789";
```

To convert that string into an array of only the names takes a lot of parsing without regular expressions before you can even use *string*.split(). However, with a regular expression as a parameter,

```
    var regexp = / - [\d-]+,?\b/;
    var newArray = nameList.split(regexp);
        // result = an array "Fred", "Jane", "Steve", ""
```

the new array entries hold only the names, and not the phone numbers or punctuation.

A second optional parameter, an integer value, allows you to specify a limit to the number of array elements generated by the method.

Example

Use The Evaluator (Chapter 4) to see how the string.split() method works. Begin by assigning a comma-delimited string to a variable:

```
    a = "Anderson,Smith,Johnson,Washington"
```

Now split the string at comma positions so that the string pieces become items in an array, saved as b:

```
b = a.split(",")
```

To prove that the array contains four items, inspect the array's `length` property:

```
b.length      // result: 4
```

Related Items: `array.join()` method

string.substr(*start* [, *length*])

Returns: String

Compatibility: WinIE4+, MacIE4+, NN4+, Moz+, Safari+, Opera+, Chrome+

The *string*.substr() method offers a variation of the *string*.substring() method that has been in the JavaScript language since the beginning. The distinction is that the *string*.substr() method's parameters specify the starting index and a number of characters to be included from that start point. In contrast, the string.substring() method parameters specify index points for the start and end characters within the main string.

As with all string methods requiring an index value, the *string*.substr() first parameter is zero-based. If you do not specify a second parameter, the returned substring starts at the indexed point and extends to the end of the string. A second parameter value that exceeds the end point of the string means that the method returns a substring to the end of the string.

Even though this method is newer than its partner, it is not part of the latest (Fifth) edition of the ECMA standard for the language. But because the method is so widely used, the standard does acknowledge it as an annex, so that other scripting contexts can implement the method, consistent with browser practice.

Example

Listing 15-6 lets you experiment with a variety of values to see how the *string*.substr() method works.

LISTING 15-6

Reading a Portion of a String

HTML: jsb-15-06.html

```
<!DOCTYPE html>
<html>
   <head>
      <meta http-equiv="content-type" content="text/html;charset=utf-8">
      <title>String Slicing and Dicing, Part II</title>
      <script type="text/javascript" src="../jsb-global.js"></script>
      <script type="text/javascript" src="jsb-15-06.js"></script>
   </head>
   <body>
      <h1>String Slicing and Dicing, Part II</h1>
```

```
        <h2>String substr() Method</h2>

        <form action="string-substr.php">
            <p>
                <label for="source">Text used for the methods:</label>
            </p>
            <p>
                <textarea id="source" name="source" cols="60" rows="1">
Electroencephalograph</textarea>
                <pre>
----|----|----|----|-
    5   10   15   20
                </pre>
            </p>

            <table>
                <thead>
                    <tr>
                        <th>Method</th>
                        <th>Parameters</th>
                        <th>Results</th>
                    </tr>
                </thead>
                <tbody>
                    <tr>
                        <td>string.substr()</td>
                        <td>(
                        <select id="parameter1" name="parameter1">
                            <option value="0">0</option>
                            <option value="1">1</option>
                            <option value="2">2</option>
                            <option value="3">3</option>
                            <option value="5">5</option>
                        </select>,
                        <select id="parameter2" name="parameter2">
                    <option>(None)</option>
                    <option value="5">5</option>
                    <option value="10">10</option>
                    <option value="20">20</option>
                        </select>
                    )</td>
                    <td>
                        <input type="text" id="result" name="result" size="25" />
                    </td>
                </tr>
            </tbody>
        </table>
    </form>
  </body>
</html>
```

continued

LISTING 15-6   *(continued)*

```javascript
JavaScript: jsb-15-06.js

// initialize when the page has loaded
addEvent(window, 'load', initialize);

function initialize()
{
   // do this only if the browser can handle DOM methods
   if (document.getElementById)
   {
      // check for critical elements
      var oSource = document.getElementById('source');
      var oParameter1 = document.getElementById('parameter1');
      var oParameter2 = document.getElementById('parameter2');
      var oResult = document.getElementById('result');

         // if they all exist...
         if (oSource && oParameter1 && oParameter2 && oResult)
         {
            // apply behaviors
            addEvent(oParameter1, 'change', showResults);
            addEvent(oParameter2, 'change', showResults);
         }
         else
         {
            alert('Critical element not found');
         }
   }
}

// execute the method and display the result
function showResults()
{
   // get source text
   var oSource = document.getElementById('source');
   var sSource = oSource.firstChild.nodeValue;

   // get paramaters
   var oParameter1 = document.getElementById('parameter1');
   var iParameter1 = parseInt(oParameter1.options[oParameter1.selectedIndex].value);

   var oParameter2 = document.getElementById('parameter2');
   var iParameter2 = parseInt(oParameter2.options[oParameter2.selectedIndex].value);

   // generate result & display it
   var oResult = document.getElementById('result');

      if (!iParameter2)
      {
         oResult.value = sSource.substr(iParameter1);
```

```
      }
      else
      {
          oResult.value = sSource.substr(iParameter1, iParameter2);
      }
}
```

Related Items: `string.substring()` method

`string.substring(indexA[, indexB])`

Returns: String of characters between index values *indexA* and *indexB*

Compatibility: WinIE3+, MacIE3+, NN2+, Moz+, Safari+, Opera+, Chrome+

The `string.substring()` method enables your scripts to extract a copy of a contiguous range of characters from any string. The parameters to this method are the starting and ending index values (the first character of the string object is index value 0) of the main string from which the excerpt should be taken. An important item to note is that the excerpt goes up to, but does not include, the character pointed to by the higher index value.

It makes no difference which index value in the parameters is larger than the other: The method starts the excerpt from the lowest value and continues to (but does not include) the highest value. If both index values are the same, the method returns an empty string; and if you omit the second parameter, the end of the string is assumed to be the endpoint.

Example

Listing 15-7 lets you experiment with a variety of values to see how the `string.substring()` method works.

LISTING 15-7

Reading a Portion of a String

HTML: jsb-15-07.html

```html
<!DOCTYPE html>
<html>
   <head>
      <meta http-equiv="content-type" content="text/html;charset=utf-8">
      <title>String Slicing and Dicing, Part III</title>
      <script type="text/javascript" src="../jsb-global.js"></script>
      <script type="text/javascript" src="jsb-15-07.js"></script>
   </head>
   <body>
      <h1>String Slicing and Dicing, Part III</h1>
      <h2>String substring() Method</h2>

      <form action="string-substring.php">
         <p>
            <label for="source">Text used for the methods:</label>
```

continued

stringObject.substring()

LISTING 15-7   *(continued)*

```
            </p>
            <p>
                <textarea id="Textarea1" name="source" cols="60" rows="1">
Electroencephalograph</textarea>
                <pre>
----|----|----|----|-
    5    10    15    20
                </pre>
            </p>

            <table>
                <thead>
                    <tr>
                        <th>Method</th>
                        <th>Parameters</th>
                        <th>Results</th>
                    </tr>
                </thead>
                <tbody>
                    <tr>
                        <td>string.substring()</td>
                        <td>(
                            <select id="parameter1" name="parameter1">
                                <option value="0">0</option>
                                <option value="1">1</option>
                                <option value="2">2</option>
                                <option value="3">3</option>
                                <option value="5">5</option>
                            </select>,
                            <select id="parameter2" name="parameter2">
                                <option>(None)</option>
                                <option value="3">3</option>
                                <option value="5">5</option>
                                <option value="10">10</option>
                            </select>
                        )</td>
                        <td>
                            <input type="text" id="result" name="result" size="25" />
                        </td>
                    </tr>
                </tbody>
            </table>
        </form>
    </body>
</html>
```

JavaScript: jsb-15-07.js

```
// initialize when the page has loaded
addEvent(window, 'load', initialize);
```

```
function initialize()
{
   // do this only if the browser can handle DOM methods
   if (document.getElementById)
   {
      // check for critical elements
      var oSource = document.getElementById('source');
      var oParameter1 = document.getElementById('parameter1');
      var oParameter2 = document.getElementById('parameter2');
      var oResult = document.getElementById('result');

         // if they all exist...
         if (oSource && oParameter1 && oParameter2 && oResult)
         {
            // apply behaviors
            addEvent(oParameter1, 'change', showResults);
            addEvent(oParameter2, 'change', showResults);
         }
         else
         {
            alert('Critical element not found');
         }
   }
}


// execute the method and display the result
function showResults()
{
   // get source text
   var oSource = document.getElementById('source');
   var sSource = oSource.firstChild.nodeValue;

   // get paramaters
   var oParameter1 = document.getElementById('parameter1');
   var iParameter1 = parseInt(oParameter1.options[oParameter1.selectedIndex].value);

   var oParameter2 = document.getElementById('parameter2');
   var iParameter2 = parseInt(oParameter2.options[oParameter2.selectedIndex].value);

   // generate result & display it
   var oResult = document.getElementById('result');

      if (!iParameter2)
      {
         oResult.value = sSource.substring(iParameter1);
      }
      else
      {
         oResult.value = sSource.substring(iParameter1, iParameter2);
      }
}
```

Related Items: `string.substr()`, `string.slice()` methods

`string.toLocaleLowerCase()`
`string.toLocaleUpperCase()`

Returns: String

Compatibility: WinIE5.5+, MacIE-, NN6+, Moz+, Safari-, Opera+, Chrome+

These two methods are variations on the standard methods for changing the case of a string. They take into account some language systems whose cases for a particular character don't necessarily map to the Latin alphabet character mappings.

Related Items: `string.toLowerCase()`, `string.toUpperCase()` methods

`string.toLowerCase()`
`string.toUpperCase()`

Returns: The string in all lower- or uppercase, depending on which method you invoke

Compatibility: WinIE3+, MacIE3+, NN2+, Moz+, Safari+, Opera+, Chrome+

A great deal of what takes place on the Internet (and in JavaScript) is case-sensitive. URLs on some servers, for instance, are case-sensitive for directory names and filenames.

These two methods, the simplest of the string methods, return a copy of a string converted to either all lowercase or all uppercase. Any mixed-case strings get converted to a uniform case. If you want to compare user input from a field against some coded string without worrying about matching case, you can convert copies of both strings to the same case for the comparison.

Example

You can use the `toLowerCase()` and `toUpperCase()` methods on literal strings, as follows:

```
var newString = "HTTP://www.Mozilla.ORG".toLowerCase();
    // result = "http://www.mozilla.org"
```

The methods are also helpful in comparing strings when case is not important, as follows:

```
if (guess.toUpperCase() == answer.toUpperCase()) {...}
    // comparing strings without case sensitivity
```

Note that these methods do not change the case of the strings themselves, but rather output modified copies, leaving the originals intact.

Related Items: `string.toLocaleLowerCase()`, `string.toLocaleUpperCase()` methods

`string.toString()`
`string.valueOf()`

Returns: String value

Compatibility: WinIE4+, MacIE4+, NN4+, Moz+, Safari+, Opera+, Chrome+

Both of these methods return string values (as opposed to full-fledged string objects). If you have created a string object via the `new String()` constructor, the type of that item is `object`. Therefore, if you want to examine more precisely what kind of value is held by the object, you can use the `valueOf()` method to get the value and then examine it via the `typeof` operator. The `toString()` method is present for this object primarily because a string object inherits the method from the root object of JavaScript.

Example

Use The Evaluator (Chapter 4) to test the `valueOf()` method. Enter the following statements into the top text box and examine the values that appear in the Results field:

```
a = new String("hello")
typeof a
b = a.valueOf()
typeof b
```

Because all other JavaScript core objects also have the `valueOf()` method, you can build generic functions that receive a variety of object types as parameters, and the script can branch its code based on the type of value that is stored in the object.

Related Items: `typeof` operator (Chapter 22)

String Utility Functions

Figuring out how to apply the various string object methods to a string manipulation challenge is not always an easy task. The situation is only made worse if you need to support legacy or mobile browsers with limited JavaScript support. It's also difficult to anticipate every possible way you may need to massage strings in your scripts. But to help you get started, Listing 15-8 contains a fully backward-compatible library of string functions for inserting, deleting, and replacing chunks of text in a string. If your audience uses browsers capable of including external `.js` library files, that would be an excellent way to make these functions available to your scripts.

LISTING 15-8

Utility String Handlers

JavaScript: `jsb-15-08.js`

```
// extract front part of string prior to searchString
function getFront(sMain, sSearch)
{
    iOffset = sMain.indexOf(sSearch);

    if (iOffset == -1)
    {
        return null;
    }
    else
```

continued

LISTING 15-8   *(continued)*

```javascript
        {
            return sMain.substring(0, iOffset);
        }
}


// extract back end of string after searchString
function getEnd(sMain, sSearch)
{
    iOffset = sMain.indexOf(sSearch);

        if (iOffset == -1)
        {
            return null;
        }
        else
        {
            return sMain.substring(iOffset + sSearch.length, sMain.length);
        }
}


// insert insertString immediately before searchString
function insertString(sMain, sSearch, sInsert)
{
    var sFront = getFront(sMain, sSearch);
    var sEnd = getEnd(sMain, sSearch);

        if (sFront == null || sEnd == null)
        {
            return null;
        }
        else
        {
            return sFront + sInsert + sSearch + sEnd;
        }
}


// remove sDelete from sMain
function deleteString(sMain, sDelete)
{
    return replaceString(sMain, sDelete, "");
}


// replace sSearch with sReplace
function replaceString(sMain, sSearch, sReplace)
{
```

```
    var sFront = getFront(sMain, sSearch);
    var sEnd = getEnd(sMain, sSearch);

        if (sFront == null || sEnd == null)
        {
            return null;
        }
        else
        {
            return sFront + sReplace + sEnd;
        }
}
```

The first two functions extract the front or end components of strings, as needed, for some of the other functions in this suite. The final three functions are the core of these string-handling functions. If you plan to use these functions in your scripts, be sure to notice the dependence that some functions have on others. Including all five functions as a group ensures that they work as designed.

A modern alternative to Listing 15-8 utilizes a combination of string and array methods to perform a global replace operation in a one-statement function:

```
        function replaceString(sMain, sSearch, sReplace)
        {
            return sMain.split(sSearch).join(sReplace);
        }
```

Going one step further, you can create a custom method to use with all string values or objects in your scripts. Simply let the following statement execute as the page loads:

```
        String.prototype.replaceString = function replaceString(sMain,
            sSearch, sReplace)
        {
            return sMain.split(sSearch).join(sReplace);
        }
```

Then, invoke this method on any string value in other scripts on the page, as in:

```
        myString = myString.replaceString(" CD ", " MP3 ");
```

(Note that global search and replace can also be accomplished using regular expressions; see Chapter 45.)

HTML markup methods

Now we come to the other group of string object methods that effectively enclose text in HTML elements. None of these methods are part of the ECMAScript Fifth Edition standard; their persistence in JavaScript implementations is clearly in support of ancient scripts. Modern web pages use stylesheets to apply cosmetic formatting to elements, and DOM methods to insert new nodes.

string.anchor("*anchorName*")	*string*.link(*locationOrURL*)
string.blink()	*string*.big()
string.bold()	*string*.small()
string.fixed()	*string*.strike()
string.fontcolor(*colorValue*)	*string*.sub()
string.fontsize(*integer1to7*)	*string*.sup()
string.italics()	

First examine the methods that don't require any parameters. You probably see a pattern: All of these methods are font-style attributes that have settings of on or off. To turn on these attributes in an HTML document, you surround the text in the appropriate tag pairs, such as `<b> ... </b>` for bold-face text. These methods take the string object, attach those tags, and return the resulting text, which is ready to be put into any HTML that your scripts are building. Therefore, the expression

```
"Good morning!".bold()
```

evaluates to

```
<b>Good morning!</b>
```

Listing 15-9 shows an example of applying these string methods to text on the page. (Internet Explorer, Chrome, and Safari do not support the `<blink>` element, so while they execute the *string*.blink() method, there is no resulting blink in the display.)

LISTING 15-9

Using Simple String Methods

HTML: `jsb-15-09.html`

```html
<!DOCTYPE html>
<html>
   <head>
      <meta http-equiv="content-type" content="text/html;charset=utf-8">
      <title>HTML by JavaScript</title>
      <script type="text/javascript" src="../jsb-global.js"></script>
      <script type="text/javascript" src="jsb-15-09.js"></script>
   </head>
<body>
   <h1>HTML by JavaScript</h1>
   <ul id="tag-list">
      <li id="anchor">anchor</li>
      <li id="big">big</li>
      <li id="blink">blink</li>
      <li id="bold">bold</li>
      <li id="fixed">fixed</li>
      <li id="fontcolor">fontcolor</li>
```

```
        <li id="fontsize">fontsize</li>
        <li id="italics">italics</li>
        <li id="link">link</li>
        <li id="small">small</li>
        <li id="strike">strike</li>
        <li>sub H<span id="sub">2</span>0</li>
        <li>sup E=mc<span id="sup">2</span></li>
    </ul>
    <form action="html-by-javascript.php">
        <p>
            <button id="apply-markup">Apply Markup</button>
        </p>
    </form>
  </body>
</html>
```

JavaScript: jsb-15-09.js

```javascript
// initialize when the page has loaded
addEvent(window, 'load', initialize);

function initialize()
{
    // do this only if the browser can handle DOM methods
    if (document.getElementById)
    {
        // check for button
        var oButton = document.getElementById('apply-markup');

            // if it exists...
            if (oButton)
            {
                // apply behavior
                addEvent(oButton, 'click', applyMarkup);
            }
    }
}


// apply markup to text elements
function applyMarkup(evt)
{
        // consolidate event handling
        if (!evt) evt = window.event;

    var oList = document.getElementById('tag-list');
    var aElements = oList.getElementsByTagName('*');

    for (var i = 0; i < aElements.length; i++)
    {
        // get this element's id & text value
        sId = aElements[i].id;
```

continued

LISTING 15-9   (continued)

```
    //var sText = aElements[i].firstChild.nodeValue;
    var sText = aElements[i].innerHTML;

    switch (sId)
    {
       case 'anchor':   sText = sText.anchor('anchor-name');   break;
       case 'big':    sText = sText.big();    break;
       case 'blink':    sText = sText.blink();    break;
       case 'bold':    sText = sText.bold();    break;
       case 'fixed':    sText = sText.fixed();    break;
       case 'fontcolor':    sText = sText.fontcolor('red');    break;
       case 'fontsize':    sText = sText.fontsize(7);    break;
       case 'italics':    sText = sText.italics();    break;
       case 'link':    sText = sText.link('http://example.com/');    break;
       case 'small':    sText = sText.small();    break;
       case 'strike':    sText = sText.strike();    break;
       case 'sub':    sText = sText.sub();    break;
       case 'sup':    sText = sText.sup();    break;
       default: continue;
    }

    // replace the element's contents with the marked-up text
    aElements[i].innerHTML = sText;
  }
  alert('Here is the modified markup:\n' + oList.innerHTML);

// cancel form submission
   // W3C DOM method (hide from IE)
   if (evt.preventDefault) evt.preventDefault();
// IE method
return false;
}
```

string.fontsize() and *string*.fontcolor() affect the font characteristics of strings displayed in the HTML page. The parameters for these items are pretty straightforward — an integer between 1 and 7, corresponding to the seven browser font sizes, and a color value (as either a hexadecimal triplet or color constant name) for the designated text.

The final two string methods let you create an anchor and a link out of a string. The *string*.anchor() method uses its parameter to create a name for the anchor. Thus, the following expression

```
    "Table of Contents".anchor("toc")
```

evaluates to

```
    <a name="toc">Table of Contents</a>
```

In a similar fashion, the *string*.link() method expects a valid location or URL as its parameter, creating a genuine HTML link out of the string:

```
"Back to Home".link("index.html")
```

This evaluates to the following:

```
<a href="index.html">Back to Home</a>
```

The primary reason that we rarely, if ever, use these methods in contemporary web site scripting is that we endeavor to separate development layers — in this case, HTML structure from CSS presentation and from JavaScript behavior. The more we keep these layers apart, the more modular and efficient development, debugging, and modification will be. For example, if all the font size and color details are specified in the style sheet, and not hard-coded in to HTML or JavaScript, then the appearance of the text on a page can be changed independently of the page's markup and behavior, and by different personnel with different skill sets. Similarly, it makes sense to keep markup in the HTML document and to enable JavaScript to operate on that markup, but not to stipulate it unless absolutely necessary.

Changing the cosmetic appearance of a page by changing its markup is a very "90s" thing to do. It relies on the default styling of the browser for a given tag, instead of taking responsibility for styling in one's own stylesheet. A modern script will change the appearance of an element by assigning an id or className, and letting the stylesheet determine how that will be presented.

URL String Encoding and Decoding

When browsers and servers communicate, some non-alphanumeric characters that we take for granted (such as spaces) cannot make the journey in their native form. Only a narrower set of letters, numbers, and punctuation is allowed. To accommodate the rest, the characters must be encoded with a special symbol (%) and their hexadecimal ASCII values. For example, the space character is hex 20 (ASCII decimal 32). When encoded, it looks like %20. You may have seen this symbol in browser history lists or URLs.

JavaScript includes two functions, encodeURIComponent() and decodeURIComponent(), that offer instant conversion of whole strings. To convert a plain string to one with these escape codes, use the escape function, as in

```
encodeURIComponent("Howdy Pardner"); // result = "Howdy%20Pardner"
```

The decodeURIComponent() function converts the escape codes into human-readable form.

Cross-Reference
Both of these functions are covered in Chapter 24, "Global Functions and Statements." ■

The Math, Number, and Boolean Objects

The introduction to data types and values in Chapter 8's tutorial scratched the surface of JavaScript's numeric and Boolean powers. In this chapter, you look more closely at JavaScript's way of working with numbers and Boolean data.

Math often frightens away budding programmers. As you've seen so far in this book, however, you don't really have to be a math genius to program in JavaScript. The powers described in this chapter are here when you need them — if you need them. So if math is not your strong suit, don't freak out over the terminology here.

An important point to remember about the objects described in this chapter is that (like string values and string objects) numbers and Booleans are both values and objects. Fortunately for script writers, the differentiation is rarely, if ever, a factor, unless you get into some very sophisticated programming. To those who actually write the JavaScript interpreters inside the browsers we use, the distinctions are vital.

For most scripters, the information about numeric data types and conversions, as well as the Math object, are important to know.

Numbers in JavaScript

More powerful programming languages have many different kinds of numbers, each related to the amount of memory the number occupies in the computer. Managing all these different types may be fun for some, but it gets in the way of quick scripting. A JavaScript number has only two possibilities. It can be an integer or a floating-point value. An *integer* is any whole number within a humongous range that does not have any fractional part. Integers never contain a decimal point in their representation. *Floating-point numbers* in JavaScript spread across the same range, but they are represented with a decimal point and some fractional value. If you are an experienced programmer, refer to the discussion about the Number object later in this chapter to see how the JavaScript number type lines up with the numeric data types you use in other programming environments.

Integers and floating-point numbers

Deep inside a computer, the microprocessor has an easier time performing math on integer values compared to any number with a decimal value tacked onto it. The microprocessor must go through extra work to add even two such floating-point numbers. We, as scripters, are unfortunately saddled with this historical baggage and must be conscious of the type of number used in certain calculations.

Most internal values generated by JavaScript, such as index values and length properties, consist of integers. Floating-point numbers usually come into play as the result of the division of numeric values, special values such as pi, and human-entered values such as dollars and cents. Fortunately, JavaScript is forgiving if you try to perform math operations on mixed numeric data types. Notice how the following examples resolve to the appropriate data type:

```
3 + 4 = 7 // integer result
3 + 4.1 = 7.1 // floating-point result
3.9 + 4.1 = 8 // integer result
```

Of the three examples, perhaps only the last result is unexpected. When two floating-point numbers yield a whole number, the result is rendered as an integer.

When dealing with floating-point numbers, be aware that not all browser versions return the precise same value down to the last digit to the right of the decimal. For example, the following table shows the result of 8/9 as calculated by various scriptable browsers, and converted for string display:

NN3 & NN4	.8888888888888888
NN6+/Moz+/Safari+/Opera+/Chrome+	0.8888888888888888
WinIE3	0.888888888888889
WinIE4+	0.8888888888888888

Clearly, from this display, you don't want to use floating-point math in JavaScript browsers to plan space flight trajectories or other highly accurate mission-critical calculations. Even for everyday math, however, you need to be cognizant of floating-point errors that accrue in PC arithmetic.

In Navigator, JavaScript relies on the operating system's floating-point math for its own math. Operating systems that offer accuracy to as many places to the right of the decimal as JavaScript displays are exceedingly rare. As you can detect from the preceding table, modern browsers agree about how many digits to display and how to perform internal rounding for this display. That's good for the math, but not particularly helpful when you need to display numbers in a specific format.

Until you get to IE5.5, Mozilla-based browsers, and other W3C-compatible browsers, JavaScript does not offer built-in facilities for formatting the results of floating-point arithmetic. (For modern browsers, see the Number object later in this chapter for formatting methods.) Listing 16-1 demonstrates a generic formatting routine for positive values, plus a specific call that turns a value into a dollar value. Remove the comments, and the routine is fairly compact.

Cross-Reference

The function to assign event handlers throughout the code in this chapter, and much of the book, is addEvent(), a cross-browser event handler explained in detail in Chapter 32, "Event Objects." ■

LISTING 16-1

A Generic Number-Formatting Routine

HTML: jsb-16-01.html

```html
<!DOCTYPE html>
<html>
  <head>
    <meta http-equiv="content-type" content="text/html;charset=utf-8">
    <title>Number Formatting</title>
    <script type="text/javascript" src="../jsb-global.js"></script>
    <script type="text/javascript" src="jsb-16-01.js"></script>
  </head>
  <body>
    <h1>How to Make Money</h1>
    <form>
      <p>
        <label for="entry">Enter a positive floating point value or arithmetic
        expression to be converted to a currency format:</label>
      </p>
      <p>
        <input type="text" id="entry" name="entry" value="1/3">
        <input type="button" id="dollars" value="&gt; Dollars and Cents &gt;">
        <input type="text" id="result" name="result">
      </p>
    </form>
  </body>
</html>
```

JavaScript: jsb-16-01.js

```javascript
// initialize when the page has loaded
addEvent(window, 'load', initialize);

function initialize()
{
   // do this only if the browser can handle DOM methods
   if (document.getElementById)
   {
      // point to critical elements
      var oButton = document.getElementById('dollars');
      var oEntry = document.getElementById('entry');
      var oResult = document.getElementById('result');

         // if they all exist...
         if (oButton && oEntry && oResult)
```

continued

LISTING 16-1   *(continued)*

```
        {
            // apply behavior to button
            oButton.onclick =
                function() { oResult.value = dollarize(oEntry.value); }
        }
    }
}
// turn incoming expression into a dollar value
function dollarize(expr)
{
    return "$" + format(expr,2);
}


// generic positive number decimal formatting function
function format(expr, decplaces)
{
    // evaluate the incoming expression
    var val = eval(expr);

    // raise the value by power of 10 times the number of decimal places;
    // round to an integer; convert to string
    var str = "" + Math.round(val * Math.pow(10, decplaces));

    // pad small value strings with zeros to the left of rounded number
    while (str.length <= decplaces)
    {
        str = "0" + str;
    }

    // establish location of decimal point
    var decpoint = str.length - decplaces;

    // assemble final result from:
    // (a) the string up to the position of the decimal point;
    // (b) the decimal point; and
    // (c) the balance of the string. Return finished product.
    return str.substring(0,decpoint) + "." + str.substring(decpoint, str.length);
}
```

This routine may seem like a great deal of work, but it's essential if your application relies on floating-point values and specific formatting for all browsers.

Note

The global `eval()` method used in this example is not a terrific choice for production work. Because `eval()` faithfully interprets all JavaScript expressions, it lays bare all the details of the script, its object and variable values, and the DOM, for the savvy visitor to peruse and act upon. The JavaScript language has deliberately been constrained to prevent security breaches on the client computer, but `XMLHttpRequest` gives access to the server. It's not appropriate to give strangers an open and unfiltered `eval()` input. ∎

You can also enter floating-point numbers with exponents. An exponent is signified by the letter *e* (upper- or lowercase), followed by a sign (+ or −) and the exponent value. Here are examples of floating-point values expressed as exponents:

```
1e6  // 1,000,000 (the "+" symbol is optional on positive exponents)
1e-4 // 0.0001 (plus some error further to the right of the decimal)
-4e-3 // -0.004
```

For values between 1e-5 and 1e15, JavaScript renders numbers without exponents (although you can force a number to display in exponential notation in modern browsers). All other values outside these boundaries return with exponential notation in all browsers.

Hexadecimal and octal integers

JavaScript enables you to work with values in decimal (base-10), hexadecimal (base-16), and octal (base-8) formats. You have only a few rules to follow when dealing with any of these values.

Decimal values cannot begin with a leading 0. Therefore, if your page asks users to enter decimal values that begin with a 0, your script must strip those zeros from the input string, or use the number parsing global functions (described in the next section), before performing any math on the values.

Hexadecimal integer values are expressed with a leading 0x or 0X. (That's a zero, not the letter *o*.) The A through F values can appear in upper- or lowercase, as you prefer. Here are some hex values:

```
0X2B
0X1a
0xcc
```

Don't confuse the hex values used in arithmetic with the hexadecimal values used in color property specifications for web documents. Those values are expressed in a special *hexadecimal triplet* format, which begins with a crosshatch symbol followed by the three hex values bunched together (such as #c0c0c0).

Octal values are represented by a leading 0 followed by any digits between 0 and 7. Octal values consist only of integers.

You are free to mix and match base values in arithmetic expressions, but JavaScript renders all results in decimal form. For conversions to other number bases, you have to employ a user-defined function in your script. Listing 16-2, for example, is a function that converts any decimal value from 0 to 255 into a JavaScript hexadecimal value.

LISTING 16-2

Decimal-to-Hexadecimal Converter Function

```
function toHex(dec)
{
    hexChars = "0123456789ABCDEF";
    if (dec > 255)
    {
```

continued

LISTING 16-2   *(continued)*

```
      return null;
   }
   var i = dec % 16;
   var j = (dec - i) / 16;
   result = "0X";
   result += hexChars.charAt(j);
   result += hexChars.charAt(i);
   return result;
}
```

The `toHex()` conversion function assumes that the value passed to the function is a decimal integer. If you simply need a hexadecimal representation of a number in string format, see the `toString()` method in Chapter 15, "The String Object."

Converting strings to numbers

What is missing so far from this discussion is a way to convert a number represented as a string to a number with which the JavaScript arithmetic operators can work. Before you get too concerned about this, be aware that most JavaScript operators and math methods gladly accept string representations of numbers and handle them without complaint. You will run into data type incompatibilities most frequently when trying to accomplish addition with the + operator (which is also the string concatenation operator). Also know that if you perform math operations on values retrieved from form text boxes, those object `value` properties are strings. Therefore, in many cases, you need to convert those string values to a number type for math operations.

Conversion to numbers requires one of two JavaScript functions:

```
parseInt(string [,radix])
parseFloat(string  [,radix])
```

These functions are inspired by the Java language. The term *parsing* has many implied meanings in programming. One meaning is the same as *extracting*. The `parseInt()` function returns whatever integer value it can extract from the string passed to it; the `parseFloat()` function returns the floating-point number that can be extracted from the string. Here are some examples and their resulting values:

```
parseInt("42")           // result = 42
parseInt("42.33")        // result = 42
parseFloat("42.33")      // result = 42.33
parseFloat("42")         // result = 42
parseFloat("fred")       // result = NaN (Not a Number)
```

Because the `parseFloat()` function can also work with an integer and return an integer value, you may prefer using this function in scripts that have to deal with either kind of number, depending on the string entered into a text field by a user.

An optional second parameter to both functions enables you to specify the base of the number represented by the string. This comes in handy particularly when you need a decimal number from a string that starts with one or more zeros. Normally, the leading zero indicates an octal value. But if you force the conversion to recognize the string value as a decimal, it is converted the way you expect:

```
parseInt("010")           // result = 8
parseInt("010",10)        // result = 10
parseInt("F2")            // result = NaN
parseInt("F2", 16)        // result = 242
```

Use these functions wherever you need the integer or floating-point value. For example:

```
var result = 3 + parseInt("3");      // result = 6
var ageVal = parseInt(document.forms[0].age.value);
```

The latter technique ensures that the string value of this property is converted to a number, although you should do more data validation — see Chapter 46, "Data-Entry Validation" (on the CD-ROM) — before trying any math on a user-entered value.

Both the parseInt() and parseFloat() methods start working on the first character of a string and continue until there are no more numbers or decimal characters. That's why you can use them on strings — such as the one returned by the navigator.appVersion property (for example, 6.0 (Windows; en-US)) — to obtain just the leading, numeric part of the string. If the string does not begin with an acceptable character, the methods return NaN (not a number).

Converting numbers to strings

If you attempt to pass a numeric data type value to many of the string methods discussed in Chapter 15, JavaScript complains. Therefore, you should convert any number to a string before, for example, you find out how many digits make up a number.

Several ways exist to force conversion from any numeric value to a string. The old-fashioned way is to precede the number with an empty string and the concatenation operator. For example, assume that a variable named dollars contains the integer value of 2500. To use the string object's length property (discussed later in this chapter) to find out how many digits the number has, use this construction:

```
("" + dollars).length     // result = 4
```

The parentheses force JavaScript to evaluate the concatenation before attempting to extract the length property.

A more elegant way is to use the toString() method. Construct such statements as you would to invoke any object's method. For example, to convert the dollars variable value to a string, use this statement:

```
dollars.toString()     // result = "2500"
```

This method has one added power in modern browsers: You can specify a number base for the string representation of the number. Called the *radix*, the base number is added as a parameter to the method name. Here is an example of creating a numeric value for conversion to its hexadecimal equivalent as a string:

```
var x = 30;
var y = x.toString(16);     // result = "1e"
```

Use a parameter of 2 for binary results and 8 for octal. The default is base 10. Be careful not to confuse these conversions with true numeric conversions. You cannot use results from the toString() method as numeric operands in other statements.

Finally, in IE5.5+, Mozilla-based browsers, and other W3C browsers, three additional methods of the Number object — toExponential(), toFixed(), and toPrecision() — return string versions of numbers formatted according to the rules and parameters passed to the methods. We describe these in detail later in this chapter.

When a number isn't a number

In a couple of examples in the previous section, you probably noticed that the result of some operations was a value named NaN. That value is not a string, but rather a special value that stands for Not a Number. For example, if you try to convert the string "joe" to an integer with parseFloat(), the function cannot possibly complete the operation. It reports back that the source string, when converted, is not a number.

When you design an application that requests user input or retrieves data from a server-side database, you cannot be guaranteed that a value you need to be numeric is, or can be converted to, a number. If that's the case, you need to see if the value is a number before performing a math operation on it. JavaScript provides a special global function, isNaN(), that enables you to test the "numberness" of a value. The function returns true if the value is not a number and false if it is a number. For example, you can examine a form field that should be a number:

```
var ageEntry = parseInt(document.forms[0].age.value);
    if (isNaN(ageEntry))
    {
        alert("Try entering your age again.");
    }
```

Math Object

Whenever you need to perform math that is more demanding than simple arithmetic, look through the list of Math object methods for the solution.

Syntax

Accessing Math object properties and methods:

```
Math.property
Math.method(value [, value])
```

Compatibility: WinIE3+, MacIE3+, NN2+, Moz+, Safari+, Opera+, Chrome+

About this object

In addition to the typical arithmetic operations (covered in detail in Chapter 22, "JavaScript Operators"), JavaScript includes more advanced mathematical powers that you can access in a way that may seem odd to you if you have not programmed in true object-oriented environments before. Although most arithmetic takes place on the fly (such as var result = 2 + 2), the rest requires use of the

JavaScript internal Math object (with a capital "M"). The Math object brings with it several properties (which behave like some other languages' constants) and many methods (which behave like some other languages' math functions).

The way you use the Math object in statements is the same way you use any JavaScript object: You create a reference beginning with the Math object's name, a period, and the name of the property or method you need:

```
Math.property | method([parameter]. . . [,parameter])
```

Property references return built-in values, such as pi. Method references require one or more values to be sent as parameters of the method. Every method returns a result.

Properties

JavaScript Math object properties represent a number of valuable constant values in math. Table 16-1 shows you those methods and their values, as displayed to 16 decimal places.

Because these property expressions return their constant values, you use them in your regular arithmetic expressions. For example, to obtain the circumference of a circle whose diameter is in variable d, employ this statement:

```
circumference = d * Math.PI;
```

Perhaps the most common mistakes scripters make with these properties are failing to capitalize the Math object name and observing the case-sensitivity of property names.

TABLE 16-1

JavaScript Math Properties

Property	Value	Description
Math.E	2.718281828459045091	Euler's constant
Math.LN2	0.6931471805599452862	Natural log of 2
Math.LN10	2.302585092994045901	Natural log of 10
Math.LOG2E	1.442695040888963387	Log base-2 of E
Math.LOG10E	0.4342944819032518167	Log base-10 of E
Math.PI	3.141592653589793116	π
Math.SQRT1_2	0.7071067811865475727	Square root of 0.5
Math.SQRT2	1.414213562373095145	Square root of 2

Methods

Methods make up the balance of JavaScript Math object powers. With the exception of the Math.random() method, all Math object methods take one or more values as parameters. Typical trigonometric methods operate on the single values passed as parameters; others determine which of the numbers passed along are the highest or lowest of the group. The `Math.random()` method takes no parameters, but returns a randomized, floating-point value between 0 and 1. Table 16-2 lists all the `Math` object methods with their syntax, and descriptions of the values they return.

TABLE 16-2

Math Object Methods

Method Syntax	Returns
`Math.abs(val)`	Absolute value of *val*
`Math.acos(val)`	Arc cosine (in radians) of *val*
`Math.asin(val)`	Arc sine (in radians) of *val*
`Math.atan(val)`	Arc tangent (in radians) of *val*
`Math.atan2(val1, val2)`	Angle of polar coordinates *x* and *y*
`Math.ceil(val)`	Next integer greater than or equal to *val*
`Math.cos(val)`	Cosine of *val*
`Math.exp(val)`	Euler's constant to the power of *val*
`Math.floor(val)`	Next integer less than or equal to *val*
`Math.log(val)`	Natural logarithm (base e) of *val*
`Math.max(val1, val2)`	The greater of *val1* or *val2*
`Math.min(val1, val2)`	The lesser of *val1* or *val2*
`Math.pow(val1, val2)`	*Val1* to the power of *val2*
`Math.random()`	Random number between 0 and 1
`Math.round(val)`	N+1 when *val* >= n.5; otherwise N
`Math.sin(val)`	Sine (in radians) of *val*
`Math.sqrt(val)`	Square root of *val*
`Math.tan(val)`	Tangent (in radians) of *val*

Although HTML may not exactly be a graphic artist's dream environment, it is possible to use JavaScript trig functions to obtain a series of values for HTML-generated charting. Since the advent of positionable elements, scripters have been able to apply their knowledge of using these functions to define fancy trajectories for flying elements. For scripters who are not trained in programming, math is often a major stumbling block. But as you've seen so far, you can accomplish a great deal with JavaScript by using simple arithmetic and a little bit of logic — leaving the heavy-duty math for those who love it.

Creating random numbers

One of the handiest methods in the `Math` object is `Math.random()`, which returns a random floating-point value between 0 and 1. If you design a script to act like a card game, you need random integers between 1 and 52; for dice, the range is 1 to 6 per die. To generate a random integer between zero and any top value (n), use the following formula (where n is the top number):

```
Math.floor(Math.random() * n)
```

This produces integers between 0 and n-1. To produce the spread between 1 and n, either add 1 or change `floor()` to `ceil()`:

```
Math.floor(Math.random() * n) + 1
Math.ceil(Math.random() * n)
```

To generate random numbers within a range that starts somewhere other than zero, use this formula:

```
Math.floor(Math.random() * (n - m + 1)) + m
```

Here, m is the lowest possible integer value of the range, and n equals the top number of the range. For the dice game, the formula for each die is

```
newDieValue = Math.floor(Math.random() * 6) + 1;
```

Math object shortcut

In Chapter 21, "Control Structures and Exception Handling," you see details about a JavaScript construction that enables you to simplify the way you address multiple `Math` object properties and methods in statements. The trick is to use the `with` statement.

In a nutshell, the `with` statement tells JavaScript that the next group of statements (inside the braces) refers to a particular object. In the case of the `Math` object, the basic construction looks like this:

```
with (Math)
{
    //statements
}
```

For all intervening statements, you can omit the specific references to the `Math` object. Compare the long reference way of calculating the area of a circle (with a radius of six units)

```
result = Math.pow(6,2) * Math.PI;
```

to the shortcut reference way:

```
with (Math)
{
    result = pow(6,2) * PI;
}
```

Though the latter occupies more lines of code, the object references are shorter and more natural to read. For a longer series of calculations involving `Math` object properties and methods, the `with` construction saves keystrokes and reduces the likelihood of a case-sensitive mistake with the object name in a reference. You can also include other full-object references within the with construction; JavaScript attempts to attach the object name only to those references lacking an object name. On the downside, the with construction is not particularly efficient in JavaScript because it must perform a lot of internal tracking in order to work. So, it's best not to use it in loops that iterate a large number of times.

Number Object

Properties	Methods
constructor	toExponential()
MAX_VALUE	toFixed()
MIN_VALUE	toLocaleString()
NaN	toString()
NEGATIVE_INFINITY	toPrecision()
POSITIVE_INFINITY	valueOf()
prototype	

Syntax

Creating a Number object:

```
var val = new Number(number);
```

Accessing number and Number object properties and methods:

```
number.property | method([parameters])
Number.property | method([parameters])
```

Compatibility: WinIE4+, MacIE4+, NN3+, Moz+, Safari+, Opera+, Chrome+

About this object

The Number object is rarely used because (for the most part) JavaScript satisfies day-to-day numeric needs with a plain number value. But the Number object contains some information and power of value to serious programmers.

First on the docket are properties that define the ranges for numbers in the language. The largest number is 1.79E+308; the smallest number is 2.22E-308. Any number larger than the maximum is POSITIVE_INFINITY; any number smaller than the minimum is NEGATIVE_INFINITY. Rarely will you accidentally encounter these values.

More to the point of a JavaScript object, however, is the `prototype` property. Chapter 15 shows how to add a method to a `string` object's prototype, such that every newly created object contains that method. The same goes for the `Number.prototype` property. If you have a need to add common functionality to every number object, this is where to do it. This prototype facility is unique to full-fledged number objects and does not apply to plain number values. For experienced programmers who care about such matters, JavaScript number objects and values are defined internally as IEEE double-precision 64-bit values.

Properties

constructor

(See `string.constructor` in Chapter 15)

MAX_VALUE
MIN_VALUE
NEGATIVE_INFINITY
POSITIVE_INFINITY

Value: Number   Read-Only

Compatibility: WinIE4+, MacIE4+, NN3+, Moz+, Safari+, Opera+, Chrome+

The `Number.MAX_VALUE` and `Number.MIN_VALUE` properties belong to the static `Number` object. They represent constants for the largest and smallest possible positive numbers that JavaScript (and ECMAScript) can work with. Their actual values are $1.7976931348623157 \infty 10^{308}$, and $5 \infty 10^{-324}$, respectively. A number that falls outside the range of allowable numbers is equal to the constant `Number.POSITIVE_INFINITY` or `Number.NEGATIVE_INFINITY`.

Example

Enter each of the four `Number` object expressions into the top text field of The Evaluator (Chapter 4, "Javascript Essentials") to see how the browser reports each value.

```
Number.MAX_VALUE
Number.MIN_VALUE
Number.NEGATIVE_INFINITY
Number.POSITIVE_INFINITY
```

Related Items: NaN property; `isNaN()` global function

NaN

Value: NaN   Read-Only

Compatibility: WinIE4+, MacIE4+, NN3+, Moz+, Safari+, Opera+, Chrome+

The `NaN` property is a constant that JavaScript uses to report when a number-related function or method attempts to work on a value other than a number, or when the result is something other than a number. You encounter the `NaN` value, most commonly as the result of the `parseInt()` and `parseFloat()` functions, whenever a string undergoing conversion to a number lacks a numeral as the first character. Use the `isNaN()` global function to see if a value is an `NaN` value.

numberObject.prototype

Example

See the discussion of the isNaN() function in Chapter 24.

Related Items: isNaN() global function

prototype

(See String.prototype in Chapter 15)

Methods

```
number.toExponential(fractionDigits)
number.toFixed(fractionDigits)
number.toPrecision(precisionDigits)
```

Returns: String

Compatibility: WinIE5.5+, MacIE-, NN6+, Moz+, Safari+, Opera+, Chrome+

These three methods let scripts control the formatting of numbers for display as string text. Each method has a unique purpose, but they all return strings. You should perform all math operations as unformatted number objects because the values have the most precision. Only after you are ready to display the results should you use one of these methods to convert the number to a string for display as body text or assignment to a text field.

The toExponential() method forces a number to display in exponential notation, even if the number is in the range in which JavaScript normally uses standard notation. The parameter is an integer specifying how many digits to the right of the decimal should be returned. All digits that far to the right of the decimal are returned, even if they are zero. For example, if a variable contains the numeric value 345, applying toExponential(3) to that value yields 3.450e+2, which is JavaScript's exponential notation for $3.45 \infty 10^2$.

Use the toFixed() method when you want to format a number with a specific number of digits to the right of the decimal. This is the method you use, for instance, to display the results of a financial calculation in units and hundredths of units (for example, dollars and cents). The parameter to the method is an integer indicating the number of digits to be displayed to the right of the decimal. If the number being formatted has more numbers to the right of the decimal than the number of digits specified by the parameter, the method rounds the rightmost visible digit — but only with respect to the unrounded value of the next digit. For example, the value 123.455 fixed to two digits to the right of the decimal is rounded up to 123.46. But if the starting value is 123.4549, the method ignores the 9 and sees that the 4 to the right of the 5 should be rounded down; therefore, the result is 123.45. Do not consider the toFixed() method to be an accurate rounder of numbers; however, it does a satisfactory job in most cases.

The final method is toPrecision(), which enables you to define how many total digits of a number (including digits to the left and right of the decimal) to display. In other words, you define the precision of a number. The following list demonstrates the results of several parameter values signifying a variety of precisions:

```
var num = 123.45
num.toPrecision(1)      // result = 1e+2
num.toPrecision(2)      // result = 1.2e+2
```

```
num.toPrecision(3)    // result = 123
num.toPrecision(4)    // result = 123.5
num.toPrecision(5)    // result = 123.45
num.toPrecision(6)    // result = 123.450
```

Notice that the same kind of rounding can occur with toPrecision() as it does for toFixed().

Example

You can use The Evaluator (see Chapter 4) to experiment with all three of these methods, with a variety of parameter values. Before invoking any method, be sure to assign a numeric value to one of the built-in global variables in The Evaluator (a through z).

```
a = 10/3
a.toFixed(4)
"$" + a.toFixed(2)
```

None of these methods works with number literals (for example, 123.toExponential(2) does not work).

Related Items: Math object

number.toLocaleString()

Returns: String

Compatibility: WinIE5.5+, MacIE5+, NN6+, Moz+, Safari+, Opera+, Chrome+

The number.toLocaleString() method returns a string value version of the current number in a format that may vary according to a browser's locale settings. According to the ECMA Edition 5 standard, browsers have some leeway in determining exactly how the toLocaleString() method should return a string value that conforms with the language standard of the client system or browser.

Related Items: number.toFixed(), number.toString() methods

number.toString([radix])

Returns: String

Compatibility: WinIE4+, MacIE4+, NN4+, Moz+, Safari+, Opera+, Chrome+

The number.toString() method returns a string value version of the current number. The default radix parameter (10) converts the value to base-10 notation if the original number isn't already of that type. Or, you can specify other number bases (for example, 2 for binary, 16 for hexadecimal) to convert the original number to the other base — as a string, not a number — for further calculation.

Example

Use The Evaluator (Chapter 4) to experiment with the toString() method. Assign the number 12 to the variable a and see how the number is converted to strings in a variety of number bases:

booleanObject

```
a = 12
a.toString()      // base 10
a.toString(2)
a.toString(16)
```

Related Items: toLocaleString() method

number.valueOf()

(See string.valueOf() in Chapter 15)

Boolean Object

Properties	Methods
constructor	toString()
prototype	valueOf()

Syntax

Creating a Boolean object:

```
var val = new Boolean(BooleanValue);
```

Accessing Boolean object properties:

```
BooleanObject.property | method
```

Compatibility: WinIE4+, MacIE4+, NN3+, Moz+, Safari+, Opera+, Chrome+

About this object

You work with Boolean values a lot in JavaScript — especially as the result of conditional tests. Just as string values benefit from association with string objects, and their properties and methods, so, too, do Boolean values receive aid from the Boolean object. For example, when you display a Boolean value in a text box, the "true" or "false" string is provided by the Boolean object's toString() method, so you don't have to invoke it directly.

The only time you need to even think about a Boolean object is if you wish to attach some property or method to Boolean objects that you create with the new Boolean() constructor. Parameter values for the constructor include the string versions of the values, numbers (0 for false; any other integer for true), and expressions that evaluate to a Boolean value. Any such new Boolean object is imbued with the new properties or methods you add to the prototype property of the core Boolean object.

For details about the properties and methods of the Boolean object, see the corresponding listings for the String object in Chapter 15.

The Date Object

P erhaps the most untapped power of JavaScript is its date and time handling. Scripters passed over the Date object with good cause in the early days of JavaScript, because in earlier versions of scriptable browsers, significant bugs and platform-specific anomalies made date and time programming hazardous without significant testing. Even with the improved bug situation, working with dates requires a working knowledge of the world's time zones and their relationships with the standard reference point, known as Greenwich Mean Time (GMT) or Coordinated Universal Time (abbreviated UTC).

Now that date- and time-handling has stabilized in modern browsers, I hope more scripters look into incorporating these kinds of calculations into their pages. In Chapter 57, "Application: Intelligent 'Updated' Flags," on the CD-ROM, for example, I show you an application that lets your web site highlight the areas that have been updated since each visitor's last surf ride through your pages — an application that relies heavily on date arithmetic and time-zone conversion.

Before getting to the JavaScript part of date discussions, however, the chapter summarizes key facts about time zones and their impact on scripting date and time on a browser. If you're not sure what GMT and UTC mean, the following section is for you.

Time Zones and GMT

By international agreement, the world is divided into distinct time zones that allow the inhabitants of each zone to say with confidence that when the Sun appears directly overhead, it is roughly noon, squarely in the middle of the day. The current time in the zone is what we set our clocks to — the local time.

That's fine when your entire existence and scope of life go no further than the width of your own time zone. But with instant communication among all parts of the world, your scope reaches well beyond local time. Periodically you must be aware of the local time in other zones. After all, if you live in New York, you don't want to wake up someone in Los Angeles before dawn with a phone call from your office.

Note
For the rest of this section, we speak of the Sun "moving" as if Earth were the center of the solar system. We do so for the convenience of our daily perception of the Sun arcing across what appears to us as a stationary sky. In point of fact, we believe Copernicus's theories, so please delete that email you were about to send us. ■

From the point of view of the time zone over which the Sun is positioned at any given instant, all time zones to the east have already had their noon, so it is later in the day for them — one hour later per time zone (except for those few time zones offset by fractions of an hour). That's why when U.S. television networks broadcast simultaneously to the eastern and central time zones, the announced schedule for a program is "10 eastern, 9 central."

Many international businesses must coordinate time schedules of far-flung events. Doing so and taking into account the numerous time zone differences (not to mention seasonal national variations, such as daylight saving time) would be a nightmare. To help everyone out, a standard reference point was devised: the time zone running through the celestial observatory at Greenwich (pronounced GREN-itch), England. This time zone is called Greenwich Mean Time, or GMT for short. The "mean" part comes from the fact that on the exact opposite side of the globe (through the Pacific Ocean) is the international date line, another world standard that decrees where the first instance of the next calendar day appears on the planet. Thus, GMT is located at the middle, or mean, of the full circuit of the day. Not that many years ago, GMT was given another abbreviation that is not based on any one language of the planet. The abbreviation is UTC (pronounced as its letters: yu-tee-see), and the English version is Coordinated Universal Time. Whenever you see UTC, it is for all practical purposes the same as GMT.

If your personal computer's system clock is set correctly, the machine ticks away in GMT time. But because you set your local time zone in the appropriate control panel, all file time stamps and clock displays are in your local time. The machine knows what the offset time is between your local time and GMT. For daylight savings time, you may have to check a preference setting so that the offset is adjusted accordingly; in Windows-based operating systems, the system knows when the changeover occurs and prompts you if changing the offset is okay. In any case, if you travel across time zones with a laptop, you should change the computer's time zone setting, not its clock.

JavaScript's inner handling of date and time works a lot like the PC clock (on which your programs rely). Date values that you generate in a script are stored internally in GMT time; however, almost all the displays and extracted values are in the local time of the visitor (not the web site server). And remember that the date values are created on the visitor's machine by virtue of your script's generating that value — you don't send "living" date objects to the client from the server. This concept is perhaps the most difficult to grasp as you work with JavaScript date and time.

Whenever you program time and date in JavaScript for a public web page, you must take the world-view. This view requires knowing that the visitor's computer settings determine the accuracy of the conversion between GMT and local time. You'll also have to do some testing by changing your PC's clock to times in other parts of the world and making believe you are temporarily in those remote locations, which isn't always easy to do. It reminds me (Danny) of the time I was visiting Sydney, Australia. I was turning in for the night and switched on the television in the hotel. This hotel received a live satellite relay of a long-running U.S. television program, *Today*. The program broadcast from New York was for the morning of the same day I was just finishing in Sydney. Yes, this time zone stuff can make your head hurt.

The Date Object

Like a handful of other objects in JavaScript and the document object models, there is a distinction between the single, static `Date` object that exists in every window (or frame) and a date object that contains a specific date and time. The static `Date` object (uppercase *D*) is used in only a few cases: Primarily to create a new instance of a date and to invoke a couple of methods that the `Date` object offers for the sake of some generic conversions.

Most of your date and time work, however, is with instances of the `Date` object. These instances are referred to generically as date objects (lowercase *d*). Each date object is a snapshot of an exact millisecond in time, whether it be for the instant at which you generate the object or for a specific time in the past or future you need for calculations. If you need to have a live clock ticking away, your scripts will repeatedly create new date objects to grab up-to-the-millisecond snapshots of your computer's clock. To show the time on the page, extract the hours, minutes, and seconds from the snapshot date object, and then display the values as you like (for example, a digital readout, a graphical bar chart, and so on). By and large, it is the methods of a date object instance that your scripts invoke to read or modify individual components of a date object (for example, the month or hour).

Despite its name, every date object contains information about date and time. Therefore, even if you're concerned only about the date part of an object's data, time data is standing by as well. As you learn in a bit, the time element can catch you off-guard for some operations.

Creating a date object

The statement that asks JavaScript to make an object for your script uses the special object construction keyword `new`. The basic syntax for generating a new date object is as follows:

```
var dateObjectName = new Date([parameters]);
```

The date object evaluates to an object data type rather than to some string or numeric value.

With the date object's reference safely tucked away in the variable name, you access all date-oriented methods in the dot-syntax fashion with which you're already familiar:

```
var result = dateObjectName.method();
```

With variables, such as `result`, your scripts perform calculations or displays of the date object's data (some methods extract pieces of the date and time data from the object). If you then want to put some new value into the date object (such as adding a year to the date object), you assign the new value to the object by way of the method that lets you set the value:

```
dateObjectName.method(newValue);
```

This example doesn't look like the typical JavaScript assignment statement, which has an equals sign operator. But this statement is the way in which methods that set date object data work.

You cannot get very far into scripting dates without digging into time zone arithmetic. Although JavaScript may render the string equivalent of a date object in your local time zone, the internal storage is strictly GMT.

Even though you haven't yet seen details of a date object's methods, here is how you use two of them to add one year to today's date:

```
var oneDate = new Date();          // creates object with current GMT date
var theYear = oneDate.getYear();   // stores the current four-digit year
```

```
theYear = theYear + 1;        // theYear now is next year
oneDate.setYear(theYear);     // the new year value now in the object
```

At the end of this sequence, the `oneDate` object automatically adjusts all the other date components for the next year's date. The day of the week, for example, will be different, and JavaScript takes care of that for you, should you need to extract that data. With next year's data in the `oneDate` object, you may now want to extract that new date as a string value for display in a field on the page or submit it quietly to a CGI program on the server.

The issue of parameters for creating a new date object is a bit complex, mostly because of the flexibility that JavaScript offers the scripter. Recall that the job of the `new Date()` statement is to create a place in memory for all data that a date needs to store. What is missing from that task is the data — what date and time to enter into that memory spot. That's where the parameters come in.

If you leave the parameters empty, JavaScript takes that to mean you want today's date and the current time to be assigned to that new date object. JavaScript isn't any smarter, of course, than the setting of the internal clock of your page visitor's personal computer. If the clock isn't correct, JavaScript won't do any better of a job identifying the date and time.

Note

Remember that when you create a new date object, it contains the current time as well. The fact that the current date may include a time of 16:03:19 (in 24-hour time) may throw off things, such as days-between-dates calculations. Be careful. ■

To create a date object for a specific date or time, you have five ways to send values as a parameter to the `new Date()` constructor function:

```
new Date("Month dd, yyyy hh:mm:ss")
new Date("Month dd, yyyy")
new Date(yy,mm,dd,hh,mm,ss)
new Date(yy,mm,dd)
new Date(milliseconds)
```

The first four variations break down into two styles — a long string versus a comma-delimited list of data — each with optional time settings. If you omit time settings, they are set to 0 (midnight) in the date object for whatever date you entered. You cannot omit date values from the parameters — every date object must have a real date attached to it, whether you need it or not.

In the long string versions, the month is spelled out in full in English. No abbreviations are allowed. The rest of the data is filled with numbers representing the date, year, hours, minutes, and seconds, even if the order is different from your local way of indicating dates. For single-digit values, you can use either a one- or two-digit version (such as 4:05:00). Colons separate hours, minutes, and seconds.

The short versions contain a non-quoted list of integer values in the order indicated. JavaScript cannot know that a 30 means the day if you accidentally place it in the month slot.

You use the last version only when you have the millisecond value of a date and time available. This generally occurs after some math arithmetic (described later in this chapter), leaving you with a date and time in millisecond format. To convert that numeric value to a date object, use the `new Date()` constructor. From the new date object created, you can retrieve more convenient values about the date and time.

Native object properties and methods

Like the String and Array objects, the Date object features a small handful of properties and methods that all native JavaScript objects have in common. On the property side, the Date object has a prototype property, which enables you to apply new properties and methods to every date object created in the current page. You can see examples of how this works in discussions of the prototype property for String and Array objects (Chapters 15 and 18, respectively). At the same time, every instance of a date object in modern browsers has a constructor property that references the constructor function that generated the object.

A date object has numerous methods that convert date object types to strings, most of which are more specific than the generic toString() one. The valueOf() method returns the millisecond integer that is stored for a particular date.

Date methods

The bulk of a date object's methods are for reading parts of the date and time information and for changing the date and time stored in the object. These two categories of methods are easily identifiable because they all begin with the word "get" or "set."

Table 17-1 lists all of the methods of both the static Date object and, by inheritance, date object instances. The list is impressive — some would say frightening — but there are patterns you should readily observe. Most methods deal with a single component of a date and time value: year, month, date, and so forth. Each block of "get" and "set" methods also has two sets of methods: one for the local date and time conversion of the date stored in the object; one for the actual UTC date stored in the object. After you see the patterns, the list should be more manageable. Unless otherwise noted, a method has been part of the Date object since the first generation of scriptable browsers, and is therefore also supported in newer browsers.

Deciding between using the UTC or local versions of the methods depends on several factors. If the browsers you must support go back to the beginning, you will be stuck with the local versions in any case. But even for newer browsers, activities, such as calculating the number of days between dates or creating a countdown timer for a quiz, won't care which set you use, but you must use the same set for all calculations. If you start mixing local and UTC versions of date methods, you'll be destined to get wrong answers. The UTC versions come in most handy when your date calculations must take into account the time zone of the client machine compared to some absolute in another time zone — calculating the time remaining to the chiming of Big Ben signifying the start of the New Year in London.

JavaScript maintains its date information in the form of a count of milliseconds (thousandths of a second) starting from January 1, 1970, in the GMT (UTC) time zone. Dates before that starting point are stored as negative values (but see the section on bugs and gremlins later in this chapter). Regardless of the country you are in or the date and time formats specified for your computer, the millisecond is the JavaScript universal measure of time. Any calculations that involve adding or subtracting times and dates should be performed in the millisecond values to ensure accuracy. Therefore, though you may never display the milliseconds value in a field or dialog box, your scripts will probably work with them from time to time in variables. To derive the millisecond equivalent for any date and time stored in a date object, use the dateObj.getTime() method, as in

```
var startDate = new Date();
var started = startDate.getTime();
```

TABLE 17-1

Date Object Methods

Method	Value Range	Description
dateObj.getFullYear()	1970–...	Specified year (NN4+, Moz1+, IE3+)
dateObj.getYear()	70–...	(See text of chapter)
dateObj.getMonth()	0–11	Month within the year (January = 0)
dateObj.getDate()	1–31	Date within the month
dateObj.getDay()	0–6	Day of week (Sunday = 0)
dateObj.getHours()	0–23	Hour of the day in 24-hour time
dateObj.getMinutes()	0–59	Minute of the specified hour
dateObj.getSeconds()	0–59	Second within the specified minute
dateObj.getTime()	0–...	Milliseconds since 1/1/70 00:00:00 GMT
dateObj.getMilliseconds()	0-999	Milliseconds since the previous full second (NN4+, Moz1+, IE3+)
dateObj.getUTCFullYear()	1970–...	Specified UTC year (NN4+, Moz1+, IE3+)
dateObj.getUTCMonth()	0–11	UTC month within the year (January = 0) (NN4+, Moz1+, IE3+)
dateObj.getUTCDate()	1–31	UTC date within the month (NN4+, Moz1+, IE3+)
dateObj.getUTCDay()	0–6	UTC day of week (Sunday = 0) (NN4+, Moz1+, IE3+)
dateObj.getUTCHours()	0–23	UTC hour of the day in 24-hour time (NN4+, Moz1+, IE3+)
dateObj.getUTCMinutes()	0–59	UTC minute of the specified hour (NN4+, Moz1+, IE3+)
dateObj.getUTCSeconds()	0–59	UTC second within the specified minute (NN4+, Moz1+, IE3+)
dateObj.getUTCMilliseconds()	0-999	UTC milliseconds since the previous full second (NN4+, Moz1+, IE3+)
dateObj.setYear(val)	1970–...	Be safe: always specify a four-digit year
dateObj.setFullYear(val)	1970–...	Specified year (NN4+, Moz1+, IE3+)
dateObj.setMonth(val)	0–11	Month within the year (January = 0)
dateObj.setDate(val)	1–31	Date within the month

Method	Value Range	Description
`dateObj.setDay(val)`	0–6	Day of week (Sunday = 0)
`dateObj.setHours(val)`	0–23	Hour of the day in 24-hour time
`dateObj.setMinutes(val)`	0–59	Minute of the specified hour
`dateObj.setSeconds(val)`	0–59	Second within the specified minute
`dateObj.setMilliseconds(val)`	0-999	Milliseconds since the previous full second (NN4+, Moz1+, IE3+)
`dateObj.setTime(val)`	0–...	Milliseconds since 1/1/70 00:00:00 GMT
`dateObj.setUTCFullYear(val)`	1970–...	Specified UTC year (NN4+, Moz1+, IE3+)
`dateObj.setUTCMonth(val)`	0–11	UTC month within the year (January = 0) (NN4+, Moz1+, IE3+)
`dateObj.setUTCDate(val)`	1–31	UTC date within the month (NN4+, Moz1+, IE3+)
`dateObj.setUTCDay(val)`	0–6	UTC day of week (Sunday = 0) (NN4+, Moz1+, IE3+)
`dateObj.setUTCHours(val)`	0–23	UTC hour of the day in 24-hour time (NN4+, Moz1+, IE3+)
`dateObj.setUTCMinutes(val)`	0–59	UTC minute of the specified hour (NN4+, Moz1+, IE3+)
`dateObj.setUTCSeconds(val)`	0–59	UTC second within the specified minute (NN4+, Moz1+, IE3+)
`dateObj.setUTCMilliseconds(val)`	0-999	UTC milliseconds since the previous full second (NN4+, Moz1+, IE3+)
`dateObj.getTimezoneOffset()`	0–...	Minutes offset from GMT/UTC
`dateObj.toDateString()`		Date-only string in a format determined by browser (WinIE5.5+)
`dateObj.toGMTString()`		Date/time string in universal format
`dateObj.toLocaleDateString()`		Date-only string in your system's localized format (NN6+, Moz1+, WinIE5.5+)
`dateObj.toLocaleString()`		Date/time string in your system's localized format
`dateObj.toLocaleTimeString()`		Time-only string in your system's localized format (NN6+, Moz1+, WinIE5.5+)

continued

TABLE 17-1 *(continued)*

Method	Value Range	Description
dateObj.toString()		Date/time string in a format determined by browser
dateObj.toTimeString()		Time-only string in a format determined by browser (WinIE5.5+)
dateObj.toUTCString()		Date/time string in universal format (NN4+, Moz1+, IE3+)
Date.parse("*dateString*")		Converts string date to milliseconds integer
Date.UTC(*date values*)		Converts GMT string date to milliseconds integer

Although the method has the word "time" in its name, the fact that the value is the total number of milliseconds from January 1, 1970, means the value also conveys a date.

Other date object get methods read a specific component of the date or time. You have to exercise some care here, because some values begin counting with 0 when you may not expect it. For example, January is month 0 in JavaScript's scheme; December is month 11. Hours, minutes, and seconds all begin with 0, which, in the end, is logical. Calendar dates, however, use the actual number that would show up on the wall calendar: the first day of the month is date value 1. For the twentieth-century years, the year value is whatever the actual year number is, minus 1900. For 1996, that means the year value is 96. But for years before 1900 and after 1999, JavaScript uses a different formula, showing the full year value. This means you have to check whether a year value is less than 100 and add 1900 to it before displaying that year.

```
var today = new Date();
var thisYear = today.getYear();
   if (thisYear < 100)
   {
      thisYear += 1900;
   }
```

This assumes, of course, you won't be working with years before A.D. 100. If you can assume that your audience is using a modern browser, which is quite likely, use only the getFullYear() method. This method returns the complete set of year digits from all ranges.

To adjust any one of the elements of a date value, use the corresponding set method in an assignment statement. If the new value forces the adjustment of other elements, JavaScript takes care of that. For example, consider the following sequence and how some values are changed for us:

```
myBirthday = new Date("July 4, 1776");
result = myBirthday.getDay(); // result = 4, a Thursday
myBirthday.setYear(1777);     // bump up to next year
result = myBirthday.getDay(); // result = 5, a Friday
```

Because the same date in the following year is on a different day, JavaScript tracks that for you.

Accommodating time zones

Understanding the `dateObj.getTimezoneOffset()` method involves both your operating system's time control panel setting and an internationally recognized (in computerdom, anyway) format for representing dates and times. If you have ignored the control panel stuff about setting your local time zone, the values you get for this property may be off for most dates and times. In the eastern part of North America, for instance, the eastern standard time zone is five hours earlier than Greenwich Mean Time. With the `getTimezoneOffset()` method producing a value of minutes' difference between GMT and the PC's time zone, the five hours difference of eastern standard time is rendered as a value of 300 minutes. On the Windows platform, the value automatically changes to reflect changes in daylight saving time in the user's area (if applicable). Offsets to the east of GMT (to the date line) are expressed as negative values.

Dates as strings

When you generate a date object, JavaScript automatically applies the `toString()` method to the object if you attempt to display that date either in a page or alert box. The format of this string varies with browser and operating system platforms. For example, in IE8 for Windows XP, the string is in the following format:

```
Sun Dec 5 16:47:20 PST 2010
```

But in Firefox 3 for Windows XP, the string is

```
Sun Dec 05 2010 16:47:20 GMT-0800 (Pacific Standard Time)
```

Other browsers return their own variations on the string. The point is not to rely on a specific format and character location of this string for the components of dates. Use the date object methods to read date object components.

JavaScript does, however, provide two methods that return the date object in more constant string formats. One, `dateObj.toGMTString()`, converts the date and time to the GMT equivalent on the way to the variable that you use to store the extracted data. Here is what such data looks like:

```
Mon, 06 Dec 2010 00:47:20 GMT
```

If you're not familiar with the workings of GMT and how such conversions can present unexpected dates, exercise great care in testing your application. A quarter to five on a Sunday afternoon on the North American west coast is well after midnight Monday morning at the Royal Observatory in Greenwich, London.

If time zone conversions make your head hurt, you can use the second string method, `dateObj.toLocaleString()`. In Firefox for North American Windows users, the returned value can look like this:

```
Sunday, December 05, 2010 4:47:20 PM
```

Ever since IE5.5 and NN6/Moz1, you can also have JavaScript convert a date object to just the date or time portions in a nicely formatted version. The best pair of methods for this are `toLocaleDateString()` and `toLocaleTimeString()`, because these methods return values that make the most sense to the user, based on the localization settings of the user's operating system and browser.

Friendly date formats for older browsers

If you don't have the luxury of writing script code only for modern browsers, you can create your own formatting function to do the job for a wide range of browsers. Listing 17-1 demonstrates one way of creating this kind of string from a date object (in a form that will work back to version 4 browsers).

Note

The function to assign event handlers throughout the code in this chapter and much of the book is addEvent(), a cross-browser event handler explained in detail in Chapter 32, "Event Objects."

The addEvent() function is part of the script file jsb-global.js located on the accompanying CD-ROM in the Content/ folder, where it is accessible to all chapters' scripts. ■

LISTING 17-1

Creating a Friendly Date String

HTML: jsb-17-01.html

```
<!DOCTYPE html>
<html>
    <head>
        <meta http-equiv="content-type" content="text/html;charset=utf-8">
        <title>Date String Maker</title>
        <script type="text/javascript" src="../jsb-global.js"></script>
        <script type="text/javascript" src="jsb-17-01.js"></script>
    </head>
    <body>
        <h1>Date String Maker</h1>
        <p id="output">Today's date</p>
    </body>
</html>
```

JavaScript: jsb-17-01.js

```
// initialize when the page has loaded
addEvent(window, 'load', initialize);

monthNames = ["January", "February", "March", "April", "May", "June", "July",
    "August", "September", "October", "November", "December"];
dayNames = ["Sunday", "Monday", "Tuesday", "Wednesday", "Thursday", "Friday",
    "Saturday"];

function initialize()
{
    // do this only if the browser can handle DOM methods
    if (document.getElementById)
    {
        // point to the paragraph to contain the date
        oOutput = document.getElementById('output');

            // if it exists, replace its contents with the date
```

```
        if (oOutput)
        {
            // remove all child nodes from the paragraph
            while (oOutput.firstChild)
            {
                oOutput.removeChild(oOutput.firstChild);
            }

            // create a text node with the date
            var sDate = customDateString(new Date());
            var oNewText = document.createTextNode(sDate);

            // insert that content into the paragraph
            oOutput.appendChild(oNewText);
        }
    }
}

// generate a formatted date
function customDateString(oDate)
{
    var theDay = dayNames[oDate.getDay()];
    var theMonth = monthNames[oDate.getMonth()];
    var theYear = oDate.getFullYear();
    return theDay + ", " + theMonth + " " + oDate.getDate() + ", " + theYear;
}
```

Assuming the user has the PC's clock set correctly (a big assumption), the date appearing just below the opening headline is the current date — making it appear as though the document had been updated today. The downside to this approach (as opposed to the newer `toLocaleDateString()` method) is that international users are forced to view dates in the format you design, which may be different from their local custom.

More conversions

The last two methods shown in Listing 17-1 are methods of the static `Date` object. These utility methods convert dates from string or numeric forms into millisecond values of those dates. The primary beneficiary of these actions is the `dateObj.setTime()` method, which requires a millisecond measure of a date as a parameter. You use this method to throw an entirely different date into an existing `date` object.

`Date.parse()` accepts as a parameter date strings similar to the ones you've seen in this section, including the internationally approved version. `Date.UTC()`, on the other hand, requires the comma-delimited list of values (in proper order: `yy,mm,dd,hh,mm,ss`) in the GMT zone. The `Date.UTC()` method gives you a backward-compatible way to hard-code a GMT time (you can do the same in version 4 browsers via the UTC methods). The following is an example that creates a new date object for 6 p.m. on October 1, 2011, GMT in WinIE8:

```
    var newObj = new Date(Date.UTC(2011, 9, 1, 18, 0, 0));
    result = newObj.toString();    // result = "Sat Oct 1 11:00:00 PDT2011"
```

The second statement returns a value in a local time zone, because all non-UTC methods automatically convert the GMT time stored in the object to the client's local time.

Date and time arithmetic

You may need to perform some math with dates for any number of reasons. Perhaps you need to calculate a date at some fixed number of days or weeks in the future or figure out the number of days between two dates. When calculations of these types are required, remember the *lingua franca* of JavaScript date values: milliseconds.

What you may need to do in your date-intensive scripts is establish some variable values representing the number of milliseconds for minutes, hours, days, or weeks, and then use those variables in your calculations. Here is an example that establishes some practical variable values, building on each other:

```
var oneMinute = 60 * 1000;
var oneHour = oneMinute * 60;
var oneDay = oneHour * 24;
var oneWeek = oneDay * 7;
```

With these values established in a script, I can use one to calculate the date one week from today:

```
var targetDate = new Date();
var dateInMs = targetDate.getTime();
dateInMs += oneWeek;
targetDate.setTime(dateInMs);
```

Another example uses components of a date object to assist in deciding what kind of greeting message to place in a document, based on the local time of the user's PC clock. Listing 17-2 adds to the scripting from Listing 17-1, bringing some quasi-intelligence to the proceedings.

LISTING 17-2

A Dynamic Welcome Message

HTML: `jsb-17-02.html`

```html
<!DOCTYPE html>
<html>
    <head>
        <meta http-equiv="content-type" content="text/html;charset=utf-8">
        <title>Date String Maker</title>
        <script type="text/javascript" src="../jsb-global.js"></script>
        <script type="text/javascript" src="jsb-17-02.js"></script>
    </head>
    <body>
        <h1>Welcome!</h1>
        <p id="date">Today's date</p>
        <p>We hope you are enjoying the <span id="day-part">day</span>.</p>
    </body>
</html>
```

JavaScript: jsb-17-02.js

```javascript
// initialize when the page has loaded
addEvent(window, 'load', initialize);

monthNames = ["January", "February", "March", "April", "May", "June", "July",
    "August", "September", "October", "November", "December"];
dayNames = ["Sunday", "Monday", "Tuesday", "Wednesday", "Thursday", "Friday",
    "Saturday"];

function initialize()
{
    // do this only if the browser can handle DOM methods
    if (document.getElementById)
    {
        // point to the target paragraphs
        var oDateDisplay = document.getElementById('date');
        var oGreeting = document.getElementById('greeting');

            // if they exist, plug in new content
            if (oDateDisplay && oGreeting)
            {
                // plug in date
                var oNow = new Date();
                var sDate = customDateString(oNow);
                replaceTextContent(oDateDisplay, sDate);

                // plug day-part into greeting
                var sDayPart = dayPart(oNow);
                replaceTextContent(oGreeting, sDayPart);
            }
    }
}

// generate a formatted date
function customDateString(oDate)
{
    var theDay = dayNames[oDate.getDay()];
    var theMonth = monthNames[oDate.getMonth()];
    var theYear = oDate.getFullYear();
    return theDay + ", " + theMonth + " " + oDate.getDate() + ", " + theYear;
}

// get the part of the day
function dayPart(oDate)
{
    var theHour = oDate.getHours();
    if (theHour < 6 )
        return "wee hours";
    if (theHour < 12)
        return "morning";
    if (theHour < 18)
```

continued

LISTING 17-2   *(continued)*

```
        return "afternoon";
    return "evening";
}

// replaces the text contents of a page element
function replaceTextContent(oElement, sContent)
{
    // if the object exists
    if (oElement)
    {
        // remove all child nodes
        while (oElement.firstChild)
        {
            oElement.removeChild(oElement.firstChild);
        }

        // create a text node with the new content
        var oNewText = document.createTextNode(sContent);

        // insert that content
        oElement.appendChild(oNewText);
    }
}
```

The script divides the day into four parts and presents a different greeting for each part of the day. The greeting that plays is based, simply enough, on the hour element of a date object representing the time the page is loaded into the browser. Because this greeting is embedded in the page, the greeting does not change no matter how long the user displays the page, but it will update each time the page is reloaded.

Counting the days . . .

You may find one or two more date arithmetic applications useful. One displays the number of shopping days left until Christmas (in the user's time zone); the other is a countdown timer to the start of the year 2100.

Listing 17-3 demonstrates how to calculate the number of days between the current day and some fixed date in the future. The assumption in this application is that all calculations take place in the user's time zone. The example shows the display of the number of shopping days before the next Christmas day (December 25). The basic operation entails converting the current date and the next December 25 to milliseconds, calculating the number of days represented by the difference in milliseconds. If you let the millisecond values represent the dates, JavaScript automatically takes care of leap years.

The only somewhat tricky part is setting the year of the next Christmas day correctly. You can't just slap the fixed date with the current year, because if the program is run on December 26, the year of the next Christmas must be incremented by one. That's why the constructor for the Christmas date object doesn't supply a fixed date as its parameters, but rather, sets individual components of the object.

Also, note that while `setDate()` accepts a counting number 1-31, `setMonth()` accepts a whole number 0-11, making December month 11 for that method call.

LISTING 17-3

How Many Days Until Christmas

HTML: jsb-17-03.html

```html
<!DOCTYPE html>
<html>
    <head>
        <meta http-equiv="content-type" content="text/html;charset=utf-8">
        <title>Christmas Countdown</title>
        <script type="text/javascript" src="../jsb-global.js"></script>
        <script type="text/javascript" src="jsb-17-03.js"></script>
    </head>
    <body>
        <h1>Christmas Countdown</h1>
        <p>You have <em id="days-left">too few</em> shopping
            <span id="day-word">days</span> until Christmas.</p>
    </body>
</html>
```

JavaScript: jsb-17-03.js

```javascript
// initialize when the page has loaded
addEvent(window, 'load', initialize);

function initialize()
{
    // do this only if the browser can handle DOM methods
    if (document.getElementById)
    {
        // point to the target paragraphs
        var oOutput = document.getElementById('days-left');
        var oDayWord = document.getElementById('day-word');

        // if they exist, plug in new content
        if (oOutput && oDayWord)
        {
            // plug in days left
            var sDaysLeft = getDaysUntilXmas();
            replaceTextContent(oOutput, sDaysLeft);
```

continued

LISTING 17-3   *(continued)*

```
            // pluralize day if not one
            var sDayWord = (sDaysLeft == 1) ? 'day' : 'days';
            replaceTextContent(oDayWord, sDayWord);
        }
    }
}

// calculate the number of days till next Christmas
function getDaysUntilXmas()
{
    var oneMinute = 60 * 1000;
    var oneHour = oneMinute * 60;
    var oneDay = oneHour * 24;

    var today = new Date();
    var nextXmas = new Date();
    nextXmas.setMonth(11);
    nextXmas.setDate(25);
        if (today.getMonth() == 11 && today.getDate() > 25)
        {
            nextXmas.setFullYear(nextXmas.getFullYear() + 1);
        }
    var diff = nextXmas.getTime() - today.getTime();
    diff = Math.floor(diff/oneDay);
    return diff;
}

// replaces the text contents of a page element
function replaceTextContent(oElement, sContent)
{
    [see listing 17-2]
}
```

The second variation on calculating the amount of time before a certain event takes time zones into account. For this demonstration, the page is supposed to display a countdown timer to the precise moment when the flame for the 2008 Summer Games in Beijing is to be lit. That event takes place in a time zone that may be different from that of the page's viewer, so the countdown timer must calculate the time difference accordingly.

Listing 17-4 shows a simplified version that simply displays the ticking timer in a text field. The output, of course, could be customized in any number of ways, depending on the amount of dynamic HTML you want to employ on a page. The time of the lighting for this demo is set at 11:00 GMT on August 8, 2008 (the date is certainly accurate, but the officials may set a different time closer to the actual event).

Because this application is implemented as a live ticking clock, the code starts by setting some global variables that should be calculated only once so that the function that gets invoked repeatedly has a minimum of calculating to do (to be more efficient). The Date.UTC() method provides the target time and date in standard time. The getTimeUntil() function accepts a millisecond value (as provided by the targetDate variable) and calculates the difference between the target date and the actual internal millisecond value of the client's PC clock.

The core of the getCountDown() function peels off the number of whole days, hours, minutes, and seconds from the total number of milliseconds difference between now and the target date. Notice that each chunk is subtracted from the total so that the next-smaller chunk can be calculated from the leftover milliseconds.

One extra touch on this page is a display of the local date and time of the actual event.

LISTING 17-4

Summer Games Countdown

HTML: jsb-17-04.html

```
<!DOCTYPE html>
<html>
   <head>
      <meta http-equiv="content-type" content="text/html;charset=utf-8">
      <title>Time Since the First Moon Landing</title>
      <script type="text/javascript" src="../jsb-global.js"></script>
      <script type="text/javascript" src="jsb-17-04.js"></script>
   </head>
   <body>
      <h1>Time Since the First Moon Landing</h1>
      <p>It is now <span id="now">the present</span> in your timezone.</p>
      <p><span id="time-since">Many days</span> have passed since the first
         moon landing on <span id="past-day">a day long ago</span>.</p>
   </body>
</html>
```

JavaScript: jsb-17-04.js

```
// initialize when the page has loaded
addEvent(window, 'load', initialize);

function initialize()
{
    // do this only if the browser can handle DOM methods
    if (document.getElementById)
    {
        // point to the target elements
        oOutputNow = document.getElementById('now');
        oOutputTimeSince = document.getElementById('time-since');
        var oOutputPastDay = document.getElementById('past-day');

        // if they exist, plug in new content
```

continued

301

LISTING 17-4   *(continued)*

```
        if (oOutputNow && oOutputTimeSince && oOutputPastDay)
        {
            // globals -- calculate only once
            // set target date to 20:17 UTC on July 20, 1969
            targetDate = Date.UTC(1969, 6, 20, 20, 17, 0, 0);
            oneSecond = 1000;
            oneMinute = oneSecond * 60;
            oneHour = oneMinute * 60;
            oneDay = oneHour * 24;

            // plug in the past date
            var sPastDay = (new Date(targetDate)).toLocaleString();
            replaceTextContent(oOutputPastDay, sPastDay);

            // plug in current time & time since
            updateCounter();
        }
    }
}

// timer loop to display changing values
function updateCounter()
{
    // plug in current time
    var sNow = (new Date()).toLocaleString();
    replaceTextContent(oOutputNow, sNow);

    // plug in days since
    var sTimeSince = formatTimeSince();
    replaceTextContent(oOutputTimeSince, sTimeSince);

    setTimeout("updateCounter()", 1000);
}

// format elapsed time
function formatTimeSince()
{
    var ms = getTimeDiff(targetDate);
    var days, hrs, mins, secs;

    days = Math.floor(ms/oneDay);
    output = days + " Day";
        if (days != 1) output += 's';

    ms -= oneDay * days;
    hrs = Math.floor(ms/oneHour);
    output += ", " + hrs + " Hour";
        if (hrs != 1) output += 's';
```

```
    ms -= oneHour * hrs;
    mins = Math.floor(ms/oneMinute);
    output += ", " + mins + " Minute";
        if (mins != 1) output += 's';

    ms -= oneMinute * mins;
    secs = Math.floor(ms/oneSecond);
    output += ", and " + secs + " Second";
        if (secs != 1) output += 's';

    return output;
}

// get the difference between two datetimes in milliseconds
function getTimeDiff(targetMS)
{
    var today = new Date();
    var diff = Math.abs(today.valueOf() - targetMS);
    return Math.floor(diff);
}

// replaces the text contents of a page element
function replaceTextContent(oElement, sContent)
{
    [see listing 17-2]
}
```

Early browser date bugs and gremlins

Each new browser generation improves the stability and reliability of scripted date objects. For example, Netscape Navigator 2 had so many bugs and crash problems that it made scripting complex world-time applications for this browser impossible. NN3 improved matters a bit, but some glaring problems still existed. And lest you think I'm picking on Netscape, rest assured that early versions of Internet Explorer also had plenty of date and time problems. IE3 couldn't handle dates before January 1, 1970 (GMT), and also completely miscalculated the time zone offset, following the erroneous pattern of NN2. Bottom line — you're asking for trouble if you must work extensively with dates and times while supporting legacy browsers.

You should be aware of one more discrepancy between Mac and Windows versions of Navigator through Version 4. In Windows, if you generate a date object for a date in another part of the year, the browser sets the time zone offset for that object according to the time zone setting for that time of year. On the Mac, the current setting of the control panel governs whether the normal or daylight savings time offset is applied to the date, regardless of the actual date within the year. This discrepancy affects Navigator 3 and 4 and can throw off calculations from other parts of the year by one hour.

It may sound as though the road to Date object scripting is filled with land mines. Although date and time scripting is far from hassle free, you can put it to good use with careful planning and a lot of testing. Better still, if you make the plausible assumption that the majority of users have a modern browser (WinIE6+, NN6+, Moz1+, FF1+, Cam1+, Safari1+, etc.), then things should go very smoothly.

Validating Date Entries in Forms

Given the bug horror stories in the previous section, you may wonder how you can ever perform data entry validation for dates in forms. The problem is not so much in the calculations as it is in the wide variety of acceptable date formats around the world. No matter how well you instruct users to enter dates in a particular format, many will follow their own habits and conventions. Moreover, how can you know whether an entry of 03/04/2010 is the North American March 4, 2010 or the European April 3, 2010? The answer: you can't.

My recommendation is to divide a date field into three components: month, day, and year. Let the user enter values into each field and validate each field individually for its valid range. Listing 17-5 shows an example of how this is done. The page includes a form that is to be validated before it is submitted. Each component field does its own range checking on-the-fly as the user enters values. But because this kind of validation can be defeated, the page includes one further check triggered by the form's onsubmit event handler. If any field is out of whack, the form submission is cancelled.

LISTING 17-5

Date Validation in a Form

HTML: jsb-17-05.html

```
<!DOCTYPE html>
<html>
    <head>
        <meta http-equiv="content-type" content="text/html;charset=utf-8">
        <title>Date Entry Validation</title>
        <script type="text/javascript" src="../jsb-global.js"></script>
        <script type="text/javascript" src="jsb-17-05.js"></script>
    </head>
    <body>
        <h1>Date Entry Validation</h1>
        <form id="birthdate" action="example.php" method="post">
            <p>Please enter your birthdate...</p>
            <p>
                <label for="month">Month:</label>
                <input type="text" id="month" name="month" value="1" size="2"
                    maxlength="2">

                <label for="day">Day:</label>
                <input type="text" id="day" name="day" value="1" size="2"
                    maxlength="2">

                <label for="year">Year:</label>
                <input type="text" id="year" name="year" value="1900" size="4"
                    maxlength="4">
            </p>
            <p>Thank you for entering <span id="fullDate">your birthdate</span>.</p>
            <p>
                <input type="submit">
```

```
            <input type="Reset">
        </p>
      </form>
   </body>
</html>
```

JavaScript: jsb-17-05.js

```
// initialize when the page has loaded
addEvent(window, 'load', initialize);

function initialize()
{
   // do this only if the browser can handle DOM methods
   if (document.getElementById)
   {
      // point to the target elements
      oForm = document.getElementById('birthdate');
      oMonth = document.getElementById('month');
      oDay = document.getElementById('day');
      oYear = document.getElementById('year');
      oFullDate = document.getElementById('fullDate');

         // if they exist, plug in new content
         if (oForm && oMonth && oDay && oYear && oFullDate)
         {
            // apply behaviors to form elements
            oForm.onsubmit = checkForm;
            oMonth.onchange = function() { return validateMonth(oMonth); }
            oDay.onchange = function() { return validateDay(oDay); }
            oYear.onchange = function() { return validateYear(oYear); }
         }
   }
}

function checkForm(evt)
{
     if (validateMonth(oMonth))
     {
        if (validateDay(oDay))
        {
           if (validateYear(oYear))
           {
              // do nothing
           }
        }
     }
   return false;
}

// validate input month
function validateMonth(oField, bBypassUpdate)
```

continued

LISTING 17-5   *(continued)*

```
{
    var sInput = oField.value;

    if (isEmpty(sInput))
    {
        alert("Be sure to enter a month value.");
        selectField(oField);
        return false;
    }
    else
    {
        sInput = parseInt(oField.value, 10);
        if (isNaN(sInput))
        {
            alert("Entries must be numbers only.");
            selectField(oField);
            return false;
        }
        else
        {
            if (!inRange(sInput,1,12))
            {
                alert("Enter a number between 1 (January) and 12 (December).");
                selectField(oField);
                return false;
            }
        }
    }

    if (!bBypassUpdate)
    {
        calcDate();
    }
    return true;
}

// validate input day
function validateDay(oField)
{
    var sInput = oField.value;

    if (isEmpty(sInput))
    {
        alert("Be sure to enter a day value.");
        selectField(oField);
        return false;
    }
    else
    {
        sInput = parseInt(oField.value, 10);
```

```
        if (isNaN(sInput))
        {
            alert("Entries must be numbers only.");
            selectField(oField);
            return false;
        }
        else
        {
            var monthField = oMonth;

                if (!validateMonth(monthField, true))
                    return false;

            var iMonthVal = parseInt(monthField.value, 10);
            var iMonthMax = new Array(31,31,29,31,30,31,30,31,31,30,31,30,31);
            var iTop = iMonthMax[iMonthVal];

                if (!inRange(sInput,1,iTop))
                {
                    alert("Enter a number between 1 and " + iTop + ".");
                    selectField(oField);
                    return false;
                }
        }
    }
    calcDate();
    return true;
}

// validate input year
function validateYear(oField)
{
    var iCurrentYear = (new Date).getFullYear();

    var sInput = oField.value;
        if (isEmpty(sInput))
        {
            alert("Be sure to enter a year value.");
            selectField(oField);
            return false;
        }
        else
        {
            sInput = parseInt(oField.value, 10);
                if (isNaN(sInput))
                {
                    alert("Entries must be numbers only.");
                    selectField(oField);
                    return false;
                }
                else
                {
                    if (!inRange(sInput, 1900, iCurrentYear))
```

continued

LISTING 17-5   (continued)

```
                        {
                            alert("Enter a number between 1900 and " + iCurrentYear + ".");
                            selectField(oField);
                            return false;
                        }
                }
        }
    calcDate();
    return true;
}
// place the edit cursor in the requested field
function selectField(oField)
{
    oField.focus();
    oField.select();
}

// format a complete date
function calcDate()
{
    var mm = parseInt(oMonth.value, 10);
    var dd = parseInt(oDay.value, 10);
    var yy = parseInt(oYear.value, 10);
    sDate = mm + "/" + dd + "/" + yy;
    replaceTextContent(oFullDate, sDate);
}
// **BEGIN GENERIC VALIDATION FUNCTIONS**
// general purpose function to see if an input value has been entered at all
function isEmpty(sInput)
{
        if (sInput == "" || sInput == null)
        {
            return true;
        }
    return false;
}

// determine if value is in acceptable range
function inRange(sInput, iLow, iHigh)
{
    var num = parseInt(sInput, 10);

        if (num < iLow || num > iHigh)
        {
            return false;
        }
    return true;
}
// **END GENERIC VALIDATION FUNCTIONS**
```

As a general rule, JavaScript validation is only the first line of defense and must be backed up by server-side validation using PHP or another server scripting language. Because some users and user agents are going to be running without JavaScript, the server-side program will need to perform the validation all over again, but for those using JavaScript the validation feedback will be immediate.

Not every date entry validation must be divided in this way. For example, an intranet application can be more demanding in the way users are to enter data. Therefore, you can have a single field for date entry, but the parsing required for such a validation is quite different from that shown in Listing 17-5. See Chapter 46 on the CD-ROM for an example of such a one-field date validation routine.

Data entry validation is also an area of scripting that can benefit from asynchronous JavaScript, also known as Ajax, when it's necessary to look up values on the server to validate input. However, the advantages should be considered carefully since every Ajax operation requires a round-trip to the server and might not be any faster than submitting the whole page.

Cross-Reference

Check out Chapter 39, "Ajax, E4X, and XML," for more on how Ajax can be used to carry out dynamic data entry validation. ■

The Array Object

An array is one of the major JavaScript structures provided for storing and manipulating ordered collections of data. But unlike some other programming languages, JavaScript's arrays are very forgiving as to the kind of data you store in each cell or entry of the array. This allows, for example, an array of arrays, providing the equivalent of multidimensional arrays customized to the kind of data your application needs.

If you have not done a lot of programming in the past, the notion of arrays may seem like an advanced topic. But if you ignore their capabilities, you set yourself up for a harder job when implementing many kinds of tasks. Whenever we approach a script, one of our first thoughts is about the data being controlled by the application and whether handling it as an array will offer some shortcuts for creating the document and handling interactivity with the user.

We hope that by the end of this chapter you will not only be familiar with the properties and methods of JavaScript arrays but you will also begin to look for ways to make arrays work for you.

IN THIS CHAPTER

Working with ordered collections of data

Simulating multidimensional arrays

Manipulating information stored in an array

New additions to JavaScript array handling

Structured Data

In programming, an *array* is defined as an ordered collection of data. You can best visualize an array as a table, not much different from a spreadsheet. In JavaScript, arrays are limited to a table holding one column of data, with as many rows as needed to hold your data. As you have seen in many chapters in Part IV, a JavaScript-enabled browser creates a number of internal arrays for the objects in your HTML documents and browser properties. For example, if your document contains five links, the browser maintains a table of those links. You access them by number (with 0 being the first link) in the array syntax: the array name is followed by the index number in square brackets, as in document.links[0], which represents the first link in the document.

For many JavaScript applications, you will want to use an array as an organized warehouse for data that users of your page access, depending on their interaction with form elements. In the application shown in Chapter 53, "Application: A Lookup Table" on the CD-ROM, for example, we demonstrate an extended version of this usage in a page that lets users search a small table of data for a match between the first three digits of their U.S. Social Security numbers and the state in which they registered with the agency. Arrays are one way JavaScript-enhanced pages can re-create the behavior of more sophisticated server-side applications such as CGI scripts and Java servlets. When the collection of data you embed in the script is no larger than a typical .gif image file, the user won't experience significant delays in loading your page; yet he or she has the full power of your small database collection for instant searching without any calls back to the server. Such database-oriented arrays are important applications of JavaScript for what we call *serverless CGIs*.

As you design an application, look for clues as to potential uses of arrays. If you have a number of objects or data points that interact with scripts the same way, you have a good candidate for array structures. For example, you can assign like names to every text field in a column of an order form. In that sequence, like-named objects are treated as elements of an array. To perform repetitive row calculations down an order form, your scripts can use array syntax to perform all the extensions within a handful of JavaScript statements, rather than perhaps dozens of statements hard-coded to each field name. Chapter 54, "Application: A 'Poor Man's' Order Form" (on the CD-ROM) shows an example of this application.

You can also create arrays that behave like the Java hash table: a lookup table that gets you to a desired data point instantaneously if you know the name associated with the entry.

If you can somehow conceive your data in a table format, an array is in your future.

Creating an Empty Array

Full-fledge array objects in JavaScript go all the way back to NN3 and IE4. It was possible to simulate some array characteristics in even earlier browsers, but since those first-generation browsers have thankfully disappeared from most users' computers, this chapter focuses on the modern array and its hefty powers.

To create a new array object, use the static `Array` object's constructor method. For example:

```
var myArray = new Array();
```

An array object automatically has a `length` property (0 for an empty array).

Should you want to presize the array (for example, preload entries with `null` values), you can specify an initial size as a parameter to the constructor. For example, here is how to create a new array to hold information about a 500-item compact disc collection:

```
var myCDCollection = new Array(500);
```

Unlike with many other programming languages, presizing a JavaScript array does not give you any particular advantage, because you can assign a value to any slot in an array at any time: The `length` property adjusts itself accordingly. For instance, if you assign a value to `myCDCollection[700]`, the array object adjusts its length upward to meet that slot (with the count starting at 0):

```
myCDCollection [700] = "The Smiths/Louder Than Bombs";
collectionSize = myCDCollection.length;    // result = 701
```

Since the count of array elements starts at 0, assigning a value to location 700 results in an array that contains 701 items.

A true array object features a number of methods and the capability to add prototype properties, described later in this chapter.

Populating an Array

Entering data into an array is as simple as creating a series of assignment statements, one for each element of the array. Listing 18-1 generates an array containing a list of the eight planets of the solar system.

LISTING 18-1

Generating and Populating a New Array

```
solarSys = new Array();
solarSys[0] = "Mercury";
solarSys[1] = "Venus";
solarSys[2] = "Earth";
solarSys[3] = "Mars";
solarSys[4] = "Jupiter";
solarSys[5] = "Saturn";
solarSys[6] = "Uranus";
solarSys[7] = "Neptune";
```

This way of populating a single array is a bit tedious when you're writing the code, but after the array is set, it makes accessing collections of information as easy as any array reference:

```
onePlanet = solarSys[4];      // result = "Jupiter"
```

A variant of this method takes advantage of the fact that, because JavaScript arrays are zero-based, the array length property always points past the end of the array at the next item to be filled. The following code produces an array identical to the one above:

```
solarSys = new Array();
solarSys[solarSys.length] = "Mercury";
solarSys[solarSys.length] = "Venus";
solarSys[solarSys.length] = "Earth";
solarSys[solarSys.length] = "Mars";
solarSys[solarSys.length] = "Jupiter";
solarSys[solarSys.length] = "Saturn";
solarSys[solarSys.length] = "Uranus";
solarSys[solarSys.length] = "Neptune";
```

This makes sense if you think about it: a newly created empty array has a length of zero, and the first item to be added to it is `array[0]`. The length is then one and the next item to be added is `array[1]`; and so on.

Assigning array elements like this makes it easy to edit the script later to add or remove elements without having to change all the subsequent subscripts:

```
solarSys = new Array();
solarSys[solarSys.length] = "Mercury";
```

```
solarSys[solarSys.length] = "Venus";
solarSys[solarSys.length] = "Earth";
solarSys[solarSys.length] = "Mars";
solarSys[solarSys.length] = "asteroid belt";
solarSys[solarSys.length] = "Jupiter";
solarSys[solarSys.length] = "Saturn";
solarSys[solarSys.length] = "Uranus";
solarSys[solarSys.length] = "Neptune";
```

A more compact way to create an array is available if you know that the data will be in the desired order (such as the preceding solarSys array). Instead of writing a series of assignment statements (as in Listing 18-1), you can create what is called a *dense array* by supplying the data as comma-delimited parameters to the Array() constructor:

```
solarSys = new Array("Mercury","Venus","Earth","Mars","Jupiter","Saturn",
    "Uranus","Neptune");
```

The term "dense array" simply means that data is packed into the array, without gaps, starting at index position 0.

The example in Listing 18-1 shows what you may call a vertical collection of data. Each data point contains the same type of data as the other data points — the name of a planet — and the data points appear in the relative order of the planets from the Sun.

JavaScript Array Creation Enhancements

JavaScript provides one more way to create a dense array and also clears up a bug in the way older browsers handled arrays. This improved approach does not require the Array object constructor. Instead, JavaScript (as of version 1.2) accepts what is called *literal notation* to generate an array. To demonstrate the difference, the following statement is the regular dense array constructor that works all the way back to NN3:

```
solarSys = new Array("Mercury","Venus","Earth","Mars","Jupiter","Saturn",
    "Uranus","Neptune");
```

While JavaScript 1.2+ fully accepts the preceding syntax, it also accepts the new literal notation:

```
solarSys = ["Mercury","Venus","Earth","Mars","Jupiter","Saturn",
    "Uranus","Neptune"];
```

The square brackets stand in for the call to the Array constructor. If you use this streamlined approach to array creation, be aware that it may stop JavaScript execution cold in old browsers.

The bug fix we mentioned has to do with how to treat the earlier dense array constructor if the scripter enters only the numeric value 1 as the parameter — new Array(1). In NN3 and IE4, JavaScript erroneously creates an array of length 1, but that element is undefined. For NN4 and all later browsers, the same statement creates that one-element array and places the value 1 in that element.

Deleting Array Entries

You can easily wipe out any data in an array element by setting the value of the array entry to `null` or an empty string. But until the `delete` operator came along in version 4 browsers, you could not completely remove an element.

Deleting an array element eliminates the index from the list of accessible index values but does not reduce the array's length, as in the following sequence of statements:

```
myArray.length      // result: 5
delete myArray[2]
myArray.length      // result: 5
myArray[2]          // result: undefined
```

The process of deleting an array entry does not necessarily release memory occupied by that data. The JavaScript interpreter's internal garbage collection mechanism (beyond the reach of scripters) is supposed to take care of such activity. See the `delete` operator in Chapter 22, "JavaScript Operators," for further details.

If you want tighter control over the removal of array elements, you might want to consider using the `splice()` method, which is supported in modern browsers. The `splice()` method can be used on any array and lets you remove an item (or sequence of items) from the array — causing the array's length to adjust to the new item count. See the `splice()` method later in this chapter.

Parallel Arrays

Using an array to hold data is frequently desirable so that a script can do a lookup to see if a particular value is in the array (perhaps verifying that a value typed into a text box by the user is permissible); however, even more valuable is if, upon finding a match, a script can look up some related information in another array. One way to accomplish this is with two or more parallel arrays: the same indexed slot of each array contains related information.

Consider the following three arrays:

```
var regionalOffices = ["New York", "Chicago", "Houston", "Portland"];
var regionalManagers = ["Shirley Smith", "Todd Gaston",
    "Leslie Jones", "Harold Zoot"];
var regOfficeQuotas = [300000, 250000, 350000, 225000];
```

The assumption for these statements is that Shirley Smith is the regional manager out of the New York office, and her office's quota is 300,000. This represents the data that is included with the document, perhaps retrieved by a server-side program that gets the latest data from a SQL database and embeds the data in the form of array constructors. Listing 18-2 shows how this data appears in a simple page that looks up the manager name and quota values for whichever office is chosen in the `select` element. The order of the items in the list of `select` is not accidental: the order is identical to the order of the array for the convenience of the lookup script.

Lookup action in Listing 18-2 is performed by the getData() function. Because the index values of the options inside the select element match those of the parallel arrays index values, the selectedIndex property of the select element makes a convenient way to get directly at the corresponding data in other arrays.

Cross-Reference

The property assignment event-handling technique employed throughout the code in this chapter and much of the book is addEvent(), a cross-browser event handler explained in detail in Chapter 32, "Event Objects."

The addEvent() function is part of the script file jsb-global.js located on the accompanying CD-ROM in the Content/ folder where it is accessible to all chapters' scripts. ∎

LISTING 18-2

A Simple Parallel Array Lookup

HTML: jsb-18-02.html

```
<!DOCTYPE html>
<html>
   <head>
      <meta http-equiv="content-type" content="text/html;charset=utf-8">
      <title>Parallel Array Lookup</title>
      <script type="text/javascript" src="../jsb-global.js"></script>
      <script type="text/javascript" src="jsb-18-02.js"></script>
   </head>
   <body>
      <h1>Parallel Array Lookup</h1>
      <form id="officeData" action="" method="post">
         <p>
            <label for="offices">Select a regional office:</label>
            <select id="offices" name="offices">
            </select>
         </p>
         <p>
            <label for="manager">The manager is:</label>
            <input type="text" id="manager" name="manager" size="35" />
         </p>
         <p>
            <label for="quota">The office quota is:</label>
            <input type="text" id="quota" name="quota" size="8" />
         </p>
      </form>
   </body>
</html>
```

JavaScript: jsb-18-02.js

```
// initialize when the page has loaded
addEvent(window, 'load', initialize);
```

```
function initialize()
{
    // do this only if the browser can handle DOM methods
    if (document.getElementById)
    {
        // set up the data in global variables (by omitting 'var')
        aRegionalOffices = ["New York", "Chicago", "Houston", "Portland"];
        aRegionalManagers = ["Shirley Smith", "Todd Gaston", "Leslie Jones",
                             "Harold Zoot"];
        aRegOfficeQuotas = [300000, 250000, 350000, 225000];

        // point to the critical input fields & save in global variables
        oSelect = document.getElementById('offices');
        oManager = document.getElementById('manager');
        oQuota = document.getElementById('quota');

            // if they all exist...
            if (oSelect && oManager && oQuota)
            {
                // build the drop-down list of regional offices
                for (var i = 0; i < aRegionalOffices.length; i++)
                {
                    oSelect.options[i] = new Option(aRegionalOffices[i]);
                }

                // set the onchange behavior
                addEvent(oSelect, 'change', getData);
            }
        // plug in data for the default select option
        getData();
    }
}


// when a new option is selected, do the lookup into parallel arrays
function getData(evt)
{
    // get the offset of the selected option
    var index = oSelect.selectedIndex;

    // get data from the same offset in the parallel arrays
    oManager.value = aRegionalManagers[index];
    oQuota.value = aRegOfficeQuotas[index];
}
```

On the other hand, if the content to be looked up is typed into a text box by the user, you have to loop through one of the arrays to get the matching index. Listing 18-3 is a variation of Listing 18-2, but instead of the select element, a text field asks users to type in the name of the region. Assuming that users will always spell the input correctly (admittedly an outrageous assumption), the version of getData() in Listing 18-3 performs actions that more closely resemble what you may think a "lookup" should be doing: looking for a match in one array, and displaying corresponding results from the parallel arrays. The for loop iterates through items in the aRegionalOffices array. An if condition compares all uppercase versions of both the input and each array entry. If there is a match, the for loop breaks, with the value of i still pointing to the matching index value. Outside the for loop, another if condition makes sure that the index value has not reached the length of the array, which means that no match is found. Only when the value of i points to one of the array entries does the script retrieve corresponding entries from the other two arrays.

LISTING 18-3

A Looping Array Lookup

HTML: jsb-18-03.html

```html
<!DOCTYPE html>
<html>
   <head>
      <meta http-equiv="content-type" content="text/html;charset=utf-8">
      <title>Parallel Array Lookup II</title>
      <script type="text/javascript" src="../jsb-global.js"></script>
      <script type="text/javascript" src="jsb-18-03.js"></script>
   </head>
   <body>
      <h1>Parallel Array Lookup II</h1>
      <form id="officeData" action="" method="post">
         <p>
            <label for="officeInput">Enter a regional office:</label>
            <input id="officeInput" name="officeInput" size="35">
            <input id="officeSearch" type="button" value="Search">
         </p>
         <p>
            <label for="manager">The manager is:</label>
            <input type="text" id="manager" name="manager" size="35" />
         </p>
         <p>
            <label for="quota">The office quota is:</label>
            <input type="text" id="quota" name="quota" size="8" />
         </p>
      </form>
   </body>
</html>
```

JavaScript: jsb-18-03.js

```javascript
// initialize when the page has loaded
addEvent(window, 'load', initialize);

function initialize()
{
   // do this only if the browser can handle DOM methods
   if (document.getElementById)
   {
      // set up the data in global variables (by omitting 'var')
```

```
      aRegionalOffices = ["New York", "Chicago", "Houston", "Portland"];
      aRegionalManagers = ["Shirley Smith", "Todd Gaston", "Leslie Jones",
                           "Harold Zoot"];
      aRegOfficeQuotas = [300000, 250000, 350000, 225000];

      // point to the critical input fields & save in global variables
      oOffice = document.getElementById('officeInput');
      oSearch = document.getElementById('officeSearch');
      oManager = document.getElementById('manager');
      oQuota = document.getElementById('quota');

         // if they all exist...
         if (oOffice && oSearch && oManager && oQuota)
         {
            // apply behavior to the search button
            addEvent(oSearch, 'click', getData);
         }
   }
}

// when the Search button is clicked, do the lookup into parallel arrays
function getData(evt)
{
   // make a copy of the text box contents
   var sInputText = oOffice.value;

      // nothing entered?
      if (!sInputText)
      {
         alert('Please enter an office location.');
      }
      else
      {
         // loop through all entries of regionalOffices array
         for (var i = 0; i < aRegionalOffices.length; i++)
         {
            // compare entered text against each item in regionalOffices
            // (make both uppercase for easy comparison)
            if (sInputText.toUpperCase() == aRegionalOffices[i].toUpperCase())
            {
               // if they're the same, then break out of the for loop
               break;
            }
         }

         // make sure the i counter hasn't exceeded the max index value
         if (i < aRegionalOffices.length)
         {
            // display corresponding entries from parallel arrays
            oManager.value = aRegionalManagers[i];
            oQuota.value = aRegOfficeQuotas[i];
         }
         // otherwise the loop went all the way with no matches
```

continued

LISTING 18-3   *(continued)*

```
        else
        {
            // empty any previous values
            oManager.value = "";
            oQuota.value = "";

            // advise user
            alert("No match found for '" + sInputText + "'.");
        }
    }
    // return the focus to the office input field
    oOffice.focus();
}
```

Multidimensional Arrays

An alternate to parallel arrays is the simulation of a multidimensional array. While it's true that JavaScript arrays are one-dimensional, you can create a one-dimensional array of arrays or other objects. A logical approach is to make an array of custom objects, because the objects easily allow for naming of object properties, making references to multidimensional array data more readable. (Custom objects are discussed at length in Chapter 23, "Function Objects and Custom Objects." See also Chapter 19, "JSON–Native JavaScript Object Notation.")

Using the same data from the examples of parallel arrays, the following statements define an object constructor for each "data record." A new object is then assigned to each of four entries in the main array.

```
        // custom object constructor
        function officeRecord(city, manager, quota)
        {
            this.city = city;
            this.manager = manager;
            this.quota = quota;
        }

        // create new main array
        var regionalOffices = new Array();

        // stuff main array entries with objects
        regionalOffices[0] = new officeRecord("New York", "Shirley Smith", 300000);
        regionalOffices[1] = new officeRecord("Chicago", "Todd Gaston", 250000);
        regionalOffices[2] = new officeRecord("Houston", "Leslie Jones", 350000);
        regionalOffices[3] = new officeRecord("Portland", "Harold Zoot", 225000);
```

The object constructor function (`officeRecord()`) assigns incoming parameter values to properties of the object. Therefore, to access one of the data points in the array, you use both array notations to get to the desired entry in the array and the name of the property for that entry's object:

```
var eastOfficeManager = regionalOffices[0].manager;
```

You can also assign string index values for this kind of array, as in:

```
regionalOffices["east"] = new officeRecord("New York", "Shirley Smith",
    300000);
```

and access the data via the same index:

```
var eastOfficeManager = regionalOffices["east"].manager;
```

But if you're more comfortable with the traditional multidimensional array (from your experience in other programming languages), you can also implement the above as an array of arrays with less code:

```
// create new main array
var regionalOffices = new Array();
// stuff main array entries with arrays
regionalOffices[0] = new Array("New York", "Shirley Smith", 300000);
regionalOffices[1] = new Array("Chicago", "Todd Gaston", 250000);
regionalOffices[2] = new Array("Houston", "Leslie Jones", 350000);
regionalOffices[3] = new Array("Portland", "Harold Zoot", 225000);
```

or with the extreme brevity of literal notation:

```
// create new main array
var regionalOffices = [
                    ["New York", "Shirley Smith", 300000],
                    ["Chicago", "Todd Gaston", 250000],
                    ["Houston", "Leslie Jones", 350000],
                    ["Portland", "Harold Zoot", 225000]
                 ];
```

Accessing a single data point of an array of arrays requires a double array reference. For example, retrieving the manager's name for the Houston office requires the following syntax:

```
var HoustonMgr = regionalOffices[2][1];
```

The first index in brackets is for the outermost array (`regionalOffices`); the second index in brackets points to the item of the array returned by `regionalOffices[2]`.

Simulating a Hash Table

Nearly all arrays shown so far in this chapter have used integers as their index values. A JavaScript array is a special type of object (the `object` type is covered in Chapter 23, "Function Objects and Custom Objects"). As a result, you can also assign values to customized properties of an array without interfering with the data stored in the array or the length of the array. In other words, you can "piggy-back" data in the array object. You may reference the values of these properties either using "dot" syntax (`array.propertyName`) or through array-looking syntax consisting of square brackets and the property name as a string inside the brackets (`array["propertyName"]`). An array used in this fashion is also known as an *associative array*. If you use the dot syntax, then you can't use characters such as hyphens, spaces, periods, and quotation marks in the `propertyName` values, whereas the only limitation on the quoted bracket syntax is that the values not contain the same type of quotation marks as you're using to quote the expressions.

These do *not* work:

```
// Dot notation:
oArray.Chris Smith          // space
oArray.Chris-Smith          // hyphen
oArray.Chris.Smith          // period
oArray.Smith,Chris          // comma
oArray.Chris"Punky"Smith    // quotes

// Quoted bracket notation:
oArray["Chris "Punky" Smith"]    // matching quotes
oArray['Chris 'Punky' Smith']    // matching quotes
```

These *do* work:

```
// Dot notation:
oArray.ChrisSmith           // one word
oArray.Chris_Smith          // underscore

// Quoted bracket notation (nearly everything works):
oArray["Chris_Smith"]
oArray["Chris.Smith"]
oArray["Chris Smith"]
oArray["Smith, Chris"]
oArray["Chris 'Punky' Smith"]    // non-matching quotes
oArray['Chris "Punky" Smith']    // non-matching quotes
```

Addressing object properties by way of string indexes is sometimes very useful. For example, the multidimensional array described in the previous section consists of four objects. If your page contains a form whose job is to look through the array to find a match for a city chosen from a `select` list, the typical array lookup would loop through the length of the array, compare the chosen value against the `city` property of each object, and then retrieve the other properties when there was a match. For a four-item list, this isn't a big deal. But for a 100-item list, the process could get time consuming. A faster approach would be to jump directly to the array entry whose `city` property is the chosen value. That's what a simulated hash table can do for you (some programming languages have formal hash table constructions especially designed to act like a lookup table).

Create a simulated hash table after the array is populated by looping through the array and assigning properties to the array object as string values. Use string values that you expect to use for lookup purposes. For example, after the `regionalOffices` array has its component objects assigned, run through the following routine to make the hash table:

```
for (var i = 0; i < regionalOffices.length; i++)
{
    regionalOffices[regionalOffices[i].city] = regionalOffices[i];
}
```

You can retrieve the manager property of the Houston office object as follows:

```
var HoustonMgr = regionalOffices["Houston"].manager;
```

With the aid of the hash table component of the array, your scripts have the convenience of both numeric lookup (if the script needs to cycle through all items) and an immediate jump to an item.

Cross-Reference

For more ways to represent data structures in JavaScript, see Chapters 19 and 20. ■

Array Object

Properties	Methods
constructor	concat()
length	every()*
prototype	filter()*
	forEach()*
	indexOf()*
	join()
	lastIndexOf()*
	map()*
	pop()
	push()
	reduce()
	reduceRight()
	reverse()
	shift()
	slice()
	some()*
	sort()
	splice()
	toLocaleString()
	toString()
	unshift()

*Items marked with an asterisk in the list of Array object properties and methods are relatively recent additions with JavaScript 1.6 and later. They are supported by Mozilla browsers such as Firefox 2.0+ but not by Internet Explorer as of version 8, which has a browser market share too large to ignore. We have provided code in this chapter that adds these new methods to the Array object if they don't already exist.

Array object properties

constructor

(See *string*.constructor in Chapter 15, "The String Object")

length

Value: Integer   Read/Write

Compatibility: WinIE4+, MacIE4+, NN3+, Moz+, Safari+, Opera+, Chrome+

A true array object's length property reflects the number of entries in the array. An entry can be any kind of JavaScript value, including null. If an entry is in the 10th cell and the rest are null, the length of that array is 10. Note that because array index values are zero-based, the index of the last cell of an array is one less than the length (9 in this case). This characteristic makes it convenient to use the property as an automatic counter to append a new item to an array:

```
myArray[myArray.length] = valueOfAppendedItem;
```

Thus, a generic function does not have to know which specific index value to apply to an additional item in the array.

prototype

Value: Variable or function   Read/Write

Compatibility: WinIE4+, MacIE4+, NN3+, Moz+, Safari+, Opera+, Chrome+

Inside JavaScript, an array object has its dictionary definition of methods and length property — items that all array objects have in common. The prototype property enables your scripts to ascribe additional properties or methods that apply to all the arrays you create in the currently loaded documents. You can override this prototype, however, for any individual object.

Example

To demonstrate how the prototype property works, Listing 18-4 creates a prototype property for all array objects generated from the static Array object. As the script generates new arrays (instances of the Array object, just as a date object is an instance of the Date object), the property automatically becomes a part of those arrays. In one array, c, you override the value of the prototype sponsor property. By changing the value for that one object, you don't alter the value of the prototype for the Array object. Therefore, another array created afterward, d, still gets the original sponsor property value.

LISTING 18-4

Adding a prototype Property

HTML: jsb-18-04.html

```
<!DOCTYPE html>
<html>
    <head>
        <meta http-equiv="content-type" content="text/html;charset=utf-8">
```

```
      <title>Array prototypes</title>
      <script type="text/javascript" src="jsb-18-04.js"></script>
   </head>
   <body>
      <h1>Array prototypes</h1>
   </body>
</html>
```

JavaScript: jsb-18-04.js

```
// add prototype to all Array objects
Array.prototype.sponsor = "DG";

// create new arrays
var a = new Array();
var b = new Array();
var c = new Array();

// override prototype property for one 'instance'
c.sponsor = "JS";

// this one picks up the original prototype
var d = new Array();

// display results
var sMsg = "Array a is brought to you by: " + a.sponsor + "\n";
sMsg += "Array b is brought to you by: " + b.sponsor + "\n";
sMsg += "Array c is brought to you by: " + c.sponsor + "\n";
sMsg += "Array d is brought to you by: " + d.sponsor;
alert(sMsg);
```

You can assign properties and functions to a prototype. To assign a function, define the function as you normally would in JavaScript. Then assign the function to the prototype by name:

```
function newFunc(param1)
{
    // statements
}
Array.prototype.newMethod = newFunc;   // omit parentheses in this reference
```

where newMethod is whatever you want to name the method (the function name will not be retained).

When you need to call upon that function (which has essentially become a new temporary method for the Array object), invoke it as you would any object method. Therefore, if an array named CDCollection has been created and a prototype method showCoverImage() has been attached to the array, the call to invoke the method for a tenth listing in the array is

```
CDCollection.showCoverImage(9);
```

arrayObject.concat()

where the parameter of the function uses the index value to perhaps retrieve an image whose URL is a property of an object assigned to the 10th item of the array.

Array object methods

After you have information stored in an array, JavaScript provides several methods to help you manage that data. These methods, all of which belong to array objects you create, have evolved over time, so pay close attention to browser compatibility if you're in need of supporting legacy (pre-version 4) browsers.

array.concat(*array2*)

Returns: Array object

Compatibility: WinIE4+, MacIE4+, NN4+, Moz+, Safari+, Opera+, Chrome+

The `array.concat()` method allows you to join two array objects into a new, third array object. The action of concatenating the arrays does not alter the contents or behavior of the two original arrays. To join the arrays, you refer to the first array object to the left of the period before the method; a reference to the second array is the parameter to the method. For example:

```
var array1 = new Array(1,2,3);
var array2 = new Array("a","b","c");
var array3 = array1.concat(array2);
    // result: array with values 1,2,3,"a","b","c"
```

If an array element is a string or number value (not a string or number object), the values are copied from the original arrays into the new one. All connection with the original arrays ceases for those items. But if an original array element is a reference to an object of any kind, JavaScript copies a reference from the original array's entry into the new array; so, if you make a change to either array's entry, the change occurs to the object, and both array entries reflect the change to the object.

Example

Listing 18-5 is a bit complex, but it demonstrates both how arrays can be joined with the `array.concat()` method and how values and objects in the source arrays do or do not propagate based on their data type. The page is shown in Figure 18-1.

After you load the page, you see readouts of three arrays. The first array consists of all string values; the second array has two string values and a reference to a form object on the page (a text box named "original" in the HTML). In the initialization routine of this page, not only are the two source arrays created, but they are joined with the `array.concat()` method, and the result is shown in the third box. To show the contents of these arrays in columns, we use the `array.join()` method, which brings the elements of an array together as a string delimited in this case by a return character — giving us an instant column of data.

Two series of fields and buttons let you experiment with the way values and object references are linked across concatenated arrays. In the first group, if you enter a new value to be assigned to `arrayThree[0]`, the new value replaces the string value in the combined array. Because regular values do not maintain a link back to the original array, only the entry in the combined array is changed. A call to `showArrays()` proves that only the third array is affected by the change.

FIGURE 18-1

Object references remain "alive" in a concatenated array.

More complex is the object relationship for this demonstration. A reference to the first text box of the second grouping has been assigned to the third entry of `arrayTwo`. After concatenation, the same reference is now in the last entry of the combined array. If you enter a new value for a property of the object in the last slot of `arrayThree`, the change goes all the way back to the original object — the first text box in the lower grouping. Thus, the text of the original field changes in response to the change of `arrayThree[5]`. And because all references to that object yield the same result, the reference in `arrayTwo[2]` points to the same text object, yielding the same new answer. The display of the array contents doesn't change, because both arrays still contain a reference to the same object (and the `value` attribute showing in the `<input>` tag of the column listings refers to the default value of the tag, not to its current algorithmically retrievable value shown in the last two fields of the page).

LISTING 18-5

Array Concatenation

HTML: `jsb-18-05.html`

```
<!DOCTYPE html>
<html>
    <head>
```

continued

arrayObject.concat()

LISTING 18-5   *(continued)*

```
        <meta http-equiv="content-type" content="text/html;charset=utf-8">
        <title>Array Prototypes</title>
        <link type="text/css" rel="stylesheet" href="jsb-18-05.css">
        <script type="text/javascript" src="../jsb-global.js"></script>
        <script type="text/javascript" src="jsb-18-05.js"></script>
    </head>
    <body>
        <h1>Array Prototypes</h1>
        <form>
            <fieldset id="arrays">
            <legend>Arrays</legend>
            <p>
                <label>arrayOne</label>
                <textarea name="array1" cols="25" rows="6"></textarea>
            </p>
            <p>
                <label>arrayTwo</label>
                <textarea name="array2" cols="25" rows="6"></textarea>
            </p>
            <p>
                <label>arrayThree</label>
                <textarea name="array3" cols="25" rows="6"></textarea>
            </p>
        </fieldset>
            <fieldset>
            <legend>Array Value Controls</legend>
            <p>
                <label class="input" for="source1">Enter new value for
                                                arrayThree[0]:</label>
                <input type="text" name="source1" value="Jerry">
                <input id="button1" type="button" value="Change arrayThree[0]">
            </p>
            <p>
                <label>Current arrayOne[0] is:</label>
                <input id="result1" type="text" disabled="disabled">
            </p>
            <p>
                <label>Current arrayThree[0] is:</label>
                <input id="result2" type="text" disabled="disabled">
            </p>
            </fieldset>

            <fieldset>
            <legend>Object Value Controls</legend>
            <p>
                <label>textObj assigned to arrayTwo[2]:</label>
                <input type="text" name="original" disabled="disabled">
            </p>
            <p>
                <label class="input">Enter new value for arrayThree[5]:</label>
```

```
        <input type="text" name="source2" value="Phoebe">
        <input id="button2" type="button" value="Change arrayThree[5].value">
    </p>
    <p>
        <label>Current arrayTwo[2].value is:</label>
        <input type="text" name="result3" disabled="disabled">
    </p>
    <p>
        <label>Current arrayThree[5].value is:</label>
        <input type="text" name="result4" disabled="disabled">
    </p>
    </fieldset>
  <p class="reset">
    <input id="buttonReset" type="button" value="Reset">
  </p>
  </form>
 </body>
</html>
```

JavaScript: jsb-18-05.js

```
// initialize when the page has loaded
addEvent(window, 'load', initialize);

// global variables
var arrayOne, arrayTwo, arrayThree, textObj;

function initialize()
{
   // do this only if the browser can handle DOM methods
   if (document.getElementById)
   {
      form = document.forms[0];

      var oButton = document.getElementById('button1');
         if (oButton) oButton.onclick = update1;

      oButton = document.getElementById('button2');
         if (oButton) oButton.onclick = update2;

      oButton = document.getElementById('buttonReset');
         if (oButton) oButton.onclick = function() { location.reload(); };

      // populate arrays
         textObj = form.original;
         arrayOne = new Array("Jerry", "Elaine", "Kramer");
         arrayTwo = new Array("Ross", "Rachel", textObj);
         arrayThree = arrayOne.concat(arrayTwo);

         // perform initial update
         update1();
         update2();
```

continued

arrayObject.concat()

LISTING 18-5   *(continued)*

```
            showArrays();
        }
}

// display current values of all three arrays
function showArrays()
{
    form.array1.value = arrayOne.join("\n");
    form.array2.value = arrayTwo.join("\n");
    form.array3.value = arrayThree.join("\n");
}

// change the value of first item in Array Three
function update1(evt)
{
    arrayThree[0] = form.source1.value;
    form.result1.value = arrayOne[0];
    form.result2.value = arrayThree[0];
    showArrays();
}

// change value of object property pointed to in Array Three
function update2(evt)
{
    arrayThree[5].value = form.source2.value;
    form.result3.value = arrayTwo[2].value;
    form.result4.value = arrayThree[5].value;
    showArrays();
}
```

Stylesheet: jsb-18-05.css

```
fieldset
{
    clear: left;
    float: left;
    margin-bottom: 1em;
    padding: .5em;
}
fieldset#arrays p
{
    float: left;
    margin: 0 .5em;
}
fieldset#arrays label
{
    display: block;
    text-align: center;
}
```

```
label.input
{
    font-weight: bold;
}
p.reset
{
    clear: left;
}
```

Related Item: `array.join()` method

array.every(*callback[, thisObject]*)
array.some(*callback[, thisObject]*)

Returns: Boolean

Compatibility: FF2+, Safari3+, Chrome1+, Opera 9.5+, WinIE−, MacIE−

`every()` and `some()` let you test the elements of an array with a callback function of your choice. (A *callback* is a function that is passed as an argument to another function.) The difference between the two methods is that `every()` returns `true` only if every array element tests true, while `some()` returns `true` if even one element tests true. The original array is not modified unless your callback function explicitly modifies it.

The callback function can contain any logic you want but in this case is required to return a Boolean value (either `true` or `false`). It takes three arguments: the value of the array element being examined, its index in the array, and a reference to the array object being traversed. `every()` uses the callback to test each member of the array in turn until a false value is returned or the end of the array is reached. `some()` uses the callback to test each member of the array until a true value is returned or the end of the array is reached. Note that if the array is empty, `every()` will return true because it hasn't encountered a value that would test false!

Here's a simple example that checks whether an array contains all positive numbers:

```
function isPositive(iValue, iIndex, aArray)
{
    return (iValue > 0);
}

var a = new Array(5, 4, 3, 2, 1);

var bResult = a.every(isPositive);
// returns true because there are no non-positive elements

bResult = a.some(isPositive);
// returns true because there is at least one positive element


a = [5, 4, 3, 2, 1, 0];

bResult = a.every(isPositive);
// returns false because zero is non-positive
```

```
bResult = a.some(isPositive);
// returns true because there is at least one positive element


a = new Array();

bResult = a.every(isPositive);
// returns true since there are no non-positive elements in an empty array!

bResult = a.some(isPositive);
// returns false because there are no positive elements in an empty array
```

The following example takes advantage of the callback function's other arguments to use other array elements to evaluate the current one. A *Fibonacci sequence* is one in which each number is the sum of the previous two. Of course, the first two numbers in the sequence are exceptions to this algorithm and are "hard-coded" as zero and one, but the rest are calculable:

```
function isFibonacci(iValue, iIndex, aArray)
{
    switch (iIndex)
    {
      case 0:
          return (iValue == 0);
      break;

      case 1:
          return (iValue == 1);
      break;

      default:
          return (iValue == aArray[iIndex-2] + aArray[iIndex-1]);
    }
}

var a = new Array(0, 1, 1, 2, 3, 5, 8, 13, 21);
var bResult = a.every(isFibonacci);
// returns true

a = [0, 1, 1, 2, 3, 5, 8, 13, 22];
var bResult = a.every(isFibonacci);
// returns false because 22 isn't 8 + 13
```

This same functionality could be gotten from a for() loop. The advantage of using every() is the encapsulation of program logic in discrete functions that can be re-used in different places in your script.

To equip browsers that don't yet support the every() method of JavaScript 1.6, you can supply that functionality to the array object using code supplied by Mozilla.org:

```
if (!Array.prototype.every)
{
    Array.prototype.every = function(fun /*, thisp*/)
```

```
    {
        var len = this.length >>> 0;
        if (typeof fun != "function")
        {
            throw new TypeError();
        }

        var thisp = arguments[1];
        for (var i = 0; i < len; i++)
        {
            if (i in this &&
                    !fun.call(thisp, this[i], i, this))
                return false;
        }

        return true;
    };
}
```

Related Items: `array.filter()`,`array.forEach()`, `array.map()` methods

array.filter(callback[, thisObject])

Returns: Array

Compatibility: FF2+, Safari3+, Chrome1+, Opera 9.5+, WinIE−, MacIE−

Similar to `every()`, the `filter()` method lets you test every element of an array with a callback function of your choice, and then returns a new array consisting of every element that tested `true`. The original array is not modified unless your callback function explicitly modifies it.

The callback function examines a single array element and returns Boolean `true` or `false`. It takes three arguments: the value of the array element being examined, its index in the array, and a reference to the array object being traversed. Every element that tests true is added to the result array.

This example uses our previous callback function to check for positive numbers:

```
function isPositive(iValue, iIndex, aArray)
{
    return (iValue > 0);
}

var a = new Array(1, -2, -3, 4, 5, -6);
var aResult = a.filter(isPositive);
// result: [1, 4, 5]
```

Mozilla suggests the following code to compensate for browsers that don't yet support the `filter()` method of JavaScript 1.6:

```
if (!Array.prototype.filter)
{
    Array.prototype.filter = function(fun /*, thisp*/)
```

arrayObject.forEach()

```
            {
                var len = this.length >>> 0;
                if (typeof fun != "function")
                    throw new TypeError();

                var res = new Array();
                var thisp = arguments[1];
                for (var i = 0; i < len; i++)
                {
                    if (i in this)
                    {
                        var val = this[i]; // in case fun mutates this
                        if (fun.call(thisp, val, i, this))
                            res.push(val);
                    }
                }

                return res;
            };
        }
```

Related Items: `array.every()`, `array.forEach()`, `array.map()`, `array.some()` methods

array.forEach(*callback[, thisObject]*)

Returns: Array

Compatibility: FF2+, Safari3+, Chrome1+, Opera 9.5+, WinIE−, MacIE−
`forEach()` executes a function on every element of an array. It does not return a value and the original array is not modified unless your callback function explicitly modifies it.

The callback function takes three arguments: the value of the array element being examined, its index in the array, and a reference to the array object being traversed.

The following example builds a message that displays the contents of an array. Note that in the callback function `buildMsg()`, the keyword `this` refers to the custom object `oMsg` that we're passing to `forEach()`:

```
function sendMessages(sValue, iIndex, aArray)
{
    sendMsg(sValue, this.text);  // where sendMsg() is defined elsewhere ...
}

var a = new Array('chris@example.com', 'pat@example.net', 'jessie@example.org');

var oMessage = {text: "Dear friend,\nYou are cordially invited..."};
a.forEach(sendMessages, oMessage);
```

Alternatively, the preceding example could be written using the more universally supported `for()` method:

```
var a = new Array('apple', 'banana', 'cardamom', 'dandelion');
var oMsg = {buffer: 'This array contains:'};
```

```
for (var i = 0; i < a.length; i++)
{
    oMsg.buffer += '\n' + i + ':' + a[i];
}
alert(oMsg.buffer);
```

Mozilla suggests the following code to equip browsers that don't yet support the `forEach()` method of JavaScript 1.6:

```
if (!Array.prototype.forEach)
{
    Array.prototype.forEach = function(fun /*, thisp*/)
    {
        var len = this.length >>> 0;
        if (typeof fun != "function")
            throw new TypeError();

        var thisp = arguments[1];
        for (var i = 0; i < len; i++)
        {
            if (i in this)
                fun.call(thisp, this[i], i, this);
        }
    };
}
```

Related Items: `array.every()`,`array.filter()`, `array.map()`, `array.some()` methods

array.indexOf(*searchString[, startFrom]*)
array.lastIndexOf(*searchString[, startFrom]*)

Returns: Index value of the array element whose value matches searchString, or −1 if not found

Compatibility: FF2+, Safari3+, Chrome1+, Opera 9.5+, WinIE−, MacIE−

These two methods search for an array element that matches `searchString` exactly and return the index of the first (or last) matching element, or return −1 if no match is found.

The principle difference between these two methods is that `indexOf()` searches from left to right, starting at the beginning of the array ascending and `lastIndexOf()` searches from right to left, from the end of the array descending. In either case, the value that's returned is the index of the found item — its offset from the beginning of the array. Therefore, if there's only one matching element in the array and `startFrom` is not specified, both `indexOf()` and `lastIndexOf()` will return the same value because they'll find the same matching element.

The optional `startFrom` argument tells the method how far from the beginning or end of the array to begin the search. If it's missing, it's assumed to be zero — that is, begin the search at the first (with `indexOf()`) or last (with `lastIndexOf()`) element. If `startFrom` is a positive number, it's used as a starting offset from the beginning of the array; if it's negative, it's used as an offset from the end of the array.

arrayObject.lastIndexOf()

Examples:

```
var a = new Array('cat', 'dog', 'cat');

// indexOf searches left to right:
a.indexOf('cat');          // result = 0 (search elements 0, 1, and 2)
a.indexOf('cat', 1);       // result = 2 (search elements 1 and 2)
a.indexOf('cat', 2);       // result = 2 (search element 2)
a.indexOf('cat', 3);       // result = -1 (no elements to search)
a.indexOf('cat', -1);      // result = 2 (search element 2)
a.indexOf('cat', -2);      // result = 2 (search elements 1 and 2)
a.indexOf('cat', -3);      // result = 0 (search elements 0, 1, and 2)

// lastIndexOf searches right to left:
a.lastIndexOf('cat');      // result = 2 (search elements 2, 1, and 0)
a.lastIndexOf('cat', 1);   // result = 0 (search elements 1 and 0)
a.lastIndexOf('cat', 2);   // result = 2 (search elements 2, 1, and 0)
a.lastIndexOf('cat', 3);   // result = 2 (search whole array)
a.lastIndexOf('cat', -1);  // result = 2 (search elements 2, 1, and 0)
a.lastIndexOf('cat', -2);  // result = 0 (search elements 1 and 0)
a.lastIndexOf('cat', -3);  // result = 0 (search element 0)
```

Mozilla suggests the following code to equip browsers that don't yet support the indexOf() method of JavaScript 1.6:

```
if (!Array.prototype.indexOf)
{
    Array.prototype.indexOf = function(elt /*, from*/)
    {
        var len = this.length >>> 0;

        var from = Number(arguments[1]) || 0;
        from = (from < 0)
                ? Math.ceil(from)
                : Math.floor(from);
        if (from < 0)
            from += len;

        for (; from < len; from++)
        {
            if (from in this &&
                    this[from] === elt)
                return from;
        }
        return -1;
    };
}
```

And the following to equip browsers that don't yet support lastIndexOf():

```
if (!Array.prototype.lastIndexOf)
{
    Array.prototype.lastIndexOf = function(elt /*, from*/)
    {
        var len = this.length;

        var from = Number(arguments[1]);
        if (isNaN(from))
        {
            from = len - 1;
        }
        else
        {
            from = (from < 0)
                    ? Math.ceil(from)
                    : Math.floor(from);
            if (from < 0)
                from += len;
            else if (from >= len)
                from = len - 1;
        }

        for (; from > -1; from--)
        {
            if (from in this &&
                    this[from] === elt)
                return from;
        }
        return -1;
    };
}
```

array.join(*separatorString*)

Returns: String of entries from the array delimited by the *separatorString* value

Compatibility: WinIE4+, MacIE4+, NN3+, Moz+, Safari+, Opera+, Chrome+

You cannot directly view data that is stored in an array. Nor can you put an array into a form element for transmittal to a server-side program that expects a string of text. To make the transition from discrete array elements to string, the array.join() method handles what would otherwise be a nasty string manipulation exercise.

The sole parameter for this method is a string of one or more characters that you want to act as a delimiter between entries. For example, if you want commas between array items in their text version, the statement is

```
var arrayText = myArray.join(",");
```

arrayObject.join

Invoking this method does not change the original array in any way. Therefore, you need to assign the results of this method to another variable or a value property of a form element.

Example

The script in Listing 18-6 converts an array of planet names into a text string. The page provides you with a field to enter the delimiter string of your choice and shows the results in a text area.

LISTING 18-6

Using the Array.join() Method

HTML: jsb-18-06.html

```html
<!DOCTYPE html>
<html>
    <head>
        <meta http-equiv="content-type" content="text/html;charset=utf-8">
        <title>Array.join()</title>
        <script type="text/javascript" src="../jsb-global.js"></script>
        <script type="text/javascript" src="jsb-18-06.js"></script>
    </head>
    <body>
        <h1>Array.join(): Converting arrays to strings</h1>
        <form>
            <p>This document contains an array of planets in our solar system.</p>
            <p>
                <label for="delimiter">Enter a string to act
                                as a delimiter between entries:</label>
                <input type="text" id="delimiter" name="delim" value="," size="5">
            </p>
            <p>
                <input id="displayButton" type="button" value="Display as String">
                <input type="reset">
            </p>
            <p>
                <textarea id="output" name="output" rows="4" cols="40"
                            wrap="virtual"></textarea>
            </p>
        </form>
    </body>
</html>
```

JavaScript: jsb-18-06.js

```javascript
// initialize when the page has loaded
addEvent(window, 'load', initialize);

function initialize()
{
    // do this only if the browser can handle DOM methods
```

```
if (document.getElementById)
{
    // point to critical elements
    oDelimiter = document.getElementById('delimiter');
    oOutput = document.getElementById('output');
    var oButton = document.getElementById('displayButton');

        // if they all exist...
        if (oDelimiter && oOutput && oButton)
        {
            // apply behavior to button
            oButton.onclick = convert;

            // set global array
            solarSys = new Array("Mercury", "Venus", "Earth", "Mars", "Jupiter",
                              "Saturn", "Uranus", "Neptune");
        }
    }
}

// join array elements into a string
function convert(evt)
{
    var delimiter = oDelimiter.value;
    oOutput.value = decodeURIComponent(solarSys.join(delimiter));
}
```

Notice that this method takes the parameter very literally. If you want to include non-alphanumeric characters, such as a newline or tab, do so with URL-encoded characters (%0D for a carriage return; %09 for a tab) instead of inline string literals. Coming up in Listing 18-7, the results of the `array.join()` method are subjected to the `decodeURIComponent()` function in order to display them in the `textarea`.

Related Items: `string.split()` method

`array.map(callback[, thisObject])`

Returns: Array

Compatibility: FF2+, Safari3+, Chrome1+, Opera 9.5+, WinIE−, MacIE−
`map()` creates a new array by running a user-provided function on each element of the original array.

The callback function returns a value that is used to build the result array. It takes three arguments: the value of the array element being examined, its index in the array, and a reference to the array object being traversed.

If provided, `thisObject` will be used as the `this` value within the callback function.

Example:

```
function square(iValue, iIndex, aArray)
{
```

339

```
        return iValue * iValue;
    }

    var a = new Array(0, 1, 2, 3, 4, 5, 6, 7);
    var b = a.map(square);
    // result: b == [0, 1, 4, 9, 16, 25, 36, 49]
```

You could also write this by creating the callback function on-the-fly:

```
    var a = new Array(0, 1, 2, 3, 4, 5, 6, 7);
    var b = a.map(function(i) { return i * i; });
```

Mozilla suggests the following code to equip browsers that don't yet support the map() method of JavaScript 1.6:

```
    if (!Array.prototype.map)
    {
        Array.prototype.map = function(fun /*, thisp*/)
        {
            var len = this.length >>> 0;
            if (typeof fun != "function")
                throw new TypeError();

            var res = new Array(len);
            var thisp = arguments[1];
            for (var i = 0; i < len; i++)
            {
                if (i in this)
                    res[i] = fun.call(thisp, this[i], i, this);
            }

            return res;
        };
    }
```

Related Items: array.every(), array.filter(),array.forEach(), array.some() methods

array.pop()
array.push(*valueOrObject*)
array.shift()
array.unshift(*valueOrObject*)

Returns: One array entry value

Compatibility: WinIE5.5+, MacIE−, NN4+, Moz+, Safari+, Opera+, Chrome+

The notion of a *stack* is well known to experienced programmers, especially those who know about the inner workings of assembly language at the CPU level. Even if you've never programmed a stack before, you have encountered the concept in real life many times. The classic analogy is the spring-loaded pile of cafeteria trays. If the pile were created one tray at a time, each tray would be pushed onto the top of the stack of trays. When a customer comes along, the topmost tray (the last one to be pushed onto the stack) gets popped off. The last one to be put on the stack is the first one to be taken off.

JavaScript in modern browsers lets you turn an array into one of these spring-loaded stacks. But instead of placing trays on the pile, you can place any kind of data at either end of the stack, depending on which method you use to do the stacking. Similarly, you can extract an item from either end.

Perhaps the most familiar terminology for this is *push* and *pop*. When you push() a value onto an array, the value is appended as the last entry in the array. When you issue the array.pop() method, the last item in the array is removed from the stack and is returned, and the array shrinks in length by one. In the following sequence of statements, watch what happens to the value of the array used as a stack:

```
var source = new Array("Homer","Marge","Bart","Lisa","Maggie");
var stack = new Array();
    // stack = <empty>
stack.push(source[0]);
    // stack = "Homer"
stack.push(source[2]);
    // stack = "Homer","Bart"
var Simpson1 = stack.pop();
    // stack = "Homer" ; Simpson1 = "Bart"
var Simpson2 = stack.pop();
    // stack = <empty> ; Simpson2 = "Homer"
```

While push() and pop() work at the end of an array, another pair of methods works at the front. Their names are not as picturesque as push() and pop(). To insert a value at the front of an array, use the array.unshift() method; to grab the first element and remove it from the array, use array.shift(). Of course, you are not required to use these methods in matching pairs. If you push() a series of values onto the back end of an array, you can shift() them off from the front end without complaint. It all depends on how you need to process the data.

Related Items: array.concat(), array.slice() method

array.reduce(*callback[, initialValue]*)
array.reduceRight(*callback[, initialValue]*)

Returns: A single value

Compatibility: FF3+, Safari4+

These methods reduce an array down to a single value. reduce() operates on the array elements starting with the first element, whereas reduceRight() begins with the last element. Both methods accept as arguments a callback function and an optional initial value (since the very first iteration will have only one array element to work on). The callback function has two arguments, (firstValue, secondValue), which it processes in some way to derive a single return value.

For example, the following code reduces an array of numbers down to their sum:

```
function addEmUp(a, b)
{
    return a + b;
}
```

```
var a = new Array(1, 2, 3, 4, 5);
var b = a.reduce(addEmUp);
// result: b == 15
```

For simple addition, it doesn't matter whether the reduction occurred frontward or backward, but look at what happens when we apply that same callback to text. (Remember that in JavaScript the plus sign adds numbers but concatenates text.)

```
var a = new Array('d', 'e', 's', 's', 'e', 'r', 't', 's');

var b = a.reduce(addEmUp);
// result: b == 'desserts'

var b = a.reduceRight(addEmUp);
// result: b == 'stressed'
```

Mozilla suggests the following code to equip browsers that don't yet support the reduce() method of JavaScript 1.8:

```
if (!Array.prototype.reduce)
{
  Array.prototype.reduce = function(fun /*, initial*/)
  {
    var len = this.length >>> 0;
    if (typeof fun != "function")
      throw new TypeError();

    // no value to return if no initial value and an empty array
    if (len == 0 && arguments.length == 1)
      throw new TypeError();

    var i = 0;
    if (arguments.length >= 2)
    {
      var rv = arguments[1];
    }
    else
    {
      do
      {
        if (i in this)
        {
          rv = this[i++];
          break;
        }

        // if array contains no values, no initial value to return
        if (++i >= len)
          throw new TypeError();
      }
      while (true);
```

```
    }

    for (; i < len; i++)
    {
      if (i in this)
        rv = fun.call(null, rv, this[i], i, this);
    }

    return rv;
  };
}
```

... and likewise for `reduceRight()`:

```
if (!Array.prototype.reduceRight)
{
  Array.prototype.reduceRight = function(fun /*, initial*/)
  {
    var len = this.length >>> 0;
    if (typeof fun != "function")
      throw new TypeError();

    // no value to return if no initial value, empty array
    if (len == 0 && arguments.length == 1)
      throw new TypeError();

    var i = len - 1;
    if (arguments.length >= 2)
    {
      var rv = arguments[1];
    }
    else
    {
      do
      {
        if (i in this)
        {
          rv = this[i--];
          break;
        }

        // if array contains no values, no initial value to return
        if (--i < 0)
          throw new TypeError();
      }
      while (true);
    }

    for (; i >= 0; i--)
    {
      if (i in this)
```

```
            rv = fun.call(null, rv, this[i], i, this);
        }

        return rv;
    };
}
```

array.reverse( )

Returns: Array of entries in the opposite order of the original

Compatibility: WinIE4+, MacIE4+, NN3+, Moz+, Safari+, Opera+, Chrome+

Occasionally, you may find it more convenient to work with an array of data in reverse order. Although you can concoct repeat loops to count backward through index values, a server-side program may prefer the data in a sequence opposite to the way it was most convenient for you to script it.

You can have JavaScript switch the contents of an array for you: Whatever element was last in the array becomes the 0 index item in the array. Bear in mind that if you do this, you're restructuring the original array, not copying it, even though the method also returns a copy of the reversed version. A reload of the document restores the order as written in the HTML document.

Example

Listing 18-7 is an enhanced version of Listing 18-6, which includes another button and function that reverse the array and display it as a string in a text area.

LISTING 18-7

Array.reverse() Method

HTML: `jsb-18-07.html`

```
<!DOCTYPE html>
<html>
    <head>
        <meta http-equiv="content-type" content="text/html;charset=utf-8">
        <title>Array.reverse()</title>
        <script type="text/javascript" src="../jsb-global.js"></script>
        <script type="text/javascript" src="jsb-18-07.js"></script>
    </head>
    <body>
        <h1>Array.reverse(): Reversing array element order</h1>
        <form>
            <p>This document contains an array of planets in our solar system.</p>
            <p>
                <label for="delimiter">Enter a string to act as
                                a delimiter between entries:</label>
                <input type="text" id="delimiter" name="delim" value="," size="5">
            </p>
            <p>
                <input type="button" id="showAsIs" value="Array as-is">
```

```
            <input type="button" id="reverseIt" value="Reverse the array">
            <input type="reset">
            <input type="button" id="reload" value="Reload">
        </p>
        <p>
            <textarea id="output" name="output" rows="4" cols="40"
                        wrap="virtual"></textarea>
        </p>
    </form>
  </body>
</html>
```

JavaScript: jsb-18-07.js

```javascript
// initialize when the page has loaded
addEvent(window, 'load', initialize);

function initialize()
{
    // do this only if the browser can handle DOM methods
    if (document.getElementById)
    {
        // point to critical elements
        oDelimiter = document.getElementById('delimiter');
        oOutput = document.getElementById('output');
        var oButtonShowAsIs = document.getElementById('showAsIs');
        var oButtonReverseIt = document.getElementById('reverseIt');
        var oReload = document.getElementById('reload');

            // if they all exist...
            if (oDelimiter && oOutput && oButtonShowAsIs && oButtonReverseIt)
            {
                // apply behaviors to buttons
                oButtonShowAsIs.onclick = showAsIs;
                oButtonReverseIt.onclick = reverseIt;
                oReload.onclick = function() { location.reload(); };

                // set global array
                solarSys = new Array("Mercury", "Venus", "Earth", "Mars", "Jupiter",
                                "Saturn", "Uranus", "Neptune");
            }
    }
}

// show array as currently in memory
function showAsIs(evt)
{
    var delimiter = oDelimiter.value;
    oOutput.value = decodeURIComponent(solarSys.join(delimiter));
}

// reverse array order, then display as string
```

continued

LISTING 18-7   *(continued)*

```
function reverseIt(evt)
{
    var delimiter = oDelimiter.value;
    solarSys.reverse();    // reverses original array
    oOutput.value = decodeURIComponent(solarSys.join(delimiter));
}
```

Notice that the solarSys.reverse() method stands by itself (meaning, nothing captures the returned value) because the method modifies the solarSys array. You then run the now-inverted solarSys array through the array.join() method for your text display.

Related Items: array.sort() method

array.slice(*startIndex* [, *endIndex*])

Returns: Array

Compatibility: WinIE4+, MacIE4+, NN4+, Moz+, Safari+, Opera+, Chrome+

Behaving as its like-named string method, array.slice() lets you extract a contiguous series of items from an array. The extracted segment becomes an entirely new array object. Values and objects from the original array have the same kind of behavior as arrays created with the array.concat() method.

One parameter is required — the starting index point for the extraction. If you don't specify a second parameter, the extraction goes all the way to the end of the array; otherwise the extraction goes to, *but does not include,* the index value supplied as the second parameter. For example, extracting Earth's neighbors from an array of planet names looks like the following:

```
var solarSys = new Array("Mercury","Venus","Earth","Mars",
    "Jupiter","Saturn","Uranus","Neptune","Pluto");
var nearby = solarSys.slice(1,4);
    // result: new array of "Venus", "Earth", "Mars"
```

Related Items: array.splice(), string.slice() methods

array.sort([*compareFunction*])

Returns: Array of entries in the order as determined by the *compareFunction* algorithm

Compatibility: WinIE4+, MacIE4+, NN3+, Moz+, Safari+, Opera+, Chrome+

JavaScript array sorting is both powerful and a bit complex to script if you haven't had experience with this kind of sorting methodology. The purpose, obviously, is to let your scripts sort entries of an array by almost any kind of criterion that you can associate with an entry. For entries consisting of strings, the criterion may be their alphabetical order or their length; for numeric entries, the criterion may be their numerical order.

Look first at the kind of sorting you can do with the array.sort() method by itself (for example, without calling a comparison function). When no parameter is specified, JavaScript takes a snapshot of the contents of the array and converts items to strings. From there, it performs a string sort of the values. ASCII values of characters govern the sort, which means that numbers are sorted by their string values, not their numeric values. This fact has strong implications if your array consists of numeric data: The value 201 sorts before 88, because the sorting mechanism compares the first characters of the strings ("2" versus "8") to determine the sort order. For simple alphabetical sorting of string values in arrays, the plain `array.sort()` method does the trick.

Fortunately, additional intelligence is available that you can add to array sorting. The key tactic is to define a function that helps the `sort()` method compare items in the array. A comparison function is passed two values from the array (what you don't see is that the `array.sort()` method rapidly sends numerous pairs of values from the array to help it sort through all entries). The comparison function lets the `sort()` method know which of the two items comes before the other, based on the value the function returns. Assuming that the function compares two values, a and b, the returned value reveals information to the `sort()` method, as shown in Table 18-1.

TABLE 18-1

Comparison Function Return Values

Return Value Range	Meaning
< 0	Value b should sort later than a.
0	The order of a and b should not change.
> 0	Value a should sort later than b.

Consider the following example:

```
myArray = new Array(12, 5, 200, 80);
function compare(a,b)
{
    return a - b;
}
myArray.sort(compare);
```

The array has four numeric values in it. To sort the items in numerical order, you define a comparison function (arbitrarily named `compare()`), which is called from the `sort()` method. Note that unlike invoking other functions, the parameter of the `sort()` method uses a reference to the function, which lacks parentheses.

When the `compare()` function is called, JavaScript automatically sends two parameters to the function in rapid succession until each element has been compared with the others. Every time `compare()` is called, JavaScript assigns two of the array's values to the parameter variables (a and b). In the preceding example, the returned value is the difference between a and b. If a is larger than b, then a positive value goes back to the `sort()` method, telling it to sort a later than b (that is, position a at a higher value index position than b). Therefore, b may end up at `myArray[0]`, whereas a ends up at a higher index-valued location. On the other hand, if a is smaller than b, the returned negative value tells `sort()` to put a in a lower index value spot than b.

Evaluations within the comparison function can go to great lengths, as long as some data connected with array values can be compared. For example, instead of numerical comparisons, as just shown, you can perform string comparisons. The following function sorts alphabetically by the last character of each array string entry:

```
function compare(a,b)
{
    // last character of array strings
    var aComp = a.charAt(a.length - 1);
    var bComp = b.charAt(b.length - 1);
    if (aComp < bComp)
        return -1;
    if (aComp > bComp)
        return 1;
    return 0;
}
```

First, this function extracts the final character from each of the two values passed to it. Then, because strings cannot be added or subtracted like numbers, you compare the ASCII values of the two characters, returning the corresponding values to the sort() method to let it know how to treat the two values being checked at that instant.

When an array's entries happen to be objects, you can even sort by properties of those objects. If you bear in mind that the a and b parameters of the sort function are references to two array entries, then by extension you can refer to properties of those objects. For example, if an array contains objects whose properties define information about employees, one of the properties of those objects can be the employee's age as a string. You can then sort the array based on the numeric equivalent of the age property of the objects by way of the following comparison function:

```
function compare(a,b) {
    return parseInt(a.age) - parseInt(b.age);
}
```

Array sorting, unlike sorting routines you may find in other scripting languages, is not a stable sort. Not being stable means that succeeding sort routines on the same array are not cumulative. Also, remember that sorting changes the sort order of the original array. If you don't want the original array harmed, make a copy of it before sorting or reload the document to restore an array to its original order. Should an array element be null, the method sorts such elements at the end of the sorted array.

JavaScript array sorting is extremely powerful stuff. Array sorting is one reason why it's not uncommon to take the time during the loading of a page containing an IE XML data island, for example, to make a JavaScript copy of the data as an array of objects (see Chapter 60, "Application: Transforming XML Data," on the CD-ROM). Converting the XML to JavaScript arrays makes the job of sorting the data much easier and faster than cobbling together your own sorting routines on the XML elements.

Example

You can look to Listing 18-8 for a few examples of sorting an array of string values (see Figure 18-2). Four buttons summon different sorting routines, three of which invoke comparison functions. This listing sorts the planet array alphabetically (forward and backward) by the last character of the planet name and also by the length of the planet name. Each comparison function demonstrates different ways of comparing data sent during a sort.

FIGURE 18-2

Sorting an array of planet names alphabetically by name length.

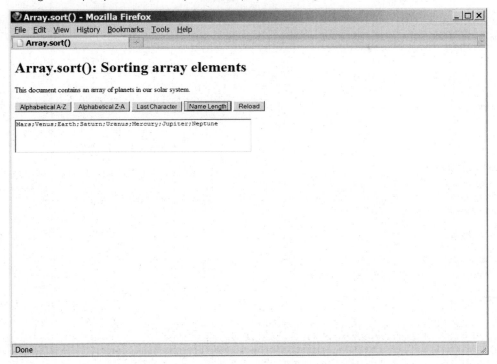

LISTING 18-8

Array.sort() Possibilities

HTML: jsb-18-08.html

```html
<!DOCTYPE html>
<html>
    <head>
        <meta http-equiv="content-type" content="text/html;charset=utf-8">
        <title>Array.sort()</title>
        <script type="text/javascript" src="../jsb-global.js"></script>
        <script type="text/javascript" src="jsb-18-08.js"></script>
    </head>
    <body>
        <h1>Array.sort(): Sorting array elements</h1>
        <form>
            <p>This document contains an array of planets in our solar system.</p>
            <p>
                <input type="button" id="sortAsc" value="Alphabetical A-Z">
                <input type="button" id="sortDesc" value="Alphabetical Z-A">
```

continued

arrayObject.sort()

LISTING 18-8   *(continued)*

```
            <input type="button" id="sortLastChar" value="Last Character">
            <input type="button" id="sortLength" value="Name Length">
            <input type="button" id="reload" value="Reload">
        </p>
        <p>
            <textarea id="output" name="output" rows="3" cols="60"
                      wrap="virtual"></textarea>
        </p>
    </form>
  </body>
</html>
```

JavaScript: jsb-18-08.js

```
// initialize when the page has loaded
addEvent(window, 'load', initialize);

function initialize()
{
    // do this only if the browser can handle DOM methods
    if (document.getElementById)
    {
        // point to critical elements
        oOutput = document.getElementById('output');
        var oButtonSortAsc = document.getElementById('sortAsc');
        var oButtonSortDesc = document.getElementById('sortDesc');
        var oButtonSortLastChar = document.getElementById('sortLastChar');
        var oButtonSortLength = document.getElementById('sortLength');
        var oReload = document.getElementById('reload');

        // if they all exist...
        if (oOutput && oButtonSortAsc && oButtonSortDesc && oButtonSortLastChar
                 && oButtonSortLength && oReload)
        {
            // apply behaviors to buttons
            oButtonSortAsc.onclick = function() { sortIt(null) };
            oButtonSortDesc.onclick = function() { sortIt(compare1) };
            oButtonSortLastChar.onclick = function() { sortIt(compare2) };
            oButtonSortLength.onclick = function() { sortIt(compare3) };
            oReload.onclick = function() { location.reload(); };

            // set global array
            solarSys = new Array("Mercury", "Venus", "Earth", "Mars", "Jupiter",
                            "Saturn", "Uranus", "Neptune");
        }
    }
}
```

```
// comparison functions
function compare1(a,b)
{
    // reverse alphabetical order
    if (a > b)
        return -1;
    if (b > a)
        return 1;
    return 0;
}

function compare2(a,b)
{
    // last character of planet names
    var aComp = a.charAt(a.length - 1);
    var bComp = b.charAt(b.length - 1);
    if (aComp < bComp)
        return -1;
    if (aComp > bComp)
        return 1;
    return 0;
}

function compare3(a,b)
{
    // length of planet names
    return a.length - b.length;
}

// sort and display array
function sortIt(compFunc)
{
    if (compFunc == null)
    {
        solarSys.sort();
    }
    else
    {
        solarSys.sort(compFunc);
    }

    // display results in field
    var delimiter = ";";
    oOutput.value = decodeURIComponent(solarSys.join(delimiter));
}
```

Related Items: `array.reverse()` method

Note

As we show you in Chapter 45, many regular expression object methods generate arrays as their result (for example, an array of matching values in a string). These special arrays have a custom set of named properties that assist your script in analyzing the findings of the method. Beyond that, these regular expression result arrays behave like all others. ∎

> `array.splice(startIndex , deleteCount[, item1[,`
> `    item2[,...itemN]]])`

Returns: Array

Compatibility: WinIE5.5+, MacIE−, NN4+, Moz+, Safari+, Opera+, Chrome+

If you need to remove items from the middle of an array, the `array.splice()` method simplifies a task that would otherwise require assembling a new array from selected items of the original array. The first of two required parameters is a zero-based index integer that points to the first item to be removed from the current array. The second parameter is another integer that indicates how many sequential items are to be removed from the array. Removing array items affects the length of the array, and those items that are removed are returned by the `splice()` method as their own array.

You can also use the `splice()` method to replace array items. Optional parameters beginning with the third let you provide data elements that are to be inserted into the array in place of the items being removed. Each added item can be any JavaScript data type, and the number of new items does not have to be equal to the number of items removed. In fact, by specifying a second parameter of zero, you can use `splice()` to insert one or more items into any position of the array.

Example

Use The Evaluator (see Chapter 4) to experiment with the `splice()` method. Begin by creating an array with a sequence of numbers:

```
a = new Array(1,2,3,4,5)
```

Next, remove the center three items, and replace them with one string item:

```
a.splice(1, 3, "two/three/four")
```

The Results box shows a string version of the three-item array returned by the method. To view the current contents of the array, enter a into the top text box.

To put the original numbers back into the array, swap the string item with three numeric items:

```
a.splice(1, 1, 2, 3, 4)
```

The method returns the single string, and the a array now has five items in it again.

Related Item: `array.slice()` method

array.toLocaleString()

Returns: String

Compatibility: WinIE5.5+, MacIE−, NN6+, Moz+, Safari+, Opera+, Chrome+

array.toString()

Returns: String

Compatibility: WinIE4+, MacIE4+, NN3+, Moz+, Safari+, Opera+, Chrome+

The array.toLocaleString() and the older, more compatible array.toString() are methods to retrieve the contents of an array in string form. Browsers use the toString() method on their own whenever you attempt to display an array in text boxes, in which case the array items are comma-delimited.

The precise string conversion of the toLocaleString() is left up to the specific browser implementation. That browsers differ in some details is not surprising, even in the U.S. English versions of operating systems and browsers. For example, if the array contains integer values, the toLocaleString() method in IE5.5+ returns the numbers comma-and-space-delimited, formatted with two digits to the right of the decimal (as if dollars and cents). Mozilla-based browsers, on the other hand, return just the integers, but these are also comma-delimited.

If you need to convert an array to a string for purposes of passing array data to other venues (for example, as data in a hidden text box submitted to a server or as search string data conveyed to another page), use the array.join() method instead. Array.join() gives you more reliable and flexible control over the item delimiters, and you are assured of the same results regardless of locale.

Related Item: array.join() method

Array Comprehensions

Compatibility: FF2+

A feature of JavaScript 1.7 is an enhancement to JavaScript syntax called *array comprehensions*, a shortcut for building a new array based on another. Comprehensions can often replace the map() and filter() methods.

Here's an example that uses a comprehension to produce a modified version of every element in an array:

```
var aIntegers = new Array(0, 1, 2, 3, 4, 5, 6, 7);
var aResults = [i * i for each (i in aIntegers)];

// result: aResults == [0, 1, 4, 9, 16, 25, 36, 49]
```

This is the equivalent of the map() syntax:

```
function square(iValue)
{
    return iValue * iValue;
}

var aIntegers = new Array(0, 1, 2, 3, 4, 5, 6, 7);
var aResults = aIntegers.map(square);
```

Array comprehensions can also be used to select certain elements from an array:

```
var aNumbers = new Array(1, -2, -3, 4, 5, -6);
var aResult = [i for each (i in aNumbers) if (i > 0)];

// result: aResult == [1, 4, 5]
```

This is the equivalent of the `filter()` syntax:

```
function isPositive(iValue, iIndex, aArray)
{
    return (iValue > 0);
}

var aNumbers = new Array(1, -2, -3, 4, 5, -6);
var aResult = aNumbers.filter(isPositive);
```

The square brackets of an array comprehension introduce an implicit block for scoping purposes. New variables (such as i in the preceding examples) have local scope (are treated as if they had been declared using `let`) and are not available outside of the comprehension.

The input to an array comprehension does not itself need to be an array; *iterators* and *generators* can also be used (see Chapter 21).

Destructuring Assignment

Compatibility: FF2+, Opera 9.5 (partial)

Destructuring assignment (introduced with JavaScript 1.7 and corrected in 1.8) makes it easy to extract an array from another array, object, or function. You can view it as setting one array equal to another:

```
[a, b, c] = [1, 2, 3]
// result: a == 1, b == 2, and c == 3
```

This syntax provides a succinct way to swap the values of variables:

```
var x = 1;
var y = 2;

[x, y] = [y, x]
// result: x == 2 and y == 1
```

... replacing the more conventional technique that employs a third temporary variable to swap two values:

```
temp = x;
x = y;
y = temp;
```

Another example is receiving an array of values from a function:

```
function fun()
{
   return [3, 'aardvark', 0];
}

[a, b, c] = fun()
// result: a == 3, b == 'aardvark', and c == 0
```

As of this writing, destructuring assignment is supported by Firefox 2.0+ and partially by Opera 9.5 but not at all by Internet Explorer 8 and other browsers. We can't use JavaScript to test a browser's ability to execute this code because an older version will simply crash trying to compile it. We can "firewall" this code with a special script tag:

```
<script type="application/javascript;version=1.8" src="scriptname.js"></script>
```

However, we question the usefulness of this if we also have to provide more conventional syntax for other browsers. Unless we're in a special circumstance in which we can guarantee that our code will be running in a browser that incorporates JavaScript 1.8, we may just have to wait until destructuring assignment syntax is more universally adopted by the other browser manufacturers.

Compatibility with Older Browsers

Some of the features described in this chapter were introduced with JavaScript 1.6 and later. They run in Firefox 2.0+ or 3.0+ and occasional others but are not supported in many other browsers, including Internet Explorer 8. New array object methods such as `every()` and `filter()` can be used in our cross-browser scripts simply by adding them to the object prototype when they're not already there, as we've listed in this chapter. However, innovations of syntax, including array comprehensions and destructuring assignment, cannot be included in blocks of script run by legacy browsers because older versions of JavaScript will simply stop cold during the compile phase and will not run any of the script on the page.

Should we then refrain from using the new syntax until it's universally supported?

As mentioned in Chapter 4, there is a way to identify a block of code so that it will run only in a given version of JavaScript or greater — for example:

```
<script type="text/javascript" src="for-everyone.js"></script>
<script type="application/javascript;version=1.7" src="new-stuff.js"></script>
```

You can isolate sections of code in this way to execute only if the browser is capable, separated safely from older user agents.

The question then comes, what alternative code will you run if the browser is older? If you have to write code that performs the same operation as an array comprehension to support older browsers, why not simply use that code for all browsers?

As with any facet of web development, and JavaScript in particular, make sure that all basic functionality on a page is intact even in the absence of JavaScript or any specific features of the language; then add enhancements when scripting and any of its advanced features are available. This principle of progressive enhancement ensures that while your pages may work better or faster for those with fancier tools, they will work fundamentally for everyone.

JSON — Native JavaScript Object Notation

J SON (JavaScript Object Notation) is a lightweight way to represent data structures that many programming languages can easily read and write. This makes it (similarly to XML) a useful data interchange format among applications written in a variety of languages, for example, between server-side PHP and client-side JavaScript. With the ECMAScript Fifth Edition standard, JSON is now formally part of the language and will be increasingly supported by more browsers over the coming years. In the meantime, there is freely available code to assist older browsers.

JSON was developed by Douglas Crockford and presented to the Internet community in 2006. It was formally made part of the ECMAScript standard, on which JavaScript is based, as of the Fifth Edition finalized in April 2010.

How JSON Works

JSON combines two aspects of JavaScript syntax for representing arrays and objects to present data structures — simple array notation using brackets [ ]:

```
[ "item1", "item2", "item3" ]
```

and the notation for objects and associative arrays using curly braces { }:

```
{ "key": "value" }
```

We have access to the embedded values by numerical index in the first case (remember that the first item has an index of zero):

```
var aItems = [ "item1", "item2", "item3" ];
// e.g., aItems[0] == "item1"
```

and by key name in the second:

```
var oExample = { "charlie": "horse" };
// oExample["charlie"] == "horse"
// oExample.charlie == "horse"
```

Using these two conventions, one can describe many data structures with sub-records having either named or numerically indexed keys:

```
var oNovelist =
{
    "firstName": "Joanna",
    "lastName": "Russ",
    "novels":
    [
        {
            "title": "And Choas Died",
            "year": "1970"
        },
        {
            "title": "The Female Man",
            "year": "1975"
        }
    ]
};
```

In this example, `firstName` and `lastName` have simple string values, while `novels` is a numerically indexed array. Here are two ways to refer to these values:

```
var sMsg = oNovelist['firstName'] + ' ' + oNovelist['lastName'] + "'s novel " +
oNovelist['novels'][0]['title'] + ' was published in ' +
oNovelist['novels'][0]['year'] + '.';

var sMsg = oNovelist.firstName + ' ' + oNovelist.lastName + "'s novel " +
oNovelist.novels[0].title + ' was published in ' +
oNovelist.novels[0].year + '.';

// result: Joanna Russ's novel And Chaos Died was published in 1970.
```

In the first example, we're treating the structure as an associative array with bracketed keys. In the second, we're using dot-notation to retrieve the object's properties. The first syntax will always work because the keys, when strings, are quoted. We got away with using dot-notation in the second example because none of these keys contained characters such as hyphens, periods, and other characters that are legal key values but would throw JavaScript a curve:

```
var sMsg = oNovelist['first-name'];   // this works
var sMsg = oNovelist.first-name;      // oh no! JavaScript tries to subtract
```

Cross-Reference

For more on this point, see the section "Simulating a Hash Table" in Chapter 18, "The Array Object." ■

Data types

Six types of data can occur as a JSON value:

- String (a collection of zero or more Unicode characters, wrapped in double quotes, using backslash escapes)
- Number (integer or real; no octal and hexadecimal formats)

- Object (a collection of key:value pairs, comma-separated and enclosed in curly braces)
- Array (an ordered sequence of values, comma-separated and enclosed in square brackets)
- Boolean (`true` or `false`)
- `null`

Whitespace can be inserted between any pair of tokens.

Sending and Receiving JSON Data

Because JSON grammar uses JavaScript's normal object and array syntax, we don't need any add-ons to the language in order to be able to build and read JSON data structures within a single script. It's when we need to share these structures between scripts that complications arise.

In order to read, write, send, and receive a JSON data object, we need to convert it to and from a string. The standard way of doing this is to read and write exactly the same syntax we'd use in JavaScript:

```
{"firstName":"Joanna","lastName":"Russ","novels":[{"title":"And Choas
Died","year":"1970"},{"title":"The Female Man","year":"1975"}]}
```

This string can then be imported into any of the programming languages that work with JSON.

Performing this conversion between object and string in JavaScript is simple enough. There are functions at `http://json.org` that we're encouraged to use for older browsers so that we don't have to reinvent the wheel.

Because the JSON data is stored in a string exactly as it is in JavaScript source code, on first glance it might seem that the most expedient way to convert it from a string back to an object is by using the JavaScript method `eval()`:

```
var sStringJSON = readJSONDataFromWhateverSource();

eval("var oJSON = " + sStringJSON);
// or:
var oJSON = eval('(' + sStringJSON + ')');
```

Now `oJSON.firstName` will yield 'Joanna' for the example above. (In the second use of `eval()`, note the necessary inclusion of parentheses around the JSON string to satisfy the JavaScript interpreter.)

However, we can't over-emphasize that `eval()` opens up a doorway for malicious exploits in JavaScript and should be avoided on any public page. A proper JSON parser will walk through the data string character by character to build the JSON object rather than yielding to the temptation to use `eval()`.

JSON goes native

The JSON object was made part of the language with the ECMAScript Fifth Edition standard, published in December 2009. Mozilla implemented this in JavaScript 1.8.1, in the Gecko layout engine version 1.9.1 that drives Firefox 3.5, Thunderbird 3, and SeaMonkey 2. Other browser development teams are sure to follow their lead.

The JSON object has two methods, `parse()` and `stringify()`. The `toJSON()` method is also added to the Date object.

JSON Object

Properties	Methods
	`parse()`
	`stringify()`

Methods

JSON.parse(*string [, translator]*)

Returns: JSON object reference

Compatibility: Moz1.9.1+, Firefox3.5+

Use the `JSON.parse()` method to convert a JSON string to a JSON object.

    object = JSON.parse(*string, translator*)

The `string` parameter is the "stringified" JSON to be converted to an object.

Related Item: `JSON.stringify()` method

JSON.stringify(*object [, replacer [, space]]*)

Returns: JSON string

Compatibility: Moz1.9.1+, Firefox3.5+

`JSON.stringify()` converts a JSON object to a JSON string.

    string = JSON.stringify(*object, replacer, space*)

The `object` parameter is the JSON object to be converted to a string.

`replacer` is an optional parameter that is either a function that alters the behavior of the stringification process or an array of String and Number objects that serve as a whitelist for selecting the properties of the object to be stringified. If this value is null or not provided, all properties of the object are included in the resulting JSON string.

`space` is a String or Number object that's used to insert white space into the output JSON string for readability purposes. If this is a Number, it indicates the number of space characters to use as white space; this number is capped at 10 if it's larger than that. Values less than 1 indicate that no space should be used. If this is a String, the string (or the first 10 characters of the string, if it's longer than that) is used as white space. If this parameter is not provided (or is null), no white space is used.

Related Item: `JSON.parse()` method

Security Concerns

Some concern has been expressed about the vulnerability JSON presents in web security. We feel that these issues can be dismissed with sufficiently careful use of the technology.

Using `eval()` to convert a JSON string to an object (or for any other purpose on a public page) is an easy pitfall to avoid. If a method (function) is embedded in serialized JSON and `eval()` is used to convert it, JavaScript code can be executed without the permission of the page author's script. The obvious solution is to use a non-`eval()` parsing algorithm, such as that published by Douglas Crockford, on older browsers and the new JSON object method `parse()` on newer browsers.

The DOM method `XMLHttpRequest()` is commonly used to exchange information between server and client. By default it permits exchanges only with the server from which the current page has originated. However, by injecting a `script` tag that links to an off-site JavaScript file, this protection can be circumvented. The solution here is to be vigilant when it comes to allowing JavaScript from third parties to execute on your page.

E4X — Native XML Processing

W ith the rise in popularity of Ajax (Asynchronous JavaScript and XML) connectivity in recent years, it's become commonplace for web developers who might otherwise never stray beyond the bounds of HTML to work with XML (Extensible Markup Language). In fact, XML has been considered so fundamental to everyday web development that the ECMA has incorporated it into the very syntactical fabric of JavaScript. We can now write unquoted XML markup right into our JavaScript statements — as permitted by the most recent browsers.

This new feature of JavaScript syntax places XML uniquely on both sides of a major divide. Every other aspect of scripting is either part of the core JavaScript language or part of the DOM (Document Object Model). XML is now a member of both camps.

We discuss techniques for transmitting XML between client and server in Chapter 39, "Ajax, E4X, and XML" (on the CD).

XML

Briefly, XML is a markup language designed to contain and transmit textual data. It consists of nested elements marked up with three types of tag — matching begin- and end-tags

```
<hobby>music</hobby>
```

and empty-element tags

```
<breathe/>
```

Elements can contain attributes, which are name/value pairs that reside within the opening or empty tag:

```
<fax location="home" call-first="true">123-456-7890</fax>;
```

Unlike HTML and XHTML, in which element and attribute name choices are constrained by the Document Type Declaration or XMLSchema, XML element and attribute names are completely arbitrary and defined by the author of the data to suit the current purpose.

For a complete formal description of XML, see the W3C specification at `http://w3.org/TR/REC-xml/`.

ECMAScript for XML (E4X)

Prior to E4X, the only way to access XML documents with JavaScript was through the DOM at the object level. With the advent of E4X, XML is treated as a primitive, at the same level as strings, numbers, and Booleans. What does this mean to us? The short story is that XML access is now simpler for us as web developers, and faster for the end user. An XML object created with the XML primitive is not part of the DOM; neither is it a DOM representation of XML. Because it is a primitive, you use it in ways similar to how you use other JavaScript objects.

Using the XML object

With E4X you declare an XML object, in much the same way that you declare a string or numeric or Boolean object, with the XML constructor:

```
var oCopyright = new XML();
```

You can initialize the object using text:

```
var sXMLText = "<copyright>"
             + "<date>2010</date>"
             + "<author>Danny Goodman</author>"
             + "</copyright>";

var oCopyright = new XML(sXMLText);
```

Remarkably, you can also use unquoted XML markup in an assignment statement, which implicitly creates the XML object:

```
var oCopyright = <copyright>
                     <date>2010</date>
                     <author>Danny Goodman</author>
                 </copyright>;
```

This type of syntax, in which specially constructed text can be assigned without quotation marks, may be reminiscent of JavaScript's native regular expression syntax, as described in Chapter 45, "The Regular Expression and RegExp Objects."

XML elements

The XML elements within the XML object are its properties. You can use both the familiar `object.property` dot-notation and the `object[property]` bracket-notation to reference elements and their values:

```
var sText = "Copyright " + oCopyright.date + " by " + oCopyright.author;
var sText = "Copyright " + oCopyright['date'] + " by " + oCopyright['author'];
```

The outermost XML element is the root of the object, so the first top-level property within our oCopyright object above is the date element:

```
alert(oCopyright.name());          // result = 'copyright'
alert(oCopyright.child(0).name()); // result = 'date'
alert(oCopyright.date);            // result = '2010'
```

Of course, as with other JavaScript objects, you won't be able to use object dot-notation successfully when an element tag name contains any characters that would confuse JavaScript. For example:

```
var oXML = <author>
              <first-name>Danny</first-name>
           </author>;

var sText = oXML['first-name'];    // result: Danny
var sText = oXML.first-name;       // result: JavaScript stops cold!
```

In the preceding example, JavaScript attempts to subtract the value of a variable called name from the value of the XML element oXML.first. If either one doesn't exist or if they do exist but don't both have numerical values that can be subtracted, JavaScript fails. The moral of the story: if you want to use dot notation and you are guaranteed to have complete control over the elements' tag names, you can restrict their character set to alphanumerics and underscores. If you're working with data coming in from a source that you might not always control, use bracket-quote notation, which will always succeed.

Adding elements

The appendChild() method of the XML object works similarly to the DOM method of the same name, inserting a child element into the referent:

```
var oBook = <book/>;
var oAuthor = <author/>;
oBook.appendChild(oAuthor);

result: <book>
           <author/>
        </book>
```

Elements can also be appended to an XML element using the same concatenation syntax that we typically use with strings:

```
oCopyright += <addendum>All rights reserved.</addendum>;
```

This results in:

```
<copyright>
   <date>2010</date>
   <author>Danny Goodman</author>
</copyright>;
<addendum>All rights reserved.<addendum>
```

In order to insert the new element inside the copyright element, we need to write:

```
oCopyright.author += <addendum>All rights reserved.</addendum>;
```

resulting in:

```
<copyright>
    <date>2010</date>
    <author>Danny Goodman</author>
    <addendum>All rights reserved.<addendum>
</copyright>
```

Embedded JavaScript expressions

E4X becomes really exciting when you want the XML object to dynamically interact with JavaScript expressions. You do this with curly braces:

```
var oDate = new Date();

var oCopyright = <copyright>
                    <date>{oDate.getFullYear()}</date>
                    <author>Danny Goodman</author>
                 </copyright>;
```

Whatever is inside the curly braces is evaluated as a JavaScript expression and its result plugged into the XML stream. In the year 2020, the preceding example will resolve to:

```
<copyright>
    <date>2020</date>
    <author>Danny Goodman</author>
</copyright>;
```

XML element attributes

Just as in XML documents, the elements in your XML objects can have attributes. Those attribute values can be set dynamically with curly brace notation as well. You can extract the value of an element's attribute by using dot notation with the @ operator in front of the attribute name, as we do with the location attribute in this example:

```
var oPhonebook = <phonebook>
                    <entry>
                        <name>Janis Joplin</name>
                        <phone location="home">123-456-7890</phone>
                    </entry>
                 </phonebook>;
var sText = oPhonebook.entry.name + "'s "
          + oPhonebook.entry.phone.@location + " phone is "
          + oPhonebook.entry.phone + ".";
// or:
var sText = oPhonebook['entry']['name'] + "'s "
          + oPhonebook['entry']['phone']['@type'] + " phone is "
          + oPhonebook['entry']['phone'] + ".";

// result == Janis Joplin's home phone is 123-456-7890.
```

You can also use the @ notation to create and modify attribute values:

```
oPhonebook.entry.phone.@location = "work";
```

The XMLList object

Most XML documents contain repeating sets of elements. You can create such sets in your XML object simply by repeating a tag name for elements with the same parent:

```
var oBook = <book>
                <title>The JavaScript Bible 7th Edition</title>
                <author>Danny Goodman</author>
                <coauthor>Michael Morrison</coauthor>
                <coauthor>Paul Novitski</coauthor>
                <coauthor>Cynthia Gustaff Rayl</coauthor>
            </book>;
```

When you point to the repeating set, you get back an XMLList object. It can be processed almost the same as you would an array. There are two primary differences: length() is a method and not a property, and therefore requires the parentheses (); and other Array object methods are not supported by XMLList.

```
var sText = "The number of co-authors is " + oBook.coauthor.length() + ".";
```

In our current example XML, oBook.coauthor comprises a list within the overall data structure because there is more than one sibling element with the same tag name.

```
// extract the XMLList of coauthor elements
var oCoauthors = oBook.coauthor;

var sText = oBook.title + ' was written by ' + oBook.author + ' with ';

// loop through co-authors
var sConj = '';
var iCoauthors = oCoauthors.length();
var sLastAuthor = oCoauthors[iCoauthors-1];

for (var i=0; i < iCoauthors; i++)
{
    // comma before item if more than two items
    if (i > 0 && iCoauthors > 2)
    {
        sConj = ', ';
    }
    // 'and' before item if last in a series
    if (i == iCoauthors-1 && iCoauthors > 1)
    {
        sConj += ' and ';
    }

    // add item to list
    sText += sConj + oCoauthors[i];
}
```

```
sText += '.';

// result == The JavaScript Bible 7th Edition was written by Danny Goodman
              with Michael Morrison, Paul Novitski, and Cynthia Gustaff Rayl.
```

The asterisk (*) can be used to represent all items in a collection. Using the preceding XML:

```
var iCount = oBook.*.length();
```

The result is 5 — the root parent has a `title`, an `author`, and three `coauthor` elements.

Adding list items

To add a new item to an `XMLList`, use the same concatenation syntax as mentioned above and name the list by its repeating element:

```
oBook.coauthor += <coauthor>John Lennon</coauthor>;
```

resulting in:

```
<book>
    <title>The JavaScript Bible 7th Edition</title>
    <author>Danny Goodman</author>
    <coauthor>Michael Morrison</coauthor>
    <coauthor>Paul Novitski</coauthor>
    <coauthor>Cynthia Gustaff Rayl</coauthor>
    <coauthor>John Lennon</coauthor>
</book>
```

Note

A cautionary note: if you extract an `XMLList` object from an `XML` object as we did above:

```
// extract the XMLList of coauthor elements
var oCoauthors = oBook.c  oauthor;
```

the list is a static copy of the XML elements with no dynamic linkage. Any subsequent change to either the `XML` object or the `XMLList` object will not be reflected in the other. In this example, adding a new `coauthor` element to the `oCoauthors` list does not modify the original `XML` object. ∎

Selecting list items

The power of E4X really shines in its ability to select `XMLList` items based on attributes and values. Consider the following example:

```
var oPhonebook = <phonebook>
                    <entry>
                        <name>Janis Joplin</name>
                        <phone location="home">123-456-7890</phone>
                        <phone location="work">234-567-8901</phone>
                        <phone location="cell">345-678-9012</phone>
                    </entry>
                    <entry>
```

```
        <name>John Lennon</name>
        <phone location="home">987-654-3210</phone>
        <phone location="work">876-543-2109</phone>
      </entry>
    </phonebook>;
```

We've seen that we can select a list of all elements of a matching name quite easily:

```
// extract a list of all the phone elements
var oPhones = oPhonebook.entry.phone;

result:
<phone location="home">123-456-7890</phone>
<phone location="work">234-567-8901</phone>
<phone location="cell">345-678-9012</phone>
<phone location="home">987-654-3210</phone>
<phone location="work">876-543-2109</phone>
```

Note that this finds the phone elements in more than one entry record. The selection statement essentially says, "Find all the phone elements whose parent is a root entry element." If we wanted to limit the search to a single entry element, we need only specify its index:

```
var oPhones = oPhonebook.entry[0].phone;
```

Similarly, we can select elements by attribute value:

```
var oWorkPhones = oPhonebook.entry.phone.(@location == 'work');

result:
<phone location="work">234-567-8901</phone>
<phone location="work">876-543-2109</phone>
```

This narrows the selection to just those phone elements that have a type attribute of "work" — when the expression in parentheses evaluates to true. Note that we're using the double equal sign == of an equality comparison, not the single = of a value assignment!

One of the handy aspects of this syntax is being able to extract the value of one element after searching for its sibling:

```
var oPhone = oPhonebook.entry.(name == 'Janis Joplin').phone.
  (@location == 'home');

result:
<phone location="home">123-456-7890</phone>
```

The selector says, "Get me the home phone number of the entry with the name 'Janis Joplin.'" The statement locates an entry with a child element name that has the value 'Janis Joplin' but then returns a phone element that is the sibling of the name element. Is that cool or what? Of course, like so many dead rock stars, Janis currently has an unlisted number, but we can always dream.

XML selector expressions can contain JavaScript functions, and without having to use curly brace syntax:

```
function checkExchange(sExchange, sPhone)
{
```

XMLObject.child()

```
        sExchange = '-' + sExchange + '-';
        return (sPhone.indexOf(sExchange) > 0);
    }
var sPhone = oPhonebook.entry.(checkExchange('543', phone.
  (@location=='work'))).name;
```

This returns "John Lennon" since we've selected the entry in which the checkExchange() function returns true.

Serializing XML objects

XML can be a handy format for keeping track of information within a script, but its primary use is communicating structured data between programs. To send an XML structure to the server, we translate the JavaScript object into a text string. The XML object has two interchangeable methods for doing this — toXMLString() and toString().These methods can operate on any subset of the object as well as the whole thing at once:

```
var sXMLText = oPhonebook.toXMLString();
var sXMLText = oPhonebook.entry.(name == 'John Lennon').toString();
```

Embedding E4X in HTML

Although you can use the standard MIME type with E4X

```
<script type="text/javascript">
```

you might end up with inexplicable syntax errors. This usually occurs for one of two reasons: you are using HTML comments to hide script from older browsers; or you are putting your scripts into XML CDATA sections. If either of these is the case, then you can add the E4X argument to the standard MIME type:

```
<script type="text/javascript;e4x=1">
```

Methods
child()

Returns: XML object

Compatibility: WinIE5-, MacIE-, NN-, FF3.5+, Safari-, Opera-, Chrome-

The child() method returns an XML element that is an immediate descendant of the referent:

```
var oPhonebook = <phonebook>
                    <person>
                        <name>Janis Joplin</name>
                        <phone location="home">123-456-7890</phone>
                    </person>
                </phonebook>;

alert(oPhonebook.person.child(1));          // result = '123-456-7890'
```

Remember that `child()` is a method, even though we use it much as we would an array, so use parentheses around the index, not brackets. Like an array, the `child()` collection is a zero-based list, so `child(1)` finds the second child element. Unlike an array, we cannot use `forEach` syntax.

Related Item: `childNodes()` DOM property

copy()

Returns: XML object

Compatibility: WinIE5-, MacIE-, NN-, FF3.5+, Safari-, Opera-, Chrome-

The `copy()` method returns a deep copy of the selected portion of an XML object. For example:

```
var oPhonebook = <phonebook>
                    <person>
                        <name>Janis Joplin</name>
                        <phone location="home">123-456-7890</phone>
                    </person>
                 </phonebook>;

var oPerson = oPhonebook.person.copy();
```

The result of this operation is the following XML object:

```
<person>
    <name>Janis Joplin</name>
    <phone location="home">123-456-7890</phone>
</person>
```

Note that this can also be accomplished using a simple assignment statement:

```
var oPerson = oPhonebook.person;
```

name()

Returns: String

Compatibility: WinIE5-, MacIE-, NN-, FF3.5+, Safari-, Opera-, Chrome-

The `name()` method returns a string that is the XML element's tag name:

```
var oPhonebook = <phonebook>
                    <person>
                        <name>Janis Joplin</name>
                        <phone location="home">123-456-7890</phone>
                    </person>
                 </phonebook>;

alert(oPhonebook.child(0).name());          // result = 'person'
alert(oPhonebook.person.child(1).name());   // result = 'phone'
alert(oPhonebook.person.child(1));          // result = '123-456-7890'
```

XMLObject.toString()

Remember that child() is a method, even though we use it much as we would an array, so use parentheses around the index, not brackets. Like an array, the child() collection is a zero-based list, so child(1) finds the second child element.

Related Item: childNodes() DOM property

toString(), toXMLString()

Returns: String

Compatibility: WinIE5-, MacIE-, NN-, FF1.5+, Safari-, Opera-, Chrome-

The toString() and toXMLString() methods return a string that is the concatenated text of all the text nodes of the XML object.

Related Item: *string*.toString()

Control Structures and Exception Handling

Y ou get up in the morning, go about your day's business, and then end the day by walking the dog, changing into comfy footwear, and relaxing. That's not much different from what a program does from the time it starts to the time it ends. But along the way, both you and a program take lots of tiny steps, not all of which advance the processing in a straight line. At times, you have to control what's going on by making a decision or repeating tasks until the whole job is finished. Control structures are the facilities that make these tasks possible in JavaScript.

Control structures in JavaScript follow along the same lines as they do in many programming languages. Basic decision-making and looping constructions satisfy the needs of just about all programming tasks.

Another vital program control mechanism — error (or exception) handling — is formally addressed in the ECMA-262 language standard. The concept of exception handling was added to the JavaScript version introduced in IE5.5 and NN6, but it is well known to programmers in many other environments. Adopting exception-handling techniques in your code can greatly enhance recovery from processing errors beyond your control, such as those caused by errant user input or network glitches.

IN THIS CHAPTER

Branching script execution down multiple paths

Looping through ordered collections of data

Applying exception handling techniques

If and If. . .Else Decisions

Compatibility: WinIE3+, MacIE3+, NN2+, Moz+, Safari+, Opera+, Chrome+

JavaScript programs frequently have to make decisions based on the current values of variables or object properties. Such decisions can have only two possible outcomes at a time. The factor that determines the path that the program takes at these decision points is if a statement evaluates to true or false. For example, when you come back from walking the dog at night, the statement under test is something such as, "Is my comfy footwear in the living room?" If that statement is false, you look for your comfy footwear; if that statement is true, you put on your comfy footwear and relax.

Simple decisions

JavaScript syntax for this kind of simple decision always begins with the keyword if, followed by the condition to test, and then the statements that execute if the condition yields a true result. JavaScript uses no "then" keyword (as some other languages do); the keyword is implied by the way parentheses and braces surround the various components of this construction. The formal syntax is:

```
if (condition)
{
    statementsIfTrue
}
```

This construction means that if the condition is true, program execution takes a detour to execute statements inside the braces. No matter what happens, the program continues executing statements beyond the closing brace (}). If a comfy footwear search were part of the scripting language, the code would look like this:

```
if (comfyFootwearInLivingRoom == false)
{
    look for them
}
```

If you're not used to C/C++, the double equals sign may have caught your eye. You learn more about this type of operator in the next chapter, but for now, know that this operator compares the equality of items on either side of it. In other words, the condition statement of an if construction must always yield a Boolean (true or false) value. Some object properties, you may recall, are Booleans, so you can stick a reference to that property into the condition statement by itself. Otherwise, the condition statement consists of two values separated by a comparison operator, such as == (equals) or != (does not equal).

Next, look at some real JavaScript. The following function receives a text input object:

```
function notTooHigh(oInput)
{
    if (parseInt(oInput.value) > 100)
    {
        alert("Sorry, the value you entered is too high. Try again.");
        return false;
    }
    return true;
}
```

The condition (in parentheses) tests the contents of the field against a hard-wired value of 100. If the entered value is larger than that, the function alerts you and returns a false value to the calling statement elsewhere in the script. But if the value is less than 100, all intervening code is skipped and the function returns true.

About (*condition*) expressions

A lot of condition testing for control structures compares a value against some very specific condition, such as a string being empty or a value being null. You can use a couple of shortcuts to take care of many circumstances. Table 21-1 details the values that evaluate to true or false (or equivalent) to satisfy a control structure's *condition* expression.

TABLE 21-1

Condition Value Equivalents

True	False
Nonempty string	Empty string
Nonzero number	0
Nonnull value	`null`
Object exists	Object doesn't exist
Property is defined	Undefined property

Instead of having to spell out an equivalency expression for a condition involving these kinds of values, you can simply supply the value to be tested. For example, if a variable named `myVal` is capable of reaching an `if` construction with a value of `null`, an empty string, or a string value for further processing, you can use the following shortcut:

```
if (myVal)
{
    // do processing on myVal
}
```

All `null` or empty string conditions evaluate to `false`, so that only the cases of `myVal` being a processable value get inside the `if` construction. This mechanism is the same that you have seen elsewhere in this book to employ object detection for browser branching. For example, the code nested inside the following code segment executes only if the `document` object has an `images` array property:

```
if (document.images)
{
    // do processing on image objects
}
```

Complex decisions

The simple type of `if` construction described earlier is fine when the decision is to take a small detour before returning to the main path. But not all decisions — in programming or in life — are like that. To present two alternate paths in a JavaScript decision, you can add a component to the construction. The syntax is

```
if (condition)
{
    // statementsIfTrue
}
else
{
    // statementsIfFalse
}
```

if . . . else

By appending the else keyword, you give the if construction a path to follow in case the condition evaluates to false. The statementsIfTrue and statementsIfFalse do not have to be balanced in any way: One statement can be one line of code, the other 100 lines. But when either one of those branches completes, execution continues after the last closing brace. To demonstrate how this construction can come in handy, the following example is a script fragment that assigns the number of days in February based on whether or not the year (the Date object is explained in Chapter 17) is a leap year (using modulo arithmetic, explained in Chapter 22, to determine if the year is evenly divisible by four, and setting aside all other leap year calculation details for the moment):

```
var howMany = 0;
var currentTime = new Date();
var theYear = currentTime.getFullYear();
  if (theYear % 4 == 0)
  {
      howMany = 29;
  }
  else
  {
      howMany = 28;
  }
```

Here is a case where execution has to follow only one of two possible paths to assign the number of days to the howMany variable. Had the else portion not been used, as in

```
var howMany = 0;
var currentTime = new Date();
var theYear = currentTime.getFullYear();
  if (theYear % 4 == 0)
  {
      howMany = 29;
  }
howMany = 28;
```

then the variable would always be set to 28, occasionally after momentarily being set to 29. The else construction is essential in this case. However, by initializing your variable to 28, it is possible to achieve the correct end without the else portion, as in

```
var howMany = 28;
var currentTime = new Date();
var theYear = currentTime.getFullYear();
  if (theYear % 4 == 0)
  {
      howMany = 29;
  }
```

Nesting if. . .else statements

Designing a complex decision process requires painstaking attention to the logic of the decisions your script must process and the statements that must execute for any given set of conditions. The need for repetitive logic disappeared with the advent of switch construction in version 4 browsers (described later in this chapter), but there may still be times when you must fashion complex decision behavior out of a series of nested if. . .else statements. Without a JavaScript-aware text editor to help keep everything properly indented and properly terminated (with closing braces), you have to monitor the authoring process very carefully. Moreover, the error messages that JavaScript provides when a mistake occurs (see Chapter 48, "Debugging Scripts," on the CD-ROM) may not point directly to the problem line, but only to the region of difficulty.

To demonstrate a nested set of if. . .else constructions, Listing 21-1 presents a simple user interface to a complex problem. A single text object asks the user to enter one of three letters — A, B, or C. The script behind that field processes a different message for each of the following conditions:

- The user enters no value.
- The user enters A.
- The user enters B.
- The user enters C.
- The user enters something entirely different.

Note

The function to assign event handlers throughout the code in this chapter and much of the book is addEvent(), a cross-browser event handler explained in detail in Chapter 32: See "A cross-browser event binding solution." ∎

What's with the Formatting?

Indentation of the if construction, and the further indentation of the statements executed on a true condition, are not required by JavaScript. What you see here, however, is a convention that most JavaScript scripters follow. As you write the code in your text editor, you can use the Tab key to establish each level of indentation; some developers prefer using a setting in their editor that converts tabs to spaces, which guarantees that indentations are consistent across different editors. The browser ignores these tab characters (and/or spaces) when loading your scripts.

There are many styles of indenting. The style we use most often in this book is known as Allman — in which opening and closing braces occupy their own lines — while many programmers prefer 1TBS (The One True Brace Style), in which the opening brace is on the same line as the control statement.

LISTING 21-1

Nested if. . .else Constructions

HTML: jsb-21-01.html

```
<!DOCTYPE html>
<html>
  <head>
    <meta http-equiv="content-type" content="text/html;charset=utf-8">
    <title>Nested if...else</title>
    <script type="text/javascript" src="../jsb-global.js"></script>
```

continued

LISTING 21-1 *(continued)*

```
    <script type="text/javascript" src="jsb-21-01.js"></script>
  </head>
  <body>
    <h1>Nested if...else</h1>
    <form id="theForm" action="validate.php" method="get">
      <fieldset>
        <label for="theText">Please enter A, B, or C: </label>
        <input id="theText" type="text">
        <input type="submit">
      </fieldset>
    </form>
  </body>
</html>
```

JavaScript: jsb-21-01.js

```
// initialize when the page has loaded
addEvent(window, 'load', initialize);

function initialize()
{
   // add an event to the form
   addEvent(document.getElementById('theForm'), 'submit',
     suppressFormSubmission);

   // add an event to the input box
   addEvent(document.getElementById('theText'), 'change', testLetter);
}

function suppressFormSubmission(evt)
{
     // consolidate event handling
     if (!evt) evt = window.event;

   // cancel default behavior
     // W3C DOM method (hide from IE)
     if (evt.preventDefault) evt.preventDefault();

   // IE method
   return false;
}

function testLetter()
{
   // assign to shorter variable name
   var inpVal = this.value;

     if (inpVal != "")
     {  // if entry is not empty then dive in...
```

```
    if (inpVal == "A")
    {  // Is it an "A"?
       alert("Thanks for the A.");
    }
    else if (inpVal == "B")
    {  // No.  Is it a "B"?
       alert("Thanks for the B.");
    }
    else if (inpVal == "C")
    {  // No.  Is it a "C"?
       alert("Thanks for the C.");
    }
    else
    { // Nope.  None of the above
       alert("Sorry, wrong character or case.");
    }
  }
  else
  {   // value was empty, so skipped all other stuff above
     alert("You did not enter anything.");
  }
}
```

Each condition executes only the statements that apply to that particular condition, even if it takes several queries to find out what the entry is. You do not need to break out of the nested construction, because when a `true` response is found, the relevant statement executes, and no other statements occur in the execution path to run.

You might have noticed the `action` on the `form` element identifies a PHP script called `validate .php`. In Chapter 7, "Scripts and HTML Documents," we talked about the advisability of always specifying a server-side program in case the user has turned off JavaScript.

Conditional Expressions

Compatibility: WinIE3+, MacIE3+, NN2+, Moz+, Safari+, Opera+, Chrome+

While we're showing you decision-making constructions in JavaScript, now is a good time to introduce a special type of expression that you can use in place of an `if...else` control structure for a common type of decision — the instance where you want to assign one of two values to a variable, depending on the outcome of some condition. The formal definition for the conditional expression is as follows:

```
variable = (condition) ? val1 : val2;
```

This expression means that if the Boolean result of the `condition` statement is `true`, JavaScript assigns `val1` to the variable; otherwise, it assigns `val2` to the variable. Like other instances of conditional expressions, this one must also be written inside parentheses. The question mark is key here, as is the colon separating the two possible values.

A conditional expression, though not particularly intuitive or easy to read inside code, is very compact. Compare an `if...else` version of an assignment decision that follows

```
var collectorStatus;
    if (CDCount > 500)
    {
        collectorStatus = "fanatic";
    }
    else
    {
        collectorStatus = "normal";
    }
```

with the conditional expression version:

```
var collectorStatus = (CDCount > 500) ? "fanatic" : "normal";
```

The latter saves a few code lines, although the internal processing is the same as that of an `if...else` construction. Of course, if your decision path contains more statements than just one setting the value of a variable, the `if...else` or `switch` construction is preferable. This shortcut, however, is a handy one to remember if you need to perform binary actions, such as setting a true-or-false flag in a script.

The switch Statement

Compatibility: WinIE4+, MacIE4+, NN4+, Moz+, Safari+, Opera+, Chrome+

In some circumstances, a binary — true or false — decision path is not enough to handle the processing in your script. An `object` property or `variable` value may contain any one of several values, and a separate execution path is required for each one. The most obvious way to establish such a decision path is with a series of `if...else` constructions. However, in addition to quickly getting unwieldy with nested code, the more conditions you must test, the less efficient the processing is, because each condition must be tested. The end result is a sequence of clauses and braces that can get very confusing.

Starting in version 4 browsers, a control structure in use by many languages was introduced to JavaScript. The implementation is similar to that of PHP, Java, and C/C++, which use the `switch` and `case` keywords. The basic premise is that you can create any number of execution paths based on the value of some expression. At the beginning of the structure, you identify what that expression is and then, for each execution path, assign a label matching a particular value.

The formal syntax for the `switch` statement is as follows:

```
switch (expression)
{
    case label1:
        [statements]
        [break;]
    case label2:
        [statements]
        [break;]
    ...
```

```
    [default:
        statements]
}
```

For example:

```
switch (TimeOfDay)
{
    case 'morning':
        meal = 'breakfast';
        break;

    case 'midday':
        meal = 'lunch';
        break;

    case 'afternoon':
    case 'evening':
        meal = 'dinner';
        break;

    default:
        meal = 'fast';
}
```

The `expression` parameter of the `switch` statement can evaluate to any string or number value. Labels are surrounded by quotes when the labels represent string values of the expression. Notice that the `break` statements are optional. A `break` statement forces the switch expression to bypass all other checks of succeeding labels against the expression value. It's important to understand that without a `break` statement at the end of each `case`, every line of code in the `switch` expression will get executed. However, since Boolean operators are not allowed (each label must be for one and only one value), you can use careful placement of the `break` statement. (In the preceding example, if the time of day is either afternoon or evening, the meal is dinner.) Another option is the `default` statement, which provides a catchall execution path when the expression value does not match any of the `case` statement labels. If you'd rather not have any execution take place with a non-matching expression value, omit the default part of the construction.

To demonstrate the syntax of a working `switch` statement, Listing 21-2 provides the skeleton of a larger application of this control structure. The page contains two separate arrays of different product categories. Each product has its name and price stored in its respective array. A `select` list displays the product names. After a user chooses a product, the script looks up the product name in the appropriate array and displays the price.

The trick behind this application is the values assigned to each product in the select list. While the displayed text is the product name, the `value` attribute of each `<option>` tag is the array category for the product. That value is the expression used to decide which branch to follow. Notice, too, that we assign a label to the entire switch construction. The purpose of that is to let the deeply nested repeat loops for each case completely bail out of the switch construction (via a labeled `break` statement) whenever a match is made. You can extend this example with any number of product category arrays with additional `case` statements to match.

381

LISTING 21-2

The switch Construction in Action

HTML: jsb-21-02.html

```html
<!DOCTYPE html>
<html>
  <head>
      <meta http-equiv="content-type" content="text/html;charset=utf-8">
      <title>Switch Statement and Labeled Break</title>
      <script type="text/javascript" src="../jsb-global.js"></script>
      <script type="text/javascript" src="jsb-21-02.js"></script>
  </head>
  <body>
      <h1>Switch Statement and Labeled Break</h1>
      <p>Select a chip for lookup in the chip price table:</p>
      <form id="theForm" action="validate.php" method="get">
        <p>
          <label for="chips">Chip:</label>
          <select id="chips">
             <option></option>
             <option value="ICs">Septium 900MHz</option>
             <option value="ICs">Septium Pro 1.0GHz</option>
             <option value="ICs">Octium BFD 750MHz</option>
             <option value="snacks">Rays Potato Chips</option>
             <option value="snacks">Cheezey-ettes</option>
             <option value="snacks">Tortilla Flats</option>
             <option>Poker Chipset</option>
          </select>
          <label for="cost">  Price:</label>
          <input type="text" id="cost" size="10">
        </p>
      </form>
  </body>
</html>
```

JavaScript: jsb-21-02.js

```javascript
// initialize when the page has loaded
addEvent(window, 'load', initialize);

function initialize()
{
   // add an event to the drop down list
   addEvent(document.getElementById('chips'), 'change', getPrice);
}

// build two product arrays with a custom object, simulating two database tables
```

```
function product(name, price)
{
   this.name = name;
   this.price = price;
}


var ICs = new Array();
ICs[0] = new product("Septium 900MHz", "$149");
ICs[1] = new product("Septium Pro 1.0GHz", "$249");
ICs[2] = new product("Octium BFD 750MHz", "$329");

var snacks = new Array();
snacks[0] = new product("Rays Potato Chips", "$1.79");
snacks[1] = new product("Cheezey-ettes", "$1.59");
snacks[2] = new product("Tortilla Flats", "$2.29");

// lookup in the 'table' the cost associated with the product
function getPrice()
{
   var chipName = this.options[this.selectedIndex].text;
   var chipType = this.options[this.selectedIndex].value;
   var outField = document.getElementById('cost');

   master:
   switch(chipType)
   {
      case "ICs":
         for (var i = 0; i < ICs.length; i++)
         {
            if (ICs[i].name == chipName)
            {
               outField.value = ICs[i].price;
               break master;
            }
         }
         break;
      case "snacks":
         for (var i = 0; i < snacks.length; i++)
         {
            if (snacks[i].name == chipName)
            {
               outField.value = snacks[i].price;
               break master;
            }
         }
         break;
      default:
         outField.value = "Not Found";
   }
}
```

Repeat (for) Loops

Compatibility: WinIE3+, MacIE3+, NN2+, Moz+, Safari+, Opera+, Chrome+

As you have seen in numerous examples throughout other chapters, the capability to cycle through every entry in an array or through every item of a form element is vital to many JavaScript scripts. Perhaps the most typical operation is inspecting a property of many similar items in search of a specific value, such as to determine which radio button in a group is selected. One JavaScript structure that allows for these repetitive excursions is the for loop, so-named after the keyword that begins the structure. Two other structures, the while loop and the do-while loop, are covered in the following sections.

The JavaScript for loop repeats a series of statements any number of times and includes an optional loop counter that can be used in the execution of the statements. The following is the formal syntax definition:

```
for ( [initial expression]; [condition]; [update expression])
{
    statements
}
```

The three statements inside the parentheses (parameters to the for statement) play a key role in the way a for loop executes.

An initial expression in a for loop is executed one time, the first time the for loop begins to run. The most common application of the initial expression is to assign a name and starting value to a loop counter variable. Thus, seeing a var statement that both declares a variable name and assigns an initial value (generally 0 or 1) to it is not uncommon. An example is

```
var i = 0;
```

You can use any variable name, but conventional usage calls for the letter i, which is short for *index*. If you prefer the word counter or another word that reminds you of what the variable represents, that's fine, too. In any case, the important point to remember about this statement is that it executes once at the outset of the for loop.

The second statement is a *condition*, precisely like the condition statement you saw in if constructions earlier in this chapter. When a loop-counting variable is established in the initial expression, the condition statement usually defines how high the loop counter should go before the looping stops. Therefore, the most common statement here is one that compares the loop counter variable against some fixed value — is the loop counter less than the maximum allowed value? If the condition is false at the start, the body of the loop is not executed. But if the loop does execute, then when execution comes back around to the top of the loop, JavaScript reevaluates the condition to determine the current result of the expression. If the loop counter increases with each loop, eventually the counter value goes beyond the value in the condition statement, causing the condition statement to yield a Boolean value of false. The instant that happens, execution drops out of the for loop entirely.

The final statement, the *update expression*, is executed at the end of each loop execution — after all statements nested inside the for construction have run. Again, the loop counter variable can be a factor here. If you want the counter value to increase by one the next time through the loop (called incrementing the value), you can use the JavaScript operator that makes that happen: the ++ operator appended to the variable name. That task is the reason for the appearance of all those i++ symbols in the for loops that you've already seen in this book. You're not limited to incrementing by one. You can increment by any multiplier you want, or even drive a loop counter backward by decrementing the value (i--).

Now, take this knowledge and beef up the formal syntax definition with one that takes into account a typical loop-counting variable, i, and the common ways to use it:

```
//incrementing loop counter
for (var i = minValue; i <= maxValue; i++)
{
    // statements
}
//decrementing loop counter
for (var i = maxValue; i >= minValue; i--)
{
    // statements
}
```

In the top loop counter, the variable, i, is initialized at the outset to a value equal to that of minValue. Variable i is immediately compared against maxValue. If i is less than or equal to maxValue, processing continues into the body of the loop. At the end of the loop, the update expression executes. The value of i is incremented by 1. Therefore, if i is initialized as 0, then the first time through the loop, the i variable maintains that 0 value during the first execution of statements in the loop. The next time around, the variable has the value of 1.

As you may have noticed in the formal syntax definition, each of the parameters to the for statement is optional. For example, the statements that execute inside the loop may control the value of the loop counter based on data that gets manipulated in the process. Therefore, the update statement would probably interfere with the intended running of the loop. But we suggest that you use all three parameters until such time as you feel absolutely comfortable with their roles in the for loop. If you omit the condition statement, for instance, and you don't program a way for the loop to exit on its own, your script may end up in an infinite loop — which does your users no good.

Putting the loop counter to work

Despite its diminutive appearance, the i loop counter (or whatever name you want to give it) can be a powerful tool for working with data inside a repeat loop. For example, examine a version of the classic JavaScript function that creates an array while initializing entries to a value of 0:

```
// initialize array with n entries
function MakeArray(n)
{
    this.length = n;
    for (var i = 0; i < n; i++)
    {
        this[i] = 0;
    }
    return this;
}
```

The loop counter, i, is initialized to a value of 0 because the first element of any JavaScript array is element zero. In the condition statement, the loop continues to execute as long as the value of the counter is less than the number of entries being created (n). (For example, if n is 10, the array is initialized with ten elements, 0–9.) After each loop, the counter increments by 1. In the nested statement that executes within the loop, you use the value of the i variable to substitute for the index value of the assignment statement:

```
this[i] = 0;
```

The first time the loop executes, the value expression evaluates to

```
this[0] = 0;
```

The next time, the expression evaluates to

```
this[1] = 0;
```

and so on, until all n entries are created and stuffed with 0.

Recall the HTML page in Listing 18-2, where a user chooses a regional office from a select list (triggering a script to look up the manager's name and sales quota for that region). Because the regional office names are stored in an array, the page could be altered so that a script populates the select element's options from the array. That way, if there is ever a change to the alignment of regional offices, there need be only one change to the array of offices, and the HTML doesn't have to be modified. As a reminder, here is the definition of the regional offices array, created while the page loads:

```
var aRegionalOffices = ["New York", "Chicago", "Houston", "Portland"];
```

Code inside the external JavaScript file can be used to dynamically generate the select list as follows:

```
for (var i = 0; i < aRegionalOffices.length; i++)
{
    oSelect.options[i] = new Option(aRegionalOffices[i]);
}

// pre-select the first option
oSelect.options[0].selected = true;
```

Notice one important point about the condition statement of the for loop: JavaScript extracts the length property from the array to be used as the loop counter boundary. From a code maintenance and stylistic point of view, this method is preferable to hard-wiring a value there. If the company added a new regional office, you would make the addition to the array "database," whereas everything else in the code would adjust automatically to those changes, including creating a longer pop-up menu in this case.

Notice, too, that the operator for the condition statement is less-than ($<$): The zero-based index values of arrays means that the maximum index value we can use is one less than the actual count of items in the array. This is vital information, because the index counter variable (i) is used as the index to the regionalOffices array each time through the loop to read the string for each item's entry. You also use the index of the first option (0) to add the selected attribute to the first option's definition.

The utility of the loop counter in for loops often influences the way you design data structures, such as two-dimensional arrays (see Chapter 18, "The Array Object") for use as databases. Always keep "the loop-counter mechanism" in the back of your mind when you begin writing JavaScript script that relies on collections of data that you embed in your documents.

Breaking out of a loop

Some loop constructions perform their job as soon as a certain condition is met, at which point they have no further need to continue looping through the rest of the values in the loop counter's range. A common scenario for this is the cycling of a loop through an entire array in search of a single entry that matches some criterion. That criterion test is set up as an `if` construction inside the loop. If that criterion is met, you break out of the loop and let the script continue with the more meaningful processing of succeeding statements in the main flow. To accomplish that exit from the loop, use the `break` statement. The following schematic shows how the `break` statement may appear in a `for` loop:

```
for (var i = 0; i < array.length; i++)
{
    if (array[i].property == magicValue)
    {
        // statements that act on entry array[i]
        break;
    }
}
```

The `break` statement tells JavaScript to bail out of the nearest `for` loop (in case you have nested `for` loops). Script execution then picks up immediately after the closing brace of the `for` statement. The variable value of `i` remains whatever it was at the time of the break, so that you can use that variable later in the same script to access, say, that same array entry.

A construction similar to this was used in Chapter 35, "Button Objects." There, the discussion of radio buttons demonstrates this construction, where, in Listing 35-6, you see a set of radio buttons whose `value` attributes contain screen sizes, in pixels. A function uses a `for` loop to find out which button was selected and then uses that item's index value — after the `for` loop breaks out of the loop — to alert the user. Listing 21-3 shows the relevant function.

LISTING 21-3

Breaking Out of a for Loop

JavaScript: jsb-21-03.js

```
function showMegapixels()
{
    var theForm = document.getElementById('sizesForm');
    if (theForm)
    {
        var sizeChoices = theForm.choices;
        for (var i = 0; i < sizeChoices.length; i++)
        {
            if (sizeChoices[i].checked)
            {
                break;
            }
        }
```

continued

while

LISTING 21-3 *(continued)*

```
        alert("That image size requires " + sizeChoices[i].value +
            " megapixels.");
    }
}
```

In this case, breaking out of the for loop is more than a matter of mere efficiency; the value of the loop counter (frozen at the break point) is used to summon a different property outside of the for loop. Starting back in version 4 browsers, the break statement gained additional powers in cooperation with the new label feature of control structures. This subject is covered later in this chapter.

Directing loop traffic with continue

One other possibility in a for loop is that you may want to skip execution of the nested statements for just one condition. In other words, as the loop goes merrily on its way round and round, executing statements for each value of the loop counter, one value of that loop counter may exist for which you don't want those statements to execute. To accomplish this task, the nested statements need to include an if construction to test for the presence of the value to skip. When that value is reached, the continue command tells JavaScript to immediately skip the rest of the body, execute the update statement, and loop back around to the top of the loop.

To illustrate this construction, take a look at an artificial example that skips over execution when the counter variable is the superstitious person's unlucky 13:

```
        for (var i = 0; i <= 20; i++)
        {
            if (i == 13)
            {
                continue;
            }
            // statements
        }
```

In this example, the statements part of the loop executes for all values of i except 13. The continue statement forces execution to jump to the i++ part of the loop structure, incrementing the value of i for the next time through the loop. In the case of nested for loops, a continue statement affects the for loop in whose immediate scope the if construction falls. The continue statement was enhanced in version 4 browsers with the label feature of control structures, which is covered later in this chapter.

The while Loop

Compatibility: WinIE3+, MacIE3+, NN2+, Moz+, Safari+, Opera+, Chrome+

The for loop is not the only kind of repeat loop you can construct in JavaScript. Another statement, called a while statement, sets up a loop in a slightly different format. Rather than providing a mechanism for modifying a loop counter, a while repeat loop assumes that your script statements will reach a condition that forcibly exits the repeat loop.

The basic syntax for a `while` loop is

```
while (condition)
{
    statements
}
```

The `condition` expression is the same kind that you saw in `if` constructions and in the middle parameter of the `for` loop. You introduce this kind of loop if some condition exists in your code (evaluates to `true`) before reaching this loop. The loop then performs some action, which affects that condition repeatedly until that condition becomes `false`. At that point, the loop exits, and script execution continues with statements after the closing brace. If the statements inside the `while` loop do not somehow affect the values being tested in `condition`, your script never exits, and it becomes stuck in an infinite loop.

Many loops can be rendered with either the `for` or `while` loops. In fact, Listing 21-4 shows a `while` loop version of the `for` loop from Listing 21-3.

LISTING 21-4

A while Loop Version of Listing 21-3

JavaScript: jsb-21-04.js

```
function showMegapixels()
{
    var theForm = document.getElementById('sizesForm');
    if (theForm)
    {
        var sizeChoices = theForm.choices;
        var i = 0;
        while (i < sizeChoices.length && !sizeChoices[i].checked)
            {
                i++;
            }
        }
        alert("That image size requires " + sizeChoices[i].value +
            " megapixels.");
    }
}
```

One point you may notice is that if the condition of a `while` loop depends on the value of a loop counter, the scripter is responsible for initializing the counter prior to the `while` loop construction and managing its value within the `while` loop.

Should you need their powers, the `break` and `continue` control statements work inside `while` loops just as they do in `for` loops. But because the two loop styles treat their loop counters and conditions differently, be extra careful (do lots of testing) when applying `break` and `continue` statements to both kinds of loops.

do-while

No hard-and-fast rules exist for which type of loop construction to use in a script. Generally, use while loops only when the data, or object, to loop through is already part of the script before the loop. In other words, by virtue of previous statements in the script, the values for any condition or loop counting (if needed) are already initialized. But if cycling through an object's properties, or an array's entries, to extract some piece of data for use later in the script is what's needed, favor the for loop. The for loop is also generally preferred when the looping involves a simple counter from one value to another.

Another point of style, particularly with the for loop, is where a scripter should declare the i variable. Some programmers prefer to declare (or initialize, if initial values are known) all variables in the opening statements of a script or function. That is why you tend to see a lot of var statements in those positions in scripts. If you have only one for loop in a function, for example, nothing is wrong with declaring and initializing the i loop counter in the initial expression part of the for loop (as demonstrated frequently in the previous sections). But if your function utilizes multiple for loops that reuse the i counter variable (that is, the loops run completely independently of one another), then you can declare the i variable once at the start of the function and simply assign a new initial value to i in each for construction.

The do-while Loop

Compatibility: WinIE4+, MacIE4+, NN4+, Moz+, Safari+, Opera+, Chrome+

JavaScript brings you one more looping construction, called the do-while loop. The formal syntax for this construction is as follows:

```
do
{
    statements
} while (condition)
```

An important difference distinguishes the do-while loop from the while loop. In the do-while loop, the statements in the construction always execute at least one time before the condition can be tested; in a while loop, the statements may never execute if the condition tested at the outset evaluates to false. So, just think of the do-while loop as a while loop where the statements get executed at least once, no matter what.

Use a do-while loop when you know for certain that the looped statements are free to run at least one time. If the condition may not be met the first time, use the while loop. For many instances, the two constructions are interchangeable, although only the while loop is compatible with legacy browsers.

Looping through Properties (for-in)

Compatibility: WinIE3+, MacIE3+, NN2+, Moz+, Safari+, Opera+, Chrome+

JavaScript includes a variation of the for loop, called a for-in loop, which has special powers of extracting the names and values of any object property currently in the browser's memory. The syntax looks like this:

```
for (varName in object)
{
```

```
    // statements
}
```

The `object` parameter is not the string name of an object but a reference to the object itself. JavaScript delivers an object reference if you provide the name of the object as an unquoted string, such as `window` or `document`, or via `getElementById`. Recall that although a legal name in HTML is case-insensitive, a legal name in JavaScript is case-sensitive, so remember to use the camelCase convention even in your HTML code. Using the `varName` variable, you can create a script that extracts and displays the range of properties for any given object.

Listings 21-5 shows a page containing a utility function that you can insert into your external JavaScript files during the authoring and debugging stages of designing a JavaScript-enhanced page. In the example, the current `window` object is examined, and its properties are presented in the page (note that Safari 1.0 doesn't expose `window` object properties).

LISTING 21-5

Property Inspector Function

HTML: jsb-21-05.html

```html
<!DOCTYPE html>
<html>
    <head>
        <meta http-equiv="content-type" content="text/html;charset=utf-8">
        <title>Property Inspector Function</title>
        <script type="text/javascript" src="../jsb-global.js"></script>
        <script type="text/javascript" src="jsb-21-05.js"></script>
        <link rel="stylesheet" href="jsb-21-05.css" type="text/css">
    </head>
    <body>
        <h1>Property Inspector Function</h1>
        <p>Here are the properties of the current window:</p>
        <ul id="propertyList"></ul>
    </body>
</html>
```

JavaScript: jsb-21-05.js

```javascript
// initialize when the page has loaded
addEvent(window, 'load', showProps);

// display all the properties of the object
function showProps()
{
    var oOutput = document.getElementById('propertyList');
    if (oOutput)
    {
        var newElem;
        var newText;
        for (var i in window)
```

continued

with

LISTING 21-5   *(continued)*

```
        {
            newElem = document.createElement('li');
            newElem.className = 'objProperty';
            newText = document.createTextNode('window.' + i + ' = ' + window[i]);

            // insert the text node into the new paragraph
            newElem.appendChild(newText);

            // insert the completed paragraph into propertyList
            oOutput.appendChild(newElem);
        }
    }
}
```

Stylesheet: jsb-21-05.css

```
ul#propertyList li
{
    white-space: pre;
}
```

For debugging purposes, you can revise the function slightly to display the results in an alert dialog box or a textarea element. Just use the \n carriage return character after each property for a nicely formatted display. If the showProps() function looks familiar to you, it is because it closely resembles the property inspector routines of The Evaluator (see Chapter 4). In Chapter 48 (on the CD-ROM), you can see how to embed functionality of The Evaluator into a page under construction so that you can view property values while debugging your scripts.

The with Statement

Compatibility: WinIE3+, MacIE3+, NN2+, Moz+, Safari+, Opera+, Chrome+

The with statement enables you to preface any number of statements by advising JavaScript on precisely which object your scripts will be talking about, so that you don't have to use full, formal addresses to access properties or invoke methods of the same object. The formal syntax definition of the with statement is as follows:

```
with (object)
{
    statements
}
```

The object reference is a reference to any valid object currently in the browser's memory. An example of this appears in Chapter 16, "The Math, Number, and Boolean Objects," when the Math object is discussed. By embracing several Math statements inside a with construction, your scripts can call the properties and methods without having to make the object part of every reference to those properties and methods. Here's an example:

```
with (Math)
{
    var randInt = round(random() * 100);
}
```

This example uses the `round()` and `random()` methods of the `Math` object to obtain a random integer between 0 and 100. The significance of the code is how the `with` statement allows you to forego using the full notation of `Math.round()` and `Math.random()`.

An advantage of the `with` structure is that it can make heavily object-dependent statements easier to read and understand. Consider this long version of a function that requires multiple calls to the same object (but different properties):

```
function seeColor(form)
{
    var newColor = (form.colorsList.options[form.colorsList.selectedIndex]
    .text);
    return newColor;
}
```

Using the `with` structure, you can shorten the long statement:

```
function seeColor(form)
{
    with (form.colorsList)
    {
        newColor = (options[selectedIndex].text);
    }
    return newColor;
}
```

When JavaScript encounters an otherwise unknown identifier inside a `with` statement, it tries to build a reference out of the object specified as its parameter and that unknown identifier. You cannot, however, nest `with` statements that build on one another. For instance, in the preceding example, you cannot have a `with (colorsList)` nested inside a `with (form)` statement and expect JavaScript to create a reference to options out of the two object names.

As clever as the `with` statement may seem, be aware that there are some cautions associated with its use. It introduces some inherent performance penalties in your script (because of the way the JavaScript interpreter must artificially generate references). You probably won't notice degradation with occasional use of this construction, but if it's used inside a loop that must iterate many times, processing speed will almost certainly be affected negatively. Additionally, some people feel that the `with` statement introduces ambiguity in your code.

Labeled Statements

Compatibility: WinIE4+, MacIE4+, NN4+, Moz+, Safari+, Opera+, Chrome+

Crafting multiple nested loops can sometimes be difficult when the final condition your script is looking for is met deep inside the nests. The problem is that the `break` or `continue` statement by itself has scope only to the nearest loop level. Therefore, even if you break out of the inner loop, the outer loop(s) continue to execute. If all you want to do is exit the function after the condition is met, a simple `return` statement performs the same job as some other languages' exit command. But if you also need some further processing within that function after the condition is met, you need the JavaScript facility supported in modern browsers that lets you assign labels to blocks of statements. Your `break` and `continue` statements can then alter their scope to apply to a labeled block other than the one containing the statement.

A *label* is any identifier (that is, a name starting with a letter and containing no spaces or odd punctuation other than underscores) followed by a colon preceding a logical block of executing statements, such as an `if...then` or loop construction. The formal syntax looks like the following:

```
labelID:
    statements
```

For a `break` or `continue` statement to apply itself to a labeled group, the label is added as a kind of parameter to each statement, as in

```
break labelID;
continue labelID;
```

Note

If you're arriving at JavaScript from another programming language that has a bit more structure, such as C++ or Java, the thought of labeled code may have you worried about the risks of creating code that is impossible to manage. This worry is likely rooted in the `goto` statement that is found in some languages, such as BASIC, and which is seriously frowned upon in modern structured languages. Labels in JavaScript are much more limited than the infamous `goto` statement in other languages; you can only use the `break` statement to target a label in which your code is nested. So, although we don't necessarily encourage the heavy usage of labels, you can rest easy knowing that they aren't on par with the much maligned `goto` statement. ■

To demonstrate how valuable labels can be in the right situation, Listing 21-6 contains two versions of the same nested loop construction. The goal of each version is to loop through two different index variables until both values equal the target values set outside the loop. When those targets are met, the entire nested loop construction should break off and continue processing afterward. To help you visualize the processing that goes on during the execution of the loops, the scripts output intermediate and final results to a `textarea`.

In the version without labels, only the simple `break` statement is issued when the targets are met. This breaks the inner loop at that point, but the outer loop picks up on the next iteration. By the time the entire construction has ended, a lot of wasted processing has gone on. Moreover, the values of the counting variables max themselves out, because the loops execute in their entirety several times after the targets are met.

But in the labeled version, the inner loop breaks out of the labeled outer loop as soon as the targets are met. Far fewer lines of code are executed, and the loop counting variables are equal to the targets, as desired. Experiment with Listing 21-6 by changing the `break` statements to `continue` statements. Then closely analyze the two results in the Results `textarea` to see how the two versions behave.

LISTING 21-6

Labeled Statements

HTML: jsb-21-06.html

```html
<!DOCTYPE html>
<html>
   <head>
      <meta http-equiv="content-type" content="text/html;charset=utf-8">
      <title>Breaking Out of Nested Labeled Loops</title>
      <script type="text/javascript" src="../jsb-global.js"></script>
      <script type="text/javascript" src="jsb-21-06.js"></script>
   </head>
   <body>
      <h1>Breaking Out of Nested Labeled Loops</h1>
      <p>Look in the Results field for traces of these button scripts:</p>
      <form id="theForm" action="validate.php" method="get">
        <p><input id="withoutLabelButton" type="button" value="Execute WITHOUT↵
             Label"></p>
        <p><input id="withLabelButton" type="button" value="Execute WITH↵
             Label"></p>
        <p>
           <label for="output">Results:</label>
           <textarea id="output" rows="43" cols="60"></textarea>
        </p>
      </form>
   </body>
</html>
```

JavaScript: jsb-21-06.js

```javascript
// initialize when the page has loaded
addEvent(window, 'load', initialize);

function initialize()
{
   // locate output field
   out = document.getElementById('output');
      // if found...
      if (out)
      {
         // add an event to the button button labeled Execute WITHOUT Label
         addEvent(document.getElementById('withoutLabelButton'), 'click', run1);

         // add an event to the button button labeled Execute WITH Label
         addEvent(document.getElementById('withLabelButton'), 'click', run2);
      }
}
```

continued

395

LISTING 21-6   *(continued)*

```javascript
var out;   // global variable for output field
var targetA = 2;
var targetB = 2;
var range = 5;

function run1()
{
    out.value = "Running WITHOUT labeled break\n";
    for (var i = 0; i <= range; i++)
    {
        out.value += "Outer loop #" + i + "\n";
        for (var j = 0; j <= range; j++)
        {
            out.value += "  Inner loop #" + j + "\n";
            if (i == targetA && j == targetB)
            {
                out.value += "**BREAKING OUT OF INNER LOOP**\n";
                break;
            }
        }
    }
    out.value += "After looping, i = " + i + ", j = " + j + "\n";
}

function run2()
{
    out.value = "Running WITH labeled break\n";
    outerLoop:
    for (var i = 0; i <= range; i++)
    {
        out.value += "Outer loop #" + i + "\n";
        innerLoop:
        for (var j = 0; j <= range; j++)
        {
            out.value += "  Inner loop #" + j + "\n";
            if (i == targetA && j == targetB)
            {
                out.value += "**BREAKING OUT OF OUTER LOOP**\n";
                break outerLoop;
            }
        }
    }
    out.value += "After looping, i = " + i + ", j = " + j + "\n";
}
```

Exception Handling

The subject of exception handling is relatively new to JavaScript. Formalized in Edition 3 of ECMA-262, parts of the official mechanism were implemented in IE5, with more complete implementations in IE6 and NN6, and, of course, in Mozilla, Firefox, Camino, Safari, Opera, and Chrome.

Exceptions and errors

If you've done any scripting, you are certainly aware of JavaScript errors, whether they be from syntax errors in your code, or what are known as *runtime* errors — errors that occur while scripts are processing information. Ideally, a program should be aware of when an error occurs and handle it as gracefully as possible. This self-healing can prevent lost data and help keep users from seeing ugly error messages. Chapter 27, "Window and Frame Objects," covers the onerror event handler and window.onerror property, which were early attempts at letting scripts gain a level of control over runtime errors. This event-driven mechanism works on a global level (that is, in the window object) and processes every error that occurs throughout the page. This event handler ends up being used primarily as a last-ditch defense against displaying any error message to the user, and is a long way from what programmers consider to be proper exception handling.

In the English language, the term "exception" can mean something out of the ordinary, or something abnormal. This definition seems quite distant from the word "error," which usually means a mistake. In the realm of programming languages, however, the two words tend to be used interchangeably, and the difference between the two depends primarily on one's point of view.

Consider, for example, a simple script whose job is to multiply numbers that the user enters into two text fields on the page. The script is supposed to display the results in a third text box. If the script contains no data entry validation, JavaScript will attempt to multiply whatever values are entered into the text boxes. If the user enters two numbers, JavaScript is smart enough to recognize that even though the value properties of the two input text fields are strings, the strings contain numbers that can be converted to number types for the proper multiplication. Without complaint, the product of the two numbers gets calculated and displayed into the results.

But what if the user types a letter into one of the text boxes? Again, without any entry validation in the script, JavaScript has a fixed way of responding to such a request: The result of the multiplication operation is the NaN (not a number) constant. If you are an untrained user, you have no idea what NaN means, but your experience with computers tells you that some kind of error has occurred. You may blame the computer or you may blame yourself — the accurate response may in fact be to blame the JavaScript developer!

To shift the point of view to the programmer, however, the script was designed to be run by a user who never makes a typing mistake, intentional or not. That, of course, is not very good programming practice. Users make mistakes. Therefore, anticipating user input that is not what would be expected is the programmer's job — input that is an exception to the rules your program wants to operate by. You must include some additional code that handles the exceptions gracefully so as to not confuse the user with unintelligible output, and perhaps even to help the user repair the input to get a result. This extra programming code handles the undesirable and erroneous input and makes your scripts considerably more user-friendly and robust.

As it turns out, JavaScript and the W3C Document Object Model liberally mix terms of exception and error within the vocabulary used to handle exceptions. As you see shortly, an exception creates an *error object*, which contains information about the exception. It is safe to say that you can think of exceptions and errors as the same things.

The exception mechanism

Newcomers to JavaScript (or any programming environment, for that matter) may at first have a difficult time creating a mental model of how all this exception stuff runs within the context of the browser. It may be easy enough to understand how pages load and create object models, and how event handlers (or listeners, in the W3C DOM terminology) cause script functions to run. But a lot of action also seems to be going on in the background. For example, the event object that is generated automatically with each event action (see Chapter 32, "Event Objects") seems to sit "somewhere," while event handler functions run so that they can retrieve details about the event. After the functions finish their processing, the event object disappears, without even leaving behind a Cheshire Cat smile. Mysterious.

Browsers equipped for exception handling have more of this "stuff" running in the background, ready for your scripts when you need it. Because you have certainly viewed the details of at least one scripting error, you have already seen some of the exception-handling mechanism that is built into browsers. If a script error occurs, the browser creates in its memory an error object, whose properties contain details about the error. The precise details (described later in this chapter) vary from one browser brand to the next, but what you see in the error details readout is the default way the browser handles exceptions/errors. As browsers have matured, their makers have gone to great lengths to tone down the intrusion of script errors. For example, in NN4+, errors appeared in a separate JavaScript Console window (which must be invoked in NN4 by typing `javascript:` into the Location field; or opened directly via the Tools menu in NN6+ and Mozilla-based browsers, including Firefox and Camino). In IE4+ for Windows, the status bar comes into play again, as the icon at the bottom-left corner turns into an alert icon: Double-clicking the icon displays more information about the error. MacIE users can turn off scripting error alerts altogether. Safari 1.0 didn't divulge any script errors but a JavaScript console was added as of version 1.3.

True exception handling, however, goes further than just displaying error messages. It also provides a uniform way to let scripts guard against unusual occurrences. Ideally, the mechanism makes sure that *all* runtime errors get funneled through the same mechanism to help simplify the scripting of exception handling. The mechanism is also designed to be used intentionally as a way for your own code to generate errors in a uniform way so that other parts of your scripts can handle them quietly and intelligently. In other words, you can use the exception handling mechanism as a kind of "back channel" to communicate from one part of your scripts to another.

The JavaScript exception handling mechanism is built around two groups of program execution statements. The first group consists of the `try-catch-finally` statement triumvirate; the second group is the single `throw` statement.

Using try-catch-finally Constructions

The purpose of the `try-catch-finally` group of related statements is to provide a controlled environment in which script statements that may encounter runtime errors can run, such that your scripts can act upon exceptions without alarming the rest of the browser's error mechanisms. Each of the three statements precedes a block of code in the following syntax:

```
try
{
    statements to run
```

```
   }

catch (errorInfo)
{
    statements to run if exception occurs in try block
}
finally
{
    statements to run whether or not an exception occurred [optional]
}
```

Each `try` block must be mated with a `catch` and/or `finally` block at the same nesting level, with no intervening statements. For example, a function can have a one-level `try-catch` construction inside it as follows:

```
function myFunc()
{
    try
    {
        // statements
    }
    catch (e)
    {
        // statements
    }
}
```

But if there were another `try` block nested one level deeper, a balancing `catch` or `finally` block would also have to be present at that deeper level:

```
function myFunc()
{
    try
    {
        // statements
        try
        {
            // statements
        }
        catch (e)
        {
            // statements
        }
    }
    catch (e)
    {
        // statements
    }
}
```

The statements inside the `try` block include statements that you believe are capable of generating a runtime error because of user input errors, the failure of some page component to load, or a similar error. The presence of the `catch` block prevents errors from appearing in the browser's regular script error reporting system (for example, the JavaScript Console of Safari1.3+, NN6+, and Mozilla-based browsers).

An important term to know about exception handling of this type is *throw*. The convention is that when an operation or method call triggers an exception, it is said to "throw an exception." For example, if a script statement attempts to invoke a method of a string object, but that method does not exist for the object (perhaps you mistyped the method name), JavaScript throws an exception. Exceptions have names associated with them — a name that sometimes, but not always, reveals important information about the exception. In the mistyped method example just cited, the name of that exception is a `TypeError` (yet more evidence of how "exception" and "error" become intertwined).

The JavaScript language supported in modern browsers is not the only entity that can throw exceptions. The W3C DOM also defines categories of exceptions for DOM objects. For example, according to the Level 2 specification, the `appendChild()` method (see Chapter 26, "Generic HTML Element Objects") can throw (or *raise*, in the W3C terminology) one of three exceptions:

Exception Name	When Thrown
HIERARCHY_REQUEST_ERR	If the current node is of a type that does not allow children of the type of the `newChild` node, or if the node to append is one of this node's ancestors
WRONG_DOCUMENT_ERR	If `newChild` was created from a different document than the one that created the current node
NO_MODIFICATION_ALLOWED_ERR	If the current node is read-only

Because the `appendChild()` method is capable of throwing exceptions, a JavaScript statement that invokes this method should ideally be inside a `try` block. If an exception is thrown, then script execution immediately jumps to the `catch` or `finally` block associated with the `try` block. Execution does not come back to the `try` block.

A `catch` block has special behavior. Its format looks similar to a function in a way, because the `catch` keyword is followed by a pair of parentheses and an arbitrary variable that is assigned a reference to the error object whose properties are filled by the browser when the exception occurs. One of the properties of that error object is the name of the error. Therefore, the code inside the `catch` block can examine the name of the error and perhaps include some branching code to take care of a variety of different errors that are caught.

To see how this construction may appear in code, look at a hypothetical generic function whose job is to create a new element and append it to some other node. Both the type of element to be created and a reference to the parent node are passed as parameters. To take care of potential misuses of this function through the passage of improper parameter values, it includes extra error handling to treat all possible exceptions from the two DOM methods: `createElement()` and `appendChild()`. Such a function looks like Listing 21-7.

LISTING 21-7

A Hypothetical try-catch Routine

```
// generic appender
function attachToEnd(theNode, newTag)
{
    try
    {
        var newElem = document.createElement(newTag);
        theNode.appendChild(newElem);
    }
    catch (e)
    {
        switch (e.name)
        {
            case "INVALID_CHARACTER_ERR" :
                // statements to handle this createElement() error
                break;
            case "HIERARCHY_REQUEST_ERR" :
                // statements to handle this appendChild() error
                break;
            case "WRONG_DOCUMENT_ERR" :
                // statements to handle this appendChild() error
                break;
            case "NO_MODIFICATION_ALLOWED_ERR" :
                // statements to handle this appendChild() error
                break;
            default:
                // statements to handle any other error
        }
        return false;
    }
    return true;
}
```

The single `catch` block in Listing 21-7 executes only if one of the statements in the `try` block throws an exception. The exceptions may be not only one of the four specific ones named in the `catch` block, but also syntax or other errors that could occur inside the `try` block. That's why you have a last-ditch case to handle truly unexpected errors. Your job as scripter is to anticipate errors and provide clean ways for the exceptions to be handled, whether it be through judiciously worded alert dialog boxes or through self-repair. For example, in the case of the invalid character error for `createElement()`, your script may attempt to salvage the data passed to the `attachToEnd()` function and reinvoke the method, passing `theNode` value as-is and the repaired value originally passed to `newTag`. If your repairs were successful, the `try` block would execute without error and carry on with the user's being completely unaware that a nasty problem had been averted. And that's really the goal of exception handling — to save the day when something "unexpected" goes wrong so that the user isn't left confused or frustrated.

A `finally` block contains code that always executes after a `try` block, whether or not the `try` block succeeds without throwing an error. Unlike the `catch` block, a `finally` block does not receive an error object as a parameter, so it operates very much in the dark about what transpires inside the `try` block. If you include both `catch` and `finally` blocks after a `try` block, the execution path depends on whether an exception is thrown. If no exception is thrown, the `finally` block executes after the last statement of the `try` block runs. But if the `try` block throws an exception, program execution runs first to the `catch` block. After all processing within the `catch` block finishes, the `finally` block executes. In development environments that give programmers complete control over resources, such as memory allocation, a `finally` block may be used to delete some temporary items generated in the `try` block, whether or not an exception occurs in the `try` block. Currently, JavaScript's automatic memory management system reduces the need for that kind of maintenance, but you should be aware of the program execution possibilities of the `finally` block in the `try-catch-finally` context.

Real-life exceptions

The example shown in Listing 21-7 is a bit idealized. The listing assumes that the browser dutifully reports every W3C DOM exception precisely as defined in the formal specification. Unfortunately, even the latest browsers have yet to fully comply with the DOM when it comes to exception reporting. Most browsers implement additional error naming conventions and layers between actual DOM exceptions and what gets reported with the error object at the time of the exception.

If you think these discrepancies make cross-browser exception handling difficult, you're right. Even simple errors are reported differently among the two major browser brands (IE and Mozilla) and the W3C DOM specification. Until the browsers exhibit a greater unanimity in exception reporting, the smoothest development road will be for those scripters who have the luxury of writing for just one of the browser platforms, such as IE for Windows or Safari for Mac.

That said, however, one aspect of exception handling can still be used in all modern browsers without a hitch. You can take advantage of `try-catch` constructions to throw your own exceptions — a practice that is quite common in advanced programming environments.

Throwing Exceptions

The last exception handling keyword not yet covered — `throw` — makes it possible to utilize exception-handling facilities for your own management of processes, such as data entry validation. At any point inside a `try` block, you can manually throw an exception that gets picked up by the associated `catch` block. The details of the specific exception are up to you.

Syntax for the `throw` statement is as follows:

```
throw value;
```

The value you throw can be of any type, but good practice suggests that the value be an error object (described more fully later in this chapter). Whatever value you throw is assigned to the parameter of the `catch` block. Look at the following two examples. In the first, the value is a string message; in the second, the value is an error object.

Listing 21-8 presents one input text box for a number between 1 and 5. Clicking a button looks up a corresponding letter in an array and displays the letter in a second text box. The lookup script has two simple data validation routines to make sure the entry is a number and is in the desired range.

Error checking here is done manually by script. If either of the error conditions occurs, throw statements force execution to jump to the catch block. The catch block assigns the incoming string parameter to the variable e. The design here assumes that the message being passed is text for an alert dialog box. Not only does a single catch block take care of both error conditions (and conceivably any others to be added later), but the catch block runs within the same variable scope as the function, so that it can use the reference to the input text box to focus and select the input text if there is an error.

LISTING 21-8

Throwing String Exceptions

HTML: jsb-21-08.html

```html
<!DOCTYPE html>
<html>
    <head>
        <meta http-equiv="content-type" content="text/html;charset=utf-8">
        <title>Throwing a String Exception</title>
        <script type="text/javascript" src="../jsb-global.js"></script>
        <script type="text/javascript" src="jsb-21-08.js"></script>
    </head>
    <body>
        <h1>Throwing a String Exception</h1>
        <form id="theForm" action="validate.php" method="get">
            <p>
                <label for="visitorInput">Enter a number from 1 to 5:</label>
                <input type="text" id="visitorInput" size="5">
                <input type="button" id="getLetterButton" value="Get Letter">
                <label for="output">Matching Letter is:</label>
                <input type="text" id="output" size="5">
            </p>
        </form>
    </body>
</html>
```

JavaScript: jsb-21-08.js

```javascript
// initialize when the page has loaded
addEvent(window, 'load', initialize);

function initialize()
{
    // add an event to the Get Letter button
    addEvent(document.getElementById('getLetterButton'), 'click', getLetter);
}

var letters = new Array("A","B","C","D","E");

function getLetter()
{
```

continued

throw

LISTING 21-8   *(continued)*

```
try
{
    var inputField = document.getElementById('visitorInput');
    var inp = parseInt(inputField.value, 10);
    var outputField = document.getElementById('output');

        if (isNaN(inp))
        {
            throw "Entry was not a number.";
        }

        if (inp < 1 || inp > 5)
        {
            throw "Enter only 1 through 5.";
        }

    outputField.value = letters[inp - 1];
}
catch (e)
{
    alert(e);
    outputField.value = "";
    inputField.focus();
    inputField.select();
}
}
```

The flaw with Listing 21-8 is that if some other kind of exception were thrown inside the `try` block, the value passed to the `catch` block would be an error object, not a string. The alert dialog box displayed to the user would be meaningless. Therefore, it is better to be uniform in your `throw-catch` constructions and pass an error object.

Listing 21-9 is an updated version of Listing 21-8, demonstrating how to create an error object that gets sent to the `catch` block via `throw` statements. The HTML code is exactly the same as for listing 21-8, so that is not repeated here.

LISTING 21-9

Throwing an Error Object Exception

JavaScript: `jsb-21-09.js`

```
// initialize when the page has loaded
addEvent(window, 'load', initialize);

function initialize()
{
    // add an event to the Get Letter button
```

```
    addEvent(document.getElementById('getLetterButton'), 'click', getLetter);
}

var letters = new Array("A","B","C","D","E");

function getErrorObj(msg)
{
    var err = new Error(msg);
    return err;
}

function getLetter()
{
    try
    {
        var inputField = document.getElementById('visitorInput');
        var inp = parseInt(inputField.value, 10);
        var outputField = document.getElementById('output');

        if (isNaN(inp))
        {
            throw getErrorObj("Entry was not a number.");
        }

        if (inp < 1 || inp > 5)
        {
            throw getErrorObj("Enter only 1 through 5.");
        }

        outputField.value = letters[inp - 1];
    }
    catch (e)
    {
        alert(e.message);
        outputField.value = "";
        inputField.focus();
        inputField.select();
    }
}
```

The only difference to the catch block is that it now reads the message property of the incoming error object. This means that if some other exception is thrown inside the try block, the browser-generated message will be displayed in the alert dialog box.

In truth, however, the job really isn't complete. In all likelihood, if a browser-generated exception is thrown, the message in the alert dialog box won't mean much to the user. The error message will probably be some kind of syntax or type error — the kind of meaningless error message you often get from your favorite operating system. A better design is to branch the catch block so that while "intentional" exceptions thrown by your code are handled through the alert dialog box messages you've put there, other types are treated differently. To accomplish this, you can take over one of the other properties of the error object — name — so that your catch block treats your custom messages separately.

throw

In Listing 21-10, the getErrorObj() function adds a custom value to the name property of the newly created error object. The name you assign can be any name, but you want to avoid exception names used by JavaScript or the DOM. Even if you don't know what all of those are, you can probably conjure up a suitably unique name for your error. Down in the catch block, a switch construction branches to treat the two classes of errors differently. In this simplified example, about the only possible problem other than the ones being trapped for explicitly in the try block would be some corruption to the page during downloading. Therefore, for this example, the branch for all other errors simply asks that the user reload the page and try again. The point is, however, that you can have as many classifications of custom and system errors as you want and handle them in a single catch block accordingly. Again, the HTML code is exactly the same as for listing 21-8, so it is not repeated here.

LISTING 21-10

A Custom Object Exception

JavaScript: jsb-21-10.js

```javascript
// initialize when the page has loaded
addEvent(window, 'load', initialize);

function initialize()
{
    // add an event to the Get Letter button
    addEvent(document.getElementById('getLetterButton'), 'click', getLetter);
}

var letters = new Array("A","B","C","D","E");

function getErrorObj(msg)
{
    var err = new Error(msg);
    err.name = "MY_ERROR";
    return err;
}

function getLetter()
{
    try
    {
        var inputField = document.getElementById('visitorInput');
        var inp = parseInt(inputField.value, 10);
        var outputField = document.getElementById('output');

        if (isNaN(inp))
        {
            throw getErrorObj("Entry was not a number.");
        }

        if (inp < 1 || inp > 5)
        {
            throw getErrorObj("Enter only 1 through 5.");
```

```
      }

    outputField.value = letters[inp - 1];
  }
catch (e)
{
    switch (e.name)
    {
      case 'MY_ERROR' :
          alert(e.message);
          outputField.value = "";
          inputField.focus();
          inputField.select();
          break;

      default :
          alert('Reload the page and try again.');
    }
  }
}
```

If you want to see how the alternative branch of Listing 21-10 looks, copy the listing file from the CD-ROM to your hard disk and modify the last line of the try block so that one of the characters is dropped from the name of the array:

```
          outputField.value = letter[inp - 1];
```

This may simulate the faulty loading of the page. If you enter one of the allowable values, the reload alert appears, rather than the actual message of the error object: letter is undefined. Your users will thank you.

All that's left now on this subject are the details of the error object.

Error Object

Properties	Methods
errorObject.prototype	errorObject.toString()
errorObject.constructor	
errorObject.description	
errorObject.filename	
errorObject.lineNumber	
errorObject.message	
errorObject.name	
errorObject.number	

errorObject.constructor

Syntax

Creating an error object:

```
var myError = new Error("message");
var myError = Error("message");
```

Accessing static `Error` object property:

```
Error.property
```

Accessing error object properties and methods:

```
errorObject.property | method([parameters])
```

Compatibility: WinIE5+, MacIE−, NN6+, Moz+, Safari+, Opera+, Chrome+

About this object

An error object instance is created whenever an exception is thrown or when you invoke either of the constructor formats for creating an error object. Properties of the error object instance contain information about the nature of the error so that `catch` blocks can inspect the error and process error handling accordingly.

IE5 implemented an error object in advance of the ECMA-262 formal error object, and the IE5 version ended up having its own set of properties that are not part of the ECMA standard. Those proprietary properties are still part of IE5.5+, which includes the ECMA properties as well. NN6, on the other hand, started with the ECMA properties and adds two proprietary properties of its own. The browser uses these additional properties in its own script error reporting. The unfortunate bottom line for cross-browser developers is that no properties in common among all browsers support the error object. However, there are two common denominators (`name` and `message`) between IE5.5+ and other browsers.

As described earlier in this chapter, you are encouraged to create an error object whenever you use the `throw` statement for your own error control.

Properties

constructor

(See Chapter 15, "The String Object.")

description

Value: String   Read/Write

Compatibility: WinIE5+, MacIE-, NN-, Moz-, Safari-, Opera-, Chrome-

The `description` property contains a descriptive string that provides some level of detail about the error. For errors thrown by the browser, the description is the same text that appears in the script error dialog box in IE. Although this property continues to be supported, the `message` property is preferred.

Related Item: `message` property

fileName
lineNumber

Value: String   Read/Write

Compatibility: WinIE-, MacIE-, NN6+, Moz+, Safari-, Opera-, Chrome-

The NN6 browser uses the `fileName` and `lineNumber` properties of an error object for its own internal script error processing — these values appear as part of the error messages that are listed in the JavaScript Console. The `fileName` is the URL of the document causing the error; the `lineNumber` is the source code line number of the statement that threw the exception. These properties are exposed to JavaScript, as well, so that your error processing may use this information if it is meaningful to your application.

See the discussion of the `window.error` property in Chapter 27 for further ideas on how to use this information for bug reporting from users.

Related Item: `window.error` property

message

Value: String   Read/Write

Compatibility: WinIE5.5+, MacIE-, NN6+, Moz+, Safari+, Opera+, Chrome+

The `message` property contains a descriptive string that provides some level of detail about the error. For errors thrown by the browser, the message is the same text that appears in the script error dialog box in IE and the JavaScript Console in Mozilla. By and large, these messages are more meaningful to scripters than to users. Unfortunately, there are no standards for the wording of a message for a given error. Therefore, it is hazardous at best to use the message content in a `catch` block as a means of branching to handle particular kinds of errors. You may get by with this approach if you are developing for a single browser platform, but you have no assurances that the text of a message for a particular exception may not change in future browser versions.

Custom messages for errors that your code explicitly throws can be in user-friendly language if you intend to display such messages to users. See Listings 21-8 through 21-10 for examples of this usage.

Related Item: `description` property

name

Value: String   Read/Write

Compatibility: WinIE5.5+, MacIE-, NN6+, Moz+, Safari+, Opera+, Chrome+

The `name` property generally contains a word that identifies the type of error that has been thrown. The most general kind of error (and the one that is created via the `new Error()` constructor) has a name `Error`. But JavaScript errors can be of several varieties: `EvalError`, `RangeError`, `ReferenceError`, `SyntaxError`, `TypeError`, and `URIError`. Some of these error types are not necessarily intended for exposure to scripters (they're used primarily in the inner workings of the JavaScript engine), but some browsers do expose them. Unfortunately, there are some discrepancies as to the specific name supplied to this property for script errors.

When JavaScript is being used in a W3C-compatible browser, some DOM exception types are returned via the `name` property. But browsers frequently insert their own error types for this property, and, as is common in this department, little uniformity exists among browser brands.

errorObject.number

For custom exceptions that your code explicitly throws, you can assign names as convenient. As shown in Listings 21-9 and 21-10, this information can assist a `catch` block in handling multiple categories of errors.

Related Item: `message` property

number

Value: Number   Read/Write

Compatibility: WinIE5+, MacIE-, NN-, Moz-, Safari-, Opera-, Chrome-

IE5+ assigns unique numbers to each error description or message. The value of the `number` property must be massaged somewhat to retrieve a meaningful error description. Following is an example of how you must apply binary arithmetic to an error number to arrive at a meaningful result:

```
var errNum = errorObj.number & 0xFFFF;
```

Related Item: `description` property

Methods

toString()

Returns: String (see text)

Compatibility: WinIE5+, MacIE-, NN6+, Moz+, Safari+, Opera+, Chrome+

The `toString()` method for an error object should return a string description of the error. In IE5+, however, the method returns a reference to the very same error object. In Mozilla-based browsers, the method returns the `message` property string, preceded by the string `Error:` (with a space after the colon). Most typically, if you want to retrieve a human-readable expression of an error object, read its `message` (or, in IE5+, `description`) property.

Related Item: `message` property

JavaScript Operators

J avaScript is rich in operators: words and symbols in expressions that perform operations on one or two values to arrive at another value. Any value on which an operator performs some action is called an operand. An expression may contain one operand and one operator (called a unary operator), as in a++, or two operands separated by one operator (called a binary operator), as in a + b. Many of the same symbols are used in a variety of operators. The combination and order of those symbols are what distinguish their powers.

IN THIS CHAPTER

Understanding operator categories

Exploring the role of operators in script statements

Recognizing operator precedence

Note
The vast majority of JavaScript operators have been in the language since the very beginning. But, as you may expect from an evolving language, some entries were added to the lexicon as the language matured and gained wider usage. In the rest of this chapter, compatibility charts typically govern an entire category of operator. If there are version anomalies for a particular operator within a category, they are covered in the text. The good news is that modern browsers support the entire set of JavaScript operators. ■

Operator Categories

To help you grasp the range of JavaScript operators, we group them into seven categories. We assign a wholly untraditional name (connubial) to the second group — but a name that we believe correctly identifies its purpose in the language. Table 22-1 shows the operator types.

Any expression that contains an operator evaluates to a value of some kind, meaning that a value always results from an operation. Sometimes the operator changes the value of one of the operands; other times the result is a new value. Even this simple expression

    5 + 5

shows two integer operands joined by the addition operator. This expression evaluates to 10. The operator (+) is what provides the instruction for JavaScript to follow in its never-ending drive to evaluate every expression in a script.

TABLE 22-1

JavaScript Operator Categories

Type	What It Does
Comparison	Compares the values of two operands, deriving a result of either `true` or `false` (used extensively in conditional statements for `if...else` and `for` loop constructions) `==  !=  ===  !==  >  >=  <  <=`
Connubial	Joins together two operands to produce a single value that is a result of an arithmetical or other operation on the two `+  -  *  /  %  ++  --  +val  -val`
Assignment	Stuffs the value of the expression of the right-hand operand into a variable name on the left-hand side, sometimes with minor modification, as determined by the operator symbol `=  +=  -=  *=  /=  %=  <<=  >=  >>=  >>>=  &=  |=  ^=  []`
Boolean	Performs Boolean arithmetic on one or two Boolean operands `&&  ||  !`
Bitwise	Performs arithmetic or column-shifting actions on the binary (base-2) representations of two operands `&	^ ~ << >> >>>`
Object	Helps scripts examine the heritage and capabilities of a particular object before they need to invoke the object and its properties or methods `.  []  ()  delete  in  instanceOf  new  this`
Miscellaneous	A handful of operators that have special behaviors `,  ?:  typeof  void`

Doing an equality comparison on two operands that, on the surface, look very different is not at all uncommon. JavaScript doesn't care what the operands look like — only how they evaluate. Two very dissimilar-looking values can, in fact, be identical when they are evaluated. Thus, an expression that compares the equality of two values, such as

```
fred == 25
```

does, in fact, evaluate to `true` if the variable `fred` has the number 25 stored in it from an earlier statement.

Comparison Operators

Compatibility: WinIE3+, MacIE3+, NN2+, Moz+, Safari+, Opera+, Chrome+

Anytime you compare two values in JavaScript, the result is a Boolean `true` or `false` value. You have a wide selection of comparison operators to choose from, depending on the kind of test you want to apply to the two operands. Table 22-2 lists all comparison operators.

TABLE 22-2

JavaScript Comparison Operators

Syntax	Name	Operand Types	Results
==	Equals	All	Boolean
!=	Does not equal	All	Boolean
===	Strictly equals	All	Boolean (IE4+, NN4+, Moz+, W3C)
!==	Strictly does not equal	All	Boolean (IE4+, NN4+, Moz+, W3C)
>	Is greater than	All	Boolean
>=	Is greater than or equal to	All	Boolean
<	Is less than	All	Boolean
<=	Is less than or equal to	All	Boolean

For numeric values, the results are the same as those you'd expect from your high school algebra class. Some examples follow, including some that may not be obvious.

```
10 == 10        // true
10 == 10.0      // true
9 != 10         // true
9 > 10          // false
9.99 <= 9.98    // false
```

Strings can also be compared on all of these levels:

```
"Fred" == "Fred"    // true
"Fred" == "fred"    // false
"Fred" > "fred"     // false
"Fran" < "Fred"     // true
```

To calculate string comparisons, JavaScript converts each character of a string to its ASCII value. Each letter, beginning with the first of the left-hand operand, is compared to the corresponding letter in the right-hand operand. With ASCII values for uppercase letters being less than those of their lowercase counterparts, an uppercase letter evaluates to being less than its lowercase equivalent. JavaScript takes case-sensitivity very seriously.

Values for comparison can also come from object properties or from values passed to functions via event handlers or other functions. A common string comparison used in data-entry validation is the one that checks whether the string has anything in it:

```
form.entry.value != ""    // true if something is in the field
```

Equality of Disparate Data Types

In versions of JavaScript before 1.2 (legacy browsers), when your script tries to compare string values consisting of numerals and real numbers (for example, "123" == 123 or "123" != 123),

JavaScript anticipates that you want to compare apples to apples. Internally, it does some data type conversion that does not affect the data type of the original values (for example, if the values are in variables). But the entire situation is more complex, because other data types, such as objects, need to be dealt with. Therefore, prior to JavaScript 1.2, the rules of comparison are as shown in Table 22-3.

TABLE 22-3

Equality Comparisons for JavaScript 1.0 and 1.1

Operand A	Operand B	Internal Comparison Treatment
Object reference	Object reference	Compare object reference evaluations
Any data type	Null	Convert non-null to its object type and compare against null
Object reference	String	Convert object to string and compare strings
String	Number	Convert string to number and compare numbers

Understanding the logic of the equality comparisons in Table 22-3 requires a lot of thought on the scripter's part, because you have to be very conscious of the particular way data types may or may not be converted for equality evaluation (even though the values themselves are not converted). Supplying the proper conversion where necessary in the comparison statement is best. This ensures that what you want to compare — for example, the string versions of two values or the number versions of two values — is compared, rather than leaving the conversion up to JavaScript.

Backward-compatible conversion from a number to string entails concatenating an empty string to a number:

```
var a = "09";
var b = 9;
a == "" + b;  // result: false, because "09" does not equal "9"
```

For converting strings to numbers, you have numerous possibilities. The simplest is subtracting zero from a numeric string:

```
var a = "09";
var b = 9;
a-0 == b;  // result: true because number 9 equals number 9
```

You can also use the parseInt() and parseFloat() functions to convert strings to numbers:

```
var a = "09";
var b = 9;
parseInt(a, 10) == b;  // result: true because number 9 equals number 9
```

Of course, the other solution is to reasonably assume that your user base has a modern web browser that supports JavaScript 1.2+. To clear up the ambiguity of JavaScript's equality internal conversions, in version 1.2 JavaScript added two more operators to force the equality comparison to be extremely literal. The strictly equals (===) and strictly does not equal (!==) operators compare both the data type and value. The only time the === operator returns true is if the two operands are of the same data type (for example, both are numbers) and the same value. Therefore, no number is ever automatically equal to a string version of that same number. Data and object types must match before their values are compared.

JavaScript 1.2+ also provides some convenient global functions for converting strings to numbers and vice versa: `String()` and `Number()`. In the following examples, the `typeof` operator shows the data type of expressions using these functions:

```
typeof 9;              // result: "number"
typeof String(9);      // result: "string"
typeof "9";            // result: "string"
typeof Number("9");    // result: "number"
```

Again, none of these functions alters the data type of the value being converted. The value of the function is what gets compared in an equality comparison:

```
var a = "09";
var b = 9;
a == String(b);    // result: false, because "09" does not equal "9"
typeof b;          // result: still "number"
Number(a) == b;    // result: true, because 9 equals 9
typeof a;          // result: still "string"
```

This discussion should impress upon you the importance of considering data types when testing the equality of two values.

Connubial Operators

Compatibility: WinIE3+, MacIE3+, NN2+, Moz+, Safari+

Connubial operators is our terminology for those operators that join two operands to yield a value related to the operands. Table 22-4 lists the connubial operators in JavaScript.

The four basic arithmetic operators for numbers are straightforward. The plus operator also works on strings to *concatenate* them (join them together), as in

```
"Scooby " + "Doo" // result = "Scooby Doo"
```

In object-oriented programming terminology, the plus sign is considered *overloaded*, meaning that it performs a different action depending on its context. Remember, too, that string concatenation does not do anything on its own to monitor or insert spaces between words. In the preceding example, the space between the names is part of the first string.

Modulo arithmetic is helpful for those times when you want to know if one number divides evenly into another. You used it in an example in Chapter 21, "Control Structures and Exception Handling," to figure out if a particular year was a leap year. Although some other leap year considerations exist for the turn of each century, the math in the example simply checked whether the year was evenly divisible by four. The result of the modulo math is the remainder after dividing the two values: When the remainder is 0, one divides evenly into the other. Here are some samples of years divided by four:

```
2002 % 4    // result = 2
2003 % 4    // result = 3
2004 % 4    // result = 0 (Bingo! Leap year!)
```

TABLE 22-4

JavaScript Connubial Operators

Syntax	Name	Operand Types	Results
+	Plus	Integer, float, string	Integer, float, string
-	Minus	Integer, float	Integer, float
*	Multiply	Integer, float	Integer, float
/	Divide	Integer, float	Integer, float
%	Modulo	Integer, float	Integer, float
++	Increment	Integer, float	Integer, float
- -	Decrement	Integer, float	Integer, float
+*val*	Positive	Integer, float, string	Integer, float
-*val*	Negation	Integer, float, string	Integer, float

Thus, we used this modulo operator in a conditional statement with an `if. . .else` structure:

```
var howMany = 0;
today = new Date();
var theYear = today.getYear();
    if (theYear % 4 == 0)
    {
        howMany = 29;
    }
    else
    {
        howMany = 28;
    }
```

The modulo operator is also handy in special cases where you need to carry out some action in a loop at certain intervals, such as every third time through the loop. Here's an example of a loop that increments a counter every third time through, while looping to 100:

```
for (var i = 1; i < 100; i++)
{
    if (i % 3 == 0)
        threeCounter++;
}
```

Just as the modulo operator gives you the remainder of a division operation, some other languages offer an operator that results in the integer part of a division: integral division, or `div`. Although JavaScript does not have an explicit operator for this behavior, you can re-create it reliably if you know that your operands are always positive numbers. Use the `Math.floor()` or `Math.ceil()` methods with the division operator, as in

```
Math.floor(4/3);    // result = 1
```

In this example, `Math.floor()` replicates integral division only with values greater than or equal to 0; `Math.ceil()` with values less than 0.

The increment operator (++) is a *unary* operator (only one operand) and displays two different behaviors, depending on the side of the operand on which the symbols lie. Both the increment and decrement (--) operators can be used in conjunction with assignment operators, which we cover next.

As its name implies, the increment operator increases the value of its operand by one. But in an assignment statement, you have to pay close attention to precisely when that increase takes place. An assignment statement stuffs the value of the right operand into a variable on the left. If the ++ operator is located in front of the right operand (prefix), the right operand is incremented before the value is assigned to the variable; if the ++ operator is located after the right operand (postfix), the previous value of the operand is sent to the variable before the value is incremented. Follow this sequence to get a feel for these two behaviors:

```
var a = 10;     // initialize a to 10
var z = 0;      // initialize z to zero
z = a;          // a = 10, so z = 10
z = ++a;        // a becomes 11 before assignment, so a = 11 and z becomes 11
z = a++;        // a is still 11 before assignment, so z = 11; then a becomes 12
z = a++;        // a is still 12 before assignment, so z = 12; then a becomes 13
```

The decrement operator behaves the same way, except that the value of the operand decreases by one.

Increment and decrement operators are used most often with loop counters in `for` and `while` loops. The simpler ++ or -- symbology is more compact than reassigning a value by adding 1 to it (such as, z = z + 1 or z += 1). Because these are unary operators, you can use the increment and decrement operators without an assignment statement to adjust the value of a counting variable within a loop:

```
function doNothing()
{
    var i = 1;
    while (i < 20)
    {
        ++i;
    }
    alert(i); // loop ends with i = 20
}
```

The last pair of connubial operators are also unary operators (operating on one operand). Both the positive and negation operators can be used as shortcuts to the `Number()` global function, converting a string operand consisting of number characters to a number data type. The string operand is not changed, but the operation returns a value of the number type, as shown in the following sequence:

```
var a = "123";
var b = +a;     // b is now 123
typeof a;       // result: "string"
typeof b;       // result: "number"
```

The negation operator (-val) has additional power. By placing a minus sign in front of any numeric value (no space between the symbol and the value), you instruct JavaScript to evaluate a positive value as its corresponding negative value, and vice versa. The operator does not change the operand's value, but the expression returns the modified value. The following example provides a sequence of statements to demonstrate:

```
var x = 2;
var y = 8;
var z = -x;          // z equals -2, but x still equals 2
z = -(x + y);        // z equals -10, but x still equals 2 and y equals 8
z = -x + y;          // z equals 6, but x still equals 2 and y equals 8
```

To negate a Boolean value, see the Not (!) operator in the discussion of Boolean operators.

Assignment Operators

Compatibility: WinIE3+, MacIE3+, NN2+, Moz+, Safari+, Opera+, Chrome+

Assignment statements are among the most common statements you write in your JavaScript scripts. These statements appear everywhere you copy a value or the results of an expression into a variable for further manipulation of that value.

You assign values to variables for many reasons, even though you could probably use the original values or expressions several times throughout a script. Here is a sampling of reasons why you should assign values to variables:

- Variable names are usually shorter
- Variable names can be more descriptive
- You may need to preserve the original value for later in the script
- The original value is a property that cannot be changed
- Invoking the same method several times in a script is not efficient

Newcomers to scripting often overlook the last reason. For instance, if a script is writing a long paragraph to a new document, it would be more efficient to assemble the paragraph as one long string of sentences before invoking the document.createTextNode() method to add that text to the document than to add each sentence at a time.

Table 22-5 shows the range of assignment operators in JavaScript.

As clearly demonstrated in the top group (see "Bitwise Operators" later in the chapter for information on the bottom group), assignment operators beyond the simple equals sign can save some characters in your typing, especially when you have a series of values that you're trying to bring together in subsequent statements. You've seen plenty of examples in previous chapters, where you used the add-by-value operator (+=) to work wonders with strings as you assemble a long string variable. Here's a bit of script that builds a paragraph listing regional offices:

```
var aRegionalOffices = ['New York', 'Paris', 'Istanbul', 'Lusaka'];
var sText = 'Our offices are located in ';
var sSuffix = ', ';

for (var i = 0; i < aRegionalOffices.length; i++)
{
    // doing penultimate office?
    if (i == aRegionalOffices.length-2)
```

```
        {
            sSuffix += 'and ';
        }
         // doing final office?
        else if (i == aRegionalOffices.length-1)
        {
            sSuffix = '.';
        }

        // add office to paragraph
        sText += aRegionalOffices[i] + sSuffix;
    }

    // create text node and add to paragraph element
    var oNewText = document.createTextNode(sText);
    var oParagraph = document.getElementById("p1");
    oParagraph.appendChild(oNewText);
```

TABLE 22-5

JavaScript Assignment Operators

Syntax	Name	Example	Means
=	Equals	x = y	x = y
+=	Add by value	x += y	x = x + y
-=	Subtract by value	x -= y	x = x - y
*=	Multiply by value	x *= y	x = x * y
/=	Divide by value	x /= y	x = x / y
%=	Modulo by value	x %= y	x = x % y
<<=	Left shift by value	x <<= y	x = x << y
>=	Right shift by value	x >= y	x = x > y
>>=	Zero fill by value	x >>= y	x = x >> y
>>>=	Right shift by value	x >>>= y	x = x >>> y
&=	Bitwise AND by value	x &= y	x = x & y
|=	Bitwise OR by value	x |= y	x = x | y
^=	Bitwise XOR by value	x ^= y	x = x ^ y
[]=	Destructuring assignment	[a,b]=[c,d]	a=c, b=d

The result is:

```
<p id="p1">Our offices are located in New York, Paris, Istanbul, and Lusaka.</p>
```

The script segment starts with a plain equals assignment operator to initialize the `sText` variable to the beginning of the paragraph. In the loop to add offices, you use the add-by-value operator to tack additional string values onto whatever is in the `sText` variable at the time. Without the add-by-value operator, you would use the plain equals assignment operator for each line of code to concatenate new string data to the existing string data, like this:

```
var sText = 'Our offices are located in ';
...
    sText = sText + aRegionalOffices[i] + sSuffix;
```

These enhanced assignment operators are excellent shortcuts that you should use at every turn.

One more bit of assignment syntax was added to JavaScript with version 1.7:

[ ] *(square brackets to indicate destructuring assignment)*

Compatibility: FF2+, Opera 9.5 (partial)

Square brackets can assign an array of values to a set of variables, including an array returned from a function:

```
[a, b, c] = [12, 23, 34];

function moveSoutheast(x, y)
{
    return [x+1, y+1];
}
[x, y] = moveSoutheast(x, y);
```

See also: Object Operators: [ ] square brackets to enumerate an object member

Boolean Operators

Compatibility: WinIE4+, MacIE4+, NN3+, Moz+, Safari+

Because a great deal of programming involves logic, it is no accident that the arithmetic of the logic world plays an important role. You've already seen dozens of instances where programs make all kinds of decisions based on whether a statement or expression is the Boolean value `true` or `false`. What you haven't seen much of yet is how to combine multiple Boolean values and expressions — a capacity that scripts with slightly above average complexity may need to have.

In the various conditional expressions required throughout JavaScript (such as in an `if` construction), the condition that the program must test for may be more complicated than, say, whether a variable value is greater than a certain fixed value or whether a field is not empty. Look at the case of validating a text field entry for whether the entry contains all the numbers that your script may want. Without some magical JavaScript function to tell you whether or not a string consists of all numbers, you have to break apart the entry, character by character, and examine whether each character falls within the range of 0 through 9. But that examination actually comprises two tests: You can test for any character whose ASCII value is less than 0 or greater than 9 (i.e., not a digit). Alternatively, you can test whether the character is greater than or equal to 0 and is less than or equal to 9 (i.e., is a digit). What you need is the bottom-line evaluation of both tests.

Boolean math

That's where the wonder of Boolean math comes into play. With just two values — `true` and `false` — you can assemble a string of expressions that yield Boolean results and then let Boolean arithmetic figure out whether the bottom line is `true` or `false`.

But you don't add or subtract Boolean values the same way you add or subtract numbers. Instead, you use one of three JavaScript Boolean operators at your disposal. Table 22-6 shows the three operator symbols. In case you're unfamiliar with the characters in the table, the symbols for the `OR` operator are created by typing Shift+\ (backslash).

TABLE 22-6

JavaScript Boolean Operators

Syntax	Name	Operands	Results
`&&`	`AND`	Boolean	Boolean
`||`	`OR`	Boolean	Boolean
`!`	`NOT`	One Boolean	Boolean

Using Boolean operators with Boolean operands gets tricky if you're not used to it, so we have you start with the simplest Boolean operator: `NOT`. This operator requires only one operand. The `NOT` operator precedes any Boolean value to switch it back to the opposite value (from `true` to `false`, or from `false` to `true`). For instance:

```
!true          // result = false
!(10 > 5)      // result = false
!(10 < 5)      // result = true
!("cat" == "bat")    // result = true
```

As shown here, enclosing the operand of a `NOT` expression inside parentheses is always a good idea. This forces JavaScript to evaluate the expression inside the parentheses before flipping it around with the `NOT` operator. Otherwise, you may accidentally perform the operation on only part of the intended expression, resulting in unexpected consequences.

The `AND` (`&&`) operator joins two Boolean values to reach a `true` or `false` value based on the results of both values. This brings up something called a *truth table,* which helps you visualize all the possible outcomes for each value of an operand. Table 22-7 is a truth table for the `AND` operator.

Only one condition yields a `true` result: Both operands must evaluate to `true`. Which side of the operator a `true` or `false` value lives on doesn't matter. Here are examples of each possibility:

```
5 > 1 && 50 > 10    // result = true
5 > 1 && 50 < 10    // result = false
5 < 1 && 50 > 10    // result = false
5 < 1 && 50 < 10    // result = false
```

Note
You may be wondering why parentheses aren't being used in this code to separate the comparison and Boolean expressions. The reason has to do with operator precedence, which you learn a great deal more about later in

the chapter. The short answer is that comparison operators are evaluated before Boolean operators. Even so, it's never a bad idea to use parentheses to group sub-expressions and make absolutely sure you're getting the desired result and to make your code easier for humans to read. ■

TABLE 22-7

Truth Table for the And **Operator**

Left Operand	AND **Operator**	Right Operand	Result
True	&&	True	True
True	&&	False	False
False	&&	True	False
False	&&	False	False

In contrast, the OR (||) operator is more lenient about what it evaluates to true. The reason is that if one or the other (or both) operands is true, the operation returns true. The OR operator's truth table is shown in Table 22-8.

TABLE 22-8

Truth Table for the Or **Operator**

Left Operand	OR **Operator**	Right Operand	Result
True	||	True	True
True	||	False	True
False	||	True	True
False	||	False	False

Therefore, if a true value exists on either side of the operator, a true value is the result. Take the previous examples and swap the AND operators with OR operators so that you can see the OR operator's impact on the results:

```
5 > 1 || 50 > 10    // result = true
5 > 1 || 50 < 10    // result = true
5 < 1 || 50 > 10    // result = true
5 < 1 || 50 < 10    // result = false
```

Only when both operands are false does the OR operator return false.

Boolean operators at work

Learning to apply Boolean operators to JavaScript just takes a little effort and some sketches on a pad of paper to help you figure out the logic of the expressions. Earlier, we talked about using a Boolean operator to see whether a character fell within a range of ASCII values for data-entry validation. Listing 22-1 is a function discussed in more depth in Chapter 46, "Data-Entry Validation" (on the CD). This function accepts any string and sees whether each character of the string has an ASCII value less than 0 or greater than 9 — meaning that the input string is not a number.

LISTING 22-1

Is the Input String a Number?

```
function isNumber(inputStr)
{
    for (var i = 0; i < inputStr.length; i++)
    {
        var oneChar = inputStr.substring(i, i + 1);
            if (oneChar < "0" || oneChar > "9")
            {
                alert("Please make sure entries are numerals only.");
                return false;
            }
    }
    return true;
}
```

This code snippet combines a number of JavaScript powers to read individual characters (substrings) from a string object within a for loop. The statement that you're interested in is the condition of the if construction:

```
(oneChar < "0" || oneChar > "9")
```

In one conditional statement, you use the OR operator to test for both possibilities. If you check the OR truth table (Table 22-8), you see that this expression returns true if either one or both tests returns true. If that happens, the rest of the function alerts the user about the problem and returns a false value to the calling statement. Only if both tests within this condition evaluate to false for all characters of the string does the function return a true value.

From the simple OR operator, we go to the opposite extreme, where the function checks — in one conditional statement — whether a number falls within several numeric ranges. The script in Listing 22-2 comes from the array lookup application in Chapter 53, "Application: A Lookup Table" (on the CD-ROM), in which a user enters the first three digits of a U.S. Social Security number.

LISTING 22-2

Is a Number within Discontiguous Ranges?

```
// function to determine if value is in acceptable range for this application
function inRange(inputStr)
{
    num = parseInt(inputStr)
        if (num < 1 || (num > 586 && num < 596) || (num > 599 && num < 700) ||
```

continued

LISTING 22-2   *(continued)*

```
       num > 728)
   {
       alert("Sorry, the number you entered is not part of our database.  Try
           another three-digit number.");
       return false;
   }
   return true;
}
```

By the time this function is called, the user's data entry has been validated enough for JavaScript to know that the entry is a number. Now the function must check whether the number falls outside of the various ranges for which the application contains matching data. The conditions that the function tests here are whether the number is

- Less than 1
- Greater than 586 and less than 596 (using the AND operator)
- Greater than 599 and less than 700 (using the AND operator)
- Greater than 728

Each of these tests is joined by an OR operator. Therefore, if any one of these conditions proves `true`, the whole `if` condition is `true`, and the user is alerted accordingly.

The alternative to combining so many Boolean expressions in one conditional statement would be to nest a series of `if` constructions. But such a construction requires not only a great deal more code but also much repetition of the alert dialog box message for each condition that could possibly fail. The combined Boolean condition is, by far, the best way to go.

Bitwise Operators

Compatibility: WinIE3+, MacIE3+, NN2+, Moz+, Safari+, Opera+, Chrome+

For scripters, bitwise operations are an advanced subject. Unless you're dealing with external processes on server-side applications or the connection to Java applets, it's rare that you will use bitwise operators. Experienced programmers who concern themselves with more specific data types (such as long integers) are quite comfortable in this arena, so we simply provide an explanation of JavaScript capabilities. Table 22-9 lists JavaScript bitwise operators.

The numeric value operands can appear in any of the JavaScript language's three numeric literal bases (decimal, octal, or hexadecimal). As soon as the operator has an operand, the value is converted to binary representation (32 bits long). For the first three bitwise operations, the individual bits of one operand are compared with their counterparts in the other operand. The resulting value for each bit depends on the operator:

- **Bitwise** AND: 1 if both digits are 1
- **Bitwise** OR: 1 if either digit is 1
- **Bitwise** Exclusive OR: 1 if only one digit is a 1

TABLE 22-9

JavaScript's Bitwise Operators

Operator	Name	Left Operand	Right Operand
&	Bitwise AND	Integer value	Integer value
|	Bitwise OR	Integer value	Integer value
^	Bitwise XOR	Integer value	Integer value
~	Bitwise NOT	(None)	Integer value
<<	Left shift	Integer value	Shift amount
>>	Right shift	Integer value	Shift amount
>>>	Zero fill right shift	Integer value	Shift amount

Bitwise NOT, a unary operator, inverts the value of every bit in the single operand. The bitwise shift operators operate on a single operand. The second operand specifies the number of positions to shift the value's binary digits in the direction of the arrows of the operator symbols.

Example

For example, the left shift (<<) operator has the following effect:

```
4 << 2 // result = 16
```

The reason for this shifting is that the binary representation for decimal 4 is 00000100 (to eight digits, anyway). The left shift operator instructs JavaScript to shift all digits two places to the left, giving the binary result 00010000, which converts to 16 in decimal format. If you're interested in experimenting with these operators, use The Evaluator to evaluate sample expressions for yourself (see Chapter 4, "JavaScript Essentials"). More advanced books on C and C++ programming are also of help.

Object Operators

The next group of operators concern themselves with objects (including native JavaScript, DOM, and custom objects) and data types. Most of these have been implemented after the earliest JavaScript browsers, so each one has its own compatibility rating.

. (dot or period)

Compatibility: WinIE3+, MacIE3+, NN2+, Moz+, Safari+, Opera+, Chrome+

The dot operator indicates that the object to its left owns or contains the resource to its right, as in `object.property` and `object.method()`. Examples:

```
native JavaScript object
var s = new String('syzygy');
```

```
var len = s.length;
var pos = s.indexOf('zyg'); // result: pos == 2
```

custom JavaScript object

```
function myMethod()
{
    // (custom code goes here)
}

function myCustomObject()
{
    this.myProperty = 'something';
    this.myMethod = myMethod;
}

var o = new myCustomObject();
var p = o.newProperty;
o.myMethod();
```

Document Object Model object

```
var sTitle = document.title;
var oThing = document.getElementById("elementID");
```

[ ] *(square brackets to enumerate object member)*

Compatibility: WinIE3+, MacIE3+, NN2+, Moz+, Safari+, Opera+, Chrome+

Square brackets enumerate a member of an object, such as an array element:

define an array:

```
var a = ['homo erectus', , 'homo sapiens'];
```

enumerate an array element:

```
a[5] = 'sixth element';
```

enumerate an object property:

```
a['color'] = 'puce';
```

See also: Assignment Operators: [ ] square brackets to indicate destructuring assignment

Delete

Compatibility: WinIE4+, MacIE4+, NN4+, Moz+, Safari+, Opera+, Chrome+

Array objects do not contain a method to remove an element from the collection, nor do custom objects offer a method to remove a property. You can always empty the data in an array item or property by setting its value to an empty string or `null`, but the array element or property remains in the object. With the `delete` operator, you can completely remove the element or property.

There is special behavior about deleting an array item that you should bear in mind. If your array uses numeric indexes, a deletion of a given index removes that index value from the total array, but without collapsing the array (which would alter index values of items higher than the deleted item).

Example

Consider the following simple dense array:

```
var oceans = new Array("Atlantic", "Pacific", "Indian","Arctic");
```

This kind of array automatically assigns numeric indices to its entries for addressing later in constructions such as `for` loops:

```
for (var i = 0; i < oceans.length; i++)
{
    if (oceans[i] == form.destination.value)
    {
        // statements
    }
}
```

If you then issue the statement

```
delete oceans[2];
```

the array undergoes significant changes. First, the third element is removed from the array. Note that the length of the array does not change. Even so, the index value (`2`) is removed from the array, such that, schematically, the array looks like the following:

```
oceans[0] = "Atlantic";
oceans[1] = "Pacific";
oceans[3] = "Arctic";
```

If you try to reference `oceans[2]` in this collection, the result is `undefined`.

The `delete` operator works best on arrays that have named indexes since there is less confusion due to deleted numeric indexes. Your scripts will have more control over the remaining entries and their values, because they don't rely on what could be a missing entry of a numeric index sequence.

One aspect of this deletion action that JavaScript doesn't provide is absolute control over memory utilization. All garbage collection is managed by the JavaScript interpreter engine, which tries to recognize when items occupying memory are no longer needed, at which time the unused browser's application memory may be recovered. But you cannot force the browser to perform its garbage collection task. So, deleting an entry from an array doesn't guarantee an immediate release of its associated memory.

in

Compatibility: WinIE5.5+, MacIE−, NN6+, Moz+, Safari+, Opera+, Chrome+

The in operator lets a script statement inspect an object to see if it has a named property or method. The operand to the left of the operator is a string reference to the property or method (just the method name, without parentheses); the operand to the right of the operator is the object being inspected. If the object knows the property or method, the expression returns true. Thus, you can use the in operator in expressions used for conditional expressions.

Example

You can experiment with this operator in The Evaluator (see Chapter 4). For example, to prove that the write() method is implemented for the document object, the expression you type into the top text box of The Evaluator is:

```
"write" in document
```

But compare the implementation of the W3C DOM document.defaultView property in IE5.5+ and modern W3C browsers:

```
"defaultView" in document
```

In NN6+, Mozilla (including Firefox and Camino), and Safari, the result is true, while in IE5.5 and IE6, the result is false.

Having this operator around for conditional expressions lets you go far beyond simple object detection for branching code. For example, if you intend to use document.defaultView in your script, you can make sure that the property is supported before referencing it (assuming your users all have browsers that know the in operator).

instanceof

Compatibility: WinIE5+, MacIE-, NN6+, Moz+, Safari+, Opera+, Chrome+

The instanceof operator lets a script test whether an object is an instance of a particular JavaScript native object or of a DOM object. The operand to the left side of the operator is the value under test; the value to the right of the operand is a reference to the root class from which the value is suspected of being constructed.

For native JavaScript classes, the kinds of object references to the right of the operator include such static objects as Date, String, Number, Boolean, Object, Array, and RegExp. You need to be mindful of how native JavaScript classes can sometimes be children of other native classes, which means that a value may be an instance of two different static objects.

Example

Consider the following sequence (which you can follow along in The Evaluator):

```
a = new Array(1,2,3);
a instanceof Array;
```

The second statement yields a result of true, because the Array constructor was used to generate the object. But the JavaScript Array is, itself, an instance of the root Object object. Therefore, both of the following statements evaluate to true:

```
a instanceof Object;
Array instanceof Object;
```

new

Compatibility: WinIE3+, MacIE3+, NN2+, Moz+, Safari+, Opera+, Chrome+

Most JavaScript core objects have constructor functions built into the language. To access those functions, you use the new operator along with the name of the constructor. The function returns a reference to the object instance, which your scripts can then use to get and set properties or invoke object methods. For example, creating a new date object requires invoking the Date object's constructor, as follows:

```
var today = new Date();
```

Some object constructor functions require parameters to help define the object. Others, as in the case of the Date object, can accept a number of different parameter formats, depending on the format of the date information with which you set the initial object. The new operator can be used with the following core language objects, as of each specified JavaScript version:

JavaScript 1.0	JavaScript 1.1	JavaScript 1.2	JavaScript 1.5
Date	Array	RegExp	Error
Object	Boolean		
(Custom object)	Function		
	Image		
	Number		
	String		

this

Compatibility: WinIE3+, MacIE3+, NN2+, Moz+, Safari+, Opera+, Chrome+

JavaScript includes an operator that allows script statements to refer to the very object in which they are located. The self-referential operator is this.

The most common application of the this operator is in event handlers that pass references of themselves to functions for further processing.

A function receiving the value assigns it to a variable that can be used to reference the sender, its properties, and its methods.

Example

Because the this operator references an object, that object's properties can be exposed with the aid of the operator. For example:

```
oInputField.onchange = validateInput;

function validateInput(evt)
{
    var sInputvalue = this.value;
}
```

When the visitor changes the contents of the input field — triggering the onchange event, which, in turn, executes the validateInput() function — the code inside that function recognizes this as being the input field object to which it belongs. In that context, this.value represents the value entered by the visitor.

In the bad old days of inline JavaScript, this would look like:

```
<input type="text" name="entry" onchange="validateInput(this)" />
```

The this operator also works inside other objects, such as custom objects. When you define a constructor function for a custom object, using the this operator to define properties of the object and assign values to those properties is common practice. Consider the following example of an object creation sequence:

```
function bottledWater(brand, ozSize, flavor)
{
    this.brand = brand;
    this.ozSize = ozSize;
    this.flavor = flavor;
}
var myWater = new bottledWater("Eau de Odio", 16, "original");
```

When the new object is created via the constructor function, the this operators define each property of the object and then assign the corresponding incoming value to that property. Using the same names for the properties and parameter variables is perfectly fine and makes the constructor easy to maintain.

By extension, if you assign a function as an object's property (to behave as a method for the object), the this operator inside that function refers to the object invoking the function, offering an avenue to the object's properties. For example, if we add the following function definition and statement to the myWater object created just above, the function can directly access the brand property of the object:

```
function adSlogan()
{
    return "Drink " + this.brand + ", it's wet and wild!";
}
myWater.getSlogan = adSlogan;
```

When a statement invokes the myWater.getSlogan() method, the object invokes the adSlogan() function, but all within the context of the myWater object. Thus, the this operator applies to the surrounding object, making the brand property available via the this operator (this.brand).

Miscellaneous Operators

The final group of operators doesn't fit into any of the previous categories, but they are no less important.

Compatibility: WinIE3+, MacIE3+, NN2+, Moz+, Safari+, Opera+, Chrome+

The comma operator indicates a series of expressions that are to be evaluated in left-to-right sequence. Most typically, this operator is used to permit multiple variable initializations. For example, you can combine the declaration of several variables in a single `var` statement, as follows:

```
var name, address, serialNumber;
```

Another situation where you could use this operator is within the expressions of a `for` loop construction. In the following example, two different counting variables are initialized and incremented at different rates. When the loop begins, both variables are initialized at zero (they don't have to be, but this example starts that way); for each subsequent trip through the loop, one variable is incremented by one, while the other is incremented by 10:

```
for (var i=0, j=0; i < someLength; i++, j+10)
{
    ...
}
```

Don't confuse the comma operator with the semicolon delimiter between statements.

?:

Compatibility: WinIE3+, MacIE3+, NN2+, Moz+, Safari+, Opera+, Chrome+

The conditional operator is a shortcut way of expressing the `if. . .else` conditional construction covered in Chapter 21, "Control Structures and Exception Handling." This operator is typically used in concert with an assignment operator to assign one of two values to a variable based on the result of a conditional expression. The formal syntax for the conditional operator is:

```
condition ? expressionIfTrue : expressionIfFalse
```

If used with an assignment operator, the syntax is:

```
var = condition ? expressionIfTrue : expressionIfFalse;
```

No matter how you use the operator, the important point to remember is that an expression that contains this operator evaluates to one of the two expressions following the question mark symbol. In truth, either expression could invoke any JavaScript, including calling other functions, or even nesting further conditional operators within one of the expressions to achieve the equivalent of nested `if. . .else` constructions. To assure proper resolution of nested conditionals, surround inner expressions with parentheses to make sure that they evaluate before the outer expression evaluates. As an example, the following statement assigns one of three strings to a variable depending on the date within a month:

```
var monthPart = (dateNum <= 10) ? "early" : ((dateNum <= 20) ?
    "middle" : "late");
```

When the statement is evaluated, the inner conditional expression at the right of the first colon is evaluated, returning either `middle` or `late`; then the outer conditional expression is evaluated, returning either `early` or the result of the inner conditional expression.

typeof

Compatibility: WinIE3+, MacIE3+, NN3+, Moz+, Safari+, Opera+, Chrome+

void

Unlike most other operators, which are predominantly concerned with arithmetic and logic, the unary `typeof` operator defines the kind of value to which a variable or expression evaluates. Typically, this operator is used to identify whether a variable value is one of the following types: `number`, `string`, `boolean`, `object`, `function`, or `undefined`.

Example

Having this investigative capability in JavaScript is helpful because variables cannot only contain any one of those data types but can change their data type on the fly. Your scripts may need to handle a value differently based on the value's type. The most common use of the `typeof` property is as part of a condition. For example:

```
if (typeof myVal == "number")
{
    myVal = parseInt(myVal);
}
```

The evaluated value of the `typeof` operation is, itself, a string.

void

Compatibility: WinIE3+, MacIE3+, NN3+, Moz+, Safari+, Opera+, Chrome+

In all scriptable browsers you can use the `javascript:` pseudo-protocol to supply the parameter for `href` and `src` attributes in HTML tags, such as links. In the process, you have to be careful that the function or statement being invoked by the URL does not return or evaluate to any values. If a value comes back from such an expression, then that value, or sometimes the directory of the client's hard disk, often replaces the page content. To avoid this possibility, use the `void` operator in front of the function or expression being invoked by the `javascript:` URL.

Example

The best way to use this construction is to place the operator before the expression or function and separate them by a space, as in

```
javascript: void doSomething();
```

On occasion, you may have to wrap the expression inside parentheses after the `void` operator. Using parentheses is necessary only when the expression contains operators of a lower precedence than the `void` operator (see the following section, "Operator Precedence"). But don't automatically wrap all expressions in parentheses, because some browsers can experience problems with these. Even so, it is common practice to assign the following URL to the `href` attribute of an a link whose `onclick` event handler does all of the work:

```
href="javascript: void (0)"
```

The `void` operator makes sure the function or expression returns no value that the HTML attribute can use. Such a link's `onclick` event handler should also inhibit the natural behavior of a clicked link (for example, by evaluating to `return false`).

Operator Precedence

When you start working with complex expressions that hold a number of operators (for example, Listing 22-2), knowing the order in which JavaScript evaluates those expressions is vital. JavaScript assigns different priorities or weights to types of operators in an effort to achieve uniformity in the way it evaluates complex expressions.

In the following expression

```
10 + 4 * 5 // result = 30
```

JavaScript uses its precedence scheme to perform the multiplication before the addition — regardless of where the operators appear in the statement. In other words, JavaScript first multiplies 4 by 5 and then adds that result to 10 to get a result of 30. That may not be the way you want this expression to evaluate. Perhaps your intention was to add the 10 and 4 first, and then to multiply that sum by 5. To make that happen, you have to override JavaScript's natural operator precedence. To do that, you must use parentheses to enclose an operator with lower precedence. The following statement shows how you adjust the previous expression to make it behave differently:

```
(10 + 4) * 5 // result = 70
```

That one set of parentheses has a great impact on the outcome. Parentheses have the highest precedence in JavaScript, and if you nest parentheses in an expression, the innermost set evaluates first.

For help in constructing complex expressions, refer to Table 22-10 for JavaScript's operator precedence. Our general practice: When in doubt about complex precedence issues, we build the expression with lots of parentheses according to the way we want the internal expressions to evaluate.

This precedence scheme is devised to help you avoid being faced with two operators from the same precedence level that often appear in the same expression. When it does happen (such as with addition and subtraction), JavaScript begins evaluating the expression from left to right.

One related fact involves a string of Boolean expressions strung together for a conditional statement (see Listing 22-2). JavaScript follows what is called *short-circuit evaluation*. As the nested expressions are evaluated left to right, the fate of the entire condition can sometimes be determined before all expressions are evaluated. Anytime JavaScript encounters an AND operator, if the left operand evaluates to false, the entire expression evaluates to false without JavaScript's even bothering to evaluate the right operand. For an Or operator, if the left operand is true, JavaScript short-circuits that expression to true. This feature can trip you up if you don't perform enough testing on your scripts: If a syntax error or other error exists in a right operand, and you fail to test the expression in a way that forces that right operand to evaluate, you may not know that a bug exists in your code. Users of your page, of course, will find the bug quickly. Do your testing to head bugs off at the pass.

TABLE 22-10

JavaScript Operator Precedence

Precedence Level	Operator	Notes
1	`()`	From innermost to outermost
	`[]`	Array index value
	`function()`	Any remote function call
2	`!`	Boolean NOT
	`~`	Bitwise NOT
	`-`	Negation
	`++`	Increment
	`--`	Decrement
	`new`	
	`typeof`	
	`void`	
	`delete`	Delete array or object entry
3	`*`	Multiplication
	`/`	Division
	`%`	Modulo
4	`+`	Addition
	`-`	Subtraction
5	`<<`	Bitwise shifts
	`>`	
	`>>`	
6	`<`	Comparison operators
	`<=`	
	`>`	
	`>=`	
7	`==`	Equality
	`!=`	
8	`&`	Bitwise AND
9	`^`	Bitwise XOR
10	`|`	Bitwise OR
11	`&&`	Boolean AND
12	`||`	Boolean OR

Precedence Level	Operator	Notes
13	?	Conditional expression
14	=	Assignment operators
	+=	
	-=	
	*=	
	/=	
	%=	
	<<=	
	>=	
	>>=	
	&=	
	^=	
	|=	
15	,	Comma (parameter delimiter)

Note

Notice, too, that all math and string concatenation is performed prior to any comparison operators. This enables all expressions that act as operands for comparisons to evaluate fully before they are compared. ■

The key to working with complex expressions is to isolate individual expressions and to try them out by themselves, if you can. See additional debugging tips in Chapter 48, "Debugging Scripts," on the CD-ROM.

Function Objects and Custom Objects

B
y now, you've seen dozens of JavaScript functions in action and probably have a pretty good feel for the way they work. This chapter provides the Function object specification and delves into the fun prospect of creating objects in your JavaScript code. If you've missed out on the object-oriented (OO) programming revolution, now is your chance to join. JavaScript is surprisingly full-featured when it comes to supporting OO and allowing you to develop scripts that rely heavily on custom objects.

Function Object

Properties	Methods	Event Handlers
arguments	apply()	
arity	call()	
caller	toString()	
constructor	valueOf()	
length		
prototype		

Syntax

Creating a Function object:

```
function functionName([arg1,...[,argN]])
{
    statement(s)
}
```

```
var funcName = new Function(["argName1",...[,"argNameN"],
        "statement1;...[;statementN]"])object.eventHandlerName =
        function([arg1,...[,argN]]) {statement(s)}
```

Accessing `Function` object properties and methods:

```
functionObject.property | method([parameters])
```

Compatibility: WinIE3+, MacIE3+, NN2+, Moz+, Safari+

About this object

JavaScript accommodates what other languages might call procedures, subroutines, and functions all in one type of structure: the *custom function*. A function may return a value (if programmed to do so with the `return` keyword), but it does not have to return any value. With the exception of JavaScript code that executes as the document loads, all deferred processing takes place in functions.

Although you can create functions that are hundreds of lines long, we recommend you break up longer processes into shorter functions. Among the reasons for doing so: smaller chunks are easier to write and debug; building blocks make it easier to visualize the entire script; you can make functions generalizable and reusable for other scripts; and other parts of the script or other open frames can use the functions.

Learning how to write good, reusable functions takes time and experience. But the earlier you understand the importance of this concept, the more you will be on the lookout for good examples in other people's scripts on the web.

Creating functions

The standard way of defining a function in your script involves following a simple pattern and then filling in the details. The formal syntax definition for a function is:

```
function functionName( [arg1] ... [, argN])
{
    statement(s)
}
```

The task of assigning a function name helps you determine the precise scope of activity of the function. If you find that you can't reduce the planned task for the function to a simple one- to three-word name (which is then condensed into one contiguous sequence of characters for the `functionName`), perhaps you're asking the function to do too much. A better idea may be to break the job into two or more functions. As you start to design a function, be on the lookout for functions that you can call from the one you're writing. If you find yourself copying and pasting lines of code from one part of a function to another because you're performing the same operation in different spots within the function, it may be time to break that segment out into its own function.

Here's a quick example of a simple function that accepts a single argument, a name, and then returns a string greeting that includes the name:

```
function sayHello(name)
{
    return ("Hello, " + name + ".");
}
```

You can also create what is called an *anonymous function* using the `new Function()` constructor. In reality, you assign a name to this anonymous function as follows:

```
var funcName = new Function(["argName1",...[,"argNameN"],
              "statement1;...[;statementN]"]);
```

This other way of building a function is particularly helpful when your scripts need to create a function after a document loads. All the components of a function are present in this definition. Each function parameter name is supplied as a string value, separated from the others by commas. The final parameter string consists of the statements that execute whenever the function is called. (Recall that quoted strings cannot be broken onto several lines; the continuation character at the end of the second line in the code segment below is used only because this book has a finite width to its pages.) Separate each JavaScript statement with a semicolon, and enclose the entire sequence of statements inside quotes, as in the following:

```
var willItFit = new Function("width","height",
             "var sx = screen.availWidth; var sy = screen.availHeight;↵
             return (sx >= width && sy >= height)");
```

The `willItFit()` function takes two parameters; the body of the function defines two local variables (`sx` and `sy`) and then returns a Boolean value of `true` if the incoming parameters are smaller than the local variables. In traditional form, this function is defined as follows:

```
function willItFit(width, height)
{
    var sx = screen.availWidth;
    var sy = screen.availHeight;
    return (sx >= width && sy >= height);
}
```

When this function exists in the browser's memory, you can invoke it like any other function:

```
if (willItFit(400,500))
{
    // statements to load image
}
```

One last function creation format is available in IE4+, NN4+, Moz, and other W3C DOM browsers. This advanced technique, called a *lambda expression,* provides a shortcut for creating a reference to an anonymous function (truly anonymous because the function has no name that you can reference later). The common application of this technique is to assign function references to event handlers when an event object also must be passed. The following is an example of how to assign an anonymous function to an `onchange` event handler for a form control:

```
document.forms[0].age.onchange = function(event)
    {isNumber(document.forms[0].age)}
```

Because an anonymous function evaluates to a reference to a function object, you can use either form of anonymous function in situations where a function reference is called for, including parameters of methods or other functions.

439

Nesting functions

Modern browsers also provide for nesting functions inside one another. In the absence of nested functions, each function definition is defined at the global level, whereby every function is exposed and available to all other script code. With nested functions, you can encapsulate the exposure of a function inside another and make that nested function private to the enclosing function. Of course, we don't recommend reusing function names with this technique, although you can create nested functions with the same name inside multiple global-level functions, as the following skeletal structure shows:

```
function outerA()
{
    // statements
    function innerA()
    {
        // statements
    }
    // statements
}
function outerB()
{
    // statements
    function innerA()
    {
        // statements
    }
    function innerB()
    {
        // statements
    }
    // statements
}
```

A good time to apply a nested function is when a sequence of statements needs to be invoked in multiple places within a large function, and those statements have meaning only within the context of the larger function. In other words, rather than break out the repeated sequence as a separate global function, you keep it all within the scope of the larger function.

Note

The premise behind nesting a function is to isolate the function and make it private from the overall script. This results in cleaner script code because nothing is exposed globally without a good reason. As an admittedly strange analogy, the water heater in your house could feasibly be placed outside (global), but it's generally safer and more organized to place it inside (local). Unlike your mailbox, which must interact with the outside (global) world, your water heater plays an internal (local) role, and therefore lives inside your house. And after all, we don't want to make our home's hot water globally available. ■

You can access a nested function only from statements in its containing function (but in any order). Moreover, all variables defined in the outer function (including parameter variables) are accessible to the inner function; but variables defined in an inner function are not accessible to the outer function. See the section "Variable scope: Globals and locals" later in this chapter for details on how variables are visible to various components of a script.

Function parameters

The function definition requires a set of parentheses after the `functionName`. If the function does not rely on any information arriving with it when invoked, the parentheses can be empty. But when some kind of data is arriving with a call to the function, you need to assign names to each parameter. Virtually any kind of value can be a parameter: strings, numbers, Boolean operators, and even complete object references such as a form or form element. Choose names for these variables that help you remember the content of those values; also, avoid reusing existing object names as variable names because it's easy to get confused when objects and variables with the same name appear in the same statements. You must avoid using JavaScript keywords (including the reserved words listed in Appendix C, on the CD) and any global variable name defined elsewhere in your script. (See more about global variables in the following sections.)

JavaScript is forgiving about matching the number of parameters in the function definition with the number of parameters passed along from the calling statement. If you define a function with three parameters and the calling statement specifies only two, the third parameter variable value in that function is assigned a `null` value. For example:

```
function saveWinners(first, second, third)
{
    // statements
}
oneFunction("George","Gracie");
```

In the preceding example, the values of `first` and `second` inside the function are `"George"` and `"Gracie"`, respectively; the value of `third` is `null`.

At the opposite end of the spectrum, JavaScript also doesn't balk if you send more parameters from the calling statement than the number of parameter variables specified in the function definition. In fact, the language includes a mechanism — the `arguments` property — that you can add to your function to gather any extraneous parameters that should read your function.

Properties
arguments (deprecated)

Value: Array of arguments   Read-Only

Compatibility: WinIE4+, MacIE4+, NN3+, Moz+, Safari+, Chrome+

When a function receives parameter values from the statement that invoked the function, those parameter values are silently assigned to the `arguments` property of the function object. This property is an array of the values, with each parameter value assigned to a zero-based index entry in the array — whether or not parameters are defined for it. You can find out how many parameters are sent by extracting `functionName.arguments.length`. For example, if four parameters are passed, `functionName.arguments.length` returns 4. Then, you can use array notation (`functionName.arguments[i]`) to extract the values of any parameter(s) you want.

Theoretically, you never have to define parameter variables for your functions because you can extract the desired arguments array entry instead. Well-chosen parameter variable names, however, are much more readable, so we recommend them over the `arguments` property in most cases. But you may run into situations in which a single function definition needs to handle multiple calls to the function when each call may have a different number of parameters. The function knows how to handle any arguments over and above the ones given names as parameter variables.

Note

It is necessary in some cases to create a function that deliberately accepts a varied number of arguments, in which case the `arguments` **property is the only way to access and process the arguments. For example, if you wanted to create a function that averages test scores, there's a good chance the number of scores may vary, in which case you would write the function so that it loops through the** `arguments` **array, adding up the scores as it carries out the calculation.** ∎

Example

See Listings 23-1 and 23-2 for a demonstration of both the `arguments` and `caller` properties.

arity (deprecated)

Value: Integer   Read-Only

Compatibility: WinIE−, MacIE−, NN4+, Moz−, Safari−, Chrome+

See the discussion of the `length` property later in this chapter.

caller

Value: Function object reference   Read-Only

Compatibility: WinIE4+, MacIE4+, NN3+, Moz+, Safari−, Chrome+

When one function invokes another, a chain is established between the two, primarily so that a returned value knows where to go. Therefore, a function invoked by another maintains a reference to the function that called it. Such information is automatically stored in a `Function` object as the `caller` property. This relationship reminds me a bit of a subwindow's `opener` property, which points to the window or frame responsible for the subwindow's creation. The value is valid only while the called function is running at the request of another function; when a function isn't running, its `caller` property is `null`.

The value of the `caller` property is a reference to a `Function` object, so you can inspect its `arguments` and `caller` properties (in case it was called by yet another function). Thus, a function can look back at a calling function to see what values it was passed.

The `functionName.caller` property reveals the contents of an entire function definition if the current function was called from another function (including an event handler). If the call for a function comes from a regular JavaScript statement not originating inside a function, the `functionName.caller` property is `null`.

Example

To help you grasp all that these two properties yield, study Listing 23-1.

Note

The function to assign event handlers throughout the code in this chapter and much of the book is `addEvent()`, **a cross-browser event handler explained in detail in Chapter 32, "Event Objects."** ∎

```
LISTING 23-1
```

A Function's arguments and caller Properties

HTML: jsb-23-01.html

```html
<!DOCTYPE html>
<html>
   <head>
      <meta http-equiv="content-type" content="text/html;charset=utf-8">
      <title>Function call information</title>
      <script type="text/javascript" src="../jsb-global.js"></script>
      <script type="text/javascript" src="jsb-23-01.js"></script>
   </head>
   <body>
      <h1>Function call information</h1>
      <div id="placeHolder"></div>
   </body>
</html>
```

JavaScript: jsb-23-01.js

```javascript
// initialize when the page has loaded
addEvent(window, "load", showArgCaller);

var newElem;
var newText;

function showArgCaller ()
{
   // Call the hansel function twice: once directly,
   // second indirectly from the gretel function.
   hansel(1, "two", 3);
   gretel(4, "five", 6, "seven");
}

function hansel(x,y)
{
   var args = hansel.arguments;
   var placeHolderElement = document.getElementById("placeHolder");

      if (placeHolderElement)
      {
         // a header line
         newElem = document.createElement("h3");
         newElem.className = "objProperty";
         newText = document.createTextNode("The caller and the arguments");
         // insert the 1st line (text node) into the new h3
         newElem.appendChild(newText);
         // insert the completed h3 into placeHolder
```

continued

functionObject.**caller()**

LISTING 23-1   *(continued)*

```
        placeHolderElement.appendChild(newElem);

        // the next line is the caller
        newElem = document.createElement("div");
        newElem.className = "objProperty";
        newText = document.createTextNode("hansel.caller is " + hansel.caller);
        newElem.appendChild(newText);
        placeHolderElement.appendChild(newElem);

        // the next line is the number or arguments
        newElem = document.createElement("div");
        newElem.className = "objProperty";
        newText = document.createTextNode("hansel.arguments.length is " +
                                    hansel.arguments.length);
        newElem.appendChild(newText);
        placeHolderElement.appendChild(newElem);

        // the rest of the lines are the arguments
        for (var i = 0; i < args.length; i++) {
            newElem = document.createElement("div");
            newElem.className = "objProperty";
            newText = document.createTextNode("argument " + i + " is " + args[i]);
            newElem.appendChild(newText);
            placeHolderElement.appendChild(newElem);
        }
    }
}

function gretel(x,y,z)
{
    today = new Date();
    thisYear = today.getFullYear();
    hansel(x,y,z,thisYear);
}
```

When you load this page, the following JavaScript results appear in the browser window:

```
The caller and the arguments
hansel.caller is function showArgCaller()
{
  hansel(1, "two", 3);
  gretel(4, "five", 6, "seven");
}
hansel.arguments.length is 3
argument 0 is 1
argument 1 is two
argument 2 is 3
The caller and the arguments
```

```
hansel.caller is function gretel(x, y, z)
{
  today = new Date();
  thisYear = today.getFullYear();
  hansel(x,y,z,thisYear);
}
hansel.arguments.length is 4
argument 0 is 4
argument 1 is five
argument 2 is 6
argument 3 is 2010 (or whatever the current year is)
```

As the document loads, the `hansel()` function is called directly in the onload event handler in the external script. It passes three arguments, even though the `hansel()` function defines only two. The `hansel.arguments` property picks up all three arguments just the same. Then the onload event handler invokes the `gretel()` function, which, in turn, calls `hansel()` again. But when `gretel()` makes the call, it passes four parameters. The `gretel()` function picks up only three of the four arguments sent by the calling statement. It also inserts another value from its own calculations as an extra parameter to be sent to `hansel()`. The `hansel.caller` property reveals the entire content of the `gretel()` function, whereas `hansel.arguments` picks up all four parameters, including the year value introduced by the `gretel()` function.

constructor

(See `object.constructor` later in this chapter.)

length

Value: Integer   Read-Only

Compatibility: WinIE4+, MacIE4+, NN4+, Moz+, Safari+

As the `arguments` property of a function proves, JavaScript is very forgiving about matching the number of parameters passed to a function with the number of parameter variables defined for the function. But a script can examine the `length` property of a `Function` object to see precisely how many parameter variables are defined for the function. A reference to the property starts with the function name representing the object. For example, consider the following function definition shell:

```
function identify(name, rank, serialNum)
{
    // ...
}
```

A script statement anywhere outside of the function can read the number of parameters with the reference:

```
identify.length
```

The value of the property in the preceding example is 3. The `length` property supercedes the NN-only `arity` property.

prototype

(See Chapter 18.)

Methods

```
apply([thisObj[, argumentsArray]])
call([thisObj[, arg1[, arg2[, ... argN]]]])
```

Returns: Nothing

Compatibility: WinIE5.5+, MacIE−, NN6+, Moz+, Safari+, Chrome+

The apply() and call() methods of a Function object invoke the function. This may seem redundant to the normal way in which script statements invoke functions by simply naming the function, following it with parentheses, passing parameters, and so on. The difference with these methods is that you can invoke the function through the apply() and call() methods using only a reference to the function. For example, if your script defines a function through the new Function() constructor (or other anonymous shortcut supported by the browser), you receive a reference to the function as a result of the constructor. To invoke the function later using only that reference (presumably preserved in a global variable), use either the apply() or call() method. Both of these methods achieve the same result, but choosing one method over the other depends on the form in which the function's parameters are conveyed (more about that in a moment).

The first parameter of both methods is a reference to the object that the function treats as the current object. For garden-variety functions defined in your script, use the keyword this, which means that the function's context becomes the current object (just like a regular function). In fact, if there are no parameters to be sent to the function, you can omit parameters to both methods altogether.

The object reference comes into play when the function being invoked is one that is normally defined as a method to a custom object. (Some of these concepts are covered later in this chapter, so you may need to return here after you are familiar with custom objects.)

Example

Consider the following code that generates a custom object and assigns a method to the object to display an alert about properties of the object:

```
// function to be invoked as a method from a 'car' object
function showCar()
{
    alert(this.make + " : " + this.color);
}
// 'car' object constructor function
function Car(make, color)
{
    this.make = make;
    this.color = color;
    this.show = showCar;
}
// create instance of a 'car' object
var myCar = new Car("Ford", "blue");
```

The normal way of getting the myCar object to display an alert about its properties is:

```
myCar.show();
```

At that point, the showCar() function runs, picking up the current Car object as the context for the this references in the function. In other words, when the showCar() function runs as a method of the object, the function treats the object as the *current object*.

With the call() or apply() methods, however, you don't have to bind the showCar() function to the myCar object. You can omit the statement in the Car() constructor that assigns the showCar function to a method name for the object. Instead, a script can invoke the showCar() method and instruct it to treat myCar as the current object:

```
showCar.call(myCar);
```

The showCar() function operates just as before, and the object reference in the call() method's first parameter slot is treated as the current object for the showCar() function.

As for succeeding parameters, the apply() method's second parameter is an array of values to be passed as parameters to the current function. The order of the values must match the order of parameter variables defined for the function. The call() method, on the other hand, enables you to pass individual parameters in a comma-delimited list. Your choice depends on how the parameters are carried along in your script. If they're already in array form, use the apply() method; otherwise, use the call() method. The (ECMA) recommended way to invoke a function through this mechanism when no parameters need to be passed is via the call() method.

Note
Remember, ECMA is the standards organization that oversees the official JavaScript language standard, which is formally known as ECMAScript. ECMAScript is the language specification, whereas JavaScript is an actual implementation. ■

toString()
valueOf()

Returns: String

Compatibility: WinIE4+, MacIE4+, NN4+, Moz+, Safari+

Scripts rarely, if ever, summon the toString() and valueOf() methods of a Function object. These methods work internally to allow debugging scripts to display a string version of the function definition. For example, when you enter the name of a function defined in The Evaluator (see Chapter 4) into the top text box, JavaScript automatically converts the function to a string so that its value can be displayed in the Results box. Using these methods or parsing the text they return has little, if any, practical application.

Function Application Notes

Understanding the ins and outs of JavaScript functions is the key to successful scripting, especially for complex applications. Additional topics covered in this section include the ways to invoke functions, variable scope in and around functions, recursion, and the design of reusable functions.

Invoking functions

A function doesn't perform any work until a script calls it by name or reference. Scripts invoke functions (that is, get functions to do something) through four routes: document object event handlers; JavaScript statements; href attributes pointing to a javascript: URL; and the more modern call() and apply() methods of the Function object. The one approach not yet discussed at length in this book is the javascript: URL (some say pseudo-URL).

Several HTML tags have href attributes that normally point to Internet URLs for navigating to another page or loading a MIME file that requires a helper application or plug-in. These HTML tags are usually tags for clickable objects, such as links and client-side image map areas.

A JavaScript-enabled browser has a special built-in URL pseudo-protocol — javascript: — that lets the href attribute point to a JavaScript function or method rather than to a URL on the Net. For example, it is common practice to use the javascript: URL to change the contents of two frames from a single link. Because the href attribute is designed to point to only a single URL, you'd be out of luck if it weren't for the convenient way that JavaScript gives you access to multiframe navigation. You implement multiframe navigation by writing a function that sets the location.href properties of the two frames; then invoke that function from the href attribute. The following example shows what the script may look like:

```
function loadPages()
{
    parent.frames[1].location.href = "page2.html";
    parent.frames[2].location.href = "instrux2.html";
}
// ...
<a href="javascript:loadPages()">Next</a>
```

These kinds of function invocations can include parameters, and the functions can do anything you want. One potential side effect to watch out for occurs when the function returns a value (perhaps the function is also invoked from other script locations where a returned value is expected). Because the href attribute sets the target window to whatever the attribute evaluates to, the returned value is assigned to the target window — probably not what you want.

To prevent the assignment of a returned value to the href attribute, prefix the function call with the void operator:

```
<a href="javascript:void loadPages()">
```

If you don't want the href attribute to do anything (that is, you want to let the onclick event handler do all the work), assign a blank function after the operator:

```
<a href="javascript:void (0)">
```

Experienced programmers of many other languages recognize this operator as a way of indicating that no values are returned from a function or procedure. The operator has that precise functionality here, but in a nontraditional location.

Variable scope: Globals and locals

A variable can have two scopes in JavaScript. As you might expect, any variable initialized within the main flow of a script (not inside a function) is a *global variable*, in that any statement in the same document's script can access it by name. You can, however, also initialize variables inside a function (in a var statement) so the variable name applies only to statements inside that function; the scope is local to the function, so they are *local variables*. By limiting the scope of the variable to a single function, you can reuse the same variable name in multiple functions, thereby enabling the variables to carry very different information in each function. Keep in mind that when you declare a variable inside of a function without the `var` keyword, you are creating a global variable and not a local variable. Listing 23-2 demonstrates the various possibilities.

LISTING 23-2

Variable Scope Workbench Page

HTML: `jsb-23-02.html`

```html
<!DOCTYPE html>
<html>
    <head>
        <meta http-equiv="content-type" content="text/html;charset=utf-8">
        <title>Variable scope</title>
        <script type="text/javascript" src="../jsb-global.js"></script>
        <script type="text/javascript" src="jsb-23-02.js"></script>
    </head>
    <body>
        <h1>Variable scope</h1>
        <h3>Charlie Brown has a global dog (Snoopy), a local dog (Gromit),
            a global toy (Gumby), and a local toy (Pokey).</h3>
        <div id="placeHolder"></div>
    </body>
</html>
```

JavaScript: `jsb-23-02.js`

```javascript
// initialize when the page has loaded
addEvent(window, "load", testValues);

var newElem;
var newText;

var toyGlobal = "Gumby";
var aBoy = "Charlie Brown";
var hisDog = "Snoopy";

function showLocal()
{
    var toyLocal = "Pokey";
    return toyLocal;
}

function showGlobal()
{
    newElem = document.createElement("div");
    newElem.className = "objProperty";
    newText = document.createTextNode("Global version of hisDog is intact: "
            + hisDog);
    // just picked up a global variable value instead
    // of the local variable in the calling function
```

continued

LISTING 23-2   *(continued)*

```
    newElem.appendChild(newText);
    placeHolderElement.appendChild(newElem);
}

function testValues()
{
    // Dangerous ground here -- declaring a global variable in a function
    placeHolderElement = document.getElementById("placeHolder");

    // Now declare the local variable
    var hisDog = "Gromit";  // initializes local version of "hisDog"

        if (placeHolderElement)
        {
            newElem = document.createElement("div");
            newElem.className = "objProperty";
            newText = document.createTextNode("aBoy is: " + aBoy);
                // just picked up a global variable value
            newElem.appendChild(newText);
            placeHolderElement.appendChild(newElem);

            newElem = document.createElement("div");
            newElem.className = "objProperty";
            newText = document.createTextNode("His toyGlobal is " + toyGlobal);
            newElem.appendChild(newText);
                // just picked up another global variable value
            placeHolderElement.appendChild(newElem);

            // Do not bother with toyLocal here because it will throw undefined

            newElem = document.createElement("div");
            newElem.className = "objProperty";
            newText = document.createTextNode(
                    "toyLocal value returned from the showLocal function is: "
                    + showLocal() );
            newElem.appendChild(newText);
            placeHolderElement.appendChild(newElem);

            newElem = document.createElement("div");
            newElem.className = "objProperty";
            newText = document.createTextNode("Local version of hisDog is: " + hisDog);
            newElem.appendChild(newText);
                // just picked up another global variable value
            placeHolderElement.appendChild(newElem);

            // now call another function that does not set the variable hisDog
            // and display the value. we'll see that the global value is intact
            showGlobal();

        }
}
```

In this page, you define a number of variables — some global, others local — that are spread out in the JavaScript file. When you load this page, it runs the `testValues()` function, which accounts for the current values of all the variable names. The script then follows up with at least one value extraction that was masked in the function. The results of the JavaScript look like this:

```
aBoy is: Charlie Brown
His toyGlobal is Gumby
toyLocal value returned from the showLocal function is: Pokey
Local version of hisDog is: Gromit
Global version of hisDog is intact: Snoopy
```

Examine the variable initialization throughout the JavaScript file. In the beginning of the script there are several lines of code that are not contained within a function; this is the immediate execution section. In that section you define the first variable (`toyGlobal`) as a global style outside of any function definition. The `var` keyword for the global variable is optional but often helpful for enabling you to see at a glance where you initialize your variables. You also define two more global variables: `aBoy` and `hisDog`.

You then create two short functions. The `showLocal()` function defines a variable (`toyLocal`) that only statements in it can use. The `showGlobal()` function defines a function that simply displays the value of a variable (more on which variable in just a bit).

There is also a `testValues()` function that is the onload event handler. The first thing you'll notice is a variable (`placeHolderElement`) declared without the `var` keyword. Since `placeHolderElement` is declared within a function, it is a global variable. The `testValues()` function calls the `showGlobal()` function that uses the `placeHolderElement` variable. Why wasn't this variable declaration made in the immediate execution section of the script? The `placeHolderElement` variable is a reference to one of the elements on the HTML page that uses these functions. The `placeHolderElement` variable cannot successfully reference the element until the page is fully loaded. The only way to guarantee that the page is loaded before you declare the variable is to place the variable declaration within the onload event handler. Since the `testValues()` function is the onload event handler, the only way to make this variable available to other functions is to declare it here globally.

Also inside the `testValues()` function (for purposes of demonstration), you reuse the `hisDog` variable name. By initializing `hisDog` with the `var` statement inside the function, you tell JavaScript to create a separate local variable whose scope is only within the function. This initialization does not disturb the global variable of the same name. It can, however, make things confusing for you as the script author.

Statements in the `testValues()` function attempt to collect the values of variables scattered around the JavaScript file. Even from within this function, JavaScript has no problem extracting global variables directly, including the one defined in the immediate execution section. But JavaScript cannot get the local variable defined in the `showLocal()` function; that `toyLocal` variable is private to its own function. If you try to reference the `showLocal()` function's variable value from within the `showGlobal()` function, you will get an error message saying that the variable name is not defined. In the eyes of everyone else outside of the `showLocal()` function, that's true. If you really need that value, you can have the function return the value to a calling statement, as you do in the `testValues()` function.

At the beginning of the `testValues()` function, the script reads the `aBoy` global value without a hitch. But because you initialized a separate version of `hisDog` inside that function, only the localized version is available to the `testValues()` function. If you reassign a global variable name inside a function, you cannot access the global version from inside that function.

As proof that the global variable — whose name was reused inside the `testValues()` function — remains untouched, the `testValues()` function calls the `showGlobal()` function. The `showGlobal()` function displays the value of the `hisDog` variable. Since we're no longer inside the `testValues()` function, we see the value of the global variable `hisDog`. Charlie Brown and his dog, Snoopy, are united.

A benefit of this variable-scoping scheme is that you can reuse throwaway variable names in any function you like. For example, you can use the `i` loop counting variable in every function that employs loops. (In fact, you can reuse it in multiple `for` loops of the same function because the `for` loop reinitializes the value at the start of the loop.) If you pass parameters to a function, you can assign the same names to those parameter variables to aid in consistency. For example, a common practice is to pass an entire form object reference as a parameter to a function (using a `this.form` parameter in the event handler). For every function that catches one of these objects, you can use the variable name `form` in the parameter:

```
function doSomething(form)
{
    // statements
}
// ...
<input type="button" value="Do Something" onclick="doSomething(this.form)">
```

If five buttons on your page pass their form objects as parameters to five different functions, each function can assign `form` (or whatever you want to use) to that parameter value.

We recommend reusing variable names only for these throwaway variables. In this case, the variables are all local to functions, so the possibility of a mix-up with global variables does not exist. But the thought of reusing a global variable name as, say, a special case inside a function sends shivers up our spines. Such a tactic is doomed to cause confusion and error.

Caution

Reusing a global variable name locally is one of the most subtle and therefore difficult bugs to find in JavaScript code. The local variable ends up temporarily hiding the global variable without making any effort to let you know. Just do yourself a favor and make sure you don't reuse a global variable name as a local variable in a function. In the same vein, declaring a global variable within a function may also create bugs that are difficult to find in JavaScript code. ∎

Some programmers devise naming conventions to avoid reusing global variables as local variables. A popular scheme puts a lowercase g in front of any global variable name. In the example from Listing 23-2, you could have named the global variables:

```
gToyGlobal
gABoy
gHisDog
gPlaceHolderElement
```

Then, if you define local variables, don't use the leading g. A similar scheme involves using an underscore character (_) global instead of a g in front of global variable names. In the example from Listing 23-2, you could have named the `local` variables:

```
_ToyLocal
_HisDog
```

Any scheme you employ to prevent the reuse of variable names in different scopes is fine, as long as it does the job. The same can be said of any scheme that clearly identifies global variables.

In a multiframe or multiwindow environment, your scripts can also access global variables from any other document currently loaded into the browser. For details about this level of access, see Chapter 27, "Window and Frame Objects."

Variable scoping rules apply equally to nested functions. Any variables defined in an outer function (including parameter variables) are exposed to all functions nested inside. But if you define a new local variable inside a nested function, that variable is not available to the outer function. Instead, you can return a value from the nested function to the statement in the outer function that invokes the nested function.

Parameter variables

When a function receives data in the form of parameters, remember that the values may be copies of the data (in the case of run-of-the-mill data values) or references to real objects (such as a form object). In the latter case, you can change the object's modifiable properties in the function when the function receives the object as a parameter, as shown in the following example:

```
function validateCountry(form)
{
    if (form.country.value == "")
    {
        form.country.value = "USA";
    }
}
```

Therefore, whenever you pass an object reference as a function parameter, be aware that the changes you make to an object you've passed into a function affect the real object.

As a matter of style, if our function needs to extract properties, or results of methods, from passed data (such as object properties or string substrings), we like to do that at the start of the function. We initialize as many variables as needed for each piece of data used later in the function. This task enables us to assign meaningful names to the data chunks, rather than rely on potentially long references within the working part of the function (such as using a variable like inputStr instead of form.entry.value). Today's machines are so incredibly fast that we don't really need to do this for machine speed; we're doing it for human speed — the code is now more readable and maintainable. Here's a quick example:

```
function updateContactInfo(form)
{
    var firstName = form.firstname.value;
    // or the preferred way:
    var lastName = document.getElementById("lastname").value;
    var address1 = document.getElementById("addr1").value;
    var address2 = document.getElementById("addr2").value;
    var phone = document.getElementById("phone").value;
    var email = document.getElementById("email").value;

    // Process contact info using local variables
}
```

Notice in this example how the form field information is first stored in local variables, which are then used to carry out the hypothetical updating of contact information. Throughout the remainder of the function you can use the local variables instead of the longer and less wieldy form fields.

Recursion in functions

In what may come as a strange surprise, it is possible for functions to call themselves — a process known as *recursion*. The classic example of programmed recursion is the calculation of the factorial (the factorial for a value of 4 is 4 * 3 * 2 * 1), shown in Listing 23-3.

In the third line of this function, the statement calls itself, passing along a parameter of the next lower value of n. As this function executes, diving ever deeper into itself, JavaScript watches intermediate values and performs the final evaluations of the nested expressions. If designed properly, a recursive function eventually stops calling itself, and the program flow eventually returns back to the original function call.

Recursive functions are dangerous in the sense that they can easily fall into an infinite state (popularly called an *infinite loop*). For this reason, it is very important that you test them carefully. In particular, make sure that the recursion is finite: that a limit exists for the number of times it can recurse. In the case of Listing 23-3, that limit is the initial value of n. Failure to watch out for this limit may cause the recursion to overpower the limits of the browser's memory and even lead to a crash.

LISTING 23-3

A JavaScript Function Utilizing Recursion

```
function factorial(n)
{
    if (n > 0)
    {
        return n * (factorial(n-1));
    } else
    {
        return 1;
    }
}
```

Turning functions into libraries

As you start writing functions for your scripts, be on the lookout for ways to make functions generalizable (written so that you can reuse the function in other instances, regardless of the object structure of the page). The likeliest candidates for this kind of treatment are functions that perform specific kinds of validation checks (see examples in Chapter 46, "Data-Entry Validation," on the CD-ROM), data conversions, or iterative math problems.

To make a function generalizable, don't let it make any references to specific objects by name. Object names generally change from document to document. Instead, write the function so that it accepts a named object as a parameter. For example, if you write a function that accepts a text object as its parameter, the function can extract the object's data or invoke its methods without knowing anything about its enclosing form or name. Look again, for example, at the factorial() function, but now as part of an entire document in Listing 23-4.

LISTING 23-4

Calling a Generalizable Function

HTML: jsb-23-04.html

```html
<!DOCTYPE html>
<html>
    <head>
        <meta http-equiv="content-type" content="text/html;charset=utf-8">
        <title>Variable Scope Trials</title>
        <script type="text/javascript" src="../jsb-global.js"></script>
        <script type="text/javascript" src="jsb-23-04.js"></script>
    </head>
    <body>
        <h1>Variable Scope Trials</h1>
        <form id="theForm" action="calc-factorial.php" method="get">
            <p>
                <label for="visitorInput">Enter an input value:</label>
                <input type="text" id="input" name="input" value="0">

                <input type="submit" value="Calc Factorial">

                <label for="output">Results:</label>
                <input type="text" id="output" value="">
            </p>
        </form>
    </body>
</html>
```

JavaScript: jsb-23-04.js

```javascript
// initialize when the page has loaded
addEvent(window, "load", initialize);

function initialize()
{
    // intercept form submission
    addEvent(document.getElementById("theForm"), "submit", calcFactorial);
}

function calcFactorial(evt)
{
    // consolidate event handling
    if (!evt) evt = window.event;

    // plug transformed input to output field
    var oInput = document.getElementById("input");
    var oOutput = document.getElementById("output");
```

continued

LISTING 23-4   *(continued)*

```
    // if they both exist
    if (oInput && oOutput)
    {
        oOutput.value = factorial(oInput.value);
    }

// cancel form submission
    // W3C DOM method (hide from IE)
    if (evt.preventDefault) evt.preventDefault();
    // IE method
    return false;
}

function factorial(n)
{
    if (n > 0)
    {
        return n * (factorial(n - 1));
    }
    else
    {
        return 1;
    }
}
```

This function is designed to be generalizable, accepting only the input value (n) as a parameter. In the form, the onsubmit event handler sends only the input value from one of the form's fields to the factorial() function. The returned value is assigned to the output field of the form. The factorial() function is totally ignorant about forms, fields, or buttons in this document. If you need this function in another script, you can copy and paste it into that script knowing that it has been pre-tested. Any generalizable function may be part of your personal library of scripts — from which you can borrow — and save time in future scripting tasks.

You cannot always generalize a function. Somewhere along the line in your scripts, you will have to have references to JavaScript or custom objects. But if you find that you're frequently writing functions that perform the same kind of actions, see how you can generalize the code and put the results in your library of ready-made functions. You should also consider placing these reusable library functions in an external .js library file, as you've seen us do in this chapter and in others. You can also see Chapter 4 for details on this convenient way to share utility functions among many documents.

Making sense of closures

A topic that has confused many an aspiring scripter is closures, which may enter the picture when you declare a function within another function. At the core of JavaScript, *closures* refer to the fact that you can keep a local variable defined in a function alive even after the function has executed — which normally signals the end of life for a local variable. That's right, it's possible for a function to return and its local variables to go on living like some kind of strange zombie data. How is this possible? Take a look at an example:

```
function countMe()
{
  var count = 1;
  var showCount = function() { alert(count); }
  count++;
  return showCount;
}
```

The unusual thing to note about this code is how the inner function assigned to the showCount variable is returned by the function. When you call the countMe() function, you receive a reference to the inner function that displays the count variable value. That wouldn't be a problem, except for the fact that the inner function acts on a variable (count) that is local to the countMe() function.

To see the closure come to life, take a look at this code that calls the countMe() function:

```
var countamatic = countMe();
countamatic();
```

The first line calls the countMe() function, which results in the local count variable being created, and a reference to the inner function being passed out and stored in the countamatic variable. The local variable count is also incremented within the countMe() function. Without knowing about closures, you would clearly be in some serious gray area at this point because the countamatic() function defined in the first line is now set to display the value of a variable that is clearly out of scope. But JavaScript works a miracle by keeping the count variable alive in a closure and still allowing the countamatic() function to access it. Thus, the second statement displays an alert with the number 2 in it.

If closures still seem a bit mysterious, just remember that a potential closure is created any time you specify a function within another function. You really only take advantage of a closure when you pass an inner function reference outside the scope of the function in which it is defined.

Okay, so closures reveal a sneaky way to manipulate scope in JavaScript, but what good are they? Closures are gaining a great deal of usage in Ajax applications because Ajax programming often uses them to work around inherent limitations in how you normally use the this keyword.

Cross-Reference
For more on Ajax, see Chapter 39, "Ajax, E4X, and XML." ■

Although we could just pawn everything closure-related off on Ajax, we can demonstrate a simple but practical application of how closures can help you carry out the seemingly impossible. Consider the scenario where you want to set a timer that calls a function after an interval of time has elapsed. You may be thinking: No problem — just create a function and pass its reference to the setTimeout() function. End of story. What we didn't mention is that you need to pass a couple of parameters to the function. See the problem?

Unless you design with anonymous functions, there is no mechanism for using parameters when you pass a function reference to another function, as in specifying a timer event handler when calling the `setTimeout()` function. Now take a look at this code that uses closures to circumvent the problem:

```
function wakeupCaller(name, roomnum)
{
    return
    (
        function()
        {
            alert("Call " + name + " in room #" + roomnum + ".");
        }
    );
}
```

By placing a zero-param function within a parameterized function, you now have the ingredients for a timer handler that can accept parameters. The next step is to create an actual function reference that uses the closure:

```
var wakeWilson = wakeupCaller("Mr. Wilson", 515);
```

At this point, you've passed parameters to a function and received a zero-param function reference in return, which can then be passed along to the `setTimeout()` function:

```
setTimeout(wakeWilson, 600000);
```

Thanks to closures, Mr. Wilson will now get his wake up call!

Caution

Before you dive into closures and begin exploiting them in all of your code, let us caution you that they can result in some tricky bugs when used incorrectly. Extensive use of closures involving references to DOM objects can also cause memory leaks (gradual increase of memory used by the browser) if the objects are not disposed of (that is, set to `null`) when they are no longer needed. Definitely spend the time to explore closures in more detail before you get too wild with them. ■

Creating Your Own Objects with Object-Oriented JavaScript

In all the previous chapters of this book, you've seen how conveniently the browser document object models organize all the information about the browser window and its document. More specifically, you learned how to use standard objects as a means of accessing different aspects of the browser window and document. What may not be obvious from the scripting you've done so far is that JavaScript enables you to create your own objects in memory — objects with properties and methods that you define. These objects are not user-interface elements on the page, but rather the kinds of objects that may contain data and script functions (behaving as methods) whose results the user can see displayed in the browser window.

You actually had a preview of this power in the discussion about arrays (Chapter 18, "The Array Object"). An array, you recall, is an ordered collection of data. An object typically contains different kinds of data. It doesn't have to be an ordered collection of data — although your scripts can use objects in constructions that strongly resemble arrays. Moreover, you can attach any number of custom functions as methods for that object. You are in total control of the object's structure, data, and behavior.

The practice of employing custom objects in your JavaScript code is known as *object-oriented programming*, or *OO programming* for short. OO has been around a long time and has been used to great success in other programming languages such as C++ and Java. However, the scripted nature of JavaScript has caused OO to catch on a bit more slowly in the JavaScript world. Even so, support for custom objects is a standard part of modern JavaScript-enabled browsers and is something you should consider taking advantage of whenever prudent.

Note

To split hairs, technically, we have to clarify that JavaScript isn't truly an object-oriented language in a strict sense. Instead, JavaScript is considered an *object-based* language. The difference between object-oriented and object-based is significant and has to do with how objects can be extended. Even so, conceptually, JavaScript's support of objects is enough akin to true OO languages that it's not unreasonable to discuss JavaScript in OO terms. You learn about some of the specific object features that allow JavaScript to approach OO languages later in the chapter. What's of further interest is that ECMAScript now supports the notions of classes, interfaces, etc., in terms that are closer to the traditional OO manner, which means that the next release(s) of JavaScript will start to support these notions as well. ■

There is no magic to knowing when to use a custom object instead of an array in your application. The more you work with and understand the way custom objects work, the more likely you will think about your data-carrying scripts in these terms — especially if an object can benefit from having one or more methods associated with it. This avenue is certainly not one for beginners, but we recommend that you give custom objects more than a casual perusal after you have gained some JavaScripting experience.

The nuts and bolts of objects

An *object* in JavaScript is really just a collection of properties. *Properties* can take on the form of data types, functions (methods), or even other objects. In fact, you might find it easier to think of a custom object as an array of values, each of which is mapped to a property (a data type, method, or object). Wait — a method can be a property of an object? We'll see how in just a bit; for now, take it on faith. A function contained in an object is known as a *method*. Methods are no different than other functions, except that they are intended to be used in the context of an object, and therefore are assumed to have access to properties of that object. This connection between properties and methods is one of the core concepts prevalent in OO.

Objects are created using a special function known as a *constructor*, which determines the name of the object — the constructor is given the same name as the object. Here's an example of a constructor function:

```
function Alien()
{
}
```

Although this function doesn't contain any code, it does nonetheless lay the groundwork for creating an Alien object. You can think of a constructor as a blueprint that is then used to create actual objects. A word about naming constructor functions: Conventionally, the constructor name is in

TitleCase, and each instance variable referencing the object is in camelCase. Here's an example of how you create an object using a constructor:

```
var myAlien = new Alien();
```

The new keyword is used, in conjunction with a constructor, to create JavaScript objects.

Creating properties for custom objects

Earlier we mentioned that properties are key to objects, so you might be wondering how you go about creating a property for a custom object. Custom object properties are created in the constructor with some help from the this keyword, as the following code reveals:

```
function Alien()
{
    this.name = "Clyde";
    this.aggressive = true;
}
```

The this keyword is used to reference the current object, which in this case is the object that is being created by the constructor. So, you use the this keyword to identify new properties for the object. The only problem with this example is that it results in all aliens that are created with the Alien() constructor having the same name and aggression. The fix is to pass in the property values to the constructor so that each alien can be customized upon creation:

```
function Alien(name, aggressive)
{
    this.name = name;
    this.aggressive = aggressive;
}
```

Now you can create different aliens that each have their own unique property values:

```
var alien1 = new Alien("Ernest", false);
var alien2 = new Alien("Wilhelm", true);
```

To get to the properties of the object (for reading or writing after the object has been created), use the same type of dot syntax you use with DOM objects. To change the name property of one of the objects, the statement would be:

```
alien1.name = "Julius";
```

Creating methods for custom objects

Properties are really only half of the JavaScript OO equation. The other half is methods, which are functions that you tie to objects so that they can access object properties. Following is an example of a method that you might use with the alien class:

```
function attack()
{
    if (this.aggressive)
    {
        // Do some attacking and return true to indicate that the attack
        // commenced
```

```
      return true;
   }
   else
   {
      // Don't attack and return false to indicate that the attack didn't
      // happen
      return false;
   }
}
```

Notice that the `attack()` method references the `this.aggressive` property to decide if the attack should take place. The only thing missing at this point is the connection between the `attack()` method and the `alien` object. Without this connection the `this` keyword would have no meaning because there would be no associated object. Here's how the connection is made:

```
function Alien(name, aggressive)
{
   // properties
   this.name = name;
   this.aggressive = aggressive;
   // methods
   this.attack = attack;
}
```

This code clearly illustrates how methods are really just properties: they are declared the same as properties, so they masquerade as properties. A new property named `attack` is created and assigned a reference to the `attack()` method. It's very important to note that the `attack()` method is specified by reference (without the parentheses). Here, then, is the creation of an `alien` object and the invocation of its `attack()` method:

```
var alien1 = new Alien("Ernest", false);
alien1.attack();
```

The way we have defined the attack method above for the alien object places it in the global namespace, which is not a good thing in terms of OO best practices (as you'll see later in this chapter when we discuss encapsulation). A better approach is to embed it in the constructor:

```
function Alien(name, aggressive)
{
   // properties
   this.name = name;
   this.aggressive = aggressive;
   // methods
   this.attack = function(name, aggressive)
   {
      if (this.aggressive)
      {
         // Do some attacking and return true to indicate that
         // the attack commenced
         return true;
      }
      else
      {
```

```
            // Don't attack and return false to indicate that
            // the attack didn't happen
            return false;
        }
    };
}
```

You're now armed with enough of the basics of JavaScript objects to move on to a more complete example, which the next section provides. This example will be progressively improved over the rest of the sections in this chapter as you build your custom object skills in a step-wise fashion.

An OO example – planetary objects

Building on your familiarity with the planetary data array created in Chapter 18, "The Array Object," this chapter shows you how convenient it is to use the data when it is constructed in the form of an OO design that utilizes custom objects. The application goal for the extended example in this section is to present a drop-down list of the nine planets of the solar system and display the properties of the selected planet.

In this chapter, instead of building arrays to hold the data, you build objects — one object for each planet. The design of your planetary object has five properties and one method. The properties of each planet are name, diameter, distance from the sun, year length, and day length. To assign more intelligence to these objects, in Listing 23-5 you give each of them the capability to display their data below the drop-down list. You can conveniently define one function that knows how to behave with any of these planet objects, rather than having to define nine separate functions. When used within the context of an object, a function is actually referred to as a *method*.

LISTING 23-5

OO Planetary Data Presentation

HTML: `jsb-23-05.html`

```html
<!DOCTYPE html>
<html>
    <head>
        <meta http-equiv="content-type" content="text/html;charset=utf-8">
        <title>OO Planetary Data Presentation</title>
        <script type="text/javascript" src="../jsb-global.js"></script>
        <script type="text/javascript" src="jsb-23-05.js"></script>
    </head>
    <body>
        <!-- Display the Planet choices to the visitor -->
        <h1>The Daily Planet</h1>
        <form>
            Select a planet to view its planetary data:
            <select name="planetsList" onchange="doDisplay(this)">
                <option>Mercury</option>
                <option>Venus</option>
                <option selected="selected">Earth</option>
                <option>Mars</option>
```

```
                <option>Jupiter</option>
                <option>Saturn</option>
                <option>Uranus</option>
                <option>Neptune</option>
                <option>Pluto</option>
            </select>
        </form>
    </body>
</html>
```

JavaScript: jsb-23-05.js

```
// definition of Planet object constructor
function Planet(name, diameter, distance, year, day)
{
    // properties
    this.name = name;
    this.diameter = diameter;
    this.distance = distance;
    this.year = year;
    this.day = day;
    // methods
    this.showPlanet = function()
    {
        var result = "<html><body><center><table border='2' cellpadding ='2'>";
        result += "<caption align='top'>Planetary data for <b>"
                + this.name + "</b></caption>";
        result += "<tr><td align='right'>Diameter</td><td>"
                + this.diameter + "</td></tr>";
        result += "<tr><td align='right'>Distance from Sun</td><td>"
                + this.distance + "</td></tr>";
        result += "<tr><td align='right'>One Orbit Around Sun</td><td>"
                + this.year + "</td></tr>";
        result += "<tr><td align='right'>One Revolution (Earth Time)</td><td>"
                + this.day + "</td></tr>";
        result += "</table></center></body></html>";
        // display results
        document.write(result);
        document.close();
    };
}


// create new Planet objects, and store in a series of reference variables
// 'new' will create a new Planet instance and insert parameter data into object
var mercury = new Planet("Mercury","3100 miles", "36 million miles",
                         "88 days", "59 days");
var venus = new Planet("Venus", "7700 miles", "67 million miles",
                         "225 days", "244 days");
var earth = new Planet("Earth", "7920 miles", "93 million miles",
                         "365.25 days","24 hours");
var mars = new Planet("Mars", "4200 miles", "141 million miles",
                         "687 days", "24 hours, 24 minutes");
```

continued

LISTING 23-5   *(continued)*

```
var jupiter = new Planet("Jupiter","88,640 miles","483 million miles",
                         "11.9 years", "9 hours, 50 minutes");
var saturn = new Planet("Saturn", "74,500 miles","886 million miles",
                        "29.5 years", "10 hours, 39 minutes");
var uranus = new Planet("Uranus", "32,000 miles","1.782 billion miles",
                        "84 years", "23 hours");
var neptune = new Planet("Neptune","31,000 miles","2.793 billion miles",
                         "165 years", "15 hours, 48 minutes");
var pluto = new Planet("Pluto", "1500 miles", "3.67 billion miles",
                       "248 years", "6 days, 7 hours");

// invoke Planet object method corresponding to the
// index of the visitor's choice
function doDisplay(popup)
{
    i = popup.selectedIndex;
    eval(popup.options[i].text.toLowerCase() + ".showPlanet()");
}
```

The first task is to define the object constructor function, which performs several important jobs. For one, everything in this function establishes the structure of your custom object: the properties available for data storage and retrieval, and any methods that the object can invoke. The name of the function is the name you use later to create new instances of the object. Therefore, choosing a name that truly reflects the nature of the object is important. And, because you probably want to stuff some data into the function's properties to get one or more instances of the object loaded and ready for the page's user, the function definition includes parameters for each of the properties defined in this object definition.

Inside the object, you use the this keyword to assign data that comes in as parameters to labeled properties. For this example, we use the same names for both the incoming parameter variables and the properties. That's primarily for convenience (and is very common practice), but you can assign any parameter and property names you want and connect them any way you like. In the Planet() constructor function, five property slots are reserved for every instance of the object, whether or not any data actually is placed in every property (any unassigned slot has a value of null).

The last entry in the Planet() constructor function is the definition of the showPlanet() method. As you do in every JavaScript method you encounter, you must invoke a method by using a reference to the object, a period, and the method name, followed by a set of parentheses. You see that syntax in a minute.

The next long block of statements creates the individual objects according to the definition established in the Planet() constructor. Just like in an array, an assignment statement and the keyword new create an object. We assign names that are the real names of planets (the mercury object reference name refers to the Mercury planet object).

The act of creating a new object sets aside space in memory (associated with the current document) for this object and its properties. An object created in memory is known as an *instance*. In this script, you create nine object instances, each with a different set of properties. Note that no parameter is sent (or expected by the function) that corresponds to the showPlanet() method. Omitting that parameter here is fine because the specification of that method in the object definition means that the script automatically attaches the method to every version (instance) of the planet object that it creates. This is important, because it links the function (method) to the object, thereby providing it access to the object's properties.

The last function definition, doDisplay(), is an event handler, invoked whenever the user makes a choice from the list of planets. The first statement extracts the index value of the selected item. Using that index value, the script extracts the text. But things get a little tricky because you need to use that text string as a variable name — the name of the planet — so that you can append to it the call to the showPlanet() method. To make the disparate data types come together, use the eval() function (see Chapter 24 for a complete discussion). Inside the parentheses, extract the string for the planet name, change it to lowercase, and concatenate a string that completes the reference to the object's showPlanet() method. The eval() function evaluates that string, which turns it into a valid method call. Therefore, if the user selects jupiter from the drop-down list, the method call becomes jupiter.showPlanet().

Now it's time to look back to the showPlanet() method definition. When that method runs in response to a user selection of the planet Jupiter, the method's only scope is of the jupiter object. Therefore, all references to this.propertyName in showPlanet() refer just to jupiter. The only possibility for this.name in the jupiter object is the value assigned to the name property for jupiter. The same goes for the rest of the properties extracted in the method.

Further encapsulation

One of the benefits of using objects in scripting is that all the "wiring" inside the object — properties and methods — are defined within the local variable scope of the object. It's a concept called *encapsulation*. Thus, when you use the this keyword to create object properties and assign values to them inside a constructor function, the property names, and any code associated with them, are private to the object and never conflict with global variable or object names.

In large scripting projects, especially when multiple programmers are involved, it's fairly easy for global names to clash. For example, in Internet Explorer, all DOM object IDs become part of the global variable space because that browser allows scripts to reference an element object simply by its ID (unlike the W3C DOM, which uses the document.getElementById() method). As a project grows in size and complexity, it is increasingly important to avoid piling up more and more objects — including function definitions — in the global variable name space.

In Listing 23-5, for example, the showPlanet() method is defined in the local name space. It's a local method to the object because the method definition is defined within the planet() constructor function. If we were to define the showPlanet() method outside of the Planet() constructor function (as shown in an earlier example in this chapter), the showPlanet() method would be taking up a global object name that might be used elsewhere.

Creating an array of objects

In Listing 23-5, each of the planet objects is assigned to a global variable whose name is that of the planet. If the idea of custom objects is new to you, this idea probably doesn't sound so bad, because it's easy to visualize each variable representing an object. But, as shown in the doDisplay() function, accessing an object by name requires use of the eval() function to convert a string representation to a valid object reference. Although it's not too important in this simple example, the eval() function is not particularly efficient in JavaScript. If you find yourself using an eval() function, look for ways to improve efficiency, such that you can reference an object directly. The way to accomplish that streamlining for this application is to place the objects in an array.

To assign the custom objects in Listing 23-5 to an array, first create an empty array and then assign the result of each object constructor call as an entry in the array. The modified code section would result in Listing 23-6. This partial listing of the code from the external JavaScript file shows just the change in the code. The HTML for Listings 23-5 and 23-6 are exactly the same, so only the code from the partial external JavaScript file is included here. Both files are complete on the CD-ROM.

LISTING 23-6
_____

Array of Planet Objects

`JavaScript: partial of jsb-23-06.js`

```
// create new Planet objects, and store in an array of reference variables
// 'new' will create a new Planet instance and insert parameter data into object
var planets = new Array
(
    new Planet("Mercury","3100 miles", "36 million miles",
            "88 days", "59 days"),
    new Planet("Venus", "7700 miles", "67 million miles",
            "225 days", "244 days"),
    new Planet("Earth", "7920 miles", "93 million miles",
            "365.25 days","24 hours"),
    new Planet("Mars", "4200 miles", "141 million miles",
            "687 days", "24 hours, 24 minutes"),
    new Planet("Jupiter","88,640 miles","483 million miles",
            "11.9 years", "9 hours, 50 minutes"),
    new Planet("Saturn", "74,500 miles","886 million miles",
            "29.5 years", "10 hours, 39 minutes"),
    new Planet("Uranus", "32,000 miles","1.782 billion miles",
            "84 years", "23 hours"),
    new Planet("Neptune","31,000 miles","2.793 billion miles",
            "165 years", "15 hours, 48 minutes"),
    new Planet("Pluto", "1500 miles", "3.67 billion miles",
            "248 years", "6 days, 7 hours")
);
}
```

The supreme advantage to this approach comes in a modified doDisplay() function, which can use the index value from the select element's selectedIndex directly:

```
function doDisplay(popup)
{
    i = popup.selectedIndex;
    planets[i].showPlanet();
}
```

The presence of so many similar objects cries out for their storage as an array. Here, we are using the numeric value of the drop-down list's selectedIndex to locate the proper array element.

Taking advantage of embedded objects

One powerful technique for using custom objects is embedding an object within another object. When you place one object inside another object, the object being placed is known as an *embedded object* or *object property*. Let's extend the planet example to help you understand the implications of using a custom object property.

Say that you want to beef up the planet page with a photo of each planet. Each photo has a URL for the photo file; each photo also contains other information, such as the copyright notice and a reference number, which displays on the page for the user. One way to handle this additional information is to create a separate object definition for a photo database. Such a definition may look like this:

```
function Photo(name, URL, copyright, refNum)
{
    this.name = name;
    this.URL = URL;
    this.copyright = copyright;
    this.refNum = refNum;
}
```

You then need to create individual photo objects for each picture. One such definition may look like this:

```
mercuryPhoto = new Photo("Planet Mercury", "/images/merc44.gif",
                    "(c)1990 NASA", 28372);
```

Attaching a photo object to a planet object requires modifying the planet constructor function to accommodate one more property — an object property. The new planet constructor looks like this:

```
function Planet(name, diameter, distance, year, day, photo)
{
    this.name = name;
    this.diameter = diameter;
    this.distance = distance;
    this.year = year;
    this.day = day;
    this.showPlanet = showPlanet;
    this.photo = photo; // add photo property
}
```

When the photo objects are created, you can then create each planet object by passing one more parameter — a photo object you want associated with that object:

```
// create new planet objects, and store in a series of variables
Mercury = new Planet("Mercury", "3100 miles", "36 million miles",
                "88 days", "59 days", mercuryPhoto);
```

To access a property of a photo object, your scripts then have to assemble a reference that works its way through the connection with the planet object:

```
copyrightData = Mercury.photo.copyright;
```

The potential of embedded objects of this type is enormous. For example, you can embed all the copy elements and image URLs for an online catalog in a single document. As the user selects items to view (or cycles through them in sequence), a new JavaScript-written page displays the information in an instant. This requires only the image to be downloaded — unless the image was pre-cached, as described in the image object discussion in Chapter 29, "The Document and Body Objects." In this case, everything works instantaneously — no waiting for page after page of catalog.

If, by now, you think you see a resemblance between this object-within-an-object construction and a relational database, give yourself a gold star. Nothing prevents multiple objects from having the same sub-object as their properties — like multiple business contacts having the same company object property.

The current way to create objects

For current browsers, you can also benefit from a shortcut literal syntax for creating a new object. You can set pairs of property names and their values inside a set of curly braces, and you can assign the whole construction to a variable that becomes the object name. The following script shows how to organize this kind of object constructor:

```
var Earth = {diameter:"7920 miles", distance:"93 million miles", year:"365.25",
             day:"24 hours", showPlanet:showPlanet};
```

Colons link name-value pairs, and commas separate multiple name-value pairs. The value portion of a name-value pair can even be an array (using the [. . .] constructor shortcut) or a nested object (using another pair of curly braces). In fact, you can nest arrays and objects to your heart's content to create exceedingly complex objects. All in all, this is a very compact way to embed data in a page for script manipulation. If your CGI, XML, and database skills are up to the task, consider using a server program to convert XML data into this compact JavaScript version, with each XML record being its own JavaScript object. For multiple records, assign the curly-braced object definitions to an array entry. Then your scripts on the client can iterate through the data and generate HTML to display the data in a variety of forms, and sorted according to different criteria (thanks to the JavaScript array-sorting powers).

Defining object property getters and setters

The idea of creating getters and setters, generally known in JavaScript as *accessors*, for an object is introduced in Chapter 25, "Document Object Model Essentials," where they are described in the context of W3C DOM objects. Here, we look at an example of using getters and setters in the context of custom objects.

The purpose of a setter is to assign a new value to a property in an object and at the same time check it for validity if necessary. A setter defines how a new value assigned to the property should apply the value to the object. We would define a getter for each property we wanted to read in the object. In our object, we would typically define a getter and setter for each property of the object. If you have a requirement for a read-only property, then you would define only a getter method.

As you can see in Listing 23-7, both getter and setter methods in the TitleCaseName object property are written in the form of methods, using the name of the corresponding property. Reading or writing an object's property value can include sophisticated processing for either operation. This is called *object literal notation*. Firefox 2.0+, Safari 3.0+, Chrome+, and Opera 9.5+ support this. As of IE8, there is no support for getters and setters for custom objects. This partial listing of the code in the external JavaScript file shows just the change in the code for Listing 23-6. The HTML for

Listings 23-5 and 23-7 are exactly the same, so only the code from the partial external JavaScript file is included here. Both files are complete on the CD-ROM.

LISTING 23-7

Planet Object Constructor Using Getters and Setters

`JavaScript: partial of jsb-23-07.js`

```javascript
// object property with accessors using object literal notation
// its property 'name', is a String value that is TitleCased when set
var TitleCaseName =
{
   _name: null,

   get name()
   {
     return this._name;
   },

   set name(value)
   {
     this._name = value.substring(0,1).toUpperCase() + value.substring(1);
   }
};

// definition of Planet object constructor
function Planet(name, diameter, distance, year, day)
{
   // properties
   TitleCaseName.name = name;
   this.name = TitleCaseName.name;
   this.diameter = diameter;
   this.distance = distance;
   this.year = year;
   this.day = day;
   // methods
   this.showPlanet = function()
   {
      // . . .
   };
}
```

In our continuing planet scenario, we want to make sure that when a Planet object is created, its name property is in TitleCase, regardless of how the developer programs the code. This is the perfect opportunity for a setter: we want to take the current value of the name property, convert its case, and then apply the new value to the name property.

The first thing in the listing is the definition of the getter and setter methods that will be used in the TitleCaseName object. You'll notice that the function keyword is not used. Once we've defined our local properties, we define the getters and/or setters. To define each getter, we only need the `get` keyword, followed by the property name we want to read. Typically, we would return the value of the corresponding property. In our case, we're only defining a getter that simply reads the current value of the object's _name property and returns it. We use the underscore prefix in _name to indicate that this property is strictly internal and should not be referenced outside its containing object.

Similarly, we use the `set` keyword to define each setter. In this case, our setter converts the `value` parameter to TitleCase, and then assigns it to the _name property.

The final piece is in the `Planet` object's constructor function. Notice the first two properties in this function. In our case, the value supplied at object instantiation for the `name` property of a planet will "call" the `TitleCaseName` getter and setter function. In the first of these two lines, we assign the name to `TitleCaseName`. This invokes the setter, converting the value to `TitleCase`. In the second line, the getter is invoked, assigning the `TitleCased` name to `Planet` name.

Object-Oriented Concepts

As mentioned previously, JavaScript is object-based rather than object-oriented. This means that instead of adhering to the class, subclass, and inheritance schemes of object-oriented languages such as Java, JavaScript uses what is called *prototype inheritance*. This scheme works not only for native and DOM objects but also for custom objects.

Adding a prototype

A custom object is frequently defined by a constructor function, which typically parcels out initial values to properties of the object, as in the following example:

```
function Car(plate, model, color)
{
    this.plate = plate;
    this.model = model;
    this.color = color;
}
var car1 = new Car("AB 123", "Ford", "blue");
```

Current browsers offer a handy shortcut to stuff default values into properties if none are provided (the supplied value is `null`, 0, or an empty string). The OR operator (`||`) can let the property assignment statement apply the passed value, if present, or a default value you hard-wire into the constructor. Therefore, you can modify the preceding function to offer default values for the properties:

```
function Car(plate, model, color)
{
    this.plate = plate || "missing";
    this.model = model || "unknown";
    this.color = color || "unknown";
}
var car1 = new Car("AB 123", "Ford", "");
```

After the preceding statements run, the `car1` object has the following properties:

```
car1.plate    // value = "AB 123"
car1.model    // value = "Ford"
car1.color    // value = "unknown"
```

You can then add a new property to the constructor's `prototype` property, as in

```
Car.prototype.companyOwned = true;
```

Any `Car` object you already created, or are about to create, automatically inherits the new `companyOwned` property and its value. You can still override the value of the `companyOwned` property for any individual `Car` object. But if you don't override the property for instances of the `Car` object, the `Car` objects whose `companyOwned` property is not overridden automatically inherit any change to the `prototype.companyOwned` value. This has to do with the way JavaScript looks for `prototype` property values. In a similar fashion, we use prototypes in Listing 23-8 in our ongoing improvements to our `Planet` object. This partial listing of the code in the external JavaScript file shows just the change in the code for Listing 23-7. The HTML for Listings 23-5 and 23-8 are exactly the same, so only the code from the partial external JavaScript file is included here. Both files are complete on the CD-ROM.

LISTING 23-8

Planet Object Constructor Using Prototype

JavaScript: partial of jsb-23-08.js

```javascript
// definition of Planet object constructor
function Planet(name, diameter, distance, year, day)
{
   // properties
   TitleCaseName.name = name;
   this.name = TitleCaseName.name;
   this.diameter = diameter;
   this.distance = distance;
   this.year = year;
   this.day = day;
}

Planet.prototype =
{
   constructor : Planet,
   // methods
   showPlanet : function()
   {
      // . . .
   }
};
```

Prototype inheritance

Each time your script attempts to read or write a property of an object, JavaScript follows a specific sequence in search of a match for the property name. The sequence is as follows:

1. If the property has a local value assigned to the current object, this is the value to use.
2. If there is no local value, check the value of the property's prototype of the object's constructor.

3. Continue up the prototype chain until either a match of the property is found (with a value assigned to it) or the search reaches the native `Object` object.

Therefore, if you change the value of a constructor's `prototype` property and you do not override the property value in an instance of that constructor, JavaScript returns the current value of the constructor's `prototype` property.

Nested objects and prototype inheritance

When you begin nesting objects, especially when one object invokes the constructor of another, there is an added wrinkle to the prototype inheritance chain. Let's continue with the `Car` object defined earlier. In this scenario, consider the `Car` object to be akin to a root object that has properties shared among two other types of objects. One of the object types is a company fleet vehicle, which needs the properties of the root `Car` object (`plate`, `model`, `color`) but also adds some properties of its own. The other object that shares the `Car` object is an object representing a car parked in the company garage — an object that has additional properties regarding the parking of the vehicle. This explains why the `Car` object is defined on its own.

Now look at the constructor function for the parking record, along with the constructor for the basic `Car` object:

```
function Car(plate, model, color)
{
    this.plate = plate || "missing";
    this.model = model || "unknown";
    this.color = color || "unknown";
}
function CarInLot(plate, model, color, timeIn, spaceNum)
{
    this.timeIn = timeIn;
    this.spaceNum = spaceNum;
    this.carInfo = car;
    this.carInfo(plate, model, color);
}
```

The `CarInLot` constructor not only assigns values to its unique properties (`timeIn` and `spaceNum`) but it also includes a reference to the `Car` constructor, arbitrarily assigned to a property called `carInfo`. This property assignment is merely a conduit that allows property values intended for the `Car` constructor to be passed within the `CarInLot` constructor function. To create a `CarInLot` object, use a statement like the following:

```
var car1 = new CarInLot("AA 123", "Ford", "blue", "10:02AM", "31");
```

After this statement, the `car1` object has the following properties and values:

```
car1.timeIn      // value = "10:02AM"
car1.spaceNum    // value = "31"
car1.carInfo     // value = reference to car object constructor function
car1.plate       // value = "AA 123"
car1.model       // value = "Ford"
car1.color       // value = "blue"
```

Let's say that five `CarInLot` objects are created in the script (`car1` through `car5`). The prototype wrinkle comes into play if, for example, you assign a new property to the `Car` constructor prototype:

```
Car.prototype.companyOwned = true;
```

Even though the `CarInLot` objects use the `Car` constructor, the instances of `CarInLot` objects do not have a prototype chain back to the `Car` object. As the preceding code stands, even though you've added a `companyOwned` property to the `Car` constructor, no `CarInLot` object inherits that property (even if you were to create a new `CarInLot` object after defining the new `prototype` property for `Car`). To get the `CarInLot` instances to inherit the `prototype.companyOwned` property, you must explicitly connect the prototype of the `CarInLot` constructor to the `Car` constructor prior to creating instances of `CarInLot` objects:

```
CarInLot.prototype = new Car();
```

The complete sequence, then, is as follows:

```
function Car(plate, model, color)
{
    this.plate = plate || "missing";
    this.model = model || "unknown";
    this.color = color || "unknown";
}
function CarsInLot(plate, model, color, timeIn, spaceNum)
{
    this.timeIn = timeIn;
    this.spaceNum = spaceNum;
    this.carInfo = car;
    this.carInfo(plate, model, color);
}
CarsInLot.prototype = new Car();
var car1 = new CarsInLot("123ABC", "Ford","blue","10:02AM", "32");
Car.prototype.companyOwned = true;
```

After this stretch of code runs, the `car1` object has the following properties and values:

```
car1.timeIn              // value = "10:02AM"
car1.spaceNum            // value = "31"
car1.carInfo             // value = reference to car object constructor function
car1.plate               // value = "AA 123"
car1.model               // value = "Ford"
car1.color               // value = "blue"
car1.companyOwned        // value = true
```

NN4+/Moz provides one extra, and proprietary, bit of syntax in this prototype world. The __proto__ property (that's with double underscores before and after the word *proto*) returns a reference to the object that is next up the prototype chain. For example, if you inspect the properties of `car1.__proto__` after the preceding code runs, you see that the properties of the object next up the prototype chain are as follows:

```
car1.__proto__.plate             // value = "AA 123"
car1.__proto__.model             // value = "Ford"
```

objectObject

```
carl.__proto__.color          // value = "blue"
carl.__proto__.companyOwned    // value = true
```

This property can be helpful in debugging custom objects and prototype inheritance chain challenges, but the property is not part of the ECMA standard. Therefore, we discourage you from using the property in your production scripts, since it isn't available in non-Mozilla-based browsers.

Object Object

Properties	Methods
constructor	hasOwnProperty()
prototype	isPrototypeOf()
	propertyIsEnumerable()
	toSource()
	toString()
	unwatch()
	valueOf()
	watch()

Syntax

Creating an Object object:

```
function constructorName([arg1,...[,argN]])
{
    statement(s)
}
var objName = new constructorName(["argName1",...[,"argNameN"]]);
var objName = new Object();
var objName = {propName1:propVal1[, propName2:propVal2[,...N]]}
```

Accessing an Object object properties and methods:

```
objectReference.property | method([parameters])
```

Compatibility: WinIE4+, MacIE4+, NN3+, Moz+, Safari+, Chrome+

About this object

Although it might sound redundant, the Object object is a vital native object in the JavaScript environment. It is the root object on which all other native objects — such as Date, Array, String, and the like — are based (see Figure 23-1). This object also provides the foundation for creating custom objects, as described earlier in this chapter.

FIGURE 23-1

The `Object` object hierarchy.

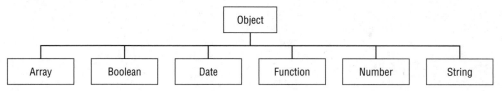

By and large, your scripts do not access the properties of the native `Object` object. The same is true for many of its methods, such as `toString()` and `valueOf()`, which internally allow debugging alert dialog boxes (and The Evaluator) to display something when referring to an object or its constructor. In the case of methods like `toString()` and `valueOf()`, you will typically override these in the child. Similarly, the `toSource()` method returns a string representation of the source code for an object, which is not something you would typically need to use in a script.

A little more practical are the `watch()` and `unwatch()` methods of the `Object` object, which provide a mechanism for taking action when a property value changes. You can call the `watch()` method and assign a function that is called when a certain property changes. This enables you to handle an internal property change as an event. When you're finished watching a property, the `unwatch()` method is used to stop the watchpoint.

Listing 23-9 contains an example of how the `watch()` and `unwatch()` methods can be used to track the value of a property.

LISTING 23-9

Watching an Object Property

HTML: `jsb-23-09.html`

```html
<!DOCTYPE html>
<html>
   <head>
      <meta http-equiv="content-type" content="text/html;charset=utf-8">
      <title>Object Watching</title>
      <script type="text/javascript" src="../jsb-global.js"></script>
      <script type="text/javascript" src="jsb-23-09.js"></script>
   </head>
   <body>
      <h1>Watching Over You</h1>
      <form id="theForm" action="validate.php" method="get">
         <div>
         <label for="theText">Enter text here: </label>
         <input id="theText" type="text" name="entry" size="50"
             value="Default Value">
         <p><input id="fourScoreButton" type="button" value="Set to Phrase I"
                 onclick="setIt('Four score and seven years ago...')"></p>
         <p><input id="whenInButton" type="button" value="Set to Phrase 2"
                 onclick="setIt('When in the course of human events...')"></p>
```

continued

objectObject.constructor

LISTING 23-9 *(continued)*

```
        <p><input id="resetButton" type="reset"
                onclick="setIt('Default value')"></p>
        <p><input id="watchButton" type="button" value="Watch It"
                onclick="watchIt(true)">
          <input id="unWatchButton" type="button" value="Don't Watch It"
                onclick="watchIt(false)"></p>
      </div>
    </form>
  </body>
</html>
```

```
JavaScript: jsb-23-09.js
```

```javascript
function setIt(msg)
{
    document.forms[0].entry.value = msg;
}

function watchIt(on)
{
    var obj = document.forms[0].entry;
      if (on)
      {
          obj.watch("value",report);
      } else
      {
          obj.unwatch("value");
      }
}

function report(id, oldval, newval)
{
    alert("The field's " + id + " property on its way from \n'" +
        oldval + "'\n to \n'" + newval + "'.");
    return newval;
}
```

You can use a trio of methods (hasOwnProperty(), isPrototypeOf(), and propertyIsEnumerable()) to perform some inspection of the prototype environment of an object instance. They are of interest primarily to advanced scripters who are building extensive, simulated, object-oriented applications.

Properties

constructor

Value: Object type   Read-Only

Compatibility: WinIE4+, MacIE4+, NN4+, Moz+, Safari+, Chrome+

This is the property that is inherited by any custom, `Array`, `String`, or other objects, when one of those objects is instantiated. It is a reference to the constructor function that was used to create the object. Be aware, though, that if a prototype were used, this property might not contain a valid value. Using the earlier car example, if you were to create a car with the `Car` constructor, then the constructor property would refer to `Car`:

```
var car1 = new Car("AA 123", "Ford", "blue");
    if (car1.constructor == Car)    // would evaluate to true
    {
        // statements dealing with the car object
    }
```

Methods

hasOwnProperty("*propName*")

Returns: Boolean.

Compatibility: WinIE5.5+, MacIE-, NN6+, Moz+, Safari-, Chrome+

The `hasOwnProperty()` method returns `true` if the current object instance has the property defined in its constructor or in a related constructor function. But if this property is defined externally, as through assignment to the object's `prototype` property, the method returns `false`.

Using the example of the `Car` and `CarInLot` objects from earlier in this chapter, the following expressions evaluate to `true`:

```
car1.hasOwnProperty("spaceNum");
car1.hasOwnProperty("model");
```

Even though the `model` property is defined in a constructor that is invoked by another constructor, the property belongs to the `car1` object. The following statement, however, evaluates to `false`:

```
car1.hasOwnProperty("companyOwned");
```

This property is defined by way of the prototype of one of the constructor functions and is not a built-in property for the object instance.

isPrototypeOf(*objRef*)

Returns: Boolean

Compatibility: WinIE5.5+, MacIE-, NN6+, Moz+, Safari-, Chrome+

The `isPrototypeOf()` method is intended to reveal whether or not the current object has a prototype relation with an object passed as a parameter. In practice, the IE and NN/Moz versions of this method operate differently and return different results.

propertyIsEnumerable("*propName*")

Returns: Boolean

Compatibility: WinIE5.5+, MacIE-, NN6+, Moz+, Safari-, Chrome+

In the terminology of the ECMA-262 language specification, a value is enumerable if constructions such as the `for...in` property inspection loop (see Chapter 21, "Control Structures and Exception

Handling") can inspect it. Enumerable properties include values such as arrays, strings, and virtually every kind of object. According to the ECMA specification, this method is not supposed to work its way up the prototype chain.

toSource()

Returns: String

Compatibility: WinIE5.5+, MacIE-, NN6+, Moz+, Safari-, Chrome+

The toSource() method obtains a string representation of the source code for an object. Unlike the toString() method, which returns a string equivalent of the value of an object, the toSource() method returns the underlying code for the object as a string. Seeing as how this is a very specialized, low-level feature, the method is typically only used internally by JavaScript, and potentially in some debugging scenarios.

toString()

Returns: String

Compatibility: WinIE5.5+, MacIE-, NN6+, Moz+, Safari-, Chrome+

The toString() method is used to obtain a string representation of the value of an object. It is fairly common to take advantage of this method in situations where an object needs to be examined as raw text. When creating custom objects, you have the ability to create your own toString() method that reveals whatever information about the object you desire to be seen.

unwatch("*propName*")

Returns: Boolean

Compatibility: WinIE-, MacIE-, NN6+, Moz+, Safari-, Chrome+

As the counterpart to the watch() method, the unwatch() method terminates a watchpoint that has been set for a particular property.

valueOf()

Returns: Object

Compatibility: WinIE5.5+, MacIE-, NN6+, Moz+, Safari-, Chrome+

The valueOf() method is used to resolve an object to a primitive data type. This may not always be possible, in which case the method simply returns the object itself. Otherwise, the method returns a primitive value that represents the object.

watch("*propName*")

Returns: Boolean

Compatibility: WinIE-, MacIE-, NN6+, Moz+, Safari-, Chrome+

The watch() method is the key to a handy little JavaScript debugging feature known as watchpoints. A watchpoint enables you to specify a function that is called whenever the value of a property is set. You can then carefully track the state of properties and take action when an important property value changes.

You set a watchpoint by calling the `watch()` method and passing the name of the property that you want to watch, like this:

```
obj.watch("count",
   function(prop, oldval, newval)
   {
      document.writeln(prop + " changed from " + oldval + " to " + newval);
      return newval;
   }
);
```

In this example, a function is created to output a property change notification and then return the new property value. Every watchpoint handler must follow this same convention of using three arguments that specify the property, old value, and new value, respectively.

Global Functions and Statements

I n addition to all the objects and other language constructs described in the preceding chapters of this reference part of the book, several language items need to be treated on a global scale. These items do not apply to any particular objects (or, in fact, to any object), and you can use them anywhere in a script. If you read earlier chapters, you were introduced to many of these functions and statements. This chapter serves as a convenient place to highlight these all-important items that are otherwise easily forgotten. At the end of the chapter, note the brief introduction to several objects that are built into the Windows-only versions of Internet Explorer.

This chapter begins with coverage of the following global functions and statements that are part of the core JavaScript language:

IN THIS CHAPTER

Converting strings into object references

Creating URL-friendly strings

Adding comments to scripts

Functions	Statements
decodeURI()	// and /*...*/ (*comment*)
decodeURIComponent()	const
encodeURI()	var
encodeURIComponent()	
escape()	
eval()	
isFinite()	
isNaN()	
Number()	
parseFloat()	
parseInt()	

decodeURI()

Functions	Statements
toString()	
unescape()	
unwatch()	
watch()	

Global functions are not tied to the document object model. Instead, they typically enable you to convert data from one type to another. The list of global statements is short, but a couple of them appear extensively in your scripting.

Functions

decodeURI("*encodedURI*")
decodeURIComponent("*encodedURIComponent*")
encodeURI("*URIString*")
encodeURIComponent("*URIComponentString*")

Returns: String

Compatibility: WinIE5.5+, MacIE−, NN6+, Moz+, Safari+, Opera+, Chrome+

The ECMA-262 standard, as implemented in IE5.5+, NN6+, and Mozilla-based browsers, provides utility functions that perform a more rigorous conversion of strings to valid URI strings, and vice versa, than was achieved earlier via the escape() and unescape() functions (described later in this chapter). In fact, the modern encodeURI(), encodeURIComponent(), decodeURI(), and decodeURIComponent() functions serve as replacements to the now deprecated escape() and unescape() functions.

The purpose of the encoding functions is to convert any string to a version that you can use as a Uniform Resource Identifier, such as a web page address or an invocation of a server CGI script. Whereas Latin alphanumeric characters pass through the encoding process untouched, you must use the encoding functions to convert some symbols and other Unicode characters into a form (hexadecimal representations of the character numbers) that the Internet can pass from place to place. The space character, for example, must be encoded to its hex version: %20.

Perhaps the biggest difference between the encodeURI() and escape() functions (and their decodeURI() and unescape() counterparts) is that the more modern versions do not encode a wide range of symbols that are perfectly acceptable as URI characters according to the syntax recommended in RFC2396 (http://www.ietf.org/rfc/rfc2396.txt). Thus, the following characters are not encoded via the encodeURI() function:

    ; / ? : @ & = + $, - _ . ! ~ * ' ( ) #

Use the encodeURI() and decodeURI() functions only on complete URIs. Applicable URIs can be relative or absolute, but these two functions are wired especially so that symbols that are part of the protocol (://), search string (? and =, for instance), and directory-level delimiters (/) are not encoded. The decodeURI() function should work with URIs that arrive from servers as page locations, but be aware that some server CGIs encode spaces into plus symbols (+) that are not decoded back into spaces by the JavaScript function. If the URIs your script needs to decode contain plus symbols in place of spaces, you need to run your decoded URI through a string replacement method to finish the job (regular expressions come in handy here). If you are decoding URI strings that your scripts encoded, use the decode functions only on URIs that were encoded via the corresponding encode function. Do not attempt to decode a URI that was created via the old escape() function, because the conversion processes work according to different rules.

The difference between a URI and a URI component is that a *component* is a single piece of a URI, generally not containing delimiter characters. For example, if you use the encodeURIComponent() function on a complete URI, almost all of the symbols (other than things such as periods) are encoded into hexadecimal versions — including directory delimiters. Therefore, you should use the component-level conversion functions only on quite granular pieces of a URI. For example, if you assemble a search string that has a name-value pair, you can use the encodeURIComponent() function separately on the name and on the value. But if you use that function on the pair that is already in the form name=value, the function encodes the equal symbol to a hexadecimal equivalent.

Since the escape() and unescape() functions were sometimes used on strings that weren't necessarily URL (URI) strings, you will generally use the encodeURIComponent() and decodeURIComponent() functions when modernizing code that utilizes escape() and unescape().

Example

Use The Evaluator (see Chapter 4, "JavaScript Essentials") to experiment with the differences between encoding a full URI and a component, and encoding and escaping a URI string. For example, compare the results of the following three statements:

```
escape("http://www.giantco.com/index.htm?code=42")
encodeURI("http://www.giantco.com/index.htm?code=42")
encodeURIComponent("http://www.giantco.com/index.htm?code=42")
```

Because the sample URI string is valid as is, the encodeURI() version makes no changes. Experiment further by making the search string value into a string with a space, and see how each function treats that character.

escape("*URIString*" [,1])
unescape("*escapedURIString*")

Returns: String

Compatibility: WinIE3+, MacIE3+, NN2+, Moz+, Safari+, Opera+, Chrome+

If you watch the content of the Location field in your browser, you may occasionally see URLs that include a lot of % symbols, plus some numbers. The format you see is *URL encoding* (more accurately called *URI encoding* — Uniform Resource Identifier rather than Uniform Resource Locator). This format allows even multiple word strings and nonalphanumeric characters to be sent as one contiguous string of a very low, common denominator character set. This encoding turns a character, such as a space, into its hexadecimal equivalent value, preceded by a percent symbol. For example, the space character (ASCII value 32) is hexadecimal 20, so the encoded version of a space is %20.

All characters, including tabs and carriage returns, can be encoded in this way and sent as a simple string that can be decoded on the receiving end for reconstruction. You can also use this encoding to preprocess multiple lines of text that must be stored as a character string in databases. To convert a plain-language string to its encoded version, use the `escape()` method. This function returns a string consisting of the encoded version. For example:

```
var theCode = escape("Hello there");
    // result: Hello%20there
```

Most, but not all, non-alphanumeric characters are converted to escaped versions with the `escape()` function. One exception is the plus sign, which URLs use to separate components of search strings. If you must encode the plus symbol, too, then add the optional second parameter to the function to make the plus symbol convert to its hexadecimal equivalent (2B):

```
var a = escape("Adding 2+2");
    // result: Adding%202+2
var a = escape("Adding 2+2",1);
    // result: Adding%202%2B2
```

Note that browser support is not consistent in the treatment of the optional second parameter; the same result could be returned whether or not the second argument is included.

The `unescape()` function was used to convert an escaped string back into plain language. We say "was" because the function is now deprecated thanks to `decodeURI()` and `decodeURIComponent()` and shouldn't be used.

The `escape()` function operates in a way that is approximately midway between the newer functions `encodeURI()` and `encodeComponentURI()`. However, the function is now deprecated in lieu of the newer functions and shouldn't be used.

eval("*string*")

Returns: Object reference

Compatibility: WinIE3+, MacIE3+, NN2+, Moz+, Safari+, Opera+, Chrome+

Expression evaluation, as you probably are well aware by now, is an important concept to grasp for scripting with JavaScript (and for programming in general). An expression evaluates to some value. But occasionally, you need to force an additional evaluation on an expression to receive the desired results. The `eval()` function acts on a string value to force an evaluation of that string expression. Perhaps the most common application of the `eval()` function is to convert a string version of an object reference to a genuine object reference.

Example

The `eval()` function can evaluate any JavaScript statement or expression stored as a string. This includes string equivalents of arithmetic expressions, object value assignments, and object method invocation. We do not recommend that you rely on the `eval()` function, however, because this function is inherently inefficient (from the standpoint of performance). Fortunately, you may not need the `eval()` function to get from a string version of an object's name to a valid object reference. For example, if your script loops through a series of objects whose names include serial numbers, you can use the object names as array indexes rather than use `eval()` to assemble the object references. The inefficient way to set the value of a series of fields named `data0`, `data1`, and so on, is as follows:

```
function fillFields()
{
    var theObj;
```

```
for (var i = 0; i < 10; i++)
{
    theObj = eval("document.forms[0].data" + i);
    theObj.value = i;
}
}
```

A more efficient way is to perform the concatenation within the index brackets for the object reference:

```
function fillFields()
{
    for (var i = 0; i < 10; i++)
    {
        document.getElementById("myForm").elements["data" + i].value = i;
    }
}
```

Tip

Whenever you are about to use an eval() **function, look for ways to use string index values of arrays of objects instead. The W3C DOM makes it even easier with the help of the** document.getElementById() **method, which takes a string as a parameter and returns a reference to the named object.** ■

isFinite(*number*)

Returns: Boolean

Compatibility: WinIE4+, MacIE4+, NN4+, Moz+, Safari+, Opera+, Chrome+

It is rare that you will ever need the isFinite() function, but its purpose is to advise whether a number is beyond the absolute minimum or maximum values that JavaScript can handle. If a number is outside of that range, the function returns false. The parameter to the function must be a number data type.

isNaN(*expression*)

Returns: Boolean

Compatibility: WinIE3+, MacIE3+, NN2+, Moz+, Safari+, Opera+, Chrome+

For those instances in which a calculation relies on data coming from a text field or other string-oriented source, you frequently need to check whether the value is a number. If the value is not a number, the calculation may result in a script error.

Example

Use the isNaN() function to test whether a value is a number, prior to passing the value onto a calculation. The most common use of this function is to test the result of a parseInt() or parseFloat() function. If the strings submitted for conversion to those functions cannot be converted to a number, the resulting value is NaN (a special symbol indicating "not a number"). The isNaN() function returns true if the value is not a number.

Number()

A convenient way to use this function is to intercept improper data before it can do damage, as follows:

```
function calc(form)
{
    var inputValue = parseInt(form.entry.value);
        if (isNaN(inputValue))
        {
            alert("You must enter a number to continue.");
        }
        else
        {
            // statements for calculation
        }
}
```

Probably the biggest mistake scripters make with this function is failing to observe the case of all the letters in the function name. The trailing uppercase "N" is easy to miss.

Number("*string*")
parseFloat("*string*")
parseInt("*string*" [,*radix*])

Returns: Number

Compatibility: WinIE3+, MacIE3+, NN2+, Moz+, Safari+, Opera+, Chrome+

All three of these functions convert a string value into a numeric value. The parseInt() and parseFloat() functions are compatible across all versions of all browsers, including very old browsers; the Number() function was introduced in version 4 browsers.

Use the Number() function when your script is not concerned with the precision of the value, and prefers to let the source string govern whether the returned value is a floating-point number or an integer. The function takes a single parameter — a string to convert to a number value.

The parseFloat() function also lets the string source value determine whether the returned value is a floating-point number or an integer. If the source string includes any non-zero value to the right of the decimal, the result is a floating-point number. But if the string value were, say, "3.00", the returned value would be an integer value.

An extra, optional parameter for parseInt() enables you to define the number base for use in the conversion. If you don't specify a radix parameter, JavaScript tries to look out for you; but in doing so, JavaScript may cause some difficulty for you. The primary problem arises when the string parameter for parseInt() starts with a zero, which a text box entry or database field might do. In JavaScript, numbers starting with zero are treated as octal (base-8) numbers. Therefore, parseInt("010") yields the decimal value 8.

When you apply the parseInt() function, always specify the radix of 10 if you are working in base-10 numbers. You can, however, specify any radix value from 2 through 36. For example, to convert a binary number string to its decimal equivalent, assign a radix of 2 as follows:

```
var n = parseInt("011",2);
    // result: 3
```

Similarly, you can convert a hexadecimal string to its decimal equivalent by specifying a radix of 16:

```
var n = parseInt("4F",16);
    // result: 79
```

Example

Both `parseInt()` and `parseFloat()` exhibit a very useful behavior: If the string passed as a parameter starts with at least one number followed by, say, letters, the functions do their jobs on the numeric part of the string and ignore the rest. This is why you can use `parseFloat()` on the `navigator.appVersion` string to extract just the reported version number without having to parse the rest of the string. For example, Firefox 1.0 for Windows reports a `navigator.appVersion` value as

```
5.0 (Windows; en-US)
```

But you can get just the numeric part of the string via `parseFloat()`:

```
var ver = parseFloat(navigator.appVersion);
```

Note
The number stored in the `navigator.appVersion` property refers to the version number of the underlying browser engine, which helps explain why the reported version in this case is 5.0, even though the Firefox browser application is considered version 1.0. ■

Because the result is a number, you can perform numeric comparisons to see, for instance, whether the version is greater than or equal to 4.

toString([*radix*])

Returns: String

Compatibility: WinIE4+, MacIE4+, NN4+, Moz+, Safari+, Opera+, Chrome+

Every JavaScript core language object and every DOM `document` object has a `toString()` method associated with it. This method is designed to render the contents of the object as a string of text that is as meaningful as possible. Table 24-1 shows the result of applying the `toString()` method on each of the convertible core `language` object types.

TABLE 24-1

toString() Method Results for Object Types

Object Type	Result
String	The same string
Number	String equivalent (but numeric literals cannot be converted)
Boolean	`true` or `false`
Array	Comma-delimited list of array contents (with no spaces after commas)
Function	Decompiled string version of the function definition

toString()

Many DOM objects can be converted to a string. For example, a `location` object returns its URL. But when an object has nothing suitable to return for its content as a string, it usually returns a string in the following format:

```
[object objectType]
```

Example

The `toString()` method is available on all versions of all browsers. By setting the optional `radix` parameter between 2 and 16, you can convert numbers to string equivalents in different number bases. Listing 24-1 calculates and draws a conversion table for decimal, hexadecimal, octal, and binary numbers between 0 and 20. In this case, the source of each value is the value of the index counter variable, each time the `for` loop's statements execute.

Note

The function to assign event handlers throughout the code in this chapter and much of the book is `addEvent()`, a cross-browser event handler explained in detail in Chapter 32, "Event Objects."

The `addEvent()` function is part of the script file `jsb-global.js` located on the accompanying CD-ROM in the `Content/` folder, where it is accessible to all chapters' scripts. ∎

LISTING 24-1

Using toString() with Radix Values

HTML: `jsp-24-01.html`

```html
<!DOCTYPE html>
<html>
    <head>
        <meta http-equiv="content-type" content="text/html;charset=utf-8">
        <title>Using toString() to convert to other number bases:</title>
        <link rel="stylesheet" type="text/css" href="jsp-24-01.css">
        <script type="text/javascript" src="../jsb-global.js"></script>
        <script type="text/javascript" src="jsb-24-01.js"></script>
    </head>
    <body>
        <h1>Using toString() to convert to other number bases:</h1>
        <table id="numberConversions">
            <tr>
                <th>Decimal</th>
                <th>Hexadecimal</th>
                <th>Octal</th>
                <th>Binary</th>
            </tr>
        </table>
    </body>
</html>
```

CSS: `jsp-24-01.css`

```css
th, td
{
    border: 5px groove black;
```

```
    text-align: center;
    padding-left: 2px;
    padding-right: 2px;
}

th
{
    font-weight: bold;
}
```

JavaScript: jsb-24-01.js

```
// initialize when the page has loaded
addEvent(window, "load", initialize);

function initialize()
{
    var theTable = document.getElementById("numberConversions");

    if (theTable)
    {
        var newRowElem;
        var newCellElem;
        var newText;
        // Insert the rows after the existing row
        var newRowPosition = 1;

        // put the converted number data into the table
        for (var i = 0; i <= 20; i++)
        {

            // create a new row
            newRowElem = theTable.insertRow(newRowPosition);

            // create the 1st new cell in the new row and its text
            newCellElem = newRowElem.insertCell(0);
            newText = document.createTextNode(i.toString(10));
            newCellElem.appendChild(newText);

            // create the next new cell in the new row and its text
            newCellElem = newRowElem.insertCell(1);
            newText = document.createTextNode(i.toString(8));
            newCellElem.appendChild(newText);

            // create the next new cell in the new row and its text
            newCellElem = newRowElem.insertCell(1);
            newText = document.createTextNode(i.toString(16));
            newCellElem.appendChild(newText);

            // create the next new cell in the new row and its text
            newCellElem = newRowElem.insertCell(2);
            newText = document.createTextNode(i.toString(2));
```

continued

LISTING 24-1   *(continued)*

```
        newCellElem.appendChild(newText);

        newRowPosition += 1;


      }
    }
  }
```

The `toString()` method of user-defined objects does not convert the object into a meaningful string, but you can create your own method to do just that. For example, if you want to make your custom object's `toString()` method behave like an array's method, define the action of the method and assign that function to a property of the object (as shown in Listing 24-2).

LISTING 24-2

Creating a Custom toString() Method

HTML: `jsp-24-02.html`

```html
<!DOCTYPE html>
<html>
  <head>
    <meta http-equiv="content-type" content="text/html;charset=utf-8">
    <title>A custom object defined toString() result:</title>
    <script type="text/javascript" src="../jsb-global.js"></script>
    <script type="text/javascript" src="jsb-24-02.js"></script>
  </head>
  <body>
    <h1>A custom object defined toString() result:</h1>
    <!-- Hard code what's in the object so we can validate
         the JavaScript visually on the page. -->
    <h3>The custom object is book and its properties are</h3>
    <h4>title:"The Aeneid", author:"Virgil", pageCount:543</h4>
    <h3>Now let's look at the results of the custom object's toString() in
        the JavaScript:</h3>
    <div id="placeHolder"></div>
  </body>
</html>
```

JavaScript: `jsb-24-02.js`

```javascript
// initialize when the page has loaded
addEvent(window, "load", initialize);

var newElem;
var newText;
```

```
// define the function that will be the method for the custom object
function customToString()
{
    var dataArray = new Array();
    var count = 0;
    for (var i in this)
    {
        dataArray[count++] = this[i];
        if (count > 2)
        {
            break;
        }
    }
    return dataArray.join(",");
}

// define a custom object
var book = { title:"The Aeneid", author:"Virgil", pageCount:543 };

// declare a method for the custom object
book.toString = customToString;

// the onload event we identified earlier
function initialize()
{

    var placeHolderElement = document.getElementById("placeHolder");

        if (placeHolderElement)
        {
            //book.toString();

            newElem = document.createElement("h4");
            newText = document.createTextNode(book.toString());
            // insert the text into the new h4
            newElem.appendChild(newText);
            // insert the completed h4 into placeholder
            placeHolderElement.appendChild(newElem);

        }


}
```

When you run Listing 24-2, you can see how the custom object's toString() handler extracts the values of all elements of the object. You can customize how the data should be labeled and/or formatted.

Keep in mind that you can provide a custom toString() method to any object that you create, not just arrays. This is a handy way to provide a glimpse at the contents of an object for debugging purposes. For example, you could craft a toString() method that carefully formats all of the properties of an object into an easily readable string of text. Then, use an alert box or browser debugging console to view the contents of the object if a problem arises.

491

unwatch()

```
unwatch(property)
watch(property, handler)
```

Returns: Nothing

Compatibility: WinIE-, MacIE-, NN4+, Moz-, Safari-, Opera-, Chrome-

To supply the right kind of information to external debuggers, JavaScript in NN4+ implements two global functions that belong to every object — including user-defined objects. The watch() function keeps an eye on a desired object and property. If that property is set by assignment, the function invokes another user-defined function that receives information about the property name, its old value, and its new value. The unwatch() function turns off the watch functionality for a particular property.

Statements

```
//
/*...*/
```

Compatibility: WinIE3+, MacIE3+, NN2+, Moz+, Safari+, Opera+, Chrome+

Comments are statements that the JavaScript interpreter (or server-side compiler) ignores. However, these statements enable authors to leave notes about how things work in their scripts. Although lavish comments are useful to authors during a script's creation and maintenance, the full content of a client-side comment is downloaded with the document. Every byte of non-operational content of the page takes a bit more time to download. Still, we recommend lots of comments — particularly as you create a script.

JavaScript offers two styles of comments. One style consists of two forward slashes (no spaces between them), and is useful for creating a comment on a single line. JavaScript ignores any characters to the right of those slashes on the same line, even if they appear in the middle of a line. You can stack as many lines of these single-line comments as is necessary to convey your thoughts. We typically place a space between the second slash and the beginning of the comment. The following are examples of valid, one-line comment formats:

```
// this is a comment line usually about what's to come
var a = "Fred";  // a comment about this line
// You may want to capitalize the first word of a comment
// sentence if it runs across multiple lines.
//
// And you can leave a completely blank line, like the one above.
```

For longer comments, it is usually more convenient to enclose the section in the other style of comment, which is fully capable of spanning multiple lines. The following comment opens with a forward slash and asterisk (/*) and ends with an asterisk and forward slash (*/). JavaScript ignores all statements in between — including multiple lines. If you want to temporarily comment out a large segment of your script for debugging purposes, it is easiest to enclose the segment with these comment symbols. To make comment blocks easier to find, we generally place the symbols on their own lines as follows:

```
/*
some
  commented-out
    statements
*/
```

If you are developing rather complex scripts, you might find using comments a convenient way to help you organize segments of your scripts and make each segment easier to find. For example, you can define a comment block above each function and describe what the function is about, as in the following example.

```
/*-----------------------------------------------
    calculate()
    Performs a mortgage calculation based on
    parameters blah, blah, blah. Called by blah
    blah blah.
-----------------------------------------------*/
function calculate(form)
{
    // statements
}
```

const

Compatibility: WinIE-, MacIE-, NN6+, Moz+, Safari+, Opera+, Chrome+

The `const` keyword initializes a constant. Unlike a variable, whose data is subject to change while a page loads, a constant's value cannot be modified once it is assigned. It is common practice in many programming languages to define constant identifiers with all uppercase letters, usually with underscore characters to delimit multiple words. This style makes it easier to quickly find constants in your code and reminds you that their values are fixed.

Example

Listing 24-3 shows how you can use a constant in any browser other than IE. The page conveys temperature data for several cities. (Presumably, this data is updated on the server and fashioned into an array of data when the user requests the page.) For temperatures below freezing, the temperature is shown in a distinctive text style. Because the freezing temperature is a constant reference point, it is assigned as a constant.

LISTING 24-3

Using the const Keyword

HTML: `jsp-24-03.html`

```
<!DOCTYPE html>
<html>
    <head>
        <meta http-equiv="content-type" content="text/html;charset=utf-8">
        <title>The const keyword</title>
```

continued

const

LISTING 24-3   *(continued)*

```
        <link rel="stylesheet" type="text/css" href="jsp-24-03.css">
        <script type="text/javascript" src="../jsb-global.js"></script>
        <script type="text/javascript" src="jsb-24-03.js"></script>
    </head>
    <body>
        <h1>The const keyword</h1>
        <table id="temps">
            <tr>
                <th>City</th>
                <th><div>Temperature</div><div>(Fahrenheit)</div></th>
            </tr>
        </table>
    </body>
</html>
```

CSS: jsp-24-03.css

```
.cold
{
    font-weight: bold;
    color: blue;
}

td
{
    text-align: center;
}
```

JavaScript: jsb-24-03.js

```
// initialize when the page has loaded
addEvent(window, "load", showData);

const FREEZING_F = 32;

var cities = ["London", "Moscow", "New York", "Tokyo", "Sydney"];

var cityTempsF = [33, 12, 20, 40, 75];

function showData()
{
    var theTable = document.getElementById("temps");

    if (theTable)
    {
        var newRowElem;
        var newCellElem;
        var newText;
        // Insert the rows after the existing row
        var newRowPosition = 1;
```

```
    // put the city temperature data in the table
    for (var i = 0; i < cities.length; i++)
    {
        // create a new row
        newRowElem = theTable.insertRow(newRowPosition);

        // create the new city cell in the new row and its text
        newCellElem = newRowElem.insertCell(0);
        newText = document.createTextNode(cities[i]);
        newCellElem.appendChild(newText);

        // create the new temp cell in the new row and its text
        newCellElem = newRowElem.insertCell(1);
        newText = document.createTextNode(cityTempsF[i]);
        newCellElem.appendChild(newText);

        // style the cells with cold data
            if (cityTempsF[i] < FREEZING_F)
            {
                newCellElem.className = "cold";
            }
        newRowPosition += 1;
    }
}
}
```

The const keyword likely will be adopted in the next version of the ECMA-262 standard and will become an official part of the JavaScript vernacular in future browsers. In the meantime, it enjoys full support in Mozilla-based browsers.

var

Compatibility: WinIE3+, MacIE3+, NN2+, Moz+, Safari+, Opera+, Chrome+

Before using any variable, you should declare it (and optionally, initialize it with a value) via the var statement. If you omit the var keyword, the variable is automatically assigned as a global variable within the current document. To keep a variable local to a function, you must declare or initialize the variable with the var keyword inside the function's braces.

If you do not assign a value to a variable, it evaluates to null. Because a JavaScript variable is not limited to one variable type during its lifetime, you don't need to initialize a variable to an empty string or zero unless that initial value helps your scripting. (For example, if you initialize a variable as an empty string, you can then use the add-by-value operator (+=) to append string values to that variable in a future statement in the document.)

To save statement lines, you can declare, and/or initialize, multiple variables with a single var statement. Separate each varName=value pair with a comma, as in

```
    var name, age, height;  // declare as null
    var color = "green", temperature = 85.6; // initialize
```

Variable names (also known as identifiers) must be one contiguous string of characters, and the first character must be a letter. Many punctuation symbols are banned, but the underscore character is valid and is often used to separate multiple words in a long variable name. All variable names (like most identifiers in JavaScript) are case-sensitive, so you must name a particular variable identically throughout the variable's scope.

By convention, variable names are written in camelCase, as in

```
var colorCode = "green";
```

WinIE Objects

Compatibility: WinIE4+, MacIE4+, NN-, Moz-, Safari-, Opera-, Chrome-

For better or worse, Microsoft prides itself on the integration between web browser functionality and the Windows operating system. The linkage between browser and OS is most apparent in IE's facilities for accessing ActiveX objects. Microsoft has fashioned several such objects for access to scripters — again, provided the deployment is intended only for Windows versions of Internet Explorer. Some objects also exist as a way to expose some Visual Basic Script (VBScript) functionality to JavaScript. Because these objects are more within the realm of Windows and ActiveX programming, the details and quirks of working with them from WinIE is best left to other venues. But in case you are not familiar with these facilities, the following discussions introduce the basic set of WinIE objects. You can find more details at the Microsoft Developer Network (MSDN) web site at `http://msdn.microsoft.com/`.

The objects mentioned here are the `ActiveXObject`, `Dictionary`, `Enumerator`, and `VBArray` objects. Microsoft documents these objects as if they were part of the native JScript language. However, you can be sure that they will remain proprietary to Internet Explorer, if not exclusively for Windows-only versions.

Note
JScript is Microsoft's proprietary take on JavaScript, supported by Internet Explorer. JScript is essentially the same as JavaScript with a few Windows-specific extras thrown in, such as support for ActiveX objects. ∎

ActiveXObject

`ActiveXObject` is a generic object that allows your script to open and access what Microsoft sometimes calls *automation objects*. An automation object is an executable program that might run on the client or be served from a server. This can include local applications, such as applications from the Microsoft Office suite, executable DLLs (dynamic-link libraries), and so on.

Use the constructor for the `ActiveXObject` to obtain a reference to the object according to the following syntax:

```
var objRef = new ActiveXObject(appName.className[, remoteServerName]);
```

This JScript syntax is the equivalent of the VBScript `CreateObject()` method. You need to know a bit about Windows programming to determine the application name and the classes or types available for that application. For example, to obtain a reference to an Excel worksheet, use this constructor:

```
var mySheet = new ActiveXObject("Excel.Sheet");
```

Once you have a reference to the desired object, you must also know the names of the properties and methods of the object you'll be addressing. You can access much of this information via Microsoft's developer tools, such as Visual Studio .NET, or the tools that come with Visual Basic .NET. These tools enable you to query an object to discover its properties and methods. Unfortunately, an `ActiveXObject`'s properties are not enumerable through a typical JavaScript `for...in` property inspector.

Accessing an `ActiveXObject`, especially one on the client, involves some serious security considerations. The typical security setup for an IE client prevents scripts from accessing client applications, at least not without asking the user if it's okay to do so. While it's foolhardy to state categorically that one cannot perform surreptitious inspection or damage to a client without the user's knowledge (hackers find holes from time to time), it is highly unlikely. In a corporate environment, where some level of access to all clients is desirable, the client may be set up to accept instructions to work with ActiveX objects when they come from trusted sources. The bottom line is that unless you are well versed in Windows programming, don't expect the `ActiveXObject` to become some kind of magic portal that enables you to invade the privacy or security of unsuspecting users.

Dictionary

Although the `Dictionary` object is very helpful to VBScript authors, JavaScript already provides the equivalent functionality natively. A `Dictionary` object behaves very much like a JavaScript array that has string index values (similar to a Java hash table), although numeric index values are also acceptable in the `Dictionary`. Indexes are called *keys* in this environment. VBScript arrays do not have this facility natively, so the `Dictionary` object supplements the language for the sake of convenience. Unlike a JavaScript array, however, you must use the various properties and methods of the `Dictionary` object to add, access, or remove items from it.

You create a `Dictionary` object via the `ActiveXObject` as follows:

```
var dict = new ActiveXObject("Scripting.Dictionary");
```

You must create a separate `Dictionary` object for each array. Table 24-2 lists the properties and methods of the `Dictionary` object. After you create a blank `Dictionary` object, populate it via the `Add()` method for each entry. For example, the following statements create a `Dictionary` object to store U.S. state capitals:

```
var stateCaps = new ActiveXObject("Scripting.Dictionary");
stateCaps.Add("Illinois", "Springfield");
```

You can then access an individual item via the `Key` property (which, thanks to its VBScript heritage, looks more like a JavaScript method). One convenience of the `Dictionary` object is the `Keys()` method, which returns an array of all the keys in the dictionary — something that a string-indexed JavaScript array could use.

Enumerator

An `Enumerator` object provides JavaScript with access to collections that otherwise do not allow direct access to their items, via index number or name. This object isn't necessary when working with DOM collections, such as `document.all`, because you can use the `item()` method to obtain a reference to any member of the collection. But if you are scripting ActiveX objects, some of these objects' methods or properties may return collections that cannot be accessed through this mechanism or the JavaScript `for...in` property inspection technique. Instead, you must wrap the collection inside an `Enumerator` object.

To wrap a collection in an `Enumerator`, invoke the constructor for the object, passing the collection as the parameter:

```
var myEnum = new Enumerator(someCollection);
```

TABLE 24-2

Dictionary Object Properties and Methods

Property	Description
Count	Integer number of entries in the dictionary (read-only)
Item("key")	Reads or writes a value for an entry whose name is key
Key("key")	Assigns a new key name to an entry

Method	Description
Add("key", value)	Adds a value associated with a unique key name
Exists("key")	Returns Boolean true if key exists in dictionary
Items()	Returns VBArray of values in dictionary
Keys()	Returns VBArray of keys in dictionary
Remove("key")	Removes key and its value
RemoveAll()	Removes all entries

This enumerator instance must be accessed, via one of its four methods, to position a "pointer" to a particular item and then extract a copy of that item. In other words, you don't access a member directly (that is, by diving into the collection with an item number to retrieve). Instead, you move the pointer to the desired position and then read the item value. As you can see from the list of methods in Table 24-3, this object is truly intended for looping through the collection. Pointer control is limited to positioning it at the start of the collection and incrementing its position along the collection by one:

```
var val;
myEnum.moveFirst();
for (; !myEnum.atEnd(); myEnum.moveNext())
{
    val = myEnum.item();
    // more statements that work on value
}
```

VBArray

The VBArray object provides JavaScript access to Visual Basic *safe arrays*. Such an array is read-only and is commonly returned by ActiveX objects. Such arrays can be composed in VBScript sections of client-side scripts. Visual Basic arrays, by their very nature, can have multiple dimensions. For example, the following code creates a three-by-two VB array:

```
<script type="text/vbscript">
    Dim myArray(2, 1)
    myArray(0, 0) = "A"
    myArray(0, 1) = "a"
```

```
        myArray(1, 0) = "B"
        myArray(1, 1) = "b"
        myArray(2, 1) = "C"
        myArray(2, 2) = "c"
    </script>
```

TABLE 24-3

Enumerator Object Methods

Method	Description
atEnd()	Returns true if pointer is at end of collection
item()	Returns value at current pointer position
moveFirst()	Moves pointer to first position in collection
moveNext()	Moves pointer to next position in collection

Once you have a valid VB array, you can convert it to an object that the JScript interpreter can't choke on:

```
    <script type="text/javascript">
        var theVBArray = new VBArray(myArray);
    </script>
```

Global variables from one script language block can be accessed by another block, even in a different language. But at this point, the array is not yet in the form of a JavaScript array. You can either convert it to such via the VBArray.toArray() method, or access information about the VBArray object through its other methods (described briefly in Table 24-4). Once you convert a VBArray to a JavaScript array, you can then iterate through the values, as with any JavaScript array.

TABLE 24-4

VBArray Object Methods

Method	Description
dimensions()	Returns number of dimensions of the original array
getItem(dim1[, dim2[,...dimN]])	Returns value at array location defined by dimension addresses
ibound(dim)	Returns lowest index value for a given dimension
toArray()	Returns JavaScript array version of VBArray
ubound(dim)	Returns highest index value for a given dimension

When you use the toArray() method, and the source array has multiple dimensions, values from dimensions after the first "row" are simply appended to the JavaScript array with no nesting structures.

Part IV

Document Objects Reference

Document Object Model Essentials

W ithout question, the biggest challenge facing client-side web scripters is the sometimes-baffling array of document object models (DOMs) that have competed for our attention throughout the short history of scriptable browsers. Netscape got the ball rolling in Navigator 2 with the first object model. By the time version 4 browsers came around, the original object model had gained not only some useful cross-browser features, but also a host of features that were unique to Navigator or Internet Explorer. The object models were diverging, causing no end of headaches for page authors whose scripts had to run on as many browsers as possible. A ray of hope emerged from the standards process of the World Wide Web Consortium (W3C) in the form of a DOM recommendation. The DOM brought forward much of the original object model, plus new ways of consistently addressing every object in a document. The goal of this chapter is to put each of the object models into perspective and help you understand how modern browsers have alleviated most of the object model compatibility problems. But before we get to those specifics, let's examine the role of the object model in designing scripted applications.

The Object Model Hierarchy

The tutorial chapters of Part II introduced the fundamental ideas behind a document object hierarchy in scriptable browsers. In other object-oriented environments, object hierarchy plays a much greater role than it does in JavaScript-able browsers. (In JavaScript, you don't have to worry about related terms, such as classes, inheritance, and instances.) Even so, you cannot ignore the hierarchy concept because some of your code relies on your ability to write references to objects that depend on their positions within the hierarchy.

Calling these objects *JavaScript objects* is not correct. They are really browser document objects: You just happen to use the JavaScript language to bring them to life. Some scripters of Microsoft Internet Explorer use the VBScript language to script the very same document objects. Technically speaking, JavaScript objects apply to data types and other core language objects separate from the document.

Hierarchy as road map

For the programmer, the primary role of the document object hierarchy is to provide a way for scripts to reference a particular object among all the objects that a browser window can contain. The hierarchy acts as a road map that the script can use to know precisely which object to address.

Consider, for a moment, a scene in which you and your friend Tony are in a high-school classroom. It's getting hot and stuffy as the afternoon sun pours in through the wall of windows on the west side of the room. You ask Tony, "Would you please open a window?" and motion your head toward a particular window in the room. In programming terms, you've issued a command to an object (whether or not Tony appreciates the comparison). This human interaction has many advantages over anything you can do in programming. First, by making eye contact with Tony before you speak, he knows that he is the intended recipient of the command. Second, your body language passes along some parameters with that command, pointing ever so subtly to a particular window on a particular wall.

If, instead, you are in the principal's office using the public address system, and you broadcast the same command ("Would you please open a window?"), no one knows what you mean. Issuing a command without directing it to an object is a waste of time, because every object thinks, "That can't be meant for me." To accomplish the same goal as your one-on-one command, the broadcast command has to be something like "Would Tony Jeffries in Room 312 please open the middle window on the west wall?"

Let's convert this last command to JavaScript *dot syntax* form (see Chapter 6, "Browser and Document Objects"). Recall from the tutorial that a reference to an object starts with the most global point of view and narrows to the most specific point of view. From the point of view of the principal's office, the location hierarchy of the target object is

```
room312.Jeffries.Tony
```

You can also say that Tony's knowledge about how to open a window is one of Tony's methods. The complete reference to Tony and his method then becomes

```
room312.Jeffries.Tony.openWindow()
```

Your job isn't complete yet. The method requires a parameter detailing which window to open. In this case, the window you want is the middle window of the west wall of Room 312. Or, from the hierarchical point of view of the principal's office, it becomes

```
room312.westWall.middleWindow
```

This object road map is the parameter for Tony's `openWindow()` method. Therefore, the entire command that comes over the PA system is

```
room312.Jeffries.Tony.openWindow(room312.westWall.middleWindow)
```

If, instead of barking out orders while sitting in the principal's office, you attempt the same task through radio from an orbiting space shuttle to all the inhabitants on Earth, imagine how laborious your object hierarchy would be. The complete reference to Tony's `openWindow()` method and the window that you want opened wolud have to be mighty long to distinguish the desired objects from the billions of objects within the space shuttle's view.

The point is that the smaller the scope of the object-oriented world you're programming, the more you can assume about the location of objects. For client-side JavaScript, the scope is no wider than the browser itself. In other words, every object that a JavaScript script can work with resides within the browser application. With few exceptions, a script does not access anything about your computer hardware, operating system, other applications, desktop, or any other stuff beyond the browser program.

The first browser document object road map

Figure 25-1 shows the lowest-common-denominator document object hierarchy that is implemented in all scriptable browsers, including scriptable legacy browsers such as IE3 and NN2. Notice that the window object is the topmost object in the entire scheme. Everything you script in JavaScript is in the browser's window.

FIGURE 25-1

The lowest-common-denominator browser document object hierarchy.

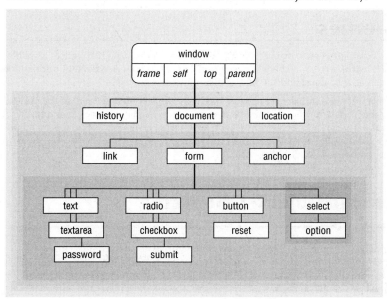

Pay attention to the shading of the concentric rectangles. Every object in the same shaded area is at the same level relative to the window object. When a line from an object extends to the next-darker shaded rectangle, that object contains all the objects in darker areas. At most, one of these lines exists between levels. The window object contains the document object; the document object contains a form object; a form object contains many different kinds of form control elements.

How Document Objects Are Born

Most of the objects that a browser creates for you are established when an HTML document loads into the browser. The same kind of HTML code you use to create links, anchors, and input elements tells a JavaScript-enhanced browser to create those objects in memory. The objects are there whether or not your scripts call them into action.

The only visible differences to the HTML code for defining those objects are the one or more optional attributes specifically dedicated to JavaScript. By and large, these attributes specify the event you want the user interface element to react to and what JavaScript should do when the user takes that action. By relying on the document's HTML code to perform the object generation, you can spend more time figuring out how to do things with those objects, or how to have them do things for you.

Bear in mind that objects are created in their load order. If you create a multiframe environment, a script in one frame cannot communicate with another frame's objects until both frames load. This trips up a lot of scripters who create multiframe and multiwindow sites (for more information, see Chapter 27, "Window and Frame Objects").

But interestingly enough, you are not confined to just those objects that the document's HTML code generates. As you'll see later in this chapter, the W3C DOM allows you to add and delete objects from the object hierarchy. In fact, if you want to create HTML code that contains no JavaScript, you'll see how you can do that as well.

Object Properties

A property generally defines a particular current setting of an object. The setting may reflect a visible attribute of an object, such as the state of a checkbox (selected or not); it may also contain information that is not so obvious, such as the action and method of a submitted form.

Document objects have most of their initial properties assigned by the attribute settings of the HTML tags that generate the objects. Thus, a property may be a word (for example, a name) or a number (for example, a size). A property can also be an array, such as an array of images contained by a document. If the HTML does not include all attributes, the browser usually fills in a default value for both the attribute and the corresponding JavaScript property.

A Note to Experienced Object-Oriented Programmers

Although the basic object model hierarchy appears to have a class/subclass relationship, many of the traditional aspects of a true object-oriented environment don't apply to the model. The original JavaScript document object hierarchy is a *containment hierarchy*, not an *inheritance hierarchy*. No object inherits properties or methods of an object higher up the chain. Neither is there any automatic message passing from object to object in any direction. Therefore, you cannot invoke a window's method by sending a message to it through the document or a form object. All object references must be explicit.

Predefined document objects are generated only when the HTML code containing their definitions loads into the browser. In Chapter 23, "Function Objects and Custom Objects," you learned how to create your own objects, but those objects do not present new visual elements on the page that go beyond what HTML, Java applets, and plug-ins can portray.

Inheritance *does* play a role, as you will see later in this chapter, in the object model defined by the W3C. This newer hierarchy is of a more general nature to accommodate requirements of XML as well as HTML. But the containment hierarchy for HTML objects, as described in this section, is still valid in W3C DOM–compatible browsers.

Property values may be changed in scripts, regardless of the DOM you are using; the difference is the code you write. Later in this chapter, we'll give you specifics for the examples you'll see now. Where applicable, we'll show the examples in DOM0 as well as the W3C DOM.

When used in script statements, property names are case-sensitive. Therefore, if you see a property name listed as bgColor, you must use it in a script statement with that exact combination of lowercase and uppercase letters. But when you set an initial value of a property by way of an HTML attribute, the attribute name (like all of HTML) is not case sensitive. Thus, <BODY BGCOLOR="white"> and <body bgcolor="white"> both set the same bgColor property value. Although XHTML won't validate correctly if you use anything but lowercase letters for tag and attribute names, most browsers will load the page anyway because they continue to be case insensitive for markup, regardless of the HTML or XHTML version you specify for the page's DOCTYPE. The case for property names is not influenced by the case of the markup attribute name. You can validate your HTML at http://validator.w3.org/.

Each property determines its own read/write status. Some properties are read-only, whereas you can change others on the fly by assigning a new value to them. For example, to put some new text into a text box object, you assign a string to the object's value property:

```
document.forms[0].phone.value = "555-1212";
```
or
```
document.getElementById("myPhoneTextBox").value = "555-1212";
```

When an object contained by the document exists (that is, its HTML is loaded into the document), you can also add one or more custom properties to that object. This can be helpful if you want to associate some additional data with an object for later retrieval. To add such a property, you may simply specify it in the same way that you assign a value to it:

```
document.forms[0].phone.delimiter = "-";
```
or
```
document.getElementById("myPhoneTextBox").value = "-";
```

You'll see later in the chapter that there are other ways to add properties to an object. Any property you set survives as long as the document remains loaded in the window and scripts do not overwrite the object. Be aware, however, that reloading the page usually destroys custom properties.

Object Methods

An object's *method* is a command that a script can give to that object. Some methods return values, but that is not a prerequisite for a method. Also, not every object has methods defined for it. In a majority of cases, invoking a method from a script causes some action to take place. The resulting action may be obvious (such as resizing a window) or something more subtle (such as sorting an array in memory).

All methods have parentheses after them, and methods always appear at the end of an object's reference. When a method accepts or requires parameters, the parameter values go inside the parentheses (with multiple parameters separated by commas).

Although an object has its methods predefined by the object model, you can also assign one or more additional methods to an object that already exists (that is, after its HTML is loaded into the document). To do this, a script in the document (or in another window or frame accessible by the document) must define a JavaScript function and then assign that function to a new property name of the object. In the following example, written to take advantage of modern browser features, the `fullScreen()` function invokes two `window` object methods. By assigning the function reference to the new `window.maximize` property, we define a `maximize()` method for the `window` object. Thus, a button's event handler can call that method directly.

```
// define the function
function fullScreen()
{
    this.moveTo(0,0);
    this.resizeTo(screen.availWidth, screen.availHeight);
}
// assign the function to a custom property
window.maximize = fullScreen;
...
<!-- invoke the custom method -->
<input type="button" value="Maximize Window" onclick="window.maximize()" />
```

In this last example, DOM0 is used. Using the W3C DOM, the function and its assignment to a custom property will be coded exactly the same. The difference is how the `onclick` event handler is identified. In DOM0, the event is defined directly as an attribute of the object in the HTML: on the `input` tag in the case above. In the W3C DOM the event may be defined within the script, rather than on the HTML element itself:

```
// initialize when the page has loaded
addEvent(window, "load", initialize);

function initialize()
{
    // add an event to the button
    addEvent(document.getElementById("theButton"), click);
}
```

Note
The function to assign event handlers throughout the code in this chapter and much of the book is `addEvent()`, a cross-browser event handler explained in detail in Chapter 32.

The `addEvent()` function is part of the script file `jsb-global.js`, which is located on the accompanying CD-ROM in the `Content/` folder, where it is accessible to all chapters' scripts. ∎

Object Event Handlers

An *event handler* specifies how an object reacts to an event that is triggered by a user action (for example, a button click) or a browser action (for example, the completion of a document load). Going back to the earliest JavaScript-enabled browser, event handlers were defined inside HTML tags as extra attributes. They included the name of the attribute, followed by an equal sign (working as an assignment operator) and a string containing the script statement(s) or function(s) to execute when the event occured (see Chapter 7, "Scripts and HTML Documents").

Although event handlers are commonly defined in an object's HTML tag, you also have the power to assign or change an event handler just as you assign or change the property of an object. The value of an event handler property looks like a function definition. For example, given this HTML definition

```
<input type="text" name="entry" onfocus="doIt()" />
```

the value of the object's `onfocus` (all lowercase) property is

```
function onfocus()
{
    doIt();
}
```

You can, however, assign an entirely different function to an event handler by assigning a function reference to the property. Such references don't include the parentheses that are part of the function's definition. (You see this again in Chapter 23 when you assign functions to object properties.)

Using the same text field definition you just looked at, you can assign a different function to the event handler, because, based on user input elsewhere in the document, you want the field to behave differently when it receives the focus. If you define a function like this

```
function doSomethingElse()
{
    //statements
}
```

You can then assign the function to the field with either:

```
document.formName.entry.onfocus = doSomethingElse;
```

or

```
document.getElementById("theEntryID").onfocus = doSomethingElse;
```

Because the new function reference is written in JavaScript, you must observe case for the function name. Additionally, you are best served across all browsers by sticking with all-lowercase event handler names as properties.

If your scripts create new element objects dynamically, you can assign event handlers to these objects by way of event handler properties. For example, the following code uses W3C DOM syntax to create a new button input element and assign an `onclick` event handler that invokes a function defined elsewhere in the script:

```
var newElem = document.createElement("input");
newElem.type = "button";
newElem.value = "Click Here";
newElem.onclick = doIt;
document.getElementById("theFormId").appendChild(newElem);
```

Object Model Smorgasbord

A survey of the entire evolution of scriptable browsers since NN2 and IE3 reveals six distinct DOM families. Even if your job entails developing content for just one current browser version, you may be surprised that family members from more than one DOM inhabit your authoring space.

Studying the evolution of the object model is extremely valuable for newcomers to scripting. It is too easy to learn the latest object model gadgets in your current browser, only to discover that your heroic scripting efforts are lost on earlier browsers accessing your pages. Even if you plan on supporting only modern browsers, a cursory knowledge of object model history is a useful part of your JavaScript knowledge base. Therefore, take a look at the six major object model types and how they came into being. Table 25-1 lists the object model families and the browser versions that support them. Note that a release number is only listed when the level of support for an object model type leaps forward (for example, going from "limited" support to "most" support). Later in this chapter are some guidelines you can follow to help you choose the object model(s) that best suit your users' appetites.

TABLE 25-1

Object Model Families

Model	Browser Support
Basic Object Model	NN2+, IE3+, Moz1+, FF2+, Safari1+, Opera+, Chrome+
Basic Plus Images	NN3+, MacIE3.01+, IE4+, Moz1+, FF2+, Safari1+, -, Opera+, Chrome+
NN4 Extensions	NN4
IE4 Extensions	IE4+ (some features in all versions require Win32 OS)
IE5 Extensions	IE5+ (some features in all versions require Win32 OS), Opera 9.62+ (very limited)
W3C DOM (I and II)	IE5+ (partial), Moz1 (most), FF2+ (most), Safari1 (partial), Safari1.3+ (most), Opera9.62+ (most), Chrome1+ (most)

It's important to realize that even though browsers have come a long way toward providing unified support for web standards, we're not quite there yet. As of this writing, no current browser fully and accurately supports Levels I and II of the W3C DOM. Firefox 2, Safari 1.3/2, Opera 9, and Chrome 1 have all closed the compatibility gap considerably, but some issues, not severely impacting HTML authoring, remain.

Basic Object Model

The first scriptable browser, Netscape Navigator 2, implemented a very basic DOM. Figure 25-1, which you saw earlier in the chapter, provides a visual guide to the objects that were exposed to scripting. The hierarchical structure starts with the window and drills inward toward the document, forms, and form control elements. A document is a largely immutable page on the screen. Only elements that are by nature interactive — links and form elements, such as text fields and buttons — are treated as objects with properties, methods, and event handlers.

The heavy emphasis on form controls opened numerous possibilities that were radical ideas at the time. Because a script could inspect the values of form controls, forms could be prevalidated on the client. If the page included a script that performed some calculations, data entry and calculated results were displayed via editable text fields.

Additional objects that exist outside the document — `window`, `history`, and `location` objects — provide scriptable access to simple yet practical properties of the browser that loads the page. The most global view of the environment is the `navigator` object, which includes properties about the browser brand and version.

When Internet Explorer 3 arrived on the scene, the short life of Navigator 2 was nearing its end. Even though NN3 was already widely available in prerelease form, Internet Explorer 3 implemented the basic object model from NN2 (plus one `window` object property from NN3). Therefore, despite the browser version number discrepancy, NN2 and IE3 were essentially the same with respect to their DOMs. For a brief moment in Internet Time, there was nearly complete harmony between Microsoft and Netscape DOMs — albeit at a very simple level.

Basic Object Model Plus Images

A very short time after Internet Explorer 3 was released, Netscape released Navigator 3 with an object model that built upon the original version. A handful of existing objects — especially the `window` object — gained new properties, methods, and/or event handlers. Scripts could also communicate with Java applets as objects. But the biggest new object on the scene was the `Image` object, along with the array of image objects exposed to the `document` object.

Most of the properties for a Navigator 3 image object gave read-only access to values typically assigned to attributes in the `<img>` tag. But you could modify one property — the `src` property — after the page loaded. Scripts could swap out images within the fixed image rectangle. Although these new image objects didn't have mouse-related event handlers, nesting an image inside a link (which had `onmouseover` and new `onmouseout` event handlers) let scripters implement image rollovers to liven up a page.

As more new scripters investigated the possibilities of adding JavaScript to their pages, frustration ensued when the image swapping they implemented for Navigator 3 failed to work in Internet Explorer 3. Although you could easily script around the lack of an image object to prevent script errors in Internet Explorer 3, the lack of this cool page feature disappointed many. Had they also taken into account the installed base of Navigator 2 in the world, they would have been disappointed there, too. To confuse matters even more, the Macintosh version of Internet Explorer 3.01 (the second release of the Internet Explorer for Mac browser) implemented scriptable image objects.

Despite these rumblings of compatibility problems to come, the object model implemented in Navigator 3 eventually became the baseline reference for future DOMs. With few exceptions, code written for this object model runs on all browsers from Navigator 3 and Internet Explorer 4, on through the latest versions of both brands and other modern browsers.

Navigator 4–Only Extensions

The next browser released to the world was Netscape Navigator 4. Numerous additions to the existing objects put more power into the hands of scripters. You could move and resize browser windows within the context of script-detectable `screen` object properties (for example, how big the user's screen was). Two concepts that represented new thinking about the object model were an enhanced event model and the layer object.

Event capture model

Navigator 4 added many new events to the repertoire. Keyboard events and more mouse events (`onmousedown` and `onmouseup`) allowed scripts to react to more user actions on form control elements and links. All of these events worked as they did in previous object models in which event handlers were typically assigned as attributes to an element's tag (although you could also assign event handlers as properties in script statements). To facilitate some of the Dynamic HTML (DHTML) potential in the rest of the Navigator 4 object model, the event model was substantially enhanced.

At the root of the system is the idea that when a user performs some physical action on an event-aware object (for example, clicking a form button), the event reaches that button from the top down, through the document object hierarchy. If you have multiple objects that share an event handler, it may be more convenient to capture that event in just one place — the window or document object level — rather than assigning the same event handler to all the elements. The default behavior of Navigator 4 allowed the event to reach the target object, just as it had in earlier browsers. But you could also turn on *event capture* in the window, document, or layer object. When captured, the event could be handled at the upper level, preprocessed before being passed onto its original target, or redirected to another object altogether.

Whether or not you capture events, the Navigator 4 event model produces an event object (with a lowercase e to distinguish it from the static Event object) for each event. That object contains properties that reveal more information about the specific event, such as the keyboard character pressed for a keyboard event or the position of a click event on the page. Any event handler can inspect event object properties to learn more about the event, and then process the event accordingly.

Layers

Perhaps the most radical addition to the Navigator 4 object model was a new object that reflected an entirely new HTML element: the layer element. A *layer* is a container that is capable of holding its own HTML document, yet it exists in a plane in front of the main document. You can move, size, and hide a layer under script control. This new element allowed, for the first time, overlapping elements in an HTML page.

To accommodate the layer object in the document object hierarchy, Netscape defined a nesting hierarchy such that a layer was contained by a document. As a result, the document object acquired a property (document.layers) that was an array of layer objects in the document. This array exposed only the first level of layer(s) in the current document object.

Each layer had its own document object because each layer could load an external HTML document if desired. As a positionable element, a layer object had numerous properties and methods that allowed scripts to move, hide, show, and change its stacking order.

Unfortunately for Netscape, the W3C did not agree to make the <layer> tag part of the HTML 4 specification. As such, it is an orphan element that exists only in Navigator 4 (not implemented in Moz1 or later). The same goes for the scripting of the layer object and its nested references.

Internet Explorer 4+ Extensions

Microsoft broke important new ground with the release of Internet Explorer 4, which came several months after the release of Navigator 4. The main improvements were in the exposure of all HTML elements, scripted support of Cascading Style Sheets (CSS), and a new event model. Some other additions were available only on Windows 32-bit operating system platforms.

HTML element objects

The biggest change to the object model world was that every HTML element became a scriptable object, while still supporting the original object model. Microsoft invented the document.all array (also called a *collection*). This array contains references to every element in the document, regardless of element nesting. If you assign a unique identifier (name) to the `id` attribute of an element, you can reference the element by the following syntax:

```
document.all.elementID
```

In most cases, you can also drop the `document.all.` part of the reference and begin with only the element ID.

Every element object has an entirely new set of properties and methods that give scripters a level of control over document content unlike anything seen before. These properties and methods are explored in more detail in Chapter 26, "Generic HTML objects," but several groups of properties deserve special mention here.

Four properties (`innerHTML`, `innerText`, `outerHTML`, and `outerText`) provide read/write access to the actual content within the body of a document. This means that you no longer have to use text boxes to display calculated output from scripts. You can modify content inside paragraphs, table cells, or anywhere, on the fly. The browser's rendering engine immediately reflows a document when the dimensions of an element's content change. That feature puts the *Dynamic* in *Dynamic HTML*. To those of us who scripted the static pages of earlier browsers, this feature — taken for granted today — was nothing short of a revelation.

The series of offset properties are related to the position of an element on the page. These properties are distinct from the kind of positioning performed by CSS. Therefore, you can get the dimensions and location of any element on the page, making it easier to move positionable content atop elements that are part of the document and that may appear in various locations due to the browser window's current size.

Finally, the `style` property is the gateway to CSS specifications defined for the element. It is important that the script can modify the numerous properties of the `style` object. Therefore, you can modify font specifications, colors, borders, and the positioning properties after the page loads. The dynamic reflow of the page takes care of any layout changes that the alteration requires (for example, adjusting to a bigger font size).

Element containment hierarchy

Although Internet Explorer 4 still recognizes the element hierarchy of the original object model (see Figure 25-1), the DOM for Internet Explorer 4 does not extend this kind of hierarchy fully into other elements. If it did, it would mean that `td` elements inside a table might have to be addressed via its next outer `tr` or `table` element (just as a form control element must be addressed through its containing `form` element). Figure 25-2 shows how all HTML elements are grouped under the `document` object. The `document.all` array flattens the containment hierarchy, as far as referencing objects goes. A reference to the most deeply nested TD element is still `document.all.cellID`. The highlighted pathway from the `window` object is the predominant reference path used when working with the Internet Explorer 4 document object hierarchy.

Element containment in Internet Explorer 4, however, is important for other reasons. Because an element can inherit some style sheet attributes from an element that contains it, you should devise a document's HTML by embedding every piece of content in a container. Paragraph elements are text containers (with start and end tags), not tall line breaks between text chunks. Internet Explorer 4 introduced the notion of a parent-child relationship between a container and elements nested within it. Also, the position of an element may be calculated relative to the position of its next outermost positioning context.

FIGURE 25-2

The Internet Explorer 4 document object hierarchy.

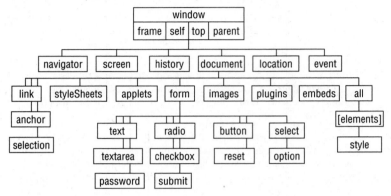

The bottom line here is that element containment doesn't have anything to do with object references (like the original object model). It has everything to do with the *context* of an element relative to the rest of the page's content.

Cascading Style Sheets

By arriving a bit later to market with its version 4 browser than Netscape, Microsoft benefited from having the CSS Level 1 specification more fully developed before the browser's release. Therefore, the implementation is far more complete than that of Navigator 4 (though it is not 100 percent compatible with the standard).

The scriptability of style sheet properties is a bit at odds with the first-generation CSS specification, which seemed to ignore the potential of scripting styles with JavaScript. Many CSS attribute names are hyphenated words (for example, `text-align`, `z-index`), even though hyphens are not allowed in identifier names in JavaScript. This necessitated conversion of the multiword CSS attribute names to camelCase JavaScript property names. Therefore, `text-align` becomes `textAlign`, and `z-index` becomes `zIndex`. You can access all of these properties through an element's `style` property:

```
document.all.elementID.style.stylePropertyName
```

or

```
document.getElementById("myElement").style.stylePropertyName
```

One byproduct of the scriptability of style sheets in Internet Explorer 4 and later is what you might call the *phantom page syndrome*. This occurs when the layout of a page is handled after the primary HTML for the page has downloaded to the browser. As the page loads, not all content may be visible, or it may be in a visual jumble. An `onload` event handler in the page then triggers scripts to set styles or content for the page. Elements jump around to get to their final resting places. This may be disconcerting to some users who at first see a link to click, but by the time the cursor reaches the click location, the page has reflowed, thereby moving the link somewhere else on the page.

Note

For Internet Explorer users with 32-bit Windows operating systems, Internet Explorer 4 includes some extra features in the object model that can enhance presentations. *Filters* **are style sheet additives that offer a variety of visual effects on body text. For example, you can add a drop shadow or a glowing effect to text simply by applying filter styles to the text, or you can create the equivalent of a slide presentation by placing the content of each slide in a positioned** div **element. Although filters follow the CSS syntax, they are not part of the W3C specification.** ■

Event bubbling

Just as Netscape invented an event model for Navigator 4, so did Microsoft for Internet Explorer 4. Unfortunately for cross-browser scripters, the two event models are quite different. Instead of events trickling down the hierarchy to the target element, an Internet Explorer event starts at the target element and, unless instructed otherwise, bubbles up through the element containment hierarchy to reach the window object eventually. At any object along the way, an event handler can perform additional processing on that event, if desired. Therefore, if you want a single event handler to process all click events for the page, assign the event handler to the body or window object so the events reach those objects (provided that the event bubbling isn't canceled by some other object along the containment hierarchy).

Internet Explorer also has an event object (a property of the window object) that contains details about the event, such as the key pressed for a keyboard event and the location of a mouse event. Names for these properties are entirely different from the event object properties of Navigator 4.

Despite what seems like incompatible, if not completely opposite, event models in Navigator 4 and Internet Explorer 4, you can make a single set of scripts handle events in both browsers; see Chapter 32, "Event Objects" and Chapter 59, "Application: Cross-Browser DHTML Map Puzzle" (on the CD-ROM) for examples. The Internet Explorer 4 event model continues to be the only model supported by Internet Explorer through version 7.

Internet Explorer 5+ Extensions

With the release of Internet Explorer 5, Microsoft built more onto the proprietary object model it launched with Internet Explorer 4. Although the range of objects remained pretty much the same, the number of properties, methods, and event handlers for the objects increased dramatically. Some of those additions were added to meet some of the specifications of the W3C DOM (discussed in the next section), occasionally causing a bit of incompatibility with Internet Explorer 4. But Microsoft also pushed ahead with features only for Windows users that may not necessarily become industry standards: DHTML behaviors and HTML applications.

A *DHTML behavior* is a chunk of script — saved as an external file — that defines some action (usually, a change of one or more style properties) that you can apply to any kind of element. The goal is to create a reusable component that you can load into any document whose elements require that behavior. As an example of a DHTML behavior, you can define a behavior that turns an element's text to red whenever the cursor rolls atop it, and reverts the text to black when the cursor rolls out. When you assign the behavior to an element in the document (through CSS-like rule syntax), the element picks up that behavior and responds to the user accordingly. You can apply that same behavior to any element(s) in the document.

Cross-Reference

You can see an example of a DHTML behavior in Chapter 26, in the description of the `addBehavior()` method; you can read an extended discussion in Chapter 50 (on the CD-ROM). ∎

HTML applications (HTAs, in Microsoft parlance) are HTML files that include an XML element known as the `hta:application` element. You can download an HTA to Internet Explorer 5 or later from the server as though it were a web page (although its file extension is `.hta` rather than `.htm` or `.html`). A user can also install an HTA on a client machine so that it behaves very much like an application, with a desktop icon and significant control over the look of the window. HTAs are granted greater security privileges on the client so that this application can behave more like a regular program. In fact, you can elect to turn off the system menu bar and use DHTML techniques to build your own menu bar for the application. Implementation details of HTAs are beyond the scope of this book, but you should be aware of their existence. More information is available at `http://msdn.microsoft.com`.

The W3C DOM

Conflicting browser object models from Netscape and Microsoft made life difficult for developers. Scripters craved a standard that would serve as a common denominator, much as HTML and CSS standards did for content and styles. The W3C took up the challenge of creating a DOM standard: the W3C DOM.

The charter of the W3C DOM working group was to create a DOM that could be applied to both HTML and XML documents. Because an XML document can have tags of virtually any name (as defined by a Document Type Definition or XML Schema), it has no intrinsic structure or fixed vocabulary of elements, as an HTML document does. As a result, the DOM specification had to accommodate the known structure of HTML (as defined in the HTML 4 specification), as well as the unknown structure of an XML document.

To make this work effectively, the working group divided the DOM specification into two sections. The first, called the *Core DOM,* defines specifications for the basic document structure that HTML and XML documents share. This includes notions of a document containing elements that have tag names and attributes; an element is capable of containing zero or more other elements. The second part of the DOM specification addresses the elements and other characteristics that apply only to HTML. The HTML portion inherits all the features of the Core DOM, while providing a measure of backward compatibility to object models already implemented in legacy browsers and providing a framework for new features.

It is important for veteran scripters to recognize that the W3C DOM does not specify all features from existing browser object models. Many features of the Internet Explorer 4 (and later) object model are not part of the W3C DOM specification. This means that if you are comfortable in the Internet Explorer environment and wish to shift your focus to writing for the W3C DOM spec, you have to change some practices, as highlighted in this chapter. In many respects, especially with regard to DHTML applications, the W3C DOM is an entirely new DOM with new concepts that you must grasp before you can successfully script in the environment.

By the same token, you should be aware that whereas Mozilla-based browsers go to great lengths to implement all of DOM Level 1 and most of Level 2, Microsoft (for whatever reason) features only a partial implementation of the W3C DOM through Internet Explorer 5.5. Although IE6 and later versions implement more W3C DOM features, some important parts — notably, W3C DOM events — are missing. Other modern browsers, such as Chrome 1+, Safari 1.3+, and Opera 9+, provide comprehensive W3C DOM support and have largely closed the gap to compete with Mozilla in terms of supporting the W3C DOM.

DOM levels

Like most W3C specifications, one version is rarely enough. The job of the DOM working group was too large to be swallowed whole in one sitting. Therefore, the DOM is a continually evolving specification. The timeline of specification releases rarely coincides with browser releases. Therefore, it is very common for any given browser release to include only some of the most recent W3C version.

The first formal specification, DOM Level 1, was released well after NN4 and IE4 shipped. The HTML portion of Level 1 includes the so-called DOM Level 0 (there is no published standard by that name). This is essentially the object model as implemented in Navigator 3 (and for the most part in Internet Explorer 3, plus image objects). Perhaps the most significant omission from Level 1 is an event model (it ignores even the simple event model implemented in NN2 and IE3).

DOM Level 2 builds on the work of Level 1. In addition to several enhancements of both the Core and HTML portions of Level 1, Level 2 adds significant new sections (published as separate modules) on the event model, ways of inspecting a document's hierarchy, XML namespaces, text ranges, style sheets, and style properties. Some modules of the Level 3 DOM have reached Recommendation status. Although IE is still a ways off from implementation to any significant degree, the other major browsers have at least partially implemented some of the modules, including some that are still in working draft status.

What stays the same

By adopting DOM Level 0 as the starting point of the HTML portion of the DOM, the W3C provided a way for a lot of existing script code to work even in a W3C DOM-compatible browser. Every object you see in the original object model, starting with the document object (see Figure 25-1) plus the image object, are in DOM Level 0. Almost all of the same object properties and methods are also available.

More important, when you consider the changes to referencing other elements in the W3C DOM, we're lucky that the old ways of referencing objects — such as forms, form control elements, and images — still work. Had the working group started with a clean slate, it is unlikely that the document object would have been given properties consisting of arrays of forms, links, and images.

The only potential problems you could encounter with your existing code have to do with a handful of properties that used to belong to the document object. In the new DOM, four style-related properties of the document object (alinkColor, bgColor, linkColor, and vlinkColor) become properties of the body object (referenced as document.body). In addition, the three link color properties pick up new names in the process (aLink, link, and vLink). It appears, however, that for now, IE6 and Moz1 maintain backward compatibility with the older document object color properties.

Also note that the DOM specification concerns itself only with the document and its content. Objects such as window, navigator, and screen are not part of the DOM specification through Level 2. Scripters are still at the mercy of browser makers for compatibility in these areas.

What isn't available

As mentioned earlier, the W3C DOM is not simply a restatement of existing browser specifications. Many convenience features of the Internet Explorer and Netscape Navigator object models do not appear in the W3C DOM. If you developed DHTML content in Internet Explorer 4 or later or in Navigator 4, you had to learn how to get along without some of these conveniences.

The Navigator 4 experiment with the `<layer>` tag was not successful in the W3C process. As a result, both the tag and the scripting conventions surrounding it do not exist in the W3C DOM. To some scripters' relief, the `document.layerName` referencing scenario (even more complex with nested layers) disappears from the object model. A positioned element is treated as just another element with some special style sheet attributes that enable you to move it anywhere on the page, stack it amid other positioned elements, or hide it from view.

Among popular Internet Explorer 4+ features missing from the W3C DOM are the `document.all` collection of HTML elements and four element properties that facilitate dynamic content: `innerHTML`, `innerText`, `outerHTML`, and `outerText`. W3C provides a new way for acquiring an array of all elements in a document, but generating HTML content to replace existing content or to be inserted in a document requires a tedious sequence of statements (see the section "New DOM concepts," later in this chapter). All the new browsers, however, have implemented the `innerHTML` property for HTML element objects, and with the exception of Firefox, have implemented the other three properties.

New HTML practices

Exploitation of DHTML possibilities in the W3C DOM relies on modern HTML practices that by now have been adopted by the majority of HTML authors. At the core of these practices (espoused by the HTML 4 specification) is making sure that all content is within an HTML container of some kind. Therefore, instead of using the `<p>` tag as a separator between blocks of running text, surround each paragraph of the running text with a `<p>...</p>` tag set. If you don't do it, the browser treats each `<p>` tag as the beginning of a paragraph and ends the paragraph element just before the next `<p>` tag or other block-level element.

Although browsers continue to accept the omission of certain end tags (for `td`, `tr`, and `li` elements, for instance) for backward compatibility, it is best to get into the habit of supplying these end tags if for no other reason than that they help you visualize where an element's sphere of influence truly begins and ends. Applying this as a best practice also means your code will validate.

Any element that you intend to script — whether to change its content or its style — should have an identifier assigned to the element's `id` attribute. The identifier should be a unique value within the context of the current web page. Form control elements still require `name` attributes if you submit the form content to a server. But you can freely assign the same or a different identifier value to a control's `id` attribute. Scripts can use either the `id` or the `document.formReference.elementName` reference to reach a control object. Identifiers are essentially the same as the values you assign to the `name` attributes of form and form input elements. Following the same rules for the `name` attribute value, an `id` identifier must be a single word (no whitespace); it cannot begin with a numeral (to prevent conflicts in JavaScript); and it should avoid punctuation symbols except for the underscore character.

New DOM concepts

With the W3C DOM comes several concepts that may be new to you unless you have worked extensively with the terminology of tree hierarchies. Concepts that have the most impact on your scripting are new ways of referencing elements and nodes.

Element referencing

Script references to objects in the DOM Level 0 are observed in the W3C DOM for backward compatibility. Therefore, a form input element whose `name` attribute is assigned the value `userName` is addressed just as it always is

```
document.forms[0].userName
```

or

```
document.formName.userName
```

But because all elements of a document are exposed to the `document` object, you can use the `document` object method designed to access any element whose ID is assigned. The method is `document.getElementById()`, and the sole parameter is a string version of the identifier of the object whose reference you want to get. To help put this in context with what you may have used with the Internet Explorer 4 object model, consider the following HTML paragraph tag:

```
<p id="myParagraph">...</p>
```

In Internet Explorer 4 or later, you can reference this element with

```
var elem = document.all.myParagraph;
```

Although the `document.all` collection is not implemented in the W3C DOM, the `document` object method (available in Internet Explorer 5 and later, Mozilla, Safari, and others) `getElementById()` enables you to access any element by its ID:

```
var elem = document.getElementById("myParagraph");
```

This method is considered the appropriate technique for referencing an element based upon its ID. Unfortunately for scripters, this method is difficult to type because it is case sensitive, so watch out for that ending lowercase *d*.

A hierarchy of nodes

The issue surrounding containers (described earlier) comes into play for the underlying architecture of the W3C DOM. Every element or free-standing chunk of text in an HTML (or XML) document is an object that is contained by its next outermost container. Let's look at a simple HTML document to see how this system works. Listing 25-1 is formatted to show the containment hierarchy of elements and string chunks.

LISTING 25-1

A Simple HTML Document

```
<html>
   <head>
      <title>
         A Simple Page
      </title>
```

continued

LISTING 25-1 *(continued)*

```
    </head>

    <body>
        <p id="paragraph1">
            This is the
            <em id="emphasis1">
                one and only
            </em>
            paragraph on the page.
        </p>
    </body>
</html>
```

What you don't see in the listing is a representation of the document object. The document object exists automatically when this page loads into a browser. It is important that the document object encompasses everything you see in Listing 25-1. Therefore, the document object has a single nested element: the html element. The html element in turn has two nested elements: head and body. The head element contains the title element, whereas the title element contains a chunk of text. Down in the body element, the p element contains three pieces: a string chunk, the em element, and another string chunk.

According to W3C DOM terminology, each container, stand-alone element (such as a br element), or text chunk is known as a *node* — a fundamental building block of the W3C DOM. Nodes have parent-child relationships when one container holds another. As in real life, parent-child relationships extend only between adjacent generations, so a node can have zero or more children. However, the number of third-generation nodes further nested within the family tree does not influence the number of children associated with a parent. Therefore, in Listing 25-1, the html node has two child nodes: head and body, which are *siblings* that have the same parent. The body element has one child (p), even though that child contains three children (two text nodes and an em element node).

If you draw a hierarchical tree diagram of the document in Listing 25-1, it should look like the illustration in Figure 25-3.

FIGURE 25-3

Tree diagram of nodes for the document in Listing 25-1.

```
document
+--<html>
    +--<head>
    |   +--<title>
    |       +--"A Simple Page"
    +--<body>
        +--<p ID="paragraph1">
            +--"This is the   "
            +--<em ID="emphasis1">
            |   +--"one and only"
            +--" paragraph on the page."
```

520

Note
If the document's source code contains a Document Type Definition (in a DOCTYPE element) above the `<html>` tag, the browser treats that DOCTYPE node as a sibling of the HTML element node. In that case, the root document node contains two child nodes. ■

The W3C DOM (through Level 2) defines 12 different types of nodes, 7 of which have direct application in HTML documents. These seven types of nodes appear in Table 25-2; the rest apply to XML. Of the 7 types, the three most common are the document, element, and text types. All W3C DOM browsers (including Internet Explorer 5 and later, Mozilla, Safari, and others) implement the three common node types, whereas Mozilla implements all of them, IE6 implements all but one, and Safari 1 implements all but two.

Applying the node types of Table 25-2 to the node diagram in Figure 25-3, you can see that the simple page consists of one document node, six element nodes, and four text nodes.

TABLE 25-2

W3C DOM HTML-Related Node Types

Type	Number	nodeName	nodeValue	Description	IE	Moz	Safari
Element	1	*tag name*	Null	Any HTML or XML tagged element	6+	1+	1+
Attribute	2	*attribute name*	*attribute value*	A name-value attribute pair in an element	6+	1+	1+
Text	3	#text	*text content*	A text fragment contained by an element	6+	1+	1+
Comment	8	#comment	*comment text*	HTML comment	6+	1+	4+
Document	9	#document	Null	Root document object	6+	1+	1+
DocumentType	10	DOCTYPE	Null	DTD specification	No	1+	4+
Fragment	11	#document-fragment	Null	Series of one or more nodes outside the document	6+	1+	1+

Node properties
A node has many properties, most of which are references to other nodes related to the current node. Table 25-3 lists all properties shared by all node types in DOM Level 2.

Note
You can find all the properties shown in Table 25-3, that also show themselves to be implemented in Internet Explorer 6+ or Moz1+, in Chapter 26, in the listing of properties that all HTML element objects have in common. That's because an HTML element, as a type of node, inherits all of the properties of the prototypical node. ■

TABLE 25-3

Node Object Properties (W3C DOM Level 2)

Property	Value	Description	IE6Win+	IE5Mac+	Moz1	Safari1
nodeName	String	Varies with node type (see Table 25-2)	Yes	Yes	Yes	Yes
nodeValue	String	Varies with node type (see Table 25-2)	Yes	Yes	Yes	Yes
nodeType	Integer	Constant representing each type	Yes	Yes	Yes	Yes
parentNode	Object	Reference to next outermost container	Yes	Yes	Yes	Yes
childNodes	Array	All child nodes in source order	Yes	Yes	Yes	Yes
firstChild	Object	Reference to first child node	Yes	Yes	Yes	Yes
lastChild	Object	Reference to last child node	Yes	Yes	Yes	Yes
previous Sibling	Object	Reference to sibling node up in source order	Yes	Yes	Yes	Yes
nextSibling	Object	Reference to sibling node next in source order	Yes	Yes	Yes	Yes
attributes	NodeMap	Array of attribute nodes	Yes	Some	Yes	Yes
ownerDocument	Object	Containing document object	Yes	Yes	Yes	Yes
namespaceURI	String	URI to namespace definition (element and attribute nodes only)	Yes	No	Yes	Yes
Prefix	String	Namespace prefix (element and attribute nodes only)	Yes	No	Yes	Yes
localName	String	Applicable to namespace-affected nodes	Yes	No	Yes	Yes

To help you see the meanings of the key node properties, Table 25-4 shows the property values of several nodes in the simple page shown in Listing 25-1. For each node column, find the node in Figure 25-3, and then follow the list of property values for that node, comparing the values against the actual node structure in Figure 25-3.

TABLE 25-4

Properties of Selected Nodes for a Simple HTML Document

Properties	Nodes			
	document	html	p	"one and only"
nodeType	9	1	1	3
nodeName	#document	html	p	#text
nodeValue	Null	null	null	"one and only"
parentNode	Null	document	body	em
previousSibling	Null	null	null	null
nextSibling	Null	null	null	null
childNodes	Html	head body	"This is the" em "paragraph on the page."	(none)
firstChild	Html	head	"This is the"	null
lastChild	Html	body	"paragraph on the page."	null

The nodeType property is an integer that is helpful in scripts that iterate through an unknown collection of nodes. Most content in an HTML document is of type 1 (an HTML element) or 3 (a text node), with the outermost container, the document, of type 9. A node's nodeName property is either the name of the node's tag (for an HTML element) or a constant value (preceded by a # [hash mark], as shown in Table 25-2). And, while it may surprise some, the nodeValue property is null except for the text node type, in which case the value is the actual string of text of the node. In other words, for HTML elements, the W3C DOM does not expose a container's HTML as a string.

The Object-Oriented W3C DOM

If you are familiar with concepts of object-oriented (OO) programming, you will appreciate the OO tendencies in the way the W3C defines the DOM. The Node object includes sets of properties (see Table 25-3) and methods (see Table 25-5) that are inherited by every object based on the Node. Most of the objects that inherit the Node's behavior have their own properties and/or methods that define their specific behaviors. Figure 25-4 shows (in W3C DOM terminology) the inheritance tree from the Node root object. Most items are defined in the Core DOM, whereas items shown in boldface are from the HTML DOM portion.

continued

continued

FIGURE 25-4

W3C DOM Node object inheritance tree.

```
Node
+--Document
|   +--HTMLDocument
+--CharacterData
|   +--Text
|   |   +--CDATASection
|   +--Comment
+--Attr
+--Element
|   +--HTMLElement
|       +-- (Each specific HTML element)
+--DocumentType
+--DocumentFragment
+--Notation
+--Entity
+--Entity Reference
+--ProcessingInstruction
```

You can see from the preceding figure that individual HTML elements inherit properties and methods from the generic HTML element, which inherits from the Core `Element` object, which in turn inherits from the basic `Node`.

It isn't important to know the `Node` object inheritance to script the DOM. But it does help in understanding the ECMA Script Language Binding appendix of the W3C DOM recommendation, as well as how a simple element object winds up with so many properties and methods associated with it.

It is doubtful that you will use all of the relationship-oriented properties of a node, primarily because there is some overlap in how you can reach a particular node from any other. The `parentNode` property is important because it is a reference to the current node's immediate container. Although the `firstChild` and `lastChild` properties point directly to the first and last children inside a container, most scripts generally use the `childNodes` property with array notation inside a `for` loop to iterate through child nodes. If there are no child nodes, the `childNodes` array has a length of zero.

Node methods

Actions that modify the HTML content of a node in the W3C DOM world primarily involve the methods defined for the prototype `Node`. Table 25-5 shows the methods and their support in the W3C DOM–capable browsers.

The important methods for modifying content are `appendChild()`, `insertBefore()`, `removeChild()`, and `replaceChild()`. Note, however, that all of these methods assume that the point of view for the action is from the parent of the nodes being affected by the methods.

For example, to delete an element (using `removeChild()`), you don't invoke that method on the element being removed, but on its parent element. This leaves open the possibility of creating a library of utility functions that obviate having to know too much about the precise containment hierarchy of an element. A simple function that lets a script appear to delete an element actually does so from its parent:

```
function removeElement(elemID)
{
    var elem = document.getElementById(elemID);
    elem.parentNode.removeChild(elem);
}
```

TABLE 25-5

Node Object Methods (W3C DOM Level 2)

Method	Description	IE5+	Moz1	Safari 1
appendChild(newChild)	Adds child node to end of current node	Yes	Yes	Yes
cloneNode(deep)	Grabs a copy of the current node (optionally with children)	Yes	Yes	Yes
hasChildNodes()	Determines whether current node has children (Boolean)	Yes	Yes	Yes
insertBefore(new, ref)	Inserts new child in front of another child	Yes	Yes	Yes
removeChild(old)	Deletes one child	Yes	Yes	Yes
replaceChild(new, old)	Replaces an old child with a new one	Yes	Yes	Yes
isSupported(feature, version)	Determines whether the node supports a particular feature	No	Yes	Yes

If this seems like a long way to go to accomplish the same result as setting the `outerHTML` property of an Internet Explorer 4 or later object to empty, you are right. Although some of this convolution makes sense for XML, the W3C working group doesn't seem to have HTML scripters' best interests in mind, unfortunately. All is not lost, however, as you see later in this chapter.

Generating new node content

The final point about the node structure of the W3C DOM focuses on the similarly gnarled way scripters must go about generating content that they want to add or replace on a page. For text-only changes (for example, the text inside a table cell), there is both an easy and a hard way to perform the task. For HTML changes, there is only the hard way (plus a handy workaround discussed later). Let's look at the hard way first and then pick up the easy way for text changes.

To generate a new node in the DOM, you look to the variety of methods that are defined for the Core DOM's document object (and are therefore inherited by the HTML document object). A node creation method is defined for nearly every node type in the DOM. The two important ones for HTML documents are createElement() and createTextNode(). The first generates an element with whatever tag name (string) you pass as a parameter; the second generates a text node with whatever text you pass.

When you first create a new element, it exists only in the browser's memory and not as part of the document containment hierarchy. Moreover, the result of the createElement() method is a reference to an empty element, except for the name of the tag. For example, to create a new p element, use

```
var newElem = document.createElement("p");
```

The new element has no ID, attributes, or any content. To assign some attributes to this element, you can use the setAttribute() method (a method of every element object) or assign a value to the object's corresponding property. For example, to assign an identifier to the new element, use either

```
newElem.setAttribute("id", "newP");
```

or

```
newElem.id = "newP";
```

Both ways are perfectly legal. Even though the element has an ID at this point, it is not yet part of the document, so you cannot retrieve it via the document.getElementById() method.

To add some content to the paragraph, you next generate a text node as a separate object:

```
var newText = document.createTextNode("This is the second paragraph.");
```

Again, this node is just sitting around in memory waiting for you to apply it as a child of some other node. To make this text the content of the new paragraph, you can append the node as a child of the paragraph element that is still in memory:

```
newElem.appendChild(newText);
```

If you were able to inspect the HTML that represents the new paragraph element, it would look like the following:

```
<p id="newP">This is the second paragraph.</p>
```

The new paragraph element is ready for insertion into a document. Using the document shown in Listing 25-1, you can append it as a child of the body element:

```
document.body.appendChild(newElem);
```

At last, the new element is part of the document containment hierarchy. Now you can reference it just like any other element in the document.

Replacing node content

The addition of the paragraph shown in the last section requires a change to a portion of the text in the original paragraph (since the first paragraph is no longer the one and only paragraph on the page). As mentioned earlier, you can perform text changes via the `replaceChild()` method or by assigning new text to a text node's `nodeValue` property. Let's see how each approach works to change the text of the first paragraph's `em` element from one and only to first.

To use `replaceChild()`, a script first must generate a valid text node with the new text:

```
var newText = document.createTextNode("first");
```

The next step is to use the `replaceChild()` method. But recall that the point of view for this method is the parent of the child being replaced. The child here is the text node inside the `em` element, so you must invoke the `replaceChild()` method on the `em` element. Also, the `replaceChild()` method requires two parameters. The first parameter is the new node; the second is a reference to the node to be replaced. Because the script statements get pretty long with the `getElementById()` method, an intermediate step grabs a reference to the text node inside the `em` element:

```
var oldChild = document.getElementById("emphasis1").childNodes[0];
```

Now the script is ready to invoke the `replaceChild()` method on the `em` element, swapping the old text node with the new:

```
document.getElementById("emphasis1").replaceChild(newText, oldChild);
```

If you want to capture the old node before it disappears, be aware that the `replaceChild()` method returns a reference to the replaced node (which is only in memory at this point and not part of the document node hierarchy). You can assign the method statement to a variable and use that old node somewhere else, if needed.

This may seem like a long way to go; it is, especially if the HTML you are generating is complex. Fortunately, you can take a simpler approach for replacing text nodes. All it requires is a reference to the text node being replaced. You can assign that node's `nodeValue` property its new string value:

```
document.getElementById("emphasis1").childNodes[0].nodeValue = "first";
```

When an element's content is entirely text (for example, a table cell that already has a text node in it), this is the most streamlined way to swap text on the fly using W3C DOM syntax. This doesn't work for the creation of the second paragraph text earlier in this chapter because the text node did not exist yet. The `createTextNode()` method had to create it explicitly.

Also remember that a text node does not have any inherent style associated with it. The style of the containing HTML element governs the style of the text. If you want to change not only the text node's text, but also how it looks, you have to modify the `style` property of the text node's parent element. Browsers that perform these kinds of content swaps and style changes automatically reflow the page to accommodate changes in the size of the content.

To summarize, Listing 25-2 is a live version of the modifications made to the original document shown in Listing 25-1. The new version includes a button and a script that makes the changes described throughout this discussion of nodes. Reload the page to start over.

LISTING 25-2

Adding/Replacing DOM Content

```html
<html>
<head>
   <title>A Simple Page</title>
   <script type="text/javascript">
   function modify()
   {
      var newElem = document.createElement("p");
      newElem.id = "newP";
      var newText = document.createTextNode("This is the second paragraph.");
      newElem.appendChild(newText);
      document.body.appendChild(newElem);
      document.getElementById("emphasis1").childNodes[0].nodeValue = "first";
   }
   </script>
</head>

<body>
   <button onclick="modify()">Add/Replace Text</button>

   <p id="paragraph1">This is the <em id="emphasis1">one and
   only</em> paragraph on the page.</p>
</body>
</html>
```

Cross-Reference

Chapter 26 details node properties and methods that are inherited by all HTML elements. Most are implemented in all modern W3C DOM browsers. Also look to the reference material for the document object in Chapter 29 for other valuable W3C DOM methods. ∎

A de facto standard: innerHTML

Microsoft was the first to implement the innerHTML property of all element objects starting with Internet Explorer 4. Although the W3C DOM has not supported this property, scripters frequently find it more convenient to modify content dynamically by way of a string containing HTML markup than by creating and assembling element and text nodes. As a result, most modern W3C DOM browsers, including Moz1 and Safari 1, support the read/write innerHTML property of all element objects as a de facto standard.

When you assign a string containing HTML markup to the innerHTML of an existing element, the browser automatically inserts the newly rendered elements into the document node tree. You may also use innerHTML with unmarked text to perform the equivalent of the Internet Explorer–only innerText property.

Despite the apparent convenience of the innerHTML property compared with the step-by-step process of manipulating element and text node objects, browsers operate on nodes much more efficiently than on assembly of long strings. This is one case where less JavaScript code does not necessarily translate to greater efficiency.

Static W3C DOM HTML objects

The Moz1+ DOM (but unfortunately, not Internet Explorer 5 or later) adheres to the core JavaScript notion of prototype inheritance with respect to the object model. When a page loads into a Moz1+ browser, the browser creates HTML objects based on the prototypes of each object defined by the W3C DOM. For example, if you use The Evaluator Sr. (discussed in Chapter 4, "JavaScript Essentials") to see what kind of object the myP paragraph object is — enter docu-ment.getElementById("myP") in the top text box and click the Evaluate button — it reports that the object is based on the HTMLParagraphElement object of the DOM. Every instance of a p element object in the page inherits its default properties and methods from HTMLParagraphEle-ment (which in turn inherits from HTMLElement, Element, and Node objects — all detailed in the JavaScript binding appendix of the W3C DOM specification).

You can use scripting to add properties to the prototypes of some of these static objects. To do so, you must use new features added to Moz1+ that are a part of JavaScript 1.5 and ECMAScript 5. Two new methods, __defineGetter__() and __defineSetter__(), enable you to assign functions to a custom property of an object.

Note

These methods are Mozilla specific. To prevent their collision with standardized implementations of these features in ECMAScript, the underscore characters on either side of the method name are pairs of underscore characters. ∎

The functions execute whenever the property is read (the function assigned via the __defineGetter__() method) or modified (the function assigned through the __defineSetter__() method). The common way to define these functions is in the form of an anonymous function (see Chapter 23). The formats for the two statements that assign these behaviors to an object prototype are as follows:

```
object.prototype.__defineGetter__("propName",
    function([param1[,...[,paramN]]]) {
  // statements
  return returnValue;
})
object.prototype.__defineSetter__("propName",
    function([param1[,...[,paramN]]]) {
  // statements
  return returnValue;
})
```

The example in Listing 25-3 demonstrates how to add a read-only property to every HTML element object in the current document. The property, called childNodeDetail, returns an object. The object has two properties: one for the number of element child nodes and one for the number of text child nodes. Note that the this keyword in the function definition is a reference to the object for which the property is calculated. And because the function runs each time a script statement reads the property, any scripted changes to the content after the page loads are reflected in the returned property value.

LISTING 25-3

Adding a Read-Only Prototype Property to All HTML Element Objects

```
<script type="text/javascript">
if (HTMLElement)
{
   HTMLElement.prototype.__defineGetter__("childNodeDetail", function()
   {
      var result = {elementNodes:0, textNodes:0 }
      for (var i = 0; i < this.childNodes.length; i++)
      {
         switch (this.childNodes[i].nodeType)
         {
            case 1:
               result.elementNodes++;
               break;
            case 3:
               result.textNodes++;
               break;
         }
      }
      return result;
   })
}
</script>
```

To access the property, use it like any other property of the object. For example:

```
var BodyNodeDetail = document.body.childNodeDetail;
```

The returned value in this example is an object, so you use regular JavaScript syntax to access one of the property values:

```
var BodyElemNodesCount = document.body.childNodeDetail.elementNodes;
```

Bidirectional event model

Despite the seemingly conflicting event models of NN4 (trickle down) and IE4 (bubble up), the W3C DOM event model (defined in Level 2) manages to employ both event propagation models. This gives the scripter the choice of where along an event's propagation path the event gets processed. To prevent conflicts with existing event model terminology, the W3C model invents many new terms for properties and new methods for events. Some coding probably requires W3C DOM–specific handling in a page aimed at multiple object models.

The W3C event model also introduces a new concept called the event listener. An *event listener* is essentially a mechanism that instructs an object to respond to a particular kind of event — very much like the way the event handler attributes of HTML tags respond to events. But the DOM recommendation points out that it prefers a more script-oriented way of assigning event listeners: the addEventListener() method available for every node in the document hierarchy. Through this method, you advise the browser whether to force an event to bubble up the hierarchy (the default behavior that is also in effect if you use the HTML attribute type of event handler) or to be captured at a higher level.

Functions invoked by the event listener receive a single parameter consisting of the event object whose properties contain contextual details about the event (details such as the position of a mouse click, character code of a keyboard key, or a reference to the target object). For example, if a form includes a button whose job is to invoke a calculation function, the W3C DOM prefers the following way of assigning the event handler:

```
document.getElementById("calcButton").addEventListener("click",
doCalc, false);
```

The addEventListener() method takes three parameters. The first parameter is a string of the event to listen for; the second is a reference to the function to be invoked when that event fires; and the third parameter is a Boolean value. When you set this Boolean value to true, it turns on event capture whenever this event is directed to this target. The function then takes its cue from the event object passed as the parameter:

```
function doCalc(evt)
{
    // get shortcut reference to input button's form
    var form = evt.target.form;
    var results = 0;
    // other statements to do the calculation //
    form.result.value = results;
}
```

To modify an event listener, you use the removeEventListener() method to get rid of the old listener, and then employ addEventListener() with different parameters to assign the new one.

Preventing an event from performing its default action is also a different procedure in the W3C event model than in Internet Explorer. In Internet Explorer 4 (as well as Navigator 3 and 4), you can cancel the default action by allowing the event handler to evaluate to return false. Although this still works in Internet Explorer 5 and later, Microsoft includes another property of the window.event object, called returnValue. Setting that property to false anywhere in the function invoked by the event handler also kills the event before it does its normal job. But the W3C event model uses a method of the event object, preventDefault(), to keep the event from its normal task. You can invoke this method anywhere in the function that executes when the event fires.

Detailed information about an event is contained in an event object that must be passed to an event handler function where details may be read. If you assign event handlers via the W3C DOM addEventListener() method or an event handler property, the event object is passed automatically as the sole parameter to the event handler function. Include a parameter variable to catch the incoming parameter:

```
function swap(evt)
{
    // statements here to work with W3C DOM event object
}
```

But if you assign events through a tag attribute, you must explicitly pass the event object in the call to the function:

```
<a href="http://www.example.com" onmouseover="swap(event)">
```

Unfortunately, as of Internet Explorer 8 for Windows and Internet Explorer 5 for Macintosh, the W3C DOM event model has yet to be supported by Microsoft. You can, however, make the Internet Explorer and W3C event models work together if you assign event handlers by way of object properties or tag attributes, and throw in a little object detection as described later in this chapter, and in more detail in Chapter 32.

Scripting Trends

Although browser scripting had humble beginnings as a way to put some intelligence into form controls, the capabilities of the JavaScript language and DOM have inspired many a web developer to create what are essentially applications. Popular implementations of web-based email systems use extensive scripting and background communication with the server to keep pages updated quickly without the need to fetch and re-render the complete page each time you delete a message from the inbox list. It's not uncommon for large projects to involve multiple scripters (along with specialists in CSS, server programming, artists, and writers). Wrangling all the code can be a chore.

Separating content from scripting

Those who use CSS to style their sites have learned that separating style definitions from the HTML markup makes a huge improvement in productivity when it comes time to change colors or font specifications throughout a site. Instead of having to modify hundreds of `<font>` tag specifications scattered around the site, all it takes is a simple tweak of a single CSS rule in one `.css` file for that change to be implemented immediately across the board.

The notion of using HTML purely for a page's structure has also impacted scripting. It is rare these days for a professional scripter to put an event handler attribute inside an HTML tag. That would be considered too much mixing of content with behavior. In other words, the HTML markup should be able to stand on its own so that those with nonscriptable browsers (including those with vision or motor disabilities who use specialized browsers) can still get the fundamental information provided by the page. Any scripting that impacts the display or behavior of the page is added to the page after the HTML markup has loaded and rendered. Even assigning events to elements is done by script after the page load.

Script code is more commonly linked into a page from an external `.js` file. This isn't part of the separation of content and scripts trend, but a practice that offers many benefits, such as the same code being instantly usable on multiple pages. Additionally, when projects involve many code chefs, scripters can work on their code while writers work on the HTML and designers work on their external CSS code.

Note
You will see lots of examples in this book that use event handler attributes inside tags, and scripts embedded within the page. This approach is used primarily for simplicity in demonstrating a language or DOM feature. ■

Using the W3C DOM where possible

Basic support for W3C DOM element referencing and content manipulation has been implemented in mainstream browsers for so long that you can be assured that composing scripts for that model will work for the bulk of your visitors. That's not to say you can assume that every visitor is equipped that way, but the hassles that scripters used to endure to support conflicting object models are behind us for the most part. The days of writing extensive branching code for IE and Netscape are not-so-fond memories.

You still want to use object detection techniques to guard against the occasional old browser that stops by. That's where the technique of assigning event handlers by scripts can save a lot of headaches.

Except for some initializations that might occur while the page loads, most script execution in a web page occurs at the instigation of an event: A user clicks a button, types something in a text box, chooses from a select element, and so on. You can prevent older browsers from tripping up on W3C DOM syntax by doing your fundamental object detection right in the event assignment code, as in the following simplified example:

```
function setUpEvents()
{
    if (document.getElementById)
    {
        // statements to bind events to elements
    }
}
window.onload = setUpEvents;
```

Now, browsers that don't have even minimum support for the W3C DOM won't generate script errors when users click or type, because those events won't be assigned for those browsers. Then scripts that survive your object detection query can also modify the page, as you saw in Listing 4-2 in Chapter 4.

Handling events

You will still find some places where the W3C DOM isn't enough. This is particularly true in processing events, where Internet Explorer (at least through version 8) does not support the W3C DOM way of getting details about an event to the event handler function. The W3C DOM automatically passes the event object as a parameter to a handler function. In the Internet Explorer model, the event object is a property of the window object. Therefore, your functions have to equalize the differences where necessary. For example, to obtain a single variable representing the event object, regardless of browser, you can use a construction similar to the following:

```
function calculate(evt)
{
    evt = (evt) ? evt : window.event;
    // more statements to process event
}
```

Additional branching is necessary to inspect important details of the event. For example, the Internet Explorer event object property pointing to the object that received the event is called srcElement, whereas the W3C DOM version is called target. Again, a little bit of equalizing code in the event handler function can handle the disparity. When your script has a reference to the element receiving the event, you can start using W3C DOM properties and methods of the element, because Internet Explorer supports those. You can find more details on event objects in Chapter 32.

Standards Compatibility Modes (DOCTYPE Switching)

Both Microsoft and Netscape/Mozilla discovered that they had, over time, implemented CSS features in ways that ultimately differed from the published standards that came later (usually after much wrangling among working-group members). To compensate for these differences and make a clean break to be compatible with the standards, the major browser makers decided to let the page author's choice of <!DOCTYPE> header element details determine whether the document was designed to follow the old way (sometimes called *quirks mode*) or the standards-compatible way. The tactic, known informally as *DOCTYPE switching,* is implemented in Internet Explorer 6 and later, Internet Explorer 5 for the Mac, all Mozilla-based browsers, and all WebKit-based browsers.

Although most of the differences between the two modes are small, there are some significant differences between the two modes in Internet Explorer 6 and later, particularly when styles or DHTML scripts rely on elements designed with borders, margins, and padding. Microsoft's original box model measured the dimensions of elements in a way that differed from the eventual CSS standard.

To place the affected browsers in CSS standards–compatible mode, you should include a <!DOC-TYPE> element at the top of every document that specifies any of the following details (the first <!DOCTYPE> statement is for HTML5):

```
<!DOCTYPE html>

<!DOCTYPE HTML PUBLIC "-//W3C//DTD HTML 4.0 Transitional//EN"
        "http://www.w3.org/TR/REC-html40/loose.dtd">

<!DOCTYPE HTML PUBLIC "-//W3C//DTD HTML 4.0 Frameset//EN"
        "http://www.w3.org/TR/REC-html40/frameset.dtd">

<!DOCTYPE HTML PUBLIC "-//W3C//DTD HTML 4.0//EN"
        "http://www.w3.org/TR/REC-html40/strict.dtd">

<!DOCTYPE html PUBLIC "-//W3C//DTD XHTML 1.0 Transitional//EN"
        "http://www.w3.org/TR/xhtml1/DTD/xhtml1-transitional.dtd">

<!DOCTYPE html PUBLIC "-//W3C//DTD XHTML 1.0 Frameset//EN"
        "http://www.w3.org/TR/xhtml1/DTD/xhtml1-frameset.dtd">

<!DOCTYPE html PUBLIC "-//W3C//DTD XHTML 1.0 Strict//EN"
        "http://www.w3.org/TR/xhtml1/DTD/xhtml1-strict.dtd">

<!DOCTYPE html PUBLIC "-//W3C//DTD XHTML 1.1//EN"
        "http://www.w3.org/TR/xhtml11/DTD/xhtml11.dtd">
```

Be aware, however, that older versions of Internet Explorer for Windows, such as Internet Explorer 5 or Internet Explorer 5.5, are ignorant of the standards-compatible mode and will use the old Microsoft quirks mode regardless of the `<!DOCTYPE>` setting. But using a standards-compliant mode DOCTYPE is more likely to force your content and style sheets to render similarly across the latest browsers.

Where to Go from Here

These past two chapters provided an overview of the core language and object model issues that anyone designing pages that use JavaScript must confront. The goal here is to stimulate your own thinking about how to embrace or discard levels of compatibility with your pages as you balance your desire to generate cool pages and serve your audience. From here on, the difficult choices are up to you.

To help you choose the objects, properties, methods, and event handlers that best suit your requirements, all the chapters in Part III and the rest of Part IV provide in-depth references to the DOM and core JavaScript language features. Observe the compatibility ratings for each language term very carefully to help you determine which features best suit your audience's browsers. Most example listings are complete HTML pages that you can load in various browsers to see how they work. Many others invite you to explore how things work through The Evaluator Sr. (see Chapter 4). Play around with the files, making modifications to build your own applications or expanding your working knowledge of JavaScript in the browser environment.

The language and object models have grown in the handful of years they have been in existence. The amount of language vocabulary has increased astronomically. It takes time to drink it all in and feel comfortable that you are aware of the powers available to you. Don't worry about memorizing the vocabulary. It's more important to acquaint yourself with the features and come back later when you need the implementation details.

Be patient. Be persistent. The reward will come.

Generic HTML Element Objects

IN THIS CHAPTER

Working with HTML element objects

Common properties and methods

Event handlers of all element objects

The object model specifications implemented in Internet Explorer 4+ and W3C (Mozilla-based and WebKit-based) browsers feature a large set of scriptable objects that represent what we often call *generic* HTML elements. Generic elements can be divided into two groups. One group, such as the `band strike` elements, defines font styles to be applied to enclosed sequences of text. The need for these elements (and the objects that represent them) is all but gone due to more page designers using style sheets. The second group of elements assigns context to content within their start and end tags. Examples of contextual elements include `h1`, `blockquote`, and the ubiquitous p element. Although browsers sometimes have consistent visual ways of rendering contextual elements by default (for example, the large bold font of an `<h1>` tag), the specific rendering is not the intended purpose of the tags. No formal standard dictates that text within an `em` element must be italicized: The style simply has become the custom since the very early days of browsers.

All of these generic elements share a large number of scriptable properties, methods, and event handlers. The sharing extends not only among generic elements, but also among virtually every renderable element — even if it has additional, element-specific properties, methods, and/or event handlers that we cover in depth in other chapters of this reference. Rather than repeat the details of these shared properties, methods, and event handlers for each object throughout this reference, we describe them in detail only in this chapter (unless there is a special behavior, bug, or trick associated with the item in some object described elsewhere). In succeeding reference chapters, each object description includes a list of the object's properties, methods, and event handlers, but we do not list shared items over and over (making it hard to find items that are unique to a particular element). Instead, you see a pointer back to this chapter for the items in common with generic HTML element objects.

Generic Objects

Table 26-1 lists all of the objects that we treat in this reference as *generic* objects. All of these objects share the properties, methods, and event handlers described in succeeding sections and have no special items that require additional coverage elsewhere in this book.

elementObject

TABLE 26-1

Generic HTML Element Objects

Formatting Objects	Contextual Objects
b	acronym
big	address
center	cite
i	code
nobr	dfn
rt	del
ruby	div
s	em
small	ins
strike	kbd
sub	listing
sup	p
tt	plaintext
u	pre
wbr	samp
	span
	strong
	var
	xmp

Properties	Methods	Event Handlers
accessKey	addBehavior()	onactivate
all[]	addEventListener()	onafterupdate
attributes[]	appendChild()	onbeforecopy
baseURI	applyElement()	onbeforecut
behaviorUrns[]	attachEvent()	onbeforedeactivate
canHaveChildren	blur()	onbeforeeditfocus
canHaveHTML	clearAttributes()	onbeforepaste

elementObject

Properties	Methods	Event Handlers
childNodes[]	click()	onbeforeupdate
children	cloneNode()	onblur
cite	compareDocumentPosition()	oncellchange
className	componentFromPoint()	onclick
clientHeight	contains()	oncontextmenu
clientLeft	createControlRange()	oncontrolselect
clientTop	detachEvent()	oncopy
clientWidth	dispatchEvent()	oncut
contentEditable	doScroll()	ondataavailable
currentStyle	dragDrop()	ondatasetchanged
dateTime	fireEvent()	ondatasetcomplete
dataFld	focus()	ondblclick
dataFormatAs	getAdjacentText()	ondeactivate
dataSrc	getAttribute()	ondrag
dir	getAttributeNode()	ondragend
disabled	getAttributeNodeNS()	ondragenter
document	getAttributeNS()	ondragleave
filters[]	getBoundingClientRect()	ondragover
firstChild	getClientRects()	ondragstart
height	getElementsByTagName()	ondrop
hideFocus	getElementsByTagNameNS()	onerrorupdate
id	getExpression()	onfilterchange
innerHTML	getFeature()	onfocus
innerText	getUserData()	onfocusin
isContentEditable	hasAttribute()	onfocusout
isDisabled	hasAttributeNS()	onhelp
isMultiLine	hasAttributes()	onkeydown
isTextEdit	hasChildNodes()	onkeypress

continued

TABLE 26-1 *(continued)*

Properties	Methods	Event Handlers
lang	insertAdjacentElement()	onkeyup
language	insertAdjacentHTML()	onlayoutcomplete
lastChild	insertAdjacentText()	onlosecapture
length	insertBefore()	onmousedown
localName	isDefaultNamespace()	onmouseenter
namespaceURI	isEqualNode()	onmouseleave
nextSibling	isSameNode()	onmousemove
nodeName	isSupported()	onmouseout
nodeType	item()	onmouseover
nodeValue	lookupNamespaceURI()	onmouseup
offsetHeight	lookupPrefix()	onmousewheel
offsetLeft	mergeAttributes()	onmove
offsetParent	normalize()	onmoveend
offsetTop	releaseCapture()	onmovestart
offsetWidth	removeAttribute()	onpaste
outerHTML	removeAttributeNode()	onpropertychange
outerText	removeAttributeNS()	onreadystatechange
ownerDocument	removeBehavior()	onresize
parentElement	removeChild()	onresizeend
parentNode	removeEventListener()	onresizestart
parentTextEdit	removeExpression()	onrowenter
prefix	removeNode()	onrowexit
previousSibling	replaceAdjacentText()	onrowsdelete
readyState	replaceChild()	onrowsinserted
recordNumber	replaceNode()	onscroll
runtimeStyle	scrollIntoView()	onselectstart
scopeName	setActive()	
scrollHeight	setAttribute()	
scrollLeft	setAttributeNode()	

Properties	Methods	Event Handlers
scrollTop	setAttributeNodeNS()	
scrollWidth	setAttributeNS()	
sourceIndex	setCapture()	
style	setExpression()	
tabIndex	setUserData()	
tagName	swapNode()	
tagUrn	tags()	
textContent	toString()	
title	urns()	
uniqueID		
unselectable		
width		

Syntax

To access element properties or methods, use this:

```
(IE4+)    [document.all.]objectID.property | method([parameters])
(IE5+/W3C) document.getElementById(objectID).property | method([parameters])
```

Note

It's important to note that unless you have the specific need of supporting IE4, which is highly unlikely at this point in time, you should rely solely on the latter approach of referencing element properties and methods via the getElementById() method. ■

About these objects

All objects listed in Table 26-1 are document object model (DOM) representations of HTML elements that influence either the font style or the context of some HTML content. The large set of properties, methods, and event handlers associated with these objects also applies to virtually every other DOM object that represents an HTML element. Discussions about object details in this chapter apply to dozens of other objects described in succeeding chapters of this reference section.

Properties
accessKey

Value: One-character string   Read/Write

Compatibility: WinIE4+, MacIE4+, NN7+, Moz-, Safari+, Opera+, Chrome+

elementObject.accessKey

For many elements, you can specify a keyboard character (letter, numeral, or punctuation symbol) that — when typed as an Alt+key combination (on the Win32 OS platform), a Ctrl+key combination (on the MacOS), or a Shift+Esc+key combination (on Opera) — brings focus to that element. An element that has focus is the one that is set to respond to keyboard activity. If the newly focused element is out of view in the document's current scroll position, the document is scrolled to bring that focused element into view (also see the `scrollIntoView()` method). The character you specify can be an uppercase or lowercase value, but these values are not case sensitive. If you assign the same letter to more than one element, the user can cycle through all elements associated with that `accessKey` value.

Internet Explorer gives some added powers to the `accessKey` property in some cases. For example, if you assign an `accessKey` value to a `label` element object, the focus is handed to the form element associated with that label. Also, when elements such as buttons have focus, pressing the spacebar acts the same as clicking the element with a mouse.

Exercise some judgment in selecting characters for `accessKey` values. If you assign a letter that is normally used to access one of the browser's built-in menus (for example, Alt+F for the File menu in IE), that `accessKey` setting overrides the browser's normal behavior. To users who rely on keyboard access to menus, your control over that key combination can be disconcerting. In other browsers your `accessKey` assignment will not override the browser's normal behavior.

Example

Listing 26-1 shows an example of how to use the `accessKey` property to manipulate the keyboard interface for navigating a web page. When you load the script in Listing 26-1, adjust the height of the browser window so that you can see nothing below the second dividing rule. Enter any character in the Settings portion of the page and press Enter. (The Enter key may cause your computer to beep.) Pressing the Enter key does not do anything visible in your browser; it just assigns the character you entered into the textbox to the appropriate element. Then hold down the Alt (Windows) or Ctrl (Mac) key (or Shift+Esc keys in Opera) while pressing the same keyboard key. The element from below the second divider should come into view.

Note

The property assignment event handling technique employed throughout the code in this chapter and much of the book is a deliberate simplification to make the code more readable. It is generally better to use the more modern approach of binding events using the `addEventListener()` **(NN6+/Moz/W3C) or** `attachEvent()` **(IE5+) method. A modern cross-browser event handling technique is explained in detail in Chapter 32.** ∎

LISTING 26-1

Controlling the accessKey Property

```
HTML: jsb26-01.html
<!DOCTYPE html>
<html>
  <head>
    <meta http-equiv="content-type" content="text/html;charset=utf-8">
    <title>accessKey Property</title>
```

```
    <script type="text/javascript" src="../jsb-global.js"></script>
    <script type="text/javascript" src="jsb26-01.js"></script>
  </head>
  <body>
    <h1>accessKey Property Lab</h1>
    <hr />
    Settings:<br />
    <form name="input">
      Assign an accessKey value to the Button below and press Return:
      <input type="text" size="2" maxlength="1"
          onkeypress="assignKey('button', this)" />
      <br />
      Assign an accessKey value to the Text Box below and press Return:
      <input type="text" size="2" maxlength="1"
          onkeypress="return assignKey('text', this)" />
      <br />
      Assign an accessKey value to the Table below (IE5.5+ only)
      and press Return:
      <input type="text" size="2" maxlength="1"
          onkeypress="return assignKey('table', this)" />
    </form>
    <br />
    Then press Alt (Windows) or Control (Mac) or ShiftESC (Opera) + the key
    <br />
    <em>Size the browser window to view nothing lower than this line.</em>
    <hr />
    <form name="output" onsubmit="return false">
      <input type="button" id="access1" value="Standard Button" />
      <input type="text" id="access2" />
    </form>
    <table id="myTable" cellpadding="10" border="2">
      <tr>
        <th>Quantity</th>
        <th>Description</th>
        <th>Price</th>
      </tr>
      <tbody bgcolor="red">
        <tr>
          <td width="100">4</td>
          <td>Primary Widget</td>
          <td>$14.96</td>
        </tr>
        <tr>
          <td>10</td>
          <td>Secondary Widget</td>
          <td>$114.96</td>
        </tr>
      </tbody>
    </table>
  </body>
</html>
```

continued

elementObject.all[]

LISTING 26-1   *(continued)*

JavaScript: jsb26-01.js

```javascript
function assignKey(type, elem)
{
    if (window.event)          // IE, Opera, Safari, Chrome
    {
        if (window.event.keyCode == 13)
        {
            switch (type)
            {
                case "button":
                    document.getElementById("access1").accessKey = elem.value;
                    break;
                case "text":
                    document.getElementById("access2").accessKey = elem.value;
                    break;
                case "table":
                    document.getElementById("myTable").accessKey = elem.value;
            }
            return false;
        }
    }
}
```

Related Item: scrollIntoView() method

all[]

Value: Array of nested element objects   Read-Only

Compatibility: WinIE4+, MacIE4+, NN-, Moz-, Safari+ (partial), Opera+, Chrome+ (partial)

Originally exclusive to Internet Explorer, the all property is a collection (array) of every HTML element and (in IE5+) XML tag within the scope of the current object. Opera now supports it fully, while WebKit-based browsers (such as Safari and Chome) support it only as a property of the document object. Even so, you should strongly consider using the document.getElementById() method (as described in Chapter 29), which is the official W3C and cross-browser approach for referencing elements. The document.getElementById() method is supported in IE5+.

Items in this array appear in source-code order, and the array is oblivious to element containment among the items. For HTML element containers, the source-code order is dependent on the position of the start tag for the element; end tags are not counted. But for XML tags, end tags appear as separate entries in the array.

Every document.all collection contains objects for the html, head, title, and body element objects even if the actual HTML source code omits the tags. The object model creates these objects for every document that is loaded into a window or frame. Although the document.all reference may be the most common usage, the all property is available for any container element. For example, document.forms[0].all exposes all elements defined within the first form of a page.

You can access any element that has an identifier assigned to its id attribute by that identifier in string form (as well as by index integer). Rather than use the performance-costly eval() function to convert a string to an object reference, use the string value of the name as an array index value:

```
var paragraph = document.all["myP"];
```

Internet Explorer enables you to use either square brackets or parentheses for single collection index values. Thus, the following two examples evaluate identically:

```
var paragraph = document.all["myP"];
var paragraph = document.all("myP");
```

In the rare case that two or more elements within the all collection have the same ID, the syntax for the string index value returns a collection of just those identically named elements. But you can use a second argument (in parentheses) to signify the integer of the initial collection and thus single out a specific instance of that named element:

```
var secondRadio = document.all("group0",1);
```

As a more readable alternative, you can use the item() method (described later in this chapter) to access the same kinds of items within a collection:

```
var secondRadio = document.all.item("group0",1);
```

Also see the tags() method (later in this chapter) as a way to extract a set of elements from an all collection that matches a specific tag name.

Example

Use The Evaluator (see Chapter 4) to experiment with the all collection. Enter the following statements one at a time in the lower text box, and review the results in the text area for each:

```
document.all
myTable.all
myP.all
```

If you encounter a numbered element within a collection, you can explore that element to see which tag is associated with it. For example, if one of the results for the document.all collection says document.all.8=[object], enter the following statement in the topmost text box:

```
document.all[8].tagName
```

Related Items: item(), tags(), document.getElementById() methods

attributes[]

Value: Array of attribute object references   Read-Only

Compatibility: WinIE5+, MacIE5+, NN6+, Moz+, Safari+, Opera+, Chrome+

The attributes property consists of an array of attributes specified for an element. In IE5+, the attributes array contains an entry for every possible property that the browser has defined for its elements — even if the attribute is not set explicitly in the HTML tag. Also, any attributes that you add later via script facilities such as the setAttribute() method are not reflected in the attributes array. In other words, the IE5+ attributes array is fixed, using default values for all properties except those that you explicitly set as attributes in the HTML tag.

Mozilla browsers' attributes property returns an array that is a named node map (in W3C DOM terminology) — an object that has its own properties and methods to read and write attribute values. For example, you can use the getNamedItem(attrName) and item(index) methods on the array returned from the attributes property to access individual attribute objects via W3C DOM syntax.

IE5 and Mozilla had different ideas about what an attribute object should be. Mozilla is dependent on the W3C DOM node inheritance model, discussed in Chapter 25. In the past, the larger set of properties in the W3C DOM node were solely supported by Mozilla. Now, as you can see, IE supports more of the W3C DOM. Table 26-2 shows the variety of properties of an attribute object as defined by the two object models. The WebKit-based browsers offer the same property support as Mozilla, while Opera lies in between.

TABLE 26-2

Attribute Object Properties

Property	IE5	Moz	Description
attributes	Yes	Yes	Array of nested attribute objects (null)
childNodes	No	Yes	Child node array
firstChild	No	Yes	First child node
lastChild	No	Yes	Last child node
localName	No	Yes	Name within current namespace
name	Yes	Yes	Attribute name
nameSpaceURI	Yes	Yes	XML namespace URI
nextSibling	Yes	Yes	Next sibling node
nodeName	Yes	Yes	Attribute name
nodeType	Yes	Yes	Node type (2)
nodeValue	Yes	Yes	Value assigned to attribute
ownerDocument	Yes	Yes	Document object reference
ownerElement	Yes	Yes	Element node reference
parentNode	Yes	Yes	Parent node reference
prefix	Yes	Yes	XML namespace prefix
previousSibling	Yes	Yes	Previous sibling node
specified	Yes	Yes	Whether attribute is explicitly specified (Boolean)
value	Yes	Yes	Value assigned to attribute

The most helpful property of an attribute object is the Boolean `specified` property. In IE, this lets you know whether the attribute is explicitly specified in the element's tag. Because Mozilla returns only explicitly specified attributes in the `attributes` array, the value in Mozilla is always `true`. Most of the time, however, you'll probably use an element object's `getAttribute()` and `setAttribute()` methods to read and write attribute values.

Example

Use The Evaluator (see Chapter 4) to examine the values of the `attributes` array for some of the elements in that document. Enter each of the following expressions in the bottom text box, and see the array contents in the Results text area for each:

```
document.body.attributes
document.getElementById("myP").attributes
document.getElementById("myTable").attributes
```

If you have both IE5+ and a W3C DOM–compatible browser, compare the results you get for each of these expressions. To view the value of a single attribute in WinIE5+ by accessing the `attributes` array, enter the following statement in the top text box:

```
document.getElementById("myForm2").attributes["name"].value
```

For W3C browsers, IE6+, and MacIE5, use the W3C DOM syntax:

```
document.getElementById("myForm2").attributes.getNamedItem("name").value
```

Related Items: `getAttribute()`, `mergeAttributes()`, `removeAttribute()`, `setAttribute()` methods

baseURI

Value: Full URI string   Read-Only

Compatibility: WinIE-, MacIE-, NN6+, Moz+, Safari+, Opera+, Chrome+

This property reveals the full path to the source from which the element was served. The property is handy in applications that import XML data, in which case the source of an XML element is likely different from the HTML page in which it is being processed.

behaviorUrns[]

Value: Array of behavior URN strings   Read-Only

Compatibility: WinIE5+, MacIE-, NN-, Moz-, Safari-, Opera-, Chrome-

The Internet Explorer `behaviorUrns` property is designed to provide a list of addresses, in the form of *URNs (Uniform Resource Names),* of all behaviors assigned to the current object. If there are no behaviors, the array has a length of zero. In practice, however, IE5+ always returns an array of empty strings. Perhaps the potential exposure of URNs by script was deemed to be a privacy risk.

Related Item: `urns()` method

canHaveChildren

Value: Boolean   Read-Only

Compatibility: WinIE5+, MacIE-, NN-, Moz-, Safari-, Opera-, Chrome-

*elementObject.*canHaveChildren

Useful in some dynamic content situations, the `canHaveChildren` property reveals whether a particular element is capable of containing a child (nested) element. Most elements that have start and end tags (particularly the generic elements covered in this chapter) can contain nested elements. A nested element is referred to as a *child* of its parent container.

Example

Listing 26-2 shows an example of how to use the `canHaveChildren` property to visually identify elements on a page that can have nested elements. This example uses color to demonstrate the difference between an element that can have children and one that cannot. The first button sets the `color` style property of every visible element on the page to red. Thus, elements (including the normally non-childbearing ones such as `hr` and `input`) are affected by the color change. But if you reset the page and click the largest button, only those elements that can contain nested elements receive the color change.

LISTING 26-2

Reading the canHaveChildren Property

HTML: jsb26-02.html

```html
<!DOCTYPE html>
<html>
    <head>
        <meta http-equiv="content-type" content="text/html;charset=utf-8">
        <title>canHaveChildren Property</title>
        <script type="text/javascript" src="../jsb-global.js"></script>
        <script type="text/javascript" src="jsb26-02.js"></script>
    </head>
    <body>
        <h1>canHaveChildren Property Lab</h1>
        <hr />
        <form name="input">
            <input type="button" value="Color All Elements" onclick="colorAll()" />
            <br />
            <input type="button" value="Reset" onclick="history.go(0)" />
            <br />
            <input type="button" value="Color Only Elements That Can Have Children"
                onclick="colorChildBearing()" />
        </form>
        <br />
        <hr />
        <form name="output">
            <input type="checkbox" checked="checked" />Your basic checkbox
            <input type="text" name="access2" value="Some textbox text." />
        </form>
        <table id="myTable" cellpadding="10" border="2">
            <tr>
                <th>Quantity</th>
                <th>Description</th>
                <th>Price</th>
            </tr>
```

```
          <tbody>
            <tr>
              <td width="100">4</td>
              <td>Primary Widget</td>
              <td>$14.96</td>
            </tr>
            <tr>
              <td>10</td>
              <td>Secondary Widget</td>
              <td>$114.96</td>
            </tr>
          </tbody>
        </table>
    </body>
</html>
```

JavaScript: jsb26-02.js

```
function colorAll()
{
    var elems = document.getElementsByTagName("*");
    for (var i = 0; i < elems.length; i++)
    {
        elems[i].style.color = "red";
    }
}

function colorChildBearing()
{
    var elems = document.getElementsByTagName("*");
    for (var i = 0; i < elems.length; i++)
    {
        if (elems[i].canHaveChildren)
        {
            elems[i].style.color = "red";
        }
    }
}
```

Related Items: childNodes, firstChild, lastChild, parentElement, parentNode properties; appendChild(), hasChildNodes(), removeChild() methods

canHaveHTML

Value: Boolean   Read-Only and Read/Write

Compatibility: WinIE5+, MacIE-, NN-, Moz-, Safari-, Opera-, Chrome-

Not all HTML elements are containers of HTML content. The canHaveHTML property lets scripts find out whether a particular object can accept HTML content, such as for insertion or replacement by object methods. The value for a p element, for example, is true. The value for a br element is false. The property is read-only for all elements except HTML Components, in which case it is read/write.

Example

Use The Evaluator (see Chapter 4) in WinIE5+ to experiment with the canHaveHTML property. Enter the following statements in the top text box, and observe the results:

```
document.getElementById("input").canHaveHTML
document.getElementById("myP").canHaveHTML
```

The first statement returns false because an input element (the top text box, in this case) cannot have nested HTML. But the myP element is a p element that gladly accepts HTML content.

Related Items: appendChild(), insertAdjacentHTML(), insertBefore() methods

childNodes[]

Value: Array of node objects   Read-Only

Compatibility: WinIE5+, MacIE5+, NN6+, Moz+, Safari+, Opera+, Chrome+

The childNodes property consists of an array of node objects contained by the current object. Note that child nodes consist of both element objects and text nodes. Therefore, depending on the content of the current object, the number of childNodes and children collections may be different.

Caution

If you use the childNodes array in a for loop that iterates through a sequence of HTML (or XML) elements, watch out for the possibility that the browser treats source-code whitespace (blank lines between elements and even simple carriage returns between elements) as text nodes. This potential problem affects MacIE5 and W3C-based browsers. If present, these extra text nodes occur primarily surrounding block elements. ■

Note

Most looping activity through the childNodes array aims to examine, count, or modify element nodes within the collection. If that is your script's goal, test each node returned by the childNodes array, and verify that the nodeType property is 1 (element) before processing that node; otherwise, skip the node. The skeletal structure of such a loop follows:

```
for (var i = 0; i < myElem.childNodes.length; i++)
{
    if (myElem.childNodes[i].nodeType == 1)
    {
        statements to work on element node i
    }
}
```

The presence of these phantom text nodes also impacts the nodes referenced by the firstChild and lastChild properties, described later in this chapter. ■

Example

Listing 26-3 contains an example of how you might code a function that walks the child nodes of a given node. The walkChildNodes() function shown in the listing accumulates and returns a hierarchical list of child nodes from the point of view of the document's HTML element (the default) or any element whose ID you pass as a string parameter. This function is embedded in The Evaluator so that you can inspect the child node hierarchy of that page or (when using `evaluator.js` for debugging as described in Chapter 48 on the CD-ROM) the node hierarchy within any page you have under construction. Try it out in The Evaluator by entering the following statements in the top text box:

```
walkChildNodes()
walkChildNodes(document.getElementById("myP"))
```

The results of this function show the nesting relationships among all child nodes within the scope of the initial object. It also shows the act of drilling down to further `childNodes` collections until all child nodes are exposed and catalogued. Text nodes are labeled accordingly. The first 15 characters of the actual text are placed in the results to help you identify the nodes when you compare the results against your HTML source code.

LISTING 26-3

Collecting Child Nodes

```
<!-- xmp tags added for display of HTML in a browser window -->
<xmp>
    function walkChildNodes(objRef, n)
    {
        var obj;
        if (objRef)
        {
            if (typeof objRef == "string")
            {
                obj = document.getElementById(objRef);
            }
            else
            {
                obj = objRef;
            }
        }
        else
        {
            obj = (document.body.parentElement) ?
                document.body.parentElement : document.body.parentNode;
        }
        var output = "";
        var indent = "";
        var i, group, txt;
        if (n)
        {
            for (i = 0; i < n; i++)
            {
                indent += "+---";
            }
        }
        else
```

continued

elementObject.children

LISTING 26-3   *(continued)*

```
        {
            n = 0;
            output += "Child Nodes of <" + obj.tagName;
            output += ">\n=====================\n";
        }
        group = obj.childNodes;
        for (i = 0; i < group.length; i++)
        {
            output += indent;
            switch (group[i].nodeType)
            {
                case 1:
                    output += "<" + group[i].tagName;
                    output += (group[i].id) ? " ID=" + group[i].id : "";
                    output += (group[i].name) ? " NAME=" + group[i].name : "";
                    output += ">\n";
                    break;
                case 3:
                    txt = group[i].nodeValue.substr(0,15);
                    output += "[Text:\"" + txt.replace(/[\r\n]/g,"<cr>");
                        if (group[i].nodeValue.length > 15)
                        {
                            output += "...";
                        }
                    output += "\"]\n";
                    break;
                case 8:
                    output += "[!COMMENT!]\n";
                    break;
                default:
                    output += "[Node Type = " + group[i].nodeType + "]\n";
            }
            if (group[i].childNodes.length > 0)
            {
                output += walkChildNodes(group[i], n+1);
            }
        }
        return output;
    }
</xmp>
```

Related Items: nodeName, nodeType, nodeValue, parentNode properties; cloneNode(), hasChildNodes(), removeNode(), replaceNode(), swapNode() methods

children

Value: Array of element objects   Read-Only

Compatibility: WinIE4+, MacIE4+, NN-, Moz+, Safari+, Opera+, Chrome+

The `children` property consists of an array of element objects contained by the current object. Unlike the `childNodes` property, `children` does not take into account text nodes, but focuses strictly on the HTML (and XML) element containment hierarchy from the point of view of the current object. Children exposed to the current object are immediate children only. If you want to get all element objects nested within the current object (regardless of how deeply nested they are), use the `all` collection instead.

Example

Listing 26-4 shows how you can use the `children` property to walk the child nodes of a given node. This function accumulates and returns a hierarchical list of child elements from the point of view of the document's HTML element (the default) or any element whose ID you pass as a string parameter. This function is embedded in The Evaluator so that you can inspect the parent–child hierarchy of that page or (when using `evaluator.js` for debugging as described in Chapter 48 on the CD-ROM) the element hierarchy within any page you have under construction. Try it out in The Evaluator by entering the following statements in the top text box:

```
walkChildren("myTable")
```

Notice in this example that the `walkChildren()` function is called with the name of an element instead of a call to `document.getElementId()`. This reveals the flexibility of the `walkChildren()` function and how it can operate on either an object or the name of an object (element). The `walkChildNodes()` function in Listing 26-3 offers the same flexibility.

The results of the `walkChildren()` function show the nesting relationships among all parent and child elements within the scope of the initial object. It also shows the act of drilling down to further `children` collections until all child elements are exposed and cataloged. The element tags also display their `id` and/or `name` attribute values if any are assigned to the elements in the HTML source code.

LISTING 26-4

Collecting Child Elements

```
<!-- xmp tags added for display of HTML in a browser window -->
<xmp>
    function walkChildren(objRef, n)
    {
       var obj;
       if (objRef)
       {
          if (typeof objRef == "string")
          {
             obj = document.getElementById(objRef);
          }
          else
          {
             obj = objRef;
          }
```

continued

LISTING 26-4   *(continued)*

```
   }
   else
   {
       obj = document.body.parentElement;
   }
   var output = "";
   var indent = "";
   var i, group;
   if (n)
   {
       for (i = 0; i < n; i++)
       {
           indent += "+---";
       }
   }
   else
   {
       n = 0;
       output += "Children of <" + obj.tagName;
       output += ">\n=====================\n";
   }
   group = obj.children;
   for (i = 0; i < group.length; i++)
   {
       output += indent + "<" + group[i].tagName;
       output += (group[i].id) ? " ID=" + group[i].id : "";
       output += (group[i].name) ? " NAME=" + group[i].name : "";
       output += ">\n";
       if (group[i].children.length > 0)
       {
           output += walkChildren(group[i], n+1);
       }
   }
   return output;
   }
</xmp>
```

Related Items: canHaveChildren, firstChild, lastChild, parentElement properties; appendChild(), removeChild(), replaceChild() methods

cite

Value: URL string   Read/Write

Compatibility: WinIE6+, MacIE-, NN6+, Moz+, Safari+, Opera+, Chrome+

The cite property contains a URL that serves as a reference to the source of an element, as in the author of a quote. The property is intended to apply to only the blockquote, q, del, and ins element objects, but IE supports it in a wider range of text content objects. This may or may not be a mistake, so it's probably not a safe bet to use the property outside its intended elements.

className

Value: String   Read/Write

Compatibility: WinIE4+, MacIE4+, NN6+, Moz+, Safari+, Opera+, Chrome+

A *class name* is an identifier that is assigned to the class attribute of an element. To associate a cascading style sheets (CSS) rule with several elements in a document, assign the same identifier to the class attributes of those elements, and use that identifier (preceded by a period) as the CSS rule's selector. An element's className property enables the application of different CSS rules to that element under script control. Listing 26-5 shows an example of such a script.

Example

The style of an element toggles between on and off in Listing 26-5 by virtue of setting the element's className property alternatively to an existing style sheet class selector name and an empty string. When you set the className to an empty string, the default behavior of the h1 element governs the display of the first header. A click of the button forces the style sheet rule to override the default behavior in the first h1 element.

LISTING 26-5

Working with the className Property

HTML: jsb26-05.html

```
<!DOCTYPE html>
<html>
    <head>
        <meta http-equiv="content-type" content="text/html;charset=utf-8">
        <title>className Property</title>
        <style type="text/css">
            .special
            {
                font-size:16pt; color:red;
            }
        </style>
        <script type="text/javascript" src="../jsb-global.js"></script>
        <script type="text/javascript" src="jsb26-05.js"></script>
    </head>
    <body>
        <h1>className Property Lab</h1>
        <hr />
        <form name="input">
            <input type="button" value="Toggle Class Name"
                    onclick="toggleSpecialStyle('head1')" />
        </form>
        <br />
```

continued

LISTING 26-5   *(continued)*

```
        <h1 id="head1">ARTICLE I</h1>
        <p>Congress shall make no law respecting an establishment of religion, or
            prohibiting the free exercise thereof; or abridging the freedom of
            speech, or of the press; or the right of the people peaceably to
            assemble, and to petition the government for a redress of grievances.
        </p>
        <h1>ARTICLE II</h1>
        <p>A well regulated militia, being necessary to the security of a free
            state, the right of the people to keep and bear arms, shall not be
            infringed.
        </p>
    </body>
</html>
```

JavaScript: jsb26-05.js

```
function toggleSpecialStyle(elemID)
{
    var elem = (document.all) ? document.all(elemID) :
                document.getElementById(elemID);
    if (elem.className == "")
    {
        elem.className = "special";
    }
    else
    {
        elem.className = "";
    }
}
```

You can also create multiple versions of a style rule with different class selector identifiers and apply them at will to a given element.

Related Items: rule, stylesheet objects (Chapter 38); id property

clientHeight
clientWidth

Value: Integer   Read-Only

Compatibility: WinIE4+, MacIE4+, NN7, Moz1.0.1+, Safari+, Opera+, Chrome+

These two properties by and large reveal the pixel height and width of the content within an element whose style sheet rule includes height and width settings. In theory, these measures do not take into account any margins, borders, or padding that you add to an element by way of style sheets. In practice, however, different combinations of borders, margins, and padding influence these values in unexpected ways. One of the more reliable applications of the clientHeight property enables you to discover, for example, where the text of an overflowing element ends. To read the rendered dimensions of an element, you are better served across browsers with the `offsetHeight` and `offsetWidth` properties.

For the `document.body` object, the `clientHeight` and `clientWidth` properties return the inside height and width of the window or frame (plus or minus a couple of pixels). These take the place of desirable, but nonexistent, window properties in IE.

Unlike earlier versions, Internet Explorer 5+ expanded the number of objects that employ these properties to include virtually all objects that represent HTML elements. Values for these properties in Mozilla-based browsers are zero except for `document.body`, which measures the browser's current content area.

Example

Listing 26-6 for IE includes an example of how to size content dynamically on a page based on the client-area width and height. This example calls upon the `clientHeight` and `clientWidth` properties of a `div` element that contains a paragraph element. Only the width of the `div` element is specified in its style sheet rule, which means that the paragraph's text wraps inside that width and extends as deeply as necessary to show the entire paragraph. The `clientHeight` property describes that depth. The `clientHeight` property then calculates where a logo image should be positioned immediately after `div`, regardless of the length of the text. As a bonus, the `clientWidth` property helps the script center the image horizontally with respect to the paragraph's text.

LISTING 26-6

Using clientHeight and clientWidth Properties

HTML: jsb26-06.html

```html
<!DOCTYPE html>
<html>
    <head>
        <meta http-equiv="content-type" content="text/html;charset=utf-8">
        <title>clientHeight and clientWidth Properties</title>
        <script type="text/javascript" src="../jsb-global.js"></script>
        <script type="text/javascript" src="jsb26-06.js"></script>
    </head>
    <body>
        <button onclick="showLogo()">Position and Show Logo Art</button>
        <div id="myDIV" style="width:200px">
            <p>Lorem ipsum dolor sit amet, consectetaur adipisicing elit, sed do
                eiusmod tempor incididunt ut labore et dolore magna aliqua. Ut enim
                adminim veniam, quis nostrud exercitation ullamco laboris nisi ut
                aliquip ex ea commodo consequat. Duis aute irure dolor in
                reprehenderit involuptate velit esse cillum dolore eu fugiat nulla
                pariatur. Excepteur sint occaecat cupidatat non proident.
            </p>
        </div>
        <div id="logo" style="position:absolute; width:120px; visibility:hidden">
            <img alt="image" src="logo.gif" />
        </div>
    </body>
</html>
```

continued

LISTING 26-6   *(continued)*

JavaScript: jsb26-01.js

```
function showLogo()
{
    var paragraphW = document.getElementById("myDIV").clientWidth;
    var paragraphH = document.getElementById("myDIV").clientHeight;
    // correct for Windows/Mac discrepancies
    var paragraphTop = (document.getElementById("myDIV").clientTop) ?
        document.getElementById("myDIV").clientTop :
        document.getElementById("myDIV").offsetTop;
    var logoW = document.getElementById("logo").style.pixelWidth;
    // center logo horizontally against paragraph
    document.getElementById("logo").style.pixelLeft = (paragraphW-logoW) / 2;
    // position image immediately below end of paragraph
    document.getElementById("logo").style.pixelTop = paragraphTop + paragraphH;
    document.getElementById("logo").style.visibility = "visible";
}
```

To assist in the vertical positioning of the logo, the offsetTop property of the div object provides the position of the start of the div with respect to its outer container (the body). Unfortunately, MacIE uses the clientTop property to obtain the desired dimension. That measure (assigned to the paragraphTop variable), plus the clientHeight of the div, provides the top coordinate of the image.

Related Items: offsetHeight, offsetWidth properties

clientLeft
clientTop

Value: Integer   Read-Only

Compatibility: WinIE4+, MacIE4+, NN-, Moz+, Safari+, Opera+, Chrome+

The purpose and names of the clientLeft and clientTop properties are confusing at best. Unlike the clientHeight and clientWidth properties, which apply to the content of an element, the clientLeft and clientTop properties return essentially no more information than the thickness of a border around an element — provided that the element is positioned. If you do not specify a border or do not position the element, the values are zero (although the document.body object can show a couple of pixels in each direction without explicit settings). If you are trying to read the left and top coordinate positions of an element, the offsetLeft and offsetTop properties are more valuable in WinIE; as shown in Listing 26-6, however, the clientTop property returns a suitable value in MacIE. Virtually all elements have the clientLeft and clientTop properties in IE5+, whereas support in MacIE is less consistent.

Related Items: offsetLeft, offsetTop properties

contentEditable

Value: Boolean   Read/Write

Compatibility: WinIE5.5+, MacIE-, NN-, Moz+, Safari+, Opera+, Chrome+

IE5.5 introduced the concept of editable HTML content on a page. Element tags can include a `contentEditable` attribute whose value is echoed via the `contentEditable` property of the element. The default value for this property is `inherit`, which means that the property inherits whatever setting this property has in the hierarchy of HTML containers outward to the body. If you set the `contentEditable` property to `true`, that element and all nested elements set to inherit the value become editable; conversely, a setting of `false` turns off the option to edit the content. Some browsers automatically provide a visual cue for editable elements by giving an editable element a glowing blue border.

Example

Listing 26-7 demonstrates how to use the `contentEditable` property to create a very simple poetry editor. When you click the button of a freshly loaded page, the `toggleEdit()` function captures the opposite of the current editable state via the `contentEditable` property of the `div` that is subject to edit. You switch on editing for that element in the next statement by assigning the new value to the `contentEditable` property of the `div`. For added impact, turn the text of the `div` to red to provide additional user feedback about what is editable on the page. The button label is also switched to one that indicates the action invoked by the next click of that button.

LISTING 26-7

Using the contentEditable Property

HTML: `jsb26-07.html`

```html
<!DOCTYPE html>
<html>
    <head>
        <meta http-equiv="content-type" content="text/html;charset=utf-8">
        <title>Editable Content</title>
        <style type="text/css">
            .normal
            {
                color: black;
            }
            .editing
            {
                color: red;
            }
        </style>
        <script type="text/javascript" src="../jsb-global.js"></script>
        <script type="text/javascript" src="jsb26-07.js"></script>
    </head>
    <body>
        <h1>Poetry Editor</h1>
        <hr />
        <p>Turn on editing to modify the following text:</p>
        <div id="noneditableText">
            Roses are red,
            <br />
            Violets are blue.
        </div>
```

continued

LISTING 26-7 *(continued)*

```
    <div id="editableText">
        Line 3,
        <br />
        Line 4.
    </div>
    <p>
        <button id="editBtn" onclick="toggleEdit()"
                onfocus="this.blur()">Enable Editing</button>
    </p>
  </body>
</html>
```

JavaScript: jsb26-07.js

```
function toggleEdit()
{
   var newState = document.getElementById("editableText").contentEditable;
   // While contentEditable is boolean, different browsers behave differently
   if (newState == false || newState == "false" || newState == "inherit")
   {
       newState = true;
   }
   else
   {
       newState = false;
   }
   document.getElementById("editableText").contentEditable = newState;
   document.getElementById("editableText").className = (newState) ?
       "editing" : "normal";
   document.getElementById("editBtn").innerHTML = (newState) ?
       "Disable Editing" : "Enable Editing";
}
```

Related Item: isContentEditable property

currentStyle

Value: style object   Read-Only

Compatibility: WinIE5+, MacIE5+, NN-, Moz-, Safari-, Opera-, Chrome-

Every element has style attributes applied to it, even if those attributes are the browser's default settings. Because an element's style object reflects only those properties whose corresponding attributes are explicitly set via CSS statements, you cannot use the style property of an element object to view default style settings applied to an element. That's where the currentStyle property comes in.

This property returns a read-only style object that contains values for every possible style property applicable to the element. If a style property is explicitly set via CSS statement or script adjustment, the current reading for that property is also available here. Thus, a script can inquire about any property to determine whether it should change to meet some scripted design goal.

For example, if you surround some text with an `<em>` tag, the browser by default turns that text into an italic font style. This setting is not reflected in the element's `style` object (`fontStyle` property) because the italic setting was not set via CSS; by contrast, the `element` object's `currentStyle.fontStyle` property reveals the true, current `fontStyle` property of the element as italic.

Example

To change a `style` property setting, access it via the element's `style` object. Use The Evaluator (see Chapter 4) to compare the properties of the `currentStyle` and `style` objects of an element. For example, an unmodified copy of The Evaluator contains an em element whose ID is "myEM". Enter `document.getElementById("myEM").style` in the bottom property listing text box and press Enter. Notice that most of the property values are empty. Now enter `document.getElementById("myEM").currentStyle` in the property listing text box and press Enter. Every property has a value associated with it.

Related Items: `runtimeStyle`, `style` objects (Chapter 38); `window.getComputedStyle()` for W3C DOM browsers (Chapter 27)

dateTime

Value: Date string   Read-Only

Compatibility: WinIE6+, MacIE-, NN6+, Moz+, Safari+, Opera+, Chrome+

The `dateTime` property contains a date/time value that is used to establish a timestamp for an element. Similar to the `cite` property, the `dateTime` property is intended to apply to a lesser number of element objects (`del` and `ins`) than is actually supported in IE. This may or may not be a mistake, so it's probably not a safe bet to use the property outside its intended elements.

dataFld
dataFormatAs
dataSrc

Value: String   Read/Write

Compatibility: WinIE4+, MacIE5, NN-, Moz-, Safari-, Opera-, Chrome-

The `dataFld`, `dataFormatAs`, and `dataSrc` properties (along with more element-specific properties such as `dataPageSize` and `recordNumber`) are part of the Internet Explorer data-binding facilities based on ActiveX controls. The Win32 versions of IE4 and later have several ActiveX objects built into the browsers that facilitate direct communication between a web page and a data source. Data sources include text files, XML data, HTML data, and external databases (MacIE supports text files only). Data binding is a very large topic, much of which extends more to discussions about Microsoft Data Source Objects (DSOs), ODBC, and JDBC — subjects well beyond the scope of this book. But data binding is a powerful tool and can be of use even if you are not a database guru. Therefore, this discussion of the three primary properties — `dataFld`, `dataFormatAs`, and `dataSrc` — briefly covers data binding through Microsoft's *Tabular Data Control DSO*. This allows any page to access, sort, display, and filter (but not update) data downloaded into a web page from an external text file (commonly, comma- or tab-delimited data).

You can load data from an external text file into a document with the help of the *Tabular Data Control* (TDC). You retrieve the data by specifying the TDC object within an `<object>` tag set and specifying additional parameters, such as the URL of the text file and field delimiter characters. The `object` element can go anywhere within the body of your document. (We tend to put it at the bottom of the code so that all normal page rendering happens before the control loads.) Retrieving the data simply brings it into the browser and does not, on its own, render the data on the page.

If you haven't worked with embedded objects in IE, the classid attribute value might seem a bit strange. The most perplexing part to some is the long value of numeric data signifying the *Globally Unique Identifier* (GUID) for the object, which is IE's way of uniquely identifying objects. You must enter this value exactly as shown in the following example for the proper ActiveX TDC to run. The HTML syntax for this object is as follows:

```
<object id="objName" classid="clsid:333C7BC4-460F-11D0-BC04-0080C7055A83">
    <param name="DataURL" value="URL">
    [additional optional parameters]
</object>
```

Table 26-3 lists the parameters available for the TDC. Only the DataURL parameter is required. Other parameters — such as FieldDelim, UseHeader, RowDelim, and EscapeChar — may be helpful, depending on the nature of the data source.

TABLE 26-3

Tabular Data Control Parameters

Parameter	Description
CharSet	Character set of the data source file. Default is latin1.
DataURL	URL of data source file (relative or absolute).
EscapeChar	Character used to escape delimiter characters that are part of the data. Default is empty. A common value is "\".
FieldDelim	Delimiter character between fields within a record. Default is comma (,). For a Tab character, use a value of 	.
Language	ISO language code of source data. Default is en-us.
TextQualifier	Optional character surrounding a field's data. Default is empty.
RowDelim	Delimiter character between records. Default is newline (NL).
UseHeader	Set to true if the first row of data in the file contains field names. Default is false.

The value you assign to the object element's id attribute is the identifier that your scripts use to communicate with the data after the page and data completely load. Therefore, you can have as many uniquely named TDCs loaded in your page as there are data source files you want to access at the same time.

The initial binding of the data to HTML elements usually comes when you assign values to the datasrc and datafld attributes of the elements. The datasrc attribute points to the dso identifier (matching the id attribute of the object element, preceded by a hash symbol), whereas the datafld attribute points to the name of the field whose data should be extracted. When you use data binding with an interactive element such as a table, multiple records are displayed in consecutive rows of the table (more about this in a moment).

Adjust the dataSrc and dataFld properties if you want the same HTML element (other than a table) to change the data that it displays. These properties apply to a subset of HTML elements that can be associated with external data: a, applet, body, button, div, frame, iframe, img, input (most types), label, marquee, object, param, select, span, and textarea objects.

In some cases, your data source may store chunks of HTML-formatted text for rendering inside an element. Unless directed otherwise, the browser renders a data source field as plain text — even if the content contains HTML formatting tags. But if you want the HTML to be observed during rendering, you can set the dataFormatAs property (or, more likely, the dataformatas attribute of the tag) to HTML. The default value is text.

Example

Listing 26-8 is a simple document that has two TDC objects associated with it. The external files are different formats of the U.S. Bill of Rights document. One file is a traditional, tab-delimited data file consisting of only two records. The first record is a tab-delimited sequence of field names (named "Article1", "Article2", and so on). The second record is a tab-delimited sequence of article content defined in HTML:

```
<h1>ARTICLE I</h1>
<p>Congress shall make...</p>
```

The second file is a raw-text file consisting of the full Bill of Rights with no HTML formatting attached.

When you load Listing 26-8, only the first article of the Bill of Rights appears in a blue-bordered box. Buttons enable you to navigate to the previous and next articles in the series. Because the data source is a traditional, tab-delimited file, the nextField() and prevField() functions calculate the name of the next source field and assign the new value to the dataFld property. All of the data is already in the browser after the page loads, so cycling through the records is as fast as the browser can reflow the page to accommodate the new content.

LISTING 26-8

Binding Data to a Page

HTML: jsb26-08.html

```
<!DOCTYPE html>
<html>
    <head>
        <meta http-equiv="content-type" content="text/html;charset=utf-8">
        <title>Data Binding</title>
        <style type="text/css">
            #display
            {
                width:500px; border:10px ridge blue; padding:20px;
            }
            .hiddenControl
```

continued

LISTING 26-8   *(continued)*

```
            {
                display:none;
            }
        </style>
        <script type="text/javascript" src="../jsb-global.js"></script>
        <script type="text/javascript" src="jsb26-08.js"></script>
    </head>
    <body>
        <h1>U.S. Bill of Rights</h1>
        <form>
            <input type="button" value="Toggle Complete/Individual"
                    onclick="toggleComplete()" />
            <span id="buttonWrapper" class="">
                <input type="button" value="Prev" onclick="prevField()" />
                <input type="button" value="Next" onclick="nextField()" />
            </span>
        </form>
        <div id="display" datasrc="#rights_html" datafld="Article1"
            dataformatas="HTML">
        </div>
        <object id="rights_html"
                classid="clsid:333C7BC4-460F-11D0-BC04-0080C7055A83">
            <param name="DataURL" value="Bill of Rights.txt" />
            <param name="UseHeader" value="True" />
            <param name="FieldDelim" value="&#09;" />
        </object>
        <object id="rights_raw"
                classid="clsid:333C7BC4-460F-11D0-BC04-0080C7055A83">
            <param name="DataURL" value="Bill of Rights (no format).txt" />
            <param name="FieldDelim" value="\" />
            <param name="RowDelim" value="\" />
        </object>
    </body>
</html>
```

JavaScript: jsb26-08.js

```
function nextField()
{
    var elem = document.getElementById("display");
    var fieldName = elem.dataFld;
    var currFieldNum = parseInt(fieldName.substring(7, fieldName.length),10);
    currFieldNum = (currFieldNum == 10) ? 1 : ++currFieldNum;
    elem.dataFld = "Article" + currFieldNum;
}
function prevField()
{
    var elem = document.getElementById("display");
    var fieldName = elem.dataFld;
    var currFieldNum = parseInt(fieldName.substring(7, fieldName.length),10);
```

```
    currFieldNum = (currFieldNum == 1) ? 10 : --currFieldNum;
    elem.dataFld = "Article" + currFieldNum;
}

function toggleComplete()
{
    if (document.getElementById("buttonWrapper").className == "")
    {
        document.getElementById("display").dataSrc = "#rights_raw";
        document.getElementById("display").dataFld = "column1";
        document.getElementById("display").dataFormatAs = "text";
        document.getElementById("buttonWrapper").className = "hiddenControl";
    }
    else
    {
        document.getElementById("display").dataSrc = "#rights_html";
        document.getElementById("display").dataFld = "Article1";
        document.getElementById("display").dataFormatAs = "HTML";
        document.getElementById("buttonWrapper").className = "";
    }
}
```

Another button on the page enables you to switch between the initial piecemeal version of the document and the unformatted version in its entirety. To load the entire document as a single record, the FieldDelim and RowDelim parameters of the second object element eliminate their default values by replacing them with characters that don't appear in the document at all. And because the external file does not have a field name in the file, the default value (column1 for the lone column in this document) is the data field. Thus, in the toggleComplete() function, the dataSrc property is changed to the desired object element ID; the dataFld property is set to the correct value for the data source; and the dataFormatAs property is changed to reflect the different intention of the source content (to be rendered as HTML or as plain text). When the display shows the entire document, you can hide the two radio buttons by assigning a className value to the span element that surrounds the buttons. The className value is the identifier of the class selector in the document's style sheet. When the toggleComplete() function resets the className property to empty, the default properties (normal inline display style) take hold.

One further example demonstrates the kind of power available to the TDC under script control. Listing 26-9 displays table data from a tab-delimited file of Academy Awards information. The data file has eight columns of data, and each column heading is treated as a field name: Year, Best Picture, Best Director, Best Director Film, Best Actress, Best Actress Film, Best Actor, and Best Actor Film. For the design of the page, only five fields from each record appear: Year, Film, Director, Actress, and Actor. Notice in the listing that the HTML for the table and its content is bound to the data source object and the fields within the data.

The dynamic part of this example is apparent in how you can sort and filter the data, after it is loaded into the browser, without further access to the original source data. The TDC object features Sort and Filter properties that enable you to act on the data currently loaded in the browser. The simplest kind of sorting indicates on which field (or fields, via a semicolon-delimited list of field names) the entire data set should be sorted. Leading the name of the sort field is either a plus (to indicate ascending) or minus (descending) symbol. After setting the data object's Sort property, invoke its

Reset() method to tell the object to apply the new property. The data in the bound table is immediately redrawn to reflect any changes.

Similarly, you can tell a data collection to display records that meet specific criteria. In Listing 26-9, two select lists and a pair of radio buttons provide the interface to the Filter property's settings. For example, you can filter the output to display only those records in which the Best Picture was the same picture of the winning Best Actress's performance. Simple filter expressions are based on field names:

```
dataObj.Filter = "Best Picture" = "Best Actress Film";
```

LISTING 26-9

Sorting Bound Data

HTML: jsb26-09.html

```html
<!DOCTYPE html>
<html>
    <head>
        <meta http-equiv="content-type" content="text/html;charset=utf-8">
        <title>Data Binding - Sorting</title>
        <style type="text/css">
            thead
            {
                background-color:yellow; text-align:center;
            }
        </style>
        <script type="text/javascript" src="../jsb-global.js"></script>
        <script type="text/javascript" src="jsb26-09.js"></script>
    </head>
    <body>
        <h1>Academy Awards 1978-2005</h1>
        <form>
          <p>Sort list by year
            <a href="javascript:sortByYear('normal')">from newest to oldest</a> or
            <a href="javascript:sortByYear('reverse')">from oldest to newest</a>.
          </p>
          <p>Filter listings for records whose
            <select name="filter1" onchange="filterInCommon(this.form)">
                <option value="Best Picture">Best Picture</option>
                <option value="Best Director Film">Best Director's Film</option>
                <option value="Best Actress Film">Best Actress' Film</option>
                <option value="Best Actor Film">Best Actor's Film</option>
            </select>
            <input type="radio" name="operator" checked="checked"
                    onclick="filterInCommon(this.form)" />is
            <input type="radio" name="operator"
                    onclick="filterInCommon(this.form)" />is not
            <select name="filter2" onchange="filterInCommon(this.form)">
```

```
            <option value="Best Picture">Best Picture</option>
            <option value="Best Director Film">Best Director's Film</option>
            <option value="Best Actress Film">Best Actress' Film</option>
            <option value="Best Actor Film">Best Actor's Film</option>
        </select>
    </p>
    </form>
    <table datasrc="#oscars" border="1" align="center">
        <thead>
            <tr>
                <td>Year</td>
                <td>Film</td>
                <td>Director</td>
                <td>Actress</td>
                <td>Actor</td>
            </tr>
        </thead>
        <tr>
            <td><div id="col1" datafld="Year"></div></td>
            <td><div id="col2" datafld="Best Picture"></div></td>
            <td><div id="col3" datafld="Best Director"></div></td>
            <td><div id="col4" datafld="Best Actress"></div></td>
            <td><div id="col5" datafld="Best Actor"></div></td>
        </tr>
    </table>
    <object id="oscars" classid="clsid:333C7BC4-460F-11D0-BC04-0080C7055A83">
        <param name="DataURL" value="Academy Awards.txt" />
        <param name="UseHeader" value="True" />
        <param name="FieldDelim" value="&#09;" />
    </object>
    </body>
</html>
```

JavaScript: jsb26-09.js

```
function sortByYear(type)
{
    oscars.Sort = (type == "normal") ? "-Year" : "+Year";
    oscars.Reset();
}
function filterInCommon(form)
{
    var filterExpr1 = form.filter1.options[form.filter1.selectedIndex].value;
    var filterExpr2 = form.filter2.options[form.filter2.selectedIndex].value;
    var operator = (form.operator[0].checked) ? "=" : "<>";
    var filterExpr = filterExpr1 + operator + filterExpr2;
    oscars.Filter = filterExpr;
    oscars.Reset();
}
```

Related Items: recordNumber, table.dataPageSize properties

dir

Value: "ltr" | "rtl"   Read/Write

Compatibility: WinIE5+, MacIE5+, NN6+, Moz+, Safari+, Opera+, Chrome+

The dir property (based on the dir attribute of virtually every text-oriented HTML element) controls whether an element's text is rendered left to right (the default) or right to left. By and large, this property (and HTML attribute) is necessary only when you need to override the default directionality of a language's character set as defined by the Unicode standard.

Example

Changing this property value in a standard U.S. version of a browser only makes the right margin the starting point for each new line of text (in other words, the characters are not rendered in reverse order). You can experiment with this in The Evaluator by entering the following statements in the expression evaluation field:

```
document.getElementById("myP").dir = "rtl"
```

Related Item: lang property

disabled

Value: Boolean   Read/Write

Compatibility: WinIE4+, MacIE4+, NN6+, Moz+, Safari+, Opera+, Chrome+

Though only form elements have a disabled property in IE4 and IE5, this property is associated with every HTML element in IE5.5+. W3C DOM browsers apply the property only to form control and style element objects. Disabling an HTML element (like form elements) usually gives the element a dimmed look, indicating that it is not active. A disabled element does not receive any events. It also cannot receive focus, either manually or by script. But a user can still select and copy a disabled body text element.

Note

If you disable a form control element, the element's data is not submitted to the server with the rest of the form elements. If you need to keep a form control locked down but still submit it to the server, use the form element's onsubmit event handler to enable the form control right before the form is submitted. ∎

Example

Use The Evaluator (see Chapter 4) to experiment with the disabled property on both form elements (IE4+ and W3C) and regular HTML elements (WinIE5.5+). For IE4+ and W3C browsers, see what happens when you disable the output text area by entering the following statement in the top text box:

```
document.forms[0].output.disabled = true
```

The text area is disabled for user entry, although you can still set the field's value property via script (which is how the true returned value got there).

If you have WinIE5.5+, disable the myP element by entering the following statement in the top text box:

```
document.getElementById("myP").disabled = true
```

The sample paragraph's text turns gray.

Related Item: isDisabled property

document

Value: document object   Read-Only

Compatibility: WinIE4+, MacIE4+, NN-, Moz-, Safari-, Opera+, Chrome-

In the context of HTML element objects as exposed in IE4+/Opera, the document property is a reference to the document that contains the object. Though it is unlikely that you will need to use this property, document may come in handy for complex scripts and script libraries that handle objects in a generic fashion and do not know the reference path to the document containing a particular object. You might need a reference to the document to inspect it for related objects. The W3C version of this property is ownerDocument.

Example

The following simplified function accepts a parameter that can be any object in a document hierarchy. The script finds out the reference of the object's containing document for further reference to other objects:

```
function getCompanionFormCount(obj)
{
    var ownerDoc = obj.document;
    return ownerDoc.forms.length;
}
```

Because the ownerDoc variable contains a valid reference to a document object, the return statement uses that reference to return a typical property of the document object hierarchy.

Related Item: ownerDocument property

filters[]

Value: Array   Read-Only

Compatibility: WinIE4+, MacIE4+, NN-, Moz-, Safari-, Opera-, Chrome-

Filters are IE-specific style sheet add-ons that offer a greater variety of font rendering (such as drop shadows) and transitions between hidden and visible elements. Each filter specification is a filter object. The filters property contains an array of filter objects defined for the current element. You can apply filters to the following set of elements: bdo, body, button, fieldset, img, input, marquee, rt, ruby, table, td, textarea, th, and positioned div and span elements. See Chapter 38 for details about style sheet filters.

elementObject.firstChild

Related Item: `filter` object

firstChild
lastChild

Value: Node object reference   Read-Only

Compatibility: WinIE5+, MacIE5+, NN6+, Moz+, Safari+, Opera+, Chrome+

W3C DOM-based DOMs are built around an architecture known as a *node map*. Each object defined by HTML is a node in the map. A node has relationships with other nodes in the document — relationships described in family terms of parents, siblings, and children.

A *child node* is an element that is contained by another element. The container is the parent of such a child. Just as an HTML element can contain any number of child elements, so can a parent object have zero or more children. A list of those children (returned as an array) can be read from an object by way of its `childNodes` property:

```
var nodeArray = document.getElementById("elementID").childNodes;
```

Though you can use this array (and its `length` property) to get a reference to the first or last child node, the `firstChild` and `lastChild` properties offer shortcuts to those positions. These are helpful when you wish to insert a new child before or after all of the others, and you need a reference point for methods that add elements to the document's node list.

Example

Listing 26-10 contains an example of how to use the `firstChild` and `lastChild` properties to access child nodes. These two properties come in handy in this example, which adds and replaces `li` elements to an existing `ol` element. You can enter any text you want to appear at the beginning or end of the list. Using the `firstChild` and `lastChild` properties simplifies access to the ends of the list. For the functions that replace child nodes, the example uses the `replaceChild()` method. Alternatively for IE4+, you can modify the `innerText` property of the objects returned by the `firstChild` or `lastChild` property. This example is especially interesting to watch when you add items to the list: The browser automatically renumbers items to fit the current state of the list.

Caution

See the discussion of the `childNodes` property earlier in this chapter for details about the presence of phantom nodes in some browser versions. The problem may influence your use of the `firstChild` and `lastChild` properties. ■

Note

As handy as it may be, in a strict W3C approach to JavaScript, you wouldn't use the `innerHTML` property because it isn't officially part of the W3C standard. However, it is often too powerful a convenience property to ignore, as much of the code throughout this book is a testament. The book does show the W3C node manipulation alternative to `innerHTML` in some examples. Refer to Chapter 29 for a thorough explanation and examples of the W3C alternative to `innerHTML`. ■

LISTING 26-10

Using firstChild and lastChild Properties

HTML: jsb26-10.html

```html
<!DOCTYPE html>
<html>
   <head>
      <meta http-equiv="content-type" content="text/html;charset=utf-8">
      <title>firstChild and lastChild Properties</title>
      <script type="text/javascript" src="../jsb-global.js"></script>
      <script type="text/javascript" src="jsb26-10.js"></script>
   </head>
   <body>
      <h1>firstChild and lastChild Property Lab</h1>
      <hr />
      <form>
         <label>Enter some text to add to or replace in the OL element:</label>
         <br />
         <input type="text" name="input" size="50" />
         <br />
         <input type="button" value="Insert at Top"
               onclick="prepend(this.form)" />
         <input type="button" value="Append to Bottom"
               onclick="append(this.form)" />
         <br />
         <input type="button" value="Replace First Item"
               onclick="replaceFirst(this.form)" />
         <input type="button" value="Replace Last Item"
               onclick="replaceLast(this.form)" />
      </form>
      <ol id="myList">
         <li>Initial Item 1</li>
         <li>Initial Item 2</li>
         <li>Initial Item 3</li>
         <li>Initial Item 4</li>
      </ol>
   </body>
</html>
```

JavaScript: jsb26-10.js

```javascript
// helper function for prepend() and append()
function makeNewLI(txt)
{
   var newItem = document.createElement("LI");
   newItem.innerHTML = txt;
   return newItem;
}
function prepend(form)
```

continued

LISTING 26-10   *(continued)*

```
{
    var newItem = makeNewLI(form.input.value);
    var firstLI = document.getElementById("myList").firstChild;
    document.getElementById("myList").insertBefore(newItem, firstLI);
}
function append(form)
{
    var newItem = makeNewLI(form.input.value);
    var lastLI = document.getElementById("myList").lastChild;
    document.getElementById("myList").appendChild(newItem);
}
function replaceFirst(form)
{
    var newItem = makeNewLI(form.input.value);
    var firstLI = document.getElementById("myList").firstChild;
    document.getElementById("myList").replaceChild(newItem, firstLI);
}
function replaceLast(form)
{
    var newItem = makeNewLI(form.input.value);
    var lastLI = document.getElementById("myList").lastChild;
    document.getElementById("myList").replaceChild(newItem, lastLI);
}
```

Related Items: nextSibling, parentElement, parentNode, previousSibling properties; appendChild(), hasChildNodes(), removeChild(), removeNode(), replaceChild(), replaceNode() methods

height
width

Value: Integer or percentage string   Read/Write and Read-Only

Compatibility: WinIE4+, MacIE4+, NN4+, Moz+, Safari+, Opera+, Chrome+

The height and width properties described here are not the identically named properties that belong to an element's style. Rather, these properties reflect the values normally assigned to height and width attributes of elements such as img, applet, table, and so on. As such, these properties are accessed directly from the object (for example, document .getElementById("myTable").width) rather than through the style object (for example, document.getElementById("myDIV").style.width). Only elements for which the HTML 4.x standard provides height and width attributes have the corresponding properties.

Values for these properties are either integer pixel values (numbers or strings) or percentage values (strings only). If you need to perform some math on an existing percentage value, use the parseInt() function to extract the numeric value for use with math calculations. If an element's height and width attributes are set as percentage values, you can use the offsetHeight and offsetWidth properties in many modern browsers to get the rendered pixel dimensions.

Property values are read/write for the image object in most recent browser versions because you can resize an image object in after the page loads. Properties are read/write for some other objects (such as the table object) — but not necessarily all others that support these properties.

In general, you cannot set the value of these properties to something less than is required to render the element. This is particularly true of a table. If you attempt to set the height value to less than the amount of pixels required to display the table as defined by its style settings, your changes have no effect (even though the property value retains its artificially low value). For other objects, however, you can set the size to anything you like, and the browser scales the content accordingly (images, for example). If you want to see only a segment of an element (in other words, to crop the element), use a style sheet to set the element's clipping region.

Example

The following example demonstrates how to use the width property by increasing the width of a table by 10 percent:

```
var tableW = parseInt(document.getElementById("myTable").width);
document.getElementById("myTable").width = (tableW * 1.1) + "%";
```

Because the initial setting for the width attribute of the table element is set as a percentage value, the script calculation extracts the number from the percentage width string value. In the second statement, the old number is increased by 10 percent and turned into a percentage string by appending the percentage symbol to the value. The resulting string value is assigned to the width property of the table.

Related Items: clientHeight, clientWidth properties; style.height, style.width properties

hideFocus

Value: Boolean   Read/Write

Compatibility: WinIE5.5+, MacIE-, NN-, Moz-, Safari-, Opera-, Chrome-

In IE for Windows, button types of form controls and links display a dotted rectangle around some part of the element whenever that element has focus. If you set the tabindex attribute or tabIndex property of any other kinds of elements in IE5+, they, too, display that dotted line when given focus. You can still let an element receive focus but hide that dotted line by setting the hideFocus property of the element object to true (default value is false).

Hiding focus does not disable the element. In fact, if the element about to receive focus is scrolled out of view, the page scrolls to bring the element into view. Form controls that respond to keyboard action (for example, pressing the spacebar to check or uncheck a checkbox control) also continue to work as normal. For some designers, the focus rectangle harms the design goals of the page. The hideFocus property gives them more control over the appearance while maintaining consistency of operation with other pages. There is no corresponding HTML attribute for a tag, so you can use an onload event handler in the page to set the hideFocus property of desired objects after the page loads.

Example

Use The Evaluator (see Chapter 4) to experiment with the hideFocus property in WinIE5.5+. Enter the following statement in the top text box to assign a tabIndex value to the myP element so that by default, the element receives focus and the dotted rectangle:

```
document.getElementById("myP").tabIndex = 1
```

Press the Tab key several times until the paragraph receives focus. Now disable the focus rectangle:

```
document.getElementById("myP").hideFocus = true
```

If you now press the Tab key several times, the dotted rectangle does not appear around the paragraph. To prove that the element still receives focus, scroll the page down to the bottom so that the paragraph is not visible (you may have to resize the window). Click one of the focusable elements at the bottom of the page and then press the Tab key slowly until the Address field toolbar has focus. Press the Tab key once. The page scrolls to bring the paragraph into view, but there is no focus rectangle around the element.

Related Items: `tabIndex` property; `srcollIntoView()` method

id

Value: String   (See text)

Compatibility: WinIE4+, MacIE4+, NN6+, Moz+, Safari+, Opera+, Chrome+

The `id` property returns the identifier assigned to an element's `id` attribute in the HTML code. A script cannot modify the ID of an existing element or assign an ID to an element that lacks one. But if a script creates a new element object, an identifier may be assigned to it by way of the `id` property.

Example

Rarely do you need to access this property in a script — unless you write an authoring tool that iterates through all elements of a page to extract the IDs assigned by the author. You can retrieve an object reference when you know the object's `id` property (via the `document.getElementById(elemID)` method). But if for some reason your script doesn't know the ID of, say, the second paragraph of a document, you can extract that ID as follows:

```
var elemID = document.getElementsByTagName("p")[1].id;
```

Related Item: `className` property

innerHTML
innerText

Value: String   Read/Write

Compatibility: WinIE4+, MacIE4+, NN6+, Moz+, Safari+, Opera+, Chrome+

One way that Internet Explorer exposes the contents of an element is through the `innerHTML` and `innerText` properties. (NN6+/Moz offer only the `innerHTML` property.) All content defined by these inner properties consists of document data that is contained by an element's start and end tags but does not include the tags themselves (see the `outerText` and `outerHTML` properties). Setting these inner properties is a common way to modify a portion of a page's content after the page loads.

The `innerHTML` property contains not only the text content for an element as seen on the page, but also every bit of HTML tagging that is associated with that content. (If there are no tags in the content, the text is rendered as is.) For example, consider the following bit of HTML source code:

```
<p id="paragraph1">"How <em>are</em> you?" he asked.</p>
```

The value of the paragraph object's `innerHTML` property (`document.getElementById`
`("paragraph1").innerHTML`) is

> `"How <em>are</em> you?" he asked.`

The browser interprets any HTML tags included in a string you assign to an element's `innerHTML`
property as tags. This also means that you can introduce entirely new nested elements (or child nodes
in the modern terminology) by assigning a slew of HTML content to an element's `innerHTML` property. The document's object model adjusts itself to the newly inserted content.

By contrast, the `innerText` property knows only about the text content of an element container.
In the example you just saw, the value of the paragraph's `innerText` property (`document`
`.getElementById("paragraph1").innerText`) is

> `"How are you?" he asked.`

It's important to remember that if you assign a string to the `innerText` property of an element, and
that string contains HTML tags, the tags and their angle brackets appear in the rendered page and are
not interpreted as live tags.

The W3C DOM Level 3 adds a `textContent` property that serves as the standard equivalent of
`innerText`. IE does not support `textContent`.

Do not modify the `innerHTML` property to adjust the HTML for `frameset`, `html`, `head`, or `title`
objects. You may modify table constructions through either `innerHTML` or the various table-related
methods that create or delete rows, columns, and cells (see Chapter 41). It is also safe to modify the
contents of a cell by setting its `innerHTML` or `innerText` property.

When the HTML you insert includes a `<script>` tag, be sure to include the `defer` attribute to the
opening tag. This goes even for scripts that contain function definitions, which you might consider to
be deferred automatically.

The `innerHTML` property is not supported by the W3C DOM, but it does share widespread support in all modern browsers. You could argue that a pure W3C DOM node manipulation approach
is more structured than just assigning HTML code to `innerHTML`, but the ease of making a single
property assignment has so far won out in the practicality of everyday scripting. Whenever possible,
the examples in this book use the W3C approach to alter the HTML code for a node, but there are
several instances where `innerHTML` is simply too concise an option to resist.

Example

Listing 26-11 contains an example of how to use the `innerHTML` and `innerText` properties to alter
dynamically the content within a page. The page generated in the listing contains an `h1` element label
and a paragraph of text. The purpose is to demonstrate how the `innerHTML` and `innerText` properties differ in their intent. Two text boxes contain the same combination of text and HTML tags that
replaces the inner content of the paragraph's label.

If you apply the default content of the first text box to the `innerHTML` property of the `label1`
object, the italic style is rendered as such for the first word. In addition, the text in parentheses is
rendered with the help of the small style sheet rule assigned by virtue of the surrounding `<span>`
tags. But if you apply that same content to the `innerText` property of the `label` object, the tags are
rendered as is.

Use this as a laboratory to experiment with some other content in both text boxes. See what happens
when you insert a `<br>` tag within some text in both text boxes.

LISTING 26-11

Using innerHTML and innerText Properties

HTML: jsb26-11.html

```
<!DOCTYPE html>
<html>
    <head>
        <meta http-equiv="content-type" content="text/html;charset=utf-8">
        <title>innerHTML and innerText Properties</title>
        <style type="text/css">
            h1
            {
                font-size:18pt; font-weight:bold;
                font-family:"Comic Sans MS", Arial, sans-serif;
            }
            .small
            {
                font-size:12pt; font-weight:400; color:gray;
            }
        </style>
        <script type="text/javascript" src="../jsb-global.js"></script>
        <script type="text/javascript" src="jsb26-11.js"></script>
    </head>
    <body>
        <form>
            <p>
                <input type="text" name="HTMLInput"
                    value="&lt;I&gt;First&lt;/I&gt; Article &lt;span↵
                        class='small'&gt;(of ten)&lt;/span&gt;"
                    size="50" />
                <input type="button" value="Change Heading HTML"
                    onclick="setGroupLabelAsHTML(this.form)" />
            </p>
            <p>
                <input type="text" name="textInput"
                    value="&lt;I&gt;First&lt;/I&gt; Article &lt;span↵
                        class='small'&gt;(of ten)&lt;/span&gt;"
                    size="50" />
                <input type="button" value="Change Heading Text"
                    onclick="setGroupLabelAsText(this.form)" />
            </p>
        </form>
        <h1 id="label1">
            ARTICLE I
        </h1>
        <p>Congress shall make no law respecting an establishment of religion, or
            prohibiting the free exercise thereof; or abridging the freedom of
            speech, or of the press; or the right of the people peaceably to
            assemble, and to petition the government for a redress of grievances.
        </p>
```

```
    </body>
</html>
```

```
JavaScript: jsb26-11.js
function setGroupLabelAsText(form)
{
    var content = form.textInput.value;
        if (content)
        {
            document.getElementById("label1").innerText = content;
        }
}
function setGroupLabelAsHTML(form)
{
    var content = form.HTMLInput.value;
        if (content)
        {
            document.getElementById("label1").innerHTML = content;
        }
}
```

Related Items: outerHTML, outerText, textContent properties; replaceNode() method

isContentEditable

Value: Boolean   Read-Only

Compatibility: WinIE5.5+, MacIE-, NN-, Moz-, Safari 1.2+, Opera+, Chrome+

The isContentEditable property returns a Boolean value indicating whether a particular element object is set to be editable (see the discussion of the contentEditable property earlier in this chapter). This property is helpful because if a parent element's contentEditable property is set to true, a nested element's contentEditable property likely is set to its default value inherit. But because its parent is editable, the isContentEditable property of the nested element returns true.

Example

Use The Evaluator (see Chapter 4) to experiment with both the contentEditable and isContentEditable properties on the myP and nested myEM elements (reload the page to start with a known version). Check the current setting for the myEM element by typing the following statement in the top text box:

        myEM.isContentEditable

This value is false because no element upward in the element containment hierarchy is set to be editable yet. Next, turn on editing for the surrounding myP element:

        myP.contentEditable = true

At this point, the entire `myP` element is editable because its child element is set, by default, to inherit the edit state of its parent. Prove it by entering the following statement in the top text box:

```
myEM.isContentEditable
```

Although the `myEM` element is shown to be editable, no change has accrued to its `contentEditable` property:

```
myEM.contentEditable
```

This property value remains the default `inherit`.

Related Item: `contentEditable` property

isDisabled

Value: Boolean   Read-Only

Compatibility: WinIE5.5+, MacIE-, NN-, Moz-, Safari-, Opera-, Chrome-

The `isDisabled` property returns a Boolean value that indicates whether a particular element object is set to be disabled (see the discussion of the `disabled` property earlier in this chapter). This property is helpful; if a parent element's `disabled` property is set to `true`, a nested element's `disabled` property likely is set to its default value of `false`. But because its parent is disabled, the `isDisabled` property of the nested element returns `true`. In other words, the `isDisabled` property returns the actual disabled status of an element regardless of its `disabled` property.

Example

Use The Evaluator (see Chapter 4) to experiment with both the `disabled` and `isDisabled` properties on the `myP` and nested `myEM` elements (reload the page to start with a known version). Check the current setting for the `myEM` element by typing the following statement in the top text box:

```
myEM.isDisabled
```

This value is `false` because no element upward in the element containment hierarchy is set for disabling yet. Next, disable the surrounding `myP` element:

```
myP.disabled = true
```

At this point, the entire `myP` element (including its children) is disabled. Prove it by entering the following statement in the top text box:

```
myEM.isDisabled
```

Although the `myEM` element is shown as disabled, no change has accrued to its `disabled` property:

```
myEM.disabled
```

This property value remains the default `false`.

Related Item: `disabled` property

isMultiLine

Value: Boolean   Read-Only

Compatibility: WinIE5.5+, MacIE-, NN-, Moz-, Safari-, Opera-, Chrome-

The isMultiLine property returns a Boolean value that reveals whether the element object is capable of occupying or displaying more than one line of text. It is important that this value does not reveal whether the element actually occupies multiple lines; rather, it indicates the potential of doing so. For example, a text input element cannot wrap to multiple lines, so its isMultiLine property is false. However, a button element can display multiple lines of text for its label, so it reports true for the isMultiLine property.

Example

Use The Evaluator (see Chapter 4) to read the isMultiLine property for elements on that page. Try the following statements in the top text box:

```
document.body.isMultiLine
document.forms[0].input.isMultiLine
myP.isMultiLine
myEM.isMultiLine
```

All but the text field form control report that they are capable of occupying multiple lines.

isTextEdit

Value: Boolean   Read-Only

Compatibility: WinIE4+, MacIE4+, NN-, Moz-, Safari-, Opera-, Chrome-

The isTextEdit property reveals whether an object can have a WinIE TextRange object created with its content (see Chapter 33 on the CD-ROM). You can create TextRange objects from only a limited selection of objects in IE4+ for Windows: body, button, button, image and radio type input, and textarea. This property always returns false in MacIE.

Example

Good coding practice dictates that your script check for this property before invoking the create-TextRange() method on any object. A typical implementation is as follows:

```
if (document.getElementById("myObject").isTextEdit)
{
    var myRange = document.getElementById("myObject").createTextRange();
    // [more statements that act on myRange]
}
```

Related Items: createRange() method; TextRange object (Chapter 33 on the CD-ROM)

lang

Value: ISO language code string   Read/Write

Compatibility: WinIE4+, MacIE4+, NN6+, Moz+, Safari+, Opera+, Chrome+

The lang property governs the written language system used to render an element's text content when overriding the default browser's language system. The default value for this property is an empty string unless the corresponding lang attribute is assigned a value in the element's tag. Modifying the property value by script control does not appear to have any effect in the current browser implementations.

elementObject.language

Example

Values for the `lang` property consist of strings containing valid ISO language codes. Such codes have, at minimum, a primary language code (for example, `"fr"` for French) plus an optional region specifier (for example, `"fr-ch"` for Swiss French). The code to assign a Swiss German value to an element looks like the following:

```
document.getElementById("specialSpan").lang = "de-ch";
```

language

Value: String   Read/Write

Compatibility: WinIE4+, MacIE4+, NN-, Moz-, Safari-

IE4+'s architecture allows for multiple scripting engines to work with the browser. Two engines are included with the basic Windows version browser: JScript (compatible with JavaScript) and Visual Basic Scripting Edition (VBScript). The default scripting engine is JScript. But if you wish to use VBScript or some other scripting language in statements that are embedded within event handler attributes of a tag, you can specifically direct the browser to apply the desired scripting engine to those script statements by way of the `language` attribute of the tag. The `language` property provides scripted access to that property. Unless you intend to modify the event handler HTML code and replace it with a statement in VBScript (or any other non-JScript-compatible language installed with your browser), you do not need to modify this property (or read it, for that matter).

Valid values include `JScript`, `javascript`, `vbscript`, and `vbs`. Third-party scripting engines have their own identifier for use with this value. Internet Explorer 5 observes `language="xml"` as well. Be aware that this attribute was deprecated in HTML4.01, so depending on the `DOCTYPE` you use, code using this attribute will not validate. You can accomplish the same objective with `type` (see Chapter 4).

Related Item: `script` element object

lastChild

(See `firstChild`)

length

Value: Integer   Read-Only and Read/Write

Compatibility: WinIE3+, MacIE3+, NN2+, Moz+, Safari+, Opera+, Chrome+

The `length` property returns the number of items in an array or collection of objects. Its most common application is as a boundary condition in a `for` loop. Though arrays and collections commonly use integer values as index values (always starting with zero), the `length` value is the actual number of items in the group. Therefore, to iterate through all items of the group, the condition expression should include a less-than (<) symbol rather than a less-than-or-equal (<=) symbol, as in the following:

```
for (var i = 0; i < someArray.length; i++)
{
  // [statements for the loop to process]
}
```

For decrementing through an array (in other words, starting from the last item in the array and working toward the first), the initial expression must initialize the counting variable as the length minus one:

```
for (var i = someArray.length - 1; i >= 0; i--)
{
   // [statements for the loop to process]
}
```

For most arrays and collections, the length property is read-only and governed solely by the number of items in the group. But in more recent versions of the browsers, you can assign values to some object arrays (areas, options, and the select object) to create placeholders for data assignments. See the discussions of the area, select, and option element objects for details. A plain JavaScript array can also have its length property value modified by script to either trim items from the end of the array or reserve space for additional assignments. See Chapter 18 for more about the Array object.

Example

You can try the following sequence of statements in the top text box of The Evaluator to see how the length property returns values (and sets them for some objects). Note that some statements work in only some browser versions.

```
(All browsers)    document.forms.length
(All browsers)    document.forms[0].elements.length
(All browsers)      document.images.length
(NN4+)            document.layers.length
(All browsers)              document.all.length
(IE5+, W3C)       document.getElementById("myTable").childNodes.length
```

All of these statements are shown primarily for completeness. Unless you have a good reason to support legacy browsers, the last technique (IE5+, W3C) should be used to access the length property.

Related Items: area, select, option, and Array objects

localName
namespaceURI
prefix

Value: String   Read-Only

Compatibility: WinIE8+, MacIE-, NN6+, Moz+, Safari+, Opera+, Chrome+

The three properties localName, namespaceURI, and prefix apply to any node in an XML document that associates a namespace URI with an XML tag. Although NN6 exposes all three properties for all element (and node) objects, the properties do not return the desired values. However, Mozilla-based browsers, including NN7+, remedy the situation. To understand better what values these three properties represent, consider the following XML content:

```
<x xmlns:bk='http://bigbooks.org/schema'>
    <bk:title>To Kill a Mockingbird</bk:title>
</x>
```

The element whose tag is `<bk:title>` is associated with the Namespace URI defined for the block, and the element's `namespaceURI` property would return the string `http://bigbooks.org/schema`. The tag name consists of a prefix (before the colon) and the local name (after the colon). In the preceding example, the `prefix` property for the element defined by the `<bk:title>` tag would be `bk`, whereas the `localName` property would return `title`. The `localName` property of any node returns the same value as its `nodeName` property value, such as `#text` for a text node.

For more information about XML Namespaces, visit `http://www.w3.org/TR/REC-xml-names`.

Related Items: `scopeName`, `tagUrn` properties

nextSibling
previousSibling

Value: Object reference   Read-Only

Compatibility: WinIE5+, MacIE5+, NN6+, Moz+, Safari+, Opera+, Chrome+

A *sibling node* is one that is at the same nested level as another node in the hierarchy of an HTML document. For example, the following p element has two child nodes (the em and span elements). Those two child nodes are siblings.

```
<p>MegaCorp is <em>the</em> source of the
    <span class="hot">hottest</span> gizmos.</p>
```

Sibling order is determined solely by the source-code order of the nodes. Therefore, in the previous example, the em node has no `previousSibling` property. Meanwhile, the span node has no `nextSibling` property (meaning that these properties return `null`). These properties provide another way to iterate through all nodes at the same level.

Example

The following function assigns the same class name to all child nodes of an element:

```
function setAllChildClasses(parentElem, className)
{
    var childElem = parentElem.firstChild;
        while (childElem.nextSibling)
        {
            childElem.className = className;
            childElem = childElem.nextSibling;
        }
}
```

This example is certainly not the only way to achieve the same results. Using a `for` loop to iterate through the `childNodes` collection of the parent element is an equally valid approach.

Related Items: `firstChild`, `lastChild`, `childNodes` properties; `hasChildNodes()`, `insertAdjacentElement()` methods

nodeName

Value: String   Read-Only

Compatibility: WinIE5+, MacIE5+, NN6+, Moz+, Safari+, Opera+, Chrome+

For HTML and XML elements, the name of a node is the same as the tag name. The `nodeName` property is provided for the sake of consistency with the node architecture specified by the formal W3C DOM standard. The value, just like the `tagName` property, is an all-uppercase string of the tag name (even if the HTML source code is written with lowercase tags).

Some nodes, such as the text content of an element, do not have a tag. The `nodeName` property for such a node is a special value: `#text`. Another kind of node is an attribute of an element. For an attribute, the `nodeName` is the name of the attribute. See Chapter 25 for more about `Node` object properties.

Example

The following function demonstrates one (not very efficient) way to assign a new class name to every p element in an IE5+ document:

```
function setAllPClasses(className)
{
    for (var i = 0; i < document.all.length; i++)
    {
        if (document.all[i].nodeName == "P")
        {
            document.all[i].className = className;
        }
    }
}
```

A more efficient approach uses the `getElementsByTagName()` method to retrieve a collection of all p elements and then iterate through them directly.

Related Item: `tagName` property

nodeType

Value: Integer   Read-Only

Compatibility: WinIE5+, MacIE5+, NN6+, Moz+, Safari+, Opera+, Chrome+

The W3C DOM specification identifies a series of constant values that denote categories of nodes. Every node has a value that identifies its type, all browsers currently support the `nodeType` property on all node types as objects, but this has not always been the case. Table 26-4 lists the `nodeType` values; all the values are considered part of the W3C DOM Level 2 specification.

The `nodeType` value is automatically assigned to a node, whether the node exists in the document's HTML source code or is generated on-the-fly via a script. For example, if you create a new element node through any of the ways available by script (for example, by assigning a string encased in HTML tags to the `innerHTML` property or by explicitly invoking the `document.createElement()` method), the new element assumes a `nodeType` of 1.

Mozilla-based browsers and Safari go one step further in supporting the W3C DOM specification by implementing a set of `Node` object property constants for each of the `nodeType` values. Table 26-5 lists the entire set as defined in the DOM Level 2 specification. Substituting these constants for `nodeType` integers can improve the readability of a script. For example, instead of

```
if (myElem.nodeType == 1)
{
    // [statements to process if true]
}
```

elementObject.nodeType

TABLE 26-4

nodeType Property Values

Value	Description
1	Element node
2	Attribute node
3	Text (#text) node
4	CDATA section node
5	Entity reference node
6	Entity node
7	Processing instruction node
8	Comment node
9	Document node
10	Document type node
11	Document fragment node
12	Notation node

TABLE 26-5

W3C DOM nodeType Constants

Reference	nodeType Value
Node.ELEMENT_NODE	1
Node.ATTRIBUTE_NODE	2
Node.TEXT_NODE	3
Node.CDATA_SECTION_NODE	4
Node.ENTITY_REFERENCE_NODE	5
Node.ENTITY_NODE	6
Node.PROCESSING_INSTRUCTION_NODE	7
Node.COMMENT_NODE	8
Node.DOCUMENT_NODE	9
Node.DOCUMENT_TYPE_NODE	10
Node.DOCUMENT_FRAGMENT_NODE	11
Node.NOTATION_NODE	12

it is much easier to see what's going on with

```
if (myElem.nodeType == Node.ELEMENT_NODE)
{
   // [statements to process if true]
}
```

Example

You can experiment with viewing nodeType property values in The Evaluator. The p element whose ID is myP is a good place to start. The p element itself is a nodeType of 1:

```
document.getElementById("myP").nodeType
```

This element has three child nodes: a string of text (nodeName #text), an em element (nodeName em), and the rest of the text of the element content (nodeName #text). If you view the nodeType of either of the text portions, the value comes back as 3:

```
document.getElementById("myP").childNodes[0].nodeType
```

Related Item: nodeName property

nodeValue

Value: Number, string, or null   Read/Write

Compatibility: WinIE5+, MacIE5+, NN6+, Moz+, Safari+, Opera+, Chrome+

For a text node, the nodeValue property consists of the actual text for that node. Such a node cannot contain any further nested elements, so the nodeValue property offers another way of reading and modifying what Internet Explorer implements as an element's innerText property (but in the W3C DOM, you must reference the child text node of an element to get or set its node value).

Of the node types implemented in the W3C DOM–capable browsers, only the text and attribute types have readable values. The nodeValue property of an element type of node returns a null value. For an attribute node, the nodeValue property consists of the value assigned to that attribute. According to the W3C DOM standard, attribute values should be reflected as strings. WinIE5, however, returns values of type Number when the value is all numeric characters. Even if you assign a string version of a number to such a nodeValue property, it is converted to a Number type internally. Other browsers return nodeValue values as strings in all cases (and convert numeric assignments to strings).

Example

You can use the nodeValue property to carry out practical tasks. As an example, nodeValue can be used to increase the width of a textarea object by 10 percent. The nodeValue is converted to an integer before performing the math and reassignment:

```
function widenCols(textareaElem)
{
   var colWidth = parseInt(textareaElem.attributes["cols"].nodeValue, 10);
   textareaElem.attributes["cols"].nodeValue = (colWidth * 1.1);
}
```

elementObject.**offsetHeight**

As another example, you can replace the text of an element, assuming that the element contains no further nested elements:

```
function replaceText(elem, newText)
{
    if (elem.childNodes.length == 1 && elem.firstChild.nodeType == 3)
    {
        elem.firstChild.nodeValue = newText;
    }
}
```

The function builds in one final verification that the element contains just one child node and that it is a text type. An alternative version of the assignment statement of the second example uses the `innerText` property in IE with identical results:

```
elem.innerText = newText;
```

You could also use the `textContent` property in any browser except IE to achieve the same concise result:

```
elem.textContent = newText;
```

Related Items: `attributes`, `innerText`, `nodeType` properties

offsetHeight
offsetWidth

Value: Integer   Read-Only

Compatibility: WinIE4+, MacIE4+, NN6+, Moz+, Safari+, Opera+, Chrome+

These properties, which ostensibly report the height and width of any element, have had a checkered history due to conflicts between interpretations of the CSS box model by Microsoft and the W3C. Both properties were invented by Microsoft for IE4. Although they are not currently part of any W3C standard (they are included in the Working Draft of the CSSOM View Module), other modern browsers, including Mozilla-based browsers, WebKit-based browsers, and Presto-based browsers, implement the properties because they're so valuable to scripters.

Assuming that you specify style sheet rules for the width or height of an inline (nonpositioned) element, the `offsetHeight` and `offsetWidth` properties act differently depending on whether the page puts the browser in standards-compatible mode (via the DOCTYPE). More specifically, when IE6+ is set to standards-compatible mode (by DOCTYPE switching, as described in Chapter 25), the properties measure the pixel dimensions of the element's content plus any padding or borders, excluding margins. This is also the default behavior for Mozilla and WebKit, which adhere to the W3C box model. In quirks mode, however, the default IE6+ behavior is to return a height and width of only the element's content, with no accounting for padding, borders, or margins. For versions of IE prior to IE6, this is the only behavior.

Note that for a normal block-level element whose height and width are not specified, the `offsetHeight` is determined by the actual height of the content after all text flows. But the `offsetWidth` always extends the full width of the containing element. Therefore, the `offsetWidth` property does not reveal the rendered width of text content that is narrower than the full parent element width. For example, a p element consisting of only a few words may report an `offsetWidth` of many hundreds of pixels because the paragraph's block extends the full width of the body element that represents the containing parent of the p element. To find out the actual width of text within a full-width, block-level element, wrap the text within an inline element (such as a span), and inspect the offsetWidth property of the span.

Example

With IE4+, you can substitute the offsetHeight and offsetWidth properties for clientHeight and clientWidth in Listing 26-6. The reason is that the two elements in question have their widths hard-wired in style sheets. Thus, the offsetWidth property follows that lead rather than observing the default width of the parent (BODY) element.

With IE5+ and W3C browsers, you can use The Evaluator to inspect the offsetHeight and offsetWidth property values of various objects on the page. Enter the following statements in the top text box:

```
document.getElementById("myP").offsetWidth
document.getElementById("myEM").offsetWidth
document.getElementById("myP").offsetHeight
document.getElementById("myTable").offsetWidth
```

Related Items: clientHeight, clientWidth properties

offsetLeft
offsetTop

Value: Integer   Read-Only

Compatibility: WinIE4+, MacIE4+, NN6+, Moz+, Safari+, Opera+, Chrome+

The offsetLeft and offsetTop properties can suffer from the same version vagaries that afflict offsetHeight and offsetWidth properties when borders, margins, and padding are associated with an element and DOCTYPE switching is a factor. However, the offsetLeft and offsetTop properties are valuable in providing pixel coordinates of an element within the positioning context of the parent element — even when the elements are not positioned explicitly.

Note

The offsetLeft and offsetTop **properties for positioned elements in MacIE do not return the same values as the** style.left **and** style.top **properties of the same element. See Listing 40-5 on the CD-ROM for an example of how to correct these discrepancies without having to hard-wire the precise pixel differences in your code.** ■

The element used as a coordinate context for these properties is whatever element the offsetParent property returns. This means that to determine the precise position of any element, you may have to add some code that iterates through the offsetParent hierarchy until that property returns null.

As with the offsetHeight and offsetWidth properties, the offsetLeft and offsetTop properties are not yet part of the W3C DOM specification; they are supported across most browsers because they are convenient for some scriptable Dynamic HTML (DHTML) tasks. Through these two properties, a script can read the pixel coordinates of any block-level or inline element. Measurements are made relative to the body element, but this may change in the future. See the discussion later in this chapter about the offsetParent property.

Example

The following IE script statements use all four offset dimensional properties to size and position a div element so that it completely covers a span element located within a p element. This can be for a fill-in-the-blank quiz that provides text entry fields elsewhere on the page. As the user gets an answer correct, the blocking div element is hidden to reveal the correct answer.

```
document.all.blocker.style.pixelLeft = document.all.span2.offsetLeft
document.all.blocker.style.pixelTop = document.all.span2.offsetTop
document.all.blockImg.height = document.all.span2.offsetHeight
document.all.blockImg.width = document.all.span2.offsetWidth
```

Because the offsetParent property for the span element is the body element, the positioned div element can use the same positioning context (it's the default context, anyway) for setting the pixelLeft and pixelTop style properties. (Remember that positioning properties belong to an element's style object.) The offsetHeight and offsetWidth properties can read the dimensions of the span element (the example has no borders, margins, or padding to worry about) and assign them to the dimensions of the image contained by the blocker div element.

This example is also a bit hazardous in some implementations. If the text of span2 wraps to a new line, the new offsetHeight value has enough pixels to accommodate both lines. But the blockImg and blocker div elements are block-level elements that render as a simple rectangle. In other words, the blocker element doesn't turn into two separate strips to cover the pieces of span2 that spread across two lines.

Related Items: clientLeft, clientTop, offsetParent properties

offsetParent

Value: Object reference   Read-Only

Compatibility: WinIE4+, MacIE4+, NN6+, Moz+, Safari+, Opera+, Chrome+

The offsetParent property returns a reference to the object that acts as a positioning context for the current element. Values for the offsetLeft and offsetTop properties are measured relative to the top-left corner of the offsetParent object.

The returned object is usually, but not always, the next outermost block-level container. For most document elements, the offsetParent object is the document.body object (with exceptions for some elements in some browsers).

Table cells, for example, have different offsetParent elements in different browsers:

Browser	td offsetParent
WinIE4	tr
WinIE5+/NN7+/Moz-based/WebKit-based/Presto-based	table
MacIE	table
NN6	body

Fortunately, the property behaves predictably for positioned elements in most modern browsers. For example, a first-level positioned element's offsetParent element is the body; the offsetParent of a nested positioned element (for example, one absolute-positioned div inside another) is the next outer container (in other words, the positioning context of the inner element).

Example

You can use the offsetParent property to help you locate the position of a nested element on the page. Listing 26-12 demonstrates how a script can walk up the hierarchy of offsetParent objects in IE for Windows to assemble the location of a nested element on a page. The goal of the exercise in Listing 26-12 is to position an image at the top-left corner of the second table cell. The entire table is centered on the page.

The onload event handler invokes the setImagePosition() function. The function first sets a Boolean flag that determines whether the calculations should be based on the client or offset sets of properties. WinIE4 and MacIE5 rely on client properties, whereas WinIE5+ works with the offset properties. The discrepancies even out, however, with the while loop. This loop traverses the offsetParent hierarchy starting with the offsetParent of the cell out to the document.body object. In IE5+ and other browsers, the while loop executes only three times (for the td, table, and body elements) because just the table element exists between the cell and the body; in IE4, the loop executes four times to account for the tr and table elements up the hierarchy. The loop terminates when the offsetParent is null. Finally, the cumulative values of left and top measures are applied to the positioning properties of the div object's style, and the image is made visible.

LISTING 26-12

Using the offsetParent Property

HTML: jsb26-12.html

```html
<!DOCTYPE html>
<html>
   <head>
      <meta http-equiv="content-type" content="text/html;charset=utf-8">
      <title>offsetParent Property</title>
      <style type="text/css">
         #myImg
         {
            position:absolute; height:12px; width:12px;
         }
      </style>
      <script type="text/javascript" src="../jsb-global.js"></script>
      <script type="text/javascript" src="jsb26-12.js"></script>
   </head>
   <body onload="setImagePosition()">
      <h1>The offsetParent Property</h1>
      <hr />
      <p>After the document loads, the script positions a small image in the
         upper left corner of the second table cell.
      </p>
      <table border="1" align="center">
         <tr>
            <td>This is the first cell</td>
            <td id="myCell">This is the second cell.</td>
```

continued

LISTING 26-12   *(continued)*

```
        </tr>
      </table>
      <img id="myImg" alt="image" src="end.gif" height="12" width="12"
           style="visibility:hidden;" />
   </body>
</html>
```

```
JavaScript: jsb26-12.js
function setImagePosition()
{
    var x = 0;
    var y = 0;
    var offsetPointer = document.getElementById("myCell"); // cElement;
        while (offsetPointer)
        {
            x += offsetPointer.offsetLeft;
            y += offsetPointer.offsetTop;
            offsetPointer = offsetPointer.offsetParent;
        }
    // correct for MacIE body margin factors
    if (navigator.userAgent.indexOf("Mac") != -1 &&
        typeof document.body.leftMargin != "undefined")
    {
        x += document.body.leftMargin;
        y += document.body.topMargin;
    }
    document.getElementById("myImg").style.left = x + "px";
    document.getElementById("myImg").style.top = y + "px";
    document.getElementById("myImg").style.visibility = "visible";
}
```

Related Items: offsetLeft, offsetTop, offsetHeight, offsetWidth properties

outerHTML
outerText

Value: String   Read/Write

Compatibility: WinIE4+, MacIE4+, NN-, Moz-, Safari 1.3+, Opera+, Chrome+

One way that Internet Explorer, WebKit-based browsers, and Presto-based browsers expose an entire element to scripting is by way of the outerHTML and outerText properties. The primary distinction between these two properties is that outerHTML includes the element's start and end tags, whereas outerText includes only rendered text that belongs to the element (including text from any nested elements).

The outerHTML property contains not only the text content for an element as seen on the page, but also every bit of HTML tagging associated with that content. For example, consider the following bit of HTML source code:

```
<p id="paragraph1">"How <em>are</em> you?" he asked.</p>
```

The value of the p object's `outerHTML` property (`document.all.paragraph1. outerHTML`) is exactly the same as that of the source code.

The browser interprets any HTML tags in a string that you assign to an element's `outerHTML` property. This means that you can delete (set the property to an empty string) or replace an entire tag with this property. The document's object model adjusts itself to whatever adjustments you make to the HTML in this manner.

In contrast, the `outerText` property knows only about the text content of an element container. In the preceding example, the value of the paragraph's `outerText` property (`document.all.paragraph1.innerText`) is

```
"How are you?" he asked.
```

If this looks familiar, it's because in most cases the `innerText` and `outerText` properties of an existing element return the same strings.

Example

Listing 26-13 demonstrates how to use the `outerHTML` and `outerText` properties to access and modify web-page content dynamically. The page generated by Listing 26-13 (WinIE4+/WebKit-or Presto-based browsers) contains an h1 element label and a paragraph of text. The purpose is to demonstrate how the `outerHTML` and `outerText` properties differ in their intent. Two text boxes contain the same combination of text and HTML tags that replaces the element that creates the paragraph's label.

If you apply the default content of the first text box to the `outerHTML` property of the `label1` object, the h1 element is replaced by a span element whose `class` attribute acquires a different style sheet rule defined earlier in the document. Notice that the ID of the new span element is the same as that of the original h1 element. This allows the script attached to the second button to address the object. But this second script replaces the element with the raw text (including tags). The element is gone, and any subsequent attempt to change the `outerHTML` or `outerText` properties of the `label1` object causes an error because there is no longer a `label1` object in the document.

Use this laboratory to experiment with some other content in both text boxes.

LISTING 26-13

Using outerHTML and outerText Properties

HTML: `jsb26-13.html`

```
<!DOCTYPE html>
<html>
    <head>
        <meta http-equiv="content-type" content="text/html;charset=utf-8">
        <title>outerHTML and outerText Properties</title>
        <style type="text/css">
            h1
            {
```

continued

elementObject.outerHTML

LISTING 26-13 *(continued)*

```
            font-size:18pt; font-weight:bold;
            font-family:"Comic Sans MS", Arial, sans-serif;
        }
        .heading
        {
            font-size:20pt; font-weight:bold;
            font-family:"Arial Black", Arial, sans-serif;
        }
    </style>
    <script type="text/javascript" src="../jsb-global.js"></script>
    <script type="text/javascript" src="jsb26-13.js"></script>
</head>
<body>
    <form>
        <p id="myP1">
            <input type="text" name="HTMLInput"
                value="&lt;span id='label1' class='heading'&gt; ↩
                    Article the First&lt;/span&gt;"
                size="55" />
            <input type="button" value="Change Heading HTML"
                onclick="setGroupLabelAsHTML(this.form)" />
        </p>
        <p id="myP2">
            <input type="text" name="textInput"
                value="&lt;span id='label1' class='heading'&gt; ↩
                    Article the First&lt;/span&gt;"
                size="55" />
            <input type="button" value="Change Heading Text"
                onclick="setGroupLabelAsText(this.form)" />
        </p>
    </form>
    <h1 id="label1">ARTICLE I</h1>
    <p>Congress shall make no law respecting an establishment of religion, or
        prohibiting the free exercise thereof; or abridging the freedom of
        speech, or of the press; or the right of the people peaceably to
        assemble, and to petition the government for a redress of grievances.
    </p>
</body>
</html>
```

JavaScript: jsb26-13.js

```
function setGroupLabelAsText(form)
{
    var content = form.textInput.value;
    if (content)
    {
        document.getElementById("label1").outerText = content;
    }
}
```

```
function setGroupLabelAsHTML(form)
{
    var content = form.HTMLInput.value;
    if (content)
    {
        document.getElementById("label1").outerHTML = content;
    }
}
```

Related Items: innerHTML, innerText properties; replaceNode() method

ownerDocument

Value: Document object reference   Read-Only

Compatibility: WinIE6+, MacIE5+, NN6+, Moz+, Safari+, Opera+, Chrome+

The ownerDocument property belongs to any element or node in the W3C DOM. The property's value is a reference to the document node that ultimately contains the element or node. If a script encounters a reference to an element or node (perhaps it has been passed as a parameter to a function), the object's ownerDocument property provides a way to build references to other objects in the same document or to access properties and methods of the document objects. IE's proprietary version of this property is simply document.

Example

Use The Evaluator (see Chapter 4) to explore the ownerDocument property. Enter the following statement in the top text box:

        document.body.childNodes[5].ownerDocument

The result is a reference to the document object. You can use that to inspect a property of the document, as shown in the following statement, which you should enter in the top text box:

        document.body.childNodes[5].ownerDocument.URL

This returns the document.URL property for the document that owns the child node.

Related Item: document object

parentElement

Value: Element object reference or null   Read-Only

Compatibility: WinIE4+, MacIE4+, NN-, Moz-, Safari 1.2+, Opera+, Chrome+

The parentElement property returns a reference to the next outermost HTML element from the current element. This parent-child relationship of elements is often, but not always, the same as a parent-child node relationship (see the parentNode property later in this chapter). The difference is that the parentElement property deals only with HTML elements as reflected as document objects, whereas a node is not necessarily an HTML element (for example, an attribute or text chunk).

There is also a distinction between `parentElement` and `offsetParent` properties. The latter returns an element that may be many generations removed from a given element but is the immediate parent with regard to positioning context. For example, a `td` element's `parentElement` property is most likely its enclosing `tr` element, but a `td` element's `offsetParent` property is its `table` element (unless you're dealing with WinIE4).

A script can walk the element hierarchy outward from an element with the help of the `parentElement` property. The top of the parent chain is the `html` element. Its `parentElement` property returns `null`.

Example

You can experiment with the `parentElement` property in The Evaluator. The document contains a `p` element named `myP`. Type each of the following statements from the left column in the top expression evaluation text box and press Enter to see the results.

Expression	IE	WebKit/Presto
`document.getElementById ("myP").tagName`	p	P
`document.getElementById ("myP").parentElement`	[object]	object HTMLHtmlElement
`document.getElementById("myP"). parentElement.tagName`	body	body
`document.getElementById("myP"). parentElement.parentElement`	[object]	object HTMLBodyElement
`document.getElementById("myP"). parentElement.parentElement.tagName`	html	html
`document.getElementById("myP"). parentElement.parentElement. parentElement`	null	null

Related Items: `offsetParent`, `parentNode` properties

parentNode

Value: Node object reference or `null`   Read-Only

Compatibility: WinIE5+, MacIE5+, NN6+, Moz+, Safari+, Opera+, Chrome+

`parentNode` is a W3C property returns a reference to the next outermost node that is reflected as an object belonging to the document. For a standard element object, the `parentNode` property is the same as IE/WebKit and Presto browser's `parentElement` because both objects happen to have a direct parent-child node relationship as well as a parent-child element relationship.

Other kinds of content, however, can be nodes, including text fragments within an element. A text fragment's `parentNode` property is the next outermost node or element that encompasses that fragment. A text node object in IE/Opera does not have a `parentElement` property.

Example

Use The Evaluator to examine the `parentNode` property values of both an element and a nonelement node. Begin with the following two statements, and watch the results of each:

```
document.getElementById("myP").parentNode.tagName
document.getElementById("myP").parentElement.tagName (IE/WebKit/Presto browsers)
```

Now examine the properties from the point of view of the first text fragment node of the `myP` paragraph element:

```
document.getElementById("myP").childNodes[0].nodeValue
document.getElementById("myP").childNodes[0].parentNode.tagName
document.getElementById("myP").childNodes[0].parentElement (WebKit only)
```

Notice in IE and Opera that the text node does not have a `parentElement` property.

Related Items: `childNodes`, `nodeName`, `nodeType`, `nodeValue`, `parentElement` properties

parentTextEdit

Value: Element object reference or `null`   Read-Only

Compatibility: WinIE4+, MacIE4+, NN-, Moz-, Safari-, Opera-, Chrome-

Only a handful of objects in IE's object model are capable of creating text ranges (see the `TextRange` object in Chapter 33 on the CD-ROM). To find an object's next outermost container capable of generating a text range, use the `parentTextEdit` property. If an element is in the hierarchy, that element's object reference is returned. Otherwise (for example, `document.body.parentTextEdit`), the value is `null`. MacIE always returns a value of `null` because the browser doesn't support the `TextRange` object.

Example

Listing 26-14 contains an example that demonstrates how to use the `parentTextEdit` property to create a text range. The page resulting from Listing 26-14 contains a paragraph of Latin text and three radio buttons that select the size of a paragraph chunk: one character, one word, or one sentence. If you click anywhere within the large paragraph, the `onclick` event handler invokes the `selectChunk()` function. The function first examines which of the radio buttons is selected to determine how much of the paragraph to highlight (select) around the point at which the user clicks.

After the script employs the `parentTextEdit` property to test whether the clicked element has a valid parent capable of creating a text range, it calls on the property again to help create the text range. From there, `TextRange` object methods shrink the range to a single insertion point, move that point to the spot nearest the cursor location at click time, expand the selection to encompass the desired chunk, and select that bit of text.

Notice one workaround for the `TextRange` object's `expand()` method anomaly: If you specify a sentence, IE doesn't treat the beginning of a p element as the starting end of a sentence automatically. A camouflaged (white text color) period is appended to the end of the previous element to force the `TextRange` object to expand only to the beginning of the first sentence of the targeted p element.

elementObject.parentTextEdit

LISTING 26-14

Using the parentTextEdit Property

HTML: jsb26-14.html

```html
<!DOCTYPE html>
<html>
    <head>
        <meta http-equiv="content-type" content="text/html;charset=utf-8">
        <title>parentTextEdit Property</title>
        <style type="text/css">
            p
            {
                cursor:hand
            }
            #placeHolder
            {
                color:white;
            }
        </style>
        <script type="text/javascript" src="../jsb-global.js"></script>
        <script type="text/javascript" src="jsb26-14.js"></script>
    </head>
    <body bgcolor="white">
        <form>
            <p>Choose how much of the paragraph is to be selected when you click
                anywhere in it:
                <br />
                <input type="radio" name="chunk" value="character"
                        checked="checked" />Character
                <input type="radio" name="chunk"
                        value="word" />Word
                <input type="radio" name="chunk"
                        value="sentence" />Sentence
                <span id="placeHolder">.</span>
            </p>
        </form>
        <p onclick="selectChunk()">Lorem ipsum dolor sit amet, consectetaur
            elit, sed do eiusmod tempor incididunt ut labore et dolore magna aliqua.
            Ut enim adminim veniam, quis nostrud exercitation ullamco laboris nisi
            ut aliquip ex ea commodo consequat. Duis aute irure dolor in
            reprehenderit involuptate velit esse cillum dolore eu fugiat nulla
            pariatur. Excepteur sint occaecat cupidatat non proident, sunt in
            culpa qui officia deserunt mollit anim id est laborum.
        </p>
    </body>
</html>
```

JavaScript: jsb26-14.js

```javascript
function selectChunk()
{
    var chunk, range;
```

```
for (var i = 0; i < document.forms[0].chunk.length; i++)
{
    if (document.forms[0].chunk[i].checked)
    {
        chunk = document.forms[0].chunk[i].value;
        break;
    }
}
var x = window.event.clientX;
var y = window.event.clientY;
if (window.event.srcElement.parentTextEdit)
{
    range = window.event.srcElement.parentTextEdit.createTextRange();
    range.collapse();
    range.moveToPoint(x, y);
    range.expand(chunk);
    range.select();
}
}
```

Related Items: isTextEdit property; TextRange object (Chapter 33, "Body Text Objects" on the CD-ROM)

prefix

(See localName)

previousSibling

(See nextSibling)

readyState

Value: String (integer for OBJECT object)   Read-Only

Compatibility: WinIE4+, MacIE4+, NN-, Moz-, Safari-, Opera-, Chrome-

A script can query an element in IE to find out whether it has loaded all ancillary data (for example, external image files or other media files) before other statements act on that object or its data. The readyState property lets you know the loading status of an element.

Table 26-6 lists the possible values and their meanings.

For most HTML elements, this property always returns complete. Most of the other states are used by elements such as img, embed, and object, which load external data and even start other processes (such as ActiveX controls) to work.

One word of caution: Do not expect the readyState property to reveal whether an object exists in the document (for example, uninitialized). If the object does not exist, it cannot have a readyState property; the result is a script error for an undefined object. If you want to run a script only after every element and its data are fully loaded, trigger the function by way of the onload event handler for the body element or the onreadystatechange event handler for the object (and check that the readyState property is complete).

597

elementObject.**recordNumber**

TABLE 26-6

readyState Property Values

HTML Value	OBJECT Value	Description
complete	4	Element and data are fully loaded.
interactive	3	Data may not be loaded fully, but user can interact with element.
loaded	2	Data is loaded, but object may be starting up.
loading	1	Data is loading.
uninitialized	0	Object has not started loading data yet.

Example

To witness a readyState property other than complete for standard HTML, you can try examining the property in a script that immediately follows an <img> tag:

```
...
<img id="myImg" src="someImage.gif">
<script type="text/javaScript">
   alert(document.getElementById("myImg").readyState);
</script>
...
```

Putting this fragment into a document that is accessible across a slow network helps. If the image is not in the browser's cache, you might get the uninitialized or loading result. The former means that the img object exists, but it has not started receiving the image data from the server. If you reload the page, chances are that the image will load instantaneously from the cache, and the readyState property will report complete.

Related Item: onreadystatechange event handler

recordNumber

Value: Integer or null   Read-Only

Compatibility: WinIE4+, MacIE4+, NN-, Moz-, Safari-, Opera-, Chrome-

Virtually every object has a recordNumber property, but it applies only to elements used in Internet Explorer data binding to represent repeated data. For example, if you display 30 records from an external data store in a table, the tr element in the table is represented only once in the HTML. However, the browser repeats the table row (and its component cells) to accommodate all 30 rows of data. If you click a row, you can use the recordNumber property of the tr object to see which record was clicked. A common application of this facility is in data binding situations that allow for updating records. For example, script a table so that clicking an uneditable row of data displays that record's data in editable text boxes elsewhere on the page. If an object is not bound to a data source, or if it is a nonrepeating object bound to a data source, the recordNumber property is null.

Example

Listing 26-15 shows how to use the `recordNumber` property to navigate to a specific record in a sequence of data. The data source is a small, tab-delimited file consisting of 20 records of Academy Awards data. Thus, the table that displays a subset of the fields is bound to the data source object. Also bound to the data source object are three `span` objects embedded within a paragraph near the top of the page. As the user clicks a row of data, three fields from that clicked record are placed in the bound `span` objects.

The script part of this page is a mere single statement. When the user triggers the `onclick` event handler of the repeated `tr` object, the function receives as a parameter a reference to the `tr` object. The data store object maintains an internal copy of the data in a `recordset` object. One of the properties of this `recordset` object is the `AbsolutePosition` property, which is the integer value of the current record that the data object points to (it can point to only one row at a time, and the default row is the first row). The statement sets the `AbsolutePosition` property of the `recordset` object to the `recordNumber` property for the row that the user clicks. Because the three `span` elements are bound to the same data source, they are immediately updated to reflect the change to the data object's internal pointer to the current record. Notice, too, that the third `span` object is bound to one of the data source fields not shown in the table. You can reach any field of a record because the data source object holds the entire data source content. However, in actual practice, it would be disconcerting for the visitor to your web site to see something like the name of the film the best actor was in when that information is not reflected in the table below (some visitor's might even start muttering "bug").

LISTING 26-15

Using the Data Binding recordNumber Property

HTML: `jsb26-15.html`

```html
<!DOCTYPE html>
<html>
  <head>
    <meta http-equiv="content-type" content="text/html;charset=utf-8">
    <title>Data Binding (recordNumber)</title>
    <style type="text/css">
      #instructions
      {
          fon-weight:bold;
      }
      .filmTitle
      {
          font-style:italic;
      }
      #columnHeaders
      {
          background-color:yellow; text-align:center;
      }
    </style>
    <script type="text/javascript" src="../jsb-global.js"></script>
    <script type="text/javascript" src="jsb26-15.js"></script>
```

continued

599

LISTING 26-15   *(continued)*

```html
</head>
<body>
 <p><span id="instructions">Academy Awards 1978-1997</span> (Click on a table
     row to extract data from one record into the following paragraph.)
 </p>
 <p>The award for Best Actor of <span datasrc="#oscars" datafld="Year"></span>
     went to <span datasrc="#oscars" datafld="Best Actor"></span>
     for his outstanding achievement in the film
    <span class="filmTitle" datasrc="#oscars" datafld="Best Actor Film"></span>.
 </p>
 <table border="1" datasrc="#oscars" align="center">
    <thead id="columnHeaders">
        <tr>
            <td>Year</td>
            <td>Film</td>
            <td>Director</td>
            <td>Actress</td>
            <td>Actor</td>
        </tr>
    </thead>
    <tr id="repeatableRow" onclick="setRecNum(this)">
        <td><div id="col1" datafld="Year"></div></td>
        <td><div class="filmTitle" id="col2" datafld="Best Picture"></div></td>
        <td><div id="col3" datafld="Best Director"></div></td>
        <td><div id="col4" datafld="Best Actress"></div></td>
        <td><div id="col5" datafld="Best Actor"></div></td>
    </tr>
 </table>
 <object id="oscars" classid="clsid:333C7BC4-460F-11D0-BC04-0080C7055A83">
    <param name="DataURL" value="Academy Awards.txt" />
    <param name="UseHeader" value="True" />
    <param name="FieldDelim" value="&#09;" />
 </object>
 </body>
</html>
```

JavaScript: jsb26-15.js

```javascript
// set recordset pointer to the record clicked on in the table.
function setRecNum(row)
{
    document.oscars.recordset.AbsolutePosition = row.recordNumber;
}
```

Related Items: dataFld, dataSrc properties; table, tr objects (Chapter 41)

runtimeStyle

Value: style object   Read-Only

Compatibility: WinIE5+, MacIE5+, NN-, Moz-, Safari-, Opera-, Chrome-

You can determine the browser default settings for style sheet attributes with the help of the `runtimeStyle` property. The `style` object that this property returns contains all style attributes and the default settings at the time the page loads. This property does not reflect values assigned to elements by style sheets in the document or by scripts. The default values returned by this property differ from the values returned by the `currentStyle` property. The latter includes data about values that are not assigned explicitly by style sheets yet are influenced by the default behavior of the browser's rendering engine. In contrast, the `runtimeStyle` property shows unassigned style values as empty or zero.

Example

To change a style property setting, access it via the element's `style` object. Use The Evaluator (see Chapter 4) to compare the properties of the `runtimeStyle` and `style` objects of an element. For example, an unmodified copy of The Evaluator contains an `em` element whose ID is `"myEM"`. Enter both

```
document.getElementById("myEM").style.color
```

and

```
document.getElementById("myEM").runtimeStyle.color
```

in the top text box in turn. Initially, both values are empty. Now assign a color to the `style` property via the top text box:

```
document.getElementById("myEM").style.color = "red"
```

If you type the two earlier statements in the top box, you can see that the `style` object reflects the change, whereas the `runtimeStyle` object holds onto its original (empty) value.

Related Items: `currentStyle` property; `style` object (Chapter 38)

scopeName
tagUrn

Value: String   Read-Only

Compatibility: WinIE5+, MacIE-, NN-, Moz-, Safari-, Opera-, Chrome-

The `scopeName` property is associated primarily with XML code that is embedded within a document. When you include XML, you can specify one or more XML Namespaces that define the owner of a custom tag name, thus aiming toward preventing conflicts of identical custom tags from different sources in a document.

The XML Namespace is assigned as an attribute of the `<html>` tag that surrounds the entire document:

```
<html xmlns:fred='http://www.someURL.com'>
```

After that, the Namespace value precedes all custom tags linked to that Namespace:

```
<fred:FIRST_Name id="fredFirstName"/>
```

elementObject.**scrollHeight**

To find out the Namespace owner of an element, you can read the scopeName property of that element. For the preceding example, the scopeName returns fred. For regular HTML elements, the returned value is always HTML. The tagURN property sits alongside scopeName and stores the URI for the namespace.

The scopeName property is available only in Win32 and UNIX flavors of IE5+. The comparable properties for scopeName and tagURN in the W3C DOM are prefix and namespaceURI.

Example

If you have a sample document that contains XML and a namespace spec, you can use document.write() or alert() methods to view the value of the scopeName property. The syntax is

```
document.getElementById("elementID").scopeName
```

Related Item: tagUrn property

scrollHeight
scrollWidth

Value: Integer   Read-Only

Compatibility: WinIE4+, MacIE4+, NN7+, Moz1.0.1+, Safari+, Opera+, Chrome+

The scrollHeight and scrollWidth properties contain the pixel measures of an object, regardless of how much of the object is visible on the page. Therefore, if the browser window displays a vertical scroll bar, and the body extends below the bottom of the viewable space in the window, the scrollHeight takes into account the entire height of the body as though you were to scroll downward and see the entire element. For most elements that don't have their own scroll bars, the scrollHeight and scrollWidth properties have the same values as the clientHeight and clientWidth properties.

Example

Use The Evaluator (see Chapter 4) to experiment with these two properties of the textarea object, which displays the output of evaluations and property listings. To begin, enter the following in the bottom one-line text box to list the properties of the body object:

```
document.body
```

This displays a long list of properties for the body object. Now enter the following property expression in the top one-line text box to see the scrollHeight property of the output textarea when it holds the dozens of lines of property listings:

```
document.getElementById("myTextArea").scrollHeight
```

The result, some number probably in the hundreds, is now displayed in the output textarea. This means that you can scroll the content of the output element vertically to reveal that number of pixels. Click the Evaluate button once more. The result, 13 or 14, is a measure of the scrollHeight property of the textarea that had only the previous result in it. The scrollable height of that content was only 13 or 14 pixels, the height of the font in the textarea. The scrollWidth property of the output textarea is fixed by the width assigned to the element's cols attribute (as calculated by the browser to determine how wide to make the text area on the page).

Related Items: `clientHeight`, `clientWidth` properties; `window.scroll()` method

scrollLeft
scrollTop

Value: Integer   Read-Only

Compatibility: WinIE4+, MacIE4+, NN7+, Moz1.0.1+, Safari+, Opera+, Chrome+

If an element is scrollable (in other words, it has its own scroll bars), you can find out how far the element is scrolled in the horizontal and vertical direction via the `scrollLeft` and `scrollTop` properties. These values are pixels. For nonscrollable elements, these values are always zero — even if they are contained by elements that are scrollable. For example, if you scroll a browser window (or frame in a multiframe environment) vertically, the `scrollTop` property of the `body` object is whatever the pixel distance is between the top of the object (now out of view) and the first visible row of pixels of the element. But the `scrollTop` value of a table that is in the document remains zero.

Netscape browsers prior to version 7 (Mozilla) treat scrolling of a `body` element from the point of view of the window. If you want to find out the scrolled offset of the current page in these browsers, use `window.scrollX` and `window.scrollY`.

Scripts that involve tracking mouse events in IE need to take into account the `scrollLeft` and `scrollTop` properties of the body to compensate for scrolling of the page. See the `Event` object in Chapter 32.

Example

Use The Evaluator (see Chapter 4) to experiment with these two properties of the `textarea` object, which displays the output of evaluations and property listings. To begin, enter the following in the bottom one-line text box to list the properties of the `body` object:

```
document.body
```

This displays a long list of properties for the `body` object. Use the `textarea`'s scroll bar to page down a couple of times. Now enter the following property expression in the top one-line text box to see the `scrollTop` property of the output `textarea` after you scroll:

```
document.getElementById("myTextArea").scrollTop
```

The result, some number, is now displayed in the output `textarea`. This means that the content of the `output` element was scrolled vertically. Click the Evaluate button once more. The result, 0, is a measure of the `scrollTop` property of the `textarea` that had only the previous result in it. There wasn't enough content in the `textarea` to scroll, so the content was not scrolled at all. The `scrollTop` property, therefore, is zero. The `scrollLeft` property of the output is always zero because the `textarea` element is set to wrap any text that overflows the width of the element. No horizontal scroll bar appears in this case, and the `scrollLeft` property never changes.

Related Items: `clientLeft`, `clientTop` properties; `window.scroll()` method

sourceIndex

Value: Integer   Read-Only

Compatibility: WinIE4+, MacIE4+, NN-, Moz-, Safari+, Opera+, Chrome+

The sourceIndex property returns the numeric index (zero-based) of the object within the entire document, which is the group of all elements in the document.

Example

Although the operation of this property is straightforward, the sequence of elements exposed by the document.all property may not be. To that end, you can use The Evaluator (see Chapter 4) to experiment in IE4+ with the values that the sourceIndex property returns to see how the index values of the document.all collection follow the source code.

To begin, reload The Evaluator. Enter the following statement in the top text box to set a preinitialized global variable:

```
a = 0
```

When you evaluate this expression, a zero should appear in the Results box. Next, enter the following statement in the top text box:

```
document.all[a].tagName + " [" + a++ + "]"
```

There are a lot of plus signs in this statement, so be sure you enter it correctly. As you successively evaluate this statement (repeatedly click the Evaluate button), the global variable (a) is incremented, enabling you to walk through the elements in source-code order. The sourceIndex value for each HTML tag appears in square brackets in the Results box. You generally begin with the following sequence:

```
html [0]
head [1]
title [2]
```

You can continue until there are no more elements, at which point an error message appears because the value of a exceeds the number of elements in the document.all array. Compare your findings against the HTML source code view of The Evaluator.

Related Item: item( ) method

style

Value: style object reference   Read/Write

Compatibility: WinIE4+, MacIE4+, NN6+, Moz+, Safari+, Opera+, Chrome+

The style property is the gateway to an element's style sheet settings. The property's value is a style object whose properties enable you to read and write the style sheet settings for the element. Although scripts do not usually manipulate the style object as a whole, it is quite common in a DHTML page for scripts to get or set multiple properties of the style object to effect animation, visibility, and all appearance parameters of the element. Note that style properties returned through this object are only those that are explicitly set by the element's style attribute or by script.

You can find significant differences in the breadth of properties of the style object in different versions of IE and NN. See Chapter 38 for more details on the style object.

Example

Most of the action with the style property has to do with the style object's properties, so you can use The Evaluator here simply to explore the lists of style object properties available on as many

DHTML-compatible browsers as you have running. To begin, enter the following statement in the bottom, one-line text box to inspect the `style` property for the `document.body` object:

```
document.body.style
```

Now inspect the `style` property of the table element that is part of the original version of The Evaluator. Enter the following statement in the bottom text box:

```
document.getElementById("myTable").style
```

In both cases, the values assigned to the `style` object's properties are quite limited by default.

Related Items: `currentStyle`, `runtimeStyle` properties; `style` object (Chapter 38)

tabIndex

Value: Integer   Read/Write

Compatibility: WinIE4+, MacIE4+, NN6+, Moz+, Safari+, Opera+, Chrome+

The `tabIndex` property controls where in the tabbing sequence the current object receives focus. This property obviously applies only to elements that can receive focus. IE5+ permits giving focus to more elements than most other browsers, but for all browsers compatible with this property, the primary elements for which you may want to control focus (namely, form input elements) are covered.

In general, browsers treat form elements as focusable elements by default. Nonform elements usually don't receive focus unless you specifically set their `tabIndex` properties (or `tabindex` tag attributes). If you set the `tabIndex` property of one form element to 1, that element is first in the tabbing order. Meanwhile, the rest fall into source-code tabbing order on successive presses of the Tab key. If you set two elements to, say, 1, the tabbing proceeds in source-code order for those two elements and then on to the rest of the elements in source-code order starting with the top of the page.

In Internet Explorer and Moz1.8+, you can remove an element from tabbing order entirely by setting its `tabIndex` property to `-1`. Users can still click those elements to make changes to form element settings, but tabbing bypasses the element.

Example

Listing 26-16 contains a sample script that demonstrates how to control the tab order of a form via the `tabIndex` property. This example demonstrates not only the way you can modify the tabbing behavior of a form on-the-fly, but also how to force form elements out of the tabbing sequence entirely. In this page, the top form (named `lab`) contains four elements. Scripts invoked by buttons in the bottom form control the tabbing sequence. Notice that the `tabindex` attributes of all bottom form elements are set to `-1`, which means that these control buttons are not part of the tabbing sequence.

When you load the page, the default tabbing order for the `lab` form control elements (default setting of zero) takes charge. If you start pressing the Tab key, the precise results at first depend on the browser you use. In IE, the Address field is first selected; next, the Tab sequence gives focus to the window (or frame, if this page were in a frameset); finally, the tabbing reaches the `lab` form. Continue pressing the Tab key, and watch how the browser assigns focus to each of the element types. In WebKit- and Presto-based browsers, as well as recent versions of Mozilla, the tabbing begins in the `lab` form. In NN6, however, you must click anywhere on the content to get the Tab key to start working on form controls.

The sample script inverts the tabbing sequence with the help of a `for` loop that initializes two variables that work in opposite directions as the looping progresses. This gives the last element the lowest tabIndex value. The skip2() function simply sets the tabIndex property of the second text box to -1, removing it from the tabbing entirely (IE used to be the only browser that supported this, but all modern browsers support it). Notice, however, that you can click in the field and still enter text. (See the disabled property earlier in this chapter to see how to prevent field editing.) NN6 does not provide a tabIndex property setting that forces the browser to skip a form control; you should disable the control instead.

LISTING 26-16

Controlling the tabIndex Property

HTML: jsb26-16.html

```
<!DOCTYPE html>
<html>
   <head>
      <meta http-equiv="content-type" content="text/html;charset=utf-8">
      <title>tabIndex Property</title>
      <script type="text/javascript" src="../jsb-global.js"></script>
      <script type="text/javascript" src="jsb26-16.js"></script>
   </head>
   <body>
      <h1>tabIndex Property Lab</h1>
      <hr />
      <form name="lab">
         Text box no. 1: <input type="text" name="text1" />
         <br />
         Text box no. 2: <input type="text" name="text2" />
         <br />
         <input type="button" value="A Button" />
         <br />
         <input type="checkbox" />And a checkbox
      </form>
      <hr />
      <form name="control">
         <input type="button" value="Invert Tabbing Order" tabindex="-1"
               onclick="invert()" />
         <br />
         <input type="button" value="Skip Text box no. 2"
               tabindex="-1" onclick="skip2()" />
         <br />
         <input type="button" value="Reset to Normal Order" tabindex="-1"
               onclick="resetTab()" />
      </form>
   </body>
</html>
```

JavaScript: jsb26-16.js

```
function invert()
{
   var form = document.lab;
   for (var i = 0, j = form.elements.length; i < form.elements.length; i++, j--)
```

```
    {
        form.elements[i].tabIndex = j;
    }
}

function skip2()
{
    document.lab.text2.tabIndex = -1;
}

function resetTab()
{
    var form = document.lab;
    for (var i = 0; i < form.elements.length; i++)
    {
        form.elements[i].tabIndex = 0;
    }
}
```

The final function, `resetTab()`, sets the `tabIndex` property value to zero for all `lab` form elements; this restores the default order.

Related Items: `blur()`, `focus()` methods

tagName

Value: String   Read-Only

Compatibility: WinIE4+, MacIE4+, NN6+, Moz+, Safari+, Opera+, Chrome+

The `tagName` property returns a string of the HTML or XML tag name belonging to the object. All `tagName` values are returned in all-uppercase characters, even if the source code is written in all-lowercase characters or a mixture. This consistency makes it easier to perform string comparisons. For example, you can create a generic function that contains a `switch` statement to execute actions for some tags and not others. The skeleton of such a function looks like the following:

```
function  processObj(objRef)
{
    switch (objRef.tagName)
    {
        case "TR":
            [statements to deal with table row object]
            break;
        case "TD":
            [statements to deal with table cell object]
            break;
        case "COLGROUP":
            [statements to deal with column group object]
            break;
        default:
            [statements to deal with all other object types]
    }
}
```

Example

You can also see the `tagName` property in action in the example associated with the `sourceIndex` property discussed earlier in the chapter. In that example, the `tagName` property is read from a sequence of objects in source-code order.

Related Items: `nodeName` property; `getElementsByTagName()` method

tagUrn

(See `scopeName`)

textContent

Value: String   Read/Write

Compatibility: WinIE-, MacIE-, NN-, Moz1.7+, Safari+, Opera+, Chrome+

This property stores the text string of a node, including any combined text nodes within an element. This means that the content of a node is reflected in the `textContent` property as a single string of text even if it has other nested elements, such as `em`. If you replace the content of a node with a string of text by setting the `textContent` property, all previous node content is replaced, including nested elements. You can think of the `textContent` property as the W3C DOM equivalent of IE's `innerText` property.

Related Item: `innerText` property

title

Value: String   Read/Write

Compatibility: WinIE4+, MacIE4+, NN6+, Moz+, Safari+, Opera+, Chrome+

The W3C standard states that you should use the `title` property (and `title` attribute) in an advisory role. Keep in mind that devices for the disabled use the `title` property and `title` attribute, so we recommend you always give them values. Most browsers interpret this role as text assigned to tooltips that pop up momentarily while the cursor rests atop an element. The advantage of having this property available for writing is that your scripts can modify an element's tooltip text in response to other user interaction on the page. A tooltip can provide brief help about the behavior of icons or links on the page. It can also convey a summary of key facts from the destination of a link, thus enabling a visitor to see vital information without having to navigate to the other page.

As with setting the status bar, we don't recommend using tooltips for conveying mission-critical information to the user. Not all users are patient enough to let the pointer pause for the tooltip to appear. On the other hand, a user may be more likely to notice a tooltip when it appears rather than a status-bar message (even though the latter appears instantaneously).

Example

Listing 26-17 provides a glimpse at how you can use the `title` property to establish tooltips for a page. A simple paragraph element has its `title` attribute set to `"First Time!"`, which is what the tooltip displays if you roll the pointer atop the paragraph and pause after the page loads. But an `onmouseover` event handler for that element increments a global variable counter in the script, and the `title` property of the paragraph object is modified with each mouseover action. The `count` value is made part of a string assigned to the `title` property. Notice that there is not a live connection between the `title` property and the variable; instead, the new value explicitly sets the `title` property.

LISTING 26-17

Controlling the title Property

HTML: jsb26-17.html

```
<!DOCTYPE html>
<html>
    <head>
        <meta http-equiv="content-type" content="text/html;charset=utf-8">
        <title>title Property</title>
        <script type="text/javascript" src="../jsb-global.js"></script>
        <script type="text/javascript" src="jsb26-17.js"></script>
    </head>
    <body>
        <h1>title Property Lab</h1>
        <hr />
        <p id="myP" title="First Time!" onmouseover="incrementCount(this)">Roll
            the mouse over this paragraph a few times.
            <br />
            Then pause atop it to view the tooltip.
        </p>
    </body>
</html>
```

JavaScript: jsb26-17.js

```
// global counting variable
var count = 0;

function setToolTip(elem)
{
    elem.title = "You have previously rolled atop this paragraph " + count + "
        time(s).";
}

function incrementCount(elem)
{
    count++;
    setToolTip(elem);
}
```

Related Item: window.status property

uniqueID

Value: String   Read-Only

Compatibility: WinIE5+, MacIE-, NN-, Moz-, Safari-, Opera-, Chrome-

You can let the WinIE5+ browser generate an identifier (id property) for a dynamically generated element on the page with the aid of the uniqueID property. You should use this feature with care, because the ID it generates at any given time may differ from the ID generated the next time the element is created in the page. Therefore, you should use the uniqueID property when your scripts *elementObject*.**uniqueID**

require an unknown element to have an `id` property, but the algorithms are not expecting any specific identifier.

To guarantee that an element gets only one ID assigned to it while the object exists in memory, assign the value via the `uniqueID` property of that same object — not some other object. After you retrieve the `uniqueID` property of an object, the property's value stays the same no matter how often you access the property again. In general, you assign the value returned by the `uniqueID` property to the object's `id` property for other kinds of processing. (For example, the parameter of a `getElementById()` method requires the value assigned to the `id` property of an object.)

Example

Listing 26-18 demonstrates the recommended syntax for obtaining and applying a browser-generated identifier for an object. After you enter some text in the text box and click the button, the `addRow()` function appends a row to the table. The left column displays the identifier generated via the table row object's `uniqueID` property. IE5+ generates identifiers in the format `"ms__idn"`, where *n* is an integer starting with zero for the current browser session. Because the `addRow()` function assigns `uniqueID` values to the row and the cells in each row, the integer for each row is three greater than the previous one. There is no guarantee that future generations of the browser will follow this format, so do not rely on the format or sequence in your scripts.

LISTING 26-18

Using the uniqueID Property

HTML: `jsb26-18.html`

```
<!DOCTYPE html>
<html>
   <head>
      <meta http-equiv="content-type" content="text/html;charset=utf-8">
      <title>Inserting an WinIE5+ Table Row</title>
      <script type="text/javascript" src="../jsb-global.js"></script>
      <script type="text/javascript" src="jsb26-18.js"></script>
   </head>
   <body>
      <table id="myTable" border="1">
         <tr>
            <th>Row ID</th>
            <th>Data</th>
         </tr>
         <tr id="firstDataRow">
            <td>firstDataRow</td>
            <td>Fred</td>
         </tr>
         <tr id="secondDataRow">
            <td>secondDataRow</td>
            <td>Jane</td>
         </tr>
      </table>
      <hr />
```

```
    <form>
        Enter text to be added to the table:
        <br />
        <input type="text" name="input" size="25" />
        <br />
        <input type='button' value='Insert Row'
               onclick='addRow(this.form.input.value)' />
    </form>
   </body>
</html>
```

JavaScript: jsb26-18.js

```
function addRow(item1)
{
    if (item1)
    {
        // assign long reference to shorter var name
        var theTable = document.getElementById("myTable");
        // append new row to the end of the table
        var newRow = theTable.insertRow(theTable.rows.length);
        // give the row its own ID
        newRow.id = newRow.uniqueID;

        // declare cell variable and data variable
        var newCell;
        var newText;

        // an inserted row has no cells, so insert the cells
        newCell = newRow.insertCell(0);
        // give this cell its own id
        newCell.id = newCell.uniqueID;
        // display the row's id as the cell text
        newText = document.createTextNode(newRow.id);
        newCell.appendChild(newText);
        newCell.bgColor = "yellow"
        // re-use cell var for second cell insertion
        newCell = newRow.insertCell(1);
        newCell.id = newCell.uniqueID;
        newText = document.createTextNode(item1);
        newCell.appendChild(newText);
    }
}
```

Related Items: id property; getElementById() method

unselectable

Value: String constant ("on" or "off")   Read/Write

Compatibility: WinIE5.5+, MacIE-, NN-, Moz-, Safari-, Opera+, Chrome-

elementObject.**addBehavior()**

This property controls the selectability of an element — that is, whether the element's content can be selected by the user. You might use this property to prevent a sensitive piece of data from being selected and copied.

Methods

addBehavior("*URL*")

Returns: Integer ID

Compatibility: WinIE5+, MacIE-, NN-, Moz-, Safari-, Opera-, Chrome-

The `addBehavior()` method imports an external Internet Explorer behavior and attaches it to the current object, thereby extending the properties and/or methods of that object. (See Chapter 51 on the CD-ROM for details on IE behaviors.) The sole parameter of the `addBehavior()` method is a URL pointer to the behavior component's code. This component may be in an external file (with an `.htc` extension), in which case the parameter can be a relative or absolute URL. IE also includes a library of built-in (default) behaviors, whose URLs are in the following format:

> `#default#behaviorName`

Here, `behaviorName` is one of the default behaviors. If the behavior is imported into the document via the `object` tag, the `addBehavior()` method parameter is the ID of that element in the following format:

> `#objectID`

When you add a behavior, the loading of the external code occurs asynchronously. This means that even though the method returns a value instantly, the behavior is not necessarily ready to work. Only when the behavior is fully loaded can it respond to events or allow access to its properties and methods. Behaviors loaded from external files observe domain security rules.

Example

Listing 26-19a shows what a behavior file looks like. It is the file used to demonstrate the `addBehavior()` method in Listing 26-19b. The behavior component and the HTML page that loads it must come from the same server and domain; they also must load via the same protocol (for example, `http://`, `https://`, and `file://` are mutually exclusive, mismatched protocols).

LISTING 26-19a

The makeHot.htc Behavior Component

```
<PUBLIC:ATTACH EVENT="onmousedown" ONEVENT="makeHot()" />
<PUBLIC:ATTACH EVENT="onmouseup" ONEVENT="makeNormal()" />
<PUBLIC:PROPERTY NAME="hotColor" />
<PUBLIC:METHOD NAME="setHotColor" />
<script type="text/jscript">
   var oldColor
   var hotColor = "red"

   function setHotColor(color)
   {
```

```
      hotColor = color
   }

   function makeHot()
   {
      if (event.srcElement == element)
      {
         oldColor = style.color
         runtimeStyle.color = hotColor
      }
   }

   function makeNormal()
   {
      if (event.srcElement == element)
      {
         runtimeStyle.color = oldColor
      }
   }
}
</script>
```

The object to which the component is attached is a simple paragraph object, shown in Listing 26-19b. When the page loads, the behavior is not attached, so clicking the paragraph text has no effect.

When you turn on the behavior by invoking the turnOn() function, the addBehavior() method attaches the code of the makeHot.htc component to the myP object. At this point, the myP object has one more property, one more method, and two more event handlers that are written to be made public by the component's code. If you want the behavior to apply to more than one paragraph in the document, you have to invoke the addBehavior() method for each paragraph object.

After the behavior file is instructed to start loading, the setInitialColor() function is called to set the new color property of the paragraph to the user's choice from the select list. But this can happen only if the component is fully loaded. Therefore, the function checks the readyState property of myP for completeness before invoking the component's function. If IE is still loading the component, the function is invoked again in 500 milliseconds.

As long as the behavior is loaded, you can change the color used to turn the paragraph hot. The function first ensures that the component is loaded by checking that the object has the new color property. If it does, the method of the component is invoked (as a demonstration of how to expose and invoke a component method). You can also simply set the property value.

LISTING 26-19b

Using addBehavior() and removeBehavior()

HTML: jsb26-19.html

```
<!DOCTYPE html>
<html>
   <head>
```

continued

elementObject.addBehavior()

LISTING 26-19b *(continued)*

```
        <meta http-equiv="content-type" content="text/html;charset=utf-8">
        <title>addBehavior() and removeBehavior() Methods</title>
        <script type="text/javascript" src="../jsb-global.js"></script>
        <script type="text/javascript" src="jsb26-19.js"></script>
    </head>
    <body>
        <h1>addBehavior() and removeBehavior() Method Lab</h1>
        <hr />
        <p id="myP">This is a sample paragraph. After turning on the behavior, it
            will turn your selected color when you mouse down anywhere in this
            paragraph.
        </p>
        <form>
            <input type="button" value="Switch On Behavior" onclick="turnOn()" />
            Choose a 'hot' color:
            <select name="colorChoice" onchange="setColor(this, this.value)">
                <option value="red">red</option>
                <option value="blue">blue</option>
                <option value="cyan">cyan</option>
            </select>
            <br />
            <input type="button" value="Switch Off Behavior"
                    onclick="turnOff()" />
            <p>
                <input type="button" value="Count the URNs"
                        onclick="showBehaviorCount()" />
            </p>
        </form>
    </body>
</html>
```

JavaScript: jsb26-19.js

```
var myPBehaviorID;

function turnOn()
{
   myPBehaviorID = document.getElementById("myP").addBehavior("makeHot.htc");
   setInitialColor();
}

function setInitialColor()
{
   if (document.getElementById("myP").readyState == "complete")
   {
      var select = document.forms[0].colorChoice;
      var color = select.options[select.selectedIndex].value;
      document.getElementById("myP").setHotColor(color);
   }
   else
```

```
    {
        setTimeout("setInitialColor()", 500);
    }
}

function turnOff()
{
    document.getElementById("myP").removeBehavior(myPBehaviorID);
}

function setColor(select, color)
{
    if (document.getElementById("myP").hotColor)
    {
        document.getElementById("myP").setHotColor(color);
    }
    else
    {
        alert("This feature is not available. Turn on the Behavior first.");
        select.selectedIndex = 0;
    }
}

function showBehaviorCount()
{
    var num = document.getElementById("myP").behaviorUrns.length;
    var msg = "The myP element has " + num + " behavior(s). ";
    alert(msg);
}
```

To turn off the behavior, the removeBehavior() method is invoked. Notice that the removeBehavior() method is associated with the myP object, and the parameter is the ID of the behavior added earlier. If you associate multiple behaviors with an object, you can remove one without disturbing the others, because each has its own unique ID.

Related Items: readyState property; removeBehavior() method; IE behaviors (Chapter 51 on the CD-ROM)

addEventListener("eventType", listenerFunc, useCapture) removeEventListener("eventType", listenerFunc, useCapture)

Returns: Nothing

Compatibility: WinIE-, MacIE-, NN6+, Moz+, Safari+, Opera+, Chrome+

The W3C DOM's event mechanism accommodates both event bubbling and trickling (see Chapter 32). Although the new mechanism supports the long-standing notion of binding an event to an element by way of HTML attributes (for example, the old onclick event handler), it encourages binding events by registering an event listener with an element. (In browsers that support the W3C event model, other ways of binding events — such as event handler attributes — are internally converted to registered events.)

elementObject.**removeEventListener()**

To tell the DOM that an element should listen for a particular kind of event, use the `addEventListener()` method on the element object. The method requires three parameters. The first is a string version of the event type for which the element should listen. Event type strings do not include the well-used `on` prefix of event handlers; instead, the names consist only of the event and are usually in all lowercase (except for some special systemwide events preceded by DOM). Table 26-7 shows all the events recognized by the W3C DOM specification (including some new DOM ones that are not yet implemented in browsers).

TABLE 26-7

W3C DOM Event Listener Types

abort	error
blur	focus
change	load
click	mousedown
DOMActivate	mousemove
DOMAttrModified	mouseout
DOMCharacterDataModified	mouseover
DOMFocusIn	mouseup
DOMFocusOut	reset
DOMNodeInserted	resize
DOMNodeInsertedIntoDocument	scroll
DOMNodeRemoved	select
DOMNodeRemovedFromDocument	submit
DOMSubtreeModified	unload

Note that the event types specified in the DOM Level 2 are more limited than the wide range of events defined in IE4+. Also, the W3C temporarily tabled the issue of keyboard events until DOM Level 3. Fortunately, most W3C-compatible browsers implement keyboard events in a fashion that likely will appear as part of the W3C DOM Level 3.

The second parameter of the `addEventListener()` method is a reference to the JavaScript function to be invoked. This is the same form used to assign a function to an event property of an object (for example, `objReference.onclick = someFunction`), and it should *not* be a quoted string. This approach also means that you cannot specify parameters in the function call. Therefore, functions that need to reference forms or form control elements must build their own references (with the help of the event object's property that says which object is the event's target).

By default, the W3C DOM event model has events bubble upward through the element container hierarchy starting with the target object of the event (for example, the button being clicked). However, if you specify `true` for the third parameter of the `addEventListener()` method, event capture is enabled for this particular event type whenever the current object is the event target. This means that any other event type targeted at the current object bubbles upward unless it, too, has an event listener associated with the object and the third parameter is set to `true`.

Using the `addEventListener()` method requires that the object to which it is attached already exists. Therefore, you most likely will use the method inside an initialization function triggered by the `onload` event handler for the page. (The `document` object can use `addEventListener()` for the load event immediately, because the `document` object exists early in the loading process.)

A script can also eliminate an event listener that was previously added by script. The `removeEventListener()` method takes the same parameters as `addEventListener()`, which means that you can turn off one listener without disturbing others. In fact, because you can add two listeners for the same event and listener function (one set to capture and one not — a rare occurrence indeed), the three parameters of the `removeEventListener()` enable you to specify precisely which listener to remove from an object.

Unlike the event capture mechanism of NN4, the W3C DOM event model does not have a global capture mechanism for an event type regardless of target. And with respect to Internet Explorer, the `addEventListener()` method is closely analogous to the IE5+ `attachEvent()` method. Also, event capture in IE5+ is enabled via the separate `setCapture()` method. Both the W3C and IE event models use their own syntaxes to bind objects to event handling functions, so the actual functions may be capable of serving both models with browser version branching required only for event binding. See Chapter 32 for more about event handling with these two event models.

Example

Listing 26-20 provides a compact workbench to explore and experiment with the basic W3C DOM event model. When the page loads, no event listeners are registered with the browser (except the control buttons, of course). But you can add an event listener for a `click` event in bubble and/or capture mode to the `body` element or the `p` element that surrounds the `span` holding the line of text. If you add an event listener and click the text, you see a readout of the element processing the event and information indicating whether the event phase is bubbling (3) or capture (1). With all event listeners engaged, notice the sequence of events being processed. Remove listeners one at a time to see the effect on event processing.

LISTING 26-20

W3C Event Lab

```
HTML: jsb26-20.html
<!DOCTYPE html>
<html>
    <head>
        <meta http-equiv="content-type" content="text/html;charset=utf-8">
        <title>W3C Event Model Lab</title>
        <style type="text/css">
            td
            {
                text-align:center
            }
        </style>
```

continued

LISTING 26-20   *(continued)*

```html
    <script type="text/javascript" src="../jsb-global.js"></script>
    <script type="text/javascript" src="jsb26-20.js"></script>
</head>
<body id="myBODY">
    <h1>W3C Event Model Lab</h1>
    <hr />
    <p id="myP"><span id="mySPAN">This paragraph (a SPAN element nested inside
        a P element) can be set to listen for "click" events.</span>
    </p>
    <hr />
    <form name="controls" id="controls">
        <p>Examine click event characteristics: 
            <input type="button" value="Clear" onclick="clearTextArea()" />
            <br />
            <textarea name="output" cols="80" rows="6" wrap="virtual"></textarea>
        </p>
        <table cellpadding="5" border="1">
            <caption style="font-weight:bold">Control Panel</caption>
            <tr style="background-color:#ffff99">
                <td rowspan="2">"Bubble"-type click listener:</td>
                <td>
                    <input type="button" value="Add to BODY"
                            onclick="addBubbleListener('myBODY')" />
                </td>
                <td>
                    <input type="button" value="Remove from BODY"
                            onclick="removeBubbleListener('myBODY')" />
                </td>
            </tr>
            <tr style="background-color:#ffff99">
                <td>
                    <input type="button" value="Add to P"
                            onclick="addBubbleListener('myP')" />
                </td>
                <td>
                    <input type="button" value="Remove from P"
                            onclick="removeBubbleListener('myP')" />
                </td>
            </tr>
            <tr style="background-color:#ff9999">
                <td rowspan="2">"Capture"-type click listener:</td>
                <td>
                    <input type="button" value="Add to BODY"
                            onclick="addCaptureListener('myBODY')" />
                </td>
                <td>
                    <input type="button" value="Remove from BODY"
                            onclick="removeCaptureListener('myBODY')" />
                </td>
            </tr>
```

```
            <tr style="background-color:#ff9999">
                <td>
                    <input type="button" value="Add to P"
                            onclick="addCaptureListener('myP')" />
                </td>
                <td>
                    <input type="button" value="Remove from P"
                            onclick="removeCaptureListener('myP')" />
                </td>
            </tr>
        </table>
    </form>
  </body>
</html>
```

JavaScript: jsb26-20.js

```javascript
// add event listeners
function addBubbleListener(elemID)
{
   document.getElementById(elemID).addEventListener("click",
     reportEvent, false);
}
function addCaptureListener(elemID)
{
   document.getElementById(elemID).addEventListener("click", reportEvent, true);
}

// remove event listeners
function removeBubbleListener(elemID)
{
   document.getElementById(elemID).removeEventListener("click",
     reportEvent, false);
}
function removeCaptureListener(elemID)
{
   document.getElementById(elemID).removeEventListener("click",
     reportEvent, true);
}

// display details about any event heard
function reportEvent(evt)
{
   var elem = (evt.target.nodeType == 3) ? evt.target.parentNode : evt.target;
   if (elem.id == "mySPAN")
   {
     var msg = "Event processed at " + evt.currentTarget.tagName +
               " element (event phase = " + evt.eventPhase + ").\n";
     document.controls.output.value += msg;
   }
}
```

continued

LISTING 26-20   *(continued)*

```
// clear the details textarea
function clearTextArea()
{
    document.controls.output.value = "";
}
```

Related Items: attachEvent(), detachEvent(), dispatchEvent(), fireEvent(), removeEventListener() methods

appendChild(*elementObject*)

Returns: Node object reference

Compatibility: WinIE5+, MacIE5+, NN6+, Moz+, Safari+, Opera+, Chrome+

The appendChild() method inserts an element or text node (defined by other code that comes before it) as the new, last child of the current element. Aside from the more obvious application of adding a new child element to the end of a sequence of child nodes, the appendChild() method is also practical for building element objects and their content before appending, replacing, or inserting the element into an existing document. The document.createElement() method generates a reference to an element of whatever tag name you assign as that method's parameter.

The appendChild() method returns a reference to the appended node object. This reference differs from the object that is passed as the method's parameter because the returned value represents the object as part of the document rather than as a freestanding object in memory.

Example

Listing 26-21 contains an example that shows how to use the appendChild() method in concert with removeChild() and replaceChild() to modify child elements in a document. Because many W3C DOM browsers treat source-code carriage returns as text nodes (and, thus, child nodes of their parent), the HTML for the affected list elements in Listing 26-21 is shown without carriage returns between elements.

The append() function creates a new li element and then uses the appendChild() method to attach the text box text as the displayed text for the item. The nested expression, document .createTextNode(newData), evaluates to a legitimate node that is appended to the new li item. All of this occurs before the new li item is added to the document. In the final statement of the function, appendChild() is invoked from the vantage point of the ul element — thus adding the li element as a child node of the ul element.

Invoking the replaceChild() method in the rplace() function uses some of the same code. The main difference is that the replaceChild() method requires a second parameter: a reference to the child element to be replaced. This demonstration replaces the final child node of the ul list, so the function takes advantage of the lastChild property of all elements to get a reference to that final nested child. That reference becomes the second parameter to replaceChild().

LISTING 26-21

Various Child Methods

HTML: jsb26-21.html

```html
<!DOCTYPE html>
<html>
   <head>
      <meta http-equiv="content-type" content="text/html;charset=utf-8">
      <title>appendChild(), removeChild(), and replaceChild() Methods</title>
      <script type="text/javascript" src="../jsb-global.js"></script>
      <script type="text/javascript" src="jsb26-21.js"></script>
   </head>
   <body>
      <h1>Child Methods</h1>
      <hr />
      Here is a list of items:
      <ul id="myUL"><li>First Item</li><li>Second Item</li></ul>
      <form>
         Enter some text to add/replace in the list:
         <input type="text" id="newListData" size="30" />
         <br />
         <input type="button" value="Append to List"
               onclick="append()" />
         <input type="button" value="Replace Final Item"
               onclick="rplace()" />
         <input type="button" value="Truncate List to 2 Items"
               onclick="truncateList()" />
      </form>
   </body>
</html>
```

JavaScript: jsb26-21.js

```javascript
function append()
{
   var newData = document.getElementById("newListData").value;
   if (newData)
   {
      var newItem = document.createElement("LI");
      newItem.appendChild(document.createTextNode(newData));
      document.getElementById("myUL").appendChild(newItem);
   }
}

// Opera throws an error when use keyword replace, so....
function rplace()
{
   var newData = document.getElementById("newListData").value;
   if (newData)
   {
```

continued

LISTING 26-21 *(continued)*

```
        var newItem = document.createElement("LI");
        var lastChild = document.getElementById("myUL").lastChild;
        newItem.appendChild(document.createTextNode(newData));
        document.getElementById("myUL").replaceChild(newItem, lastChild);
    }
}

function truncateList()
{
    var oneChild;
    var mainObj = document.getElementById("myUL");
    while (mainObj.childNodes.length > 2)
    {
        oneChild = mainObj.lastChild;
        mainObj.removeChild(oneChild);
    }
}
```

The final part of the demonstration uses the removeChild() method to peel away all children of the ul element until just two items are left standing. Again, the lastChild property comes in handy as the truncateList() function keeps removing the last child until only two remain.

Related Items: removeChild(), replaceChild() methods; nodes and children (Chapter 25)

applyElement(*elementObject*[, *type*])

Returns: Nothing

Compatibility: WinIE5+, MacIE-, NN-, Moz-, Safari-, Opera-, Chrome-

The applyElement() method enables you to insert a new element as the parent or child of the current object. An important feature of this method is that the new object is wrapped around the current object (if the new element is to become the parent) or the current object's content (if the new element is to become a child). When the new element becomes a child, all previous children are nested further by one generation to become immediate children of the new element. You can imagine how the resulting action of this method affects the containment hierarchy of the current element, so you must be careful how you use the applyElement() method.

One parameter, a reference to the object to be applied, is required. This object may be generated from constructions such as document.createElement() or from one of the child or node methods that returns an object. The second parameter is optional, and it must be one of the following values:

Parameter Value	Description
outside	New element becomes the parent of the current object.
inside	New element becomes the immediate child of the current object.

If you omit the second parameter, the default value (outside) is assumed. Listing 26-22 shows how the applyElement() method is used both with and without default values.

Example

To help you visualize the impact of the applyElement() method with its different parameter settings, Listing 26-22 enables you to apply a new element (an em element) to a span element inside a paragraph. At any time, you can view the HTML of the entire p element to see where the em element is applied, as well as its impact on the element containment hierarchy for the paragraph.

After you load the page, inspect the HTML for the paragraph before doing anything else. Notice the span element and its nested code element, both of which surround the one-word content. If you apply the em element inside the span element (click the middle button), the span element's first (and only) child element becomes the em element; the code element is now a child of the new em element.

LISTING 26-22

Using the applyElement() Method

HTML: jsb26-22.html

```
<!DOCTYPE html>
<html>
   <head>
      <meta http-equiv="content-type" content="text/html;charset=utf-8">
      <title>applyElement() Method</title>
      <style type="text/css">
         #mySpan
         {
            font-size:x-large;
         }
      </style>
      <script type="text/javascript" src="../jsb-global.js"></script>
      <script type="text/javascript" src="jsb26-22.js"></script>
   </head>
   <body>
      <h1>applyElement() Method</h1>
      <hr />
      <p id="myP">A simple paragraph with a <span id="mySpan"><code>
      special</code></span> word in it. How special? Click an apply button,
         then click the show button.
      </p>
      <form>
         <input type="button" value="Apply &lt;EM&gt; Outside"
               onclick="applyOutside()" />
         <input type="button" value="Apply &lt;EM&gt; Inside"
               onclick="applyInside()" />
         <input type="button" value="Show &lt;P&gt; HTML..."
               onclick="showHTML()" />
         <br />
         <input type="button" value="Restore Paragraph"
               onclick="location.reload()" />
```

continued

623

LISTING 26-22   *(continued)*

```
        </form>
    </body>
</html>
```

```
JavaScript: jsb26-22.js
function applyOutside()
{
    var newItem = document.createElement("EM");
    newItem.id = newItem.uniqueID;
    // no 2nd argument--use default: outside
    document.getElementById("mySpan").applyElement(newItem);
}

function applyInside()
{
    var newItem = document.createElement("EM");
    newItem.id = newItem.uniqueID;
    document.getElementById("mySpan").applyElement(newItem, "inside");
}

function showHTML()
{
    alert(document.getElementById("myP").outerHTML);
}
```

The visible results of applying the em element inside and outside the span element in this case are the same. But you can see from the HTML results that each element impacts the element hierarchy quite differently.

Related Items: insertBefore(), appendChild(), insertAdjacentElement() methods

attachEvent("*eventName*", *functionRef*)
detachEvent("*eventName*", *functionRef*)

Returns: Boolean

Compatibility: WinIE5+, MacIE-, NN-, Moz-, Safari-, Opera+, Chrome-

The attachEvent() method originated as a means to bind events for IE behaviors (see Chapter 51 on the CD-ROM). But the method has gained acceptance as an IE alternative to the W3C addEventListener() event binding method. To illustrate the method's usage, we want you to first consider the following example of the typical property assignment approach to binding an event handler:

```
myObject.onmousedown = setHilite;
```

The version with attachEvent() is as follows:

```
myObject.attachEvent("onmousedown", setHilite);
```

Both parameters are required. The first parameter is a string version (case insensitive) of the event name. The second is a reference to the function to be invoked when the event fires for this object. A *function reference* is an unquoted, case-sensitive identifier for the function without any parentheses (which also means that you cannot pass parameters in this function call).

There is a subtle benefit to using attachEvent() over the event property binding approach. When you use attachEvent(), the method returns a Boolean value of true if the event binding succeeds. IE triggers a script error if the function reference fails, so don't rely on a returned value of false to catch these kinds of errors. Also, there is no validation that the object recognizes the event name.

If you have used attachEvent() to bind an event handler to an object's event, you can disconnect that binding with the detachEvent() method. The parameters are the same as for attachEvent(). The detachEvent() method cannot unbind events whose associations are established via tag attributes or event property settings.

The W3C DOM event model provides functionality similar to these IE-only methods: addEventListener() and removeEventListener().

Example

Use The Evaluator (see Chapter 4) to create an anonymous function that is called in response to an onmousedown event of the first paragraph on the page. Begin by assigning the anonymous function to global variable a (already initialized in The Evaluator) in the top text box:

```
a = new Function("alert('Function created at " + (new Date()) + "')")
```

The quote marks and parentheses can get jumbled easily, so enter this expression carefully. When you enter the expression successfully, the Results box shows the function's text. Now assign this function to the onmousedown event of the myP element by entering the following statement in the top text box:

```
document.getElementById("myP").attachEvent("onmousedown", a)
```

The Results box displays true when successful. If you mouse down on the first paragraph after the evaluator panel, an alert box displays the date and time when the anonymous function was created (when the new Date() expression was evaluated).

Now disconnect the event relationship from the object by entering the following statement in the top text box:

```
document.getElementById("myP").detachEvent("onmousedown", a)
```

Related Items: addEventListener(), detachEvent(), dispatchEvent(), fireEvent(), removeEventListener() methods; event binding (Chapter 32)

blur()
focus()

Returns: Nothing

Compatibility: WinIE3+, MacIE3+, NN2+, Moz+, Safari+, Opera+, Chrome+

The blur() method removes focus from an element, whereas the focus() method gives focus to an element. Even though the blur() and focus() methods have been around since the earliest scriptable browsers, not every focusable object has enjoyed these methods since the beginning.

elementObject.blur()

Browsers before IE4 and NN6 limited these methods primarily to the `window` object and form control elements.

Windows

For window objects, the `blur()` method (NN3+, IE4+, Opera) pushes the referenced window to the back of all other open windows. If other browser suite windows (such as email or newsreader windows) are open, the window receiving the `blur()` method is placed behind these windows as well.

In Safari and Firefox, the `blur()` method pushes the referenced window only behind the window that opened it. In Chrome, the `window.blur()` method does not work, as demonstrated if you click the Put Me in Back button in Listing 26-23a. For that matter, the `window.focus()` method does not work in Chrome either, as demonstrated if you click the Bring Main to Front button in Listing 26-23a. The window.focus() method does not work in IE8 either.

Caution

When it works, the `window.blur()` **method does not consistently adjust the stacking order of the current window in the different browsers. But a script in a window can invoke the** `focus()` **method of another window to bring that other window to the front (provided that a scriptable linkage, such as the** `window.opener` **property, exists between the two windows).** ∎

The minute you create another window for a user in your web-site environment, you must pay attention to window layer management. With browser windows so easily activated by the slightest mouse click, a user can lose a smaller window behind a larger one in a snap. Most inexperienced users don't think to check the Windows taskbar or browser menu bar (if the browser is so equipped) to see whether a smaller window is still open and then activate it. If that subwindow is important to your site design, you should present a button or other device in each window that enables users to switch among windows safely. The `window.focus()` method brings the referenced window to the front of all the windows.

Rather than supply a separate button on your page to bring a hidden window forward, you should build your window-opening functions in such a way that if the window is already open, the function automatically brings that window forward (as shown in Listing 26-23a). This removes the burden of window management from your visitors.

The key to success with this method is making sure that your references to the desired windows are correct. Therefore, be prepared to use the `window.opener` property to refer to the main window if a subwindow needs to bring the main window back into focus.

Form control elements

The `blur()` and `focus()` methods apply primarily to text-oriented form controls: text input, `select`, and `textarea` elements.

Just as a camera lens blurs when it goes out of focus, a text object blurs when it loses focus — when someone clicks or tabs out of the field. Under script control, `blur()` deselects whatever may be selected in the field, and the text insertion pointer leaves the field. The pointer does not proceed to the next field in tabbing order, as it does if you perform a blur by tabbing out of the field manually.

For a text object, having focus means that the text insertion pointer is flashing in that text object's field. Giving a field focus is like opening it up for human editing.

Setting the focus of a text box or `textarea` does not by itself enable you to place the cursor at any specified location in the field. The cursor usually appears at the beginning of the text. To prepare a field for entry to remove the existing text, use both the `focus()` and `select()` methods in series.

There is a caveat about using `focus()` and `select()` together to preselect the content of a text box for immediate editing: Many versions of Internet Explorer fail to achieve the desired results due to an internal timing problem. You can work around this problem (and remain compatible with other browsers) by initiating the focus and selection actions through a `setTimeout()` method.

A common design requirement is to position the insertion pointer at the end of a text box or `textarea` so that a user can begin appending text to existing content immediately. This is possible in IE4+ with the help of the `TextRange` object. The following script fragment moves the text insertion pointer to the end of a `textarea` element whose ID is `myTextarea`:

```
var range = document.getElementById("myTextarea").createTextRange();
range.move("textedit");
range.select();
```

You should be very careful in combining `blur()` or `focus()` methods with `onblur` and `onfocus` event handlers — especially if the event handlers display alert boxes. Many combinations of these events and methods can cause an infinite loop in which it is impossible to dismiss the alert dialog box completely. On the other hand, there is a useful combination for older browsers that don't offer a `disabled` property for text boxes. The following text box event handler can prevent users from entering text in a text box:

```
onfocus = "this.blur()";
```

Some operating systems and browsers enable you to give focus to elements such as buttons (including radio and checkbox buttons) and hypertext links (encompassing both `a` and `area` elements). Typically, once such an element has focus, you can accomplish the equivalent of a mouse click on the element by pressing the spacebar. This is helpful for accessibility to those who have difficulty using a mouse.

An unfortunate side effect of button focus in Win32 environments is that the focus highlight (a dotted rectangle) remains around the button after a user clicks it and until another object gets focus. You can eliminate this artifact for browsers and objects that implement the `onmouseup` event handler by including the following event handler in your buttons:

```
onmouseup = "this.blur()";
```

IE5.5+ recognizes the often undesirable effect of that dotted rectangle and lets scripts set the `hideFocus` property of an element to `true` to keep that rectangle hidden while giving the element focus. It is a trade-off for the user, however, because there is no visual feedback about which element has focus.

Other elements

For other kinds of elements that support the `focus()` method, you can bring an element into view in lieu of the `scrollIntoView()` method. Link (a) and `area` elements in Windows versions of IE *elementObject*.blur()

display the dotted rectangle around them after a user brings focus to them. To eliminate that artifact, use the same

```
onmouseup = "this.blur()";
```

event handler (or IE5.5+ hideFocus property) just described for form controls.

Example

Listing 26-23a contains an example of using the focus() and blur() methods to tinker with changing the focus of windows. This example creates a two-window environment; from each window, you can bring the other window to the front. The main window uses the object returned by window.open() to assemble the reference to the new window. In the subwindow (whose content is created entirely on-the-fly by JavaScript), self.opener is summoned to refer to the original window, whereas self.blur() operates on the subwindow itself. Blurring one window and focusing on another window yields the same result of sending the window to the back of the pile.

LISTING 26-23a

The window.focus() and window.blur() Methods

HTML: jsb26-23.html

```
<!DOCTYPE html>
<html>
   <head>
      <meta http-equiv="content-type" content="text/html;charset=utf-8">
      <title>Window Focus() and Blur()</title>
      <script type="text/javascript" src="../jsb-global.js"></script>
      <script type="text/javascript" src="jsb26-23.js"></script>
   </head>
   <body>
      <h1>Window focus() and blur() Methods</h1>
      <hr />
      <form>
         <input type="button" name="newOne" value="Show New Window"
               onclick="makeNewWindow()" />
      </form>
   </body>
</html>
```

JavaScript: jsb26-23.js

```
// declare global variable name
var newWindow = null;

function makeNewWindow()
{
   // check if window already exists
   if (!newWindow || newWindow.closed)
   {
      // store new window object in global variable
      newWindow = window.open("","","width=250,height=250");
      // pause briefly to let IE3 window finish opening
```

```
        setTimeout("fillWindow()",100);
    }
    else
    {
        // window already exists, so bring it forward
        newWindow.focus();
    }
}

// assemble new content and write to subwindow
function fillWindow()
{
    var newContent = "<html><head><title>Another Sub Window<\/title><\/head>";
    newContent += "<body bgColor='salmon'>";
    newContent += "<h1>A Salmon-Colored Subwindow.<\/h1>";
    newContent += "<form><input type='button' value='Bring Main to Front'
        onclick='self.opener.focus()'>";
    newContent += "<input type='button' value='Put Me in Back'
        onclick='self.blur()'>";
    newContent += "<\/form><\/body><\/html>";
    // write HTML to new window document
    newWindow.document.write(newContent);
    newWindow.document.close();
}
```

A key ingredient to the success of the `makeNewWindow()` function in Listing 26-23a is the first conditional expression. Because `newWind` is initialized as a `null` value when the page loads, that is its value the first time through the function. But after you open the subwindow the first time, `newWind` is assigned a value (the subwindow object) that remains intact even if the user closes the window. Thus, the value doesn't revert to `null` by itself. To catch the possibility that the user has closed the window, the conditional expression also sees whether the window is closed. If it is, a new subwindow is generated, and that new window's reference value is reassigned to the `newWind` variable. On the other hand, if the window reference exists and the window is not closed, the `focus()` method brings that subwindow to the front.

In Listing 26-23a you can see where the subwindow's content is created entirely on-the-fly by JavaScript. One of the nice little tools in IE and Firefox is the ability to view generated source. It's a little ugly, in that all the code is on a single line. We've formatted the generated source for you in Listing 26-23b so that you can see just what was created entirely on-the-fly in Listing 26.23a.

LISTING 26-23b

The Source Code Generated On-the-Fly in Listing 26-23a

```
<html>
    <head>
        <title>Another Sub Window</title>
    </head>
    <body bgcolor="salmon">
```

continued

elementObject.clearAttributes()

LISTING 26-23b   *(continued)*

```
    <h1>A Salmon-Colored Subwindow.</h1>
    <form>
        <input value="Bring Main to Front" onclick="self.opener.focus()"
               type="button">
        <input value="Put Me in Back" onclick="self.blur()" type="button">
    </form>
  </body>
</html>
```

You can see the `focus()` method for a text object in action in the description of the `select()` method for text objects in Chapter 36.

Related Items: `window.open()`, `document.formObject.textObject.select()` methods

clearAttributes()

Returns: Nothing

Compatibility: WinIE5+, MacIE-, NN-, Moz-, Safari-, Opera-, Chrome-

The `clearAttributes()` method removes all attributes from an element except the `name` and `id` values. Thus, styles and event handlers are removed, as are custom attributes assigned in either the HTML source code or later by script. You should know that the `clearAttributes()` method does not alter the length of the element's `attributes` collection, because the collection always contains all possible attributes for an element. (See the `attributes` property for elements earlier in this chapter.)

This method is handy if you wish to construct an entirely new set of attributes for an element and prefer to start out with a blank slate. Be aware, however, that unless your scripts immediately assign new attributes to the element, the appearance of the element reverts to its completely unadorned form until you assign new attributes. This means that even positioned elements find their way back to their source-code order until you assign a new positioning style. If you simply want to change the value of one or more attributes of an element, it is faster to use the `setAttribute()` method or adjust the corresponding properties.

To accomplish a result in NN6+/Moz that simulates that of IE5+'s `clearAttributes()`, you must iterate through all attributes of an element and remove those attributes (via the `removeAttribute()` method) whose names are other than `id` and `name`.

Example

Use The Evaluator (see Chapter 4) to examine the attributes of an element before and after you apply `clearAttributes()`. To begin, display the HTML for the table element on the page by entering the following statement in the top text box:

```
    myTable.outerHTML
```

Notice the attributes associated with the `<table>` tag. Look at the rendered table to see how attributes such as `border` and `width` affect the display of the table. Now enter the following statement in the top text box to remove all removable attributes from this element:

```
    myTable.clearAttributes()
```

First, look at the table. The border is gone, and the table is rendered only as wide as is necessary to display the content with no cell padding. Finally, view the results of the `clearAttributes()` method in the `outerHTML` of the table again:

```
myTable.outerHTML
```

The source-code file has not changed, but the object model in the browser's memory reflects the changes you made.

Related Items: `attributes` property; `getAttribute()`, `setAttribute()`, `removeAttribute()`, `mergeAttributes()`, and `setAttributeNode()` methods

click()

Returns: Nothing

Compatibility: WinIE4+, MacIE4+, NN2+, Moz+, Safari+, Opera+, Chrome+

The `click()` method lets a script perform nearly the same action as clicking an element. Before NN4 and IE4, the `click()` method invoked on a button did not trigger the `onclick` event handler for the object. This has significant impact if you expect the `onclick` event handler of a button to function even if a script performs the click. For earlier browser versions, you have to invoke the event handler statements directly. Also, just because a script is clicking a button, not all buttons in all platforms change their appearance in response. For example, NN4 on the Mac does not change the state of a checkbox clicked remotely.

If you want to script the action of clicking a button, you can safely invoke the resulting event handler function directly. And if the element is a radio button or checkbox, handle the change of state directly (for example, set the `checked` property of a checkbox) rather than expect the browser to take care of it for you.

Example

Use The Evaluator (see Chapter 4) to experiment with the `click()` method. The page includes various types of buttons at the bottom. You can click the checkbox, for example, by entering the following statement in the top text box:

```
document.myForm2.myCheckbox.click()
```

If you use a recent browser version, you most likely can see the checkbox change states between checked and unchecked each time you execute the statement.

Related Item: `onclick` event handler

cloneNode(*deepBoolean*)

Returns: Node object reference

Compatibility: WinIE5+, MacIE5+, NN6+, Moz+, Safari+, Opera+, Chrome+

The `cloneNode()` method makes an exact copy of the current node object. This copy does not have a parent node or other relationship with any element after the copy exists (of course, the original node remains in place). The clone also does not become part of the document's object model (the node tree) unless you explicitly insert or append the node somewhere on the page. The copy includes all element attributes, including the `id` attribute. Because the value returned by the `cloneNode()` method is a genuine `Node` object, you can operate on it with any `Node` object methods while it is still in the nondocument object state.

The Boolean parameter of the `cloneNode()` method controls whether the copy of the node includes all child nodes (`true`) or just the node itself (`false`). For example, if you clone a paragraph element by itself, the clone consists only of the raw element (equivalent of the tag pair, including attributes in the start tag) and none of its content. But including child nodes makes sure that all content within that paragraph element is part of the copy. This parameter is optional in IE5 (defaulting to `false`), but it is required in other W3C-compatible browsers.

Example

Use The Evaluator (see Chapter 4) to clone, rename, and append an element found in The Evaluator's source code. Begin by cloning the paragraph element named `myP` along with all of its content. Enter the following statement in the top text box:

```
a = document.getElementById("myP").cloneNode(true)
```

The variable `a` now holds the clone of the original node, so you can change its `id` attribute at this point by entering the following statement:

```
a.setAttribute("id", "Dolly")
```

If you want to see the properties of the cloned node, enter `a` in the bottom text box. The precise listing of properties you see depends on the browser you're using; in either case, you should be able to locate the `id` property, whose value is now `Dolly`.

As a final step, append this newly named node to the end of the `body` element by entering the following statement in the top text box:

```
document.body.appendChild(a)
```

You can now scroll down to the bottom of the page and see a duplicate of the content. But because the two nodes have different `id` attributes, they cannot confuse scripts that need to address one or the other.

Related Items: `Node` object (Chapter 25); `appendChild()`, `removeChild()`, `removeNode()`, `replaceChild()`, and `replaceNode()` methods

compareDocumentPosition(nodeRef)

Returns: Integer

Compatibility: WinIE-, MacIE-, NN6+, Moz1.4+, Safari+, Opera+, Chrome+

This method determines the tree position of one node with respect to another node. More specifically, the `nodeRef` object provided as a parameter (Node B) is compared with the object on which the method is called (Node A). The result is returned from the method as an integer value that can contain one or more of the comparison masks listed in Table 26-8.

The integer value returned by the `compareDocumentPosition()` method is actually a bitmask, which explains why the values in Table 26-8 are powers of 2. This allows the method to return multiple comparison values simply by adding them together. For example, a return value of `20` indicates that Node B is contained by Node A (16) and also that Node B follows Node A (4).

TABLE 26-8

Comparison Return Flags

Integer Value	Constant	Description
0		Node B and Node A are one and the same.
1	DOCUMENT_POSITION_DISCONNECTED	No connection exists between the nodes.
2	DOCUMENT_POSITION_PRECEDING	Node B precedes Node A.
4	DOCUMENT_POSITION_FOLLOWING	Node B follows Node A.
8	DOCUMENT_POSITION_CONTAINS	Node B contains Node A (and therefore precedes it).
16	DOCUMENT_POSITION_CONTAINED_BY	Node B is contained by Node A (and therefore follows it).
32	DOCUMENT_POSITION_IMPLEMENTATION_ SPECIFIC	The comparison is determined by the browser.

Related Item: contains() method

componentFromPoint(*x,y*)

Returns: String

Compatibility: WinIE5+, MacIE-, NN-, Moz-, Safari-, Opera-, Chrome-

The componentFromPoint() method assists in some event-related tasks. You can use it for a kind of collision detection (in other words, to determine whether an event occurs inside or outside a particular element). If the element has scroll bars, the method can provide additional information about the event, such as which component of the scroll bar the user activates.

A key aspect of this method is that you invoke it on any element that you want to use as the point of reference. For example, if you want to find out whether a mouseup event occurs in an element whose ID is myTable, invoke the method as follows:

```
var result = document.getElementById("myTable").componentFromPoint(↵
    event.clientX, event.clientY);
```

Parameters passed to the method are *x* and *y* coordinates. These coordinates do not have to come from an event, but the most likely scenario links this method with an event of some kind. Mouse events (other than onclick) work best.

The value returned by the method is a string that provides details about where the coordinate point is with respect to the current element. If the coordinate point is inside the element's rectangle, the returned value is an empty string. Conversely, if the point is completely outside the element, the returned value is the string "outside". For scroll-bar pieces, the list of possible returned values is quite lengthy (as shown in Table 26-9).

elementObject.componentFromPoint()

TABLE 26-9

Returned Values for componentFromPoint()

Returned String	Element Component at Coordinate Point
(empty)	Inside the element content area
outside	Outside the element content area
handleBottom	Resize handle at bottom
handleBottomLeft	Resize handle at bottom left
handleBottomRight	Resize handle at bottom right
handleLeft	Resize handle at left
handleRight	Resize handle at right
handleTop	Resize handle at top
handleTopLeft	Resize handle at top left
handleTopRight	Resize handle at top right
scrollbarDown	Scroll-bar down arrow
scrollbarHThumb	Scroll-bar thumb on horizontal bar
scrollbarLeft	Scroll-bar left arrow
scrollbarPageDown	Scroll-bar page-down region
scrollbarPageLeft	Scroll-bar page-left region
scrollbarPageRight	Scroll-bar page-right region
scrollbarPageUp	Scroll-bar page-up region
scrollbarRight	Scroll-bar right arrow
scrollbarUp	Scroll-bar up arrow
scrollbarVThumb	Scroll-bar thumb on vertical bar

You do not have to use this method for most collision or event detection, however. The event object's srcElement property returns a reference to whatever object receives the event.

Example

Listing 26-24 demonstrates how the componentFromPoint() method can be used to determine exactly where a mouse event occurred. As presented, the method is associated with a textarea object that is specifically sized to display both vertical and horizontal scroll bars. As you click various areas of the textarea and the rest of the page, the status bar displays information about the location of the event with the help of the componentFromPoint() method.

The script uses a combination of the `event.srcElement` property and the `componentFrom-Point()` method to help you distinguish how you can use each one for different types of event processing. The `srcElement` property is used initially as a filter to decide whether the status bar will reveal further processing about the `textarea` element's event details.

The `onmousedown` event handler in the `body` element triggers all event processing. IE events bubble up the hierarchy (and no events are canceled in this page), so all `mousedown` events eventually reach the `body` element. Then the `whereInWorld()` function can compare each `mousedown` event from any element against the text area's geography.

LISTING 26-24

Using the componentFromPoint() Method

HTML: `jsb26-24.html`

```
<!DOCTYPE html>
<html>
    <head>
        <meta http-equiv="content-type" content="text/html;charset=utf-8">
        <title>componentFromPoint() Method</title>
        <script type="text/javascript" src="../jsb-global.js"></script>
        <script type="text/javascript" src="jsb26-24.js"></script>
    </head>
    <body onmousedown="whereInWorld()">
        <h1>componentFromPoint() Method</h1>
        <hr />
        <p>Tracking the mouseDown event relative to the textarea object. View
            results in status bar.
        </p>
        <form>
            <textarea id="myTextarea" wrap="off" cols="12" rows="4">
                This is Line 1
                This is Line 2
                This is Line 3
                This is Line 4
                This is Line 5
                This is Line 6
            </textarea>
        </form>
    </body>
</html>
```

JavaScript: `jsb26-24.js`

```
function whereInWorld(elem)
{
  var x = event.clientX;
  var y = event.clientY;
  var component = document.getElementById("myTextarea").componentFromPoint(x,y);
  if (window.event.srcElement == document.getElementById("myTextarea"))
  {
```

continued

elementObject.contains()

LISTING 26-24 *(continued)*

```
   if (component == "")
   {
      status = "mouseDown event occurred inside the element";
   }
   else
   {
      status = "mouseDown occurred on the element\'s " + component;
   }
}
else
{
   status = "mouseDown occurred " + component + " of the element";
}
}
```

Related Item: event object

contains(*elementObjectReference*)

Returns: Boolean

Compatibility: WinIE4+, MacIE4+, NN-, Moz-, Safari+-, Opera+, Chrome+

The contains() method reports whether the current object contains another known object within its HTML containment hierarchy. Note that this is not geographical collision detection of overlapping elements, but the determination of whether one element is nested somewhere within another.

The scope of the contains() method extends as deeply within the current object's hierarchy as is necessary to locate the object. In essence, the contains() method examines all of the elements that are part of an element's all array. Therefore, you can use this method as a shortcut replacement for a for loop that examines each nested element of a container for the existence of a specific element.

The parameter to the contains() method is a reference to an object. If you have only the element's ID as a string to go by, you can use the document.getElementById() method to generate a valid reference to the nested element.

Note

An element always contains itself. ■

Example

Using The Evaluator (Chapter 4), see how the contains() method responds to the object combinations in each of the following statements as you enter them in the top text box:

```
document.body.contains(document.getElementById("myP"))
document.getElementById("myP").contains(document.getElementById("myEM"))
document.getElementById("myEM").contains(document.getElementById("myEM"))
document.getElementById("myEM").contains(document.getElementById("myP"))
```

Feel free to test other object combinations within this page.

Related Items: `item()`, `document.getElementById()` methods

createControlRange("*param*")

Returns: Integer ID

Compatibility: WinIE5+, MacIE-, NN-, Moz-, Safari-, Opera-, Chrome-

The `createControlRange()` method is used to create a control range for a selection of text. Although the method is implemented for several elements, it is intended solely for the `selection` object and, therefore, should be used only on that object.

Related Item: `selection` object

detachEvent()

(See `attachEvent()`)

dispatchEvent(*eventObject*)

Returns: Boolean

Compatibility: WinIE-, MacIE-, NN6+, Moz+, Safari+, Opera+, Chrome+

The `dispatchEvent()` method allows a script to fire an event aimed at any object capable of supporting that event. This is the W3C event model way of generalizing mechanisms that earlier browsers sometimes mimic with object methods such as `click()` and `focus()`.

The process of generating one of these events is similar to the way a script generates a new node and inserts that node somewhere into the DOM. For events, however, the object that is created is an `Event` object, which is generated via the `document.createEvent()` method. An event generated in this manner is simply a specification about an event. Use properties of an event object to supply specifics about the event, such as its coordinates or mouse button. Then dispatch the event to a target object by invoking that target object's `dispatchEvent()` method and passing the newly created `Event` object as the sole parameter.

Interpreting the meaning of the Boolean value that the `dispatchEvent()` method returns is not straightforward. The browser follows the dispatched event through whatever event propagation is in effect for that object and event type (either bubbling or capture). If any of the event listener functions triggered by this dispatched event invokes the `preventDefault()` method, the `dispatchEvent()` method returns `false` to indicate that the event did not trigger the native action of the object; otherwise, the method returns `true`. Notice that this returned value indicates nothing about propagation type or how many event listeners run as a result of dispatching this event.

Caution

Although the `dispatchEvent()` method was implemented in NN6, the browser does not yet provide a way to generate new events from scratch. And if you attempt to redirect an existing event to another object via the `dispatchEvent()` method, the browser is prone to crashing. In other words, Mozilla-based browsers are much better candidates for scripts that use `dispatchEvent()`. ■

elementObject.dispatchEvent()

Example

Listing 26-25 demonstrates how to fire events programmatically using the W3C DOM `dispatchEvent()` method. Notice the syntax in the `doDispatch()` function for creating and initializing a new mouse event, supported most reliably in Mozilla-based browsers. The behavior is identical to that of Listing 26-26 later in this chapter, which demonstrates the IE5.5+ equivalent: `fireEvent()`.

LISTING 26-25

Using the dispatchEvent() Method

HTML: `jsb26-25.html`

```html
<!DOCTYPE html>
<html>
  <head>
    <meta http-equiv="content-type" content="text/html;charset=utf-8">
    <title>Using the dispatchEvent() Method</title>
    <style type="text/css">
        #mySPAN
        {
          font-style:italic;
        }
        #ctrlPanel
        {
          font-weight:bold;
        }
    </style>
    <script type="text/javascript" src="../jsb-global.js"></script>
    <script type="text/javascript" src="jsb26-25.js"></script>
  </head>
<body id="myBODY" onload="init()">
 <h1>dispatchEvent() Method</h1>
 <hr />
 <p id="myP">This is a paragraph <span id="mySPAN">(with a nested SPAN)</span>
            that receives click events.
 </p>
 <hr />
 <p>
    <span id="ctrlPanel">Control Panel</span>
 </p>
 <form name="controls">
    <p>
        <input type="checkbox" name="bubbleOn"
                onclick="event.stopPropagation()" />Cancel event bubbling.
    </p>
    <p>
        <input type="button" value="Fire Click Event on BODY"
                onclick="doDispatch('myBODY', event)" />
    </p>
    <p>
```

```
        <input type="button" value="Fire Click Event on myP"
               onclick="doDispatch('myP', event)" />
    </p>
    <p>
        <input type="button" value="Fire Click Event on mySPAN"
               onclick="doDispatch('mySPAN', event)" />
    </p>
  </form>
 </body>
</html>
```

JavaScript: jsb26-25.js

```javascript
// assemble a couple event object properties
function getEventProps(evt)
{
   var msg = "";
   var elem = evt.target;
   msg += "event.target.nodeName: " + elem.nodeName + "\n";
   msg += "event.target.parentNode: " + elem.parentNode.id + "\n";
   msg += "event button: " + evt.button;
   return msg;
}

// onClick event handlers for body, myP, and mySPAN
function bodyClick(evt)
{
   var msg = "Click event processed in BODY\n\n";
   msg += getEventProps(evt);
   alert(msg);
   checkCancelBubble(evt);
}
function pClick(evt)
{
   var msg = "Click event processed in P\n\n";
   msg += getEventProps(evt);
   alert(msg);
   checkCancelBubble(evt);
}
function spanClick(evt)
{
   var msg = "Click event processed in SPAN\n\n";
   msg += getEventProps(evt);
   alert(msg);
   checkCancelBubble(evt);
}

// cancel event bubbling if checkbox is checked
function checkCancelBubble(evt)
{
   if (document.controls.bubbleOn.checked)
   {
      evt.stopPropagation();
```

continued

elementObject.doScroll()

LISTING 26-25 *(continued)*

```
    }
}

// assign onClick event handlers to three elements
function init()
{
    document.body.onclick = bodyClick;
    document.getElementById("myP").onclick = pClick;
    document.getElementById("mySPAN").onclick = spanClick;
}

// invoke dispatchEvent() on object whose ID is passed as parameter
function doDispatch(objID, evt)
{
    // create empty mouse event
    var newEvt = document.createEvent("MouseEvents");
    // initialize as click with button ID 3
    newEvt.initMouseEvent("click", true, true, window, 0, 0, 0, 0, 0, false,
        false, false, false, 3, null);
    // send event to element passed as param
    document.getElementById(objID).dispatchEvent(newEvt);
    // don't let button clicks bubble
    evt.stopPropagation();
}
```

Related Item: fireEvent() method

doScroll("*scrollAction*")

Returns: Nothing

Compatibility: WinIE5+, MacIE-, NN-, Moz-, Safari-, Opera-, Chrome-

The doScroll() method is used to control the scrolling of an element by triggering its scroll bars. Although a subtle distinction, doScroll() doesn't move the scroll bars to a specific position; instead, it simulates a scroll-bar click. The end result is an onscroll event being fired, which is what you would expect from a simulated scroll.

The string parameter to doScroll() can be one of the following values to indicate what kind of scrolling is to take place: scrollbarUp, scrollbarDown, scrollbarLeft, scrollbarRight, scrollbarPageUp, scrollbarPageDown, scrollbarPageLeft, scrollbarPageRight, scrollbarHThumb, or scrollbarVThumb.

dragDrop()

Returns: Boolean

Compatibility: WinIE5.5+, MacIE-, NN-, Moz-, Safari-, Opera-, Chrome-

The dragDrop() method initiates a mouse drag-and-drop sequence by triggering an ondragstart event. The return value is a Boolean that indicates when the user releases the mouse button (true).

fireEvent("*eventType*"[, *eventObjectRef*])

Returns: Boolean

Compatibility: WinIE5.5+, MacIE-, NN-, Moz-, Safari-, Opera-, Chrome-

Although some objects have methods that emulate physical events (for example, the click() and focus() methods), WinIE5.5+ generalizes the mechanism by letting a script direct any valid event to any object. The fireEvent() method is the vehicle.

One required parameter is the event type, formatted as a string. IE event types are coded just like the property names for event handlers (for example, onclick, onmouseover, and so on).

A second, optional parameter is a reference to an existing event object. This object can be an event that some user or system action triggers (meaning that the fireEvent() method is in a function invoked by an event handler). The existing event can also be an object created by the IE5.5+ document.createEventObject() method. In either case, the purpose of providing an existing event object is to set the properties of the event object that the fireEvent() method creates. The event type is defined by the method's first parameter, but if you have other properties to set (for example, coordinates or a keyboard key code), those properties are picked up from the existing object. Here is an example of a sequence that creates a new mousedown event, stuffs some values into its properties, and then fires the event at an element on the page:

```
var newEvent = document.createEventObject();
newEvent.clientX = 100;
newEvent.clientY = 30;
newEvent.cancelBubble = false;
newEvent.button = 1;
document.getElementById("myElement").fireEvent("onmousedown", newEvent);
```

Events generated by the fireEvent() method are just like regular IE window.event objects, and they have several important event object properties that the browser presets. It is important that cancelBubble is set to false and returnValue is set to true — just like a regular user- or system-induced event. This means that if you want to prevent event bubbling and/or prevent the default action of the event's source element, the event handler functions must set these event object properties just like normal event handling in IE.

The fireEvent() method returns a Boolean value that the returnValue property of the event determines. If the returnValue property is set to false during event handling, the fireEvent() method returns false. Under normal processing, the method returns true.

The W3C DOM (Level 2) event model includes the dispatchEvent() method to accommodate script-generated events (and Event object methods to create event objects), which is roughly the W3C equivalent of the fireEvent() method.

Example

Listing 26-26 contains script code that shows how to fire events programmatically using the fireEvent() method. Three buttons in the example page enable you to direct a click event to each of the three elements that have event handlers defined for them. The events fired this way are artificial, generated via the createEventObject() method. For demonstration purposes, the button property of these scripted events is set to 3. This property value is assigned to the event *elementObject*.fireEvent()

object that eventually gets directed to an element. With event bubbling left on, the events sent via fireEvent() behave just like the physical clicks on the elements. Similarly, if you disable event bubbling, the first event handler to process the event cancels bubbling, and no further processing of that event occurs. Notice that event bubbling is canceled within the event handlers that process the event. To prevent the clicks of the checkbox and action buttons from triggering the body element's onclick event handlers, event bubbling is turned off for the buttons right away.

LISTING 26-26

Using the fireEvent() Method

HTML: jsb26-26.html

```html
<!DOCTYPE html>
<html>
  <head>
    <meta http-equiv="content-type" content="text/html;charset=utf-8">
    <title>Using the fireEvent() Method</title>
    <style type="text/css">
        #mySPAN
        {
            font-style:italic;
        }
        #ctrlPanel
        {
            font-weight:bold;
        }
    </style>
    <script type="text/javascript" src="../jsb-global.js"></script>
    <script type="text/javascript" src="jsb26-26.js"></script>
  </head>
  <body id="myBODY" onload="init()">
    <h1>fireEvent() Method</h1>
    <hr />
    <p id="myP">This is a paragraph <span id="mySPAN">(with a nested SPAN)</span>
             that receives click events.
    </p>
    <hr />
    <p>
        <span id="ctrlPanel">Control Panel</span>
    </p>
    <form name="controls">
        <p>
            <input type="checkbox" name="bubbleOn"
                 onclick="event.cancelBubble=true" />Cancel event bubbling.
        </p>
        <p>
            <input type="button" value="Fire Click Event on BODY"
                 onclick="doFire('myBODY')" />
        </p>
        <p>
            <input type="button" value="Fire Click Event on myP"
```

```
                    onclick="doFire('myP')" />
        </p>
        <p>
            <input type="button" value="Fire Click Event on mySPAN"
                    onclick="doFire('mySPAN')" />
        </p>
    </form>
  </body>
</html>
```

JavaScript: jsb26-26.js

```
// assemble a couple event object properties
function getEventProps()
{
    var msg = "";
    var elem = event.srcElement;
    msg += "event.srcElement.tagName: " + elem.tagName + "\n";
    msg += "event.srcElement.id: " + elem.id + "\n";
    msg += "event button: " + event.button;
    return msg;
}

// onClick event handlers for body, myP, and mySPAN
function bodyClick()
{
    var msg = "Click event processed in BODY\n\n";
    msg += getEventProps();
    alert(msg);
    checkCancelBubble();
}
function pClick()
{
    var msg = "Click event processed in P\n\n";
    msg += getEventProps();
    alert(msg);
    checkCancelBubble();
}
function spanClick()
{
    var msg = "Click event processed in SPAN\n\n";
    msg += getEventProps();
    alert(msg);
    checkCancelBubble();
}

// cancel event bubbling if checkbox is checked
function checkCancelBubble()
{
    event.cancelBubble = document.controls.bubbleOn.checked;
}

// assign onClick event handlers to three elements
```

continued

elementObject.getAdjacentText()

LISTING 26-26   *(continued)*

```
function init()
{
   document.getElementById("myBODY").onclick = bodyClick;
   document.getElementById("myP").onclick = pClick;
   document.getElementById("mySPAN").onclick = spanClick;
}

// invoke fireEvent() on object whose ID is passed as parameter
function doFire(objID)
{
   var newEvt = document.createEventObject();
   newEvt.button = 3;
   document.all(objID).fireEvent("onclick", newEvt);
   // don't let button clicks bubble
   event.cancelBubble = true;
}
```

Related Item: dispatchEvent() method

focus()

(See blur())

getAdjacentText("*position*")

Returns: String

Compatibility: WinIE5+, MacIE-, NN-, Moz-, Safari-, Opera-, Chrome-

The getAdjacentText() method enables you to extract copies of plain-text components of an element object (in other words, without any HTML tag information). The sole parameter is one of four case-insensitive string constant values that indicate from where, in relation to the current object, the text should be extracted. The values are:

Parameter Value	Description
beforeBegin	Text immediately in front of the element's tag, back to the preceding tag
afterBegin	Text that begins inside the element tag, up to the next tag (whether it be a nested element or the element's end tag)
beforeEnd	Text immediately in front of the element's end tag, back to the preceding tag (whether it be a nested element or the element's start tag)
afterEnd	Text immediately following the element's end tag, forward until the next tag

If the current object has no nested elements, both the `afterBegin` and `beforeEnd` versions return the same as the object's `innerText` property. When the current object is encased immediately within another element (for example, a `td` element inside a `tr` element), there is no text before the element's beginning or after the element's end, so these values are returned as empty strings.

The strings returned from this method are roughly equivalent to values of text fragment nodes in the W3C DOM, but IE5+ treats these data pieces as string data types rather than as text node types. W3C DOM equivalents for the four versions are

```
document.getElementById("objName").previousSibling.nodeValue
document.getElementById("objName").firstChild.nodeValue
document.getElementById("objName").lastChild.nodeValue
document.getElementById("objName").nextSibling.nodeValue
```

Example

Use The Evaluator (see Chapter 4) to examine all four adjacent text possibilities for the `myP` and nested `myEM` elements in that document. Enter each of the following statements in the top text box, and view the results:

```
document.getElementById("myP").getAdjacentText("beforeBegin")
document.getElementById("myP").getAdjacentText("afterBegin")
document.getElementById("myP").getAdjacentText("beforeEnd")
document.getElementById("myP").getAdjacentText("afterEnd")
```

The first and last statements return empty strings because the `myP` element has no text fragments surrounding it. The `afterBegin` version returns the text fragment of the `myP` element up to, but not including, the EM element nested inside. The `beforeEnd` string picks up after the end of the nested EM element and returns all text to the end of `myP`.

Now see what happens with the nested `myEM` element:

```
document.getElementById("myEM").getAdjacentText("beforeBegin")
document.getElementById("myEM").getAdjacentText("afterBegin")
document.getElementById("myEM").getAdjacentText("beforeEnd")
document.getElementById("myEM").getAdjacentText("afterEnd")
```

Because this element has no nested elements, the `afterBegin` and `beforeEnd` strings are identical — the same value as the `innerText` property of the element.

Related Items: `childNodes`, `data`, `firstChild`, `lastChild`, `nextSibling`, `nodeValue`, and `previousSibling` properties

getAttribute("*attributeName*"[, *caseSensitivity*])

Returns: (See text)

Compatibility: WinIE4+, MacIE4+, NN6+, Moz+, Safari+, Opera+, Chrome+

The `getAttribute()` method returns the value assigned to a specific attribute of the current object. You can use this method as an alternative to retrieving properties of an object, particularly when your script presents you the attribute name as a string (in contrast to a fully formed reference to an object and its property). Thus, the following example statements yield the same data:

```
var mult = document.getElementById("mySelect").multiple;
var mult = document.getElementById("mySelect").getAttribute("multiple");
```

Returned value types from `getAttribute()` are either strings (including attribute values assigned as unquoted numeric values) or Booleans (for example, the `multiple` property of a `select` element object).

Note

The W3C DOM Level 2 standard recommends `getAttribute()` **and** `setAttribute()` **for reading and writing element object attribute values, rather than reading and writing those values by way of their corresponding properties. Although using these methods is certainly advisable for XML elements, the same DOM standard sends conflicting signals by defining all kinds of properties for HTML element objects. Browsers, of course, will support access via properties well into the future, so don't feel obligated to change your ways just yet.** ■

All browsers that support the `getAttribute()` method require one parameter, which is a string of the attribute name. By default, this parameter is not case sensitive. Note that this has impact on custom attributes that you might assign to HTML or XML elements in your documents. Attribute names are automatically converted to lowercase when they are turned into properties of the object. Therefore, you must avoid reusing attribute names, even if you use different case letters in the source-code assignments.

IE includes an optional extension to the method in the form of a second parameter that enables you to be more specific about the case sensitivity of the first parameter. The default value of the second parameter is `false`, which means that the first parameter is not case sensitive. A value of `true` makes the first parameter case sensitive. This matters only if you use `setAttribute()` to add a parameter to an existing object and if the IE version of that method insists on case sensitivity. The default behavior of `setAttribute()` respects the case of the attribute name. See also the discussion of the `setAttribute()` method later in this chapter with regard to `setAttribute()`'s influence on the IE `attributes` property.

Example

Use The Evaluator (see Chapter 4) to experiment with the `getAttribute()` method for the elements in the page. You can enter the following sample statements in the top text box to view attribute values:

```
document.getElementById("myTable").getAttribute("cellpadding")
document.getElementById("myTable").getAttribute("border")
```

Related Items: `attributes` property; `document.createAttribute()`, `setAttribute()` methods

getAttributeNode("*attributeName*")

Returns: Attribute node object

Compatibility: WinIE6+, MacIE-, NN6+, Moz+, Safari+, Opera+, Chrome+

In the W3C DOM, an attribute is an object that inherits all the properties of a `Node` object (see Chapter 25). As its name implies, an attribute object represents a name-value pair of an attribute that is explicitly defined inside an element's tag. The ability to treat attributes as node objects is far more important when working with XML than HTML, but it is helpful to understand attribute nodes within the context of the W3C DOM object-oriented view of a document. It is important that attribute nodes specifically are not recognized as nodes of a document hierarchy. Therefore, an attribute node is not a child node of the element that defines the attribute.

The nodeness of attributes comes into play when addressing the contents of an object's `attributes` property. The W3C `attributes` property builds on the DOM's formal structure by returning an object known (internally) as a *named node map*. Like an array, the named node map has a `length` property (facilitating `for` loop iteration through the map), plus several methods that allow for inserting, removing, reading, or writing attribute name-value pairs within the node map.

An attribute object inherits all the properties of the `Node` object. Table 26-10 lists the properties of an attribute object.

All of this is a long way to explain the W3C DOM `getAttributeNode()` method, which returns a W3C DOM attribute object. The sole parameter of the method is a case-insensitive string version of the attribute's name. Then you can use any of the properties shown in Table 26-10 to get or set attribute values. Of course, HTML attributes are generally exposed as properties of HTML elements, so it is usually easier to read or write the object's properties directly.

TABLE 26-10

Attribute Object Properties of W3C DOM–Compatible Browsers

`attributes`
`childNodes`
`firstChild`
`lastChild`
`name`
`nextSibling`
`nodeName`
`nodeType`
`nodeValue`
`ownerDocument`
`parentNode`
`previousSibling`
`specified`
`value`

Example

Use The Evaluator (see Chapter 4) to explore the `getAttributeNode()` method. The Results `textarea` element provides several attributes to check out. Because the method returns an object, enter the following statements in the bottom text box so you can view the properties of the attribute node object returned by the method:

```
document.getElementById("myTextArea").getAttributeNode("cols")
document.getElementById("myTextArea").getAttributeNode("rows")
document.getElementById("myTextArea").getAttributeNode("wrap")
document.getElementById("myTextArea").getAttributeNode("style")
```

All (except the last) statements display a list of properties for each attribute node object. The last statement, however, returns nothing because the `style` attribute is not specified for the element.

You can also use The Evaluator to explore the properties of the attribute object returned by the `getAttributeNode()` method. Enter the following statement in the top text box:

```
document.getElementById("myTextArea").getAttributeNode("cols").value
```

Related Items: `attributes` property; `getAttribute()`, `removeAttributeNode()`, `setAttributeNode()` methods

getAttributeNodeNS("*namespaceURI*", "*localName*")

Returns: Attribute node object

Compatibility: WinIE-, MacIE-, NN6+, Moz+, Safari+-, Opera+, Chrome_

This method returns a W3C DOM attribute object. The first parameter of the method is a URI string matching a URI assigned to a label in the document. The second parameter is the local name portion of the attribute you are getting.

Related Items: `attributes`, `namespaceURI`, `localName` properties; `getAttributeNode()`, `setAttributeNodeNS()` methods

getAttributeNS("*namespaceURI*", "*localName*")

Returns: (See text)

Compatibility: WinIE-, MacIE-, NN6+, Moz+, Safari+-, Opera+, Chrome+

This method returns the value assigned to a specific attribute of the current object when that attribute's name is defined by way of an XML namespace definition within the document. The first parameter of the method is a URI string matching a URI assigned to a namespace label in a tag defined earlier in the document. The second parameter is the local name portion of the attribute whose value you are getting.

Returned value types from `getAttributeNS()` are either strings (including attribute values assigned as unquoted numeric values) or Booleans (for example, the `multiple` property of a `select` element object). In the W3C DOM, Netscape, Safari, and Opera, return values are always strings.

Related Items: `attributes`, `namespaceURI`, `localName` properties; `getAttribute()`, `getAttributeNodeNS()`, `setAttributeNodeNS()` methods

getBoundingClientRect()
getClientRects()

Returns: getBoundingClientRect() returns a TextRectangle object; getClientRects() returns an array of TextRectangle objects

Compatibility: WinIE5+, MacIE-, NN-, Moz+-, Safari+-, Opera+, Chrome+

Original with IE5+, most modern browsers assign to every content-holding element a rectangle that describes the space that the element occupies on the page. This rectangle is called a *bounding rectangle,* and it is expressed as a TextRectangle object (even when the content is an image or some other kind of object). A TextRectangle object has four properties (top, left, bottom, and right) that are the pixel coordinates that define the rectangle. You can get the same information from older browsers that do not support the TextRectangle object with offsetTop, offsetLeft, offsetHeight, and offsetWidth. The getBoundingClientRect() method returns a TextRectangle object that describes the bounding rectangle of the current object. You can access an individual measure of an object's bounding rectangle, as in the following example:

```
var parTop = document.getElementById("myP").getBoundingClientRect().top;
```

For elements that consist of text, such as paragraphs, the dimensions of individual TextRectangles for each line of text in the element influence the dimensions of the bounding rectangle. For example, if a paragraph contains two lines, and the second line extends only halfway across the width of the first line, the width of the second line's TextRectangle object is only as wide as the actual text in the second line. But because the first line extends close to the right margin, the width of the encompassing bounding rectangle is governed by that wider, first line TextRectangle. Therefore, an element's bounding rectangle is as wide as its widest line and as tall as the sum of the height of all TextRectangle objects in the paragraph.

The method getClientRects() enables you to obtain a collection of line-by-line TextRectangle objects for an element. It returns an array of all TextRectangle objects that fall within the current object the moment the method is invoked. Each TextRectangle object has its own top, left, bottom, and right coordinate properties. You can then, for example, loop through all objects in this array to calculate the pixel width of each line. If you want to find out the aggregate height and/or maximum width of the entire collection, you can use the getBoundingClientRect() method as a shortcut.

The length of the collection returned by getClientRects() is where you'll see differences between the browsers. WebKit-based browsers and earlier releases of Mozilla-based browsers have only one TextRectangle object in the collection returned by getClientRects() for each block element found in the argument passed to it. IE and the most recent releases of Mozilla-based browsers will do the same only if a width is specified for a block element. Presto-based browsers always return a collection of one regardless of how many elements, block or not, are involved. All that we've said so far just pertains to an argument that is not identified by a block element (for example, the argument passed to getClientRects() in Listing 26-27a is a span element). If the argument is a block element (for example a div), then the only browser that returns a collection of TextRectangle objects for each line is IE. Obviously, this can be very frustrating for scripters. Keep this in mind when looking at Listings 26-27a and 26-27b in the various browsers.

Example

Listing 26-27a employs only the getClientRects() method. (We'll look at both methods in Listing 26-27b in a moment.) The element passed to the getClientRects() method is a span and it contains two paragraphs and an ordered list. The area contained by it is colored blue. There is a button that generates an alert about the length of the collection that is returned by the method.

elementObject.getClientRects()

LISTING 26-27a

Using getClientRects()

HTML: jsb26-27a.html

```
<!DOCTYPE html>
<html>
   <head>
      <meta http-equiv="content-type" content="text/html;charset=utf-8">
      <title>getClientRects() Method</title>
      <style type="text/css">
         #main
         {
            color:blue;
         }
      </style>
      <script type="text/javascript" src="../jsb-global.js"></script>
      <script type="text/javascript" src="jsb26-27a.js"></script>
   </head>
   <body>
      <h1>getClientRects() Method</h1>
      <hr />
      <p>The area we're interested in is colored blue.</p>
      <form>
         <button onclick="howMany();">How many TextRectangle objects
                                 are in the collection?</button>
      </form>
      <span id="main">
         <p>Lorem ipsum dolor sit amet, consectetaur adipisicing
            elit, sed do eiusmod tempor incididunt ut labore et dolore magna
            aliqua. Ut enim adminim veniam, quis nostrud exercitation
            ullamco:
         </p>
         <ul>
            <li>laboris</li>
            <li>nisi</li>
            <li>aliquip ex ea commodo</li>
         </ul>
         <p>Duis aute irure dolor in reprehenderit involuptate velit esse cillum
            dolore eu fugiat nulla pariatur. Excepteur sint occaecat cupidatat
            non proident, sunt in culpa qui officia deseruntmollit anim id est
            laborum. Et harumd und lookum like Greek to me, dereud facilis est
            er expedit distinct.
         </p>
      </span>
   </body>
</html>
```

JavaScript: jsb26-27a.js

```
function howMany()
{
    var clientRects = document.getElementById("main").getClientRects();
    alert("The length of the rectangle returned by getClientRects() is ="
        + clientRects.length + ".");
}
```

Listing 26-27b employs both the getBoundingClientRect() and getClientRects() methods in a demonstration of how they differ. While the listing works in all major browsers, due to the differences you've already since in the collection returned by the getClientRects() method, you'll only really see anything meaningful in IE, and you'll only really want to use it in IE anyway. Keep in mind, though, that you don't have to use the two methods together; there are many things you can do regardless of the browser with just the getBoundingClientRect() method.

As with Listing 26-27a, a set of elements is grouped within a span element named main. The group consists of two paragraphs and an unordered list, all of whose text is colored blue.

Two controls enable you to set the position of an underlying highlight rectangle to any line of your choice. A checkbox enables you to set whether the highlight rectangle should be only as wide as the line or the full width of the bounding rectangle for the entire span element.

All the code is located in the hilite() function. The select and checkbox elements invoke this function. Early in the function, the getClientRects() method is invoked for the main element to capture a snapshot of all TextRectangles for the entire element. This array comes in handy when the script needs to get the coordinates of a rectangle for a single line, as chosen in the select element.

Whenever the user chooses a number from the select list, and the value is less than the total number of TextRectangle objects in clientRects, the function begins calculating the size and location of the underlying yellow highlighter. When the Full Width checkbox is checked, the left and right coordinates are obtained from the getBoundingClientRect() method because the entire span element's rectangle is the space you're interested in; otherwise, you pull the left and right properties from the chosen rectangle in the clientRects array.

Next comes the assignment of location and dimension values to the hiliter object's style property. The top and bottom are always pegged to whatever line is selected, so the clientRects array is polled for the chosen entry's top and bottom properties. The previously calculated left value is assigned to the hiliter object's pixelLeft property, whereas the width is calculated by subtracting the left from the right coordinates. Notice that the top and left coordinates also take into account any vertical or horizontal scrolling of the entire body of the document. If you resize the window smaller, line wrapping throws off the original line count. However, an invocation of hilite() from the onresize event handler applies the currently chosen line number to whatever content falls in that line after resizing.

Because the z-index style property of the hiliter element is set to -1, the element always appears beneath the primary content on the page. If the user selects a line number beyond the current number of lines in the main element, the hiliter element is hidden.

elementObject.getBoundingClientRect()

LISTING 26-27b

Using getBoundingClientRect()

HTML: jsb26-27b.html

```html
<html>
   <head>
      <meta http-equiv="content-type" content="text/html;charset=utf-8">
      <title>getClientRects() and getBoundClientRect() Methods</title>
      <style type="text/css">
         #main
         {
            color:blue;
         }
      </style>
      <script type="text/javascript" src="../jsb-global.js"></script>
      <script type="text/javascript" src="jsb26-27b.js"></script>
   </head>
   <body id="myBody" onresize="hilite()">
      <h1>getClientRects() and getBoundClientRect() Methods</h1>
      <hr />
      <form>
         Choose a line to highlight:
         <select id="choice" onchange="hilite()">
            <option value="1">1</option>
            <option value="2">2</option>
            <option value="3">3</option>
            <option value="4">4</option>
            <option value="5">5</option>
            <option value="6">6</option>
            <option value="7">7</option>
            <option value="8">8</option>
            <option value="9">9</option>
            <option value="10">10</option>
            <option value="11">11</option>
            <option value="12">12</option>
            <option value="13">13</option>
            <option value="14">14</option>
            <option value="15">15</option>
         </select>
         <br />
         <input name="fullWidth" type="checkbox" onclick="hilite()" />
         Full Width (bounding rectangle)
      </form>
      <span id="main">
         <p>Lorem ipsum dolor sit amet, consectetaur adipisicing
            elit, sed do eiusmod tempor incididunt ut labore et dolore magna
            aliqua. Ut enim adminim veniam, quis nostrud exercitation
            ullamco:
         </p>
```

```
       <ul>
           <li>laboris</li>
           <li>nisi</li>
           <li>aliquip ex ea commodo</li>
       </ul>
       <p>Duis aute irure dolor in reprehenderit involuptate velit esse cillum
           dolore eu fugiat nulla pariatur. Excepteur sint occaecat cupidatat
           non proident, sunt in culpa qui officia deseruntmollit anim id est
           laborum Et harumd und lookum like Greek to me, dereud facilis est
           er expedit distinct.
       </p>
    </span>
    <div id="hiliter"
    style="position:absolute; background-color:yellow; ↵
           z-index:-1; visibility:hidden">
    </div>
  </body>
</html>
```

JavaScript: jsb26-27b.js

```
function hilite()
{
    var hTop, hLeft, hRight, hBottom, hWidth;
    var selectList = document.getElementById("choice");
    var n = parseInt(selectList.options[selectList.selectedIndex].value) - 1;
    var clientRects = document.getElementById("main").getClientRects();
    var mainElem = document.getElementById("main");

    if (n >= 0 && n < clientRects.length)
    {
        if (document.forms[0].fullWidth.checked)
        {
            hLeft = mainElem.getBoundingClientRect().left;
            hRight = mainElem.getBoundingClientRect().right;
        }
        else
        {
            hLeft = clientRects[n].left;
            hRight = clientRects[n].right;
        }
        document.getElementById("hiliter").style.pixelTop =
            clientRects[n].top + document.getElementById("myBody").scrollTop;
        document.getElementById("hiliter").style.pixelBottom
            = clientRects[n].bottom;
        document.getElementById("hiliter").style.pixelLeft = hLeft
            + document.getElementById("myBody").scrollLeft;
        document.getElementById("hiliter").style.pixelWidth = hRight - hLeft;
        document.getElementById("hiliter").style.visibility = "visible";
    }
    else if (n > 0)
    {
```

continued

LISTING 26-27b   *(continued)*

```
        alert("The content does not have that many lines.");
        document.getElementById("hiliter").style.visibility = "hidden";
    }
}
```

Related Item: `TextRectangle` object (Chapter 33, on the CD-ROM)

getElementsByTagName("*tagName*")

Returns: Array of element objects

Compatibility: WinIE5+, MacIE5+, NN6+, Moz+, Safari+, Opera+, Chrome+

The `getElementsByTagName()` method returns an array of all elements contained by the current object whose tags match the tag name supplied as the sole parameter to the method. The tag name parameter must be in the form of a string and is case insensitive. The group of elements returned in the array includes only those elements that are within the containment scope of the current object. Therefore, if you have two table objects in a document, and you invoke the `getElementsByTag-Name("td")` method on one of them, the list of returned table cell elements is confined to those cells within the current table object. The current element is not included in the returned array.

For MacIE5, WinIE6+, and all other supporting browsers, the method accepts a wildcard character (`"*"`) for matching descendent elements regardless of tag name. The resulting array of elements is nearly identical to what IE4+ returns via the `document.all` collection.

Example

Use The Evaluator (see Chapter 4) to experiment with the `getElementsByTagName()` method. Enter the following statements one at a time in the top text box, and study the results:

```
document.body.getElementsByTagName("div")
document.body.getElementsByTagName("div").length
document.getElementById("myTable").getElementsByTagName("td").length
```

Because the `getElementsByTagName()` method returns an array of objects, you can use one of those returned values as a valid element reference:

```
document.getElementsByTagName("form")[0].getElementsByTagName("input").length
```

Related Items: `getElementByTagNameNS()`, `getElementById()`, `tags()` methods

getElementsByTagNameNS("*namespaceURI*", "*localName*")

Returns: Array of element objects

Compatibility: WinIE-, MacIE-, NN6+, Moz+, Safari+, Opera+, Chrome+

This method returns an array of all elements contained by the current object (within an XML document) as specified in the two parameters. The first parameter of the method is a URI string matching a URI assigned to a label in the document. The second parameter is the local name portion of the attribute whose value you are getting.

Returned value types from getAttributeNS() are either strings (including attribute values assigned as unquoted numeric values) or Booleans (for example, the multiple property of a select element object).

Related Items: attributes, namespaceURI, localName properties; getElementsByTagNameNS(), getElementById(), tags() methods

getExpression("*attributeName*")

Returns: String

Compatibility: WinIE5+, MacIE-, NN-, Moz-, Safari-, Opera-, Chrome-

The getExpression() method returns the text of the expression that was assigned to an element's attribute via the setExpression() method. The returned value is not the value of the expression, but the expression itself. If you want to find out the current value of the expression (assuming that the variables used are within the scope of your script), you can use the eval() function on the call to getExpression(). This action converts the string to a JavaScript expression and returns the evaluated result.

One parameter, a string version of the attribute name, is required.

Example

See Listing 26-32 for the setExpression() method. This listing demonstrates the kinds of values returned by getExpression().

Related Items: document.recalc(), removeExpression(), setExpression() methods

getFeature("*feature*", "*version*")

Returns: Object

Compatibility: WinIE-, MacIE-, NN-, Moz1.7.2+, Safari-, Opera+, Chrome-

According to the W3C DOM specification, the getFeature() method accepts a scripting feature and version, and returns an object that implements the APIs for the feature. Examples of possible feature parameters to this method are Core and Events, which correspond to DOM modules.

As recently as Mozilla 1.8.1 (Firefox 2.0), the getFeature() method returns an object but the object exposes no API features to the script.

Related Item: implementation.hasFeature() method

getUserData("*key*")

Returns: Object

Compatibility: WinIE-, MacIE-, NN6-, Moz1.7.2+, Safari+-, Opera-, Chrome+

The getUserData() method enables you to access custom user data that has been associated with a node. A given node can have multiple objects of user data, in which case each one is identified through a text key. This key is the parameter that you pass into getUserData() to obtain a user data object. As of Mozilla 1.8.1 (Firefox 2.0), the method is only partially implemented and, therefore, still not useful.

hasAttribute("*attributeName*")

Returns: Boolean

Compatibility: WinIE+, MacIE-, NN6+, Moz+, Safari+, Opera+, Chrome+

The hasAttribute() method returns true if the current object has an attribute whose name matches the sole parameter; it returns false otherwise.

Related Items: hasAttributeNS(), hasAttributes() methods

hasAttributeNS("*namespaceURI*", "*localName*")

Returns: Boolean

Compatibility: WinIE-, MacIE-, NN6+, Moz+, Safari+, Opera+, Chrome+

The hasAttributeNS() method returns true if the current object has an attribute as identified by the two parameters; it returns false otherwise. The first parameter of the method is a URI string matching a URI assigned to a label in the document. The second parameter is the local name portion of the attribute whose value you are getting.

Related Items: attributes, namespaceURI, localName properties; hasAttribute(), hasAttributes() methods

hasAttributes()

Returns: Boolean

Compatibility: WinIE+, MacIE-, NN6+, Moz+, Safari+, Opera+, Chrome+

The hasAttributes() method returns true if the current object has any attributes explicitly assigned within the tag; it returns false otherwise.

Related Items: hasAttribute(), hasAttributeNS() methods

hasChildNodes()

Returns: Boolean

Compatibility: WinIE5+, MacIE5+, NN6+, Moz+, Safari+, Opera+, Chrome+

The hasChildNodes() method returns true if the current object has child nodes nested within; it returns false otherwise. A child node is not necessarily the same as a child element, so the following two expressions return true when the current object has at least one child node:

```
document.getElementById("myObject").hasChildNodes()
document.getElementById("myObject").childNodes.length > 0
```

You cannot use the second expression interchangeably with the following statement (which uses the children property):

```
document.getElementById("myObject").children.length > 0
```

You generally use the hasChildNodes() method in a conditional expression to make sure such nodes exist before performing operations on them:

```
if (document.getElementById("myObject").hasChildNodes()
{
    // [statements that apply to child nodes]
}
```

Example

Use The Evaluator (see Chapter 4) to experiment with the hasChildNodes() method. If you enter the following statement in the top text box

```
document.getElementById("myP").hasChildNodes()
```

the returned value is true. You can find out how many nodes there are by getting the length of the childNodes array:

```
document.getElementById("myP").childNodes.length
```

This expression reveals a total of three nodes: the two text nodes and the em element between them. Check out whether the first text node has any children:

```
document.getElementById("myP").childNodes[0].hasChildNodes()
```

The response is false because text fragments do not have any nested nodes. But check out the em element, which is the second child node of the myP element:

```
document.getElementById("myP").childNodes[1].hasChildNodes()
```

The answer is true because the em element has a text fragment node nested within it. Sure enough, the statement

```
document.getElementById("myP").childNodes[1].childNodes.length
```

yields a node count of 1. You can also go directly to the em element in your references:

```
document.getElementById("myEM").hasChildNodes()
document.getElementById("myEM").childNodes.length
```

If you want to see the properties of the text fragment node inside the em element, enter the following in the bottom text box:

```
document.getElementById("myEM").childNodes[0]
```

You can see that the data and nodeValue properties for the text fragment return the text "all".

Related Items: childNodes property; appendChild(), removeChild(), replaceChild() methods.

insertAdjacentElement("*location*", *elementObject*)

Returns: Object

Compatibility: WinIE5+, MacIE-, NN-, Moz-, Safari+, Opera+, Chrome+

elementObject.**insertAdjacentHTML()**

The `insertAdjacentElement()` method inserts an element object (coming from a variety of sources) into a specific position relative to the current object. Both parameters are required. The first must be one of four possible case-insensitive locations for the insertion, shown in the following table:

Location	Description
beforeBegin	Before the current element's start tag
afterBegin	After the start tag but before any nested content
beforeEnd	Before the end tag but after all other nested content
afterEnd	After the end tag

These locations are relative to the current object. The element type of the current object (a block-level or inline element) has great bearing on how the inserted element is rendered. For example, suppose that you create a b element (using `document.createElement()`) and assign some inner text to it. You then use `insertAdjacentElement()` in an effort to insert this b element before some text in a p element. Because a p element is a block-level element, the location `beforeBegin` places the new b element before the start tag of the p element. This means, however, that the bold text appears in a text line above the start of the p element because a `<p>` tag begins a new block at the left margin of its container (unless instructed otherwise by style sheets). The resulting HTML looks like the following:

```
<b>The new element.</b><p>The original paragraph element.</p>
```

To make the new b element a part of the p element — but in front of the existing p element's content — use the `afterBegin` location. The resulting HTML looks like the following:

```
<p><b>The new element.</b>The original paragraph element.</p>
```

To complete the demonstration of the four location types, the following is the result of the `beforeEnd` location:

```
<p>The original paragraph element. <b>The new element.</b></p>
```

And this is the result of the `afterEnd` location:

```
<p>The original paragraph element.</p><b>The new element.</b>
```

The object to be inserted is a reference to an element object. The object reference can come from any expression that evaluates to an element object or, more likely, from the result of the `document.createElement()` method. Bear in mind that the object generated by `document.createElement()` initially has no content, and all attribute values are set to default values. Moreover, the object is passed to `insertAdjacentElement()` by reference, which means that there is only one instance of that object. If you attempt to insert that object in two places with two statements, the object is moved from the first location to the second. If you need to copy an existing object so that the original is not moved or otherwise disturbed by this method, use the `cloneNode()` method to specify the `true` parameter to capture all nested content of the node.

Example

Use The Evaluator (see Chapter 4) in WinIE5+ to experiment with the `insertAdjacentElement()` method. The goal of the experiment is to insert a new `h1` element above the `myP` element.

All actions require you to enter a sequence of statements in the top text box. Begin by storing a new element in the global variable `a`:

```
a = document.createElement("h1")
```

Give the new object some text:

```
a.innerText = "New Header"
```

Now insert this element before the start of the `myP` object:

```
myP.insertAdjacentElement("beforeBegin", a)
```

Notice that you have not assigned an `id` property value to the new element. But because the element was inserted by reference, you can modify the inserted object by changing the object stored in the `a` variable:

```
a.style.color = "red"
```

The inserted element is also part of the document hierarchy, so you can access it through hierarchy references such as `myP.previousSibling`.

The parent element of the newly inserted element is the `body`. Thus, you can inspect the current state of the HTML for the rendered page by entering the following statement in the top text box:

```
document.body.innerHTML
```

If you scroll down past the first form, you can find the `<h1>` element that you added along with the `style` attribute.

Related Items: `document.createElement()`, `applyElement()` methods

insertAdjacentHTML("*location*", "*HTMLtext*")
insertAdjacentText("*location*", "*text*")

Returns: Nothing

Compatibility: WinIE4+, MacIE4+, NN-, Moz-, Safari+, Opera+, Chrome+

These two methods insert HTML or straight text at a location relative to the current element. They are intended for use after a page loads, rather than inserting content while the page loads (in which case you can use `document.write()` wherever you need evaluated content to appear on the page).

659

elementObject.**insertAdjacentText()**

The first parameter must be one of four possible case-insensitive locations for the insertion, shown in the following table:

Location	Description
beforeBegin	Before the current element's start tag
afterBegin	After the start tag but before any nested content
beforeEnd	Before the end tag but after all other nested content
afterEnd	After the end tag

These locations yield the same results as described in the insertAdjacentElement() function discussed earlier in this chapter.

Whether you use insertAdjacentHTML() or insertAdjacentText() depends on the nature of your content and what you want the browser to do with it. If the content contains HTML tags that you want the browser to interpret and render as though it were part of the page source code, use the insertAdjacentHTML() method. All tags become objects in the document's object model. But if you want only to display some text (including HTML tags in their raw form), use insertAdjacent-Text(). The rendering engine does not interpret any tags included in the string passed as the second parameter. Instead, these tags are displayed as characters on the page. This distinction is identical to the one between the innerHTML and innerText properties.

The difference between insertAdjacentHTML() and insertAdjacentElement() is the nature of the content that you insert. The former enables you to accumulate the HTML as a string, whereas the latter requires the creation of an element object. Also, the two methods in this section work with IE4+ (including Mac versions), whereas insertAdjacentElement() requires the newer object model of WinIE5+.

If the HTML you pass as the second parameter of insertAdjacentHTML() contains <script> tags, you must set the defer attribute in the opening tag. This prevents script statements from executing as you insert them.

Example

Use The Evaluator (see Chapter 4) to experiment with these two methods. The example here demonstrates the result of employing both methods in an attempt to add some HTML to the beginning of the myP element.

Begin by assigning a string of HTML code to the global variable a:

```
a = "<b id='myB'>Important News!</b>"
```

Because this HTML is to go on the same line as the start of the myP paragraph, use the afterBegin parameter for the insert method:

```
myP.insertAdjacentHTML("afterBegin", a)
```

Notice that there is no space after the exclamation mark of the inserted HTML. But to prove that the inserted HTML is genuinely part of the document's object model, now you can insert the text of a space after the b element whose ID is myB:

```
myB.insertAdjacentText("afterEnd", " ")
```

Each time you evaluate the preceding statement (by repeatedly clicking the Evaluate button or pressing Enter with the cursor in the top text box), another space is added.

You should also see what happens when the string to be inserted with insertAdjacentText() contains HTML tags. Reload The Evaluator, and enter the following two statements in the top text box, evaluating each one in turn:

```
a = "<b id='myB'>Important News!</b>"
myP.insertAdjacentText("afterBegin", a)
```

The HTML is not interpreted but is displayed as plain text. There is no object named myB after executing this latest insert method.

Related Items: innerText, innerHTML, outerText, outerHTML properties; insertAdjacentElement(), replaceAdjacentText() methods

insertBefore(*newChildNodeObject, referenceChildNode*)

Returns: Node object

Compatibility: WinIE5+, MacIE5+, NN6+, Moz+, Safari+, Opera+, Chrome+

The insertBefore() method is the W3C DOM syntax for inserting a new child node into an existing element. Node references for both parameters must be valid Node objects (including those that document.createElement() generates).

The behavior of this method might seem counterintuitive at times. If you include the second parameter (a reference to an existing child node of the current element — optional in IE), the new child node is inserted before that existing one. But if you omit the second parameter (or its value is null), the new child node is inserted as the last child of the current element — in which case the method acts the same as the appendChild() method. The true power of this method is summoned when you specify that second parameter; from the point of view of a parent element, you can drop a new child into any spot among its existing children. If an inserted node already exists in the document tree, it will be removed from its previous position.

Bear in mind that the insertBefore() method works from a parent element. Internet Explorer provides additional methods, such as insertAdjacentElement(), to operate from the perspective of what will become a child element.

Example

Listing 26-28 demonstrates how the insertBefore() method can insert child elements (li) inside a parent (ol) at different locations, depending on the second parameter. A text box enables you to enter your choice of text and/or HTML for insertion at various locations within the ol element. If you don't specify a position, the second parameter of insertBefore() is passed as null — meaning that the new child node is added to the end of the existing children. But choose a spot from the select *elementObject*.insertBefore()

list where you want to insert the new item. The value of each `select` list option is an index of one of the first three child nodes of the `ol` element.

LISTING 26-28

Using the insertBefore() Method

HTML: jsb26-28.html

```
<!DOCTYPE html>
<html>
    <head>
        <meta http-equiv="content-type" content="text/html;charset=utf-8">
        <title>insertBefore() Method</title>
        <script type="text/javascript" src="../jsb-global.js"></script>
        <script type="text/javascript" src="jsb26-28.js"></script>
    </head>
    <body>
        <h1>insertBefore() Method</h1>
        <hr />
        <form onsubmit="return false">
            <p>Enter text or HTML for a new list item:
                <input type="text"
                       name="newText" size="40" value="" />
            </p>
            <p>Before which existing item?
                <select name="itemIndex">
                    <option value="null">None specified</option>
                    <option value="0">1</option>
                    <option value="1">2</option>
                    <option value="2">3</option>
                </select>
            </p>
            <input type="button" value="Insert Item"
                   onclick="doInsert(this.form)" />
        </form>
        <ol id="myUL">
            <li>Originally the First Item</li>
            <li>Originally the Second Item</li>
            <li>Originally the Third Item</li>
        </ol>
    </body>
</html>
```

JavaScript: jsb26-28.js

```
function doInsert(form)
{
    if (form.newText)
    {
        var newChild = document.createElement("LI");
        newChild.innerHTML = form.newText.value;
```

```
var choice = form.itemIndex.options[form.itemIndex.selectedIndex].value;
var insertPoint = (isNaN(choice)) ?
    null : document.getElementById("myUL").childNodes[choice];
document.getElementById("myUL").insertBefore(newChild, insertPoint);
    }
}
```

Related Items: `appendChild()`, `replaceChild()`, `removeChild()`, `insertAdjacentElement()` methods

isDefaultNamespace("*namespaceURI*")

Returns: Boolean

Compatibility: WinIE-, MacIE-, NN6-, Moz1.7.2+, Safari+, Opera+, Chrome+

This method checks whether the specified namespace matches the default namespace of the current node.

isEqualNode(*nodeRef*)
isSameNode(*nodeRef*)

Returns: Integer ID

Compatibility: WinIE-, MacIE-, NN-, Moz1.7.2+, Safari+, Opera+, Chrome+

When it comes to nodes, there is a distinct difference between a node being equal to another node and a node being the same as another node. Equality has a very specific meaning with respect to nodes: Two nodes are considered equal if they have the same values for the `attributes`, `childNodes`, `localname`, `namespaceURI`, `nodeName`, `nodeType`, `nodeValue`, and `prefix` properties. Together, these properties essentially reflect the content of a node. What they don't reflect is the relative position of a node within a document, which means that nodes can be equal and reside in different locations in the node tree. Two nodes are considered the same if ... well, they are the same identical node. The `isEqualNode()` method checks for node equality, whereas `isSameNode()` checks whether two nodes are the same. Both methods expect a node reference as their only parameter. Currently, Opera does not support the `isEqualNode()` method.

isSupported("*feature*", "*version*")

Returns: Boolean

Compatibility: WinIE-, MacIE-, NN6+, Moz+, Safari+, Opera+, Chrome+

The `isSupported()` method returns `true` if the current node supports required portions of the specified W3C DOM module and version; it returns `false` otherwise. The first parameter accepts any of the following case-sensitive DOM module name strings: `Core`, `XML`, `HTML`, `Views`, `StyleSheets`, `CSS`, `CSS2`, `Events`, `UIEvents`, `MouseEvents`, `MutationEvents`, `HTMLEvents`, `Range`, and `Traversal`. The second parameter accepts a string representation of the major and minor DOM module version, such as `"2.0"` for DOM Level 2.

elementObject.item()

Example

Use The Evaluator (see Chapter 4) to experiment with the isSupported() method. If you have multiple versions of NN6 or later and Mozilla, try the following (and others) to see how the support for various modules has evolved:

```
document.body.isSupported("CSS", "2.0")
document.body.isSupported("CSS2", "2.0")
document.body.isSupported("Traversal", "2.0")
```

If you have access to Safari, Opera, or Chrome, try the same methods there to see the differences in modules supported compared with Mozilla-based browsers.

item(*index* | "*index*" [, *subIndex*])

Returns: Object

Compatibility: WinIE4+, MacIE4+, NN6+, Moz+, Safari+, Opera+, Chrome+

The item() method works with most objects that are themselves collections of other objects. In W3C DOM terminology, these kinds of objects are known as *named node lists* (for objects such as nodes and attributes) or *HTML collections* (for objects such as elements of a form). You may call the item() method with a single numeric parameter that is the index value of the desired object within the collection. If you know the index number of the item, you can use JavaScript array syntax instead. The following two statements return the same object reference:

```
document.getElementById("myTable").childNodes.item(2)
document.getElementById("myTable").childNodes[2]
```

The method also supports a string of the ID of an object within the collection. (Integer values are required for the attributes, rules, and TextRectangle objects, however.) Additionally, if the collection has more than one object with the same ID (never a good idea except when necessary), a second numeric parameter enables you to select which identically named group you want (using zero-based index values within that subgroup). This obviously does not apply to collections, such as attributes and rules, which have no ID associated with them.

The method returns a reference to the object specified by the parameters.

Example

Use The Evaluator (see Chapter 4) to experiment with the item() method. Type the following statements in the top text box, and view the results for each.

W3C and IE5:

```
document.getElementById("myP").childNodes.length
document.getElementById("myP").childNodes.item(0).data
document.getElementById("myP").childNodes.item(1).nodeName
```

W3C, IE4, and IE5:

```
document.forms[1].elements.item(0).type
```

The first approach is helpful when your script is working with a string version of an object's name. If your script already knows the object reference, the second approach is more efficient and compact.

Related Items: All object element properties that return collections (arrays) of other objects

lookupNamespaceURI("*prefix*")
lookupPrefix("*namespaceURI*")

Returns: Namespace or prefix string (see description)

Compatibility: WinIE-, MacIE-, NN-, Moz1.7.2+, Safari+, Opera+, Chrome+

These two methods use one piece of information to look up the other. The lookupNamespaceURI() method accepts a prefix as its only parameter and returns a URI string for the node if the prefix matches a previously defined namespace. Operating in the reverse, the lookupPrefix() method accepts a namespace URI string and returns a prefix string for the node if the namespace parameter matches a previously defined namespace.

mergeAttributes("*sourceObject*")

Returns: Nothing

Compatibility: WinIE5+, MacIE-, NN-, Moz-, Safari-, Opera-, Chrome-

The mergeAttributes() method is a convenient way to propagate attributes in newly created elements without painstakingly adding attributes one at a time. When you have an object whose attributes can function as a prototype for other elements, those attributes (except for the id attribute) can be applied to a newly created element instantaneously. The default action of this method is not to duplicate the id or name attributes of the element. However, IE5.5+ introduced an extra Boolean parameter, preserveIDs, that enables you to duplicate these two attributes by setting the parameter to false (true is the default).

Example

Listing 26-29 demonstrates the usage of mergeAttributes() in the process of replicating the same form input field while assigning a unique ID to each new field. So that you can see the results as you go, we display the HTML for each input field in the field.

The doMerge() function begins by generating two new elements: a p element and an input element. Because these newly created elements have no properties associated with them, a unique ID is assigned to the input element through the uniqueID property. Attributes from the field in the source code (field1) are merged into the new input element. Thus, all attributes except name and id are copied to the new element. The input element is inserted into the p element, and the p element is appended to the document's form element. Finally, the outerHTML of the new element is displayed in its field. Notice that except for the name and id attributes, all others are copied. This includes style sheet attributes and event handlers. To prove that the event handler works in the new elements, you can add a space to any one of them and press Tab to trigger the onchange event handler that changes the content to all-uppercase characters.

elementObject.mergeAttributes()

LISTING 26-29

Using the mergeAttributes() Method

HTML: jsb2-29.html

```html
<!DOCTYPE html>
<html>
    <head>
        <meta http-equiv="content-type" content="text/html;charset=utf-8">
        <title>mergeAttributes() Method</title>
        <script type="text/javascript" src="../jsb-global.js"></script>
        <script type="text/javascript" src="jsb26-29.js"></script>
    </head>
    <body
    onload="document.expandable.field1.value = ↵
            document.expandable.field1.outerHTML">
        <h1>mergeAttributes() Method</h1>
        <hr />
        <form name="expandable" onsubmit="return false">
            <p>
                <input type="button" value="Append Field 'Clone'"
                    onclick="doMerge(this.form)" />
            </p>
            <p>
                <input type="text" name="field1" id="FIELD1" size="120" value=""
                    style="font-size:9pt" onchange="upperMe(this)" />
            </p>
        </form>
    </body>
</html>
```

JavaScript: jsb26-29.js

```javascript
function doMerge(form)
{
    var newPElem = document.createElement("p");
    var newInputElem = document.createElement("input");
    newInputElem.id = newInputElem.uniqueID;
    newInputElem.mergeAttributes(form.field1);
    newPElem.appendChild(newInputElem);
    form.appendChild(newPElem);
    newInputElem.value = newInputElem.outerHTML;
}

// called by onChange event handler of fields
function upperMe(field)
{
    field.value = field.value.toUpperCase();
}
```

Related Items: clearAttributes(), cloneNode(), removeAttributes() methods

normalize()

Returns: Nothing

Compatibility: WinIE6+, MacIE5+, NN7+, Moz+, Safari1.2+, Opera+, Chrome+

In the course of appending, inserting, removing, and replacing child nodes of an element, it is conceivable that two text nodes can end up adjacent to each other. Although this typically has no effect on the rendering of the content, some XML-centric applications that rely heavily on the document node hierarchy to interpret content properly may not like having two text nodes sitting next to each other. The proper form of a node hierarchy is for a single text node to be bounded by other node types. The normalize() method sweeps through the child nodes of the current node object and combines adjacent text nodes into a single text node. The effect obviously impacts the number of child nodes of an element, but it also cleanses the nested node hierarchy.

Example

Use The Evaluator (see Chapter 4) to experiment with the normalize() method. The following sequence adds a text node adjacent to one in the myP element. A subsequent invocation of the normalize() method removes the division between the adjacent text nodes.

Begin by confirming the number of child nodes of the myP element:

```
document.getElementById("myP").childNodes.length
```

Three nodes initially inhabit the element. Next, create a text node, and append it as the last child of the myP element:

```
a = document.createTextNode("This means you!")
document.getElementById("myP").appendChild(a)
```

With the new text now rendered on the page, the number of child nodes increases to four:

```
document.getElementById("myP").childNodes.length
```

You can see that the last child node of myP is the text node you just created:

```
document.getElementById("myP").lastChild.nodeValue
```

But by invoking normalize() on myP, all adjacent text nodes are accumulated into single nodes:

```
document.getElementById("myP").normalize()
```

You can see that the myP element is back to three child nodes, and the last child is a combination of the two previously distinct, but adjacent, text nodes:

```
document.getElementById("myP").childNodes.length
document.getElementById("myP").lastChild.nodeValue
```

Related Items: document.createTextNode(), appendChild(), insertBefore(), removeChild(), replaceChild() methods

releaseCapture()
setCapture(containerBoolean)

Returns: Nothing

Compatibility: WinIE5+, MacIE-, NN-, Moz-, Safari-, Opera-, Chrome-

You can instruct a single object on a page to capture all mouse events (onmousedown, onmouseup, onmousemove, onmouseout, onmouseover, onclick, and ondblclick) via the WinIE-specific setCapture() method. A primary scenario for mouse event capture is when some content appears on the page that you wish to leave as the center of user focus — items such as pull-down menus, context menus, or simulated modal window areas. When such items appear onscreen, you want the effect of blocking all mouse events except those that apply to the menu or currently visible pseudowindow. When the region disappears, mouse events can be released so that individual elements (such as buttons and links elsewhere on the page) respond to mouse events.

Event capture does not block the events. Instead, the events are redirected to the object set to capture all mouse events. Events bubble up from that point unless explicitly canceled (see Chapter 32). For example, consider a document that has a <body> tag containing an onclick event handler that governs the entire document at all times. If you turn on event capture for a div somewhere in the document, the click event first goes to the div. That div might have an onclick event handler that looks to process click events when they occur in some of its child elements. If the event handler for the div does not also cancel the bubbling of that click event, the body element's onclick event handler eventually receives and processes the event, even though the div initially captured the event.

Deciding which object should capture events is an important design issue to confront. With event capture engaged, all mouse events (no matter where they occur) get funneled to the object set to capture the events. Therefore, if you design an application whose entire interface consists of clicking and dragging positionable elements, you can set one of those elements (or even the document object) to perform the capturing. For pop-up regions, however, it is generally more logical and convenient for your coding to assign the capture mechanism to the primary container of the pop-up content (usually, a positioned div).

The setCapture() method has one optional Boolean parameter. The parameter controls whether mouse events on child elements within the capturing object are under control of the event capture mechanism. The default value (true) means that all mouse events targeted at elements within the current object go to the current object rather than to the original target — the most likely way you will use setCapture() for things such as pop-up and context menus. But if you specify false as the parameter, mouse events occurring in child elements of the capturing container receive their events directly. From there, regular event bubbling upward from the target ensues (see Chapter 32).

You may encounter odd behavior when the region you set up to capture mouse events contains form elements such as text input fields and select lists. Because these elements require mouse events to gain focus for interaction, the event capture mechanism inhibits access to these items. To work around this behavior, you can examine the click event's srcElement property to see whether the click was on one of these elements and script the focus of that element (or instruct the user to press the Tab key until the element gets focus manually).

After an object is set to capture events, your other code must define which events actually do something and decide whether events should bubble up beyond the capturing element. You need to worry about bubbling only if your design includes mouse event handlers in elements higher up the element containment hierarchy. You may not want those event handlers to fire while event capture is on; in this case, you need to cancel the bubbling of those events in the capturing object.

If your application design requires that the pop-up area be hidden and event handling be returned to normal (such as after the user makes a pop-up menu selection), use the releaseCapture() method in conjunction with hiding the container. Because event capture can be engaged for only one element at a time, you can release capture by invoking the releaseCapture() method from the container or from the document object.

Event capture is automatically disengaged when the user performs any of the following actions:

- Gives focus to any other window
- Displays any system modal dialog window (for example, alert window)
- Scrolls the page
- Opens a browser context menu (by right-clicking)
- Tabs to give focus to the Address field in the browser window

Therefore, you may want to set the document object's onlosecapture event handler to hide any container that your script displays in concert with event capture.

Also be aware that even though mouse events may be captured to prevent mouse access to the rest of the page, keyboard events are not captured. Thus, using the event capture mechanism to simulate modal windows is not foolproof: A user can tab to any form element or link in the page and press the spacebar or Enter key to activate that element.

Event capture, as defined in the W3C DOM, operates differently from WinIE event capture. In the W3C DOM, you can instruct the browser to substitute event capture of any kind of event for the normal event bubbling behavior. For example, you can attach an event listener to the body element in such a way that it sees all click events aimed at elements contained by the body element before the events reach their target elements. (See Chapter 25 and Chapter 32, for more on the W3C DOM event model and how to integrate it into cross-browser applications.)

Example

Listing 26-30 demonstrates the usage of setCapture() and releaseCapture() in a quick-and-dirty context menu for WinIE5+. The job of the context menu is to present a list of numbering styles for the ordered list of items on the page. Whenever the user brings up the context menu atop the ol element, the custom context menu appears. Event capture is turned on in the process to prevent mouse actions elsewhere on the page from interrupting the context menu choice. Even a click of the link set up as the title of the list is inhibited while the context menu is visible. A click anywhere outside the context menu hides the menu. Clicking a choice in the menu changes the listStyleType property of the ol object and hides the menu. Whenever the context menu is hidden, event capture is turned off so that clicking the page (such as the link) works as normal.

For this design, onclick, onmouseover, and onmouseout event handlers are assigned to the div element that contains the context menu. To trigger the display of the context menu, the ol element has an oncontextmenu event handler. This handler invokes the showContextMenu() function. In this function, event capture is assigned to the context menu div object. The div is also positioned at the location of the click before it is set to be visible. To prevent the system's regular context menu from also appearing, the event object's returnValue property is set to false.

Now that all mouse events on the page go through the contextMenu div object, let's examine what happens with different kinds of events triggered by user action. As the user rolls the mouse, a flood of mouseover and mouseout events fires. The event handlers assigned to the div manage these events. But notice that the two event handlers, highlight() and unhighlight(), perform action only when the srcElement property of the event is one of the menu items in the div. Because the page has no other onmouseover or onmouseout event handlers defined for elements up the containment hierarchy, you do not have to cancel event bubbling for these events.

elementObject.releaseCapture()

When a user clicks the mouse button, different things happen, depending on whether event capture is enabled. Without event capture, the `click` event bubbles up from wherever it occurred to the `onclick` event handler in the `body` element. (An alert dialog box displays to let you know when the event reaches the `body`.) But with event capture turned on (the context menu is showing), the `handleClick()` event handler takes over to apply the desired choice whenever the click is atop one of the context menu items. For all `click` events handled by this function, the context menu is hidden, and the `click` event is canceled from bubbling up any higher (no alert dialog box appears). This takes place whether the user makes a choice in the context menu or clicks anywhere else on the page. In the latter case, all you need is for the context menu to go away as the real context menu does. For added insurance, the `onlosecapture` event handler hides the context menu when a user performs any of the actions just listed that cancel capture.

LISTING 26-30

Using setCapture() and releaseCapture()

HTML: jsb26-30.html

```html
<!DOCTYPE html>
<html>
  <head>
    <meta http-equiv="content-type" content="text/html;charset=utf-8">
    <style type="text/css">
      #contextMenu
      {
        position:absolute; background-color:#cfcfcf;
        border-style:solid; border-width:1px;
        border-color:#EFEFEF #505050 #505050 #EFEFEF;
        padding:3px 10px; font-size:8pt; font-family:Arial, Helvetica;
        line-height:150%; visibility:hidden;
      }
      .menuItem
      {
        color:black;
      }
      .menuItemOn
      {
        color:white
      }
      ol
      {
        list-style-position:inside; font-weight:bold; cursor:hand;
      }
      li
      {
        font-weight:normal;
      }
    </style>
    <script type="text/javascript" src="../jsb-global.js"></script>
    <script type="text/javascript" src="jsb26-30.js"></script>
  </head>
```

```html
<body onclick="alert('You reached the document object.')">
  <ol id="shapesList" oncontextmenu="showContextMenu()">
    <li style="list-style: none"><a
     href="javascript:alert('A%20sample%20link.')">Three-DimensionalShapes</a>
    </li>
    <li value="1">Circular Cylinder</li>
    <li>Cube</li>
    <li>Rectangular Prism</li>
    <li>Regular Right Pyramid</li>
    <li>Right Circular Cone</li>
    <li>Sphere</li>
  </ol>
  <div id="contextMenu" onlosecapture="hideMenu()" onclick="handleClick()"
      onmouseover="highlight()" onmouseout="unhighlight()">
    <span id="menuItem1" class="menuItem"
          listtype="upper-alpha">A,B,C,...</span>
    <br />
    <span id="menuItem2" class="menuItem"
          listtype="lower-alpha">a,b,c,...</span>
    <br />
    <span id="menuItem3" class="menuItem"
          listtype="upper-roman">I,II,III,...</span>
    <br />
    <span id="menuItem4" class="menuItem"
          listtype="lower-roman">i,ii,iii,...</span>
    <br />
    <span id="menuItem5" class="menuItem"
          listtype="decimal">1,2,3,...</span>
  </div>
</body>
</html>
```

JavaScript: jsb26-30.js
```javascript
function showContextMenu()
{
   contextMenu.setCapture();
   contextMenu.style.pixelTop = event.clientY + document.body.scrollTop;
   contextMenu.style.pixelLeft = event.clientX + document.body.scrollLeft;
   contextMenu.style.visibility = "visible";
   event.returnValue = false;
}

function revert()
{
   document.releaseCapture();
   hideMenu();
}

function hideMenu()
{
   contextMenu.style.visibility = "hidden";
}
```

continued

elementObject.removeAttribute()

LISTING 26-30   *(continued)*

```
function handleClick()
{
    var elem = window.event.srcElement;
    if (elem.id.indexOf("menuItem") == 0)
    {
        document.getElementById("shapesList").style.listStyleType = elem.listtype;
    }
    revert();
    event.cancelBubble = true;
}

function highlight()
{
    var elem = event.srcElement;
    if (elem.className == "menuItem")
    {
        elem.className = "menuItemOn";
    }
}

function unhighlight()
{
    var elem = event.srcElement
    if (elem.className == "menuItemOn")
    {
        elem.className = "menuItem";
    }
}
```

Related Items: addEventListener(), dispatchEvent(), fireEvent(), removeEventLis-
tener() methods; onlosecapture event; Event object (Chapter 32)

removeAttribute("*attributeName*"[, *caseSensitivity*])

Returns: Boolean (IE), nothing (NN/DOM)

Compatibility: WinIE4+, MacIE4+, NN6+, Moz+, Safari+, Opera+, Chrome+

If you create an attribute with the setAttribute() method, you can eliminate that attribute from
the element object via the removeAttribute() method. The required parameter is the name of
the attribute. Internet Explorer permits you to set and remove attributes such that the attribute names
are case sensitive. The default behavior of removeAttribute() in IE (the second parameter is a
Boolean value) is false. Therefore, if you supply a value of true for the case-sensitivity parameter
in setAttribute(), you should set the parameter to true in removeAttribute() to ensure a
proper balance between created and removed attributes.

The W3C DOM (NN/Moz-/WebKit-based) version of the removeAttribute() method has a single
parameter (a case-insensitive attribute name) and returns no value. The returned value in IE is true

if the removal succeeds and `false` if it doesn't succeed (or if the attribute is one that you set in some other manner).

Example

Use The Evaluator (see Chapter 4) to experiment with the `removeAttribute()` method for the elements in the page. See the examples for the `setAttribute()` method later in this chapter, and enter the corresponding `removeAttribute()` statements in the top text box. Interlace statements using `getAttribute()` to verify the presence or absence of each attribute.

Related Items: `attributes` property; `document.createAttribute()`, `getAttribute()`, `setAttribute()` methods

removeAttributeNode(*attributeNode*)
setAttributeNode(*attributeNode*)

Returns: `Attribute` object

Compatibility: WinIE6+, MacIE-, NN6+, Moz+, Safari+, Opera+, Chrome+

As discussed in the coverage of the `getAttributeNode()` method earlier in this chapter, the W3C DOM treats a name–value attribute pair as an attribute object. An attribute object is a distinct node within a named node map — a collection of attribute objects belonging to an element. Understanding named node maps and attribute objects is more useful in an XML environment, where attributes can not only contain valuable data, but also are not exposed to the DOM as properties you can access via script. Instead of accessing an object's properties, you work with the actual attributes.

If you want to insert an attribute in the formal W3C methodology, you can use `document.createAttribute()` to generate a new attribute object. Subsequent script statements assign values to the `nodeName` and `nodeValue` properties to give the attribute its traditional name–value pair. You can then insert that new attribute object into the attribute list of an object via the `setAttributeNode()` method. The sole parameter is an attribute object, and the return value is a reference to the newly inserted attribute object.

To remove an attribute node from an element using this syntax, employ the `removeAttributeNode()` method. Again, the sole parameter is an attribute object. If your script knows only the attribute's name, you can use `getAttributeNode()` to obtain a valid reference to the attribute object. The `removeAttributeNode()` method returns a reference to the removed attribute object. That object remains in the browser's memory, but it is not part of the document hierarchy. By capturing this removed attribute object in a variable, you have the flexibility to modify and assign it to another object elsewhere in the document.

In practice, you may rarely, if ever, need to address attributes as nodes. Other methods — notably `getAttribute()`, `removeAttribute()`, and `setAttribute()` — do the job when your scripts have only the name (as a string) of an attribute belonging to an element.

Example

Use The Evaluator (see Chapter 4) to experiment with the `setAttributeNode()` and `removeAttributeNode()` methods for the p element in the page. The task is to create and add a `style` attribute to the p element. Begin by creating a new attribute and storing it temporarily in the global variable `a`:

```
a = document.createAttribute("style")
```

Assign a value to the `attribute` object:

```
a.nodeValue = "color:red"
```

Now insert the new attribute into the p element:

```
document.getElementById("myP").setAttributeNode(a)
```

The paragraph changes color in response to the newly added attribute.

Due to the NN6 bug that won't allow the method to return a reference to the newly inserted attribute node, you can artificially obtain such a reference:

```
b = document.getElementById("myP").getAttributeNode("style")
```

Finally, use the reference to the newly added attribute to remove it from the element:

```
document.getElementById("myP").removeAttributeNode(b)
```

Upon the removal of the attribute, the paragraph resumes its initial color. See the example for the `setAttribute()` method later in this chapter to discover how you can perform this same kind of operation with `setAttribute()`.

Related Items: `attributes` property; `document.createAttribute()`, `getAttribute()`, `getAttributeNode()`, `setAttribute()` methods

removeAttributeNS("*namespaceURI*", "*localName*")

Returns: Nothing

Compatibility: WinIE-, MacIE-, NN6+, Moz+, Safari+, Opera+, Chrome+

This method removes the attribute specified in the two parameters. The first parameter of the method is a URI string matching a URI assigned to a label in the document. The second parameter is the local name portion of the attribute whose value you are removing.

Related Items: `attributes`, `namespaceURI`, `localName` properties; `removeAttribute()`, `getAttributeNS()`, `setAttributeNS()` methods

removeBehavior(*ID*)

Returns: Boolean

Compatibility: WinIE5+, MacIE-, NN-, Moz-, Safari-, Opera-, Chrome-

The `removeBehavior()` method detaches a behavior from an object. It assumes that the behavior was added to the object via the `addBehavior()` method. The return value of the `addBehavior()` method is a unique identifier for that particular behavior. This identifier is the required parameter for the `removeBehavior()` method. Thus, you can add two behaviors to an object and remove just one of them if you so desire. If the removal succeeds, the `removeBehavior()` method returns `true`; otherwise, it returns `false`.

Example

See Listing 26-19a and Listing 26-19b earlier in this chapter for examples of how to use `addBehavior()` and `removeBehavior()`.

Related Item: `addBehavior()` method

removeChild(*nodeObject*)

Returns: `Node` object reference

Compatibility: WinIE5+, MacIE5+, NN6+, Moz+, Safari+, Opera+, Chrome+

The `removeChild()` method erases a child element from the current element. Content associated with the child element is no longer visible on the page, and the object is no longer part of the document object hierarchy.

As destructive as that sounds, the specifications for the deleted object are not necessarily lost to the ether. The `removeChild()` method returns a reference to the removed node. By assigning this value to a variable, you can hold on to that object specification for insertion later in the session. You are free to use this value as a parameter to such methods as `appendChild()`, `replaceChild()`, `swapNode()`, and `insertBefore()`.

Remember that `removeChild()` is invoked from the point of view of a parent element. If you simply want to remove an element, you can do so more directly (in WinIE5+ only) with the `removeNode()` method. The IE `removeNode()` method also allows a node to remove itself, which isn't possible via the `removeChild()` method.

Example

You can see an example of `removeChild()` as part of Listing 26-21 earlier in this chapter.

Related Items: `appendChild()`, `replaceChild()`, `removeNode()` methods

removeEventListener()

(See `addEventListener()`)

removeExpression("*propertyName*")

Returns: Boolean

Compatibility: WinIE5+, MacIE-, NN-, Moz-, Safari-, Opera-, Chrome-

If you assign an expression to an object property (including an object's `style` object) via the `setExpression()` method, you can remove it under script control with the `removeExpression()` method. The sole parameter is the name of the property in string form. Property names are case sensitive.

The method returns `true` if the removal succeeds; otherwise, `false` is returned. Be aware that removing an expression does not alter the value that is currently assigned to the property. In other words, you can use `setExpression()` to set a property's value and then remove the expression so that no further changes are made when the document recalculates expressions. If this is your goal, however, you are probably better served by simply setting the property directly via scripting.

Example

You can experiment with all three expression methods in The Evaluator (Chapter 4). The following sequence adds an expression to a style sheet property of the `myP` element on the page and then removes it.

elementObject.removeNode()

To begin, enter the number 24 in the bottom one-line text box in The Evaluator (but don't press Enter or click the List Properties button). This is the value used in the expression to govern the fontSize property of the myP object. Next, assign an expression to the myP object's style object by entering the following statement in the top text box:

```
myP.style.setExpression("fontSize","document.forms[0]. ↵
inspector.value","JScript")
```

Now you can enter different font sizes in the bottom text box and have the values immediately applied to the fontSize property. (Keyboard events in the text box automatically trigger the recalculation.) The default unit is px, but you can also append other units (such as pt) to the value in the text box to see how different measurement units influence the same numeric value.

Before proceeding to the next step, enter a value other than 16 (the default fontSize value). Finally, enter the following statement in the top text box to disconnect the expression from the property:

```
myP.style.removeExpression("fontSize")
```

Notice that although you can no longer adjust the font size from the bottom text box, the most recent value assigned to it sticks to the element. To prove it, enter the following statement in the top text box to see the current value:

```
myP.style.fontSize
```

Related Items: document.recalc(), getExpression(), setExpression() methods

removeNode(*removeChildrenFlag*)

Returns: Node object reference

Compatibility: WinIE5+, MacIE-, NN-, Moz-, Safari-, Opera-, Chrome-

You can use the removeNode() method to delete the current node from an element hierarchy in WinIE5+. The sole parameter is a Boolean value that directs the method to remove only itself (without its child nodes) or the node and all of its children (value of true). The method returns a reference to the node object removed. This removed object is no longer accessible to the DOM. But the returned value contains all properties of the object as it existed before you removed it (including properties such as outerHTML and explicitly set style sheet rules). Thus, you can use this value as a parameter to insert the node elsewhere in the document.

Although the W3C DOM does not have a removeNode() method, the cross-browser method whose behavior most closely resembles removeNode() is the removeChild() method. The scope of the removeChild() method is one level up the object hierarchy from the object you use for the removeNode() method.

Example

Examine Listing 26-21 for the appendChild() method to understand the difference between removeChild() and removeNode(). In the restore() function, you can replace this statement

```
mainObj.removeChild(oneChild);
```

in IE5+ with

```
oneChild.removeNode(true);
```

The difference is subtle, but it is important to understand. See Listing 26-31 later in this chapter for another example of the `removeNode()` method.

Related Items: Node object; `appendChild()`, `cloneChild()`, `removeChild()`, `replaceChild()`, `replaceNode()` methods

replaceAdjacentText("*location*", "*text*")

Returns: String

Compatibility: WinIE5+, MacIE-, NN-, Moz-, Safari-, Opera-, Chrome-

The `replaceAdjacentText()` method enables you to replace one chunk of document text with another in a specific position relative to the current object. Be aware that this method works only for plain text and not HTML tags. The returned value is the string of the text that you replace.

Both parameters are required. The first must be one of four possible case-insensitive locations for the insertion, shown in the following table:

Location	Description
beforeBegin	Before the current element's start tag
afterBegin	After the start tag but before any nested content
beforeEnd	Before the end tag but after all other nested content
afterEnd	After the end tag

This method is best used with inline (rather than block) elements when specifying the `beforeBegin` and `afterEnd` parameters. For example, if you attempt to use `replaceAdjacentText()` with `beforeBegin` on the second of two consecutive paragraph elements, the replacement text is inserted into the end of the first paragraph. You can think of the `replaceAdjacentText()` method in terms of text fragment nodes. The method replaces the text fragment node (given any one of the four position parameters) with new text. Replacing the text of a simple element with either the `afterBegin` or `beforeEnd` locations is the same as assigning that text to the object's `innerText` property.

Example

Use The Evaluator (see Chapter 4) to experiment with the `replaceAdjacentText()` method. Enter each of the following statements in the top text box, and watch the results in the `myP` element (and its nested `myEM` element) below the solid rule:

```
document.getElementById("myEM").replaceAdjacentText("afterBegin", "twenty")
```

Notice that the `myEM` element's new text picks up the behavior of the element. In the meantime, the replaced text (`all`) is returned by the method and displayed in the Results box:

```
document.getElementById("myEM").replaceAdjacentText("beforeBegin", "We need")
```

elementObject.replaceChild()

All characters of the text fragment, including spaces, are replaced. Therefore, you may need to supply a trailing space, as shown here, if the fragment you replace has a space:

```
document.getElementById("myP").replaceAdjacentText("beforeEnd", "good people.")
```

This is another way to replace the text fragment following the myEM element, but it is also relative to the surrounding myP element. If you now attempt to replace text after the end of the myP block-level element

```
document.getElementById("myP").replaceAdjacentText("afterEnd", "Hooray!")
```

the text fragment is inserted after the end of the myP element's tag set. The fragment is just kind of floating in the DOM as an unlabeled text node.

Related Items: innerText, outerText properties; getAdjacentText(), insertAdjacentHTML(), insertAdjacentText() methods

replaceChild(*newNodeObject, oldNodeObject*)

Returns: Node object reference

Compatibility: WinIE5+, MacIE5+, NN6+, Moz+, Safari+, Opera+, Chrome+

The replaceChild() method enables you to swap an existing child node object for a new node object. Parameters for the replaceChild() method are node object references, and they must be in the order of the new object followed by the object you want to replace. The old object must be an immediate child node of the parent used to invoke the method, and the new object must also be a legal child element within the document containment hierarchy.

The method returns a reference to the child object that you replaced with the new object. This reference can be used as a parameter to any of the node-oriented insertion or replacement methods.

Remember that replaceChild() is invoked from the point of view of a parent element. If you simply want to change an element, you can do so more directly in WinIE5+ with the swapNode() or replaceNode() method.

Example

You can see an example of replaceChild() as part of Listing 26-21 (for the appendChild property) earlier in this chapter.

Related Items: appendChild(), removeChild(), replaceNode(), swapNode() methods

replaceNode("*newNodeObject*")

Returns: Node object reference

Compatibility: WinIE5+, MacIE-, NN-, Moz-, Safari-, Opera-, Chrome-

The replaceNode() method is related to the replaceChild() method, but you invoke this method on the actual node you want to replace (instead of the object's parent). The sole parameter is a reference to a valid node object, which you can generate via the document.createElement() method or copy from an existing node. The value returned from the method is a reference to the object that you replace. Thus, you can preserve a copy of the replaced node by storing the results in a variable for use later.

If the node you replace contains other nodes, the replaceNode() method removes all contained nodes of the original from the document. Therefore, if you want to change a wrapper node but want to maintain the original children, your script must capture the children and put them back into the new node as shown in the following example.

Example

Listing 26-31 demonstrates three node-related methods: removeNode(), replaceNode(), and swapNode(). These methods work in WinIE5+ only.

The page rendered from Listing 26-31 begins with a ul type list of four items. Four buttons control various aspects of the node structure of this list element. The first button invokes the replace() function, which changes the ul type to ol. To do this, the function must temporarily tuck away all child nodes of the original ul element so that they can be added back into the new ol element. At the same time, the old ul node is stored in a global variable (oldNode) for restoration in another function.

To replace the ul node with an ol, the replace() function creates a new, empty ol element and assigns the myOL ID to it. Next, the children (li elements) are stored en masse as an array in the variable innards. The child nodes are then inserted into the empty ol element, using the insert-Before() method. Notice that as each child element from the innards array is inserted into the ol element, the child element is removed from the innards array. That's why the loop to insert the child nodes is a while loop that constantly inserts the first item of the innards array to the new element. Finally, the replaceNode() method puts the new node in the old node's place, and the old node (just the ul element) is stored in oldNode.

The restore() function operates in the inverse direction of the replace() function. The same juggling of nested child nodes is required.

The third button invokes the swap() function, whose script exchanges the first and last nodes. The swapNode() method, like the others in this discussion, operates from the point of view of the node. Therefore, the method is attached to one of the swapped nodes, and the other node is specified as a parameter. Because of the nature of the ol element, the number sequence remains fixed, but the text of the li node swaps.

To demonstrate the removeNode() method, the fourth function removes the last child node of the list. Each call to removeNode() passes the true parameter to guarantee that the text nodes nested inside each li node are also removed. Experiment with this method by setting the parameter to false (the default). Notice how the parent-child relationship changes when you remove the li node.

LISTING 26-31

Using Node-Related Methods

HTML: jsb26-31.html

```
<!DOCTYPE html>
<html>
  <head>
```

continued

elementObject.replaceNode()

LISTING 26-31   *(continued)*

```
   <meta http-equiv="content-type" content="text/html;charset=utf-8">
   <title>removeNode(), replaceNode(), and swapNode() Methods</title>
   <script type="text/javascript" src="../jsb-global.js"></script>
   <script type="text/javascript" src="jsb26-31.js"></script>
 </head>
 <body>
  <h1>Node Methods</h1>
  <hr />
  Here is a list of items:
  <ul id="myUL">
   <li>First Item</li>
   <li>Second Item</li>
   <li>Third Item</li>
   <li>Fourth Item</li>
  </ul>
  <form>
   <input type="button" value="Change to OL List"
          onclick="replace()" />  
   <input type="button"
          value="Restore LI List" onclick="restore()" />  
   <input type="button" value="Swap First/Last" onclick="swap()" />  
   <input type="button" value="Remove Last" onclick="remove()" />
  </form>
 </body>
</html>
```

JavaScript: jsb26-31.js

```
// store original node between changes
var oldNode;

// replace UL node with OL
function replace()
{
   if (document.getElementById("myUL"))
   {
      var newNode = document.createElement("OL");
      newNode.id = "myOL";
      var innards = document.getElementById("myUL").children;
      while (innards.length > 0)
      {
         newNode.insertBefore(innards[0]);
      }
      oldNode = document.getElementById("myUL").replaceNode(newNode);
   }
}

// restore OL to UL
function restore()
{
```

```
    if (document.getElementById("myOL") && oldNode)
    {
        var innards = document.getElementById("myOL").children;
        while (innards.length > 0)
        {
            oldNode.insertBefore(innards[0]);
        }
        document.getElementById("myOL").replaceNode(oldNode);
    }
}

// swap first and last nodes
function swap()
{
    if (document.getElementById("myUL"))
    {
        document.getElementById("myUL").firstChild.swapNode(
            document.getElementById("myUL").lastChild);
    }
    if (document.getElementById("myOL"))
    {
        document.getElementById("myOL").firstChild.swapNode(
            document.getElementById("myOL").lastChild);
    }
}

// remove last node
function remove()
{
    if (document.getElementById("myUL"))
    {
        document.getElementById("myUL").lastChild.removeNode(true);
    }
    if (document.getElementById("myOL"))
    {
        document.getElementById("myOL").lastChild.removeNode(true);
    }
}
```

You can accomplish the same functionality shown in Listing 26-31 in a cross-browser fashion using the W3C DOM. In place of the removeNode() and replaceNode() methods, use removeChild() and replaceChild() methods to shift the point of view (and object references) to the parent of the ul and ol objects: the document.body. Also, you need to change the document.all references to document.getElementById().

Related Items: removeChild(), removeNode(), replaceChild(), swapNode() methods

scrollIntoView(*topAlignFlag*)

Returns: Nothing

Compatibility: WinIE4+, MacIE4+, NN7+, Moz+, Safari 2.02, Opera+, Chrome+

The `scrollIntoView()` method scrolls the page (vertically and/or horizontally as needed) such that the current object is visible within the window or frame that contains it. A single parameter, a Boolean value, controls the location of the element within the viewable space. A value of `true` (the default) causes the element to be displayed so that its top is aligned with the top of the window or frame (provided that the document beneath it is long enough to allow this amount of scrolling). But a value of `false` causes the bottom of the element to align with the bottom of the viewable area. In most cases, you want the former so that the beginning of a page section is at the top of the viewable area. But if you don't want a user to see content below a certain element when you jump to the new view, use the `false` parameter.

For form elements, you must use the typical form element reference (`document.formName .elementName.scrollIntoView()`) unless you also specify an ID attribute for the element (`document.getElementById("elementID").scrollIntoView()`).

Example

Use The Evaluator (see Chapter 4) to experiment with the `scrollIntoView()` method. Resize the browser window height so that you can see only the top text box and the Results text area. Enter each of the following statements in the top text box, and see where the `myP` element comes into view:

```
myP.scrollIntoView()
myP.scrollIntoView(false)
```

Expand the height of the browser window until you can see part of the table lower on the page. If you enter

```
myTable.scrollIntoView(false)
```

in the top text box, the page scrolls to bring the bottom of the table to the bottom of the window. But if you use the default parameter (`true` or empty)

```
myTable.scrollIntoView()
```

the page scrolls as far as it can in an effort to align the top of the element as closely as possible to the top of the window. The page cannot scroll beyond its normal scrolling maximum (although if the element is a positioned element, you can use dynamic positioning to place it wherever you want — including off the page). Also, if you shrink the window and try to scroll the top of the table to the top of the window, be aware that the `table` element contains a `caption` element, so the caption is flush with the top of the window.

Related Items: `window.scroll()`, `window.scrollBy()`, `window.scrollTo()` methods

setActive()

Returns: Nothing

Compatibility: WinIE5.5+, MacIE-, NN-, Moz-, Safari-, Opera-, Chrome-

The `setActive()` method lets a script designate an element object as the active element. However, unlike in the `focus()` method, the window does not scroll the active element into view. Any `onFocus` event handler defined for the element fires when `setActive()` is invoked without the browser's giving the element focus.

elementObject.setAttribute()

Example

Use The Evaluator (see Chapter 4) to compare the setActive() and focus() methods. With the page scrolled to the top and the window sized so that you cannot see the sample checkbox near the bottom of the page, enter the following statement in the top text box:

```
document.getElementById("myCheckbox").setActive()
```

Scroll down to see that the checkbox has operational focus (press the spacebar to see). Now scroll back to the top, and enter the following:

```
document.getElementById("myCheckbox").focus()
```

This time, the checkbox gets focus, and the page automatically scrolls the object into view.

Related Item: focus() method

setAttribute("*attributeName*", *value*[, *caseSensitivity*])

Returns: Nothing

Compatibility: WinIE4+, MacIE4+, NN6+, Moz+, Safari+, Opera+, Chrome+

The setAttribute() method assigns a new value to an existing attribute of the current object or inserts an entirely new attribute name–value pair among the attributes of the current object. This method represents an alternative syntax to setting a property of the object directly.

Note

The W3C DOM Level 2 standard recommends getAttribute() and setAttribute() for reading and writing element object attribute values, rather than reading and writing those values by way of their corresponding properties. Although using these methods is certainly advisable for XML elements, the same DOM standard sends conflicting signals by defining all kinds of properties for HTML element objects. Browsers, of course, will support access via properties well into the future, so don't feel obligated to change your ways just yet. ■

The first two parameters of setAttribute() are required. The first is the name of the attribute. The default behavior of this method respects the case of the attribute name. Therefore, if you use setAttribute() to adjust the value of an existing attribute in default mode, the first parameter must match the case of the attribute as known by the object model for the current document. Remember that all names of all attributes assigned as inline source-code attributes are automatically converted to lowercase letters.

A value you assign to the attribute is the second parameter. For cross-browser compatibility, the value should be either a string or Boolean data type.

IE provides an optional third parameter to control the case-sensitivity issue for the attribute name. The default value (true) has a different impact on your object depending on whether you use setAttribute() to assign a new attribute or reassign an existing one. In the former case, the third parameter as true means that the attribute name assigned to the object observes the case of the first parameter. In the latter case, the third parameter as true means that the attribute isn't reassigned unless the first parameter matches the case of the attribute currently associated with the object. Instead, a new attribute with a different case sequence is created.

Attempting to manage the case sensitivity of newly created attributes is fraught with peril, especially if you try to reuse names but with different case sequences. We strongly recommend using default case-sensitivity controls for setAttribute() and getAttribute().

683

See also the W3C DOM facilities for treating attributes as node objects in the discussions of the getAttributeNode() and removeAttributeNode() methods earlier in this chapter.

Example

Use The Evaluator (see Chapter 4) to experiment with the setAttribute() method for the elements in the page. Setting attributes can have immediate impact on the layout of the page (just as setting an object's properties can). Enter the following sample statements in the top text box to view attribute values.

```
document.getElementById("myTable").setAttribute("width", "80%")
document.getElementById("myTable").setAttribute("border", "5")
```

Related Items: attributes property; document.createAttribute(), getAttribute(), getAttributeNode(), removeAttribute(), removeAttributeNode(), setAttributeNode() methods

setAttributeNode()

(See removeAttributeNode())

setAttributeNodeNS("*attributeNode*")

Returns: Attribute object

Compatibility: WinIE-, MacIE-, NN6+, Moz+, Safari+, Opera+, Chrome+

This method inserts or replaces an attribute in the current element. The sole parameter is an attribute object, and the return value is a reference to the newly inserted attribute object. When the method is invoked, the browser looks for a pairing of local name and namespace URI between the nodes. If there is a match, the node replaces the matched node; otherwise, the node is inserted.

Related Items: attributes, namespaceURI, localName properties; removeAttributeNS(), getAttributeNS(), and setAttributeNS() methods

setAttributeNS("*namespaceURI*", "*qualifiedName*", "*value*")

Returns: Nothing

Compatibility: WinIE-, MacIE-, NN6+, Moz+, Safari+, Opera+, Chrome+

This method inserts or replaces an attribute in the current element, as specified in the three parameters. The first parameter of the method is a URI string matching a URI assigned to a label in the document. The second parameter is the local name portion of the attribute whose value you are getting. If a match is found among these parameters, the value in the third parameter is assigned to the existing attribute; otherwise, the value is inserted as a new attribute.

Related Items: attributes, namespaceURI, localName properties; removeAttributeNS(), getAttributeNS(), and setAttributeNodeNS() methods

setCapture(*containerBoolean*)

(See releaseCapture())

setExpression("*propertyName*", "*expression*",["*language*"])

Returns: Nothing

Compatibility: WinIE5+, MacIE-, NN-, Moz-, Safari-, Opera-, Chrome-

Use the setExpression() method to assign the result of an executable expression to the value of an element object property. This method can assign values to both HTML element objects and style objects that belong to them.

The setExpression() method is a scripted way of assigning expressions to attributes. But you can also assign expressions directly to style sheet definitions in the HTML tag of an element using the expression() syntax, as in the following example:

```
<p style="width:expression(document.body.style.width * 0.75)">
```

The setExpression() method requires three parameters. The first parameter is the name of the property (in string form) to which you assign the expression. Property names are case sensitive. The second parameter is a string form of the expression to be evaluated to supply a value for the property. Expressions can refer to global variables or properties of other objects in the same document (provided that the property is anything other than an array). An expression may also contain math operators.

Pay close attention to the data type of the evaluated value of the expression. The value must be a valid data type for the property. For example, the URL of the body background image must be a string. But for numeric values, you can generally use number and string types interchangeably because the values are converted to the proper type for the property. Even for expressions that evaluate to numbers, encase the expression inside quotes. It may not be necessary in all cases, but if you get into the habit of using quotes, you'll have fewer problems for strings or complex expressions that require them.

You are not limited to using JavaScript as the language for the expression because you can also specify the scripting language of the expression in the optional third parameter. Acceptable parameter values for the language are

```
JScript
JavaScript
VBScript
```

For all intents and purposes, JScript and JavaScript are the same. Both languages are ECMA-262 compatible. JScript is the default value for the language parameter.

One reason to use setExpression() for dynamic properties is to let the property always respond to the current conditions on the page. For example, if you set a property that is dependent on the current width of the body, you want a recalculation that is applied to the property if the user resizes the window. The browser automatically responds to many events and updates any dynamic properties. In essence, the browser recalculates the expressions and applies the new values to the property. Keyboard events in particular trigger this kind of automatic recalculation for you. But if your scripts perform actions on their own (in other words, not triggered by events), your scripts need to force the recalculation of the expressions. The document.recalc() method takes care of this, but you must invoke it to force the recalculation of dynamic properties in these cases.

Example

Listing 26-32 shows the `setExpression()`, `recalc()`, and `getExpression()` methods at work in a DHTML-based clock. Figure 26-1 shows the clock. As time clicks by, the bars for hours, minutes, and seconds adjust their widths to reflect the current time. At the same time, the `innerHTML` of `span` elements to the right of each bar display the current numeric value for the bar.

FIGURE 26-1

A bar-graph clock created with dynamic expressions

The dynamically calculated values in this example are based on the creation of a new `Date` object over and over again to get the current time from the client computer clock. It is from the `Date` object (stored in the variable called `now`) that the hour, minute, and second values are retrieved. Some other calculations are involved so that a value for one of these time components is converted to a pixel value for the width of the bars. The bars are divided into 24 (for the hours) and 60 (for the minutes and seconds) parts, so the scale for the two types differs. For the 60-increment bars in this application, each increment is set to 5 pixels (stored in `shortWidth`); the 24-increment bars are 2.5 times the `shortWidth`.

As the document loads, the three `span` elements for the colored bars are given no width, which means that they assume the default width of zero. But after the page loads, the `onload` event handler invokes the `init()` function, which sets the initial values for each bar's width and the text (`innerHTML`) of the three labeled spans. After these initial values are set, the `init()` function invokes the `updateClock()` function.

In the `updateClock()` function, a new `Date` object is created for the current instant. The `document.recalc()` method is called, instructing the browser to recalculate the expressions that were set in the `init()` function and assign the new values to the properties. To keep the clock ticking, the `setTimeout()` method is set to invoke this same `updateClock()` function in 1 second.

To see what the `getExpression()` method does, you can click the button on the page. It simply displays the returned value for one of the attributes that you assign using `setExpression()`.

LISTING 26-32

Dynamic Properties

HTML: `jsb26-32.html`

```html
<html>
   <head>
      <meta http-equiv="content-type" content="text/html;charset=utf-8">
      <title>getExpression(), setExpression(), and recalc() Methods</title>
      <style type="text/css">
         th
         {
            text-align:right;
         }
         span
         {
            vertical-align:bottom;
         }
      </style>
      <script type="text/javascript" src="../jsb-global.js"></script>
      <script type="text/javascript" src="jsb26-32.js"></script>
   </head>
   <body onload="init()">
      <h1>getExpression(), setExpression(), recalc() Methods</h1>
      <hr />
      <p>This clock uses Dynamic Properties to calculate bar width and time
         numbers:
      </p>
      <table border="0">
         <tr>
            <th>Hours:</th>
            <td>
               <span id="hoursBlock" style="background-color:red"></span>
                <span id="hoursLabel"></span>
            </td>
         </tr>
         <tr>
            <th>Minutes:</th>
            <td>
               <span id="minutesBlock" style="background-color:yellow"></span>
                <span id="minutesLabel"></span>
            </td>
```

continued

elementObject.setExpression()

LISTING 26-32　　*(continued)*

```
          </tr>
          <tr>
              <th>Seconds:</th>
              <td>
                  <span id="secondsBlock" style="background-color:green"></span>
                   <span id="secondsLabel"></span>
              </td>
          </tr>
      </table>
      <hr />
      <form>
          <input type="button" value="Show 'Hours' number innerHTML Expression"
                 onclick="showExpr()" />
      </form>
   </body>
</html>
```

JavaScript: jsb26-32.js

```
var now = new Date();
var shortWidth = 5;
var multiple = 2.5;

function init()
{
    with (document.all)
    {
        hoursBlock.style.setExpression("width",
            "now.getHours() * shortWidth * multiple","jscript");
        hoursLabel.setExpression("innerHTML",
            "now.getHours()","jscript");
        minutesBlock.style.setExpression("width",
            "now.getMinutes() * shortWidth","jscript");
        minutesLabel.setExpression("innerHTML",
            "now.getMinutes()","jscript");
        secondsBlock.style.setExpression("width",
            "now.getSeconds() * shortWidth","jscript");
        secondsLabel.setExpression("innerHTML",
            "now.getSeconds()","jscript");
    }

    updateClock();
}

function updateClock()
{
    now = new Date();
    document.recalc();
    setTimeout("updateClock()",1000);
}
```

```
function showExpr()
{
    alert("Expression for the \'Hours\' innerHTML property is:\r\n" +
       document.getElementById("hoursLabel").getExpression("innerHTML") +
       ".");
}
```

Related Items: document.recalc(), removeExpression(), setExpression() methods

setUserData("*key*", *dataObj*, *dataHandler*)

Returns: Object

Compatibility: WinIE-, MacIE-, NN-, Moz1.7.2+, Safari+, Opera-, Chrome+

The setUserData() method is designed to allow for the addition of user data to a node. This user data comes in the form of an object and is associated with a node through a string key. By requiring a key for an object of user data, the setUserData() method allows you to set multiple pieces of data (objects) on a single node. The last parameter to the method is an event handler function reference that is called whenever the data object is cloned, imported, deleted, renamed, or adopted.

Although some support for the setUserData() method was added in Moz1.7.2, the method still isn't supported to the degree that you can actually use it, as of Moz1.8.1.

swapNode(*otherNodeObject*)

Returns: Node object reference

Compatibility: WinIE5+, MacIE-, NN-, Moz-, Safari-, Opera-, Chrome-

The swapNode() method exchanges the positions of two nodes within an element hierarchy. Contents of both nodes are preserved in their entirety during the exchange. The single parameter must be a valid node object (perhaps created with document.createElement() or copied from an existing node). A return value is a reference to the object whose swapNode() method was invoked.

Example

See Listing 26-31 (the replaceNode() method) for an example of the swapNode() method in action.

Related Items: removeChild(), removeNode(), replaceChild(), replaceNode() methods

tags("*tagName*")

Returns: Array of element objects

Compatibility: WinIE4+, MacIE4+, NN-, Moz-, Safari+, Opera+, Chrome+

The tags() method does not belong to every element, but it is a method of every collection of objects (such as all, forms, and elements). The method is best thought of as a kind of filter for the elements that belong to the current collection. For example, to get an array of all p elements inside a document, use this expression:

```
document.all.tags("P")
```

689

You must pass a parameter string consisting of the tag name you wish to extract from the collection. The tag name is case insensitive.

The return value is an array of references to the objects within the current collection whose tags match the parameter. If there are no matches, the returned array has a length of zero. If you need cross-browser compatibility, use the getElementsByTagName() method described earlier in this chapter, and pass a wildcard value of "*".

Example

Use The Evaluator (see Chapter 4) to experiment with the tags() method. Enter the following statements one at a time in the top text box, and study the results:

```
document.all.tags("div")
document.all.tags("div").length
myTable.all.tags("td").length
```

Because the tags() method returns an array of objects, you can use one of those returned values as a valid element reference:

```
document.all.tags("form")[1].elements.tags("input").length
```

The browsers that support tags do not all support it for the same HTML elements. For example, WebKit-based browsers do not support tags as part of table.

Related Item: getElementsByTagName() method

toString("*param*")

Returns: String

Compatibility: WinIE4+, MacIE4+, NN6+, Moz+, Safari+, Opera+, Chrome+

The toString() method returns a string representation of the element object, which unfortunately can mean different things to different browsers. Don't expect entirely consistent results across browsers, especially when you consider that IE simply returns a generic "[object]" string.

urns("*behaviorURN*")

Returns: Array of element objects

Compatibility: WinIE5+, MacIE-, NN-, Moz-, Safari-, opera-, Chrome-

The urns() method does not belong to every element, but it is a method of every collection of objects. You must pass a parameter string consisting of the URN (Uniform Resource Name) of a behavior resource (most typically .htc) assigned to one or more elements of the collection. The parameter does not include the extension of the filename. If there is no matching behavior URN for the specified parameter, the urns() method returns an array of zero length. This method is related to the behaviorUrns property, which contains an array of behavior URNs assigned to a single element object.

Example

In case the urns() method is reconnected in the future, you can add a button and function to Listing 26-19b that reveals whether the makeHot.htc behavior is attached to the myP element. Such a function looks like this:

```
function behaviorAttached()
{
    if (document.all.urns("makeHot"))
    {
        alert("There is at least one element set to \'makeHot\'.");
    }
}
```

Related Item: `behaviorUrns` property

Event handlers

onactivate
ondeactivate

Compatibility: WinIE5.5+, MacIE-, NN-, Moz-, Safari-, Opera-, Chrome-

The `onactivate` and `ondeactivate` event handlers are similar to the `onfocus` and `onblur` event handlers, respectively, as well as to the IE5.5+ `onfocusin` and `onfocusout` events. Starting with IE5.5+, it is possible to manage the activation of an element and the focus of an element separately. The `onactivate` and `ondeactivate` events correspond to the activation of an element, whereas `onfocusin` and `onfocusout` deal with focus. In many cases, activation and focus go hand in hand, but not always.

If an element receives activation, the `onactivate` event fires for that element just before the activation takes hold; conversely, just before the element loses activation, events fire in the sequence `onbeforedeactivate`, `ondeactivate`, `onblur`. Only elements that by their nature can accept activation (for example, links and form input controls) or that have a `tabindex` attribute set can become the active element (and, therefore, fire these events).

WinIE5.5+ maintains the original `onfocus` and `onblur` event handlers. But because the behaviors are so close to those of the `onactivate` and `ondeactivate` events, we don't recommend mixing the old and new event handler names in your coding style. If you script exclusively for WinIE5.5+, which is unlikely in this day and age, you can use the newer terminology throughout. And if you truly want to track the focus of an element in IE, consider using `onfocusin` and `onfocusout` instead.

Example

You can modify Listing 26-34 later in this chapter by substituting `onactivate` for `onfocus` and `ondeactivate` for `onblur`.

Use The Evaluator (see Chapter 4) to experiment with the `onbeforedeactivate` event handler. To begin, set the `myP` element so it can accept focus:

```
myP.tabIndex = 1
```

If you repeatedly press the Tab key, the `myP` paragraph will eventually receive focus — indicated by the dotted rectangle around it. To see how you can prevent the element from losing focus, assign an anonymous function to the `onbeforedeactivate` event handler, as shown in the following statement:

```
myP.onbeforedeactivate = new Function("event.returnValue=false")
```

Now you can press Tab all you like or click other focusable elements all you like, and the myP element will not lose focus until you reload the page (which clears away the event handler). Please do not do this on your pages unless you want to infuriate and alienate your site visitors.

Related Items: onblur, onfocus, onfocusin, onfocusout event handlers

onafterupdate
onbeforeupdate

Compatibility: WinIE4+, MacIE5+, NN-, Moz-, Safari-, Opera-, Chrome-

The onafterupdate and onbeforeupdate event handlers fire on a bound data object in IE whenever the data in the object is being updated. The onbeforeupdate event is fired just before the update occurs, whereas onafterupdate is fired after the data has been successfully updated.

onbeforecopy

Compatibility: WinIE5+, MacIE-, NN-, Moz-, Safari1.3+, Opera-, Chrome+

The onbeforecopy event handler fires before the actual copy action takes place whenever the user initiates a content copy action via the Edit menu (including the Ctrl+C, for Windows, and Command+C, for Mac, keyboard shortcuts) or the right-click context menu. In all browsers, if the user copies with a keyboard shortcut, the copy operation will be completed. If the user accesses the Copy command via the Edit or context menu different browsers behave differently. In WebKit-based browsers, the menu displays, the user selects copy and then the onbeforecopy event fires. The onbeforecopy event fires before either menu can display in IE. In practice, the event may fire twice even though you expect it only once. Just because the onbeforecopy event fires, it does not guarantee that a user will complete the copy operation (for example, the context menu may close before the user makes a selection).

Unlike paste-related events, the onbeforecopy event handler does not work with form input elements. Just about any other HTML element is fair game, however.

Example

In Listing 26-33, the function invoked by the "Latin" paragraph element's onbeforecopy event handler merely issues an alert. If your audience is limited in their browser use, you could use the onbeforecopy event handler to preprocess information prior to an actual copy action.

LISTING 26-33

The onbeforecopy Event Handler

HTML: jsb26-33.html

```
<!DOCTYPE html>
<html>
    <head>
        <meta http-equiv="content-type" content="text/html;charset=utf-8">
        <title>onbeforecopy event handler</title>
        <style type="text/css">
            .keyword
```

```
            {
                color: blue; font-weight:bold;
            }
        </style>
        <script type="text/javascript" src="../jsb-global.js"></script>
        <script type="text/javascript" src="jsb26-33.js"></script>
    </head>
    <body>
        <h1>onbeforecopy event handler</h1>
        <hr />
        <p>Select one or more characters in the Latin paragraph.
            then execute a copy command:
            <ul>
                <li>edit menu</li>
                <li>context menu</li>
                <li>ctrl-c (on Windows)</li>
                <li>command-c (on Mac)</li>
            </ul>
            Browsers that support <span class="keyword">onbeforecopy</span>,
            do not behave consistently. You may not be able to use all
            of the copy commands normally available to you. Test all the
            different ways to copy text and see what happens.
        </p>
        <p>
            Browsers that do not support <span class="keyword">onbeforecopy</span>
            will still allow you to copy -- you just won't see an alert.
        </p>
        <p id="myp" onbeforecopy="beforeCopy()">lorem ipsum dolor sit amet.
            consectetaur adipisicing elit, sed do eiusmod tempor incididunt ut
            labore et dolore magna aliqua. ut enim adminim veniam, quis nostrud
            exercitation ullamco laboris nisi ut aliquip ex commodo consequat.</p>
        <form>
            <p>paste results here:<br />
                <textarea name="output" cols="60" rows="5"></textarea>
            </p>
        </form>
    </body>
</html>
```

JavaScript: jsb26-33.js

```
function beforeCopy()
{
    alert("onbeforecopy is supported by your browser");
}
```

Related Items: onbeforecut, oncopy event handlers

onbeforecut

Compatibility: WinIE5+, MacIE-, NN-, Moz-, Safari 1.3+, Opera-, Chrome+

The onbeforecut event handler fires before the actual cut action takes place whenever the user initiates a content cut via the Edit menu (including the Ctrl+X keyboard shortcut) or the right-click context menu. If you add the onbeforecut event handler to an HTML element, the context menu usually disables the Cut menu item. But assigning a JavaScript call to this event handler brings the Cut menu item to life. If the user accesses the Cut command via the Edit or context menu, different browsers behave differently. In WebKit-based browsers, the menu displays, the user selects cut and then the onbeforecut event fires. In IE the onbeforecut event fires before either menu displays. In practice, the event may fire twice even though you expect it only once. Just because the onbeforecut event fires, it does not guarantee that a user will complete the cut operation (for example, the context menu may close before the user makes a selection).

Example

You can use the onbeforecut event handler to preprocess information prior to an actual cut action. You can try this by editing a copy of Listing 26-33, changing the onbeforecopy event handler to onbeforecut.

Related Items: onbeforecopy, oncut event handlers

onbeforedeactivate

Compatibility: WinIE5.5+, MacIE-, NN-, Moz-, Safari-

(See onactivate event handler)

onbeforeeditfocus

Compatibility: WinIE5+, MacIE-, NN-, Moz-, Safari-, Opera-, Chrome-

The onbeforeeditfocus event handler is triggered whenever you edit an element on a page in an environment such as Microsoft's DHTML Editing ActiveX control or with the editable page content feature of IE5.5+. This discussion focuses on the latter scenario because it is entirely within the scope of client-side JavaScript. The onbeforeeditfocus event fires just before the element receives its focus. (There may be no onscreen feedback that editing is turned on unless you script it yourself.) The event fires each time a user clicks the element, even if the element just received edit focus elsewhere in the same element.

Example

Use The Evaluator (see Chapter 4) to explore the onbeforeeditfocus in WinIE5.5+. In the following sequence, you assign an anonymous function to the onbeforeeditfocus event handler of the myP element. The function turns the text color of the element to red when the event handler fires:

```
document.getElementById("myP").onbeforeeditfocus = new
Function("document.getElementById('myP').style.color='red'")
```

Now turn on content editing for the myP element:

```
document.getElementById("myP").contentEditable = true
```

Now if you click inside the myP element on the page to edit its content, the text turns red before you begin editing. In a page scripted for this kind of user interface, you would include some control that turns off editing and changes the color to normal.

Related Items: `document.designMode`, `contentEditable`, `isContentEditable` properties

onbeforepaste

Compatibility: WinIE5+, MacIE-, NN-, Moz-, Safari 1.3+, Opera-, Chrome+

Like `onbeforecopy` and `onbeforecut`, the `onbeforepaste` event occurs differently in different browsers. In WebKit-based browsers, the menu displays, the user selects paste and then the `onbeforepaste` event fires. In IE, the `onbeforepaste` event fires just prior to the display of either the context or menu-bar Edit menu when the current object is selected (or has a selection within it). The primary value of this event comes when you use scripts to control the copy-and-paste process of a complex object. Such an object may have multiple kinds of data associated with it, but your script captures only one of the data types. Or you may want to put some related data about the copied item (for example, the `id` property of the element) into the clipboard. By using the `onbeforepaste` event handler to set the `event.returnValue` property to `false`, you guarantee that the pasted item is enabled in the context or Edit menu (provided that the clipboard is holding some content). A handler invoked by `onpaste` should then apply the specific data subset from the clipboard to the currently selected item.

Example

See Listing 26-44 for the `onpaste` event handler (later in this chapter) to see how the `onbeforepaste` and `onpaste` event handlers work together.

Related Items: `oncopy`, `oncut`, `onpaste` event handlers

onbeforeupdate

(See `onafterupdate`)

onblur

Compatibility: WinIE3+, MacIE3+, NN2+, Moz+, Safari+, Opera+, Chrome+

The `onblur` event fires when an element that has focus is about to lose focus because some other element is about to receive focus. For example, a text input element fires the `onblur` event when a user tabs from that element to the next one inside a form. The `onblur` event of the first element fires before the `onfocus` event of the next element.

The availability of the `onblur` event has expanded with succeeding generations of script-capable browsers. In the earlier versions, blur and focus were largely confined to text-oriented input elements (including the `select` element). These are safe to use with all scriptable browser versions. The `window` object received the `onblur` event handler starting with NN3 and IE4. IE4 also extended the event handler to more form elements, predominantly on the Windows operating system because that OS has a user interface clue (the dotted rectangle) when items such as buttons and links receive focus (so that you may act upon them by pressing the spacebar). For IE5+, the `onblur` event handler is available to virtually every HTML element. For most of those elements, however, blur and focus are not possible unless you assign a value to the `tabindex` attribute of the element's tag. For example, if you assign `tabindex="1"` inside a `<p>` tag, the user can bring focus to that paragraph (highlighted with the dotted rectangle in Windows in some of the browsers) by clicking the paragraph or pressing the Tab key until that item receives focus in sequence.

If you plan to use the `onblur` event handler on window or text-oriented input elements, be aware that there might be some unexpected and undesirable consequences of scripting for the event. For example, in IE, a `window` object that has focus loses focus (and triggers the `onblur` event) if the user brings focus to any element on the page (or even clicks a blank area on the page). Similarly, the interaction between `onblur`, `onfocus`, and the `alert()` dialog box can be problematic with text input elements. This is why we generally recommend using the `onchange` event handler to trigger form validation routines. If you should employ both the `onblur` and `onchange` event handler for the same element, the `onchange` event fires before `onblur`. For more details about using this event handler for data validation, see Chapter 46 on the CD-ROM.

WinIE5.5+ added the `ondeactivate` event handler, which fires immediately before the `onblur` event handler. Both the `onblur` and `ondeactivate` events can be blocked if the `onbeforedeactivate` event handler function sets `event.returnValue` to `false`.

Example

More often than not, a page author uses the `onblur` event handler to exert extreme control over the user, such as preventing a user from exiting a text box unless that user types something in the box. This is not a web-friendly practice, and it is one that we discourage because there are intelligent ways to ensure that a field has something typed into it before a form is submitted (see Chapter 46 on the CD-ROM). Listing 26-34 simply demonstrates the impact of the `tabindex` attribute with respect to the `onblur` and `onfocus` events. Notice that as you press the Tab key, only the second paragraph issues the events, even though all three paragraphs have event handlers assigned to them.

LISTING 26-34

onblur and onfocus Event Handlers

HTML: `jsb26-34.html`

```html
<!DOCTYPE html>
<html>
   <head>
      <meta http-equiv="content-type" content="text/html;charset=utf-8">
      <title>onblur and onfocus Event Handlers</title>
      <script type="text/javascript" src="../jsb-global.js"></script>
      <script type="text/javascript" src="jsb26-34.js"></script>
   </head>
   <body>
      <h1 id="H1" tabindex="2">onblur and onfocus Event Handlers</h1>
      <h2>Start tabbing and see what happens</h2>
      <hr />
      <p id="P1" onblur="showBlur()" onfocus="showFocus()">Lorem ipsum dolor
         sit amet, consectetaur adipisicing elit, sed do eiusmod tempor
         incididunt ut labore et dolore magna aliqua. Ut enim adminim veniam,
         quis nostrud exercitation ullamco laboris nisi ut aliquip ex ea
         commodo consequat.
      </p>
      <p id="P2" tabindex="1" onblur="showBlur()" onfocus="showFocus()">Bis
         nostrud exercitation ullam mmodo consequet. Duis aute involuptate
         velit esse cillum dolore eu fugiat nulla pariatur. At vver eos et
         accusam dignissum qui blandit est praesent luptatum delenit
         aigueexcepteur sint occae.
      </p>
      <p id="P3" onblur="showBlur()" onfocus="showFocus()">Unte af phen
```

```
                neigepheings atoot Prexs eis phat eit sakem eit vory gast te Plok
                peish ba useing phen roxas. Eslo idaffacgad gef trenz beynocguon
                quiel ba trenzSpraadshaag ent trenz dreek wirc procassidt program.
        </p>
    </body>
</html>
```

JavaScript: jsb26-34.js
```
function showBlur()
{
    var id = event.srcElement.id;
    alert("Element \"" + id + "\" has blurred.");
}

function showFocus()
{
    var id = event.srcElement.id;
    alert("Element \"" + id + "\" has received focus.");
}
```

Related Items: blur(), focus() methods; ondeactivate, onbeforedeactivate, onfocus, onactivate event handlers

oncellchange

Compatibility: WinIE5+, MacIE-, NN-, Moz-, Safari-, Opera-, Chrome-

The oncellchange event handler is part of the data binding of IE and fires when data changes in the data provider, which is usually a bound control. When responding to this event, you can analyze the dataFld property to find out which field in the recordset has changed.

onclick

Compatibility: WinIE3+, MacIE3+, NN2+, Moz+, Safari+, Opera+, Chrome+

The onclick event fires when a user presses down (with the primary mouse button) and releases the button with the pointer atop the element (both the down and up strokes must be within the rectangle of the same element). The event also fires with non-mouse-click equivalents in operating systems such as Windows. For example, you can use the keyboard to give focus to a clickable object and then press the spacebar or Enter key to perform the same action as clicking the element. In IE, if the element object supports the click() method, the onclick event fires with the invocation of that method (notice that this does not apply to Navigator or other browsers).

The onclick event is closely related to other mouse events. The other related events are onmouse-down, onmouseup, and ondblclick. The onmousedown event fires when the user makes contact with the mouse switch on the downstroke of a click action. Next comes the onmouseup event (when the contact breaks). Only then does the onclick event fire — provided that the onmousedown and onmouseup events have fired in the same object. See the discussions on the onmousedown and onmouseup events later in this chapter for examples of their usage.

elementObject.**onclick**

Interaction with the ondblclick event is simple: The onclick event fires (after the first click), followed by the ondblclick event (after the second click). See the discussion of the ondblclick event handler later in this chapter for more about the interaction of these two event handlers.

When used with objects that have intrinsic actions when users click them (namely, links and areas), the onclick event handler can perform all of the actions — including navigating to the destination normally assigned to the href attribute of the element. For example, to be compatible with all scriptable browsers, you can make an image clickable if you surround its tag with an <a> link tag. This lets the onclick event of that tag substitute for the missing onclick event handler of earlier <img> tags. If you assign an onclick event handler without special protection, the event handler will execute, and the intrinsic action of the element will be carried out. Therefore, you need to block the intrinsic action. To accomplish this, the event handler must evaluate to the statement return false. You can do this in two ways. The first is to append a return false statement to the script statement assigned to the event handler:

```
<a href="#" onclick="yourFunction(); return false"><img...></a>
```

As an alternative, you can let the function invoked by the event handler supply the false part of the return false statement, as shown in the following sequence:

```
function yourFunction()
{
    // [statements that do something here]
    return false;
}
...
<a href="#" onclick="return yourFunction()"><img...></a>
```

Either methodology is acceptable. A third option is to not use the onclick event handler at all but assign a javascript: pseudo-URL to the href attribute (see the Link object in Chapter 30).

The event model in IE4+ provides one more way to prevent the intrinsic action of an object from firing when a user clicks it. If the onclick event handler function sets the returnValue property of the event object to false, the intrinsic action is canceled. Simply include the following statement in the function invoked by the event handler:

```
event.returnValue = false;
```

The event model of the W3C DOM has a different approach to canceling the default action. In the event handler function for an event, invoke the eventObj.cancelDefault() method.

A common mistake made by scripting beginners is to use a submit type input button as a button intended to perform some script action rather than submitting a form. The typical scenario is an input element of type submit assigned an onclick event handler to perform some local action. The submit input button has an intrinsic behavior, just like links and areas. Although you can block the intrinsic behavior, as just described, you should use an input element of type button.

If you are experiencing difficulty with an implementation of the onclick event handler (such as trying to find out which mouse button was used for the click), it may be that the operating system or default browser behavior is getting in the way of your scripting. But you can usually get what you need via the onmousedown event handler. (The onmouseup event may not fire when you use the secondary mouse button to click an object.) Use the onclick event handler whenever possible to capture user clicks, because this event behaves most like users are accustomed to in their daily computing work. But fall back on onmousedown in an emergency.

Example

The `onclick` event handler is one of the simplest to grasp and use. Listing 26-35 demonstrates its interaction with the `ondblclick` event handler and shows you how to prevent a link's intrinsic action from activating when combined with `click` events. As you click and/or double-click the link, the text in the `span` element displays a message associated with each event. Notice that if you double-click, the `click` event fires first, with the first message immediately replaced by the second. For demonstration purposes, we show both backward-compatible ways of canceling the link's intrinsic action. In practice, decide on one style and stick with it.

LISTING 26-35

Using onclick and ondblclick Event Handlers

HTML: jsb26-35.html

```
<!DOCTYPE html>
<html>
   <head>
      <meta http-equiv="content-type" content="text/html;charset=utf-8">
      <title>onclick and ondblclick Event Handlers</title>
      <script type="text/javascript" src="../jsb-global.js"></script>
      <script type="text/javascript" src="jsb26-35.js"></script>
   </head>
   <body>
      <h1>onclick and ondblclick Event Handlers</h1>
      <hr />
      <a href="#" onclick="showClick();return false"
         ondblclick="return showDblClick()">A sample link.</a>
      (Click type: <span id="clickType"></span>)
   </body>
</html>
```

JavaScript: jsb26-35.js

```
var timeout;
function clearOutput()
{
   document.getElementById("clickType").innerHTML = "";
}
function showClick()
{
   document.getElementById("clickType").innerHTML = "single";
   clearTimeout(timeout);
   timeout = setTimeout("clearOutput()", 3000);
}
function showDblClick()
{
   document.getElementById("clickType").innerHTML = "double";
   clearTimeout(timeout);
   timeout = setTimeout("clearOutput()", 3000);
   return false;
}
```

Related Items: `click()` method; `oncontextmenu`, `ondblclick`, `onmousedown`, `onmouseup` event handlers

oncontextmenu

Compatibility: WinIE5+, MacIE-, NN7+, Moz+, Safari+, Opera-, Chrome+

The `oncontextmenu` event fires when the user clicks an object with the secondary (usually the right) mouse button. The only click-related events that fire with the secondary button are `onmousedown` and `oncontextmenu`.

To block the intrinsic application menu display of the `oncontextmenu` event, use any of the event cancellation methodologies available in for your browser (as just described in the `onclick` event handler description: two variations of evaluating the event handler to `return false`; assigning `false` to the `event.returnValue` property). It is not uncommon to wish to block the context menu from appearing so that users are somewhat inhibited from downloading copies of images or viewing the source code of a frame. Be aware, however, that if a user turns Active Scripting off in WinIE5+, the event handler cannot prevent the context menu from appearing.

Another possibility for this event is to trigger the display of a custom context menu constructed with other DHTML facilities. In this case, you must also disable the intrinsic context menu so that both menus do not display at the same time.

Example

See Listing 26-30 earlier in this chapter for an example of using the `oncontextmenu` event handler with a custom context menu.

Related Items: `releaseCapture()`, `setCapture()` methods

oncontrolselect

Compatibility: WinIE5.5+, MacIE-, NN-, Moz-, Safari-, Opera-, Chrome-

The `oncontrolselect` event fires just before a user makes a selection on an editable element while the page is in edit mode. It's important to note that it is the element itself that is selected to trigger this event, not the content within the element.

Related Items: `onresizeend`, `onresizestart` event handlers

oncopy
oncut

Compatibility: WinIE5+, MacIE4+, NN-, Moz+, Safari1.3+, Opera-, Chrome+

The `oncopy` and `oncut` events fire immediately after the user or script initiates a copy or cut edit action on the current object. Each event is preceded by its associated before event, which fires before any Edit or context menu appears (or before the copy or cut action, if initiated by keyboard shortcut).

Use these event handlers to provide edit functionality to elements that don't normally allow copying or cutting. In such circumstances, you need to enable the Copy or Cut menu items in the context or Edit menu by setting the `event.returnValue` for the `onbeforecopy` or `onbeforecut` event handlers to `false`. Then your `oncopy` or `oncut` event handlers must manually stuff a value into the clipboard by way of the `setdata()` method of the IE `clipboardData` object. If you use the `setdata()` method in your `oncopy` or `oncut` event handler, you must also set the `event.returnValue` property to `false` in the handler function to prevent the default copy or cut action from wiping out your clipboard contents.

Because you are in charge of what data is stored in the clipboard, you are not limited to a direct copy of the data. For example, you might wish to store the value of the `src` property of an image object so that the user can paste it elsewhere on the page.

In the case of the `oncut` event handler, your script is also responsible for cutting the element or selected content from the page. To eliminate all of the content of an element, you can set the element's `innerHTML` or `innerText` property to an empty string. For a selection, use the `selection.createRange()` method to generate a `TextRange` object whose contents you can manipulate through the `TextRange` object's methods.

Example

Listing 26-36 shows both the `onbeforecut` and `oncut` event handlers in action (as well as `onbeforepaste` and `onpaste`). Notice that the `handleCut()` function not only stuffs the selected word into the IE `clipboardData` object, but also erases the selected text from the table cell element from where it came. If you replace the `onbeforecut` and `oncut` event handlers with `onbeforecopy` and `oncopy` (and change `handleCut()` to not eliminate the inner text of the event source element), the operation works with copy and paste instead of cut and paste. We demonstrate this later in the chapter in Listing 26-44.

LISTING 26-36

Cutting and Pasting under Script Control

HTML: `jsb26-36.html`

```
<html>
   <head>
      <meta http-equiv="content-type" content="text/html;charset=utf-8">
      <title>onbeforecut and oncut Event Handlers Using a range object</title>
      <style type="text/css">
         td
         {   text-align:center;
         }
         th
         {   text-decoration:underline;
         }
         .blanks
         {   text-decoration:underline;
         }
      </style>
      <script type="text/javascript" src="../jsb-global.js"></script>
      <script type="text/javascript" src="jsb26-36.js"></script>
   </head>
   <body>
      <h1>onbeforecut and oncut Event Handlers</h1>
      <hr />
      <p>Your goal is to cut and paste one noun and one adjective from the
         following table into the blanks of the sentence. Select a word from
```

continued

LISTING 26-36   *(continued)*

```
        the table and use the Edit or context menu to cut it from the table.
        Select one or more spaces of the blanks in the sentence and choose
        Paste to replace the blank with the clipboard contents.
    </p>
    <table cellpadding="5" onbeforecut="selectWhole()" oncut="handleCut()">
        <tr>
            <th>Nouns</th>
            <th>Adjectives</th>
        </tr>
        <tr>
            <td>truck</td>
            <td>round</td>
        </tr>
        <tr>
            <td>doll</td>
            <td>red</td>
        </tr>
        <tr>
            <td>ball</td>
            <td>pretty</td>
        </tr>
    </table>
    <p id="myP" onbeforepaste="handleBeforePaste()" onpaste="handlePaste()">
        Pat said, "Oh my, the <span id="blank1"
        class="blanks">     </span> is so <span
        id="blank2" class="blanks">     </span> !"
    </p>
    <button onclick="location.reload()">Reset</button>
    </body>
</html>
```

JavaScript: jsb26-36.js

```
function selectWhole()
{
    var obj = window.event.srcElement;
    var range = document.body.createTextRange();
    range.moveToElementText(obj);
    range.select();
    event.returnValue = false;
}

function handleCut()
{
    var rng = document.selection.createRange();
    clipboardData.setData("Text",rng.text);
    var elem = event.srcElement;
    elem.innerText = "";
    event.returnValue = false;
}
```

```
function handlePaste()
{
    var elem = window.event.srcElement;
        if (elem.className == "blanks")
        {
            elem.innerHTML = clipboardData.getData("Text");
        }
    event.returnValue = false;
}

function handleBeforePaste()
{
    var elem = window.event.srcElement;
        if (elem.className == "blanks")
        {
            event.returnValue = false;
        }
}
```

Related Items: onbeforecopy, onbeforecut, onbeforepaste, and onpaste event handlers

ondataavailable
ondatasetchanged
ondatasetcomplete

Compatibility: WinIE4+, MacIE-, NN-, Moz-, Safari-, Opera-, Chrome-

These three events are part of the data binding of IE and are fired to help reflect the state of data that is being transmitted. The ondataavailable event fires when data is transmitted from the data source, whereas the ondatasetcomplete event indicates that the recordset has completely downloaded from the data source. The ondatasetchanged event is fired when the recordset of a data source has somehow changed.

ondblclick

Compatibility: WinIE4+, MacIE4+, NN4+, Moz+, Safari+, Opera+, Chrome+

The ondblclick event fires after the second click of a double-click sequence. The timing between clicks depends on the client's mouse control panel settings. The onclick event also fires, but only after the first of the two clicks.

In general, it is rarely a good design to have an element perform one task when the mouse is single-clicked and a different task if double-clicked. With the event sequence employed in modern browsers, this isn't practical anyway (the onclick event always fires, even when the user double-clicks). But it is not uncommon to have the mouse down action perform some helper action. You see this in most icon-based file systems: If you click a file icon, it is highlighted at mouse down to select the item; you can double-click the item to launch it. In either case, one event's action does not impede the other nor confuse the user.

Example

See Listing 26-35 (for the onclick event handler) to see the ondblclick event in action.

elementObject.**ondrag**

Related Items: `onclick`, `onmousedown`, `onmouseup` event handlers

ondrag, ondragend, ondragstart

Compatibility: WinIE5+, MacIE-, NN-, Moz+, Safari 1.3+, Opera-, Chrome+

The `ondrag` event fires after the `ondragstart` event and continues firing repeatedly while the user drags a selection or object onscreen. Unlike the `onmousemove` event, which fires only as the cursor moves onscreen, the `ondrag` event continues to fire even when the cursor is stationary. In most browsers, users can drag objects to other browser windows or other applications. The event fires while the dragging extends beyond the browser window.

Because the event fires regardless of what is underneath the dragged object, you can use it in a game or training environment in which the user has only a fixed amount of time to complete a dragging operation (for example, matching similar pairs of objects). If the browser accommodates downloadable cursors, the `ondrag` event could cycle the cursor through a series of cursor versions to resemble an animated cursor.

Understanding the sequence of drag-related events during a user drag operation can be helpful if your scripts need to micromanage the actions (usually not necessary for basic drag-and-drop operations). Consider the drag-and-drop operation shown in Figure 26-2.

FIGURE 26-2

A typical drag-and-drop operation

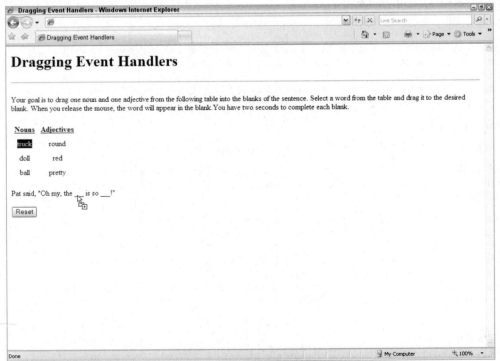

It helps to imagine that the cells of the table with draggable content are named like spreadsheet cells: truck is cell A1; round is B1; doll is A2; and so on. During the drag operation, many objects are the targets of a variety of drag-related events. Table 26-11 lists the event sequence and the event targets.

In practice, some of the events shown in Table 26-11 may not fire. Much has to do with how many event handlers you trap that need to execute scripts along the way. The other major factor is the physical speed at which the user performs the drag-and-drop operation (which interacts with the CPU processing speed). The kinds of events that are most likely to be skipped are the ondragenter and ondragleave events, and perhaps some ondragover events if the user flies over an object before its ondragover event has a chance to fire.

Despite this uncertainty about drag-related event reliability, you can count on several important ones to fire all the time. The ondragstart, ondrop (if over a drop target), and ondragend events — as well some interstitial ondrag events — will definitely fire in the course of dragging onscreen. All but ondrop direct their events to the source element, whereas ondrop fires on the target.

Example

Listing 26-37 shows several drag-related event handlers in action. The page resembles the example in Listing 26-36, but the scripting behind the page is quite different. In this example, the user is encouraged to select individual words from the Nouns and Adjectives columns and drag them to the blanks of the sentence. To beef up the demonstration, Listing 26-37 shows you how to pass the equivalent of array data from a drag source to a drag target. At the same time, the user has a fixed amount of time (2 seconds) to complete each drag operation.

The ondragstart and ondrag event handlers are placed in the <body> tag because those events bubble up from any element that the user tries to drag. The scripts invoked by these event handlers filter the events so that the desired action is triggered only by the hot elements inside the table. This approach to event handlers prevents you from having to duplicate event handlers for each table cell.

The ondragstart event handler invokes setupDrag(). This function cancels the ondragstart event except when the target element (the one about to be dragged) is one of the td elements inside the table. To make this application smarter about what kind of word is dragged to which blank, it passes not only the word's text, but also some extra information about the word. This lets another event handler verify that a noun has been dragged to the first blank, whereas an adjective has been dragged to the second blank. To help with this effort, class names are assigned to the td elements to distinguish the words from the Nouns column from the words of the Adjectives column. The setup-Drag() function generates an array consisting of the innerText of the event's source element plus the element's class name. But the event.dataTransfer object cannot store array data types, so the Array.join() method converts the array to a string with a colon separating the entries. This string, then, is stuffed into the event.dataTransfer object. The object is instructed to render the cursor display during the drag-and-drop operation so that when the cursor is atop a drop target, the cursor is the copy style. Finally, the setupDrag() function is the first to execute in the drag operation, so a timer is set to the current clock time to time the drag operation.

The ondrag event handler (in the body) captures the ondrag events that are generated by whichever table cell element is the source element for the action. Each time the event fires (which is a lot during the action), the timeIt() function is invoked to compare the current time against the reference time (global timer) set when the drag starts. If the time exceeds 2 seconds (2,000 milliseconds), an alert dialog box notifies the user. To close the alert dialog box, the user must unclick the mouse button to end the drag operation.

elementObject.ondrag

TABLE 26-11

Events and Their Targets during a Typical Drag-and-Drop Operation

Event	Target	Discussion
ondragstart	cell A1	The very first event that fires during a drag-and-drop operation.
ondrag	cell A1	Fires continually on this target throughout the entire operation. Other events get interspersed, however.
ondragenter	cell A1	Even though the cursor hasn't moved from cell A1 yet, the ondragenter event fires upon first movement within the source element.
ondragover	cell A1	Fires continually on whatever element the cursor rests on at that instant. If the user simply holds the mouse button down and does not move the cursor during a drag, the ondrag and ondragover events fire continually, alternating between the two.
(repetition)	cell A1	ondrag and ondragover events fire alternately while the cursor remains atop cell A1.
ondragenter	table	The table element, represented by the border and/or cell padding, receives the ondragenter event when the cursor touches its space.
ondragleave	cell A1	Notice that the ondragleave event fires after the ondragenter event fires on another element.
ondrag	cell A1	Still firing away.
ondragover	table	The source element for this event shifts to the table because that's what the cursor is over at this instant. If the cursor doesn't move from this spot, the ondrag (cell A1) and ondragover (table) events continue to fire in turn.
ondragenter	cell B1	The drag is progressing from the table border space to cell B1.
ondragleave	table	The table element receives the ondragleave event when the cursor exits its space.
ondrag	cell A1	The ondrag event continues to fire on the cell A1 object.
ondragover	cell B1	The cursor is atop cell B1 now, so the ondragover event fires for that object. Fires multiple times (depending on the speed of the computer and the user's drag action), alternating with the previous ondrag event.
		More of the same as the cursor progresses from cell B1 through the table border again to cell B2, the table again, cell B3, and the outermost edge of the table.
ondragenter	body	Dragging is free of the table and is floating free on the bare body element.
ondragleave	table	Yes, you just left the table.
ondrag	cell A1	Still alive and receiving this event.

Event	Target	Discussion
ondragover	body	That's where the cursor is now. Fires multiple times (depending on the speed of the computer and the user's drag action), alternating with the previous ondrag event.
ondragenter	blank1	The cursor reaches the span element whose ID is blank1, where the empty underline is.
ondragleave	body	Just left the body for the blank.
ondrag	cell A1	Still kicking.
ondragover	blank1	That's where the cursor is now. Fires multiple times (depending on the speed of the computer and the user's drag action), alternating with the previous ondrag event.
ondrop	blank1	The span element gets the notification of a recent drop.
ondragend	cell A1	The original source element gets the final word that dragging is complete. This event fires even if the drag does not succeed because the drag does not end on a drop target.

To turn the blank span elements into drop targets, their ondragenter, ondragover, and ondrop event handlers must set event.returnValue to false; also, the event.dataTransfer.dropEffect property should be set to the desired effect (copy, in this case). These event handlers are placed in the p element that contains the two span elements, again for simplicity. Notice, however, that the cancelDefault() functions do their work only if the target element is one of the span elements whose ID begins with blank.

As the user releases the mouse button, the ondrop event handler invokes the handleDrop() function. This function retrieves the string data from event.dataTransfer and restores it to an array data type (using the String.split() method). A little bit of testing makes sure that the word type (noun or adjective) is associated with the desired blank. If so, the source element's text is set to the drop target's innerText property; otherwise, an error message is assembled to help the user know what went wrong.

LISTING 26-37

Using Drag-Related Event Handlers

HTML: jsb26-37.html

```
<!DOCTYPE html>
<html>
    <head>
        <meta http-equiv="content-type" content="text/html;charset=utf-8">
        <title>Dragging Event Handlers</title>
        <style type="text/css">
            td
            {
                text-align:center;
```

continued

LISTING 26-37 *(continued)*

```
        }
        th
        {
            text-decoration:underline;
        }
        .blanks
        {
            text-decoration:underline;
        }
    </style>
    <script type="text/javascript" src="../jsb-global.js"></script>
    <script type="text/javascript" src="jsb26-37.js"></script>
</head>
<body ondragstart="setupDrag()" ondrag="timeIt()">
    <h1>Dragging Event Handlers</h1>
    <hr />
    <p>Your goal is to drag one noun and one adjective from the following
        table into the blanks of the sentence. Select a word from the table
        and drag it to the desired blank. When you release the mouse, the word
        will appear in the blank. You have two seconds to complete each blank.
    </p>
    <table cellpadding="5">
        <tr>
            <th>Nouns</th>
            <th>Adjectives</th>
        </tr>
        <tr>
            <td class="noun">truck</td>
            <td class="adjective">round</td>
        </tr>
        <tr>
            <td class="noun">doll</td>
            <td class="adjective">red</td>
        </tr>
        <tr>
            <td class="noun">ball</td>
            <td class="adjective">pretty</td>
        </tr>
    </table>
    <p id="myP" ondragenter="cancelDefault()" ondragover="cancelDefault()"
        ondrop="handleDrop()">Pat said, "Oh my, the <span id="blank1"
        class="blanks">     </span> is so <span
        id="blank2" class="blanks">     </span> !"
    </p>
    <button onclick="location.reload()">Reset</button>
</body>
</html>
```

JavaScript: jsb26-37.js

```
var timer;
```

```
function setupDrag()
{
   if (event.srcElement.tagName != "TD")
   {
      // don't allow dragging for any other elements
      event.returnValue = false;
   }
   else
   {
      // setup array of data to be passed to drop target
      var passedData = [event.srcElement.innerText, event.srcElement.className];
      // store it as a string
      event.dataTransfer.setData("Text", passedData.join(":"));
      event.dataTransfer.effectAllowed = "copy";
      timer = new Date();
   }
}

function timeIt()
{
   if (event.srcElement.tagName == "TD" && timer)
   {
      if ((new Date()) - timer > 2000)
      {
         alert("Sorry, time is up. Try again.");
         timer = 0;
      }
   }
}

function handleDrop()
{
   var elem = event.srcElement;
   var passedData = event.dataTransfer.getData("Text");
   var errMsg = "";
      if (passedData)
      {
         // reconvert passed string to an array
         passedData = passedData.split(":");
         if (elem.id == "blank1")
         {
            if (passedData[1] == "noun")
            {
               event.dataTransfer.dropEffect = "copy";
               event.srcElement.innerText = passedData[0];
            }
            else
            {
               errMsg = "You can't put an adjective into the noun placeholder.";
            }
         }
         else if (elem.id == "blank2")
```

continued

LISTING 26-37   *(continued)*

```
        {
            if (passedData[1] == "adjective")
            {
                event.dataTransfer.dropEffect = "copy";
                event.srcElement.innerText = passedData[0];
            }
            else
            {
                errMsg = "You can't put a noun into the adjective placeholder.";
            }
        }
        if (errMsg)
        {
            alert(errMsg);
        }
    }
}

function cancelDefault()
{
    if (event.srcElement.id.indexOf("blank") == 0)
    {
        event.dataTransfer.dropEffect = "copy";
        event.returnValue = false;
    }
}
```

One event handler not shown in Listing 26-37 is `ondragend`. You can use this event to display the elapsed time for each successful drag operation. Because the event fires on the drag source element, you can implement it in the `<body>` tag and filter events similar to the way the `ondragstart` or `ondrag` event handlers filter events for the `td` element.

Related Items: `event.dataTransfer` object; `ondragenter`, `ondragleave`, `ondragover`, `ondrop` event handlers

ondragenter
ondragleave
ondragover

Compatibility: WinIE5+, MacIE-, NN-, Moz+, Safari 1.3+, Opera-, Chrome+

These events fire during a drag operation. When the cursor enters the rectangular space of an element on the page, the `ondragenter` event fires on that element. Immediately thereafter, the `ondragleave` event fires on the element from which the cursor came. Although this may seem to occur out of sequence from the physical action, the events always fire in this order. Depending on the speed of the client computer's CPU and the speed of the user's dragging action, one or the other of these events may not fire — especially if the physical action outstrips the computer's capability to fire the events in time.

The `ondragover` event fires continually while a dragged cursor is atop an element. In the course of dragging from one point on the page to another, the `ondragover` event target changes with the element beneath the cursor. If no other drag-related events are firing (the mouse button is still down in the drag operation, but the cursor is not moving), the `ondrag` and `ondragover` events fire continually, alternating between the two.

You should have the `ondragover` event handler of a drop target element set the `event` `.returnValue` property to `false`. See the discussion of the `ondrag` event handler earlier in this chapter for more details on the sequence of drag-related events.

Example

Listing 26-38 shows the `ondragenter` and `ondragleave` event handlers in use. The simple page displays (via the status bar) the time of entry to one element of the page. When the dragged cursor leaves the element, the `ondragleave` event handler hides the status-bar message. No drop target is defined for this page, so when you drag the item, the cursor remains the no-drop cursor.

LISTING 26-38

Using ondragenter and ondragleave Event Handlers

HTML: `jsb26-38.html`

```
<!DOCTYPE html>
<html>
    <head>
        <meta http-equiv="content-type" content="text/html;charset=utf-8">
        <title>ondragenter and ondragleave Event Handlers</title>
        <script type="text/javascript" src="../jsb-global.js"></script>
        <script type="text/javascript" src="jsb26-38.js"></script>
    </head>
    <body>
        <h1 ondragenter="showEnter()" ondragleave="clearMsg()">
            ondragenter and ondragleave Event Handlers
        </h1>
        <hr />
        <p>Select any character(s) from this paragraph, and slowly drag it around
            the page. When the dragging action enters the large header above, the
            status bar displays when the onDragEnter event handler fires. When you
            leave the header, the message is cleared via the onDragLeave event
            handler.
        </p>
    </body>
</html>
```

JavaScript: `jsb26-38.js`

```
function showEnter()
{
    status = "Entered at: " + new Date();
    event.returnValue = false;
}
```

continued

LISTING 26-38   *(continued)*

```
function clearMsg()
{
    status = "";
    event.returnValue = false;
}
```

Related Items: ondrag, ondragend, ondragstart, ondrop event handlers

ondragstart

(See ondrag)

ondrop

Compatibility: WinIE5+, MacIE-, NN-, Moz+, Safari 1.3+, Opera-, Chrome+

The ondrop event fires on the drop target element as soon as the user releases the mouse button at the end of a drag-and-drop operation. For IE, Microsoft recommends that you denote a drop target by applying the ondragenter, ondragover, and ondrop event handlers to the target element. In each of those event handlers, you should set the dataTransfer.dropEffect to the transfer effect you wish to portray in the drag-and-drop operation (signified by a different cursor for each type). These settings should match the dataTransfer.effectAllowed property that is usually set in the ondragstart event handler. Each of the three drop-related handlers should also override the default event behavior by setting the event.returnValue property to false. See the discussion of the ondrag event handler earlier in this chapter for more details on the sequence of drag-related events.

Example

See Listing 26-37 of the ondrag event handler to see how to apply the ondrop event handler in a typical drag-and-drop scenario.

Related Items: event.dataTransfer object; ondrag, ondragend, ondragenter, ondragleave, ondragover, ondragstart event handlers

onerrorupdate

Compatibility: WinIE4+, MacIE5+, NN-, Moz-, Safari-, Opera-, Chrome-

The onerrorupdate event handler is part of the data binding of IE and fires when an error occurs while updating the data in the data source object.

onfilterchange

Compatibility: WinIE4+, MacIE-, NN-, Moz-, Safari-, Opera-, Chrome-

The onfilterchange event fires whenever an object's visual filter switches to a new state or a transition completes (a transition may be extended over time). Only objects that accommodate filters and transitions in IE (primarily block elements and form controls) receive the event.

A common usage of the `onfilterchange` event is to trigger the next transition within a sequence of transition activities. This may include an infinite loop transition, for which the object receiving the event toggles between two transition states. If you don't want to get into a loop of that kind, place the different sets of content in their own positionable elements, and use the `onfilterchange` event handler in one to trigger the transition in the other.

Example

Listing 26-39 demonstrates how the `onfilterchange` event handler can trigger a second transition effect after another one completes. The `onload` event handler triggers the first effect. Although the `onfilterchange` event handler works with most of the same objects in IE4 as IE5, the filter object transition properties are not reflected in a convenient form. The syntax shown in Listing 26-39 uses the more modern ActiveX filter control found in IE5.5+ (described in Chapter 38).

LISTING 26-39

Using the onFilterChange Event Handler

HTML: jsb26-39.html

```
<!DOCTYPE html>
<html>
    <head>
        <meta http-equiv="content-type" content="text/html;charset=utf-8">
        <title>onfilterchange  Event Handler</title>
        <style type="text/css">
            #image1
            {
                position:absolute; top:150px; left:150px;
                filter:progID:DXImageTransform.Microsoft.Iris(irisstyle='CIRCLE',
                    motion='in')
            }
            #image2
            {
                position:absolute; top:150px; left:150px;
                filter:progID:DXImageTransform.Microsoft.Iris(irisstyle='CIRCLE',
                    motion='out')
            }
            .anImage
            {
                height:90px; width:120px;
            }
        </style>
        <script type="text/javascript" src="../jsb-global.js"></script>
        <script type="text/javascript" src="jsb26-39.js"></script>
    </head>
    <body onload="init()">
        <h1>onfilterchange  Event Handler</h1>
        <hr />
        <p>The completion of the first transition ("circle-in") triggers the
            second ("circle-out").
            <button onclick="location.reload()">Play It Again</button>
```

continued

LISTING 26-39 *(continued)*

```
      </p>
      <div id="image1" style="visibility:visible;"
           onfilterchange="finish()">
        <img class="anImage" alt="image" src="desk1.gif" />
      </div>
      <div id="image2" style="visibility:hidden;" >
        <img class="anImage" alt="image" src="desk3.gif" />
      </div>
   </body>
</html>
```

JavaScript: jsb26-39.js

```
function init()
{
   image1.filters[0].apply();
   image2.filters[0].apply();
   start();
}

function start()
{
   image1.style.visibility = "hidden";
   image1.filters[0].play();
}

function finish()
{
   // verify that first transition is done (optional)
   if (image1.filters[0].status == 0)
   {
       image2.style.visibility = "visible";
       image2.filters[0].play();
   }
}
```

Related Item: filter object

onfocus

Compatibility: WinIE3+, MacIE3+, NN2+, Moz+, Safari+, Opera+, Chrome+

The onfocus event fires when an element receives focus, usually following some other object's losing focus. (The element losing focus receives the onblur event before the current object receives the onfocus event.) For example, a text input element fires the onfocus event when a user tabs to that element while navigating through a form via the keyboard. Clicking an element also gives that element focus, as does making the browser the frontmost application on the client desktop.

The availability of the `onfocus` event has expanded with succeeding generations of script-capable browsers. In earlier versions, blur and focus were largely confined to text-oriented input elements such as the `select` element. The `window` object received the `onfocus` event handler starting with NN3 and IE4. IE4 also extended the event handler to more form elements, predominantly on the Windows operating system because that OS has a user interface clue (the dotted rectangle) when items such as buttons and links receive focus (so that users may act on them by pressing the spacebar). For IE5+, the `onfocus` event handler is available to virtually every HTML element. For most of those elements, however, you cannot use blur and focus unless you assign a value to the `tabindex` attribute of the element's tag. For example, if you assign `tabindex="1"` inside a `<p>` tag, the user can bring focus to that paragraph (highlighted with the dotted rectangle in Windows) by clicking the paragraph or pressing the Tab key until that item receives focus in sequence.

WinIE5.5 adds the `onfocusin` event handler, which fires immediately before the `onfocus` event handler. You can use one or the other, but there is little need to include both event handlers for the same object unless you wish to block an item temporarily from receiving focus. To prevent an object from receiving focus in IE5.5+, include an `event.returnValue=false` statement in the `onfocusin` event handler for the same object. In other browsers, you can usually get away with assigning `onfocus="this.blur()"` as an event handler for elements such as form controls. However, this is not a foolproof way to prevent a user from changing a control's setting. Unfortunately, there are few reliable alternatives short of disabling the control.

Example

See Listing 26-34 earlier in this chapter for an example of the `onfocus` and `onblur` event handlers.

Related Items: `onactivate`, `onblur`, `ondeactivate`, `onfocusin`, `onfocusout` event handlers

onfocusin
onfocusout

Compatibility: WinIE6+, MacIE-, NN-, Moz-, Safari-, Opera-, Chrome-

The `onfocusin` and `onfocusout` events fire to indicate that an element is about to receive focus or has just lost focus. These events are closely related to `onactivate` and `ondeactivate` except that in IE5.5+ activation and focus can be distinguished from each other. For example, if you set an element as the active element through `setActive()`, the element becomes active, but it does not gain the input focus. However, if you set the focus of an element with a call to `focus()`, the element is activated and gains input focus.

Related Items: `onactivate`, `onblur`, `ondeactivate`, `onfocus` event handlers

onhelp

Compatibility: WinIE4+, MacIE5+, NN-, Moz-, Safari-, Opera-, Chrome-

The `onhelp` event handler fires in Windows whenever an element of the document has focus and the user presses the F1 function key on a Windows PC. As of MacIE5, the event fires only on the window (in other words, event handler specified in the `<body>` tag) and does so via the dedicated Help key on a Mac keyboard. Browser Help menu choices do not activate this event. To prevent the browser's Help window from appearing, the event handler must evaluate to `return false` (for IE4+) or set the `event.returnValue` property to `false` (IE5+). Because the event handler can be associated with individual elements of a document in the Windows version, you can create a context-sensitive help system. However, if the focus is in the Address field of the browser window, you cannot intercept the event. Instead, the browser's Help window appears.

elementObject.onhelp

Example

Listing 26-40 is a rudimentary example of a context-sensitive help system that displays help messages tailored to the kind of text input required by different text boxes. When the user gives focus to either of the text boxes, a small legend appears to remind the user that help is available by a press of the F1 help key. MacIE5 provides only generic help.

LISTING 26-40

Creating Context-Sensitive Help

HTML: jsb26-40.html

```html
<!DOCTYPE html>
<html>
    <head>
        <meta http-equiv="content-type" content="text/html;charset=utf-8">
        <title>onhelp Event Handler</title>
        <style type="text/css">
            #legend
            {
                font-size:10px;
            }
        </style>
        <script type="text/javascript" src="../jsb-global.js"></script>
        <script type="text/javascript" src="jsb26-40.js"></script>
    </head>
    <body onload="init()" onhelp="return showGenericHelp()">
        <h1>onhelp Event Handler</h1>
        <hr />
        <p id="legend" style="visibility:hidden;"> </p>
        <form>
            Name:
            <input type="text" name="name" size="30"
                    onfocus="showLegend()" onblur="hideLegend()"
                    onhelp="return showNameHelp()" />
            <br />
            Year of Birth:
            <input type="text" name="YOB" size="30"
                    onfocus="showLegend()" onblur="hideLegend()"
                    onhelp="return showYOBHelp()" />
        </form>
    </body>
</html>
```

JavaScript: jsb26-40.js

```javascript
function showNameHelp()
{
    alert("Enter your first and last names.");
    event.cancelBubble = true;
```

```
   return false;
}
function showYOBHelp()
{
   alert("Enter the four-digit year of your birth. For example: 1972");
   event.cancelBubble = true;
   return false;
}
function showGenericHelp()
{
   alert("All fields are required.");
   event.cancelBubble = true;
   return false;
}
function showLegend()
{
   document.getElementById("legend").style.visibility = "visible";
}
function hideLegend()
{
   document.getElementById("legend").style.visibility = "hidden";
}
function init()
{
   var msg = "";
     if (navigator.userAgent.indexOf("Mac") != -1)
     {
        msg = "Press \'help\' key for help.";
     }
     else if (navigator.userAgent.indexOf("Win") != -1)
     {
        msg = "Press F1 for help.";
     }
   document.getElementById("legend").style.visibility = "hidden";
   document.getElementById("legend").innerHTML = msg;
}
```

Related Items: `window.showHelp()`, `window.showModalDialog()` methods

onkeydown
onkeypress
onkeyup

Compatibility: WinIE4+, MacIE4+, NN4+, Moz+, Safari+, Opera+, Chrome+

When someone presses and releases a keyboard key, a sequence of three events fires in quick succession. The onkeydown event fires when the key makes its first contact. This is followed immediately by the onkeypress event. When contact is broken by the key release, the onkeyup event fires.

If you hold a character key down until it begins autorepeating, the onkeydown and onkeypress events fire with each repetition of the character.

The sequence of events can be crucial in some keyboard event handling. Consider the scenario that wants the focus of a series of text boxes to advance automatically after the user enters a fixed number of characters (for example, date, month, and two-digit year). By the time the onkeyup event fires, the character associated with the key-press action is already added to the box and you can accurately determine the length of text in the box, as shown in this simple example:

```html
<!DOCTYPE html>
<html>
    <head>
        <meta http-equiv="content-type" content="text/html;charset=utf-8">
        <title>Simple entry form</title>
        <script type="text/javascript">
            function jumpNext(fromFld, toFld)
            {
                if (fromFld.value.length == 2)
                {
                    document.dateForm.elements[toFld].focus();
                    document.dateForm.elements[toFld].select();
                }
            }
        </script>
    </head>
    <body>
        <form name="dateForm">
            Month: <input name="month" type="text" size="3" value=""
                        onkeyup="jumpNext(this, 'day')" maxlength="2" />
            Day: <input name ="day" type="text" size="3" value=""
                        onkeyup ="jumpNext(this, 'year')" maxlength="2" />
            Year: <input name="year" type="text" size="3" value=""
                        onkeyup ="jumpNext(this, 'month')" maxlength="2" />
        </form>
    </body>
</html>
```

These three events do not fire for all keys of the typical PC keyboard on all browser versions that support keyboard events. The only keys that you can rely on supporting the events in all browsers shown in the preceding compatibility chart are the alphanumeric keys represented by ASCII values, including the spacebar and Enter (Return on the Mac), but excluding all function keys, arrow keys, and other navigation keys. Modifier keys, such as Shift, Ctrl (PC), Alt (PC), Command (Mac), and Option (Mac), generate some events on their own (depending on browser and version). However, functions invoked by other key events can always inspect the pressed states of these modifier keys.

Caution

The onkeydown **event handler works in Mozilla-based browsers only starting with Mozilla 1.4 (and Netscape 7.1).** ■

Scripting keyboard events almost always entails examining which key is pressed so that some processing or validation can be performed on that key press. This is where the situation gets very complex if you are writing for cross-browser implementation. In some cases, even writing just for Internet

Explorer gets tricky because nonalphanumeric keys generate only the `onkeydown` and `onkeyup` events.

In fact, to comprehend keyboard events fully, you need to make a distinction between *key codes* and *character codes*. Every PC keyboard key has a key code associated with it. This key code is always the same regardless of what other keys you press at the same time. Only the alphanumeric keys (letters, numbers, spacebar, and so on), however, generate character codes. The code represents the typed character produced by that key. The value might change if you press a modifier key. For example, if you press the A key by itself, it generates a lowercase *a* character (character code 97); if you also hold down the Shift key, that same key produces an uppercase *A* character (character code 65). The key code for that key (65 for Western-language keyboards) remains the same no matter what.

That brings us, then, to where these different codes are made available to scripts. In all cases, the code information is conveyed as one or two properties of the browser's `event` object. IE's `event` object has only one such property: `keyCode`. It contains key codes for `onkeydown` and `onkeyup` events but character codes for `onkeypress` events. The NN6+/Moz event object, on the other hand, contains two separate properties: `charCode` and `keyCode`. You can find more details and examples about these `event` object properties in Chapter 32.

The bottom-line script consideration is to use either `onkeydown` or `onkeyup` event handlers when you want to look for nonalphanumeric key events (for example, function keys, arrow and page-navigation keys, and so on). To process characters as they appear in text boxes, use the `onkeypress` event handler. You can experiment with these events and codes in Listing 26-41, as well as in examples from Chapter 32.

Common keyboard event tasks

WinIE4+ enables you to modify the character that a user who is editing a text box enters. The `onkeypress` event handler can modify the `event.keyCode` property and allow the event to continue (in other words, don't evaluate to `return false` or set the `event.returnValue` property to `false`). The following IE function (invoked by an `onkeypress` event handler) makes sure that text entered in a text box is all uppercase, even if you type it as lowercase:

```
function assureUpper()
{
    if (event.keyCode >= 97 && event.keyCode <= 122)
    {
        event.keyCode = event.keyCode - 32;
    }
}
```

Doing this might confuse (or frustrate) users, so think carefully before implementing such a plan.

To prevent a key press from becoming a typed character in a text box, the `onkeypress` event handler prevents the default action of the event. For example, the following HTML page shows how to inspect a text box's entry for numbers only:

```
<!DOCTYPE html>
<html>
    <head>
        <meta http-equiv="content-type" content="text/html;charset=utf-8">
        <title>Keyboard Capture</title>
        <script type="text/javascript">
```

```
            function checkIt(evt)
            {
                var charCode = (evt.charCode) ?
                    evt.charCode : ((evt.which) ? evt.which : evt.keyCode);
                if (charCode > 31 && (charCode < 48 || charCode > 57))
                {
                    alert("Please make sure entries are numbers only.");
                    return false;
                }
                return true;
            }
        </script>
    </head>
    <body>
        <form>
            Enter any positive integer:
            <input type="text" name="numeric" onkeypress="return checkIt(event)">
        </form>
    </body>
</html>
```

Whenever a user enters a non-number, the user receives a warning, and the character is not appended to the text box's text.

Keyboard events also enable you to script the submission of a form when a user presses the Enter (Return on the Mac) key within a text box. The ASCII value of the Enter/Return key is 13. Therefore, you can examine each key press in a text box and submit the form whenever value 13 arrives, as shown in the following function:

```
function checkForEnter(evt)
{
    evt = (evt) ? evt : event;
    var charCode = (evt.charCode) ?
            evt.charCode : ((evt.which) ? evt.which : evt.keyCode);

    if (charCode == 13)
        {
        document.forms[0].submit();
        return false;
        }
        return true;
}
```

By assigning the checkForEnter() function to each box's onkeypress event handler, you suddenly add some extra power to a typical HTML form.

You can intercept Ctrl+keyboard combinations (letters only) in HTML pages most effectively in IE, but only if the browser itself does not use the combination. In other words, you cannot redirect Ctrl+key combinations that the browser uses for its own control. The onkeypress keyCode value for Ctrl+key combinations ranges from 1 through 26 for letters A through Z (except for those used by the browser, in which case no keyboard event fires).

Example

Listing 26-41 is a working laboratory that you can use to better understand the way keyboard event codes and modifier keys work in IE5+ and W3C browsers. The actual code of the listing is less important than watching the page while you use it. For every key or key combination that you press, the page shows the keyCode value for the onkeydown, onkeypress, and onkeyup events. If you hold down one or more modifier keys while performing the key press, the modifier-key name is highlighted for each of the three events. Note that when run in NN6+/Moz-based browsers/WebKit-based browsers, the keyCode value is not the character code. In older browsers, you may need to click the page for the document object to recognize the keyboard events.

The best way to watch what goes on during keyboard events is to press and hold a key to see the key codes for the onkeydown and onkeypress events. Then release the key to see the code for the onkeyup event. Notice, for instance, that if you press the A key without any modifier key, the onkeydown event key code is 65 (A), but the onkeypress key code in IE (and the charCode property in NN6+/Moz-based browsers/WebKit-based browsers) is 97 (a). If you then repeat the exercise but hold the Shift key down, all three events generate the 65 (A) key code (and the Shift modifier labels are highlighted). Releasing the Shift key causes the onkeyup event to show the key code for the Shift key.

In another experiment, press any of the four arrow keys. No key code is passed for the onkeypress event because those keys don't generate those events. They do, however, generate onkeydown and onkeyup events.

LISTING 26-41

Keyboard Event Handler Laboratory

HTML: jsb26-41.html

```html
<!DOCTYPE html>
<html>
    <head>
        <meta http-equiv="content-type" content="text/html;charset=utf-8">
        <title>Keyboard Event Handler Lab</title>
        <style type="text/css">
            td
            {
                text-align:center;
            }
        </style>
        <script type="text/javascript" src="../jsb-global.js"></script>
        <script type="text/javascript" src="jsb26-41.js"></script>
    </head>
    <body onload="init()">
        <h1>Keyboard Event Handler Lab</h1>
        <hr />
        <form>
            <table border="2" cellpadding="2">
                <tr>
                    <th></th>
```

continued

elementObject.onkeyup

LISTING 26-41   *(continued)*

```
            <th>onKeyDown</th>
            <th>onKeyPress</th>
            <th>onKeyUp</th>
        </tr>
        <tr>
            <th>Key Codes</th>
            <td id="downKeyCode">0</td>
            <td id="pressKeyCode">0</td>
            <td id="upKeyCode">0</td>
        </tr>
        <tr>
            <th>Char Codes (IE5/Mac; Moz; WebKit)</th>
            <td id="downCharCode">0</td>
            <td id="pressCharCode">0</td>
            <td id="upCharCode">0</td>
        </tr>
        <tr>
            <th rowspan="3">Modifier Keys</th>
            <td><span id="shiftDown">Shift</span></td>
            <td><span id="shift">Shift</span></td>
            <td><span id="shiftUp">Shift</span></td>
        </tr>
        <tr>
            <td><span id="ctrlDown">Ctrl</span></td>
            <td><span id="ctrl">Ctrl</span></td>
            <td><span id="ctrlUp">Ctrl</span></td>
        </tr>
        <tr>
            <td><span id="altDown">Alt</span></td>
            <td><span id="alt">Alt</span></td>
            <td><span id="altUp">Alt</span></td>
        </tr>
    </table>
  </form>
 </body>
</html>
```

JavaScript: jsb26-41.js

```
function init()
{
    document.onkeydown = showKeyDown;
    document.onkeyup = showKeyUp;
    document.onkeypress = showKeyPress;
}


function showKeyDown(evt)
{
```

```
    evt = (evt) ? evt : window.event;
    document.getElementById("pressKeyCode").innerHTML = 0;
    document.getElementById("upKeyCode").innerHTML = 0;
    document.getElementById("pressCharCode").innerHTML = 0;
    document.getElementById("upCharCode").innerHTML = 0;
    restoreModifiers("");
    restoreModifiers("Down");
    restoreModifiers("Up");
    document.getElementById("downKeyCode").innerHTML = evt.keyCode;
        if (evt.charCode)
        {
            document.getElementById("downCharCode").innerHTML = evt.charCode;
        }
    showModifiers("Down", evt);
}

function showKeyUp(evt)
{
    evt = (evt) ? evt : window.event;
    document.getElementById("upKeyCode").innerHTML = evt.keyCode;
        if (evt.charCode)
        {
            document.getElementById("upCharCode").innerHTML = evt.charCode;
        }
    showModifiers("Up", evt);
    return false;
}

function showKeyPress(evt)
{
    evt = (evt) ? evt : window.event;
    document.getElementById("pressKeyCode").innerHTML = evt.keyCode;
        if (evt.charCode)
        {
            document.getElementById("pressCharCode").innerHTML = evt.charCode;
        }
    showModifiers("", evt);
    return false;
}

function showModifiers(ext, evt)
{
    restoreModifiers(ext);
    if (evt.shiftKey)
    {
        document.getElementById("shift" + ext).style.backgroundColor = "#ff0000";
    }
    if (evt.ctrlKey)
    {
        document.getElementById("ctrl" + ext).style.backgroundColor = "#00ff00";
    }
```

continued

723

elementObject.**onlayoutcomplete**

LISTING 26-41 *(continued)*

```
  if (evt.altKey)
  {
      document.getElementById("alt" + ext).style.backgroundColor = "#0000ff";
  }
}

function restoreModifiers(ext)
{
    document.getElementById("shift" + ext).style.backgroundColor = "#ffffff";
    document.getElementById("ctrl" + ext).style.backgroundColor = "#ffffff";
    document.getElementById("alt" + ext).style.backgroundColor = "#ffffff";
}
```

Spend some time with this lab, and try all kinds of keys and key combinations until you understand the way the events and key codes work.

Related Item: `String.fromCharCode()` method

onlayoutcomplete

Compatibility: WinIE5.5+, MacIE-, NN-, Moz-, Safari-, Opera-, Chrome-

The `onlayoutcomplete` event handler fires when a print or print-preview layout operation completes on the current layout rectangle (`LayoutRect` object). This event is primarily used as the basis for overflowing content from one page to another during printing. In response to the `onlayoutcomplete` event, the `contentOverflow` property can be inspected to determine whether page content has indeed overflowed the current layout rectangle.

onlosecapture

Compatibility: WinIE5+, MacIE-, NN-, Moz-, Safari-, Opera-, Chrome-

The `onlosecapture` event handler fires whenever an object that has event capture turned on no longer has that capture. Event capture is automatically disengaged when the user performs any of the following actions:

- Gives focus to any other window
- Displays any system modal dialog box (for example, alert window)
- Scrolls the page
- Opens a browser context menu (right-clicking)
- Tabs to give focus to the Address field in the browser window

A function associated with the `onlosecapture` event handler should perform any cleanup of the environment due to an object's no longer capturing mouse events.

Example

See Listing 26-30 earlier in this chapter for an example of how to use `onlosecapture` with an event-capturing scenario for displaying a context menu. The `onlosecapture` event handler hides the context menu when the user performs any action that causes the menu to lose mouse capture.

Related Items: `releaseCapture()`, `setCapture()` methods

onmousedown
onmouseup

Compatibility: WinIE4+, MacIE4+, NN4+, Moz+, Safari+, Opera+, Chrome+

The `onmousedown` event handler fires when the user presses any button on a mouse. The `onmouseup` event handler fires when the user releases the mouse button, provided that the object receiving the event also received an `onmousedown` event. When a user performs a typical click of the mouse button atop an object, mouse events occur in the following sequence: `onmousedown`, `onmouseup`, and `onclick`. But if the user presses the mouse atop an object and then slides the cursor away from the object, only the `onmousedown` event fires.

These events enable authors and designers to add more applicationlike behavior to images that act as action or icon buttons. If you notice the way most buttons work, the appearance of the button changes while you press the mouse button and reverts to its original style when you release the mouse button (or you drag the cursor out of the button). These events enable you to emulate that behavior.

The event object created with every mouse button action has a property that reveals which mouse button the user pressed. NN4's event model called that property the `which` property. IE4+ and NN6+/Moz-based browsers/WebKit-based browsers call it the `button` property (but with different values for the buttons). It is most reliable to test for the mouse button number on either the `onmousedown` or `onmouseup` event rather than on `onclick`. The `onclick` event object does not always contain the button information.

Example

To demonstrate a likely scenario of changing button images in response to rolling atop an image, pressing down on it, releasing the mouse button, and rolling away from the image, Listing 26-42 presents a pair of small navigation buttons (left- and right-arrow buttons). Images are preloaded into the browser cache as the page loads so that response to the user is instantaneous the first time the user calls upon new versions of the images.

LISTING 26-42

Using onmousedown and onmouseup Event Handlers

HTML: `jsb26-42.html`

```
<!DOCTYPE html>
<html>
   <head>
      <meta http-equiv="content-type" content="text/html;charset=utf-8">
      <title>onmousedown and onmouseup Event Handlers</title>
      <style type="text/css">
         #imgHolder
         {
```

continued

LISTING 26-42   *(continued)*

```
            text-align:center;
        }
        .images
        {
            height:16px; width:16px; border:0px;
        }
    </style>
    <script type="text/javascript" src="../jsb-global.js"></script>
    <script type="text/javascript" src="jsb26-42.js"></script>
</head>
<body>
    <h1>onmousedown and onmouseup Event Handlers</h1>
    <hr />
    <p>Roll atop and click on the buttons to see how the link event handlers
        swap the subtlety different images:
    </p>
    <div id="imgHolder">
        <img alt="image" class="images"
            name="Left" src="LeftNorm.gif"
            onmouseover="return setImage('Left','Up')"
            onmousedown="return setImage('Left','Down')"
            onmouseup="return setImage('Left','Up')"
            onmouseout="return setImage('Left','Norm')" />
          
        <img alt="image" class="images"
            name="Right" src="RightNorm.gif"
             onmouseover="return setImage('Right','Up')"
            onmousedown="return setImage('Right','Down')"
            onmouseup="return setImage('Right','Up')"
            onmouseout="return setImage('Right','Norm')" />
    </div>
</body>
</html>
```

JavaScript: jsb26-42.js

```
var RightNormImg = new Image(16,16);
var RightUpImg = new Image(16,16);
var RightDownImg = new Image(16,16);
var LeftNormImg = new Image(16,16);
var LeftUpImg = new Image(16,16);
var LeftDownImg = new Image(16,16);

RightNormImg.src = "RightNorm.gif";
RightUpImg.src = "RightUp.gif";
RightDownImg.src = "RightDown.gif";
LeftNormImg.src = "LeftNorm.gif";
LeftUpImg.src = "LeftUp.gif";
LeftDownImg.src = "LeftDown.gif";
```

```
function setImage(imgName, type)
{
    var imgFile = eval(imgName + type + "Img.src");
    document.images[imgName].src = imgFile;
    return false;
}
```

Related Item: onclick event handler

onmouseenter
onmouseleave

Compatibility: WinIE5.5+, MacIE-, NN-, Moz-, Safari-, Opera-, Chrome-

WinIE5.5 introduced the onmouseenter and onmouseleave event handlers. Both event handlers operate just like the onmouseover and onmouseout event handlers, respectively. Microsoft simply offers an alternative terminology. The old and new events continue to fire in IE5.5+. The old ones fire just before the new ones for each act of moving the cursor atop, and exiting from atop, the object. If you are scripting exclusively for IE5.5+, you should use the new terminology; otherwise, stay with the older versions.

Example

You can modify Listing 26-43 with the IE5.5 syntax by substituting onmouseenter for onmouseover and onmouseleave for onmouseout. The effect is the same.

Related Items: onmouseover, onmouseout event handlers

onmousemove

Compatibility: WinIE4+, MacIE4+, NN4+, Moz+, Safari+, Opera+, Chrome+

The onmousemove event handler fires whenever the cursor is atop the current object and the mouse is moved, even by a single pixel. You do not have to press the mouse button for the event to fire, although the event is most commonly used in element dragging — especially in NN/FF3.4-/Opera, where no ondrag event handler is available.

Even though the granularity of this event can be at the pixel level, you should not use the number of event firings as a measurement device. Depending on the speed of cursor motion and the performance of the client computer, the event may not fire at every pixel location.

In IE4+ and W3C DOM-compatible browsers, you can assign the onmousemove event handler to any element (although you can drag only with positioned elements). When designing a page that encourages users to drag multiple items on a page, it is most common to assign the onmousemove event handler to the document object and let all such events bubble up to the document for processing.

Example

See Chapter 43 and Chapter 59 on the CD-ROM for examples of using mouse events to control element dragging on a page.

Related Items: ondrag, onmousedown, onmouseup event handlers

```
onmouseout
onmouseover
```

Compatibility: WinIE3+, MacIE3+, NN2+, Moz+, Safari+, Opera+, Chrome+

The `onmouseover` event fires for an object whenever the cursor rolls into the rectangular space of the object on the screen. The `onmouseout` event handler fires when you move the cursor outside the object's rectangle. These events most commonly display explanatory text about an object in the window's status bar and effect image swapping (so-called mouse rollovers). Use the `onmouseover` event handler to change the state to a highlighted version; use the `onmouseout` event handler to restore the image or status bar to its normal setting.

Although these two events have been in object models of scriptable browsers since the beginning, they were not available to most objects in earlier browsers. IE4+ and W3C DOM-compatible browsers provide support for these events on every element that occupies space onscreen. IE5.5+ includes an additional pair of event handlers — `onmouseenter` and `onmouseleave` — that duplicates the `onmouseover` and `onmouseout` events but with different terminology. The old event handlers fire just before the new versions.

Note

The `onmouseout` **event handler commonly fails to fire if the event is associated with an element that is near a frame or window edge and the user moves the cursor quickly outside the current frame.** ∎

Example

Listing 26-43 uses the U.S. Pledge of Allegiance with four links to demonstrate how to use the `onmouseover` and `onmouseout` event handlers. Notice that for each link, the handler runs a general-purpose function that sets the window's status message. The function returns a `true` value, which the event handler call evaluates to replicate the required `return true` statement needed for setting the status bar. In one status message, we supply a URL in parentheses to let you evaluate how helpful you think it is for users.

LISTING 26-43

Using onmouseover and onmouseout Event Handlers

HTML: `jsb26-43.html`

```html
<!DOCTYPE html>
<html>
    <head>
        <meta http-equiv="content-type" content="text/html;charset=utf-8">
        <title>onmouseover and onmouseout Event Handlers</title>
        <script type="text/javascript" src="../jsb-global.js"></script>
        <script type="text/javascript" src="jsb26-43.js"></script>
    </head>
    <body>
        <h1>onmouseover and onmouseout Event Handlers</h1>
        <hr />
        <h1>Pledge of Allegiance</h1>
        <hr />
        I pledge
        <a href="javascript:emulate()"
```

```
              onmouseover="return setStatus('View dictionary definition')"
              onmouseout="return setStatus('')">allegiance</a>
    to the
    <a href="javascript:emulate()"
       onmouseover="return setStatus('Learn about the U.S. flag↵
          (http://lcweb.loc.gov)')"
       onmouseout="return setStatus('')">flag</a>
    of the
    <a href="javascript:emulate()"
       onmouseover="return setStatus('View info about the U.S. government')"
       onmouseout="return setStatus('')">United States of America</a>,
    and to the Republic for which it stands, one nation
    <a href="javascript:emulate()"
       onmouseover="return setStatus('Read about the history of this phrase↵
          in the Pledge')"
       onmouseout="return setStatus('')">under God</a>,
    indivisible, with liberty and justice for all.
  </body>
</html>
```

JavaScript: jsb26-43.js

```
function setStatus(msg)
{
   window.status = msg;
   return true;
}

// destination of all link HREFs
function emulate()
{
   alert("Not going there in this demo.");
}
```

Related Items: onmouseenter, onmouseleave, onmousemove event handlers

onmousewheel

Compatibility: WinIE6+, MacIE-, NN-, Moz+, Safari+, Opera+, Chrome+

The onmousewheel event handler fires in response to the user's rotating the mouse wheel. When responding to the onmousewheel event, you can check the wheelDelta property to find out how far the mouse wheel has been rotated. The wheelDelta property expresses mouse wheel rotations in multiples of 120, with positive values indicating a rotation away from the user and negative values corresponding to a rotation toward the user. The W3C equivalent is DOMMouseScroll.

Related Item: onmousemove event handler

onmove

Compatibility: WinIE5.5+, MacIE-, NN-, Moz-, Safari-, Opera-, Chrome-

Not to be confused with onmousemove, the onmove event has nothing to do with the mouse. Instead, the onmove event is fired whenever a positionable *element* is moved. For example, if a div element is created as an absolutely positioned moveable element, you can track its movement by responding to the onmove event. The offsetLeft and offsetTop properties can be used within this event handler to determine the exact location of the element as it is moving.

Related Items: onmoveend, onmovestart event handlers

onmoveend
onmovestart

Compatibility: WinIE5.5+, MacIE-, NN-, Moz-, Safari-, Opera-, Chrome-

The onmovestart and onmoveend event handlers fire in response to a positionable element's being moved on a page. More specifically, the onmovestart event is triggered when an element first starts moving and the onmoveend event fires when the element stops moving. In between the onmovestart and onmoveend events firing, multiple onmove events may be sent out to indicate the movement of the element.

Related Item: onmove event handler

onpaste

Compatibility: WinIE5+, MacIE-, NN-, Moz+, Safari 1.3+, Opera-, Chrome+

The onpaste event fires immediately after the user or script initiates a paste edit action on the current object. The event is preceded by the onbeforepaste event, which fires prior to any edit or context menu that appears (or before the paste action if initiated by keyboard shortcut).

Use this event handler to provide edit functionality to elements that don't normally allow pasting. In such circumstances, you need to enable the Paste menu item in the context or Edit menu by setting the event.returnValue for the onbeforepaste event handler to false. Then your onpaste event handler must manually retrieve data from the clipboard (by way of the getData() method of the IE clipboardData object) and handle the insertion into the current object.

Because you are in charge of what data is stored in the clipboard, you are not limited to a direct copy of the data. For example, you might wish to store the value of the src property of an image object so that you can paste it elsewhere on the page.

Example

Listing 26-44 demonstrates how to use the onbeforepaste and onpaste event handlers (in conjunction with onbeforecopy and oncopy) to let scripts control the data-transfer process during a copy-and-paste user operation. A table contains words to be copied (one column of nouns, one column of adjectives) and then pasted into blanks in a paragraph. The onbeforecopy and oncopy event handlers are assigned to the table element because the events from the td elements bubble up to the table container and there is less HTML code to contend with.

Inside the paragraph, two span elements contain underscored blanks. To paste text into the blanks, the user must first select at least one character of the blanks. (See Listing 26-37, which gives a drag-and-drop version of this application.) The onbeforepaste event handler in the paragraph (which gets the event as it bubbles up from either span) sets the event.returnValue property to false, thus allowing the Paste item to appear in the context and Edit menus (not a normal occurrence in HTML body content).

At paste time, the `innerHTML` property of the target `span` is set to the text data stored in the clipboard. The `event.returnValue` property is set to `false` here as well to prevent normal system pasting from interfering with the controlled version.

LISTING 26-44

Using onbeforepaste and onpaste Event Handlers

HTML: `jsb26-44.html`

```html
<!DOCTYPE html>
<html>
    <head>
        <meta http-equiv="content-type" content="text/html;charset=utf-8">
        <title>onbeforepaste and onpaste Event Handlers</title>
        <style type="text/css">
            td
            {
                text-align:center;
            }
            th
            {
                text-decoration:underline;
            }
            .blanks
            {
                text-decoration:underline;
            }
        </style>
        <script type="text/javascript" src="../jsb-global.js"></script>
        <script type="text/javascript" src="jsb26-44.js"></script>
    </head>
    <body>
        <h1>onbeforepaste and onpaste Event Handlers</h1>
        <h6>Be very precise when selecting characters</h6>
        <hr />
        <p>Your goal is to copy and paste one noun and one adjective from the
            following table into the blanks of the sentence. Select a word from
            the table and use a menu to copy it to the clipboard. Select one or
            more spaces of the blanks in the sentence and choose Paste from a
            menu to replace the blank with the clipboard contents.
        </p>
        <table cellpadding="5" onbeforecopy="selectWhole()"
                oncopy="handleCopy()">
            <tr>
                <th>Nouns</th>
                <th>Adjectives</th>
            </tr>
            <tr>
                <td>truck</td>
                <td>round</td>
```

continued

elementObject.onpaste

LISTING 26-44   *(continued)*

```
            </tr>
            <tr>
               <td>doll</td>
               <td>red</td>
            </tr>
            <tr>
               <td>ball</td>
               <td>pretty</td>
            </tr>
      </table>
      <p id="myP" onbeforepaste="handleBeforePaste()" onpaste="handlePaste()">
         Pat said, "Oh my, the <span id="blank1" class="blanks">
              </span>
         is so <span id="blank2" class="blanks">
              </span> !"
      </p>
      <button onclick="location.reload()">Reset</button>
   </body>
</html>
```

JavaScript: jsb26-44.js

```
function selectWhole()
{
   var obj = window.event.srcElement;
   var range = document.body.createTextRange();
   range.moveToElementText(obj);
   range.select();
   event.returnValue = false;
}
function handleCopy()
{
   var rng = document.selection.createRange();
   clipboardData.setData("Text",rng.text);
   event.returnValue = false;
}

function handlePaste()
{
   var elem = window.event.srcElement;
      if (elem.className == "blanks")
      {
         elem.innerHTML = clipboardData.getData("Text");
      }
   event.returnValue = false;
}
function handleBeforePaste()
{
   var elem = window.event.srcElement;
```

```
if (elem.className == "blanks")
{
    event.returnValue = false;
}
}
```

Related Items: oncopy, oncut, onbeforepaste event handlers

onpropertychange

Compatibility: WinIE5+, MacIE-, NN-, Moz-, Safari-, Opera-, Chrome-

The onpropertychange event fires in WinIE5+ whenever a script modifies an object's property. This includes changes to the properties of an object's style. Changing properties by way of the setAttribute() method also triggers this event.

A script can inspect the nature of the property change because the event.propertyName property contains the name (as a string) of the property that was just changed. In the case of a change to an object's style object, the event.propertyName value begins with "style." as in style.backgroundcolor.

You can use this event handler to localize any object-specific postprocessing of changes to an object's properties. Rather than include the postprocessing statements inside the function that makes the changes, you can make that function generalized (perhaps to modify properties of multiple objects).

Example

Listing 26-45 shows how you can respond programmatically to an object's properties being changed. The page generated by the listing contains four radio buttons that alter the innerHTML and style.color properties of a paragraph. The paragraph's onpropertychange event handler invokes the showChange() function, which extracts information about the event and displays the data in the status bar of the window. Notice that the property name includes style. when you modify the style sheet property.

LISTING 26-45

Using the onPropertyChange Property

HTML: jsb26-45.html

```
<!DOCTYPE html>
<html>
   <head>
     <meta http-equiv="content-type" content="text/html;charset=utf-8">
     <title>onpropertychange Event Handler</title>
     <script type="text/javascript" src="../jsb-global.js"></script>
     <script type="text/javascript" src="jsb26-45.js"></script>
   </head>
   <body onload="init()";>
     <h1>onpropertychange Event Handler</h1>
```

continued

733

LISTING 26-45 *(continued)*

```
        <hr />
        <p id="myP" onpropertychange="showChange()">This is a sample paragraph.</p>
        <form>
            Text:
            <input type="radio" name="btn1" checked="checked"
                   onclick="normalText()" />Normal
            <input type="radio" name="btn1"
                   onclick="shortText()" />Short
            <br />
            Color:
            <input type="radio" name="btn2" checked="checked"
                   onclick="normalColor()" />Black
            <input type="radio" name="btn2"
                   onclick="hotColor()" />Red
        </form>
    </body>
</html>
```

JavaScript: jsb26-45.js

```
function init()
{
    elem = document.getElementById("myP");
}
function normalText()
{
    if (elem.textContent)
    {
        elem.textContent = "This is a sample paragraph.";
    }
    else
    {
        elem.innerText = "This is a sample paragraph.";
    }
}
function shortText()
{
    if (elem.textContent)
    {
        elem.textContent = "Short stuff.";
    }
    else
    {
        elem.innerText = "Short stuff.";
    }
}
function normalColor()
{
    elem.style.color = "black";
}
```

```
function hotColor()
{
    elem.style.color = "red";
}
function showChange()
{
    var objID = event.srcElement.id;
    var propName = event.propertyName;
    var newValue = eval(objID + "." + propName);
    var msg = "The " + propName + " property of the " + objID;
    msg += " object has changed to \"" + newValue + "\".";
    alert(msg);
}
```

Related Items: `style` property; `setAttribute()` method

onreadystatechange

Compatibility: WinIE4+, MacIE-, NN7+, Moz1.0.1+, Safari 1.2+, Opera+, Chrome+

The `onreadystatechange` event handler fires whenever the ready state of an object changes. See details about these states in the discussion of the `readyState` property earlier in this chapter (and notice the limits for IE4). The change of state does not guarantee that an object is in fact ready for script statements to access its properties. Always check the `readyState` property of the object in any script that the `onreadystatechange` event handler invokes.

This event fires for objects that are capable of loading data: `applet`, `document`, `frame`, `frameset`, `iframe`, `img`, `link`, `object`, `script`, and XML objects. The event doesn't fire for other types of objects unless a Microsoft DHTML behavior is associated with the object. The `onreadystatechange` event does not bubble; neither can you cancel it.

Related Item: `readyState` property

onresize

Compatibility: WinIE4+, MacIE4+, NN4+, Moz+, Safari+, Opera+, Chrome+

The `onresize` event handler fires whenever an object is resized in response to a variety of user or scripted actions. Most elements include this event handler, provided that the object has dimensional style attributes (for example, height, width, or position) assigned to it.

The `onresize` event does not bubble. Resizing the browser window or frame does not cause the window's `onload` event handler to fire.

Example

If you want to capture the user's resizing of the browser window (or frame), you can assign a function to the `onresize` event handler either via script

```
window.onresize = handleResize;
```

elementObject.onresizeend

or by an HTML attribute of the body element:

```
<body onresize="handleResize()">
```

Related Item: window.resize() method

onresizeend
onresizestart

Compatibility: WinIE5.5+, MacIE-, NN-, Moz-, Safari-, Opera-, Chrome-

The onresizeend and onresizestart event handlers fire only on a resizable object in Windows edit mode.

Related Item: oncontrolselect event handler

onrowenter
onrowexit

Compatibility: WinIE4+, MacIE-, NN-, Moz-, Safari-, Opera-, Chrome-

The onrowenter and onrowexit events fire in response to changes in the current row of recordset data in IE data binding. More specifically, onrowenter is triggered when the data for the current row of data has changed and new data is available on the data source object. The onrowexit event is triggered when the current row is changing, meaning that another row of data is being selected; the event is fired just before the row changes.

Related Items: onrowsdelete, onrowsinserted event handlers

onrowsdelete
onrowsinserted

Compatibility: WinIE5+, MacIE-, NN-, Moz-, Safari-, Opera-, Chrome-

The onrowsdelete event fires when one or more rows of data are about to be deleted from the recordset in IE data binding. Conversely, the onrowsinserted event is triggered when one or more rows of data have been inserted into the recordset.

Related Items: onrowenter, onrowexit event handlers

onscroll

Compatibility: WinIE4+, MacIE4+, NN-, Moz+, Safari+, Opera_, Chrome+

The onscroll event handler fires whenever the scroll box within a scroll bar of an element is repositioned. In simpler terms, when the user clicks and drags the scroll box with the mouse, the onscroll event is fired. That's not the only action that triggers the event, however. An onscroll event is also fired in response to the user's clicking the scroll arrow, clicking the scroll bar, or pressing any of the following keys: Home, End, Space, Page Up, or Page Down. A call to the doScroll() method also triggers the event, as does the user's holding down the Up Arrow or Down Arrow key.

Related Item: doScroll() method

onselectstart

Compatibility: WinIE4+, MacIE4+, NN-, Moz-, Safari 1.3+, Opera-, Chrome+

The `onselectstart` event handler fires when a user begins to select content on the page. Selected content can be inline text, images, or text within an editable text box. If the user selects more than one object, the event fires in the first object affected by the selection.

Example

Use the page from Listing 26-46 to see how the `onselectstart` event handler works when a user selects across multiple elements on a page. As the user begins a selection anywhere on the page, the ID of the object receiving the event appears in the status bar. Notice that the event doesn't fire until you actually make a selection. When no other element is under the cursor, the `body` element fires the event.

LISTING 26-46

Using the onselectstart Event Handler

HTML: `jsb26-46.html`

```html
<!DOCTYPE html>
<html>
    <head>
        <meta http-equiv="content-type" content="text/html;charset=utf-8">
        <title>onselectstart Event Handler</title>
        <style type="text/css">
            h1, th
            {
                padding:5px;
            }
            td
            {
                text-align:center;
            }
        </style>
        <script type="text/javascript" src="../jsb-global.js"></script>
        <script type="text/javascript" src="jsb26-46.js"></script>
    </head>
    <body id="myBody" onselectstart="showObj()">
        <h1 id="myH1">
            onselectstart Event Handler
        </h1>
        <hr id="myHR" />
        <p id="myP">This is a sample paragraph.</p>
        <table border="1">
            <tr id="row1">
                <th id="header1">Column A</th>
                <th id="header2">Column B</th>
                <th id="header3">Column C</th>
            </tr>
            <tr id="row2">
                <td id="cellA2">text</td>
                <td id="cellB2">text</td>
```

continued

*elementObject.***onselectstart**

LISTING 26-46   *(continued)*

```
            <td id="cellC2">text</td>
        </tr>
        <tr id="row3">
            <td id="cellA3">text</td>
            <td id="cellB3">text</td>
            <td id="cellC3">text</td>
        </tr>
    </table>
  </body>
</html>
```

JavaScript: jsb26-46.js

```
function showObj()
{
    var objID = event.srcElement.id;
    alert("Selection started with object: " + objID);
}
```

Related Item: onselect event handler for a variety of objects

Window and Frame Objects

A quick look at the basic document object model diagram in Chapter 25, "Document Object Model Essentials," (refer to Figure 25-1) reveals that the window object is the outermost global container of all document-related objects that you script with JavaScript. All HTML and JavaScript activity takes place inside a window. That window may be a standard Windows, Mac, or XWindows application-style window, complete with scroll bars, toolbars, and other chrome; you can also generate windows that have only some of a typical window's chrome. A frame is also a window, even though a frame doesn't have many accoutrements beyond scroll bars. The window object is where everything begins when JavaScript references objects. Modern browsers treat the frameset as a special kind of window object, so it is also covered in this chapter.

Of all the objects associated with browser scripting, the window and window-related objects have by far the most object-specific terminology associated with them. This necessitates a rather long chapter to keep the whole discussion in one place.

Window Terminology

The window object is often a source of confusion when you first learn about the document object model. A number of synonyms for window objects muck up the works: top, self, parent, and frame. Aggravating the situation is the fact that these terms are also properties of a window object. Under some conditions, a window is its own parent, but if you define a frameset with two frames, you have only one parent among a total of three window objects. It doesn't take long before the whole subject can make your head hurt.

If you do not use frames in your web applications, these headaches never appear. But if frames are part of your design plan, you should get to know how frames affect the object model.

Frames

The application of frames has become a religious issue among web designers: Some swear by them; others swear at them. We believe, after careful consideration, that there can be compelling reasons to use frames at times. Historically, any humungous document with a hierarchy, or that depends on a file system, might be a good candidate. For example, if you have a document that requires considerable scrolling to get through, you may want to maintain a static set of navigation controls that are visible at all times. By placing those controls — be they links or image maps — in a separate frame, you have made the controls available for immediate access, regardless of the scrolled condition of the main document. However, you could use an Ajax framework to provide such navigational controls instead of using HTML frames. Be aware that creating bookmarks and printing documents in frames can range anywhere from impossible to difficult. Frames can be a problem for folks with disabilities. Most web designers provide an alternative flat HTML document with links for those types of situations.

Creating frames

The task of defining frames in a document remains the same whether or not you're using JavaScript. The simplest framesetting document consists of tags that are devoted to setting up the frameset, as follows:

```html
<html>
    <head>
        <title>My Frameset</title>
    </head>
<frameset>
    <frame name="Frame1" src="document1.html">
    <frame name="Frame2" src="document2.html">
</frameset>
</html>
```

The preceding HTML document, which the user never sees, defines the frameset for the entire browser window. Each frame must have a URL reference (specified by the `src` attribute) for a document to load into that frame. Assigning a name to each frame with the `name` attribute greatly simplifies the scripting of frame content.

The frame object model

Perhaps the key to successful frame scripting is understanding that the object model in the browser's memory at any given instant is determined by the HTML tags in the currently loaded documents. All canned object model graphics in this book, such as Figure 27-1, do not reflect the precise object model for your document or document set.

For a single, frameless document, the object model starts with just one `window` object, which contains one document, as shown in Figure 27-1. In this simple structure, the `window` object is the starting point for all references to any loaded object. Because the window is always there — it must be there for a document to load into — a reference to any object in the document can omit a reference to the current window.

In a simple two-framed frameset model (see Figure 27-2), the browser treats the container of the initial, framesetting, document as the parent window. The only visible evidence that the document exists is the framesetting document's title in the browser window title bar.

FIGURE 27-1

The simplest window-document relationship.

FIGURE 27-2

The parent and frames are part of the object model.

Each <frame> tag inside the <frameset> tag set creates another window object into which a document is loaded. Each of those frames, then, has a document object associated with it. From the point of view of a given document, it has a single window container, just as in the model shown in Figure 27-1. And although the parent object is not visible to the user, it remains in the object model in memory. The presence of the parent often makes it a convenient repository for variable data that needs to be shared by multiple child frames, or that must persist between loading different documents inside a child frame.

In even more complex arrangements, as shown in Figure 27-3, a child frame itself may load a framesetting document. In this situation, the difference between the parent and top objects starts to come into focus. The top window is the only one in common with all frames in Figure 27-3. As you see in a moment, when frames need to communicate with other frames (and their documents), you must fashion references to the distant object via the window object that they all have in common.

FIGURE 27-3

Three generations of window objects.

Referencing frames

The purpose of an object reference is to help JavaScript locate the desired object in the object model currently held in memory. A reference is a road map for the browser to follow so that it can track down, say, the value of a particular text field in a particular document. Therefore, when you construct a reference, think about where the script appears in the object model and how the reference can help the browser determine where it should go to find the distant object. In a two-generation scenario, such as the one shown in Figure 27-2, three intergenerational references are possible:

- Parent-to-child
- Child-to-parent
- Child-to-child

Assuming that you need to access an object, function, or variable in the relative's frame, the following are the corresponding reference structures: `frameName.objFuncVarName`, `parent.objFuncVarName.` and `parent.frameName.objFuncVarName.`

The rule is this: Whenever a reference must point to another frame, begin the reference with the `window` object that the two destinations have in common. To demonstrate that rule on the complex model in Figure 27-3, if the left child frame's document needs to reference the document at the bottom right of the map, the reference structure is

```
top.frameName.frameName.document. ...
```

Follow the map from the top `window` object, down through two frames, to the final document. JavaScript has to take this route, so your reference must help it along.

Top versus parent

After seeing the previous object maps and reference examples, you may be wondering, Why not use top as the leading object in all transframe references? From an object model point of view, you'll have no problem doing that: A parent in a two-generation scenario is also the top window. What you can't count on, however, is your framesetting document's always being the top window object in someone's browser. Take the instance where a web site loads other web sites into one of its frames. At that instant, the top window object belongs to someone else. If you always specify top in references intended just for your parent window, your references won't work, and will probably lead to script errors for the user. Our advice, then, is to use parent in references whenever you mean one generation above the current document.

Preventing framing

You can use your knowledge of top and parent references to prevent your pages from being displayed inside another web site's frameset. Your top-level document must check whether it is loaded into its own top, or parent, window. When a document is in its own top window, a reference to the top property of the current window is equal to a reference to the current window (the window synonym self seems most grammatically fitting here). If the two values are not equal, you can script your document to reload itself as a top-level document. When it is critical that your document be a top-level document, include the script in Listing 27-1 in the head portion of your document:

LISTING 27-1

Preventing a Document from Getting Framed

```
<script type="text/javascript">
    if (top != self)
    {
        top.location = location;
    }
</script>
```

Your document may appear momentarily inside the other site's frameset, but then the slate is wiped clean, and your top-level document rules the browser window.

Ensuring framing

When you design a web application around a frameset, you may want to make sure that a page always loads the complete frameset. Consider the possibility that a visitor adds only one of your frames to a bookmarks list. On the next visit, only the bookmarked page appears in the browser, without your frameset, which may contain valuable navigation aids to the site.

A script can make sure that a page always loads into its frameset by comparing the URLs of the top and self windows. If the URLs are the same, it means that the page needs to load the frameset. Listing 27-2 shows the simplest version of this technique, which loads a fixed frameset. For a more complete implementation that passes a parameter to the frameset so that it opens a specific page in one of the frames, see the location.search property in Chapter 28, "Location and History Objects."

LISTING 27-2

Forcing a Frameset to Load

```
<script type="text/javascript">
    if (top.location.href == window.location.href)
    {
        top.location.href = " myFrameset.html";
    }
</script>
```

Switching from frames to frameless

Some sites load themselves in a frameset by default, and offer users the option of getting rid of the frames. Modern browsers let you modify a frameset's `cols` or `rows` properties on the fly to simulate adding or removing frames from the current view (see the `frameset` element object later in this chapter). Legacy browsers, on the other hand, don't allow you to change the makeup of a frameset dynamically after it has loaded, but you can load the content page of the frameset into the main window. The workaround for older browsers is to include a button or link whose action loads that document into the `top` window object:

```
top.location.href = "mainBody.html";
```

A switch back to the frame version entails nothing more complicated than loading the framesetting document.

Inheritance versus containment

Scripters who have experience in object-oriented programming environments probably expect frames to inherit properties, methods, functions, and variables, defined in a parent object. That's not the case with scriptable browsers. You can, however, still access those parent items when you make a call to the item with a complete reference to the parent. For example, if you want to define a deferred function in the framesetting parent document that all frames can share, the scripts in the frames refer to that function with this reference:

```
parent.myFunc()
```

You can pass arguments to such functions and expect returned values.

Frame synchronization

A pesky problem for some scripters' plans is that including immediate scripts in the framesetting document is dangerous. Such scripts tend to rely on the presence of documents in the frames being created by this framesetting document. But if the frames have not yet been created, and their documents have not yet loaded, the immediate scripts will likely crash and burn.

One way to guard against this problem is to trigger all such scripts from the frameset's `onload` event handler. In theory, this handler won't trigger until all documents have successfully loaded into the child frames defined by the frameset. At the same time, be careful with `onload` event handlers in the documents that go into a frameset's frames. If one of those scripts relies on the presence of a document in another frame (one of its brothers or sisters), you're doomed to eventual failure. Anything coming from a slow network or server to a slow modem can get in the way of other documents loading into frames in the ideal order.

One way to work around these problems is to create a Boolean variable in the parent document to act as a flag for the successful loading of subsidiary frames. When a document loads into a frame, its onload event handler can set that flag to true to indicate that the document has loaded. Any script that relies on a page being loaded should use an if construction to test the value of that flag before proceeding.

It is best to construct the code so that the parent's onload event handler triggers all the scripts that you want to run after loading. You should also test your pages thoroughly for any residual effects that may accrue if someone resizes a window or clicks Reload.

Blank frames

Often, you may find it desirable to create a frame in a frameset, but not put any document in it until the user has interacted with various controls or other user interface elements in other frames. Most modern browsers have a somewhat empty document in one of their internal URLs (about:blank). However, this URL is not guaranteed to be available on all browsers. If you need a blank frame, let your framesetting document write a generic HTML document to the frame directly from the src attribute for the frame, as shown in the skeletal code in Listing 27-3. Loading an empty HTML document requires no additional transactions.

LISTING 27-3

Creating a Blank Frame

```
<html>
    <head>
        <script type="text/javascript">
        <! —
            function blank()
            {
                return "<html></html>";
            }
        // — >
        </script>
    </head>
    <frameset>
        <frame name="Frame1" src="someURL.html">
        <frame name="Frame2" src="javascript:parent.blank()">
    </frameset>
</html>
```

Viewing frame source code

Studying other scripters' work is a major tool for learning JavaScript (or any programming language). With most scriptable browsers, you can easily view the source code for any frame, including those frames whose content is generated entirely, or in part, by JavaScript. Click the desired frame to activate it (a subtle border may appear just inside the frame on some browser versions, but don't be alarmed if the border doesn't appear). Then select Frame Source (or equivalent) from the View menu (or from the right-click submenu). You can also print or save a selected frame.

Frames versus frame element objects

With the expansion of object models that expose every HTML element to scripting, a terminology conflict comes into play. Everything that you have read about frames thus far in the chapter refers to the original object model, where a frame is just another kind of window with a slightly different referencing approach. That still holds true, even in the latest browsers.

But when the object model also exposes HTML elements, the notion of the `frame` element object is somewhat distinct from the frame object of the original model. The `frame` element object represents an object whose properties are dominated by the attributes you set inside the `<frame>` tag. This provides access to settings, such as the frame border and scrollability — the kinds of properties that are not exposed to the original frame object.

References to the frame and `frame` element objects are also different. You've seen plenty of examples of how to reference an old-fashioned frame earlier in this chapter. But access to a `frame` element object is either via the element's `id` attribute or through the child node relationship of the enclosing `frameset` element (you cannot use the `parentNode` property to back your way out of the current document to the `frame` element that encloses the document). The strategy we prefer is assigning an `id` attribute to `<frame>` tags and accessing the `frame` element object by way of the `document` object that lives in the parent (or top) of the frameset hierarchy. Therefore, to access the `frameBorder` property of a `frame` element object from a script living in any frame of a frameset, the syntax is

```
parent.document.all.frame1ID.frameBorder
```

or (for IE5+/Moz/W3C)

```
parent.document.getElementById("frame1ID").frameBorder
```

When the reference goes through the `frame` element object, you can still reach the document object in that frame via the element object's `contentWindow` or `contentDocument` properties (see the `frame` element object later in this chapter).

window Object

Properties	Methods	Event Handlers
appCore	addEventListener()[†]	onabort[††]
clientInformation	alert()	onafterprint
clipboardData	attachEvent()[†]	onbeforeprint
closed	back()	onbeforeunload

windowObject

Properties	Methods	Event Handlers
components[]	blur()[†]	onblur[†]
content	clearInterval()	onchange[††]
controllers[]	clearTimeout()	onclick[††]
crypto	close()	onclose[††]
defaultStatus	confirm()	onerror
dialogArguments	createPopup()	onfocus[†]
dialogHeight	detachEvent()[†]	onhelp
dialogLeft	dispatchEvent()[†]	onkeydown[††]
dialogTop	dump()	onkeypress[††]
dialogWidth	execScript()	onkeyup[††]
directories	find()	onload
document	fireEvent()[†]	onmousedown[††]
event Event	focus()[†]	onmousemove[††]
external	forward()	onmouseout[††]
frameElement	geckoActiveXObject()	onmouseover[††]
frames[]	getComputedStyle()	onmouseup[††]
fullScreen	getSelection()	onmove
history	home()	onreset[††]
innerHeight	moveBy()	onresize
innerWidth	moveTo()	onscroll
length	navigate()	onselect[††]
location	open()	onsubmit[††]
locationbar	openDialog()	onunload
menubar	print()	
name	prompt()	
navigator	removeEventListener()[†]	
netscape	resizeBy()	
offscreenBuffering	resizeTo()	
opener	scroll()	
outerHeight	scrollBy()	

windowObject

Properties	Methods	Event Handlers
outerWidth	scrollByLines()	
pageXOffset	scrollByPages()	
pageYOffset	scrollTo()	
parent	setActive()[†]	
personalbar	setInterval()	
pkcs11	setTimeout()	
prompter	showHelp()	
returnValue	showModalDialog()	
screen	showModelessDialog()	
screenLeft	sizeToContent()	
screenTop	stop()	
screenX		
screenY		
scrollbars		
scrollMaxX		
scrollMaxY		
scrollX		
scrollY		
self		
sidebar		
status		
statusbar		
toolbar		
top		
window		

[†] See Chapter 26, "Generic HTML Element Objects."

[††] To handle captured or bubbled events of other objects in IE4+ and W3C DOM browsers.

Syntax

Creating a window:

```
var windowObject = window.open([parameters]);
```

Accessing window properties or methods:

```
window.property | method([parameters])

self.property | method([parameters])

windowObject.property | method([parameters])
```

Compatibility: WinIE3+, MacIE3+, NN2+, Moz+, Safari+, Opera+, Chrome+

About this object

The `window` object has the unique position of being at the top of the object hierarchy, encompassing even the almighty `document` object. This exalted position gives the `window` object a number of properties and behaviors unlike those of any other object.

Chief among its unique characteristics is that because everything takes place in a window, you can usually omit the `window` object from object references. You've seen this behavior in previous chapters when we invoked document methods, such as `document.write()`. The complete reference is `window.document.write()`. But because the activity was taking place in the window that held the document running the script, that window was assumed to be part of the reference. For single-frame windows, this concept is simple enough to grasp.

As previously stated, among the list of properties for the `window` object is one called `self`. This property is synonymous with the `window` object itself (which is why it shows up in hierarchy diagrams as an object). Having a property of an object that is the same name as the object may sound confusing, but this situation is not that uncommon in object-oriented environments. We discuss the reasons why you may want to use the `self` property as the window's object reference in the `self` property description that follows.

As indicated earlier in the syntax definition, you don't always have to create a `window` object specifically in JavaScript code. Your browser usually opens a window after you start it up. That window is a valid `window` object, even if the window is blank. Therefore, after a user loads your page into the browser, the `window` object part of that document is automatically created for your script to access as it pleases.

One conceptual trap to avoid is believing that a `window` object's event handler or custom property assignments outlive the document whose scripts make the assignments. Except for some obvious physical properties of a window, each new document that loads into the window starts with a clean slate of window properties and event handlers.

Your script's control over an existing (already open) window's user interface elements varies widely with the browser and browser version for which your application is intended. Before the version 4 browsers, the only change you could make to an open window was to the status line at the bottom of the browser window. Version 4 browsers added the ability to control such properties as the size, location, and (with signed scripts in Navigator and Mozilla) the presence of chrome elements (toolbars and scroll bars, for example) on the fly. Many of these properties can be changed beyond specific safe limits only if you cryptographically sign the scripts (see Chapter 49, "Security and Netscape Signed Scripts," on the CD-ROM) and/or the user grants permission for your scripts to make those modifications.

Window properties are far more flexible on all browsers when your scripts generate a new window (with the `window.open()` method): You can influence the size, toolbar, or other view options of a window. Recent browser versions provide even more options for new windows, including the position of the window and whether the window should display a title bar. Again, if an option can conceivably be used to deceive a user (for example, silently hiding one window that monitors activity in another window), signed scripts and/or user permission are necessary.

The `window` object is also the level at which a script asks the browser to display any of three styles of dialog boxes (a plain alert dialog box, an OK/Cancel confirmation dialog box, or a prompt for user text entry). Although dialog boxes are extremely helpful for cobbling together debugging tools for your own use (see Chapter 48, "Debugging Scripts," on the CD-ROM), they can be very disruptive to visitors who navigate through web sites. Because most JavaScript dialog boxes are modal (that is, you cannot do anything else in the browser until you dismiss the dialog box), use them sparingly, if at all. Remember that some users may create macros on their computers to visit sites unattended. Should such an automated visitor to your site encounter a modal dialog box, it is trapped on your page until a human intervenes.

All dialog boxes generated by JavaScript identify themselves as being generated by JavaScript. This is primarily a security feature to prevent deceitful scripts from creating system- or application-style dialog boxes that convince visitors to enter private information. It should also discourage dialog box usage in web-page design. And that's good, because dialog boxes tend to annoy users.

With the exception of the IE- and Safari-specific modal, and IE-specific modeless, dialog boxes (see the `window.showModalDialog()` and `window.showModeless()` methods), JavaScript dialog boxes are not particularly flexible in letting you fill them with text or graphic elements beyond the basics. In fact, you can't even change the text of the dialog-box buttons or add buttons. With Dynamic HTML (DHTML)-capable browsers, you can use positioned `div` or `iframe` elements to simulate dialog-box behavior in a cross-browser way.

With respect to the W3C DOM, the window is outside the scope of the standard through DOM Level 2. The closest that the standard comes to acknowledging a window at all is the `document.defaultView` property, which evaluates to the `window` object in today's browsers (predominantly Mozilla). But the formal DOM standard specifies no properties or methods for this view object.

Properties

```
appCore
components[]
content
controllers[]
prompter
sidebar
```

Values: (See text)   Read-Only

Compatibility: WinIE-, MacIE-, NN6+, Moz+, Safari-, Opera-, Chrome-

NN6+/Mozilla provide scriptable access to numerous services that are part of the xpconnect package (*xp* stands for *cross-platform*), which is part of the larger NPAPI (Netscape Plugin Application Programming Interface). The xpconnect services allow scripts to work with COM objects and the mozilla.org XUL (XML-based User Interface Language) facilities — lengthy subjects that extend well beyond the scope of this book. You can begin to explore this subject within the context of Mozilla-based browsers and scripting at `http://www.mozilla.org/scriptable/`.

clientInformation

Value: navigator object   Read-Only

Compatibility: WinIE4+, MacIE4+, NN-, Moz-, Safari 1.2+, Opera-, Chrome+

In an effort to provide scriptable access to browser-level properties while avoiding reference to the Navigator browser brand, Microsoft created the clientInformation property. Its value is identical to that of the navigator object — an object name that is also available in IE. Although Safari 1.2 adopted usage of the clientInformation property, you should use the navigator object for cross-browser applications. (See Chapter 42, "The Navigator and Other Environment Objects," on the CD-ROM.)

Related Item: navigator object

clipboardData

Value: Object   Read/Write

Compatibility: WinIE5+, MacIE-, NN-, Moz-, Safari-, Opera-, Chrome-

Use the clipboardData object to transfer data for such actions as cutting, copying, and pasting under script control. The object contains data of one or more data types associated with a transfer operation. Use this property only when editing processes via the Edit menu (or keyboard equivalents) or the context menu controlled by script — typically in concert with edit-related event handlers.

Working with the clipboardData object requires knowing about its three methods, shown in Table 27-1. Familiarity with the edit-related event handlers (before and after versions of cut, copy, and paste) is also helpful (see Chapter 26).

TABLE 27-1

window.clipboardData Object Methods

Method	Returns	Description
clearData([*format*])	Nothing	Removes data from the clipboard. If no format parameter is supplied, all data is cleared. Data formats can be one or more of the following strings: Text, URL, File, HTML, Image.
getData(*format*)	String	Retrieves data of the specified format from the clipboard. The format is one of the following strings: Text, URL, File, HTML, Image. The clipboard is not emptied when you get the data so that the data can be retrieved in several sequential operations.
setData(*format*, *data*)	Boolean	Stores string data in the clipboard. The format is one of the following strings: Text, URL, File, HTML, Image. For nontext data formats, the data must be a string that specifies the path or URL to the content. Returns true if the transfer to the clipboard is successful.

You cannot use the clipboardData object to transfer data between pages that originate from different domains or arrive via different protocols (http versus https).

Example

See Listings 26-36 and 26-44 in Chapter 26, "Generic HTML Element Objects," to see how the `clipboardData` object is used with a variety of edit-related event handlers.

Related Items: `event.dataTransfer` property; `onbeforecopy`, `onBeforeCut`, `onbeforepaste`, `oncopy`, `oncut`, `onpaste` event handlers

closed

Value: Boolean   Read-Only

Compatibility: WinIE4+, MacIE4+, NN3+, Moz+, Safari+, Opera+, Chrome+

When you create a subwindow with the `window.open()` method, you may need to access object properties from that subwindow, such as setting the value of a text field. Access to the subwindow is via the `window` object reference that is returned by the `window.open()` method, as in the following code fragment:

```
var newWind = window.open("someURL.html","subWind");
...
newWind.document.entryForm.ZIP.value = "00000";
```

In this example, the `newWind` variable is not linked live to the window, but is only a reference to that window. If the user should close the window, the `newWind` variable still contains the reference to the now-missing window. Thus, any script reference to an object in that missing window will likely cause a script error. What you need to know before accessing items in a subwindow is whether the window is still open.

The `closed` property returns `true` if the `window` object has been closed, either by script or by the user. Any time you have a script statement that can be triggered after the user has an opportunity to close the window, test for the `closed` property before executing that statement.

Example

Listing 27-4 is a basic window-opening and window-closing example. The script begins by initializing a global variable, `newWind`, which is used to hold the object reference to the second window. This value needs to be global so that other functions can reference the window for tasks, such as closing.

For this example, the new window contains some HTML code written dynamically to it, rather than loading an existing HTML file into it. Therefore, the URL parameter of the `window.open()` method is left as an empty string. Next comes a brief delay to allow Internet Explorer (especially versions 3 and 4) to catch up with opening the window, so that content can be written to it. The delay (using the `setTimeout()` method described later in this chapter) invokes the `finishNewWindow()` function, which uses the global `newWind` variable to reference the window for writing. The `document.close()` method closes writing to the document — a different kind of close from a window close. A separate function, `closeWindow()`, is responsible for closing the subwindow.

As a final test, an `if` condition looks at two conditions: (1) whether the `window` object has ever been initialized with a value other than `null` (in case you click the window-closing button before ever having created the new window) and (2) whether the window's `closed` property is `null` or `false`. If either condition is true, the `close()` method is sent to the second window.

Note

This is a simple example, so the property assignment event-handling technique employed uses the more modern approach of binding events, using the `addEventListener()` **(NN6+/Moz/W3C)** or `attachEvent()` **(IE5+)** methods. This modern, cross-browser event-handling technique is explained in detail in Chapter 32, "Event Objects." The event-handling technique employed throughout most of the code in this chapter and much of the book is a deliberate simplification to make the code more readable. It is generally better to use the more modern approach of binding events, as we do in this example. ■

LISTING 27-4

Checking Before Closing a Window

HTML: jsb27-04.html

```html
<!DOCTYPE html>
<html>
    <head>
        <meta http-equiv="content-type" content="text/html;charset=utf-8">
        <title>window.closed Property</title>
        <script type="text/javascript" src="../jsb-global.js"></script>
        <script type="text/javascript" src="jsb27-04.js"></script>
    </head>
    <body>
        <h1>window.closed Property</h1>
        <hr />
        <p>The new window might open behind this window.</p>
        <form id="newWinForm" name="newWinForm">
            <input id="openNewWin" name="openNewWin" type="button"
                    value="Open Window" />
            <br />
            <input id="closeNewWin" name="closeNewWin" type="button"
                    value="Close it if Still Open" />
        </form>
    </body>
</html>
```

JavaScript: jsb27-04.js

```javascript
// initialize when the page has loaded
addEvent(window, "load", initialize);

// global variables
    var oNewWinForm;
    var oOpenNewWin;
    var oCloseNewWin;

// initialize global var for new window object
// so it can be accessed by all functions on the page
var newWind;
```

continued

LISTING 27-4   *(continued)*

```
function initialize ()
{
   // get IE4+ or W3C DOM reference for an ID
   if (document.getElementById)
   {
      oNewWinForm = document.getElementById("newWinForm");
      oOpenNewWin = document.getElementById("openNewWin");
      oCloseNewWin = document.getElementById("closeNewWin");
   }
   else
   {
      oNewWinForm = document.newWinForm;
      oOpenNewWin = document.oNewWinForm.openNewWin;
      oCloseNewWin = document.oNewWinForm.closeNewWin;
   }
   addEvent(oOpenNewWin, 'click', newWindow);
   addEvent(oCloseNewWin, 'click', closeWindow);
}

// make the new window and put some stuff in it
function newWindow()
{
   newWind = window.open("","subwindow","height=200,width=200");
   setTimeout("finishNewWindow()", 100);
}
function finishNewWindow()
{
   var output = "";
   output += "<html><body><h1>A Sub-window</h1>";
   output += "<form><input type='button' value='Close Main Window'";
   output +="onclick='window.opener.close()'></form></body></html>";
   newWind.document.write(output);
   newWind.document.close();
}

// close subwindow
function closeWindow()
{
   if (newWind && !newWind.closed)
   {
      newWind.close();
   }
   else
   {
      alert("The window is no longer open");
   }
}
```

To complete the example of the window opening and closing, notice that the subwindow is given a button whose `onclick` event handler (bound in the `initialization()` function) closes the main window/tab. In some modern browsers, the user is presented with an alert asking to confirm the closure of the main browser window/tab. Other browsers simply ignore the request with, in some cases, a warning in the error console. Safari closes the main window/tab without any warning.

Related Items: `window.open()`, `window.close()` methods

components

(See `appCore`)

controllers

(See `appCore`)

crypto
pkcs11

Values: Object references   Read-Only

Compatibility: WinIE-, MacIE-, NN6+, Moz+, Safari-, Opera-, Chrome-

The `crypto` and `pkcs11` properties return references to browser objects that are relevant to internal public-key cryptography mechanisms. These subjects are beyond the scope of this book, but you can read more about Netscape's efforts on this front at `http://www.mozilla.org/projects/security/`.

defaultStatus

Value: String   Read/Write

Compatibility: WinIE3+, MacIE3+, NN2+, Moz+, Safari+, Opera+, Chrome-

After a document is loaded into a window or frame, the status bar's message field can display a string that is visible any time the mouse pointer is not atop an object that takes precedence over the status bar (such as a link object or an image map). The `window.defaultStatus` property is normally an empty string, but you can set this property at any time. Any setting of this property will be temporarily overridden when a user moves the mouse pointer on top of a link object (see `window.status` property for information about customizing this temporary status-bar message).

Probably the most common time to set the `window.defaultStatus` property is when a document loads into a window. You can do this as an immediate script statement that executes from the `head` or `body` portion of the document or as part of a document's `onload` event handler.

Example

Unless you plan to change the default status-bar text while a user spends time at your web page, the best time to set the property is when the document loads. In Listing 27-5, notice that we also read this property to reset the status bar in an `onmouseout` event handler. Setting the `status` property to empty also resets the status bar to the `defaultStatus` setting. When testing, remember that even though modern browsers support the `status` property, some of them do not display scripted status-bar text associated with links, in order to prevent link spoofing.

```
LISTING 27-5
```

Setting the Default Status Message

```html
<!DOCTYPE html>
<html>
    <head>
        <meta http-equiv="content-type" content="text/html;charset=utf-8">
        <title>window.defaultStatus property</title>
        <script type="text/javascript">
            window.defaultStatus = "Welcome to my Web site.";
        </script>
    </head>
    <body>
        <h1>window.defaultStatus property</h1>
        <hr />
        <p><a href="http://www.microsoft.com"
            onmouseover="window.status = 'Visit Microsoft\'s Home page.'; return true;"
            onmouseout="window.status = '';return true;">Microsoft</a>
        </p>
        <p><a href="http://mozilla.org"
            onmouseover="window.status = 'Visit Mozilla\'s Home page.'; return true;"
            onmouseout="window.status = window.defaultStatus;return true;">Mozilla</a>
        </p>
    </body>
</html>
```

If you need to display single or double quotes in the status bar (as in both links in Listing 27-5), use escape sequences (\' and \") as part of the strings being assigned to these properties.

Related Item: `window.status` property

dialogArguments

Value: Varies   Read-Only

Compatibility: WinIE4+, MacIE4+, NN-, Moz+, Safari+, Opera-, Chrome+

The `dialogArguments` property is available only in a window that is generated by the `showModalDialog()` or the IE-specific `showModelessDialog()` methods. Those methods allow a parameter to be passed to the dialog-box window, and the `dialogArguments` property lets the dialog box window's scripts access that parameter value. The value can be in the form of a string, number, or JavaScript array (convenient for passing multiple values).

Example

See Listing 27-36 for the `window.showModalDialog()` method, to see how arguments can be passed to a dialog box and retrieved via the `dialogArguments` property.

Related Items: `window.showModalDialog()`, `window.showModelessDialog()` methods

dialogHeight
dialogWidth

Value: String   Read/Write

Compatibility: WinIE4+, MacIE-, NN-, Moz-, Safari-, Opera-, Chrome-

Scripts in a document located inside a modal or IE-specific modeless dialog box (generated by showModalDialog() or showModelessDialog()) can read or modify the height and width of the dialog-box window via the dialogHeight and dialogWidth properties. Scripts can access these properties from the main window only for modeless dialog boxes, which remain visible while the user can control the main window contents.

Values for these properties are strings and include the unit of measure, the pixel (px).

Example

Dialog boxes sometimes provide a button or icon that reveals more details or more complex settings for advanced users. You can create a function that handles the toggle between two sizes. The following function assumes that the document in the dialog box has a button whose label also toggles between Show Details and Hide Details. The button's onclick event handler invokes the function as toggleDetails(this):

```
function toggleDetails(btn)
{
    if (dialogHeight == "200px")
    {
        dialogHeight = "350px";
        btn.value = "Hide Details";
    }
    else
    {
        dialogHeight = "200px";
        btn.value = "Show Details";
    }
}
```

In practice, you also have to toggle the display style sheet property of the extra material between none and block to make sure that the dialog box does not display scroll bars in the smaller dialog-box version.

Related Items: window.dialogLeft, window.dialogTop properties

dialogLeft
dialogTop

Value: String   Read/Write

Compatibility: WinIE4+, MacIE4+, NN-, Moz-, Safari-, Opera-, Chrome-

Scripts in a document located inside a modal or IE-specific modeless dialog box (generated by show-ModalDialog() or showModelessDialog()) can read or modify the left and top coordinates of the dialog-box window via the dialogLeft and dialogTop properties. Scripts can access these properties from the main window only for modeless dialog boxes, which remain visible while the user can control the main window contents.

Values for these properties are strings and include the unit of measure, the pixel (px). If you attempt to change these values so that any part of the dialog-box window would be outside the video monitor, the browser overrides the settings to keep the entire window visible.

Example

Although usually not a good idea because of the potentially jarring effect on a user, you can reposition a dialog-box window that has been resized by script (or by the user if you let the dialog box be resizable). The following statements in a dialog-box window document's script re-center the dialog-box window:

```
dialogLeft = (screen.availWidth/2) - (parseInt(dialogWidth)/2) + "px";
dialogHeight = (screen.availHeight/2) - (parseInt(dialogHeight)/2) + "px";
```

Note that the parseInt() functions are used to read the numeric portion of the dialogWidth and dialogHeight properties so that the values can be used for arithmetic.

Related Items: window.dialogHeight, window.dialogTopWidth properties

```
directories
locationbar
menubar
personalbar
scrollbars
statusbar
toolbar
```

Value: Object   Read/Write (with signed scripts)

Compatibility: WinIE-, MacIE-, NN4+, Moz+, Safari-, Opera-, Chrome-

Beyond the rectangle of the content region of a window (where your documents appear), the Netscape browser window displays an amalgam of bars and other features known collectively as *chrome*. All browsers can elect to remove these chrome items when creating a new window (as part of the third parameter of the window.open() method), but until signed scripts were available in Navigator 4, these items could not be turned on and off in the main browser window, or in any existing window.

Navigator 4 promoted these elements to first-class objects contained by the window object. Navigator 6 added one more feature, called the *directories bar* — a framelike device that can be opened or hidden from the left edge of the browser window. At the same time, however, NN6+/Mozilla browsers no longer permit hiding and showing the browser window's scroll bars. Chrome objects have but one property: visible. Reading this Boolean value (possible without signed scripts) lets you inspect the visitor's browser window for the elements currently engaged.

Changing the visibility of these items on the fly alters the relationship between the inner and outer dimensions of the browser window. If you must carefully size a window to display content, you should adjust the chrome elements before sizing the window. But before you start changing chrome visibility before the eyes of your page visitors, weigh the decision carefully. Experienced users have fine-tuned the look of their browser windows to just the way they like them. If you mess with that look, you may anger your visitors. Fortunately, changes you make to a chrome element's visibility are not stored to the user's preferences. However, the changes you make survive an unloading of the page. If you change the settings, be sure that you first save the initial settings and restore them with an `onunload` event handler.

Tip

The Macintosh menu bar is not part of the browser's window chrome. Therefore, its visibility cannot be adjusted from a script. ■

Example

In Listing 27-6, you can experiment with the look of a browser window with any of the chrome elements turned on or off. To run this script, you must either sign the scripts or turn on codebase principals (see Chapter 49, "Security and Netscape Signed Scripts," on the CD-ROM). Java must also be enabled to use the signed script statements.

As the page loads, it stores the current state of each chrome element. One button for each chrome element triggers the `toggleBar()` function. This function inverts the visible property for the chrome object passed as a parameter to the function. Finally, the Restore button returns the visibility properties to their original settings. Notice that the `restore()` function is also called by the `onunload` event handler for the document.

LISTING 27-6

Controlling Window Chrome

HTML: `jsb27-06.html`

```html
<!DOCTYPE html>
<html>
   <head>
      <meta http-equiv="content-type" content="text/html;charset=utf-8">
      <title>Bars Bars Bars</title>
      <script type="text/javascript" src="jsb27-06.js"></script>
   </head>
   <body onunload="restore()">
      <h1>Bars Bars Bars</h1>
      <hr />
      <form>
         <b>Toggle Window Bars</b>
         <br />
         <input type="button" value="Location Bar"
                onclick="toggleBar(window.locationbar)" />
         <br />
         <input type="button" value="Menu Bar"
                onclick="toggleBar(window.menubar)" />
         <br />
         <input type="button" value="Personal Bar"
                onclick="toggleBar(window.personalbar)" />
         <br />
         <input type="button" value="Scrollbars"
                onclick="toggleBar(window.scrollbars)" />
         <br />
         <input type="button" value="Status Bar"
```

continued

LISTING 27-6   *(continued)*

```
                onclick="toggleBar(window.statusbar)" />
        <br />
        <input type="button" value="Tool Bar"
                onclick="toggleBar(window.toolbar)" />
        <br />
        <hr />
        <input type="button" value="Restore Original Settings"
                onclick="restore()" />
    </form>
  </body>
</html>
```

JavaScript: jsb27-06.js

```
// store original outer dimensions as page loads
var originalLocationbar = window.locationbar.visible;
var originalMenubar = window.menubar.visible;
var originalPersonalbar = window.personalbar.visible;
var originalScrollbars = window.scrollbars.visible;
var originalStatusbar = window.statusbar.visible;
var originalToolbar = window.toolbar.visible;

// generic function to set inner dimensions
function toggleBar(bar)
{
   netscape.security.PrivilegeManager.enablePrivilege("UniversalBrowserWrite");
   bar.visible = !bar.visible;
   netscape.security.PrivilegeManager.revertPrivilege("UniversalBrowserWrite");
}
// restore settings
function restore()
{
   netscape.security.PrivilegeManager.enablePrivilege("UniversalBrowserWrite");
   window.locationbar.visible = originalLocationbar;
   window.menubar.visible = originalMenubar;
   window.personalbar.visible = originalPersonalbar;
   window.scrollbars.visible = originalScrollbars;
   window.statusbar.visible = originalStatusbar;
   window.toolbar.visible = originalToolbar;
   netscape.security.PrivilegeManager.revertPrivilege("UniversalBrowserWrite");
}
```

Related Item: window.open() method

document

Value: Object   Read-Only

Compatibility: WinIE3+, MacIE3+, NN2+, Moz+, Safari+, Opera+, Chrome+

We list the `document` property here primarily for completeness. Each `window` object contains a single `document` object. The value of the `document` property is the `document` object, which is not a displayable value. Instead, you use the `document` property as you build references to properties and methods of the document and to other objects contained by the document, such as a form and its elements. To load a different document into a window, use the `location` object (see Chapter 28, "Location and History Objects"). The `document` object is described in detail in Chapter 29, "Document and Body Objects."

Related Item: `document` object

event
Event

Value: Object   Read/Write

Compatibility: WinIE4+, MacIE4+, NN+, Moz+, Safari 1+, Opera+, Chrome+

IE4+ treats the `event` object as a property of the `window` object. The W3C DOM passes an instance of the `Event` object as an argument to event handler functions. The connection with the `window` object is relatively inconsequential because all action involving the `event` object occurs in event handler functions. The only difference is that the object can be treated as a more global object when one event handler function invokes another. Instead of having to pass the `event` object parameter to the next function, functions can access the `event` object directly (with or without the `window.` prefix in the reference).

For complete details about the `event` object in all browsers, see Chapter 32, "Event Objects."

Related Item: `event` object

external

Value: Object   Read-Only

Compatibility: WinIE4+, MacIE-, NN-, Moz+, Safari-, Opera-, Chrome-

The `external` property is useful only when the browser window is a component in another application. The property provides a gateway between the current browser window and the application that acts as a host to the browser window component.

With WinIE4+ acting as a component to the host operating system, the `external` property can be used to access several methods that influence behaviors outside the browser. Perhaps the three most useful methods to regular web-page scripters are `AddDesktopComponent()`, `AddFavorite()`, and `NavigateAndFind()`. The first two methods display the same kind of alert dialog box that users get after making these choices from the browser or desktop menus, so that you won't be able to sneak your web site onto desktops or Favorites listings without the visitor's approval. IE7 and Firefox2+ allow `AddSearchProvider()` for installing search plug-ins. As with the first two methods, an alert is displayed asking the user permission to install the search plug-in. You can find information about OpenSearch and the format for the XML file passed to the method at `http://www.opensearch.org/Specifications/OpenSearch/1.1`. Table 27-2 describes the parameters for these methods.

TABLE 27-2

Popular window.external Object Methods

Method	Description
AddDesktopComponent("URL", "type"[, left, top, width, height])	Adds a web site or image to the Active Desktop (if turned on in the user's copy of Windows). The type parameter value is either website or image. Dimensional parameters (optional) are all integer values.
AddFavorite("URL"[, "title"])	Adds the specified URL to the user's Favorites list. The optional title string parameter is how the URL should be listed in the menu (if missing, the URL appears in the list).
AddSearchProvider("URL")	Adds the search provider, specified in the URL with an OpenSearchDescription XML file.
NavigateAndFind("URL", "findString", "target")	Navigates to the URL in the first parameter and opens the page in the target frame (an empty string opens in the current frame). The findString is text to be searched for on that page and highlighted when the page loads.

Example

The first example asks the user whether it is okay to add a web site to the Active Desktop. If Active Desktop is not enabled, the user is given the choice of enabling it at this point:

```
external.AddDesktopComponent("http://www.nytimes.com","website", 200,
    100, 400, 400);
```

In the next example, the user is asked to approve the addition of a URL to the Favorites list. The user can follow the normal procedure for filing the item in a folder in the list:

```
external.AddFavorite("http://www.dannyg.com/support/update13.html",
    "JSBible 6 Support Center");
```

The final example assumes that a user makes a choice from a select list of items. The onchange event handler of the select list invokes the following function to navigate to a fictitious page and locate listings for a chosen sports team on the page:

```
function locate(list)
{
    var choice = list.options[list.selectedIndex].value;
    external.NavigateAndFind("http://www.collegesports.net/scores.html",
        choice, "scores");
}
```

frameElement

Values: frame or iframe object reference   Read-Only

Compatibility: WinIE5.5+, MacIE-, NN7+, Moz1.0.1+, Safari 1.2+, Opera+, Chrome+

If the current window exists as a result of a `<frame>` or `<iframe>` tag, the window's `frameEle-ment` property returns a reference to the hosting element. As is made clear in the discussion about the `frame` element object later in this chapter, a reference to a `frame` or `iframe` element object provides access to the properties that echo the attributes of the HTML element object. For a window that is not part of a frameset, the `frameElement` property returns `null`.

The convenience of this property becomes apparent when a single document is loaded into multiple framesets. A script in the document can still refer to the containing `frame` element, even when the ID of the element changes from one frameset to another. The `frameset` element is also accessible via the `parentElement` property of the `frameElement` property:

```
var frameSetObj = self.frameElement.parentElement;
```

A reference to the `frameset` element opens possibilities for adjusting frame sizes.

Related Items: `frame`, `iframe` objects

frames

Value: Array   Read-Only

Compatibility: WinIE3+, MacIE3+, NN2+, Moz+, Safari+, Opera+, Chrome+

In a multiframe window, the top or parent window contains any number of separate frames, each of which acts as a full-fledged `window` object. The `frames` property (note the plural use of the word as a property name) plays a role when a statement must reference an object located in a different frame. For example, if a button in one frame is scripted to load a document in another frame, the button's event handler must be able to tell JavaScript precisely where to display the new HTML document. The `frames` property assists in that task.

To use the `frames` property to communicate from one frame to another, it should be part of a reference that begins with the `parent` or `top` property. This lets JavaScript make the proper journey through the hierarchy of all currently loaded objects to reach the desired object. To find out how many frames are currently active in a window, use this expression:

```
parent.frames.length
```

This expression returns a number indicating how many frames the parent window defines. This value does not, however, count further nested frames, should a third generation of frame be defined in the environment. In other words, no single property exists that you can use to determine the total number of frames in the browser window if multiple generations of frames are present.

The browser stores information about all visible frames in a numbered (indexed) array, with the first frame (that is, the topmost `<frame>` tag defined in the framesetting document) as number 0:

```
parent.frames[0]
```

Therefore, if the window shows three frames (whose indexes are `frames[0]`, `frames[1]`, and `frames[2]`, respectively), the reference for retrieving the `title` property of the document in the second frame is

```
parent.frames[1].document.title
```

This reference is a road map that starts at the parent window and extends to the second frame's document and its `title` property. Other than the number of frames defined in a parent window and each frame's name (`top.frames[i].name`), no values from the frame definitions are directly available from the frame object via scripting until you get to IE4 and NN6/Moz/W3C (see the `frame` element object later in this chapter). In these browsers, individual `frame` element objects have several properties that reveal `<frame>` tag attributes.

Using index values for frame references is not always the safest tactic, however, because your frameset design may change over time, in which case the index values will also change. Instead, you should take advantage of the `name` attribute of the `<frame>` tag, and assign a unique, descriptive name to each frame. A value you assign to the `name` attribute is also the name that you use for `target` attributes of links in order to force a linked page to load in a frame other than the one containing the link. You can use a frame's name as an alternative to the indexed reference. For example, in Listing 27-7, two frames are assigned distinctive names. To access the title of a document in the `JustAKid2` frame, the complete object reference is

```
parent.JustAKid2.document.title
```

with the frame name (case sensitive) substituting for the `frames[1]` array reference. Or, in keeping with JavaScript flexibility, you can use the object name in the array index position:

```
parent.frames["JustAKid2"].document.title
```

The supreme advantage to using frame names in references is that no matter how the frameset structure may change over time, a reference to a named frame will always find that frame, even though its index value (that is, its position in the frameset) may change.

Example

Listing 27-7 and Listing 27-8 demonstrate how JavaScript treats values of frame references from objects inside a frame. The same document is loaded into each frame. A script in that document extracts information about the current frame and the entire frameset.

LISTING 27-7

Framesetting Document for Listing 27-8

```
<!DOCTYPE html>
<html>
   <head>
      <meta http-equiv="content-type" content="text/html;charset=utf-8">
<title>window.frames property</title>
   </head>
   <frameset cols="50%,50%">
      <frame name="JustAKid1" src="jsb27-08.html" />
      <frame name="JustAKid2" src="jsb27-08.html" />
   </frameset>
</html>
```

A call to determine the number (length) of frames returns 0, from the point of view of the current frame referenced. That's because each frame here is a window that has no nested frames within it. But add the `parent` property to the reference, and the scope zooms out to take into account all frames generated by the parent window's document.

LISTING 27-8

Showing Various Window Properties

```html
<!DOCTYPE html>
<html>
    <head>
        <meta http-equiv="content-type" content="text/html;charset=utf-8">
        <title>Window Revealer II</title>
        <script type="text/javascript">
            function gatherWindowData()
            {
                var msg = "";
                msg += "<p><b>From the point of view of this frame:</b><br />";
                msg += "window.frames.length: " + window.frames.length + "<br />";
                msg += "window.name: " + window.name + "</p>";
                msg += "<p><b>From the point of view of the framesetting ↵
                            document:</b><br />";
                msg += "parent.frames.length: " + parent.frames.length + "<br />";
                msg += "parent.frames[0].name: " + parent.frames[0].name + "</p>";
                return msg;
            }
        </script>
    </head>
    <body>
        <script type="text/javascript">
            document.write(gatherWindowData());
        </script>
    </body>
</html>
```

The last statement in the example shows how to use the array syntax (brackets) to refer to a specific frame. All array indexes start with 0 for the first entry. Because the document asks for the name of the first frame (parent.frames[0]), the response is JustAKid1 for both frames.

Related Items: frame, frameset objects; window.parent, window.top properties

fullScreen

Values: Boolean   Read-Only

Compatibility: WinIE-, MacIE-, NN7.1+, Moz1.4+, Safari-, Opera-, Chrome-

The intent of the fullScreen property is to indicate whether the browser is in full-screen mode, which can be set in Mozilla browsers through the Full Screen command in the View menu. Unfortunately, the property isn't reliable (as of Mozilla 1.8.1) and always returns false, regardless of the browser's actual full-screen setting.

history

Value: Object   Read-Only

Compatibility: WinIE3+, MacIE3+, NN2+, Moz+, Safari+, Opera+, Chrome+

windowObject.innerHeight

(See the discussion of the `history` object in Chapter 28, "Location and History Objects.")

```
innerHeight
innerWidth
outerHeight
outerWidth
```

Value: Integer   Read/Write (see text)

Compatibility: WinIE-, MacIE-, NN4+, Moz+, Safari+, Opera+, Chrome+

NN4+/Moz/WebKit- and Presto-based browers let scripts adjust the height and width of any window, including the main browser window, by setting properties. This adjustment can be helpful if your page shows itself best with the browser window sized to a particular height and width. Rather than relying on the user to size the browser window for optimum viewing of your page, you can dictate the size of the window (although the user can always resize the main window manually). And because you can examine the operating system of the visitor via the `navigator` object (see Chapter 42), you can size a window to adjust for the differences in font and form element rendering on different platforms.

Supporting browsers provide two different points of reference for measuring the height and width of a window: inner and outer. Both are measured in pixels. The inner measurements are that of the active document area of a window (sometimes known as a window's content region). If the optimum display of your document depends on the document display area being a certain number of pixels high and/or wide, the `innerHeight` and `innerWidth` properties are the ones to set.

By contrast, the outer measurements reference the outside boundary of the entire window, including whatever chrome is showing in the window: scroll bars, status bar, and so on. Setting the `outerHeight` and `outerWidth` is generally done in concert with a reading of `screen` object properties (see Chapter 42). Perhaps the most common use of the outer properties is to set the browser window to fill the available screen area of the visitor's monitor.

A more efficient way of modifying both outer dimensions of a window is with the `window.resizeTo()` method, which is also available in IE4+. The method takes pixel width and height (as integer values) as parameters, thus accomplishing a window resizing in one statement. Be aware that resizing a window does not adjust the location of a window. Therefore, just because you set the outer dimensions of a window to the available space returned by the `screen` object, you can't count on the window suddenly filling the available space on the monitor. Application of the `window.moveTo()` method is necessary to ensure that the top-left corner of the window is at screen coordinates 0,0.

Despite the freedom that these properties afford the page author, Netscape and Mozilla-based browsers have built in a minimum size limitation for scripts that are not cryptographically signed. You cannot set these properties such that the outer height and width of the window is smaller than 100 pixels on a side. This limitation is to prevent an unsigned script from setting up a small or nearly invisible window that monitors activity in other windows. With signed scripts, however, windows can be made smaller than 100×100 pixels, with the user's permission. IE4+ maintains a smaller minimum size to prevent resizing a window to zero size.

Caution

Users may dislike your scripts messing with their browser window sizes and positions. NN7+/Moz/WebKit- and Presto-based browsers do not allow scripts to resize windows unless the script is signed. ∎

Example

In Listing 27-9, several buttons let you see the results of setting the `innerHeight`, `innerWidth`, `outerHeight`, and `outerWidth` properties. Safari ignores scripted adjustments to these properties, whereas Mozilla users can set preferences that prevent scripts from moving and resizing windows.

LISTING 27-9

Setting Window Height and Width

HTML: jsb27-09.html

```html
<!DOCTYPE html>
<html>
    <head>
        <meta http-equiv="content-type" content="text/html;charset=utf-8">
        <title>Window Sizer</title>
        <script type="text/javascript" src="jsb27-09.js"></script>
    </head>
    <body>
        <h1>Window Sizer</h1>
        <hr />
        <form>
            <b>Setting Inner Sizes</b><br />
            <input type="button" value="600 Pixels Square"
                    onclick="setInner(600,600)" /><br />
            <input type="button" value="300 Pixels Square"
                    onclick="setInner(300,300)" /><br />
            <input type="button" value="Available Screen Space"
                    onclick="setInner(screen.availWidth, screen.availHeight)" /><br />
            <hr />
            <b>Setting Outer Sizes</b><br />
            <input type="button" value="600 Pixels Square"
                    onclick="setOuter(600,600)" /><br />
            <input type="button" value="300 Pixels Square"
                    onclick="setOuter(300,300)" /><br />
            <input type="button" value="Available Screen Space"
                    onclick="setOuter(screen.availWidth, screen.availHeight)" /><br />
            <hr />
            <input type="button" value="Cinch up for Win95"
                    onclick="setInner(273,304)" /><br />
            <input type="button" value="Cinch up for Mac"
                    onclick="setInner(273,304)" /><br />
            <input type="button" value="Restore Original"
                    onclick="restore()" /><br />
        </form>
    </body>
</html>
```

continued

windowObject.location

LISTING 27-9   *(continued)*

```
JavaScript: jsb27-09.js

// store original outer dimensions as page loads
var originalWidth = window.outerWidth;
var originalHeight = window.outerHeight;
alert("original dimensions: \nwindow.outerWidth="
      + window.outerWidth
      + ". \nwindow.outerHeight ="
      + window.outerHeight
      + ". \nwindow.innerWidth = "
      + window.innerWidth
      + ". \nwindow.outerHeight = "
      + window.outerHeight);

// generic function to set inner dimensions
function setInner(width, height)
{
   window.innerWidth = width;
   window.innerHeight = height;
}

// generic function to set outer dimensions
function setOuter(width, height)
{
   window.outerWidth = width;
   window.outerHeight = height;
}

// restore window to original dimensions
function restore()
{
   window.outerWidth = originalWidth;
   window.outerHeight = originalHeight;
}
```

Related Items: window.resizeTo(), window.moveTo() methods; screen object; navigator object

location

Value: Object   Read/Write

Compatibility: WinIE3+, MacIE3+, NN2+, Moz+, Safari+, Opera+, Chrome+

(See the discussion of the location object in Chapter 28, "Location and History Objects.")

locationbar

(See directories)

name

Value: String   Read/Write

Compatibility: WinIE3+, MacIE3+, NN2+, Moz+, Safari+, Opera+, Chrome+

All window objects can have names assigned to them. Names are particularly useful for working with frames, because a good naming scheme for a multiframe environment can help you determine precisely which frame you're working with in references coming from other frames.

The main browser window, however, has no name attached to it by default. Its value is an empty string. There aren't many reasons to assign a name to the window, because JavaScript and HTML provide plenty of other ways to refer to the window object (the top property, the _top constant for target attributes, and the opener property from subwindows).

If you want to attach a name to the main window, you can do so by setting the window.name property at any time. But be aware that because this is one window property whose life extends beyond the loading and unloading of any given document, chances are that your scripts would use the reference in only one document or frameset. Unless you restore the default empty string, your programmed window name will be present for any other document that loads later. Our suggestion in this regard is to assign a name in a window's or frameset's onload event handler and then reset it to empty in a corresponding onunload event handler:

```
<body onload="self.name = 'Main'" onunload="self.name = ''">
```

You can see an example of this application in Listing 27-15, where setting a parent window name is helpful for learning the relationships between parent and child windows.

Related Items: top property; window.open(), window.sizeToContent() methods

navigator

Value: Object   Read-Only

Compatibility: WinIE4+, MacIE4+, NN6+, Moz+, Safari+, Opera+, Chrome+

Although the navigator object appears as a property of the window object only in modern browsers, this object has been around since the very beginning (see Chapter 42). In previous browsers, the navigator object was referenced as a stand-alone object. And because you can omit any reference to the window object for a window object's properties, you can use the same windowless reference syntax for compatibility across all scriptable browsers (at least for the navigator object properties that exist across all browsers). That's the way we recommend referring to the navigator object.

Example

This book is littered with examples of using the navigator object, primarily for performing browser detection. You can find examples of specific navigator object properties in Chapter 42.

Related Item: navigator object

netscape

Value: Object   Read-Only

Compatibility: WinIE-, MacIE-, NN3+, Moz+, Safari-, Opera-, Chrome-

Given its name, you might think that the `netscape` property somehow works in tandem with the `navigator` property, but this is not the case. The `netscape` property is unique to NN/Moz browsers and provides access to functionality that is specific to the Netscape family of browsers, such as the privilege manager.

Example

The `netscape` property is commonly used as a means of accessing the NN/Moz-specific `PrivilegeManager` object to enable or disable security privileges. Following is an example of how this access is carried out:

```
netscape.security.PrivilegeManager.enablePrivilege("UniversalBrowserRead");
```

offscreenBuffering

Value: Boolean or string   Read/Write

Compatibility: WinIE4+, MacIE4+, NN-, Moz-, Safari 1.2+, Opera-, Chrome+

IE4+/Safari 1.2+ by default initially render a page in a buffer (a chunk of memory) before it is blasted to the video screen. You can control this behavior explicitly by modifying the `window.offscreenBuffering` property.

The default value of the property is the string `auto`. You can also assign Boolean `true` or `false` to the property to override the normal automatic handling of this behavior.

Example

If you want to turn off buffering for an entire page, include the following statement at the beginning of your script statements:

```
window.offscreenBuffering = false;
```

onerror

Value: Function   Read/Write

Compatibility: WinIE4+, MacIE4+, NN3+, Moz+, Safari-, Opera-, Chrome-

The `onerror` property is an exception to this book's rule of not describing event handlers as properties within object reference sections. The reason is that the `onerror` event brings along some special properties that are useful to control by setting the event handler property in scripts.

Modern browsers (IE5+, NN4+, and W3C) are designed to prevent script errors from being intrusive if a user encounters a script error while loading or interacting with a page. But even the subtle hints about problems (messages or icons in the status bar) can be confusing for users who have no idea what JavaScript is. JavaScript lets you turn off the display of script error windows or messages as someone executes a script on your page. The question is: When should you turn off these messages?

Script errors generally mean that something is wrong with your script. The error may be the result of a coding mistake or, conceivably, a bug in JavaScript (perhaps on a platform version of the browser that you haven't been able to test). If such errors occur, often the script won't continue to do what you intended. Hiding the script error from yourself during development would be foolhardy, because you'd never know whether unseen errors are lurking in your code. It can be equally dangerous to turn off error dialog boxes for users who may believe that the page is operating normally, when in fact it's not. Some data values may not be calculated or displayed correctly.

That said, we can see some limited instances of when you may want to keep such dialog-box windows from appearing. For example, if you know for a fact that a platform-specific bug trips the error message without harming the execution of the script, you may want to prevent that error alert dialog box from appearing in the files posted to your web site. You should do this only after extensive testing to ensure that the script ultimately behaves correctly, even with the bug or error.

Note

IE fires the `onerror` event handler only for runtime errors. This means that if you have a syntactical error in your script that trips the browser as the page loads, the `onerror` event doesn't fire, and you cannot trap that error message. Moreover, if the user has the IE script debugger installed, any code you use to prevent browser error messages from appearing will not work. ■

When the browser starts, the `window.onerror` property is `<undefined>`. In this state, all errors are reported via the normal JavaScript error window or message. To turn off error alerts, set the `window.onerror` property to invoke a function that does absolutely nothing:

```
function doNothing() { return true; }
window.onerror = doNothing;
```

To restore the error messages, reload the page.

You can, however, also assign a custom function to the `window.onerror` property. This function then handles errors in a more friendly way under your script control. Whenever error messages are turned on (the default behavior), a script error (or Java applet or class exception) invokes the function assigned to the `onerror` property, passing three parameters:

- Error message
- URL of the document causing the error
- Line number of the error

You can essentially trap for all errors and handle them with your own interface (or no user notification at all). The last statement of this function must be `return true` if you do not want the JavaScript script error message to appear.

If you are using the NPAPI to communicate with a Java applet directly from your scripts, you can use the same scheme to handle any exception that Java may throw. A Java exception is not necessarily a mistake kind of error: Some methods assume that the Java code will trap for exceptions to handle special cases — for example, reacting to a user's denial of access when prompted by a signed script dialog box. See Chapter 47, "Scripting Java Applets and Plug-Ins" (on the CD-ROM), for an example of trapping for a specific Java exception. Also, see Chapter 21, "Control Stuctures and Exception Handling," for JavaScript exception handling introduced for W3C DOM–compatible browsers.

Example

In Listing 27-10, one button triggers a script that contains an error. We added an error-handling function to process the error so that it opens a separate window and fills in a `textarea` form element (see Figure 27-4). A Submit button is also provided to mail the bug information to a support center email address — an example of how to handle the occurrence of a bug in your scripts.

windowObject.**onerror**

FIGURE 27-4

An example of a self-reporting error window.

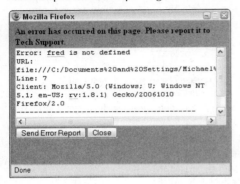

LISTING 27-10

Controlling Script Errors

HTML: jsb27-10.html

```html
<!DOCTYPE html>
<html>
    <head>
        <meta http-equiv="content-type" content="text/html;charset=utf-8">
        <title>Error Dialog Control</title>
        <script type="text/javascript" src="jsb27-10.js"></script>
    </head>
    <body>
        <h1>Error Dialog Control</h1>
        <hr />
        <form name="myform">
            <input type="button" value="Cause an Error" onclick="goWrong()" />
            <p><input type="button" value="Turn Off Error Dialogs"
                    onclick="errOff()" />
                <input type="button" value="Turn On Error Dialogs"
                    onclick="errOn()" />
            </p>
        </form>
    </body>
</html>
```

JavaScript: jsb27-10.js

```javascript
// function with invalid variable value
function goWrong()
{
    var x = fred;
```

```
}
// turn off error dialogs
function errOff()
{
    window.onerror = doNothing;
}
// turn on error dialogs with hard reload
function errOn()
{
    window.onerror = handleError;
}

// assign default error handler
window.onerror = handleError;

// error handler when errors are turned off...prevents error dialog
function doNothing() { return true; }

function handleError(msg, URL, lineNum)
{
    var errWind = window.open("","errors","height=270,width=400");
    var wintxt = "<html><body bgcolor=red>";
    wintxt += "<b>An error has occurred on this page. "
            + "Please report it to Tech Support.</b>";
    wintxt += "<form method=POST enctype='text/plain' "
            + "action=mailTo:support4@dannyg.com >";
    wintxt += "<textarea name='errMsg' cols=45 rows=8 wrap=VIRTUAL>";
    wintxt += "Error: "
            + msg + "\n";
    wintxt += "URL: "
            + URL + "\n";
    wintxt += "Line: "
            + lineNum + "\n";
    wintxt += "Client: "
            + navigator.userAgent + "\n";
    wintxt += "-----------------------------------------\n";
    wintxt += "Please describe what you were doing when the error occurred:";
    wintxt += "</textarea><br />";
    wintxt += "<input type=SUBMIT value='Send Error Report'>";
    wintxt += "<input type=button value='Close' onclick='self.close()'>";
    wintxt += "</form></body></html>";
    errWind.document.write(wintxt);
    errWind.document.close();
    return true;
}
```

We provide a button that performs a hard reload, which in turn resets the `window.onerror` property to its default value. With error dialog boxes turned off, the error handling function does not run.

Related Items: `location.reload()` method; JavaScript exception handling (Chapter 21, "Control Structures and Exception Handling"); debugging scripts (Chapter 48, "Debugging Scripts," on the CD-ROM)

opener

Value: Window object reference

Read/Write

Compatibility: WinIE3+, MacIE3+, NN3+, Moz+, Safari+, Opera+, Chrome+

Many scripters make the mistake of thinking that a new browser window created with the `window.open()` method has a child-parent relationship similar to the one that frames have with their parents. That's not the case at all. New browser windows, when created, have a very slim link to the window from whence they came: via the `opener` property. The purpose of the `opener` property is to provide scripts in the new window with a valid reference back to the original window. For example, the original window may contain some variable values or general-purpose functions that a new window at this web site wants to use. The original window may also have form elements whose settings are of value to the new window, or that get set by user interaction in the new window.

Because the value of the `opener` property is a reference to a genuine `window` object, you can begin references with the property name. Or, you may use the more complete `window.opener` or `self.opener` reference. But then the reference must include some object or property of that original window, such as a window method or a reference to something contained by that window's document.

If a subwindow opens yet another subwindow, the chain is still valid, albeit one step longer. The third window can reach the main window with a reference that begins

```
opener.opener....
```

It's a good idea for the third window to store in a global variable the value of `opener.opener` while the page loads. Then, if the user closes the second window, the variable can be used to start a reference to the main window.

When a script that generates a new window is within a frame, the `opener` property of the subwindow points to that frame. Therefore, if the subwindow needs to communicate with the main window's parent or another frame in the main window, you have to very carefully build a reference to that distant object. For example, if the subwindow needs to get the `checked` property of a checkbox in a sister frame of the one that created the subwindow, the reference is

```
opener.parent.sisterFrameName.document.formName.checkboxName.checked
```

It is a long way to go, indeed, but building such a reference is always a case of mapping out the path from where the script is, to where the destination is, step by step.

Example

To demonstrate the importance of the `opener` property, take a look at how a new window can define itself from settings in the main window (see Listing 27-11). The `doNew()` function generates a small subwindow and loads the file in Listing 27-12 into the window. Notice the initial conditional statements in `doNew()` that make sure that if the new window already exists, it comes to the front, by invoking the new window's `focus()` method.

LISTING 27-11

Contents of a Main Window Document That Generates a Second Window

HTML: jsb27-11.html

```html
<!DOCTYPE html>
<html>
   <head>
      <meta http-equiv="content-type" content="text/html;charset=utf-8">
      <title>Master of all Windows</title>
      <script type="text/javascript" src="jsb27-11.js"></script>
   </head>
   <body>
      <form name="input">
         Select a color for a new window:
         <input type="radio" name="color" value="red" checked="checked" />Red
         <input type="radio" name="color" value="yellow" />Yellow
         <input type="radio" name="color" value="blue" />Blue
         <input type="button" name="storage" value="Make a Window" onclick="doNew()"/>
         <hr />
         This field will be filled from an entry in another window:
         <input type="text" name="entry" size="25" />
      </form>
   </body>
</html>
```

JavaScript: jsb27-11.js

```javascript
var myWind;
function doNew()
{
   if (!myWind || myWind.closed)
   {
      myWind = window.open("jsb27-12.html","subWindow","height=200, ↵
            width=350,resizable");
   }
   else
   {
      // bring existing subwindow to the front
      myWind.focus();
   }
}
```

LISTING 27-12

References to the opener Property

HTML: jsb27-12.html

```html
<!DOCTYPE html>
<html>
   <head>
      <meta http-equiv="content-type" content="text/html;charset=utf-8">
      <title>New Window on the Block</title>
      <script type="text/javascript" src="jsb27-12.js"></script>
      <script type="text/javascript">
         document.write("<body bgcolor='" + getColor() + "'>")
      </script>
   </head>
   <body>
      <form>
         <input type="button" value="Who's in the Main window?"
                onclick="alert(self.opener.document.title)" />
         <p>Type text here for the main window:
            <input type="text" size="25"
                   onchange="self.opener.document.forms[0].entry.value ↵
                   = this.value" />
         </p>
      </form>
   </body>
</html>
```

JavaScript: jsb27-12.js

```javascript
function getColor()
{
   // shorten the reference
   colorButtons = self.opener.document.forms[0].color;
   // see which radio button is checked
   for (var i = 0; i < colorButtons.length; i++)
   {
      if (colorButtons[i].checked)
      {
         return colorButtons[i].value;
      }
   }
   return "white";
}
```

In the `getColor()` function, the multiple references to the radio-button array can be very long. To simplify the references, the `getColor()` function starts by assigning the radio-button array to a variable we arbitrarily call `colorButtons`. That shorthand now stands in for lengthy references as we loop through the radio buttons to determine which button is checked, and retrieve its value property.

A button in the second window simply fetches the title of the opener window's document. Even if another document loads in the main window in the meantime, the `opener` reference still points to the main window: Its `document` object, however, will change.

Finally, the second window contains a text input object. Enter any text there that you like and then either tab or click out of the field. The `onchange` event handler updates the field in the opener's document (provided that the document is still loaded).

Related Items: `window.open()`, `window.focus()` methods

outerHeight
outerWidth

(See `innerHeight` and `innerWidth`, earlier in this chapter)

pageXOffset
pageYOffset

Value: Integer   Read-Only

Compatibility: WinIE-, MacIE-, NN4+, Moz+, Safari+, Opera+, Chrome+

The top-left corner of the content (inner) region of the browser window is an important geographical point for scrolling documents. When a document is scrolled all the way to the top and flush left in the window (or when a document is small enough to fill the browser window without displaying scroll bars), the document's location is said to be `0,0`, meaning zero pixels from the top and zero pixels from the left. If you were to scroll the document, some other coordinate point of the document would be under that top-left corner. That measure is called the *page offset,* and the `pageXOffset` and `pageYOffset` properties let you read the pixel value of the document at the inner window's top-left corner: `pageXOffset` is the horizontal offset, and `pageYOffset` is the vertical offset.

The value of these measures becomes clear if you design navigation buttons in your pages to carefully control paging of content being displayed in the window. For example, you might have a two-frame page in which one of the frames features navigation controls and the other displays the primary content. The navigation controls take the place of scroll bars, which, for aesthetic reasons, are turned off in the display frame. Scripts connected to the simulated scrolling buttons can determine the `pageYOffset` value of the document, and then use the `window.scrollTo()` method to position the document precisely to the next logical division in the document for viewing.

IE has corresponding values as `body` object properties: `body.scrollLeft` and `body.scrollTop` (see Chapter 29).

Related Items: `window.innerHeight`, `window.innerWidth`, `body.scrollLeft`, `body.scrollTop` properties; `window.scrollBy()`, `window.scrollTo()` methods

parent

Value: Window object reference   Read-Only

Compatibility: WinIE3+, MacIE3+, NN2+, Moz+, Safari+, Opera+,Chrome+

The `parent` property (and the `top` property, discussed later in this section) comes into play primarily when a document is to be displayed as part of a multiframe window. The HTML documents that users see in the frames of a multiframe browser window are distinct from the document that specifies the frameset for the entire window. That document, though still in the browser's memory (and appearing as the URL in the location field of the browser), is not otherwise visible to the user (except in source view).

If scripts in your visible documents need to reference objects or properties of the frameset window, you can reference those frameset window items with the `parent` property. (Do not, however, expand the reference by preceding it with the `window` object, as in `window.parent.propertyName`, because this causes problems in early browsers.) In a way, the `parent` property seems to violate the object hierarchy because, from a single frame's document, the property points to a level seemingly higher in precedence. If you didn't specify the `parent` property, or instead specified the `self` property from one of these framed documents, the object reference is to the frame only, rather than to the outermost framesetting `window` object.

A nontraditional but perfectly legal way to use the `parent` object is as a means of storing temporary variables. Thus, you could set up a holding area for individual variable values, or even an array of data. Then these values can be shared among all documents loaded into the frames, even when documents change inside the frames. You have to be careful, however, when storing data in the parent on the fly (that is, in response to user action in the frames). In early browsers, variables can revert to their default values (the values set by the parent's own script) if the user resizes the window.

A child window can also call a function defined in the parent window. The reference for such a function is

```
parent.functionName([parameters])
```

At first glance, it may seem as though the `parent` and `top` properties point to the same framesetting `window` object. In an environment consisting of one frameset window and its immediate children, that's true. But if one of the child windows was itself another framesetting window, you wind up with three generations of windows. From the point of view of the youngest child (for example, a window defined by the second frameset), the `parent` property points to its immediate parent, whereas the `top` property points to the first framesetting window in this chain.

On the other hand, a new window created via the `window.open()` method has no parent–child relationship to the original window. The new window's `top` and `parent` point to that new window. You can read more about these relationships in the "Frames" section earlier in this chapter.

Example

To demonstrate how various `window` object properties refer to window levels in a multiframe environment, use your browser to load the Listing 27-13 document. It in turn sets each of two equal-size frames to the same document: Listing 27-14. This document extracts the values of several window properties, plus the `document.title` properties of two different window references.

LISTING 27-13

Framesetting Document for Listing 27-14

```html
<!DOCTYPE html>
<html>
   <head>
      <meta http-equiv="content-type" content="text/html;charset=utf-8">
      <title>The Parent Property Example</title>
      <script type="text/javascript">
         self.name = "Framesetter";
      </script>
   </head>
   <frameset cols="50%,50%" onunload="self.name = ''">
      <frame name="JustAKid1" src="jsb27-14.html" />
      <frame name="JustAKid2" src="jsb27-14.html" />
   </frameset>
</html>
```

LISTING 27-14

Revealing Various Window-Related Properties

```html
<!DOCTYPE html>
<html>
   <head>
      <meta http-equiv="content-type" content="text/html;charset=utf-8">
      <title>Window Revealer II</title>
      <script type="text/javascript">
         function gatherWindowData()
         {
            var msg = "";
            msg += "top name: "
               + top.name + "<br />";
            msg += "parent name: "
               + parent.name + "<br />";
            msg += "parent.document.title: "
               + parent.document.title + "<br />";
            msg += "window name: "
               + window.name + "<br />";
            msg += "self name: "
               + self.name + "<br />";
            msg += "self.document.title: "
               + self.document.title;
            return msg;
         }
      </script>
   </head>
```

continued

LISTING 27-14   *(continued)*

```
<body>
    <script type="text/javascript">
        document.write(gatherWindowData());
    </script>
</body>
</html>
```

In the two frames, the references to the `window` and `self` object names return the name assigned to the frame by the frameset definition (`JustAKid1` for the left frame, `JustAKid2` for the right frame). In other words, from each frame's point of view, the `window` object is its own frame. References to `self.document.title` refer only to the document loaded into that window frame. But references to the top and parent windows (which are one and the same in this example) show that those object properties are shared between both frames.

A couple of other fine points are worth highlighting. First, the name of the framesetting window is set as Listing 27-13 loads, rather than in response to an `onload` event handler in the `<frameset>` tag. The reason for this is that the name must be set in time for the documents loading in the frames to get that value. If we had waited until the frameset's `onload` event handler, the name wouldn't be set until after the frame documents had loaded. Second, we restore the parent window's name to an empty string when the framesetting document unloads. This is to prevent future pages from getting confused about the window name.

Related Items: `window.frames`, `window.self`, `window.top` properties

personalbar

(See `directories`)

returnValue

Value: Any data type   Read/Write

Compatibility: WinIE4+, MacIE5+, NN-, Moz+, Safari+, Opera-, Chrome-

Scripts use the `returnValue` property in a document that loads into the originally IE-specific modal dialog box. A modal dialog box is generated via the `showModalDialog()` method, which returns whatever data has been assigned to the `returnValue` property of the dialog-box window before it closes. This is possible because script processing in the main window freezes while the modal dialog box is visible. As the dialog box closes, a value can be returned to the main window's script right where the modal dialog box was invoked, and the main window's script resumes executing statements.

Example

See Listing 27-36 for the `showModalDialog()` method, for an example of how to get data back from a dialog box.

Related Item: `showModalDialog()` method

screen

Value: screen object   Read-Only

Compatibility: WinIE4+, MacIE4+, NN6+, Moz+, Safari+, Opera+, Chrome+

Although the screen object appears as a property of the window object in modern browsers, the screen object is also available in NN4 (see Chapter 42), but as a stand-alone object. Because you can omit any reference to the window object for a window object's properties, the same windowless reference syntax can be used for compatibility with legacy browsers that support the screen object.

Example

See Chapter 42 for examples of using the screen object to determine the video-monitor characteristics of the computer running the browser.

Related Item: screen object

screenLeft
screenTop

Value: Integer   Read-Only

Compatibility: WinIE5+, MacIE-, NN-, Moz-, Safari 1.2+, Opera+, Chrome+

WinIE5+ originally provided the screenLeft and screenTop properties of the window object to let you read the pixel position (relative to the top-left 0,0 coordinate of the video monitor) of what Microsoft calls the *client area* of the browser window. The client area excludes most window chrome, such as the title bar, address bar, and the window-sizing bar. Therefore, when the browser window is maximized (meaning that no sizing bars are exposed), the screenLeft property of the window is 0, whereas the screenTop property varies, depending on the combination of toolbars the user has elected to display. For nonmaximized windows, if the window has been positioned so that the top and/or left parts of the client area are out of view, their property values will be negative integers.

These two properties are read-only. You can position the browser window via the window.moveTo() and window.moveBy() methods, but these methods position the top-left corner of the entire browser window, not the client area. IE browsers through version 7 do not provide properties for the position of the entire browser window.

Example

Use The Evaluator (Chapter 4, "JavaScript Essentials") to experiment with the screenLeft and screenTop properties. Start with the browser window maximized (if you are using Windows). Enter the following property name in the top text box:

```
window.screenLeft
```

Click the Evaluate button to see the current setting. Unmaximize the window, and drag it around the screen. Each time you finish dragging, click the Evaluate button again to see the current value. Do the same for window.screenTop.

Related Items: window.moveTo(), window.moveBy() methods

screenX
screenY

Value: Integer   Read/Write

Compatibility: WinIE-, MacIE-, NN6+, Moz+, Safari 1.2+, Opera+, Chrome+

NN6+/Moz/W3C provide the screenX and screenY properties to read the position of the outer boundary of the browser window relative to the top-left coordinates (0,0) of the video monitor. The browser window includes the 4-pixels-wide window-sizing bars that surround Win32 windows. Therefore, when the WinNN6+ browser window is maximized, the value for both screenX and screenY is -4. NN/Moz/W3C do not provide the equivalent measures of the browser window client area as found in the screenLeft and screenTop properties of IE5+. You can, however, find out whether various toolbars are visible in the browser window (see window.directories).

Although you can assign a value to either property, current versions of supporting browsers do not adjust the window position in response, if the user has set the preference that prevents window movement and resizing. Moving and resizing windows by script is considered by many web surfers to be unacceptable behavior.

Example

Use The Evaluator (Chapter 4, "JavaScript Essentials") to experiment with the screenX and screenY properties. Start with the browser window maximized (if you are using Windows). Enter the following property name in the top text box:

        window.screenY

Click the Evaluate button to see the current setting. Unmaximize the window, and drag it around the screen. Each time you finish dragging, click the Evaluate button again to see the current value. Do the same for window.screenY.

Related Items: window.moveTo(), window.moveBy() methods

scrollbars

(See directories)

scrollMaxX
scrollMaxY

Value: Integer   Read/Write

Compatibility: WinIE-, MacIE-, NN7.1+, Moz1.4+, Safari-, Opera-, Chrome-

The NN7.1+/Moz1.4+ scrollMaxX and scrollMaxY properties let you determine the maximum horizontal and vertical scrolling extents of a window. Scrolling is possible only if the window displays scroll bars along the desired axis. Values are pixel integers.

Related Items: scrollX, scrollY properties

scrollX
scrollY

Value: Integer   Read-Only

Compatibility: WinIE-, MacIE-, NN6+, Moz+, Safari+, Opera+, Chrome+

The NN6+/Mozilla/Safari `scrollX` and `scrollY` properties let you determine the horizontal and vertical scrolling of a window. Scrolling is possible only if the window displays scroll bars along the desired axis. Values are pixel integers.

Although the IE DOM does not provide similar properties for the window, the same information can be derived from the `body.scrollLeft` and `body.scrollTop` properties.

Example

Use The Evaluator (Chapter 4, "JavaScript Essentials") to experiment with the `scrollX` and `scrollY` properties. Enter the following property in the top text box:

```
window.scrollY
```

Now manually scroll the page down so that you can still see the Evaluate button. Click the button to see how far the window has scrolled along the *y*-axis.

Related Items: `body.scrollLeft`, `body.scrollTop` properties

self

Value: Window object reference   Read-Only

Compatibility: WinIE3+, MacIE3+, NN2+, Moz+, Safari+, Opera+, Chrome+

Just as the `window` object reference is optional, so is the `self` property when the object reference points to the same window as the one containing the reference. In what may seem to be an unusual construction, the `self` property represents the same object as the `window`. For instance, to obtain the title of the document in a single-frame window, you can use any of the following three constructions:

```
window.document.title
self.document.title
document.title
```

Although `self` is a property of a window, you should not combine the references within a single-frame window script (for example, don't begin a reference with `window.self`, which has been known to cause numerous scripting problems). Specifying the `self` property, though optional for single-frame windows, can help make an object reference crystal clear to someone reading your code (and to you, for that matter). Multiple-frame windows are where you need to pay particular attention to this property.

JavaScript is pretty smart about references to a statement's own window. Therefore, you can generally omit the `self` part of a reference to a same-window document element. But when you intend to display a document in a multiframe window, complete references (including the `self` prefix) to an object make it much easier on anyone who reads or debugs your code to track who is doing what to whom. You are free to retrieve the `self` property of any window. The value that comes back is a `window` object reference.

Example

Listing 27-15 uses the same operations as Listing 27-5 but substitutes the `self` property for all `window` object references. The application of this reference is entirely optional, but it can be helpful for reading and debugging scripts if the HTML document is to appear in one frame of a multiframe window — especially if other JavaScript code in this document refers to documents in other frames. The `self` reference helps anyone reading the code know precisely which frame was being addressed. When testing, remember that even though modern browsers support the `status` property, some of them do not display scripted status-bar text associated with links, in order to prevent link spoofing.

LISTING 27-15

Using the self Property

```
<!DOCTYPE html>
<html>
    <head>
        <meta http-equiv="content-type" content="text/html;charset=utf-8">
        <title>self Property</title>
        <script type="text/javascript">
            self.defaultStatus = "Welcome to my Website.";
        </script>
    </head>
    <body>
        <h1>self Property</h1>
        <hr />
        <p><a href="http://www.microsoft.com"
            onmouseover="self.status = 'Visit Microsoft\'s Home page.';return true;"
            onmouseout="self.status = '';return true;">Microsoft</a>
        </p>
        <p><a href="http://mozilla.org"
            onmouseover="self.status = 'Visit Mozilla\'s Home page.';return true;"
            onmouseout="self.status = self.defaultStatus;
            return true;">Mozilla</a></p>
    </body>
</html>
```

Related Items: `window.frames`, `window.parent`, `window.top` properties

sidebar

(See appCore)

status

Value: String   Read/Write

Compatibility: WinIE3+, MacIE3+, NN2+, Moz+, Safari+, Opera+, Chrome-

At the bottom of the browser window is a status bar. Part of that bar includes an area that normally discloses the document loading progress or the URL of a link that the mouse is pointing to at any given instant. You can control the temporary content of that field by assigning a text string to the `window` object's `status` property. You should adjust the `status` property only in response to events that have a temporary effect, such as a link or image map area object's `onmouseover` event handler. When the `status` property is set in this situation, it overrides any other setting in the status bar. If the user then moves the mouse pointer away from the object that changes the status bar, the bar returns to its default setting (which may be empty on some pages). To prevent link spoofing, however, not all modern browsers display scripted status-bar text associated with links.

Use this window property as a friendlier alternative to displaying the URL of a link as a user rolls the mouse around the page. For example, if you'd rather use the status bar to explain the nature of the destination of a link, put that text into the status bar in response to the onmouseover event handler. But be aware that experienced web surfers like to see URLs down there. Therefore, consider creating a hybrid message for the status bar that includes a friendly description followed by the URL in parentheses. In multiframe environments, you can set the window.status property without having to worry about referencing the individual frame.

Example

In Listing 27-16, the status property is set in a handler embedded in the onmouseover attribute of two HTML link tags. Notice that the handler requires a return true statement (or any expression that evaluates to return true) as the last statement of the handler. This statement is required; otherwise, the status message will not display in all browsers. When testing, remember that even though modern browsers support the status property, some of them do not display scripted status-bar text associated with links, in order to prevent link spoofing.

LISTING 27-16

Links with Custom Status-Bar Messages

```
<!DOCTYPE html>
<html>
    <head>
        <meta http-equiv="content-type" content="text/html;charset=utf-8">
        <title>window.status Property</title>
    </head>
    <body>
        <h1>window.status Property</h1>
        <hr />
        <a href="http://www.dannyg.com"
            onmouseover="window.status = 'Go to my Home page. (www.dannyg.com)';  ↵
            return true">
            Home</a>
        <p>
            <a href = "http://mozilla.org"
                onmouseover="window.status = 'Visit Mozilla Home page. (mozilla.org)';  ↵
                return true">
            Mozilla</a>
        </p>
    </body>
</html>
```

As a safeguard against platform-specific anomalies that affect the behavior of onmouseover event handlers and the window.status property, you should also include an onmouseout event handler for links and client-side image map area objects. Such onmouseout event handlers should set the status property to an empty string. This setting ensures that the status-bar message returns to the defaultStatus setting when the pointer rolls away from these objects. If you want to write a generalizable function that handles all window status changes, you can do so, but word the onmouseover attribute carefully so that the event handler evaluates to return true. Listing 27-17 shows such an alternative. Again, when testing, remember that some modern browsers do not display scripted status-bar text associated with links, in order to prevent link spoofing.

LISTING 27-17

Handling Status Message Changes

```html
<!DOCTYPE html>
<html>
    <head>
        <meta http-equiv="content-type" content="text/html;charset=utf-8">
        <title>Generalizable window.status Property</title>
        <script type="text/javascript">
            function showStatus(msg)
            {
                window.status = msg;
                return true;
            }
        </script>
    </head>
    <body>
        <h1>Generalizable window.status Property</h1>
        <hr />
        <a href="http://www.dannyg.com"
            onmouseover="return showStatus('Go to my Home page.')"
            onmouseout="return showStatus('')">Home</a>
        <p>
            <a href="http://mozilla.org"
                onmouseover="return showStatus('Visit Mozilla Home page.')"
                onmouseout="return showStatus('')">Mozilla</a></p>
    </body>
</html>
```

Notice how the event handlers return the results of the showStatus() method to the event handler, allowing the entire handler to evaluate to return true.

One final example of setting the status bar (shown in Listing 27-18) also demonstrates how to create a simple scrolling banner in the status bar.

LISTING 27-18

Creating a Scrolling Banner

```
HTML: jsb27-18.html
```

```html
<!DOCTYPE html>
<html>
    <head>
        <meta http-equiv="content-type" content="text/html;charset=utf-8">
```

```
       <title>Message Scroller</title>
       <script type="text/javascript" src="jsb27-18.js"></script>
   </head>
   <body onload="scrollMsg()">
       <h1>Message Scroller</h1>
       <hr />
   </body>
</html>
```

JavaScript: jsb27-18.js

```
var msg = "Welcome to my world...";
var delay = 150;
var timerId;
var maxCount = 0;
var currCount = 1;

function scrollMsg()
{
   // set the number of times scrolling message is to run
   if (maxCount == 0)
   {
      maxCount = 3 * msg.length;
   }
   window.status = msg;

   // keep track of how many characters have scrolled
   currCount++;

   // shift first character of msg to end of msg
   msg = msg.substring (1, msg.length) + msg.substring (0, 1);

   // test whether we've reached maximum character count
   if (currCount >= maxCount)
   {
      timerID = 0;   // zero out the timer
      window.status = "";   // clear the status bar
      return;   // break out of function
   }
   else
   {
      // recursive call to this function
      timerId = setTimeout("scrollMsg()", delay);
   }
}
```

Because the status bar is being set by a stand-alone function (rather than by an onmouseover event handler), you do not have to append a return true statement to set the status property. The scrollMsg() function uses more advanced JavaScript concepts, such as the window.setTimeout() method (covered later in this chapter) and string methods (covered in

Chapter 15, "The String Object"). To speed the pace at which the words scroll across the status bar, reduce the value of `delay`.

Many web surfers (including us) don't care for these scrollers that run forever in the status bar. Rolling the mouse over links disturbs the banner display. Use scrolling bars sparingly or design them to run only a few times after the document loads.

Tip

Setting the `status` **property with** `onmouseover` **event handlers has had checkered results along various implementations in Navigator. A script that sets the status bar is always in competition against the browser itself, which uses the status bar to report loading progress. When a hot spot on a page is at the edge of a frame, many times the** `onmouseout` **event fails to fire, preventing the status bar from clearing itself. Be sure to torture-test any such implementations before declaring your page ready for public access.** ∎

Related Items: `window.defaultStatus` property; `onmouseover`, `onmouseout` event handlers; `link` object

statusbar
toolbar

(See `locationbar`)

top

Value: Window object reference   Read-Only

Compatibility: WinIE3+, MacIE3+, NN2+, Moz+, Safari+, Opera+, Chrome+

The `window` object's `top` property refers to the topmost window in a frameset object hierarchy. For a single-frame window, the reference is to the same object as the window itself (including the `self` and `parent` properties), so do not include `window` as part of the reference. In a multiframe window, the top window is the one that defines the first frameset (in case of nested framesets). Users don't ever really see the top window in a multiframe environment, but the browser stores it as an object in its memory. The reason is that the top window has the road map to the other frames (in case one frame should need to reference an object in a different frame), and its child frames can call upon it. Such a reference looks like this:

```
top.functionName([parameters])
```

For more about the distinction between the `top` and `parent` properties, see the in-depth discussion about scripting frames at the beginning of this chapter. See also the example of the `parent` property for listings that demonstrate the values of the `top` property.

Related Items: `window.frames`, `window.self`, `window.parent` properties

window

Value: Window object   Read-Only

Compatibility: WinIE3+, MacIE3+, NN2+, Moz+, Safari+, Opera+, Chrome+

Listing the window property as a separate property may be more confusing than helpful. The window property is the same object as the window object. You do not need to use a reference that begins with window.window. Although the window object is assumed for many references, you can use window as part of a reference to items in the same window or frame as the script statement that makes that reference. You should not, however, use window as a part of a reference involving items higher up in the hierarchy (top or parent).

Methods

alert("*message*")

Returns: Nothing

Compatibility: WinIE3+, MacIE3+, NN2+, Moz+, Safari+, Opera+, Chrome+

An *alert dialog box* is a modal window that presents a message to the user with a single OK button to dismiss the dialog box. As long as the alert dialog box is showing, no other application or window can be made active. The user must dismiss the dialog box before proceeding with any more work in the browser.

The single parameter to the alert() method can be a value of any data type, including representations of some unusual data types whose values you don't normally work with in JavaScript (such as complete objects). This makes the alert dialog box a handy tool for debugging JavaScript scripts. Any time you want to monitor the value of an expression, use that expression as the parameter to a temporary alert() method in your code. The script proceeds to that point and then stops to show you the value. (See Chapter 48 for more tips on debugging scripts.)

What is often disturbing to application designers is that all JavaScript-created modal dialog boxes (via the alert(), confirm(), and prompt() methods) identify themselves as being generated by JavaScript or the browser. The purpose of this identification is to act as a security precaution against unscrupulous scripters who might try to spoof system or browser alert dialog boxes, inviting a user to reveal passwords or other private information. These identifying words cannot be overwritten or eliminated by your scripts. You can simulate a modal dialog-box window in a cross-browser fashion with regular browser windows, but it is not as robust as a genuine modal window, which you can create in IE4+, and some of the other modern browsers, via the window.showModalDialog() method.

Because the alert() method is of a global nature (that is, no particular frame in a multiframe environment derives any benefit from laying claim to the alert dialog box), a common practice is to omit all window object references from the statement that calls the method. Restrict the use of alert dialog boxes in your HTML documents and site designs. The modality of the windows is disruptive to the flow of a user's navigation around your pages. Communicate with users via forms or by writing to separate document window frames. Of course, alert boxes can still be very handy as a quick debugging aid.

Example

The parameter for the example in Listing 27-19 is a concatenated string. It joins two fixed strings and the value of the browser's navigator.appName property. Loading this document causes the alert dialog box to appear, as shown in several configurations in Figure 27-5. The JavaScript Alert line cannot be deleted from the dialog box in earlier browsers, while the title bar can't be changed in later browsers.

windowObject.back()

LISTING 27-19

Displaying an Alert Dialog Box

```html
<!DOCTYPE html>
<html>
    <head>
        <meta http-equiv="content-type" content="text/html;charset=utf-8">
        <title>window.alert() Method</title>
    </head>
    <body>
        <h1>window.alert() Method</h1>
        <hr />
        <script type="text/javascript">
            alert("You are running the " + navigator.appName + " browser.");
        </script>
    </body>
</html>
```

FIGURE 27-5

Results of the alert() method in Listing 27-19 in Firefox and Internet Explorer.

Related Items: window.confirm(), window.prompt() methods

back()
forward()

Returns: Nothing

Compatibility: WinIE+, MacIE-, NN4+, Moz+, Safari+, Opera+, Chrome+

The purpose of the window.back() and window.forward() methods that began in NN4 is to offer a scripted version of the global back and forward navigation buttons while allowing the history object to control navigation strictly within a particular window or frame — as it should. Even though IE now supports these window methods, they did not catch on (and the window object is out of the scope of the W3C DOM Level 2), so you are better off staying with the history object's methods for navigating browser history. For more information about version compatibility and about back and forward navigation, see the `history` object in Chapter 28.

Related Items: `history.back()`, `history.forward()`, `history.go()` methods

clearInterval(*intervalIDnumber*)

Returns: Nothing

Compatibility: WinIE4+, MacIE4+, NN4+, Moz+, Safari+, Opera+, Chrome+

Use the `window.clearInterval()` method to turn off an interval loop action started with the `window.setInterval()` method. The parameter is the ID number returned by the `setInterval()` method. A common application for the JavaScript interval mechanism is animation of an object on a page. If you have multiple intervals running, each has its own ID value in memory. You can turn off any interval by its ID value. As soon as an interval loop stops, your script cannot resume that interval: It must start a new one, which generates a new ID value.

Example

See Listing 27-33 and Listing 27-34 later in this chapter for an example of how `setInterval()` and `clearInterval()` are used together on a page.

Related Items: `window.setInterval()`, `window.setTimeout()`, `window.clearTimeout()` methods

clearTimeout(*timeoutIDnumber*)

Returns: Nothing

Compatibility: WinIE3+, MacIE3+, NN2+, Moz+, Safari+, Opera+, Chrome+

Use the `window.clearTimeout()` method in concert with the `window.setTimeout()` method, as described later in this chapter, when you want your script to cancel a timer that is waiting to run its expression. The parameter for this method is the ID number that the `window.setTimeout()` method returns when the timer starts ticking. The `clearTimeout()` method cancels the specified timeout. A good practice is to check your code for instances where user action may negate the need for a running timer — and to stop that timer before it goes off.

Example

The page in Listing 27-20 features one text box and two buttons. One button starts a countdown timer coded to last 1 minute (easily modifiable for other durations); the other button interrupts the timer at any time while it is running. When the minute is up, an alert dialog box lets you know.

LISTING 27-20

A Countdown Timer

HTML: `jsb27-20.html`

```
<!DOCTYPE html>
<html>
  <head>
```

continued

LISTING 27-20 *(continued)*

```
      <meta http-equiv="content-type" content="text/html;charset=utf-8">
      <title>Count Down Timer</title>
      <script type="text/javascript" src="jsb27-20.js"></script>
   </head>
   <body>
      <form>
         <input type="button" name="startTime" value="Start 1 min. Timer"
               onclick="startTimer()" />
         <input type="button" name="clearTime"
               value="Clear Timer" onclick="stopTimer()" />
         <p><input type="text" name="timerDisplay" value="" /></p>
      </form>
   </body>
</html>
```

JavaScript: jsb27-20.js

```
var running = false;
var endTime = null;
var timerID = null;

function startTimer()
{
   running = true;
   now = new Date();
   now = now.getTime();
   // change last multiple for the number of minutes
   endTime = now + (1000 * 60 * 1);
   showCountDown();
}

function showCountDown()
{
   var now = new Date();
   now = now.getTime();
      if (endTime - now <= 0)
      {
         stopTimer();
         alert("Time is up.  Put down your pencils.");
      }
      else
      {
         var delta = new Date(endTime - now);
         var theMin = delta.getMinutes();
         var theSec = delta.getSeconds();
         var theTime = theMin;
         theTime += ((theSec < 10) ? ":0" : ":") + theSec;
         document.forms[0].timerDisplay.value = theTime;
         if (running)
```

```
        {
            timerID = setTimeout("showCountDown()",1000);
        }
    }
}

function stopTimer()
{
    clearTimeout(timerID);
    running = false;
    document.forms[0].timerDisplay.value = "0:00";
}
```

Notice that the script establishes three variables with global scope in the window: running, end-Time, and timerID. These values are needed inside multiple functions, so they are initialized outside the functions.

In the startTimer() function, you switch the running flag on, meaning that the timer should be going. Using some date functions (see Chapter 17, "The Date Object"), you extract the current time in milliseconds and add the number of milliseconds for the next minute (the extra multiplication by 1 is the place where you can change the amount to the desired number of minutes). With the end time stored in a global variable, the function now calls another function that compares the current and end times, and displays the difference in the text box.

Early in the showCountDown() function, check to see whether the timer has wound down. If so, you stop the timer and alert the user. Otherwise, the function continues to calculate the difference between the two times, and formats the time in mm:ss format. As long as the running flag is set to true, the function sets the 1-second timeout timer before repeating itself. To stop the timer before it has run out (in the stopTimer() function), the most important step is to cancel the timeout running inside the browser. The clearTimeout() method uses the global timerID value to do that. Then the function turns off the running switch and zeros out the display.

When you run the timer, you may occasionally notice that the time skips a second. It's not cheating. It just takes slightly more than 1 second to wait for the timeout and then finish the calculations for the next second's display. What you're seeing is the display catching up with the real time left.

Related Item: window.setTimeout() method

close()

Returns: Nothing

Compatibility: WinIE3+, MacIE3+, NN2+, Moz+, Safari+, Opera+, Chrome+

The window.close() method closes the browser window referenced by the window object. Most likely, you will use this method to close subwindows created from a main document window. If the call to close the window comes from a window other than the new subwindow, the original window object must maintain a record of the subwindow object. You accomplish this by storing the value returned from the window.open() method in a global variable that will be available to other objects later (for example, a variable not initialized inside a function). If, on the other hand, an object inside the new subwindow calls the window.close() method, the window or self reference is sufficient.

Be sure to include a window as part of the reference to this method. Failure to do so may cause JavaScript to regard the statement as a `document.close()` method, which has a different behavior (see Chapter 29). Only the `window.close()` method can close the window via a script. Closing a window, of course, forces the window to trigger an `onunload` event handler before the window disappears from view, but after you've initiated the `window.close()` method, you cannot stop it from completing its task. Moreover, `onunload` event handlers that attempt to execute time-consuming processes (such as submitting a form in the closing window) may not complete because the window can easily close before the process completes — a behavior that has no workaround (with the exception of the `onbeforeunload` event handler in IE4+).

While we're on the subject of closing windows, a special case exists when a subwindow tries to close the main window (via a statement such as `self.opener.close()`) when the main window has more than one entry in its session history. As a safety precaution against scripts closing windows they did not create, modern browsers ask the user whether he or she wants the main window to close (via a browser-generated dialog box). This security precaution cannot be overridden except in NN4+/Moz via a signed script, when the user grants permission to control the browser (see Chapter 49).

Example

See Listing 27-4 (for the `window.closed` property), which provides a cross-platform example of applying the `window.close()` method across multiple windows.

Related Items: `window.open()`, `document.close()` methods

confirm(*"message"*)

Returns: Boolean

Compatibility: WinIE3+, MacIE3+, NN2+, Moz+, Safari+, Opera+, Chrome+

A confirm dialog box presents a message in a modal dialog box along with OK and Cancel buttons. Such a dialog box can be used to ask a question of the user, usually prior to a script's performing actions that will not be undoable. Querying a user about proceeding with typical web navigation in response to user interaction on a form element is generally a disruptive waste of the user's time and attention. But for operations that may reveal a user's identity or send form data to a server, a JavaScript confirm dialog box may make a great deal of sense. Users may also accidentally click buttons, so you should provide avenues for backing out of an operation before it executes.

Because this dialog box returns a Boolean value (OK = `true`; Cancel = `false`), you can use this method as a comparison expression or as an assignment expression. In a comparison expression, you nest the method within any other statement where a Boolean value is required. For example:

```
if (confirm("Are you sure?"))
{
    alert("OK");
}
else
{
    alert("Not OK");
}
```

Here, the returned value of the confirm dialog box provides the desired Boolean value type for the `if...else` construction (see Chapter 21).

This method can also appear on the right side of an assignment expression, as in:

```
var adult = confirm("Do you certify that you are over 18 years old?");
if (adult)
{
    //statements for adults
}
else
{
    //statements for children
}
```

You cannot specify other alert icons or labels for the two buttons in JavaScript confirm dialog-box windows.

The example in Listing 27-21 shows the user interface part of how you can use a confirm dialog box to query a user before clearing a table full of user-entered data. The text in the title bar, as shown in Figure 27-6, cannot be removed from the dialog box.

LISTING 27-21

The Confirm Dialog Box

```
<!DOCTYPE html>
<html>
    <head>
        <meta http-equiv="content-type" content="text/html;charset=utf-8">
        <title>window.confirm() Method</title>
        <script type="text/javascript">
            function clearTable()
            {
                if (confirm("Are you sure you want to empty the table?"))
                {
                    alert("Emptying the table...");   // for demo purposes
                    //statements that actually empty the fields
                }
            }
        </script>
    </head>
    <body>
        <h1>window.confirm() Method</h1>
        <hr />
        <form>
            <h3>A large table with data would be here.</h3>
            <input type="button" name="clear" value="Reset Table"
                    onclick="clearTable()" />
        </form>
    </body>
</html>
```

windowObject.createPopup()

FIGURE 27-6

A JavaScript confirm dialog box in Internet Explorer.

Related Items: `window.alert()`, `window.prompt()`, `form.submit()` methods

createPopup()

Returns: Pop-up object reference

Compatibility: WinIE5.5+, MacIE-, NN-, Moz-, Safari-, Opera-, Chrome-

An IE pop-up window is a chromeless rectangular space that overlaps the current window. Unlike the dialog boxes generated by the `showModalDialog()` and `showModelessDialog()` methods, the pop-up window's entire content must be explicitly controlled by script. That also goes for the size and location of the window. Generating the window via the `createPopup()` method simply creates the object in memory without displaying it. You can then use the reference to the pop-up window that is returned by the method to position the window, populate its content, and make it visible. See details in the description of the `popup` object later in this chapter.

Example

See Listing 27-46 later in this chapter for an example of the `createPopup()` method.

Related Item: `popup` object

dump("*message*")

Returns: Nothing

Compatibility: WinIE-, MacIE-, NN7.1+, Moz1.4+, Safari-, Opera-, Chrome-

The `window.dump()` method is a debugging/diagnostic method that you can use to output a string of text to *standard output*, which is typically the operating system's console window. The `dump()` method provides a less intrusive alternative to displaying debugging messages via the `alert()` method.

execScript("*exprList*"[, *language*])

Returns: Nothing

Compatibility: WinIE4+, MacIE4+, NN-, Moz-, Safari-, Opera-, Chrome-

The IE-specific `window.execScript()` method executes one or more script statements that are passed as string expressions. The first parameter is a string version of one or more script statements (multiple statements must be separated by semicolons). The second, optional, parameter is the language interpreter the browser should use to execute the script statement. Acceptable values for the language are JavaScript, JScript, VBS, and VBScript. The default value is JScript, so you can omit the second parameter when supplying expressions in JavaScript.

Unlike the JavaScript core language eval() function (which also executes string versions of JavaScript statements), the execScript() method returns no values. Even so, the method operates within the global variable space of the window holding the current document. For example, if a document's script declares a global variable as follows

```
var myVar;
```

the execScript() method can read or write to that variable:

```
window.execScript("myVar = 10; myVar += 5");
```

After this statement runs, the global variable myVar has a value of 15.

Example

Use The Evaluator (Chapter 4, "JavaScript Essentials") to experiment with the execScript() method. The Evaluator has predeclared global variables for the lowercase letters *a* through *z*. Enter each of the following statements in the top text box, and observe the results for each.

```
a
```

When first loaded, the variable is declared, but assigned no value, so it is undefined:

```
window.execScript("a = 5")
```

The method returns no value, so the mechanism inside The Evaluator says that the statement is undefined:

```
a
```

The variable is now 5.

```
window.execScript("b = a * 50")
b
```

The b global variable has a value of 250. Continue exploring with additional script statements. Use semicolons to separate multiple statements within the string parameter.

Related Item: eval() function

find(["*searchString*" [, *matchCaseBoolean*, *searchUpBoolean*]])

Returns: Boolean value for non-dialog-box searches

Compatibility: WinIE-, MacIE-, NN4+, Moz1.0.1+, Safari+, Opera-, Chrome+

The window.find() method introduced in NN4 mimics the powers of the browser's Find dialog box, accessible from the Find button in the toolbar. This method was deactivated in NN6, but reactivated in NN7/Moz1.0.1.

If you specify no parameters, the browser's Find dialog box appears, just as though the user had clicked the Find button in the toolbar. With no parameters, this function does not return a value.

You can specify a search string as a parameter to the function. The search is based on simple string matching, and is not in any way connected with the regular-expression kind of search (see Chapter 45, "The Regular Expression and RegExp Objects"). If the search finds a match, the browser scrolls to that matching word and highlights the word, just as though it were using the browser's own Find dialog box. The function also returns a Boolean true after a match is found. If no match is found in the document, or no more matches occur in the current search direction (the default direction is from top to bottom), the function returns false.

Table 27-3 lists the optional parameters you can use; in all cases, the default value is false. These choices are identical to the ones that appear in NN4+'s Find dialog box.

TABLE 27-3

window.find() Method Attributes Controllable via Script

Attribute	Description
caseSensitive	Boolean; true specifies that the search is case sensitive
backwards	Boolean; true specifies that the search is backwards
wraparound	Boolean; true specifies that the search will wrap to the top of the document when the bottom is reached.
wholeWord	Boolean; true specifies that the search is a whole word search.
searchInFrames	Boolean; true specifies to search in frames.
showDialog	Boolean; true specifies to display the browser's find dialog.

Some modern browsers such as Firefox have evolved to forego the Find dialog box in favor of an integrated find feature that appears at the bottom of the browser window. This approach to find can be applied to the entire page at the same time, in which case all the text matches are highlighted.

IE4+ also has a scripted text search facility, but it is implemented in an entirely different way (using the TextRange object described in Chapter 33, "Body Text Objects"). The visual behavior also differs in that it does not highlight and scroll to a matching string in the text.

Example

A simple call to the window.find() method looks as follows:

```
var success = window.find("contract");
```

And if you want the search to be case sensitive, add at least one of the optional parameters:

```
success = window.find(matchString,caseSensitive);
```

In many ways, the window.find() method is a remnant of NN4. Refer to discussions of the TextRange and Range objects in Chapter 33 for more modern implementations of body-text searching.

Related Items: TextRange, Range objects (Chapter 33)

forward()

(See `window.back()`)

geckoActiveXObject(*"progID"*)

Returns: WMP control object

Compatibility: WinIE-, MacIE-, NN7.1+, Moz1.4+, Safari-, Opera-, Chrome-

One interesting result of the NN/IE browser wars is Microsoft's victory in establishing Windows Media Player as the PC media player of choice in the Windows operating system. Because WMP is implemented as an ActiveX control, NN/Moz browsers were somewhat left out in the cold in terms of scriptability. The `window.geckoActiveXObject()` method was added to Moz1.4 browsers to give them the capability of accessing WMP as an ActiveX control. Although the name of the method suggests generic support for ActiveX controls, it currently enables you to open only the WMP control.

The only parameter to `geckoActiveXObject()` is a programmatic ID, which for WMP is currently `MediaPlayer.MediaPlayer.1`. So, to grab a WMP control reference for media playback using the `geckoActiveXObject()` method, use code such as this:

```
var player = new GeckoActiveXObject("MediaPlayer.MediaPlayer.1");
```

getComputedStyle(elementNodeRef, "pseudoElementName")

Returns: CSS style object

Compatibility: WinIE-, MacIE-, NN-, Moz+, Safari+, Opera+, Chrome+

The `window.getComputedStyle()` method enables you to access the cascading style sheet (CSS) style object associated with a given element. You specify an element node reference as the first parameter to the method, along with the optional name of a specific pseudoelement to which the style applies. We say *optional* because you can pass an empty string as the second parameter to obtain a style object with no pseudoelement implications.

Note
Although various browsers support the `getComputedStyle()` **method, the values returned could be in different formats, depending on the style specified for the element. For example, if you requested the style of an element that had a background color, Opera would return the color in hex format, and Firefox, Safari, and Chrome would return it in** `rgb()` **format.** ■

Although the `getComputedStyle()` method is defined (and works) for the `window` object, the W3C DOM prefers `document.defaultView.getComputedStyle()` as the standard means of accessing a style object for an element. It's the same method that's ultimately being called; the way it's accessed is what differs.

getSelection()

Returns: Selection object

Compatibility: WinIE-, MacIE-, NN6+, Moz+, Safari+, Opera+, Chrome+

This method takes the place of the deprecated method of the same name that appeared in the `document` object. The method offers a scripted way of capturing the text selected by a user in a page, which is a common task involving the selection and copying of body text in a document for pasting into other application documents. The `window.getSelection()` method returns the string of text *windowObject*.**getSelection()**

selected by the user. If nothing is selected, an empty string is the result. Returned values consist only of the visible text on the page and not the underlying HTML or style of the text.

The WinIE4+ equivalent involves the `document.selection` property, which returns an IE `selection` object. To derive the text from this object, you must create a `TextRange` object from it and then inspect the `text` property:

```
var selectedText = document.selection.createRange().text;
```

Example

The document in Listing 27-22 provides a cross-browser (but not MacIE5) solution to capturing text that a user selects in the page. Selected text is displayed in the text area. The script uses browser detection and branching to account for the differences in event handling between Mozilla and Internet Explorer.

LISTING 27-22

Retrieving Selected Text

HTML: jsb27-22.html

```
<!DOCTYPE html>
<html>
    <head>
        <meta http-equiv="content-type" content="text/html;charset=utf-8">
        <title>Getting Selected Text</title>
        <script type="text/javascript" src="../jsb-global.js"></script>
        <script type="text/javascript" src="jsb27-22.js"></script>
    </head>
    <body>
        <h1>Getting Selected Text</h1>
        <hr />
        <p>Select some text and see how JavaScript can capture the selection:</p>
        <h2>ARTICLE I</h2>
        <p>Congress shall make no law respecting an establishment of religion, or
            prohibiting the free exercise thereof; or abridging the freedom of
            speech, or of the press; or the right of the people peaceably to
            assemble, and to petition the government for a redress of grievances.
        </p>
        <form>
            <textarea name="selectedText" rows="3" cols="40" wrap="virtual">
            </textarea>
        </form>
    </body>
</html>
```

JavaScript: jsb27-22.js

```
addEvent(document, "mouseup", showSelection);
```

```
function showSelection()
{
    if (window.getSelection)
    {
        document.forms[0].selectedText.value = window.getSelection();
    }
    else if (document.selection)
    {
        document.forms[0].selectedText.value = document.selection.createRange().text;
        event.cancelBubble = true;
    }
}
```

Related Item: document.selection property

home()

Returns: Nothing

Compatibility: WinIE-, MacIE-, NN4+, Moz+, Safari-, Opera+, Chrome-

Like many of the window methods originally introduced in Navigator 4, the window.home() method provides a scripted way of replicating the action of a toolbar button: the Home button. The action navigates the browser to whatever URL is set in the browser preferences for home-page location. You cannot control the default home page of a visitor's browser.

Related Items: window.back(), window.forward() methods; window.toolbar property

moveBy(*deltaX,deltaY*)
moveTo(*x,y*)

Returns: Nothing

Compatibility: WinIE4+, MacIE4+, NN4+, Moz+, Safari+, Opera+, Chrome-

Version 4 browsers introduced the capability of allowing JavaScript to adjust the location of a browser window onscreen. This applies to the main window or any subwindow generated by script. NN/Moz regard the possibility of a window moved out of screen view as a potential security hole, so signed scripts are needed in NN4+/Moz to move a window offscreen. While these methods are compatible with Chrome, Chrome ignores them.

You can move a window to an absolute position onscreen or adjust it along the horizontal and/or vertical axis by any number of pixels, irrespective of the absolute pixel position. The coordinate space for the *x* (horizontal) and *y* (vertical) position is the entire screen, with the top-left corner representing 0,0. The point of the window you set with the moveBy() and moveTo() methods is the top-left corner of the outer edge of the browser window. Therefore, when you move the window to point 0,0, the window is set flush with the top-left corner of the screen. This may not be the equivalent of a truly maximized window for all browsers and operating systems, however, because a maximized window's coordinates may be negative by a handful of pixels.

The difference between the moveTo() and moveBy() methods is that one is an absolute move, whereas the other is relative with respect to the current window position. Parameters you specify for moveTo() are the precise horizontal and vertical pixel counts onscreen where you want the top-left corner of the window to appear. By contrast, the parameters for moveBy() indicate how far to adjust the window location in either direction. If you want to move the window 25 pixels to the right, you must still include both parameters, but the y value will be zero:

```
window.moveBy(25,0);
```

To move to the left, the first parameter must be a negative number.

Example

Several examples of using the window.moveTo() and window.moveBy() methods are shown in Listing 27-23. The page presents four buttons, each of which performs a different kind of browser-window movement.

LISTING 27-23

Window Boogie

HTML: jsb27-23.html

```html
<!DOCTYPE html>
<html>
    <head>
        <meta http-equiv="content-type" content="text/html;charset=utf-8">
        <title>Window Gymnastics</title>
        <script type="text/javascript" src="jsb27-23.js"></script>
    </head>
    <body onload="init()">
        <h1>Window Gymnastics</h1>
        <hr />
        <form name="buttons">
            <ul>
                <li><input name="offscreen" type="button"
                        value="Disappear a Second"
                        onclick="moveOffScreen()" />
                </li>
                <li><input name="circles" type="button"
                        value="Swift and Tiny Circular Motion"
                        onclick="revolve()" />
                </li>
                <li><input name="bouncer" type="button"
                        value="Zig Zag"
                        onclick="zigzag()" />
                </li>
                <li><input name="expander" type="button"
                        value="Maximize"
                        onclick="maximize()" />
                </li>
            </ul>
        </form>
```

```
        </body>
</html>
```

JavaScript: jsb27-23.js

```
// wait in onload for page to load and settle in IE
function init()
{
    // fill missing IE properties
    if (!window.outerWidth)
    {
        window.outerWidth = document.body.clientWidth;
        window.outerHeight = document.body.clientHeight + 30;
    }
}

// function to run when window captures a click event
function moveOffScreen()
{
    // branch for NN security
    if (window.netscape)
    {
        // will also get here if in Opera, but Opera will throw error, so...
        try
        {
          netscape.security.PrivilegeManager.enablePrivilege("UniversalBrowserWrite");
        }
        catch (e)
        {
            null;
        }
    }
    var maxX = screen.width;
    var maxY = screen.height;
    window.moveTo(maxX+1, maxY+1);
    setTimeout("window.moveTo(0,0)",500);
    if (window.netscape)
    {
        // will also get here if in Opera, but Opera will throw error, so...
        try
        {
          netscape.security.PrivilegeManager.disablePrivilege("UniversalBrowserWrite");
        }
        catch (e)
        {
            null;
        }
    }
}

// moves window in a circular motion
function revolve()
```

continued

LISTING 27-23   *(continued)*

```
{
    var winX = (screen.availWidth - window.outerWidth) / 2;
    var winY = 50;
    window.resizeTo(400,300);
    window.moveTo(winX, winY);
    for (var i = 1; i < 36; i++)
    {
        winX += Math.cos(i * (Math.PI/18)) * 5;
        winY += Math.sin(i * (Math.PI/18)) * 5;
        window.moveTo(winX, winY);
    }
}

// moves window in a horizontal zig-zag pattern
function zigzag()
{
    window.resizeTo(400,300);
    window.moveTo(0,80);
    var incrementX = 2;
    var incrementY = 2;
    var floor = screen.availHeight - window.outerHeight;
    var rightEdge = screen.availWidth - window.outerWidth;
    for (var i = 0; i < rightEdge; i += 2)
    {
        window.moveBy(incrementX, incrementY);
        if (i%60 == 0)
        {
            incrementY = -incrementY;
        }
    }
}

// resizes window to occupy all available screen real estate
function maximize()
{
    window.moveTo(0,0);
    window.resizeTo(screen.availWidth, screen.availHeight);
}
```

To run successfully in NN/Moz, the first button requires that you have codebase principals turned on (see Chapter 49 to take advantage of what would normally be a signed script). The moveOff-Screen() function momentarily moves the window entirely out of view. Interestingly, Opera recognizes window.netscape but throws an error if an attempt is made to turn on the codebase principals. A try catch gets around that problem. Notice how the script determines the size of the screen before deciding where to move the window. After the journey offscreen, the window comes back into view at the top-left corner of the screen.

If using the web sometimes seems like going around in circles, the second function, `revolve()`, should feel just right. After reducing the size of the window and positioning it near the top center of the screen, the script uses a bit of math to position the window along 36 spots around a perfect circle (at 10-degree increments). This is an example of how to control a window's position dynamically based on math calculations. IE complicates the job a bit by not providing properties that reveal the outside dimensions of the browser window.

To demonstrate the `moveBy()` method, the third function, `zigzag()`, uses a `for` loop to increment the coordinate points to make the window travel in a sawtooth pattern across the screen. The *x* coordinate continues to increment linearly until the window is at the edge of the screen (also calculated on the fly to accommodate monitors of any size). The *y* coordinate must increase and decrease as that parameter changes direction as it moves around the screen.

In the fourth function, you see some practical code (finally) that demonstrates how best to simulate maximizing the browser window to fill the entire available screen space on the visitor's monitor.

Related Items: `window.outerHeight`, `window.outerWidth` properties; `window.resizeBy()`, `window.resizeTo()` methods

navigate("*URL*")

Returns: Nothing

Compatibility: WinIE4+, MacIE4+, NN-, Moz-, Safari-, Opera+, Chrome-

The `window.navigate()` method is an IE-original method that lets you load a new document into a window or frame. This method's action is the same as assigning a URL to the `location.href` property — a property that is available on all scriptable browsers. If your audience is entirely IE or Opera based, this method is safe. Otherwise, we recommend the `location.href` property as the best navigation approach.

Example

Supply any valid URL as the parameter to the method, as in:

```
window.navigate("http://www.dannyg.com");
```

Related Item: `location` object

open("*URL*", "*windowName*" [, "*windowFeatures*"] [,*replaceFlag*])

Returns: A window object representing the newly created window; `null` if method fails

Compatibility: WinIE3+, MacIE3+, NN2+, Moz+, Safari+, Opera+, Chrome+

With the `window.open()` method, a script provides a web-site designer an immense range of options for the way a second or third web browser window looks on the user's computer screen. Moreover, most of this control can work with all JavaScript-enabled browsers without the need for signed scripts. Because the interface elements of a new window are easier to envision, we cover those aspects of the `window.open()` method parameters first.

Setting new window features

The optional windowFeatures parameter is one string consisting of a comma-separated list of assignment expressions (behaving something like HTML tag attributes). *Important:* For the best browser compatibility, do not put spaces after the commas. If you omit the third parameter, JavaScript creates the same type of new window you get from the New Web Browser menu choice in the File menu. But you can control which window elements appear in the new window with the third parameter. Remember this important rule: If you specify even one of the method's original set of third parameter values, all other features are turned off unless the parameters specify the features to be switched on. Table 27-4 lists the attributes that you can control for a newly created window in all browsers. Except where noted, all Boolean values default to yes if you do not specify the third parameter.

TABLE 27-4

window.open() Method Attributes Controllable via Script

Attribute	Browsers	Description
alwaysLowered[3]	NN4+/Moz+	(Boolean) Always behind other browser windows
alwaysRaised[3]	NN4+/Moz+	(Boolean) Always in front of other browser windows
channelMode	IE4+	(Boolean) Theater mode with channel band (default is no)
chrome[3]	NN7.2+/Moz1.7+	(Boolean) Browser user interface features
close	NN4+/Moz+	(Boolean) System close command icon and menu item at top of dialog window
dependent[6]	NN4+/Moz+	(Boolean) Subwindow closes if the opener window closes
directories[7]	NN2+/Moz+, IE3–6	(Boolean) Displays personal/bookmarks/links toolbar
fullscreen[5]	IE4+	(Boolean) No title bar or menus (default is no)
height	NN2+/Moz+, IE3+, Safari+, Opera+, Chrome+	(Integer) Content region height in pixels
innerHeight[4]	NN4+/Moz+, Safari+, Chrome+	(Integer) Content region height; same as old height property
innerWidth[4]	NN4+/Moz+, Safari+, Chrome+	(Integer) Content region width; same as old width property
left	NN6+/Moz+, IE4+, Safari+, Opera+, Chrome+	(Integer) Horizontal position of top-left corner onscreen
location[8]	NN2+/Moz+, IE3+, Safari	(Boolean) Field displaying the current URL
menubar[1]	NN2+/Moz+, IE3+, Safari	(Boolean) Menu bar at top of window

Attribute	Browsers	Description
minimizable	NN7.1+/Moz1.2+	(Boolean) Minimize command icon at top of dialog windows only
modal[3]	NN7.1+/Moz1.2+	(Boolean) Modality of window, as in preventing access to the main window until the opened window is closed
outerHeight[4]	NN4+/Moz+	(Integer) Visible window height
outerWidth[4]	NN4+/Moz+	(Integer) Visible window width
personalBar[7]	NN4+/Moz+	(Boolean) Mozilla-specific version of the directories attribute
resizable[2,9]	NN2+/Moz0−1.4, IE3+	(Boolean) Interface elements that allow resizing by dragging
screenX[4]	NN4+/Moz+	(Integer) Horizontal position of top-left corner onscreen
screenY[4]	NN4+/Moz+	(Integer) Vertical position of top-left corner onscreen
scrollbars	NN2+/Moz+, IE3+, Opera+	(Boolean) Displays scroll bars if document is larger than window
status	NN2+/Moz+, IE3+, Safari	(Boolean) Status bar at bottom of window
titlebar[3]	NN4+/Moz+	(Boolean) Title bar and all other border elements
toolbar	NN2+/Moz+, IE3+, Safari	(Boolean) Back, Forward, and other buttons in the row
top	NN6+/Moz+, IE4+, Safari+, Opera+, Chrome+	(Integer) Vertical position of top-left corner onscreen
width	NN2+/Moz+, IE3+, Safari+, Opera+, Chrome+	(Integer) Content region width in pixels
z-lock[3]	NN4+/Moz+	(Boolean) Window layer is fixed below browser windows

[1]Not on Macintosh because the menu bar is not in the browser window; when off in MacNN4, displays an abbreviated Mac menu bar.
[2]Macintosh windows are always resizable.
[3]Requires a signed script.
[4]Requires a signed script to size or position a window beyond safe threshold. Left and Top have precedence over these two features, respectively.
[5]Behavior changed in IE6+. Its use is not recommended and, except in a kiosk type situation, we strongly concur as its use has always upset users.
[6]Behavior changed in Moz5. It was never implemented on Mac OS. It is currently under revision to be removed.
[7]In Mozilla based browsers, this feature only works if toolbar is also set to yes.
[8]In Safari, if toolbar is checked, then location always behaves as checked.
[9]In IE7+ this feature disables tabs in the new window. In FF3+ new windows are always resizable.

Boolean values are handled a bit differently than you might expect. The value for true can be yes, 1, or just the feature name by itself; for false, use a value of no or 0. If you omit any Boolean attributes, they are rendered as false. Therefore, if you want to create a new window that shows only the toolbar and status bar and is resizable, the method looks like this:

```
window.open("newURL","NewWindow", "toolbar,status,resizable");
```

A new window whose height and width has not been specified is set to the default size of the browser window that the browser creates from a File menu's New Web Browser command. In other words, a new window does not automatically inherit the size of the window making the window.open() method call. A new window created via a script is positioned somewhat arbitrarily unless you use the window positioning attributes available in modern browsers. Notice that the position attributes are different for each browser (screenX and screenY for NN/Moz/W3C; left and top for IE). You can include both sets of attributes in a single parameter string because the browser ignores attributes that it doesn't recognize.

Note

The ability to invoke window.open() via a window's onload and onunload event handlers has led to severe abuse in the form of unwanted pop-up advertising windows. Browsers that include pop-up blockers (such as IE6+, and Mozilla/WebKit/Presto-based browsers) prevent the method from being invoked by these event handlers. With more browsers and users employing pop-up blockers every day, you should not even think about blasting pop-up ads to web surfers. ∎

Netscape/Mozilla-only signed scripts

Many NN/Moz-specific attributes are deemed to be security risks, and thus require signed scripts and the user's permission before they are recognized. If the user fails to grant permission, the secure parameter is ignored.

To apply signed scripts to opening a new window with the secure window features, you must enable UniversalBrowserWrite privileges as you do for other signed scripts (see Chapter 49). A code fragment that generates an alwaysRaised style window follows:

```
<script type="text/javaScript" archive="myJar.jar" id="1">
function newRaisedWindow()
{
  netscape.security.PrivilegeManager.enablePrivilege("UniversalBrowserWrite");
  var newWindow = window.open("","","height=100,width=300,alwaysRaised=yes");
  netscape.security.PrivilegeManager.disablePrivilege("UniversalBrowserWrite");
  var newContent = "<html><body><b> "On top of spaghetti!"</b>";
  newContent += "<form><center><input type='button' value='OK'";
  newContent += "onclick='self.close()'></center></form></body></html>";
  newWindow.document.write(newContent);
  newWindow.document.close();
}
</script>
```

You can experiment with the look and behavior of new windows with any combination of attributes with the help of the script in Listing 27-24. This page presents a table of new window Boolean attributes and creates a new 300×300 pixel window based on your choices. This page assumes that if you are using NN/Moz, you have codebase principals turned on for signed scripts (see Chapter 49).

Be careful with turning off the title bar. With the title bar off, the content appears to float in space because absolutely no borders are displayed. However, hotkeys are always turned on, so you can use Ctrl+W to close this borderless window (except on the Mac, for which the hotkeys are always disabled with the title bar off). In browsers that support the `titlebar` feature, you can turn a computer into a kiosk by sizing a window to the screen's dimensions and setting the window options to `"titlebar=no"`. In IE you can also add `fullscreen=yes` to the feature list.

LISTING 27-24

New Window Laboratory

HTML: jsb27-24.html

```html
<!DOCTYPE html>
<html>
    <head>
        <meta http-equiv="content-type" content="text/html;charset=utf-8">
        <title>window.open() Options</title>
        <style type="text/css">
            .colHeaders
            {
                background-color:yellow; text-align:center;
            }
        </style>
        <script type="text/javascript" src="jsb27-24.js"></script>
    </head>
    <body>
        <h1>Select new window options:</h1>
        <hr />
        <form>
            <table border="2">
                <tr>
                    <td class="colHeaders" colspan="2">
                        Browser Features:
                    </td>
                </tr>
                <tr>
                    <td>
                        <input type="checkbox" name="toolbar" />
                        toolbar
                    </td>
                    <td>
                        <input type="checkbox" name="location" />
                        location
                    </td>
                </tr>
                <tr>
                    <td>
                        <input type="checkbox" name="directories" />
                        directories
                    </td>
```

continued

windowObject.open()

LISTING 27-24   *(continued)*

```html
                    <td>
                        <input type="checkbox" name="status" />
                        status
                    </td>
                </tr>
                <tr>
                    <td>
                        <input type="checkbox" name="menubar" />
                        menubar
                    </td>
                    <td>
                        <input type="checkbox" name="scrollbars" />
                        scrollbars
                    </td>
                </tr>
                <tr>
                    <td>
                        <input type="checkbox" name="resizable" />
                        resizable
                    </td>
                    <td>
                        <input type="checkbox" name="titlebar" checked="checked" />
                        titlebar
                    </td>
                </tr>
                <tr>
                    <td colspan="2" align="middle">
                        <input type="button" name="forAll" value="Make New Window"
                            onclick="makeNewWind(this.form)" />
                    </td>
                </tr>
            </table>
        </form>
        <br />
    </body>
</html>
```

JavaScript: jsb27-24.js

```javascript
function makeNewWind(form)
{
    if (window.netscape)
    {
        // will also get here if in Opera, but Opera will throw error, so...
        try
        {
        netscape.security.PrivilegeManager.enablePrivilege("UniversalBrowserWrite");
        }
        catch(e)
```

```
    {
        null;
    }
}
var attr = "width=300,height=300";
for (var i = 0; i < form.elements.length; i++)
{
    if (form.elements[i].type == "checkbox")
    {
        attr += "," + form.elements[i].name + "=";
        attr += (form.elements[i].checked) ? "yes" : "no";
    }
}
var newWind = window.open("bofright.html","subwindow",attr);
if (window.netscape)
{
    try
    {
        netscape.security.PrivilegeManager.revertPrivilege("CanvasAccess");
    }
    catch(e)
    {
        null;
    }
}
}
```

Specifying a window name

Getting back to the other parameters of `window.open()`, the second parameter is the name for the new window. Don't confuse this parameter with the document's title, which normally would be set by whatever HTML text determines the content of the window. A window name must be the same style of the one-word identifier that you use for other object names and variables. This name is also an entirely different entity from the `window` object that the `open()` method returns. You don't use the name in your scripts. At most, the name can be used for `target` attributes of links and forms.

Loading content into a new window

A script generally populates a window with one of two kinds of information:

- An existing HTML document whose URL is known beforehand
- An HTML page created on the fly

To create a new window that displays an existing HTML document, supply the URL as the first parameter of the `window.open()` method. If your page is having difficulty loading a URL into a new page, try specifying the complete URL of the target document (instead of just the filename).

Leaving the first parameter as an empty string forces the window to open with a blank document, ready to have HTML written to it by your script (or loaded separately by another statement that sets that window's location to a specific URL). If you plan to write the content of the window on the fly, assemble your HTML content as one long string value and then use the `document.write()` method to post that content to the new window. If you plan to append no further writing to the page, also include a `document.close()` method at the end to tell the browser that you're finished with the layout (so that the `Layout:Complete` or `Done` message appears in the status bar, if your new window has one).

A call to the `window.open()` method returns a reference to the new window's object if the window opens successfully. This value is vitally important if your script needs to address elements of that new window (such as when writing to its document).

To allow other functions in your script to reference the subwindow, you should assign the result of a `window.open()` method to a global variable. Before writing to the new window the first time, test the variable to make sure that it is not a `null` value; the window may have failed to open because of low memory, for instance. If everything is okay, you can use that variable as the beginning of a reference to any property or object within the new window. For example:

```
var newWindow
//...
function createNewWindow()
{
    newWindow = window.open("","");
    if (newWindow != null)
    {
        newWindow.document.write("<html><head><title>Hi!</title></head>");
    }
}
```

That global variable reference continues to be available for another function — perhaps one that closes the subwindow (via the `close()` method).

When scripts in the subwindow need to communicate with objects and scripts in the originating window, you must make sure that the subwindow has an `opener` property if the level of JavaScript in the visitor's browser doesn't automatically supply one. See the discussion about the `window.opener` property earlier in this chapter.

Invoking multiple `window.open()` methods with the same window name parameter (the second parameter) does not create additional copies of that window in Netscape browsers (although it does in Internet Explorer). JavaScript prevents you from creating two windows with the same name. Also be aware that a `window.open()` method does not bring an existing window of that name to the front of the window layers: Use `window.focus()` for that.

Internet Explorer idiosyncrasies

Creating subwindows in IE can sometimes be complicated by undesirable behavior by the browser. One of the most common problems occurs when you attempt to use `document.write()` to put content into a newly created window. IE, including some of the latest versions, fails to complete the window opening job before the script statement that uses `document.write()` executes. This causes a script error because the reference to the subwindow is not yet valid. To work around this, you should put the HTML assembly and `document.write()` statements in a separate function that gets invoked via a `setTimeout()` method after the window is created. You can see an example of this in Listing 27-25.

Another problem that affects IE is the occasional security violation ("access denied") warning when a script attempts to access a subwindow. This problem goes away when the page that includes the script for opening and accessing the subwindow is served from an HTTP server rather than accessed from a local hard disk.

Example

The page rendered by Listing 27-25 displays a single button that generates a new window of a specific size that has only the status bar turned on. The script here shows all the elements necessary to create a new window that has all the right stuff on most platforms. The new window object reference is assigned to a global variable, newWindow. Before a new window is generated, the script looks to see whether the window has never been generated before (in which case newWindow would be null) or, for newer browsers, the window is closed. If either condition is true, the window is created with the open() method; otherwise, the existing window is brought forward with the focus() method.

Due to the timing problem that afflicts all IE generations, the HTML assembly and writing to the new window are separated into their own function, which is invoked after a 50-millisecond delay (other browsers go along for the ride even if they could accommodate the assembly and writing without the delay). To build the string that is eventually written to the document, we use the += (add-by-value) operator, which appends the string on the right side of the operator to the string stored in the variable on the left side. In this example, the new window is handed an <h1>-level line of text to display.

LISTING 27-25

Creating a New Window

HTML: jsb27-25.html

```html
<!DOCTYPE html>
<html>
    <head>
        <meta http-equiv="content-type" content="text/html;charset=utf-8">
        <title>New Window</title>
        <script type="text/javascript" src="jsb27-25.js"></script>
    </head>
    <body>
        <h1>Creating a New Window</h1>
        <hr />
        <form>
            <input type="button" name="newOne" value="Create New Window"
                onclick="makeNewWindow()" />
        </form>
    </body>
</html>
```

JavaScript: jsb27-25.js

```javascript
var newWindow;

function makeNewWindow()
{
    if (!newWindow || newWindow.closed)
    {
        newWindow = window.open("","","status,height=200,width=300");
        // force small delay for IE to catch up
        setTimeout("writeToWindow()", 50);
```

continued

windowObject.openDialog()

LISTING 27-25   *(continued)*

```
    }
    else
    {
        // window's already open; bring to front
        newWindow.focus();
    }
}

function writeToWindow()
{
    // assemble content for new window
    var newContent = "<html><head><title>One Sub Window<\/title><\/head>";
    newContent += "<body><h1>This window is brand new.<\/h1>";
    newContent += "<\/body><\/html>";
    // write HTML to new window document
    newWindow.document.write(newContent);
    newWindow.document.close();   // close layout stream
}
```

The window.open() method can potentially create problems in browsers such as IE7+ and FF2+ that support tabbed browsing where multiple pages are opened as different tabs within the same browser instance. The default response to window.open() is to open a new tab for the new window, as opposed to a new browser window, which can be a problem if the script is truly expecting a completely new browser window.

Related Items: window.close(), window.blur(), window.focus(), window.openDialog() methods; window.closed property

openDialog("*URL*", "*windowName*" [, "*windowFeatures*"] [, *arg1*][, *arg2*] ...)

Returns: A window object representing the newly created dialog box (window); null if method fails

Compatibility: WinIE-, MacIE-, NN7+, Moz1.0.1+, Safari-, Opera-, Chrome-

The window.openDialog() method is a Mozilla-specific method that serves as a XUL counterpart to the window.open() method. XUL is Mozilla's XML-based user interface description language that is used throughout the Mozilla application suite. The openDialog() method offers a few extra window features, along with the ability to pass a varying number of arguments, which can be handy when creating custom windows.

The parameters to the openDialog() method are similar to those found in the open() method, except for the optional arg1, arg2, and so on. One notable difference is the addition of the all window feature, which is used to show (all=yes) or hide (all=no) all window features except chrome, dialog, and modal; these excluded features can still be shown or hidden individually.

Related Item: window.open() method

print()

Returns: Nothing

Compatibility: WinIE5+, MacIE5+, NN4+, Moz+, Safari+, Opera+, Chrome+

The print() method provides a scripted way of sending the window or a frame from a frameset to the printer. In all cases, the Print dialog box appears for the user to make the printer choices typical of printing manually. This prevents a rogue print() command from tying up a printer without the user's permission. Rather disconcertingly, the user has to reload the page to see the page content after sending the page to the printer.

WinIE5 introduced some print-specific event handlers that are triggered by scripted printing as well as manual printing. The events begin to fire after the user has accepted the Print dialog box. An onbeforeprint event handler can be used to show content that might be hidden from view but should appear in the printout. After the content has been sent to the print spooler, the onafterprint event can restore the page.

Example

Listing 27-26 is a frameset that loads Listing 27-27 into the top frame, and a copy of the Bill of Rights into the bottom frame.

LISTING 27-26

Print Example Frameset

```
<!DOCTYPE html>
<html>
   <head>
      <meta http-equiv="content-type" content="text/html;charset=utf-8">
      <title>window.print() method</title>
   </head>
   <frameset rows="25%,75%">
      <frame name="controls" src="jsb27-27.html" />
      <frame name="display" src="bofright.html" />
   </frameset>
</html>
```

Two buttons in the top control panel (see Listing 27-27) let you print the whole frameset (in those browsers and OS's that support it) or just the bottom frame. To print the entire frameset, the reference includes the parent window; to print the bottom frame, the reference is directed at the parent.display frame.

LISTING 27-27

Printing Control

```
<!DOCTYPE html>
<html>
   <head>
      <meta http-equiv="content-type" content="text/html;charset=utf-8">
```

continued

windowObject.prompt()

LISTING 27-27 *(continued)*

```
    <title>Print()</title>
  </head>
  <body>
    <h1>Print()</h1>
    <hr />
    <form>
      <input type="button" name="printWhole"
             value="Print Entire Frameset"
             onclick="parent.print()" />
      <p><input type="button" name="printFrame"
             value="Print Bottom Frame Only"
             onclick="parent.display.print()" />
      </p>
    </form>
  </body>
</html>
```

If you don't like some facet of the printed output, blame the browser's print engine, not JavaScript. The print() method merely invokes the browser's regular printing routines.

Related Items: window.back(), window.forward(), window.home(), window.find() methods

prompt("*message*", "*defaultReply*")

Returns: String of text entered by user, or null

Compatibility: WinIE3+, MacIE3+, NN2+, Moz+, Safari+, Opera+, Chrome+

The third kind of dialog box that JavaScript can display includes a message from the script author, a field for user entry, and two buttons (OK and Cancel). The script writer can supply a prewritten answer so that a user confronted with a prompt dialog box can click OK (or press Enter) to accept that answer without further typing. Supplying both parameters to the window.prompt() method is important. Even if you don't want to supply a default answer, enter an empty string as the second parameter:

```
        prompt("What is your postal code?","");
```

If you omit the second parameter, JavaScript inserts the string undefined into the dialog box's field. This message is disconcerting to most web-page visitors.

The value returned by this method is a string in the dialog box's field when the user clicks the OK button. If you're asking the user to enter a number, remember that the value returned by this method is a string. You may need to perform data-type conversion with the parseInt() or parseFloat() function (see Chapter 24, "Global Functions and Statements") to use the returned values in math calculations.

When the user clicks the prompt dialog box's OK button without entering any text in a blank field, the returned value is an empty string (""). Clicking the Cancel button, however, makes the method return a null value. Therefore, the scripter must test for the type of returned value to make sure that the user entered some data that can be processed later in the script, as in:

```
var entry = prompt("Enter a number between 1 and 10:","");
if (entry != null)
{
    //statements to execute with the value
}
```

This script excerpt assigns the results of the prompt dialog box to a variable and executes the nested statements if the returned value of the dialog box is not null (if the user clicked the OK button). The rest of the statements then include data validation to make sure that the entry is a number within the desired range (see Chapter 46, "Data-Entry Validation," on the CD-ROM).

It may be tempting to use the prompt dialog box as a handy user input device. But as with the other JavaScript dialog boxes, the modality of the prompt dialog box is disruptive to the user's flow through a document and can also trap automated macros that some users activate to capture web sites. In forms, HTML fields are better user interface elements for attracting user text entry. Perhaps the safest way to use a prompt dialog box is to have it appear when a user clicks a button element on a page — and then only if the information you require of the user can be provided in a single prompt dialog box. Presenting a sequence of prompt dialog boxes is downright annoying to users.

Example

The function that receives values from the prompt dialog box in Listing 27-28 (see the dialog box in Figure 27-7) does some data-entry validation (but certainly not enough for a commercial site). The function first checks to make sure that the returned value is neither null (Cancel) nor an empty string (the user clicked OK without entering any values). See Chapter 46 for more about data-entry validation.

LISTING 27-28

The Prompt Dialog Box

```
<!DOCTYPE html>
<html>
    <head>
        <meta http-equiv="content-type" content="text/html;charset=utf-8">
        <title>window.prompt() Method</title>
        <script type="text/javascript">
            function populateTable()
            {
                var howMany = prompt("Fill in table for how many factors?","");
                if (howMany != null && howMany != "")
                {
                    alert("Filling the table for " + howMany);    // for demo
                    //statements that validate the entry and
                    //actually populate the fields of the table
                }
            }
        </script>
```

continued

LISTING 27-28   *(continued)*

```
</head>
<body>
    <h1>window.prompt() Method</h1>
    <hr />
    <form>
        <h3>Other statements that display and populate a large table
            would be here.</h3>
        <input type="button" name="fill" value="Fill Table..."
            onclick="populateTable()" />
    </form>
</body>
</html>
```

FIGURE 27-7

The prompt dialog box from Listing 27-28 displayed in Internet Explorer.

Notice one important user interface element in Listing 27-28. Because clicking the button leads to a dialog box that requires more information from the user, the button's label ends in an ellipsis (or, rather, three periods acting as an ellipsis character). The ellipsis is a common courtesy to let users know that a user interface element leads to a dialog box of some sort. Consistent with stand-alone applications, the user should be able to cancel out of that dialog box and return to the same screen state that existed before the button was clicked.

Related Items: `window.alert()`, `window.confirm()` methods

resizeBy(*deltaX,deltaY*)
resizeTo(*outerwidth,outerheight*)

Returns: Nothing

Compatibility: WinIE4+, MacIE4+, NN4, Moz+, Safari 1+, Opera-, Chrome-

Starting with version 4 browsers, scripts can control the size of the current browser window on the fly (no longer available in Mozilla-based browsers). Although you can set the individual inner and (in NN4) outer width and height properties of a window, the `resizeBy()` and `resizeTo()` methods let you adjust both axis measurements in one statement. In both instances, all adjustments affect the bottom-right corner of the window. To move the top-left corner, use the `window.moveBy()` or `window.moveTo()` methods.

Each resize method requires a different kind of parameter. The `resizeBy()` method adjusts the window by a certain number of pixels along one or both axes. Therefore, it is not concerned with the specific size of the window beforehand — only by how much each axis is to change. For example, to increase the current window size by 100 pixels horizontally and 50 pixels vertically, the statement is

```
window.resizeBy(100, 50);
```

Both parameters are required, but if you want to adjust the size in only one direction, set the other to zero. You may also shrink the window by using negative values for either or both parameters.

You may find a greater need for the `resizeTo()` method, especially when you know that on a particular platform, the window needs adjustment to a specific width and height to best accommodate that platform's display of form elements. Parameters for the `resizeTo()` method are the actual pixel width and height of the outer dimension of the window — the same as NN4's `window.outerWidth` and `window.outerHeight` properties.

To resize the window so that it occupies all screen real estate (except for the Windows taskbar and Macintosh menu bar), use the `screen` object properties that calculate the available screen space:

```
window.resizeBy(screen.availWidth, screen.availHeight);
```

This action, however, is not precisely the same in Windows as maximizing the window. To achieve that same effect, you must move the window to coordinates -4, -4 and add 8 to the two parameters of `resizeBy()`:

```
window.moveTo(-4,-4);
window.resizeTo(screen.availWidth + 8, screen.availHeight + 8);
```

This hides the window's own 4-pixels-wide border, as occurs during OS-induced window maximizing. See also the `screen` object discussion (see Chapter 41, "Table and List Objects") for more OS-specific details.

On some platforms, the dimensions are applied to the inner width and height rather than outer. If a specific outer size is necessary, use the NN-specific `window.outerHeight` and `window.outerWidth` properties instead.

Navigator 4 imposes some security restrictions for maximum and minimum size for a window. For both methods, you are limited to the viewable area of the screen and visible minimums unless the page uses signed scripts (see Chapter 49). With signed scripts and the user's permission, for example, you can adjust windows beyond the available screen borders.

Example

You can experiment with the resize methods with the page in Listing 27-29. Two parts of a form let you enter values for each method. The one for `window.resize()` also lets you enter several repetitions to better see the impact of the values. Enter zero and negative values to see how those affect the method. Also test the limits of different browsers.

windowObject.resizeTo()

LISTING 27-29

Window Resize Methods

```html
<!DOCTYPE html>
<html>
    <head>
        <meta http-equiv="content-type" content="text/html;charset=utf-8">
        <title>Window Resize Methods</title>
        <style type="text/css">
            .instructions
            {
                font-weight:bold;
            }
        </style>
        <script type="text/javascript">
            function doResizeBy(form)
            {
                var x = parseInt(form.resizeByX.value);
                var y = parseInt(form.resizeByY.value);
                var count = parseInt(form.count.value);
                for (var i = 0; i < count; i++)
                {
                    window.resizeBy(x, y);
                }
            }
            function doResizeTo(form)
            {
                var x = parseInt(form.resizeToX.value);
                var y = parseInt(form.resizeToY.value);
                window.resizeTo(x, y);
            }
        </script>
    </head>
    <body>
        <h1>Window Resize Methods</h1>
        <hr />
        <form>
            <div class="instructions">Enter the x and y increment,
                plus how many times the window should
                be resized by these increments:
            </div>
            Horiz:<input type="text" name="resizeByX" size="4" />
            Vert:<input type="text" name="resizeByY" size="4" />
            How Many:<input type="text" name="count" size="4" />
            <input type="button" name="ResizeBy" value="Show resizeBy()"
                    onclick="doResizeBy(this.form)" />
            <hr />
            <div class="instructions">Enter the desired width
                and height of the current window:</div>
            Width:<input type="text" name="resizeToX" size="4" />
```

```
        Height:<input type="text" name="resizeToY" size="4" />
        <input type="button" name="ResizeTo" value="Show resizeTo()"
               onclick="doResizeTo(this.form)" />
    </form>
  </body>
</html>
```

Related Items: window.outerHeight, window.outerWidth properties; window.moveTo(), window.sizeToContent() methods

scroll (*horizontalCoord, verticalCoord*)

Returns: Nothing

Compatibility: WinIE4+, MacIE4+, NN3+, Moz+, Safari+, Opera+, Chrome+

The window.scroll() method was introduced in NN3 and has been implemented in all scriptable browsers since then. But in the meantime, the method has been replaced by the window.scrollTo() method, which is in more syntactic alliance with many other window methods.

The window.scroll() method takes two parameters: the horizontal (x) and vertical (y) coordinates of the document that is to be positioned at the top-left corner of the window or frame. You must realize that the window and document have two similar, but independent, coordinate schemes. From the window's point of view, the top-left pixel (of the content area) is point 0,0. All documents also have a 0,0 point: the very top left of the document. The window's 0,0 point doesn't move, but the document's 0,0 point can move — via manual or scripted scrolling. Although scroll() is a window method, it seems to behave more like a document method, as the document appears to reposition itself within the window. Conversely, you can also think of the window moving to bring its 0,0 point to the designated coordinate of the document.

Although you can set values beyond the maximum size of the document or to negative values, the results vary from platform to platform. For the moment, the best usage of the window.scroll() method is as a means of adjusting the scroll to the very top of a document (window.scroll(0,0)) when you want the user to be at a base location in the document. For vertical scrolling within a text-heavy document, an HTML anchor may be a better alternative for now (though it doesn't readjust horizontal scrolling).

Related Items: window.scrollBy(), window.scrollTo() methods

Unwanted User Scrolling

Wheeled mice have become increasingly popular. These mice include a scroll wheel that is activated by pressing down on the wheel and spinning the wheel. Be aware that even if your page design loads into frames or new windows that intentionally lack scroll bars, the page will be scrollable via this wheel if the document or its background image is larger than the window or frame. Users may not even be aware that they have scrolled the page (because there are no scroll-bar visual clues). If this affects your design, you may need to build in a routine (via setTimeout()) that periodically sets the scroll of the window to 0,0.

windowObject.scrollBy()

```
scrollBy(deltaX,deltaY)
scrollTo(x,y)
```

Returns: Nothing

Compatibility: WinIE4+, MacIE4+, NN4+, Moz+, Safari+, Opera+, Chrome+

Modern browsers provide a related pair of window scrolling methods. The window.scrollTo() method is the newer version of the window.scroll() method. The two work identically to position a specific coordinate point of a document at the top-left corner of the inner window region.

By contrast, the window.scrollBy() method allows for relative positioning of the document. Parameter values indicate by how many pixels the document should scroll in the window (horizontally and vertically). Negative numbers are allowed if you want to scroll to the left and/or up. The scrollBy() method comes in handy if you elect to hide the scroll bars of a window or frame and offer other types of scrolling controls for your users. For example, to scroll down one entire screen of a long document, you can use the window.innerHeight (in NN/Moz) or document.body.clientHeight (in IE) properties to determine what the offset from the current position would be:

```
// assign IE body clientHeight to window.innerHeight
if (document.body && document.body.clientHeight)
{
    window.innerHeight = document.body.clientHeight;
}
window.scrollBy(0, window.innerHeight);
```

To scroll up, use a negative value for the second parameter:

```
window.scrollBy(0, -window.innerHeight);
```

The window scroll methods are not the ones to use to produce the scrolling effect of a positioned element. That kind of animation is accomplished by adjusting style position properties (see Chapter 43, "Positioned Objects").

Example

To work with the scrollTo() method, you can use Listing 27-30, Listing 27-31, and Listing 27-32. The code in Listing 27-34 includes a control panel frame (similar to Listing 27-32) that provides input to experiment with the scrollBy() method.

LISTING 27-30

Frameset for ScrollBy Controller

```
<!DOCTYPE html>
<html>
    <head>
        <meta http-equiv="content-type" content="text/html;charset=utf-8">
        <title>window.scrollBy() Method</title>
    </head>
```

```
   <frameset rows="50%,50%">
      <frame src="jsb27-31.html" name="display" />
      <frame src="jsb27-32.html" name="control" />
   </frameset>
</html>
```

LISTING 27-31

The Image to Be Scrolled

```
<!DOCTYPE html>
<html>
   <head>
      <meta http-equiv="content-type" content="text/html;charset=utf-8">
      <title>Arch</title>
   </head>
   <body>
      <h1>
         A Picture is Worth...
      </h1>
      <hr />
      <center>
         <table border="3">
            <caption align="bottom">
               A Splendid Arch
            </caption>
            <tr>
               <td>
                  <img alt="image" src="arch.gif" />
               </td>
            </tr>
         </table>
      </center>
   </body>
</html>
```

Notice in Listing 27-32 that all references to window properties and methods are directed to the `display` frame. String values retrieved from text fields are converted to numbers with the `parseInt()` global function.

LISTING 27-32

ScrollBy Controller

```
<!DOCTYPE html>
<html>
   <head>
      <meta http-equiv="content-type" content="text/html;charset=utf-8">
      <title>ScrollBy Controller</title>
      <script type="text/javascript">
```

continued

windowObject.**scrollByLines()**

LISTING 27-32   *(continued)*

```
        function page(direction)
        {
            var pixFrame = parent.display;
            var deltaY = (pixFrame.innerHeight) ? pixFrame.innerHeight :
                pixFrame.document.body.scrollHeight;
            if (direction == "up")
            {
                deltaY = -deltaY;
            }
            parent.display.scrollBy(0, deltaY);
        }
        function customScroll(form)
        {
            parent.display.scrollBy(parseInt(form.x.value), parseInt(form.y.value));
        }
    </script>
</head>
<body>
    <h1>ScrollBy Controller</h1>
    <hr />
    <form name="custom">
        Enter an Horizontal increment
        <input type="text" name="x" value="0" size="4" />
        and Vertical
        <input type="text" name="y" value="0" size="4" /> value.
        <br />
        Then
        <input type="button" value="click to scrollBy()"
                onclick="customScroll(this.form)" />
        <hr />
        <input type="button" value="PageDown" onclick="page('down')" />
        <input type="button" value="PageUp" onclick="page('up')" />
    </form>
</body>
</html>
```

Related Items: window.pageXOffset, window.pageYOffset properties; window.scroll() method

scrollByLines(*intervalCount*)
scrollByPages(*intervalCount*)

Returns: Nothing

Compatibility: WinIE-, MacIE-, NN6+, Moz+, Safari-, Opera-, Chrome-

The window.scrollByLines() and window.scrollByPages() methods scroll the document by a specified number of lines or pages, respectively. You can think of these methods as the script equivalents to clicking the arrow (scrollByLines()) and page (scrollByPages()) regions of the browser's vertical scroll bar. The argument to each method determines how many lines or pages to scroll, with positive values resulting in downward scrolling, and negative values resulting in upward scrolling.

```
setInterval("expr", msecDelay [, language])
setInterval(funcRef, msecDelay [, funcarg1, ... ,
funcargn])
```

Returns: Interval ID integer

Compatibility: WinIE4+, MacIE4+, NN4+, Moz+, Safari+, Opera+, Chrome+

It is important to understand the distinction between the setInterval() and setTimeout() methods. Before the setInterval() method was part of JavaScript, authors replicated the behavior with setTimeout(), but the task often required reworking scripts a bit.

Use setInterval() when your script needs to call a function or execute some expression repeatedly with a fixed time delay between calls to that function or expression. The delay is not at all like a wait state in some languages: Other processing does not halt while the delay is in effect. Typical applications include animation by moving an object around the page under controlled speed (instead of letting the JavaScript interpreter whiz the object through its path at CPU-dependent speeds). In a kiosk application, you can use setInterval() to advance slides that appear in other frames or as layers, perhaps changing the view every 10 seconds. Clock displays and countdown timers would also be suitable uses of this method (even though you see examples in this book that use the old-fashioned setTimeout() way to perform timer and clock functions).

By contrast, setTimeout() is best suited for those times when you need to carry out a function or expression once in the future — even if that future is only a second or two away. In other words, setTimeout() gives you a one-shot timer, whereas setInterval() gives you a recurring timer. See the discussion of the setTimeout() method later in this chapter for details on this application.

Although the primary functionality of the setInterval() method is the same in all browsers, NN/Moz and IE offer some extra possibilities depending on the way you use parameters to the method. For simple invocations of this method, the same parameters work in all browsers that support the method. First, we address the parameters that all browsers have in common.

The first parameter of the setInterval() method is the name of the function or expression to run after the interval elapses. This item must be a quoted string. If the parameter is a function, no function arguments are allowed inside the function's parentheses unless the arguments are literal strings (but see the next section, "Passing function parameters").

The second parameter of this method is the number of milliseconds (1,000 per second) that JavaScript should use as the interval between invocations of the function or expression. Even though the measure is in extremely small units, don't rely on 100 percent accuracy of the intervals. Various other internal processing delays may throw off the timing just a bit.

Just like setTimeout(), setInterval() returns an integer value that is the ID for the interval process. That ID value lets you turn off the process with the clearInterval() method, which takes the ID value as its sole parameter. This mechanism allows for the setting of multiple running interval processes and gives your scripts the power to stop individual processes at any time without interrupting the others.

IE4+ uses the optional third parameter to specify the scripting language of the statement or function being invoked in the first parameter. As long as you are scripting exclusively in JavaScript (the same as JScript), there is no need to include this parameter.

Passing function parameters

NN4+/Moz provides a mechanism for easily passing evaluated parameters to a function invoked by setInterval(). To use this mechanism, the first parameter of setInterval() must not be a string, but a reference to the function (no trailing parentheses). The second parameter remains the amount of delay. But beginning with the third parameter, you can include evaluated function arguments as a comma-delimited list:

```
intervalID = setInterval(cycleAnimation, 500, "figure1");
```

The function definition receives those parameters in the same form as any function:

```
function cycleAnimation(elemID) {...}
```

For use with a wider range of browsers, you can also cobble together the ability to pass parameters to a function invoked by setInterval(). Because the call to the other function is a string expression, you can use computed values as part of the strings, via string concatenation. For example, if a function uses event handling to find the element that a user clicked (to initiate some animation sequence), that element's ID, referenced by a variable, can be passed to the function invoked by setInterval():

```
function findAndCycle()
{
    var elemID;
    // statements here that examine the event info
    // and extract the ID of the clicked element,
    // assigning that ID to the elemID variable
    intervalID = setInterval("cycleAnimation(" + elemID + ")", 500);
}
```

If you need to pass ever-changing parameters with each invocation of the function from setInterval(), look instead to using setTimeout() at the end of a function to invoke that same function again.

Example

The demonstration of the setInterval() method entails a two-framed environment. The framesetting document is shown in Listing 27-33.

LISTING 27-33

SetInterval() Demonstration Frameset

```
<!DOCTYPE html>
<html>
    <head>
        <meta http-equiv="content-type" content="text/html;charset=utf-8">
<title>setInterval() Method</title>
    </head>
    <frameset rows="50%,50%">
        <frame src="jsb27-34.html" name="control" />
        <frame src="bofright.html" name="display" />
    </frameset>
</html>
```

In the top frame is a control panel with several buttons that control the automatic scrolling of the Bill of Rights text document in the bottom frame. Listing 27-34 shows the control-panel document. Many functions here control the interval, scrolling jump size, and direction, and they demonstrate several aspects of applying setInterval().

Notice that in the beginning the script establishes several global variables. Three of them are parameters that control the scrolling; the last one is for the ID value returned by the setInterval() method. The script needs that value to be a global value so that a separate function can halt the scrolling with the clearInterval() method.

All scrolling is performed by the autoScroll() function. For the sake of simplicity, all controlling parameters are global variables. In this application, placement of those values in global variables helps the page restart autoscrolling with the same parameters as it had when it last ran.

LISTING 27-34

SetInterval() Control Panel

HTML: jsb27-34.html

```html
<!DOCTYPE html>
<html>
    <head>
        <meta http-equiv="content-type" content="text/html;charset=utf-8">
        <title>ScrollBy Controller</title>
        <script type="text/javascript" src="jsb27-34.js"></script>
    </head>
    <body onload="startScroll()">
        <h1>AutoScroll by setInterval() Controller</h1>
        <hr />
        <form name="custom">
            <input type="button" value="Start Scrolling"
                    onclick="startScroll()" />
            <input type="button" value="Stop Scrolling"
                    onclick="stopScroll()" />
            <p>
                <input type="button" value="Shorter Time Interval"
                        onclick="reduceInterval()" />
                <input type="button" value="Longer Time Interval"
                        onclick="increaseInterval()" />
            </p>
            <p><input type="button" value="Bigger Scroll Jumps"
                        onclick="increaseJump()" />
                <input type="button" value="Smaller Scroll Jumps"
                        onclick="reduceJump()" />
            </p>
            <p><input type="button" value="Change Direction"
                        onclick="swapDirection()" />
            </p>
        </form>
    </body>
</html>
```

continued

windowObject.setInterval()

LISTING 27-34   *(continued)*

```javascript
JavaScript: jsb27-34.js

var scrollSpeed = 500;
var scrollJump = 1;
var scrollDirection = "down";
var intervalID;

function autoScroll()
{
   if (scrollDirection == "down")
   {
      scrollJump = Math.abs(scrollJump);
   }
   else if (scrollDirection == "up" && scrollJump > 0)
   {
      scrollJump = -scrollJump;
   }
   parent.display.scrollBy(0, scrollJump);
   if (parent.display.pageYOffset <= 0)
   {
      clearInterval(intervalID);
   }
}

function reduceInterval()
{
   stopScroll();
   scrollSpeed -= 200;
   startScroll();
}
function increaseInterval()
{
   stopScroll();
   scrollSpeed += 200;
   startScroll();
}
function reduceJump()
{
   scrollJump -= 2;
}
function increaseJump()
{
   scrollJump += 2;
}
function swapDirection()
{
   scrollDirection = (scrollDirection == "down") ? "up" : "down";
}
function startScroll()
```

```
{
    parent.display.scrollBy(0, scrollJump);
    if (intervalID)
    {
        clearInterval(intervalID);
    }
    intervalID = setInterval("autoScroll()",scrollSpeed);
}
function stopScroll()
{
    clearInterval(intervalID);
}
```

The setInterval() method is invoked inside the startScroll() function. This function initially burps the page by one scrollJump interval so that the test in autoScroll() for the page being scrolled all the way to the top doesn't halt a page from scrolling before it gets started. Notice, too, that the function checks for the existence of an interval ID. If one is there, it is cleared before the new one is set. This is crucial within the design of the example page, because repeated clicking of the Start Scrolling button triggers multiple interval timers inside the browser. Only the most recent one's ID would be stored in intervalID, allowing no way to clear the older ones. But this little side trip makes sure that only one interval timer is running. One of the global variables, scrollSpeed, is used to fill the delay parameter for setInterval(). To change this value on the fly, the script must stop the current interval process, change the scrollSpeed value, and start a new process.

The intensely repetitive nature of this application is nicely handled by the setInterval() method.

Related Items: window.clearInterval(), window.setTimeout() methods

setTimeout("*expr*", *msecDelay* [, *language*])
setTimeout(*functionRef*, *msecDelay* [, *funcarg1*, ... , *funcargn*])

Returns: ID value for use with window.clearTimeout() method

Compatibility: WinIE3+, MacIE3+, NN2+, Moz+, Safari+, Opera+, Chrome+

The name of this method may be misleading, especially if you have done other kinds of programming involving timeouts. In JavaScript, a *timeout* is an amount of time (in milliseconds) before a stated expression evaluates. A timeout is not a wait or script delay, but a way to tell JavaScript to hold off executing a statement or function for a desired amount of time. Other statements following the one containing setTimeout() execute immediately.

Suppose that you have a web page designed to enable users to interact with a variety of buttons or fields within a time limit (this is a web page running at a freestanding kiosk). You can turn on the timeout of the window so that if no interaction occurs with specific buttons or fields lower in the document after, say, 2 minutes (120,000 milliseconds), the window reverts to the top of the document or to a help screen. To tell the window to switch off the timeout after a user does navigate within the allotted time, you need to have any button that the user interacts with call the other side of a setTimeout() method — the clearTimeout() method — to cancel the current timer. (The clearTimeout() method is explained earlier in this chapter.) Multiple timers can run concurrently and are completely independent of one another.

windowObject.setTimeout()

Although the primary functionality of the setTimeout() method is the same in all browsers, NN/Moz and IE offer some extra possibilities depending on the way you use parameters to the method. For simple invocations of this method, the same parameters work in all browsers that support the method. We first address the parameters that all browsers have in common.

The expression that comprises the first parameter of the method window.setTimeout() is a quoted string that can contain either a call to any function or method, or a stand-alone JavaScript statement. The expression evaluates after the time limit expires.

Understanding that this timeout does not halt script execution is very important. In fact, if you use a setTimeout() method in the middle of a script, the succeeding statements in the script execute immediately; after the delay time, the expression in the setTimeout() method executes. Therefore, we've found that the best way to design a timeout in a script is to plug it in as the last statement of a function: Let all other statements execute and then let the setTimeout() method appear to halt further execution until the timer goes off. In truth, however, although the timeout is holding, the user is not prevented from performing other tasks. And after a timeout timer is ticking, you cannot adjust its time. Instead, clear the timeout and start a new one.

If you need to use setTimeout() as a delay inside a function, break the function into two parts, using the setTimeout() method as a bridge between the two functions. You can see an example of this in Listing 27-25, where IE needs a little delay to finish opening a new window before content can be written for it. If it weren't for the required delay, the HTML assembly and writing would have been accomplished in the same function that opens the new window.

It is not uncommon for a setTimeout() method to invoke the very function in which it lives. For example, if you have written a Java applet to perform some extra work for your page, and you need to connect to it via the NPAPI, your scripts must wait for the applet to load and carry out its initializations. Although an onload event handler in the document ensures that the applet object is visible to scripts, it doesn't know whether the applet has finished its initializations. A JavaScript function that inspects the applet for a clue might need to poll the applet every 500 milliseconds until the applet sets some internal value indicating that all is ready, as shown here:

```
var t;
function autoReport()
{
    if (!document.myApplet.done)
    {
        t = setTimeout("autoReport()",500);
    }
    else
    {
        clearTimeout(t);
        // more statements using applet data //
    }
}
```

JavaScript provides no built-in equivalent for a wait command. The worst alternative is to devise a looping function of your own to trap script execution for a fixed amount of time. Unfortunately, this approach prevents other processes from being carried out, so you should consider reworking your code to rely on a setTimeout() method instead.

NN4+/Moz provides a mechanism for passing parameters to functions invoked by setTimeout(). See the section "Passing function parameters" in the discussion of window.setInterval() for details on this topic, and on passing parameters in other browser versions.

As a note to experienced programmers, neither `setInterval()` nor `setTimeout()` spawns new threads in which to run its invoked scripts. When the timer expires and invokes a function, the process gets at the end of the pending script processing queue in the JavaScript execution thread.

Example

When you load the HTML page in Listing 27-35, it triggers the `updateTime()` function, which displays the time (in hh:mm am/pm format) in the status bar. Instead of showing the seconds incrementing one by one (which may be distracting to someone trying to read the page), this function alternates the last character of the display between an asterisk and nothing, like a visual heartbeat.

LISTING 27-35

Display the Current Time

```html
<html>
    <head>
        <meta http-equiv="content-type" content="text/html;charset=utf-8">
        <title>Status Bar Clock</title>
        <script type="text/javascript" src="../jsb-global.js"></script>
        <script type="text/javascript">
            // initialize when the page has loaded
            addEvent(window, "load", updateTime);

            var flasher = false;
            // calculate current time, determine flasher state,
            // and insert time into status bar every second
            function updateTime()
            {
                var now = new Date();
                var theHour = now.getHours();
                var theMin = now.getMinutes();
                var theTime = "" + ((theHour > 12) ? theHour - 12 : theHour);
                theTime += ((theMin < 10) ? ":0" : ":") + theMin;
                theTime += (theHour >= 12) ? " pm" : " am";
                theTime += ((flasher) ? " " : "*");
                flasher = !flasher;
                window.status = theTime;
                // recursively call this function every second to keep timer going
                timerID = setTimeout("updateTime()",1000);
            }
        </script>
    </head>
    <body>
        <h1>Status Bar Clock</h1>
        <hr />
    </body>
</html>
```

In this function, the `setTimeout()` method works in the following way: When the current time (including the flasher status) appears in the status bar, the function waits approximately 1 second

(1,000 milliseconds) before calling the same function again. You don't have to clear the `timerID` value in this application because JavaScript does it for you every time the 1,000 milliseconds elapse.

A logical question to ask is whether this application should be using `setInterval()` instead of `setTimeout()`. This is a case in which either one does the job. Using `setInterval()` here would require that the interval process start outside the `updateTime()` function, because you need only one process running that repeatedly calls `updateTime()`. It would be a cleaner implementation instead of the numerous timeout processes spawned by Listing 27-35. On the other hand, the application would not run in legacy browsers, as Listing 27-35 does. That's likely not a problem at this point in time, but this application remains a decent example of the `setTimeout()` function.

To demonstrate passing parameters, you can modify the `updateTime()` function to add the number of times it gets invoked to the display in the status bar. For that to work, the function must have a parameter variable so that it can catch a new value each time it is invoked by `setTimeout()`'s expression. For all browsers, the function would be modified as follows (unchanged lines are represented by the ellipsis):

```
function updateTime(i)
{
    //...
    window.status = theTime + "  (" + i + ")";
    // pass updated counter value with next call to this function
    timerID = setTimeout("updateTime(" + i+1 + ")",1000);
}
```

If you were running this exclusively in NN4+/Moz, you could use its more convenient way of passing parameters to the function:

```
timerID = setTimeout(updateTime, 1000, i+1);
```

In either case, the `onload` event handler would also have to be modified to get the ball rolling with an initial parameter:

```
onload = "updateTime(0)";
```

Related Items: `window.clearTimeout()`, `window.setInterval()`, `window.clearInterval()` methods

showHelp(*"URL"*,[*"contextID"*])

Returns: Nothing

Compatibility: WinIE4+, MacIE-, NN-, Moz-, Safari-, Opera-, Chrome-

The IE-specific `showHelp()` method lets a script open a Winhelp window with a particular `.hlp` file. This method is specific to Win32 operating systems.

If your Winhelp file has context identifiers specified in various places, you can pass the ID as an optional second parameter. This lets the call to `showHelp()` navigate to the particular area of the `.hlp` file that applies to a specific element on the page.

See the Microsoft Visual Studio authoring environment for details on building Winhelp files.

```
showModalDialog("URL"[, arguments][, features])
showModelessDialog("URL"[, arguments][, features])
```

Returns: `returnValue` (modal) or `window` object (modeless)

Compatibility: WinIE4+, MacIE4+, NN-, Moz+, Safari 2.01+, Opera-, Chrome+

IE, Safari, Chrome, and Mozilla-based browsers such as Firefox, provide methods for opening a modal dialog-box window, which always stays in front of the main browser window, while making the main window inaccessible to the user. In WinIE5, Microsoft added the modeless type of dialog box, which is not supported by Safari, Chrome and Mozilla-based browsers such as Firefox. The modeless type of dialog box also stays in front but allows user access to whatever can be seen in the main window. You can load any HTML page or image that you like into the dialog-box window by providing a URL as the first parameter. Optional parameters let you pass data to a dialog box and give you considerable control over the look of the window. A similar type of dialog-box window is available in NN/Moz via the `window.openDialog()` method.

The windows generated by both methods are (almost) full-fledged `window` objects, with some extra properties that are useful for what these windows are intended to do. Perhaps the most important property is the `window.dialogArgument` property. This property lets a script read the data that is passed to the window via the second parameter of both `showModalDialog()` and `show-ModelessDialog()`. Passed data can be in any valid JavaScript data type, including objects and arrays.

Displaying a modal dialog box has some ramifications for scripts. In particular, script execution in the main window halts at the statement that invokes the `showModalDialog()` method as long as the modal dialog box remains visible. Scripts are free to run in the dialog-box window during this time. The instant the user closes the dialog box, execution resumes in the main window. A call to show a modeless dialog box, on the other hand, does not halt processing because scripts in the main page or dialog-box window are allowed to communicate live with the other window.

Retrieving dialog-box data

To send data back to the main window's script from a modal dialog-box window, a script in the dialog-box window can set the `window.returnValue` property to any JavaScript value. It is this value that gets assigned to the variable receiving the returned value from the `setModelDialog()` method, as shown in the following example:

```
var specifications = window.showModalDialog("preferences.html");
```

The makeup and content of the returned data are in the hands of your scripts. No data is automatically returned for you.

Because a modeless dialog box coexists with your live main page window, returning data is not as straightforward as for a modal dialog box. The second parameter of the `showModelessDialog()` method takes on a special task that isn't exactly the same as passing parameters to the dialog box. Instead, if you define a global variable or a function in the main window's script, pass a reference to that variable or function as the second parameter to display the modeless dialog box. A script in the modeless dialog box can then point to that reference as the way to send data back to the main window before the dialog box closes (or when a user clicks something, such as an Apply button). This mechanism even allows for passing data back to a function in the main window. For example, say that the main window has a function defined as the following:

```
function receivePrefsDialogData(a, b, c)
{
    // statements to process incoming values //
}
```

Then pass a reference to this function when opening the window:

```
dlog = showModelessDialog("prefs.html", receivePrefsDialogData);
```

A script statement in the dialog-box window's document can pick up that reference so that other statements, such as a function for an Apply button's `onclick` event handler, can use it:

```
var returnFunc = window.dialogArguments;
//...
function apply(form)
{
    returnFunc(form.color.value, form.style.value, form.size.value);
}
```

Although this approach seems to block ways of getting parameters to the dialog box when it opens, you can always reference the dialog box in the main window's script and set form or variable values directly:

```
dlog = showModelessDialog("prefs.html", receivePrefsDialogData);
dlog.document.forms[0].userName.value = GetCookie("userName");
```

Be aware that a dialog-box window opened with either of these methods does not maintain a connection to the originating window via the `opener` property. The `opener` property for both dialog-box types is undefined.

Dialog-box window features

Both methods provide an optional third property that lets you specify visible features of the dialog-box window. Omitting the property sets all features to their default values. All parameters are to be contained by a single string, and each parameter's name–value pair is in the form of CSS `attribute:value` syntax. Table 27-5 lists all the window features available for the two window styles. If you are designing for backward compatibility with IE4, you are restricted to the modal dialog box and a subset of features, as noted in the table. All values listed as Boolean take only the following four values: `yes`, `no`, `1`, and `0`.

The CSS-type of syntax for these features lets you thread multiple features together by separating each pair with a semicolon within the string. For example:

```
var dlogData = showModalDialog("prefs.html", defaultData,
    "dialogHeight:300px; dialogWidth:460px; help:no");
```

Although they are not explicitly listed among the window features, scroll bars are normally displayed in the window if the content exceeds the size assigned or available to the dialog box. If you don't want scroll bars to appear, have your dialog-box document's script set the `document.body.scroll` property to `false` as the page opens.

TABLE 27-5

IE Dialog-Box Window Features

Feature	Type	Default	Description
center	Boolean	yes	Whether to center dialog box (overridden by dialogLeft and/or dialogTop).
dialogHeight	Length	Varies	Outer height of the dialog-box window. IE4 default length unit is em; IE5+/Moz/Safari/Chrome is pixel (px).
dialogLeft	Integer	Varies	Pixel offset of dialog box from left edge of screen.
dialogTop	Integer	Varies	Pixel offset of dialog box from top edge of screen.
dialogWidth	Length	Varies	Outer width of the dialog-box window. IE4 default length unit is em; IE5+/Moz/Safari/Chrome is pixel (px).
edge	String	raised | sunken	Border style (IE only).
resizable	Boolean	no	Dialog box is resizable.
scroll	Boolean	yes	Display scrollbars
status	Boolean	Varies	Display status bar at window bottom (IE5+/Safari/Chrome only). Default is yes for untrusted dialog box, no for trusted dialog box.

Dialog-box cautions

A potential user problem to watch for is that typically, a dialog-box window does not open until the HTML file for the dialog box has loaded. Therefore, if there is substantial delay before a complex document loads, the user does not see any action indicating that something is happening. You may want to experiment with setting the cursor style sheet property and restoring it when the dialog box's document loads.

Example

To demonstrate the two styles of dialog boxes, we have implemented the same functionality (setting some session visual preferences) for both modal and modeless dialog boxes. This tactic shows you how to pass data back and forth between the main page and both styles of dialog-box windows.

The first example demonstrates how to use a modal dialog box. In the process, data is passed into the dialog-box window, and values are returned. Listing 27-36 is the HTML and scripting for the main page. A button's onclick event handler invokes a function that opens the modal dialog box. The dialog box's document (see Listing 27-37) contains several form elements for entering a user name and selecting a few color styles for the main page. Data from the dialog box is fashioned into an array to be sent back to the main window. That array is initially assigned to a local variable, prefs, as the dialog box closes. If the user cancels the dialog box, the returned value is an empty string, so nothing more in getPrefsData() executes. But when the user clicks OK, the array comes back. Each of the array items is read and assigned to its respective form value or style property. These values are also preserved in the global `currPrefs` array. This allows the settings to be sent to the modal dialog box (as the second parameter to `showModalDialog()`) the next time the dialog box is opened.

LISTING 27-36

Main Page for showModalDialog()

HTML: jsb27-36.html

```html
<html>
    <head>
        <title>window.setModalDialog() Method</title>
        <script type="text/javascript" src="jsb27-36.js"></script>
    </head>
    <body bgcolor="#EEEEEE" style="margin:20px" onload="init()">
        <h1>window.setModalDialog() Method</h1>
        <hr />
        <h2 id="welcomeHeader">Welcome, <span id="firstName">.</span>!</h2>
        <hr />
        <p>Use this button to set style preferences for this page:
            <button id="prefsButton" onclick="getPrefsData()">Preferences</button>
        </p>
    </body>
</html>
```

JavaScript: jsb27-36.js

```javascript
var currPrefs = new Array();
var nameHolder;

function getPrefsData()
{
    var prefs = showModalDialog("jsb27-37.html", currPrefs,
                "dialogWidth:400px; dialogHeight:300px;");
    if (prefs)
    {
        if (prefs["name"])
        {
            if (nameHolder.textContent == "friend")
            {
                nameHolder.textContent = prefs["name"];
            }
            else
            {
                //IE
                nameHolder.innerText = prefs["name"];
            }
            currPrefs["name"] = prefs["name"];
        }
```

836

```
    if (prefs["bgColor"])
    {
        document.body.style.backgroundColor = prefs["bgColor"];
        currPrefs["bgColor"] = prefs["bgColor"];
    }
    if (prefs["textColor"])
    {
        document.body.style.color = prefs["textColor"];
        currPrefs["textColor"] = prefs["textColor"];
    }
    if (prefs["h1Size"])
    {
        if (document.all)
        {
            document.all.welcomeHeader.style.fontSize = prefs["h1Size"];
        }
        else
        {
            document.getElementById("welcomeHeader").style.fontSize
            = prefs["h1Size"];
        }
        currPrefs["h1Size"] = prefs["h1Size"];
    }
  }
}
function init()
{
    nameHolder = document.getElementById("firstName");
    if (nameHolder.textContent == ".")
    {
        nameHolder.textContent = "friend";
    }
    else
    {
        //IE
        nameHolder.innerText = "friend";
    }
}
```

The dialog box's document, shown in Listing 27-37, is responsible for reading the incoming data (and setting the form elements accordingly) and assembling form data for return to the main window's script. Notice when you load the example that the `title` element of the dialog box's document appears in the dialog-box window's title bar.

When the page loads into the dialog-box window, the `init()` function examines the `window.dialogArguments` property. If it has any data, the data is used to preset the form elements to mirror the current settings of the main page. A utility function, `setSelected()`, preselects the option of a `select` element to match the current settings.

Buttons at the bottom of the page are explicitly positioned to be at the bottom-right corner of the window. Each button invokes a function to do what is needed to close the dialog box. In the case of the OK button, the `handleOK()` function sets the `window.returnValue` property to the data that comes back from the getFormData() function. This latter function reads the form element values and packages them in an array using the form elements' names as array indices. This helps keep everything straight back in the main window's script, which uses the index names, and therefore is not dependent upon the precise sequence of the form elements in the dialog-box window.

LISTING 27-37

Document for the Modal Dialog Box

HTML: jsb27-37.html

```html
<html>
    <head>
        <title>User Preferences</title>
        <script type="text/javascript" src="jsb27-37.js"></script>
    </head>
    <body bgcolor="#EEEEEE" onload="init()">
        <h2>Web Site Preferences</h2>
        <hr />
        <form name="prefs" onsubmit="return false">
            <table>
                <tr>
                    <td>Enter your first name:
                        <input name="name" type="text" value=""
                               size="20" onkeydown="checkEnter()" />
                    </td>
                </tr>
                <tr>
                    <td>Select a background color:
                        <select name="bgColor">
                            <option value="beige">Beige</option>
                            <option value="antiquewhite">Antique White</option>
                            <option value="goldenrod">Goldenrod</option>
                            <option value="lime">Lime</option>
                            <option value="powderblue">Powder Blue</option>
                            <option value="slategray">Slate Gray</option>
                        </select>
                    </td>
                </tr>
                <tr>
                    <td>Select a text color:
                        <select name="textColor">
                            <option value="black">Black</option>
                            <option value="white">White</option>
                            <option value="navy">Navy Blue</option>
                            <option value="darkorange">Dark Orange</option>
                            <option value="seagreen">Sea Green</option>
                            <option value="teal">Teal</option>
                        </select>
                    </td>
                </tr>
                <tr>
                    <td>Select "Welcome" heading font point size:
```

```
            <select name="h1Size">
                <option value="12">12</option>
                <option value="14">14</option>
                <option value="18">18</option>
                <option value="24">24</option>
                <option value="32">32</option>
                <option value="48">48</option>
            </select>
        </td>
    </tr>
</table>
</form>
<div style="position:absolute; left:200px; top:220px">
    <button style="width:80px"
            onclick="handleOK()">OK</button>
      
    <button style="width:80px"
            onclick="handleCancel()">Cancel</button>
</div>
</body>
</html>
```

JavaScript: jsb27-37.js

```
// Close the dialog
function closeme()
{
    window.close();
}


// Handle click of OK button
function handleOK()
{
    window.returnValue = getFormData();
    closeme();
}


// Handle click of Cancel button
function handleCancel()
{
    window.returnValue = "";
    closeme();
}


// Generic function converts form element name-value pairs
// into an array
function getFormData()
{
    var form = document.prefs;
    var returnedData = new Array();
    // Harvest values for each type of form element
    for (var i = 0; i < form.elements.length; i++)
```

continued

windowObject.**showModalDialog()**

LISTING 27-37   *(continued)*

```
    {
        if (form.elements[i].type == "text")
        {
            returnedData[form.elements[i].name] = form.elements[i].value;
        }
        else if (form.elements[i].type.indexOf("select") != -1)
        {
            returnedData[form.elements[i].name] =
                form.elements[i].options[form.elements[i].selectedIndex].value;
        }
        else if (form.elements[i].type == "radio")
        {
            returnedData[form.elements[i].name] = form.elements[i].value;
        }
        else if (form.elements[i].type == "checkbox")
        {
            returnedData[form.elements[i].name] = form.elements[i].value;
        }
        else
        {
            continue;
        }
    }
    return returnedData;
}

// Initialize by setting form elements from passed data
function init()
{
    if (window.dialogArguments)
    {
        var args = window.dialogArguments;
        var form = document.prefs;
        if (args["name"])
        {
            form.name.value = args["name"];
        }
        if (args["bgColor"])
        {
            setSelected(form.bgColor, args["bgColor"]);
        }
        if (args["textColor"])
        {
            setSelected(form.textColor, args["textColor"]);
        }
        if (args["h1Size"])
        {
            setSelected(form.h1Size, args["h1Size"]);
        }
```

```
    }
}

// Utility function to set a SELECT element to one value
function setSelected(select, value)
{
    for (var i = 0; i < select.options.length; i++)
    {
        if (select.options[i].value == value)
        {
            select.selectedIndex = i;
            break;
        }
    }
    return;
}

// Utility function to accept a press of the
// Enter key in the text field as a click of OK
function checkEnter()
{
    if (window.event.keyCode == 13)
    {
        handleOK();
    }
}
```

One last convenience feature of the dialog-box window is the onkeypress event handler in the text box. The function it invokes looks for the Enter key. If that key is pressed while the box has focus, the same handleOK() function is invoked, as though the user had clicked the OK button. This feature makes the dialog box behave as though the OK button is an automatic default, just as in real dialog boxes.

You should observe several important structural changes that were made to turn the modal approach into a modeless one. Listing 27-38 shows a version of the main window modified for use with a modeless dialog box. Another global variable, prefsDlog, is initialized to eventually store the reference to the modeless window returned by the showModelessWindow() method. The variable gets used to invoke the init() function inside the modeless dialog box, but also as a condition in an if construction surrounding the generation of the dialog box. The reason this is needed is to prevent multiple instances of the dialog box from being created (the button is still alive while the modeless window is showing). The dialog box won't be created again as long as there is a value in prefsDlog and the dialog-box window has not been closed (picking up the window.closed property of the dialog-box window).

The showModelessDialog() method's second parameter is a reference to the function in the main window that updates the main document. As you see in a moment, that function is invoked from the dialog box when the user clicks the OK or Apply button.

windowObject.showModelessDialog()

LISTING 27-38

Main Page for showModelessDialog()

HTML: jsb27-38.html

```html
<!DOCTYPE html>
<html>
   <head>
      <meta http-equiv="content-type" content="text/html;charset=utf-8">
      <title>window.setModelessDialog() Method</title>
      <script type="text/javascript" src="jsb27-38.js"></script>
   </head>
   <body bgcolor="#EEEEEE" style="margin:20px" onload="init()">
      <h1>window.setModelessDialog() Method</h1>
      <hr />
      <h2 id="welcomeHeader">Welcome, <span id="firstName"> </span>!</h2>
      <hr />
      <p>Use this button to set style preferences for this page:
      <button id="prefsButton"
              onclick="getPrefsData()">Preferences</button>
      </p>
   </body>
</html>
```

JavaScript: jsb27-38.js

```javascript
var currPrefs = new Array();
var prefsDlog;
function getPrefsData()
{
   if (!prefsDlog || prefsDlog.closed)
   {
      prefsDlog = showModelessDialog("jsb27-39.html", setPrefs,
                 "dialogWidth:400px; dialogHeight:300px");
      prefsDlog.init(currPrefs);
   }
}

function setPrefs(prefs)
{
   if (prefs["bgColor"])
   {
      document.body.style.backgroundColor = prefs["bgColor"];
      currPrefs["bgColor"] = prefs["bgColor"];
   }
   if (prefs["textColor"])
   {
      document.body.style.color = prefs["textColor"];
      currPrefs["textColor"] = prefs["textColor"];
   }
   if (prefs["h1Size"])
```

```
    {
        document.all.welcomeHeader.style.fontSize = prefs["h1Size"];
        currPrefs["h1Size"] = prefs["h1Size"];
    }
    if (prefs["name"])
    {
        document.all.firstName.innerText = prefs["name"];
        currPrefs["name"] = prefs["name"];
    }
}

function init()
{
    document.all.firstName.innerText = "friend";
}
```

Changes to the dialog-box window document for a modeless version (see Listing 27-39) are rather limited. A new button is added to the bottom of the screen for an Apply button. As in many dialog-box windows you see in Microsoft products, the Apply button lets current settings in dialog boxes be applied to the current document, but without closing the dialog box. This approach makes experimenting with settings easier.

The Apply button invokes a handleApply() function, which works the same as handleOK(), except that the dialog box is not closed. But these two functions communicate back to the main window differently from a modal dialog box. The main window's processing function is passed as the second parameter of showModelessDialog() and is available as the window.dialogArguments property in the dialog-box window's script. That function reference is assigned to a local variable in both functions, and the remote function is invoked, passing the results of the getFormData() function as parameter values back to the main window.

LISTING 27-39

Document for the Modeless Dialog Box

HTML: jsb27-39.html

```
<!DOCTYPE html>
<html>
    <head>
        <meta http-equiv="content-type" content="text/html;charset=utf-8">
        <title>User Preferences</title>
        <script type="text/javascript" src="jsb27-39.js"></script>
    </head>
    <body bgcolor="#EEEEEE" onload="init()">
        <h2>Web Site Preferences</h2>
        <hr />
        <form name="prefs" onsubmit="return false">
            <table>
                <tr>
                    <td>Enter your first name:
```

continued

LISTING 27-39   *(continued)*

```
                        <input name="name" type="text" value=""
                                size="20" onkeydown="checkEnter()" />
                    </td>
                </tr>
                <tr>
                    <td>Select a background color:
                        <select name="bgColor">
                            <option value="beige">Beige</option>
                            <option value="antiquewhite">Antique White</option>
                            <option value="goldenrod">Goldenrod</option>
                            <option value="lime">Lime</option>
                            <option value="powderblue">Powder Blue</option>
                            <option value="slategray">Slate Gray</option>
                        </select>
                    </td>
                </tr>
                <tr>
                    <td>Select a text color:
                        <select name="textColor">
                            <option value="black">Black</option>
                            <option value="white">White</option>
                            <option value="navy">Navy Blue</option>
                            <option value="darkorange">Dark Orange</option>
                            <option value="seagreen">Sea Green</option>
                            <option value="teal">Teal</option>
                        </select>
                    </td>
                </tr>
                <tr>
                    <td>Select "Welcome" heading font point size:
                        <select name="h1Size">
                            <option value="12">12</option>
                            <option value="14">14</option>
                            <option value="18">18</option>
                            <option value="24">24</option>
                            <option value="32">32</option>
                            <option value="48">48</option>
                        </select>
                    </td>
                </tr>
            </table>
        </form>
        <div style="position:absolute; left:120px; top:220px">
            <button style="width:80px"
                    onclick="handleOK()">OK</button>
              
            <button style="width:80px"
                    onclick="handleCancel()">Cancel</button>
              
            <button style="width:80px"
```

```
                    onclick="handleApply()">Apply</button>
        </div>
    </body>
</html>
```

JavaScript: jsb27-39.js

```
// Close the dialog
function closeme()
{
    window.close();
}

// Handle click of OK button
function handleOK()
{
    var returnFunc = window.dialogArguments;
    returnFunc(getFormData());
    closeme();
}

// Handle click of Apply button
function handleApply()
{
    var returnFunc = window.dialogArguments;
    returnFunc(getFormData());
}

// Handle click of Cancel button
function handleCancel()
{
    window.returnValue = "";
    closeme();
}

// Generic function converts form element name-value pairs
// into an array
function getFormData()
{
    var form = document.prefs;
    var returnedData = new Array();
    // Harvest values for each type of form element
    for (var i = 0; i < form.elements.length; i++)
    {
        if (form.elements[i].type == "text")
        {
            returnedData[form.elements[i].name] = form.elements[i].value;
        }
        else if (form.elements[i].type.indexOf("select") != -1)
        {
            returnedData[form.elements[i].name] =
                form.elements[i].options[form.elements[i].selectedIndex].value;
```

continued

LISTING 27-39 *(continued)*

```
        }
        else if (form.elements[i].type == "radio")
        {
            returnedData[form.elements[i].name] = form.elements[i].value;
        }
        else if (form.elements[i].type == "checkbox")
        {
            returnedData[form.elements[i].name] = form.elements[i].value;
        }
        else
        {
            continue;
        }
    }
    return returnedData;
}

// Initialize by setting form elements from passed data
function init(currPrefs)
{
    if (currPrefs)
    {
        var form = document.prefs;
        if (currPrefs["name"])
        {
            form.name.value = currPrefs["name"];
        }
        if (currPrefs["bgColor"])
        {
            setSelected(form.bgColor, currPrefs["bgColor"]);
        }
        if (currPrefs["textColor"])
        {
            setSelected(form.textColor, currPrefs["textColor"]);
        }
        if (currPrefs["h1Size"])
        {
            setSelected(form.h1Size, currPrefs["h1Size"]);
        }
    }
}

// Utility function to set a SELECT element to one value
function setSelected(select, value)
{
    for (var i = 0; i < select.options.length; i++)
    {
        if (select.options[i].value == value)
        {
            select.selectedIndex = i;
```

```
        break;
    }
  }
  return;
}

// Utility function to accept a press of the
// Enter key in the text field as a click of OK
function checkEnter()
{
  if (window.event.keyCode == 13)
  {
    handleOK();
  }
}
```

The biggest design challenge you probably face with respect to these windows is deciding between a modal and modeless dialog-box style. Some designers insist that modality has no place in a graphical user interface; others say that there are times when you need to focus the user on a very specific task before any further processing can take place. That's where a modal dialog box makes perfect sense.

Related Item: window.open() method

sizeToContent()

Returns: Nothing

Compatibility: WinIE-, MacIE-, NN6+, Moz+, Safari-, Opera-, Chrome-

The NN6+/Moz window.sizeToContent() method can be a valuable aid in making sure that a window (especially a subwindow) is sized for the optimum display of the window's content. But you must be cautious with this method, or it will do more harm than good.

Invoking the sizeToContent() method resizes the window so that all content is visible. Concerns about variations in OS-specific rendering become a thing of the past. Naturally, you should perform this action only on a window whose content occupies, at the most, a space smaller than the smallest video monitor running your code (typically 640×480 pixels, but conceivably much smaller for future versions of the browser used on handheld computers).

You can get the user in trouble, however, if you invoke the method twice on the same window that contains the resizing script. This action can cause the window to expand to a size that may exceed the pixel size of the user's video monitor. Successive invocations fail to cinch up the window's size to fit its content again. Multiple invocations are safe, however, on subwindows when the resizing script statement is in the main window.

Example

Use The Evaluator (Chapter 4, "JavaScript Essentials") in NN6+/Moz to try the sizeToContent() method. Assuming that you are running The Evaluator from the Chap13 directory on the CD-ROM (or the directory copied as is to your hard disk), you can open a subwindow with one of the other files in the directory and then size the subwindow. Enter the following statement in the top text box:

```
a = window.open("jsb13-02.html","")
```

windowObject.stop()

You might, depending on where you installed the CD-ROM, have to alter the path in the above statement to something like this:

```
a = window.open("../../Chap13/lst13-02.htm","")
```

The file will open, depending on the browser version and your browser configuration settings, in either a new tab or a new subwindow. Enter the following statement in the top text box:

```
a.sizeToContent()
```

The resized window (if a new tab was opened) or subwindow is at the minimum recommended width for a browser window and at a height tall enough to display the little bit of content in the document.

As with any method that changes the size of the browser window, problems arise in browsers such as Firefox 2 that support tabbed browsing where multiple pages are opened as different tabs within the same browser instance. In a tabbed browser, it is impossible to resize the window of one page without altering all others. It's certainly still possible to open multiple browser instances to resolve this problem, but the default response to `window.open()` is to open a new tab, not a new browser window.

Related Item: `window.resizeTo()` method

stop()

Returns: Nothing

Compatibility: WinIE-, MacIE-, NN4+, Moz+, Safari+, Opera+, Chrome-

The NN/Moz original `stop()` method offers a scripted equivalent of clicking the Stop button in the toolbar. The availability of this method allows you to create your own toolbar on your page and hide the toolbar (in the main window with signed scripts, or in a subwindow). For example, if you have an image representing the Stop button in your page, you can surround it with a link whose action stops loading, as in the following:

```
<a href="javascript: void stop()"><img src="myStop.gif" border="0"></a>
```

A script cannot stop its own document from loading, but it can stop the loading of another frame or window. Similarly, if the current document dynamically loads a new image or a multimedia MIME type file as a separate action, the `stop()` method can halt that process. Even though the `stop()` method is a window method, it is not tied to any specific window or frame: Stop means stop.

Related Items: `window.back()`, `window.find()`, `window.forward()`, `window.home()`, `window.print()` methods

Event handlers
onafterprint
onbeforeprint

Compatibility: WinIE5+, MacIE-, NN-, Moz-, Safari-, Opera-, Chrome-

Each of these event handlers fires after the user has clicked the OK button in IE's Print dialog box. This goes for printing that is invoked manually (via menus and browser shortcut buttons) and the `window.print()` method.

Although printing is usually WYSIWYG, it is conceivable that you may want the printed version of a document to display more, or less, of the document than is showing at that instant. For example, you may have a special copyright notice that you want appended to the end of a page whenever it goes to the printer. In that case, the element with that content can have its display style sheet property set to none when the page loads. Before the document is sent to the printer, a script needs to adjust that style property to display the element as a block item; after printing, have your script revert the setting to none.

Immediately after the user clicks the OK button in the Print dialog box, the onbeforeprint event handler fires. As soon as the page is sent to the printer or spooler, the onafterprint event handler fires.

Example

The following script fragment assumes that the page includes a div element whose style sheet includes a setting of display:none as the page loads. Somewhere in the head, the print-related event handlers are set as properties:

```
function showPrintCopyright()
{
    document.all.printCopyright.style.display = "block";
}
function hidePrintCopyright()
{
    document.all.printCopyright.style.display = "none";
}
window.onbeforeprint = showPrintCopyright;
window.onafterprint = hidePrintCopyright;
```

onbeforeunload

Compatibility: WinIE4+, MacIE5+, NN-, Moz+, Safari+, Opera-, Chrome+

Any user or scripted action that normally forces the current page to be unloaded or replaced causes the onbeforeunload event handler to fire. Unlike the onunload event handler, however, onbeforeunload is a bit better behaved when it comes to allowing complex scripts to finish before the actual unloading takes place. Moreover, you can assign a string value to the event.returnValue property in the event handler function. That string becomes part of a message in an alert window that gives the user a chance to stay on the page. If the user agrees to stay, the page does not unload, and any action that caused the potential replacement is canceled.

Example

The simple page in Listing 27-40 shows you how to give the user a chance to stay on the page.

LISTING 27-40

Using the onbeforeunload Event Handler

```
<html>
   <head>
      <title>onbeforeunload Event Handler</title>
```

continued

LISTING 27-40 *(continued)*

```
    <script type="text/javascript">
        function verifyClose()
        {
            return "We really like you and hope you will stay longer.";
        }
    </script>
</head>
<body onbeforeunload="return verifyClose()">
    <h1>onbeforeunload Event Handler</h1>
    <hr />
    <p>Use this button to navigate to the previous page:
        <button id="go"
                onclick="history.back()">Go Back</button>
    </p>
</body>
</html>
```

Related Item: onunload event handler

onerror

Compatibility: WinIE4+, MacIE4+, NN3+, Moz+, Safari-, Opera-, Chrome-

(See the discussion of the window.onerror property earlier in this chapter.)

onhelp

Compatibility: WinIE4+, MacIE4+, NN-, Moz-, Safari-, Opera-, Chrome-

The generic onhelp event handler, discussed in Chapter 26, also fires when the user activates the context-sensitive help within a modal or modeless dialog box. In the latter case, a user can click the Help icon in the dialog box's title bar, at which time the cursor changes to a question mark. The user can then click any element in the window. At that second click, the onhelp event handler fires, and the event object contains information about the element clicked (the event.srcElement is a reference to the specific element), allowing a script to supply help about that element.

To prevent the browser's built-in help window from appearing, the event handler must evaluate to return false (IE4+) or set the event.returnValue property to false (IE5+).

Example

The following script fragment can be used to provide context-sensitive help within a dialog box. Help messages for only two form elements are shown here, but in a real application, you could easily add more messages.

```
        function showHelp()
        {
            switch (event.srcElement.name)
```

```
{
    case "bgColor" :
        alert("Choose a color for the main window\'s background.");
        break;
    case "name" :
        alert("Enter your first name for a friendly greeting.");
        break;
    default :
        alert("Make preference settings for the main page styles.");
    }
    event.returnValue = false;
}
window.onhelp = showHelp;
```

Because this page's help focuses on form elements, the switch construction cases are based on the name properties of the form elements. For other kinds of pages, the id properties may be more appropriate.

Related Items: event object (Chapter 32, "Event Objects"); switch construction (Chapter 21, "Control Structures and Exception Handling")

onload

Compatibility: WinIE3+, MacIE3+, NN2+, Moz+, Safari+, Opera+, Chrome+

The onload event handler fires in the current window at the end of the document loading process (after all text and image elements have been transferred from the source file server to the browser, and after all plug-ins and Java applets have loaded and started running). At that point, the browser's memory contains all the objects and script components in the document that the browser can possibly know about.

The onload handler is an attribute of a <body> tag for a single-frame document, or of the <frameset> tag for the top window of a multiple-frame document. When the handler is an attribute of a <frameset> tag, the event triggers only after all frames defined by that frameset have completely loaded.

Use either of the following scenarios to insert an onload handler into a document the old way:

```
<html>
    <head>
    </head>
    <body [other attributes] onload="statementOrFunction">
        [body content]
    </body>
</html>

<html>
    <head>
    </head>
    <frameset [other attributes] onload="statementOrFunction">
        <frame [frame specification attributes] />
    </frameset>
</html>
```

Alternatively, you can bind an event listener to the `window` object using the W3C `addEventListener()` method. Chapter 32 explains the modern cross-browser event-handling technique.

This handler has a special capability when it's part of a frameset definition: The handler won't fire until the `onload` event handlers of all child frames in the frameset have fired. Therefore, if some initialization scripts depend on components existing in other frames, trigger them from the frameset's `onload` event handler. This brings up a good general rule of thumb for writing JavaScript: Scripts that execute during a document's loading should contribute to the process of generating the document and its objects. To act immediately on those objects, design additional functions that are called by the `onload` event handler for that window.

The type of operations suited for an `onload` event handler are those that can run quickly and without user intervention. Users shouldn't be penalized by having to wait for considerable postloading activity to finish, before they can interact with your pages. At no time should you present a modal dialog box as part of an `onload` handler. Users who design macros on their machines to visit sites unattended may get hung up on a page that automatically displays an alert, confirm, or prompt dialog box. On the other hand, an operation such as setting the `window.defaultStatus` property is a perfect candidate for an `onload` event handler, as is initializing event handlers as properties of element objects in the page.

Note

Browsers equipped with pop-up window blockers ignore all `window.open()` method calls in `onload` event handler functions. ■

Related Items: `onunload` event handler; `window.defaultStatus` property

onresize

Compatibility: WinIE4+, MacIE4+, NN4+, Moz+, Safari+, Opera+, Chrome+

If a user resizes a window, the action causes the `onresize` event handler to fire for the `window` object. When you assign a function to the event (for example, `window.onresize = handleResizes`), the NN/Moz event object conveys `width` and `height` properties that reveal the outer width and height of the entire window. A window resize should not reload the document such that an `onload` event handler fires (although some early Navigator versions did fire the extra event).

Related Item: `event` object (Chapter 32, "Event Objects")

onscroll

Compatibility: WinIE4+, MacIE4+, NN7+, Moz+, Safari 1.3+, Opera+, Chrome+

The `onscroll` event handler fires for the `body` element object as the result of manual scrolling of the document (via scroll bars or navigation keyboard keys) and scripted scrolling via the `doScroll()` method, via the `scrollIntoView()` method, or by adjusting the `scrollTop` and/or `scrollLeft` properties of the `body` element object. For manual scrolling and scrolling by `doScroll()`, the event seems to fire twice in succession. Moreover, the `event.srcElement` property is `null` even when the `body` element is handling the `onscroll` event handler.

Example

Listing 27-41 is a highly artificial demonstration of what can be a useful tool for some page designs. Consider a document that occupies a window or frame but that you don't want scrolled, even by accident with a mouse wheel. (Be aware that the `onscroll` event is not fired if the user scrolls the page with a mouse wheel in Safari and Chrome in some versions of Windows, but is fired on the Mac.) If scrolling of the content would destroy the appearance or value of the content, you want to make sure that the page always zips back to the top. The `onscroll` event handler in Listing 27-41 does just that. Notice that the event handler is set as a property of the `window` object.

LISTING 27-41

Preventing a Page from Scrolling

```
<!DOCTYPE html>
<html>
    <head>
        <meta http-equiv="content-type" content="text/html;charset=utf-8">
        <title>onscroll Event Handler</title>
        <script type="text/javascript" src="../jsb-global.js"></script>
        <script type="text/javascript">
            addEvent(window, "scroll", zipBack);
            //window.onscroll = zipBack;

            function zipBack()
            {
                window.scroll(0,0);
            }
        </script>
    </head>
    <body>
        <h1>onscroll Event Handler</h1>
        <hr />
        <div>This page always zips back to the top if you try to scroll it.</div>
        <p>
            <iframe frameborder="0" scrolling="no" height="1000"
                    src="bofright.html"></iframe>
        </p>
    </body>
</html>
```

Related Items: `scrollBy()`, `scrollByLines()`, `scrollByPages()` methods

onunload

Compatibility: WinIE3+, MacIE3+, NN2+, Moz+, Safari+, Opera-, Chrome+

An `unload` event reaches the current window just before a document is cleared from view. The most common ways windows are cleared are when new HTML documents are loaded into them, when the user clicks the `back` button or the `reload` button, or when the user does the reload keyboard shortcut, when a script begins writing new HTML on the fly for the window or frame. Be aware that in Safari the unload event is not fired when closing the tab/browser in some versions of Windows.

Limit your use of the `onunload` event handler to quick operations that do not inhibit the transition from one document to another. Do not invoke any methods that display dialog boxes. You specify `onunload` event handlers in the same places in an HTML document as the `onload` handlers:

as a `<body>` tag attribute for a single-frame window or as a `<frameset>` tag attribute for a multiframe window. Both `onload` and `onunload` event handlers can appear in the same `<body>` or `<frameset>` tag without causing problems. The `onunload` event handler merely stays safely tucked away in the browser's memory, waiting for the `unload` event to arrive for processing as the document gets ready to clear the window.

One caution about the `onunload` event handler: Even though the event fires before the document goes away, don't burden the event handler with time-consuming tasks, such as generating new objects or submitting a form. The document will probably go away before the function completes, leaving the function looking for objects and values that no longer exist. The best defense is to keep your `onunload` event handler processing to a minimum.

Note
Browsers equipped with pop-up window blockers ignore all `window.open()` method calls in `onunload` event handler functions. ■

Related Item: `onload` event handler

frame Element Object

For HTML element properties, methods, and event handlers, see Chapter 26, "Generic HTML Element Objects."

Properties	Methods	Event Handlers
allowTransparency		
borderColor		
contentDocument		
contentWindow		
frameBorder		
height		
longDesc		
marginHeight		
marginWidth		
name		
noResize		
scrolling		
src		
width		

Syntax

Accessing properties or methods of a `frame` element object from a `frameset`:

```
(IE4+)     document.all.frameID. property | method([parameters])
(IE5+/W3C) document.getElementById("frameID"). property |
           method([parameters])
```

Accessing properties or methods of a `frame` element from a frame document:

```
(IE4+)     parent.document.all.frameID. property | method([parameters])
(IE5+/W3C) parent.document.getElementById("frameID"). property |
           method([parameters])
```

Compatibility: WinIE4+, MacIE4+, NN6+, Moz+, Safari+, Opera+, Chrome+

About this object

As noted in the opening section of this chapter, a `frame` element object is distinct from the frame object that acts as a `window` object in a document hierarchy. The `frame` element object is available to scripts only when all HTML elements are exposed in the object model.

Because the `frame` element object is an HTML element, it shares the properties, methods, and event handlers of all HTML elements, as described in Chapter 26. By and large, you access the `frame` element object to set or modify an attribute value in the `<frame>` tag. If so, you simplify matters if you assign an identifier to the `id` attribute of the tag. Your tag still needs a `name` attribute if your scripts refer to frames through the original object model (a `parent.frameName` reference). Although there is no law against using the same identifier for both `name` and `id` attributes, using different names to prevent potential conflict with references in browsers that recognize both attributes is best.

To modify the dimensions of a frame, you must go to the `frameset` element object that defines the `cols` and `rows` attributes for the frameset. These properties can be modified on the fly in modern browsers.

Properties

allowTransparency

Value: Boolean   Read/Write

Compatibility: WinIE6+, MacIE-, NN-, Moz-, Safari-, Opera-, Chrome-

The `allowTransparency` property indicates whether the frame's background is transparent. This property applies primarily to the `iframe` object, because framesets don't have background colors or images to show through a transparent frame.

borderColor

Value: Hexadecimal triplet or color name string   Read/Write

Compatibility: WinIE4+, MacIE4+, NN-, Moz-, Safari-, Opera-, Chrome-

If a frame displays a border (as determined by the `frameborder` attribute of the `frame` element, or `border` attribute of the `frameset` element), it can have a color set separately from the rest of the frames. The initial color (if different from the rest of the frameset) is usually set by the `bordercolor` attribute of the `<frame>` tag. After that, scripts can modify settings as needed.

Modifying a single frame's border can be risky at times, depending on your color combinations. In practice, different browsers appear to follow different rules when it comes to negotiating conflicts or defining just how far a single frame's border extends into the border space. Color changes to individual frame borders do not always render. Verify your designs on as many browsers and operating system variations as you can to test your combinations.

Example

Although you may experience problems changing the color of a single frame border, the W3C DOM syntax would look like the following if the script were inside the framesetting document:

```
document.getElementById("contentsFrame").borderColor = "red";
```

The IE-only version would be

```
document.all["contentsFrame"].borderColor = "red";
```

These examples assume that the frame name arrives to a script function as a string. If the script is executing in one of the frames of the frameset, add a reference to `parent` in the preceding statements.

Related Items: `frame.frameBorder`, `frameset.frameBorder` properties

contentDocument

Value: document object reference   Read-Only

Compatibility: WinIE8+, MacIE-, NN6+, Moz+, Safari+, Opera+, Chrome+

The `contentDocument` property of a `frame` element object is nothing more than a reference to the document contained by that frame. This property bridges the gap between the `frame` element object and the `frame` object. Both of these objects contain the same `document` object, but from a scripting point of view, references most typically use the frame object to reach the document inside a frame, whereas the `frame` element is used to access properties equated with the `frame` tag's attributes. But if your script finds that it has a reference to the `frame` element object, you can use the `contentDocument` property to get a valid reference to the document and, therefore, any other content of the frame.

Example

A framesetting document script might be using the ID of a `frame` element to read or adjust one of the element properties, and then need to perform some action on the content of the page through its `document` object. You can get the reference to the `document` object via a statement such as the following:

```
var doc = document.getElementById("Frame3").contentDocument;
```

Then your script can, for example, dive into a form in the document:

```
var val = doc.mainForm.entry.value;
```

Related Items: `contentWindow` property; `document` object

contentWindow

Value: `document` object reference   Read-Only

Compatibility: WinIE5.5+, MacIE-, NN7+, Moz1.0.1+, Safari+, Opera+, Chrome+

The `contentWindow` property of a `frame` element object is simply a reference to the window generated by that frame. This property provides access to the frame's window, which can then be used to
reach the document inside the frame.

Example

You can get the reference to the `window` object associated with a frame via a statement such as the
following:

```
var win = document.getElementById("Frame3").contentWindow;
```

Related Item: `window` object

frameBorder

Value: `yes | no | 1 | 0` as strings   Read/Write

Compatibility: WinIE4+, MacIE4+, NN6+, Moz+, Safari+, Opera+, Chrome+

The `frameBorder` property offers scripted access to a `frame` element object's `frameborder`
attribute setting. Except for IE, none of the browsers we tested responded well to modifying this
property after the page has loaded.

Values for the `frameBorder` property are strings that substitute for Boolean values. Value `yes` or `1`
means that the border is (supposed to be) turned on; `no` or `0` (supposedly) turns off the border. There
is no consistent default behavior among the browsers.

Example

The default value for the `frameBorder` property is `yes`. You can use this setting to create a toggle
script (which, unfortunately, does not change the border's appearance in IE). The W3C-compatible
version looks like the following:

```
function toggleFrameScroll(frameID)
{
    var theFrame = document.getElementById(frameID);
    if (theFrame.frameBorder == "yes")
    {
        theFrame.frameBorder = "no";
    }
    else
    {
        theFrame.frameBorder = "yes";
    }
}
```

Related Items: `frameset.frameBorder` properties

857

height
width

Value: Integer   Read-Only

Compatibility: WinIE4+, MacIE4+, NN-, Moz-, Safari+, Opera-, Chrome+

These two properties enable you to retrieve the height and width of a `frame` element
object. These values are not necessarily the same as `document.body.clientHeight` and
`document.body.clientWidth`, because the frame dimensions include chrome associated with
the frame, such as scroll bars. These values are read-only. If you need to modify the dimensions of
a frame, do so via the `frameset` element object's `rows` and/or `cols` properties. Reading integer
values for a frame's height and width properties is much easier than trying to parse the `rows` and
`cols` string properties.

Example

The following fragment assumes a frameset defined with two frames set up as two columns within the
frameset. The statements here live in the framesetting document. They retrieve the current width of
the left frame and increase the width of that frame by 10 percent. Syntax shown here is for the W3C
DOM, but can easily be adapted to IE-only terminology.

```
var frameWidth = document.getElementById("leftFrame").width;
document.getElementById("mainFrameset").cols =
    (Math.round(frameWidth * 1.1)) + ",*";
```

Notice that the numeric value of the existing frame width is first increased by 10 percent and then
concatenated to the rest of the string property assigned to the frameset's `cols` property. The asterisk
after the comma means that the browser should figure out the remaining width and assign it to the
right frame.

Related Item: `frameset` object

longDesc

Value: URL string   Read/Write

Compatibility: WinIE6+, MacIE5+, NN6+, Moz+, Safari+, Opera+, Chrome+

The `longDesc` property is the scripted equivalent of the `longdesc` attribute of the `<frame>` tag.
This HTML 4 attribute is intended to provide browsers a URL to a document that contains a long
description of the element. Future browsers can use this feature to provide information about the
frame for visually impaired site visitors.

marginHeight
marginWidth

Value: Integer   Read/Write

Compatibility: WinIE6+, MacIE5+, NN6+, Moz+, Safari+, Opera+, Chrome+

Browsers tend to insert content within a frame automatically by adding a margin between the
content and the edge of the frame. These values are represented by the `marginHeight` (top and
bottom edges) and `marginWidth` (left and right edges) properties. Although the properties are not
read-only, changing the values after the frameset has loaded does not alter the appearance of the

document in the frame. If you need to alter the margin(s) of a document inside a frame, adjust the `document.body.style` margin properties.

Also be aware that although the default values of these properties are empty (meaning when no `marginheight` or `marginwidth` attributes are set for the `<frame>` tag), margins are built into the page. The precise pixel count of those margins varies with operating system.

Related Item: `style` object (Chapter 38, "Style Sheet and Style Objects")

name

Value: String   Read/Write

Compatibility: WinIE4+, MacIE4+, NN6+, Moz+, Safari+, Opera+, Chrome+

The `name` property is the identifier associated with the frame for use as a reference. Scripts can reference the frame through the `name` property (for example, `top.frames["myFrame"]`), which is typically assigned via the `name` attribute.

noResize

Value: Boolean   Read/Write

Compatibility: WinIE6+, MacIE5+, NN6+, Moz+, Safari+, Opera+, Chrome+

Web designers commonly fix their framesets so that users cannot resize the frames (by dragging any divider border between frames). The `noResize` property lets you read and adjust that behavior of a frame after the page has loaded. For example, during some part of the interaction with a user on a page, you may allow the user to modify the frame size manually while in a certain mode. Or you may grant the user one chance to resize the frame. When the `onresize` event handler fires, a script sets the `noResize` property of the `frame` element to `false`. If you turn off resizing for a frame, all edges of the frame become nonresizable, regardless of the `noResize` value setting of adjacent frames. Turning off resizability has no effect on the ability of scripts to alter the sizes of frames via the `frameset` element object's `cols` or `rows` properties.

Example

The following statement turns off the ability for a frame to be resized:

```
parent.document.getElementById("myFrame1").noResize = true;
```

Because of the negative nature of the property name, it may be difficult to keep the logic straight (setting `noResize` to `true` means that resizability is turned off). Keep a watchful eye on your Boolean values.

Related Items: `frameset.cols`, `frameset.rows` properties

scrolling

Value: yes | no | 1 | 0 as strings   Read/Write

Compatibility: WinIE6+, MacIE5+, NN6+, Moz+, Safari+, Opera+, Chrome+

The `scrolling` property lets scripts turn scroll bars on and off inside a single frame of a frameset. By default, scrolling is turned on unless overridden by the `scroll` attribute of the `<frame>` tag.

Values for the `scrolling` property are strings that substitute for Boolean values. Value `yes` or `1` means that scroll bars are visible (provided that there is more content than can be viewed without *frameObject*.scrolling

scrolling); no or 0 hides scroll bars in the frame. IE also recognizes (and sets as default) the auto value.

Note
Although this property is read/write, changing its value by script does not alter a frame's appearance in WinIE, Mozilla browsers, or Safari. ■

Example

Listing 27-42 produces a frameset consisting of eight frames. The content for the frames is generated by a script within the frameset (via the fillFrame() function). Event handlers (onclick) in the body of each frame invoke the toggleFrameScroll() function. Both ways of referencing the frame element object are shown, with the IE-only version commented out.

In the toggleFrameScroll() function, the if condition checks whether the property is set to something other than no. This allows the condition to evaluate to true if the property is set to either auto (the first time) or yes (as set by the function). Note that the scroll bars don't disappear from the frames in IE, NN6+, Safari, Opera, or Chrome.

LISTING 27-42

Controlling the frame.scrolling Property

```
<!DOCTYPE html>
<html>
   <head>
      <meta http-equiv="content-type" content="text/html;charset=utf-8">
      <title>frame.scrolling Property</title>
      <script type="text/javascript">
         function toggleFrameScroll(frameID)
         {
            // IE5+/W3C version
            var theFrame = document.getElementById(frameID);

            if (theFrame.scrolling != "no")
            {
               theFrame.scrolling = "no";
            }
            else
            {
               theFrame.scrolling = "yes";
            }
         }

         // generate content for each frame
         function fillFrame(frameID)
         {
            var page = "<html><body onclick='parent.toggleFrameScroll(\""
                  +  frameID
```

```
                    + "\")'><span style='font-size:24pt'>";
            page += "<p>This frame has the ID of:<\/p><p>"
                    + frameID
                    + ".<\/p>";
            page += "<\/span><\/body><\/html>";
            return page;
        }
    </script>
</head>
<frameset id="outerFrameset" cols="50%,50%">
    <frameset id="innerFrameset1" rows="25%,25%,25%,25%">
        <frame id="myFrame1" src="javascript:parent.fillFrame('myFrame1')" />
        <frame id="myFrame2" src="javascript:parent.fillFrame('myFrame2')" />
        <frame id="myFrame3" src="javascript:parent.fillFrame('myFrame3')" />
        <frame id="myFrame4" src="javascript:parent.fillFrame('myFrame4')" />
    </frameset>
    <frameset id="innerFrameset2" rows="25%,25%,25%,25%">
        <frame id="myFrame5" src="javascript:parent.fillFrame('myFrame5')" />
        <frame id="myFrame6" src="javascript:parent.fillFrame('myFrame6')" />
        <frame id="myFrame7" src="javascript:parent.fillFrame('myFrame7')" />
        <frame id="myFrame8" src="javascript:parent.fillFrame('myFrame8')" />
    </frameset>
</frameset>
</html>
```

src

Value: URL string   Read/Write

Compatibility: WinIE6+, MacIE5+, NN6+, Moz+, Safari+, Opera+, Chrome+

The src property of a frame element object offers an additional way of navigating to a different page within a frame (meaning other than assigning a new URL to the location.href property of the frame object). For backward compatibility with older browsers, however, continue using location.href for scripted navigation. Remember that the src property belongs to the frame element object, not the window object it represents. Therefore, references to the src property must be via the element's ID and/or node hierarchy.

Example

For best results, use fully formed URLs as values for the src property, as shown here:

```
parent.document.getElementById("mainFrame").src = "http://www.dannyg.com";
```

Relative URLs and javascript: pseudo-URLs will also work most of the time.

Related Item: location.href property

frameset Element Object

For HTML element properties, methods, and event handlers, see Chapter 26, "Generic HTML Element Objects."

Properties	Methods	Event Handlers
border		
borderColor		
cols		
frameBorder		
frameSpacing		
rows		

Syntax

Accessing properties or methods of a `frameset` element object from a `frameset`:

```
(IE4+)     document.all.framesetID. property | method([parameters])
(IE5+/W3C) document.getElementById("framesetID"). property |
           method([parameters])
```

Accessing properties or methods of a `frameset` element from a frame document:

```
(IE4+)     parent.document.all.framesetID. property | method([parameters])
(IE5+/W3C) parent.document.getElementById("framesetID"). property |
           method([parameters])
```

Compatibility: WinIE4+, MacIE4+, NN6+, Moz+, Safari+, Opera+, Chrome+

About this object

The `frameset` element object is the script-accessible equivalent of the element generated via the `<frameset>` tag. This element is different from the parent (window-type) object of the original object model. A `frameset` element object has properties and methods that impact the HTML element; by contrast, the `window` object referenced from documents inside frames via the `parent` or `top` window references, contains a document and all the content that goes along with it.

When framesets are nested in side one another, a node parent–child relationship exists between containing and contained framesets. For example, consider the following skeletal nested frameset structure:

```
<frameset id="outerFrameset" cols="30%, 70%">
    <frame id="frame1">
        <frameset id="innerFrameset" rows="50%,50%">
```

```
            <frame id="frame2">
            <frame id="frame3">
        </frameset>
    </frameset>
```

When writing scripts for documents that go inside any of the frames of this structure, references to the framesetting window and frames are a flatter hierarchy than the HTML signifies. A script in any frame references the framesetting window via the `parent` reference; a script in any frame references another frame via the `parent.frameName` reference. In other words, the `window` objects of the frameset defined in a document are all siblings, and have the same parent.

Such is not the case when viewing the preceding structure from the perspective of W3C node terminology. Parent–child relationships are governed by the nesting of HTML elements, irrespective of whatever windows get generated by the browser. Therefore, `frame2` has only one sibling: `frame3`. Both of those share one parent: `innerFrameset`. Both `innerFrameset` and `frame1` are children of `outerFrameset`. If your script were sitting on a reference to `frame2`, and you wanted to change the `cols` property of `outerFrameset`, you would have to traverse two generations of nodes:

```
    frame2Ref.parentNode.parentNode.cols = "40%,60%";
```

What might confuse matters ever more in practice is that a script belonging to one of the frames must use window object terminology to jump out of the current `window` object to the frameset that generated the frame window for the document. In other words, there is no immediate way to jump directly from a document to the `frame` element object that defines the frame in which the document resides. The document's script accesses the node hierarchy of its frameset via the `parent.document` reference. But this reference is to the `document` object that contains the entire frameset structure. Fortunately, the W3C DOM provides the `getElementById()` method to extract a reference to any node nested within the document. Thus, a document inside one of the frames can access the `frame` element object just as though it were any element in a typical document (which it is):

```
    parent.document.getElementById("frame2")
```

No reference to the containing `frameset` element object is necessary. To make that column width change from a script inside one of the frame windows, the statement would be

```
    parent.document.getElementById("outerFrame").cols = "40%,60%";
```

The inner frameset is equally accessible by the same syntax.

Properties

border

Value: Integer   Read/Write

Compatibility: WinIE4+, MacIE4+, NN-, Moz-, Safari-, Opera-, Chrome-

The `border` property of a `frameset` element object lets you read the thickness (in pixels) of the borders between frames of a frameset. If you do not specify a `border` attribute in the frameset's tag, the property is empty, rather than reflecting the actual border thickness applied by default.

framesetObject.borderColor

Example

Even though the property is read/write, changing the value does not change the thickness of the border you see in the browser. If you need to find the thickness of the border, a script reference from one of the frame's documents would look like the following:

```
var thickness = parent.document.all.outerFrameset.border;
```

Related Item: `frameset.frameBorder` property

borderColor

Value: Hexadecimal triplet or color name string   Read/Write

Compatibility: WinIE4+, MacIE4+, NN-, Moz-, Safari-, Opera-, Chrome-

The `borderColor` property lets you read the value of the color assigned to the `bordercolor` attribute of the frameset's tag. Although the property is read/write, changing the color by script does not alter the border colors rendered in the browser window. Attribute values set as color names are returned as hexadecimal triplets when you read the property value.

Example

To retrieve the current color setting in a frameset, a script reference from one of the frame's documents would look like the following:

```
var borderColor = parent.document.all.outerFrameset.borderColor;
```

Related Items: `frame.borderColor`, `frameset.frameBorder` properties

cols
rows

Value: String   Read/Write

Compatibility: WinIE4+, MacIE4+, NN6+, Moz+, Safari+, Opera+, Chrome+

The `cols` and `rows` properties of a `frameset` element object let you read and modify the sizes of frames after the frameset has loaded. These two properties are defined in the W3C DOM. Values for both properties are strings, which may include percent symbols or asterisks. Therefore, if you are trying to increase or decrease the size of a frame column or row gradually, you must parse the string for the necessary original values before performing any math on them (or, in IE4+, use the `frame` element object's `height` and `width` properties to gauge the current frame size in pixels).

Adjusting these two properties lets you modify the frameset completely, including adding or removing columns or rows in the frameset grid. Because a change in the frameset structure could impact scripts by changing the size of the frames array associated with the parent window or unloading documents that contain needed data, be sure to test your scripts with both states of your frameset. If you want to remove a frame from a frameset view, you might be safer to specify the size of zero for that particular row or column in the frameset. Of course, a size of zero still leaves a 1-pixel frame, but it is essentially invisible if borders are not turned on and the 1-pixel frame has the same background color as the other frames. Another positive byproduct of this technique is that you can restore the other frame with its document state identical from when it was hidden.

When you have nested framesets defined in a single document, be sure to reference the desired `frameset` element object. One object may be specifying the columns, and another (nested) one specifies the rows for the grid. Assign a unique ID to each `frameset` element so that references can be reliably directed to the proper object.

Example

Listings 27-43, 27-44, and 27-45 show the HTML for a frameset and two of the three documents that go into the frameset. The final document is an HTML version of the U.S. Bill of Rights, which is serving here as a content frame for the demonstration.

The frameset listing (see Listing 27-43) shows a three-frame setup. Down the left column is a table of contents (see Listing 27-44). The right column is divided into two rows. In the top row is a simple control (see Listing 27-45) that hides and shows the table-of-contents frame. As the user clicks the hot spot of the control (located inside a `span` element), the `onclick` event handler invokes the `toggleTOC()` function in the frameset.

LISTING 27-43

Frameset and Script for Hiding/Showing a Frame

```html
<!DOCTYPE html>
<html>
    <head>
        <meta http-equiv="content-type" content="text/html;charset=utf-8">
        <title>Hide/Show Frame Example</title>
        <script type="text/javascript">
            var origCols;
            function toggleTOC()
            {
                if (origCols)
                {
                    showTOC();
                }
                else
                {
                    hideTOC();
                }
            }
            function hideTOC()
            {
                var frameset = document.getElementById("outerFrameset");
                origCols = frameset.cols;
                frameset.cols = "0,*";
            }
            function showTOC()
            {
                if (origCols)
                {
                    document.getElementById("outerFrameset").cols = origCols;
                    origCols = null;
                }
            }
        </script>
```

continued

framesetObject.borderColor

LISTING 27-43   *(continued)*

```
    </head>
    <frameset id="outerFrameset" frameborder="no" cols="150,*">
        <frame id="TOC" name="TOCFrame" src="jsb27-44.html" />
        <frameset id="innerFrameset1" rows="80,*">
            <frame id="controls" name="controlsFrame" src="jsb27-45.html" />
            <frame id="content" name="contentFrame" src="bofright.html" />
        </frameset>
    </frameset>
</html>
```

When a user clicks the hot spot to hide the frame, the script copies the original cols property settings to a global variable. The variable is used in showTOC() to restore the frameset to its original proportions. This allows a designer to modify the HTML for the frameset without also having to dig into scripts to hard-wire the restored size.

LISTING 27-44

Table of Contents Frame Content

```
<!DOCTYPE html>
<html>
    <head>
        <meta http-equiv="content-type" content="text/html;charset=utf-8">
        <title>Table of Contents</title>
        <style type="text/css">
            body
            {
            background-color:#EEEEEE;
            }
        </style>
    </head>
    <body>
        <h3>
            Table of Contents
        </h3>
        <hr />
        <ul style="font-size:10pt">
            <li><a href="bofright.htm#article1"
                target="contentFrame">Article I</a></li>
            <li><a href="bofright.htm#article2"
                target="contentFrame">Article II</a></li>
            <li><a href="bofright.htm#article3"
                target="contentFrame">Article III</a></li>
            <li><a href="bofright.htm#article4"
                target="contentFrame">Article IV</a></li>
            <li><a href="bofright.htm#article5"
                target="contentFrame">Article V</a></li>
            <li><a href="bofright.htm#article6"
```

```
            target="contentFrame">Article VI</a></li>
      <li><a href="bofright.htm#article7"
            target="contentFrame">Article VII</a></li>
      <li><a href="bofright.htm#article8"
            target="contentFrame">Article VIII</a></li>
      <li><a href="bofright.htm#article9"
            target="contentFrame">Article IX</a></li>
      <li><a href="bofright.htm#article10"
            target="contentFrame">Article X</a></li>
    </ul>
  </body>
</html>
```

LISTING 27-45

Control Panel Frame

```
<html>
  <head>
    <title>Control Panel</title>
    <style type="text/css">
      span
      {
          text-decoration:underline; cursor:pointer;
      }
    </style>
  </head>
  <body>
    <p><span id="tocToggle"
            onclick="parent.toggleTOC()">
          &lt;&lt;Hide/Show&gt;&gt;</span> Table of Contents
    </p>
  </body>
</html>
```

Related Item: frame object

frameBorder

Value: yes | no | 1 | 0 as strings   Read/Write

Compatibility: WinIE4+, MacIE4+, NN-, Moz-, Safari-, Opera-, Chrome-

The frameBorder property offers scripted access to a frameset element object's frameborder attribute setting. IE4+ does not respond well to modifying this property after the page has loaded.

Values for the frameBorder property are strings that substitute for Boolean values. Value yes or 1 means that the border is (supposed to be) turned on; no or 0 turns off the border.

Example

The default value for the frameBorder property is yes. You can use this setting to create a toggle script (which, unfortunately, does not change the appearance in IE). The IE5+ version looks like the following:

```
function toggleFrameScroll(framesetID)
{
    var theFrameset = document.getElementById(framesetID);
    if (theFrameset.frameBorder == "yes")
    {
        theFrameset.frameBorder = "no";
    }
    else
    {
        theFrameset.frameBorder = "yes";
    }
}
```

Related Item: frame.frameBorder property

frameSpacing

Value: Integer   Read/Write

Compatibility: WinIE4+, MacIE4+, NN-, Moz-, Safari-, Opera-, Chrome-

The frameSpacing property of a frameset element object lets you read the spacing (in pixels) between frames of a frameset. If you do not specify a framespacing attribute in the frameset's tag, the property is empty, rather than reflecting the actual border thickness applied by default (usually 2).

Example

If you need to change the spacing, a script reference would look like the following:

```
document.getElementById("outerFrameset").frameSpacing = "10";
```

Related Item: frameset.border property

iframe Element Object

For HTML element properties, methods, and event handlers, see Chapter 26, "Generic HTML Element Objects."

Properties	Methods	Event Handlers
align		
allowTransparency		
contentDocument		
contentWindow		

Properties	Methods	Event Handlers
frameBorder		
frameSpacing		
height		
hspace		
longDesc		
marginHeight		
marginWidth		
name		
noResize		
scrolling		
src		
vspace		
width		

Syntax

Accessing properties or methods of an iframe element object from a containing document:

```
(IE4+)     document.all.iframeID. property | method([parameters])
(IE4+/NN6) window.frames["iframeName"]. property | method([parameters])
(IE5+/W3C) document.getElementById("iframeID"). property |
           method([parameters])
```

Accessing properties of methods of an iframe element from a document inside the iframe element:

```
(IE4+)     parent.document.all.iframeID. property | method([parameters])
(IE5+/W3C) parent.document.getElementById("iframeID"). property |
           method([parameters])
```

Compatibility: WinIE4+, MacIE4+, NN6+, Moz+, Safari+, Opera+, Chrome+

About this object

An iframe element allows HTML content from a separate source to be loaded within the body of another document. In some respects, the NN4 layer element was a precursor to the iframe concept, but unlike the layer, an iframe element is not inherently positionable. It is positionable the same way as any other HTML element: by assigning positioning attributes to a style sheet associated with the iframe. Without explicit positioning, an iframe element appears in the body of a *iframeObject*.align

document in the normal source-code order of elements. Unlike a frame of a frameset, an iframe can be placed arbitrarily in the middle of any document. If the iframe changes size under script control, the surrounding content moves out of the way or cinches up.

What truly sets the iframe apart from other HTML elements is its ability to load and display external HTML files and, with the help of scripts, have different pages loaded into the iframe without disturbing the rest of the content of the main document. Pages loaded into the iframe can also have scripts and any other features that you may like to put into an HTML document (including XML, in IE for Windows).

The iframe element has a rich set of attributes that lets the HTML author control the look, size (height and width), and, to some degree, behavior of the frame. Most of these attributes are accessible to scripts as properties of an iframe element object.

It is important to bear in mind that an iframe element is in many respects like a frame element, especially when it comes to window kinds of relationships. If you plant an iframe element in a document of the main window, that element shows up in the main window's object model as a frame, accessible via common frames terminology:

```
window.frames[i]
window.frames[frameName]
```

Within that iframe frame object is a document and all its contents. All references to the document objects inside the iframe must flow through the portal of the iframe frame.

Conversely, scripts in the document living inside an iframe can communicate with the main document via the parent reference. Of course, you cannot replace the content of the main window with another HTML document (using location.href, for instance) without destroying the iframe that was in the original document.

Properties

align

Value: String   Read/Write

Compatibility: WinIE4+, MacIE4+, NN6+, Moz+, Safari+, Opera+, Chrome+

The align property governs how an iframe element aligns itself with respect to surrounding content on the page. Two of the possible values (left and right) position the iframe along the left and right edge (respectively) of the iframe's containing element (usually the body). Just as with an image, when an iframe is floated along the left and right edges of a container, other content wraps around the element. Table 27-6 shows all possible values and their meanings.

As your script changes the value of the align property, the page automatically reflows the content to suit the new alignment.

Example

The default setting for an iframe alignment is baseline. A script can shift the iframe to be flush with the right edge of the containing element as follows:

```
document.getElementById("iframe1").align = "right";
```

TABLE 27-6

Values of the align Property

Value	Description
absbottom	Aligns the bottom of the iframe with the imaginary line that extends along character descenders of surrounding text
absmiddle	Aligns the middle of the iframe with the center point between the surrounding text's top and absbottom
baseline	Aligns the bottom of the iframe with the baseline of surrounding text
bottom	Aligns the bottom of the iframe with the bottom of the surrounding text
left	Aligns the iframe flush with left edge of the containing element
middle	Aligns the imaginary vertical center line of surrounding text with the same for the iframe element
right	Aligns the iframe flush with the right edge of the containing element
texttop	Aligns the top of the iframe element with the imaginary line that extends along the tallest ascender of surrounding text
top	Aligns the top of the iframe element with the surrounding element's top

Related Items: iframe.hspace, iframe.vspace properties

allowTransparency

Value: Boolean   Read/Write

Compatibility: WinIE6+, MacIE-, NN-, Moz-, Safari-, Opera-, Chrome-

The allowTransparency property indicates whether the frame's background is transparent. By setting this property to true, you allow a background color or image to show through the transparent frame.

contentDocument

Value: document object reference   Read-Only

Compatibility: WinIE8+, MacIE-, NN6+, Moz+, Safari+, Opera+, Chrome+

The contentDocument property of an iframe element object is nothing more than a reference to the document contained by that frame. If your script finds that it has a reference to an iframe element object, you can use the contentDocument property to get a valid reference to the document and, therefore, any other content of the frame.

Example

A document script might be using the ID of an iframe element to read or adjust one of the element properties; then it needs to perform some action on the content of the page through its document object. You can get the reference to the document object via a statement such as the following:

```
var doc = document.getElementById("Frame3").contentDocument;
```

Then your script can, for example, dive into a form in the document:

```
var val = doc.mainForm.entry.value;
```

Related Items: contentWindow property; document object

contentWindow

Value: document object reference   Read-Only

Compatibility: WinIE5.5+, MacIE-, NN7+, Moz1.0.1+, Safari+, Opera+, Chrome+

The contentWindow property of an iframe element object serves as a reference to the window object generated by the frame. You can then use this window object as a means of accessing the document object and any document elements.

Related Items: contentDocument property; window object

frameBorder

(See frame.frameBorder() and frameset.frameBorder())

frameSpacing

(See frameset.frameSpacing())

height
width

Value: Integer   Read/Write

Compatibility: WinIE4+, MacIE4+, NN6+, Moz+, Safari+, Opera+, Chrome+

The height and width properties provide access to the height and width of the iframe object, and allow you to alter the size of the frame. Both properties are specified in pixels.

hspace
vspace

Value: Integer   Read/Write

Compatibility: WinIE4+, MacIE4+, NN-, Moz-, Safari-, Opera-, Chrome-

These IE-specific properties allow for margins to be set around an iframe element. In general, hspace and vspace properties (and their HTML attributes) have been replaced by CSS margins and padding. These properties and their attributes are not recognized by any W3C standard (including HTML 4).

Values for these properties are integers representing the number of pixels of padding between the element and surrounding content. The hspace value assigns the same number of pixels to the left and right sides of the element; the `vspace` value is applied to both the top and bottom edges. Scripted changes to these values have no effect in WinIE5+.

Related Item: `style.padding` property

longDesc

Value: URL string   Read/Write

Compatibility: WinIE6+, MacIE5+, NN6+, Moz+, Safari+, Opera+, Chrome+

The `longDesc` property is the scripted equivalent of the `longdesc` attribute of the `<iframe>` tag. This HTML 4 attribute is intended to provide browsers a URL to a document that contains a long description of the element. Future browsers can use this feature to provide information about the frame for visually impaired site visitors.

marginHeight
marginWidth

Value: Integer   Read/Write

Compatibility: WinIE4+, MacIE4+, NN6+, Moz+, Safari+, Opera+, Chrome+

Browsers tend to insert content within a frame automatically by adding a margin between the content and the edge of the frame. These values are represented by the `marginHeight` (top and bottom edges) and `marginWidth` (left and right edges) properties. Although the properties are not read-only, changing the values after the frameset has loaded does not alter the appearance of the document in the frame. If you need to alter the margin(s) of a document inside a frame, adjust the `document.body.style` margin properties.

Also be aware that although the default values of these properties are empty (that is, when no `marginheight` or `marginwidth` attributes are set for the `<iframe>` tag), margins are built into the page. The precise pixel count of those margins varies with different operating systems.

Related Item: `style` object (Chapter 38, "Style Sheet and Style Objects")

name

Value: String   Read/Write

Compatibility: WinIE4+, MacIE4+, NN6+, Moz+, Safari+, Opera+, Chrome+

The `name` property is the identifier associated with the frame for use as a reference. Scripts can reference the frame through the `name` property (for example, `window.frames["myIframe"]`), which is typically assigned via the `name` attribute.

noResize

(See `frame.noResize()`)

scrolling

Value: yes | no | 1 | 0 as strings   Read/Write

Compatibility: WinIE4+, MacIE4+, NN6+, Moz+, Safari+, Opera+, Chrome+

iframeObject.src

The `scrolling` property lets scripts turn scroll bars on and off inside an `iframe` element. By default, scrolling is turned on unless overridden by the `scroll` attribute of the `<iframe>` tag.

Values for the `scrolling` property are strings that substitute for Boolean values. Value `yes` or `1` means that scroll bars are visible (provided that there is more content than can be viewed without scrolling); `no` or `0` hides scroll bars in the frame. IE4+ also recognizes (and sets as default) the `auto` value.

Example

The following `toggleIFrameScroll()` function accepts a string of the `iframe` element's ID as a parameter, and switches between on and off scroll bars in the `iframe`. The `if` condition checks whether the property is set to something other than `no`. This test allows the condition to evaluate to `true` if the property is set to either `auto` (the first time) or `yes` (as set by the function).

```
function toggleFrameScroll(frameID)
{
    // IE5 & NN6 version
    var theFrame = document.getElementById(frameID);

    if (theFrame.scrolling != "no")
    {
        theFrame.scrolling = "no";
    }
    else
    {
        theFrame.scrolling = "yes";
    }
}
```

Related Item: `frame.scrolling` property

src

Value: URL string   Read/Write

Compatibility: WinIE4+, MacIE4+, NN6+, Moz+, Safari+, Opera+, Chrome+

The `src` property of an `iframe` element object offers an additional way of navigating to a different page within an inline frame (that is, other than assigning a new URL to the `location.href` property of the frame object). Remember that the `src` property belongs to the `iframe` element object, not the `window` object it represents. Therefore, references to the `src` property must be via the element's ID and/or node hierarchy.

Example

For best results, use fully formed URLs as values for the `src` property, as shown here:

```
document.getElementById("myIframe").src = "http://www.dannyg.com";
```

Relative URLs and `javascript:` pseudo-URLs also work most of the time.

Related Item: `location.href` property

popup Object

Properties	Methods	Event Handlers
document	hide()	
isOpen	show()	

Syntax

Creating a popup object:

```
var popupObj = window.createPopup()
```

Accessing properties or methods of a popup object from a document in the window that created the pop-up:

```
popupObj.property | method([parameters])
```

Compatibility: WinIE5.5+, MacIE-, NN-, Moz-, Safari-, Opera-, Chrome-

About this object

A popup object is a chromeless window space that overlaps the window whose document generates the pop-up. A pop-up also appears in front of any dialog boxes. Unlike the dialog-box windows generated via showModalDialog() and showModelessDialog() methods, your scripts must not only create the window, but also put content in it, and then define where on the screen, and how big, it will be. Because the pop-up window IE creates is a window and not a dialog box, there is no exact W3C equivalent. However, with the ability to add and delete elements to the node tree using the W3C DOM, you can achieve the same type of functionality. See Chapter 25, "Document Object Model Essentials," for more information.

Because the pop-up window has no chrome (title bar, resize handles, and so on), you should populate its content with a border and/or background color so that it stands out from the main window's content. The following statements reflect a typical sequence of creating, populating, and showing a popup object:

```
var popup = window.createPopup();
var popupBody = popup.document.body;
popupBody.style.border = "solid 2px black";
popupBody.style.padding = "5px";
popupBody.innerHTML = "<p>Here is some text in a popup window</p>";
popup.show(200,100, 200, 50, document.body);
```

Note

As handy as it may be, in a strict W3C approach to JavaScript, you wouldn't use the innerHTML property, because it isn't officially part of the W3C standard. However, it is often too powerful a convenience property to ignore, as much of the code throughout this book is a testament. The book does show the W3C node manipulation alternative to innerHTML in some examples. Refer to Chapter 29 for a thorough explanation and examples of the W3C alternative to innerHTML. ∎

popupObject.**document**

The pop-up window that IE creates is, in fact, a window, but only from the point of view of the document that it contains. In other words, although the number of properties and methods for the popup object is small, the parentWindow property of the document inside the pop-up points to a genuine window property. Even so, be aware that this pop-up does not appear as a distinct window among those listed in the Windows Taskbar. If a user clicks outside the pop-up or switches to another application, the pop-up disappears, and you must reinvoke the show() method by script (complete with dimension and position parameters) to force the pop-up to reappear.

When you assign content to a pop-up, you are also responsible for making sure that the content fits the size of the pop-up you specify. If the content runs past the rectangular space (body text word wraps within the pop-up's rectangle), no scroll bars appear.

Properties

document

Value: document object reference   Read-Only

Compatibility: WinIE5.5+, MacIE-, NN-, Moz-, Safari-, Opera-, Chrome-

Use the document property as a gateway to the content of a pop-up window. This property is the only access point available from the script that creates the pop-up, to the pop-up itself. The most common application of this property is to set document properties governing the content of the pop-up window. For example, to give the pop-up a border (because the pop-up itself has no window chrome), the script that creates the window can assign values to the style property of the document in the pop-up window, as follows:

```
myPopup.document.body.style.border = "solid 3px gray";
```

Be aware that the document object of a pop-up window may not implement the full flexibility you're used to with primary window document objects. For example, you are not allowed to assign a URL to the document.URL property in a pop-up window.

Example

Use The Evaluator (Chapter 4, "JavaScript") to experiment with the popup object and its properties. Enter the following statements in the top text box. The first statement creates a pop-up window whose reference is assigned to the a global variable. Next, a reference to the body of the pop-up's document is preserved in the b variable for the sake of convenience. Further statements work with these two variables.

```
a = window.createPopup()
b = a.document.body
b.style.border = "solid 2px black"
b.style.padding = "5px"
b.innerHTML = "<p>Here is some text in a popup window</p>"
a.show(200,100, 200, 50, document.body)
```

See the description of the show() method for details on the parameters.

Related Item: document object

isOpen

Value: Boolean   Read-Only

Compatibility: WinIE5.5+, MacIE-, NN-, Moz-, Safari-, Opera-, Chrome-

While a pop-up window is visible, its isOpen property returns true; otherwise, the property returns false. Because any user action in the browser causes the pop-up to hide itself, the property is useful only for script statements that are running on their own after the pop-up is made visible.

Example

Use The Evaluator (Chapter 4, "JavaScript Essentials") to experiment with the isOpen property. Enter the following statements in the top text box. The sequence begins with a creation of a simple pop-up window, whose reference is assigned to the a global variable. Note that the final statement is actually two statements, designed so that the second statement executes while the pop-up window is still open.

```
a = window.createPopup();
a.document.body.innerHTML = "<p>Here is a popup window</p>";
a.show(200,100, 200, 50, document.body); alert("Popup is open:" + a.isOpen);
```

If you then click in the main window to hide the pop-up, you will see a different result if you enter the following statement in the top text box by itself:

```
alert("Popup is open:" + a.isOpen);
```

Related Item: popup.show() method

Methods
```
hide()
show(left, top, width, height[, positioningElementRef])
```

Returns: Nothing

Compatibility: WinIE5.5+, MacIE-, NN-, Moz-, Safari-, Opera-, Chrome-

After you have created a popup object with the window.createPopup() method and populated it with content, you must explicitly show the window via the show() method. If the window is hidden because a user clicked the main browser window somewhere, the show() method (and all its parameters) must be invoked again. To have a script hide the window, invoke the hide() method for the popup object.

The first four parameters of the show() method are required; they define the pixel location and size of the pop-up window. By default, the coordinate space for the left and top parameters is the video display. Thus, a left and top setting of zero places the pop-up in the top-left corner of the video screen. But you can define a different coordinate space by adding an optional fifth parameter. This parameter must be a reference to an element on the page. To confine the coordinate space to the content region of the browser window, specify the document.body object as the positioning element reference.

popupObject.show()

Example

Listing 27-46 demonstrates the show() and hide() methods for a popup object. A click of the button on the page invokes the selfTimer() function, which acts as the main routine for this page.
The goal is to produce a pop-up window that self-destructs 5 seconds after it appears. Along the way,
a message in the pop-up counts down the seconds.

A reference to the pop-up window is preserved as a global variable called popup. After the popup
object is created, the initContent() function stuffs the content into the pop-up by way of assigning style properties, and some innerHTML, for the body of the document that is automatically
created when the pop-up is generated. A span element is defined so that another function later on
can modify the content of just that segment of text in the pop-up. Notice that the assignment of content to the pop-up is predicated on the pop-up window's having been initialized (by virtue of the
popup variable's having a value assigned to it) and that the pop-up window is not showing. Although
invoking initContent() under any other circumstances is probably impossible, the validation of
the desired conditions is good programming practice.

Back in selfTimer(), the popup object is displayed. Defining the desired size requires some trial
and error to make sure that the pop-up window comfortably accommodates the text that is put into
the pop-up in the initContent() function.

With the pop-up window showing, now is the time to invoke the countDown() function. Before
the function performs any action, it validates that the pop-up has been initialized and is still visible.
If a user clicks the main window while the counter is counting down, this changes the value of the
isOpen property to false, and nothing inside the if condition executes.

This countDown() function grabs the inner text of the span and uses paresInt() to extract
just the integer number (using base 10 numbering, because we're dealing with zero-leading numbers
that can potentially be regarded as octal values). The condition of the if construction decreases the
retrieved integer by one. If the decremented value is zero, the time is up, and the pop-up window is
hidden with the popup global variable returned to its original, null value. But if the value is other
than zero, the inner text of the span is set to the decremented value (with a leading zero), and the
setTimeout() method is called upon to reinvoke the countDown() function in 1 second (1,000
milliseconds).

LISTING 27-46

Hiding and Showing a Pop-Up

HTML: jsb27-46.html

```
<!DOCTYPE html>
<html>
    <head>
        <meta http-equiv="content-type" content="text/html;charset=utf-8">
        <title>popup Object</title>
        <script type="text/javascript" src="jsb27-46.js"></script>
    </head>
    <body>
        <form>
```

```
            <input type="button" value="Impossible Mission"
                   onclick="selfTimer()" />
        </form>
    </body>
</html>
```

JavaScript: jsb27-46.js

```
var popup;
function initContent()
{
    if (popup && !popup.isOpen)
    {
        var popBody = popup.document.body;
        popBody.style.border = "solid 3px red";
        popBody.style.padding = "10px";
        popBody.style.fontSize = "24pt";
        popBody.style.textAlign = "center";
        var bodyText = "<P>This popup will self-destruct in ";
        bodyText += "<span id='counter'>05<\/span>";
        bodyText += " seconds...<\/P>";
        popBody.innerHTML = bodyText;
    }
}
function countDown()
{
    if (popup && popup.isOpen)
    {
        var currCount = parseInt(popup.document.all.counter.innerText, 10);
        if (--currCount == 0)
        {
            popup.hide();
            popup = null;
        }
        else
        {
            popup.document.all.counter.innerText = "0" + currCount;
            setTimeout("countDown()", 1000);
        }
    }
}
function selfTimer()
{
    popup = window.createPopup();
    initContent();
    popup.show(200,200,400,100,document.body);
    setTimeout("countDown()", 1000);
}
```

879

popupObject.show()

The `hide()` method here is invoked by a script that is running while the pop-up window is show-ing. Because a pop-up window automatically goes away if a user clicks the main window, it is highly unlikely that the `hide()` method would ever be invoked by itself in response to user action in the main window. If you want a script in the pop-up window to close the pop-up, use `parentWin-dow.close()`.

Related Items: `popup.isOpen` property; `window.createPopup()` method

Location and History Objects

N ot all objects in the document object model (DOM) are things you can see in the content area of the browser window. Each browser window or frame maintains a bunch of other information about the page you are currently visiting and where you have been. The URL of the page you see in the window is called the *location,* and browsers store this information in the `location` object. As you surf the Web, the browser stores the URLs of your past pages in the `history` object. You can manually view what that object contains by looking in the browser menu for the item that enables you to jump back to a previously visited page. This chapter is all about these two nearly invisible, but important, objects.

These objects are not only valuable to your browser, but also valuable to snoopers who might want to write scripts to see what URLs you're viewing in another frame, or the URLs of other sites you've visited in the past dozen mouse clicks. As a result, security restrictions built into browsers limit access to some of these objects' properties (unless you use signed scripts in NN4+/Moz). For older browsers, these properties simply are not available from a script.

IN THIS CHAPTER

Loading new pages and other media types via the location object

Security restrictions across frames

Navigating through the browser history under script control

location Object

Properties	Methods	Event Handlers
hash	assign()	None
host	reload()	
hostname	replace()	
href		
pathname		

locationObject

Properties	Methods	Event Handlers
port		
protocol		
search		

Syntax

Loading a new document into the current window:

```
[window.]location.href = "URL";
```

Accessing location object properties or methods:

```
[window.]location.property | method([parameters])
```

About this object

In its place one level below window-style objects in the original document object hierarchy, the location object represents information about the URL of any currently open window, or of a specific frame. To display the URL of the current web page, you can reference the location object like this:

```
document.write(location.href);
```

In this example, the href property evaluates to the URL, which is written to the current page in its entirety. The location object also allows you to access individual parts of the URL, as you will see in a moment.

When you reference the location object in the framesetting document of a multiple-frame window, the location is given as the parent window's URL, which appears in the Location (or Address) field of the browser. Each frame also has a location associated with it, although you may not see any overt reference to the frame's URL in the browser. To get URL information about a document located in another frame, the reference to the location object must include the window frame reference. For example, if you have a window consisting of two frames, Table 28-1 shows the possible references to the location objects for all frames comprising the web presentation.

Note

Scripts cannot alter the URL displayed in the browser's Location/Address box. For security and privacy reasons, that text box cannot display anything other than the URL of a current page or URL in transit. ■

Most properties of a location object deal with network-oriented information. This information involves various data about the physical location of the document on the network, including the host server, the protocol being used, and other components of the URL. Given a complete URL for a typical World Wide Web page, the window.location object assigns property names to various segments of the URL, as shown here:

```
http://www.example.com:80/promos/newproducts.html#giantGizmo
```

882

locationObject

Property	Value
protocol	"http:"
hostname	"www.example.com"
port	"80"
host	"www.example.com:80"
pathname	"/promos/newproducts.html"
hash	"#giantGizmo"
href	"http://www.example.com:80/promos newproducts.html#giantGizmo"

TABLE 28-1

Location Object References in a Two-Frame Browser Window

Reference	Description
location (or window.location)	URL of frame displaying the document that runs the script statement containing this reference
parent.location	URL information for parent window that defines the <frameset>
parent.frames[0].location	URL information for first visible frame
parent.frames[1].location	URL information for second visible frame
parent.otherFrameName.location	URL information for another named frame in the same frameset

The window.location object is handy when a script needs to extract information about the URL, perhaps to obtain a base reference on which to build URLs for other documents to be fetched as the result of user action. This object can eliminate a nuisance for web authors who develop sites on one machine and then upload them to a server (perhaps at an Internet service provider) with an entirely different directory structure. By building scripts to construct base references from the directory location of the current document, you can construct the complete URLs for loading documents. You don't have to change the base reference data manually in your documents as you shift the files from computer to computer or from directory to directory. To extract the segment of the URL and place it in the enclosing directory, use the following:

```
var baseRef = location.href.substring(0,location.href.lastIndexOf("/") + 1);
```

Caution

Security alert: To allay fears of Internet security breaches and privacy invasions, scriptable browsers prevent your script in one frame from retrieving location object properties from other frames whose domain and server are not your own (unless you use signed scripts in NN4+/Moz or the user has set the IE browser to trust your site). This restriction puts a damper on many scripters' well-meaning designs and aids for web watchers and visitors. If you attempt such property accesses, however, you receive an "access denied" (or similar) security warning dialog box. ■

locationObject.hash

Setting the value of some `location` properties is the preferred way to control which document gets loaded into a window or frame. Though you may expect to find a method somewhere in JavaScript that contains a plain-language *Go* or *Open* word (to simulate what you see in the browser menu bar), you point your browser to another URL by setting the `window.location.href` property to that URL, as in:

```
window.location.href = "http://www.dannyg.com/";
```

The equals assignment operator (=) in this kind of statement is a powerful weapon. In fact, setting the `location.href` object to a URL of a different MIME type, such as one of the variety of sound and video formats, causes the browser to load those files into the plug-in or helper application designated in your browser's settings. The `location.assign()` method was originally intended for internal use by the browser, but it is available for scripters (although I don't recommend using it for navigation). Internet Explorer's object model includes a `window.navigate()` method that also loads a document into a window, but you can't use it for cross-browser applications.

Two other methods complement the `location` object's capability to control navigation. One method is the script equivalent of clicking Reload; the other method enables you to replace the current document's entry in the history with that of the next URL of your script's choice.

Properties

hash

Value: String   Read/Write

Compatibility: WinIE3+, MacIE3+, NN2+, Moz+, Safari+, Opera+, Chrome+

The *hash mark* (#) is a URL convention that directs the browser to an anchor located in the document. Any name you assign to an anchor (with the `<a name="...">  ...</a>` tag pair) becomes part of the URL after the hash mark. A `location` object's `hash` property is the name of the anchor part of the current URL (which consists of the hash mark and the name).

If you have written HTML documents with anchors and directed links to navigate to those anchors, you have probably noticed that although the destination location shows the anchor as part of the URL (for example, in the Location field), the window's anchor value does not change as the user manually scrolls to positions in the document where other anchors are defined. An anchor appears in the URL only when the window has navigated there as part of a link or in response to a script that adjusts the URL.

Just as you can navigate to any URL by setting the `window.location.href` property, you can navigate to another hash in the same document by adjusting only the `hash` property of the location without the hash mark (as shown in the following example).

Listing 28-1 demonstrates how to use the `hash` property to access the anchor part of a URL. When you load the script in Listing 28-1, adjust the height of the browser window so that only one section is visible at a time. When you click a button, the script navigates to the next logical section in the progression and eventually takes you back to the top. The page won't scroll any farther than the bottom of the document. Therefore, an anchor near the bottom of the page may not appear at the top of the browser window.

LISTING 28-1

A Document with Anchors

```
<!DOCTYPE html>
<html>
    <head>
        <meta http-equiv="content-type" content="text/html;charset=utf-8">
        <title>location.hash Property</title>
        <script type="text/javascript">
        function goNextAnchor(where)
        {
            window.location.hash = where;
        }
        </script>
    </head>
    <body>
        <h1><a id="start" name="start">Top</a></h1>
        <form>
            <input type="button" name="next" value="NEXT"
            onclick="goNextAnchor('sec1')" />
        </form>
        <hr /><br /><br /><br /><br /><br />
        <h1><a id="sec1" name="sec1">Section 1</a></h1>
        <form>
            <input type="button" name="next" value="NEXT"
            onclick="goNextAnchor('sec2')" />
        </form>
        <hr /><br /><br /><br /><br /><br />
        <h1><a id="sec2" name="sec2">Section 2</a></h1>
        <form>
            <input type="button" name="next" value="NEXT"
            onclick="goNextAnchor('sec3')" />
        </form>
        <hr /><br /><br /><br /><br /><br />
        <h1><a id="sec3" name="sec3">Section 3</a></h1>
        <form>
            <input type="button" name="next" value="BACK TO TOP"
            onclick="goNextAnchor('start')" />
        </form>
    </body>
</html>
```

locationObject.host

Note

The property assignment event handling technique used in the previous example and throughout the chapter is a deliberate simplification to make the code more readable. It is generally better to use the more modern approach of binding events using the `addEventListener()` **(NN6+/Moz/W3C) or** `attachEvent()` **(IE5+) methods. A modern cross-browser event handling technique is explained in detail in Chapter 32, "Event Objects." Several other chapters use the modern technique extensively. ∎**

Anchor names are passed as parameters with each button's `onclick` event handler. Instead of going through the work of assembling a `window.location` value in the function by appending a literal hash mark and the value for the anchor, here we simply modify the `hash` property of the current window's location. This is the preferred, cleaner method.

If you attempt to read back the `window.location.hash` property in an added line of script, however, the window's actual URL probably will not have been updated yet, and the browser will appear to be giving your script false information. To prevent this problem in subsequent statements of the same function, construct the URLs of those statements from the same variable values you use to set the `window.location.hash` property; don't rely on the browser to give you the values you expect.

Related Item: `location.href` property

host

Value: String   Read/Write

Compatibility: WinIE3+, MacIE3+, NN2+, Moz+, Safari+, Opera+, Chrome+

The `location.host` property describes both the hostname and port of a URL. The port is included in the value only when the port is an explicit part of the URL. If you navigate to a URL that does not display the port number in the Location field of the browser, the `location.host` property returns the same value as the `location.hostname` property. As with the `location.hostname` property, the `location.host` property will likely come up blank for pages that you open from your local hard drive (localhost) in some browsers — for example, IE and WebKit browsers such as Chrome.

Use the `location.host` property to extract the `hostname:port` part of the URL of any document loaded in the browser. This capability may be helpful for building a URL to a specific document that you want your script to access on-the-fly.

Use the documents in Listing 28-2, Listing 28-3, and Listing 28-4 as tools to help you learn the values that the various `window.location` properties return. In the browser, open the file for Listing 28-2. This file creates a two-frame window. The left frame contains a temporary placeholder (see Listing 28-4) that displays some instructions. The right frame has a document (see Listing 28-3) that enables you to load URLs into the left frame and get readings on three different windows available: the parent window (which creates the multiframe window), the left frame, and the right frame.

LISTING 28-2

Frameset for the Property Picker

```
<!DOCTYPE html>
<html>
    <head>
        <meta http-equiv="content-type" content="text/html;charset=utf-8">
```

```
    <title>window.location Properties</title>
    </head>
    <frameset cols="50%,50%" border="1" bordercolor="black">
        <frame name="Frame1" src="jsb28-04.html" />
        <frame name="Frame2" src="jsb28-03.html" />
    </frameset>
</html>
```

LISTING 28-3

Property Picker

```
<!DOCTYPE html>
<html>
    <head>
        <meta http-equiv="content-type" content="text/html;charset=utf-8">
        <title>Property Picker</title>
        <script type="text/javascript">
        var isNav = (typeof netscape != "undefined") ? true : false;

        function fillLeftFrame()
        {
            newURL = prompt("Enter the URL of a document to show in the left
                frame:","");
            if (newURL != null && newURL != "")
            {
                parent.frames[0].location = newURL;
            }
        }
        function showLocationData(form)
        {
            for (var i = 0; i <3; i++)
            {
                if (form.whichFrame[i].checked)
                {
                    var windName = form.whichFrame[i].value;
                    break;
                }
            }
            var theWind = "" + windName + ".location";
            if (isNav)
            {
                netscape.security.PrivilegeManager.enablePrivilege(
                    "UniversalBrowserRead");
            }
            var theObj = eval(theWind);
            form.windName.value = windName;
            form.windHash.value = theObj.hash;
            form.windHost.value = theObj.host;
            form.windHostname.value = theObj.hostname;
```

continued

LISTING 28-3   *(continued)*

```
        form.windHref.value = theObj.href;
        form.windPath.value = theObj.pathname;
        form.windPort.value = theObj.port;
        form.windProtocol.value = theObj.protocol;
        form.windSearch.value = theObj.search;
        if (isNav)
        {
            netscape.security.PrivilegeManager.disablePrivilege(
                "UniversalBrowserRead");
        }
    }
}
    </script>
</head>
<body>
    Click the "Open URL" button to enter the location of an HTML document to
    display in the left frame of this window.
    <form>
        <input type="button" name="opener" value="Open URL..."
        onclick="fillLeftFrame()" />
        <hr />
        <center>
            Select a window/frame. Then click the "Show Location Properties"
            button to view each window.location property value for the desired
            window.
            <p><input type="radio" name="whichFrame" value="parent"
                checked="checked" />Parent window <input type="radio"
                name="whichFrame" value="parent.frames[0]" />Left frame <input
                type="radio" name="whichFrame" value="parent.frames[1]" />This
                frame</p>
            <p><input type="button" name="getProperties"
                value="Show Location Properties"
                onclick="showLocationData(this.form)" /> <input type="reset"
                value="Clear" /></p>
            <table border="2">
                <tr>
                    <td align="right">Window:</td>
                    <td><input type="text" name="windName" size="30" /></td>
                </tr>
                <tr>
                    <td align="right">hash:</td>
                    <td><input type="text" name="windHash" size="30" /></td>
                </tr>
                <tr>
                    <td align="right">host:</td>
                    <td><input type="text" name="windHost" size="30" /></td>
                </tr>
                <tr>
                    <td align="right">hostname:</td>
                    <td><input type="text" name="windHostname" size="30" /></td>
                </tr>
```

```
            <tr>
                <td align="right">href:</td>
                <td><textarea name="windHref" rows="3" cols="30" wrap="soft">
                    </textarea></td>
            </tr>
            <tr>
                <td align="right">pathname:</td>
                <td><textarea name="windPath" rows="3" cols="30" wrap="soft">
                    </textarea></td>
            </tr>
            <tr>
                <td align="right">port:</td>
                <td><input type="text" name="windPort" size="30" /></td>
            </tr>
            <tr>
                <td align="right">protocol:</td>
                <td><input type="text" name="windProtocol" size="30" /></td>
            </tr>
            <tr>
                <td align="right">search:</td>
                <td><textarea name="windSearch" rows="3" cols="30"
                    wrap="soft"></textarea></td>
            </tr>
        </table>
    </center>
  </form>
  </body>
</html>
```

LISTING 28-4

Placeholder Document for Listing 28-2

```
<!DOCTYPE html>
<html>
    <head>
        <meta http-equiv="content-type" content="text/html;charset=utf-8">
    <title>Opening Placeholder</title>
    </head>
    <body>
        Initial placeholder. Experiment with other URLs for this frame (see
        right).
    </body>
</html>
```

For the best results, open a URL to a web document on the network from the same domain and server from which you load the listings (perhaps your local hard disk). If you open a URL to a web document that is not from the same domain and server, be sure to specify the fully qualified URL. If possible, load a document that includes anchor points to navigate through a long document. Click

889

the Left frame radio button and then click the button that shows all properties. This action fills the table in the right frame with all the available `location` properties for the selected window.

Related Items: `location.port, location.hostname` properties

hostname

Value: String

Read/Write

Compatibility: WinIE3+, MacIE3+, NN2+, Moz+, Safari+, Opera+, Chrome+

The hostname of a typical URL is the name of the server on the network that stores the document you view in the browser. For most web sites, the server name includes not only the domain name, but also the `www.` prefix. The hostname does not, however, include the port number if the URL specifies such a number. Keep in mind that the `hostname` property will likely come up blank for pages that you open from your local hard drive (localhost) in some browsers — for example, IE and WebKit browsers such as Chrome.

See Listing 28-2, Listing 28-3, and Listing 28-4 for a set of related pages to help you view the hostname data for a variety of other pages.

Related Items: `location.host, location.port` properties

href

Value: String

Read/Write

Compatibility: WinIE3+, MacIE3+, NN2+, Moz+, Safari+, Opera+, Chrome+

Of all the `location` object properties, `href` (hypertext reference) is probably the one most often called upon in scripting. The `location.href` property supplies a string of the entire URL of the specified `window` object.

Using this property on the left side of an assignment statement is the JavaScript way of opening a URL for display in a window. Any of the following statements can load my web site's index page into a single-frame browser window:

```
window.location = "http://www.dannyg.com";
window.location.href = "http://www.dannyg.com";
```

At times, you may encounter difficulty by omitting a reference to a window. JavaScript may get confused and reference the `document.location` property. To prevent this confusion, the `document.location` property was deprecated (put on the no-no list) and replaced by the `document.URL` property. In the meantime, you can't go wrong by always specifying a window in the reference.

Note

You should be able to omit the `href` property name when assigning a new URL to the `location` object (for example, `location = "http://www.dannyg.com"`). Although this works in most browsers most of the time, some early browsers behave more reliably if you assign a URL explicitly to the `location.href` property. If you want to play it safe, use `location.href` at all times. ∎

Sometimes, you must extract the name of the current directory in a script so that another statement can append a known document to the URL before loading it into the window. Although the other `location` object properties yield an assortment of a URL's segments, none of them provides the full URL to the current URL's directory. But you can use JavaScript string manipulation techniques to accomplish this task. Listing 28-5 shows such a possibility.

Depending on your browser, the values for the `location.href` property may be encoded with ASCII equivalents of nonalphanumeric characters. Such an ASCII value includes the % symbol and the ASCII numeric value. The most common encoded character in a URL is the space: %20. If you need to extract a URL and display that value as a string in your documents, you can safely pass all such potentially encoded strings through the JavaScript `unescape()` function. For example, if a URL is `http://www.example.com/product%20list`, you can convert it by passing it through the `unescape()` function, as in the following example.

```
var plainURL = unescape(window.location.href);
// result = "http://www.example.com/product list";
```

The inverse function, `escape()`, is available for sending encoded strings to server applications, such as CGI scripts. See Chapter 24, "Global Functions and Statements," for more details on these functions.

Listing 28-5 shows how the `href` property can be used to view the directory URL of the current page. This example includes the `unescape()` function in front of the part of the script that captures the URL. This function serves cosmetic purposes by displaying the pathname in alert dialog boxes for browsers that normally display the ASCII-encoded version.

Note

Although Listing 28-5 uses the `unescape()` global function for backward compatibility, that function (and its partner, `escape()`) have been removed from the ECMAScript standard as of version 3. These functions have been replaced by more modern versions, `decodeURI()` and `encodeURI()`. See Chapter 24 for details. ∎

LISTING 28-5

Extracting the Directory of the Current Document

```
<!DOCTYPE html>
<html>
   <head>
      <meta http-equiv="content-type" content="text/html;charset=utf-8">
      <title>Extract pathname</title>
      <script type="text/javascript">
      // general purpose function to extract URL of current directory
      function getDirPath(URL)
      {
          var result = unescape(URL.substring(0,(URL.lastIndexOf("/")) + 1));
          return result;
      }

      // handle button event, passing work onto general purpose function
      function showDirPath(URL)
      {
          alert(getDirPath(URL));
      }
      </script>
   </head>
```

continued

locationObject.pathname

LISTING 28-5   *(continued)*

```
<body>
    <form>
        <input type="button" value="View directory URL"
        onclick="showDirPath(window.location.href)" />
    </form>
</body>
</html>
```

Related Items: location.pathname, document.location properties; String object (Chapter 15, "The String Object")

pathname

Value: String   Read/Write

Compatibility: WinIE3+, MacIE3+, NN2+, Moz+, Safari+, Opera+, Chrome+

The pathname component of a URL consists of the directory structure relative to the server's root volume. In other words, the root (the server name in an http: connection) is not part of the pathname. If the URL's path is to a file in the root directory, the location.pathname property is a single slash (/) character. Any other pathname starts with a slash character, indicating a directory nested within the root. The value of the location.pathname property also includes the document name.

See Listing 28-2, Listing 28-3, and Listing 28-4 earlier in this chapter for a multiple-frame example you can use to view the location.pathname property for a variety of URLs of your choice.

Related Item: location.href property

port

Value: String   Read/Write

Compatibility: WinIE3+, MacIE3+, NN2+, Moz+, Safari+, Opera+, Chrome+

These days, few consumer-friendly web sites need to include the port number as part of their URLs. You see port numbers mostly in the less-popular protocols, in URLs to sites used for private development purposes, or in URLs to sites that have no assigned domain names. You can retrieve the value with the location.port property. If you extract the value from one URL and intend to build another URL with that component, be sure to include the colon delimiter between the server's IP address and port number.

If you have access to URLs containing port numbers, use the documents in Listing 28-2, Listing 28-3, and Listing 28-4 to experiment with the output of the location.port property.

Related Item: location.host property

protocol

Value: String   Read/Write

Compatibility: WinIE3+, MacIE3+, NN2+, Moz+, Safari+, Opera+, Chrome+

The first component of any URL is the protocol used for the particular type of communication. For World Wide Web pages, the Hypertext Transfer Protocol (http) is the standard. Other common protocols you may see in your browser include HTTP-Secure (https), File Transfer Protocol (ftp), File (file), and Mail (mailto); web pages opened from your local hard drive use the file protocol. Values for the location.protocol property include not only the name of the protocol, but also the trailing colon delimiter. Thus, for a typical web-page URL, the location.protocol property is

```
http:
```

Notice that the usual slashes after the protocol in the URL are not part of the location. protocol value. Of all the location object properties, only the full URL (location.href) reveals the slash delimiters between the protocol and other components.

See Listing 28-2, Listing 28-3, and Listing 28-4 for a multiple-frame example you can use to view the location.protocol property for a variety of URLs. Notice that the protocol shows up initially as file: to indicate that the first page in the left frame is stored locally and accessed via the File protocol. Also try loading an FTP site to see the location.protocol value for that type of URL.

Related Item: location.href property

search

Value: String   Read/Write

Compatibility: WinIE3+, MacIE3+, NN2+, Moz+, Safari+, Opera+, Chrome+

Perhaps you've noticed the long, cryptic URL that appears in the Location/Address field of your browser whenever you ask one of the World Wide Web search services to look up matches for items you enter in the keyword field. The URL starts the regular way — with protocol, host, and pathname values. But following the more traditional URL are search commands that are submitted to the search engine (typically, a CGI program running on the server). You can retrieve or set that trailing search query by using the location.search property.

Each search engine has its own formula for query submissions based on the designs of the HTML forms that obtain details from users. These search queries come in an encoded format that appears in anything but plain language. If you plan to script a search query, be sure you fully understand the search engine's format before you start assembling a string to assign to the location.search property of a window.

The most common format for search data is a series of name/value pairs. An equal symbol (=) separates a name and its value. Multiple name/value pairs have ampersands (&) between them. You should use the escape() function to convert the data to URL-friendly format, especially when the content includes spaces.

The location.search property also applies to any part of a URL after the filename, including parameters being sent to CGI programs on the server.

Passing data between pages via URLs

It is not uncommon to want to preserve some pieces of data that exist in one page so that a script in another page can pick up where the script processing left off in the first page. You can achieve persistence across page loads without any server programming through one of three techniques: the document.cookie (see Chapter 29, "Document and Body Objects"), variables in framesetting documents, and the search string of a URL. That's really what happens when you visit search and e-commerce sites that return information to your browser. Rather than store, say, your search criteria on the server, they

893

locationObject.search

spit the criteria back to the browser as part of the URL. The next time you activate that URL, the values are sent to the server for processing (for example, to send you the next page of search results for a particular query).

Passing data between pages is not limited to client/server communication. You can use the search string strictly on the client side to pass data from one page to another. Unless some CGI process on the server is programmed to do something with the search string, a web server regurgitates the search string as part of the location data that comes back with a page. A script in the newly loaded page can inspect the search string (via the `location.search` property) and tear it apart to gather the data and put it into script variables. Take a look at Listing 28-6, Listing 28-7, and Listing 28-8 to see a powerful application of this technique.

As mentioned in Chapter 27, "Window and Frame Objects," you can force a particular HTML page to open inside the frameset for which it is designed. But with the help of the search string, you can reuse the same framesetting document to accommodate any number of content pages that go into one of the frames (rather than specifying a separate frameset for each possible combination of pages in the frameset). The listings in this section create a simple example of how to force a page to load in a frameset by passing some information about the page to the frameset. Thus, if a user has a URL to one of the content frames (perhaps it has been bookmarked by right-clicking the frame, or it comes up as a search-engine result), the page appears in its designated frameset the next time the user visits the page.

The fundamental task in this scheme has two parts. The first is in each of the content pages, where a script checks whether the page is loaded inside a frameset. If the frameset is missing, a search string is composed and appended to the URL for the framesetting document. The framesetting document has its own short script that looks for the presence of the search string. If the string is there, the script extracts the search string data and uses it to load that specific page into the content frame of the frameset.

Listing 28-6 is the framesetting document. The `getSearchAsArray()` function is more complete than necessary for this simple example, but you can use it in other instances to convert any number of name/value pairs passed in the search string (in traditional format of `name1=value1&name2=value2&etc.`) into an array whose indexes are the names (making it easier for scripts to extract a specific piece of passed data).

LISTING 28-6

A Smart Frameset

```html
<!DOCTYPE html>
<html>
    <head>
        <meta http-equiv="content-type" content="text/html;charset=utf-8">
        <title>Example Frameset</title>
        <script type="text/javascript">
        // Convert location.search into an array of values
        // indexed by name.
        function getSearchAsArray()
        {
            var results = new Array();
            var input = unescape(location.search.substr(1));
```

```
        if (input)
        {
            var srchArray = input.split("&");
            var tempArray = new Array();
            for (var i = 0; i < srchArray.length; i++)
            {
                tempArray = srchArray[i].split("=");
                results[tempArray[0]] = tempArray[1];
            }
        }
        return results;
    }

    function loadFrame()
    {
        if (location.search)
        {
            var srchArray = getSearchAsArray();
            if (srchArray["content"])
            {
                self.content.location.href = srchArray["content"];
            }
        }
    }
    </script>
</head>
<frameset cols="250,*" onload="loadFrame()">
    <frame name="toc" src="jsb28-07.html" />
    <frame name="content" src="jsb28-08.html" />
</frameset>
</html>
```

Listing 28-7 is the HTML for the table-of-contents frame. Nothing elaborate goes on here, but you can see how normal navigation works for this simplified frameset. You can also see how this example could be easily built upon to provide a handy table-of-contents feature to a site with multiple sections or pages.

LISTING 28-7

The Table of Contents

```
<!DOCTYPE html>
<html>
    <head>
        <meta http-equiv="content-type" content="text/html;charset=utf-8">
    <title>Table of Contents</title>
    </head>
    <body bgcolor="#EEEEEE">
        <h3>Table of Contents</h3>
```

continued

LISTING 28-7   *(continued)*

```
        <hr />
        <ul>
            <li><a href="jsb28-08.html" target="content">Page 1</a></li>
            <li><a href="jsb28-08a.html" target="content">Page 2</a></li>
            <li><a href="jsb28-08b.html" target="content">Page 3</a></li>
        </ul>
    </body>
</html>
```

Listing 28-8 shows one of the content pages. As the page loads, the checkFrameset() function is invoked. If the window does not load inside a frameset, the script navigates to the framesetting page, passing the current content URL as a search string. Notice that the loading of this page on its own does not get recorded to the browser's history and isn't accessed if the user clicks the Back button.

LISTING 28-8

A Content Page

```
<!DOCTYPE html>
<html>
    <head>
        <meta http-equiv="content-type" content="text/html;charset=utf-8">
        <title>Page 1</title>
        <script type="text/javascript">
        function checkFrameset()
        {
            if (parent == window)
            {
                // Use replace() to keep current page out of history
                location.replace("jsb28-06.html?content=" + escape(location.href));
            }
        }

        // Invoke the function
        checkFrameset();
        </script>
    </head>
    <body>
        <h1>Page 1</h1>
        <hr />
    </body>
</html>
```

In practice, we recommend placing the code for the checkFrameset() function and the call to it inside an external .js library, and linking that library to each content document of the frameset. That's why the function assigns the generic location.href property to the search string: You can use it on any content page.

The code in Listing 28-6, Listing 28-7, and Listing 28-8 establishes a frameset containing two frames. In the left frame is a table of contents that allows you to navigate among three different pages, the first of which is initially displayed in the right frame. The interesting thing about the example is how you can specify a new page in the `content` parameter of the search property; the page is then opened within the frameset. For example, the following URL would result in the page `hello.html` being opened in the right frame:

```
jsb28-06.html?content=hello.html
```

In this example URL, the frameset page is first opened due to the inclusion of the file `jsb28-06.html`, whereas the `hello.html` file is specified as the value of the `content` parameter.

Note

While this frameset example is an easy way to demonstrate the uses of the various location object properties, keep in mind that the use of framesets is no longer common programming practice. First, it does not support accessibility. Second, CSS Positioning is the standard for placing content on a webpage. ∎

Related Item: `location.href` property

Methods

assign("*URL*")

Returns: Nothing

Compatibility: WinIE3+, MacIE3+, NN2+, Moz+, Safari+, Opera+, Chrome+

In earlier discussions about the `location` object, I said that you navigate to another page by assigning a new URL to the `location` object or `location.href` property. The `location.assign()` method does the same thing. In fact, when you set the `location` object to a URL, JavaScript silently applies the `assign()` method. No particular penalty or benefit comes from using the `assign()` method except perhaps making your code more understandable to others.

Related Item: `location.href` property

reload(*unconditionalGETBoolean*)

Returns: Nothing

Compatibility: WinIE4+, MacIE4+, NN3+, Moz+, Safari+, Opera+, Chrome+

The `location.reload()` method may be named inappropriately because it makes you think of the Reload/Refresh button in the browser toolbar. The `reload()` method is actually more powerful than the Reload/Refresh button in that it clears form control values that otherwise might survive the Reload/Refresh button. Note that IE for the Mac, Opera, and WebKit browsers such as Safari and Chrome do not preserve form control settings even with a soft reload.

Most form elements retain their screen states when you click Reload/Refresh. Text and `textarea` objects maintain whatever text is inside them; radio buttons and checkboxes maintain their checked status; `select` objects remember which item is selected. About the only items the Reload/Refresh button destroys are global variable values and any settable, but not visible, property (for example, the value of a `hidden input` object). I call this kind of reload a *soft reload*. A *hard reload*, on the other hand, should reset all data associated with a page, including default form selections.

locationObject.reload()

Browsers are frustratingly irregular about the ways they reload a document in the memory cache. In theory, an application of the `location.reload()` method should retrieve the page from the cache if the page is still available there (and the `history.go(0)` method should be even gentler, preserving form element settings). Adding a `true` parameter to the method is supposed to force an *unconditional GET* to the server, ignoring the cached version of the page. Yet when it is crucial for your application to get a page from the cache (for speed) or from the server (to guarantee a fresh copy), the browser behaves just the opposite of the way you want it to behave. Meta tags supposedly designed to prevent caching of a page rarely, if ever, work. Some scripters have had success in reloading the page from the server by setting `location.href` to the URL of the page, plus a slightly different search string (for example, based on a string representation of the `Date` object), so that there is no match for the URL in the cache.

The bottom line is that you should be prepared to try different schemes to achieve the effect you want. Also be prepared not to get the results you want. In other words, learn to live with the fact that you don't really have exacting control over retrieving a fresh page.

Listing 28-9 provides a means of testing the different outcomes of a soft reload versus a hard reload. Open this example page in a browser, and click a radio button. Then enter some new text, and make a choice in the `select` object. Clicking the Soft Reload/Refresh button invokes a method that reloads the document as though you had clicked the browser's Reload/Refresh button. It also preserves the visible properties of form elements. The Hard Reload button invokes the `location.reload()` method, which resets all objects to their default settings.

LISTING 28-9

Hard versus Soft Reloading

```
<!DOCTYPE html>
<html>
    <head>
        <meta http-equiv="content-type" content="text/html;charset=utf-8">
        <title>Reload Comparisons</title>
        <script type="text/javascript">
        function hardReload()
        {
            location.reload(true);
        }
        function softReload()
        {
            history.go(0);
        }
        </script>
    </head>
    <body>
        <form name="myForm">
            <input type="radio" name="rad1" value="1" />Radio 1<br />
            <input type="radio" name="rad1" value="2" />Radio 2<br />
            <input type="radio" name="rad1" value="3" />Radio 3
            <p><input type="text" name="entry" value="Original" /></p>
            <p><select name="theList">
```

```
        <option>Red</option>
        <option>Green</option>
        <option>Blue</option>
      </select></p>
    <hr />
    <input type="button" value="Soft Reload" onclick="softReload()" />
    <input type="button" value="Hard Reload" onclick="hardReload()" />
  </form>
 </body>
</html>
```

Related Item: history.go() method

replace("*URL*")

Returns: Nothing

Compatibility: WinIE4+, MacIE4+, NN3+, Moz+, Safari+, Opera+, Chrome+

In a complex web site, you may have pages that you do not want to appear in the user's history list. For example, a registration sequence may lead the user to one or more intermediate HTML documents that won't make much sense to the user later. Or you may have a one-time introduction page that appears only the first time a user visits your site. You especially don't want users to see these pages again if they use the Back button to return to a previous URL. The location.replace() method navigates to another page, but it does not let the current page stay in the queue of pages accessible via the Back button.

Although you cannot prevent a document from appearing in the history list while the user views that page, you can instruct the browser to load another document into the window and replace the current history entry with the entry for the new document. This trick does not empty the history list but removes the current item from the list before the next URL is loaded. Removing the item from the history list prevents users from seeing the page again by clicking the Back button later.

Listing 28-10 shows how to use the replace() method to direct a web browser to a new URL. Calling the location.replace() method navigates to another URL, similarly to assigning a URL to the location. The difference is that the document doing the calling doesn't appear in the history list after the new document loads. You can verify this by trying to click the Back button to return to the page after clicking Replace Me in Listing 28-10; the button is dimmed because the page no longer exists in the browser history. Also check the history listing (in your browser's usual spot for this information) before and after clicking Replace Me.

LISTING 28-10

Invoking the location.replace() Method

```
<!DOCTYPE html>
<html>
  <head>
    <meta http-equiv="content-type" content="text/html;charset=utf-8">
    <title>location.replace() Method</title>
```

continued

LISTING 28-10   *(continued)*

```
    <script type="text/javascript">
    function doReplace()
    {
        location.replace("jsb28-01.html");
    }
    </script>
</head>
<body>
    <form name="myForm">
        <input type="button" value="Replace Me" onclick="doReplace()" />
    </form>
</body>
</html>
```

Related Item: history object

history Object

Properties	Methods	Event Handler
current	back()	(None)
length	forward()	
next	go()	
previous		

Syntax

Accessing history object properties or methods:

> [window.]history.*property* | *method*([*parameters*])

About this object

As a user surfs the web, the browser maintains a list of URLs for the most recent stops. This list is represented in the scriptable object model by the history object. A script cannot surreptitiously extract actual URLs maintained in this list unless you use signed scripts (in NN4+/Moz; see Chapter 49, "Security and Netscape Signed Scripts" on the CD-ROM), and the user grants permission. Under unsigned conditions, a script can methodically navigate to each URL in the history (by relative number or by stepping back one URL at a time), in which case the user sees the browser navigating on its own as though possessed by a spirit. Good Netiquette dictates that you do not navigate a user outside your web site without the user's explicit permission.

One application for the `history` object and its `back()` or `go()` methods is to provide the equivalent of a Back button in your HTML documents. That button triggers a script that checks for any items in the history list and then goes back one page. Your document doesn't have to know anything about the URL from which the user lands at your page; it delegates the specifics of the navigation back to the browser.

The behavior of the Back and Forward buttons is also available through a pair of window methods: `window.back()` and `window.forward()`. The `history` object methods are specific to a frame that is part of the reference. When the `parent.frameName.history.back()` method reaches the end of history for that frame, further invocations of that method are ignored.

IE's history mechanism is not localized to a particular frame of a frameset. Instead, the `history.back()` and `history.forward()` methods mimic the physical act of clicking the toolbar buttons. If you want to ensure cross-browser, if not cross-generational, behavior in a frameset, address references to the `history.back()` and `history.forward()` methods to the parent window.

Opera's history mechanism is also interesting. Let's say that you are developing a web page. You load it into Opera and observe how it behaves. You then edit the page, save it, and go back to Opera to observe the behavior. If you were to click the back button or use any of the methods described in this chapter, you would go back to the previous version of the web page you just edited.

You should use the `history` object and its methods with extreme care. Your design must be smart enough to watch what the user is doing with your pages (for example, by checking the current URL before navigating with these methods). Otherwise, you run the risk of confusing your user by navigating to unexpected places. Your script can also get into trouble because it cannot detect where the current document is in the Back/Forward sequence in history. Your script is also at the mercy of how the browser's history mechanism operates.

Properties
`current`
`next`
`previous`

Value: String   Read-Only

Compatibility: WinIE-, MacIE-, NN4+, Moz+, Safari-, Opera+ (current only), Chrome-

To determine where to go when you click the Back and Forward buttons, the browser maintains a list of URLs visited. To someone trying to invade your privacy and see what sites and pages you frequent, this information is valuable. That's why the three properties that expose the actual URLs in the history list are restricted to pages with signed scripts (NN4+/Moz), and whose visitors have given permission to read sensitive browser data (see Chapter 49 on the CD-ROM).

With signed scripts and permission, you can look through the entire array of history entries in any frame or window. Because the list is an array, you can extract individual items by index value. For example, if the array has 10 entries, you can see the fifth item by using normal array indexing methods:

```
var fifthEntry = window.history[4];
```

No property or method exists that directly reveals the index value of the currently loaded URL, but you can script an educated guess by comparing the values of the current, next, and previous properties of the `history` object against the entire list.

historyObject.**length**

We personally don't like some unknown entity watching over our shoulders while we're on the Net, so we respect that same feeling in others and therefore discourage the use of these powers, unless the user is given adequate warning. The signed script permission dialog box does not offer enough detail about the consequences of revealing this level of information. This means that you should explicitly notify users of the fact that you are accessing their history, even when you have implicit permission via a signed script.

Related Item: `history.length` property

length

Value: Number   Read-Only

Compatibility: WinIE3+, MacIE3+, NN2+, Moz+, Safari+, Opera+, Chrome+

Use the `history.length` property to count the items in the history list. Unfortunately, this nugget of information is not particularly helpful in scripting navigation relative to the current location because your script cannot extract anything from the place in the history queue where the current document is located. If the current document is at the top of the list (the most recently loaded), you can calculate relative to that location. But users can use the Go/View menu to jump around the history list as they like. The position of a listing in the history list does not change by virtue of navigating back to that document. A `history.length` of 1, however, indicates that the current document is the first one the user has loaded since starting the browser software.

Listing 28-11 shows how to use the `length` property to notify users of how many pages they've visited.

LISTING 28-11

A Browser History Count

```
<!DOCTYPE html>
<html>
    <head>
        <meta http-equiv="content-type" content="text/html;charset=utf-8">
        <title>History Object</title>
        <script type="text/javascript">
        function showCount()
        {
            var histCount = window.history.length;
            if (histCount > 5)
            {
                alert("My, my, you\'ve been busy. You have visited " + histCount +
                    " pages so far.");
            }
            else
            {
                alert("You have been to " + histCount + " Web pages this
                    session.");
            }
```

```
        }
    </script>
</head>
<body>
    <form>
        <input type="button" name="activity" value="My Activity"
        onclick="showCount()" />
    </form>
</body>
</html>
```

Related Items: None

Methods
`back()`
`forward()`

Returns: Nothing

Compatibility: WinIE3+, MacIE3+, NN2+, Moz+, Safari+, Opera+, Chrome+

Although the names might lead you to believe that these methods mimic the buttons on a browser's toolbar, they do not. The `history.back()` method is window/frame specific, meaning that if you direct successive `back()` methods to a frame within a frameset, the method is ignored when it reaches the first document to be loaded into that frame. The Back button and the `window.back()` method unload the frameset and continue taking you back through the browser's global history.

If you deliberately lead a user to a dead end in your web site, you should make sure that the HTML document provides a way to navigate back to a recognizable spot. Because you can easily create a new window that has no toolbar or menu bar (non-Macintosh browsers), you may end up stranding your users because they have no way of navigating out of a cul-de-sac in such a window. A button in your document should give the user a way back to the last location.

Unless you need to perform some additional processing prior to navigating to the previous location, you can simply place this method as the parameter to the event handler attribute of a button definition. To guarantee compatibility across all browsers, direct this method at the parent document when it's used from within a frameset.

Less likely to be scripted than the `history.back()` action is the method that performs the opposite action: navigating forward one step in the browser's history list. The only time you can confidently use the `history.forward()` method is in balancing the use of the `history.back()` method in the same script — where your script closely keeps track of how many steps the script heads in either direction. Use the `history.forward()` method with extreme caution, and only after performing extensive user testing on your web pages to make sure that you've covered all user possibilities. Similar to navigating backward via `history.back()`, forward progress when using `history.forward()` extends only through the history listing for a given window or frame, not the entire browser history list.

Listing 28-12 and Listing 28-13 provide a little workshop in which you can test the behavior of a variety of forms of backward and forward navigation in different browsers.

historyObject.forward()

LISTING 28-12

Navigation Lab Frameset

```
<!DOCTYPE html>
<html>
    <head>
        <meta http-equiv="content-type" content="text/html;charset=utf-8">
    <title>Back and Forward</title>
    </head>
    <frameset cols="45%,55%">
        <frame name="controller" src="jsb28-13.html" />
        <frame name="display" src="jsb28-01.html" />
    </frameset>
</html>
```

LISTING 28-13

Navigation Lab Control Panel

```
<!DOCTYPE html>
<html>
  <head>
    <meta http-equiv="content-type" content="text/html;charset=utf-8">
    <title>Lab Controls</title>
  </head>
  <body>
    <b>Load a series of documents into the right frame by clicking some
    of these links (make a note of the sequence you click on):</b>
    <p><a href="jsb28-01.html" target="display">Listing 28-1</a><br />
        <a href="jsb28-05.html" target="display">Listing 28-5</a><br />
        <a href="jsb28-09.html" target="display">Listing 28-9</a><br /></p>
    <hr />
    <form name="input">
        <b>Click on the various buttons below to see the results in this
        frameset:</b>
        <ul>
            <li><tt>history.back()</tt> and <tt>history.forward()</tt> for
                righthand frame:<input type="button" value="Back"
                onclick="parent.display.history.back()" /><input type="button"
                value="Forward" onclick="parent.display.history.forward()" />
                </li>
            <li><tt>history.back()</tt> for this frame:<input type="button"
                value="Back" onclick="history.back()" /></li>
            <li><tt>history.back()</tt> for parent:<input type="button"
                value="Back" onclick="parent.history.back()" /></li>
        </ul>
    </form>
  </body>
</html>
```

Related Items: history.go() method

go(*relativeNumber* | *"URLOrTitleSubstring"*)

Returns: Nothing

Compatibility: WinIE3+, MacIE3+, NN2+, Moz+, Safari+, Opera+, Chrome+

Use the history.go() method to script navigation within the history list currently stored in the browser. If you elect to use a URL as a parameter, however, that precise URL must already exist in the history listing. Therefore, do not regard this method as an alternative to setting the window.location object to a brand-new URL.

For navigating n steps in either direction along the history list, use the relativeNumber parameter of the history.go() method. This number is an integer value that indicates which item in the list to use, relative to the current location. For example, if the current URL is at the top of the list (that is, the Forward button in the toolbar is dimmed), you need to use the following method to jump to the URL two items backward in the list:

```
history.go(-2);
```

In other words, the current URL is the equivalent of history.go(0) (a method that reloads the window). A positive integer indicates a jump that many items forward in the history list. Thus, history.go(-1) is the same as history.back(), whereas history.go(1) is the same as history.forward().

Alternatively, you can specify one of the URLs or document titles stored in the browser's history list (titles appear in the Go/View menu). As security and privacy concerns have increased over time, this variant of the go() method has been reined in. It's best not to use the string parameter in your scripting; in fact, none of the current browser versions support this variant.

Like most other history methods, your script finds it difficult to manage the history list or the current URL's spot in the queue. That fact makes it even more difficult for your script to determine intelligently how far to navigate in either direction, or to which specific URL or title matches it should jump. Use this method only for situations in which your web pages are in strict control of the user's activity (or for designing scripts for yourself that automatically crawl around sites according to a fixed regimen). When you give the user control over navigation, you have no guarantee that the history list will be what you expect, and any scripts you write that depend on a history object will likely break.

In practice, this method mostly performs a soft reload of the current window using the 0 parameter.

Tip

If you are developing a page for all scriptable browsers, be aware that the reloading of a page with history.go(0) **in IE often returns to the server to reload the page rather than reloading from the cache.** ∎

Listing 28-14 contains sample code that demonstrates how to navigate the history list via the go() method. Fill in either the number or text field of the page in Listing 28-14, and then click the associated button. The script passes the appropriate kind of data to the go() method. Unless you are using an older browser version, using the matching string text box and its button will do nothing. Be sure to use negative numbers for visiting a page earlier in the history.

historyObject.go

Note
Mozilla browsers respond only to the integer offset approach to using the `history.go()` method. ∎

LISTING 28-14

Navigating to an Item in History

```html
<!DOCTYPE html>
<html>
    <head>
        <meta http-equiv="content-type" content="text/html;charset=utf-8">
        <title>history.go() Method</title>
        <script type="text/javascript">
        function doGoNum(form) {
            window.history.go(parseInt(form.histNum.value));
        }
        function doGoTxt(form) {
            window.history.go(form.histWord.value);
        }
        </script>
    </head>
    <body>
        <form>
            <b>Calling the history.go() method:</b>
            <hr />
            Enter a number (+/-):<input type="text" name="histNum" size="3"
            value="0" /> <input type="button" value="Go to Offset"
            onclick="doGoNum(this.form)" />
            <p><div>Enter either a word found in a document title in your
                    history, or a word in a document URL in your history
                    (remember, this will only work if your browser version is
                    older):</div>
            <input type="text" name="histWord" />
                <input type="button" value="Go to Match"
                onclick="doGoTxt(this.form)" /></p>
        </form>
    </body>
</html>
```

Related Items: `history.back()`, `history.forward()`, `location.reload()` methods

Document and Body Objects

IN THIS CHAPTER

Accessing arrays of objects contained by the document object

Writing new document content to a window or frame

Using the body element for IE window measurements

U ser interaction is a vital aspect of client-side JavaScript scripting, and most of the communication between script and user takes place by way of the document object and its components. Understanding the scope of the document object within each of the object models you support is key to implementing successful cross-browser applications.

Review the document object's place within the original object hierarchy. Figure 29-1 shows that the document object is a pivotal point for a large percentage of objects. In the W3C DOM, the document object plays an even more important role as the container of all element objects delivered with the page: The document object is the root of the entire document tree.

In fact, the document object and all that it contains is so big that we have divided its discussion into many chapters, each focusing on related object groups. This chapter looks at the document object and body object (which have conceptual relationships), whereas each of the succeeding chapters in this part of the book details objects contained by the document object.

documentObject

FIGURE 29-1

The basic document object model hierarchy.

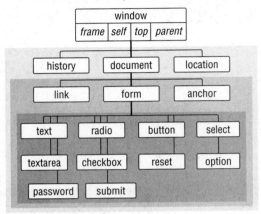

document Object

Compatibility: WinIE3+, MacIE3+, NN2+, Moz+, Safari+, Opera+, Chrome+

Properties	Methods	Event Handlers
activeElement	attachEvent()[†]	onactivate[†]
alinkColor	captureEvents()	onbeforecut[†]
all[†]	clear()	onbeforedeactivate[†]
anchors[]	clearAttributes()[†]	onbeforeeditfocus[†]
applets[]	close()	onbeforepaste[†]
attributes[†]	createAttribute()	onclick[†]
baseURI	createCDATASection()	oncontextmenu[†]
bgColor	createComment()	oncontrolselect[†]
body	createDocumentFragment()	oncut[†]
charset	createElement()	ondblclick[†]
characterSet	createElementNS()	ondrag[†]
childNodes[†]	createEvent()	ondragend[†]
compatMode	createEventObject()	ondragenter[†]
contentType	createNSResolver()	ondragleave[†]
cookie	createRange()	ondragover[†]

Properties	Methods	Event Handlers
defaultCharset	createStyleSheet()	ondragstart[†]
defaultView	createTextNode()	ondrop[†]
designMode	createTreeWalker()	onhelp[†]
doctype	detachEvent()[†]	onkeydown[†]
documentElement	elementFromPoint()	onkeypress[†]
documentURI	evaluate()	onkeyup[†]
domain	execCommand()	onmousedown[†]
embeds[]	focus()[†]	onmousemove[†]
expando	getElementById()	onmouseout[†]
fgColor	getElementsByName()	onmouseover[†]
fileCreatedDate	getElementsByTagName()[†]	onmouseup[†]
fileModifiedDate	getElementsByTagNameNS()[†]	onpaste[†]
fileSize	hasFocus()	onpropertychange[†]
firstChild[†]	importNode()	onreadystatechange[†]
forms[]	mergeAttributes()[†]	onresizeend[†]
frames[]	open()	onresizestart[†]
height	queryCommandEnabled()	onselectionchange
id[†]	queryCommandIndterm()	onstop
images[]	queryCommandState()	
implementation	queryCommandSupported()	
inputEncoding	queryCommandText()	
lastChild[†]	queryCommandValue()	
lastModified	recalc()	
layers[]	releaseCapture()[†]	
linkColor	releaseEvents()	
links[]	routeEvent()	
location	setActive()[†]	
media	write()	
mimeType	writeln()	
nameProp		
namespaces[]		

documentObject

Properties	Methods	Event Handlers
namespaceURI[†]		
nextSibling[†]		
nodeName[†]		
nodeType[†]		
ownerDocument[†]		
parentNode[†]		
parentWindow		
plugins[]		
previousSibling[†]		
protocol		
readyState[†]		
referrer		
scripts[]		
security		
selection		
strictErrorChecking		
styleSheets[]		
tags[]		
title		
uniqueID[†]		
URL		
URLUnencoded		
vlinkColor		
width		
xmlEncoding		
xmlStandalone		
xmlVersion		

[†]See Chapter 26, "Generic HTML Element Objects."

Syntax

Accessing document object properties or methods:

```
[window.]document.property | method([parameters])
```

About this object

A document object encompasses the totality of what exists inside the content region of a browser window or window frame (excluding toolbars, status lines, and so on). The document is a combination of the content and interface elements that make the web page worth visiting. In modern browsers the document object also serves as the root node of a page's hierarchical tree of nodes — that from which all other nodes grow.

Because the document object isn't explicitly represented in an HTML document by tags or any other notation, the original designers of JavaScript and object models decided to make the document object the portal to many settings that were represented in HTML as belonging to the body element. Therefore, the body element's tag contains attributes for document-wide attributes, such as background color (bgcolor) and link colors in various states (alink, link, and vlink). The original designers decided to have the body element also serve as an HTML container for forms, links, and anchors. The document object, therefore, assumed a majority of the role of the body element. But even then, the document object became the most convenient place to bind some properties that extend beyond the body element, such as the title element and the URL of the link that referred the user to the page. When viewed within the context of the HTML source code, the original document object is somewhat schizophrenic. Even so, the document object has worked well as the basis for references to original object model objects, such as forms, images, and applets.

This, of course, was before every HTML element, including the body element, was exposed as an object through modern object models. Amazingly, even with the IE4+ object model and W3C DOM — both of which treat the body element as an object separate from the document object — script compatibility with the original object model is quite easily accomplished. The document object has assumed a new schizophrenia, splitting its personality between the original object model and the one that places the document object at the root of the hierarchy, quite separate from the body element object it contains. The object knows which face to put on based on the rest of the script syntax that follows it. This means that quite often there are multiple ways to achieve the same reference. For example, you can use the following statement in all scriptable browsers to get the number of form objects in a document:

```
document.forms.length
```

In IE4+, you can also use

```
document.tags["form"].length
```

And in the W3C DOM as implemented in IE5+ and NN6+/Moz/Safari/Opera/Chrome, you can use

```
document.getElementsByTagName("form").length
```

Modern browsers provide a generic approach to accessing elements (getElementsByTagName() method in the W3C DOM) to meet the requirements of object models that expose every HTML (and XML) element as an object.

Promoting the body element to the ranks of exposed objects presented its own challenges to the new object model designers. The body element is the true owner of some properties that the original document object had to take on by default. Most properties that belonged to the original document object were renamed in their transfer to the body element. For example, the original document.alinkColor property is the body.aLink property in the modern model. But the bgColor property has not been renamed. For the sake of code compatibility, modern browsers recognize both properties, even though the W3C DOM has removed the old versions of the properties for the newly conceived document object. Considering the fact that modern browsers are now prevalent, you should be able to stick with the new properties from here on.

Properties
activeElement

Value: Object reference

Read-Only

Compatibility: WinIE4+, MacIE4+, NN-, Moz+, Safari+, Opera+, Chrome+

Originally just in IE4+, a script can examine the document.activeElement property to see which element currently has focus. The value returned is an element object reference. You can use any of the properties and methods listed in Chapter 26 to find out more about the object.

Although the element used to generate a mouse or keyboard event will most likely have focus, don't rely on the activeElement property to find out which element generated an event. The IE event.srcElement property is far more reliable.

Example

Use The Evaluator (see Chapter 4, "JavaScript Essentials") with IE4+ to experiment with the activeElement property. Type the following statement into the top text box:

```
document.activeElement.value
```

After you press the Enter key, the Results box shows the value of the text box you just typed into (the very same expression you just typed). But if you then click the Evaluate button, you will see the value property of that button object appear in the Results box.

Related Item: event.srcElement property

alinkColor
bgColor
fgColor
linkColor
vlinkColor

Value: Hexadecimal triplet or color name string

Mostly Read/Write

Compatibility: WinIE3+, MacIE3+, NN2+, Moz+, Safari+, Opera+, Chrome+

These five properties are the script equivalent of the <body> tag attributes of the same name (although the property names are case-sensitive). All five settings can be read via the document .body object in modern browsers. Values for all color properties can be either the common HTML hexadecimal triplet value (for example, "#00FF00") or any of the standard color names.

Example

We select some color values at random to plug into three settings of the group of ugly colors for Listing 29-1. The smaller window displays a dummy button so that you can see how its display contrasts with color settings. Notice that the script sets the colors of the smaller window by rewriting the entire window's HTML code. After changing colors, the script displays the color values in the original window's textarea. Even though some colors are set with the color constant values, properties come back in the hexadecimal triplet values. You can experiment to your heart's content by changing color values in the listing. Every time you change the values in the script, save the HTML file and reload it in the browser.

LISTING 29-1

Tweaking the Color of Page Elements

```
<!DOCTYPE html>
<html>
    <head>
        <meta http-equiv="content-type" content="text/html;charset=utf-8">
        <title>Color Me</title>
        <script type="text/javascript">
            // may be blocked at load time by browser popup blockers
            var newWindow = window.open("","","height=150,width=300");

            function defaultColors()
            {
                return "bgcolor='#c0c0c0' vlink='#551a8b' link='#0000ff'";
            }

            function uglyColors()
            {
                return "bgcolor='yellow' vlink='pink' link='lawngreen'";
            }

            function showColorValues()
            {
                var result = "";
                result += "bgColor: " + newWindow.document.bgColor + "\n";
                result += "vlinkColor: " + newWindow.document.vlinkColor + "\n";
                result += "linkColor: " + newWindow.document.linkColor + "\n";
                document.forms[0].results.value = result;
            }

            // dynamically writes contents of another window
            function drawPage(colorStyle)
            {
                // work around popup blockers
                if (!newWindow || newWindow.closed)
                {
                    newWindow = window.open("","","height=150,width=300");
                }
                var thePage = "";
                thePage += "<html><head><title>Color Sampler<\/title><\/head><body ";
                if (colorStyle == "default")
                {
                    thePage += defaultColors();
                }
                else
                {
```

continued

LISTING 29-1   *(continued)*

```
              thePage += uglyColors();
      }
      thePage += ">Just so you can see the variety of items and colors, <a ";
      thePage += "href='http://www.nowhere.com'>here\'s a link<\/a>, and <a ";
      href='http://home.netscape.com'> here is another link <\/a> you can
      use on-line to visit and see how its color differs from the standard
      link.";
      thePage += "<form>";
      thePage += "<input type='button' name='sample' value='Just a Button'>";
      thePage += "<\/form><\/body><\/html>";
      newWindow.document.write(thePage);
      newWindow.document.close();
      showColorValues();
}

// the following works properly only in Windows Navigator
function setColors(colorStyle)
{
      if (colorStyle == "default")
      {
          document.bgColor = "#c0c0c0";
      }
      else
      {
          document.bgColor = "yellow";
      }
}

// bind the event handlers
function addEvent(elem, evtType, func)
{
      if (elem.addEventListener)
      {
          elem.addEventListener(evtType, func, false);
      }
      else if (elem.attachEvent)
      {
          elem.attachEvent("on" + evtType, func);
      }
      else
      {
          elem["on" + evtType] = func;
      }
}
addEvent(window, "load", function()
{
      addEvent(document.getElementById("default1"), "click",
          function(evt) {drawPage("default")});
      addEvent(document.getElementById("weird1"), "click",
          function(evt) {drawPage("ugly")});
```

```
              addEvent(document.getElementById("default2"), "click",
                  function(evt) {setColors("default")});
              addEvent(document.getElementById("weird2"), "click",
                  function(evt) {setColors("ugly")});
          });
      </script>
  </head>
  <body>
      Try the two color schemes on the document in the small window.
      <form>
          <input type="button" id="default1" name="default" value='Default Colors' />
          <input type="button" id="weird1" name="weird" value="Ugly Colors" />
          <p>
              <textarea name="results" rows="3" cols="20"></textarea>
          </p>
          <hr />
          These buttons change the current document.
          <p>
              <input type="button" id="default2" name="default"
                  value='Default Colors' />
              <input type="button" id="weird2" name="weird" value="Ugly Colors" />
          </p>
      </form>
  </body>
</html>
```

Note
The examples in this chapter take advantage of the modern approach to event handling, which involves the addEventListener() **(NN6+/Moz/W3C) and** attachEvent() **(IE5+) methods. This event-handling technique is explained in detail in Chapter 32, "Event Objects."** ■

Related Items: body.aLink, body.bgColor, body.link, body.text, body.vLink properties

anchors[]

Value: Array of anchor objects   Read-Only

Compatibility: WinIE3+, MacIE3+, NN2+, Moz+, Safari+, Opera+, Chrome+

Anchor objects (described in Chapter 30, "Link and Anchor Objects") are points in an HTML document marked with <a name=""> tags. Anchor objects are referenced in URLs by a hash value between the page URL and anchor name. Like other object properties that contain a list of nested objects, the document.anchors property delivers an indexed array of anchors in a document. Use the array references to pinpoint a specific anchor for retrieving any anchor property.

Anchor arrays begin their index counts with 0: The first anchor in a document, then, has the reference document.anchors[0]. And, as is true with any built-in array object, you can find out how many entries the array has by checking the length property. For example:

```
    alert("This document has " + document.anchors.length + " anchors.");
```

documentObject.anchors[]

The document.anchors property is read-only. To script navigation to a particular anchor, assign a value to the window.location or window.location.hash object, as described in the location object discussion in Chapter 28, "Location and History Objects."

Example

In Listing 29-2, we append an extra script to Listing 28-1 to demonstrate how to extract the number of anchors in the document. The document dynamically writes the number of anchors found in the document. You will not likely ever need to reveal such information to users of your page, and the document.anchors property is not one that you will call frequently. The object model defines it automatically as a document property while defining actual anchor objects.

LISTING 29-2

Using Anchors to Navigate Through a Page

```
<!DOCTYPE html>
<html>
    <head>
        <meta http-equiv="content-type" content="text/html;charset=utf-8">
        <title>document.anchors Property</title>
        <script type="text/javascript">
            function goNextAnchor(where)
            {
                window.location.hash = where;
            }

            // bind the event handlers
            function addEvent(elem, evtType, func)
            {
                if (elem.addEventListener) {
                    elem.addEventListener(evtType, func, false);
                }
                else if (elem.attachEvent)
                {
                    elem.attachEvent("on" + evtType, func);
                }
                else
                {
                    elem["on" + evtType] = func;
                }
            }
            addEvent(window, "load", function()
            {
                addEvent(document.getElementById("next1"), "click",
                    function(evt) {goNextAnchor("sec1")});
                addEvent(document.getElementById("next2"), "click",
                    function(evt) {goNextAnchor("sec2")});
                addEvent(document.getElementById("next3"), "click",
                    function(evt) {goNextAnchor("sec3")});
                addEvent(document.getElementById("next4"), "click",
```

```
                 function(evt) {goNextAnchor("start")});
        });
    </script>
  </head>
  <body>
    <h1><a id="start" name="start">Top</a></h1>
    <form>
       <input type="button" id="next1" name="next" value="NEXT" />
    </form>
    <hr />
    <h1><a id="sec1" name="sec1">Section 1</a></h1>
    <form>
       <input type="button" id="next2" name="next" value="NEXT" />
    </form>
    <hr />
    <h1><a id="sec2" name="sec2">Section 2</a></h1>
    <form>
       <input type="button" id="next3" name="next" value="NEXT" />
    </form>
    <hr />
    <h1><a id="sec3" name="sec3">Section 3</a></h1>
    <form>
       <input type="button" id="next4" name="next" value="BACK TO TOP" />
    </form>
    <hr />
    <p>
       <script type="text/javascript">
         document.write("<i>There are " +
                     document.anchors.length +
                     " anchors defined for this document<\/i>")
       </script>
    </p>
  </body>
</html>
```

Related Items: `anchor`, `location` objects; `document.links` property

applets[]

Value: Array of applet objects   Read-Only

Compatibility: WinIE3+, MacIE3+, NN2+, Moz+, Safari+, Opera+, Chrome+

The `applets` property refers to Java applets defined in a document by the `<applet>` tag. An applet is not officially an object in the document until the applet loads completely.

Most of the work you do with Java applets from JavaScript takes place through the methods and variables defined inside the applet. Although you can reference an applet according to its indexed array position within the `applets` array, you will more likely use the applet object's name in the reference to avoid any confusion.

Example

The document.applets property is defined automatically as the browser builds the object model for a document that contains applet objects. You will rarely access this property, except to determine how many applet objects a document has, as in this example:

```
var numApplets = document.applets.length;
```

Related Item: applet object

baseURI

Value: String   Read-Only

Compatibility: WinIE-, MacIE-, NN7+, Moz+, Safari+, Opera+, Chrome+

The baseURI property reveals the absolute base URI of the document. You can check the base URI of a document in the Evaluator (see Chapter 4, "JavaScript Essentials") by entering the following:

```
document.baseURI
```

Related Item: document.documentURI property

bgColor

(See alinkColor)

body

Value: body element object   Read/Write

Compatibility: WinIE4+, MacIE4+, NN6+, Moz+, Safari+, Opera+, Chrome+

The document.body property is a shortcut reference to the body element object in modern object models. As you can see in the discussion of the body element object later in this chapter, that object has many key properties that govern the look of the entire page. Because the document object is the root of all references within any window or frame, the document.body property is easier to use to get to the body properties than the longer references normally used to access HTML element objects in both the IE4+ and W3C object models.

Example

Use The Evaluator (see Chapter 4, "JavaScript Essentials") to examine properties of the body element object. First, to prove that the document.body is the same as the element object that comes back from longer references, enter the following statement into the top text box with either IE5+, NN6+/Moz, or some other W3C browser:

```
document.body == document.getElementsByTagName("body")[0]
```

Next, check out the body object's property listings later in this chapter and enter the listings into the top text box to review their results. For example:

```
document.body.bgColor
document.body.tagName
```

The main point to take from this example is that the `document.body` reference provides a simpler and more direct means of accessing a document's `body` object without having to use the `getElementsByTagName()` method.

Related Item: `body element` object

charset

Value: String   Read/Write

Compatibility: WinIE4+, MacIE4+, NN-, Moz-, Safari+, Opera+, Chrome+

The `charset` property reveals the character set originally used by the browser (IE4+) to render the current document (the NN6+/Moz version of this property is called `characterSet`). You can find possible values for this property at

    ftp://ftp.isi.edu/in-notes/iana/assignments/character-sets

Each browser and operating system has its own default character set. Values may also be set through a `<meta>` tag.

Example

Use The Evaluator (Chapter 4, "JavaScript Essentials") to experiment with the `charset` property. To see the default setting applied to the page, enter the following statement into the top text box:

    document.charset

If you are running IE5+ for Windows and you enter the following statement, the browser will apply a different character set to the page:

    document.charset = "iso-8859-2"

If your version of Windows does not have that character set installed in the system, the browser may ask permission to download and install the character set.

Related Items: `characterSet, defaultCharset` properties

characterSet

Value: String   Read/Write

Compatibility: WinIE-, MacIE-, NN6+, Moz+, Safari+, Opera+, Chrome+

The `characterSet` property reveals the character set used by the browser to render the current document (the IE version of this property is called `charset`). You can find possible values for this property at

    http://www.iana.org/assignments/character-sets

Each browser and operating system has its own default character set. Values may also be set through a `<meta>` tag.

Example

Use The Evaluator (Chapter 4, "JavaScript Essentials") to experiment with the `characterSet` property in NN6+/Moz. To see the default setting applied to the page, enter the following statement into the top text box:

```
document.characterSet
```

Related Item: `charset` property

compatMode

Value: String   Read-Only

Compatibility: WinIE6+, MacIE6+, NN7+, Moz+, Safari+, Opera+, Chrome+

The `compatMode` property reveals the compatibility mode for the document, as determined by the `DOCTYPE` element's content. The value for this property can be one of the following string constants: `BackCompat` or `CSS1Compat`. The default setting for the `compatMode` property is `BackCompat`, which means that the document is not W3C standards-compliant; in other words, the document is in Quirks mode. Otherwise the document is in Strict mode and is W3C standards-compliant. By *standards-compliant* I'm referring to the CSS1 standard.

Example

You may find it useful to check the compatibility mode of a document in order to carry out processing specific to one of the modes. Following is an example of how you might branch to carry out processing for backward-compatible documents:

```
if (document.compatMode == "BackCompat") {
    // perform backward compatible processing
}
```

Related Items: *Standards Compatibility Modes* (see Chapter 4, "JavaScript Essentials")

contentType

Value: String   Read-Only

Compatibility: WinIE-, MacIE-, NN7+, Moz+, Safari-, Opera-, Chrome-

The `contentType` property holds the content type (MIME type) of the document. For a normal HTML document, the value of this property is `text/html`.

cookie

Value: String   Read/Write

Compatibility: WinIE3+, MacIE3+, NN2+, Moz+, Safari+, Opera+, Chrome+

The cookie mechanism in a web browser lets you store small pieces of information on the client computer in a reasonably secure manner. In other words, when you need some tidbit of information to persist at the client level while either loading diverse HTML documents or moving from one session to another, the cookie mechanism saves the day. The cookie is commonly used as a means to store the username and password you enter into a password-protected web site. The first time you enter this information into a form, the server-side form processing program has the browser write the information back to a cookie on your hard disk (usually after encrypting the password). Rather than bothering you to enter the username and password the next time you access the site, the server searches the cookie data stored for that particular server and extracts the username and password for automatic validation processing behind the scenes.

Other applications of the cookie include storing user preferences and information about the user's previous visit to the site. Preferences may include font styles or sizes and whether the user prefers viewing content inside a frameset or not. As shown in Chapter 57, "Application: Intelligent 'Updated' Flags" (on the CD-ROM), a time stamp of the previous visit can allow a coded HTML page to display highlighted images next to content that has changed since the user's last visit, even if you have updated the page several times in the interim. Rather than hard-wiring new flags for *your* last visit, the scripts highlight what's new for the visitor.

The cookie file

Allowing some foreign server program to read from and write to your hard disk may give you pause, but browser cookie mechanisms don't just open up your drive's directory for the world to see (and to corrupt). Instead, the cookie mechanism provides access to a type of text file (Internet Explorer) or just one special text file (browsers other than IE) located in a platform-specific spot on your drive.

In Mozilla-based browsers, for example, the cookie file is named `cookies.txt` and is located in a directory (whose name ends in `.slt`) within the browser's profile area. In Windows, that location is `C:\\Windows\Application Data\Mozilla\Profiles\[profilename]\`; in Mac OSX, the location is `[user]/Library/Mozilla/Profiles/[profilename]/`. Internet Explorer for Windows uses a different filing system: all cookies for each domain are saved in a domain-specific file inside the `C:\\Windows\Temporary Internet Files\` directory. Filenames begin with `Cookie:` and include the username and domain of the server that wrote the cookie. Safari cookies are recorded in an XML file named `Cookies.plist` within the `[user]/Library/Cookies/` directory. Opera cookies are recorded in a binary file named `cookies4.dat` within the `[user]\Application Data\Opera\Opera` directory. Google Chrome cookies are recorded in a SQLite database file named `Cookies` within the `[user]\Local Settings\Application Data\Google\Chrome\User Data\Default` directory. Be aware that if you are testing with Google Chrome, your code will not work unless the files are coming from an HTTP server. Chrome intentionally disables cookies on `file:///` documents.

A cookie file is a text file. If curiosity drives you to open a cookie file, we recommend that you do so only with a copy saved in another directory or folder. Any alteration to the existing file can mess up whatever valuable cookies are stored there for sites you regularly visit. The data format for cookie files differs across browsers, in line with the different methodologies used for filing cookies. Inside the Mozilla file (after a few comment lines warning you not to manually alter the file) are lines of tab-delimited text. Each return-delimited line contains one cookie's information. The cookie file is just like a text listing of a database. In each of the IE cookie files, the same data points are stored for a cookie as for Mozilla, but the items are in a return-delimited list. The structure of these files is of no importance to scripting cookies, because all browsers utilize the same syntax for reading and writing cookies through the `document.cookie` property.

Note
As you experiment with browser's cookies, you will be tempted to look into the cookie file after a script writes some data to the cookie. The cookie file usually will not contain the newly written data, because in most browsers cookies are transferred to disk only when the user quits the browser; conversely, the cookie file is read into the browser's memory when it is launched. While you read, write, and delete cookies during a browser session, all activity is performed in memory (to speed up the process) to be saved later. ∎

documentObject.cookie

A cookie record

Among the fields of each cookie record are the following (not necessarily in this order):

- Domain of the server that created the cookie
- Information on whether you need a secure HTTP connection to access the cookie
- Pathname of URL(s) capable of accessing the cookie
- Expiration date of the cookie
- Name of the cookie entry
- String data associated with the cookie entry

Note that cookies are domain-specific. In other words, if one domain creates a cookie, another domain cannot access it through the browser's cookie mechanism behind your back. That reason is why it's generally safe to store what we call *throwaway passwords* (the username/password pairs required to access some free registration-required sites) in cookies. Moreover, sites that store passwords in a cookie usually do so as encrypted strings, making it more difficult for someone to hijack the cookie file from your unattended PC and figure out what your personal password scheme may be.

Cookies also have expiration dates. Because some browsers may allow no more than a fixed number of cookies (1000 in Firefox), the cookie file can get pretty full over the years. Therefore, if a cookie needs to persist past the current browser session, it should have an expiration date established by the cookie writer. Browsers automatically clean out any expired cookies.

Not all cookies have to last beyond the current session, however. In fact, a scenario in which you use cookies temporarily while working your way through a web site is quite typical. Many shopping sites employ one or more temporary cookie records to behave as the shopping cart for recording items you intend to purchase. These items are copied to the order form at checkout time. But after you submit the order form to the server, that client-side data has no particular value. As it turns out, if your script does not specify an expiration date, the browser keeps the cookie fresh in memory without writing it to the cookie file. When you quit the browser, that cookie data disappears as expected.

JavaScript access

Scripted access to cookies from JavaScript is limited to setting the cookie (with a number of optional parameters) and getting the cookie data (but with none of the parameters).

The original object model defines cookies as properties of documents, but this description is somewhat misleading. If you use the default path to set a cookie (that is, the current directory of the document whose script sets the cookie in the first place), all documents in that same server directory have read and write access to the cookie. A benefit of this arrangement is that if you have a scripted application that contains multiple documents, all documents served from the same directory can share the cookie data. Modern browsers, however, impose a limit of 20 named cookie entries (that is, one name/value pair) for any domain. If your cookie requirements are extensive, you need to fashion ways of concatenating cookie data. (We do this in the Decision Helper application in Chapter 58 on the CD-ROM.)

Saving cookies

To write cookie data to the cookie file, you use a simple JavaScript assignment operator with the `document.cookie` property. But the formatting of the data is crucial to achieving success. Here is the syntax for assigning a value to a cookie (optional items are in brackets; placeholders for data you supply are in italics):

```
document.cookie = "cookieName=cookieData
        [; expires=timeInGMTString]
```

```
[; path=pathName]
[; domain=domainName]
[; secure]"
```

Let's examine each of the properties individually.

Name/Data

Each cookie must have a name and a string value (even if that value is an empty string). Such name/value pairs are fairly common in HTML, but they look odd in an assignment statement. For example, if you want to save the string "Fred" to a cookie named "userName," the JavaScript statement is

```
document.cookie = "userName=Fred";
```

If the browser sees no existing cookie in the current domain with this name, it automatically creates the cookie entry for you; if the named cookie already exists, the browser replaces the old data with the new data. Retrieving the document.cookie property at this point yields the following string:

```
userName=Fred
```

You can omit all the other cookie-setting properties, in which case the browser uses default values, as explained in a following section. For temporary cookies (those that don't have to persist beyond the current browser session), the name/value pair is usually all you need.

The entire name/value pair must be a single string with no semicolons, commas, or character spaces. To take care of spaces between words, preprocess the value with the JavaScript encodeURIComponent() function, which URI-encodes the spaces as %20 — and then be sure to convert the value to restore the human-readable spaces (through decodeURIComponent()) when you retrieve the cookie later.

You cannot save a JavaScript array or object to a cookie. But with the help of the Array.join() method, you can convert an array to a string; use String.split() to re-create the array after reading the cookie at a later time.

Expires

Expiration dates, when supplied, must be passed as Greenwich Mean Time (GMT) strings (see Chapter 17, "The Date Object," about time data). To calculate an expiration date based on today's date, use the JavaScript Date object as follows:

```
var exp = new Date();
var oneYearFromNow = exp.getTime() + (365 * 24 * 60 * 60 * 1000);
exp.setTime(oneYearFromNow);
```

Since the getTime() and setTime() methods operate in milliseconds, the year you're adding to the current date must be converted to milliseconds. After making the calculation, the date is converted to the accepted GMT string format:

```
document.cookie = "userName=Fred; expires=" + exp.toGMTString();
```

In the cookie file, the expiration date and time is stored as a numeric value (in seconds), but to set it, you need to supply the time in GMT format. You can delete a cookie before it expires by setting the

923

documentObject.cookie

named cookie's expiration date to a time and date earlier than the current time and date. The safest expiration parameter is

```
expires=Thu, 01-Jan-70 00:00:01 GMT;
```

Omitting the expiration date signals to the browser that this cookie is temporary. The browser never writes it to the cookie file and forgets it when you quit the browser.

Path

For client-side cookies, the default path setting (the current directory) is usually the best choice. You can, of course, create a duplicate copy of a cookie with a separate path (and domain) so that the same data is available to a document located in another area of your site (or the Web).

Domain

To help synchronize cookie data with a particular document (or group of documents), the browser matches the domain of the current document with the domain values of cookie entries in the cookie file. Therefore, if you were to display a list of all cookie data contained in a `document.cookie` property, you would get back all the name-value cookie pairs from the cookie file whose domain parameter matches that of the current document.

Unless you expect the document to be replicated in another server within your domain, you can usually omit the `domain` parameter when saving a cookie. Default behavior automatically supplies the domain of the current document to the cookie file entry. Be aware that a domain setting must have at least two periods, such as

```
.google.com
.hotwired.com
```

Or, you can write an entire URL to the domain, including the `http://` protocol.

SECURE

If you omit the `SECURE` parameter when saving a cookie, you imply that the cookie data is accessible to any document or server-side program from your site that meets the other domain- and path-matching properties. For client-side scripting of cookies, you should omit this parameter when saving a cookie.

Retrieving cookie data

Cookie data retrieved through JavaScript arrives as one string, which contains the whole name-data pair. Even though the cookie file stores other parameters for each cookie, you can retrieve only the name-data pairs through JavaScript. Moreover, when two or more (up to a maximum of 20) cookies meet the current domain criteria, these cookies are also lumped into that string, delimited by a semicolon and space. For example, a `document.cookie` string may look like this:

```
userName=Fred; password=NikL2sPacU
```

In other words, you cannot treat named cookies as objects. Instead, you must parse the entire cookie string, extracting the data from the desired name-data pair.

When you know that you're dealing with only one cookie (and that no more will ever be added to the domain), you can customize the extraction based on known data, such as the cookie name. For example, with a cookie name that is seven characters long, you can extract the data with a statement such as this:

```
var data = decodeURIComponent(document.cookie.substring
    (7,document.cookie.length));
```

The first parameter of the substring() method includes the equal sign to separate the name from the data; this is where the 7 comes from in the code. This example works with single cookies only because it assumes that the cookie starts at the beginning of the cookie file, which may not be the case if the file contains multiple cookies.

A better approach to cookie extraction is to create a general-purpose function that can work with single- or multiple-entry cookies. For example:

```
function getCookieData(labelName) {
    var labelLen = labelName.length;
    // read cookie property only once for speed
    var cookieData = document.cookie;
    var cLen = cookieData.length;
    var i = 0;
    var cEnd;
    while (i < cLen) {
        var j = i + labelLen;
        if (cookieData.substring(i,j) == labelName) {
            cEnd = cookieData.indexOf(";",j);
            if (cEnd == -1) {
                cEnd = cookieData.length;
            }
            return decodeURIComponent(cookieData.substring(j+1, cEnd));
        }
        i++;
    }
    return "";
}
```

Calls to this function pass the label name of the desired cookie as a parameter. The function parses the entire cookie string, chipping away any mismatched entries (through the semicolons) until it finds the cookie name.

If all of this cookie code still makes your head hurt, you can turn to a set of functions devised by experienced JavaScripter and web site designer Bill Dortch of hIdaho Design. His cookie functions provide generic access to cookies that you can use in all of your cookie-related pages. Listing 29-3 shows Bill's cookie functions, which include a variety of safety nets for date calculation bugs that appeared in some legacy versions of Netscape Navigator. The code is updated with modern URL encoding and decoding methods. Don't be put off by the length of the listing: Most of the lines are comments.

documentObject.cookie

LISTING 29-3

Bill Dortch's Cookie Functions

```
<html>
   <head>
      <title>Cookie Functions</title>
   </head>
   <body>
      <script type="text/javascript">
      //
      // Cookie Functions -- "Night of the Living Cookie" Version (25-Jul-96)
      //
      // Written by:  Bill Dortch, hIdaho Design
      // The following functions are released to the public domain.
      //
      // This version takes a more aggressive approach to deleting
      // cookies.  Previous versions set the expiration date to one
      // millisecond prior to the current time; however, this method
      // did not work in Netscape 2.02 (though it does in earlier and
      // later versions), resulting in "zombie" cookies that would not
      // die.  DeleteCookie now sets the expiration date to the earliest
      // usable date (one second into 1970), and sets the cookie's value
      // to null for good measure.
      //
      // Also, this version adds optional path and domain parameters to
      // the DeleteCookie function.  If you specify a path and/or domain
      // when creating (setting) a cookie**, you must specify the same
      // path/domain when deleting it, or deletion will not occur.
      //
      // The FixCookieDate function must now be called explicitly to
      // correct for the 2.x Mac date bug.  This function should be
      // called *once* after a Date object is created and before it
      // is passed (as an expiration date) to SetCookie.  Because the
      // Mac date bug affects all dates, not just those passed to
      // SetCookie, you might want to make it a habit to call
      // FixCookieDate any time you create a new Date object:
      //
      //    var theDate = new Date();
      //    FixCookieDate (theDate);
      //
      // Calling FixCookieDate has no effect on platforms other than
      // the Mac, so there is no need to determine the user's platform
      // prior to calling it.
      //
      // This version also incorporates several minor coding improvements.
      //
      // **Note that it is possible to set multiple cookies with the same
      // name but different (nested) paths.  For example:
      //
      //    SetCookie ("color","red",null,"/outer");
      //    SetCookie ("color","blue",null,"/outer/inner");
```

```
//
// However, GetCookie cannot distinguish between these and will return
// the first cookie that matches a given name.  It is therefore
// recommended that you *not* use the same name for cookies with
// different paths.  (Bear in mind that there is *always* a path
// associated with a cookie; if you don't explicitly specify one,
// the path of the setting document is used.)
//
// Revision History:
//
//    "JavaScript Bible 6th Edition" Version (28-July-2006)
//      - Replaced deprecated escape()/unescape() functions with
//        encodeURI() and decodeURI() functions
//
//    "Toss Your Cookies" Version (22-Mar-96)
//      - Added FixCookieDate() function to correct for Mac date bug
//
//    "Second Helping" Version (21-Jan-96)
//      - Added path, domain and secure parameters to SetCookie
//      - Replaced home-rolled encode/decode functions with
//        new (then) escape/unescape functions
//
//    "Free Cookies" Version (December 95)
//
//
// For information on the significance of cookie parameters,
// and on cookies in general, please refer to the official cookie
// spec, at:
//
//      http://www.netscape.com/newsref/std/cookie_spec.html
//
//********************************************************************
//
// "Internal" function to return the decoded value of a cookie
//
function getCookieVal (offset)
{
  var endstr = document.cookie.indexOf (";", offset);
    if (endstr == -1)
    {
      endstr = document.cookie.length;
    }
  return decodeURI(document.cookie.substring(offset, endstr));
}


//
// Function to correct for 2.x Mac date bug.  Call this function to
// fix a date object prior to passing it to SetCookie.
// IMPORTANT:  This function should only be called *once* for
// any given date object!  See example at the end of this document.
//
```

continued

documentObject.cookie

LISTING 29-3   *(continued)*

```
function FixCookieDate (date)
{
  var base = new Date(0);
  var skew = base.getTime(); // dawn of (Unix) time - should be 0
    if (skew > 0)
    {  // Except on the Mac - ahead of its time
       date.setTime (date.getTime() - skew);
    }
}


//
//   Function to return the value of the cookie specified by "name".
//     name - String object containing the cookie name.
//     returns - String object containing the cookie value, or null if
//        the cookie does not exist.
//
function GetCookie (name)
{
    var arg = name + "=";
    var alen = arg.length;
    var clen = document.cookie.length;
    var i = 0;
    while (i < clen)
    {
      var j = i + alen;
        if (document.cookie.substring(i, j) == arg)
        {
            return getCookieVal (j);
        }
      i = document.cookie.indexOf(" ", i) + 1;
        if (i == 0)
        {
            break;
        }
    }
    return null;
}


//
//   Function to create or update a cookie.
//     name - String object containing the cookie name.
//     value - String object containing the cookie value.  May contain
//       any valid string characters.
//     [expires] - Date object containing the expiration data of the
//       cookie.  If omitted or null, expires the cookie at the end of the
//       current session.
//     [path] - String object indicating the path for which the cookie is
//       valid.
//       If omitted or null, uses the path of the calling document.
```

```
//    [domain] - String object indicating the domain for which the cookie
//       is valid. If omitted or null, uses the domain of the calling
//       document.
//    [secure] - Boolean (true/false) value indicating whether cookie
//       transmission requires a secure channel (HTTPS).
//
//  The first two parameters are required.  The others, if supplied, must
//  be passed in the order listed above.  To omit an unused optional
//  field, use null as a place holder.  For example, to call SetCookie
//  using name, value and path, you would code:
//
//      SetCookie ("myCookieName", "myCookieValue", null, "/");
//
//  Note that trailing omitted parameters do not require a placeholder.
//
//  To set a secure cookie for path "/myPath", that expires after the
//  current session, you might code:
//
//      SetCookie (myCookieVar, cookieValueVar, null, "/myPath", null,
//          true);
//
function SetCookie (name,value,expires,path,domain,secure)
{
    document.cookie = name + "=" + encodeURIComponent (value) +
        ((expires) ? "; expires=" + expires.toGMTString() : "") +
        ((path) ? "; path=" + path : "") +
        ((domain) ? "; domain=" + domain : "") +
        ((secure) ? "; secure" : "");
}


//  Function to delete a cookie. (Sets expiration date to start of epoch)
//    name -    String object containing the cookie name
//    path -    String object containing the path of the cookie to delete.
//              This MUST be the same as the path used to create the
//              cookie, or null/omitted if
//              no path was specified when creating the cookie.
//    domain - String object containing the domain of the cookie to
//              delete.  This MUST be the same as the domain used to
//              create the cookie, or null/omitted if no domain was
//              specified when creating the cookie.
//
function DeleteCookie (name,path,domain)
{
    if (GetCookie(name))
    {
        document.cookie = name + "=" +
            ((path) ? "; path=" + path : "") +
            ((domain) ? "; domain=" + domain : "") +
            "; expires=Thu, 01-Jan-70 00:00:01 GMT";
    }
}
```

continued

documentObject.cookie

LISTING 29-3   *(continued)*

```
//
//  Examples
//
var expdate = new Date ();
FixCookieDate (expdate); // Correct for Mac date bug (call only once)
expdate.setTime (expdate.getTime() + (24 * 60 * 60 * 1000)); // 24 hrs
SetCookie ("ccpath", "http://www.hidaho.com/colorcenter/", expdate);
SetCookie ("ccname", "hIdaho Design ColorCenter", expdate);
SetCookie ("tempvar", "This is a temporary cookie.");
SetCookie ("ubiquitous", "This cookie will work anywhere in this ↵
    domain",null,"/");
SetCookie ("paranoid", "This cookie requires secure ↵
    communications",expdate,"/",null,true);
SetCookie ("goner", "This cookie must die!");
document.write (document.cookie + "<br>");
DeleteCookie ("goner");
document.write (document.cookie + "<br>");
document.write ("ccpath = " + GetCookie("ccpath") + "<br>");
document.write ("ccname = " + GetCookie("ccname") + "<br>");
document.write ("tempvar = " + GetCookie("tempvar") + "<br>");
</script>
</body>
</html>
```

Extra batches

You may design a site that needs more than 20 cookies for a given domain. For example, in a shopping site, you never know how many items a customer may load into the shopping cart cookie.

Because each named cookie stores plain text, you can create your own text-based data structures to accommodate multiple pieces of information per cookie. (But also watch out for a practical limit of 2,000 characters per name/value pair within the 4,000 character maximum for any domain's combined cookies.) The trick is determining a delimiter character that won't be used by any of the data in the cookie. In Decision Helper (in Chapter 58), for example, we use a period to separate multiple integers stored in a cookie.

With the delimiter character established, you must then write functions that concatenate these "subcookies" into single cookie strings and extract them on the other side. It's a bit more work, but well worth the effort, to have the power of persistent data on the client.

Example

Experiment with the last group of statements in Listing 29-3 to create, retrieve, and delete cookies. You can also experiment with The Evaluator by assigning a name/value pair string to `document.cookie`, and then examining the value of the `cookie` property.

Related Items: `String` object methods (see Chapter 15, "The String Object")

defaultCharset

Value: String   Read/Write

Compatibility: WinIE4+, MacIE4+, NN-, Moz-, Safari+, Opera-, Chrome+

The `defaultCharset` property reveals the character set used by the browser to render the current document. You can find possible values for this property at

        http://www.iana.org/assignments/character-sets

Each browser and operating system has its own default character set. Values may also be set through a `<meta>` tag. The difference between the `defaultCharset` and `charset` properties is not clear, especially because both are read/write (although modifying the `defaultCharset` property has no visual effect on the page). However, if your scripts temporarily modify the `charset` property, you can use the `defaultCharset` property to return to the original character set:

        document.charset = document.defaultCharset;

Example

Use The Evaluator (Chapter 4, "JavaScript Essentials") to experiment with the `defaultCharset` property. To see the default setting applied to the page, enter the following statement into the top text box:

        document.defaultCharset

Related Items: `charset`, `characterSet` properties

defaultView

Value: `window` or `frame` object reference   Read-Only

Compatibility: WinIE-, MacIE-, NN6+, Moz+, Safari+, Opera+, Chrome+

The `defaultView` property returns a reference to the object serving as the viewer for the document. The viewer is responsible for rendering the document, and in Mozilla the object returned in the `defaultView` property is the `window` or `frame` object that contains the document. This W3C DOM Level 2 property provides access to the computed CSS values being applied to any HTML element (through the `document.defaultView.getComputedStyle()` method).

Related Items: `window` and `frame` properties; `window.getComputedStyle()` method

designMode

Value: String   Read/Write

Compatibility: WinIE5+, MacIE-, NN7.1, Moz1.4+, Safari+, Opera+, Chrome+

The `designMode` property is applicable for IE only when WinIE5+ technology is being used as a component in another application. The property controls whether the browser module is being used for HTML editing. Modifying the property from within a typical HTML page in the IE5+ browser has no effect. But on the Mozilla side, the property can be used to turn an `iframe` element's `document` object into an HTML editable document. Visit `http://www.mozilla.org/editor` for current details and examples.

doctype

Value: `DocumentType` object reference   Read-Only

Compatibility: WinIE+, MacIE5+, NN6+, Moz+, Safari+, Opera+, Chrome+

The `doctype` property comes from the W3C Core DOM and returns a `DocumentType` object — a representation of the Document Type Definition (DTD) information for the document. The `DocumentType` object (if one is explicitly defined in the source code) is the first child node of the root document node (and is thus a sibling to the `HTML` element). In IE, this property is only supported in XML documents; HTML documents always return `null`.

Table 29-1 shows the typical `DocumentType` object property list and values for a generic HTML page. Future DOM specifications will allow these properties to be read/write.

Related Items: `Node` object (see Chapter 25, "Document Object Model Essentials")

Example

Take a look at the `document.doctype` object by entering the following line of code in the bottom text field of the Evaluator web page (see Chapter 4):

```
document.doctype
```

TABLE 29-1

DocumentType Object in NN6+/Moz

Property	Value
baseURI	http://www.dannyg.com/index.html
entities	null
internalSubset	null
name	HTML
nodeName	HTML
nodeType	10
notations	null
publicId	-//W3C//DTD XHTML 1.0 Transitional//EN
systemId	http://www.w3.org/TR/xhtml1/DTD/xhtml1-transitional.dtd

If you pay close attention you'll notice that the `publicId` property is actually set to `-//W3C//DTD HTML 4.01 Transitional//EN`, which is different from the value shown in Table 29-1. This reveals the fact that the Evaluator page declares itself as an HTML 4.01 document.

documentElement

Value: HTML or XML element object reference   Read-Only

Compatibility: WinIE5+, MacIE5+, NN6+, Moz+, Safari+, Opera+, Chrome+

The documentElement property returns a reference to the HTML (or XML) element object that contains all of the content of the current document. The naming of this property is a bit misleading, because the root document node is not an element, but its only child node is the HTML (or XML) element for the page. At best, you can think of this property as providing scripts with an *element face* to the document object and document node associated with the page currently loaded in the browser.

The document.documentElement object represents the html element for a page, whereas docoument.body represents the body element. This explains why document.body is a child of the document.documentElement object.

Example

Use The Evaluator (Chapter 4, "JavaScript Essentials") to examine the behavior of the documentElement property. In IE5+/W3C, enter the following statement into the top text field:

```
document.documentElement.tagName
```

The result is HTML, as expected.

Related Item: ownerDocument property (see Chapter 26, "Generic HTML Element Objects")

documentURI

Value: String   Read-Only

Compatibility: WinIE-, MacIE-, NN8+, Moz1.7+, Safari+, Opera+, Chrome+

The documentURI property contains the location of the document. This is the W3C DOM Level 3 equivalent of the non-W3C DOM location.href property. Use The Evaluator (Chapter 4) to view the document URI by entering the following:

```
document.documentURI
```

Related Item: document.baseURI property

domain

Value: String   Read/Write

Compatibility: WinIE4+, MacIE4+, NN3+, Moz+, Safari+, Opera+, Chrome+

Security restrictions can get in the way of sites that have more than one server at their domain. Because some objects, especially the location object, prevent access to properties of other servers displayed in other frames, legitimate access to those properties is blocked. For example, it's not uncommon for popular sites to have their usual public access site on a server named something such as www.popular.com. If a page on that server includes a front end to a site search engine located at search.popular.com, visitors who use browsers with these domain restrictions security restrictions are denied access.

To guard against that eventuality, a script in documents from two servers can instruct the browser to think both servers are the same. In the preceding example, you would set the `document.domain` property in both documents to `popular.com`. Without specifically setting the property, the default value includes the server name as well, thus causing a mismatch between hostnames.

Before you start thinking that you can spoof your way into other servers, be aware that you can set the `document.domain` property only to servers with the same domain (following the two-dot rule) as the document doing the setting. Therefore, documents originating only from *xxx*.`popular.com` can set their `document.domain` properties to `popular.com` server.

Related Items: `window.open()` method; `window.location` object; security (see Chapter 49, "Security and Netscape Signed Scripts" on the CD-ROM)

embeds[]

Value: Array of embed element objects   Read-Only

Compatibility: WinIE4+, MacIE4+, NN3+, Moz+, Safari+, Opera+, Chrome+

Although now supplanted by the `<object>` tag, the `<embed>` tag used to be the markup that loaded data requiring a plug-in application to play or display. The `document.embeds` property is an array of embed element objects within the document:

```
var count = document.embeds.length;
```

Related Item: embed element object (see Chapter 44, "Embedded Objects")

expando

Value: Boolean   Read/Write

Compatibility: WinIE4+, MacIE4+, NN-, Moz-, Safari-, Opera-, Chrome-

Microsoft calls any custom property that is not a native property of the `document` object an *expando* property. By default, most objects in recent generations of browsers allow scripts to add new properties of objects as a way to temporarily store data without explicitly defining global variables. For example, if you want to maintain an independent counter of how often a function is invoked, you can create a custom property of the `document` object and use it as the storage facility:

```
document.counter = 0;
```

IE4+ enables you to control whether the `document` object is capable of accepting `expando` properties. The default value of the `document.expando` property is `true`, thus allowing custom properties. But the potential downside to this permissiveness, especially during the page construction phase, is that a misspelled native property name is gladly accepted by the `document` object. You may not be aware of why the title bar of the browser window doesn't change when you assign a new string to the `document.Title` property (which, in the case-sensitive world of JavaScript, is distinct from the native `document.title` property).

Example

Use The Evaluator (Chapter 4, "JavaScript Essentials") to experiment with the `document.expando` property in IE4+. Begin by proving that the `document` object can normally accept custom properties. Type the following statement into the top text field:

```
document.spooky = "Boo!"
```

This property is now set and stays that way until the page is either reloaded or unloaded.

Now freeze the `document` object's properties with the following statement:

```
document.expando = false
```

If you try to add a new property, such as the following, you receive an error:

```
document.happy = "tra la"
```

Interestingly, even though `document.expando` is turned off, the first custom property is still accessible and modifiable.

Related Item: `prototype` property of custom objects (see Chapter 23, "Function Objects and Custom Objects")

fgColor

(See `alinkColor`)

fileCreatedDate
fileModifiedDate
fileSize

Value: String, Integer (fileSize)   Read-Only

Compatibility: WinIE4+, MacIE4+, NN-, Moz-, Safari-, Opera-, Chrome-

These three IE-specific properties return information about the file that holds the current document. The first two properties (not implemented in MacIE) reveal the dates on which the current document's file was created and modified. For an unmodified file, its creation and modified dates are the same. The `fileSize` property reveals the number of bytes of the file.

Date values returned for the first two properties are in a format similar to mm/dd/yyyy. Note, however, that the values contain only the date and not the time. In any case, you can use the values as the parameter to a `new Date()` constructor function. You can then use date calculations for such information as the number of days between the current day and the most recent modification.

Not all servers may provide the proper date or size information about a file, or in a format that IE can interpret. Test your implementation on the deployment server to ensure compatibility.

Also, be aware that these properties can be read-only for a file that is loaded in the browser. JavaScript by itself cannot get this information about files that are on the server, but not loaded into the browser.

Example

Listing 29-4 dynamically generates several pieces of content relating to the creation and modification dates of the file, as well as its size. More importantly, the listing demonstrates how to turn a value returned by the file date properties into a genuine date object that can be used for date calculations. In the case of Listing 29-4, the calculation is the number of full days between the creation date and the day someone views the file. Notice that the dynamically generated content is added very simply through the `innerText` properties of carefully located `span` elements in the body content.

documentObject.fileSize

LISTING 29-4

Displaying File Information for a Web Page

```html
<!DOCTYPE html>
<html>
    <head>
        <meta http-equiv="content-type" content="text/html;charset=utf-8">
        <title>fileCreatedDate and fileModifiedDate Properties</title>
        <script type="text/javascript">
            function fillInBlanks()
            {
                var created = document.fileCreatedDate;
                var modified = document.fileModifiedDate;
                document.getElementById("created").innerText = created;
                document.getElementById("modified").innerText = modified;
                var createdDate = new Date(created).getTime();
                var today = new Date().getTime();
                var diff = Math.floor((today - createdDate) / (1000*60*60*24));
                document.getElementById("diff").innerText = diff;
                document.getElementById("size").innerText = document.fileSize;
            }

            // bind the event handlers
            function addEvent(elem, evtType, func)
            {
                if (elem.addEventListener)
                {
                    elem.addEventListener(evtType, func, false);
                }
                else if (elem.attachEvent)
                {
                    elem.attachEvent("on" + evtType, func);
                }
                else
                {
                    elem["on" + evtType] = func;
                }
            }
            addEvent(window, "load", function()
            {
                fillInBlanks();
            });
        </script>
    </head>
    <body>
        <h1>fileCreatedDate and fileModifiedDate Properties</h1>
        <hr />
        <p>This file (<span id="size"> </span> bytes) was created on
            <span id="created"> </span> and most recently modified on
            <span id="modified"> </span>.
```

```
    </p>
    <p>It has been <span id="diff"> </span> days since this file was
       created.
    </p>
  </body>
</html>
```

Related Item: lastModified property

forms[]

Value: Array   Read-Only

Compatibility: WinIE3+, MacIE3+, NN2+, Moz+, Safari+, Opera+, Chrome+

As we show in Chapter 34, "Form and Related Objects," which is dedicated to the form object, an HTML form (anything defined inside a <form>...</form> tag pair) is a JavaScript object unto itself. You can create a valid reference to a form according to its name (assigned through a form's name attribute). For example, if a document contains the following form definition:

```
<form name="phoneData">
    input item definitions
</form>
```

then your scripts can refer to the form object by name:

```
document.phoneData
```

However, a document object also tracks its forms in another way: as an array of form objects. The first item of a document.forms array is the form that loaded first (it was foremost from the top of the HTML code). If your document defines one form, the forms property is an array one entry in length; with three separate forms in the document, the array is three entries long.

Use standard array notation to reference a particular form from the document.forms array. For example, the first form in a document (the zeroth entry of the document.forms array) is referenced as

```
document.forms[0]
```

Any of the form object's properties or methods are available by appending the desired property or method name to the reference. For example, to retrieve the value of an input text field named homePhone from the second form of a document, the reference you use is

```
document.forms[1].homePhone.value
```

One advantage to using the document.forms property for addressing a form object or element instead of the actual form name is that you may be able to generate a library of generalizable scripts that know how to cycle through all available forms in a document and then hunt for a form that has some special element and property. The following script fragment (part of a *repeat loop* described more

***documentObject*.forms[]**

fully in Chapter 21, "Control Structures and Exception Handling") uses a loop-counting variable (i) to help the script check all forms in a document:

```
for (var i = 0; i < document.forms.length; i++) {
    if (document.forms[i]. ... ) {
        statements
    }
}
```

One more variation on forms array references enables you to substitute the name of a form (as a string) for the `forms` array index. For example, the form named `phoneData` can be referenced as:

```
document.forms["phoneData"]
```

If you take a lot of care in assigning names to objects, you will likely prefer the `document.formName` style of referencing forms. In this book, you see both indexed array and form name style references. The advantage of using name references is that even if you redesign the page and change the order of forms in the document, references to the named forms will still be valid, whereas the index numbers of the forms will have changed. Also see the discussion in Chapter 34, "Form and Related Objects," of the `form` object and how to pass a form's data to a function.

Example

The document in Listing 29-5 is set up to display an alert dialog box that simulates navigation to a particular music site, based on the selected status of the blues check box. The user input here is divided into two forms: one form with the check box and the other form with the button that does the navigation. A block of copy fills the space in between. Clicking the bottom button (in the second form) triggers the function that fetches the checked property of the blues check box by using the `document.forms[i]` array as part of the address.

LISTING 29-5

A Simple Form Example

```html
<!DOCTYPE html>
<html>
    <head>
        <meta http-equiv="content-type" content="text/html;charset=utf-8">
        <title>document.forms example</title>
        <script type="text/javascript">
            function goMusic()
            {
                if (document.forms[0].bluish.checked)
                {
                    alert("Now going to the Blues music area...");
                }
                else
                {
                    alert("Now going to the Rock music area...");
                }
            }
```

```
        // bind the event handlers
        function addEvent(elem, evtType, func)
        {
            if (elem.addEventListener)
            {
                elem.addEventListener(evtType, func, false);
            }
            else if (elem.attachEvent)
            {
                elem.attachEvent("on" + evtType, func);
            }
            else
            {
                elem["on" + evtType] = func;
            }
        }
        addEvent(window, "load", function()
        {
            addEvent(document.getElementById("visit"), "click", goMusic);
        });
    </script>
</head>
<body>
    <form name="theBlues">
        <input type="checkbox" name="bluish" />Check here if you've got the
        blues.
    </form>
    <hr />
    M<br />
    o<br />
    r<br />
    e<br />
    <br />
    C<br />
    o<br />
    p<br />
    y<br />
    <hr />
    <form name="visit">
        <input type="button" id="visit" value="Visit music site" />
    </form>
</body>
</html>
```

Related Item: form object (see Chapter 34, "Form and Related Objects")

frames[]

Value: Array   Read-Only

Compatibility: WinIE4+, MacIE4+, NN-, Moz-, Safari-, Opera+, Chrome-

documentObject.**height**

The document.frames property is similar to the window.frames property, but its association with the document object may seem a bit illogical at times. The objects contained by the array returned from the property are window objects, which means they are the window objects of any defined frame elements (from a framesetting document) or iframe elements (from a plain HTML document). Distinguishing the window objects from the iframe element objects is important. Window objects have different properties and methods from the frame and iframe element objects. The latter's properties typically represent the attributes for those element's tags. If a document contains no iframe elements, the document.frames array length is zero.

Although you can access an individual frame object through the typical array syntax (for example, document.frames[0]), you can also use alternate syntax that Microsoft provides for collections of objects. The index number can also be placed inside parentheses, as in:

```
document.frames(0)
```

Moreover, if the frames have values assigned to their name attributes, you can use the name (in string form) as a parameter:

```
document.frames("contents")
```

And if the collection of frames has more than one frame with the same name, you must take special care. Using the duplicated name as a parameter forces the reference to return a collection of frame objects that share that name. Or, you can limit the returned value to a single instance of the duplicate-named frames by specifying an optional second parameter indicating the index. For example, if a document has two iframe elements with the name contents, a script could reference the second window object as:

```
document.frames("contents", 1)
```

For the sake of cross-browser compatibility, my preference for referencing frame window objects is through the window.frames property.

Example

See Listings 27-7 and 27-8 for examples of using the frames property with window objects.

Related Item: window.frames property

`height`
`width`

Value: Integer   Read-Only

Compatibility: WinIE-, MacIE-, NN4+, Moz+, Safari+, Opera-, Chrome+

The height and width properties provide the pixel dimensions of the content within the current window (or frame). If the document's content is smaller than the size of the browser's content region, the dimensions returned by these properties include the blank space to the right or bottom edges of the content area of the window. But if the content extends beyond the viewable edges of the content region, the dimensions include the unseen content as well. The corresponding measures in Internet Explorer are the document.body.scrollHeight and document.body.scrollWidth properties. These IE properties are also supported by most modern browsers.

Example

Use The Evaluator (Chapter 4, "JavaScript Essentials") to examine the height and width properties of that document. Enter the following statement into the top text box and click the Evaluate button:

```
"height=" + document.height + "; width=" + document.width
```

Resize the window so that you see both vertical and horizontal scroll bars in the browser window and click the Evaluate button again. If either or both numbers get smaller, the values in the Results box are the exact size of the space occupied by the document. But if you expand the window to well beyond where the scroll bars are needed, the values extend to the number of pixels in each dimension of the window's content region.

Related Items: document.body.scrollHeight, document.body.scrollWidth properties

images[]

Value: Array   Read-Only

Compatibility: WinIE4+, MacIE3+, NN3+, Moz+, Safari+, Opera+, Chrome+

With images treated as first-class objects, beginning with NN3 and IE4, it's only natural for a document to maintain an array of all the image tags defined on the page (just as it does for links and anchors). The primary importance of having images as objects is that you can modify their content (the source file associated with the rectangular space of the image) on-the-fly. You can find details about the image object in Chapter 31, "Image, Area, Map, and Canvas Objects."

Use image array references to pinpoint a specific image for the retrieval of any image property, or for assigning a new image file to its src property. Image arrays begin their index counts with 0: The first image in a document has the reference document.images[0]. And, as with any array object, you can find out how many images the array contains by checking the length property. For example:

```
var imageCount = document.images.length;
```

Images can also have names, so if you prefer, you can refer to the image object by its name, as in

```
var imageLoaded = document.imageName.complete;
```

or

```
var imageLoaded = document.images[imageName].complete;
```

The document.images array is a useful guide to knowing whether a browser supports swappable images. Any browser that treats an img element as an object always forms a document.images array in the page. If no images are defined in the page, the array is still there, but its length is zero. The array's existence, however, is the clue about image object compatibility. Because the document.images array evaluates to an array object when present, the expression can be used as a conditional expression for branching to statements that involve image swapping:

```
if (document.images) {
    // image swapping or precaching here
}
```

Browsers that don't have this property (legacy and, potentially, mobile) evaluate document.images as undefined, and thus the condition is treated as a false value.

941

documentObject.implementation

Example

The `document.images` property is defined automatically as the browser builds the object model for a document that contains image objects. See the discussion about the `Image` object in Chapter 31, for reference examples.

Related Item: `Image` object (see Chapter 31, "Image, Area, Map, and Canvas Objects")

implementation

Value: Object   Read-Only

Compatibility: WinIE6+, MacIE5+, NN6+, Moz+, Safari+, Opera+, Chrome+

The Core W3C DOM defines the `document.implementation` property as an avenue to let scripts find out what DOM features (that is, modules of the DOM standard) are implemented for the current environment. Although the object returned by the property (a `DOMImplementation` object) has no properties, it has a method, `hasFeature()`, which lets scripts find out, for example, whether the environment supports HTML or just XML. The first parameter of the `hasFeature()` method is the feature in the form of a string. The second parameter is a string form of the version number. The method returns a Boolean value.

The "Conformance" section of the W3C DOM specification governs the module names. (The standard also allows browser-specific features to be tested through the `hasFeature()` method.) Module names include strings such as `HTML`, `XML`, `MouseEvents`, and so on.

Version numbering for W3C DOM modules corresponds to the W3C DOM level. Thus, the version for the XML DOM module in DOM Level 2 is known as `2.0`. Note that versions refer to DOM modules and not, for example, the separate HTML standard.

Example

Use The Evaluator (Chapter 4, "JavaScript Essentials") to experiment with the `document.implementation.hasFeature()` method. Enter the following statements one at a time into the top text field and examine the results:

```
document.implementation.hasFeature("HTML","1.0")
document.implementation.hasFeature("HTML","2.0")
document.implementation.hasFeature("HTML","3.0")
document.implementation.hasFeature("CSS","2.0")
document.implementation.hasFeature("CSS2","2.0")
```

Feel free to try other values. For some reason, as of version 7, Internet Explorer returns false for some features that it indeed supports, such as CSS 2.0. In other words, it's probably not a good idea to place a lot of trust in the IE results of the `hasFeature()` method, at least for the time being.

inputEncoding

Value: String   Read-Only

Compatibility: WinIE-, MacIE-, NN-, Moz1.8+, Safari+, Opera-, Chrome+

The input encoding of a document is the character encoding that is in effect at the time when the document is parsed. For example, ISO-8859-1 is a common character encoding that you may see reported by the `inputEncoding` property.

lastModified

Value: Date string   Read-Only

Compatibility: WinIE3+, MacIE3+, NN2+, Moz+, Safari+, Opera+, Chrome+

Every disk file maintains a modified time stamp, and most (but not all) servers are configured to expose this information to a browser accessing a file. This information is available by reading the `document.lastModified` property. If your server supplies this information to the client, you can use the value of this property to present this information for readers of your web page. The script automatically updates the value for you, rather than requiring you to hand-code the HTML line every time you modify the home page. Be aware that if you are testing with Safari or Google Chrome, your code will not work unless the files are coming from an HTTP server.

If the value returned to you displays itself as a date in 1969, it means that you are positioned somewhere west of GMT, or Greenwich Mean Time (some number of time zones west of GMT at 1 January 1970), and the server is not providing the proper data when it serves the file. Sometimes server configuration can fix the problem, but not always.

The returned value is not a date object, but rather a straight string consisting of the time and date, as recorded by the document's file system. The format of the string varies from browser to browser and version to version. You can, however, usually convert the date string to a JavaScript date object and use the date object's methods to extract selected elements for recompilation into readable form. Listing 29-6 shows an example.

Even local file systems don't necessarily provide the correct data for every browser to interpret. But put that same file on a UNIX or Windows web server, and the date appears correctly when accessed through the Net.

Example

Experiment with the `document.lastModified` property with Listing 29-6. But also be prepared for inaccurate readings depending on the location of the file.

LISTING 29-6
___

Putting a Time Stamp on a Page

```
<!DOCTYPE html>
<html>
   <head>
      <meta http-equiv="content-type" content="text/html;charset=utf-8">
      <title>Time Stamper</title>
   </head>
   <body>
      <center>
         <h1>GiantCo Home Page</h1>
      </center>
      <script type="text/javascript">
         update = new Date(document.lastModified);
         theMonth = update.getMonth() + 1;
         theDate = update.getDate();
```

continued

documentObject.layers[]

LISTING 29-6   *(continued)*

```
        theYear = update.getFullYear();
        document.writeln("<I>Last updated:" +
                         theMonth + "/" + theDate +
                         "/" + theYear + "<\/I>");
    </script>
    <hr />
  </body>
</html>
```

As noted at great length in the `Date` object discussion in Chapter 17, you should be aware that date formats vary greatly from country to country. Some of these formats use a different order for date elements. When you hard-code a date format, it may take a form that is unfamiliar to other users of your page.

Related Item: `Date` object (see Chapter 17, "The Date Object")

layers[]

Value: Array   Read-Only

Compatibility: WinIE-, MacIE-, NN4, Moz-, Safari-, Opera-, Chrome-

The `layer` object is the NN4 way of exposing positioned elements to the object model. Thus, the `document.layers` property is an array of positioned elements in the document. The `layer` object and `document.layers` property are orphaned in NN4, and their importance is all but gone now that Mozilla has taken over. Chapter 43 includes several examples of how to carry out similar functionality as the `document.layers` property using the standard W3C DOM.

Related Item: `layer` object (see Chapter 43, "Positioned Objects")

linkColor

(See `alinkColor`)

links[]

Value: Array   Read-Only

Compatibility: WinIE3+, MacIE3+, NN2+, Moz+, Safari+, Opera+, Chrome+

The `document.links` property is similar to the `document.anchors` property, except that the objects maintained by the array are link objects — items created with `<a href="">` tags. Use the array references to pinpoint a specific link for retrieving any link property, such as the target window specified in the link's HTML definition.

Link arrays begin their index counts with 0: The first link in a document has the reference `document.links[0]`. And, as with any array object, you can find out how many entries the array has by checking the `length` property. For example:

```
    var linkCount = document.links.length;
```

Entries in the document.links property are full-fledged location objects, which means you have the same properties available to each member of the links[] array as you do in the location object.

Example

The document.links property is defined automatically as the browser builds the object model for a document that contains link objects. You rarely access this property, except to determine the number of link objects in the document.

Related Items: link object; document.anchors property

location
URL

Value: String   Read/Write and Read-Only (see text)

Compatibility: WinIE4+, MacIE4+, NN3+, Moz+, Safari+, Opera+, Chrome+

The document.URL property is similar to the window.location property. A location object, you may recall from Chapter 28, "Location and History Objects," consists of a number of properties regarding the document currently loaded in a window or frame. Assigning a new URL to the location object (or location.href property) tells the browser to load the page from that URL into the frame. The document.URL property, on the other hand, is simply a string (read-only in Navigator, Mozilla, and Safari) that reveals the URL of the current document. The value may be important to your script, but the property does not have the object power of the window.location object. You cannot change (assign another value to) this property value because a document has only one URL: its location on the Net (or your hard disk) where the file exists, and what protocol is required to get it.

This may seem like a fine distinction, and it is. The reference you use (window.location object or document.URL property) depends on what you are trying to accomplish specifically with the script. If the script is changing the content of a window by loading a new URL, you have no choice but to assign a value to the window.location object. Similarly, if the script is concerned with the component parts of a URL, the properties of the location object provide the simplest avenue to that information. To retrieve the URL of a document in string form (whether it is in the current window or in another frame), you can use either the document.URL property or the window.location.href property.

Note

The document.URL **property replaces the old** document.location **property, which is still supported in most browsers.** ■

Example

HTML documents in Listings 29-7 through 29-9 create a test lab that enables you to experiment with viewing the document.URL property for different windows and frames in a multiframe environment. Results are displayed in a table, with an additional listing of the document.title property to help you identify documents being referred to. The same security restrictions that apply to retrieving window.location object properties also apply to retrieving the document.URL property from another window or frame.

documentObject.URL

LISTING 29-7

A Simple Frameset for the URL Example

```html
<!DOCTYPE html>
<html>
    <head>
        <meta http-equiv="content-type" content="text/html;charset=utf-8">
        <title>document.URL Reader</title>
    </head>
    <frameset rows="60%,40%">
        <frame name="Frame1" src="jsb29-09.html" />
        <frame name="Frame2" src="jsb29-08.html" />
    </frameset>
</html>
```

LISTING 29-8

Showing Location Information for Different Contexts

```html
<!DOCTYPE html>
<html>
    <head>
        <meta http-equiv="content-type" content="text/html;charset=utf-8">
        <title>URL Property Reader</title>
        <script type="text/javascript">
            function fillTopFrame()
            {
                newURL=prompt("Enter the URL of a document to show in the top frame:","");
                if (newURL != null && newURL != "")
                {
                    top.frames[0].location = newURL;
                }
            }

            function showLoc(item)
            {
                var windName = item.value;
                var theRef = windName + ".document";
                item.form.dLoc.value = decodeURIComponent(eval(theRef + ".URL"));
                item.form.dTitle.value = decodeURIComponent(eval(theRef + ".title"));
            }

            // bind the event handlers
            function addEvent(elem, evtType, func)
            {
                if (elem.addEventListener)
                {
```

```
            elem.addEventListener(evtType, func, false);
        }
        else if (elem.attachEvent)
        {
            elem.attachEvent("on" + evtType, func);
        }
        else
        {
            elem["on" + evtType] = func;
        }
    }
    addEvent(window, "load", function()
    {
        addEvent(document.getElementById("opener"), "click", fillTopFrame);
        addEvent(document.getElementById("parent"), "click",
            function(evt) {showLoc(document.getElementById("parent"));});
        addEvent(document.getElementById("upper"), "click",
            function(evt) {showLoc(document.getElementById("upper"));});
        addEvent(document.getElementById("this"), "click",
            function(evt) {showLoc(document.getElementById("this"));});
    });
    </script>
</head>
<body>
    Click the "Open URL" button to enter the location of an HTML document to
    display in the upper frame of this window.
    <form>
        <input type="button" id="opener" name="opener" value="Open URL..." />
    </form>
    <hr />
    <form>
        Select a window or frame to view each document property values.
        <p>
            <input type="radio" id="parent" name="whichFrame" value="parent" />
            Parent window
            <input type="radio" name="whichFrame" id="upper"
                value="top.frames[0]" />
            Upper frame
            <input type="radio" name="whichFrame" id="this" value="top.frames[1]" />
            This frame
        </p>
        <table border="2">
            <tr>
                <td align="right">document.URL:</td>
                <td><textarea name="dLoc" rows="3" cols="30" wrap="soft">
                    </textarea>
                </td>
            </tr>
            <tr>
                <td align="right">document.title:</td>
                <td><textarea name="dTitle" rows="3" cols="30" wrap="soft">
                    </textarea>
```

continued

947

LISTING 29-8   *(continued)*

```
            </td>
          </tr>
        </table>
      </form>
    </body>
</html>
```

LISTING 29-9

A Placeholder Page for the URL Example

```html
<!DOCTYPE html>
<html>
    <head>
        <meta http-equiv="content-type" content="text/html;charset=utf-8">
        <title>Opening Placeholder</title>
    </head>
    <body>
        Initial place holder. Experiment with other URLs for this frame (see
        below).
    </body>
</html>
```

Related Items: `location` object; `location.href`, `URLUnencoded` properties

media

Value: String   Read/Write

Compatibility: WinIE5.5+, MacIE-, NN-, Moz-, Safari-, Opera-, Chrome-

The `document.media` property indicates the output medium for which content is formatted. The property actually returns an empty string as of IE7, but the intention appears to be to provide a way to use scripting to set the equivalent of the CSS2 `@media` rule (one of the so-called *at* rules because of the at symbol). This style sheet rule allows browsers to assign separate styles for each type of output device on which the page is rendered (for example, perhaps a different font for a printer versus the screen). In practice, however, this property is not modifiable, at least through IE8.

Related Items: None

mimeType

Value: String   Read-Only

Compatibility: WinIE5+, MacIE-, NN-, Moz-, Safari-, Opera-, Chrome-

Although this property is readable in WinIE5+, its value is not, strictly speaking, a MIME type, at least not in traditional MIME format. Moreover, the results are inconsistent between IE versions 5, 6,

7, and 8. Perhaps this property will be of more use in an XML, rather than an HTML, document environment. In any case, this property in no way exposes supported MIME types in the current browser.

nameProp

Value: String   Read-Only

Compatibility: WinIE6+, MacIE-, NN-, Moz-, Safari-, Opera-, Chrome-

The nameProp property returns a string containing the title of the document, which is the same as document.title. If the document doesn't have a title, nameProp contains an empty string.

Related Item: title property

namespaces[]

Value: Array of namespace objects   Read-Only

Compatibility: WinIE5.5+, MacIE-, NN-, Moz-, Safari-, Opera-, Chrome-

A namespace object can dynamically import an XML-based IE Element Behavior. The namespaces property returns an array of all namespace objects defined in the current document.

Related Items: None

parentWindow

Value: window object reference   Read-Only

Compatibility: WinIE4+, MacIE4+, NN-, Moz-, Safari-, Opera+, Chrome-

The document.parentWindow property returns a reference to the window object containing the current document. The value is the same as any reference to the current window.

Example

To prove that the parentWindow property points to the document's window, you can enter the following statement into the top text field of The Evaluator (see Chapter 4, "JavaScript Essentials"):

```
document.parentWindow == self
```

This expression evaluates to true only if both references are of the same object.

Related Item: window object

plugins[]

Value: Array   Read-Only

Compatibility: WinIE4+, MacIE4+, NN4+, Moz+, Safari+, Opera+, Chrome+

The document.plugins property returns the same array of embed element objects that you get from the document.embeds property. This property has been deprecated in favor of document.embeds.

Related Item: document.embeds property

documentObject.protocol

protocol

Value: String

Read/Write

Compatibility: WinIE4+, MacIE4+, NN-, Moz-, Safari-, Opera-, Chrome-

The IE-specific `document.protocol` property returns the plain-language version of the protocol that was used to access the current document. For example, if the file is accessed from a web server, the property returns `Hypertext Transfer Protocol`. This property differs from the `location.protocol` property, which returns the portion of the URL that includes the often more cryptic protocol abbreviation (for example, `http:`). As a general rule, you want to hide all of this stuff from a web application user.

Example

If you use The Evaluator (Chapter 4, "JavaScript Essentials") to test the `document.protocol` property, you will find that it displays `File Protocol` in the results because you are accessing the listing from a local hard disk or CD-ROM. However, if you upload the Evaluator web page to a web server and access it from there, you will see the expected `Hypertext Transfer Protocol` result.

Related Item: `location.protocol` property

referrer

Value: String

Read-Only

Compatibility: WinIE3+, MacIE3+, NN2+, Moz+, Safari+, Opera+, Chrome+

When a link from one document leads to another, the second document can, under JavaScript control, reveal the URL of the document containing the link. The `document.referrer` property contains a string of that URL. This feature can be a useful tool for customizing the content of pages based on the previous location the user was visiting within your site. A referrer contains a value only when the user reaches the current page through a link. Any other method of navigation (such as through the history, bookmarks, or by manually entering a URL) sets this property to an empty string.

Caution

The `document.referrer` **property usually returns an empty string unless the files are retrieved from a web server.** ∎

Example

This demonstration requires two documents (and you'll need to access the documents from a web server). The first document, in Listing 29-10, simply contains one line of text as a link to the second document. In the second document, shown in Listing 29-11, a script verifies the document from which the user came through a link. If the script knows about that link, it displays a message relevant to the experience the user had at the first document. Also try opening Listing 29-11 in a new browser window from the Open File command in the File menu to see how the script won't recognize the referrer.

LISTING 29-10

An Example Referrer Page

```
<!DOCTYPE html>
<html>
   <head>
      <meta http-equiv="content-type" content="text/html;charset=utf-8">
      <title>document.referrer Property 1</title>
   </head>
   <body>
      <h1><a href="jsb29-11.html">Visit my sister document</a></h1>
   </body>
</html>
```

LISTING 29-11

Determining the Referrer when a Page Is Visited Through a Link

```
<!DOCTYPE html>
<html>
   <head>
      <meta http-equiv="content-type" content="text/html;charset=utf-8">
      <title>document.referrer Property 2</title>
   </head>
   <body>
      <h1>
         <script type="text/javascript">
            alert(document.referrer.length + "    :    " + document.referrer);
               if (document.referrer.length > 0 &&
                  document.referrer.indexOf("jsb29-10.html") != -1)
               {
                  document.write("How is my brother document?");
               }
               else
               {
                  document.write("Hello, and thank you for stopping by.");
               }
         </script>
      </h1>
   </body>
</html>
```

Related Item: link object

scripts[]

Value: Array   Read-Only

Compatibility: WinIE4+, MacIE4+, NN-, Moz-, Safari+, Opera+, Chrome+

Originally IE-specific, the document.scripts property returns an array of all script element objects in the current document. You can reference an individual script element object to read not only the properties it shares with all HTML element objects (see Chapter 26, "Generic HTML Element Objects"), but also script-specific properties, such as defer, src, and htmlFor. The actual scripting is accessible through either the innerText or text properties for any script element object.

Although the document.scripts array is read-only, many properties of individual script element objects are modifiable. Adding or removing script elements impacts the length of the document.scripts array. Don't forget, too, that if your scripts need to access a specific script element object, you can assign an id attribute to it and reference the element directly.

This property is the same as the W3C browser expression document .getElementsByTagName("script"), which returns an array of the same objects.

Example

You can experiment with the document.scripts array in The Evaluator (Chapter 4, "JavaScript Essentials"). For example, you can see that only one script element object is in the Evaluator page if you enter the following statement into the top text field:

```
document.scripts.length
```

If you want to view all of the properties of that lone script element object, enter the following statement into the bottom text field:

```
document.scripts[0]
```

Among the properties are both innerText and text. If you assign an empty string to either property, the scripts are wiped out from the object model, but not from the browser. The scripts disappear because after they were loaded, they were cached outside of the object model. Therefore, if you enter the following statement into the top field:

```
document.scripts[0].text = ""
```

the script contents are gone from the object model, yet subsequent clicks of the Evaluate and List Properties buttons (which invoke functions of the script element object) still work.

Related Item: script element object (Chapter 40, "HTML Directive Objects")

security

Value: String   Read-Only

Compatibility: WinIE5.5+, MacIE-, NN-, Moz-, Safari-, Opera-, Chrome-

The security property reveals information about a security certificate, if one is associated with the current document.

Related Items: none

selection

Value: Object   Read-Only

Compatibility: WinIE4+, MacIE4+, NN-, Moz-, Safari-, Opera+, Chrome-

The document.selection property returns a selection object whose content is represented in the browser window as a body text selection. That selection can be explicitly performed by the user (by clicking and dragging across some text) or created under script control through the WinIE `TextRange` object (see Chapter 33). Because script action on a selection (for example, finding the next instance of selected text) is performed through the `TextRange` object, converting a selection to a `TextRange` object using the `document.selection.createRange()` method is common practice. See the `selection` object in Chapter 33 for more details.

Be aware that you cannot script interaction with text selections through user interface elements, such as buttons. Clicking a button gives focus to the button and deselects the selection. Use other events, such as `document.onmouseup` to trigger actions on a selection.

Example

Refer to Listings 26-36 and 26-44 in Chapter 26 to see the `document.selection` property in action for script-controlled copying and pasting (WinIE only).

Related Items: `selection`, `TextRange` objects

strictErrorChecking

Value: String   Read-Only

Compatibility: WinIE-, MacIE-, NN-, Moz1.8+, Safari-, Opera-, Chrome-

The `strictErrorChecking` property reveals the error-checking mode for the document. More specifically, if the property is set to `true` (the default), exceptions and errors related to DOM operations are reported. Otherwise, DOM-related exceptions may not be thrown, and errors may not be reported.

styleSheets[]

Value: Array   Read-Only

Compatibility: WinIE4+, MacIE4+, NN6+, Moz+, Safari+, Opera+, Chrome+

The `document.styleSheets` array consists of references to all `style` element objects in the document. Not included in this array are style sheets that are assigned to elements by way of the `style` attribute inside a tag, or linked in through `link` elements. See Chapter 38 for details about the `styleSheet` object.

Related Item: `styleSheet` object (see Chapter 38, "Style Sheet and Style Objects")

title

Value: String   Read-Only and Read/Write

Compatibility: WinIE3+, MacIE3+, NN2+, Moz+, Safari+, Opera+, Chrome+

A document's title is the text that appears between the `<title>...</title>` tag pair in an HTML document's `head` portion. The title usually appears in the title bar of the browser window in a single-frame presentation, or in a tabbed pane within a multi-paned browser window. Only the title of the topmost framesetting document appears as the title of a multiframe window. Even so, the `title` property for an individual document within a frame is available through scripting. For example, if two frames are available (`UpperFrame` and `LowerFrame`), a script in the document occupying the `LowerFrame` frame can reference the `title` property of the other frame's document, such as this:

```
parent.UpperFrame.document.title
```

The document.title property is a holdover from the original document object model. HTML elements in recent browsers have an entirely different application of the title property (see Chapter 26). In modern browsers (IE4+/W3C/Moz/Safari/Opera/Chrome), you should address the document's title by way of the title element object directly.

Related Items: history object

URL

(See location)

URLUnencoded

Value: String   Read-Only

Compatibility: WinIE5.5+, MacIE-, NN-, Moz+, Safari+, Opera+, Chrome+

The document.URL property returns a URL-encoded string, meaning that non-alphanumeric characters in the URL are converted to URL-friendly characters (for example, a space becomes %20). You can always use the decodeURI() function on the value returned by the document.URL property, although in IE the URLUnencoded property does that for you. If there are no URL-encoded characters in the URL, then both properties return identical strings.

Related Items: document.URL property

vlinkColor

(See alinkColor)

width

(See height)

xmlEncoding
xmlStandalone
xmlVersion

Value: String   Read-Only

Compatibility: WinIE-, MacIE-, NN-, Moz1.8+, Safari+, Opera-, Chrome+

These three properties reveal information about the document as it pertains to XML. More specifically, they convey the XML encoding of the document, whether or not the document is a standalone XML document, and the XML version number of the document, respectively. If any of the property values cannot be determined, their values remain null.

Methods

captureEvents(*eventTypeList*)

Returns: Nothing

Compatibility: WinIE-, MacIE-, NN4+, Moz-, Safari-, Opera-, Chrome-

In Navigator 4 only, the natural propagation of an event is downward from the window object, through the document object, and eventually reaching its target. For example, if you click a button, the click event first reaches the window object; then it goes to the document object; if the button is defined within a layer, the event also filters through that layer; eventually (in a split second) the event reaches the button, where an onclick event handler is ready to act on that click.

Event capture with different syntax has been standardized in the W3C DOM and is implemented in W3C browsers, such as Firefox and Camino (Mozilla). More specifically, the W3C event capture model introduces the concept of an event listener, which enables you to bind an event handler function to an event. See the addEventListener() method in Chapter 26 for the W3C counterpart to the NN4 captureEvents() method. Also, see Chapter 32 for more details on the combination of event capture and event bubbling in the W3C DOM.

clear()

Returns: Nothing

Compatibility: WinIE3+, MacIE3+, NN2+, Moz+, Safari+, Opera+, Chrome+

Ever since NN2, the document.clear() method was intended to clear the current document from the browser window. This method is quite impractical, because you typically need some further scripts to execute after you clear the document, but if the scripts are gone, nothing else happens.

In practice, the document.clear() method never did what it was supposed to do (and in earlier browsers easily caused browser crashes). We strongly recommend against using document.clear(), even in preparation for generating a new page's content with document.write(). The document.write() method clears the original document from the window before adding new content. If you truly want to empty a window or frame, then use document.write() to write a blank HTML document or to load an empty HTML document from the server.

Related Items: document.close(), document.write(), document.writeln() methods

close()

Returns: Nothing

Compatibility: WinIE3+, MacIE3+, NN2+, Moz+, Safari+, Opera+, Chrome+

Whenever a layout stream is opened to a window through the document.open() method or through either of the document writing methods (which also open the layout stream), you must close the stream after the document is written. This causes the Layout:Complete and Done messages to appear in the status line (although you may experience some bugs in the status message on some platforms). The document-closing step is very important to prepare the window for the next potential round of replenishment with new script-assembled HTML. If you don't close the document, subsequent writing is appended to the bottom of the document.

Some or all of the data specified for the window won't display properly until you invoke the document.close() method, especially when images are being drawn as part of the document stream. A common symptom is the momentary appearance and then disappearance of the document parts. If you see such behavior, look for a missing document.close() method after the last document.write() method.

Fixing the Sticky Wait Cursor

From time to time, various browsers fail to restore the cursor to normal after `document.write()` and `document.close()` (and some other content-modifying scripts). The cursor stubbornly remains in the wait mode, or the progress bar keeps spinning when, in truth, all processing has been completed. Albeit ugly, one workaround that we have found effective is to force an extra `document.close()` via a `javascript:` pseudo-URL (just adding another `document.close()` to your script doesn't do the trick). For use within a frameset, the `javascript:` URL must be directed to the top of the frameset hierarchy, whereas the `document.close()` method is aimed at the frame that had its content changed. For example, if the change is made to a frame named `content`, create a function, such as the following:

```
function recloseDoc() {
    top.location.href =
        "javascript:void (parent.content.document.close())";
}
```

If you place this function in the framesetting document, scripts that modify the content frame can invoke this script after any operation that prevents the normal cursor from appearing.

Example

Before you experiment with the `document.close()` method, be sure you understand the `document.write()` method described later in this chapter. After that, make a separate set of the three documents for that method's example (Listings 29-14 through 29-16 in a different directory or folder). In the `takePulse()` function listing, comment out the `document.close()` statement, as shown here:

```
msg += "<p>Make it a great day!</body></html>";
parent.frames[1].document.write(msg);
//parent.frames[1].document.close();
```

Now try the pages on your browser. You see that each click of the upper button appends text to the bottom frame, without first removing the previous text. The reason is that the previous layout stream was never closed. The document thinks that you're still writing to it. Also, without properly closing the stream, the last line of text may not appear in the most recently written batch.

Related Items: `document.open()`, `document.clear()`, `document.write()`, `document.writeln()` methods

createAttribute("*attributeName*")

Returns: Attribute object reference

Compatibility: WinIE6+, MacIE5+, NN6+, Moz+, Safari+, Opera+, Chrome+

The `document.createAttribute()` method generates an attribute node object (formally known as an `Attr` object in W3C DOM terminology) and returns a reference to the newly created object. Invoking the method assigns only the name of the attribute, so it is up to your script to assign a value to the object's `nodeValue` property and then plug the new attribute into an existing element through that element's `setAttributeNode()` method (described in Chapter 26). The following sequence generates an attribute that becomes an attribute of a `table` element:

```
var newAttr = document.createAttribute("width");
newAttr.nodeValue = "80%";
document.getElementById("myTable").setAttributeNode(newAttr);
```

Attributes do not always have to be attributes known to the HTML standard, because the method also works for XML elements, which have custom attributes.

Example

To create an attribute and inspect its properties, enter the following text into the top text box of The Evaluator (Chapter 4, "JavaScript Essentials"):

```
a = document.createAttribute("author")
```

Now enter a into the bottom text box to inspect the properties of an `Attr` object.

Related Items: `setAttributeNode()` method (see Chapter 26, "Generic HTML Element Objects")

createCDATASection("*data*")

Returns: CDATA section object reference

Compatibility: WinIE-, MacIE5, NN7+, Moz+, Safari+, Opera+, Chrome+

The `document.createCDATASection()` method generates a CDATA section node for whatever string you pass as the parameter. The value of the new node becomes the string that you pass.

createComment("*commentText*")

Returns: Comment object reference

Compatibility: WinIE6+, MacIE5+, NN6+, Moz+, Safari+, Opera+, Chrome+

The `document.createComment()` method creates an instance of a comment node. Upon creation, the node is in memory and available to be inserted into the document via any node's `appendChild()` or `insertBefore()` method.

Related Items: `appendChild()`, `insertBefore()` methods

createDocumentFragment()

Returns: Document fragment object reference

Compatibility: WinIE6+, MacIE5+, NN6+, Moz+, Safari+, Opera+, Chrome+

The `document.createDocumentFragment()` method creates an instance of an empty document fragment node. This node serves as a holder that can be used to assemble a sequence of nodes in memory. After creating and assembling nodes into the document fragment, the entire fragment can be inserted into the document tree.

A document fragment is particularly helpful when your scripts assemble an arbitrary sequence of element and text nodes. By providing a parent node for all content within, the fragment node supplies the necessary parent node context for W3C DOM node methods, such as `appendChild()`, during the content assembly process. If you then append or insert the document fragment node to an element in the rendered document tree, the fragment wrapper disappears, leaving just its content in the desired location in the document. Therefore, a typical usage pattern for a document fragment is to begin by creating an empty fragment node (through the `createDocumentFragment()` method), populate it at will with newly created element or text nodes or both, and then use the appropriate node method on a document tree's element to append, insert, or replace, using the fragment node as the source material.

Related Items: None

createElement("tagName")
createElementNS("namespaceURI", "*tagName*")

Returns: Element object reference

Compatibility: WinIE4+, MacIE4+, NN6+, Moz+, Safari+, Opera+, Chrome+

The `document.createElement()` and `document.createElementNS()` methods generate an element object for whatever HTML (or XML) tag name you pass as the parameter. An object created in this manner is not officially part of the current document node tree because it has not yet been placed into the document. But these methods are the way you begin assembling an element object that eventually gets inserted into the document. The `createElementNS()` method is identical to `createElement()`, except that the latter method accepts an extra parameter that you use to pass a namespace URI for the element. Additionally, the tag name that you specify when creating an element via `createElementNS()` must be a qualified name. Note, however, that `createElementNS()` is not supported in Internet Explorer through version 8.

The returned value is a reference to the object. Properties of that object include all properties (set to default values) that the browser's object model defines for that element object. Your scripts can then address the object through this reference to set the object's properties. Typically, you do this before the object is inserted into the document, especially because otherwise read-only properties can be modified before the element is inserted into the document.

After the object is inserted into the document, the original reference (for example, a global variable used to store the value returned from the `createElement()` method) still points to the object, even while it is in the document and being displayed for the user. To demonstrate this effect, consider the following statements that create a simple paragraph element containing a text node:

```
var newText = document.createTextNode("Four score and seven years ago...");
var newElem = document.createElement("p");
newElem.id = "newestP";
newElem.appendChild(newText);
document.body.appendChild(newElem);
```

At this point, the new paragraph is visible in the document. But you can now modify, for example, the style of the paragraph by addressing either the element in the document object model or the variable that holds the reference to the object you created:

```
newElem.style.fontSize = "20pt";
```

or

```
document.getElementById("newestP").style.fontSize = "20pt";
```

The two references are inextricably connected and always point to the exact same object. Therefore, if you want to use a script to generate a series of similar elements (for example, a bunch of li list item elements), then you can use `createElement()` to make the first one and set all properties that the items have in common. Then use `cloneNode()` to make a new copy, which you can then treat as a separate element (and probably assign unique IDs to each element).

When scripting in the W3C DOM environment, you may rely on `document.createElement()` frequently to generate new content for a page or portion thereof (unless you prefer to use the convenience `innerHTML` property to add content in the form of strings of HTML). In a strict W3C DOM environment, creating new elements is not a matter of assembling HTML strings, but rather creating genuine element (and text node) objects.

Example

Chapter 26, "Generic HTML Element Objects," contains numerous examples of the `document` `.createElement()` method in concert with methods that add or replace content to a document. See Listings 26-10, 26-21, 26-22, 26-28, 26-29, and 26-31.

Related Item: `document.createTextNode()` method

createEvent("*eventType*")

Returns: Event object reference

Compatibility: WinIE-, MacIE-, NN6+, Moz+, Safari+, Opera+, Chrome+

The `document.createEvent()` method creates an instance of a W3C DOM `Event` object of the specified event category. Upon creation, the generic event must be initialized as a particular event type, and any other relevant properties set for the event. After successfully initializing the event, you can fire it through a call to the `dispatchEvent()` method.

Event types recognized by Mozilla are `KeyEvents`, `MouseEvents`, `MutationEvents`, and `UIEvents`. Beginning with Mozilla 1.7.5, the following additional types may also be used: `Event`, `KeyboardEvent`, `MouseEvent`, `MutationEvent`, `MutationNameEvent`, `TextEvent`, `UIEvent`. The process of initializing each of these event types requires its own series of parameters in the associated `initEvent()` method. See Chapter 32 for more details.

Example

Following is an example of how you might create an event, initialize it to a specific event type, and send it to a given element:

```
var evt = document.createEvent("MouseEvents");
evt.initEvent("mouseup", true, true);
document.getElementById("myButton").dispatchEvent(evt);
```

Related Items: `createEventObject()` method; W3C DOM event object (see Chapter 32, "Event Objects")

createEventObject([*eventObject*])

Returns: `event` object

Compatibility: WinIE5.5+, MacIE-, NN-, Moz-, Safari-, Opera-, Chrome-

The IE-specific `createEventObject()` method creates an `event` object, which can then be passed as a parameter to the `fireEvent()` method of any element object. The `event` object created by this event is just like an `event` object created by a user or system action.

An optional parameter enables you to base the new event on an existing event object. In other words, the properties of the newly created event object pick up all the properties of the event object passed as a parameter, which then enables you to modify properties of your choice. If you provide no parameter to the method, then you must fill the essential properties manually. For more about the properties of an event object, see Chapter 32.

Example

See the discussion of the fireEvent() method in Chapter 26 for an example of the sequence to follow when creating an event to fire on an element.

Related Items: createEvent() method; fireEvent() method (see Chapter 26); event object (see Chapter 32)

createNSResolver(*nodeResolver*)

Returns: XPath namespace resolver object reference

Compatibility: WinIE-, MacIE-, NN7+, Moz+, Safari+, Opera+, Chrome+

The createNSResolver() method is used in the context of XPath to alter a node so that it can resolve namespaces. This is necessary as part of the evaluation of an XPath expression. The only parameter is the node that is to serve as the basis for the namespace resolver.

Related Item: evaluate() method

createRange()

Returns: Range object reference

Compatibility: WinIE-, MacIE-, NN6+, Moz+, Safari+, Opera+, Chrome+

The document.createRange() method creates an empty W3C DOM Range object with the boundary points of the range collapsed to the point before the first character of the rendered body text.

Related Item: Range object

createStyleSheet(["*URL*"[, *index*]])

Returns: styleSheet object reference

Compatibility: WinIE4+, MacIE4, NN-, Moz-, Safari-, Opera-, Chrome-

The IE-specific createStyleSheet() method creates a styleSheet object, a type of object that includes style element objects as well as style sheets that are imported into a document through the link element. Thus, you can dynamically load an external style sheet even after a page has loaded.

Unlike the other create methods entering W3C DOM usage, the createStyleSheet() method not only creates the style sheet, but it inserts the object into the document object model immediately. Thus, any style sheet rules that belong (or are assigned to) that object take effect on the page right away. If you'd rather create a style sheet and delay its deployment, you should use the createElement() method and element object assembly techniques.

If you don't specify any parameters to the method in WinIE, an empty styleSheet object is created. It is assumed that you will then use styleSheet object methods, such as addRule() to add the details to the style sheet. To link in an external style sheet file, assign the file's URL to the first parameter of the method. The newly imported style sheet is appended to the end of the `document.styleSheets` array of `styleSheet` objects. An optional second parameter lets you specify precisely where in the sequence of style sheet elements the newly linked style sheet should be inserted. A style sheet rule for any given selector is overridden by a style sheet for the same selector that appears later in the sequence of style sheets in a document.

Example

Listing 29-12 demonstrates adding an internal and external style sheet to a document. For the internal addition, the `addStyle1()` function invokes `document.createStyleSheet()` and adds a rule governing the p elements of the page. In the `addStyle2()` function, an external file is loaded. That file contains the following two style rules:

```
h2 {font-size:20pt; color:blue;}
p  {color:blue;}
```

Notice that by specifying a position of zero for the imported style sheet, the addition of the internal style sheet always comes afterward in `styleSheet` object sequence. Thus, except when you deploy only the external style sheet, the red text color of the p elements override the blue color of the external style sheet. If you remove the second parameter of the `createStyleSheet()` method in `addStyle2()`, the external style sheet is appended to the end of the list. If it is the last style sheet to be added, the blue color prevails. Repeatedly clicking the buttons in this example continues to add the style sheets to the document.

LISTING 29-12

Creating and Applying Style Sheets

```html
<!DOCTYPE html>
<html>
    <head>
        <meta http-equiv="content-type" content="text/html;charset=utf-8">
        <title>document.createStyleSheet() Method</title>
        <script type="text/javascript">
            function addStyle1()
            {
                var newStyle = document.createStyleSheet();
                newStyle.addRule("P", "font-size:16pt; color:red");
            }

            function addStyle2()
            {
                var newStyle = document.createStyleSheet("jsb29-12.css",0);
            }

            // bind the event handlers
            function addEvent(elem, evtType, func)
            {
                if (elem.addEventListener)
                {
                    elem.addEventListener(evtType, func, false);
```

continued

LISTING 29-12 *(continued)*

```
        }
        else if (elem.attachEvent)
        {
            elem.attachEvent("on" + evtType, func);
        }
        else
        {
            elem["on" + evtType] = func;
        }
    }
    addEvent(window, "load", function()
    {
        addEvent(document.getElementById("addint"), "click", addStyle1);
        addEvent(document.getElementById("addext"), "click", addStyle2);
    });
    </script>
</head>
<body>
    <h1>document.createStyleSheet() Method</h1>
    <hr />
    <form>
        <input type="button" id="addint" value="Add Internal" /> 
        <input type="button" id="addext" value="Add External" />
    </form>
    <h2>Section 1</h2>
    <p>Lorem ipsum dolor sit amet, consectetaur adipisicing elit, sed do
        eiusmod tempor incididunt ut labore et dolore magna aliqua. Ut enim
        adminim veniam, quis nostrud exercitation ullamco laboris nisi ut
        aliquip ex ea commodo consequat.</p>
    <h2>Section 2</h2>
    <p>Duis aute irure dolor in reprehenderit involuptate velit esse cillum
        dolore eu fugiat nulla pariatur. Excepteur sint occaecat cupidatat non
        proident, sunt in culpa qui officia deseruntmollit anim id est
        laborum.</p>
</body>
</html>
```

Related Item: styleSheet object (see Chapter 38, "Style Sheet and Style Objects")

createTextNode("*text*")

Returns: Object

Compatibility: WinIE5+, MacIE5+, NN6+, Moz+, Safari+, Opera+, Chrome+

A text node is a W3C DOM object that contains body text without any HTML (or XML) tags, but is usually contained by (meaning, is a child of) an HTML (or XML) element. Without the IE innerText convenience property for modifying the text of an element, the W3C DOM relies on the node hierarchy of a document (Mozilla exceeds the W3C DOM by providing an innerHTML property, which you can use to replace text in an element). To insert or replace text inside an HTML element in the W3C DOM way, you create the text node and then use methods of the parent element (for example, `appendChild()`, `insertBefore()`, and `replaceChild()`, all described in Chapter 26) to modify the document's content. To generate a fresh text node, use `document.createTextNode()`.

The sole parameter of the `createTextNode()` method is a string whose text becomes the `nodeValue` of the text node object returned by the method. You can also create an empty text node (passing an empty string) and assign a string to the `nodeValue` of the object later. As soon as the text node is present in the document object model, scripts can simply change the `nodeValue` property to modify the text of an existing element. For more details on the role of text nodes in the W3C DOM, see Chapter 25, "Document Object Model Essentials."

Example

Although Chapters 25 and 26 (Listing 26-21, for instance) provide numerous examples of the `createTextNode()` method at work, using The Evaluator is instructive to see just what the method generates in IE5+/W3C. You can use one of the built-in global variables of The Evaluator to hold a reference to a newly generated text node by entering the following statement into the top text field:

```
a = document.createTextNode("Hello")
```

The Results box shows that an object was created. Now, look at the properties of the object by entering a into the bottom text field. The precise listings of properties varies between IE5+ and W3C browsers, but the W3C DOM properties that they share in common indicate that the object is a node type 3 with a node name of #text. No parents, children, or siblings exist yet because the object created here is not part of the document hierarchy tree until it is explicitly added to the document.

To see how insertion works, enter the following statement into the top text field to append the text node to the `myP` paragraph:

```
document.getElementById("myP").appendChild(a)
```

The word *Hello* appears at the end of the simple paragraph lower on the page. Now you can modify the text of that node either through the reference, from the point of view of the containing p element, or through the global variable reference for the newly created node:

```
document.getElementById("myP").lastChild.nodeValue = "Howdy"
```

or

```
a.nodeValue = "Howdy"
```

Related Item: `document.createElement()` method

createTreeWalker(*rootNode, whatToShow, filterFunction, entityRefExpansion*)

Returns: TreeWalker object reference

Compatibility: WinIE-, MacIE-, NN7+, Moz1.4+, Safari+, Opera+, Chrome+

The `document.createTreeWalker()` method creates an instance of a TreeWalker object that can be used to navigate the document tree. The first parameter to the method indicates the node in the document that is to serve as the root node of the tree. The second parameter is an integer constant that specifies one of several built-in filters for selecting nodes to be included in the tree. Following are the possible acceptable values for this parameter:

NodeFilter.SHOW_ALL	NodeFilter.SHOW_ATTRIBUTE
NodeFilter.SHOW_CDATA_SECTION	NodeFilter.SHOW_COMMENT
NodeFilter.SHOW_DOCUMENT	NodeFilter.SHOW_DOCUMENT_FRAGMENT
NodeFilter.SHOW_DOCUMENT_TYPE	NodeFilter.SHOW_ELEMENT
NodeFilter.SHOW_ENTITY	NodeFilter.SHOW_ENTITY_REFERENCE
NodeFilter.SHOW_NOTATION	NodeFilter.SHOW_PROCESSING_INSTRUCTION
NodeFilter.SHOW_TEXT	

The third parameter to the createNodeIterator() method is a reference to a filter function that can filter nodes even further than the whatToShow parameter. This function must accept a single node and return an integer value based upon one of the following constants: Node-Filter.FILTER_ACCEPT, NodeFilter.FILTER_REJECT, or NodeFilter.FILTER_SKIP. The idea is that you code the function to perform a test on each node and return an indicator value that lets the node iterator know whether or not to include the node in the tree. Your function doesn't loop through nodes. The TreeWalker object mechanism repetitively invokes the function as needed to look for the presence of whatever characteristic you wish to use as a filter.

The final parameter to the method is a Boolean value that determines whether or not the content of entity reference nodes should be treated as hierarchical nodes. This parameter applies primarily to XML documents.

Related Items: TreeWalker object

elementFromPoint(*x, y*)

Returns: Element object reference

Compatibility: WinIE4+, MacIE4+, NN-, Moz+, Safari+, Opera+, Chrome+

Originally IE-specific, the elementFromPoint() method returns a reference to whatever element object occupies the point whose integer coordinates are supplied as parameters to the method. The coordinate plane is that of the document, whose top-left corner is at point 0,0. This coordinate plane can be very helpful in interactive designs that need to calculate collision detection between positioned objects or mouse events.

When more than one object occupies the same point (for example, one element is positioned atop another), the element with the highest z-index value is returned. A positioned element always wins when placed atop a normal body-level element. And if multiple overlapping positioned elements have the same z-index value (or none by default), the element that comes last in the source code order is returned for the coordinate that they share in common.

Example

Listing 29-13 is a document that contains many different types of elements, each of which has an ID attribute assigned to it. The onmouseover event handler for the document object invokes a function that finds out which element the cursor is over when the event fires. Note that the event coordinates are `event.clientX` and `event.clientY`, which use the same coordinate plane as the page for their point of reference. As you roll the mouse over every element, its ID appears on the page. Some elements, such as `br` and `tr`, occupy no space in the document, so you cannot get their IDs to appear. On a typical browser screen size, a positioned element rests atop one of the paragraph elements so that you can see how the `elementFromPoint()` method handles overlapping elements. If you scroll the page, the coordinates for the event and the page's elements stay in sync.

LISTING 29-13

Tracking the Mouse as It Passes over Elements

```
<!DOCTYPE html>
<html>
    <head>
        <meta http-equiv="content-type" content="text/html;charset=utf-8">
        <title>document.elementFromPoint() Method</title>
        <script type="text/javascript">
            function replaceHTML(elem, text)
            {
                while(elem.firstChild)
                {
                    elem.removeChild(elem.firstChild);
                }
                elem.appendChild(document.createTextNode(text));
            }

            function showElemUnderneath(evt)
            {
                var elem
                elem = document.elementFromPoint(evt.clientX, evt.clientY);
                replaceHTML(document.getElementById("mySpan"), elem.id);
            }

        </script>
    </head>
    <body id="myBody" onmousemove="showElemUnderneath(event)">
        <h1 id="header">document.elementFromPoint() Method</h1>
        <hr id="myHR" />
        <p id="instructions">Roll the mouse around the page. The coordinates
            of the mouse pointer are currently atop an element
            whose ID is: "<span id='mySpan' style='font-weight:bold;'></span>".</p>
        <br id="myBR" />
        <form id="myForm">
            <input id="myButton" type="button" value="Sample Button" /> 
        </form>
        <table border="1" id="myTable">
            <tr id="tr1">
                <td id="td_A1">Cell A1</td>
                <td id="td_B1">Cell B1</td>
            </tr>
```

continued

LISTING 29-13   *(continued)*

```
        <tr id="tr2">
            <td id="td_A2">Cell A2</td>
            <td id="td_B2">Cell B2</td>
        </tr>
    </table>
    <h2 id="sec1">Section 1</h2>
    <p id="p1">Lorem ipsum dolor sit amet, consectetaur adipisicing elit, sed
        do eiusmod tempor incididunt ut labore et dolore magna aliqua. Ut enim
        adminim veniam, quis nostrud exercitation ullamco laboris nisi ut
        aliquip ex ea commodo consequat.</p>
    <h2 id="sec2">Section 2</h2>
    <p id="p2">Duis aute irure dolor in reprehenderit involuptate velit esse
        cillum dolore eu fugiat nulla pariatur. Excepteur sint occaecat
        cupidatat non proident, sunt in culpa qui officia deseruntmollit anim
        id est laborum.</p>
    <div id="myDIV"
        style="position:absolute; top:340px; left:300px; background-color:yellow;">
        Here is a positioned element.
    </div>
    </body>
</html>
```

Related Items: event.clientX, event.clientY properties; positioned objects (see Chapter 43, "Positioned Objects")

evaluate("expression", contextNode, resolver, type, result)

Returns: XPath result object reference

Compatibility: WinIE-, MacIE-, NN7+, Moz+, Safari+, Opera+, Chrome+

The document.evaluate() method evaluates an XPath expression and returns an XPath result object (XPathResult). The most important parameter to this method is the first one, which contains the actual XPath expression as a string. The second parameter is the context node to which the expression applies, whereas the third parameter is the namespace resolver (see the createNSResolver() method). The resolver parameter can be specified as null as long as there aren't any namespace prefixes used within the expression.

The type parameter determines the type of the result of the expression and is specified as one of the XPath result types, such as 0 for any type, 1 for number, 2 for string, and so forth. Finally, a reusable result object can be specified in the last parameter, which will then be modified and returned from the method as the result of the expression.

Related Item: createNSResolver() method

execCommand("commandName"[, UIFlag] [, param])

Returns: Boolean

Compatibility: WinIE4+, MacIE-, NN7.1+, Moz1.3+, Safari1.3+, Opera+, Chrome+

The execCommand() method is the JavaScript gateway to a set of commands that is outside of the methods defined for objects in the object model. A series of related methods (queryCommandEnable() and others) also facilitate management of these commands.

The syntax for the execCommand() method requires at least one parameter, a string version of the command name. Command names are not case-sensitive. An optional second parameter is a Boolean flag to instruct the command to display any user interface artifacts that may be associated with the command. The default is false. For the third parameter, some commands require that an attribute value be passed for the command to work. For example, to set the font size of a text range, the syntax is

```
myRange.execCommand("FontSize", true, 5);
```

The execCommand() method returns Boolean true if the command is successful; false if not successful. Some commands can return values (for example, finding out the font name of a selection), but those are accessed through the queryCommandValue() method.

In Internet Explorer, most of these commands operate on body text selections that are TextRange objects. As described in Chapter 33, a TextRange object must be created under script control. But a TextRange object can be created in response to a user selecting some text in the document. Because a TextRange object is independent of the element hierarchy (indeed, a TextRange can spread across multiple nodes), it cannot respond to style sheet specifications. Thus, many of the commands that can operate on a TextRange object have to do with formatting or modifying the text. For a list of commands that work exclusively on TextRange objects, see the TextRange.execCommand() method in Chapter 33.

Although many of the commands intended for the TextRange also work when invoked from the document object, in this section the focus is on those commands that have scope over the entire document. Table 29-2 lists those few commands that work with the document. Also listed are many commands that work exclusively on text selections in the document, whether the selections are made manually by the user or with the help of the TextRange object (see Chapter 33).

Mozilla 1.4 and Safari 1.3 added a feature that allows scripts to turn an iframe element's document object into an HTML editable document. Here is an example of how to center the selected text in an iframe with an ID of msg:

```
document.getElementById("msg").contentDocument.execCommand("JustifyCenter");
```

Note that the contentDocument property is used to access the iframe as a document. Visit http://www.mozilla.org/editor for additional details and examples of the document.execCommand() method.

Example

You can find many examples of the execCommand() method for the TextRange object in Chapter 33. But you can try out the document-specific commands in The Evaluator (see Chapter 4) in Internet Explorer if you like. Try each of the following statements in the top text box and click the Evaluate button:

```
document.execCommand("Refresh")
document.execCommand("SelectAll")
document.execCommand("Unselect")
```

TABLE 29-2

document.execCommand() Commands

Command	Parameter	Description
BackColor	Color String	Encloses the current selection with a font element whose style attribute sets the background-color style to the parameter value.
CreateBookmark	Anchor String	Encloses the current selection (or text range) with an anchor element whose name attribute is set to the parameter value.
CreateLink	URL String	Encloses the current selection with an a element whose href attribute is set to the parameter value.
decreaseFontSize	none	Encloses the current selection with a small element.
Delete	none	Deletes the current selection from the document.
FontName	Font Face(s)	Encloses the current selection with a font element whose face attribute is set to the parameter value.
FontSize	Size String	Encloses the current selection with a font element whose size attribute is set to the parameter value.
foreColor	Color String	Encloses the current selection with a font element whose color attribute is set to the parameter value.
FormatBlock	Block Element String	Encloses the current selection with the specified block element. IE only supports the h1 through h6, address and pre block elements. Other browsers support all block elements.
increaseFontSize	none	Encloses the current selection with a big element.
Indent	None	Indents the current selection.
InsertHorizontalRule	Id String	Encloses the current selection in an hr element, whose id attribute is set to the parameter value.
InsertImage	Id String	Encloses the current selection in an img element, whose id attribute is set to the parameter value.
InsertParagraph	Id String	Encloses the current selection in an p element, whose id attribute is set to the parameter value.
JustifyCenter	None	Centers the current selection.
JustifyFull	None	Full-justifies the current selection.
JustifyLeft	None	Left-justifies the current selection.
JustifyRight	None	Right-justifies the current selection.
Outdent	None	Outdents the current selection.

TABLE 29-2	*(continued)*	
Command	**Parameter**	**Description**
Refresh	None	Reloads the page.
RemoveFormat	None	Removes formatting for the current selection.
SelectAll	None	Selects all text of the document.
UnBookmark	None	Removes anchor tags that surround the current selection.
Unlink	None	Removes link tags that surround the current selection.
Unselect	None	Deselects the current selection anywhere in the document.

All methods return `true` in the Results box.

Because any way you can evaluate a statement in The Evaluator forces a body selection to become de-selected before the evaluation takes place, you can't experiment this way with the selection-oriented commands.

Related Items: `queryCommandEnabled()`, `queryCommandIndterm()`, `queryCommand-State()`, `queryCommandSupported()`, `queryCommandText()`, `queryCommandValue()` methods

getElementById("*elementID*")

Returns: Element object reference

Compatibility: WinIE5+, MacIE5+, NN6+, Moz+, Safari+, Opera+, Chrome+

The `document.getElementById()` method is the W3C DOM syntax for retrieving a reference to any element in a document that has a unique identifier assigned to its `id` attribute. If the document contains more than one instance of an ID, the method returns a reference to the first element in source code order with that ID. Because this method is such an important avenue to writing references to objects that are to be modified under script control, you can see how important it is to assign unique IDs to elements.

This method's name is quite a finger twister for scripters, especially compared to the IE4+ convention of letting a reference to any element begin simply with the object's ID. However, the `getElementById()` method is the modern way of acquiring an element's reference for W3C DOM-compatible browsers, including IE. When you type this method, be sure to use a lowercase d as the last character of the method name.

Unlike some other element-oriented methods (for example, `getElementsByTagName()`), which can be invoked on any element in a document, the `getElementById()` method works exclusively with the `document` object.

Example

You can find many examples of this method in use throughout this book, but you can take a closer look at how it works by experimenting in The Evaluator (Chapter 4, "JavaScript Essentials"). A number of elements in The Evaluator have IDs assigned to them, so that you can use the method to inspect the objects and their properties. Enter the following statements into both the top and bottom text fields of The Evaluator. Results from the top field are references to the objects; results from the bottom field are lists of properties for the particular object.

```
document.getElementById("myP")
document.getElementById("myEM")
document.getElementById("myTitle")
document.getElementById("myScript")
```

Related Item: getElementsByTagName() method (see Chapter 26, "Generic HTML Element Objects")

getElementsByName("*elementName*")

Returns: Array

Compatibility: WinIE5+, MacIE5+, NN6+, Moz+, Safari+, Opera+, Chrome+

The document.getElementsByName() method returns an array of references to objects whose name attribute is assigned the element name passed as the method's attribute. Although other browsers recognize name attributes even for elements that don't have them by default, IE does not. Therefore, for maximum cross-browser compatibility, use this method only to locate elements that have name attributes defined for them by default, such as form control elements. If the element does not exist in the document, the method returns an array of zero length.

For the most part, you are best served by using IDs on elements and the getElementById() method to unearth references to individual objects. But some elements, especially the input element of type radio, use the name attribute to group elements together. In that case, a call to getElementsByName() returns an array of all elements that share the name — facilitating perhaps a for loop that inspects the checked property of a radio button group. Thus, instead of using the old-fashioned approach by way of the containing form object:

```
var buttonGroup = document.forms[0].radioGroupName;
```

you can retrieve the array more directly:

```
var buttonGroup = document.getElementsByName(radioGroupName);
```

In the latter case, you operate independently of the containing form object's index number or name. This assumes, of course, that a group name is not shared elsewhere on the page, which would certainly lead to confusion.

Example

Use The Evaluator (Chapter 4, "JavaScript Essentials") to test out the getElementsByName() method. All form elements in the upper part of the page have names associated with them. Enter the following statements into the top text field and observe the results:

```
document.getElementsByName("output")
document.getElementsByName("speed").length
document.getElementsByName("speed")[0].value
```

You can also explore all of the properties of the text field by typing the following expression into the bottom field:

```
document.getElementsByName("speed")[0]
```

Related Items: document.getElementsById(), getElementsByTagName() methods

importNode(node, deep)

Returns: Node object reference

Compatibility: WinIE-, MacIE-, NN7+, Moz+, Safari+, Opera+, Chrome+

The document.importNode() method imports a node from another document object into the current document object. A copy of the original node is made when the node is imported, meaning that the original node remains unchanged. The second parameter to the method is a Boolean value that determines whether or not the node's entire subtree is imported (true) or just the node itself (false).

open(["*mimeType*"] [,"*replace*"])

Returns: Nothing

Compatibility: WinIE3+, MacIE3+, NN2+, Moz+, Safari+, Opera+, Chrome+

Opening a document is different from opening a window. In the case of a window, you're creating a new object, both on the screen and in the browser's memory. Opening a document, on the other hand, tells the browser to get ready to accept some data for display in the window named or implied in the reference to the document.open() method. (For example, parent.frames[1] .document.open() may refer to a different frame in a frameset, whereas document.open() implies the current window or frame.) Therefore, the method name may mislead newcomers because the document.open() method has nothing to do with loading documents from the web server or hard disk. Rather, this method is a prelude to sending data to a window through the document.write() or document.writeln() methods. In a sense, the document.open() method merely opens the valve of a pipe; the other methods send the data down the pipe like a stream, and the document.close() method closes that valve as soon as the page's data has been sent in full.

The document.open() method is optional because a document.write() method that attempts to write to a closed document automatically clears the old document and opens the stream for a new one. Whether or not you use the document.open() method, be sure to use the document.close() method after all the writing has taken place.

An optional parameter to the document.open() method enables you to specify the nature of the data being sent to the window. A MIME (Multipurpose Internet Mail Extension) type is a specification for transferring and representing multimedia data on the Internet (originally for mail transmission, but now applicable to all Internet data exchanges). You've seen MIME depictions in the list of helper applications in your browser's preferences settings. A pair of data type names separated by a slash represents a MIME type (such as text/html and image/gif). When you specify a MIME type as a parameter to the document.open() method, you're instructing the browser about the kind of data it is about to receive, so that it knows how to render the data. Common values that most browsers accept are:

```
text/html
text/plain
image/gif
image/jpeg
image/xbm
```

documentObject.queryCommandEnabled()

If you omit the parameter, JavaScript assumes the most popular type, text/html — the kind of data you typically assemble in a script prior to writing to the window. The text/html type includes any images that the HTML references. Specifying any of the image types means that you have the raw binary representation of the image that you want to appear in the new document — possible, but unlikely.

Another possibility is to direct the output of a write() method to a plug-in. For the mimeType parameter, specify the plug-in's MIME type (for example, application/x-director for Shockwave). Again, the data you write to a plug-in must be in a form that it knows how to handle. The same mechanism also works for writing data directly to a helper application.

Note

IE accepts only the text/html MIME type parameter. ∎

Modern browsers include a second, optional parameter to the method: replace. This parameter does for the document.open() method what the replace() method does for the location object. For document.open(), it means that the new document you are about to write replaces the previous document in the window or frame, with the end result that the replaced window or frame's history is not recorded.

Example

You can see an example of where the document.open() method fits in the scheme of dynamically creating content for another frame in the discussion of the document.write() method later in this chapter.

Related Items: document.close(), document.clear(), document.write(), document.writeln() methods

queryCommandEnabled("*commandName*")
queryCommandIndterm("*commandName*")
queryCommandState("*commandName*")
queryCommandSupported("*commandName*")
queryCommandText("*commandName*")
queryCommandValue("*commandName*")

Returns: Various values

Compatibility: WinIE4+, MacIE-, NN7.1, Moz1.3+, Safari+, Opera+, Chrome+

These six methods lend further support to the execCommand() method for document and TextRange objects. If you choose to use the execCommand() method to achieve some stylistic change on a text selection, you can use some of these query methods to make sure the browser supports the desired command and to retrieve any returned values. Table 29-3 summarizes the purpose and returned values for each of the query methods. Note that browser support for these seven methods is uneven.

Because the execCommand() method cannot be invoked on a page while it is still loading, any such invocations that may collide with the loading of a page should check with queryCommandEnabled() prior to invoking the command. Validating that the browser version running the script supports the desired command is also a good idea. Therefore, you may want to wrap any command call with the following conditional structure:

```
if (document.queryCommandEnabled(commandName) &&
    document.queryCommandSupported(commandName)) {
    // ...
}
```

TABLE 29-3

Query Commands

queryCommand	Returns	Description
Enabled	Boolean	Reveals whether the document or TextRange object is in a suitable state to be invoked.
Indterm	Boolean	Reveals whether the command is in an indeterminate state.
CommandState	Boolean | null	Reveals whether the command has been completed (true), is still working (false), or is in an indeterminate state (null).
Supported	Boolean	Reveals whether the command is supported in the current browser.
Text	String	Returns any text that may be returned by a command.
Value	Varies	Returns whatever value (if any) is returned by a command.

When using a command to read information about a selection, use the queryCommandText() or queryCommandValue() methods to catch that information (recall that the execCommand() method itself returns a Boolean value regardless of the specific command invoked).

Example

See the examples for these methods covered under the TextRange object in Chapter 33, "Body Text Objects."

Related Items: TextRange object (see Chapter 33); execCommand() method

recalc([allFlag])

Returns: Nothing

Compatibility: WinIE5+, MacIE-, NN-, Moz-, Safari-, Opera-, Chrome-

IE5 introduced the concept of dynamic properties. With the help of the setExpression() method of all elements and the expression() style sheet value, you can establish dependencies between object properties and potentially dynamic properties, such as a window's size or a draggable element's location. After those dependencies are established, the document.recalc() method causes those dependencies to be recalculated — usually in response to some user action, such as resizing a window or dragging an element.

The optional parameter is a Boolean value. The default value, false, means that the recalculations are performed only on expressions for which the browser has detected any change since the last recalculation. If you specify true, however, all expressions are recalculated, whether they have changed or not.

Mozilla 1.4 includes a feature that allows scripts to turn an iframe element's document object into an HTML editable document. Part of the scripting incorporates the document.execCommand() and related methods. Visit http://www.mozilla.org/editor for current details and examples.

Example

You can see an example of recalc() in Listing 26-32 for the setExpression() method. In that example, the dependencies are between the current time and properties of standard element objects.

Related Items: getExpression(), removeExpression(), setExpression() methods (see Chapter 26, "Generic HTML Element Objects")

releaseEvents(*eventTypeList*)

Returns: Nothing

Compatibility: WinIE-, MacIE-, NN4+, Moz-, Safari-, Opera-, Chrome-

In NN4+, as soon as you enable event capture for a particular event type in a document, that capture remains in effect until the page unloads or you specifically disable the capture. You can turn off event capture for each event via the releaseEvents() method. See Chapter 32, "Event Objects," for more details on event capture and release.

Related Items: captureEvents(), routeEvent() methods

routeEvent([*eventObject*])

Returns: Nothing

Compatibility: WinIE-, MacIE-, NN4+, Moz-, Safari-, Opera-, Chrome-

If you capture a particular event type in NN4, your script may need to perform some limited processing on that event before letting it reach its intended target. To let an event pass through the object hierarchy to its target, you use the routeEvent() method, passing as a parameter the event object being handled in the current function. See Chapter 32, "Event Objects," for more details on event processing.

Related Items: captureEvents(), releaseEvents() methods

write("*string1*" [,"*string2*" ... [, "*stringn*"]])
writeln("*string1*" [,"*string2*" ... [, "*stringn*"]])

Returns: Boolean true if successful

Compatibility: WinIE3+, MacIE3+, NN2+, Moz+, Safari+, Opera+, Chrome+

Both of these methods send text to a document for display in its window. The only difference between the two methods is that `document.writeln()` appends a carriage return to the end of the string it sends to the document. This carriage return is helpful for formatting source code when viewed through the browser's source view window. For new lines in rendered HTML that is generated by these methods, you must still write a `<br>` to insert a line break.

A common, incorrect conclusion that many JavaScript newcomers make is that these methods enable a script to modify the contents of an existing document, which is not true. As soon as a document has loaded into a window (or frame), the only fully backward-compatible text that you can modify without reloading or rewriting the entire page is the content of `text` and `textarea` objects. In IE4+, you can modify HTML and text through the `innerHTML`, `innerText`, `outerHTML`, and `outerText` properties of any element. For W3C DOM–compatible browsers, you can modify an element's text by setting its `nodeValue` or `innerHTML` properties. The preferred approach for modifying the content of a node involves strict adherence to the W3C DOM, which requires creating and inserting or replacing new elements, as described in Chapter 26, and demonstrated in examples throughout this chapter and the rest of the book.

The two safest ways to use the `document.write()` and `document.writeln()` methods are to:

- Write some or all of the page's content by way of scripts embedded in the document
- Send HTML code either to a new window or to a separate frame in a multiframe window

For the first case, you essentially interlace script segments within your HTML. The scripts run as the document loads, writing whatever scripted HTML content you like. This task is exactly what you did in `script1.html` in Chapter 3, "Selecting and Using Your Tools." This task is also how you can have one page generate browser-specific HTML when a particular class of browser requires unique syntax.

In the latter case, a script can gather input from the user in one frame and then algorithmically determine the layout and content destined for another frame. The script assembles the HTML code for the other frame as a string variable (including all necessary HTML tags). Before the script can write anything to the frame, it can optionally open the layout stream (to close the current document in that frame) with the `parent.frameName.document.open()` method. In the next step, a `parent.frameName.document.write()` method pours the entire string into the other frame. Finally, a `parent.frameName.document.close()` method ensures that the total data stream is written to the window. Such a frame looks just the same as if it were created by a source document on the server rather than on-the-fly in memory. The `document` object of that window or frame is a full citizen as a standard `document` object. You can, therefore, even include scripts as part of the HTML specification for one of these temporary HTML pages.

After an HTML document (containing a script that is going to write via the `write()` or `writeln()` methods) loads completely, the page's incoming stream closes automatically. If you then attempt to apply a series of `document.write()` statements, the first `document.write()` method completely removes all vestiges of the original document. That includes all of its objects and scripted variable values. Therefore, if you try to assemble a new page with a series of `document.write()` statements, the script and variables from the original page will be gone before the second `document.write()` statement executes. To get around this potential problem, assemble the content for the new screen as one string variable, and then pass that variable as the parameter to a single `document.write()` statement. Also be sure to include a `document.close()` statement in the next line of script.

Assembling HTML in a script to be written via the `document.write()` method often requires skill in concatenating string values and nesting strings. A number of JavaScript `String` object shortcuts facilitate the formatting of text with HTML tags (see Chapter 15, "The String Object," for details).

If you are writing to a different frame or window, you are free to use multiple `document.write()` statements if you like. Whether your script sends lots of small strings via multiple `document .write()` methods, or assembles a larger string to be sent through one `document.write()` method, depends partly on the situation and partly on your own scripting style. From a performance standpoint, a fairly standard procedure is to do more preliminary work in memory and place as few I/O (input/output) calls as possible. On the other hand, making a difficult-to-track mistake is easier in string concatenation when you assemble longer strings. You should use the system that's most comfortable for you.

You may see another little-known way of passing parameters to these methods. Instead of concatenating string values with the plus (+) operator, you can also bring string values together by separating them with commas, in which case the strings appear to be arguments to the `document.write()` method. For example, the following two statements produce the same results:

```
document.write("Today is " + new Date());
document.write("Today is ",new Date());
```

Neither form is better than the other, so use the one that feels more comfortable to your existing programming style.

Note

Dynamically generating scripts requires an extra trick, especially in NN. The root of the problem is that if you try code such as `document.write("<script></script>")`**, the browser interprets the end script tag as the end of the script that is doing the writing. You have to trick the browser by separating the end tag into a couple of components. Escaping the forward slash also helps. For example, if you want to load a different** `.js` **file for each class of browser, the code looks similar to the following:**

```
// variable 'browserVer' is a browser-specific string
// and 'page' is the HTML your script is accumulating
// for document.write()
page += "<script type='text/javascript' src='" +
        browseVer + ".js'><" + "\/script>"; ■
```

Using the `document.open()`, `document.write()`, and `document.close()` methods to display images in a document requires some small extra steps. First, any URL assignments that you write via `document.write()` must be complete (not relative) URL references. Alternatively, you can write the `<base>` tag for the dynamically generated page so that its `href` attribute value matches that of the file that is writing the page.

The other image trick is to be sure to specify `height` and `width` attributes for every image, scripted or otherwise. Document-rendering performance is improved on all platforms, because the values help the browser lay out elements even before their details are loaded.

In addition to the `document.write()` example that follows (see Listings 29-14 through 29-16), you can find fuller implementations that use this method to assemble images and bar charts in many of the applications in Chapters 52 through 61 on the CD-ROM. Because you can assemble any valid HTML as a string to be written to a window or frame, a customized, on-the-fly document can be as elaborate as the most complex HTML document that you can imagine.

Example

The example in Listings 29-14 through 29-16 demonstrates several important points about using the `document.write()` and `document.writeln()` methods for writing to another frame. First is the fact that you can write any HTML code to a frame, and the browser accepts it as if the source code came from an HTML file somewhere. In the example, we assemble a complete HTML document, including basic HTML tags for completeness.

LISTING 29-14

A Frameset for the Document Writing Example

```
<!DOCTYPE html>
<html>
    <head>
        <meta http-equiv="content-type" content="text/html;charset=utf-8">
        <title>Writin' to the doc</title>
    </head>
    <frameset rows="50%,50%">
        <frame name="Frame1" src="jsb29-15.html" />
        <frame name="Frame2" src="jsb29-16.html" />
    </frameset>
</html>
```

LISTING 29-15

Writing a Document Based upon User Input

```
<!DOCTYPE html>
<html>
    <head>
        <meta http-equiv="content-type" content="text/html;charset=utf-8">
        <title>Document Write Controller</title>
        <script type="text/javascript">
            function takePulse(form)
            {
                var msg = "<html><head><title>On The Fly with " +
                        form.yourName.value + "<\/title><\/head>";
                msg += "<body bgcolor='salmon'><h1>Good Day " +
                        form.yourName.value +
                        "!<\/h1><hr />";
                for (var i = 0; i < form.how.length; i++)
                {
                    if (form.how[i].checked)
                    {
                        msg += form.how[i].value;
                        break;
                    }
                }
                msg += "<br />Make it a great day!<\/body><\/html>";
                parent.Frame2.document.write(msg);
                parent.Frame2.document.close();
            }
```

continued

documentObject.writeln

LISTING 29-15   *(continued)*

```
        function getTitle()
        {
          alert("Lower frame document.title is now:" + parent.Frame2.document.title);
        }

        // bind the event handlers
        function addEvent(elem, evtType, func)
        {
          if (elem.addEventListener)
          {
            elem.addEventListener(evtType, func, false);
          }
          else if (elem.attachEvent)
          {
            elem.attachEvent("on" + evtType, func);
          }
          else
          {
            elem["on" + evtType] = func;
          }
        }
      addEvent(window, "load", function()
      {
        addEvent(document.getElementById("enter"), "click",
                function(evt)
                {takePulse(document.getElementById("enter").form)
                });
        addEvent(document.getElementById("peek"), "click", getTitle);
      });
    </script>
  </head>
  <body>
    Fill in a name, and select how that person feels today. Then click "Write
    To Below" to see the results in the bottom frame.
    <form>
      Enter your first name:
      <input type="text" name="yourName" value="Dave" />
      <p>How are you today?
        <input type="radio" name="how"
                value="I hope that feeling continues forever."
                checked="checked" />
        Swell
        <input type="radio" name="how"
                value="You may be on your way to feeling Swell" />
        Pretty Good
        <input type="radio" name="how"
                value="Things can only get better from here." />So-So
      </p>
      <p><input type="button" id="enter" name="enter" value="Write To Below" /></p>
```

```
        <hr />
        <input type="button" id="peek" name="peek" value="Check Lower Frame Title" />
    </form>
  </body>
</html>
```

LISTING 29-16

A Placeholder Page for the Document Writing Example

```
<!DOCTYPE html>
<html>
  <head>
    <meta http-equiv="content-type" content="text/html;charset=utf-8">
    <title>Placeholder</title>
  </head>
  <body>
  </body>
</html>
```

It is important to note that this example customizes the content of the document based on user input. This customization makes the experience of working with your web page feel far more interactive to the user — yet you're doing it without any server-side programs.

The second point we want to bring home is that the document created in the separate frame by the document.write() method is a genuine document object. In this example, the <title> tag of the written document changes if you redraw the lower frame after changing the entry of the name field in the upper frame. If you click the lower button after updating the bottom frame, you see that the document.title property has, indeed, changed to reflect the <title> tag written to the browser in the course of displaying the frame's page. The fact that you can artificially create full-fledged, JavaScript document objects on the fly represents one of the most important powers of serverless CGI scripting (for information delivery to the user) with JavaScript. You have much to take advantage of here if your imagination is up to the task.

Note that you can easily modify Listing 29-15 to write the results to the same frame as the document containing the field and buttons. Instead of specifying the lower frame:

```
        parent.frames[1].document.open();
        parent.frames[1].document.write(msg);
        parent.frames[1].document.close();
```

The code simply can use:

```
        document.open();
        document.write(msg);
        document.close();
```

This code would replace the form document with the results and not require any frames in the first place. Because the code assembles all of the content for the new document into one variable value, that data survive the one document.write() method.

The frameset document (see Listing 29-14) creates a blank frame by loading a blank document (see Listing 29-16). An alternative that we highly recommend is to have the framesetting document fill the frame with a blank document of its own creation. See the section "Blank frames" in Chapter 27, "Window and Frame Objects," for further details about this technique.

Related Items: `document.open()`; `document.close()`; `document.clear()` methods

Event handlers

onselectionchange

Compatibility: WinIE5.5+, MacIE-, NN-, Moz-, Safari-, Opera-, Chrome-

The `onselectionchange` event can be triggered by numerous user actions, although all of those actions occur on elements that are under the influence of the WinIE5.5+ edit mode.

Related Item: `oncontrolselect` event handler

onstop

Compatibility: WinIE5+, MacIE-, NN-, Moz-, Safari-, Opera-, Chrome-

The `onstop` event fires in WinIE5+ when the user clicks the browser's Stop button. Use this event handler to stop potentially runaway script execution on a page, because the Stop button does not otherwise control scripts after a page has loaded. If you are having a problem with a runaway repeat loop during development, you can temporarily use this event handler to let you stop the script for debugging.

Example

Listing 29-17 provides a simple example of an intentional infinitely looping script. In case you load this page into a browser other than IE5+, you can click the Halt Counter button to stop the looping. The Halt Counter button, as well as the `onstop` event handler, invokes the same function.

LISTING 29-17

Stopping a Script Using the onstop Event Handler

```
<!DOCTYPE html>
<html>
    <head>
        <meta http-equiv="content-type" content="text/html;charset=utf-8">
        <title>onStop Event Handler</title>
        <script type="text/javascript">
            var counter = 0;
            var timerID;
            function startCounter()
            {
                document.forms[0].display.value = ++counter;
                //clearTimeout(timerID)
                timerID = setTimeout("startCounter()", 10);
            }
            function haltCounter()
```

```
        {
            clearTimeout(timerID);
            counter = 0;
        }

        // bind the event handlers
        function addEvent(elem, evtType, func)
        {
            if (elem.addEventListener)
            {
                elem.addEventListener(evtType, func, false);
            }
            else if (elem.attachEvent)
            {
                elem.attachEvent("on" + evtType, func);
            }
            else
            {
                elem["on" + evtType] = func;
            }
        }
        addEvent(window, "load", function()
        {
            addEvent(document, "stop", haltCounter);
            addEvent(document.getElementById("start"), "click", startCounter);
            addEvent(document.getElementById("halt"), "click", haltCounter);
        });
    </script>
</head>
<body>
    <h1>onStop Event Handler</h1>
    <hr />
    <p>Click the browser's Stop button (in IE) to stop the script counter.</p>
    <form>
        <p><input type="text" name="display" /></p>
        <input type="button" id="start" value="Start Counter" />
        <input type="button" id="halt" value="Halt Counter" />
    </form>
</body>
</html>
```

Related Items: Repeat loops (Chapter 21, "Control Structures and Exception Handling")

body Element Object

Compatibility: WinIE4+, MacIE4+, NN6+, Moz+, Safari+, Opera+, Chrome+

For HTML element properties, methods, and event handlers, see Chapter 26, "Generic HTML Element Objects."

Properties	Methods	Event Handlers
alink	createControlRange()	onafterprint
background	createTextRange()	onbeforeprint
bgColor	doScroll()	onscroll
bgProperties		
bottomMargin		
leftMargin		
link		
noWrap		
rightMargin		
scroll		
scrollLeft		
scrollTop		
text		
topMargin		
vLink		

Syntax

Accessing body element object properties or methods:

```
[window.] document.body.property | method([parameters])
```

About this object

In object models that reveal HTML element objects, the body element object is the primary container of the content that visitors see on the page. The body contains all rendered HTML. This special place in the node hierarchy gives the body object some unique powers, especially in the IE object model.

As if to signify the special relationship, both the IE and W3C object models provide the same shortcut reference to the body element: document.body. As a first-class HTML element object (as evidenced by the long lists of properties, methods, and event handlers covered in Chapter 26), you are also free to use other syntaxes to reach the body element.

You are certainly familiar with several body element attributes that govern body-wide content appearance, such as link colors (in three states) and background (color or image). But IE and NN/Mozilla (and the W3C so far) have some very different ideas about the body element's role in scripting documents. Many methods and properties that NN/Mozilla considers to be the domain of the window (for example, scrolling, inside window dimensions, and so forth), IE puts into the hands of the body element object. Therefore, whereas NN/Mozilla scrolls the window (and whatever it may contain), IE scrolls the body (inside whatever window it lives). And because the body element fills the entire viewable area of a browser window or frame, that viewable rectangle is determined in IE by the body's `scrollHeight` and `scrollWidth` properties, whereas NN4+/Moz features `window.innerHeight` and `window.innerWidth` properties. This distinction is important to point out because when you are scripting window- or document-wide appearance factors, you may have to look for properties and methods for the `window` or `body` element object, depending on your target browser(s).

Note

Use caution when referencing the `document.body` object while the page is loading. The object may not officially exist until the page has completely loaded. If you need to set some initial properties through scripting, do so in response to the `onload` event handler located in the `<body>` tag. Attempts at setting `body` element object properties in immediate scripts inside the `head` element may result in error messages about the object not being found. ■

Properties

```
alink
bgColor
link
text
vLink
```

Value: Hexadecimal triplet or color name string   Read/Write

Compatibility: WinIE4+, MacIE4+, NN6+, Moz+, Safari+, Opera+, Chrome+

The `aLink`, `link`, and `vLink` properties replaced the ancient `document` properties `alinkColor`, `linkColor`, and `vlinkColor`. The `bgColor` property is the same as the old `document.bgColor` property, while the `text` property replaced the `document.fgColor` property. These properties serve as the scripted equivalents of the HTML attributes for the `body` element — the new property names more closely align themselves with the HTML attributes than the old property names.

We use past tense when referring to these properties because CSS has largely made them obsolete. Granted, they still work, but will likely fall into disuse as web developers continue to embrace style sheets as the preferred means of altering color in web pages. Link colors that are set through pseudo-class selectors in style sheets (as `style` attributes of the `body` element) must be accessed through the `style` property for the `body` object.

background

Value: URL string   Read/Write

Compatibility: WinIE4+, MacIE4+, NN6+, Moz+, Safari+, Opera+, Chrome+

The `background` property enables you to set or get the URL for the background image (if any) assigned to the `body` element. A `body` element's background image overlays the background color in case both attributes or properties are set. To remove an image from the document's background, set the `document.body.background` property to an empty string.

Similar to the properties that provide access to colors on the page, the background image in modern web pages should be set through style sheets, as opposed to the `body.background` property. In that case, you access the background programmatically through the `style` property of the `body` object.

bgColor

(See aLink)

bgProperties

Value: String constant   Read/Write

Compatibility: WinIE4+, MacIE4+, NN-, Moz-, Safari-, Opera-, Chrome-

The IE-specific bgProperties property is an alternative way of adjusting whether the background image should remain fixed when the user scrolls the document or scroll with the document. Initial settings for this behavior should be done through the background-attachment CSS attribute and modified under script control by way of the body element's style.backgroundAttachment property.

No matter which way you reference this property, the only allowable values are the string constants scroll (the default) or fixed.

Example

Both of the following statements change the default behavior of background image scrolling in IE4+:

```
document.body.bgProperties = "fixed";
```

or

```
document.body.style.backgroundAttachment = "fixed";
```

The added benefit of using the style sheet version is that it also works in NN6+/Moz and other W3C browsers.

Related Item: body.background property

bottomMargin
leftMargin
rightMargin
topMargin

Value: Integer   Read/Write

Compatibility: WinIE4+, MacIE4+, NN-, Moz-, Safari-, Opera-, Chrome-

The four IE-specific margin properties are alternatives to setting the corresponding four margin style sheet attributes for the body element (body.style.marginBottom, and so on). Style sheet margins represent blank space between the edge of an element's content and its next outermost container. In the case of the body element, that container is an invisible document container.

Of the four properties, only the one for the bottom margin may be confusing, if the content does not fill the vertical space of a window or frame. The margin value is not automatically increased to accommodate the extra blank space.

Example

Both of the following statements change the default left margin in IE4+. The style sheet version has an added benefit — it also works in NN6+/Moz and other W3C browsers.

```
document.body.leftMargin = 30;
```

and

```
document.body.style.marginLeft = 30;
```

Related Item: style object

leftMargin

(See bottomMargin)

link

(See aLink)

noWrap

Value: Boolean   Read/Write

Compatibility: WinIE4+, MacIE4+, NN-, Moz-, Safari-, Opera-, Chrome-

The nowrap property enables you to modify the body element behavior normally set through the HTML nowrap attribute. Because the property name is a negative, the Boolean logic needed to control it can get confusing.

The default behavior for a body element is for text to wrap within the width of the window or frame. This behavior occurs when the value of noWrap is its default value of false. By turning noWrap to true, a line of text continues to render past the right edge of the window or frame until the HTML contains a line break (or end of paragraph). If the text continues on past the right edge of the window, the window (or frame) gains a horizontal scroll bar (unless, of course, a frame is set to not scroll).

By and large, users don't like to scroll in any direction if they don't have to. Unless you have a special need to keep single lines intact, let the default behavior rule the day.

Example

To change the word-wrapping behavior from the default, the statement is:

```
document.body.noWrap = true;
```

Related Items: None

rightMargin

(See bottomMargin)

scroll

Value: Constant string   Read/Write

Compatibility: WinIE4+, MacIE4+, NN-, Moz-, Safari-, Opera-, Chrome-

The IE-specific scroll property provides scripted access to the IE-specific scroll attribute of a body element. By default, an IE body element displays a vertical scroll bar even if the height of the content does not warrant it; a horizontal scroll bar appears only when the content is forced to be wider than the window or frame. You can make sure that both scroll bars are hidden by setting the scroll attribute to no or changing it through a script. Possible values for this property are the constant strings yes and no.

Except for `frame` attributes and NN4+/Moz-signed scripts, other browsers do not provide facilities for turning off scroll bars under script control. You can generate a new window (via the `window.open()` method) and specify that its scroll bars be hidden.

Example

To change the scroll bar appearance from the default, the statement is:

```
document.body.scroll = "no";
```

Related Items: `window.scrollbars` property; `window.open()` method

scrollLeft
scrollTop

Value: Integer   Read/Write

Compatibility: WinIE4+, MacIE4+, NN7+, Moz+, Safari+, Opera+, Chrome+

Even though the `scrollLeft` and `scrollTop` properties of the `body` object are the same as those for generic HTML element objects, they play an important role in determining the placement of positioned elements (described more fully in Chapter 43). Because the mouse event and element position properties tend to be relative to the visible content region of the browser window, you must take the scrolling values of the `document.body` object into account when assigning an absolute position. Values for both of these properties are integers representing pixels.

Example

Listing 29-18 is an unusual construction that creates a frameset and the content for each of the two frames, all within a single HTML document. In the left frame of the frameset are two fields that are ready to show the pixel values of the right frame's `xOffset` and `yOffset` properties. The content of the right frame is a 30-row table of fixed width (800 pixels). Mouse-click events are captured by the document level (see Chapter 32), allowing you to click any table or cell border, or outside the table, to trigger the `showOffsets()` function in the right frame. That function is a simple script that displays the page offset values in their respective fields in the left frame.

LISTING 29-18

Determining Scroll Values

```
<!DOCTYPE html>
<html>
    <head>
        <meta http-equiv="content-type" content="text/html;charset=utf-8">
        <title>Master of all Windows</title>
        <script type="text/javascript">
            function leftFrame()
            {
                var output = "<html><body><h3>Body Scroll Values<\/h3><hr />\n";
                output += "<form>body.scrollLeft:<input type='text' ";
                output += "name='xOffset' size=4 /><br />\n";
                output += "body.scrollTop:<input type='text' ";
                output += "name='yOffset' size=4 /><br />\n";
                output += "<\/form><\/body><\/html>";
```

```
        return output;
    }

    function rightFrame()
    {
        var output = "<html><head><script type='text/javascript'>\n";
        output += "function showOffsets() {\n";
        output += "parent.readout.document.forms[0].xOffset.value ";
        output += "= document.body.scrollLeft\n";
        output += "parent.readout.document.forms[0].yOffset.value ";
        output += "= document.body.scrollTop\n}\n";
        output += "document.onclick = showOffsets\n";
        output += "<\/script><\/head><body><h3>Content Page<\/h3>\n";
        output += "Scroll this frame and click on a table border to view ";
        output += "page offset values.<br /><hr />\n";
        output += "<table border=5 width=800>";
        var oneRow = "<td>Cell 1<\/td><td>Cell 2<\/td><td>Cell ";
        oneRow += "3<\/td><td>Cell 4<\/td><td>Cell 5<\/td>";
        for (var i = 1; i <= 30; i++)
        {
            output += "<tr><td><b>Row " + i + "<\/b><\/td>" + oneRow + "<\/tr>";
        }
        output += "<\/table><\/body><\/html>";
        return output;
    }
    </script>
</head>
<frameset cols="30%,70%">
    <frame name="readout" src="javascript:parent.leftFrame()" />
    <frame name="display" src="javascript:parent.rightFrame()" />
</frameset>
</html>
```

Related Items: `window.pageXOffset`, `window.pageYOffset` properties

text

(See `aLink`)

topMargin

(See `bottomMargin`)

vLink

(See `aLink`)

Methods
createControlRange()

Returns: Array

Compatibility: WinIE5+, MacIE-, NN-, Moz-, Safari-, Opera-, Chrome-

bodyObject.createTextRange()

This method creates a control range in WinIE5+ browsers. Control ranges are used for control-based selection, as opposed to text-based selection made possible by text ranges. The method only applies to documents in edit mode. In regular document view mode, the createControlRange() method returns an empty array.

createTextRange()

Returns: Object

Compatibility: WinIE4+, MacIE-, NN-, Moz-, Safari-, Opera-, Chrome-

The body element object is the most common object used to generate a TextRange object in IE4+, especially when the text you are about to manipulate is part of the document's body text. The initial TextRange object returned from the createTextRange() method encompasses the entire body element's HTML and body text. Further action on the returned object is required to set the start and end point of the range. See the discussion of the TextRange object in Chapter 33 for more details.

Example

See Listing 30-10 for an example of the createTextRange() method in action.

Related Item: TextRange object (see Chapter 33, "Body Text Objects")

doScroll(["*scrollAction*"])

Returns: Nothing

Compatibility: WinIE5+, MacIE-, NN-, Moz-, Safari-, Opera-, Chrome-

Use the doScroll() method to simulate user action on the scroll bars inside a window or frame that holds the current document. This method comes in handy if you are creating your own scroll bars in place of the standard system scroll bars. Scrolling is instantaneous, however, rather than animated, even if the Display control panel is set for animated scrolling. The parameter for this method is one of the string constant values shown in Table 29-4. Occasionally, in practice, the longer scroll action names more closely simulate an actual click on the scroll bar component, whereas the shortcut versions may scroll at a slightly different increment.

Unlike scrolling to a specific pixel location (by setting the body element's scrollTop and scrollLeft properties), the doScroll() method depends entirely on the spatial relationship between the body content and the window or frame size. Also, the doScroll() method triggers the onscroll event handler for the body element object.

Be aware that scripted modifications to body content can alter these spatial relationships. IE is prone to being sluggish in updating all of its internal dimensions after content has been altered. Should you attempt to invoke the doScroll() method after such a layout modification, the scroll may not be performed as expected. You may find the common trick of using setTimeout() to delay the invocation of the doScroll() method by a fraction of a second.

Example

Use The Evaluator (Chapter 4, "JavaScript Essentials") to experiment with the doScroll() method in IE5+. Size the browser window so that at least the vertical scroll bar is active (meaning it has a thumb region). Enter the following statement into the top text field and press the Enter key a few times to simulate clicking the PgDn key:

```
document.body.doScroll()
```

Return to the top of the page, and now do the same for scrolling by the increment of the scroll bar down arrow:

```
document.body.doScroll("down")
```

TABLE 29-4

document.body.doScroll() Parameters

Long Parameter	Short Parameter	Scroll Action Simulates
scrollbarDown	down	Clicking the down arrow.
scrollbarHThumb	n/a	Clicking the horizontal scroll bar thumb (no scrolling action).
scrollbarLeft	left	Clicking the left arrow.
scrollbarPageDown	pageDown	Clicking the page down area or pressing PgDn (default).
scrollbarPageLeft	pageLeft	Clicking the page left area.
scrollbarPageRight	pageRight	Clicking the page right area.
scrollbarPageUp	pageUp	Clicking the page up area or pressing PgUp.
scrollbarRight	right	Clicking the right arrow.
scrollbarUp	up	Clicking the up arrow.
scrollbarVThumb	n/a	Clicking the vertical scroll bar thumb (no scrolling action).

You can also experiment with upward scrolling. Enter the desired statement in the top text field and leave the text cursor in the field. Manually scroll to the bottom of the page and then press Enter to activate the command.

Related Items: `body.scroll`, `body.scrollTop`, `body.scrollLeft` properties; `window.scroll()`, `window.scrollBy()`, `window.scrollTo()` methods

Event handlers
onafterprint
onbeforeprint
onscroll

(See these event handlers for the `window` object, Chapter 27, "Window and Frame Objects.")

TreeWalker Object

Property	Method	Event Handler
currentNode	firstChild()	
expandEntityReference	lastChild()	
filter	nextNode()	
root	nextSibling()	
whatToShow	parentNode()	
	previousNode()	
	previousSibling()	

Syntax

Creating a TreeWalker object:

```
var treewalk = document.createTreeWalker(document, whatToShow,
    filterFunction, entityRefExpansion);
```

Accessing TreeWalker object properties and methods:

```
TreeWalker.property | method([parameters])
```

Compatibility: WinIE-, MacIE-, NN7+, Moz+, Safari+, Opera+, Chrome+

About this object

The TreeWalker object serves as a container for a list of nodes that meet the criteria defined by the document.createTreeWalker() method, which is used to create the object. The list of nodes contained by a TreeWalker object conforms to the same hierarchical structure of the document from which they are referenced. The TreeWalker object provides a means of navigating through this list of nodes based on their inherent tree-like structure.

You can think of the TreeWalker object as somewhat of an iterator object since its main purpose is to provide a means of stepping through nodes in a list. However, in this case the list is a hierarchical tree, as opposed to a linear list. The TreeWalker object maintains a pointer inside the list of nodes that always points to the current node. Whenever you navigate through the list using the TreeWalker object, the navigation is always relative to the pointer. For example, referencing the previous or next node through calls to the previousNode() or nextNode() methods depends upon the current position of the node pointer in the tree.

Use the document.createTreeWalker() method to create a TreeWalker object for a particular document. This method requires a user function that serves as a filter for nodes selected to be part of the tree. A reference to the function is the third parameter of the method call. The return value of this user function can be one of three constant values, which indicate the status of the current node: NodeFilter.FILTER_ACCEPT, NodeFilter.FILTER_REJECT, or NodeFilter.FILTER_SKIP. The difference between NodeFilter.FILTER_REJECT and NodeFilter.FILTER_SKIP is that descendents of skipped nodes may still qualify as part of the tree, whereas rejected nodes and their descendents are excluded altogether. Following is an example of a user function you could use to create a TreeWalker object:

```
function ratingAttrFilter(node)
{
    if (node.hasAttribute("rating"))
    {
        return NodeFilter.FILTER_ACCEPT;
    }
    return NodeFilter.FILTER_REJECT;
}
```

In this example function, only nodes containing an attribute named rating are allowed through the filter, which means that only those nodes will get added to the list (tree). With this function in place, you then call the document.createTreeWalker() method to create the TreeWalker object:

```
var myTreeWalker = document.createTreeWalker(document, NodeFilter.SHOW_ELEMENT,
                        ratingAttrFilter, false);
```

Now that the TreeWalker object is created, you can use its properties and methods to access individual nodes and navigate through the list.

Properties
currentNode

Value: Node reference   Read/Write

Compatibility: WinIE-, MacIE-, NN7+, Moz+, Safari+, Opera+, Chrome+

The currentNode property returns a reference to the current node, which sits at the location of the tree's node pointer. Although you can use the currentNode property to access the current node, you can also use it to set the current node.

Example

To assign a node to the current position in the tree, just create an assignment statement using the currentNode property:

```
myTreeWalker.currentNode = document.getElementById("info");
```

Related Item: root property

expandEntityReference
filter
root
whatToShow

Value: See text   Read-Only

Compatibility: WinIE-, MacIE-, NN7+, Moz+, Safari+, Opera+, Chrome+

These properties reflect the parameter values passed into the `document.createTreeWalker()` method upon the creation of the `TreeWalker` object.

Related Item: `document.createTreeWalker()` method

Methods
```
firstChild()
lastChild()
nextSibling()
parentNode()
previousSibling()
```

Returns: Node reference

Compatibility: WinIE-, MacIE-, NN7+, Moz+, Safari+, Opera+, Chrome+

These methods return references to nodes within the hierarchy of the tree-like list of nodes contained by the `TreeWalker` object. There is a parent-child relationship among all of the nodes in the tree, and these functions are used to obtain node references based upon this relationship. The node pointer within the tree moves to the new node whenever you use one of these methods to navigate to a given node. This means you can access the new node as the current node after calling one of these navigation methods.

Example

The following code shows how to obtain the tag name of the parent node of the current node in the `TreeWalker` object:

```
if (myTreeWalker.parentNode())
{
    var parentTag = myTreeWalker.currentNode.tagName;
}
```

Related Items: `nextNode()`, `previousNode()` methods

```
nextNode()
previousNode()
```

Returns: Node reference

Compatibility: WinIE-, MacIE-, NN7+, Moz+, Safari+, Opera+, Chrome+

The `nextNode()` and `previousNode()` methods navigate back and forth in the list of nodes contained by the `TreeWalker` object. It's important to note that these methods operate on the node list as if it had been flattened from a tree into a linear sequence of nodes. Both methods move the internal node pointer to the next or previous node, respectively.

Example

The following code demonstrates both the node filter function and a typical function you could use to display (in a series of alert windows, perhaps for debugging purposes) the IDs of all elements inside the body that have id attributes assigned. The nextNode() method is called first to advance the TreeWalker's node pointer to the first node of the collection, and then iteratively (inside a do-while construction) to obtain the next node that passes the node filter's test.

```
function idFilter(node)
{
    if (node.hasAttribute("id"))
    {
        return NodeFilter.FILTER_ACCEPT;
    }
    return NodeFilter.FILTER_SKIP;
}

function showIds()
{
    var tw =
    document.createTreeWalker(document.body, NodeFilter.SHOW_ELEMENT,
        idFilter, false);
    // make sure TreeWalker contains at least one node, and go to it if true
    if (tw.nextNode())
    {
        do
        {
            alert(tw.currentNode.id);
        } while (tw.nextNode());
    }
}
```

Related Item: parentNode() method

Link and Anchor Objects

T he Web is based on the notion that the world's information can be strung
together by way of the *hyperlink* — the clickable hunk of text or image
that enables an inquisitive reader to navigate to a further explanation or
related material. Of all the document objects you work with in JavaScript, the
link is the one that makes that connection. Anchors provide guideposts to specific locations within documents.

As scriptable objects going back to the first scriptable browsers, links and
anchors are comparatively simple devices. But this simplicity belies their
significance in the entire scheme of the Web. Under script control, links can be
far more powerful than mere tethers to locations on the Web.

In modern browsers, the notion of separating links and anchors as similar yet
distinctly different objects begins to fade. The association of the word *link* with
objects is potentially confused by the newer browsers' recognition of the link
element (see Chapter 40, "HTML Directive Objects"), which has an entirely different purpose as a scriptable object. Taking the place of the anchor and link
objects is an HTML element object representing the element created by the <a>
tag. As an element object, the a element assumes all the properties, methods, and
event handlers are associated with all HTML element objects in modern object
models. To begin making that transition, this chapter treats all three types of
objects at the same time.

Anchor, Link, and a Element Objects

For HTML element properties, methods, and event handlers, see Chapter 26,
"Generic HTML Element Objects."

Properties	Methods	Event Handlers
charset		
coords		
hash		
host		
hostname		
href		
hreflang		
methods		
mimeType		
name		
nameProp		
pathname		
port		
protocol		
rel		
rev		
search		
shape		
target		
type		
urn		

Syntax

Accessing Link Object Properties:

```
(all)     [window.]document.links[index].property
```

Accessing a element object properties:

```
(IE4+)    [window.]document.all.elemID.property | method([parameters])
(IE5+/W3C) [window.]document.getElementById("elemID").property |
    method([parameters])
```

Compatibility: WinIE4+, MacIE4+, NN6+, Moz+, Safari+, Opera+, Chrome+

About this object

A little scripting history can help you understand where the link and anchor objects came from and how the a element object evolved from them.

Using the terminology of the original object model, the anchor and link objects are both created in the object model from the <a> tag. What distinguishes a link from an anchor is the presence of the href attribute in the tag. Without an href attribute, the element is an anchor object, which has only a single property (name) in modern browsers. A link, on the other hand, is much more alive as an object — all because of the inclusion of an href attribute, which usually points to a URL to load into a window or frame.

When object models treat HTML elements as objects, both the anchor and link objects are subsumed by the a element object. Even so, one important characteristic from the original object holds true: All a element objects that behave as link objects (by virtue of the presence of an href attribute) are members of the document.links property array. Therefore, if your scripts need to inspect or modify properties of all link objects on a page, they can do so by way of a for loop through the array of link objects. This is true even if you script solely for modern browsers and want to, say, change a style attribute of all links (for example, change their style.textDecoration property from none to underline). The fact that the same element can have different behaviors depending on the existence of one attribute makes us think of the a element object as potentially two different animals. Therefore, when you see separate references to the link and anchor objects, you know the distinction between the two is important.

Scripting newcomers are often confused about the purpose of the target attribute of an a element when they want a scripted link to act on a different frame or window. Under plain HTML, the target attribute points to the frame or window into which the new document (the one assigned to the href attribute) is to load, leaving the current window or frame intact. But if you intend to use event handlers to navigate (by setting the location.href property), the target attribute does not apply to the scripted action. Instead, assign the new URL to the location.href property of the desired frame or window. For example, if one frame contains a table of contents consisting entirely of links, the onclick event handlers of those links can load other pages into the main frame by assigning the URL to the parent.main.location.href property. You must also cancel the default behavior of any link, as described in the discussion of the generic onclick event handler in Chapter 26.

When you want a click of the link (whether the link consists of text or an image) to initiate an action without actually navigating to another URL, you can use a special technique — the javascript: pseudo-URL — to direct the URL to a JavaScript function. The URL javascript:functionName() is a valid parameter for the href attribute (and not just in the link object). You can also add a special void operator that guarantees that the called function does not trigger any true linking action (href="javascript: void someFunction()"). Specifying an empty string for the href attribute yields an FTP-like file listing for the client computer — an undesirable artifact. Don't forget, too, that if the URL leads to a type of file that initiates a browser helper application (for example, playing a QuickTime movie), the helper app or plug-in loads and plays without changing the page in the browser window.

Note

Usage of the javascript: pseudo-URL is controversial. There is no published industry standard that supports it, even though most browsers do. It is also unfriendly to users who visit the page with scripting disabled or unavailable (for example, browsers designed for visually impaired users), because the links won't do anything, leading to frustration. You should also be aware that search engines won't follow these types of links when they work their way through a site. ■

A single link can change the content of more than one frame at the same time with the help of JavaScript. If you want only JavaScript-enabled browsers to act on such links, one approach is to use a `javascript:` pseudo-URL to invoke a function that changes the `location.href` properties of multiple frames. For example, consider the following function, which changes the content of two frames:

```
function navFrames(url1, url2)
{
    parent.product.location.href = url1;
    parent.accessories.location.href = url2;
}
```

Then you can have a `javascript:` pseudo-URL invoke this multipurpose function, and pass the specifics for the link as parameters:

```
<a href="javascript: void navFrames('products/gizmo344.html',
    'access/access344.html')">Deluxe Super Gizmo</a>
```

Or, if you want one link to do something for everyone, but something extra for JavaScript-enabled browsers (an approach that is desirable when designing a page for accessibility), you can combine the standard link behavior with an `onclick` event handler to take care of both situations:

```
function setAccessFrame(url)
{
    parent.accessories.location.href = url;
}
...
<a href="products/gizmo344.html" target="product"
onclick="setAccessFrame('access/access344.html')">Deluxe Super Gizmo</a>
```

Note
The property assignment event handling technique in the previous example is a deliberate simplification to make the code more readable. It is generally better to use the more modern approach of binding events using the `addEventListener()` **(NN6+/Moz/W3C)** or `attachEvent()` **(IE5+)** method. A modern cross-browser event handling technique is explained in detail in Chapter 32, "Event Objects." ■

Notice here that the `target` attribute is necessary for the standard link behavior, whereas the script assigns a URL to a frame's `location.href` property.

One additional technique allows a single link tag to operate for both scriptable and nonscriptable browsers. For nonscriptable browsers, establish a genuine URL to navigate from the link. Then make sure that the link's `onclick` event handler evaluates to `return false` or cancels the default action. At click time, a scriptable browser executes the event handler and ignores the `href` attribute; a nonscriptable browser ignores the event handler and follows the link. See the discussion of the generic `onclick` event handler in Chapter 26 for more details.

Properties
charset

Value: String   Read/Write

Compatibility: WinIE6+, MacIE6+, NN6+, Moz+, Safari+, Opera+, Chrome+

The `charset` property represents the HTML 4 `charset` attribute of an a element. It advises the browser of the character set used by the document to which the `href` attribute points. The value is a string of one of the character set codes from the registry at `http://www.iana.org/assignments/character-sets`. The most commonly used character set on the Web is called `ISO-8859-5`.

coords
shape

Value: Strings   Read/Write

Compatibility: WinIE6+, MacIE6+, NN6+, Moz+, Safari+, Opera+, Chrome+

HTML 4 provides specifications for a elements that accommodate different shapes (`rect`, `circle`, and `poly`) and coordinates when the link surrounds an image. Although the `coords` and `shape` properties are present for a element objects in all W3C DOM−compatible browsers, active support for the feature is not present in NN6.

hash
host
hostname
pathname
port
protocol
search

Value: Strings   Read/Write

Compatibility: WinIE3+, MacIE3+, NN2+, Moz+, Safari+, Opera+, Chrome+

This large set of properties is identical to the same-named properties of the `location` object (see Chapter 28, "Location and History Objects"). All properties are components of the URL that is assigned to the link object's `href` attribute. Although none of these properties appears in the W3C DOM specification for the a element object, the properties survive in modern browsers for backward compatibility. If you want to script the change of the destination for a link, try modifying the value of the object's `href` property, rather than modifying individual components of the URL.

Related Item: `location` object

href

Value: String   Read/Write

Compatibility: WinIE3+, MacIE3+, NN2+, Moz+, Safari+, Opera+, Chrome+

The `href` property (included in the W3C DOM) is the URL of the destination of an a element equipped to act as a link. URLs can be relative or absolute.

In W3C DOM−compatible browsers, you can turn an anchor object into a link object by assigning a value to the `href` property, even if the a element has no `href` attribute in the HTML that loads from the server. Naturally, this conversion is temporary, and it lasts only as long as the page is loaded in the browser. When you assign a value to the `href` property of an a element that surrounds text, the text assumes the appearance of a link (either the default appearance or whatever style you assign to links).

Related Item: `location` object

hreflang

Value: String   Read/Write

Compatibility: WinIE6+, MacIE6+, NN6+, Moz+, Safari+, Opera+, Chrome+

The hreflang property advises the browser (if the browser takes advantage of it) about the written language used for the content to which the a element's href attribute points. Values for this property must be in the form of the standard language codes (for example, en-us for U.S. English).

Methods

Value: String   Read/Write

Compatibility: WinIE4+, MacIE4+, NN-, Moz-, Safari-, Opera-, Chrome-

The Methods property (note the uppercase M) represents the HTML 4 methods attribute for an a element. Values for this attribute and property serve as advisory instructions to the browser about which HTTP method(s) to use for accessing the destination document. This is a rare case in which an HTML 4 attribute is not echoed in the W3C DOM. In any case, although IE4+ supports the property, the IE browsers do nothing special with the information.

mimeType

Value: String   Read-Only

Compatibility: WinIE4+, MacIE-, NN-, Moz-, Safari-, Opera-, Chrome-

This property is used to obtain the MIME type of the document linked to by the a element. The HTML 4 and W3C DOM specifications define a type attribute and type property, instead of mimeType. The property is a read-only property and, therefore, has no control over the MIME type of the destination document. Interestingly, the IE8 MSDN documentation for the a object does not list this attribute, although IE8 does continue to support it.

Related Item: a.type property

name

Value: String   Read/Write

Compatibility: WinIE3+, MacIE3+, NN2+, Moz+, Safari+, Opera+, Chrome+

Although a name attribute is optional for an a element serving solely as a link object, it is required for an anchor object. This value is exposed to scripting via the name property. Although it is unlikely that you will need to change the value by scripting, you can use this property as a way to identify a link object from among the document.links arrays in a repeat loop. For example:

```
for (var i = 0; i < document.links.length; i++)
{
    if (document.links[i].name == "bottom")
    {
        // statements dealing with the link named "bottom"
    }
}
```

If this code makes it inside the if clause, you know you've found a link with the name bottom.

nameProp

Value: String

Read-Only

Compatibility: WinIE4+, MacIE4+, NN-, Moz-, Safari-

The IE-specific nameProp property is a convenience property that retrieves the segment of the href to the right of the rightmost forward slash character of the URL. Most typically, this value is the name of the file from a URL. But if the URL also includes a port number, that number is returned as part of the nameProp value.

rel
rev

Value: String

Read/Write

Compatibility: WinIE4+, MacIE4+, NN6+, Moz+, Safari+, Opera+, Chrome+

The rel and rev properties define relationships in the forward and back directions with respect to the destination document of the a element. In other words, you're describing how a link relates to the document to which it points, as well as how the document relates back. For example, in a table-of-contents page, each link to a chapter might have its rel attribute set to chapter, whereas its rev attribute might be set to contents. Browsers have yet to exploit most of the potential of these attributes and properties.

A long list of values is predefined for these properties, based on the corresponding attribute values specified in HTML 4. If the browser does nothing with a particular value, the value is ignored. You can string together multiple values in a space-delimited list inside a single string. Accepted values are as follows:

alternate	contents	index	start
appendix	copyright	next	stylesheet
bookmark	glossary	prev	subsection
chapter	help	section	

target

Value: String

Read/Write

Compatibility: WinIE3+, MacIE3+, NN2+, Moz+, Safari+, Opera+, Chrome+

An important property of the link object is the target. This value reflects the window name supplied to the target attribute in the a element.

You can temporarily change the target for a link. But as with most transient object properties, the setting does not survive soft reloads. Rather than alter the target this way, you can safely force the target change by letting the href attribute call a javascript:functionName() psuedo-URL in which the function assigns a document to the desired window.location. If you have done extensive HTML authoring before, you will find it hard to break the habit of relying on the target attribute.

Another drawback to the target attribute is the fact that it isn't supported by the strict XHTML DTD. So if you develop XHTML pages that must validate with the strict DTD, you will not be able to include a `target` attribute in your `<a>` tags. Instead, use the page's `onload` event handler or the `a` element's `onclick` event handler to invoke a function that assigns the desired value to the `target` property. In this case, you are using a JavaScript property to sidestep a limitation associated with an HTML attribute.

Related Item: `document.links` property

type

Value: String   Read/Write

Compatibility: WinIE6+, MacIE6+, NN6+, Moz+, Safari+, Opera+, Chrome+

The `type` property represents the HTML 4 `type` attribute, which specifies the MIME type for the content of the destination document to which the element's `href` attribute points. This is primarily an advisory property for browsers that wish to, say, display different cursor styles based on the anticipated type of content at the other end of the link. Thus far, browsers do not take advantage of this feature. However, you can assign MIME type values to the attribute (for example, `video/mpeg`) and let scripts read those values for making style changes to the link text after the page loads. IE4+ also implements a similar property in the `mimeType` property.

Related Item: `a.mimeType` property

urn

Value: String   Read/Write

Compatibility: WinIE4+, MacIE4+, NN-, Moz-, Safari-, Opera-, Chrome-

The `urn` property represents the IE-specific URN attribute, which enables authors to use a URN (Uniform Resource Name) for the destination of the a element. (See `http://www.ietf.org/rfc/rfc2141.txt` for information about URNs.) This property is not in common use.

Image, Area, Map, and Canvas Objects

F or modern web browsers, images and areas — those items created by the `<img>` and `<area>` tags — are first-class objects that you can script for enhanced interactivity. You can swap the image displayed in an `<img>` tag with other images, perhaps to show the highlighting of an icon button when the cursor rolls atop it. And with scriptable client-side area maps, pages can be smarter about how they respond to users' clicks on image regions.

One further benefit afforded scripters is that they can preload images into the browser's image cache as the page loads. With cached images, the user experiences no delay when the first swap occurs. The need for this capability has diminished slightly with higher bandwidth connections, but it still isn't a bad idea for those users who still rely on connections with speed limitations.

New on the graphical JavaScript scene is the notion of a canvas, which is a graphical region that you can use to carry out graphics operations via JavaScript code. A few browsers already support canvases, so you can get started tinkering with them now.

Image and img Element Objects

For HTML element properties, methods, and event handlers, see Chapter 26, "Generic HTML Element Objects."

Properties	Methods	Event Handlers
align		onabort
alt		onerror
border		onload
complete		

imageObject

Properties	Methods	Event Handlers
dynsrc		
fileCreatedDate		
fileModifiedDate		
fileSize		
fileUpdatedDate		
height		
href		
hspace		
isMap		
loop		
longDesc		
lowsrc		
mimeType		
name		
nameProp		
naturalHeight		
naturalWidth		
protocol		
src		
start		
useMap		
vspace		
width		
x		
y		

Syntax

Creating an Image object:

```
imageObject = new Image([pixelWidth, pixelHeight]);
```

Accessing `img` element and `Image` object properties or methods:

```
(NN3+/IE4+)    [window.]document.imageName. property | method([parameters])
(NN3+/IE4+)    [window.]document.images[index]. property | method([parameters])
(NN3+/IE4+)    [window.]document.images["imageName"]. property |
               method([parameters])
(IE4+)         [window.]document.all.elemID.property | method([parameters])
(IE5+/W3C)     [window.]document.getElementById("elemID").property |
               method([parameters])
```

Compatibility: WinIE4+, MacIE4+, NN3+, Moz+, Safari+, Opera+, Chrome+

About this object

Before getting into detail about images as objects, it's important to understand the distinction between instances of the static `Image` object and `img` element objects. The former exist only in the browser's memory without showing anything to the user; the latter are the elements on the page generated via the `<img>` (or nonsanctioned, but accepted, `<image>`) tag. Scripts use instances of the `Image` object to pre-cache images for a page, but `Image` object instances obviously have fewer applicable properties, methods, and event handlers because they are neither visible on the page nor influenced by tag attributes.

The primary advantage of treating `img` elements as objects is that scripts can change the image that occupies the `img` object's space on the page, even after the document has loaded and displayed an initial image. The key to this scriptability is the `src` property of an image.

In a typical scenario, a page loads with an initial image. That image's tags specify any of the extra attributes, such as `height` and `width` (which help speed the rendering of the page), and specify whether the image uses a client-side image map to make it interactive. (See the `area` object later in this chapter.) As the user spends time on the page, the image can then change (perhaps in response to user action or some timed event in the script), replacing the original image with a new one in the same space. In legacy browsers that support the `img` element object, the height and width of the initial image that loads into the element establishes a fixed-sized rectangular space for the image. Attempts to fit an image of another size into that space forces the image to scale (up or down, as the case may be) to fit the rectangle. But in modern browsers (IE4+/Moz/W3C), a change in the image's size is reflected by an automatic reflow of the page content around the different size. Of course, you might not consider this desirable and choose to pre-size your images to the same size to avoid the automatic reflow of the page content.

The benefit of separate instances of the `Image` object is that a script can create a virtual image to hold a preloaded image. (The image is loaded into the image cache but the browser does not display the image.) The hope is that one or more unseen images will load into memory while the user is busy reading the page or waiting for the page to download. Then, in response to user action on the page, an image can change instantaneously rather than forcing the user to wait for the image to load on demand.

To preload an image, begin by assigning a new, empty `Image` object to a global variable. The new image is created via the constructor function available to the `Image` object:

```
var imageVariable = new Image(width, height);
```

You help the browser allocate memory for the image if you provide the pixel height and width of the pre-cached image as parameters to the constructor function. All that this statement does is create an object in memory whose properties are all empty. To force the browser to load the image into the cache, assign an image file URL to the object's src property:

```
var oneImage = new Image(55,68);
oneImage.src = "neatImage.gif";
```

As this image loads, you see the progress in the status bar, just like you would with any image. Later, assign the src property of this stored image to the src property of the img element object that appears on the page:

```
document.images["someImage"].src = oneImage.src;
```

Depending on the type and size of image, you will be amazed at the speedy response of this kind of loading. With small-palette graphics, the image displays instantaneously.

A popular user-interface technique is to change the appearance of an image that represents a clickable button when the user rolls the mouse pointer atop the art. This action assumes that a mouse event fires on an element associated with the object. Image rollovers are most commonly accomplished in two different image states: normal and highlighted. But you may want to increase the number of states to more closely simulate the way clickable buttons work in application programs. In some instances, a third state signifies that the button is switched on. For example, if you use rollovers in a frame for navigational purposes, and the user clicks a button to navigate to the Products area, that button stays selected but in a different style than the rollover highlights. Some designers go one step further by providing a fourth state that appears briefly when the user mouses down an image. Each one of these states requires the download of yet another image, so you have to gauge the effect of the results against the delay in loading the page.

The speed with which image swapping takes place may lead you to consider using this approach for animation. Though this approach may be practical for brief bursts of animation, the many other ways of introducing animation to your web page (such as via GIF89a-standard images, Flash animations, Java applets, and a variety of plug-ins) produce animation that offers better speed control. In fact, swapping preloaded JavaScript image objects for some cartoon-like animations may be too fast. You can build a delay mechanism around the setInterval() method, but the precise timing between frames varies with client processor performance.

All browsers that implement the img element object also implement the document.images array. You can (and probably should) use the availability of this array as a conditional switch before any script statements that work with the img element or Image object. The construction to use is as follows:

```
if (document.images)
{
   // statements working with images as objects
}
```

Earlier browsers treat the absence of this array as the equivalent of false in the if clause's conditional statement.

Most of the properties discussed here mirror attributes of the img HTML element. For more details on the meanings and implications of attribute values on the rendered content, consult the HTML 4.01 specification (http://www.w3.org/TR/html4/), the HTML 5 specification (http://www.w3.org/TR/html5/), and Microsoft's extensions for IE (http://msdn.microsoft.com/en-us/library/ms535259%28VS.85%29.aspx).

Properties

align

Value: String   Read/Write

Compatibility: WinIE4+, MacIE4+, NN6+, Moz+, Safari+, Opera+, Chrome+

The align property defines how the image is oriented in relation to surrounding text content. It is a double-duty property because you can use it to control the vertical or horizontal alignment, depending on the value (and whether the image is influenced by a float style attribute). Values are string constants, as follows:

```
absbottom    middle
absmiddle    right
baseline     texttop
bottom       top
left
```

The default alignment for an image is bottom. Increasingly, element alignment is handed over to style sheet control. (This is reflected in the corresponding alignment attribute's deprecation in HTML 4.01 and nonexistence in HTML 5.) In modern web pages, designers are encouraged to use style sheets, as opposed to element attributes, for presentation details such as alignment.

Listing 31-1 enables you to choose from the different align property values as they influence the layout of an image whose HTML is embedded inline with some other text. Resize the window to see different perspectives on word-wrapping on a page and their effects on the alignment choices. Not all browsers provide distinctive alignments for each choice, so experiment in multiple supported browsers.

LISTING 31-1

Testing an Image's align Property

```
<!DOCTYPE html>
<html>
   <head>
      <meta http-equiv="content-type" content="text/html;charset=utf-8">
      <title>img align Property</title>
      <script type="text/javascript">
      function setAlignment(sel)
      {
         document.getElementById("myIMG").align =
            sel.options[sel.selectedIndex].value;
      }
      </script>
   </head>
   <body>
      <h1>img align Property</h1>
      <hr />
      <form>
         Choose the image alignment: <select onchange="setAlignment(this)">
            <option value="absbottom">absbottom</option>
            <option value="absmiddle">absmiddle</option>
```

continued

LISTING 31-1   *(continued)*

```
        <option value="baseline">baseline</option>
        <option value="bottom" selected="selected">bottom</option>
        <option value="left">left</option>
        <option value="middle">middle</option>
        <option value="right">right</option>
        <option value="texttop">texttop</option>
        <option value="top">top</option>
    </select>
  </form>
  <hr />
  <p>Lorem ipsum dolor sit amet, consectetaur adipisicing elit, sed do
     eiusmod tempor incididunt ut labore et dolore magna aliqua.
     <img alt="image" id="myIMG" src="desk1.gif" height="90" width="120" />
     Ut enim adminim veniam, quis nostrud exercitation ullamco laboris nisi ut
     aliquip ex ea commodo consequat.</p>
  </body>
</html>
```

Related Items: text-align, float style sheet attributes

alt

Value: String   Read/Write

Compatibility: WinIE4+, MacIE4+, NN6+, Moz+, Safari+, Opera+, Chrome+

The alt property enables you to set or modify the text that the browser displays in the image's
rectangular space (if height and width are specified in the tag) before the image downloads
to the client. Also, if a browser has images turned off (or is incapable of displaying images),
the alt text helps users identify what is normally displayed in that space. In IE, the alt text
is displayed when you mouse over the image. You can modify this alt text even after the
page loads.

Example

Use The Evaluator (Chapter 4, "JavaScript Essentials") to assign a string to the alt property of the
document.myIMG image on the page. First, assign a nonexistent image to the src property to
remove the existing image:

```
document.myIMG.src = "fred.gif"
```

Scroll down to the image, and you can see that the original image has been replaced with a space for
the new, nonexistent, image. Now, assign a string to the alt property:

```
document.myIMG.alt = "Fred\'s face"
```

The extra backslash is required to escape the apostrophe inside the string. Scroll down to see the
new alt text in the image space. This simple test in The Evaluator will work in most browsers.
In some browsers, such as Firefox, it will appear to not work. Browsers such as Firefox support

the properties in question, but since the new image is nonexistent, it doesn't replace the original image; because the original image isn't broken, you won't see the effect of changing the `alt` property.

Related Item: `title` property

border

Value: Integer   Read/Write

Compatibility: WinIE4+, MacIE4+, NN3+, Moz+, Safari+, Opera+, Chrome+

The `border` property defines the thickness in pixels of a border around an image. Remember that if you wrap an image inside an `a` element to make use of the mouse events (for rollovers and such), be sure to set the `border=0` attribute of the `<img>` tag to prevent the browser from generating the usual link type of border around the image. Even though the default value of the attribute is zero, surrounding the image with an `a` element or attaching the image to a client-side image map puts a border around the image.

As with the `alignment` property, an element's border is increasingly handed over to style sheet control. (This is reflected in the corresponding `border` attribute's nonexistence in HTML 5.) In modern web pages, designers are encouraged to use style sheets as opposed to element attributes for presentation details such as borders.

Example

Feel free to experiment with the `document.myIMG.border` property for the image in The Evaluator (Chapter 4, "JavaScript Essentials") by assigning different integer values to the property.

Related Items: `isMap`, `useMap` properties

complete

Value: Boolean   Read-Only

Compatibility: WinIE4+, MacIE4+, NN3+, Moz+, Safari+, Opera+, Chrome+

Sometimes you may want to make sure that an image is not still in the process of loading before allowing another process to take place. This situation is different from waiting for an image to load before triggering some other process (which you can do via the `Image` object's `onload` event handler). To verify that the `img` object displays a completed image, check for the Boolean value of the `complete` property. To verify that a particular image file has loaded, first find out whether the `complete` property is `true`; then compare the `src` property against the desired filename.

An image's `complete` property switches to `true` even if only the specified `lowsrc` image has finished loading. Do not rely on this property alone for determining whether the `src` image has loaded if both `src` and `lowsrc` attributes are specified in the `<img>` tag.

One of the best ways to use this property is in an `if` construction's conditional statement:

```
if (document.myImage.complete)
{
    // statements that work with document.myImage
}
```

imageObject.complete

To experiment with the image.complete property, run Listing 31-2. Click the Load NASA Image button. As the image loads, click the Is "it loaded yet?" button to see the status of the complete property for the Image object. The value is false until the loading finishes; then, the value becomes true. We deliberately chose to load a large image directly from the NASA web site so that you would have plenty of time to click the "Is it loaded yet?" button several times in order to see the behavior of the complete property. You may have to quit and relaunch your browser between trials to clear the image from the cache (or empty the browser's memory cache) if you've been visiting the NASA web site's image gallery.

LISTING 31-2

Scripting image.complete

```
<!DOCTYPE html>
<html>
    <head>
        <meta http-equiv="content-type" content="text/html;charset=utf-8">
        <title>The Complete Property</title>
        <script type="text/javascript">
        function loadIt()
        {
            document.getElementById("result").value = "";
            document.getElementById("theImage").src =
                "http://www.nasa.gov/images/content/402217main_ssc2008-01b_full.jpg" ;
        }
        function checkLoad()
        {
            document.getElementById("result").value =
                document.getElementById("theImage").complete;
        }
        </script>
    </head>
    <body>
        <img id="theImage" alt="image" width="120" height="90" />
        <form>
            <input type="button" value="Load NASA image"
                    onclick="loadIt();" />
            <p><input type="button" value="Is it loaded yet?"
                    onclick="checkLoad();" />
                <input id="result" type="text" />
            </p>
            <input type="reset" />
        </form>
    </body>
</html>
```

Note

The property assignment event handling technique in the previous example is a deliberate simplification to make the code more readable. It is generally better to use the more modern approach of binding events using the addEventListener() **(NN6+/Moz/W3C)** or attachEvent() **(IE5+)** methods. A modern cross-browser event handling technique is explained in detail in Chapter 32, "Events Objects." ∎

Related Items: `img.src`, `img.lowsrc`, `img.readyState` properties; `onload` event handler

dynsrc

Value: URL string   Read/Write

Compatibility: WinIE4-6, MacIE4+, NN-, Moz-, Safari-, Opera-, Chrome-

The `dynsrc` property is a URL to a video source file, which (in IE) you can play through an `img` element. You can turn a space devoted to a static image into a video viewer by assigning a URL of a valid video source (for example, an `.avi` or `.mpg` file) to the `dynsrc` property of the image element object. Unlike the `src` property of image objects, assigning a URL to the `dynsrc` property does not pre-cache the video.

You may experience buggy behavior in various IE versions when you assign a value to an image's `dynsrc` property after the `img` element renders a `.gif` or `.jpg` image. In WinIE5, the status bar indicates that the video file is still downloading, even though the download is complete. Clicking the Stop button has no effect. WinIE5.5+ may not even load the video file, leaving a blank space, although the property does store the value of the URL. MacIE5 changes between static and motion images with no problems, but playing the video file multiple times causes the `img` element to display black space beyond the element's rectangle.

Related Items: `img.loop`, `img.start` properties

fileCreatedDate
fileModifiedDate
fileUpdatedDate
fileSize

Value: String, Integer (`fileSize`)   Read-Only

Compatibility: WinIE4+, MacIE5+, NN-, Moz-, Safari-, Opera-, Chrome-

These four IE-specific properties return information about the file displayed in the `img` element (whether it's a still or animated image). Three of the properties reveal the dates on which the current image's file was created, modified, and updated. For an unmodified file, its creation and modified dates are the same. The updated date of an image is the date on which the image file was last uploaded to the server; the `fileUpdatedDate` property is only supported on WinIE5.5+ and MacIE5. The `fileSize` property reveals the number of bytes of the file.

Date values returned for the first two properties are formatted differently between IE4 and IE5. The former provides a full readout of the day and date; the latter returns a format similar to mm/dd/yyyy. Note, however, that the values contain only the date and not the time. In any case, you can use the values as the parameter to a `new Date()` constructor function. This enables you to then use date calculations for such information as the number of days between the current day and the most recent modification.

Not all servers provide the proper date or size information about a file or in a format that IE can inter-pret. Test your implementation on the deployment server to ensure compatibility.

Also, be aware that these properties can be read-only for a file that is loaded in the browser. JavaScript by itself cannot get this information about files on the server.

imageObject.height

Note
All of these file-related properties are present in the Mac version of IE, but the values are empty. ■

Example

These properties are similar to the same-named properties of the `document` object. You can see these properties in action in Listing 29-4. Make a copy of that listing, and supply an image before modifying the references from the `document` object to the `Image` object to see how these properties work with the `img` element object.

Or, just test them out one at a time using an existing image in the Evaluator (Chapter 4, "JavaScript Essentials"):

```
document.getElementById("myIMG").fileSize
```

Related Items: None

height
width

Value: Integer   Read/Write (see text)

Compatibility: WinIE4+, MacIE4+, NN3+, Moz+, Safari+, Opera+, Chrome+

The `height` and `width` properties return and control the pixel height and width of an image object. The property is read/write in all modern browsers that support the `img` element object. However, the net effect of changing these properties varies from browser to browser. For example, if you adjust the `height` property of an image in Mozilla, the browser automatically scales the image within the same proportions as the original. But adjusting the `width` property has no effect on the `height` property. In IE7, the opposite effect is true in regard to `width` and `height`. Any time an image is scaled dynamically, unwanted pixelation can occur in the image, so modify an image's size with extreme care.

Example

Use The Evaluator (Chapter 4, "JavaScript Essentials") to experiment with the `height` and `width` properties. Begin retrieving the default values by entering the following two statements into the top text box:

```
document.myIMG.height
document.myIMG.width
```

Increase the height of the image from its default 90 to 180:

```
document.myIMG.height = 180
```

Next, exaggerate the width:

```
document.myIMG.width = 400
```

View the resulting image.

Related Items: `hspace`, `vspace` properties

href

(See src property)

hspace
vspace

Value: Integer   Read/Write

Compatibility: WinIE4+, MacIE4+, NN3+, Moz+, Safari+, Opera+, Chrome+

The hspace and vspace properties control the pixel width of a transparent margin surrounding an image. Specifically, hspace controls the margins at the left and right of the image; vspace controls the top and bottom margins. Images, by default, have margins of zero pixels.

Example

Use The Evaluator (Chapter 4, "JavaScript Essentials") to experiment with the hspace and vspace properties. Begin by noticing that the image near the bottom of the page has no margins specified for it and is flush left with the page. Now assign a horizontal margin spacing of 30 pixels:

    document.myIMG.hspace = 30

The image has shifted to the right by 30 pixels. An invisible margin also exists to the right of the image.

Related Items: height, width properties

isMap

Value: Boolean   Read/Write

Compatibility: WinIE4+, MacIE4+, NN6+, Moz+, Safari+ Opera+, Chrome+

The isMap property enables you to set whether the image should act as a server-side image map. When set as a server-side image map, pixel coordinates of the click are passed as parameters to whatever link href surrounds the image. For client-side image maps, see the useMap property later in this chapter.

Example

The image in The Evaluator page is not defined as an image map. Thus, if you type the following statement into the top text box, the property returns false:

    document.myIMG.isMap

Related Item: img.useMap property

longDesc

Value: URL string   Read/Write

Compatibility: WinIE6+, MacIE5+, NN6+, Moz+, Safari+, Opera+, Chrome+

The longDesc property is a URL of a file that is intended to provide a detailed description of the image associated with the img element. Current browsers recognize this property, but do not do anything special with the information — whether specified by script or the longdesc attribute.

Related Item: `alt` property

loop

Value: Integer   Read/Write

Compatibility: WinIE4-6, MacIE4+, NN-, Moz-, Safari-, Opera-, Chrome-

The `loop` property represents the number of times a video clip playing through the `img` element object should run. After the video plays that number of times, only the first frame of the video appears in the image area. The default value is 1; but if you set the value to `-1`, the video plays continuously. Unfortunately, setting the property to 0 prior to assigning a URL to the `dynsrc` property does not prevent the movie from playing at least once (except on the Mac, as noted in the `dynsrc` property discussion earlier in this chapter).

Related Item: `dynsrc` property

lowsrc
lowSrc

Value: URL string   Read/Write

Compatibility: WinIE4+, MacIE4+, NN3+, Moz-, Safari-, Opera-, Chrome-

For image files that take several seconds to load, modern browsers enable you to specify a lower-resolution image, or some other quick-loading placeholder, to stand in while the big image crawls to the browser. You assign this alternate image via the `lowsrc` attribute in the `<img>` tag. The attribute is reflected in the `lowsrc` property of an image object. While all modern browsers enable you to specify this property or its corresponding HTML attribute, only IE actually displays the specified image.

All compatible browsers recognize the all-lowercase version of this property. NN6 also recognizes a camelCase "S" version of the property, `lowSrc`.

Be aware that in some browsers if you assign a URL to the `lowsrc` attribute, the `complete` property switches to `true` and the `onLoad` event handler fires when the alternate file finishes loading: The browser does not wait for the main `src` file to load.

Example

See Listing 31-4 for the `Image` object's `onload` event handler to see how the source-related properties affect event processing.

Related Items: `img.src`, `img.complete` properties

mimeType

Value: String   Read-Only

Compatibility: WinIE6+, MacIE-, NN-, Moz-, Safari-, Opera-, Chrome-

The `mimeType` property returns a plain-language description of the MIME type for the image, such as `JPEG Image` or `GIF Image`.

Example

You can use the `mimeType` property in Internet Explorer to determine the format of an image, as the following example demonstrates:

```
if (document.myIMG.mimeType.indexOf("JPEG") != -1) {
    // Carry out JPEG-specific processing
}
```

In this example, the `indexOf()` method is used to check for the presence of the phrase `"JPEG"` anywhere in the MIME type string. This works because the string returned in the `mimeType` property for JPEG images is `JPEG Image`.

Related Items: None

name

Value: Identifier string   Read/Write

Compatibility: WinIE3+, MacIE3+, NN2+, Moz+, Safari+ Opera+, Chrome+

The `name` property returns the value assigned to the `name` attribute of an `img` element. Modern browsers allow you to use the ID of the element (`id` attribute) to reference the `img` element object via `document.all` (IE) and `document.getElementById()`. But references in the form of `document.imageName` and `document.images[imageName]` must use only the value assigned to the `name` attribute.

In some designs, it may be convenient to assign numerically sequenced names to `img` elements, such as `img1`, `img2`, and so on. As with any scriptable identifier, the name cannot begin with a numeric character. Rarely, if ever, will you need to change the name of an `img` element object.

Example

You can use The Evaluator (Chapter 4, "JavaScript Essentials") to examine the value returned by the `name` property of the image on that page. Enter the following statement into the top text box:

```
document.myIMG.name
```

Of course, this is redundant because the name is part of the reference to the object.

Related Item: `id` property

nameProp

Value: Filename string   Read-Only

Compatibility: WinIE5+, MacIE-, NN-, Moz-, Safari-, Opera-, Chrome-

Unlike the `src` property, which returns a complete URL in IE, the IE `nameProp` property returns only the filename, exclusive of protocol and path. If your image-swapping script needs to read the name of the file currently assigned to the image (to determine which image to show next), the `nameProp` property makes it easier to get the actual filename without having to perform extensive parsing of the URL.

Example

You can use The Evaluator Sr. (Chapter 4, "JavaScript Essentials") to compare the results of the `src` and `nameProp` properties in WinIE5+. Enter each of the following statements into the top text box:

```
document.myIMG.src
document.myIMG.nameProp
```

Related Item: `img.src` property

naturalHeight
naturalWidth

Value: Integer   Read-Only

Compatibility: WinIE-, MacIE-, NN6+, Moz+, Safari+, Opera-, Chrome+

The `naturalHeight` and `naturalWidth` properties return the unscaled height and width of the image, in pixels. These properties are useful in situations where script code or `img` element attributes have scaled an image and you wish to know the image's original size.

Example

Use The Evaluator (Chapter 4, "JavaScript Essentials") to experiment with the `naturalHeight` and `naturalWidth` properties in a Mozilla-based or WebKit-based browser. Begin retrieving the default values by entering the following statement into the top text box:

```
document.myIMG.width
```

Increase the width of the image from its default 120 to 200:

```
document.myIMG.width = 200
```

If you scroll down to the image, you see that the image has scaled in proportion. You can now find out the natural width of the original image by taking a look at the `naturalWidth` property:

```
document.myIMG.naturalWidth
```

The Evaluator will reveal 120 as the natural image width even though the image is currently scaled to 200.

Related Items: `img.height`, `img.width` properties

protocol

Value: String   Read-Only

Compatibility: WinIE4+, MacIE5+, NN-, Moz-, Safari-, Opera-, Chrome-

The IE `protocol` property returns only the protocol portion of the complete URL returned by the `src` property. This allows your script, for example, to see if the image is sourced from a local hard drive or a web server. Values returned are not the actual protocol strings; rather, they are descriptions thereof: `HyperText Transfer Protocol` or `File Protocol`.

Example

You can use The Evaluator Sr. (Chapter 4, "JavaScript Essentials") to examine the `protocol` property of the image on the page. Enter the following statement into the top text box:

```
document.myIMG.protocol
```

Related Items: `img.src`, `img.nameProp` properties

src

Value: URL string   Read/Write

Compatibility: WinIE4+, MacIE4+, NN3+, Moz+, Safari+, Opera+, Chrome+

The `src` property is the gateway to precaching images (in instances of the `Image` object that are stored in memory) and performing image swapping (in `img` element objects). Assigning a URL to the `src` property of an image object in memory causes the browser to load the image into the browser's cache (provided the user has the cache turned on). Assigning a URL to the `src` property of an `img` element object causes the element to display the new image. To take advantage of this powerful combination, you preload alternate versions of swappable images into image objects in memory and then assign the `src` property of the `Image` object to the `src` property of the desired `img` element object.

In legacy browsers, the size of the image defined by the original `img` element governs the rectangular space devoted to that image. An attempt to assign an image of a different size to that `img` element object causes the image to rescale to fit the rectangle (usually resulting in a distorted image). In all modern browsers, however, the `img` element object resizes itself to accommodate the image, and the page content reflows around the new size.

Note that when you read the `src` property, it returns a fully formed URL of the image file, including protocol and path. This often makes it inconvenient to let the name of the file guide your script in swapping images in a sequence of your choice. Some other mechanism (such as storing the current filename in a global variable) may be easier to work with (also see the WinIE5+ `nameProp` property).

Example

In the following example (see Listing 31-3), you see a few applications of image objects. Of prime importance is a comparison of how pre-cached versus images rendered on-the-fly feel to the user. As a bonus, you see an example of how to set a timer to automatically change the images displayed in an image object. This feature is a popular request among sites that display advertising banners or slide shows.

As the page loads, a global variable is handed an array of image objects. Entries of the array are assigned string names as index values (`"desk1"`, `"desk2"`, and so on). The intention is that these names ultimately will be used as addresses to the array entries. Each image object in the array has a URL assigned to it, which pre-caches the image.

The page (see Figure 31-1) includes two `img` elements: one that displays noncached images and one that displays cached images. Under each image is a `select` element that you can use to select one of four possible image files for each element. The `onchange` event handler for each `select` list invokes a different function to change the noncached (`loadIndividual()`) or cached (`loadCached()`) images. Both of these functions take as their single parameter a reference to the form that contains the `select` elements.

FIGURE 31-1

The image object demonstration page.

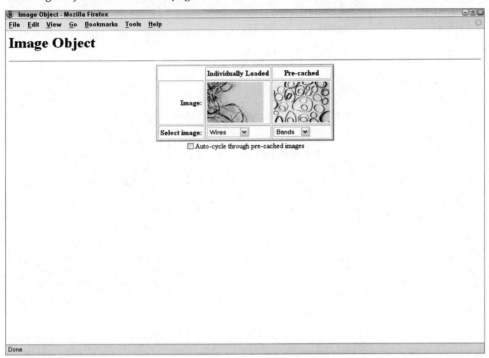

To cycle through images at five-second intervals, the checkTimer() function looks to see if the timer check box is selected. If so, the selectedIndex property of the cached image select control is copied and incremented (or reset to zero if the index is at the maximum value). The select element is adjusted, so you can now invoke the loadCached() function to read the currently selected item and set the image accordingly.

For some extra style points, the <body> tag includes an onunload event handler that invokes the resetSelects() function. This general-purpose function loops through all forms on the page and all elements within each form. For every select element, the selectedIndex property is reset to zero. Thus, if a user reloads the page, or returns to the page via the Back button, the images start in their original sequence. An onload event handler makes sure that the images are in sync with the select choices and the checkTimer() function is invoked with a five-second delay. Unless the timer check box is checked, however, the cached images don't cycle.

LISTING 31-3

A Scripted Image Object and Rotating Images

```
<!DOCTYPE html>
<html>
    <head>
        <meta http-equiv="content-type" content="text/html;charset=utf-8">
        <title>Image Object</title>
        <script type="text/javascript">
        // global declaration for 'desk' images array
        var imageDB;
        // pre-cache the 'desk' images
        if (document.images)
        {
            // list array index names for convenience
            var deskImages = new Array("desk1", "desk2", "desk3", "desk4");
            // build image array and pre-cache them
            imageDB = new Array(4);
            for (var i = 0; i < imageDB.length ; i++)
            {
                imageDB[deskImages[i]] = new Image(120,90);
                imageDB[deskImages[i]].src = deskImages[i] + ".gif";
            }
        }
        // change image of 'individual' image
        function loadIndividual(form)
        {
            if (document.images)
            {
                var gifName =
                    form.individual.options[form.individual.selectedIndex].value;
                document.getElementById("thumbnail1").src = gifName + ".gif";
            }
        }
        // change image of 'cached' image
        function loadCached(form)
        {
            if (document.images)
            {
                var gifIndex =
                    form.cached.options[form.cached.selectedIndex].value;
                document.getElementById("thumbnail2").src = imageDB[gifIndex].src;
            }
        }
        // if switched on, cycle 'cached' image to next in queue
        function checkTimer()
```

continued

imageObject.src

LISTING 31-3   *(continued)*

```
    {
        if (document.images & document.Timer.timerBox.checked)
        {
            var gifIndex = document.selections.cached.selectedIndex;
            if (++gifIndex > imageDB.length - 1)
            {
                gifIndex = 0;
            }
            document.selections.cached.selectedIndex = gifIndex;
            loadCached(document.selections);
            var timeoutID = setTimeout("checkTimer()",5000);
        }
    }
    // reset form controls to defaults on unload
    function resetSelects()
    {
        for (var i = 0; i < document.forms.length; i++)
        {
            for (var j = 0; j < document.forms[i].elements.length; j++)
            {
                if (document.forms[i].elements[j].type == "select-one")
                {
                    document.forms[i].elements[j].selectedIndex = 0;
                }
            }
        }
    }
    // get things rolling
    function init()
    {
        loadIndividual(document.selections);
        loadCached(document.selections);
        setTimeout("checkTimer()",5000);
    }
    </script>
</head>
<body onload="init()" onunload="resetSelects ()">
    <h1>Image Object</h1>
    <hr />
    <center>
        <table border="3" cellpadding="3">
            <tr>
                <th></th>
                <th>Individually Loaded</th>
                <th>Pre-cached</th>
            </tr>
            <tr>
                <td align="right"><b>Image:</b></td>
                <td><img alt="image" src="cpu1.gif" id="thumbnail1"
                    height="90" width="120" /></td>
```

```
            <td><img alt="image" src="desk1.gif" id="thumbnail2"
                height="90" width="120" /></td>
        </tr>
        <tr>
            <td align="right"><b>Select image:</b></td>
            <form name="selections">
            <td><select name="individual"
                onchange="loadIndividual(this.form)">
                    <option value="cpu1">Wires</option>
                    <option value="cpu2">Keyboard</option>
                    <option value="cpu3">Discs</option>
                    <option value="cpu4">Cables</option>
                </select></td>
            <td><select name="cached" onchange="loadCached(this.form)">
                <option value="desk1">Bands</option>
                <option value="desk2">Clips</option>
                <option value="desk3">Lamp</option>
                <option value="desk4">Erasers</option>
            </select></td>
            </form>
        </tr>
    </table>
    <form name="Timer">
        <input type="checkbox" name="timerBox"
        onclick="checkTimer()" />Auto-cycle through pre-cached images
    </form>
    </center>
</body>
</html>
```

Related Items: `img.lowsrc`, `img.nameProp` properties

start

Value: String   Read/Write

Compatibility: WinIE4-6, MacIE4+, NN-, Moz-, Safari-, Opera-, Chrome-

The `start` property works in conjunction with video clips viewed through the `img` element in IE4+. By default, a clip starts playing (except on the Macintosh) when the image file opens. This follows the default setting of the `start` property: `"fileopen"`. Another recognized value is `"mouseover"`, which prevents the clip from running until the user rolls the mouse pointer atop the image.

Related Items: `img.dynsrc`, `img.loop` properties

useMap

Value: Identifier string   Read/Write

Compatibility: WinIE4+, MacIE4+, NN6+, Moz+, Safari+, Opera+, Chrome+

The `useMap` property represents the `usemap` attribute of an `img` element, pointing to the name assigned to the `map` element in the page (see Listing 31-6). This `map` element contains the details about the client-side image map (described later in this chapter). The value for the useMap property must include the hash mark that defines an internal HTML reference on the page. If you need to switch between two or more image maps for the same img element (for example, you swap images or the user is in a different mode), you can define multiple map elements with different names. Then, change the value of the useMap property for the img element object to associate a different map with the image.

Related Item: isMap property

vspace

(See hspace)

width

(See height)

x
y

Value: Integer   Read-Only

Compatibility: WinIE-, MacIE-, NN4, Moz1+, Safari1+, Opera-, Chrome+

A script can retrieve the x and y coordinates of an img element (the top-left corner of the rectangular space occupied by the image) via the x and y properties. These properties are read-only. They are generally not used, in favor of the offsetLeft and offsetTop properties of any element, which are also supported in IE.

Related Items: img.offsetLeft, img.offsetTop properties; img.scrollIntoView(), window.scrollTo() methods

Event handlers

onabort
onerror

Compatibility: WinIE4+, MacIE4+, NN3+, Moz-, Safari-, Opera-, Chrome-

Your scripts may need to be proactive when a user clicks the Stop button while an image loads or when a network or server problem causes the image transfer to fail. Use the onabort event handler to activate a function in the event of a user clicking the Stop button; use the onerror event handler for the unexpected transfer snafu. Be aware that while onerror works in all browsers, onabort does not.

In practice, these event handlers don't supply all the information you may like to have in a script, such as the filename of the image that's loading at the time. If such information is critical to your scripts, the scripts need to store the name of a currently loading image to a variable before they set the image's src property. You also don't know the nature of the error that triggers an error event. You can treat such problems by forcing a scripted page to reload or by navigating to an entirely different spot in your web site.

Example

Listing 31-4 includes an onabort event handler. If the images already exist in the cache, you must quit and relaunch the browser to try to stop the image from loading. In that example, we provide a reload option for the entire page. How you handle the exception depends a great deal on your page design. Do your best to smooth over any difficulties that users may encounter.

onload

Compatibility: WinIE3+, MacIE3+, NN2+, Moz+, Safari+, Opera+, Chrome+

An img object's onload event handler fires when one of three actions occurs: an image's lowsrc image finishes loading; in the absence of a lowsrc image specification, the src image finishes loading; or when each frame of an animated GIF (GIF89a format) appears.

It's important to understand that if you define a lowsrc file inside an <img> tag, the img object receives no further word about the src image having completed its loading. If this information is critical to your script, verify the current image file by checking the src property of the Image object.

Be aware, too, that an img element's onload event handler may fire before the other elements on the page have completed loading. If the event handler function refers to other elements on the page, the function should verify the existence of other elements prior to addressing them.

Quit and restart your browser, or clear your cache, to get the most from Listing 31-4. As the document first loads, the lowsrc image file (the picture of pencil erasers) loads ahead of the NASA image. (Recall that the lowsrc property is not supported by all browsers, so you won't necessarily see the pencil erasers loaded ahead of the NASA image.) Again, we deliberately chose to load a large image directly from the NASA web site so that you would have more time to see the behavior of the onload event handler. When the erasers are loaded, the onload event handler writes "done" to the text field, even though the main image (the NASA image) is not loaded yet.

LISTING 31-4

The Image onload Event Handler

```
<!DOCTYPE html>
<html>
    <head>
        <meta http-equiv="content-type" content="text/html;charset=utf-8">
        <title>The Image onload Event Handler</title>
        <script type="text/javascript">
        function loadIt(theImage,form)
        {
            if (document.images)
            {
                form.result.value = "";
                document.images[0].lowsrc = "desk1.gif";
                document.images[0].src = theImage;
            }
        }
        function checkLoad(form)
        {
            if (document.images)
            {
                form.result.value = document.images[0].complete;
            }
```

continued

areaObject

LISTING 31-4   *(continued)*

```
      }
      function signal()
      {
          if(confirm("You have stopped the image from loading. Do you want to try again?"))
          {
              location.reload();
          }
      }
      </script>
  </head>
  <body>
      <h1>The Image onload Event Handler</h1>
      <h3>Click the browser's STOP button to invoke the onabort event handler</h3>
      <img alt="image" width="120" height="90" lowsrc="desk4.gif"
          src="http://www.nasa.gov/images/content/406570main_s129e007575_hires_full.jpg"
          onload="if (document.forms[0].result) document.forms[0].result.value='done'"
          onabort="signal()" />
      <form>
          <p><input type="button" value="Is it loaded yet?"
                  onclick="checkLoad(this.form)" />
              <input type="text" name="result" />
              <input type="hidden" />
          </p>
      </form>
  </body>
</html>
```

Related Items: `img.src`, `img.lowsrc` properties

area Element Object

For HTML element properties, methods, and event handlers, see Chapter 26, "Generic HTML Element Objects."

Properties	Methods	Event Handlers
alt		
coords		
hash		
host		
hostname		
href		

Properties	Methods	Event Handlers
noHref		
pathname		
port		
protocol		
search		
shape		
target		

Syntax

Accessing area element object properties:

```
(NN3+/IE4+)    [window.]document.links[index].property
(IE4+)         [window.]document.all.elemID.property | method([parameters])
(IE4+)         [window.]document.all.MAPElemID.areas[index].property |
               method([parameters])
(IE5+/W3C)     [window.]document.getElementById("MAPElemID).areas
               [index].property | method([parameters])
(IE5+/W3C)     [window.]document.getElementById("elemID").property |
               method([parameters])
```

Compatibility: WinIE4+, MacIE4+, NN3+, Moz+, Safari+, Opera+, Chrome+

About this object

Document object models treat an image map area object as one of the link (a element) objects in a document (see the anchor object in Chapter 30, "Link and Anchor Objects"). When you think about it, such treatment is not illogical at all because clicking a map area generally leads the user to another document or anchor location in the same document — a hyperlinked reference.

Although the HTML definitions of links and map areas differ greatly, the earliest scriptable implementations of both kinds of objects had nearly the same properties and event handlers. Starting with IE4, NN6/Moz, and W3C-compatible browsers, all area element attributes are accessible as scriptable properties. Moreover, you can change the makeup of client-side image map areas by way of the map element object. The map element object contains an array of area element objects nested inside. You can remove, modify, or add to the area elements inside the map element.

Client-side image maps are fun to work with, and they have been well documented in HTML references since Netscape Navigator 2 introduced the feature. Essentially, you define any number of areas within the image, based on shape and coordinates. Many graphics tools can help you capture the coordinates of images that you need to enter into the coords attribute of the <area> tag.

Tip

If one gotcha exists that trips up most HTML authors, it's the tricky link between the <img> and <map> tags. You must assign a name to the <map>; in the <img> tag, the usemap attribute requires a hash symbol (#) and the map name. If you forget the hash symbol, you can't create a connection between the image and its map. ■

areaObject

Listing 31-5 contains an example of a client-side image map that allows you to navigate through different geographical features of the Middle East. As you drag the mouse around an aerial image, certain regions cause the mouse pointer to change, indicating that there is a link associated with the region. Clicking a region results in an alert box indicating which region you clicked.

LISTING 31-5

A Simple Client-Side Image Map

```
<!DOCTYPE html>
<html>
    <head>
        <meta http-equiv="content-type" content="text/html;charset=utf-8">
        <title>Image Maps</title>
        <script type="text/javascript">
        function show(msg)
        {
            window.status = msg;
            return true;
        }
        function go(where)
        {
            alert("We're going to " + where + "!");
        }
        function clearIt()
        {
            window.status = "";
            return true;
        }
        </script>
    </head>
    <body>
        <h1>Sinai and Vicinity</h1>
        <img alt="image" src="nile.gif" width="320" height="240"
            usemap="#sinai" />
        <map id="sinai" name="sinai" >
            <area href="javascript:go('Cairo')" coords="12,152,26,161"
                shape="rect" onmouseover="return show('Cairo')"
                onmouseout="return clearIt()" />
            <area href="javascript:go('the Nile River')"
                shape="poly" onmouseover="return show('Nile River')"
                onmouseout="return clearIt()"
                coords="1,155,6,162,0,175,3,201,61,232,109,227,167,238,274,239,292,220,307,
                220,319,230,319,217,298,213,282,217,267,233,198,228,154,227,107,
                221,71,225,21,199,19,165,0,149" />
            <area href="javascript:go('Israel')" coords="95,69,201,91"
                shape="rect" onmouseover="return show('Israel')"
                onmouseout="return clearIt()" />
            <area href="javascript:go('Saudi Arabia')"
                coords="256,57,319,121"
                shape="rect" onmouseover="return show('Saudi Arabia')"
                onmouseout="return clearIt()" />
            <area href="javascript:go('the Mediterranean Sea')"
```

```
        coords="1,55,26,123" shape="rect"
        onmouseover="return show('Mediterranean Sea')"
        onmouseout="return clearIt()" />
   <area href="javascript:go('the Mediterranean Sea')"
        coords="27,56,104,103" shape="rect"
        onmouseover="return show('Mediterranean Sea')"
        onmouseout="return clearIt()" />
</map>
</body>
</html>
```

Properties

alt

Value: String   Read/Write

Compatibility: WinIE4+, MacIE4+, NN6+, Moz+, Safari+, Opera+, Chrome+

The `alt` property represents the `alt` attribute of an `area`. Internet Explorer displays the `alt` text in a tiny pop-up window (tool tip) above an area when you pause (hover) the mouse pointer over it. There is debate among web developers about Microsoft's usage of tool tips for `alt` text, both in image maps and regular images.

Future browsers may implement this attribute to provide additional information about the link associated with the `area` element. For the time being, Internet Explorer is the only mainstream browser to use the `alt` property in any noticeable way, although all the browsers recognize it.

Related Item: `title` property

coords
shape

Value: String   Read/Write

Compatibility: WinIE4+, MacIE4+, NN6+, Moz+, Safari+, Opera+, Chrome+

The `coords` and `shape` properties control the location, size, and shape of the image hot spot governed by the `area` element. Shape values that you can use for this property control the format of the `coords` property values, as follows:

Shape	Coordinates	Example
`circ`	center-x, center-y, radius	`"30, 30, 20"`
`circle`	center-x, center-y, radius	`"30, 30, 20"`
`poly`	x1, y1, x2, y2, ...	`"0, 0, 0, 30, 15, 30, 0, 0"`
`polygon`	x1, y1, x2, y2, ...	`"0, 0, 0, 30, 15, 30, 0, 0"`
`rect`	left, top, right, bottom	`"10, 20, 60, 40"`
`rectangle`	left, top, right, bottom	`"10, 20, 60, 40"`

areaObject.**hash**

The default shape for an `area` is a `rectangle`.

Related Items: None

```
hash
host
hostname
href
pathname
port
protocol
search
target
```

(See corresponding properties of the `link` object in Chapter 30, "Link and Anchor Objects.")

noHref

Value: Boolean   Read/Write

Compatibility: WinIE4+, MacIE4+, NN6+, Moz+, Safari+, Opera+, Chrome+

The `noHref` property is used to enable or disable a particular area within a map. The values of the property may be `true`, which means an area is enabled, or `false` to prevent the area from serving as a link within the map. The actual behavior in any of the browsers may be unpredictable, so test carefully.

shape

(See `coords`)

map Element Object

For HTML element properties, methods, and event handlers, see Chapter 26, "Generic HTML Element Objects."

Properties	Methods	Event Handlers
areas[]		onscroll[†]
name		

[†]See Chapter 29

Syntax

Accessing `map` element object properties:

```
(IE4+)       [window.]document.all.elemID.property | method([parameters])
(IE5+/W3C)   [window.]document.getElementById("elemID").property |
             method([parameters])
```

Compatibility: WinIE4+, MacIE4+, NN6+, Moz+, Safari+, Opera+, Chrome+

About this object

The map element object is an invisible HTML container for all area elements, each of which defines a "hot" region for an image. Client-side image maps associate links (and targets) to rectangular, circular, or polygonal regions of the image.

By far, the most important properties of a map element object are the areas array and, to a lesser extent, the name. It is unlikely that you will change the name of a map. (It is better to define multiple map elements with different names, and then assign the desired name to an img element object's useMap property.) But you can use the areas array to change the makeup of the area objects inside a given client-side map.

Properties

areas[]

Value: Array of area element objects   Read/Write

Compatibility: WinIE4+, MacIE4+, NN6+, Moz+, Safari+, Opera+, Chrome+

Use the areas array to iterate through all area element objects within a map element. Whereas Mozilla-based and WebKit-based browsers adhere closely to the document node structure of the W3C DOM, IE4+ provides more direct access to the area element objects nested inside a map. If you want to rewrite the area elements inside a map, you can clear out the old ones by setting the length property of the areas array to zero. Then assign area element objects to slots in the array to build that array.

Listing 31-6 demonstrates how to use scripting to replace the area element objects inside a map element. The scenario is that the page loads with one image of a computer keyboard. This image is linked to the keyboardMap client-side image map, which specifies details for three hot spots on the image. If you then switch the image displayed in that img element, scripts change the useMap property of the img element object to point to a second map that has specifications more suited to the desk lamp in the second image. Roll the mouse pointer atop the images, and view the URLs associated with each area in the status bar (for this example, the URLs do not lead to other pages).

Another button on the page, however, invokes the makeAreas() function (not supported by MacIE5), which creates four new area element objects and (through DOM-specific pathways) adds those new area specifications to the image. If you roll the mouse atop the image after the function executes, you can see that the URLs now reflect those of the new areas. Also note the addition of a fourth area, whose status bar message appears in Figure 31-2.

LISTING 31-6

Modifying area Elements On-the-Fly

```
<!DOCTYPE html>
<html>
    <head>
        <meta http-equiv="content-type" content="text/html;charset=utf-8">
        <title>map Element Object</title>
        <script type="text/javascript">
        // generate area elements on-the-fly
        function makeAreas()
```

continued

mapObject.areas[]

LISTING 31-6   *(continued)*

```
    {
        document.getElementById("myIMG").src = "desk3.gif";
        // build area element objects
        var area1 = document.createElement("area");
        area1.href = "Script-Made-Shade.html";
        area1.shape = "polygon";
        area1.coords = "52,28,108,35,119,29,119,8,63,0,52,28";
        var area2 = document.createElement("area");
        area2.href = "Script-Made-Base.html";
        area2.shape = "rect";
        area2.coords = "75,65,117,87";
        var area3 = document.createElement("area");
        area3.href = "Script-Made-Chain.html";
        area3.shape = "polygon";
        area3.coords = "68,51,73,51,69,32,68,51";
        var area4 = document.createElement("area");
        area4.href = "Script-Made-Emptyness.html";
        area4.shape = "rect";
        area4.coords = "0,0,50,120";
        // stuff new elements into MAP child nodes
        var mapObj = document.getElementById("lamp_map");
        while (mapObj.childNodes.length)
        {
            mapObj.removeChild(mapObj.firstChild);
        }
        mapObj.appendChild(area1);
        mapObj.appendChild(area2);
        mapObj.appendChild(area3);
        mapObj.appendChild(area4);
        // workaround NN6 display bug
        document.getElementById("myIMG").style.display = "inline";
    }
    function changeToKeyboard()
    {
        document.getElementById("myIMG").src = "cpu2.gif";
        document.getElementById("myIMG").useMap = "#keyboardMap";
    }
    function changeToLamp()
    {
        document.getElementById("myIMG").src = "desk3.gif";
        document.getElementById("myIMG").useMap = "#lampMap";
    }
    </script>
</head>
<body>
    <h1>map Element Object</h1>
    <hr />
    <img alt="image" id="myIMG" src="cpu2.gif" width="120" height="90"
        usemap="#keyboardMap" />
    <map id="keyboardMap" name="keyboardMap">
        <area href="AlpaKeys.htm" shape="rect" coords="0,0,26,42" />
```

```
        <area href="ArrowKeys.htm" shape="polygon"
              coords="48,89,57,77,69,82,77,70,89,78,84,89,48,89" />
        <area href="PageKeys.htm" shape="circle" coords="104,51,14" />
    </map>
    <map name="lampMap" id="lamp_map">
        <area href="Shade.htm" shape="polygon"
              coords="52,28,108,35,119,29,119,8,63,0,52,28" />
        <area href="Base.htm" shape="rect" coords="75,65,117,87" />
        <area href="Chain.htm" shape="polygon"
              coords="68,51,73,51,69,32,68,51" />
    </map>
    <form>
        <p><input type="button" value="Load Lamp Image"
                  onclick="changeToLamp()" />
            <input type="button" value="Write Map on-the-Fly"
                  onclick="makeAreas()" />
        </p>
        <p><input type="button" value="Load Keyboard Image"
                  onclick="changeToKeyboard()" />
        </p>
    </form>
    </body>
</html>
```

FIGURE 31-2

Scripts created a special client-side image map for the image.

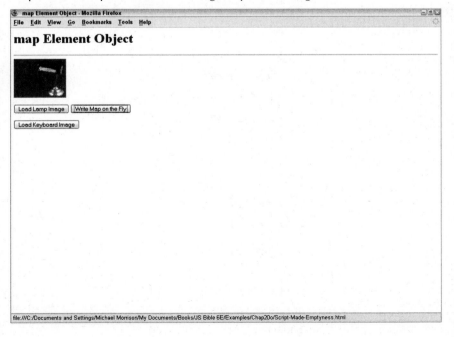

mapObject.name

Related Items: area element object

name

Value: String   Read/Write

Compatibility: WinIE4+, MacIE4+, NN6+, Moz+, Safari+, Opera+, Chrome+

A relationship between the image map and the image needs to be created. We do this with the value of the name property for an image map: it matches the value of the corresponding image's useMap property.

Related Item: useMap property of the corresponding image

canvas Element Object

For HTML element properties, methods, and event handlers, see Chapter 26, "Generic HTML Element Objects."

Properties	Methods	Event Handlers
fillStyle	arc()	
globalAlpha	arcTo()	
globalCompositeOperation	bezierCurveTo()	
lineCap	beginPath()	
lineJoin	clearRect()	
lineWidth	clip()	
miterLimit	closePath()	
shadowBlur	createLinearGradient()	
shadowColor	createPattern()	
shadowOffsetX	createRadialGradient()	
shadowOffsetY	drawImage()	
strokeStyle	fill()	
	fillRect()	
	getContext()	
	lineTo()	
	moveTo()	
	quadraticCurveTo()	
	rect()	
	restore()	

Properties	Methods	Event Handlers
	rotate()	
	save()	
	scale()	
	stroke()	
	strokeRect()	
	translate()	

Syntax

Accessing canvas element object properties:

> (W3C) [window.]document.getElementById("*canvasID*").*property* |
> *method*([*parameters*])

Compatibility: WinIE-, MacIE-, NN-, Moz1.8+, Safari1.3+, Opera+, Chrome+

About this object

A *canvas* is a relatively new construct that enables you to create a rectangular region on a page that can be drawn to programmatically through JavaScript. Relative to a web page, a canvas appears as an image since it occupies a rectangular space. Unlike images, however, canvas content is generated programmatically using a series of methods defined on the canvas object. Support for canvases first appeared in the Safari browser in version 1.3, and then spread to Mozilla browsers in Mozilla version 1.8, which corresponds to Firefox 1.5. While the current version of IE does not natively support this object, there are third-party libraries that allow you to use this object in IE.

Canvas objects are created and positioned on the page using the <canvas> tag, which supports only two unique attributes: width and height. After the canvas is created, the remainder of the work associated with creating a canvas graphic falls to JavaScript code. You'll typically want to create a special draw function that takes on the task of drawing to the canvas, upon the page loading. The job of the draw function is to use the methods of the canvas object to render the canvas graphic.

Listing 31-7 contains a skeletal page for placing a basic canvas with a border. Notice that there is a draw() function that is ready to receive the code for rendering the canvas graphic.

LISTING 31-7

A Skeletal Canvas

```
<!DOCTYPE html>
<html>
   <head>
      <meta http-equiv="content-type" content="text/html;charset=utf-8">
      <title>canvas Object</title>
      <script type="text/javascript">
```

continued

canvasObject

LISTING 31-7   *(continued)*

```
    function draw()
    {
        // Draw some stuff
    }
    </script>
    <style type="text/css">
        canvas { border: 1px solid black; }
    </style>
  </head>
  <body onload="draw();">
    <h1>canvas Object</h1>
    <hr />
    <canvas width="350" height="250"></canvas>
  </body>
</html>
```

Listing 31-8 contains a more interesting canvas example that builds on the skeletal page by adding some actual canvas drawing code. The properties and methods in the `canvas` object provide you with the capability to do some amazing things, so consider this example a rudimentary scratching of the canvas surface.

LISTING 31-8

A Canvas Containing a Simple Chart

```
<!DOCTYPE html>
<html>
    <head>
        <meta http-equiv="content-type" content="text/html;charset=utf-8">
        <title>canvas Object</title>
        <script type="text/javascript">
        function draw()
        {
            var canvas = document.getElementById('chart');
                if (canvas.getContext)
                {
                    var context = canvas.getContext('2d');
                    context.lineWidth = 20;
                    // First bar
                    context.strokeStyle = "red";
                    context.beginPath();
                    context.moveTo(20, 90);
                    context.lineTo(20, 10);
                    context.stroke();
                    // Second bar
                    context.strokeStyle = "green";
                    context.beginPath();
                    context.moveTo(50, 90);
```

```
              context.lineTo(50, 50);
              context.stroke();
              // Third bar
              context.strokeStyle = "yellow";
              context.beginPath();
              context.moveTo(80, 90);
              context.lineTo(80, 25);
              context.stroke();
              // Fourth bar
              context.strokeStyle = "blue";
              context.beginPath();
              context.moveTo(110, 90);
              context.lineTo(110, 75);
              context.stroke();
          }
      }
      </script>
      <style type="text/css">
          canvas { border: 1px solid black; }
      </style>
  </head>
  <body onload="draw();">
      <h1>canvas Object</h1>
      <hr />
      <canvas id="chart" width="130" height="100"></canvas>
  </body>
</html>
```

Figure 31-3 shows this canvas example in action, which involves the display of a simple bar chart. The thing to keep in mind is that this bar chart is being rendered programmatically using vector graphics, which is quite powerful.

This example reveals a few more details about how canvases work. Notice that you must first obtain a context in order to perform operations on the canvas. (In reality, you perform graphics operations on a canvas context, not the canvas element itself.) The job of a context is to provide you with a virtual surface on which to draw. You obtain a canvas context by calling the getContext() method on the canvas object and specifying the type of context; currently, only the 2d (two-dimensional) context is supported in browsers.

When you have a context, canvas drawing operations are carried out relative to the context. You are then free to tinker with stroke and fill colors, create paths and fills, and do most of the familiar graphical things that go along with vector drawing.

You can find a more complete tutorial and examples dedicated to drawing with the canvas element at http://developer.mozilla.org/en/docs/Canvas_tutorial.

Properties
fillStyle

Value: String   Read/Write

Compatibility: WinIE-, MacIE-, NN-, Moz1.8+, Safari1.3+, Opera+, Chrome+

1035

FIGURE 31-3

A simple bar chart created using a vector canvas.

The fillStyle property sets the fill for the brush used in filling a region of a canvas is with a color or pattern. Although you can create gradients and other interesting patterns for use in filling shapes, the most basic usage of the fillStyle property is creating a solid color fill by setting the property to an HTML-style color (#RRGGBB). All fill operations that follow the fillStyle setting will use the new fill style.

Example

Setting a fill color simply involves assigning an HTML-style color to the fillStyle property:

```
context.fillStyle = "#FF00FF";
```

Related Item: strokeStyle property

globalAlpha

Value: Float   Read/Write

Compatibility: WinIE-, MacIE-, NN-, Moz1.8+, Safari1.3+, Opera+, Chrome+

The globalAlpha property is a floating-point property that establishes the transparency (or opacity, depending on how you think about it) of the content drawn on a canvas. Acceptable values for this property range from 0.0 (fully transparent) to 1.0 (fully opaque). The default setting is 1.0, which means that all canvases initially have no transparency.

Example

To set the transparency of a canvas to 50 percent transparency, set the globalAlpha property to 0.5:

```
context.globalAlpha = 0.5;
```

Related Item: None

globalCompositeOperation

Value: String   Read/Write

Compatibility: WinIE-, MacIE-, NN-, Moz1.8+, Safari1.3+, Opera+, Chrome+

The globalCompositeOperation property determines how the canvas appears in relation to background content on a web page. This is a powerful property because it can dramatically affect the manner in which canvas content appears with respect to any underlying web page content. The default setting is source-over, which means opaque areas of the canvas are displayed, but transparent areas are not. Other popular settings include copy, lighter, and darker, among others.

Example

If you want a canvas to always fully cover the background web page, regardless of any transparent areas it may have, you should set the globalCompositeOperation property to copy:

```
context.globalCompositeOperation = "copy";
```

Related Item: None

lineCap
lineJoin
lineWidth

Value: String, Float (lineWidth)   Read/Write

Compatibility: WinIE-, MacIE-, NN-, Moz1.8+, Safari1.3+, Opera+, Chrome+

These properties all impact the manner in which lines are drawn on a canvas. The lineCap property determines the appearance of line end points (butt, round, or square). Similar to lineCap is the lineJoin property, which determines how lines are joined to each other (bevel, miter, or round). By default, lines terminate with no special end point (butt) and are joined cleanly with no special joint graphic (miter).

The lineWidth property establishes the width of lines and is expressed as an integer value greater than 0 in the canvas coordinate space. When a line is drawn, its width appears centered over the line coordinates.

Example

You'll often want to change the lineWidth property to get different effects when assembling a canvas graphic. Here's an example of setting a wider line width (10 in this case):

```
context.lineWidth = 10;
```

Related Items: `miterLimit`, `strokeStyle` properties

miterLimit

Value: Float   Read/Write

Compatibility: WinIE-, MacIE-, NN-, Moz1.8+, Safari1.3+, Opera+, Chrome+

The `miterLimit` property is a floating-point value that determines more specifically how lines are joined together. The `miterLimit` property works in conjunction with the `lineJoin` property to cleanly and consistently join lines in a path.

Related Item: `lineJoin` property

shadowBlur
shadowColor
shadowOffsetX
shadowOffsetY

Value: Integer, String (`shadowColor`)   Read/Write

Compatibility: WinIE-, MacIE-, NN-, Moz1.8+, Safari1.3+, Opera+, Chrome+

These properties all work in conjunction to establish a shadow around canvas content. The `shadowBlur` property determines the width of the shadow itself, whereas `shadowColor` sets the color of the shadow as an HTML-style RGB value (#RRGGBB). Finally, the `shadowOffsetX` and `shadowOffsetY` properties specify exactly how far the shadow is offset from a graphic. The `shadowBlur`, `shadowOffsetX`, and `shadowOffsetY` properties are all expressed in units of the canvas coordinate space.

Example

The following code creates a shadow that is 5 units wide, light gray in color (#BBBBBB), and offset 3 units in both the X and Y directions:

```
context.shadowBlur = 5;
context.shadowColor = "#BBBBBB";
context.shadowOffsetX = 3;
context.shadowOffsetY = 3;
```

Related Item: None

strokeStyle

Value: String   Read/Write

Compatibility: WinIE-, MacIE-, NN-, Moz1.8+, Safari1.3+, Opera+, Chrome+

The `strokeStyle` property controls the style of strokes used to draw on the canvas. You are free to set the stroke style to a gradient or pattern using more advanced canvas features, but the simpler approach is to just set a solid colored stroke as an HTML-style color value (#RRGGBB). The default stroke style is a solid black stroke.

Example

To change the stroke style to a solid green brush, set the `strokeStyle` property to the color green:

```
context.strokeStyle = "#00FF00";
```

Related Item: `fillStyle` property

Methods
```
arc(x, y, radius, startAngle, endAngle, clockwise)
arcTo(x1, y1, x2, y2, radius)
bezierCurveTo(cp1x, cp1y, cp2x, cp2y, x, y)
quadraticCurveTo(cpx, cpy, x, y)
```

Returns: Nothing

Compatibility: WinIE-, MacIE-, NN-, Moz1.8+, Safari1.3+, Opera+, Chrome+

These methods are all responsible for drawing curves in one way or another. If you have any experience with drawing vector graphics, then you're probably familiar with the difference between arcs, Bezier curves, and quadratic curves.

The `arc()` method draws a curved line based upon a center point, a radius, and start and end angles. You can think of this method as tracing the curve of a circle from one angle to another. The angles are expressed in radians, not degrees, so you'll probably need to convert degrees to radians:

```
var radians = (Math.PI / 180) * degrees;
```

The last argument to `arc()` is a Boolean value that determines whether or not the arc is drawn in the clockwise (`true`) or counterclockwise (`false`) direction.

The `arcTo()` method draws an arc along a curve based upon tangent lines of a circle. This method is not implemented in Mozilla until version 1.8.1.

Finally, the `bezierCurveTo()` and `quadraticCurveTo()` methods draw a curved line based upon arguments relating to Bezier and quadratic curves, respectively, which are a bit beyond this discussion. To learn more about Bezier and quadratic curves, check out `en.wikipedia.org/wiki/Bézier_curve`.

```
beginPath()
closePath()
```

Returns: Nothing

Compatibility: WinIE-, MacIE-, NN-, Moz1.8+, Safari1.3+, Opera+, Chrome+

These two methods are used to manage paths. Call the `beginPath()` method to start a new path, into which you can then add shapes. When you're finished, call `closePath()` to close up the path. The only purpose of `closePath()` is to close a subpath that is still open, meaning that you want to finish connecting an open shape back to its start. If you've created a path that is already closed, there is no need to call the `closePath()` method. Listing 31-8 contains a good example of where the `closePath()` method is unnecessary because the bar shapes don't need to be closed.

clip()

Returns: Nothing

Compatibility: WinIE-, MacIE-, NN-, Moz1.8+, Safari1.3+, Opera+, Chrome+

The `clip()` method recalculates the clipping path based upon the current path and the clipping path that already exists. Subsequent drawing operations rely on the newly calculated clipping path.

createLinearGradient(*x1, y1, x2, y2*)
createRadialGradient(*x1, y1, radius1, x2, y2, radius2*)
createPattern(*image, repetition*)

Returns: Gradient object reference, pattern object reference (`createPattern()`)

Compatibility: WinIE-, MacIE-, NN-, Moz1.8+, Safari1.3+, Opera+, Chrome+

These methods are used to create special patterns and gradients for fill operations. A linear gradient is specified as a smooth color transition between two coordinates, whereas a radial gradient is specified based upon two circles with similar radii. You set the actual color range of a gradient by calling the `addColorStop()` method on the gradient object returned from the `createLinear-Gradient()` and `createRadialGradient()` methods. The `addColorStop()` method accepts a floating-point offset and a string color value as its only two arguments.

The `createPattern()` method is used to create a fill pattern based upon an image. You provide an image object and a repetition argument for how the image is tiled when filling a region. Repetition options include `repeat`, `repeat-x`, `repeat-y`, and `no-repeat`.

drawImage(*image, x, y*)
drawImage(*image, x, y, width, height*)
drawImage(*image, srcX, srcY, srcWidth, srcHeight, destX, destY, destWidth, destHeight*)

Returns: Nothing

Compatibility: WinIE-, MacIE-, NN-, Moz1.8+, Safari1.3+, Opera+, Chrome+

These `drawImage()` methods all draw an image to the context. The difference between them has to do with if and how the image is scaled as it is drawn. The first version draws the image at a coordinate with no scaling, whereas the second version scales the image to the specified target width and height. Finally, the third version enables you to draw a portion of the image to a target location with a scaled width and height.

fill()
fillRect(*x, y, width, height*)
clearRect(*x, y, width, height*)

Returns: Nothing

Compatibility: WinIE-, MacIE-, NN-, Moz1.8+, Safari1.3+, Opera+, Chrome+

These methods are used to fill and clear areas. The `fill()` method fills the area within the current path, whereas the `fillRect()` method fills a specified rectangle independent of the current path. The `clearRect()` method is used to clear (erase) a rectangle.

getContext(*contextID*)

Returns: Context object reference

Compatibility: WinIE-, MacIE-, NN-, Moz1.8+, Safari1.3+, Opera+, Chrome+

The `getContext()` method operates on a canvas element object, not a context, and is used to obtain a context for further graphical operations. You must call this method to obtain a context before you can draw to a canvas since all of the canvas drawing methods are actually called relative to a context, not a canvas. For the standard two-dimensional canvas context, specify `"2d"` as the sole parameter to the method.

lineTo(*x, y*)
moveTo(*x, y*)

Returns: Nothing

Compatibility: WinIE-, MacIE-, NN-, Moz1.8+, Safari1.3+, Opera+, Chrome+

These two methods are used to draw lines and adjust the stroke location. The `moveTo()` method simply moves the current stroke location without adding anything to the path. The `lineTo()` method, on the other hand, draws a line from the current stroke location to the specified point. It's worth pointing out that drawing a line with the `lineTo()` method only adds a line to the current path; the line doesn't actually appear on the canvas until you call the `stroke()` method to carry out the actual drawing of the path.

rect(*x, y, width, height*)

Returns: Nothing

Compatibility: WinIE-, MacIE-, NN-, Moz1.8+, Safari1.3+, Opera+, Chrome+

The `rect()` method adds a rectangle to the current path. Similar to other drawing methods, the rectangle is actually just added to the current path, which isn't truly visible until you render it using the `stroke()` method.

restore()
save()

Returns: Nothing

Compatibility: WinIE-, MacIE-, NN-, Moz1.8+, Safari1.3+, Opera+, Chrome+

It's possible to save and restore the state of the graphic context, in which case you can make changes and then return to a desired state. The context state includes information such as the clip region, line width, fill color, and so forth. Call the `save()` and `restore()` methods to save and restore the context state.

canvasObject.scale()

```
rotate(angle)
scale(x, y)
translate(x, y)
```

Returns: Nothing

Compatibility: WinIE-, MacIE-, NN-, Moz1.8+, Safari1.3+, Opera+, Chrome+

All of the drawing operations that you perform on a canvas are expressed in units relative to the coordinate system of the canvas. These three methods enable you to alter the canvas coordinate system by rotating, scaling, or translating its origin. Rotating the coordinate system affects how angles are expressed in drawing operations that involve angles. Scaling the coordinate system impacts the relative size of units expressed in the system. And finally, translating the coordinate system alters the location of the origin, which affects where positive and negative values intersect on the drawing surface.

```
stroke()
strokeRect(x, y, width, height)
```

Returns: Nothing

Compatibility: WinIE-, MacIE-, NN-, Moz1.8+, Safari1.3+, Opera+, Chrome+

Most of the drawing operations on a canvas impact the current path, which you can think of as a drawing you've committed to memory but have yet to put on paper. You render a path to the canvas by calling the stroke() method. If you want to draw a rectangle to the canvas without dealing with the current path, call the strokeRect() method.

Event Objects

Prior to version 4 browsers, user and system actions — events — were captured predominantly by event handlers defined as attributes inside HTML tags. For instance, when a user clicked a button, the clickevent triggered the onclick event handler in the tag. That handler may invoke a separate function or perform some inline JavaScript script. Even so, the events themselves were rather dumb: Either an event occurred or it didn't. Where an event occurred (that is, the screen coordinates of the pointer at the moment the mouse button was clicked) and other pertinent event tidbits (for example, whether a keyboard modifier key was pressed at the same time) were not part of the equation — until version 4 browsers, that is.

While remaining fully backward compatible with the event handler mechanism of old, version 4 browsers had the first event model that turn events into first-class objects whose properties automatically carry a lot of relevant information about the event when it occurs. These properties are fully exposed to scripts, allowing pages to respond more intelligently about what the user does with the page and its elements.

Another new aspect of version 4 event models was the notion of "event propagation." It was possible to have an event processed by an object higher up the element containment hierarchy whenever it made sense to have multiple objects share one event handler. That the event being processed carried along with it information about the intended target, plus other golden information nuggets, made it possible for event handler functions to be smart about processing the event without requiring an event handler call to pass all kinds of target-specific information.

Unfortunately, the joy of this newly found power is tempered by the forces of object model incompatibility. Event object models are clearly divided along two fronts:

- The IE4+ model
- The model adopted by the W3C DOM Level 2, as implemented in NN6+/Moz and Gecko-, WebKit-, and Presto-based browsers

Many of these distinctions are addressed in the overviews of the object models in Chapter 26, "Generic HTML Element Objects." In this chapter, you find out more about the actual event objects that contain all the "goodies." Where possible, cross-browser concerns are addressed.

Why "Events"?

Graphical user interfaces are more difficult to program than the "old-fashioned" command-line interface. With a command-line or menu-driven system, users were intentionally restricted in the types of actions they could take at any given moment. The world was very modal, primarily as a convenience to programmers who led users through rigid program structures.

That all changes in a graphical user interface, such as Windows, Mac OS, XWindow System, or any other derived from the pioneering work of the Xerox Star system. The challenge for programmers is that a good user interface in this realm must make it possible for users to perform all kinds of actions at any given moment: roll the mouse, click a button, type a key, select text, choose a pull-down menu item, and so on. To accommodate this, a program (or, better yet, the operating system) must be on the lookout for any possible activity coming from all input ports, whether it be the mouse, keyboard, or network connection.

A common methodology to accomplish this at the operating system level is to look for any kind of event, whether it comes from user action or some machine-generated activity. The operating system or program then looks up how it should process each kind of event. Such events, however, must have some smarts about them so that the program knows what, and where on the screen, the event is.

What an event knows (and when it knows it)

Although the way to reference an event object varies a bit among the three event models, the one concept they all share is that an event object is created the instant the event action occurs. For instance, if you click a button, an event object is created in the browser's memory. As the object is created, the browser assigns values to the object's properties — properties that reflect numerous characteristics of that specific event. For a click event, that information includes the coordinates of the click, and which mouse button was used to generate the event. To be even more helpful, the browser does some quick calculations to determine that the coordinates of the click event coincide with the rectangular space of a button element on the screen. Therefore, the event object has as one of its properties a reference to the "screen thing" that you clicked on.

Most event object properties are read-only (in some even models, all the properties are), because an event object is like a snapshot of an event action. If the event model were to allow modification of event properties, performing both potentially useful and potentially unfriendly actions would be possible. For example, how frustrating would it be to a user to attempt to type into a text box, only for a keystroke to be modified after the actual key press and a totally different character to appear in the text box? On the other hand, perhaps it may be useful in some situations to make sure that anything typed into a text box is converted to uppercase characters, no matter what is typed. Each event model brings its own philosophy to the table in this regard. For example, the IE4+ event model allows keyboard character events to be modified by script; the W3C DOM event model does not.

Perhaps the most important aspect of an event object to keep in mind is that it exists only as long as scripts process the event. An event can trigger an event handler — usually a function. That function, of course, can invoke other functions. As long as statements are still executing in response to the event handler, the event object and all its properties are still "alive" and available to your scripts. But after the last script statement runs, the event object reverts to an empty object.

The reason an event object has such a brief life is that there can be only one event object at a time. In other words, no matter how complex your event handler functions are, or how rapidly events fire, they are executed serially (for experienced programmers: there is one execution thread). The operating system buffers events that start to bunch up on each other. Except in rare cases in which the buffer gets full and events are not recorded, event handlers are executed in the order in which the events occur.

The static Event object

Up to this point, the discussion has been about the event object (with a lowercase "e"), which is one instance of an event, with all the properties associated with that specific event action. In the W3C DOM event model, there is also a static Event object (with an uppercase "E") that includes additional subcategories within it. These subcategories are all covered later in this chapter, but they are introduced here to illustrate the contrast between the event and Event objects. The former, as you've seen, is a transient object with details about a specific event action; the latter serves primarily as a holder of event-related constant values that scripts can use. The static Event object is always available to scripts inside any window or frame. For a list of all Event object properties in NN6+/Moz and Gecko-, WebKit-, and Presto-based browsers, use The Evaluator (see Chapter 4, 'JavaScript Essentials'): enter **Event** into the bottom text box (also check out the KeyEvent object in NN6+/Moz).

The static Event object also turns out to be the object from which event objects are cloned. Thus, the static Event object has a number of properties and methods that apply to (are inherited by) the event objects created by event actions. These relationships are more important in the W3C DOM event model, which builds upon the DOM's object-oriented tendencies to implement the event model.

Event Propagation

Prior to version 4 browsers, an event fired on an object. If an event handler was defined for that event and that object, the handler executed; if there was no event handler, the event just disappeared into the ether. Newer browsers, however, send events on a longer ride, causing them to propagate through the document object models. As you know by now, two propagation models exist, one for each of the event models in use today: IE4+ and W3C DOM, as implemented in NN6+/Moz and Gecko-, WebKit-, and Presto-based browsers. It's also worth mentioning the event model that is unique to NN4, which served as a third model prior to NN4 succumbing to modern browsers. The NN4 event model has historical relevance because it aids in understanding the latter two models. Conceptually, the NN4 and IE4+ propagation models are diametrically opposite each other — any NN4 event propagates inward toward the target, whereas an IE event starts at the target and propagates outward. But the W3C DOM model manages to implement both models simultaneously, albeit with all new syntax so as not to step on the older models.

At the root of all three models is the notion that every event has a target. For user-initiated actions, this is fairly obvious. If you click a button or type in a text box, that button is the target of your mouse-related event; the text box is the target of your keyboard event. System-generated events are not so obvious, such as the onload event that fires after a page finishes loading. In all event models, this event fires on the window object. What distinguishes the event propagation models is how an event reaches its target, and what, if anything, happens to the event after it finishes executing the event handler associated with the target.

NN4-only event propagation

Although NN4 has given way to newer browsers, its propagation model initiated some concepts that are found in the modern W3C DOM event propagation model. The name for the NN4 model is *event capture*.

In NN4, all events propagate from the top of the document object hierarchy (starting with the window object) downward to the target object. For example, if you click a button in a form, the click event passes through the window and document (and, if available, layer) objects before reaching the button (the form object is not part of the propagation path). This propagation happens instantaneously, so that there is no performance penalty by this extra journey.

The event that passes through the window, document, and layer objects is a fully formed event object, complete with all properties relevant to that event action. Therefore, if the event were processed at the window level, one of the event object's properties is a reference to the target object, so that the event handler scripts at the window level can find out information, such as the name of the button, and even get a reference to its enclosing form.

By default, event capture is turned off. To instruct the window, document, or layer object levels to process that passing click object, requires turning on event capture for the window, document, and/or layer object.

Enabling NN4 event capture

All three objects just mentioned — window, document, and layer — have a captureEvents() method. You use this method to enable event capture at any of those object levels. The method requires one or more parameters, which are the event types (as supplied by Event object constants) that the object should capture, while letting all others pass untouched. For example, if you want the window object to capture all keypress events, you include the following statement in a script that executes as the page loads:

```
window.captureEvents(Event.KEYPRESS);
```

Defining event handlers in the intended targets is also a good idea, even if they are empty (for example, onkeypress="") to help NN4 generate the event in the first place. If you want the window to capture multiple event types, string the event type constants together, separated by the pipe character:

```
window.captureEvents(Event.KEYPRESS | Event.CLICK);
```

Now you must assign an action to the event, at the window's level, for each event type. More than likely, you have defined functions to execute for the event. Assign a function reference to the event handler by setting the handler property of the window object:

```
window.onkeypress = processKeyEvent;
window.onclick = processClickEvent;
```

Hereafter, if a user clicks a button or types into a field inside that window, the events are processed by their respective window-level event handler functions.

Turning off event capture

As soon as you enable event capture for a particular event type in a document, that capture remains in effect until the page unloads or you specifically disable the capture. You can turn off event capture for each event via the window, document, or layer releaseEvents() method. The releaseEvents() method takes the same kind of parameters — Event object type constants — as the captureEvents() method.

The act of releasing an event type simply means that events go directly to their intended targets without stopping elsewhere for processing, even if an event handler for the higher-level object is still defined. And because you can release individual event types based on parameters set for the `releaseEvents()` method, other events being captured are not affected by the release of others.

Passing events toward their targets

If you capture a particular event type in NN4, your script may need to perform some limited processing on that event before letting it reach its intended target. For example, perhaps you want to do something special if a user clicks an element with the Shift meta key pressed. In that case, the function that handles the event at the document level inspects the event's `modifiers` property to determine if the Shift key was pressed at the time of the event. If the Shift key was not pressed, you want the event to continue on its way to the element that the user clicked.

To let an event pass through the object hierarchy to its target, you use the `routeEvent()` method, passing as a parameter the event object being handled in the current function. A `routeEvent()` method does not guarantee that the event will reach its intended destination, because another object in between may have event capturing for that event type turned on and will intercept the event. That object, too, can let the event pass through with its own `routeEvent()` method.

In some cases, your scripts need to know if an event that is passed onward by the `routeEvent()` method activated a function that returns a value. This knowledge is especially valuable if your event must return a `true` or `false` value to let an object know if it should proceed with its default behavior (for example, whether a link should activate its `href` attribute URL or cancel after the event handler evaluates to `return true` or `return false`). When a function is invoked by the action of a `routeEvent()` method, the return value of the destination function is passed back to the `routeEvent()` method. That value, in turn, can be returned to the object that originally captured the event.

Event traffic cop

The last scenario is one in which a higher-level object captures an event and directs the event to a particular object elsewhere in the hierarchy. For example, you could have a document-level event handler function direct every `click` event whose `modifiers` property indicates that the Alt key was pressed, to a Help button object whose own `onclick` event handler displays a help panel (perhaps showing an otherwise hidden layer).

You can redirect an event to any object via the `handleEvent()` method. This method works differently from the others described in this chapter, because the object reference of this method is the reference of the object to handle the event (with the event object being passed as a parameter, such as one of the other methods). As long as the target object has an event handler defined for that event, it will process the event as if it had received the event directly from the system (even though the event object's target property may be some other object entirely).

IE4+ event propagation

IE's event propagation model is called *event bubbling*, since events "bubble" upward from the target object through the HTML element containment hierarchy. It's important to distinguish between the old-fashioned document object hierarchy (followed in the NN4 event capture model) and the more modern notion of HTML element containment — a concept that carries over to the W3C DOM as well.

A good way to demonstrate the effect of event bubbling — a behavior that is turned on by default — is to populate a simple document with lots of event handlers to see which ones fire and in what order. Listing 32-1 has onclick event handlers defined for a button inside a form, the form itself, and other elements and objects, all the way up the hierarchy to the window.

LISTING 32-1

Event Bubbling Demonstration

```
<!DOCTYPE html>
<html onclick="alert('Event is now at the HTML element.')">
   <head>
      <meta http-equiv="content-type" content="text/html;charset=utf-8">
      <title>Event Bubbles</title>
      <script type="text/javascript">
      function init()
      {
         window.onclick = winEvent
         document.onclick = docEvent;
         document.body.onclick = docBodEvent;
      }
      function winEvent()
      {
         alert("Event is now at the window object level.");
      }
      function docEvent()
      {
         alert("Event is now at the document object level.");
      }
      function docBodEvent()
      {
         alert("Event is now at the BODY element.");
      }
      </script>
   </head>
   <body onload="init()">
      <h1>Event Bubbles</h1>
      <hr />
      <form onclick="alert('Event is now at the FORM element.')">
         <input type="button" value="Button 'main1'" name="main1"
               onclick="alert('Event started at Button: ' + this.name)" />
      </form>
   </body>
</html>
```

You can try this listing in IE4+ and even NN6+/Moz , Safari, Opera, or Chrome because W3C DOM browsers also observe event bubbling. But you will notice differences in the precise propagation among WinIE4+, MacIE4+, and W3C DOM browsers. But notice that after you click the button in Listing 32-1, the event first fires at the target: the button. Then the event bubbles upward through the HTML containment to fire at the enclosing form element, next to the enclosing body element, and so on. Where the differences occur are after the body element. Table 32-1 shows the objects for which event handlers are defined in Listing 32-1, and to which objects the click event bubbles in the three classes of browsers.

Despite the discrepancies in Table 32-1, events do bubble through the most likely HTML containers that come to mind. The object level with the most global scope, and that works in all browser categories shown in the table, is the `document` object.

Preventing IE event bubbling

Because bubbling occurs by default, there are times when you may prefer to prevent an event from bubbling up the hierarchy. For example, if you have one handler at the `document` level whose job is to deal with the `click` event from a related series of buttons, any other object that receives `click` events will allow those events to bubble upward to the `document` level unless the bubbling is cancelled. Having the event bubble up could conflict with the document-level event handler.

TABLE 32-1

Event Bubbling Variations for Listing 32-1

Event Handler Location	WinIE4+/Opera	MacIE4+	NN6+/Moz/Safari/Chrome
`button`	Yes	Yes	Yes
`form`	Yes	Yes	Yes
`body`	Yes	Yes	Yes
`HTML`	Yes	No	Yes
`document`	Yes	Yes	Yes
`window`	No	No	Yes

Each `event` object in IE has a property called `cancelBubble`. The default value of this property is `false`, which means that the event bubbles to the next outermost container that has an event handler for that event. But if, in the execution of an event handler, that property is set to `true`, the event does not bubble up any higher when the processing of that handler finishes its job. Therefore, to stop an event from bubbling beyond the current event handler, include the following statement somewhere in the handler function:

```
event.cancelBubble = true;
```

You can prove this to yourself by modifying the page in Listing 32-1 to cancel bubbling at any level. For example, if you change the event handler of the `form` element to include a statement that cancels bubbling, the event goes no further than the `form` in IE (while the WebKit engine and recent versions of the Mozilla/Gecko engine support some of the IE syntax, the syntax is different for NN6+/Moz browsers, as discussed later in this chapter):

```
<form onclick="alert('Event is now at the form element.');
    event.cancelBubble=true">
```

Preventing IE event default action

In the days when events were almost always bound to elements by way of attributes in tags, the technique to block the event's default action was to make sure the event handler evaluated to return false. This is how, for instance, a form element's onsubmit event handler could prevent the form from carrying out the submission if client-side form validation failed.

To enhance that capability — especially when events are bound by other means, such as object element properties — IE's event object includes a returnValue property. Assign false to this property in the event handler function to block the element's default action to the event:

```
event.returnValue = false;
```

This way of blocking default actions in IE is often more effective than the old return false technique.

Redirecting events

Starting with IE5.5, you can redirect an event to another element, but with some limitations. The mechanism that makes this possible is the fireEvent() method of all HTML element objects (see Chapter 26). This method isn't so much redirecting an event as causing a brand-new event to be fired. But you can pass most of the properties of the original event object with the new event by specifying a reference to the old event object as the optional second parameter to the fireEvent() method.

The big limitation in this technique, however, is that the reference to the target element gets lost in this hand-off to the new event. The srcElement property of the old event gets overwritten with a reference to the object that is the target of the call to fireEvent(). For example, consider the following onclick event handler function for a button inside a form element:

```
function buttonEvent() {
    event.cancelBubble = true;
    document.body.fireEvent("onclick", event);
}
```

By cancelling event bubbling, the event does not propagate upward to the enclosing form element. Instead, the event is explicitly redirected to the body element, passing the current event object as the second parameter. When the event handler function for the body element runs, its event object has information about the original event, such as the mouse button used for the click and the coordinates. But the event.srcElement property points to the document.body object. As the event bubbles upward from the body element, the srcElement property continues to point to the document.body object. You can see this at work in Listing 32-2 for IE5.5+.

LISTING 32-2

Cancelling and Redirecting Events in IE5.5+

```
<!DOCTYPE html>
<html onclick="revealEvent('HTML', event)">
    <head>
        <meta http-equiv="content-type" content="text/html;charset=utf-8">
        <title>Event Cancelling & Redirecting</title>
        <script type="text/javascript">
            // display alert with event object info
            function revealEvent(elem, evt)
```

```
        {
            var msg = "Event (from " + evt.srcElement.tagName + " at ";
            msg += event.clientX + "," + event.clientY + ") is now at the ";
            msg += elem + " element.";
            alert(msg);
        }
        function init()
        {
            document.onclick = docEvent;
            document.body.onclick = docBodEvent;
        }
        function docEvent()
        {
            revealEvent("document", event);
        }
        function docBodEvent()
        {
            revealEvent("BODY", event);
        }
        function buttonEvent(form)
        {
            revealEvent("BUTTON", event);
            // cancel if checked (IE4+)
            event.cancelBubble = form.bubbleCancelState.checked;
            // redirect if checked (IE5.5+)
            if (form.redirect.checked)
            {
                document.body.fireEvent("onclick", event);
            }
        }
    </script>
</head>
<body onload="init()">
    <h1>Event Cancelling &amp; Redirecting</h1>
    <hr />
    <form onclick="revealEvent('FORM', event)">
        <p><button name="main1" onclick="buttonEvent(this.form)">Button
            'main1'</button>
        </p>
        <p><input type="checkbox" name="bubbleCancelState"
                onclick="event.cancelBubble=true" />Cancel Bubbling at BUTTON
            <br />
            <input type="checkbox" name="redirect"
                onclick="event.cancelBubble=true" />Redirect Event to BODY
        </p>
    </form>
</body>
</html>
```

Listing 32-2 is a modified version of Listing 32-1. Major additions are enhanced event handlers at each level so that you can see the tag name of the event that is regarded as the srcElement of the event, as well as the coordinates of the click event. With both check boxes unchecked, events bubble upward from the button, and the button element is then shown to be the original target all the way up the bubble hierarchy. If you check the Cancel Bubbling check box, the event goes no further than the button element, because that's where event bubbling is turned off. If you then check the "Redirect Event to Body" check box, the original event is cancelled at the button level, but a new event is fired at the body element. But notice that by passing the old event object as the second parameter, the click location properties of the old event are applied to the new event directed at the body. This event then continues to bubble upward from the body.

As a side note, if you uncheck the Cancel Bubbling check box but leave the Redirect Event box checked, you can see how the redirection is observed at the end of the button's event handler, and that something special goes on. The original event is held aside by the browser while the redirected event bubbles upward. As soon as that event-processing branch finishes, the original bubbling propagation carries on with the form. Notice, though, that the event object still knows that it was targeted at the button element, and the other properties are intact. This means that for a time, two event objects were in the browser's memory, but only one is "active" at a time. While the redirected event is propagating, the window.event object refers to that event object only.

Applying event capture

WinIE 5 and later also provide a kind of event capture, which overrides all other event propagation. Intended primarily for temporary capture of mouse events, it is controlled not through the event object but via the setCapture() and releaseCapture() methods of all HTML element objects (described in Chapter 26).

When you engage capture mode, all mouse events are directed to the element object that invoked the setCapture() method, regardless of the actual target of the event. This action facilitates such activities as element dragging, so that mouse events that might fire outside of the intended target (for example, when dragging the cursor too fast for the animation to track) continue to go to the target. When the drag mode is no longer needed, invoke the releaseCapture() method to allow mouse events to propagate normally.

W3C event propagation

Yielding to arguments in favor of both NN4's event capture and IE's event bubbling, the W3C DOM group managed to assemble an event model that employs both propagation systems. Although forced to use new syntax so as not to conflict with older browsers, the W3C DOM propagation model works like the NN4 model for capture and like IE4+ for bubbling. In other words, an event bubbles by default, but you can also turn on event capture if you want. Thus, an event first trickles down the element containment hierarchy to the target; then it bubbles up through the reverse path.

Event bubbling is on by default, just as in IE4+. To enable capture, you must apply a W3C DOM event listener to an object at some higher container. Use the addEventListener() method (see Chapter 26) for any visible HTML element or node. One of the parameters of the addEventListener() method determines whether the event listener function should be triggered while the event is bubbling or while it is captured.

Listing 32-3 is a simplified example for NN6+/Moz/W3C that demonstrates how a click event aimed at a button can be both captured and allowed to bubble. Most event handling functions are assigned inside the init() function. Borrowing code from Listing 32-1, event handlers are assigned to the window, document, and body objects as property assignments. These are automatically treated as bubble-type event listeners. Next, two objects — document and form — are given capture-type event listeners for the click event. The document object event listener invokes the same function as the bubble-type event handler (the alert text includes some asterisks to remind you that it is the same alert being displayed in both the capture and bubble phases of the event). For the form object, however, the capture-type event listener is directed to one function, while a bubble-type listener for the same object is directed at a separate function. In other words, the form object invokes one function as the event trickles down to the target, and another function when the event starts bubbling back up. Many of the event handler functions dynamically read the eventPhase property of the event object to reveal which phase of event propagation is in force at the instance the event handler is invoked (although an apparent bug reports the incorrect phase at the document object during event capture).

LISTING 32-3

W3C Event Capture and Bubble

```
<!DOCTYPE html>
<html>
    <head>
        <meta http-equiv="content-type" content="text/html;charset=utf-8">
        <title>W3C DOM Event Propagation</title>
        <script type="text/javascript">
            function init()
            {
                // using old syntax to assign bubble-type event handlers
                window.onclick = winEvent;
                document.onclick = docEvent;
                document.body.onclick = docBodEvent;
                // turn on click event capture for two objects
                document.addEventListener("click", docEvent, true);
                document.forms[0].addEventListener("click", formCaptureEvent, true);
                // set event listener for bubble
                document.forms[0].addEventListener("click", formBubbleEvent, false);
            }
            function winEvent(evt)
            {
                alert("Event is now at the window object level
                    (" + getPhase(evt) + ").");
            }
            function docEvent(evt)
            {
                alert("Event is now at the **document** object level
                    (" + getPhase(evt) + ").");
            }
            function docBodEvent(evt)
            {
                alert("Event is now at the BODY level (" + getPhase(evt) + ").");
            }
            function formCaptureEvent(evt)
            {
                alert("This alert triggered by FORM only on CAPTURE.");
            }
            function formBubbleEvent(evt)
            {
                alert("This alert triggered by FORM only on BUBBLE.");
```

continued

LISTING 32-3   *(continued)*

```
      }
      // reveal event phase of current event object
      function getPhase(evt)
      {
         switch (evt.eventPhase)
         {
            case 1:
               return "CAPTURING";
               break;
            case 2:
               return "AT TARGET";
               break;
            case 3:
               return "BUBBLING";
               break;
            default:
               return "";
         }
      }
   </script>
</head>
<body onload="init()">
   <h1>W3C DOM Event Propagation</h1>
   <hr />
   <form>
      <input type="button" value="Button 'main1'" name="main1"
            onclick="alert('Event is now at the button object level ('
                        + getPhase(event)
                        + ').')" />
   </form>
</body>
</html>
```

If you want to remove event capture after it has been enabled, use the removeEventListener() method on the same object as the event listener that was originally added (see Chapter 26). And, because multiple event listeners can be attached to the same object, specify the exact same three parameters to the removeEventListener() method that were applied to the addEventListener() method.

Preventing W3C event bubbling or capture

Corresponding to the cancelBubble property of the IE4+ event object is an event object method in the W3C DOM. The method that prevents propagation in any event phase is the stopPropagation() method. Invoke this method anywhere within an event listener function. The current function executes to completion, but the event propagates no further.

Listing 32-4 extends the example of Listing 32-3 to include two check boxes that let you stop propagation at the form element in your choice of the capture or bubble phase.

LISTING 32-4

Preventing Bubble and Capture

```html
<!DOCTYPE html>
<html>
    <head>
        <meta http-equiv="content-type" content="text/html;charset=utf-8">
        <title>W3C DOM Event Propagation</title>
        <script type="text/javascript">
            function init()
            {
                // using old syntax to assign bubble-type event handlers
                window.onclick = winEvent;
                document.onclick = docEvent;
                document.body.onclick = docBodEvent;
                // turn on click event capture for two objects
                document.addEventListener("click", docEvent, true);
                document.forms[0].addEventListener("click", formCaptureEvent, true);
                // set event listener for bubble
                document.forms[0].addEventListener("click", formBubbleEvent, false);
            }
            function winEvent(evt)
            {
                if (evt.target.type == "button")
                {
                    alert("Event is now at the window object level ↵
                        (" + getPhase(evt) + ").");
                }
            }
            function docEvent(evt)
            {
                if (evt.target.type == "button")
                {
                    alert("Event is now at the **document** object level ↵
                        (" + getPhase(evt) + ").");
                }
            }
            function docBodEvent(evt)
            {
                if (evt.target.type == "button")
                {
                    alert("Event is now at the BODY level (" + getPhase(evt) + ").");
                }
            }
            function formCaptureEvent(evt)
```

continued

LISTING 32-4 *(continued)*

```
        {
            if (evt.target.type == "button")
            {
                alert("This alert triggered by FORM only on CAPTURE.");
                if (document.forms[0].stopAllProp.checked)
                {
                    evt.stopPropagation();
                }
            }
        }
        function formBubbleEvent(evt)
        {
            if (evt.target.type == "button")
            {
                alert("This alert triggered by FORM only on BUBBLE.");
                if (document.forms[0].stopDuringBubble.checked)
                {
                    evt.stopPropagation();
                }
            }
        }
        // reveal event phase of current event object
        function getPhase(evt)
        {
            switch (evt.eventPhase)
            {
                case 1:
                    return "CAPTURING";
                    break;
                case 2:
                    return "AT TARGET";
                    break;
                case 3:
                    return "BUBBLING";
                    break;
                default:
                    return "";
            }
        }
    </script>
</head>
<body onload="init()">
    <h1>W3C DOM Event Propagation</h1>
    <hr />
    <form>
        <input type="checkbox" name="stopAllProp" />Stop all propagation at FORM
        <br />
```

```
        <input type="checkbox" name="stopDuringBubble" />Prevent bubbling past FORM
        <hr />
        <input type="button" value="Button 'main1'" name="main1"
            onclick="alert('Event is now at the button object level ('
                    + getPhase(event)
                    + ').')" />
    </form>
  </body>
</html>
```

In addition to the W3C DOM stopPropagation() method, NN6+, Moz, Safari, Opera, and Chrome also support IE's cancelBubble property for syntactical convenience.

Preventing W3C event default action

The W3C DOM counterpart to IE's returnValue property is the event object's preventDefault() method. Invoke this method in an event handler function when you wish to block the element's default action to the event:

```
        evt.preventDefault();
```

Redirecting W3C DOM events

The mechanism for sending an event to an object outside the normal propagation pattern in W3C is similar to that of IE4+, although with different syntax and an important requirement. In place of the IE4+ fireEvent() method, NN6+/Moz and Gecko-, WebKit-, and Presto-based browsers use the W3C DOM dispatchEvent() method. The sole parameter of the method is an event object, but it cannot be an event object that is already propagating through the element hierarchy. Instead, you must create a new event object via a W3C DOM event object constructor (described later in this chapter). Listing 32-5 is the same as the IE4+ Listing 32-2, but with just a few modifications to run in the W3C event model. Notice that the dispatchEvent() method passes a newly created event object as its sole parameter.

LISTING 32-5

Cancelling and Redirecting Events in the W3C DOM

```
<!DOCTYPE html>
<html onclick="revealEvent('HTML', event)">
  <head>
    <meta http-equiv="content-type" content="text/html;charset=utf-8">
    <title>Event Cancelling & Redirecting</title>
    <script type="text/javascript">
      // display alert with event object info
      function revealEvent(elem, evt)
      {
        var msg = "Event (from " + evt.target.tagName + " at ";
        msg += evt.clientX + "," + evt.clientY + ") is now at the ";
        msg += elem + " element.";
        alert(msg);
```

continued

LISTING 32-5 *(continued)*

```
        }
        function init()
        {
           document.onclick = docEvent;
           document.body.onclick = docBodEvent;
        }
        function docEvent(evt)
        {
           revealEvent("document", evt);
        }
        function docBodEvent(evt)
        {
           revealEvent("BODY", evt);
        }
        function buttonEvent(form, evt)
        {
           revealEvent("BUTTON", evt);
           // redirect if checked
              if (form.redirect.checked)
              {
                 document.body.dispatchEvent(evt);
              }
           // cancel if checked
              if (form.bubbleCancelState.checked)
              {
                 evt.stopPropagation();
              }
        }
     </script>
  </head>
  <body onload="init()">
     <h1>Event Cancelling & Redirecting</h1>
     <hr />
     <form onclick="revealEvent('FORM', event)">
        <p><button name="main1" onclick="buttonEvent(this.form, event)">Button
           'main1'</button>
        </p>
        <p><input type="checkbox" name="bubbleCancelState"
                 onclick="event.stopPropagation()" />Cancel Bubbling at BUTTON
           <br />
           <input type="checkbox" name="redirect"
                 onclick="event.stopPropagation()" /> Redirect Event to BODY
        </p>
     </form>
  </body>
</html>
```

Referencing the event Object

Just as there are two different event object models in today's browsers, the way your scripts access those objects is divided into two camps: the IE way and the W3C way. We start with the simpler, IE way.

In IE4+, the `event` object is accessible as a property of the `window` object:

```
window.event
```

But, as you are well aware, the `window` part of references is optional, so your scripts can treat the `event` object as if it were a global reference:

```
event.propertyName
```

Thus, any statement in an event handler function can access the `event` object without any special preparation or initializations.

The situation is a bit more complicated in the W3C event model. In some cases you must explicitly pass the event object as a parameter to an event handler function, whereas in other cases, the event object is delivered as a parameter automatically. The difference depends on how the event handler function is bound to the object.

Binding Events

Perhaps the most important facet of event handling in any script is binding an event to an element on the page. There are several different ways that you can carry out this event binding, and as you might expect, they aren't all compatible across different browsers. Furthermore, some of the techniques are considered passé in the sense that they have been improved upon by more modern approaches. Following are the four main techniques that can be used to bind events to elements:

- Assignment through tag attributes
- Assignment through object properties
- Attachment in IE
- Event listeners in NN/Moz/W3C

The following sections explore these event binding options in more detail, with an emphasis on showing you how to craft a modern, cross-browser event binding function based upon the last two techniques listed.

Binding events through tag attributes

Dating back to some of the earliest JavaScript-powered browsers, the original way of binding event handlers to objects is through an attribute in the element's tag. To bind an event in this manner, you simply assign inline JavaScript code in the attribute of an element, as in the following:

```
<input type="button" value="Click Me" onclick="handleClick();" />
```

The attribute name is the name of the event being handled, and its value is inline JavaScript code that is executed upon the event firing. You can include multiple statements in the event attribute, as this code reveals:

```
<input type="button" value="Click Me"
onclick="doSomething(this); doSomethingElse(this.form);" />
```

For modern browsers that support the W3C event model (NN6+/Moz and Gecko, WebKit- and Presto-based browsers), if you intend to inspect properties of the event within the event handler function, you must specify the event object as a parameter by passing event as a parameter, as in:

```
<input type="button" value="Click Me" onclick="handleClick(event);" />
```

This is the only time in the W3C model that you see an explicit reference to the event (lowercase e) object as if it were a global reference. This reference does not work in any other context — only as a parameter to an event handler function. If you have multiple parameters, the event reference can go in any order, but we tend to put it last:

```
<input type="button" value="Click Me" onclick="doSomething(this, event);" />
```

The function definition that is bound to the element should therefore have a parameter variable in place to catch the event object parameter:

```
function doSomething(widget, evt) {...}
```

You have no restrictions on how you name this parameter variable. In some examples of this book, you may see the variable assigned as event or, more commonly, evt. When working with cross-browser scripts, avoid using event as a parameter variable name so as not to interfere with the Internet Explorer window.event property.

The good news is that binding an event through an event tag attribute works well across all browsers. The bad news is that it goes against the prevailing trend in web design, which is to separate HTML content from the code that makes it interactive. In other words, there is a concerted effort among web developers to clearly delineate JavaScript code from HTML code.

This concept is closely related to the notion of separating content from presentation, which is afforded by style sheets. In this way, you could think of a web page as having three distinct components: HTML content, CSS, and JavaScript code. Keeping these three components as compartmentalized as possible results in cleaner, more manageable code.

Note

You see many examples of event tag attribute binding throughout this book during demonstrations of various objects, properties, and methods. The usage is intentional because it is generally easier to understand the concepts under discussion when the events are bound closely to the elements. ■

The trick to maintaining a clean separation between JavaScript event binding and HTML code is to bind the events purely within script code as opposed to within attributes of HTML elements. The latter three event binding approaches mentioned earlier all offer this separation.

Binding events through object properties

Dating back as far as NN3 and IE4, element objects have event properties that can be used to bind events by assignment. For every event that an element is capable of receiving and responding to, there is a suitably named property, in all lowercase. For example, the button element object has a property named onclick that corresponds to the onclick event. You can bind an event handler to a button element by assigning a function reference to the onclick property:

```
document.forms[0].myButton.onclick = handleClick;
```

Note
Although event properties should be specified in all lowercase (onclick), some browsers also recognize mixed case event names (onClick). ■

One catch to binding events as object properties is that at first glance it doesn't appear to be possible to pass your own parameters to the invoked handler functions. W3C browsers pass an event object as the only parameter to event handler functions, and this doesn't exactly leave room for you to include your own parameters. Without any further trickery, this means that your functions should receive the passed event object in a parameter variable:

```
function doSomething(evt) {...}
```

Recall that the event object contains a reference to the object that was the target of the event. From that, you can access any properties of that object, such as the form object that contains a form control object.

It is in fact perfectly possible to pass along your own parameters; it just takes an intermediary anonymous function to do the go-between work. For example, the following code demonstrates how to pass a single custom parameter along with the standard event object:

```
document.forms[0].myButton.onclick =
    function(evt) {doSomething("Cornelius", evt);};
```

In this example, a name string is passed along as the first parameter to the event handler, whereas the event object (automatically passed to the anonymous function as its sole parameter, and assigned to the parameter variable evt) is routed along as the second parameter. The actual handler code would look something like this:

```
function doSomething(firstName, evt) {...}
```

The evt parameter variable in the doSomething() event handler function acts as a reference to the event object for statements within the function. If you need to invoke other functions from there, you can pass the event object reference further along as needed. The event object retains its properties as long as the chain of execution triggered by the event action continues.

Binding events through IE attachments

In IE5 Microsoft set out to establish a new means of binding events to elements through attachments, which were originally intended for use with IE behaviors (see Chapter 51, "Internet Explorer Behaviors," on the CD-ROM). Eventually, the attachment approach to event binding expanded beyond behaviors and became the de facto IE standard for event binding. Seeing as how IE (as of version 8) still does not support the W3C approach to binding events, which you see in the next section, you should consider attachments the preferred way of handling events in IE for the foreseeable future.

IE event attachments are managed through the attachEvent() and detachEvent() methods, which are supported by all element objects that are capable of receiving events. By using both of these methods, you can bind and unbind events throughout the course of an application as needed.

The attachEvent() method takes the following form:

```
elementReference.attachEvent("event", functionReference);
```

To put this form in perspective, the following is an example of binding an event using the attachEvent() method in IE:

```
document.getElementById("myButton").attachEvent("onclick", doSomething);
```

The first parameter to the attachEvent() is the string name of the event, including the on prefix, as in "onclick". The second parameter is a reference to the event handler function for the event.

One new power afforded by IE event attachment is the ability to attach the same event to the same element multiple times (presumably pointing to different event handler functions). Just remember that if you choose to bind multiple events of the same type to the same element, they will be processed in the reverse order that they were assigned. This means the first event added is processed last.

Since the IE event model is predicated on the event object, which is a property of the window object, there is no event object passed into the event handler function. To access event properties, you simply access the window's event object using either window.event or just event. The latter approach works because the window object is always assumed in client-side scripting. The upcoming section "event Object Compatibility" shows how to reconcile the IE window.event property and the W3C event event handler parameter.

The IE event binding approach also offers the ability to unbind an event, which means the targeted element will no longer receive event notifications. You unbind an IE event by calling the detachEvent() method on the element, like this:

```
document.getElementById("myButton").detachEvent("onclick", doSomething);
```

This example reveals how the detachEvent() method relies on the exact same syntax as attachEvent().

Binding events through W3C listeners

The W3C approach to binding events is logically similar to IE event attachment in that it revolves around two methods: addEventListener() and removeEventListener(). These two methods give elements the ability to listen for events and then respond accordingly. Also similarly to the IE attachEvent() and detachEvent() methods, addEventListener() and removeEventListener() work as a pair for adding and removing event listeners, respectively.

The addEventListener() method takes the following form:

```
elementReference.addEventListener("eventType", functionReference,
    captureSwitch);
```

The following example should help to reveal the practical usage of the method:

```
document.getElementById("myButton").addEventListener("click", doSomething,
    false);
```

Note how the event name is specified without the on prefix, which is different from the name used in IE event attachments. The other notable difference in W3C event listeners as compared to IE event attachments involves the third parameter to addEventListener(), captureSwitch, which determines whether the element should listen for the event during the capture phase of event propagation. Later in the chapter you learn about event propagation and how this parameter might be used to tweak the propagation of an event. For now, just know that the parameter is typically set to false.

Similar to IE event attachments, you can add the same event listener to the same element multiple times. Unlike the IE approach, however, is the fact that W3C events added in this manner are processed in the same order that they were assigned. This means that the first event added is processed first.

Another similarity the W3C event model has to IE event handling is the ability to unbind an event from an element. The W3C version of event unbinding involves the removeEventListener() method, which is demonstrated in this example:

```
document.getElementById("myButton").removeEventListener("click", doSomething,
    false);
```

This example shows how the removeEventListener() method accepts the same parameters as addEventListener().

A cross-browser event binding solution

Pulling together what you've learned about modern event handling, you know it must be possible to reconcile the IE and W3C approaches to event binding. In fact, it doesn't take all that much extra code to bind events in a manner that cleanly attempts to use the latest event binding techniques while still gracefully falling back on an older technique (object properties) for legacy browsers.

Following is a cross-browser function you can use to add an event binding to an element:

```
function addEvent(elem, evtType, func)
{
    if (elem.addEventListener)
    {
        elem.addEventListener(evtType, func, false);
    }
    else if (elem.attachEvent)
    {
        elem.attachEvent("on" + evtType, func);
    }
    else
    {
        elem["on" + evtType] = func;
    }
}
```

Parameters for the function are a reference to the element, a string of the event type (that is, the version without the on prefix), and a reference to the function to be invoked when the event fires on the element. The addEvent() function first attempts to use the addEventListener() method on the supplied element, which satisfies modern W3C browsers (NN6+/Mozilla/Safari/Opera/Chrome). If that fails, attachEvent() is tried, which accommodates modern IE browsers (IE5+). If that's a bust, the function falls back on simply assigning the event handler function to the event object property, which works on the vast majority of browsers.

Note

You could easily extend the addEvent() **function to allow for the** captureSwitch **parameter of the** addEventListener() **method by adding a fourth parameter and passing it to** addEventListener(), **instead of passing** false. ■

Of course, the addEvent() function has to get called in order to bind events for a page. The onload event provides a great opportunity for binding events but, as you know, it's not a good idea to just call the addEvent() function in the onload HTML attribute. That would go against everything you've just learned. The trick is to first add an anonymous event handler for the onload event, and then carry out your other event bindings within that function. Here's an example of how you might do this:

```
addEvent(window, "load", function()
{
    addEvent(document.getElementById("myButton"), "click", handleClick);
    addEvent(document.body, "mouseup",
        function(evt) {handleClick(evt);});
});
```

In case you need to unbind an event, here is a suitable cross-browser function for unbinding events:

```
function removeEvent(elem, evtType, func)
{
    if (elem.removeEventListener)
    {
        elem.removeEventListener(evtType, func, false);
    }
    else if (elem.detachEvent)
    {
        elem.detachEvent("on" + evtType, func);
    }
    else
    {
        elem["on" + evtType] = null;
    }
}
```

event Object Compatibility

Despite the incompatible ways that W3C DOM and IE event objects arrive at an event handler function, you can easily stuff the object into one variable that both browser types can use. For example, the following function fragment receives a W3C DOM event object but also accommodates the IE event object:

```
function doSomething(evt)
```

```
    {
        evt = (evt) ? evt : ((window.event) ? window.event : null);
        if (evt)
        {
            // browser has an event to process
            ...
        }
    }
```

If an `event` object arrives as a parameter, it continues to be available as `evt`; but if not, the function makes sure that a `window.event` object is available and assigns it to the `evt` variable; finally, if the browser doesn't know about an `event` object, the `evt` variable is made `null`. Processing continues only if `evt` contains an event object.

That's the easy part. The madness comes in the details: reading properties of the event object when the property names can vary widely across the two event object models. Sections later in this chapter provide specifics of each property and method of both event object models, but seeing an overview of the property terminology on a comparative basis is helpful. Table 32-2 lists the common information bits and actions you are likely to want from an event object, and the property or method names used in the event object models.

TABLE 32-2

Common event Object Properties and Methods

Property/Action	IE4+	W3C DOM
Target element	`srcElement`	`target`
Event type	`type`	`type`
X coordinate in element	`offsetX`	n/a[†]
Y coordinate in element	`offsetY`	n/a[†]
X coordinate on page	n/a[†]	`pageX`[††]
Y coordinate on page	n/a[†]	`pageY`[††]
X coordinate in window	`clientX`	`clientX`
Y coordinate in window	`clientY`	`clientY`
X coordinate on screen	`screenX`	`screenX`
Y coordinate on screen	`screenY`	`screenY`
Mouse button	`button`	`button`
Keyboard key	`keyCode`	`keyCode`
Shift key pressed	`shiftKey`	`shiftKey`
Alt key pressed	`altKey`	`altKey`
Ctrl key pressed	`ctrlKey`	`ctrlKey`

TABLE 32-2	*(continued)*	
Property/Action	**IE4+**	**W3C DOM**
Previous Element	`fromElement`	`relatedTarget`
Next Element	`toElement`	`relatedTarget`
Cancel bubbling	`cancelBubble`	`stopPropagation()`
Prevent default action	`returnValue`	`preventDefault()`

†Value can be derived through calculations with other properties.
††Not an official W3C DOM property, but is supported in Mozilla, Safari, Opera, and Chrome.

As you can see in Table 32-2, properties for the IE4+ and W3C event objects have a lot in common. Perhaps the most important incompatibility to overcome is referencing the element that is the intended target of the event. This, too, can be branched in your code to achieve a common variable that references the element. For example, embedded within the previous function fragment can be a statement, such as the following:

```
var elem = (evt.target) ? evt.target : ((evt.srcElement) ?
    evt.srcElement : null);
```

Each event model has additional properties that are not shared by the other. Details about these are covered in the rest of this chapter.

Dueling Event Models

Despite the sometimes widely divergent ways event object models treat their properties, accommodating a wide range of browsers for event manipulation is not difficult. In this section, you see two scripts that examine important event properties. The first script reveals which, if any, modifier keys are held down during an event; the second script extracts the codes for both mouse buttons and keyboard keys. Both scripts work with all modern browsers that have event objects.

Cross-platform modifier key check

Listing 32-6 demonstrates branching techniques for examining the modifier key(s) being held down while an event fires. You can find details of the event object properties, such as `modifiers` and `altKey`, later in this chapter. To see the page in action, click a link, type into a text box, and click a button while holding down any combination of modifier keys. A series of four check boxes representing the four modifier keys is at the bottom. As you click or type, the check box(es) of the pressed modifier key(s) become checked.

LISTING 32-6

Checking Events for Modifier Keys

```
<!DOCTYPE html>
<html>
    <head>
        <meta http-equiv="content-type" content="text/html;charset=utf-8">
```

```
<title>Event Modifiers</title>
<script type="text/javascript">
    function checkMods(evt)
    {
        evt = (evt) ? evt : ((window.event) ? window.event : null);
            if (evt)
            {
                var elem = (evt.target) ? evt.target : evt.srcElement;
                var form = document.output;
                form.modifier[0].checked = evt.altKey;
                form.modifier[1].checked = evt.ctrlKey;
                form.modifier[2].checked = evt.shiftKey;
                form.modifier[3].checked = false;
            }
        return false;
    }

    // bind the event handlers
    function addEvent(elem, evtType, func)
    {
        if (elem.addEventListener)
        {
            elem.addEventListener(evtType, func, false);
        }
        else if (elem.attachEvent)
        {
            elem.attachEvent("on" + evtType, func);
        }
        else
        {
            elem["on" + evtType] = func;
        }
    }

    addEvent(window, "load", function()
    {
        addEvent(document.getElementById("link"), "mousedown",
            function(evt) {return checkMods(evt);});
        addEvent(document.getElementById("text"), "keyup",
            function(evt) {checkMods(evt);});
        addEvent(document.getElementById("button"), "click",
            function(evt) {checkMods(evt);});
    });
</script>
</head>
<body>
    <h1>Event Modifiers</h1>
    <hr />
    <p>Hold one or more modifier keys and click on
        <a id="link" href="javascript:void(0)">this link</a>
        while looking at the checkboxes to see which keys you are holding.
    </p>
    <form name="output">
```

continued

1067

LISTING 32-6   *(continued)*

```
        <p>Enter some text with uppercase and lowercase letters
            (while looking at the checkboxes):
            <input id="text" type="text" size="40" />
        </p>
        <p>
            <input id="button" type="button"
            value="Click Here With Modifier Keys" />
        </p>
        <p>
            <input type="checkbox" name="modifier" />Alt
            <input type="checkbox" name="modifier" />Control
            <input type="checkbox" name="modifier" />Shift
            <input type="checkbox" name="modifier" />Meta
        </p>
    </form>
  </body>
</html>
```

The script checks the event object property for each of three modifiers to determine which, if any, modifier keys are being pressed.

Cross-platform key capture

To demonstrate keyboard events in both event capture models, Listing 32-7 captures the key character being typed into a text box, as well as the mouse button used to click a button.

LISTING 32-7

Checking Events for Key and Mouse Button Pressed

```
<!DOCTYPE html>
<html>
  <head>
    <meta http-equiv="content-type" content="text/html;charset=utf-8">
    <title>Button and Key Properties</title>
    <script type="text/javascript">
        function checkWhich(evt)
        {
          evt = (evt) ? evt : ((event) ? event : null);
            if (evt)
            {
                var thingPressed = "";
                var elem = (evt.target) ? evt.target : evt.srcElement;
                  if (elem.type == "textarea")
                  {
                      thingPressed = (evt.charCode) ? evt.charCode : evt.keyCode;
                  }
                  else if (elem.type == "button")
                  {
                      thingPressed = (typeof evt.button !=
```

```
                      "undefined") ? evt.button : "n/a";
              }
          alert(thingPressed);
      }
  return false;
}

// bind the event handlers
function addEvent(elem, evtType, func)
{
    if (elem.addEventListener)
    {
        elem.addEventListener(evtType, func, false);
    }
    else if (elem.attachEvent)
    {
        elem.attachEvent("on" + evtType, func);
    }
    else
    {
        elem["on" + evtType] = func;
    }
}

addEvent(window, "load", function()
{
    addEvent(document.getElementById("button"), "mousedown",
            function(evt) {checkWhich(evt);});
    addEvent(document.getElementById("text"), "keypress",
            function(evt) {checkWhich(evt);});
});
</script>
</head>
<body>
    <h1>Button and Key Properties</h1>
    <hr />
    <form>
        <p>Mouse down atop this
            <input id="button" type="button" value="Button" />
            with either mouse button (if you have more than one).
        </p>
        <p>Enter some text with uppercase and lowercase letters:
            <textarea id="text" cols="40" rows="4" wrap="virtual"></textarea>
        </p>
    </form>
</body>
</html>
```

The codes displayed for each keyboard event are equivalent to the ASCII values of character keys. If you need the codes of other keys, the onkeydown and onkeyup event handlers provide Unicode values for any key that you press on the keyboard. See the charCode and keyCode property listings for event objects later in this chapter for more details.

Event Types

Although browsers prior to version 4 did not have an accessible event object, this is a good time to summarize the evolution of what in today's browsers is known as the `type` property. The `type` property reveals the kind of event that generates an event object (the event handler name minus the "on"). Object models in IE4+ and NN6+/W3C provide event handlers for virtually every HTML element, so that it's possible, for example, to define an `onclick` event handler for not only a clickable button, but also for a `p` or even an arbitrary `span` element.

Older Browsers

Earlier browsers tended to limit the number of event handlers for any particular element to just those that made sense for the kind of element it was. Even so, many scripters wanted more event handlers on more objects. But until that became a reality in IE4+ and NN6+/W3C, authors had to know the limits of the object models. Table 32-4 shows the event handlers available for objects within three generations of early browsers. Each column represents the version in which the event type was introduced. For example, the `window` object started out with four event types, and gained three more when NN4 was released. In contrast, the `area` object was exposed as an object for the first time in NN3, which is where the first event types for that object are listed.

With the exception of the NN4 `layer` object, all objects shown in Table 32-4 have survived into the newer browsers, so that you can use these event handlers with confidence. Again, keep in mind that of the browsers listed in Table 32-4, only NN4 has an `event` object of any kind exposed to scripts.

TABLE 32-3

Event Types through the Early Ages

Object	NN2/IE3	NN3	NN4
window	blur		dragdrop
	focus		move
	load		resize
	unload		
layer			blur
			focus
			load
			mouseout
			mouseover
			mouseup

Object	NN2/IE3	NN3	NN4
link	click	mouseout	dblclick
	mouseover		mousedown
			onmouseup
area		mouseout	click
		mouseover	
image		abort	
		error	
		load	
form	submit	reset	
text, textarea, password			
	blur		keydown
	change		keypress
	focus		keyup
	select		
all buttons	click		mousedown
			mouseup
select	blur		
	change		
	focus		
fileupload		blur	
		focus	
		select	

Event types in IE4+ and NN6+/W3C

By now you should have at least scanned the list of event handlers defined for elements in common, as shown in Chapter 26. This list of event types is enormous. A sizable number of the event types are unique to IE4, IE5, and IE5.5+, and in some cases, just the Windows version at that.

If you compose pages for both IE4+ and NN6+/W3C, however, you need to know which event types these browser families and generations have in common. Event types for NN6+/Moz and Gecko-, WebKit-, and Presto-based browsers, are based primarily on the W3C DOM Level 2 specification, although they also include keyboard events, whose formal standards are still under development for DOM Level 3. Table 32-4 lists a common denominator of event types for modern browsers and the

TABLE 32-4

IE4+ and W3C DOM Event Types in Common

Event Type	Applicable Elements
abort	object
blur	window, button, text, password, label, select, textarea
change	text, password, textarea, select
click	All elements
error	window, frameset, object
focus	window, button, text, password, label, select, textarea
keydown	text, password, textarea
keypress	text, password, textarea
keyup	text, password, textarea
load	window, frameset, object
mousedown	All elements
mousemove	All elements
mouseout	All elements
mouseover	All elements
mouseup	All elements
reset	form
resize	window
scroll	window
select	text, password, textarea
submit	form
unload	window, frameset
IE4+ event Object	
altKey	
altLeft	
behaviorCookie	
behaviorPart	

IE4+ event Object
bookmarks
boundElements
button
cancelBubble
clientX
clientY
contentOverflow
ctrlKey
ctrlLeft
dataFld
dataTransfer
fromElement
keyCode
nextPage
offsetX
offsetY
propertyName
qualifier
reason
recordset
repeat
returnValue
saveType
screenX
screenY
shiftKey
shiftLeft
srcElement

continued

TABLE 32-4	*(continued)*
IE4+ event Object	
srcFilter	
srcUrn	
toElement	
type	
wheelData	
X	
Y	

objects that support them. Although not as long as the IE event list, the event types in Table 32-4 are the basic set you should get to know for all browsers.

Syntax

Accessing IE4+ event object properties:

```
[window.]event.property
```

Compatibility: WinIE4+, MacIE4+, NN-, Moz-, Safari-, Opera-, Chrome-

About this object

The IE4+ event object is a property of the window object. Its basic operation is covered earlier in this chapter.

You can see a little of what the event object is about with the help of The Evaluator (see Chapter 4, "JavaScript Essentials"). If you type event into the bottom text box, you can examine the properties of the event object for the event that triggers the function that displays the event object properties. If you press the Enter key in the text box, you see properties of the keypress event that caused the internal script to run; click the List Properties button to see the properties of the click event fired at the button. Hold down some of the modifier keys while clicking to see how this affects some of the properties.

As you review the properties for the event object, make special note of the compatibility rating for each property. The list of properties for this object has grown over the evolution of the IE4+ event object model. Also, most properties are listed here as being read-only, which they were in IE4. But for IE5+, these properties are also Read/Write if the event is created artificially via methods, such as IE5.5+'s document.createEventObject() method. Event objects that are created by user or system action have very few properties that can be modified on the fly (to prevent your scripts from altering user actions). Notice, too, that some properties are the same as for the W3C DOM event object, as revealed in the compatibility ratings.

Properties
`altKey`
`ctrlKey`
`shiftKey`

Value: Boolean   Read-Only

Compatibility: WinIE4+, MacIE4+, NN6+, Moz+, Safari+, Opera+, Chrome+

When an `event` object is created in response to a user or system action, these three properties are set based on whether their corresponding keys were being held down at the time — a Shift-click, for example. If the key was held down, the property is assigned a value of `true`; otherwise the value is `false`.

Most commonly, you use expressions consisting of this property as `if` construction conditional statements. Because these are Boolean values, you can combine multiple properties in a single condition. For example, if you have a branch of a function that is to execute only if the event occurred with both the Shift and Control keys held down, the condition looks as the following:

```
if (event.shiftKey && event.ctrlKey)
{
    // statements to execute
}
```

Conversely, you can take a more user-friendly approach to provide special processing if the user holds down any one of the three modifier keys:

```
if (event.shiftKey || event.ctrlKey || event.altKey)
{
    // statements to execute
}
```

The rationale behind this approach is to offer perhaps some shortcut operation for users, but not force them to memorize a specific modifier key combination.

Example
See Listing 32-6, where the values of these three properties are used to set the `checked` properties of corresponding check boxes for a variety of event types.

Related Items: `altLeft`, `ctrlLeft`, `shiftLeft` properties

`altLeft`
`ctrlLeft`
`shiftLeft`

Value: Boolean   Read-Only

Compatibility: WinIE5.5+, MacIE-, NN-, Moz-, Safari-, Opera-, Chrome-

Some versions of Windows allow events to be modified by only the left-hand Alt, Ctrl, and Shift keys when using IE5.5+. For these modifiers to be recorded by the `event` object, focus must be on the document (body), and not in any form control. If the left-key version is `false` and the regular version is `true`, then your script knows that the right-hand key had been held down during the event.

Related Items: `altKey`, `ctrlKey`, `shiftKey` properties

behaviorCookie
behaviorPart

Value: Integer   Read-Only

Compatibility: WinIE6+, MacIE-, NN-, Moz-, Safari-, Opera-, Chrome-

These two properties are related to a Windows technology that Microsoft calls *rendering behaviors*. Unlike the behaviors discussed under the addBehavior() method in Chapter 26, rendering behaviors are written in C++ and provide services for custom drawing on your web page. For more details, consult the document "Implementing Rendering Behaviors" at http://msdn.microsoft.com/en-us/library/aa753628%28VS.85%29.aspx.

bookmarks
boundElements
dataFld
qualifier
reason
recordset

Value: See text   Read-Only

Compatibility: WinIE6+, MacIE-, NN-, Moz-, Safari-, Opera-, Chrome-

---

TABLE 32-5

ADO-Related event Object Properties

Property	Value	First Implemented	Description
bookmarks	Array	IE4	Array of ADO bookmarks (saved positions) for records within a recordset associated with the object that received the event.
boundElements	Array	IE5	Array of element references for all elements bound to the same data set that was touched by the current event.
dataFld	String	IE5	Name of the data source column that is bound to a table cell that receives a cellchange event.
qualifier	String	IE5	Name of the data member associated with a data source that receives a data-related event. Available only if the data source object (DSO) allows multiple-named data members or a qualifier has been explicitly set via the datasrc attribute of the bound element. Read-write in IE5+.
reason	Integer	IE4	Set only from onDataSetComplete event, provides the result code of the data set loading (0=successful; 1=transfer aborted; 2=other error).
recordset	Object	IE4	Reference to the current recordset in a data source object.

eventObject.button

This group of `event` object properties is tied to using Data Binding in Windows versions of IE4+. Extensive details of Data Binding lie outside the scope of this book, but Table 32-5 provides a summary of these `event` object properties within that context (much of the terminology is used in Data Binding, but doesn't affect other scripting). For more details, search for ActiveX Data Objects (ADO) at `http://msdn.microsoft.com/en-us/library/default.aspx`.

Note

Although still supported in IE, Microsoft's original ADO technology has given way to ADO.NET, which is designed for tighter integration with Microsoft's .NET architecture. To learn more about the differences between the two technologies, visit `http://msdn.microsoft.com/library/en-us/dndotnet/html /adonetprogmsdn.asp.` ■

button

Value: Integer   Read-Only

Compatibility: WinIE4+, MacIE4+, NN6+, Moz+, Safari+, Opera+, Chrome+

The `button` property reveals which button or buttons were pressed to activate a mouse event. If no mouse button is pressed to generate an event, this property is zero in IE. But integers 1 through 7 reveal single and multiple button presses, including the actions of three-button mice when they are recognized by the operating system. Integer values in IE correspond to buttons according to the following scheme:

Value	Description
0	No button
1	Left (primary) button
2	Right button
3	Left and right buttons together
4	Middle button
5	Left and middle buttons together
6	Right and middle buttons together
7	Left, middle, and right buttons together

Mouse buttons other than the primary one are easier to look for in `mousedown` or `mouseup` events rather than in `onclick` events. Be aware that as the user works toward pressing multiple buttons, each press fires a `mousedown` event. Therefore, if the user presses the left button first, the `mousedown` event fires, with the `event.button` property bearing the 1 value; as soon as the right button is pressed, the `mousedown` event fires again, but this time with an `event.button` value of 3. If your script intends to perform special action with both buttons pressed, it should ignore and not perform any action for a single mouse button, because that one-button event will very likely fire in the process, disturbing the intended action.

Exercise caution when scripting the `event.button` property for both IE4+ and NN6+/Moz/W3C. The W3C DOM event model defines different button values for mouse buttons (0, 1, and 2 for left, middle, and right) and no values for multiple buttons.

Example

See Listing 32-7, where the `event.button` property is revealed in the status bar. Try pressing individual mouse buttons on, for example, the screen button. Then try combinations, watching the results very closely in the status bar.

Related Items: None

cancelBubble

Value: Boolean   Read/Write

Compatibility: WinIE4+, MacIE4+, NN6+, Moz+, Safari+, Opera+, Chrome+

The `cancelBubble` property (which sounds more as if it should be a method name) determines whether the current `event` object bubbles up any higher in the element containment hierarchy of the document. By default, this property is `false`, meaning that if the event is supposed to bubble, it will do so automatically.

To prevent event bubbling for the current event, set the property to `true` anywhere within the event handler function. As an alternative, you can cancel bubbling directly in an element's event handler attribute, as in the following:

```
onclick="doButtonClick(this); event.cancelBubble = true"
```

Cancelling event bubbling works only for the current event. The very next event to fire will have bubbling enabled (provided the event bubbles).

Example

See Listing 32-2 to see the `cancelBubble` property in action. Even though that listing has some features that apply to IE5.5+, the bubble cancelling demonstration works all the way back to IE4.

Related Item: `returnValue` property

clientX
clientY
offsetX
offsetY
screenX
screenY
x
y

Value: Integer   Read/Write

Compatibility: WinIE4+, MacIE4+, NN6+, Moz+, Safari+, Opera+, Chrome+

An IE `event` object provides coordinates for an event in as many as four coordinate spaces: the element itself, the parent element of the event's target, the viewable area of the browser window, and the entire video screen. Unfortunately, misleading values can be returned by some of the properties that correspond to these coordinate spaces, as discussed in this section. Note that no properties provide the explicit position of an event relative to the entire page, in case the user has scrolled the window.

Starting with the innermost space — that of the element that is the target of the event — the `offsetX` and `offsetY` properties should provide pixel coordinates within the target element. This is how, for example, you could determine the click point on an image, regardless of whether the image is embedded in the body or floating around in a positioned div. Windows versions through IE8 produce the correct values in most cases. But for some elements that are child elements of the body element, the vertical (y) value may be relative to the viewable window, rather than just the element itself. You can see an example of this when you work with Listing 32-8 and click the h1 or p elements near the top of the page. This problem does not affect MacIE, but there is another problem on Mac versions: If the page is scrolled away from its normal original position, the scrolled values are subtracted from the clientX and clientY values. This is an incompatibility bug, and you must take this error into account if you need click coordinates inside an element for a potentially scrolled page. This error correction must be done only for the Mac, because in Windows it works as is.

Extending scope to the offset parent element of the event's target, the x and y properties in IE5+ for Windows should return the coordinates for the event relative to the target's offset parent element (the element that can be found via the offsetParent property). For most non-positioned elements, these values are the same as the clientX and clientY properties because, as discussed in a moment, the offset parent element has a zero offset with *its* parent, the body. Observe an important caution about the x and y properties: In WinIE4 and through MacIE5, the properties do not take into account any offset parent locations other than the body. Even in WinIE5+, this property can give false readings in some circumstances. By and large, these two properties should not be used.

The next set of coordinates, clientX and clientY, are relative to the visible document area of the browser window. When the document is scrolled all the way to the top (or the document doesn't scroll at all), these coordinates are the same as the coordinates on the entire page. But because the page can scroll "underneath" the viewable window, the coordinates on the page can change if the page scrolls. Also, in the Windows versions of IE, you can actually register mouse events that are up to 2 pixels outside of the body element, which is weird, but true. Therefore, in WinIE, if you click the background of the body, the event fires on the body element, but the clientX/clientY values will be 2 pixels greater than offsetX/offsetY (they're equal in MacIE). Despite this slight discrepancy, you should rely on the clientX and clientY properties if you are trying to get the coordinates of an event that may be in a positioned element, but have those coordinates relative to the entire viewable window, rather than just the positioning context.

Taking the page's scrolling into account for an event coordinate is often important. After all, unless you generate a fixed-size window for a user, you don't know how the browser window will be oriented. If you're looking for a click within a specific region of the page, you must take page scrolling into account. The scrolling factor can be retrieved from the document.body.scrollLeft and document.body.scrollTop properties. When reading the clientX and clientY properties, be sure to add the corresponding scroll properties to get the position on the page:

```
var coordX = event.clientX + document.body.scrollLeft;
var coordY = event.clientY + document.body.scrollTop;
```

Do this in your production work without fail.

Finally, the screenX and screenY properties return the pixel coordinates of the event on the entire video screen. These properties would be more useful if IE provided more window dimension properties. In any case, because mouse events fire only when the cursor is somewhere in the content region of the browser window, don't expect to get the screen values of any place outside this region.

If these descriptions seem confusing to you, you are not alone. Throw in a few bugs, and it may seem like quite a mess. But think how you may use event coordinates in scripts. By and large, you want to know one of two types of mouse event coordinates: within the element itself and within the page. Use the offsetX/offsetY properties for the former; use clientX/clientY (plus the scroll property values) for the latter.

Although the coordinate properties are used primarily for mouse events, there is a little quirk that may let you determine if the user has resized the window via the maximize icon in the title bar *eventObject*.clientX

(on the Mac, this is called the zoom box) or the resize handle at the bottom-right corner of the screen. Mouse event coordinates are recorded in the event object for a resize event. In the case of the maximize icon, the clientY coordinate is a negative value (above the client space) and the clientX coordinate is within about 45 pixels of the previous width of the window (document.body.clientWidth). This, of course, happens after the window has resized, so it is not a way to prevent window resizing.

Example

Listing 32-8 provides readings of all event coordinate properties in an interactive way. An onmousedown event handler triggers all event handling, and you can click the mouse anywhere on the page to see what happens. You see the tag of the element targeted by the mouse event to help you visualize how some of the coordinate properties are determined. An image is encased inside a positioned div element to help you see what happens to some of the properties when the event is targeted inside a positioned element.

LISTING 32-8

IE4+ Event Coordinate Properties

```
<!DOCTYPE html>
<html>
    <head>
        <meta http-equiv="content-type" content="text/html;charset=utf-8">
        <title>X and Y Event Properties (IE4+ Syntax)</title>
        <script type="text/javascript">
            function checkCoords(evt)
            {
                evt = (evt) ? evt : ((window.event) ? window.event : null);
                    if (evt)
                    {
                        var elem = (evt.target) ? evt.target : evt.srcElement;
                        var form = document.forms[0];
                        form.srcElemTag.value = "<" + elem.tagName + ">";
                        form.clientCoords.value = evt.clientX + "," + evt.clientY;
                            if (typeof document.body.scrollLeft != "undefined")
                            {
                                form.pageCoords.value = (evt.clientX +
                                document.body.scrollLeft) +
                                    "," + (evt.clientY + document.body.scrollTop);
                            }
                        form.offsetCoords.value = evt.offsetX + "," + evt.offsetY;
                        form.screenCoords.value = evt.screenX + "," + evt.screenY;
                        form.xyCoords.value = evt.x + "," + evt.y;
                            if (elem.offsetParent)
                            {
                                form.parElem.value = "<" + elem.offsetParent.tagName + ">";
                            }
                        return false;
                    }
            }
            function handleSize(evt)
```

```
    {
        evt = (evt) ? evt : ((window.event) ? window.event : null);
            if (evt)
            {
                document.forms[0].resizeCoords.value =
                    evt.clientX + "," + evt.clientY;
            }
    }

    // bind the event handlers
    function addEvent(elem, evtType, func)
    {
        if (elem.addEventListener)
        {
            elem.addEventListener(evtType, func, false);
        }
        else if (elem.attachEvent)
        {
            elem.attachEvent("on" + evtType, func);
        }
        else
        {
            elem["on" + evtType] = func;
        }
    }
    addEvent(window, "load", function()
    {
        addEvent(document.body, "mousedown",
                function(evt) {checkCoords(evt);});
        addEvent(document.body, "resize",
                function(evt) {handleSize(evt);});
    });
</script>
</head>
<body>
    <h1>X and Y Event Properties (IE4+ Syntax)</h1>
    <hr />
    <p>Click on any element to see the coordinate values
        for the event object.
    </p>
    <form name="output">
        <table>
            <tr>
                <td colspan="2">IE Mouse Event Coordinates:</td>
            </tr>
            <tr>
                <td align="right">srcElement:</td>
                <td>
                    <input type="text" name="srcElemTag" size="10" />
                </td>
            </tr>
            <tr>
                <td align="right">clientX, clientY:</td>
```

continued

LISTING 32-8   *(continued)*

```
        <td>
            <input type="text" name="clientCoords" size="10" />
        </td>
        <td align="right">...With scrolling:</td>
        <td>
            <input type="text" name="pageCoords" size="10" />
        </td>
    </tr>
    <tr>
        <td align="right">offsetX, offsetY:</td>
        <td>
            <input type="text" name="offsetCoords" size="10" />
        </td>
    </tr>
    <tr>
        <td align="right">screenX, screenY:</td>
        <td>
            <input type="text" name="screenCoords" size="10" />
        </td>
    </tr>
    <tr>
        <td align="right">x, y:</td>
        <td>
            <input type="text" name="xyCoords" size="10" />
        </td>
        <td align="right">...Relative to:</td>
        <td>
            <input type="text" name="parElem" size="10" />
        </td>
    </tr>
    <tr>
        <td align="right">
            <input type="button" value="Click Here" />
        </td>
    </tr>
    <tr>
        <td colspan="2"><hr /></td>
    </tr>
    <tr>
        <td colspan="2">Window Resize Coordinates:</td>
    </tr>
    <tr>
        <td align="right">clientX, clientY:</td>
        <td>
            <input type="text" name="resizeCoords" size="10" />
        </td>
    </tr>
    </table>
</form>
```

```
    <div id="display" style="position:relative; left:100">
        <img alt="image" src="nile.gif" width="320" height="240" border="0" />
    </div>
  </body>
</html>
```

Here are some tasks to try in IE with the page that loads from Listing 32-8 to help you understand the relationships among the various pairs of coordinate properties:

1. Click the dot above the "i" on the "Click Here" button label. The target element is the button (input) element, whose offsetParent is a table cell element. The offsetY value is very low because you are near the top of the element's own coordinate space. The client coordinates (and x and y), however, are relative to the viewable area in the window. If your browser window is maximized in Windows, the screenX and clientX values will be the same; the difference between screenY and clientY is the height of all the window chrome above the content region. With the window not scrolled at all, the client coordinates are the same with and without scrolling taken into account.

2. Jot down the various coordinate values and then scroll the page down slightly (clicking the scrollbar fires an event), and click the dot on the button again. The clientY value shrinks because the page has moved upward relative to the viewable area, making the measure between the top of the area smaller with respect to the button. The Windows version does the right thing with the offset properties, by continuing to return values relative to the element's own coordinate space; the Mac, unfortunately, subtracts the scrolled amount from the offset properties.

3. Click the large image. The client properties perform as expected for both Windows and Mac, as do the screen properties. For Windows, the x and y properties correctly return the event coordinates relative to the img element's offsetParent, which is the div element that surrounds it. Note, however, that the browser "sees" the div as starting 10 pixels to the left of the image. In WinIE5.5+, you can click within those 10 transparent pixels to the left of the image to click the div element. This padding is inserted automatically and impacts the coordinates of the x and y properties. A more reliable measure of the event inside the image is the offset properties. The same is true in the Macintosh version, as long as the page isn't scrolled, in which case the scroll, just as in Step 2, affects the values above.

4. Click the top hr element under the heading. It may take a couple of tries to actually hit the element (you've made it when the hr element shows up in the srcElement box). This is to reinforce the way the client properties provide coordinates within the element itself (again, except on the Mac when the page is scrolled). Clicking at the very left end of the rule, you eventually find the 0,0 coordinate.

Finally, if you are a Windows user, here are two examples to try to see some of the unexpected behavior of coordinate properties.

1. With the page not scrolled, click anywhere along the right side of the page, away from any text, so that the body element is srcElement. Because the body element theoretically fills the entire content region of the browser window, all coordinate pairs except for the screen coordinates should be the same. But offset properties are 2 pixels less than all the others. By and large, this difference won't matter in your scripts, but you should be aware of this potential discrepancy if precise positioning is important. For inexplicable reasons, the offset properties are measured in a space that is inset 2 pixels from the left and top of the window. This is not the case in the Macintosh version, where all value pairs are the same from the body perspective.

2. Click the text of the h1 or p elements (just above and below the long horizontal rule at the top of the page). In theory, the offset properties should be relative to the rectangles occupied by these elements (they're block elements, after all). But instead, they're measured in the same space as the client properties (plus the 2 pixels). This unexpected behavior doesn't have anything to do with the cursor being a text cursor, because if you click inside any of the text box elements, their offset properties are properly relative to their own rectangles. This problem does not afflict the Macintosh version.

Many of these properties are also in the W3C DOM and are therefore supported in W3C DOM browsers. Unsupported properties display their values as undefined when you run Listing 32-8 in those browsers.

You can see further examples of important event coordinate properties in action in the discussion of dragging elements around the IE page in Chapter 43, "Positioned Objects."

Related Items: fromElement, toElement properties

contentOverflow

Value: Boolean   Read-Only

Compatibility: WinIE5.5+, MacIE-, NN-, Moz-, Safari-, Opera-, Chrome-

The value indicates whether page content has overflowed the current layout rectangle. This property is primarily used during printing as the basis for overflowing content from one page to another.

dataTransfer

Value: Object   Read-Only

Compatibility: WinIE5+, MacIE-, NN-, Moz-, Safari-, Opera-, Chrome-

The dataTransfer property is a reference to the dataTransfer object. Use this object in drag-and-drop operations (that is, with drag-and-drop-related events) to control not only the data that gets transferred from the source to the target, but also to control the look of the cursor along the way.

Table 32-6 lists the properties and methods of the dataTransfer object.

The dataTransfer object acts as a conduit and controller of the data that your scripts need to transfer from one element to another in response to a user's drag-and-drop action. You need to adhere to a well-defined sequence of actions triggered by a handful of event handlers. This means that the object is invoked on different instances of the event object as different events fire in the process of dragging and dropping.

The sequence begins at the source element, where an ondragstart event handler typically assigns a value to the dropEffect property and uses the getData() method to explicitly capture whatever data regarding the source object gets transferred to the eventual target. For example, if you drag an image, the information being transferred may simply be the URL of the image — data that is extractable from the event.srcElement.src property of that event (the src property of the image, that is).

At the target element(s), three event handlers must be defined: ondragenter, ondragover, and ondrop. Most commonly, the first two event handlers do nothing more than mark the element for a particular dropEffect (which must match the effectAllowed set at the source during the drag's start) and set event.returnValue to false so the desired cursor is displayed. These actions are also carried out in the `ondrop` event handler, but that is also the handler that does the processing of the destination action at the target element. This is when the `dataTransfer` object's `getData()` method is invoked to pick up the data that has been "stored" away by `getData()` at the start of the drag. If you also want to make sure that the data is not picked up accidentally by another event, invoke the `clearData()` method to remove that data from memory.

TABLE 32-6

dataTransfer object Properties and Methods

Property/Method	Returns	Description
`dropEffect`	String	An element that is a potential recipient of a drop action can use the `ondragenter`, `ondragover`, or `ondrop` event handler to set the cursor style to be displayed when the cursor is atop the element. Before this can work, the source element's `ondragstart` event handler must assign a value to the `event.effectAllowed` property. Possible string values for both properties are `copy`, `link`, `move`, or `none`. These properties correspond to the Windows system cursors for the operations users typically do with files and in other documents. You must also cancel the default action (meaning set `event.returnValue` to `false`) for all of these drop element event handlers: `ondragenter`, `ondragover`, and `ondrop`.
`effectAllowed`	String	Set in response to an `ondragstart` event of the source element, this property determines which kind of drag-and-drop action will be taking place. Possible string values are `copy`, `link`, `move`, or `none`. This property value must match the `dropEffect` property value for the target element's event object. Also, cancel the default action (meaning, set `event.returnValue` to `false`) in the `ondragstart` event handler.
`clearData([format])`	Nothing	Removes data in the clipboard. If no format parameters are supplied, all data are cleared. Data formats can be one or more of the following strings: `Text`, `URL`, `File`, `HTML`, `Image`.
`getData(format)`	String	Retrieves data of the specified format from the clipboard. The format is one of the following strings: `Text`, `URL`, `File`, `HTML`, `Image`. The clipboard is not emptied after you get the data, so it can be retrieved in several sequential operations.
`setData(format, data)`	Boolean	Stores string data in the clipboard. The format is one of the following strings: `Text`, `URL`, `File`, `HTML`, `Image`. For non-text data formats, the data must be a string that specifies the path or URL to the content. Returns `true` if the transfer to the clipboard is successful.

Note that the style of dragging being discussed here is not the kind in which you see the source element actually moving on the screen (although you could script it that way). The intention is to treat drag-and-drop operations just as Windows does in, say, the Windows Explorer window or on the Desktop. To the user, the draggable component becomes encapsulated in the cursor. That's why the properties of the `dataTransfer` object control the appearance of the cursor at the drop point as a way of conveying to the user the type of action that will occur with the impending drop. Apple implements the same behavior in Safari 2.

Example

An extensive example of the `dataTransfer` property in action can be found in Listing 26-37 in the section for the `ondrag` event handler.

Related Items: `ondragend`, `ondragenter`, `ondragleave`, `ondragover`, `ondragstart`, `ondrop` event handlers

fromElement
toElement

Value: Element object   Read-Only

Compatibility: WinIE4+, MacIE4+, NN-, Moz-, Safari+, Opera+, Chrome+

The `fromElement` and `toElement` properties allow an element to uncover where the cursor rolled in from or has rolled out to. These properties extend the power of the `onmouseover` and `onmouseout` event handlers by expanding their scope to outside the current element (usually to an adjacent element).

When the `onmouseover` event fires on an element, the cursor had to be over some other element just beforehand. The `fromElement` property holds a reference to that element. Conversely, when the `onmouseout` event fires, the cursor is already over some other element. The `toElement` property holds a reference to that element.

Example

Listing 32-9 provides an example of how the `fromElement` and `toElement` properties can reveal the life of the cursor action before and after it rolls into an element. When you roll the cursor to the center box (a table cell), its `onmouseover` event handler displays the text from the table cell from which the cursor arrived.

LISTING 32-9

Using the toElement and fromElement Properties

```
<!DOCTYPE html>
<html>
   <head>
      <meta http-equiv="content-type" content="text/html;charset=utf-8">
      <title>fromElement and toElement Properties</title>
      <style type="text/css">
         .direction {background-color:#00FFFF; width:100; height:50;
                     text-align:center;}
```

```
        #main {background-color:#FF6666; text-align:center;}
    </style>
    <script type="text/javascript">
        function showArrival(evt)
        {
            evt = (evt) ? evt : ((event) ? event : null);
            var direction = (event.fromElement.innerText) ?
                event.fromElement.innerText :
                "parts unknown";
            status = "Arrived from: " + direction;
        }
        function showDeparture(evt)
        {
            evt = (evt) ? evt : ((event) ? event : null);
            var direction = (event.toElement.innerText) ?
                event.toElement.innerText :
                "parts unknown";
            status = "Departed to: " + direction;
        }


        // bind the event handlers
        function addEvent(elem, evtType, func)
        {
            if (elem.addEventListener)
            {
                elem.addEventListener(evtType, func, false);
            }
            else if (elem.attachEvent)
            {
                elem.attachEvent("on" + evtType, func);
            }
            else
            {
                elem["on" + evtType] = func;
            }
        }
        addEvent(window, "load", function()
        {
            addEvent(document.getElementById("main"), "mouseover",
                    function(evt) {showArrival(evt);});
            addEvent(document.getElementById("main"), "mouseout",
                    function(evt) {showDeparture(evt);});
        });
    </script>
</head>
<body>
    <h1>fromElement and toElement Properties</h1>
    <hr />
    <p>Roll the mouse to the center box and look for arrival information in
        the status bar. Roll the mouse away from the center box and look for
        departure information in the status bar.</p>
    <table cellspacing="0" cellpadding="5">
        <tr>
```

continued

LISTING 32-9 *(continued)*

```
        <td></td>
        <td class="direction">North</td>
        <td></td>
      </tr>
      <tr>
        <td class="direction">West</td>
        <td id="main" onmouseover="showArrival()"
            onmouseout="showDeparture()">Roll</td>
        <td class="direction">East</td>
      </tr>
      <tr>
        <td></td>
        <td class="direction">South</td>
        <td></td>
      </tr>
    </table>
  </body>
</html>
```

This is a good example to experiment with in the browser, because it also reveals a potential limitation. The element registered as the `toElement` or `fromElement` must fire a mouse event to register itself with the browser. If not, the next element in the sequence that registers itself is the one acknowledged by these properties. For example, if you roll the mouse into the center box, and then extremely quickly roll the cursor to the bottom of the page, you may bypass the South box entirely. The text that appears in the status bar is actually the inner text of the `body` element, which is the element that caught the first mouse event to register itself as the `toElement` for the center table cell.

Related Item: `srcElement` property

keyCode

Value: Integer   Read-Only

Compatibility: WinIE4+, MacIE4+, NN6+, Moz+, Safari+, Opera+, Chrome+

For keyboard events, the `keyCode` property returns an integer corresponding to the Unicode value of the character (for `onkeypress` events) or the keyboard character key (for `onkeydown` and `onkeyup` events). There is a significant distinction between these numbering code systems.

If you want the Unicode values (the same as ASCII values for the Latin character set) for the key that a user pressed, get the `keyCode` property from the `onkeypress` event handler. For example, a lowercase "a" returns 97, whereas an uppercase "A" returns 65. Non-character keys, such as arrows, page navigation, and function keys, return a `null` value for the `keyCode` property during `onkeypress` events. In other words, the `keyCode` property for `onkeypress` events is more like a character code than a key code.

To capture the exact keyboard key that the user presses, use either the `onkeydown` or `onkeyup` event handler. For these events, the `event` object captures a numeric code associated with a particular key on the keyboard. For the character keys, this varies with the language assigned as the system language. Importantly, there is no distinction between uppercase or lowercase: The "A" key on the Latin keyboard returns a value of 65, regardless of the state of the Shift key. At the same time, however, the press of the Shift key fired its own onkeydown and onkeyup events, setting the key-Code value to 16. Other non-character keys — arrows, page navigation, function, and similar — have their own codes as well. This gets very detailed, and involves special key codes for the numeric keyboard keys that are different from their corresponding numbers along the top row of the alphanumeric keyboard.

Cross-Reference

Be sure to see the extensive section on keyboard events in Chapter 26 for examples of how to apply the key-Code property in applications. ■

Example

Listing 32-10 provides an additional play area to view the keyCode property for all three keyboard events while you type into a textarea. You can use this page later as an authoring tool to grab the precise codes for keyboard keys you may not be familiar with.

LISTING 32-10

Displaying keyCode Property Values

```
<html>
<!DOCTYPE html>
<html>
    <head>
        <meta http-equiv="content-type" content="text/html;charset=utf-8">
        <title>keyCode Property</title>
        <style type="text/css">
            td {text-align:center}
        </style>
        <script type="text/javascript">
            function showCode(which, evt)
            {
                evt = (evt) ? evt : ((event) ? event : null);
                    if (evt)
                    {
                        document.forms[0].elements[which].value = evt.keyCode;
                    }
            }

            function clearEm()
            {
                for (var i = 1; i < document.forms[0].elements.length; i++)
                {
                    document.forms[0].elements[i].value = "";
                }
            }

            // bind the event handlers
```

continued

eventObject.**keyCode**

LISTING 32-10 *(continued)*

```
        function addEvent(elem, evtType, func)
        {
            if (elem.addEventListener)
            {
                elem.addEventListener(evtType, func, false);
            }
            else if (elem.attachEvent)
            {
                elem.attachEvent("on" + evtType, func);
            }
            else
            {
                elem["on" + evtType] = func;
            }
        }
        addEvent(window, "load", function()
        {
            addEvent(document.getElementById("scratchpad"), "keydown",
                    function(evt) {clearEm(); showCode("down", evt);});
            addEvent(document.getElementById("scratchpad"), "keypress",
                    function(evt) {showCode("press", evt);});
            addEvent(document.getElementById("scratchpad"), "keyup",
                    function(evt) {showCode("up", evt);});
        });
    </script>
</head>
<body>
    <h1>keyCode Property</h1>
    <hr />
    <form>
        <p>
            <textarea id="scratchpad" name="scratchpad"
             cols="40" rows="5" wrap="hard"></textarea>
        </p>
        <table cellpadding="5">
            <tr>
                <th>Event</th>
                <th>event.keyCode</th>
            </tr>
            <tr>
                <td>onKeyDown:</td>
                <td><input type="text" name="down" size="3" /></td>
            </tr>
            <tr>
                <td>onKeyPress:</td>
                <td><input type="text" name="press" size="3" /></td>
            </tr>
            <tr>
                <td>onKeyUp:</td>
```

```
            <td><input type="text" name="up" size="3" /></td>
         </tr>
       </table>
     </form>
   </body>
</html>
```

The following are some specific tasks to try with the page to examine key codes (if you are not using a browser set for English, and a Latin-based keyboard, your results may vary):

1. Enter a lowercase **a**. Notice how the onkeypress event handler shows the code to be 97, which is the Unicode (and ASCII) value for the first of the lowercase letters of the Latin alphabet. But the other two events record just the key's code: 65.

2. Type an uppercase **A** via the Shift key. If you watch closely, you see that the Shift key itself generates the code 16 for the onkeydown and onkeyup events. But the character key then shows the value 65 for all three events, because the ASCII value of the uppercase letter happens to match the keyboard key code for that letter.

3. Press and release the Down Arrow key (be sure the cursor still flashes in the textarea, because that's where the keyboard events are being monitored). As a non-character key, it does not fire an onkeypress event. But it does fire the other events, and assigns 40 as the code for this key.

4. Poke around with other non-character keys. Some may produce dialog boxes or menus, but their key codes are recorded nonetheless. Note that not all keys on a Macintosh keyboard register with MacIE.

Notice also that the keyCode property doesn't work properly for the onkeypress event in Mozilla-based browsers. This is because Mozilla uses the charCode property for the onkeypress event instead of keyCode. You could make the code in the listing work for all modern browsers with the following modification in the showCode() function:

```
if (evt)
{
   var charCode = (evt.charCode) ? evt.charCode : evt.keyCode;
   document.forms[0].elements[which].value = charCode;
}
```

Related Items: onkeydown, onkeypress, onkeyup event handlers

nextPage

Value: String   Read-Only

Compatibility: WinIE5.5+, MacIE-, NN-, Moz-, Safari-, Opera-, Chrome-

The nextPage property is applicable only if your WinIE5.5+ page uses a TemplatePrinter behavior. Values of this property are one of the following strings: left, right, or an empty string.

propertyName

Value: String   Read-Only

Compatibility: WinIE5+, MacIE-, NN-, Moz-, Safari-, Opera-, Chrome-

The propertyName property is filled only after an onpropertychange event fires.

If a script modifies a property, the onpropertychange event handler fires, and the string name of the property is stuffed into the event.propertyName property. If the property happens to be a property of the style object associated with the element, the propertyName is the full property reference, as in style.backgroundColor.

Example

See Listing 26-45 in the section about the onpropertychange event handler for an example of the values returned by this property.

Related Item: onpropertychange event handler (Chapter 26, "Generic HTML Element Objects")

repeat

Value: Boolean   Read-Only

Compatibility: WinIE5+, MacIE-, NN-, Moz-, Safari-, Opera-, Chrome-

The repeat property reveals for onkeydown events only whether the key is in repeat mode (as determined by the keyboard control panel settings in the system). With this information, you can prevent the automatic triggering of repeat mode from causing multiple characters from being recognized by the browser. This property can come in handy if users accidentally hold down a key too long. The following script fragment in an onkeydown event handler for a text box or textarea prevents multiple characters from appearing even if the system goes into repeat mode:

```
if (event.repeat)
{
    event.returnValue = false;
}
```

By disabling the default action while in repeat mode, no further characters reach the text box until repeat mode goes away (with the press of another key).

Related Item: onkeydown event handler

returnValue

Value: Boolean   Read-Only

Compatibility: WinIE4+, MacIE4+, NN-, Moz-, Safari1.2+, Opera+, Chrome+

While IE4+ continues to honor the original way of preventing default action for an event handler (that is, having the last statement of the event handler evaluate to return false), the IE4+ event model provides a property that lets the cancellation of default action take place entirely within a function invoked by an event handler. By default, the returnValue property of the event object is true, meaning that the element processes the event after the scripted handler completes its job, just as if the script weren't there. Normal processing, for example, is displaying a typed character, navigating to a link's href URL upon being clicked, or submitting a form after the Submit button is clicked.

But you don't always want the default action to occur. For example, consider a text box that is supposed to allow only numbers to be typed in it. The onkeypress event handler can invoke a function that inspects each typed character. If the character is not a numeric character, it should not reach the text box for display. The following validation function may be invoked from the `onkeypress` event handler of just such a text box:

```
function checkIt()
{
   var charCode = event.keyCode;
      if (charCode < 48 || charCode > 57)
      {
         alert("Please make sure entries are numerals only.");
         event.returnValue = false;
      }
}
```

By using this event handler, the errant character won't appear in the text box.

Note that this property is not a substitute for the `return` statement of a function. If you need a value to be returned to the invoking statement, you can use a `return` statement in addition to setting the `event.returnValue` property.

Example

You can find several examples of the `returnValue` property at work in Chapters 1 and 26. Specifically, refer to Listings 26-30, 26-33, 26-36, 26-37, 26-38, and 26-44. Moreover, many of the other examples in Chapter 26 can substitute the `returnValue` property way of cancelling the default action if the scripts were to be run exclusively on IE4+.

Related Item: `return` statement (Chapter 23, "Function Objects and Custom Objects")

saveType

Value: String   Read-Only

Compatibility: WinIE5.5+, MacIE-, NN-, Moz-, Safari-, Opera-, Chrome-

The `saveType` property is assigned a value only when an `oncontentsave` event is bound to a WinIE DHTML behavior file. For more information about behaviors, see `http://msdn.microsoft.com/en-us/library/ms531079%28VS.85%29.aspx`.

Related Item: `addBehavior()` method

srcElement

Value: Element object reference   Read-Only

Compatibility: WinIE4+, MacIE4+, NN-, Moz-, Safari1.2+, Opera+, Chrome+

The `srcElement` property is a reference to the HTML element object that is the original target of the event. Because an event may bubble up through the element containment hierarchy and be processed at any level along the way, having a property that points back to the element from which the event originated is comforting. After you have a reference to that element, you can read or write any properties that belong to that element or invoke any of its methods.

eventObject.**srcElement**

Example

As a simplified demonstration of the power of the srcElement property, Listing 32-11 has but two event handlers defined for the body element, each invoking a single function. The idea is that the onmousedown and onmouseup events will bubble up from whatever their targets are, and the event handler functions will find out which element is the target and modify the color style of that element.

An extra flair is added to the script in that each function also checks the className property of the target element. If the className is bold — a class name shared by three span elements in the paragraph — the stylesheet rule for that class is modified so that all items share the same color. Your scripts can do even more in the way of filtering objects that arrive at the functions to perform special operations on certain objects or groups of objects.

Notice that the scripts don't have to know anything about the objects on the page to address each clicked one individually. That's because the srcElement property provides all of the specificity needed for acting on the target element.

LISTING 32-11

Using the srcElement Property

```
<!DOCTYPE html>
<html>
    <head>
        <meta http-equiv="content-type" content="text/html;charset=utf-8">
        <title>srcElement Property</title>
        <style type="text/css">
            .bold {font-weight:bold}
            .ital {font-style:italic}
        </style>
        <script type="text/javascript">
            function highlight()
            {
                var elem = event.srcElement;
                if (elem.className == "bold")
                {
                    document.styleSheets[0].rules[0].style.color = "red";
                }
                else
                {
                    elem.style.color = "#FFCC00";
                }
            }
            function restore()
            {
                var elem = event.srcElement;
                if (elem.className == "bold")
                {
                    document.styleSheets[0].rules[0].style.color = "";
                }
                else
                {
```

```
                elem.style.color = "";
            }
        }

        // bind the event handlers
        function addEvent(elem, evtType, func)
        {
            if (elem.addEventListener)
            {
                elem.addEventListener(evtType, func, false);
            }
            else if (elem.attachEvent)
            {
                elem.attachEvent("on" + evtType, func);
            }
            else
            {
                elem["on" + evtType] = func;
            }
        }
        addEvent(window, "load", function()
        {
            addEvent(document.body, "mousedown", highlight);
            addEvent(document.body, "mouseup", restore);
        });
    </script>
</head>
<body>
    <h1>srcElement Property</h1>
    <hr />
    <p>Click on the bolded text, then click on the unbolded text.
        What do you see happen?
    </p>
    <p>One event handler...</p>
    <ul>
        <li>Can</li>
        <li>Cover</li>
        <li>Many</li>
        <li>Objects</li>
    </ul>
    <p>Lorem ipsum dolor sit amet, consectetaur adipisicing elit,
        <span class="bold">sed do</span>
        eiusmod tempor incididunt
        <span class="ital">ut labore et</span>
        dolore magna aliqua. Ut enim adminim veniam,
        <span class="bold">quis nostrud exercitation</span>
        ullamco laboris nisi ut aliquip ex ea
        <span class="bold">commodo consequat</span>.
    </p>
</body>
</html>
```

Related Items: `fromElement`, `toElement` properties

srcFilter

Value: String   Read-Only

Compatibility: WinIE4+, MacIE-, NN-, Moz-, Safari-, Opera-, Chrome-

According to Microsoft, the `srcFilter` property should return a string of the name of the filter that was applied to trigger an `onfilterchange` event handler. While the property exists in the `event` object, its value is always `null`, at least through WinIE8.

Related Items: `onfilterchange` event handler; `style.filter` object

srcUrn

Value: String   Read-Only

Compatibility: WinIE5+, MacIE-, NN-, Moz-, Safari-, Opera-, Chrome-

If an event is fired in a WinIE behavior attached to an element, and the behavior has a URN identifier defined for it, the `srcUrn` property returns the string from the URN identifier. For more information about behaviors, see `http://msdn.microsoft.com/en-us/library/ms531079%28VS.85%29.aspx`.

Related Item: `addBehavior()` method

toElement

(See `fromElement`)

type

Value: String   Read-Only

Compatibility: WinIE4+, MacIE4+, NN4+, Moz+, Safari+, Opera+, Chrome+

You can find out what kind of event fired to create the current `event` object by way of the `type` property. The value is a string version of the event name — just the name of the event without the "on" prefix that is normally associated with event names in IE. This property can be helpful when you designate one event handler function to process different kinds of events. For example, both the `onmousedown` and `onclick` event handlers for an object can invoke one function. Inside the function, a branch is written for whether the type comes in as `mousedown` or `click`, with different processing for each event type. That is not to endorse such event handler function sharing, but for you to be aware of this power should your script constructions find the property helpful.

This property and its values are fully compatible with the NN6+/Moz/W3C event models.

Example

Use The Evaluator (Chapter 4, "JavaScript Essentials") to see values returned by the `type` property. Enter the following object name into the bottom text box and press Enter/Return:

    event

If necessary, scroll the Results box to view the `type` property, which should read `keypress`. Now click the List Properties button. The type changes to `click`. The reason for these types is that the event object whose properties are being shown here is the event that triggers the function to show the properties. From the text box, an onkeypress event handler triggers that process; from the button, an onclick event handler does the job.

Related Items: All event handlers (Chapter 26, "Generic HTML Element Objects")

wheelData

Value: Integer   Read-Only

Compatibility: WinIE5.5+, MacIE-, NN-, Moz-, Safari-, Opera-, Chrome-

The wheelData property returns an integer indicating which direction the mouse wheel was rolled for an onmousewheel event. The values returned are typically either 120 or −120, with a positive value indicating that the mouse wheel was rolled toward the screen and a negative value indicating that the wheel was rolled the opposite direction.

NN6+/Moz event Object

Properties	Methods	Event Handlers
altKey	initEvent()	
bubbles	initKeyEvent()	
button	initMouseEvent()	
cancelable	initMutationEvent()	
cancelBubble	initUIEvent()	
charCode	preventDefault()	
clientX	stopPropagation()	
clientY		
ctrlKey		
currentTarget		
detail		
eventPhase		
isChar		
isTrusted		
keyCode		
layerX		
layerY		

Properties	Methods	Event Handlers
metaKey		
originalTarget		
pageX		
pageY		
screenX		
screenY		
shiftKey		
target		
timeStamp		
type		
view		

Syntax

Accessing NN6+/Moz event object properties and methods:

```
eventObject.property | method([parameters])
```

Compatibility: WinIE-, MacIE-, NN6+, Moz+, Safari+, Opera+, Chrome+

About this object

Although it is based largely on the event object as defined by the W3C DOM Level 2, the NN6+/Moz event object also carries forward several characteristics from the NN4 event object. A few properties are continued primarily for backward compatibility. But because future Mozilla development will likely forego the peculiarities of the NN4 DOM and event models, you should ignore these items (as high-lighted below). Wherever possible, look forward and embrace the W3C DOM aspects of the event model. Safari, Opera, and Chrome, for example, implement a lot of the W3C DOM event model, but exclude all old NN4 properties.

Although the NN6+/Moz event model provides a bubbling event propagation model just as IE4+ does the incompatibility of referencing event objects between the event models is still there. In the W3C DOM (as in NN4), an event object is explicitly passed as a parameter to event handler (or, rather, event listener) functions. But after you have a browser-specific event object assigned to a variable inside a function, a few important properties have the same names between the IE4+ and W3C DOM event models. If Microsoft adopts more of the W3C DOM event model in future versions of IE, the compatibility situation should improve.

The event object discussed in this section is the instance of an event that is created as the result of a user or system event action. The W3C DOM includes an additional static Event object. Many of the properties of the static Event object are inherited by the event instances, so the detailed coverage of those shared properties is in this section because it is the event object you'll be scripting for the most part.

In many code fragments in the following detail sections, you will see references that begin with the evt reference. This assumes that the statement(s) resides inside a function that has assigned the incoming event object to the evt parameter variable:

```
function myFunction(evt) {...}
```

As shown earlier in this chapter, you can equalize W3C DOM and IE4+ event object references when it is practical to do so because the scripts work on identical (or similar) event object properties. The results of this equalization are typically stored in the evt variable.

Properties

altKey
ctrlKey
metaKey
shiftKey

Value: Boolean   Read-Only

Compatibility: WinIE4+, MacIE4+, NN6+, Moz+, Safari+, Opera+, Chrome+

When an event object is created in response to a user or system action, these four properties are set based on whether their corresponding keys were being held down at the time — a Shift-click, for example. If the key was held down, the property is assigned a value of true; otherwise the value is false. The metaKey property corresponds to the Command key on the Macintosh keyboard but does not register for the Windows key on Wintel computers.

Most commonly, you use expressions consisting of this property as if construction conditional statements. Because these are Boolean values, you can combine multiple properties in a single condition. For example, if you have a branch of a function that is to execute only if the event occurred with both the Shift and Control keys held down, the condition looks like the following:

```
if (evt.shiftKey && evt.ctrlKey)
{
    // statements to execute
}
```

Conversely, you can take a more user-friendly approach to provide special processing if the user holds down any one of the four modifier keys:

```
if (evt.shiftKey || evt.ctrlKey || evt.metaKey || evt.altKey)
{
    // statements to execute
}
```

The rationale behind this approach is to offer perhaps some shortcut operation for users, but not force them to memorize a specific modifier key combination.

1099

Example

See Listing 32-6, where the values of these properties are used to set the `checked` properties of corresponding check boxes for a variety of event types.

Related Items: None

bubbles

Value: Boolean   Read-Only

Compatibility: WinIE-, MacIE-, NN6+, Moz+, Safari+, Opera+, Chrome+

Not every event bubbles. For example, an `onsubmit` event propagates no further than the form object with which the event is associated. Events that do not bubble have their event object's `bubbles` property set to `false`; all others have the property set to `true`. You use this property in the rare circumstance of a single event handler function processing a wide variety of events. You may want to perform special operations only on events that can bubble, and handle the others without special treatment. For this branch, you can use the property in an `if` conditional statement:

```
if (evt.bubbles)
{
    // special processing for bubble-able events
}
```

You do not have to branch, however, just to cancel bubbling. A non-propagating event doesn't mind if you tell it not to propagate.

Related Item: `cancelBubble` property

button

Value: Integer   Read-Only

Compatibility: WinIE4+, MacIE4+, NN6+, Moz+, Safari+, Opera8+, Chrome+

The `button` property reveals the button that was pressed to activate the mouse event. In the W3C DOM, the left (primary) button returns a value of `0`. If the mouse is a three-button mouse, the middle button returns `1`. The right button (on any multi-button mouse) returns a value of `2`.

Mouse buttons other than the primary one are easier to look for in `mousedown` or `mouseup` events, rather than `onclick` events. In the case of a user pressing multiple buttons, only the most recent button is registered.

Exercise caution when scripting the `button` property across browsers. The respective event models define different button values for mouse buttons.

Example

See Listing 32-7, where the `button` property is revealed in the status bar. Try pressing individual mouse buttons on, say, the screen button.

Related Items: None

cancelable

Value: Boolean   Read-Only

Compatibility: WinIE-, MacIE-, NN6+, Moz+, Safari+, Opera+, Chrome+

If an event is cancelable, then its default action can be prevented from occurring with the help of a script. Although most events are cancelable, some are not. The cancelable property lets you inquire about a particular event object to see if its event type is `cancelable`. Values for the property are Booleans. You may want to perform special operations only on events that are cancelable and handle the others without special treatment. For this branch, you can use the property in an `if` conditional statement:

```
if (evt.cancelable)
{
    // special processing for cancelable events
}
```

You do not have to branch, however, just to prevent an event's default action. A non-cancelable event doesn't mind if you tell it to prevent the default action.

Related Item: `preventDefault()` method

cancelBubble

Value: Boolean   Read/Write

Compatibility: WinIE4+, MacIE4+, NN6+, Moz+, Safari+, Opera+, Chrome+

The `cancelBubble` property is a rare instance of an IE4+ event property being implemented in NN6+/Moz and Gecko-, WebKit-, and Presto-based browsers, even though the property is not defined in the W3C DOM. The property operates the same as in IE4+ in that it determines whether the current event object bubbles up any higher in the element containment hierarchy of the document. By default, this property is `false`, meaning that if the event is supposed to bubble, it will do so automatically.

To prevent event bubbling for the current event, set the property to `true` anywhere within the event handler function. Cancelling event bubbling works only for the current event. The very next event to fire will have bubbling enabled (provided the event bubbles).

If you are trying to migrate your code as much as possible to the W3C DOM, use the `stopPropagation()` method instead of `cancelBubble`. For cross-browser compatibility, however, `cancelBubble` is a safe bet.

Example

See Listing 32-2 to see the `cancelBubble` property in action in an IE environment. Even though that listing has some features that apply to WinIE5.5+, the bubble cancelling demonstration works all the way back to IE4.

Related Item: `stopPropagation()` method

charCode
keyCode

Value: Integer   Read-Only

Compatibility: WinIE-, MacIE-, NN6+, Moz+, Safari+, Opera-, Chrome+

*eventObject.***keyCode**

The W3C DOM event object model clearly distinguishes between the Unicode character attached to the alphanumeric keys of the keyboard and the code attached to each of the keyboard keys (regardless of character). To inspect the character of a key, use the onkeypress event to create the event object, and then look at the event object's charCode property. This is the property that returns 97 for "a" and 65 for "A" because it's concerned with the character associated with the key action. This property's value is zero for onkeydown and onkeyup events.

In contrast, the keyCode property is filled with a non-zero value only from onkeydown and onkeyup events (onkeypress sets the property to zero) when alphanumeric keys are pressed; for most other non-character keys, all three events fill the keyCode property. Through this property you can look for non-character keys, such as arrows, page navigation, and function keys. For the character keys, there is no distinction between uppercase and lowercase: The "A" key on the Latin keyboard returns a value of 65, regardless of the state of the Shift key. At the same time, however, the press of the Shift key fires its own onkeydown and onkeyup events, setting the keyCode value to 16 (except in Safari, which does not register modifier keys in this way). Other non-character keys — arrows, page navigation, function, and similar — have their own codes as well. This gets very detailed, and involves special key codes for the numeric keyboard keys that are different from their corresponding numbers along the top row of the alphanumeric keyboard.

Cross-Reference

Be sure to see the extensive section on keyboard events in Chapter 26, "Generic HTML Element Objects," for examples of how to apply the keyCode property in applications. ∎

Example

Listing 32-12 provides a play area to view the charCode and keyCode properties for all three keyboard events while you type into a textarea. You can use this later as an authoring tool to grab the precise codes for keyboard keys you may not be familiar with.

LISTING 32-12

Displaying charCode and keyCode Property Values

```
<!DOCTYPE html>
<html>
   <head>
      <meta http-equiv="content-type" content="text/html;charset=utf-8">
      <title>charCode and keyCode Properties</title>
      <style type="text/css">
         td {text-align:center}
      </style>
      <script type="text/javascript">
         function showCode(which, evt)
         {
            document.forms[0].elements[which + "Char"].value = evt.charCode;
            document.forms[0].elements[which + "Key"].value = evt.keyCode;
         }
         function clearEm()
         {
            for (var i = 1; i < document.forms[0].elements.length; i++)
```

```
            {
                document.forms[0].elements[i].value = "";
            }
        }

    // bind the event handlers
    function addEvent(elem, evtType, func)
    {
        if (elem.addEventListener)
        {
            elem.addEventListener(evtType, func, false);
        }
        else if (elem.attachEvent)
        {
            elem.attachEvent("on" + evtType, func);
        }
        else
        {
            elem["on" + evtType] = func;
        }
    }
    addEvent(window, "load", function()
    {
        addEvent(document.getElementById("scratchpad"), "keydown",
                function(evt) {clearEm(); showCode("down", evt);});
        addEvent(document.getElementById("scratchpad"), "keypress",
                function(evt) {showCode("press", evt);});
        addEvent(document.getElementById("scratchpad"), "keyup",
                function(evt) {showCode("up", evt);});
    });
    </script>
</head>
<body>
    <h1>charCode and keyCode Properties</h1>
    <hr />
    <form>
        <p>
            <textarea id="scratchpad" name="scratchpad"
             cols="40" rows="5" wrap="hard"></textarea>
        </p>
        <table cellpadding="5">
            <tr>
                <th>Event</th>
                <th>event.charCode</th>
                <th>event.keyCode</th>
            </tr>
            <tr>
                <td>onKeyDown:</td>
                <td><input type="text" name="downChar" size="3" /></td>
                <td><input type="text" name="downKey" size="3" /></td>
            </tr>
            <tr>
                <td>onKeyPress:</td>
```

continued

LISTING 32-12 *(continued)*

```
            <td><input type="text" name="pressChar" size="3" /></td>
            <td><input type="text" name="pressKey" size="3" /></td>
          </tr>
          <tr>
            <td>onKeyUp:</td>
            <td><input type="text" name="upChar" size="3" /></td>
            <td><input type="text" name="upKey" size="3" /></td>
          </tr>
        </table>
      </form>
    </body>
</html>
```

Here are some specific tasks to try with the page in NN6+/Moz to examine key codes (if you are not using a browser set for English and a Latin-based keyboard, your results may vary):

1. Enter a lowercase **a**. Notice how the onkeypress event handler shows the charCode to be 97, which is the Unicode (and ASCII) value for the first of the lowercase letters of the Latin alphabet. But the other two event types record just the key's code: 65.

2. Type an uppercase **A** via the Shift key. If you watch closely, you see that the Shift key, itself, generates the key code 16 for the onkeydown and onkeyup events. But the character key then shows the value 65 for all three events (until you release the Shift key), because the ASCII value of the uppercase letter happens to match the keyboard key code for that letter.

3. Press and release the Down Arrow key (be sure the cursor still flashes in the textarea, because that's where the keyboard events are being monitored). As a non-character key, all three events stuff a value into the keyCode property, but zero into charCode. The keyCode value for this key is 40.

4. Poke around with other non-character keys. Some may produce dialog boxes or menus, but their key codes are recorded nonetheless.

Related Items: onkeydown, onkeypress, onkeyup event handlers

clientX
clientY
layerX
layerY
pageX
pageY
screenX
screenY

Value: Integer   Read-Only

Compatibility: WinIE4+, MacIE4+, NN6+, Moz+, Safari+, Opera+, Chrome+

The W3C DOM `event` object borrows mouse coordinate properties from both the NN4 and the IE4+ event models. If you have worked with event coordinates in these other browsers, you have nothing new to learn for W3C DOM-compatible browsers.

Like the IE4+ `event` object, the W3C DOM `event` object's `clientX` and `clientY` properties are the coordinates within the viewable content region of the window. These values are relative to the window space, not the document. But unlike IE4+, you don't have to calculate the position of the coordinates within the document because another pair of NN/Moz properties, `pageX` and `pageY`, provide that information automatically. If the page has not scrolled, the values of the client and page coordinates are the same. Because it is usually more important to know an event's coordinates with respect to the document than the window, the `pageX` and `pageY` properties are used most often.

Another NN/Moz property pair, `layerX` and `layerY`, borrow terminology from the now defunct layer schemes of NN4, but the properties can still be quite valuable nonetheless. These coordinates are measured relative to the positioning context of the element that received the event. For regular, unpositioned elements in the `body` part of a document, that positioning context is the `body` element. Thus, for those elements, the values of the page and layer coordinates will be the same. But if you create a positioned element, the coordinate space is measured from the top-left corner of that space. Thus, if you are using the coordinates to assist in scripted dragging of positioned elements, you can confine your scope to just the positioned element.

One coordinate system missing from the NN6+/Moz repertoire, but present in Safari, is that of the target element itself (comparable to the `offsetX` and `offsetY` properties of IE4+). These values, however, can be calculated in NN/Moz by subtracting from the page coordinate properties the `offsetLeft` and `offsetTop` properties of both the target element and its positioning context. For example, if you want to get the coordinates of a mouse event inside an image, the event handler can calculate those values as follows:

```
var clickOffsetX = evt.pageX - evt.target.offsetLeft -
    document.body.offsetLeft;
var clickOffsetY = evt.pageY - evt.target.offsetTop -
    document.body.offsetTop;
```

The last set of coordinate properties, `screenX` and `screenY`, provide values relative to the entire video display. Of all these properties, only the client and screen coordinates are defined in the W3C DOM Level 2 standard.

Keep in mind that in most W3C DOM–compatible browsers, event targets include text nodes inside elements. Because nodes do not have all the properties of elements (for example, they have no offset properties signifying their location in the document), you may sometimes have to go to the target node's parent node to get an element object whose offset properties provide the necessary page geography. This matters, of course, only if your scripts need to concern themselves with mouse events on text.

Example

You can see the effects of the coordinate systems and associated NN6+/Moz properties with the page in Listing 32-13. You can view coordinate values for all four measuring systems, as well as some calculated value. Two clickable objects are provided so that you can see the differences between an object not in any layer and an object residing within a layer (although anything you see is clickable, including text nodes). Figure 32-1 shows the results of a click inside the positioned layer.

One of the calculated fields applies window scrolling values to the client coordinates. But, as you will see, these calculated values are the same as the more convenient page coordinates. The other calculated field shows the coordinates relative to the rectangular space of the target element. Notice in the code that if the nodeType of the target indicates a text node, that node's parent node (an element) is used for the calculation.

LISTING 32-13

NN6+/Moz Event Coordinate Properties

```html
<!DOCTYPE html>
<html>
    <head>
        <meta http-equiv="content-type" content="text/html;charset=utf-8">
        <title>X and Y Event Properties (NN6+/Moz)</title>
        <script type="text/javascript">
            function checkCoords(evt)
            {
                var form = document.forms["output"];
                var targText, targElem;
                    if (evt.target.nodeType == 3)
                    {
                        targText = "[textnode] inside <" +
                                        evt.target.parentNode.tagName + ">";
                        targElem = evt.target.parentNode;
                    }
                    else
                    {
                        targText = "<" + evt.target.tagName + ">";
                        targElem = evt.target;
                    }
                form.srcElemTag.value = targText;
                form.clientCoords.value = evt.clientX + "," + evt.clientY;
                form.clientScrollCoords.value = (evt.clientX + window.scrollX) +
                                        "," + (evt.clientY + window.scrollY);
                form.layerCoords.value = evt.layerX + "," + evt.layerY;
                form.pageCoords.value = evt.pageX + "," + evt.pageY;
                form.inElemCoords.value =
                    (evt.pageX - targElem.offsetLeft - document.body.offsetLeft) +
                    "," + (evt.pageY - targElem.offsetTop - document.body.offsetTop);
                form.screenCoords.value = evt.screenX + "," + evt.screenY;
                return false;
            }

            // bind the event handler
            function addEvent(elem, evtType, func)
            {
                if (elem.addEventListener)
                {
                    elem.addEventListener(evtType, func, false);
                }
                else if (elem.attachEvent)
                {
                    elem.attachEvent("on" + evtType, func);
                }
```

```
            else
            {
                elem["on" + evtType] = func;
            }
        }
        addEvent(window, "load", function()
        {
            addEvent(document.body, "mousedown",
                    function(evt) {checkCoords(evt);});
        });
    </script>
</head>
<body>
    <h1>X and Y Event Properties (NN6+/Moz)</h1>
    <hr />
    <p>Click on the button and in the DIV/image to see the coordinate values
        for the event object.
    </p>
    <form name="output">
        <table>
            <tr>
                <td colspan="2">NN6 Mouse Event Coordinates:</td>
            </tr>
            <tr>
                <td align="right">target:</td>
                <td colspan="3"><input type="text" name="srcElemTag"
                <td size="25" /></td>
            </tr>
            <tr>
                <td align="right">clientX, clientY:</td>
                <td><input type="text" name="clientCoords" size="10" /></td>
                <td align="right">...With scrolling:</td>
                <td><input type="text" name="clientScrollCoords" size="10" /></td>
            </tr>
            <tr>
                <td align="right">layerX, layerY:</td>
                <td><input type="text" name="layerCoords" size="10" /></td>
            </tr>
            <tr>
                <td align="right">pageX, pageY:</td>
                <td><input type="text" name="pageCoords" size="10" /></td>
                <td aligh="right">Within Element:</td>
                <td><input type="text" name="inElemCoords" size="10" /></td>
            </tr>
            <tr>
                <td align="right">screenX, screenY:</td>
                <td><input type="text" name="screenCoords" size="10" /></td>
            </tr>
            <tr>
                <td align="right"><input type="button" value="Click Here" /></td>
            </tr>
        </table>
    </form>
```

continued

LISTING 32-13 *(continued)*

```
    <div id="display" style="position:relative; left:100">
        <img alt="image" src="nile.gif" width="320" height="240" border="0" />
    </div>
  </body>
</html>
```

FIGURE 32-1

NN6+/Moz event coordinates for a click inside a positioned element.

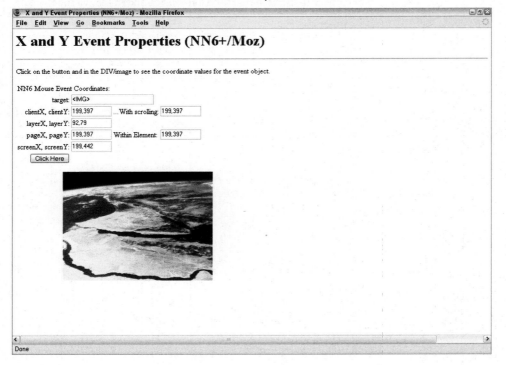

Related Item: `target` property

currentTarget

Value: Element object reference   Read-Only

Compatibility: WinIE-, MacIE-, NN6+, Moz+, Safari+, Opera+, Chrome+

As an event courses its way through its propagation paths, an event listener may process that event along the way. Though the event knows what the target is, it can also be helpful for the event listener function to know which element's event listener is now processing the event. The `currentTarget` property provides a reference to the element object whose event listener is processing the event. This allows one listener function to potentially process the event from different levels, branching the code to accommodate different element levels that process the event.

A valuable companion piece of information about the event is the `eventPhase` property, which helps your event listener function determine if the event is in capture mode, bubble mode, or is at the target. This property is demonstrated in the next section.

Example

Listing 32-14 shows the power of the `currentTarget` property in revealing the element that is processing an event during event propagation. Similar to the code in Listing 32-3, this example is made simpler because it lets the event object's properties do more of the work to reveal the identity of each element that processes the event. Event listeners assigned for various propagation modes are assigned to a variety of nodes in the document. After you click the button, each listener in the propagation chain fires in sequence. The alert dialog box shows which node is processing the event. And, as in Listing 32-3, the `eventPhase` property is used to help display the propagation mode in force at the time the event is processed by each node.

LISTING 32-14

currentTarget and eventPhase Properties

```
<!DOCTYPE html>
<html>
    <head>
        <meta http-equiv="content-type" content="text/html;charset=utf-8">
        <title>currentTarget and eventPhase Properties</title>
        <script type="text/javascript">
            function processEvent(evt)
            {
                var currTargTag, msg;
                    if (evt.currentTarget.nodeType == 1)
                    {
                        currTargTag = "<" + evt.currentTarget.tagName + ">";
                    }
                    else
                    {
                        currTargTag = evt.currentTarget.nodeName;
                    }
                msg = "Event is now at the " + currTargTag + " level ";
                msg += "(" + getPhase(evt) + ").";
                alert(msg);
            }
            // reveal event phase of current event object
            function getPhase(evt)
            {
```

continued

LISTING 32-14   *(continued)*

```
            switch (evt.eventPhase)
            {
                case 1:
                    return "CAPTURING";
                    break;
                case 2:
                    return "AT TARGET";
                    break;
                case 3:
                    return "BUBBLING";
                    break;
                default:
                    return "";
            }
        }

        // bind the event handlers
        function addEvent(elem, evtType, func)
        {
            if (elem.addEventListener)
            {
                elem.addEventListener(evtType, func, false);
            }
            else if (elem.attachEvent)
            {
                elem.attachEvent("on" + evtType, func);
            }
            else
            {
                elem["on" + evtType] = func;
            }
        }
        addEvent(window, "load", function()
        {
            // using old syntax to assign bubble-type event handlers
            document.onclick = processEvent;
            document.body.onclick = processEvent;
            // turn on click event capture for document and form
            document.addEventListener("click", processEvent, true);
            document.forms[0].addEventListener("click", processEvent, true);
            // set bubble event listener for form
            document.forms[0].addEventListener("click", processEvent, false);
            // turn on event capture for the button
            document.getElementById("main1").addEventListener("click",
            processEvent, true);
        });
    </script>
</head>
<body>
```

```
        <h1>currentTarget and eventPhase Properties</h1>
        <hr />
        <form>
            <input type="button" value="A Button" id="main1" name="main1" />
        </form>
    </body>
</html>
```

You can also click other places on the page. For example, if you click to the right of the button, you will be clicking the form element. Event propagation and processing adjusts accordingly. Similarly, if you click the header text, the only event listeners that see the event are in the document and body levels.

Related Item: eventPhase property

detail

Value: Integer   Read-Only

Compatibility: WinIE-, MacIE-, NN6+, Moz+, Safari2+, Opera8+, Chrome+

The detail property is included in the W3C DOM specification as an extra property whose purpose can be determined by the browser maker. Mozilla-, WebKit-, and Presto-based browsers increment a numeric value for rapid instances of click events on an object.

Related Items: None

eventPhase

Value: Integer   Read-Only

Compatibility: WinIE-, MacIE-, NN6+, Moz+, Safari+, Opera+, Chrome+

An event fires in one of three possible event phases: at event capture, at the target, or during bubbling. Because the same event listener function may be processing an event in multiple phases, it can inspect the value of the eventPhase property of the event object to see in which phase the event was when the function was invoked. Values for this property are integers 1 (capture), 2 (at target), or 3 (bubbling).

Example

Refer to Listing 32-14, earlier in this chapter, for an example of how you can use a switch construction to branch function processing based on the event phase of the current event object.

Related Item: currentTarget property

isChar

Value: Boolean   Read-Only

Compatibility: WinIE-, MacIE-, NN6+, Moz+, Safari-, Opera-, Chrome-

You can find out from each keyboard event whether the key being pressed is a character key by examining the isChar property. Most typically, however, you are already filtering for character or non-character keys by virtue of the event handlers used to capture keyboard actions: `onkeypress` for character keys; `onkeydown` or `onkeyup` for non-character keys. Be aware that the `isChar` property returns inconsistent values (even for the same key) in the first release of NN6.

Related Items: `charCode`, `keyCode` properties

isTrusted

Value: Boolean   Read-Only

Compatibility: WinIE-, MacIE-, NN8+, Moz1.7.5+, Safari-, Opera-, Chrome-

Because an event can be generated by user action or script, the `isTrusted` property enables you to determine how the event was created. Any event triggered by user action is considered to be trusted from a security point of view. Therefore, when this property returns `true`, it means that the event came to life as the result of user activity (clicking, keyboarding, and so on).

originalTarget

Value: Node object reference   Read-Only

Compatibility: WinIE-, MacIE-, NN6+, Moz+, Safari-, Opera-, Chrome-

The `originalTarget` property provides a reference to the node object that serves as the genuine first target of the event. This information is typically associated with the internal construction of certain elements, which makes it less useful for scripting purposes. Additionally, in many cases the `originalTarget` property holds the same value as the `target` property.

relatedTarget

Value: Element object   Read-Only

Compatibility: WinIE-, MacIE-, NN6+, Moz+, Safari+, Opera+, Chrome+

The `relatedTarget` property allows an element to uncover where the cursor rolled in from or has rolled out to. This property extends the power of the `onmouseover` and `onmouseout` event handlers by expanding their scope to outside the current element (usually to an adjacent element). This one W3C DOM property does the same duty as the `fromElement` and `toElement` properties of the IE4+ `event` object.

When the `onmouseover` event fires on an element, the cursor had to be over some other element just beforehand. The `relatedTarget` property holds a reference to that element. Conversely, when the `onmouseout` event fires, the cursor is already over some other element. The `relatedTarget` property holds a reference to that element.

Example

Listing 32-15 provides an example of how the `relatedTarget` property can reveal the life of the cursor action before and after it rolls into an element. When you roll the cursor to the center box (a table cell), its `onmouseover` event handler displays the text from the table cell from which the cursor arrived (the `nodeValue` of the text node inside the table cell). If the cursor comes in from one of the corners (not easy to do), a different message is displayed.

The two functions that report the results employ a bit of filtering to make sure that they process the event object only if the event occurs on an element and if the `relatedTarget` element is anything other than a nested text node of the central table cell element. Because nodes respond to events in W3C DOM browsers, this extra filtering prevents processing whenever the cursor makes the transition from the central td element to its nested text node.

LISTING 32-15

Using the relatedTarget Property

```
<!DOCTYPE html>
<html>
    <head>
        <meta http-equiv="content-type" content="text/html;charset=utf-8">
        <title>relatedTarget Properties</title>
        <style type="text/css">
            .direction {background-color:#00FFFF; width:100; height:50;
                                 text-align:center;}
            #main {background-color:#FF6666; text-align:center;}
        </style>
        <script type="text/javascript">
            function showArrival(evt)
            {
                if (evt.target.nodeType == 1)
                {
                    if (evt.relatedTarget != evt.target.firstChild)
                    {
                        var direction = (evt.relatedTarget.firstChild) ?
                            evt.relatedTarget.firstChild.nodeValue : "parts unknown";
                        window.status = "Arrived from: " + direction;
                    }
                }
            }
            function showDeparture(evt)
            {
                if (evt.target.nodeType == 1)
                {
                    if (evt.relatedTarget != evt.target.firstChild)
                    {
                        var direction = (evt.relatedTarget.firstChild) ?
                            evt.relatedTarget.firstChild.nodeValue : "parts unknown";
                        window.status = "Departed to: " + direction;
                    }
                }
            }

            // bind the event handlers
            function addEvent(elem, evtType, func)
            {
                if (elem.addEventListener)
                {
                    elem.addEventListener(evtType, func, false);
                }
                else if (elem.attachEvent)
```

continued

`LISTING 32-15`   *(continued)*

```
            {
                elem.attachEvent("on" + evtType, func);
            }
            else
            {
                elem["on" + evtType] = func;
            }
        }
        addEvent(window, "load", function()
        {
            addEvent(document.getElementById("main"), "mouseover",
                    function(evt) {showArrival(evt);});
            addEvent(document.getElementById("main"), "mouseout",
                    function(evt) {showDeparture(evt);});
        });
    </script>
</head>
<body>
    <h1>relatedTarget Properties</h1>
    <hr />
    <p>Roll the mouse to the center box and look for arrival information in
        the status bar. Roll the mouse away from the center box and look for
        departure information in the status bar.
    </p>
    <table cellspacing="0" cellpadding="5">
        <tr>
            <td></td>
            <td class="direction">North</td>
            <td></td>
        </tr>
        <tr>
            <td class="direction">West</td>
            <td id="main">Roll</td>
            <td class="direction">East</td>
        </tr>
        <tr>
            <td></td>
            <td class="direction">South</td>
            <td></td>
        </tr>
    </table>
</body>
</html>
```

Related Item: target property

target

Value: Element object reference   Read-Only

Compatibility: WinIE-, MacIE-, NN6+, Moz+, Safari+, Opera+, Chrome+

The `target` property is a reference to the HTML element object that is the original target of the event. Because an event may trickle down and bubble up through the element containment hierarchy and be processed at any level along the way, having a property that points back to the element from which the event originated is comforting. As soon as you have a reference to that element, you can read or write any properties that belong to that element, or invoke any of its methods.

Example

As a simplified demonstration of the power of the `target` property, Listing 32-16 has but two event handlers defined for the `body` element, each invoking a single function. The idea is that the `onmousedown` and `onmouseup` events will bubble up from whatever their targets are, and the event handler functions will find out which element is the target and modify the color style of that element.

An extra flair is added to the script in that each function also checks the `className` property of the target element. If the `className` is `bold` — a class name shared by three `span` elements in the paragraph — the stylesheet rule for that class is modified so that all items share the same color. Your scripts can do even more in terms of filtering objects that arrive at the functions by performing special operations on certain objects or groups of objects.

Notice that the scripts don't have to know anything about the objects on the page to address each clicked one individually. That's because the `target` property provides all of the specificity needed for acting on the target element.

LISTING 32-16

Using the target Property

```
<!DOCTYPE html>
<html>
    <head>
        <meta http-equiv="content-type" content="text/html;charset=utf-8">
        <title>target Property</title>
        <style type="text/css">
            .bold {font-weight:bold;}
            .ital {font-style:italic;}
        </style>
        <script type="text/javascript">
            function highlight(evt)
            {
                var elem = (evt.target.nodeType == 3) ?
                        evt.target.parentNode : evt.target;
                if (elem.className == "bold")
                {
                    document.styleSheets[0].cssRules[0].style.color = "red";
                }
                else
                {
                    elem.style.color = "#FFCC00";
                }
```

continued

LISTING 32-16   *(continued)*

```
      }
      function restore(evt)
      {
          var elem = (evt.target.nodeType == 3) ?
                     evt.target.parentNode : evt.target;
              if (elem.className == "bold")
              {
                  document.styleSheets[0].cssRules[0].style.color = "black";
              }
              else
              {
                  elem.style.color = "black";
              }
      }

      // bind the event handlers
      function addEvent(elem, evtType, func)
      {
          if (elem.addEventListener)
          {
              elem.addEventListener(evtType, func, false);
          }
          else if (elem.attachEvent)
          {
              elem.attachEvent("on" + evtType, func);
          }
          else
          {
              elem["on" + evtType] = func;
          }
      }
      addEvent(window, "load", function()
      {
          addEvent(document.body, "mousedown",
                   function(evt) {highlight(evt);});
          addEvent(document.body, "mouseup",
                   function(evt) {restore(evt);});
      });
    </script>
</head>
<body>
    <h1>target Property</h1>
    <hr />
    <p>One event handler...</p>
    <ul>
        <li>Can</li>
        <li>Cover</li>
        <li>Many</li>
        <li>Objects</li>
    </ul>
```

```
    <p>Lorem ipsum dolor sit amet, consectetaur adipisicing elit,
        <span class="bold">sed do</span>
        eiusmod tempor incididunt
        <span class="ital">ut labore et</span>
        dolore magna aliqua. Ut enim adminim veniam,
        <span class="bold">quis nostrud exercitation</span>
        ullamco laboris nisi ut aliquip ex ea
        <span class="bold">commodo consequat</span>.
    </p>
    </body>
</html>
```

Related Item: relatedTarget property

timeStamp

Value: Integer   Read-Only

Compatibility: WinIE-, MacIE-, NN6+, Moz+, Safari+, Opera-, Chrome+

Each event receives a time stamp in milliseconds, based on the same date epoch as the Date object (1 January 1970). Just as with the Date object, accuracy is wholly dependent on the accuracy of the system clock of the client computer.

Although the precise time of an event may be of value in only some situations, the time between events can be useful for applications, such as timed exercises or action games. You can preserve the time of the most recent event in a global variable, and compare the time of the current time stamp against the stored value to determine the elapsed time between events.

Example

Listing 32-17 uses the timeStamp property to calculate the instantaneous typing speed when you type into a textarea. The calculations are pretty raw, and work only on intra-keystroke times without any of the averaging or smoothing that a more sophisticated typing tutor might perform. Calculated values are rounded to the nearest integer.

LISTING 32-17

Using the timeStamp Property

```
<!DOCTYPE html>
<html>
    <head>
        <meta http-equiv="content-type" content="text/html;charset=utf-8">
        <title>timeStamp Property</title>
        <script type="text/javascript">
            var stamp;
            function calcSpeed(evt)
            {
```

continued

LISTING 32-17   *(continued)*

```
        if (stamp)
        {
            var gross = evt.timeStamp - stamp;
            var wpm = Math.round(6000/gross);
            document.getElementById("wpm").firstChild.nodeValue = wpm + " wpm.";
        }
        stamp = evt.timeStamp;
    }

    // bind the event handlers
    function addEvent(elem, evtType, func)
    {
        if (elem.addEventListener)
        {
            elem.addEventListener(evtType, func, false);
        }
        else if (elem.attachEvent)
        {
            elem.attachEvent("on" + evtType, func);
        }
        else
        {
            elem["on" + evtType] = func;
        }
    }
    addEvent(window, "load", function()
    {
        addEvent(document.getElementById("scratchpad"), "keypress",
                function(evt) {calcSpeed(evt);});
    });
    </script>
</head>
<body>
    <h1>timeStamp Property</h1>
    <hr />
    <p>Start typing, and watch your instantaneous typing speed below:</p>
    <p><textarea id="scratchpad" cols="60" rows="10" wrap="hard"></textarea></p>
    <p>Typing Speed: <span id="wpm"> </span></p>
</body>
</html>
```

Related Item: Date object

type

Value: String   Read-Only

Compatibility: WinIE4+, MacIE4+, NN6+, Moz+, Safari+, Opera+, Chrome+

You can find out what kind of event fired to create the current event object by way of the `type` property. The value is a string version of the event name — just the name of the event without the "on" prefix that is normally associated with event listener names in NN6+/Moz/W3C. This property can be helpful when you designate one event handler function to process different kinds of events. For example, both the `onmousedown` and `onclick` event listeners for an object can invoke one function. Inside the function, a branch is written for whether the type comes in as `mousedown` or `click`, with different processing for each event type. That is not to endorse such event handler function sharing, but to be aware of this power should your script constructions find the property helpful.

This property and its values are fully compatible with the NN4 and IE4+ event models.

Caution
Keyboard events in earlier versions of Safari reported their types as `khtml_keydown`, `khtml_keypress`, **and** `khtml_keyup`. **This was probably to avoid committing to an unfinished W3C DOM Level 3 keyboard event specification. The current version of Safari reports the keyboard events without the** `khtml` **prefix.** ∎

Related Items: All event handlers (Chapter 26, "Generic HTML Element Objects")

view

Value: Window object reference   Read-Only

Compatibility: WinIE-, MacIE-, NN6+, Moz+, Safari+, Opera+, Chrome+

The closest that the W3C DOM Level 2 specification comes to acknowledging the browser window is an abstract object called an *abstract view* (AbstractView class). The object's only property is a reference to the document that it contains — the root document node that you've come to know and love. User events always occur within the confines of one of these views, and this is reflected in the `event` object's `view` property. This property holds a reference to the `window` object (which can be a frame) in which the event occurs. This reference allows an event object to be passed to scripts in other frames, and those scripts can then gain access to the `document` object of the target element's window.

Related Item: `window` object

Methods
`initEvent("eventType", bubblesFlag, cancelableFlag)`

`initKeyEvent("eventType", bubblesFlag, cancelableFlag, view, ctrlKeyFlag, altKeyFlag, shiftKeyFlag, metaKeyFlag, keyCode, charCode)`

`initMouseEvent("eventType", bubblesFlag, cancelableFlag, view, detailVal, screenX, screenY, clientX, clientY, ctrlKeyFlag, altKeyFlag, shiftKeyFlag, metaKeyFlag, buttonCode, relatedTargetNodeRef)`

`initMutationEvent("eventType", bubblesFlag, cancelableFlag, relatedNodeRef, prevValue, newValue, attrName, attrChangeCode)`

`initUIEvent("eventType", bubblesFlag, cancelableFlag, view, detailVal)` *eventObject*.**preventDefault()**

Returns: Nothing

Compatibility: WinIE-, MacIE-, NN6+, Moz+, Safari+, Opera+, Chrome+

The W3C DOM `event` object initialization methods provide a means of initializing a newly-created event with a complete set of property values associated with that particular event. The parameters to each of the initialization methods vary according to the type of event being initialized. However, all of the initialization methods share the first three parameters: `eventType`, `bubblesFlag`, and `cancelableFlag`. The `eventType` parameter is a string identifier for the event's type, such as `mousedown` or `keypress`. The `bubblesFlag` parameter is a Boolean value that specifies whether the event's default propagation behavior is to bubble (`true`) or not (`false`). The `cancelable-Flag` parameter is also a Boolean value, and its job is to specify if the event's default action may be prevented with a call to the `preventDefault()` method (`true`) or not (`false`).

A few of the methods also include `view` and `detailVal` parameters, which correspond to the window or frame in which the event occurred, and the integer code of detail data associated with the event, respectively. Additional parameters are specified for some of the methods, and are unique to the event being initialized.

You don't have to use the more detailed methods if you need a simple event. For example, if you want a simple `mouseup` event, you can initialize a generic event with `initEvent()`, and dispatch the event to the desired element, without having to fill in all of the coordinate, button, and other parameters of the `initMouseEvent()` method:

```
var evt = document.createEvent("MouseEvents");
evt.initEvent("mouseup", true, true);
document.getElementById("myButton").dispatchEvent(evt);
```

For more details about W3C DOM event types and the values expected for each of the more complex initialization methods, visit `http://www.w3.org/TR/DOM-Level-2-Events/events.html#Events-eventgroupings`.

Related Item: `document.createEvent()` method

`preventDefault()`

Returns: Nothing

Compatibility: WinIE-, MacIE-, NN6+, Moz+, Safari+, Opera+, Chrome+

While NN6+ continues to honor the original way of preventing default action for an event handler (that is, having the last statement of the event handler evaluate to `return false`), the W3C DOM event model provides a method that lets the cancellation of default action take place entirely within a function invoked by an event handler. For example, consider a text box that is supposed to allow only numbers to be typed in it. The `onkeypress` event handler can invoke a function that inspects each typed character. If the character is not a numeric character, it does not reach the text box for display. The following validation function may be invoked from the `onkeypress` event handler of just such a text box:

```
function checkIt(evt)
{
    var charCode = evt.charCode;
        if (charCode < 48 || charCode > 57)
        {
```

```
        alert("Please make sure entries are numbers only.");
        evt.preventDefault();
    }
}
```

This way, the errant character won't appear in the text box.

Invoking the `preventDefault()` method in NN6+/Moz and Gecko-, WebKit-, and Presto-based browsers, is the equivalent of assigning `true` to `event.returnValue` in IE5+.

Related Item: `cancelable` property

stopPropagation()

Returns: Nothing

Compatibility: WinIE-, MacIE-, NN6+, Moz+, Safari+, Opera+, Chrome+

Use the `stopPropagation()` method to stop events from trickling down or bubbling up further through the element containment hierarchy. A statement in the event listener function that invokes the following is all that is needed:

```
    evt.stopPropagation();
```

As an alternative, you can cancel bubbling directly in an element's event handler attribute, as in the following:

```
    onclick="doButtonClick(this); event.stopPropagation()"
```

If you are writing cross-browser scripts, you also have the option of using the `cancelBubble` property, which is compatible with IE4+.

Related Items: `bubbles`, `cancelBubble` properties

Part V

Appendixes

JavaScript and Browser Objects Quick Reference

JavaScript and Browser Objects Quick Reference

String · 15

constructor	anchor("*anchorName*")
length	big()
prototype	blink()
	bold()
	charAt(*index*)
	charCodeAt([*i*])
	concat(*string2*)
	fixed()
	fontcolor(#*rrggbb*)
	fontsize(*1 to 7*)
	fromCharCode(*n1*...)*
	indexOf("*str*" [,*i*])
	italics()
	lastIndexOf("*str*" [,*i*])
	link(*url*)
	localeCompare()
	match(*regexp*)
	replace(*regexp,str*)
	search(*regexp*)
	slice(i,j)
	small()
	split(*char*)
	strike()
	sub()
	substr(*start,length*)
	substring(*intA, intB*)
	sup()
	toLocaleLowerCase()
	toLocaleUpperCase()
	toLowerCase()
	toString()
	toUpperCase()
	valueOf()

*Method of the static String object.

Regular Expressions · 45

global	compile(*regexp*)
ignoreCase	exec("*string*")*
input[ESC]	test("*string*")
lastIndex	
multiline[EMSC]	
lastMatch[EMSC]	
lastParen[EMSC]	
leftContext	
prototype	
rightContext	
source	
$1...$9	

*Returns array with properties: index, input, [0],...[n].

Array · 18

constructor	concat(*array2*)
length	every(*func*[, *thisObj*])[M1.8S3O9.5C]
prototype	filter(*func*[, *thisObj*])[M1.8S3O9.5C]
	forEach(*func*[, *thisObj*])[M1.8S3O9.5C]
	indexOf(*func*[, *thisObj*])[M1.8S3O9.5C]
	join("*char*")
	lastIndexOf(*func*[, *thisObj*])[M1.8S3O9.5C]
	map(*func*[, *thisObj*])[M1.8S3O9.5C]
	pop()
	push()
	reduce()[MS4]
	reduceRight()[MS4]
	reverse()
	shift()
	slice(i,[j])
	some(*func*[, *thisObj*])[M1.8S3O9.5C]
	sort(*compareFunc*)
	splice(i,j[,*items*])
	toLocaleString()
	toString()
	unshift()

Function · 23

arguments	apply(*this*, *argsArray*)
caller	call(*this*[,*arg1*[,...*argN*]])
constructor	toString()
length	valueOf()
prototype	

Date · 17

constructor	getFullYear()
prototype	getYear()
	getMonth()
	getDate()
	getDay()
	getHours()
	getMinutes()
	getSeconds()
	getTime()
	getMilliseconds()
	getUTCFullYear()
	getUTCMonth()
	getUTCDate()
	getUTCDay()
	getUTCHours()
	getUTCMinutes()
	getUTCSeconds()
	getUTCMilliseconds()
	setYear(*val*)
	setFullYear(*val*)
	setMonth(*val*)
	setDate(*val*)
	setDay(*val*)
	setHours(*val*)
	setMinutes(*val*)
	setSeconds(*val*)
	setMilliseconds(*val*)
	setTime(*val*)
	setUTCFullYear(*val*)
	setUTCMonth(*val*)
	setUTCDate(*val*)
	setUTCDay(*val*)
	setUTCHours(*val*)
	setUTCMinutes(*val*)
	setUTCSeconds(*val*)
	setUTCMilliseconds(*val*)
	getTimezoneOffset()
	toDateString()
	toGMTString()
	toLocaleDateString()
	toLocaleString()
	toLocaleTimeString()
	toString()
	toTimeString()
	toUTCString()
	parse("*dateString*")*
	UTC(*dateValues*)*

*Method of the static Date object.

Math* · 16

E	abs(*val*)
LN2	acos(*val*)
LN10	asin(*val*)
LOG2E	atan(*val*)
LOG10E	atan2(*val1*, *val2*)
PI	ceil(*val*)
SQRT1_2	cos(*val*)
SQRT2	exp(*val*)
	floor(*val*)
	log(*val*)
	max(*val1*, *val2*)
	min(*val1*, *val2*)
	pow(*val1*, *power*)
	random()
	round(*val*)
	sin(*val*)
	sqrt(*val*)
	tan(*val*)

*All properties and methods are of the static Math object.

Error · 21

prototype	toString()
constructor	
description[E]	
fileName[M]	
lineNumber[M]	
message	
name	
number[E]	

Control Statements · 21

```
if (condition) {
    statementsIfTrue
}

if (condition) {
    statementsIfTrue
} else {
    statementsIfFalse
}

result = condition ? expr1 : expr2

for ([init expr]; [condition]; [update expr]) {
    statements
}

for (var in object) {
    statements
}

for each ([var] varName in objectRef) {
    statements
}M1.8.1

with (objRef) {
    statements
}

do {
    statements
} while (condition)

while (condition) {
    statements
}

return [value]

switch (expression) {
    case labelN :
        statements
        [break]
    ...
    [default :
        statements]
}

label :
continue [label]
break [label]

try {
    statements to test
}
catch (errorInfo) {
    statements if exception occurs in try block
}
[finally {
    statements to run, exception or not
}]

throw value
```

Number · 16

constructor	toExponential(n)
MAX_VALUE	toFixed(n)
MIN_VALUE	toLocaleString()
NaN	toString([*radix*])
NEGATIVE_INFINITY	toPrecision(n)
POSITIVE_INFINITY	valueOf()
prototype	

Boolean · 16

constructor	toString()
prototype	valueOf()

JavaScript and Browser Objects Quick Reference

Globals 24

Functions
atob()^M
btoa()^M
decodeURI("encodedURI")
decodeURIComponent("encComp")
encodeURI("URIString")
encodeURIComponent("compString")
escape("string" [,1])
eval("string")
isFinite(number)
isNaN(expression)
Number("string")
parseFloat("string")
parseInt("string" [,radix])
toString([radix])
unescape("string")
unwatch(prop)
watch(prop, handler)

Statements
// /*...*/
const
var

Appendix A
JavaScript Bible, 7th Edition
by Danny Goodman

How to Use This Quick Reference

This guide contains quick reference info for the core JavaScript language and browser object models starting with IE 5.5, Mozilla, and Safari.

Numbers in the upper right corners of object squares are chapter numbers in which the object is covered in detail.

Each term is supported by all baseline browsers unless noted with a superscript symbol indicating browser brand and version:

E—Internet Explorer M—Mozilla S—Safari
O—Opera C—Google Chrome

For example, M1.4 means the term is supported only by Mozilla 1.4 or later; E means the terms is supported only by Internet Explorer.

Operators 22

Comparison
==	Equals
===	Strictly equals
!=	Does not equal
!==	Strictly does not equal
>	Is greater than
>=	Is greater than or equal to
<	Is less than
<=	Is less than or equal to

Arithmetic/Connubial
+	Plus (and string concat.)
-	Minus
*	Multiply
/	Divide
%	Modulo
++	Increment
--	Decrement
+val	Positive
-val	Negation

Assignment
=	Equals
+=	Add by value
-=	Subtract by value
*=	Multiply by value
/=	Divide by value
%=	Modulo by value
<<=	Left shift by value
>>=	Right shift by value
>>>=	Zero fill by value
&=	Bitwise AND by value
|=	Bitwise OR by value
^=	Bitwise XOR by value
[]=	Destructuring assignment

Boolean
&&	AND
||	OR
!	NOT

Bitwise
&	Bitwise AND
		Bitwise OR
^	Bitwise XOR
~	Bitwise NOT
<<	Left shift
>>	Right shift
>>>	Zero fill right shift

Miscellaneous
,	Series delimiter
delete	Property destroyer
in	Item in object
instanceof	Instance of
new	Object creator
this	Object self-reference
? :	Conditional operator
typeof	Value type
void	Return no value

frameset 27

border^E (None)
borderColor^E
cols
frameBorder^E
frameSpacing^E
rows

iframe 27

align
allowTransparency^E
contentDocument^{E8MSOC}
contentWindow
frameBorder^E
frameSpacing^E
height
hspace^E
longDesc
marginHeight^{E6MSOC}
marginWidth^{E6MSOC}
name
noResize
scrolling
src
vspace^E
width

frame 27

allowTransparency^E
borderColor^E
contentDocument^{E8MSOC}
contentWindow
frameBorder
height^{ESC}
longDesc
marginHeight
marginWidth
name
noResize
scrolling
src
width^{ESC}

popup^E 27

document   hide()
isOpen   show()

location 28

hash   assign("url")
host   reload([unconditional])
hostname   replace("url")
href
pathname
port
protocol
search

history 28

current$^{M(signed)O}$ back()
length   forward()
next$^{M(signed)}$ go(int | "url")
previous$^{M(signed)}$

treeWalker^{MSOC} 29

currentNode   firstChild()
expandEntityReference   lastChild()
filter   nextNode()
root   nextSibling()
whatToShow   parentNode()
                         previousNode()
                         previousSibling()

window 27

appCore^M
clientInformation$^{ES1.2C}$
clipboardData^E
closed
Components[]^M
content^M
controllers[]^M
crypto^M
defaultStatus^{EMSO}
dialogArguments^{EMSC}
dialogHeight^E
dialogLeft^E
dialogTop^E
dialogWidth^E
directories^M
document
event/Event
external^{EM}
frameElement$^{EMS1.2OC}$
frames[]
fullScreen$^{M1.4}$
history
innerHeight^{MSOC}
innerWidth^{MSOC}
length
location
locationbar^M
menubar^M
name
navigator
netscape$^{S1.2C}$
offscreenBuffering$^{ES1.2C}$
opener
outerHeight^{MSOC}
outerWidth^{MSOC}
pageXOffset^{MSOC}
pageYOffset^{MSOC}
parent
personalbar^M
pkcs11^M
prompter^M
returnValue^{EMS}
screen
screenLeft$^{ES1.2OC}$
screenTop$^{ES1.2OC}$
screenX$^{MS1.2OC}$
screenY$^{MS1.2OC}$
scrollbars^M
scrollMaxX$^{M1.4}$
scrollMaxY$^{M1.4}$
scrollX^{MSOC}
scrollY^{MSOC}
self
sidebar^M
status^{EMSO}
statusbar^M
toolbar^M
top
window

addEventListener("evt", func,capt)^{MS}
alert("msg")
attachEvent("evt", func)^E
back()^M
blur()
clearInterval(ID)
clearTimeout(ID)
close()
confirm("msg")
createPopup()^E
detachEvent("evt", func)^E
dispatchEvent()^{MS}
dump("msg")$^{M1.4}$
execScript("exprList"[, lang])^E
find(["str"[, case[, up]])^{MSC}
fireEvent("evt"[, evtObj])^E
focus()
forward()^M
geckoActiveXObject(ID)$^{M1.4}$
getComputedStyle(node, "")^{MSOC}
getSelection()^{MSOC}
home()^{MO}
moveBy(Δx, Δy)^{EMSO}
moveTo(x, y)^{EMSO}
navigate("url")^{EO}
open("url","name"[, specs])
openDialog("url","name"[, specs])^M
print()
prompt("msg", "reply")
removeEventListener("evt", func,capt)^{MS}
resizeBy(Δx, Δy)^{EMS1}
resizeTo(width, height)^{EMS1}
scroll()
scrollBy(Δx, Δy)
scrollByLines(n)^M
scrollByPages(n)^M
scrollTo(x, y)
setInterval(func, msecs[, args])
setTimeout(func, msecs[, args])
showHelp("url")^E
showModalDialog("url"[, args][, features])$^{EMS2.01C}$
showModelessDialog("url"[, args][, features])^E
sizeToContent()^M
stop()^{MSOC}

onabort^M
onafterprint^E
onbeforeprint^E
onbeforeunload^{EMSC}
onblur
onclick
onclose
onerror^{EM}
onfocus
onhelp^E
onkeydown
onkeypress
onkeyup
onload
onmousedown
onmousemove
onmouseout
onmouseover
onmouseup
onmove
onreset
onresize
onscroll$^{EMS1.3OC}$
onselect
onsubmit
onunload

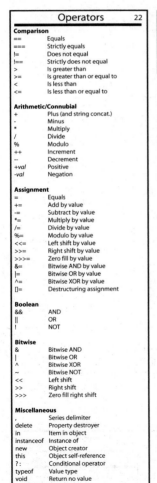

JavaScript and Browser Objects Quick Reference

document 29

activeElement	clear()	onselectionchange[E]
alinkColor	close()	onstop[E]
anchors[]	createAttribute("name")[E6MSOC]	
applets[]	createCDATASection("data")[MSOC]	
baseURI[M]	createComment("text")[E6MSOC]	
bgColor	createDocumentFragment()[E6MSOC]	
body	createElement("tagname")	
charset[ESOC]	createElementNS("uri","tagname")	
characterSet[MSOC]	createEvent("evtType")[MSOC]	
compatMode	createEventObject([evtObj])[E]	
contentType[M]	createNSResolver(nodeResolver)[MSOC]	
cookie	createRange()[MSOC]	
defaultCharset[ESC]	createStyleSheet(["url"[, index]])[E]	
defaultView[MSOC]	createTextNode("text")	
designMode	createTreeWalker(root, what, filterfunc, exp)[M1.4SOC]	
doctype	elementFromPoint(x, y)	
documentElement	evaluate("expr", node, resolver, type, result)[MSOC]	
documentURI[M1.7SOC]	execCommand("cmd"[, UI][, param])[EM1.3S1.3OC]	
domain	getElementById("ID")	
embeds[]	getElementsByName("name")	
expando[E]	hasFocus()[EMSC]	
fgColor	importNode(node, deep)[MSOC]	
fileCreatedDate[E]	open(["mimetype"][, "replace"])	
fileModifiedDate[E]	queryCommandEnabled("commandName")[EM1.3SOC]	
fileSize[E]	queryCommandIndterm("commandName")[EM1.3SC]	
forms[]	queryCommandState("commandName")[EM1.3SOC]	
frames[]	queryCommandSupported("commandName")[ESOC]	
height[MSC]	queryCommandText("commandName")[E]	
images[]	queryCommandValue("commandName")[EM1.3SOC]	
implementation[E6MSOC]	recalc([all])[E]	
inputEncoding[M1.8SOC]	write("string")	
lastModified	writeln("string")	
linkColor		
links[]		
location		
media[E]		
mimeType[E]		
nameProp[E6]		
namespaces[][E]		
parentWindow[EO]		
plugins[]		
protocol[E]		
referrer		
scripts[][ESOC]		
security[E]		
selection[EO]		
strictErrorChecking[M1.8]		
styleSheets[]		
title		
URL		
URLUnencoded		
vlinkColor		
width[MSC]		
xmlEncoding[M1.8SC]		
xmlStandalone[M1.8SC]		
xmlVersion[M1.8SC]		

All HTML Element Objects 26

accessKey	addBehavior("url")[E]	onactivate[E]
all[][EO]	addEventListener("evt", func,capt)[MSOC]	onafterupdate[E]
attributes[]	appendChild(node)	onbeforecopy[ES1.3]
baseURI[MSOC]	applyElement(elem[, type])[E]	onbeforecut[ES1.3]
behaviorUrns[][E]	attachEvent("evt", func)[EO]	onbeforedeactivate[E]
canHaveChildren[E]	blur()	onbeforeeditfocus[E]
canHaveHTML[E]	click()	onbeforepaste[ES1.3C]
childNodes[]	cloneNode(deep)	onbeforeupdate[E]
children[EMS1.2OC]	compareDocumentPosition(node)[M1.4SOC]	onblur
cite[E6MSOC]	componentFromPoint(x, y)[E]	oncellchange[E]
className	contains(elem)[ESOC]	onclick
clientHeight	createControlRange()[E]	oncontextmenu[EMSC]
clientLeft	detachEvent("evt", func)[EO]	oncontrolselect[E]
clientTop	dispatchEvent(evtObj)[MSOC]	oncopy[EMS1.3]
clientWidth	doScroll("action")[E]	oncut[EMS1.3]
contentEditable[EMS1.2OC]	dragDrop()[E]	ondataavailable[E]
currentStyle[E]	fireEvent("evtType"[, evtObj])[E]	ondatasetchanged[E]
dateTime[E6MSOC]	focus()	ondatasetcomplete[E]
dataFld[E]	getAdjacentText("where")[E]	ondblclick
dataFormatAs[E]	getAttribute("name"[, case])	ondeactivate[E]
dataSrc[E]	getAttributeNode("name")[E6MSOC]	ondrag[EMS1.3C]
dir	getAttributeNodeNS("uri","name")[M]	ondragend[EMS1.3C]
disabled	getAttributeNS("uri","name")[MSOC]	ondragenter[EMS1.3C]
document[ES1.2O]	getBoundingClientRect()[E]	ondragleave[EMS1.3C]
filters[][E]	getClientRects()[E]	ondragover[EMS1.3C]
firstChild	getElementsByTagName("tagname")	ondragstart[EMS1.3C]
height	getElementsByTagNameNS("uri","name")[MSOC]	ondrop[EMS1.3C]
hideFocus[E]	getExpression("attrName")[E]	onerrorupdate[E]
id	getFeature("feature","version")[M1.7.2O]	onfilterchange[E]
innerHTML	getUserData("key")[M1.7.2SC]	onfocus
innerText[ESOC]	hasAttribute("attrName")	onfocusin[E]
isContentEditable[ES1.2OC]	hasAttributeNS("uri","name")[MSOC]	onfocusout[E]
isDisabled[E]	hasAttributes()	onhelp[E]
isMultiLine[E]	hasChildNodes()	onkeydown
isTextEdit[E]	insertAdjacentElement("where", obj)[ESOC]	onkeypress
lang	insertAdjacentHTML("where","HTML")[ESOC]	onkeyup
language[E]	insertAdjacentText("where", "text")[ESOC]	onlayoutcomplete[E]
lastChild	insertBefore(newNode, refNode)	onlosecapture[E]
length	isDefaultNamespace("uri")[M1.7.2SOC]	onmousedown
localName[E8MSOC]	isEqualNode(node)[M1.7.2SOC]	onmouseenter[E]
namespaceURI[E8MSOC]	isSameNode(node)[M1.7.2SOC]	onmouseleave[E]
nextSibling	isSupported("feature","version")[MSOC]	onmousemove
nodeName	item(index)	onmouseout
nodeType	lookupNamespaceURI("prefix")[M1.7.2SOC]	onmouseover
nodeValue	lookupPrefix("uri")[M1.7.2SOC]	onmouseup
offsetHeight	mergeAttributes(srcObj)[E]	onmousewheel
offsetLeft	normalize()	onmove[E]
offsetParent	releaseCapture()[E]	onmoveend[E]
offsetTop	removeAttribute("attrName"[, case])	onmovestart[E]
offsetWidth	removeAttributeNode(attrNode)[E6MSOC]	onpaste[EMS1.3C]
outerHTML[ES1.3OC]	removeAttributeNS("uri","name")[MSOC]	onpropertychange[E]
outerText[ES1.3OC]	removeBehavior(ID)[E]	onreadystatechange[EMS1.2OC]
ownerDocument	removeChild(node)	onresize
parentElement[ES1.2OC]	removeEventListener("evt", func,capt)[MSOC]	onresizeend[E]
parentNode	removeExpression("propName")[E]	onresizestart[E]
parentTextEdit[E8MSOC]	removeNode(childrenFlag)[E]	onrowenter[E]
prefix[E8MSOC]	replaceAdjacentText("where","text")[E]	onrowexit[E]
previousSibling	replaceChild(newNode, oldNode)	onrowsdelete[E]
readyState[E]	replaceNode(newNode)[E]	onrowsinserted[E]
recordNumber[E]	scrollIntoView(topFlag)[EMS2.02OC]	onscroll
runtimeStyle[E]	setActive()[E]	onselectstart[ES1.3C]
scopeName[E]	setAttribute("name","value"[, case])	
scrollHeight	setAttributeNode(attrNode)[E6MSOC]	
scrollLeft	setAttributeNodeNS("uri","name")[MSOC]	
scrollTop	setAttributeNS("uri","name","value")[MSOC]	
scrollWidth	setCapture(containerFlag)[E]	
sourceIndex[ESOC]	setExpression("propName","expr")[E]	
style	setUserData("key", data, handler)[M1.7.2SC]	
tabIndex	swapNode(nodeRef)[E]	
tagName	tags("tagName")[ESOC]	
tagUrn[E]	textContent[M1.7SOC]	toString()
title	urns("behaviorURN")[E]	
uniqueID[E]		
unselectable[EO]		
width		

link 40

charset	(None)	onload[E]
disabled		
href		
hreflang[E6MSOC]		
media		
rel		
rev		
sheet[E]		
styleSheet[E]		
target		
type		

html 40

version[E6MSOC]

head 40

profile

meta 40

charset[E]
content
httpEquiv
name
url[E]

script 40

defer[E]
event[E]
htmlFor[E]
src
text
type

title 40

text

base 40

href
target

JavaScript and Browser Objects Quick Reference

body 29
alink, background, bgColor, bgProperties[E], bottomMargin[E], leftMargin[E], link, noWrap[E], rightMargin[E], scroll[E], scrollLeft, scrollTop, text, topMargin[E], vLink
createControlRange()[E], createTextRange()[E], doScroll("scrollAction")[E]
onafterprint[E], onbeforeprint[E], onscroll

h1...h6 33
align

br 33
clear

blockquote, q 33
cite[E6MSOC]

font 33
color, face, size

marquee 33
behavior, bgColor, direction, height, hspace, loop[EMO], scrollAmount, scrollDelay, trueSpeed[EM], vspace, width
start(), stop()
onbounce[EM], onfinish[EM], onstart[EM]

ol 41
start, type

ul 41
type

li 41
type, value

hr 33
align, color, noShade, size, width

dl, dt, dd 41
compact

Range 33
collapsed[MSOC], commonAncestorContainer[MSOC], endContainer[MSOC], endOffset[MSOC], startContainer[MSOC], startOffset[MSOC]
cloneContents()[MSOC], cloneRange()[MSOC], collapse([start])[MSOC], compareBoundaryPoints(type,src)[MSOC], compareNode(node)[MSC], comparePoint(node, offset)[MSOC], createContextualFragment("text")[MSOC], deleteContents()[MSOC], detach()[MSOC], extractContents()[MSOC], insertNode(node)[MSOC], intersectsNode(node)[MSOC], isPointInRange(node, offoffsetset)[MSC], selectNode(node)[MSOC], selectNodeContents(node)[MSOC], setEnd(node,offset)[MSOC], setEndAfter(node)[MSOC], setEndBefore(node)[MSOC], setStart(node,offset)[MSOC], setStartAfter(node)[MSOC], setStartBefore(node)[MSOC], surroundContents(node)[MSOC], toString()[MSOC]

TextRange[E] 33
boundingHeight, boundingLeft, boundingTop, boundingWidth, htmlText, text
collapse([start]), compareEndPoints("type",range), duplicate(), execCommand("cmd"[,UI[,val]]), expand("unit"), findText("str"[,scope,flags]), getBookmark(), inRange(range), isEqual(range), move("unit"[,count]), moveEnd("unit"[,count]), moveStart("unit"[,count]), moveToBookmark("bookmark"), moveToElementText(elem), moveToPoint(x,y), parentElement(), pasteHTML("HTMLText"), queryCommandEnabled("cmd"), queryCommandIndeterm("cmd"), queryCommandState("cmd"), queryCommandSupported("cmd"), queryCommandText("cmd"), queryCommandValue("cmd"), select(), setEndPoint("type",range)

canvas[M1.8S1.3OC] 31
fillStyle, globalAlpha, globalCompositeOperation, lineCap, lineJoin, lineWidth, miterLimit, shadowBlur, shadowColor, shadowOffsetX, shadowOffsetY, strokeStyle, target
arc(x, y, radius, start, end, clockwise), arcTo(x1, y1, x2, y2, radius), bezierCurveTo(cp1x, cp1y, cp2x, cp2y, x, y), beginPath(), clearRect(x, y, width, height), clip(), closePath(), createLinearGradient(x1, y1, x2, y2), createPattern(img, repetition), createRadialGradient(x1, y1, radius1, x2, y2, radius2), drawImage(img, x, y), drawImage(img, x, y, width, height), fill(), fillRect(x, y, width, height), getContext(contextID), lineTo(x, y), moveTo(x, y), quadraticCurveTo(cpx, cpy, x, y), rect(x, y, width, height), restore(), rotate(angle), save(), scale(x, y), stroke(), strokeRect(x, y, width, height), translate(x, y)

img 31
align, alt, border, complete, dynsrc[E], fileCreatedDate[E], fileModifiedDate[E], fileSize[E], fileUpdatedDate[E], height, href, hspace, isMap, longDesc[E6MSOC], loop[E], lowsrc[E], mimeType[E6], name, nameProp[E], naturalHeight[MSC], naturalWidth[MSC], protocol[E], src, start[E], useMap, vspace, width, x[MSC], y[MSC]
(None)
onabort[E], onerror, onload

selection 33
anchorNode[MSOC], anchorOffset[MSOC], focusNode[MSOC], focusOffset[MSOC], isCollapsed[MSOC], rangeCount[MSOC], type[E], typeDetail[E]
addRange(range)[MSOC], clear()[E], collapse(node, offset)[MSOC], collapseToEnd()[MSOC], collapseToStart()[MSOC], containsNode(node, entireFlag)[MSOC], createRange()[EO], deleteFromDocument()[MSOC], empty()[EO], extend(node, offset)[MSOC], getRangeAt(rangeIndex)[MSOC], removeAllRanges()[MSOC], removeRange(range)[MSOC], selectAllChildren(elementRef)[MSOC], toString()[MSOC]

TextNode, Text 33
data
appendData("text"), deleteData(offset, count), insertData(offset, "text"), replaceData(offset, count, "text"), splitText(offset), substringData(offset, count)

TextRectangle[ES4O9.5C3] 33
bottom, left, right, top

map 31
areas[], name

area 31
alt, coords, hash, host, hostname, href, noHref, pathname, port, protocol, search, shape, target

a 30
charset[E6MSOC], coords[E6MSOC], hash, host, hostname, href, hreflang[E6MSOC], methods[E], mimeType[E], name, nameProp[E], pathname, port, protocol, rel, rev, search, shape[E6MSOC], target, type[E6MSOC], urn[E]

JavaScript and Browser Objects Quick Reference

form — 34

acceptCharset	reset()	onreset
action	submit()	onsubmit
autocomplete^E		
elements[]		
encoding^{E6MSOC}		
enctype^{E6MSOC}		
length		
method		
name		
target		

input — 35/36/37

checked$^{(†)}$	blur()$^{(†††)}$	onafterupdate$^{E(†††)}$
complete$^{E(image)}$	click()$^{(††)}$	onbeforeupdate$^{E(†††)}$
defaultChecked$^{(†)}$	focus()$^{(†††)}$	onblur$^{(†††)}$
defaultValue$^{(††††)}$	select()$^{(††††)}$	onchange$^{(††††)}$
form		onclick$^{(††)}$
maxLength$^{(††††)}$		onerrorupdate$^{E(†††)}$
name		onfocus$^{(†††)}$
readOnly$^{(††††)}$		onmousedown$^{(button)}$
size$^{(††††)}$	† checkbox, radio	onmouseup$^{(button)}$
src$^{(image)}$	†† button, checkbox, radio	onselect$^{(†††)}$
type	††† text, password, hidden	
value	†††† text, password, hidden, file	

textarea — 36

cols	createTextRange()^E	onafterupdate^E
form	select()	onbeforeupdate^E
name		onchange
readOnly		onerrorupdate^E
rows		
type		
value		
wrap^E		

select — 37

form	add(newOption[, index])^E	onchange
length	add(newOption, optionRef)^{MS}	
multiple	item(index)^{EM5O9}	
name	namedItem("optionID")^{EM5O9}	
options[]	options[i].add(elementRef[, index])^{ESOC}	
options[i].defaultSelected	options[i].remove()	
options[i].index	remove(index)	
options[i].selected		
options[i].text		
options[i].value		
selectedIndex		
size		
type		
value		

option — 37

defaultSelected
form
label^{E6MSOC}
selected
text
value

fieldset, legend — 33/34

align
form

label — 33/34

accessKey
form
htmlFor

optgroup^{E6MSOC} — 37

form
label

table — 41

align	createCaption()
background^E	createTFoot()
bgColor	createTHead()
border	deleteCaption()
borderColor^E	deleteRow(i)
borderColorDark^E	deleteTFoot()
borderColorLight^E	deleteTHead()
caption	firstPage()^E
cellPadding	insertRow(i)
cells^E	lastPage()^E
cellSpacing	moveRow(srcIndex, destIndex)^E
cols^E	nextPage()^E
datePageSize^E	previousPage()^E
frame	refresh()^E
height	
rows	
rules	
summary^{E6MSOC}	
tBodies	
tFoot	
tHead	
width	

tbody, tfoot, thead — 41

align	deleteRow(i)
bgColor	insertRow(i)
ch^{E6MSOC}	moveRow(srcIndex, destIndex)^E
chOff^{E6MSOC}	
rows	
vAlign	

tr — 41

align	deleteCell(i)
bgColor	insertCell(i)
borderColor^E	
borderColorDark^E	
borderColorLight^E	
cells	
ch^{E6MSOC}	
chOff^{E6MSOC}	
height^{EO}	
rowIndex	
sectionRowIndex	
vAlign	

col, colgroup — 41

align
ch^{E6MSOC}
chOff^{E6MSOC}
span
vAlign
width

td, th — 41

abbr^{E6MSOC}
align
axis^{E6MSOC}
background
bgColor
borderColor^E
borderColorDark^E
borderColorLight^E
cellIndex
ch^{E6MSOC}
chOff^{E6MSOC}
colSpan
headers^{E6MSOC}
height
noWrap
rowSpan
vAlign
width

caption — 41

align
vAlign

navigator — 42

appCodeName	javaEnabled()^{MSOC}
appMinorVersion^{EO}	preference(name[, val])$^{M(signed)}$
appName	
appVersion	
browserLanguage^{EO}	
cookieEnabled	
cpuClass^E	
language^{MSOC}	
mimeTypes^{MSOC}	
onLine	
oscpu^M	
platform	
plugins^{MSOC}	
product^{MSC}	
productSub^{MSC}	
securityPolicy^M	
systemLanguage^{EO}	
userAgent	
userLanguage^{EO}	
userProfile^E	
vendor^{MSC}	
vendorSub^{MSC}	

screen — 42

availHeight
availLeft^{MSC}
availTop^{MSC}
availWidth
bufferDepth^E
colorDepth
fontSmoothingEnabled^E
height
pixelDepth
updateInterval^E
width

JavaScript and Browser Objects Quick Reference

event   32

altKey	initEvent()[MS]
altLeft[E]	initKeyEvent()[MS]
behaviorCookie[E6]	initMouseEvent()[MS]
behaviorPart[E6]	initMutationEvent()[MS]
bookmarks[E6]	initUIEvent()[MS]
boundElements[E6]	preventDefault()[MS]
bubbles[MS]	stopPropagation()[MS]
button	
cancelable[MSOC]	
cancelBubble	
charCode[MSC]	
clientX	
clientY	
contentOverflow[E5.5]	
ctrlKey	
ctrlLeft[E]	
currentTarget[MSOC]	
dataFld[E6]	
dataTransfer[E]	
detail[MS2O8C]	
eventPhase[MSOC]	
fromElement[ESOC]	
isChar[M]	
isTrusted[M1.7.5]	
keyCode[MSC]	
layerX[MSC]	
layerY[MSC]	
metaKey	
nextPage[E]	
offsetX[ESOC]	
offsetY[ESOC]	
originalTarget[M]	
pageX[MSOC]	
pageY[MSOC]	
propertyName[E]	
qualifier[E6]	
reason[E6]	
recordset[E6]	
relatedTarget[MSOC]	
repeat[E]	
returnValue[ES1.2OC]	
saveType[E]	
screenX	
screenY	
shiftKey	
shiftLeft[E]	
srcElement[ES1.2OC]	
srcFilter[E]	
srcUrn[E]	
target[MSOC]	
timeStamp[MSC]	
toElement[ESOC]	
type	
view[MSOC]	
wheelData[E]	
x[ESOC]	
y[ESOC]	

XMLHttpRequest[EMS1.2OC]   39

readyState	abort()	onreadystatechange
responseText	getAllResponseHeaders()	
responseXML	getResponseHeader("headerName")	
status	open("method","url"[, asyncFlag])	
statusText	send(data)	
	setRequestHeader("name","value")	

xml[E]   39

src
XMLDocument

applet   44

align	(Applet methods)
alt[E6MSOC]	
altHTML[E]	
archive[E6MSOC]	
code	
codeBase	
height	
hspace	
name	
object[E]	
vspace	
width	
(Applet variables)	

embed   44

align[MSOC]	(Object methods)	onload()
height		onscroll()
hidden[E]		
name		
pluginspage[E]		
src		
units[E]		
width		
(Object variables)		

mimeType[MSOC]   42

description
enabledPlugin
type
suffixes

plugin[MSOC]   42

name	refresh()
filename	
description	
length	

object (element)   44

align[ESOC]	(Object methods)	oncellchange
alt[E6]		ondataavailable
altHTML[E]		ondatasetchanged
archive[E6MSOC]		ondatasetcomplete
baseHref[E]		onload
baseURI[MSOC]		onrowenter
border[E6MSOC]		onrowexit
classid[E]		onrowsdelete
code		onrowsinserted
codeBase		onscroll
codeType		
contentDocument[MSOC]		
data		
declare[E6MSOC]		
form		
height		
hspace		
name		
object[E]		
standby[E6MSOC]		
type		
useMap[E6MSOC]		
vspace		
width		
(Object variables)		

object (object)   23

constructor	hasOwnProperty("propName")
prototype	isPrototypeOf(objRef)
	propertyIsEnumerable("propName")
	toSource()[M]
	toString()
	unwatch("propName")[M]
	valueOf()
	watch("propName")[M]

Notes

JavaScript and Browser Objects Quick Reference

style, currentStyle, runtimeStyle 38

Text & Fonts	Borders & Edges	Inline Display & Layout
color	border	clear
font	borderBottom	clip
fontFamily	borderLeft	clipBottom[E]
fontSize	borderRight	clipLeft[E]
fontSizeAdjust[M]	borderTop	clipRight[E]
fontStretch[M]	borderBottomColor	clipTop[E]
fontStyle	borderLeftColor	content[MS1.3OC]
fontVariant[EMS1.3OC]	borderRightColor	counterIncrement[M1.8SOC]
fontWeight	borderTopColor	counterReset[M1.8SO9C]
letterSpacing	borderBottomStyle	cssFloat[MSOC]
lineBreak[E]	borderLeftStyle	cursor[EMS1.3OC]
lineHeight	borderRightStyle	direction
quotes[MO]	borderTopStyle	display
rubyAlign[E]	borderBottomWidth	filter[E]
rubyOverhang[E]	borderLeftWidth	layoutGrid[E]
rubyPosition[E]	borderRightWidth	layoutGridChar[E]
textAlign	borderTopWidth	layoutGridLine[E]
textAlignLast[E]	borderColor	layoutGridMode[E]
textAutospace[E]	borderStyle	layoutGridType[E]
textDecoration	borderWidth	markerOffset[M]
textDecorationBlink[E]	margin	marks[M]
textDecorationLineThrough[E]	marginBottom	maxHeight[E7MSOC]
textDecorationNone[E]	marginLeft	maxWidth[MSOC]
textDecorationOverline[E]	marginRight	minHeight[MSOC]
textDecorationUnderline[E]	marginTop	minWidth[MSOX]
textIndent	mozBorderRadius[M]	mozOpacity[M]
textJustify[E]	mozBorderRadiusBottomLeft[M]	opacity[M1.7.2S1.2OC]
textJustifyTrim[E]	mozBorderRadiusBottomRight[M]	overflow
textKashidaSpace[E]	mozBorderRadiusTopLeft[M]	overflowX[EM1.8S1.2OC]
textOverflow[E6S1.3C]	mozBorderRadiusTopRight[M]	overflowY[EM1.8S1.2OC]
textShadow[MS1.2OC]	outline[M1.8.1S1.2OC]	styleFloat[EO]
textTransform	outlineColor[M1.8.1S1.2OC]	verticalAlign[EMS1.2OC]
textUnderlinePosition[E]	outlineOffset[M1.8.1S1.2OC]	visibility
unicodeBidi	outlineStyle[M1.8.1S1.2OC]	width
whiteSpace	outlineWidth[M1.8.1S1.2OC]	zoom[E]
wordBreak[ESC]	padding	
wordSpacing[E6MSOC]	paddingBottom	**Page and Printing**
wordWrap[ES1.3C]	paddingLeft	orphans[MO]
writingMode[E]	paddingRight	page[M]
	paddingTop	pageBreakAfter[EMS1.3OC]
Positioning		pageBreakBefore[EMS1.3OC]
bottom	**Tables**	pageBreakInside[E8MSOC]
height	borderCollapse[EMS1.3OC]	size[MO]
left	borderSpacing	widows[MO]
pixelBottom[ESOC]	captionSide[MSOC]	
pixelHeight[ESOC]	emptyCells[MS1.3OC]	**Miscellaneous**
pixelLeft[ESOC]	tableLayout	accelerator[E]
pixelRight[ESOC]		behavior[E]
pixelTop[ESOC]	**Lists**	cssText[EMS1.3OC]
pixelWidth[ESOC]	listStyle	imeMode[EM]
posBottom[ESOC]	listStyleImage	
posHeight[ESOC]	listStylePosition	**Scrollbars**
posLeft[ESOC]	listStyleType	scrollbar3dLightColor[EO]
posRight[ESOC]		scrollbarArrowColor[EO]
posTop[ESOC]	**Background**	scrollbarBaseColor[EO]
posWidth[ESOC]	background	scrollbarDarkShadowColor[EO]
position	backgroundAttachment[EMS1.2OC]	scrollbarFaceColor[EO]
right	backgroundColor	scrollbarHighlightColor[EO]
top	backgroundImage	scrollbarShadowColor[EO]
width	gackgroundPosition	scrollbarTrackColor[EO]
zIndex	backgroundPositionX[ES1.3OC]	
	backgroundPositionY[ES1.3OC]	
	backgroundRepeat	

styleSheet 38

cssRules[MSO9C]	addImport("url"[, index])[E]
cssText[E]	addRule("selector","spec"[, index])[ESC]
disabled	deleteRule(index)[MSOC]
href[EMSO9C]	insertRule("rule", index)[MSOC]
id[E]	removeRule(index)[ESC]
imports[E]	
media	
ownerNode[MSOC]	
ownerRule[MSOC]	
owningElement[E]	
pages[E]	
parentStyleSheet[EMS]	
readOnly[E]	
rules[ESC]	
title	
type	

style (element) 38

media
type

cssRule, rule 38

cssText[MSOC]
parentStyleSheet[MSOC]
readOnly[E]
selectorText
style
type[MSOC]

JavaScript Bible, 7th Edition. ©2010 Danny Goodman (dannyg.com). All Rights Reserved.

What's on the CD-ROM

The accompanying Windows–Macintosh CD-ROM contains additional chapters that include many more JavaScript examples, an electronic version of the Quick Reference shown in Appendix A for printing, a complete, searchable version of the entire book, and the Adobe Reader.

System Requirements

To derive the most benefit from the example listings, you should have a Mozilla-based browser (for example, Firefox 3.6+, -, or Camino 2+), Internet Explorer 8+, a WebKit-based browser (for example, Safari 4+, or Google Chrome 5+) or a Presto-based browser (for example, Opera 10+) installed on your computer. Although many scripts run in these and other browsers, several scripts demonstrate features that are available on only a limited range of browsers. To write scripts, you can use a simple text editor, word processor, or dedicated HTML editor.

To use the Adobe Reader (version 7.0), you need the following:

- For Windows XP Pro/Home, or Windows XP Table PC Edition, you should be using a Pentium computer with 128 MB of RAM and 90 MB of hard disk space.

- Macintosh users require a PowerPC G3, G4, or G5 processor, OS X v10.2.8 or later, at least 128 MB of RAM, and 110 MB of disk space.

Disc Contents

When you view the contents of the CD-ROM, you will see files tailored for your operating system. The contents include the following items.

JavaScript listings for text editors

Starting with Part III of the book, almost all example listings are on the CD-ROM in the form of complete HTML files, which you can load into a browser to see the JavaScript item in operation. A directory called Listings contains the example files, with nested folders named for each chapter. The name of each HTML file is keyed to the listing number in the book. For example, the file for Listing 26-1 is named jsb26-01.html. Note that no listing files are provided for the tutorial chapters of Part II, because you are encouraged to enter HTML and scripting code manually.

For your convenience, the _index.html file in the Listings folder provides a front-end table of contents to the HTML files for the book's program listings. Open that file from your browser whenever you want to access the program listing files. If you intend to access that index page frequently, you can bookmark it in your browser(s). Using the index file to access the listing files can be very important in some cases, because several individual files must be opened within their associated framesets to work properly. Accessing the files through the _index.html file ensures that you open the frameset. The _index.html file also shows browser compatibility ratings for all the listings. This saves you time from opening listings that are not intended to run on your browser. To examine and modify the HTML source files, open them from your favorite text editor program (for Windows editors, be sure to specify the .html file extension in the Open File dialog box).

You can open all example files directly from the CD-ROM, but if you copy them to your hard drive, access is faster and you will be able to experiment with modifying the files more readily. Copy the folder named Listings from the CD-ROM to any location on your hard drive.

Printable version of the JavaScript and Browser Object Quick Reference from Appendix A

If you like the quick reference in Appendix A, you can print it out with the help of the Adobe Reader, included with the CD-ROM.

Adobe Reader

The Adobe Reader is a helpful program that enables you to view the Quick Reference from Appendix A and the searchable version of this book, both of which are in PDF format on the CD-ROM. To install and run Adobe Reader, follow these steps:

For Windows

1. Navigate to the Adobe_Reader folder on the CD-ROM.
2. In the Adobe_Reader folder, double-click the lone executable file and follow the instructions presented on-screen for installing Adobe Acrobat Reader.

For Macintosh

1. Open the Adobe_Reader folder on the CD-ROM.
2. In the Adobe_Reader folder, double-click the Adobe Reader disk image icon; this will mount the disk image on your computer. Then open the mounted image and copy the Adobe Reader folder to the Applications directory of your computer.

PDF version of book with topical references

In many places throughout the reference chapters of Parts III and IV, you see notations directing you to the CD-ROM for a particular topic being discussed. All these topics are located in the chapters as they appear in complete Adobe Acrobat form on the CD-ROM. A single PDF file is located on the CD-ROM, and it serves as an electronic version of the entire book, complete with full topics that are listed as CD-ROM references in the printed book. For the fastest access to these topics, copy the entire PDF file for the book to your hard disk.

Like any PDF document, the PDF version of the book is searchable. Recent versions of Adobe Reader should automatically load the index file (with the `.pdx` extension) to supply indexed search capabilities (which is much faster than Acrobat's Find command).

To begin an actual search, click the Search icon (binoculars in front of a sheet of paper). Enter the text for which you're searching. To access the index and search facilities in future sessions, the CD-ROM must be in your CD-ROM drive — unless, of course, you've copied both the `.pdx` and `.pdf` files to your hard drive.

Troubleshooting

If you have difficulty installing or using the CD-ROM programs, try the following solutions:

- **Turn off any anti-virus software that you may have running.** Installers sometimes mimic virus activity and can make your computer incorrectly believe that a virus is infecting it. (Be sure to turn the anti-virus software back on later.)

- **Close all running programs.** The more programs you're running, the less memory is available to other programs. Installers also typically update files and programs; if you keep other programs running, installation may not work properly.

- **Reference the ReadMe file.** Refer to the ReadMe file located at the root of the CD-ROM for the latest product information at the time of publication.

Customer Care

If you have trouble with the CD-ROM, please call the Customer Support phone number at (800) 762-2974. Outside the United States, call 1(317) 572-3994. You can also contact Wiley Product Technical Support at `http://support.wiley.com`. John Wiley & Sons will provide technical support only for installation and other general quality control items. For technical support on the applications themselves, consult the program's vendor or author.

To place additional orders or to request information about other Wiley products, please call (877) 762-2974.

Index

SYMBOLS

: (colon)
date/time, 288
document.all, 91
identifiers, 85
name, 147

, (comma)
for, 431
cookies, 923
operator, 431
parameters, 91
regular expressions, BC482

. (dot, period)
document.all, 91
dot syntax form, 86, 504
identifiers, 85
name, 147
object operator, 425
regular expressions
metacharacter, BC468

?: (question mark/colon)
if...else, 431
operator, 431

; (semicolon)
cookies, 923
onevent, BC626
statements, 99

:// (colon/slash-double),
encodeURI(), 482

& (ampersand)
bitwise AND operator, 425
operator precedence, 434
XHTML, 43

&& (ampersand - double)
Boolean AND operator, 175, 421
operator precedence, 434

&= (ampersand/equals sign)
assignment operator, 419
operator precedence, 435

* (asterisk)

multiplication connubial
operator, 416
operator precedence, 434
regular expressions
metacharacter, BC469
XML, 368

*= (asterisk/equals sign)
assignment operator, 419
operator precedence, 435

*/ (asterisk/slash), 66
statements, 492–493

@ (at symbol)
e-mail, 77, 189
XML elements, 366

\ (backslash), regular expressions, 245

\\ (backslash - double), inline character, 227

\' (backslash/apostrophe), apostrophe inline character, 227

\" (backslash/quotation mark), double quote inline character, 227

^ (caret sign)
bitwise XOR operator, 425
operator precedence, 434
regular expressions
metacharacter, BC470

^= (caret sign/equals sign)
assignment operator, 419
operator precedence, 435

{} (curly brackets), 128–129
if...else, BC571
JSON, 357

$ (dollar sign), regular expressions
metacharacter, BC470

= (equals sign)
assignment operator, 111, 116, 419
encodeURI(), 482

operator precedence, 434–435

== (equals sign - double)
comparison operator, 117, 132, 374, 413
condition, 374
operator precedence, 434

=== (equals sign - triple), strictly equals comparison operator, 413

! (exclamation mark), 68
Boolean operator, 421
operator precedence, 434

!= (exclamation mark/equals sign)
comparison operator, 374
operator precedence, 434

!== (exclamation mark/equals sign -double), strictly does not equal comparison operator, 413

> (greater than)
comparison operator, 117, 413
operator precedence, 434

>> (greater than - double)
bitwise operator, 425
operator precedence, 434

>>= (greater than - double/equals sign)
assignment operator, 419
operator precedence, 435

>>> (greater than - triple), bitwise operator, 425

>>>= (greater than - triple/equals sign), assignment operator, 419

>= (greater than or equal to)
assignment operator, 419
comparison operator, 117, 413
operator precedence, 434–435

 # (hash symbol), usemap, 1025

- (hyphen)
document.all, 91

1137

SYMBOLS

C

I

O

Wiley Publishing, Inc.
End-User License Agreement

READ THIS. You should carefully read these terms and conditions before opening the software packet(s) included with this book "Book". This is a license agreement "Agreement" between you and Wiley Publishing, Inc. "WPI". By opening the accompanying software packet(s), you acknowledge that you have read and accept the following terms and conditions. If you do not agree and do not want to be bound by such terms and conditions, promptly return the Book and the unopened software packet(s) to the place you obtained them for a full refund.

1. **License Grant.** WPI grants to you (either an individual or entity) a nonexclusive license to use one copy of the enclosed software program(s) (collectively, the "Software," solely for your own personal or business purposes on a single computer (whether a standard computer or a workstation component of a multi-user network). The Software is in use on a computer when it is loaded into temporary memory (RAM) or installed into permanent memory (hard disk, CD-ROM, or other storage device). WPI reserves all rights not expressly granted herein.

2. **Ownership.** WPI is the owner of all right, title, and interest, including copyright, in and to the compilation of the Software recorded on the physical packet included with this Book "Software Media". Copyright to the individual programs recorded on the Software Media is owned by the author or other authorized copyright owner of each program. Ownership of the Software and all proprietary rights relating thereto remain with WPI and its licensers.

3. **Restrictions On Use and Transfer.**

    (a) You may only (i) make one copy of the Software for backup or archival purposes, or (ii) transfer the Software to a single hard disk, provided that you keep the original for backup or archival purposes. You may not (i) rent or lease the Software, (ii) copy or reproduce the Software through a LAN or other network system or through any computer subscriber system or bulletin-board system, or (iii) modify, adapt, or create derivative works based on the Software.

    (b) You may not reverse engineer, decompile, or disassemble the Software. You may transfer the Software and user documentation on a permanent basis, provided that the transferee agrees to accept the terms and conditions of this Agreement and you retain no copies. If the Software is an update or has been updated, any transfer must include the most recent update and all prior versions.

4. **Restrictions on Use of Individual Programs.** You must follow the individual requirements and restrictions detailed for each individual program in the About the CD-ROM appendix of this Book or on the Software Media. These limitations are also contained in the individual license agreements recorded on the Software Media. These limitations may include a require-ment that after using the program for a specified period of time, the user must pay a registration fee or discontinue use. By opening the Software packet(s), you will be agreeing to abide by the licenses and restrictions for these individual programs that are detailed in the About the CD-ROM appendix and/or on the Software Media. None of the material on this Software Media or listed in this Book may ever be redistributed, in original or modified form, for commercial purposes.

5. **Limited Warranty.**

    (a) WPI warrants that the Software and Software Media are free from defects in materials and workmanship under normal use for a period of sixty (60) days from the date of purchase of this Book. If WPI receives notification within the warranty period of defects in materials or workmanship, WPI will replace the defective Software Media.

(b) WPI AND THE AUTHOR(S) OF THE BOOK DISCLAIM ALL OTHER WARRANTIES, EXPRESS OR IMPLIED, INCLUDING WITHOUT LIMITATION IMPLIED WARRANTIES OF MERCHANTABILITY AND FITNESS FOR A PARTICULAR PURPOSE, WITH RESPECT TO THE SOFTWARE, THE PROGRAMS, THE SOURCE CODE CONTAINED THEREIN, AND/OR THE TECHNIQUES DESCRIBED IN THIS BOOK. WPI DOES NOT WARRANT THAT THE FUNCTIONS CONTAINED IN THE SOFTWARE WILL MEET YOUR REQUIREMENTS OR THAT THE OPERATION OF THE SOFTWARE WILL BE ERROR FREE.

(c) This limited warranty gives you specific legal rights, and you may have other rights that vary from jurisdiction to jurisdiction.

6. Remedies.

(a) WPI's entire liability and your exclusive remedy for defects in materials and workmanship shall be limited to replacement of the Software Media, which may be returned to WPI with a copy of your receipt at the following address: Software Media Fulfillment Department, Attn.: *JavaScript Bible, 7e*, Wiley Publishing, Inc., 10475 Crosspoint Blvd., Indianapolis, IN 46256, or call 1-800-762-2974. Please allow four to six weeks for delivery. This Limited Warranty is void if failure of the Software Media has resulted from accident, abuse, or mis-application. Any replacement Software Media will be warranted for the remainder of the original warranty period or thirty (30) days, whichever is longer.

(b) In no event shall WPI or the author be liable for any damages whatsoever (including without limitation damages for loss of business profits, business interruption, loss of business information, or any other pecuniary loss) arising from the use of or inability to use the Book or the Software, even if WPI has been advised of the possibility of such damages.

(c) Because some jurisdictions do not allow the exclusion or limitation of liability for consequential or incidental damages, the above limitation or exclusion may not apply to you.

7. U.S. Government Restricted Rights. Use, duplication, or disclosure of the Software for or on behalf of the United States of America, its agencies and/or instrumentalities "U.S. Government" is subject to restrictions as stated in paragraph (c)(1)(ii) of the Rights in Technical Data and Computer Software clause of DFARS 252.227-7013, or subparagraphs (c) (1) and (2) of the Commercial Computer Software - Restricted Rights clause at FAR 52.227-19, and in similar clauses in the NASA FAR supplement, as applicable.

8. General. This Agreement constitutes the entire understanding of the parties and revokes and supersedes all prior agreements, oral or written, between them and may not be modified or amended except in a writing signed by both parties hereto that specifically refers to this Agreement. This Agreement shall take precedence over any other documents that may be in conflict herewith. If any one or more provisions contained in this Agreement are held by any court or tribunal to be invalid, illegal, or otherwise unenforceable, each and every other provision shall remain in full force and effect.

The books you read to succeed.

Get the most out of the latest software and leading-edge technologies with a Wiley Bible—your one-stop reference.

978-0-470-45264-6

978-0-470-50909-8

978-0-470-43640-0

978-0-470-47191-3

Available wherever books are sold.

Wiley and the Wiley logo are registered trademarks of John Wiley & Sons, Inc. All other trademarks are the property of their respective owners.

WILEY
Now you know.
wiley.com